"In this day and age, any serious student (

of men and women. Featuring meticulous research in an easy question and answer format, Wayne Grudem's book is an invaluable resource."

Mary A. Kassian, Professor of Women's Studies, The Southern Baptist Theological Seminary; author, *The Feminist Mistake*

"After the Bible, I cannot imagine a more useful book for finding reliable help in understanding God's will for manhood and womanhood in the church and the home. The practical design of this book will help laypeople find answers without having to read eight hundred pages. But the rigor of scholarship, the amazing thoroughness, and the unparalleled clarity (which Wayne Grudem is justly famous for!) will make this book the standard complementarian manifesto for many years to come. I thank God and stand in respectful awe of Grudem's achievement."

John Piper, Pastor for Preaching and Vision, Bethlehem Baptist Church, Minneapolis, Minnesota

"The entire body of Christ owes an enormous debt of gratitude to Wayne Grudem for his effort in producing this outstanding, comprehensive work; for his courage in taking on what has become a Goliath within the camp of modern-day evangelicalism; and for his noncombative, gracious spirit in doing so. Those who love the truth will find here an invaluable resource in a user-friendly format that is both scholarly and accessible. They cannot help but appreciate this fair, thorough, warmhearted treatment of one of the most significant issues facing the church today."

Nancy Leigh DeMoss, Radio host; author *Revive Our Hearts*

"The gender issue may well be the critical fault line for contemporary theology. Controversies over these issues involve basic questions of biblical authority, God's order and design for creation, and Christ's purpose for the church. Wayne Grudem cuts through the confusion, making *Evangelical Feminism and Biblical Truth* an important book that is urgently needed. This book belongs in the hands of every pastor, seminary student, and thinking person."

R. Albert Mohler Jr., President, The Southern Baptist Theological Seminary

"In a troubling debate, resolution of which is currently out of sight, this extended monograph is a must-read for all who care about biblical authority, Christian relationships, and well-ordered church life. Laboriously and exhaustively, with clarity, charity and a scholar's objectivity, Wayne Grudem sifts through 118 current challenges to the Bible's apparent teaching on men and women. This is the fullest and most informative analysis available, and no one will be able to deny the cumulative strength of the case this author makes, as he vindicates the older paths."

J. I. Packer, Board of Governors' Professor of Theology, Regent College; author, *Knowing God*

"God's beautiful plan for manhood and womanhood is under attack today, Wayne Grudem's response to the onslaught of misinformation and distortion from evangelical feminists is clear, biblically sound, scholarly, and yet easy to grasp. If you've been sitting on the sidelines, if you've been indifferent on this issue, it's time to care. The stakes are too high to remain uninformed and silent. This book will equip you with truth and inspire you to stand your ground."

JOSHUA HARRIS, SENIOR PASTOR, COVENANT LIFE CHURCH, GAITHERSBURG, MARYLAND

"Wayne Grudem has produced an invaluable resource for refuting the confusing and tortured arguments evangelical feminists are using to redefine women's roles in the church and home. His masterful work helps clarify what is at risk in this life-and-death issue—nothing less than the doctrine of God and the doctrine of Scripture. I highly recommend it."

BARBARA HUGHES, AUTHOR, *DISCIPLINES OF A GODLY WOMAN*; COAUTHOR, *DISCIPLINES OF A GODLY FAMILY*

"*Evangelical Feminism and Biblical Truth* is a tour de force. Over the last twenty years, no one has articulated, clarified, specified, and defended the Bible's teaching on male and female role relationships in the home and church better than Wayne Grudem, and he once again shows that he is master of this field. Grudem faithfully and carefully sets out God's instruction on this important aspect of Christian discipleship and then answers the whole range of questions and excuses that are raised against the plain teaching of Scripture. His analysis is trenchant, his presentation persuasive, his scope comprehensive, his grasp magisterial. In the old days, mathematicians and logicians would often place three letters at the end of a completed equation or proof: QED, an abbreviation of the Latin phrase *quod erat demonstrandum* (literally "that which was to be demonstrated") indicating that the problem had been solved and the matter settled definitively. Well, you can write a QED at the end of this book. The debate is over. The only question now is whether we will bow our hearts to the authority of the Lord's inspired, inerrant, perspicuous Word on the matter of biblical manhood and womanhood."

J. LIGON DUNCAN III, SENIOR MINISTER, FIRST PRESBYTERIAN CHURCH, JACKSON, MISSISSIPPI; PRESIDENT, ALLIANCE OF CONFESSING EVANGELICALS

"If you love truth more than feminism, you will treasure this book. If you love feminism more than truth, you will despise it."

STEVE FARRAR, AUTHOR, *POINT MAN* AND *FINISHING STRONG*

"In his exhaustive treatment of the evangelical feminist debate, Wayne Grudem proves that the Word of God is still authoritative for all issues of faith and practice. His through scholarship, combined with a direct approach in an easy-to-read style, makes this work a vital reference for every Christian library."

Alistair Begg, Senior Pastor, Parkside Church, Cleveland, Ohio

"Forty years of feminist indoctrination has replaced a sound Christian worldview in many of our churches and seminaries. Wayne Grudem explores some of the most contentious issues in the church today and bases his studied responses upon Scripture and sound Christian doctrine. I recommend this book highly, especially to those women who have endured feminist studies in our colleges and universities and are trying to evaluate that teaching in light of their Christian profession of faith."

Diane Passno, Executive Vice President, Focus on the Family; author, *Feminism: Mystique or Mistake?*

"As an evangelical woman dedicated to standing under Scripture, and more especially as a professor of theology in women's studies, I am deeply indebted to Wayne Grudem for his careful research, clear exegesis, and faithful theological foundations. In *Evangelical Feminism and Biblical Truth*, he has provided another valuable resource for women and men who want to remain faithful to biblical guidelines while keeping their hearts turned to humble service to Christ. I will be adding this volume to my personal desk resources, recommending it to my students to consider in their spiritual journeys, and encouraging anyone seeking answers to difficult questions to examine the proposals found in this timely work."

Dorothy Kelley Patterson, Homemaker; Professor of Theology in Women's Studies, Southwestern Baptist Theological Seminary

"Wayne Grudem provides evangelical churches with a reverent, kind, thoughtful, and ultimately decisive answer to the shaky logic and questionable exegesis often advocated by feminists, who wish to overturn twenty centuries of Christian history and the clear witness of Holy Scripture."

Paige Patterson, President, Southwestern Baptist Theological Seminary

"With diplomacy and world-class scholarship, Wayne Grudem has taken on not just some of the thorny questions, but the entire briar patch! This book will be used and referenced by scholars, church leaders, and laymen and laywomen for decades."

Dennis Rainey, President, FamilyLife

"While our culture is careening out of control in its understanding of what it means to be a man or a woman, the winds of change have swept into evangelical circles and caused no little controversy. Many are confused by the streams of books and articles from evangelical feminists. In this magnificently clear and comprehensive work, Wayne Grudem calls the church of Jesus Christ back to the Scriptures, showing that the Bible itself prescribes different roles for men and women. Remarkably, almost every question a reader might have on this subject is answered here. This book is a treasure and a resource demonstrating that the complementarian view is biblical and beautiful."

Thomas R. Schreiner, James Buchanan Harrison Professor of New Testament Interpretation, The Southern Baptist Theological Seminary

"This book is the most thorough refutation of evangelical feminism you can get. Not only is it well organized and easy to navigate, but it provide the most up-to-date research on nearly every conceivable argument being put forth by egalitarians. And it is written with the superior precision and clarity we have come to expect from Wayne Grudem. Every Christian who is concerned about the negative impact of evangelical feminism, or who just wants to get up to speed on the debate, should take advantage of this great resource."

Randy Stinson, Senior Fellow, Council on Biblical Manhood and Womanhood

"The evangelical world has waiting a long time for such a comprehensive work on what has become, sadly, a controversial topic. This is the most thorough, balanced, and biblically accurate treatment of feminism and the Bible I have seen. It also exudes kindness and grace, qualities sorely needed for meaningful dialogue on this foundational issue."

Stu Weber, Author, *Tender Warrior*

"This is an indispensable reference work. Wayne Grudem's repeated call for upholding the equal worth, sanctity, and spiritual giftedness of both sexes should be welcomed by all sides. A major contribution to an increasingly crucial discussion."

Robert W. Yarbrough, Professor of New Testament, Covenant Theological Seminary

"The major strength of this work is that it engages with the best egalitarian writing over the past twenty years. This is a massive work which is unique in its breadth and detail."

Sharon James, *Evangelical Quarterly*

"Though the [book's] contents reflect Grudem's commendable scholarly research and clear thinking, he also presents the material in an extraordinarily well-organized format and in highly readable prose. . . . Grudem proves masterful in his refutation of the arguments [of egalitarianism]. Yet, he maintains an unusually irenic and charitable spirit in so doing, for which he is to be commended. . . . [This book] should be read by anyone who wants to understand both Scripture and the current debate on this theme. I highly recommend this new volume by Dr. Grudem as the appropriate follow-up to and extension of the discussion in the earlier volume, *Recovering Biblical Manhood and Womanhood."*

Richard L. Mayhue, *The Master's Seminary Journal*

"Impressive. . . . Leaves no stone unturned. Grudem deals with every question imaginable that is connected with the biblical texts on the topic from Genesis 1 to 1 Timothy 2. . . . In all cases Grudem tries to argue in the best way possible, taking into account the most recent research and literature on each topic. . . . The book is meant to be used as a reference book when looking for answers to a specific argument in the debate."

Jürg Buchegger, *Evangelical Review of Theology*

Evangelical Feminism & Biblical Truth

An Analysis of More Than One Hundred Disputed Questions

WAYNE GRUDEM

CROSSWAY
WHEATON, ILLINOIS

Evangelical Feminism and Biblical Truth:
An Analysis of More Than One Hundred Disputed Questions

Published by Crossway
1300 Crescent Street
Wheaton, Illinois 60187

Originally published 2004 by Multnomah Publishers, a division of Random House, Inc.

Cover design and image: Tyler Deeb

First printing of Crossway reprint edition 2012

Printed in the United States of America

All emphases in Scripture quotations have been added by the author.

Trade paperback ISBN: 978-1-4335-3261-0
PDF ISBN:978-1-4335-3262-7
Mobipocket ISBN: 978-1-4335-3263-4
ePub ISBN: 978-1-4335-3264-1

Library of Congress Cataloging-in-Publication Data

Grudem, Wayne A.
Evangelical feminism and biblical truth : an analysis of more than one hundred disputed questions / Wayne Grudem.
p. cm.
Originally published: Sisters, Or. : Multnomah Publishers, c2004.
Includes bibliographical references and index.
ISBN 978-1-4335-3261-0
1. Feminism—Religious aspects—Christianity. 2. Bible—Feminist criticism. 3. Evangelicalism. I. Title.
BT704.G78 2012
270.8'2082—dc23 2012015398

Crossway is a publishing ministry of Good News Publishers.

SH 21 20 19 18 17 16 15 14 13 12
14 13 12 11 10 9 8 7 6 5 4 3 2 1

This book is dedicated to three friends
who have played a significant role in this book,
and in the controversy over
biblical manhood and womanhood,
and in my life:

AUSTIN CHAPMAN,
retired businessman,
Minneapolis, Minnesota,

ROBERT LEWIS,
pastor-at-large of Fellowship Bible Church,
Little Rock, Arkansas,

and

C. J. MAHANEY,
president of Sovereign Grace Ministries,
Gaithersburg, Maryland.

Male and female he created them....

And behold, it was very good.

GENESIS 1:27, 31

Contents

Preface to the Crossway Reprint Edition

I wrote this book as an all-purpose reference work to reply to every argument I have ever heard favoring evangelical feminism (the view that all leadership roles in the home and the church should be open to men and women equally). I am glad that Crossway is reprinting the book, because I think of it as a sort of timeless "encyclopedia" of evangelical feminist arguments. I poured into it everything I learned in twenty-seven years of research and writing (1977–2004) on the biblical teachings about gender roles.

This book responds to 118 specific arguments regarding the roles of men and women. My recent reading suggests that these same arguments continue to be used by evangelical feminists today, and I don't expect that to change for a long time to come.

For example, at about the same time that *Evangelical Feminism and Biblical Truth* was first published in 2004, InterVarsity Press published *Discovering Biblical Equality*, edited by Ronald W. Pierce and Rebecca Groothuis, which took the evangelical feminist view. Because of their simultaneous publication, neither book took account of the other. Upon reading the IVP book, however, I found that nearly every argument in it was similar to something that had been published elsewhere, mostly by the same authors, and I had already answered their arguments in this book, *Evangelical Feminism and Biblical Truth*.

I have designed this book for use as a reference tool. Everything is arranged within fourteen broad chapters, the first eight covering different parts of the Bible and the last six covering more general topics such as "fairness" and methods of interpretation. I suggest you take a few minutes to get an overview of the book by reading the fourteen main chapter headings in the Table of Contents.

Is "evangelical feminism" an important topic? I think it is crucial. When churches adopt an evangelical feminist (or "egalitarian") position, they adopt viewpoints that undermine the effective authority of Scripture and thus start down a path toward liberalism, as I explain in chapter 13. Soon they begin to refer to God as "Mother" and eventually they endorse "faithful" homosexual relationships as morally right.

Sadly, this trend continues today. For example, when this book was first published in 2004, I noted (p. 513) that there were still three large denominations that had not yet approved the ordination of homosexuals even though they had approved the ordination of women and adopted a more liberal view of the Bible. These were the United Methodist Church, the Evangelical Lutheran Church in America (ELCA), and the Presbyterian Church–USA (PCUSA). Predictably, however, the ELCA eventually voted to ordain homosexuals (August 21, 2009), and the PCUSA did the same on May 10, 2011. (For more detail on this inevitable trend from feminism to liberalism, see my book *Evangelical Feminism: A New Path to Liberalism?* [Crossway, 2006].) Feminism continues to be the first step toward liberalism in many churches, colleges, seminaries, and denominations.

Margaret and I have been married now for forty-three years, and some readers might be interested in how the Bible's teachings work out in our own marriage. I think we would both say that we have never been happier together than we are now, for God has given much blessing to our marriage. There is a video available where Pastor Mark Driscoll interviews Margaret and me (mostly Margaret!) about our marriage. It is easily found by Googling "Margaret Grudem," or else at this link: http://theresurgence.com/2010/06/14/pastor-mark-interviews-wayne-and-margaret-grudem.

In addition, Dennis Rainey and Bob Lepine at FamilyLife Today interviewed me at length about a decision to change jobs for the sake of Margaret's health, and that interview is here: http://www.oneplace.com/ministries/familylife-today/listen/what-a-loving-husband-looks-like-152782.html.

I am grateful to Crossway for agreeing to reissue this book. I hope that readers will find it to be accurate, clear, and persuasive, as they seek to be faithful to the teachings of the Bible—in particular, that God created men and women equal in personhood and importance but different in the roles for which He created us, roles in which we discover His greatest blessing.

—Wayne Grudem
July 2012

Preface

In 1991, John Piper and I published a collection of essays by twenty-two authors titled *Recovering Biblical Manhood and Womanhood: A Response to Evangelical Feminism* (Wheaton, IL: Crossway Books, 1991). We are grateful to God for the positive response it received: It was named *Christianity Today*'s "Book of the Year" in 1992 and it continues to be widely read. It remains the standard defense of the complementarian[1] position on manhood and womanhood.

Yet for some time I have thought that another book was needed to supplement *Recovering Biblical Manhood and Womanhood* in several ways:

1. to answer new arguments made by evangelical feminists since 1991;
2. to summarize the results of new scholarly research in one place and in a form that can be understood by non-specialists;
3. to adopt a user-friendly format that would enable readers quickly to find a fair summary of egalitarian[2] arguments from the last thirty years, references to the best egalitarian literature supporting each argument, and clearly written answers to each of those arguments;
4. to provide an updated assessment of where the evangelical world is heading on this issue, along with actual policy statements about men and women in leadership from dozens of denominations and parachurch groups; and
5. to warn about troubling trends in the evangelical feminist camp that indicate increasing movement toward theological liberalism through various types of interpretation that imply a rejection of the effective authority of Scripture in our lives.

For these reasons, I have written this book.

The first two chapters contain a positive view of men and women in our similarities and differences as created by God. They can be read on their own, even if someone does not read the rest

---

1. We chose *complementarian* to stand for our view that men and women are equal and different—equal in value and personhood, but different in roles in marriage and the church. (See also 639–40.)
2. Throughout this book I use *egalitarian* and *evangelical feminist* as synonyms that both refer to the view that the Bible does not teach different roles for men and women in marriage or the church that are based on gender alone (apart from our obvious physical differences). An egalitarian would say that there is no unique leadership role that belongs to the husband in a marriage, and that all governing and teaching roles in the church should be open to both men and women alike.

of the book. Chapters 3–12 then answer 118 arguments that evangelical feminists have made in an attempt to deny that any unique leadership role is reserved for men in marriage or in the church.

In chapter 13 I argue that many of these egalitarian arguments reveal a dismaying trend to deny the full authority of the Bible. This makes evangelical feminism a new path into liberalism as it leads to an increasing rejection of the authority of Scripture in our lives. I am troubled that even those egalitarian authors who do not explicitly deny the Bible's authority still refrain from renouncing the approaches of those who do, and that the influential egalitarian organization Christians for Biblical Equality promotes on its website all of the authors that I quote who deny the authority of Scripture in the ways I list in that chapter.

In chapter 14 I survey the current positions of many evangelical denominations and parachurch organizations on this issue and attempt to explain why many have adopted an egalitarian position. My conclusion at the end of the discussion is that evangelicals who believe the Bible will ultimately have to choose between evangelical feminism and biblical truth.

The appendices contain important material that cannot easily be found elsewhere, such as a collection of policy statements on women in ministry from several dozen denominations and parachurch groups, a list of over fifty ancient texts where the Greek word *kephalē* ("head") means "person in authority," and a complete list of quotations of all eighty-two examples of the word *authenteō* ("to exercise authority") from ancient literature (in English translation). I included these lists of actual examples of disputed words because they give all readers fair access to the original data upon which to base a decision about the meanings of those words.

The appendices also include a recent review I wrote of the influential book by William Webb, *Slaves, Women, and Homosexuals* (Downers Grove, IL: InterVarsity Press, 2001), three reviews of the book *I Suffer Not a Woman* by Richard and Catherine Kroeger (Grand Rapids: Baker Book House, 1992), a recounting of procedures used by egalitarians to gain approval of women's ordination in the church of England (written by a bishop who opposed that action), and a reprint of a detailed scholarly article I wrote in 2001 on the meaning of the much-disputed Greek word *kephalē* ("head") in ancient literature.

I intend this book to be useful for all Christians who are wondering what to believe about biblical manhood and womanhood. It should especially be useful for college and seminary students, church study committees, and pastors and Bible study leaders looking for a summary of arguments on both sides of this issue. It will also provide a useful handbook for Christians to consult when they seek answers to arguments from their egalitarian friends.

But I think the book will also be useful for those who are not engaged in any controversy but who simply want to understand more deeply what the Bible teaches about men and women and about our similarities and differences as created by God in His infinite wisdom.

Controversy is never easy, but God in His grace often allows controversies to bring us to deeper understanding of His Word and deeper love and trust for Him. This has been true throughout history as Christians have grown in their understanding of the Bible when they had to ponder and seek to answer controversial viewpoints on topics such as the Trinity, the person of Christ, justification by faith, the inerrancy of the Bible, and so forth. And so it has been in this controversy as well. As I have taught and written and debated about this topic for the past twenty-seven years, I know that God has given me a deeper love and appreciation for my wife, Margaret, a deeper respect for the wisdom that God gives to both women and men, a deeper desire to see women as well as men using all the gifts God has given them for the good of the church, and a deeper appreciation for the amazing wisdom of God in creating men and women so wonderfully equal in many ways, yet so delightfully different in many other ways.

One danger of controversy is that it can overwhelm us to the point that we lose our joy. With regard to this issue, there is a risk of being so entangled in controversy that we lose the joy of being men and women. I hope this book will enable women to rejoice once again that God has made them women, and men to rejoice once again that God has made them men. I hope that we will be able to look at each other once again as brothers and sisters in God's family and feel something of the joy that God felt just after He first created us male and female: "And God saw everything that he had made, and behold, *it was very good*" (Genesis 1:31).

Another danger of controversy is that we can lose our tempers or lash out in anger at those with whom we disagree. When we do this we forget what the New Testament teaches us about how we are to disagree with others:

> And the Lord's servant must not be quarrelsome but kind to everyone, able to teach, patiently enduring evil, correcting his opponents with gentleness. God may perhaps grant them repentance leading to a knowledge of the truth.
> (2 Timothy 2:24–25)

> Who is wise and understanding among you? By his good conduct let him show his works in the meekness of wisdom.... But the wisdom from above is first pure, then peaceable, gentle, open to reason, full of mercy and good fruits, impartial and sincere. And a harvest of righteousness is sown in peace by those who make peace (James 3:13, 17–18).

I have tried to follow these principles even when I disagree very directly with my egalitarian brothers and sisters in this book. I hope others who read this book will seek to obey these verses as well, and I hope readers will call it to my attention if I have been unfaithful to these verses in anything I wrote in this book.

Another danger of controversy is the temptation to passivity and to avoidance of an important issue that the Lord is asking us to deal with in our generation. I have been saddened to hear of churches and institutions that decide not to take any position regarding roles of men and women in marriage and the church. "It's too controversial," people have told me.

But this was not the practice of the apostle Paul. He was the greatest evangelist in the history of the world, but his concern to reach the lost did not lead him to shrink back from declaring unpopular doctrines if they were part of the Word of God. He told the elders of the church at Ephesus: "I testify to you this day that I am innocent of the blood of all of you, for I did not shrink from declaring to you the whole counsel of God" (Acts 20:26–27).

The implication is that if he had avoided some unpopular teachings in the Word of God, he would have to answer to the Lord for his negligence on the Last Day (see 2 Corinthians 5:10).

There is a parallel today. If a pastor or other ministry leader decides not to teach about male headship in the home, and if marriages in his church begin to experience the conflict and disintegration that result from the dominant feminist mindset of our secular culture, then he cannot say like Paul, "I am innocent of the blood of all of you." He cannot say at the end of his life that he has been a faithful steward of the responsibility entrusted to him (1 Corinthians 4:1–5). Those who avoid teaching on unpopular topics that are taught in God's Word have forgotten their accountability before God for their congregations: "They are keeping watch over your souls, as those who will have to give account" (Hebrews 13:17).

Churches and institutions that decide not to take any position on this issue are in fact taking a position anyway. They are setting themselves up for continual leftward movement and continual erosion of their obedience to Scripture (see chapters 13 and 14 for several examples). A church or organization that decides to have no policy on this issue will keep ratcheting left one cog at a time, in the direction of the main pressures of the culture. I hope this book will keep that process from happening in many churches and parachurch organizations.

I have dedicated this book to Austin Chapman, a retired businessman from Minneapolis, Minnesota, who has been a trusted board member and supporter of the Council on Biblical Manhood and Womanhood for many years, and has also been a wise mentor, advisor, and friend for me personally.

I have also dedicated this book to Robert Lewis, pastor-at-large of Fellowship Bible Church in Little Rock, Arkansas, who first encouraged me to write this book during a conversation at a restaurant in Dallas, Texas, in 1999. Robert has been a friend, advisor, example, and encouragement to me for many years. I am grateful to Robert's church, Fellowship Bible Church, for providing a grant that enabled me to take a leave of absence for one term from Trinity Evangelical Divinity School in order to work on this book.

And I have dedicated this book to C. J. Mahaney, president of Sovereign Grace Ministries in Gaithersburg, Maryland, who has been a friend, example, and wise counselor for me for several years. I am also grateful to Sovereign Grace Ministries for providing me with an excellent computer and with additional funding for research support in this project.

I wish to thank the Board of Regents of Trinity Evangelical Divinity School, Deerfield, Illinois, for granting me a sabbatical and a leave of absence in the spring and fall of 2000 to work on this book. I also wish to thank the Board of Directors of Phoenix Seminary for granting me a sabbatical in the fall of 2003, during which I completed this manuscript.

Many others have had a significant role. My parents, Arden and Jean Grudem, provided additional funding for my leave of absence in 2000, and they have continued to pray for me and give me wise counsel for my entire fifty-five years. Stu Weber first put me in touch with Multnomah Publishers to inquire if they would publish this book. David Jones and Jeff Purswell, friends and former students from Trinity Evangelical Divinity School, helped me write the first proposal and outline for the book and then worked many hours summarizing, classifying, and providing initial answers to the arguments in several influential egalitarian books.

At Phoenix Seminary, Travis Buchanan, my administrative assistant, and Steve Eriksson, my teaching assistant, gave excellent help in research and manuscript preparation, in proofreading, and in compiling the indices. Travis also spent many hours compiling the appendix with policy statements from various denominations. David Dickerson also helped with research, organization of information, and indexing and proofreading. Paul Wegner helped me with some details of Hebrew grammar, and Paul Wegner and Fred Chay (who are Phoenix Seminary colleagues and good friends) interacted with my critique of William Webb's writings. David Instone-Brewer at the Tyndale House Library in Cambridge, England, helped set up my computer when I spent research time there in 2002 and 2004. Chris Cowan at the Southern Baptist Theological Seminary in Louisville and Justin Taylor at Bethlehem Baptist Church in Minneapolis helped track down obscure library materials not available to me in Arizona, and Chris Cowan also compiled the list of examples of *kephalē* in Appendix 3. Gary C. Johnson called my attention to additional denominational policy material. Sarah Affleck and Heidi Frye compiled the bibliography. Tracey Miller, Sharon Sullivan, Travis Buchanan, and Susanne Henry typed various portions of the manuscript at different times, and Sarah Walker photocopied and mailed copies several times. Ron Dickison fixed my computer several times, including helping me recover from two crashed hard drives. Steve and Barb Uhlmann gave me a backup computer that protected my work and saved me countless hours.

Several longtime friends gave me advice on specific parts of the manuscript from time to time, including Vern Poythress, John Piper, Bruce Ware, Randy Stinson, and Tom Schreiner (who read the whole manuscript and made helpful suggestions at a number of points).

Rod Morris of Multnomah Publishers did an excellent job of shortening the manuscript and editing it for consistency and clarity.

As with all my other books, my wife, Margaret, has been my greatest encouragement and support as she prays for me, talks with me, keeps me from distractions, sacrifices some of her time so that I can write, and continues to remind me that I have to finish the book! I thank God for giving me such a wonderful wife.

—Wayne Grudem
Phoenix Seminary, Scottsdale, Arizona
January 2004

"Male and female he created them...and behold, it was very good" (Genesis 1:27, 31).

How to Use This Book

Chapters 1 and 2 give a positive picture of men and women in creation, marriage, and the church, and they should be read first. Many readers may then wish to skim the 118 arguments found in chapters 3–12 and read only those sections that they find of interest. These chapters contain detailed section headings to enable readers to see the argument quickly and skip over the details if they wish. Chapters 13 and 14 contain my conclusions about the state of evangelicalism on this subject, and they assume the conclusions I reached in chapters 1–12, but they may be read at any time.

However, some readers may just want to find an answer to a specific egalitarian book or argument, and this book is written in such a way that they can find the specific argument or author in the table of contents or indices. In every section of the book, I have provided frequent cross-references to other sections where appropriate.

Note regarding references in the footnotes: In order to save some space in what were already lengthy footnotes, the publisher decided to use an abbreviated form of references for the books I cite in the footnotes (giving only the author, a short form of the title, and, for the first instance in each chapter, the date). Full bibliographic information in each case can be found in the bibliography (pp. 767–81).

Note on future arguments, additions, and corrections: I have attempted to include in this book every major claim made in every influential evangelical feminist book up to 2003. However, it is possible that I will discover, after this book is published, that I have missed some claims. It is also possible that evangelical feminists will make additional claims in new books after 2003. Therefore I intend from time to time to post additional claims and answers, additional arguments, and any needed corrections to this book at a special web site that has been established for this book, www.EFBT100.com.

Abbreviations

ANF: *Ante-Nicene Fathers*, 5th ed., ed. Alexander Roberts, James Donaldson, et. al., 10 vols. (Grand Rapids: Wm. B. Eerdmans, 1969; first published 1885).

BDAG: *A Greek-English Lexicon of the New Testament and Other Early Christian Literature*, 3rd ed., rev. and ed. Frederick William Danker, based on Walter Bauer's *Griechisch-deutsches Wörterbuch...*, 6th ed., and on previous English editions by W. F. Arndt, F. W. Gingrich, and F. W. Danker (Chicago and London: University of Chicago Press, 2000).

BDB: Francis Brown, S. R. Driver, and Charles A. Briggs, *A Hebrew and English Lexicon of the Old Testament* (Oxford: Clarendon Press, 1968).

DNTB: *Dictionary of New Testament Background*, ed. Craig A. Evans and Stanley E. Porter (Downers Grove, IL: InterVarsity Press, 2000).

DPL: *Dictionary of Paul and His Letters*, ed. Gerald F. Hawthorne, Ralph P. Martin, and Daniel G. Reid (Downers Grove, IL: InterVarsity Press, 1993).

EDT: *Evangelical Dictionary of Theology*, ed. Walter Elwell (Grand Rapids: Baker Book House, 1984).

HALOT: *The Hebrew and Aramaic Lexicon of the Old Testament*, Ludwig Koehler and Walter Baumgartner, rev. and ed. Walter Baumgartner and Johann Stamm, 2 vols. (Leiden: Brill, 2001).

ICC: *The International Critical Commentary*, ed. J. A. Emerton, C. E. B. Cranfield, and G.N. Stanton (Edinburgh: T & T Clark).

JBMW: *Journal for Biblical Manhood and Womanhood.*

JETS: *Journal of the Evangelical Theological Society.*

LS: *Greek-English Lexicon with a Revised Supplement*, ed. Liddell, H. G. and R. Scott (Oxford: Clarendon Press, 1996).

NIGTC: *The New International Greek Testament Commentary*, ed. I. Howard Marshall, W. Ward Gasque, and Donald Hagner (Grand Rapids: Wm. B. Eerdmans).

NIDOTTE: *The New International Dictionary of Old Testament Theology and Exegesis*, ed. Willem A. VanGemeren, 10 vols. (Grand Rapids: Zondervan, 1997).

NPNF: *The Nicene and Post-Nicene Fathers*, Series 1 and 2, ed. Philip Schaff, et. al., 26 vols. (Grand Rapids: Wm. B. Eerdmans, 1974).

TDNT: *Theological Dictionary of the New Testament,* ed. Gerhard Kittel and Gerhard Freidrich, trans. and ed. Geoffrey W. Bromiley, 9 vols. (Grand Rapids: Wm. B. Eerdmans Publishing Co., 1964–1974).

TrinJ: *Trinity Journal.*

WTJ: *Westminster Theological Journal.*

Chapter One

A Biblical Vision of Manhood and Womanhood as Created by God[1]

Most of this book contains answers to 118 claims that have come from evangelical feminism. But before I can interact with those claims, I must first present a clear statement of what I stand for. Just what is a "complementarian" view of biblical manhood and womanhood? How does it work in the home and in the church?

In this chapter, I consider six key issues related to a complementarian view of men and women in creation and in marriage. In the next chapter, I present a complementarian view of men and women in the church.

Key Issue #1: Men and Women Are Equal in Value and Dignity

On the first page of the Bible we read that both men and women are "in the image of God." In fact, the very first verse that tells us that God created human beings also tells us that both "male and female" are in the image of God:

> So God created man in his own image, in the image of God he created him; *male and female he created them.* (Genesis 1:27)

To be in the image of God is an incredible privilege. It means *to be like God* and *to represent God.*[2] No other creatures in all of creation, not even the powerful angels, are said to be in the image of God. It is a privilege given only to us as men and women.[3]

1. This chapter is taken and modified from *Biblical Foundations for Manhood and Womanhood* ed. Wayne Grudem, © 2002. Used by permission of Crossway Books, a division of Good News Publishers, Wheaton, IL.
2. For further discussion, see Grudem, *Systematic Theology* (1994), 442–50.
3. God created us so that our likeness to Him would be seen in our moral judgment and actions; in our spiritual life and ability to relate to God, who is spirit; in our reasoning ability; in our use of language; in our awareness of the distant past and future; in our creativity; in the complexity and variety of our emotions; in the depth of our interpersonal relationships; in our equality and differences in marriage and other interpersonal relationships; in our rule over the rest of creation; and in other ways. All of these aspects are distorted by sin and manifest themselves in ways that are *unlike* God and are displeasing to Him, but all of these areas of our lives are also

Any discussion of manhood and womanhood in the Bible must start here. Every time we talk to each other as men and women, we should remember that the person we are talking to is a creature of God who is *more like God than anything else in the universe*, and men and women share that status equally. Therefore we should treat men and women with equal dignity and we should think of men and women as having equal value. We are *both* in the image of God, and we have been so since the very first day that God created us. "In the image of God he created him; *male and female he created them*" (Genesis 1:27). Nowhere does the Bible say that men are more in God's image than women.[4] Men and women share equally in the tremendous privilege of being in the image of God.

The Bible thus corrects the errors of male dominance and male superiority that have come as the result of sin and that have been seen in nearly all cultures in the history of the world. Wherever men are thought to be better than women, wherever husbands act as selfish "dictators," wherever wives are forbidden to have their own jobs outside the home or to vote or to own property or to be educated, wherever women are treated as inferior, wherever there is abuse or violence against women or rape or female infanticide or polygamy or harems, the biblical truth of equality in the image of God is being denied. To all societies and cultures where these things occur, we must proclaim that the very first page of God's Word bears a fundamental and irrefutable witness against these evils.[5]

---

being progressively restored to greater Godlikeness through the salvation that is ours in Christ, and they will be completely restored in us when Christ returns.

For a fuller discussion on what it means to be in the image of God, see Bruce Ware, "Male and Female Complementarity and the Image of God" in Grudem, *Biblical Foundations for Manhood and Womanhood*, (2002), 71–92.

4. In 1 Corinthians 11:7, Paul says, "For a man ought not to cover his head, since he is the image and glory of God, but woman is the glory of man." He is not denying here that woman was created in the image of God, for that is clearly affirmed in Genesis 1:27. Nor does he say that woman is the image of man. Rather, Paul is simply saying that *in the relationship between man and woman*, man in particular reflects something of the excellence of the God who created him, and woman *in that relationship* reflects something of the excellence of the man from whom she was created. Yet Paul goes on almost immediately to say that men and women are interdependent (see vv. 11–12) and that we could not exist without each other. He does not say in this passage that man is more in the image of God than woman is, nor should we derive any such idea from this passage.

5. A tragic example of male dominance was reported on the front page of *USA Today: International Edition* (September 6, 1994). "No girls allowed: abortion for sex selection raises moral questions" was the caption on a photo of a doctor performing an ultrasound on a pregnant woman in India. The cover story, "Asians' Desire for Boys Leaves a Deadly Choice," reported that according to Dr. Datta Pai, a Bombay obstetrician, "Ninety-nine percent of those found to be carrying female fetuses aborted their unborn children" (2A). The story explained that "modern technology, the strong cultural desire for boys and pressure to reduce population have joined forces in a deadly combination in India, China and much of Asia to produce a booming business in sex selection.... The practice of aborting female fetuses appears common judging by emerging statistics that show lopsided sex ratios throughout Asia and into North Africa. Nor is the practice of sex selection limited to abortion. Female infanticide, the abandonment of baby girls, and the preferential feeding and health care of boys contribute greatly to the imbalanced ratios" (1A–2A). The story goes on to quote Harvard professor Amartya Sen as saying that there are now more than 100 million women "missing" in the population of the world, including 44 million fewer women in China and 37 million fewer in India than should be alive, according to normal sex ratios at birth (2A).

This is a tragedy of unspeakable proportions. In addition to the harm of these lost lives, we must think of

Yet we can say even more. If men and women are equally in the image of God, then we are equally important and equally valuable *to God*. We have equal worth before Him *for all eternity*, for this is how we were created. This truth should exclude all our feelings of pride or inferiority, and should exclude any idea that one sex is better or worse than the other. In contrast to many non-Christian cultures and religions, no one should feel proud or superior because he is a man, and no one should feel disappointed or inferior because she is a woman. If God thinks us to be equal in value, then that settles forever the question of personal worth, for God's evaluation is the true standard of personal value for all eternity.

Further evidence of our equality in the image of God is seen in the New Testament church, where the Holy Spirit is given in new fullness to both men and women (Acts 2:17–18), where both men and women are baptized into membership in the body of Christ (Acts 2:41),[6] and where both men and women receive spiritual gifts for use in the life of the church (1 Corinthians 12:7, 11; 1 Peter 4:10). The apostle Paul reminds us that we are not to be divided into factions that think of themselves as superior and inferior (such as Jew and Greek, or slave and free, or male and female), but rather that we should think of ourselves as united because we "are all one in Christ Jesus" (Galatians 3:28).

Whenever husbands and wives do not listen respectfully and thoughtfully to each other's viewpoints, do not value the wisdom that might be arrived at differently and expressed differently from the other person, or do not value the other person's different gifts and preferences as much as their own, they neglect this teaching on equality in the image of God.

Speaking personally for a moment, I do not think I listened very well to my wife, Margaret, early in our marriage. I did not value her different gifts and preferences as much as my own, or her wisdom that was arrived at differently (often, it seemed, quickly and instinctively) and that she expressed differently from how I expressed things. Later we made much progress in this area, but, looking back, Margaret told me that early in our marriage it felt as though her voice was taken away, and as though my ears were closed. I wonder if there are other couples where God needs to open the husband's ears to listen, and needs to restore the wife's voice to speak.[7]

---

the destructive consequences in the lives of those women who survive. From their earliest age, they receive the message from their families and indeed from their whole society that "boys are better than girls" and "I wish you were a boy." The devastation to their own sense of self-worth must be immense. Yet all of this comes about as the result of a failure to realize that men and women, boys and girls, have equal value in God's sight and should have equal value in our sight as well. The first chapter of the Bible corrects this practice, and corrects any lurking sense in our own hearts that boys are more valuable than girls, when it says we are both created in the image of God.

6. The fact that both men and women are baptized stands in contrast to the Old Testament, where the outward sign of inclusion in the community of God's people was circumcision. But circumcision by its nature was administered only to men. By contrast, both men and women are baptized in the New Testament church. In this way, every baptism should remind us of our equality in the image of God.

7. I realize that there is an opposite mistake in which the husband listens so much and the wife has so great a voice that she becomes the governing partner in the relationship. I am not advocating that mistake either, and in what follows I will argue for the necessity of a male leadership role in decision-making within marriage.

A healthy perspective on the way that equality manifests itself in marriage was summarized as part of a "Marriage and Family Statement" issued by Campus Crusade for Christ in July of 1999. After three paragraphs discussing both equality and differences between men and women, the statement says:

> In a marriage lived according to these truths, the love between husband and wife will show itself in listening to each other's viewpoints, valuing each other's gifts, wisdom, and desires, honoring one another in public and in private, and always seeking to bring benefit, not harm, to one another.[8]

Why do I list this as a key issue in the manhood–womanhood controversy? Not because we differ with egalitarians[9] on this question, but because we differ at this point with sinful tendencies in our own hearts and with the oppressive male chauvinism and male dominance that has marred most cultures throughout most of history.

Anyone preaching or teaching on manhood and womanhood has to start here—where the Bible starts—not with our differences, but with our *equality* in the image of God.

If you're a pastor and you don't start here in your preaching on biblical manhood and womanhood, affirming our equality in the image of God, you simply will not get a hearing from many people in your church. And if you don't start here, your heart won't be right on this issue.

There is yet one more reason why I think this is a key issue, one that speaks especially to men. I personally think that one reason God has allowed this controversy on manhood and womanhood to come into the church at this time is so that we could correct some mistakes, change some wrongful traditions, and become more faithful to Scripture in treating our wives and all women with dignity and respect. The first step in correcting these mistakes is to be fully convinced in our hearts that women share equally with us men in the value and dignity that belongs to being made in the image of God.

---

8. Policy statement announced and distributed to Campus Crusade staff members at a biannual staff conference on July 28, 1999, at Colorado State University, Fort Collins, Colorado. The statement was reported in a Religion News Service dispatch July 30, 1999; a Baptist Press story by Art Toalston on July 29, 1999 (www.baptistpress.com); an article in *World*, September 11, 1999, p. 32; and it was also quoted in full in James Dobson's monthly newsletter *Family News from Dr. James Dobson*, September 1999, 1–2. The statement is also reproduced and discussed in Rainey, *Ministering to Twenty-First Century Families* (2001), 39–56.

   Carolyn Custis James misrepresents my position when she attributes to John Piper and me the view that "a man is abdicating his headship when he listens to his wife" (James, *When Life and Beliefs Collide* [2001], 192). The book she quotes, *Recovering Biblical Manhood and Womanhood,* refutes that view on pp. 62, 195, 482, n. 50 and elsewhere. (Carolyn James assures me this will be corrected in future printings.)

9. Throughout this chapter, I use the word *egalitarian* to refer to those within the evangelical world who say that no differences in the roles of men and women should be based on their gender alone. In particular, egalitarians deny that there is any unique male leadership role in marriage or in the church. Sometimes I use *evangelical feminist* to mean the same thing as *egalitarian.*

KEY ISSUE #2: MEN AND WOMEN HAVE DIFFERENT ROLES IN MARRIAGE AS PART OF THE CREATED ORDER

When the members of the Council on Biblical Manhood and Womanhood wrote the "Danvers Statement" in 1987, we included the following affirmations:

1. Both Adam and Eve were created in God's image, equal before God as persons and distinct in their manhood and womanhood.
2. Distinctions in masculine and feminine roles are ordained by God as part of the created order, and should find an echo in every human heart.
3. Adam's headship in marriage was established by God before the Fall, and was not a result of sin.[10]

The statement adopted by the Southern Baptist Convention in June 1998 and affirmed (with one additional paragraph) by Campus Crusade in July 1999 also acknowledges God-given differences:

> The husband and wife are of equal worth before God, since both are created in God's image. The marriage relationship models the way God relates to his people. A husband is to love his wife as Christ loved the church. He has the God-given responsibility *to provide for, to protect, and to lead his family.* A wife is to submit herself graciously to the servant leadership of her husband even as the church willingly submits to the headship of Christ. She, being in the image of God as is her husband and thus equal to him, has the God-given responsibility *to respect her husband and serve as his helper* in managing the household and nurturing the next generation.[11]

By contrast, egalitarians do not affirm such created differences. In fact, the statement on "Men, Women and Biblical Equality" published by Christians for Biblical Equality (CBE) says:

1. The Bible teaches that both man and woman were created in God's image, had a direct relationship with God, and shared jointly the responsibilities of bearing and rearing children and having dominion over the created order (Gen. 1:26–28).

5. The Bible teaches that the rulership of Adam over Eve resulted from the Fall and was, therefore, *not a part of the original created order....*

10. The Bible defines the function of leadership as the empowerment of others for service rather than as the exercise of power over them (Matt. 20:25–28, 23:8; Mark 10:42–45; John 13:13–17; Gal. 5:13; 1 Pet. 5:2–3).

---

10. The Danvers Statement was prepared by several evangelical leaders at a CBMW meeting in Danvers, Massachusetts, in December 1987. It was first published in final form by the CBMW in Wheaton, IL, in November 1988. See Appendix 1 for the full text of this statement.
11. The entire statement in the form adopted by Campus Crusade for Christ is available at www.baptistpress.com, in the archives for July 29, 1999 (italics added).

11. The Bible teaches that husbands and wives are heirs together of the grace of life and that they are bound together in a relationship of mutual submission and responsibility (1 Cor. 7:3–5; Eph. 5:21; 1 Pet. 3:1–7; Gen. 21:12). The husband's function as "head" (*kephalē*) is to be understood as self-giving love and service within this relationship of mutual submission (Eph. 5:21–33; Col. 3:19; 1 Pet. 3:7).[12]

So which position is right? Does the Bible really teach that men and women had different roles from the beginning of Creation?

When we look carefully at Scripture, we can see at least ten arguments indicating that God gave men and women distinct roles before the Fall, and particularly, that there was male headship in marriage before the Fall.

A. Ten arguments showing male headship in marriage before the Fall

1. The order: Adam was created first, then Eve (note the sequence in Genesis 2:7 and Genesis 2:18–23). We may not think of this as very important today, but it was important to the original readers of this text, and the apostle Paul sees it as important: he bases his argument for different roles in the assembled New Testament church on the fact that Adam was created prior to Eve. He says, "I do not permit a woman to teach or to exercise authority over a man.... For Adam was formed first, then Eve" (1 Timothy 2:12–13).

According to Scripture itself, then, the fact that Adam was created first and then Eve has implications not just for Adam and Eve, but for the relationships between men and women throughout the church age.[13]

2. The representation: Adam, not Eve, had a special role in representing the human race.

Looking at the Genesis narrative, we find that Eve sinned first, and then Adam sinned: "She took of its fruit and ate, and she also gave some to her husband who was with her, and he ate" (Genesis 3:6). Since Eve sinned first, we might expect that the New Testament would tell us that we inherit a sinful nature because of Eve's sin, or that we are counted guilty because of Eve's sin. But this is not the case. The New Testament does not say, "as *in Eve* all die," but rather, "For as *in Adam* all die, so also *in Christ* shall all be made alive" (1 Corinthians 15:22).

This is further seen in the parallel between Adam and Christ, where Paul views Christ as the "last Adam":

12. The entire statement is available from the website of Christians for Biblical Equality (CBE), www.cbeinternational.org (italics added to the statement as quoted above). The CBE statement regularly portrays a non-egalitarian position in pejorative language such as "the rulership of Adam over Eve" and fails to even mention a third alternative, namely, loving, humble headship. (For a discussion of repeated ambiguities in the CBE statement, see Piper and Grudem, "Charity, Clarity, and Hope," in Piper and Grudem, *Recovering Biblical Manhood and Womanhood* [1991], 403–22.)

13. Bruce Ware adds yet another reason related to this temporal priority in creation, namely, that woman was created "from" or "out of" man. See his discussion in Grudem, *Biblical Foundations for Manhood and Womanhood*, 82–84. Although I have not listed it separately here, it could be counted as an eleventh reason along with the ten I list.

Thus it is written, "The first man Adam became a living being"; the last Adam became a life-giving spirit.... The first man was from the earth, a man of dust; the second man is from heaven.... Just as we have borne the image of the man of dust, we shall also bear the image of the man of heaven. (1 Corinthians 15:45–49; see also Romans 5:12–21, where another relationship between Adam and Christ is developed.)

It is unmistakable then that Adam had a leadership role in representing the entire human race, a leadership role that Eve did not have. Nor did Adam and Eve *together* represent the human race. *Adam alone* represented the human race, because he had a particular leadership role that God had given him, a role Eve did not share.

3. The naming of woman: When God made the first woman and "brought her to the man," the Bible tells us, "Then the man said,

"'This at last is bone of my bones
and flesh of my flesh;
she shall be called Woman,
because she was taken out of Man.'" (Genesis 2:23)

When Adam says, "she shall be called Woman," he is giving a name to her. This is important because in the context of Genesis 1–2, the original readers would have recognized that the person doing the "naming" of created things is always the person who has authority over those things.

Some egalitarians (such as Gilbert Bilezikian and Stanley Grenz) deny that Adam gives a name to his wife in Genesis 2:23.[14] But this objection is hardly convincing when we see how Genesis 2:23 fits into the pattern of naming activities throughout these first two chapters of Genesis. We see this when we examine the places where the same verb (the Hebrew verb *qārā'*, "to call") is used in contexts of naming in Genesis 1–2:

---

14. See Bilezikian, *Beyond Sex Roles* (1985), 259, where he says, "No mention of 'giving a name' is made in reference to the woman in verse 23." He also says, "The contrast between Genesis 2:23 and 3:20 bears out the fact that there was no act of naming in the first instance. When Eve actually receives her *name*, the text uses that very word, 'The man called his wife's *name* Eve'" (261).

Bilezikian apparently thinks that where *name* (the Hebrew noun *shēm*) is not used, no act of naming occurs. But he takes no account of the fact that the noun *shēm* is not used in Genesis 1:5, 8, or 10 either, where God names the Day and the Night and Heaven and Earth and Seas. The idea of naming can be indicated by the verb *qārā'* without the noun *shēm* being used.

Grenz, *Women in the Church* (1995), 163, says, "The usual Hebrew construction for the act of naming is not present in the Genesis 2:23 text. Phyllis Trible points out that in order to denote naming, the Hebrew verb 'call' must be followed by an actual name.... In the Genesis 2:23 text, however, no actual name is present, only the designation *woman*.... The narrator does not state that the man did in fact name his wife when God brought her to him.... It is not until after the Fall that Adam calls her Eve."

But Grenz (and Trible) are incorrect in this because they wrongly assume that *woman* (Hebrew *'ishshāh*) is not a name—it is surely taken as a name here in Genesis, and is parallel to the other naming verses in this context, and with Genesis 5:2 where it is said that "God blessed them and *named (qārā')* them Man when [literally ("on the day")] they were created." Grenz and Trible fail to account for the special nature of Genesis 1–2, where this same naming pattern is used of whole broad categories of the created order and an individual personal name (like Eve) would not yet be expected.

- Genesis 1:5: "God *called* the light Day, and the darkness he *called* Night."
- Genesis 1:8: "And God *called* the expanse Heaven."
- Genesis 1:10: "God *called* the dry land Earth, and the waters that were gathered together he *called* Seas."
- Genesis 2:19: "So out of the ground the LORD God formed every beast of the field and every bird of the heavens and brought them to the man to see what he would *call* them. And whatever the man *called* every living creature, that was its name."
- Genesis 2:20: "The man *gave names* to all livestock and to the birds of the heavens and to every beast of the field."

In each of these verses prior to Genesis 2:23, the same verb, the Hebrew verb *qārā'*, had been used. Just as God demonstrated His sovereignty over day and night, heavens, earth, and seas by assigning them names, so Adam demonstrated his authority over the animal kingdom by assigning every living creature its name. The original readers would have easily recognized the pattern and they would have seen a continuation of the pattern when Adam said, "she shall be *called* Woman."

The original readers of Genesis and of the rest of the Old Testament would have been familiar with this pattern, a pattern whereby people who have authority over another person or thing have the ability to assign a name to that person or thing, a name that often indicates something of the character or quality of the person. Thus, parents give names to their children (see Genesis 4:25, 26; 5:3, 29; 16:15; 19:37, 38; 21:3). And God is able to change the names of people when He wishes to indicate a change in their character or role (see Genesis 17:5, 15, where God changes Abram's name to Abraham and Sarai's name to Sarah). In each of these passages we have the same verb (*qārā'*) as is used in Genesis 2:23, and in each case the person who gives the name has authority over the person who receives the name. Therefore when Adam gives to his wife the name "Woman," this indicates a kind of authority that God gave to Adam, a leadership function that Eve did not have with respect to her husband.[15]

George W. Ramsey, "Is Name-Giving an Act of Domination in Genesis 2:23 and Elsewhere?" (*Catholic Biblical Quarterly* 50, 1988), argues against Trible's claim, saying, "It is an error to argue that Genesis 2:23 is not an instance of name-giving.... The use of the noun *shēm* is not absolutely essential to the naming formula. *Qārā'* plus *lāmed* with an object indicates naming just as well as *qārā'* plus *shēm*" (29). Ramsey points out similar examples, such as the naming of Ichabod in 1 Samuel 4:21, "And she named the child Ichabod," where the word *shēm* ("name") is not used, but the verb *qārā'* is used plus *lāmed* with an object, as in Genesis 2:23.

15. William Webb claims that when Adam calls the woman (*'ishshāh*) in Genesis 2:23, it shows her role as an equal partner with Adam, because her name is similar to the name for man (*'îsh*) (Webb, *Slaves, Women and Homosexuals* [2001], 116). This argument is not convincing because the names for "man" and "woman" are similar but they are not identical (*'îsh* and *'ishshāh*), so they are somewhat the same and somewhat different.

The words mean different things: *'îsh* means "man" or "husband" (BDB, 35), and *'ishshāh* means "woman, wife, female" (BDB, 61), and though the words look similar they are related to different roots (the BDB *Lexicon* speaks of "the impossibility of deriving *'îsh* and *'ishshāh* from the same root," 35).

For Webb to say that this name *only* indicates equality is simply reductionistic—it is taking part of the truth and making it the whole truth. The names signify *both* similarity *and* difference.

Linda Belleville objects that naming in the Old Testament "was not an act of control or power."[16] But this misses the point. The point is not that in the act of naming the person controls or exercises power over someone else (in a sort of magical way). The point is that the authority to give a name in itself assumes that the person giving the name *already has authority* over the person or thing receiving that name.[17]

We should notice here that Adam does not give the personal name Eve to his wife until Genesis 3:20 ("the man *called* [*qārā'*] his wife's name Eve, because she was the mother of all living"). This is because in the creation story in Genesis 2, Adam is giving a broad category name to his wife, indicating the name that would be given to women generally; he is not giving specific personal names designating the character of the individual person.[18]

---

16. Linda Belleville, "Women in Ministry," in *Two Views on Women in Ministry* [2001], 143. Belleville refers to Anthony Thiselton, "Supposed Power of Words in the Biblical Writings," *Journal of Theological Studies*, N.S., vol. XXV, pt. 2 (October 1974) 283–99, and also to an article by Ramsey (see footnotes 14 and 17 for a discussion of Ramsey's article).

   Thiselton's article does not really address the question under discussion here in Genesis 2:23, however, because his concern is to show that name-giving does not have some sort of automatic or magical power in the biblical writings. That of course is not what I am claiming here, but rather that the right to give someone a name implies that the name-giver has authority over that person or thing.

17. Ramsey, "Name-Giving?" 24–35, provides evidence that enables us to make a helpful qualification, however, between what we may term "private" and "public" names (this is my distinction, not his). Ramsey points out that Hagar gave a name to God in Genesis 16:13: "So she called the name of the LORD who spoke to her, 'You are a God of seeing.'" He rightly says, "It is difficult to imagine that the narrator intended us to understand that this woman...is exercising some sort of control over God" (34). I agree, but what this verse demonstrates is simply a common human activity whereby people can make up all sorts of "private names" by which they refer to someone else, even someone great or famous (for example, someone who admires a current president of the United States might often refer to him as "our great president," while someone who opposes his policies might frequently refer to "that dummy in the White House"). Such private names do not change the public or official or widely used name of that person, and Ramsey is right to see that in a case such as this there is no indication of authority over the person named. Ramsey is wrong, however, to take this unusual example and from it derive a general conclusion that name-giving does not indicate power or authority over the person or thing named.

   The example of Hagar is not like the many other biblical examples of giving a public or official name to someone, a name commonly used by other people and a name by which the recipient of the name henceforth identifies himself or herself. In the Old Testament, that kind of bestowal of a public or official name is regularly done by those in authority over the person or thing named (as the many Genesis passages cited in my earlier paragraphs clearly demonstrate, as do the passages Ramsey cites [32] in which kings bestow names, and warriors who conquer territories bestow names). God gives public and official names frequently in Genesis, and parents also give such names, and they are able to do so because of their authority over the person named.

   Ramsey's citation of Genesis 26:17–21 as a counterexample is hardly persuasive, for in that very context there is significant evidence that the act of bestowing a name on a well is an act of asserting dominion over that well. Note Genesis 26:18: "And Isaac dug again the wells of water that had been dug in the days of Abraham his father, which the Philistines had stopped after the death of Abraham. And he gave them the names that his father had given them." The fact that Isaac names two more wells Esek ("contention") and Sitnah ("enmity") before he leaves them for a third well (which he names!) shows that he is still asserting an inherent right to dominion over them, though he is temporarily relinquishing the exercise of that right for the sake of peace. Note that all of this contention over wells is carried out in the light of Genesis 26:3, where God had promised him, "To you and to your offspring I will give all these lands."

18. Similarly, because God is having Adam examine and name the entire animal kingdom, it is likely that Adam gave names to one representative of each broad category or type of animal in Genesis 2:19–20 (such as dog, cat, deer, or lion, to use English equivalents). We hardly expect that he would have given individual, personal names (such as Rover, Tabby, Bambi, or Leo), because those names would not have applied to others of the same kind. This distinction is missed by Bilezikian (*Beyond Sex Roles*, 259–61), and Grenz (*Women in the Church*

4. The naming of the human race: God named the human race "Man," not "Woman." Because the idea of naming is so important in the Old Testament, it is significant to notice what name God chose for the human race as a whole. We read,

> When God created man, he made him in the likeness of God. Male and female he created them, and he blessed them and *named them Man* when they were created. (Genesis 5:1–2)

The word that is translated "Man" is the Hebrew word *'ādām*. But this is by no means a gender-neutral term in the eyes of the Hebrew reader, because in the four chapters prior to Genesis 5:2, *'ādām* has been used many times to speak of a male human being in distinction from a female human being. In the following list, the italicized word *man* represents the Hebrew word *'ādām* in every case:

- Genesis 2:22: "And the rib that the LORD God had taken from the *man* he made into a woman and brought her to the *man*." (It does not say that God made the rib into another *'ādām*, another "man," but that he made the rib into a woman, which is a different Hebrew word.)
- Genesis 2:23: "Then the *man* said, 'This at last is bone of my bone and flesh of my flesh; she shall be called Woman.'"
- Genesis 2:25: "And the *man* and his wife were both naked and were not ashamed."
- Genesis 3:8: "And the *man* and his wife hid themselves from the presence of the LORD God."
- Genesis 3:9: "But the LORD God called to the *man* and said to him, 'Where are you?'"
- Genesis 3:12: "The *man* said, 'The woman whom you gave to be with me, she gave me fruit of the tree, and I ate.'"
- Genesis 3:20: "The *man* called his wife's name Eve."

When we come, then, to the naming of the human race in Genesis 5:2 (reporting an event before the Fall), it was evident to the original readers that God was using a name that had clear male overtones or nuances. In the first four chapters of Genesis the word *'ādām* was used thirteen times to refer not to a human being in general but to a male human being. In addition to the eight examples mentioned above, it was used an additional five times as a proper name for Adam in distinction from Eve (Genesis 3:17, 21; 4:1, 25; 5:1).[19]

[1995], 163) when they object that Adam did not name Eve until Genesis 3:20, after the Fall. (See also Brown, *Women Ministers According to Scripture* [1996], 31.) He did give her a specific personal name ("Eve") after the Fall, but he also gave her the general category name "woman" before the Fall. The one does not exclude the other, for the Bible reports both events.

19. There are actually more than thirteen instances where the Hebrew word *'ādām* refers to a male human being, because prior to the creation of Eve there are twelve additional instances where references to "the man" spoke only of a male person God had created (see Genesis 2:5, 7 [twice], 8, 15, 16, 18, 19 [twice], 20 [twice], 21). If we add these instances, there are twenty-five examples of *'ādām* used to refer to a male human being prior to Genesis 5:2. The male connotations of the word could not have been missed by the original readers.

I am not saying that *'ādām* in the Hebrew Bible always refers to a male human being, for sometimes it has a broader sense, and means something like "person." But in the early chapters of Genesis, the connection with the man in distinction from the woman is a very clear pattern. God gave the human race a name which, like the English word *man*, can either mean a male human being or can refer to the human race in general.[20]

Does this make any difference? It does give a hint of male leadership, which God suggested in choosing this name. It is significant that God did not call the human race "Woman." (I am speaking of Hebrew equivalents to these English words.) Nor did He give the human race a name such as "humanity," which would have no male connotations and no connection with the man in distinction from the woman. Rather, He called the race "man." Raymond C. Ortlund rightly says, "God's naming of the race 'man' whispers male headship."[21]

When Genesis 5:2 reports this naming process, it refers to an event prior to sin and the Fall:

> When God created man, he made him in the likeness of God. Male and female he created them, and he blessed them and named them Man *when they were created.* (Genesis 5:1–2)

And, in fact, the name is already indicated in Genesis 1:27, "So God created *man* in his own image, in the image of God he created him; male and female he created them."

If the name "man" in English (as in Hebrew) did not suggest male leadership or headship

---

20. Linda Belleville denies that God's use of *'ādām* indicates male headship, because there were other male-oriented words available. She says, "*'ādām* is not a term that denotes gender. It...is properly translated with a generic term like *human* or *humankind*. When gender comes into play, the Hebrew terms *zākār* ('male') and *neqēbāh* ('female') are used.... That *'ādām* is a gender-inclusive term is clear from the repeated reference to *'ādām* as 'them' (Genesis 1:26–27; 5:2). The Septuagint's consistent choice of the generic term *anthrōpos* ('person,' 'human') to translate *'ādām* points to the same thing" (*Women Leaders and the Church* [2000], 102).

Belleville here misses the point: The Hebrew word *'ādām* is not exclusively male-oriented (as *zākār* is), but can be used in four senses: (1. to refer to the human race as a whole, (2. to refer to a human being or a person, (3. to refer to a man in distinction from a woman (especially in the early chapters of Genesis), and (4. as a proper name for Adam (see Brown, Driver, and Briggs *Hebrew and English Lexicon of the Old Testament* [BDB], 9). The Septuagint's term *anthrōpos* is therefore a useful translation of *'ādām*, because it can mean either person or man, depending on context. Belleville surprisingly gives readers only half the relevant evidence at this point, neglecting to mention that *anthrōpos* can also mean "a male person; *man*" (see BDAG, 81).

Belleville says nothing about the most significant evidence in these chapters: the male connotations that readers would pick up from the use of *'ādām* twenty-five times in the early chapters of Genesis to refer to Adam or to a male human being in distinction from a woman.

Aida Spencer, on the other hand, tries to deny the male nuance in *'ādām* by making it always collective, saying, "'The Adam' is a 'they'.... 'The Adam' is a 'male and female.' Thus 'the Adam' could be translated 'human' or 'humanity.'" She even goes so far as to speak of "Adam, the female" (*Beyond the Curse* [1985], 21). But her argument will not work, because it is contradicted by many verses in Genesis 2–3, where *'ādām* has to refer to Adam alone, not Adam and Eve together (and it is never used of Eve alone). Spencer's attempt to squeeze all examples of the word into one meaning would yield absurd sentences like, "And *the humanity* and his wife were both naked and were not ashamed" (Genesis 2:25) and "*The humanity* and his wife hid themselves from the presence of the LORD God" (Genesis 3:8).

21. Raymond C. Ortlund Jr., "Male-Female Equality and Male Headship," in Piper and Grudem, *Recovering Biblical Manhood and Womanhood,* 98.

in the human race, there would be no objection to using *man* to refer to the human race today. But it is precisely the hint of male leadership in the word that has led some people to object to this use of *man* and to attempt to substitute other terms instead.[22] Yet it is that same hint of male leadership that makes this precisely the best translation of Genesis 1:27 and 5:2.

5. The primary accountability: God spoke to Adam first after the Fall.

After Adam and Eve sinned, they hid from the Lord among the trees of the Garden. Then we read, "But the LORD God called to *the man* and said to *him*, 'Where are *you*?'" (Genesis 3:9).

In the Hebrew text, the expression "the man" and the pronouns "him" and "you" are all singular. Even though Eve had sinned first, God first summoned Adam to give account for what had happened in his family. Adam was the one primarily accountable.

An analogy to this is seen in the life of a contemporary human family. When a parent comes into a room where several children have been misbehaving and have left the room in chaos, the parent will probably summon the oldest and say, "What happened here?" Though all are responsible for their behavior, the oldest child bears the primary responsibility.

In a similar way, when God summoned Adam to give an account, it indicated a primary responsibility for Adam in the conduct of his family. This is similar to the situation in Genesis 2:15–17, where God gave commands to Adam alone before the Fall, indicating there also a primary responsibility that belonged to Adam.[23] By contrast, the serpent spoke to Eve first (Genesis 3:1), trying to get her to take responsibility for leading the family into sin, and inverting the order that God had established at Creation.

6. The purpose: Eve was created as a helper for Adam, not Adam as a helper for Eve.

After God had created Adam and given him directions concerning his life in the Garden of Eden, we read, "Then the LORD God said, 'It is not good that the man should be alone; I will make him a helper fit for him'" (Genesis 2:18).

It is true that the Hebrew word here translated "helper" *(ʿēzer)* is often used elsewhere in the Bible of God who is our helper. (See for example Psalm 33:20; 70:5; 115:9.) But *helper* does

---

22. Several gender-neutral Bible translations have changed the word *man,* which was standard in earlier English translations. *Humankind* is used in the New Revised Standard Version of Genesis 1:26–27. The New Living Translation uses *people*, while the inclusive language edition of the New International Version uses *human beings*. In Genesis 5:2, various gender-neutral substitutes replace the name *man*: *humankind* (NRSV), *human* (NLT), or *human beings* (NIV–Inclusive Language Edition, CEV, NCV).

23. Gilbert Bilezikian claims that when God approached Adam first, it did not indicate any greater accountability for Adam as leader, but was only because God had earlier spoken to Adam alone: "As the sole recipient of God's original order prohibiting consumption from the tree, God asked Adam to give an account of himself. That order had been given to Adam as a personal prohibition (2:17 is also in the second-person singular) when Eve was not yet formed.... God did not ask him any questions about Eve. Her turn would come" (*Beyond Sex Roles* (1985), 51).

I agree with Bilezikian that God had earlier commanded Adam alone regarding the forbidden tree, but this just reinforces the point that God's actions in both cases imply a leadership role for Adam with respect to Eve. Just as God gave the command first to Adam alone, but Eve was also responsible to obey as soon as Adam told her of the command, so now God speaks to Adam first and holds him primarily accountable for disobeying the command he had received directly from God. This does not deny Eve's personal accountability (God also speaks to her), but it does assume Adam's leadership.

not by itself decide what God intended the relationship to be between Adam and Eve. The activity of helping is so broad that it can be done by someone who has greater authority, someone who has equal authority, or someone who has lesser authority than the person being helped. For example, I can help my son do his homework.[24] Or I can help my neighbor to move his sofa. Or my son can help me clean the garage. Yet the fact remains that *in the situation under consideration*, the person doing the helping puts himself in a subordinate role to the person who has primary responsibility for carrying out the activity. Even if I help my son with his homework, the primary responsibility for the homework remains his and not mine. I am the helper. And even when God helps us, He still holds us primarily responsible for the activity, and He holds us accountable for what we do.

But Genesis 2 does not merely say that Eve functions as Adam's helper in one or two specific events. Rather, it says that God made Eve to provide Adam with a helper, one who *by virtue of creation* would function as Adam's helper.

> Then the LORD God said, "It is not good that the man should be alone; I will make him a helper fit for him." (v. 18)

The Hebrew text can be translated literally as, "I will make *for him* (Hebrew, *lô*) a helper fit for him." The apostle Paul understands this accurately, because in 1 Corinthians 11 he writes, "for indeed man was not created for the woman's sake, but woman for the man's sake" (v. 9, NASB). Eve's role, and the purpose that God had in mind when He created her, was that she would be "for him...a helper."

Yet in the same sentence God emphasizes that she is not to help him as one who is inferior to him. Rather, she is to be a helper "fit for him" and here the Hebrew word *kenegdô* means "a help corresponding to him," that is "equal and adequate to himself."[25] So Eve was created as a helper, but as a helper who was Adam's equal. She was created as one who differed from him, but who differed from him in ways that exactly complemented who Adam was.

7. *The conflict:* The curse brought a distortion of previous roles, not the introduction of new roles. After Adam and Eve sinned, God spoke the following words of judgment to Eve:

> To the woman he said,
> "I will surely multiply your pain in childbearing;
> in pain you shall bring forth children.
> Your desire shall be for your husband,
> and he shall rule over you." (Genesis 3:16)

The word translated "desire" is an unusual Hebrew word, *teshûqāh*. In this context and *in this specific construction* it probably implies an aggressive desire, perhaps a desire to conquer

24. I am taking this analogy from Ortlund, "Male-Female Equality," 104.
25. This is the definition given in BDB, 617.

or rule over, or else an urge or impulse the woman has to oppose her husband, an impulse to act against him. This sense is seen in the only other occurrence of *teshûqāh* in all the books of Moses and the only other occurrence of *teshûqāh* plus the preposition *'el* in the whole Bible. That occurrence is in the very next chapter of Genesis, in Genesis 4:7. God says to Cain, "Sin is crouching at the door. Its *desire* is for you, but you must rule over it."

Here the sense is very clear. God pictures sin like a wild animal waiting outside Cain's door, waiting to pounce on him and overpower him. In that sense, sin's "desire" or "instinctive urge" is "against" him.[26]

What a remarkable parallel this is to Genesis 3:16! In the Hebrew text, six words are the same words and found in the same order in both verses. It is almost as if this other usage is put here by the author so that we would know how to understand the meaning of the term in Genesis 3:16. The expression in 4:7 has the sense, "desire, urge, impulse *against*" (or perhaps "desire to conquer, desire to rule over"). And that sense fits very well in Genesis 3:16 also.[27]

---

26. The ESV provides an alternative translation *"against"* for *teshûqāh* + *'el* in Genesis 3:16 and 4:7. This seems to be the most accurate rendering. The preposition *'el* can take the meaning "against," as is clear from the next verse, Genesis 4:8, where "Cain rose up against *('el)* his brother Abel, and killed him." BDB give sense 4 for *'el* as: "Where the motion or direction implied appears from the context to be of a hostile character, *'el* = against." They cite Genesis 4:8 and several other verses.

27. The only other occurrence of *teshûqāh* in the entire Hebrew Old Testament (apart from Genesis 3:16 and 4:7) is found in Song of Solomon 7:10 (v. 11 in Hebrew), "I am my beloved's, and his *desire* is for me." In this context the word does not indicate a hostile or aggressive desire, but indicates the man's sexual desire for his wife.

I had previously argued that a positive kind of "desire to conquer" could be understood in Song of Solomon 7:10, indicating the man's desire to have a kind of influence over his beloved that is appropriate to initiating and consummating the sexual relationship, an influence such that she would receive and yield to his amorous advances. This sense would be represented by the paraphrase, "His desire is to have me yield to him."

However, I am now inclined to think that *teshûqāh* itself does not signify anything so specific as "desire to conquer" but rather something more general such as "urge, impulse." (The word takes that sense in Mishnaic Hebrew, as indicated by David Talley in footnote 30 below.) In that case, Genesis 3:16 and 4:7 have the sense "desire, urge, impulse *against*" and Song of Solomon 7:10 has the sense "desire, urge, impulse *for*." This seems to me to fit better with the context of Song of Solomon 7:10.

The difference in meaning may also be signaled by a different construction. The Genesis and Song of Solomon examples are not exactly parallel linguistically, because a different preposition follows the verb in Song of Solomon, and therefore the sense may be somewhat different. In Song of Solomon 7:11 (Hebrew), *teshûqāh* is followed by *'al*, but it is followed by *'el* in Genesis 3:16 and 4:7.

(The preposition *'al* is misprinted as *'el* in Song of Solomon 7:11 as cited in BDB, 1003. BDB apparently do this because they follow the *Biblia Hebraica Stuttgartensia* editors [1334] who in the margin suggest changing the Hebrew text to *'el*, but this is mere conjecture with no manuscript support. The LXX confirms the difference, translating with *pros* for *'el* in Genesis 3:16 and 4:7, but with *epi* for *'al* in Song of Solomon 7:11, which is what we would expect with a literal translation.)

In any case, while the sense in Song of Solomon 7:10 (11) is different, both the context and the construction are different, and this example is removed in time and authorship from Genesis 3:16 and must be given lower importance in understanding the meaning of the word in Genesis. Surely the sense cannot be "sexual desire" in Genesis 4:7, and it seems very unlikely in the context of Genesis 3:16 as well.

Kaiser, *Hard Sayings of the Old Testament* (1988), 34–35, argues that *teshûqāh* in Genesis 3:16 means "turning" and the passage means that Eve's "turning" would be away from God and toward her husband. The problem is that the text has no hint of any sense of "away from God," and Kaiser has to import that idea into the verse. In addition, the lexicons show no support for even considering Kaiser's meaning for *teshûqāh* as a possibility (see BDB and *Hebrew and Aramaic Lexicon [HALOT]*, as well as *New International Dictionary of Old Testament Theology [NIDOTTE]*, under *teshûqāh*). However, Kaiser rightly argues that the meaning "sexual desire" is contrary both to the context in Genesis 3:16 and to the rest of the Old Testament.

Some have assumed that the "desire" in Genesis 3:16 refers to sexual desire.[28] But that is highly unlikely because (1) the entire Bible views sexual desire within marriage as something positive, not as something evil or something that God imposed as a judgment; and (2) surely Adam and Eve had sexual desire for one another prior to their sin, for God had told them to "be fruitful and multiply" (Genesis 1:28), and certainly He would have given the desire that corresponded to the command. So "your desire shall be for your husband" cannot refer to sexual desire. It is much more appropriate to the context of a curse to understand this as an aggressive desire *against* her husband, one that would bring her into conflict with him.

Then God says that Adam, "shall *rule* over you" (Genesis 3:16).[29] The word here—translated "rule"—is the Hebrew term *māshal*, a common term in the Old Testament that regularly if not always refers to ruling by greater power or force or strength. It is used of human military or political rulers, such as Joseph ruling over the land of Egypt (Genesis 45:26), or the Philistines ruling over Israel (Judges 14:4; 15:11), or Solomon ruling over all the kingdoms he had conquered (1 Kings 4:21). It is also used to speak of God ruling over the sea (Psalm 89:9) or God ruling over the earth generally (Psalm 66:7). Sometimes it refers to oppressive rulers who cause the people under them to suffer (Nehemiah 9:37; Isaiah 19:4). In any case, the word does not signify one who leads among equals, but rather one who rules by virtue of power and strength, and sometimes even rules harshly and selfishly.

Once we understand these two terms, we can see much more clearly what was involved in the curse that God brought to Adam and Eve as punishment for their sins. One aspect of the curse was imposing *pain on Adam's particular area of responsibility*, raising food from the ground:

> Cursed is the ground because of you;
> in pain you shall eat of it all the days of your life;
> thorns and thistles it shall bring forth for you;
> and you shall eat the plants of the field.
> By the sweat of your face
> you shall eat bread,
> till you return to the ground. (Genesis 3:17–19)

Another aspect of the curse was to impose *pain on Eve's particular area of responsibility*, the bearing of children:

28. See, for example, Belleville, *Women Leaders and the Church,* 106. She claims the use of *teshûqāh* in Song of Solomon 7:10 (11), but she fails to discuss the different construction in that distant context, where *teshûqāh* is followed by *'al* rather than by *'el* as in Genesis 3:16 and 4:7.

29. Belleville says a "plausible" suggestion that "nicely fits the context" is "to read the pronoun *hû'* as *it* (neuter), rather than *he* (masculine). The wife's desire will be for her husband, and *it* (the desire) will rule her" (107). Belleville shows no awareness that the word for "desire" (*teshûqāh*) is not masculine or neuter but feminine, and it would ordinarily require a feminine pronoun (*hî'*) for such a meaning. The pronoun *hû'* and the verb *yimshāl* ("he shall rule") are both masculine, and there is a corresponding masculine noun ("your husband") that makes good sense in the immediate context. Belleville's suggestion simply does not match the Hebrew grammar of the verse.

"I will surely multiply your pain in childbearing;
in pain you shall bring forth children." (Genesis 3:16)

And a third aspect of the curse was to introduce *pain and conflict into the relationship* between Adam and Eve. Prior to their sin, they had lived in the Garden of Eden in perfect harmony, yet with a leadership role belonging to Adam as the head of his family. But after the Fall, God introduced conflict in that Eve would have an inward urging and impulse to oppose Adam, to resist Adam's leadership (the verb *teshûqāh +'el*). "Your impulse, desire will be *against* your husband." And Adam would respond with a rule over Eve that came from his greater strength and aggressiveness, a rule that was forceful and at times harsh (the verb *māshal*). "And he, because of his greater strength, will *rule* over you." There would be pain in tilling the ground, pain in bearing children, and pain and conflict in their relationship.

It is crucial at this point for us to realize that *we are never to try to increase or perpetuate the results of the curse*. We should never try to promote Genesis 3:16 as something good! In fact, the entire Bible after Genesis 3 is the story of God's working to overcome the effects of the curse that He in His justice imposed. Eventually God will bring in a new heaven and a new earth in which crops come forth abundantly from the ground (Isaiah 35:1–2; Amos 9:13; Romans 8:20–21) and in which there is no more pain or suffering (Revelation 21:4).

So we should *never* try to perpetuate the elements of the curse! We should not plant thorns and weeds in our garden, but rather overcome them. We should do everything we can to alleviate the pain of childbirth for women. And we should do everything we can to undo the conflict that comes about through women desiring to oppose or even control their husbands, and husbands ruling harshly over them.

Therefore Genesis 3:16 should never be used as a direct argument for male headship in marriage. But it does show us that the Fall brought about a *distortion* of previous roles, not the introduction of new roles. The distortion was that Eve would now rebel against her husband's authority and Adam would misuse that authority to rule forcefully and even harshly over Eve.[30]

8. The restoration: When we come to the New Testament, salvation in Christ reaffirms the creation order.

If the previous understanding of Genesis 3:16 is correct, as I believe it is, then what we would expect to find in the New Testament is a reversal of this curse. We would expect to find an *undoing* of the wife's hostile or aggressive impulses against her husband and the husband's response of harsh rule over his wife. In fact, that is exactly what we find. We read in the New Testament,

30. The understanding of Genesis 3:16 as a hostile desire, or even a desire to rule over, has gained significant support among Old Testament commentators. It was first suggested by Susan T. Foh, "What Is the Woman's Desire?" *WTJ*, 37 (1975): 376–83. David Talley says the word is attested in Samaritan and Mishnaic Hebrew "with the meaning urge, craving, impulse," and says of Foh, "Her contention that the desire is a contention for leadership, a negative usage, seems probable for Genesis 3:16" (*NIDOTTE*, 4:341, with reference to various commentators).

> Wives, ***submit to your husbands***, as is fitting in the Lord. Husbands, ***love your wives***, and ***do not be harsh with them***. (Colossians 3:18–19)

This command is an undoing of the impulse to oppose (Hebrew *teshûqāh +'el*) and the harsh rule (Hebrew *māshal*) that God imposed at the curse.

God reestablishes in the New Testament the beauty of the relationship between Adam and Eve that existed from the moment they were created. Eve was subject to Adam as the head of the family. Adam loved his wife and was not harsh with her in his leadership. That is the pattern that Paul commands husbands and wives to follow.[31]

9. The mystery: Marriage from the beginning of Creation was a picture of the relationship between Christ and the church.

When the apostle Paul discusses marriage and wishes to speak of the relationship between husband and wife, he does not look back to any sections of the Old Testament telling about the situation after sin came into the world. Rather, he looks all the way back to Genesis 2, prior to the Fall, and uses that creation order to speak of marriage:

> "Therefore a man shall leave his father and mother and hold fast to his wife, and the two shall become one flesh." This mystery is profound, and I am saying that *it refers to Christ and the church.* (Ephesians 5:31–32)

Now a "mystery" in Paul's writing is something that was understood only faintly if at all in the Old Testament, but which is now made clearer in the New Testament. Here Paul makes clear the meaning of the "mystery" of marriage as God created it in the Garden of Eden. Paul is saying that the "mystery" of Adam and Eve, the meaning that was not previously understood, was that marriage "refers to Christ and the church."

Although Adam and Eve did not know it, *their relationship represented the relationship between Christ and the church.* They were *created* to represent that relationship, and that is what *all marriages* are supposed to do. In that relationship, Adam represents Christ and Eve represents the church, because Paul says, "for the husband is the head of the wife *even as Christ is the head of the church*" (Ephesians 5:23).

Now the relationship between Christ and the church is not culturally variable. It is the same for all generations. And it is not reversible. There is a leadership or headship role that belongs to Christ and that the church does not have. Similarly, in marriage as God created it to be, there is a leadership role for the husband that the wife does not have. This relationship was there from the beginning of Creation, in the beautiful marriage between Adam and Eve in the Garden.

31. There was a foreshadowing of these New Testament commands in several godly marriages found in the Old Testament and the honor given to women in passages such as Ruth, Esther, and Proverbs 31. But in the unfolding of God's plan of redemption, He waited until the New Testament to give the full and explicit directions for the marriage relationship that we find in Ephesians 5, Colossians 3, and 1 Peter 3.

10. The parallel with the Trinity: The equality, differences, and unity between men and women reflect the equality, differences, and unity in the Trinity.

Though I list this here as the tenth argument why there were differences in roles between men and women from Creation, I will not explain it at this point because it constitutes "Key Issue #3" that I discuss further on.

Conclusion: Here then are ten arguments showing differences in the roles of men and women before the Fall. Some arguments are not as forceful as others, though all have some force. Some of them whisper male headship and some shout it clearly. But they form a cumulative case showing that Adam and Eve had distinct roles before the Fall, and this was God's purpose in creating them.

B. But how does it work in practice?

I would like to say something at this point about how male-female equality together with male headship work out in actual practice. The situation I know best is my own marriage, so I will speak about that briefly.

In our marriage, Margaret and I talk frequently and at length about many decisions. Sometimes these are large decisions (such as buying a house or a car), and sometimes they are small decisions (such as where we should go for a walk together). I often defer to her wishes, and she often defers to mine, because we love each other. In almost every case, each of us has some wisdom and insight that the other does not have, and we have learned to listen to each other and to place much trust in each other's judgment. Usually we reach agreement on the decision. Very seldom will I do something that she does not think to be wise. She prays, she loves God, she is sensitive to the Lord's leading and direction, and I greatly respect her and the wisdom God gives her.

But in every decision, whether large or small, and whether we have reached agreement or not, the responsibility to make the decision still rests with me. (I am speaking here of the decisions that involve the both of us, not the individual decisions we each make about our personal spheres of responsibility.) I do not agree with those who say that male headship only makes a difference once in ten years or so when a husband and wife can't reach agreement. I think that male headship makes a difference in every decision that the couple makes every day of their married life. If there is genuine male headship, there is a quiet, subtle acknowledgment that the focus of the decision-making process is the husband, not the wife. And even though there will often be much discussion, and there should be much mutual respect and consideration of each other, yet ultimately the responsibility to make the decision rests with the husband. And so in our marriage, the responsibility to make the decision rests with me.

This is not because I am wiser or a more gifted leader. It is because I am the husband, and God has given me that responsibility. In the face of cultural pressures to the contrary, I will not forsake this male headship; I will not deny this male headship; I will not be embarrassed by it.

This is God-given. It is very good. It brings peace and joy to our marriage, and both Margaret and I are thankful for it.

Yet there are dangers of distortion. Putting this biblical pattern into practice is a challenge, because we can err in one direction or the other. There are errors of passivity, and there are errors of aggressiveness. This can be seen in the following chart:

	Errors of passivity	Biblical ideal	Errors of aggressiveness
Husband	Wimp	Loving, humble headship	Tyrant
Wife	Doormat	Joyful, intelligent submission	Usurper

The biblical ideal, in the center column, is loving, humble headship on the part of the husband, following Ephesians 5:23–33. The biblical ideal on the part of the wife is joyful, intelligent submission to and support of her husband's leadership, in accordance with Ephesians 5:22–24 and 31–33.

On the right side of the chart, the errors of aggressiveness are those that had their beginning, as we saw, in Genesis 3:16. The husband can become selfish, harsh, and domineering and act like a "tyrant." This is not biblical headship, but a tragic distortion of it. A wife can also demonstrate errors of aggressiveness when she resists her husband's leadership, not supporting it but fighting against it and creating conflict every step of the way. She can become a "usurper," something that is a tragic distortion of the biblical pattern of equality in the image of God.

On the left side of the chart are the opposite errors, the errors of passivity. A husband can abdicate his leadership and neglect his responsibilities. The children are not disciplined and he sits and watches TV and does nothing. The family is not going to church regularly and he is passive and does nothing. The family keeps going further in debt and he closes his eyes to it and does nothing. Some relative or friend is verbally harassing his wife and he does nothing. This also is a tragic distortion of the biblical pattern. He has become a "wimp."

A wife can also commit errors of passivity. Rather than participating actively in family decisions, rather than contributing her wisdom and insight that is so much needed, her only response to every question is, "Yes, dear, whatever you say." She knows her husband and her children are doing wrong and she says nothing. Or her husband becomes verbally or physically abusive, and she never objects to him, never seeks church discipline or civil intervention to bring about an end to the abuse. Or she never expresses her preferences about friendships or family vacations, or her opinions about people or events. She thinks what is required of her is to be "submissive" to her husband. But this also is a tragic distortion of biblical patterns. She has become a "doormat."

Now we all have different backgrounds, personalities, and temperaments. We also have different areas of life in which sanctification is less complete. Some of us are more prone toward errors of aggressiveness, and others are more prone toward errors of passivity. We can even fall into errors of aggressiveness in our homes and errors of passivity when we visit our in-laws. Or it can be just the other way around. In order to maintain a healthy, biblical balance, we need to keep reading God's Word each day and continue to pray for God's help to obey His Word as best we can.

C. The man's responsibility to provide for and protect, and the woman's responsibility to care for the home and to nurture children

There are other differences in roles in addition to headship and submission. Two other aspects of a husband's headship in marriage are the responsibility to *provide for* and to *protect* his wife and family. A corresponding responsibility for the wife is to have primary responsibility to care for *home* and *children*. Each can help the other, but there remains a primary responsibility that is not shared equally.

These responsibilities are mentioned in both the Danvers Statement and the Southern Baptist Convention/Campus Crusade for Christ statement. I will not discuss these in detail at this point, but simply note that these additional aspects of differing roles are established in Scripture. Biblical support for the husband having the primary responsibility to provide for his family and the wife having primary responsibility to care for the household and children is found in Genesis 2:15, along with 2:18–23; 3:16–19 (Eve is assumed to have the primary responsibility for childbearing, but Adam for tilling the ground to raise food, and pain is introduced into both of their areas of responsibility); Proverbs 31:10–31, especially verses 15, 21, 27; Isaiah 4:1 (shame at the tragic undoing of the normal order); 1 Timothy 5:8 (the Greek text does not specify "any man," but in the historical context that would have been the assumed referent except for unusual situations like a household with no father); 1 Timothy 5:10; 1 Timothy 5:3–16 (widows, not widowers, are to be supported by the church); Titus 2:5.

Biblical support for the idea that the man has the primary responsibility to protect his family is found in Deuteronomy 20:7–8 (men go forth to war, not women, here and in many Old Testament passages); 24:5; Joshua 1:14; Judges 4:8–10 (Barak does not get the glory because he insisted that a woman accompany him into battle); Nehemiah 4:13–14 (the people are to fight for their brothers, homes, wives, and children, but it does not say they are to fight for their husbands!); Jeremiah 50:37 (it is the disgrace of a nation when its warriors become women); Nahum 3:13 ("Behold, your troops are women in your midst" is a taunt of derision); Matthew 2:13–14 (Joseph is told to protect Mary and baby Jesus by taking them to Egypt); Ephesians 5:25 (a husband's love should extend even to a willingness to lay down his life for his wife, something many soldiers in battle have done throughout history to protect their families and homelands); 1 Peter 3:7 (a wife is a "weaker vessel," and therefore the husband, as generally stronger, has a greater responsibility to use his strength to protect his wife).

In addition, there is the complete absence of evidence from the other side. Nowhere can we find Scripture encouraging women to be the primary means of support while their husbands care for the house and children. Nowhere can we find Scripture encouraging women to be the primary protectors of their husbands. Certainly women can help in these roles as time and circumstances allow (see Genesis 2:18–23), but they are not the ones primarily responsible for them.

Finally, there is the internal testimony from both men's and women's hearts. There is something in a man that says, "I don't want to be dependent on a woman to provide for me in the long term. I want to be the one responsible to provide for the family, the one my wife looks to and depends on for support." I have never met a man who does not feel some measure of shame at the idea of being supported by his wife in the long term.

I recognize that in many families there is a temporary reversal of roles due to involuntary unemployment or while the husband is getting further education, and in those circumstances these are entirely appropriate arrangements; yet the longer they go on, the more strain they put on a marriage. I also recognize that a husband's permanent disability, or the absence of a husband in the home, can create a necessity for the wife to be the primary provider, but families in which that happens often testify to the unusual stress it brings and that they wish it did not have to be so.

On the other hand, there is something in a woman that says, "I want my husband to provide for me, to give me the security of knowing that we will have enough to buy groceries and pay the bills. It feels right to me to look to him and depend on him for that responsibility." I have never met a woman who did not want her husband to provide that sense of security for her.[32]

Key Issue #3: The Equality and Differences Between Men and Women Reflect the Equality and Differences in the Trinity

This point is at the heart of the controversy, and it shows why much more is at stake than the meaning of one or two words or one or two verses in the Bible. Much more is at stake even than how we live in our marriages. Here we are talking about the nature of God Himself.

In 1 Corinthians 11, Paul writes,

> But I want you to understand that the *head* of every man is Christ, the *head* of a wife is her husband, and the *head* of Christ is God. (v. 3)

In this verse, "head" refers to one who is in a position of authority over the other, as this Greek word (*kephalē*) uniformly does whenever it is used in ancient literature to say that one

32. For some further discussion, see Piper, "A Vision of Biblical Complementarity," in *Recovering Biblical Manhood and Womanhood,* 31–59. See also Dorothy Patterson, "The High Calling of Wife and Mother in Biblical Perspective," 364–77, in the same volume.

person is "head of" another person or group.[33] So Paul is here referring to a relationship of authority between God the Father and God the Son, and he is making a parallel between that relationship in the Trinity and the relationship between the husband and wife in marriage. This is an important parallel because it shows that there can be equality and differences between persons at the same time. We can illustrate that in the following diagram, where the arrows indicate authority over the person to whom the arrow points:

DIAGRAM 1A

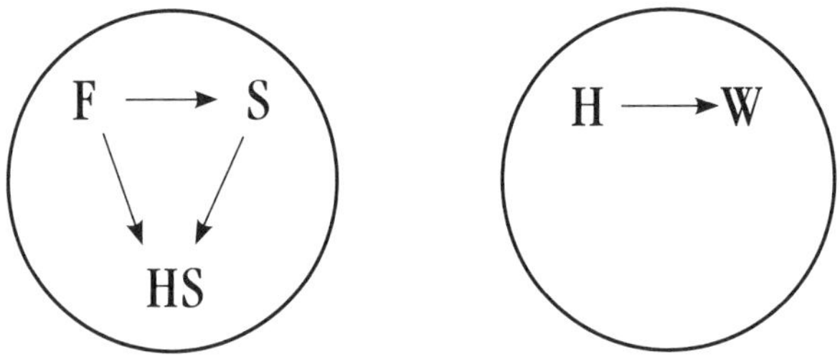

Just as the Father and Son are equal in deity and equal in all their attributes, but different in role, so husband and wife are equal in personhood and value, but they are different in the roles God has given them. Just as God the Son is eternally subject to the authority of God the Father, so God has planned that wives be subject to the authority of their husbands.

Scripture frequently speaks of the Father–Son relationship within the Trinity, a relationship in which the Father "gave" His only Son (John 3:16) and "sent" the Son into the world (John 3:17, 34; 4:34; 8:42; Galatians 4:4), a relationship in which the Father "predestined us" to be conformed to the image of His Son (Romans 8:29; cf. 1 Peter 1:2) and "chose us" in the Son "before the foundation of the world" (Ephesians 1:4). The Son is obedient to the commands of the Father (John 12:49), and says that He comes to do "the will of him who sent me" (John 4:34; 6:38).

These relationships are never reversed. Never does Scripture say that the Son sends the Father into the world, or that the Holy Spirit sends the Father or the Son into the world, or that the Father obeys the commands of the Son or of the Holy Spirit. Never does Scripture say that the Son predestined us to be conformed to the image of the Father. The role of planning, directing, sending, and commanding the Son belongs to the Father only.

And these relationships are eternal, for the Father predestined us in the Son "before the foundation of the world" (Ephesians 1:4), requiring that the Father has eternally been Father, and the Son has eternally been Son. If the Father's love is seen in that He "gave his only Son" (John 3:16), then the Father had to be Father and the Son had to be Son before He came into

33. See my extended discussion of the meaning of *kephalē* in Appendix 4, pp. 552–99.

the world. The Father did not give someone who was just another divine person in the Trinity, but He gave the one who was His only Son, one who eternally had been His Son.

It was also this way in the Creation of the world, where the Father initiated and commanded and created "through" the Son. The Son was the powerful Word of God who carried out the commands of the Father, for "all things were made through him" (John 1:3). The Son is the one "through whom" God created the world (Hebrews 1:2). All things were created by the Father working through the Son, for "there is one God, the Father, *from* whom are all things...and one Lord, Jesus Christ, *through* whom are all things" (1 Corinthians 8:6). Nowhere does Scripture reverse this and say that the Son created "through" the Father.

The Son sits at the Father's right hand (Romans 8:34; Hebrews 1:3, 13; 1 Peter 3:22); the Father does not sit at the Son's right hand. And for all eternity, the Son will be subject to the Father, for after the last enemy, death, is destroyed, "the Son himself will also be subjected to him who put all things in subjection under him, that God may be all in all" (1 Corinthians 15:28).

We see from these passages then that *the idea of headship and submission within a personal relationship* did not begin with the Council on Biblical Manhood and Womanhood in 1987. Nor did it begin with some writings of the apostle Paul in the first century. Nor did it begin with a few patriarchal men in a patriarchal society in the Old Testament. Nor did the idea of headship and submission begin with Adam and Eve's fall into sin in Genesis 3. In fact, the idea of headship and submission did not even begin with the creation of Adam and Eve in Genesis 1 and 2.

No, the idea of headship and submission existed *before Creation*. It began in the relationship between the Father and Son in the Trinity. The Father has eternally had a leadership role, an authority to initiate and direct, that the Son does not have. Similarly, the Holy Spirit is subject to both the Father and Son and plays yet a different role in Creation and in the work of salvation.

When did the idea of headship and submission begin, then? *The idea of headship and submission never began!* It has *always existed* in the eternal nature of God Himself. And in this most basic of all authority relationships, authority is not based on gifts or ability (for the Father, Son, and Holy Spirit are equal in attributes and perfections). It is just there. Authority belongs to the Father, not because He is wiser or because He is a more skillful leader, but just because He is the Father.

Authority and submission between the Father and the Son, and between Father and Son and the Holy Spirit, is a fundamental difference (or probably *the* fundamental difference) between the persons of the Trinity. They don't differ in any attributes, but only in how they relate to each other. And that relationship is one of leadership and authority on the one hand and voluntary, willing, joyful submission to that authority on the other hand.

We can learn from this relationship among the members of the Trinity that submission to a rightful authority is a noble virtue. It is a privilege. It is something good and desirable. It is the virtue that the eternal Son of God has demonstrated *forever*. It is His glory, the glory of the Son as He relates to His Father.

In modern society, we tend to think if you are a person who has authority over another, that's a good thing. If you are someone who has to submit to an authority, that's a bad thing. But that is the world's viewpoint, and it is not true. Submission to a rightful authority is a good and noble and wonderful thing, because it reflects the interpersonal relationships within God Himself.

We can say then that a relationship of authority and submission between equals, with mutual giving of honor, is the most fundamental and most glorious interpersonal relationship in the universe. Such a relationship allows there to be interpersonal differences without "better" or "worse," without "more important" and "less important."

And when we begin to dislike the very idea of authority and submission—not distortions and abuses, but *the very idea*—we are tampering with something very deep. We are beginning to dislike God Himself.

Now this truth about the Trinity creates a problem for egalitarians. They try to force people to choose between equality and authority. They say, "If you have male headship, then you can't be equal. Or if you are equal, then you can't have male headship." And our response is that you can have both: just look at the Trinity. Within the being of God, you have both equality and authority.

In reply to this, egalitarians should have said, "Okay, we agree on this much. In God you *can* have equality and differences at the same time." In fact, some egalitarians have said this very thing.[34] But some prominent egalitarians have taken a different direction, one that is very troubling. Both Gilbert Bilezikian and Stanley Grenz have now written that they think there is "mutual submission" within the Trinity. They say that the Father also submits to the Son.[35] This is their affirmation even though no passage of Scripture affirms such a relationship, and even though this has never been the orthodox teaching of the church throughout two thousand years. But so deep is their commitment to an egalitarian view of men and women within marriage, that they will modify the doctrine of the Trinity, and remake the Trinity in the image of egalitarian marriage, if it seems necessary to maintain their position.

---

34. See Craig Keener's affirmation of an eternal subordination of the Son to the Father in "Is Subordination Within the Trinity Really Heresy? A Study of John 5:18 in Context," *TrinJ* 20 NS (1999): 39–51.
35. For a fuller discussion of egalitarian tampering with the doctrine of the Trinity, see Ware, "Tampering with the Trinity: Does the Son Submit to His Father?" in Grudem, *Biblical Foundations for Manhood and Womanhood* (2002), 233–53. The primary statements by Bilezikian and Grenz are found in Bilezikian, "Hermeneutical Bungee-Jumping: Subordination in the Godhead," *Journal of the Evangelical Theological Society*, 40/1 (March 1997): 57–68; and Grenz, "Theological Foundations for Male-Female Relationships," *Journal of the Evangelical Theological Society*, 41/4 (December 1998): 615–30.

    A survey of historical evidence showing affirmation of the eternal subordination of the Son to the authority of the Father is found in Stephen D. Kovach and Peter R. Schemm Jr., "A Defense of the Doctrine of the Eternal Subordination of the Son," *Journal of the Evangelical Theological Society*, 42/3 (September 1999): 461–76. See also Grudem, *Systematic Theology*, 248–52.

    See also my discussion of egalitarian claim 10.3, "mutual submission in the Trinity," in chapter 10 (429–33; see also 405–29).

KEY ISSUE #4: THE EQUALITY AND DIFFERENCES BETWEEN MEN AND WOMEN ARE VERY GOOD

In today's hostile culture, we might be embarrassed to talk about God-given differences between men and women. We don't want to be attacked or laughed at by others. Perhaps we fear that someone will take offense if we talk clearly about God-given differences between men and women. (However, there is more acknowledgment of male/female differences in the general culture today than there was a few years ago. A number of secular books, such as John Gray's *Men Are from Mars, Women Are from Venus*, have once again made it acceptable to talk about *at least some* differences between men and women, though the idea of the husband's authority and the wife's submission within marriage still seems to be taboo in the general culture.)[36]

The fundamental statement of the excellence of the way God made us as men and women is found in Genesis 1:31: "And God saw everything that he had made, and behold, *it was very good*." Just four verses after the Bible tells us that God made us "male and female," it tells us that God looked at everything He had made, *including Adam and Eve created in His image*, and His evaluation of what He saw was that it was "very good." The way God created us as men and women, equal in His image and different in roles, was very good. And if it is very good, then we can make some other observations about the created order.

This created order is *fair*. Our egalitarian friends argue that it's "not fair" for men to have a leadership role in the family simply because they are men. But if this difference is based on God's assignment of roles from the beginning, then it is fair. Does the Son say to the Father, "It's not fair for You to be in charge simply because You are the Father"? Does the Son say to the Father, "You've been in charge for fifteen billion years, and now it's My turn for the next fifteen billion"? No! Absolutely not! Rather, He fulfilled the psalm that said, "I desire to do your will, O my God; your law is within my heart" (Psalm 40:8; compare Hebrews 10:7). And of His relationship with the Father, He said, "I always do the things that are pleasing to him" (John 8:29). He said, "I have come down from heaven, not to do my own will but the will of him who sent me" (John 6:38). The order of relationships within the Trinity is fair. And the order of relationships established by God for marriage is fair.

This created order is also *best for us*, because it comes from an all-wise Creator. This created order truly honors men and women. It does not lead to abuse, but guards against it, because both men and women are equal in value before God. It does not suppress women's gifts and wisdom and insight, as people sometimes have done in the past, but it encourages them.

---

36. See Gray, *Men Are from Mars, Women Are from Venus* (1992), and several other books written by Gray on a similar theme; see also Tannen, *You Just Don't Understand* (1990). I am not, of course, endorsing everything in these books.

This created order is also a *mystery*. I have been married to one very wonderful woman for thirty-four years. I cannot understand her. Just when I think I understand her, she surprises me again. Marriage is a challenge! And it's also very fun. But in our relationships with each other as men and women, there will always be elements of surprise, always elements of mystery, always aspects of difference that we cannot fully understand but simply enjoy.

This created order is also *beautiful*. God took delight in it and thought it was "very good." When it is functioning in the way that God intended, we will enjoy this relationship and delight in it, because there is a Godlike quality about it. And though some elements of society have been pushing in the opposite direction for several decades, there is much evidence from "natural law"—from our observation of the world and our inner sense of right and wrong—that different roles within marriage are *right*. This is what we meant when we said in the Danvers Statement, "Distinctions in masculine and feminine roles are ordained by God and should find an echo in every human heart" (Affirmation 2). God's created order for marriage is beautiful because it is God's way to bring amazing *unity* to people who are as *different* as men and women are.

The beauty of God's created order for marriage finds expression in our sexuality within marriage. "Therefore a man shall leave his father and his mother and hold fast to his wife, and they shall become one flesh" (Genesis 2:24). From the beginning, God designed our sexuality so that it reflects unity and differences and beauty all at the same time. As husband and wife, we are most attracted to the parts of each other that are the most different. Our deepest unity—including a physical and emotional and spiritual unity—comes at the point where we are most different. In our physical union as God intended it, there is no dehumanization of women and no emasculation of men, but there is equality and honor for both the husband and the wife. And there is our deepest human joy, and our deepest expression of unity.

This means that sexuality within marriage is precious to God. It is designed by Him to show *equality* and *difference* and *unity* all at the same time. It is a great mystery how this can be so, and it is also a great blessing and joy. Moreover, God has ordained that from that sexual union comes the most amazing, the most astounding event—the creation of a new human being in the image of God!

Within this most intimate of human relationships, we show equality and difference and unity and much Godlikeness all at once. Glory be to God!

KEY ISSUE #5: THIS IS A MATTER OF OBEDIENCE TO THE BIBLE

Why did the Southern Baptist Convention in June 1998, for the first time since 1963, add to their statement of faith that men and women are equal in God's image but different in their roles in marriage?[37] Why, shortly after that, did over one hundred Christian leaders sign a full-page ad

37. This is the text of the June 1998 addition to the Southern Baptist Convention's statement, "The Baptist Faith and Message": XVIII. The Family

God has ordained the family as the foundational institution of human society. It is composed of persons related to one another by marriage, blood, or adoption.

in *USA Today* saying, "Southern Baptists, you are right. We stand with you."[38] Why did Campus Crusade for Christ, after forty years of no change in their doctrinal policies, endorse a similar statement as the policy of their organization in 1999?[39]

I think these things indicate that many Christian leaders are beginning to say, "The egalitarian view just *cannot* be proven from Scripture."

Thirty years ago there were many questions about differences in interpretation, and both the egalitarian position and the complementarian position were found within evangelical groups. Over the last thirty years, we have seen extensive discussion and argument, and we have seen hundreds of articles and books published.

But now people are beginning to look at the situation differently. The egalitarian viewpoint, which was novel within evangelicalism twenty-five years ago, has had great opportunity to defend itself. The arguments are all out on the table, and the detailed word studies, the technical questions of grammar, and the extensive studies of background literature and history have been carried out. There are dozens and dozens of egalitarian books denying differences in male and female roles within marriage, but they now seem to be repeating the same arguments over and over. The egalitarians have not had any new breakthroughs, any new discoveries that lend substantial strength to their position.

So now many people in leadership are deciding that the egalitarian view is just not what the Bible teaches. And they are deciding that it will not be taught in their churches. Then they add to their statements of faith, and the controversy is essentially over, for that group at least, for the next ten or twenty years.

Marriage is the uniting of one man and one woman in covenant commitment for a lifetime. It is God's unique gift to reveal the union between Christ and His church and to provide for the man and the woman in marriage the framework for intimate companionship, the channel of sexual expression according to biblical standards, and the means for procreation of the human race.

The husband and wife are of equal worth before God since both are created in God's image. The marriage relationship models the way God relates to His people. A husband is to love his wife as Christ loved the church. He has the God-given responsibility to provide for, to protect, and to lead his family. A wife is to submit herself graciously to the servant leadership of her husband even as the church willingly submits to the headship of Christ. She, being in the image of God as is her husband and thus equal to him, has the God-given responsibility to respect her husband and to serve as his helper in managing the household and nurturing the next generation.

Children, from the moment of conception, are a blessing and heritage from the Lord. Parents are to demonstrate to their children God's pattern for marriage. Parents are to teach their children spiritual and moral values and to lead them, through consistent lifestyle example and loving discipline, to make choices based on biblical truth. Children are to honor and obey their parents.

Genesis 1:26–28; 2:15–25; 3:1–20; Exodus 20:12; Deuteronomy 6:4–9; Joshua 24:15; 1 Samuel 1:26–28; Psalms 51:5; 78:1–8; 127–128; 139:13–16; Proverbs 1:8; 5:15–20; 6:20–22; 12:4; 13:24; 14:1; 17:6; 18:22; 22:6, 15; 23:13–14; 24:3; 29:15, 17; 31:10–31; Ecclesiastes 4:9–12; 9:9; Malachi 2:14–16; Matthew 5:31–32; 18:2–5; 19:3–9; Mark 10:6–12; Romans 1:18–32; 1 Corinthians 7:1–16; Ephesians 5:21–33; 6:1–4; Colossians 3:18–21; 1 Timothy 5:8, 14; 2 Timothy 1:3–5; Titus 2:3–5; Hebrews 13:4; 1 Peter 3:1–7.

In June 2000, the SBC added the following sentence to Article VI, "The Church": "While both men and women are gifted for service in the church, the office of pastor is limited to men as qualified by Scripture."

38. *USA Today*, August 26, 1998.

39. See above, 28–29, for a discussion of the Campus Crusade policy statement.

James Dobson saw the wisdom of this. After Campus Crusade announced its policy in June 1999, in affirming and adding to the Southern Baptist statement, Dr. Dobson said on the front page of his September 1999 newsletter, "We applaud our friends at Campus Crusade for taking this courageous stance." Then he quoted the statement in full and added,

> It is our prayer that additional denominations and parachurch organizations will join with SBC in adopting this statement on marriage and the family. Now is the time for Christian people to identify themselves unreservedly with the truths of the Bible, whether popular or not.[40]

Our egalitarian friends were greatly troubled by Dr. Dobson's statement. In the Spring 2000 issue of their newsletter, *Mutuality*, Kim Pettit objected that "endorsement of the SBC statement by an increasing number of Christian organizations means dissenters are excluded as this becomes a confessional issue."[41]

I do not think that the SBC statement or others like it will mean that people who hold another view will be excluded from fellowship in the church. But I do think that people who hold an egalitarian view will be excluded from many teaching and governing positions. Because I think that the egalitarian view is both harmful and contrary to Scripture, I think this is an appropriate result, and I think it is the one that was intended by those who added this statement to the "Baptist Faith and Message" in 1998.

People in the middle of turning points in history do not always realize it. I believe that today we are right in the middle of a turning point in the history of the Church. Christian organizations right now are deciding these issues. They are making commitments and establishing those commitments in their policies. Some organizations are affirming biblical principles, as the Southern Baptists did. Others are establishing egalitarian principles as part of their policies, as Willow Creek Community Church has done.[42] There is a sifting, a sorting, a dividing going on within the evangelical world, and I believe that institutions that adopt an egalitarian position will drift further and further from faithfulness to the Bible on other issues as well.

What is "the way forward" for biblical manhood and womanhood? I believe the way forward is to add a clear statement to the governing document of your church, your denomination, or your parachurch organization.

Why should we do this? First, because it affects so much of life. As Christians, we can differ over the tribulation or the millennium and still live largely the same way. But differences over this issue affect people's lives and result in "increasingly destructive consequences in our families, our churches, and the culture at large," to use the words of the Danvers Statement (Affirmation 10). Where biblical patterns are not followed, husbands and wives have no clear

40. *Family News from Dr. James Dobson*, September 1999, 1–2.
41. Kim Pettit, "Why I Disagree with Dobson and the SBC," *Mutuality* (Spring 2000), 17.
42. See Grudem, "Willow Creek Enforces Egalitarianism," in *CBMW News* 1, 3–6 (available at www.cbmw.org).

guidance on how to act within their marriages, and there is increasing stress that brings harmful and even destructive consequences to families.

Second, egalitarians have run out of new exegetical arguments, and they simply are not winning the arguments on the basis of the biblical text (for details see chapters 3–12). Their books increasingly deal not with detailed analyses of biblical texts, but with broad generalizations about Scripture, then with arguments from experience or arguments from philosophical concepts like fairness, or from the supposed negative results of a complementarian position (such as spousal abuse, which we strongly oppose and condemn as well).[43] But it seems to me, and increasingly it seems to many others, that egalitarians have simply lost the key arguments on the meaning of the biblical text, and they have no more arguments to make.

A third reason why I think organizations should add a statement on biblical manhood and womanhood to their governing documents is that I believe this is a watershed issue. Many years ago Francis Schaeffer called the doctrine of biblical inerrancy a watershed issue because the position that people took on inerrancy determined where their teachings would lead in succeeding years. Schaeffer said that the first people who make a mistake on a watershed issue take only a very small step, and in all other areas of life they are godly and orthodox. This was the case with a number of scholars who denied inerrancy in principle but did not change their beliefs on much of anything else. However, the next generation of leaders and scholars who come after them take the error much further. They see the implications of the change, and they are consistent in working it out in other matters of doctrine and practice, and they fall into greater and greater deviation from the teachings of the Bible.

I believe it is the same with this issue today. This controversy is the key to deeper issues and deeper commitments that touch every part of life (a number of these will be discussed later in this book). Though many of our egalitarian friends today do not adopt the other implications of their view, their followers will, and the next generation of leaders will go much further in the denial of the truths of Scripture or in their failure to be subject to Scripture in other parts of life.

I said earlier that I believe one reason God allowed this controversy into the church at this time is so that we could correct wrongful male chauvinism in our churches and families. I think another reason God has allowed this controversy into the church is to test our hearts. Will we be faithful to Him and obey His Word or not? God often allows false teaching to spread among His people as a means of testing us, to see what our response will be.

In the Old Testament, God allowed false prophets to come among the people, but He had told them, "you shall not listen to the words of that prophet or that dreamer of dreams. *For the*

43. I still regret, and still cannot understand, why the board of directors of CBE declined to issue a joint statement with the CBMW on the issue of abuse. CBMW adopted the statement in November 1994 and has continued to distribute it widely through its literature and on its website. The letter from CBE in which they declined to issue a statement jointly with us can be found in *CBMW News* 1:1 (August 1995), 3, and is available at www.cbmw.org.

	THE EFFEMINATE LEFT	
	No Differences: "all is one"	*Egalitarianism:* removing or denying many differences between men and women
God	God equals creation, God as mother, Sophia worship, New Age worship	mutual submission in the Trinity 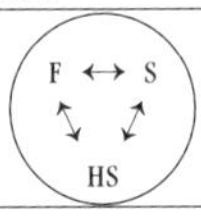
Man, Woman	emasculation of men, defeminization of women	no gender-based role differences in marriage
Marriage	same-sex marriages approved	mutual submission, often husband as wimp and wife as usurper
Children	children murdered, abortion supported by women who reject feminine roles	children raised with too little discipline, little respect for authority
Family Responsibilities	no family—just "society"	all responsibilities shared equally between husband and wife or divided according to gifts and interests
Sex	homosexuality, lesbianism;	men become unmasculine, unattractive to women; women become unfeminine, unattractive to men;
	violent opposition to God's plan for sex as only between a man and woman	ambivalence toward sex
Natural Desires	temptation: unlimited same-sex activity	moving "contrary to nature" (Romans 1:26) ←
Religion	feminized religion in churches; pantheism	no governing or teaching roles in church reserved for men
Authority	hatred of authority	suspicion of authority
Sports	no competition: "everybody wins"	anticompetition
Crime	no respect for authority, rampant crime, especially by frustrated, angry men	criminal seen as victim to be helped, not punished; punishment long delayed
Property	no private property: all possessions equalized	no one is allowed to be very rich; large-scale dependence on welfare state and government
Education	all-male schools prohibited by law; prohibitions against educating boys and girls separately	systematic pressure to make boys and girls do equally well in all subjects

Please note: This chart contains many generalizations and is only meant to show broad tendencies. Most people and many religious
from adopting all aspects of non-biblical views. Therefore this chart certainly does not imply that every person or religious

	THE COMPLEMENTARIAN MIDDLE		THE VIOLENT RIGHT
	Equality and Differences and Unity: emphasizing both equality and differences between men and women	*Male Dominance:* overemphasizing the differences between men and women	*No Equality:* "might makes right"
	God as Trinity Father, Son, Holy Spirit are of equal value with different roles 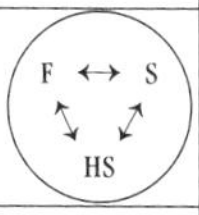	Arianism: Son and Holy Spirit are not fully God	God as one person, not a Trinity, not three persons; harsh, unloving warrior-god (Allah)
	husband and wife have equal value but different roles 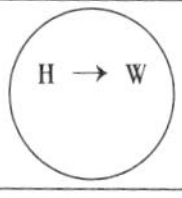	men are better than women; excessive competitiveness to show women are inferior	men as brutes; women as objects; dehumanization of women
	husband: loving, humble headship; wife: intelligent, joyful submission to husband	husband as harsh, selfish dictator; wife as doormat	polygamy, harems, female infanticide
	children loved, cared for, valued, raised with discipline and love	children raised with harsh discipline, little love or compassion	children murdered, abortion supported by men who reject masculine responsibility for family
	husband: responsible to lead, provide for, protect; wife: responsible to help husband by managing household and nurturing children	wives forbidden to have a job outside the home or to vote or own property	men have all power; women and children are to serve them
	monogamous, equally fulfilling intercourse as the deepest expression of a great "mystery": equality and differences and unity!	pornography, lust, adultery	violence against women, rape
	positive delight in sex as a gift from God	excessive attention to sex	violent opposition to God's plan for sex as only within marriage
	natural desires fulfilled; men and women have deep sense of acting as God made them to act	moving in exaggeration and distortion of nature →	temptation: unlimited, unequal sexual activity
	some governing and teaching roles in church restricted to men	all ministry done by men; women's gifts squelched; Crusades	militant forms of Islam; religion advanced by violence
	authority exercised within boundaries	overuse of authority	abuse of authority
	competition with fairness and rules: winners honored, losers respected	excessive competition: losers humiliated	violent harm to opponents; gladiators fight to the death
	punishment is speedy, fair; aims at justice plus restoration of criminal	repressive government, little freedom, debtor's prisons	excessive punishment, dehumanization of criminals (cut off hand of thief); little crime, but no freedom
	laws protect private property and care for poor; more work and skill earns more wealth; equal opportunity for all	women cannot own property	slavery; dehumanization of the poor and weak; all property in the hands of few
	boys and girls both educated, but different preferences, abilities, and sense of calling respected	boys given preferential treatment in schools	girls not allowed to be educated

systems hold mixed views and have inconsistencies in thinking. Moreover, conscience, social pressure, and the Bible often restrain people
system within each column holds to everything in that column. This chart may be duplicated for teaching purposes without charge.

LORD your God is testing you, to know whether you love the LORD your God with all your heart and with all your soul" (Deuteronomy 13:3). Now I am certainly not saying that egalitarians are the same as those who advocated the serving of other gods in the Old Testament, for egalitarians within evangelicalism do worship Jesus Christ as their Savior. But I am saying that there is a principle of God's actions in history that we can see in Deuteronomy 13:3, and that is that God often allows various kinds of false teaching to exist in the church, probably in every generation, and by these false teachings God tests His people to see whether they will be faithful to His Word or not. In this generation, one of those tests is whether we will be faithful to God in the teaching of His Word on matters of manhood and womanhood.

A similar idea is found in 1 Corinthians 11:19: "For there must be factions among you in order that those who are genuine among you may be recognized." When divisions and controversies arise in the church, people who make the right choices about the division eventually become "recognized" or are made "evident" (NASB). Others make wrong choices and thereby disqualify themselves from leadership. Charles Hodge wrote about this verse, "By the prevalence of disorders and other evils in the church, God puts his people to the test. They are tried as gold in the furnace, and their genuineness is made to appear."[44]

Today, by the controversy over manhood and womanhood, God is testing all of His people, all of His churches. The egalitarian alternative would be so easy to adopt in today's culture, and it can appear on the surface to make so little difference. But will we remain faithful to the Word of God?

KEY ISSUE #6: THIS CONTROVERSY IS MUCH BIGGER THAN WE REALIZE, BECAUSE IT TOUCHES ALL OF LIFE

The question of biblical manhood and womanhood is the focal point in a tremendous battle of worldviews. In that battle, biblical Christianity is being attacked simultaneously by two opponents representing the dominant ideas in the cultures of the world. The opponent on the "Effeminate Left" may be called "No Differences," and its slogan is, "all is one." The opponent on the "Violent Right," may be called "No Equality," and its slogan is, "might makes right."[45]

The chart on pages 54–55 shows how a biblical view of men and women, the "Complementarian Middle," stands in contrast to these opponents. For example, a biblical view of God includes equality and differences and unity. God is a Trinity where the Father, Son, and Holy Spirit have equal value and different roles, and they have absolute unity in the one being of God.

---

44. Hodge, *An Exposition of 1 and 2 Corinthians* (1972), 125.
45. The groundbreaking ideas of Peter Jones and Dan Heimbach, fellow members of the CBMW, provided the fundamental concepts that led to this material. I am grateful for their contributions, though the specific applications that follow are my own. See the chapters by Jones and Heimbach in Grudem, *Biblical Foundations for Manhood and Womanhood.*

The Effeminate Left Column: On the far left, the differences in the persons of God are abolished and the differences between God and the Creation are abolished because "all is one." God then is viewed as equal to the Creation, and people will worship the earth or parts of the earth as God (or as our "Mother"). Much New Age worship takes this form, as does much eastern religion, where the goal is to seek unity with the universe.

When we follow the theme that there are "No Differences" into the area of manhood and womanhood, the attempt to obliterate differences leads to the emasculation of men and the defeminization of women. Men become more like women and women become more like men, because "all is one."

Within marriage, if there are no differences, then same sex "marriages" are approved. Women who reject feminine roles will support abortion. Since there are no distinct roles for a child's father and mother, there's no longer any need to have children raised by the family, but rather "society" can take care of raising children. Within the realm of sexuality, homosexuality and lesbianism are approved. The chart details how the idea that there should be "No Differences" but that "all is one" will also work out in feminized religion within churches, in hatred of authority (for if someone has more authority, then all is not one), in no competition in sports (for if we have "winners" and "losers" then all is not one), in no respect for authority in the civil realm (with an increase in rampant crime), with attempts to abolish private property and equalize possessions (for no one can be different, but all should be one), and with attempts to prohibit all-male schools or prohibit educating boys and girls separately. These are the tendencies that follow once we adopt the conviction that "all is one." From this perspective, there are no differences between persons in the being of God, and there should be no differences between men and women either.

The Egalitarianism Column: The egalitarian viewpoint within evangelicalism tends toward this direction in many areas. It tends to remove or deny many differences between men and women. Egalitarians have begun to deny eternal personal distinctions among the Father, Son, and Holy Spirit, and to argue rather for "mutual submission" within the Trinity. They deny that there are any gender-based role differences in marriage.[46] Within marriage, an egalitarian view tends toward abolishing differences and advocates "mutual submission," which often results in the husband acting as a wimp and the wife as a usurper. Because this perspective tends in the direction of a deep-seated opposition to most authority, the drive toward "sameness" often results in children

46. There was an amusing, but very revealing, suggestion for a new title to the book *Men Are from Mars, Women Are from Venus* in the CBE publication *Mutuality*: In an imaginary conversation in a bookstore, the writer suggested that a better title for a book about men and women would be, *Men Are from Mars, Women Are from Venus, But Some Men Are from Venus and Some Women Are from Mars, and All of God's Children Have Both Mars and Venus Qualities Within Them So Why Not Just Say that Men and Women Are from the Earth, and Let's Get About the Business of Developing the Unique God-given Mars/Venus Qualities That God Has Given All of Us for the Sake of the Kingdom* (Jim Banks, *Mutuality* [May 1998], 3). What was so revealing about this humorous suggestion was the way it showed that egalitarians seem compelled to oppose any differences between men and women other than those that are purely physical.

being raised with too little discipline and too little respect for authority. Within the family, there will be a tendency toward sharing all responsibilities equally between husband and wife, or toward dividing responsibilities according to gifts and interests, not according to roles as specified by Scripture. Within the realm of human sexuality, tendencies to deny the differences between men and women will often result in men becoming unmasculine and unattractive to women and women becoming unfeminine and unattractive to men. There will often be ambivalence toward sex.

The chart shows how within the realm of religion the egalitarian view supports the idea that no governing or teaching roles within the church should be reserved for men (for there should be "No Differences"). Within sports, this viewpoint that attempts to deny differences would tend to oppose competition and think of it as evil rather than good. With respect to crime, the criminal is seen as a victim to be helped and not punished, and punishment is long delayed. As far as private property is concerned, because there are tendencies to abolish differences, no one would be allowed to be very rich, and there would be large-scale dependence on the welfare state and on government. Within education, there would be systematic pressure to make boys and girls participate equally and do equally well in all subjects and all activities, attempting to forcibly eradicate any patterns of natural preferences and aptitudes for some kinds of activities by boys, and some kinds by girls. All of this tends to deny differences between men and women.

The Violent Right Column: But there are opposite errors as well. The opponent on the far right side of the chart is "No Equality," and the dominant idea from this perspective is that there is no equality between persons who are different. Rather, the stronger person is more valuable, and the weaker person is devalued, for "might makes right." In this view, God is not viewed as a Trinity but as one person who is all-powerful. Often God is viewed as a harsh, unloving warrior God, as in a common Islamic view of Allah. Since "might makes right" and the weaker person is considered inferior, the relationships between men and women are distorted as well. Men begin to act as brutes and they treat women as objects. This view results in a dehumanizing of women. Whereas the "No Differences" error on the far left results in the destruction of men, this "No Equality" error on the far right results in the destruction of women.

Within marriage, the idea that there is no equality in value between men and women will lead to polygamy and harems in which one man will have many wives. There is no concern to value women equally, for "might makes right," and men are stronger. This view will also lead to female infanticide in which girls are put to death because people prefer to have boys. With regard to children, in this "No Equality" viewpoint, men who reject masculine responsibility to care for their families will support abortion and encourage the murder of unborn children. Within the family, if there is no equality in value before God, men will have all the power, and women and children will simply exist to serve them. Within the realm of sexuality, the "No Equality" error results in violence against women and rape.

The chart explains how this viewpoint also works out in religion, where religion is advanced by violence and force (as in militant forms of Islam). The view that there need be no equality of value between persons results in the destruction of people who have less power or less authority, so authority is abused as a result. Within sports, this viewpoint leads to violent harm to opponents, and even to gladiators fighting to the death. (The increasing popularity of violent and harmful interpersonal combat programs on television is a manifestation of this tendency.) As for criminal justice, this viewpoint will lead to excessive punishment and dehumanization of criminals (such as cutting off the hand of a thief, or putting people to death for expressing different religious beliefs). There will often be little outward crime in the society, but there will be little freedom for people as well. As far as private property is concerned, there will be slavery and dehumanization of the poor and weak, while all property is held in the hands of a powerful few. In education, the "No Equality" viewpoint would result in girls not being allowed to obtain an education.

The Male Dominance Column: Whenever a "Male Dominance" view is expressed within the church or society, there are disturbing tendencies leading in the direction of "No Equality," and advocating that "might makes right." This viewpoint overemphasizes the differences between men and women and does not treat women as having equal value to men, nor does it treat those under authority as having equal value to those who have authority. With respect to a view of God, this view, that might be called the "domineering right," would be parallel to Arianism (the view that the Son and Holy Spirit are not fully God in the sense that the Father is God, but are lesser beings that were created at one time). In relationships between men and women, this viewpoint would have an attitude that men are better than women and it would result in excessive competitiveness in which a man feels he always has to win in any sport or any argument, in order to show that women are inferior.

Within marriage, this "Male Dominance" error would result in a husband being harsh and selfish and acting as a dictator or a tyrant, and the wife acting as a doormat.

Because there is too great an emphasis on authority, this viewpoint would tend toward a system where children are raised with harsh discipline but with little love or compassion. As far as family responsibilities, wives would be forbidden to have jobs outside the home, or to vote, or to own property, for there is no thought of treating them as equal.

Within the realm of sexuality, a male dominance view would result in pornography and adultery and hearts filled with lust. There would be too much attention given to sex, with men focusing excessively on their own sexual desires. People may wonder why involvement with pornography often leads to violence against women, but this chart makes the connection clear: Pornography encourages men to look at women as objects for sexual gratification, not as persons equal in God's sight; violence against women just takes that idea one step further as men begin to treat women as objects unworthy of dignity and respect.

The chart goes on to point out how "Male Dominance," the view that overemphasizes differences between men and women, would work out in a religious system where all ministry is done by men, and women's gifts are suppressed and squelched. This view would also lead to things like the Crusades, the mistaken military expeditions in the eleventh, twelfth, and thirteenth centuries to regain control of the Holy Land from the Muslims by force. Within sports, there would be excessive competition, and losers would be humiliated. Within crime, there would be a repressive government with little freedom, and things like debtors' prisons would dehumanize the poor. Within such a viewpoint, women would not be permitted to own property, and boys would be given preferential treatment in schools.

The Complementarian Middle: In contrast to these errors in both directions, the biblical picture is one that emphasizes "Equality and Differences and Unity" at the same time. In parallel to the equality and differences among the members of the Trinity, within a complementarian view, men and women are equal in value but have different roles. Within marriage, a husband manifests loving, humble headship, and a wife manifests intelligent, joyful submission to her husband's leadership. Children are cared for and valued, and raised with both discipline and love. Children respect the authority of their parents, but their parents respect the children as having equal value because they are persons created in the image of God. Within the family, the husband is primarily responsible to lead, provide for, and protect his family, and the wife is primarily responsible to help her husband by managing the household and nurturing the children. But both husband and wife often willingly help the other person with his or her area of primary responsibility.

In the realm of sexuality, a complementarian view yields monogamous, lifelong marriage, and equally fulfilling experiences of sex as the deepest expression of a great "mystery" created by God: We are equal, and we are different, and we are one! There is a delight in God's plan for sexual expression, but it is restrained by the bonds of lifelong marriage and lifelong faithfulness to one's marriage partner. Men and women will then have a deep sense of acting in the way that God created them to act in all these areas.

The lower rows of the chart explain how a complementarian viewpoint works out in religion, where some governing and teaching roles in the church are restricted to men, but women's gifts are also honored and used fully in the ministries of the church. In all areas of life, authority is exercised within boundaries so that the person under authority is treated with respect and dignity, and treated as someone who shares equally in the image of God. Within sports, there is an appreciation for competition with fairness and rules, and winners are honored while losers are respected. Equality. Differences. Unity.

As far as crime is concerned, punishment will be speedy and fair, and will aim at the satisfaction of justice as well as the restoration of the criminal. As far as private property, laws will protect private property but will also reflect care for the poor. People will be rewarded according to their work and skill, and there will be a desire to have equal opportunity for all in the economic realm. Within education, boys and girls will both be educated, but the different preferences and abilities and senses of calling that boys and girls may have should be respected and no quotas will be imposed to force an artificial equality in number of participants in every activity where that would not have resulted from allowing boys and girls to choose activities freely of their own accord. Equality. Differences. Unity.

I realize, of course, that any chart like this has generalizations. People who hold one viewpoint within a particular column on the chart may not hold all the viewpoints represented within that column. Nevertheless, the chart has significant value in showing that we continually face two opposing challenges in trying to uphold a biblical viewpoint of manhood and womanhood. People on the domineering right think of us as weak and yielding too much to the demands of feminism. People on the egalitarian left see us as harsh and overemphasizing the differences between men and women. We must steadfastly and patiently hold to the middle, with the help of God.

Now I think it is plain why I say that this controversy is much bigger than we realize. The struggle to uphold equality *and* differences *and* unity between men and women has implications for all areas of life.

Moreover, there are strong spiritual forces invisibly warring against us. I am not now focusing on the egalitarian left or the domineering right, but on the far left column and the far right column, the effeminate left and the violent right. We cannot look at those two columns for long without realizing that behind the attempt to abolish all differences and make everything "one," and behind the attempt to destroy those who are weaker and make the stronger always "right," there is a deep spiritual evil. At both extremes we see the hand of the enemy seeking to destroy God's idea of sex, of marriage, and of manhood and womanhood. We see the hand of the enemy seeking to destroy everything that glorifies God and especially seeking to destroy the beauty of our sexual differences that wonderfully reflect God's glory. We see the hand of the enemy who hates everything that God created as good, and hates everything that brings glory to God Himself.

So in the end, this controversy is really about God and how His character is reflected in the beauty and excellence of manhood and womanhood as He created it. Will we glorify God through manhood and womanhood lived according to His Word? Or will we deny His Word and give in to the pressures of modern culture? That is the choice we have to make.

CHAPTER TWO

A Biblical Vision of Manhood and Womanhood in the Church

In the previous chapter, I discussed a biblical vision of manhood and womanhood as they were created by God from the beginning and as they should function in marriage, in obedience to God's Word today. But how will this picture of manhood and womanhood work itself out in the life of the church? What does the Bible teach about the roles of men and women in the church, and how should this teaching be applied in the practical details of church life?

This chapter will discuss the many ways churches can encourage women's ministries, while retaining male leadership in certain roles. The remainder of the book will interact with challenges and objections that egalitarians have brought against the views expressed in these first two chapters.

2.1: EQUALITY IN VALUE AND DIGNITY

We must reaffirm that when God created us in His image, the Bible says, "*male and female* he created them" (Genesis 1:27). *Both* men and women are in God's image, and we share that status equally. We are equally valuable to God and equally important to God's work in the world and in the church.

In the New Testament, the Holy Spirit is poured out in a new kind of fullness on both men and women. On the day of Pentecost, Peter says that the prophecy of Joel is fulfilled,

> "And in the last days it shall be, God declares,
> that I will pour out my Spirit on all flesh,
> and *your sons and your daughters* shall prophesy,
> and your young men shall see visions,
> and your old men shall dream dreams;
> even on my male servants and female servants
> in those days I will pour out my Spirit, and they shall prophesy." (Acts 2:17–18)

From Pentecost onward, this New Covenant work of the Holy Spirit would involve giving spiritual gifts to both men *and women*, and to sons *and daughters*. All will have spiritual gifts for various kinds of ministries.

When Paul discusses the work of the Holy Spirit in giving spiritual gifts, he says, "*To each* is given the manifestation of the Spirit for the common good" (1 Corinthians 12:7). He repeats this idea a few verses later, after listing several kinds of spiritual gifts: "All these are empowered by one and the same Spirit, who apportions to *each one* individually as he wills" (v. 11).

The practical implication of this is that Paul expects *every believer* will have at least one spiritual gift to be used for the benefit of others in the church. Therefore women as well as men will have such gifts.

Peter has a similar emphasis when he says, "As *each* has received a gift, use it to serve one another, as good stewards of God's varied grace" (1 Peter 4:10).

A very visible testimony to the equality of men and women in their importance to God is seen in baptism. We read in Acts: "But when they believed Philip as he preached good news about the kingdom of God and the name of Jesus Christ, they were baptized, *both men and women"* (8:12).

In the Old Covenant, the physical, outward sign of membership among God's people was circumcision. But circumcision by its very nature was received only by men. Now in the New Covenant, the physical, outward sign of becoming a member of God's people is baptism. And baptism is administered to both men and women. Therefore every time we witness a baptism today, it should be a reminder that both men and women are equally valuable to God, and equally valuable as members of His people.

Yet another reminder of our equal value before God is Paul's affirmation of our unity in the body of Christ, rather than being divided into groups who are "more important" and "less important," or who have higher or lower status. Paul says, "There is neither Jew nor Greek, there is neither slave nor free, *there is neither male nor female, for you are all one* in Christ Jesus" (Galatians 3:28).

These passages should cause us to ask whether our churches have rightly and fully utilized the gifts and ministries of women in the past. I hope that many church leaders reading this chapter will decide that they have not done enough to encourage various kinds of ministries by women. Although I argue below that God restricts the office of elder or pastor to men, there are many other activities in the church in which women should be actively involved.

I discuss a number of these activities under the heading "But What *Should* Women Do in the Church?" in the last part of this chapter. But at this point, we can consider a couple of common examples.

To take one example, nothing in Scripture prohibits women from chairing various committees within the church, as long as that does not involve functioning as an elder with authority over the whole church. And though I think that only men should be elders, elders will make better decisions if they regularly seek their wives' insight and wisdom.

I was part of two different elder boards at different times in the past, and in each case we agreed that everything discussed in the elders' meeting was confidential, except that we could share all of it with our wives to hear their viewpoints. In addition, every few months we scheduled a social evening with our wives and encouraged them to share with us their thoughts about what was going on in the church. These meetings were always very helpful.

Now someone might object that our wives were actually functioning as elders. But they were not functioning as elders, for they did not attend the elder board meetings and they did not vote on the matters that we dealt with. Nevertheless, on the analogy of a wise husband who listens to his wife's counsel and wisdom, though he remains the head of the household, we thought it wise for us regularly to seek and give careful attention to the wisdom God had given our wives. In both of the churches in which this procedure was in place, the expectations of confidentiality were honored fully, so that no confidential information "leaked" out.

What about women serving communion? In some denominations, there is a strong tradition that only elders (or the equivalent to elders) help in serving the Lord's supper. In such churches, I understand that it would not be possible to have women serving communion unless the policy that allows only elders to serve communion is changed. And that is a matter for an individual church or denomination to decide.

But I see no persuasive reason why only church officers should serve communion. In churches where there is no such restriction, surely it would be appropriate that both men and women join in serving communion together, (as they do at Scottsdale Bible Church in Arizona, where I am a member), though the pastor or some other elder should officiate. Where this is done, it becomes a regular, highly visible testimony to our equal value and dignity before God.

There is also nothing in Scripture that prohibits a woman from being a paid full-time staff member in a church. Many churches that restrict the office of pastor and elder to men are still willing to have a woman in a paid staff position, such as a director of educational ministries, or a women's ministry director, or in a youth ministry position, or in a role as a part-time or full-time counselor. *We should not make rules that the Bible does not support*, and *we should not add restrictions to ministry positions when the Bible does not justify these restrictions*. Where the Bible allows freedom, we should encourage ministries by women as well by men.

In the current controversy, God has provided us with an excellent opportunity to reexamine the Scriptures to see if they really do support all the restrictions we have inherited from tradition.[1]

---

1. Egalitarian literature contains many real-life stories of wrongful repression of women's gifts and viewpoints, such as Ruth Tucker's carefully stated but evidently painful memory of trying to serve as a pastor's wife when her husband would repeatedly put her down by quoting "Women should be silent in the churches" whenever she said something in a Bible study or church business meeting (Tucker, *Women in the Maze* [1992], 121–22). I appreciated Ruth as a colleague when I was at Trinity Evangelical Divinity School, and I know that God has gifted her with wisdom and compassion and significant gifts for the benefit of the church. Though I differ with Ruth and with other egalitarians at several places throughout this book, I hope that I and my fellow complementarians will continually be mindful of the hurt that has been caused, and the damage that has been done, by harsh advocates

2.2: Biblical passages that restrict some governing and teaching roles in the church to men

In this section I examine a number of biblical passages that restrict some governing and teaching roles in the church to men. The biblical passage that addresses this situation most directly is 1 Timothy 2:11–15, so I examine that first and then treat several other passages as well.

1 Timothy 2:11–15

> Let a woman learn quietly with all submissiveness. I do not permit a woman to teach or to exercise authority over a man; rather, she is to remain quiet. For Adam was formed first, then Eve; and Adam was not deceived, but the woman was deceived and became a transgressor. Yet she will be saved through childbearing—if they continue in faith and love and holiness, with self-control.

Overview

The setting for this passage is ***the assembled church***. Just a few verses earlier, Paul says,

> I desire then that in every place the men should pray, lifting holy hands without anger or quarreling; likewise also that women should adorn themselves in respectable apparel, with modesty and self-control, not with braided hair and gold or pearls or costly attire, but with what is proper for women who profess godliness—with good works. (1 Timothy 2:8–10)

This is a setting in which men lift "holy hands" to pray, and they do so "without anger or quarreling," which implies that Paul is thinking of them in a group, when they get together as an assembled church. Similarly, the demand that women dress "with modesty" implies that Paul is thinking about a time when other people are present, as when the church gathers together. The phrase "in every place" in verse 8 indicates that it applies wherever groups of Christians might meet for prayer, worship, and instruction.

In fact, Paul's instructions in this section generally have to do with the church, because in 1 Timothy 3:1–7, he talks about the requirements for elders, and then in verses 8–13, he talks about the requirements for deacons, and both of these offices pertain to the entire church. Then immediately after that, Paul says he is writing these things to Timothy "so that, if I delay, you may know how one ought to behave in the household of God, which is the church of the living God, a pillar and buttress of truth" (v. 15).

Therefore, according to the context of this passage, the setting in which Paul does not allow

---

of male headship, people that do not hold to a balanced complementarian view but rather to a repressive "male dominance" view. And I hope that we will resolve also to oppose such a harsh, repressive view whenever we encounter it, and thus fully honor the wisdom and gifting that God has given to women in His church.

a woman to teach and have authority over a man is the assembled church, where Bible teaching would be done.[2]

What kind of "teaching" does Paul have in mind? Certainly this passage does not exclude women from teaching men mathematics or geography or a foreign language or any hundreds of other subjects. That is not what the verb "teach" (*didaskō*) would have meant in this context to the Christians who read Paul's letter. Paul was talking about what should happen when the whole church came together, and in such a setting, *the kind of "teaching" that would be done was Bible teaching*. For example, when Paul and Barnabas were at Antioch, we read that they were "teaching and preaching *the word of the Lord*" (Acts 15:35). Or when Paul was at Corinth, "he stayed a year and six months, *teaching the word of God* among them" (Acts 18:11). In other cases, Paul commands Timothy to "teach" what Paul himself has written or taught, since such apostolic teachings had the same status as Scripture, and in fact Paul's written words had the authority of Scripture (see 1 Corinthians 14:37; 1 Timothy 4:11; 6:2; 2 Timothy 2:2). Using the related noun *didaskalia*, "teaching, instruction," Paul says that "all Scripture is breathed out by God and *profitable for teaching*" (2 Timothy 3:16).

The conclusion is that Paul did not allow women to do Bible teaching or have governing authority over the assembled church.

Detailed analysis

But does Paul's command regarding women not preaching or having authority over a man apply to Christians today as it did in the first century? Or was this just a temporary command given for a specific local situation?

In chapter 8 of this book, I examine different arguments that this is just a temporary command, something given to a specific situation at Ephesus.[3] But at this point we should realize that Paul's words do not at all give the appearance of a temporary command for a specific situation, for he grounds his instructions in the situation of Adam and Eve before the Fall:

> Let a woman learn quietly with all submissiveness. I do not permit a woman to teach or to exercise authority over a man; rather, she is to remain quiet. For *Adam was*

---

2. Sumner, *Men and Women in the Church* (2003), ignores the need to interpret verses of Scripture in their context when she makes the astounding claim about 1 Timothy 2:12: "There's no way to interpret this verse at face value unless we're ready to say that it is sinful for a man to learn about God from a woman" (210). She apparently assumes that "face value" does not include the immediate context of the verse. She goes on to say that those who claim that this verse restricts women from teaching the Bible "publicly at the main church service in a pulpit on Sunday morning" are guilty of adding "extra phrases to the biblical text in order to make sense of the verse." She fails even to mention the complementarian literature on 1 Timothy 2:12 that argues *from the immediate context* that Paul is talking about meetings of the assembled congregation. Though Sumner's book is promoted as an important academic study of this topic (the cover names the author as "Sarah Sumner, PhD" and an InterVarsity Press advertisement for the book in *World* [July 16, 2003, p. 31] prominently claimed that it was written by "the first woman to earn a PhD in systematic theology from Trinity Evangelical Divinity School"), such a failure even to mention significant opposing arguments (which happens frequently in her book) seriously mars the credibility of the book.
3. See 280–302; also 329–61.

> ***formed first, then Eve; and Adam was not deceived, but the woman was deceived*** and became a transgressor. Yet she will be saved through childbearing—if they continue in faith and love and holiness, with self-control. (1 Timothy 2:11–15)

Paul's first reason is the order of Creation: "For Adam was formed first, then Eve." Paul does not use some local situation in Ephesus for a reason, such as saying, "For women aren't as well educated there in Ephesus," or "For you have some disruptive women teaching false doctrine there in Ephesus." No, he points back to the original time of Creation, before there was any sin in the world, and sees that there was a purpose of God indicated in the order of Creation: "For Adam was formed first, then Eve." Paul simply assumes that his readers will understand that when God created Adam first, and then gave commands to him alone (Genesis 2:7, 15–17), and then later created Eve (v. 22), that God was giving a leadership role to Adam.[4]

People in the ancient world, where the firstborn son had a leadership role in the family, would have understood this. But we do not need to assume that Paul was endorsing the entire system of "primogeniture," at least not in all its details. It is enough simply to say that people who were familiar with that system would have had no trouble understanding Paul's reasoning: The firstborn male in any family is assumed to be the leader in that family in his generation, and Adam was the firstborn in his generation, so he was the leader.

It does not really matter whether we think such a system is right today, or whether we practice some elements of such a system in families today, in order for this text of Scripture to be true. What matters is that Paul the apostle, writing under the guidance of the Holy Spirit, sees a leadership function that God indicated by creating Adam first, and then Eve. This leadership function had implications even for Christian churches in the first century, because Paul gives it as a reason why a woman should not teach or have authority over a man in the assembled congregation.

We can understand Paul's reasoning in an example from ordinary life: Suppose a man tells his seventeen-year-old son that he would like him to trim and prune the trees behind their house. Then he walks out with the son, gives him the necessary tools, and explains how he wants each tree trimmed. An hour later, the father realizes that the job is bigger than he had expected, so he sends his fifteen-year-old son out to help.

Who is in charge? The seventeen-year-old. He was put on the job first, he is older, and he received instructions directly from the father, while the younger son was sent to be the older son's "helper." The father will hold the older son responsible for completing the task, and will hold the younger son responsible for helping in that task. If the fifteen-year-old tried to take over

---

4. Some have objected that 1 Timothy 2:13 does not give a reason for verse 12, but is simply an illustration. But William Mounce argues convincingly that the conjunction "for" (Greek *gar*) is a reason or ground for Paul's command in verse 12. See Mounce, *Pastoral Epistles* (2000), 131–32, where he shows that in more than 98 percent of Paul's 454 uses of the word *gar,* he uses it to give a reason for his previous statement. Mounce quotes Douglas Moo (in *TrinJ* 2 [1981], 203) as saying that in the Pastoral Epistles alone the word *gar* is found twenty-one times following an imperative or an imperatival idea, and in every case *gar* has a "causal" sense, which is the grammatical category for giving a reason for the command.

and give orders to his older brother on how the job should be done, he would be usurping his brother's authority and acting outside the boundaries of the father's expectations.

Or to use another analogy, suppose a plant manager tells a senior employee to drive across town to get a part for a certain machine, and then, before the employee leaves, realizes that the employee will need help loading and unloading the part. If he then sends a junior employee along as a helper, it is evident who is in charge. The senior employee who was first given the task has leadership authority in deciding how the task is to be done.

These analogies help us to understand Paul's reasoning in 1 Timothy 2. By virtue of the order of Creation, Paul sees that God gave to Adam a leadership role that Eve did not have. And he also sees (under the guidance of the Holy Spirit in writing Scripture) that this pattern is fundamental to manhood and womanhood in such a way that God wants it reflected in the leadership positions He entrusts to people in the church. When men have governing and teaching authority over the church, they reflect something of the character of manhood in the way God intended it to function, and this is right and appropriate and pleasing to God. When women support men in these leadership positions, they reflect something of the excellence of their creation as women in the image of God, and this is right and appropriate and pleasing in God's sight as well. *In this way, the beauty of both manhood and womanhood is reflected in the conduct of the church.*

Sometimes egalitarians object, "If being created first means that one is a leader, then the animals should have authority over human beings!" But that objection fails to understand that authority relationships among human beings apply only to human beings. It would be foolishness to think otherwise, because God gave to human beings the responsibility to rule over the Creation and to subdue the earth for His glory (see Genesis 1:28). That egalitarian objection is similar to saying, "If the older son is in charge of pruning trees because he was there first, then squirrels and rabbits should have authority over him, because they were in the backyard before he arrived!" Such a suggestion is foolish, of course, because we realize that authority relationships among humans apply only to humans.

Another objection egalitarians make is to say, "If we say that Adam had authority because he was created first, then we should say that the Old Testament concept of primogeniture, which gave a greater inheritance and larger authority to the eldest son, should be followed by societies today as well." But Paul does not mention any Old Testament system of inheritance rights or any developed system of primogeniture. His reasoning is much simpler than that: Adam was created first, was put in the garden and given commands by God, and Eve was created as a helper for Adam; in that sequence of events God gave to Adam a leadership role. This should be evident to anyone whether he has heard of an Old Testament concept of primogeniture or not (though that Old Testament concept is consistent with this idea, and it may be an analogy that would help readers understand it more readily).

The larger problem with both of these objections is that they imply that the apostle Paul was wrong. Someone today may have the opinion that the statement, "Adam was formed first, then

Eve," is not a good reason to prohibit women from teaching or having authority over men in the congregation. But the fact remains that Paul thought it was a good reason, and the Bible itself, inspired by the Holy Spirit, says it is a good reason. Therefore we should not object that the reasoning is incorrect.

When Paul bases his argument on the order of creation of Adam and Eve, it indicates that his command about women not teaching or having authority in the assembled congregation transcends cultures and societies. It applies to men and women as they were created by God at the beginning, and it is not due to any distortion brought on by sin or the Fall. It applies, then, to all churches for all time, and it is a means by which the beauty of manhood and womanhood as God created them to be can be manifested in the life of the church.

Paul gives a second reason in verse 14:"And Adam was not deceived, but the woman was deceived and became a transgressor" (1 Timothy 2:14).

We should not understand this to mean that Paul was punishing women for something that Eve did, as if Paul were saying, "Eve made a mistake and now all women forever have to suffer the consequences and pay the penalty for it." We should not think that, because the New Testament authors do not try to perpetuate the punishments of the curse in Genesis 3, but work to bring redemption and alleviate the punishments that came as a result of the Fall. The goal of the gospel is redemption, not punishment. And life in the New Testament church is to be lived as a life under God's grace and a life that experiences God's forgiveness, not as a life that subjects people to continual punishment.

There is a better explanation for verse 14. When Paul says, "And Adam was not deceived, but the woman was deceived and became a transgressor," he must have in mind something about the way the first sins of Adam and Eve came about, and he must be trying to avoid having a similar kind of disobedience in the New Testament church. Therefore, Paul must be pointing to something in the nature of Adam and Eve, or something in the roles in which God created them, that was violated when "Adam was not deceived, but the woman was deceived and became a transgressor." What was that?

There are two main interpretations of 1 Timothy 2:14.[5] The first interpretation says that verse 14 refers to a *role reversal* in the Fall. The idea is that Eve took the initiative and made the decision to eat the forbidden fruit on her own, but in doing this she took a leadership role that belonged to Adam. In this way, Paul is pointing out what happens when women take the leadership role that God has reserved for men.

We could paraphrase this "role reversal" interpretation as follows: "Women should not teach or have authority over men because Adam was not the first one deceived, but Eve was first

5. For further discussion, see especially the detailed studies by Mounce, *Pastoral Epistles*, 135–43, and Thomas R. Schreiner, "An Interpretation of 1 Timothy 2:9–15: A Dialogue with Scholarship," in Köstenberger, *Women in the Church* (1995), 140–46, and for a history of interpretation of the passage, see Doriani, "A History of the Interpretation of 1 Timothy 2," in *Women in the Church,* 213–67, and especially his summary on pp. 262–67.

deceived by the serpent when she took leadership instead of deferring to the leadership of her husband." Paul is not saying anything about the natural abilities of men and women or about their natural tendencies or preferences, but is simply saying that tragic results follow when people abandon God's plan for male leadership, and Eve is an example of that.

While this interpretation has some able defenders,[6] Paul does not specify that he is talking about who was deceived first and who was deceived second. He does not say, "And Adam was not deceived first, but the woman was deceived first."[7] He says that Adam was not deceived *at all*: "And Adam *was not deceived*."[8] If Paul simply meant that Eve was deceived first and then Adam was deceived second, it seems unlikely that he would have started this clause by emphasizing that "Adam was not deceived." Rather, Paul is saying that Eve was convinced to believe something false, and she sinned as a result, but that Adam knew it was wrong, and went ahead and sinned intentionally. Paul is not excusing either Adam or Eve, for both sinned, but he identifies a difference in the way their sins came about.

This "role reversal" interpretation would be more likely if the Genesis story were somewhat different, so that Paul could argue that the Genesis story shows that "Women should not teach or have authority over a man because Eve taught Adam to eat the forbidden fruit" or "because Eve commanded Adam to eat the forbidden fruit," but neither of those things is said, and we have no reason to think that either one happened. Eve did not teach or govern Adam, but she simply "gave some to her husband who was with her, and he ate" (Genesis 3:6). So this interpretation does not seem to give enough weight to Paul's emphasis on deception, and on the fact that Eve was deceived and Adam was not.

The second major interpretation of verse 14 is that Paul is saying something about the nature of men and women as God created them. This is by far the most common viewpoint in the history of interpretation of this passage.[9] While some authors have wrongly understood this text to be teaching the intellectual inferiority of women, that misunderstanding is certainly not necessary to the passage, nor am I aware of any modern author who holds that view today.

Rather, this interpretation says that while God made men and women (in general) with equal intellectual abilities, there are still differences in preferences and inclinations, and those differences are consistent or "congruent" with God's purposes in entrusting leadership in the church to men. Daniel Doriani expresses this view in the following words:

---

6. See, for example, Moo, "What Does It Mean Not to Teach or Have Authority over Men?" in Piper and Grudem, *Recovering Biblical Manhood and Womanhood* (1991).
7. Unless the sense of "first" is carried over from the previous verse, as Paul Barnett argues in *Evangelical Quarterly* 61 (1989), 234. This is possible, but I think it doubtful; it is not made explicit, and it is difficult to see how readers would catch this sense.
8. Two related words are translated "deceived" in this passage. When Paul says Adam *was not deceived* he uses the word *apataō*, which means "deceive, mislead" (*A Greek-English Lexicon of the New Testament* [BDAG], 98), and when he says "The woman was deceived," he uses a compound form of the same word, *exapataō*, which means "to cause someone to accept false ideas about something, deceive, cheat, lead astray" (BDAG, 345), and is probably in this context just a stronger or more emphatic form of the first word.
9. See Doriani, "A History of the Interpretation of 1 Timothy 2," 213–68.

> Men lead in home and church because God desired an ordered creation. He sovereignly chose to order it through male headship, a headship given to them without a view to any merit on their part. Yet God established a coherence or congruence between his decree and his creation...God shaped the minds, proclivities and perhaps even the bodies of humans to reflect his decree.[10]

Doriani notes that modern feminist analyses of differences between men's and women's behaviors converge in part with some traditionalist interpretations of 1 Timothy 2:14:

> Both sides note that women tend toward enmeshment, which entails an unwillingness to see and condemn harsh truths about loved ones. Mindful of many individual exceptions to the rule, they sometimes say that women generally have more interest in persons and less interest in detached rational analysis of ideas. But the capacity for detached, critical assessment is absolutely essential for discerning and rooting out heresy, for carrying out discipline in the church.... If, as analysts past and present maintain, men can more easily "forget" that the heretic before them is their neighbor, then we can see one reason why Paul said men should promulgate and guard doctrine. Their greater willingness to disagree openly, while no intrinsic virtue, does suit them for the task of guarding doctrine and condemning error....
>
> We can also recognize variety in human nature, without labeling anything inferior or superior. In this view, because women generally focus on relationships more than abstract rational analysis, enmeshment in relationships could compromise a woman's willingness to uproot heresy in the church. (264–265)

While agreeing that there are many individual exceptions, Doriani suggests that in general God has "etched traces of his sovereign decree concerning male leadership into the nature of men and women. These reflections of his decree allow men to seek leadership more readily and allow women to follow them" (265).

Thomas Schreiner adopts a similar position in understanding 1 Timothy 2:14.

> God's order of creation is mirrored in the nature of men and women. Satan approached the woman first not only because of the order of creation but also because of the different inclinations present in Adam and Eve. Generally speaking, women are more relational and nurturing and men are more given to rational analysis and objectivity.... Appointing women to the teaching office is prohibited because they are less likely to draw a line on doctrinal non-negotiables, and thus deception and false teaching will more easily enter the church. This is not to say women are intellectually deficient or inferior to men.... Their kinder and gentler

10. Ibid., 263.

> nature inhibits them from excluding people for doctrinal error. There is the danger of stereotyping here, for obviously some women are more inclined to objectivity and are "tougher" and less nurturing than other women. But as a general rule women are more relational and caring than men. This explains why most women have many more close friends than men. The different inclinations of women (and men!) do not imply that they are inferior or superior to men. It simply demonstrates that men and women are profoundly different. Women have some strengths that men do not have, and men have some strengths that are generally lacking in women.[11]

This explanation seems to me to best suit the wording in 1 Timothy 2:14. Paul is saying that women should not teach or have authority over men in the congregation of God's people for two reasons: (1) Because God gave Adam a leadership role when He created him first and Eve second (v. 13), and (2) God gave men, in general, a disposition that is better suited to teaching and governing in the church, a disposition that inclines more to rational, logical analysis of doctrine and a desire to protect the doctrinal purity of the church, and God gave women, in general, a disposition that inclines more toward a relational, nurturing emphasis that places a higher value on unity and community in the church (v. 14). Both emphases are needed, of course, and both men and women have some measure of both tendencies. But Paul understands the kinder, gentler, more relational nature of women as something that made Eve less inclined to oppose the deceptive serpent and more inclined to accept his words as something helpful and true.

To say this is not at all to say that men are better than women or that women are inferior to men. That would be contrary to the entire biblical testimony. But if in fact God has created us to be different, then it is inevitable that women will be better at some things (in general) and men will be better at other things (in general).

To take an obvious example, women are better at bearing and nursing children than men (for men cannot do these things!). This does not make women better than men, but it does make them better than men *at some things*. Similarly, because of their size and strength, men (in general) are better boxers and wrestlers and football players, for no women are able to compete against men at a professional level in these sports. This does not mean that men are better than women, but they are better *at some things* than women. Similarly, academic achievement tests regularly show that women (in general) are better than men in verbal skills, while men (in general) are better than women in mathematical skills and skills having to do with spatial concepts. While there are numerous exceptions, these things are true of men and women in general, and they say something about our nature. Similarly, men tend to be more aggressive and to gravitate toward positions of leadership and dominance, and women tend to be more relational and to gravitate toward community and cooperation. These things are neither "better" nor "worse," but they are different.

In the same way, it seems that 1 Timothy 2:14 is saying that men are better suited for the

---

11. Schreiner, "Interpretation of 1 Timothy 2:9–15," 145–46.

task of governing and of safeguarding the doctrine of the church. This does not mean that women *could not* do this task, and do it well, at least in certain cases. But it does mean that God has both established men in that responsibility and has given inclinations and abilities that are well suited to that responsibility.

Yet we must be cautious at this point. We should not say, "Since Paul's reasoning is based on different general tendencies in men and women, there will be some unusual women who can be elders because they don't fit the generalizations but reason and relate more like men." We should not say that because Paul does not say that; he prohibits *all women* from teaching and governing the assembled congregation, not just those with certain abilities and tendencies.[12] And he does so first because of the order in which God created Adam and Eve (v. 13), and second because he sees something in Eve that is representative of womanhood generally (v. 14) and therefore applies broadly and in principle to all women as they are representatives of womanhood as well.

What then is the meaning of verse 15: "Yet she will be saved through childbearing—if they continue in faith and love and holiness, with self-control"?

The general force of the sentence is clear, although people differ about the details. Paul has just finished saying that "the woman was deceived and became a transgressor." In this final comment his purpose is to assure readers that Eve's sin was not the final word regarding women! Though Eve sinned, salvation is now possible through Christ.

The phrase "through childbearing" is probably best understood as an example of being obedient to God's calling on one's life. Women are not to teach or govern the church, but God has given them a special responsibility, the awesome responsibility of bearing and raising children. Paul understands that not all women will be able to have children (for the Old Testament and life experience both testify to that fact), and he also gives a long section on widows in 1 Timothy 5:3–16, so he knows there are many women in the church at Ephesus who do not have husbands. But Paul is speaking of "childbearing" as a representative example of how a woman should be obedient to God's calling on her life and fulfill the role or roles God has called her to do, whether that includes bearing and raising of children, or showing "hospitality" (1 Timothy 5:10), or caring for the afflicted (v. 10), or managing their households (v. 14), or ministering through "supplications and prayers" (v. 5), or training younger women (Titus 2:4–5), or any mixture of these or other callings. Paul takes "childbearing" as one obvious and representative example of a woman's distinctive role and calling from God.

What does it mean then to say that "she will be saved through childbearing"? It surely does not mean that a woman is justified or forgiven of her sins because of childbearing or fulfilling other tasks to which God calls her, for Paul clearly teaches that salvation in this sense is a "gift of God, not a result of works, so that no one would boast" (Ephesians 2:8–9) and it comes

12. In the same way, all men have a responsibility for leadership in their marriages, even though some men are not as naturally inclined or gifted for leadership.

"through faith" (v. 8). "Salvation" in that sense is what Paul refers to when he says "the free gift of God is eternal life in Christ Jesus our Lord" (Romans 6:23), and when he says that we "are justified by his grace as a gift, through the redemption that is in Christ Jesus" (3:24).

But Paul can use *salvation* and related terms in another sense, to refer to the Christian life from initial conversion until our death, a life in which we live in increasing obedience to God and see more and more good works as a consequence and as an evidence of the change that God has brought about in our lives. It is this sense of *salvation* that Paul uses when he tells believers to "work out your own *salvation* with fear and trembling, for it is God who works in you, both to will and to work for his good pleasure" (Philippians 2:12–13). In theological terms, this aspect of salvation is often called "perseverance." After our initial conversion, we continue or "persevere" in the Christian faith until the day of our death.[13]

So Paul means that a woman will be "saved"—she will continue to work out the results of her salvation—"through childbearing," that is, through being obedient to God in the various tasks and roles that He calls her to, rather than attempting to teach or govern the church, a role God has not called women to.

In the last part of the verse, Paul switches from a singular example of a woman who will be saved ("yet she will be saved") to a plural statement about all women who are Christians. Though the sentence forms a rather irregular construction in Greek, and is therefore a bit difficult to translate due to the shift from singular to plural, Paul is making a general statement that persevering in the Christian life and working out the results and implications of one's "salvation" (in the sense of perseverance) depends on continuing in faith and obedience. He says, "*if they* continue in faith and love and holiness, with self-control" (1 Timothy 2:15). This is consistent with Paul's teaching elsewhere that Christians, if they are genuine Christians, must continue trusting in Christ and being obedient to Him throughout their lives. For example, he says that Christ's purpose is to "present you holy and blameless and above reproach before him," but he adds that Christians must continue believing, for he says, "*if indeed you continue in the faith*, stable and steadfast, not shifting from the hope of the gospel that you heard" (Colossians 1:22–23).

So the point of 1 Timothy 2:15 is that women are not eternally lost because of Eve's sin, but they will be saved and will experience the outworking of their salvation throughout their Christian lives if they follow the roles God has given to them and continue in faith and obedience.[14]

---

13. Another possible explanation of "saved" here is "kept safe from Satan's deception." See Andreas Köstenberger, "Saved Through Childbearing: A Fresh Look at 1 Timothy 2:15 Points to Protection from Satan's Deception," *CBMW News* 2:4 (September 1997): 1–5.

14. Some other interpretations of 1 Timothy 2:15 have been proposed, and it is beyond the purpose of this book to analyze every one of them. One view is that "childbearing" refers to the birth of the Messiah, Jesus, who was the descendent of Eve and who brought salvation to us. Another view is that "saved" means "kept safe from straying after Satan's deceptions" (see previous note). Although these interpretations are not impossible, I think them to be less likely. For an explanation for these and other views of 1 Timothy 2:15, see Mounce, *Pastoral Epistles*, 143–47; also, on the whole of 1 Timothy 2:8–15, see the detailed exegesis of Knight, *The Pastoral Epistles* (1992), 130–49. However, on any of these interpretations, the main point of verse 15 is still clear: Though Eve sinned, salvation for women is still possible, and thus Paul ends the chapter on a positive and reassuring note.

Not all teaching is prohibited: Other kinds of teaching and speaking by women that Scripture views positively

Acts 18:26: Explaining Scripture privately, outside the context of the assembled congregation

It is important to understand 1 Timothy 2:12 in the light of other passages that view some kinds of teaching by women in a positive way. For example, we read in Acts 18:26 concerning Apollos, a man competent in the Scriptures but who did not understand fully the good news of salvation in Christ (Acts 18:24–25), that both Aquila and Priscilla explained the way of God more accurately to him:

> He began to speak boldly in the synagogue, but when Priscilla and Aquila heard him, *they* took him and *explained to him* the way of God more accurately. (Acts 18:26)

The word translated "explained" (Greek *ektithēmi*) is plural and it indicates *both* Aquila and Priscilla were involved in explaining the way of God more fully to Apollos.

This incident is viewed with approval in the book of Acts, for there is no indication that anything was wrong with this conduct as it fits the ongoing narrative of the spread of the gospel to many Gentile cities. Therefore *this passage gives warrant for women and men to talk together about the meaning of biblical passages and to "teach" one another in such settings*. A parallel example in modern church life would be a home Bible study where both men and women contribute to the discussion of the meaning and application of Scripture. In such discussions, everyone is able to "teach" everyone else in some sense, for such discussions of the meaning of the Word of God are not the authoritative teaching that would be done by a pastor or elder to an assembled congregation, as in 1 Timothy 2.[15]

Another modern parallel to the private conversation between Priscilla and Aquila and Apollos would be *the writing of books on the Bible and theology by women*. When I read a Bible commentary written by a woman, for example, it is as if the author were talking privately to me, explaining her interpretation of the Bible, much as Priscilla talked to Apollos in Acts 18:26. Reading a book by a woman author is much like having a private conversation with a woman author. The woman author does not have teaching authority over an assembled congregation or a group of men.[16]

---

15. Belleville, "Women in Ministry," 99–100, makes much of the fact that Priscilla "expounded" the way of God to Apollos, but she fails to consider the single most important difference: Acts 18:26 records a private conversation, whereas 1 Timothy 2:12 and related passages talk about the responsibility of Bible teaching and governing over an assembled church.
16. There is another point of difference: Preaching to a church is generally endorsed by the church, while publishing a book is not. We can see this in the fact that churches carefully guard the responsibility of preaching to the congregation, so that, in general, the congregation knows that those who preach from the pulpit have the endorsement and approval of the church leadership. But we all read many things we disagree with, and churches do not usually try to keep their members from reading a variety of viewpoints. Bible teaching to the assembled congregation has the general endorsement of that church (and thus carries authority over that church) in a way publishing a book does not.

1 Corinthians 11:4–5: Praying and prophesying in the assembled congregation

Another example of an activity in the church that Scripture approves is *praying and prophesying aloud before the assembled congregation*, because Paul says,

> Every man who prays or prophesies with his head covered dishonors his head, but every wife who *prays or prophesies* with her head uncovered dishonors her head—it is the same as if her head were shaven. (1 Corinthians 11:4–5)

Paul implies that it would be normal and natural in the church at Corinth for women to pray and to prophesy aloud. If it were wrong for women to pray or prophesy in the church service, Paul would not have said they should have their heads covered when they do so!

This passage also implies that giving prophecies aloud in the assembled congregation is appropriate for women (in churches that allow this gift today). As I explain more fully later in this book, giving prophecy is simply reporting something that God has spontaneously brought to mind.[17] Prophecy is always listed as a separate gift from teaching in the New Testament, and prophecy is always to be subject to the governing authority of the elders and is to be tested for its conformity to Scripture (see 1 Corinthians 14:29; 1 Thessalonians 5:20–21).

Titus 2:3–5: Women teaching women

Paul encourages another kind of teaching activity by women when he says:

> Older women. . .are to teach what is good, and so *train the young women* to love their husbands and children, to be self-controlled, pure, working at home, kind, and submissive to their own husbands, that the word of God may not be reviled. (Titus 2:3–5)

All kinds of Bible teaching ministries from women to other women are encouraged by this passage. Organizations such as Bible Study Fellowship have outstanding ministries in training women in the knowledge of the Word of God, and in the United States at least, some excellent women Bible teachers will speak to conferences of several thousand women at one time. These are valuable ministries that should be encouraged. They are not the kind of teaching or having authority over men that Paul prohibits in 1 Timothy 2.

John 4:28–30 and Matthew 28:5–10: Evangelism

Evangelism of all kinds is another activity not restricted to men alone but open to men and women alike. For example, the woman at the well in Samaria went and told her village about Jesus:

> So the woman left her water jar and went away into town and said to the people, "Come, see a man who told me all that I ever did. Can this be the Christ?" They went out of the town and were coming to him. (John 4:28–30)

17. See below, pp. 78–80 and 227–32, on the reasons why women can prophesy but not teach. See also Grudem, *The Gift of Prophecy in the New Testament and Today* (2000).

The women at the tomb became the first eyewitnesses of the resurrection, and Jesus sent them to tell His disciples about the resurrection. This was an affirmation of the principle of women as evangelists in the New Covenant age:

> But the angel said to the women, "Do not be afraid, for I know that you seek Jesus who was crucified. He is not here, for he has risen, as he said. Come, see the place where he lay. Then go quickly and tell his disciples that he has risen from the dead, and behold, he is going before you to Galilee; there you will see him. See, I have told you." So they departed quickly from the tomb with fear and great joy, and ran to tell his disciples. And behold, Jesus met them and said, "Greetings!" And they came up and took hold of his feet and worshiped him. Then Jesus said to them, "Do not be afraid; go and tell my brothers to go to Galilee, and there they will see me." (Matthew 28:5–10)

These passages seem to indicate that it would be appropriate for women to do evangelism in any setting, whether privately or in large groups. In speaking to non-Christians,[18] they are not having the kind of teaching or governing authority over the church that Paul prohibits in 1 Timothy 2, because the unbelievers who hear the gospel message are not a congregation of assembled believers.

The history of missions has many stories of courageous women who went by themselves to proclaim the gospel to unreached people. For example, Wycliffe Bible translator Joanne Shetler tells a beautiful story of her work with the Balangao people in the Philippines, and her interaction with a man in the village (her "daddy") who had adopted her into his family and who was reading pages of the New Testament for her as she produced it:

> I continued translating in Timothy with my daddy. And we came to a verse where Paul says to Timothy, "I don't allow women to teach men." My daddy didn't bat an eyelash. But that afternoon, after we'd finished work, he said to me, "Now what is that we're going to study on Sunday?" I thought he was just curious. I didn't know what was on his mind since fathers don't report to their children. So I told him. Sunday morning came, and before I could stand up to start, he stood up and said, "My daughter here knows more about this than I do, but we found in the Bible that women aren't supposed to teach men. So I guess I have to be the one!" And that was the end of my career, and the beginning of their teaching.[19]

18. One qualification is necessary here: In some evangelical churches, an "evangelistic service" may have 1 percent or fewer non-Christians and 99 percent Christians. Preaching to such an assembled group in the church is exactly what Paul said not to do in 1 Timothy 2:12. What I have in mind in this section is an audience that is primarily non-Christians (though some Christians may be in attendance), and the message is addressed to non-Christians. There will no doubt be borderline cases where people in the situation will need wisdom to decide what is right, but the distinction between evangelism and Bible teaching to the church is still a valid one and is not disproved by the existence of mixed situations.

19. Joanne Shetler, "Faithful in Obedience," can be found at www.urbana.org/_today.cfm (accessed January 28, 2004).

It was a beautiful picture of a key turning point in the transition from an informal group of new Christians to an established congregation with indigenous male leadership naturally taking charge.

Situations similar to this have probably occurred hundreds of times throughout the history of the church, and no doubt God gives much grace as new Christians seek to be faithful to His Word, even when it might be difficult to say exactly what point a transition should occur without being present in the actual situation. The important point is that the transition does occur, and male leadership is established in the church.

Other kinds of speech activities by women are also appropriate in the assembled church. Examples include giving a personal testimony of God's work in a woman's own life or in the lives of others (such as in youth work or in a mission activity), reading Scripture, singing a solo or singing in a group, acting as part of a dramatic presentation—whatever goes on in the assembled church other than what is explicitly prohibited by Scripture (Bible teaching and governing over the congregation of God's people).

1 Corinthians 14:33–35: Women should remain silent when prophecies are being judged

Paul writes:

> As in all the churches of the saints, the women should keep silent in the churches. For they are not permitted to speak, but should be in submission, as the Law also says. If there is anything they desire to learn, let them ask their husbands at home. For it is shameful for a woman to speak in church. (1 Corinthians 14:33b–35)

Paul cannot mean that women are to be completely silent at all times in church, for he had just finished saying in 1 Corinthians 11:5 that they should not pray or prophesy unless they had a head covering.[20] And surely women along with men should join in congregational singing (see Colossians 3:16), which is not exactly being silent! So then what kind of silence does Paul mean?

The best explanation is that Paul means "women should keep silent in the churches" *with respect to the topic under discussion in this context*. This section begins at verse 29, where Paul says, "Let two or three prophets speak, and let the others weigh what is said." In verses 30–33a, Paul gives an explanation for the first half of verse 29 ("Let two or three prophets speak"). But now in verses 33b[21]–36 Paul goes on to explain the judging of prophecies, some-

---

20. A few interpreters have tried to say that Paul is not speaking about the assembled church in 1 Corinthians 11:5, but about private prayer of some kind. Such explanations have not been persuasive, however, because there is no convincing indication in the context of 1 Corinthians 11 that Paul has any such restrictive meaning in mind. He is dealing with the assembled congregation, and he goes on to talk about celebrating the Lord's supper in the verses immediately following (vv. 17–34), and then to talk about the functioning of spiritual gifts in the congregation (chapters 12–14). See also p. 233, n.31.

21. Verse numbers were not in what Paul wrote, but were added for the first time in 1551 in the fourth edition of the Greek text that was published by Stephanus (also referred to as Robert Estienne, 1503–1559). He inserted

thing he had mentioned in the second half of verse 29: "And let the others weigh what is said."

Paul says that when people are weighing and evaluating a prophetic message, the women should be silent and not speak up to judge the prophecies. This understanding fits the context well because it relates to the topic that is already under discussion, namely, prophesying and judging prophecies.

This understanding of 1 Corinthians 14:33b–36 is consistent with the teachings of the rest of the New Testament on appropriate roles for women in the church. Speaking out and judging prophecies before the assembled congregation is a governing role over the assembled church, and Paul reserves that role for men.

What then shall we say about verse 35, "If there is anything they desire to learn, let them ask their husbands at home. For it is shameful for a woman to speak in church"? If we have understood verse 34 correctly, then verse 35 is understandable. Suppose that some women in Corinth had wanted to evade the force of Paul's directive. The easy way to do this would be to say, "We'll do just as Paul says. We won't speak up and criticize prophecies. But surely no one would mind if we asked a few questions! We just want to learn more about what these prophets are saying." Then such questioning could be used as a platform for expressing in none-too-veiled form the very criticisms Paul forbids. If a "prophet" proclaimed that "Jesus is coming back ten days from now," rather than saying, "That is contrary to what Jesus taught," a woman could ask a question: "You said that Jesus is coming back in ten days, but didn't Jesus say that no one can know the day or the hour of His return?"[22]

Paul anticipates this possible evasion and writes, "If there is anything they desire to learn, let them ask their husbands at home." Of course, some women were unmarried and would not have had a husband to ask. But there would have been other men within their family circles, or within the fellowship of the church, with whom they could discuss the content of the prophecies. Paul's general guideline is clear, even though he did not make pedantic qualifications to deal with each specific case.

To apply this to a hypothetical modern situation, if Fred stands up in a church service and says, "I believe the Lord has said to me that He is coming back next Thursday," then it would not be right for a woman to stand up and say, "Fred's prophecy is wrong, because Jesus says in Matthew 25:13 that we can know neither the day nor the hour of His return." Rather, it would be the role of some man in the congregation to do this. In this way, Paul reserves for men the function of governing and protecting doctrine in the church, and this is similar to what he says in 1 Timothy 2:12. (See further discussion of 1 Corinthians 14:34–35 on pp. 227–46.)

---

the verse divisions while on a journey from Paris to Lyons. For discussion, see Metzger, *Text of the New Testament* (1968), 104n270.

22. See Matthew 25:13.

1 Timothy 3:2 and Titus 1:6: Elders are to be the husband of one wife[23]

In two different places, Paul affirms that the office of elder (which he also calls the office of "overseer" or "bishop") should be filled by someone who is the "*husband of one wife.*"

> Therefore an overseer must be above reproach, *the husband of one wife*. (1 Timothy 3:2)

> This is why I left you in Crete, so that you might put what remained into order, and appoint elders in every town as I directed you—if anyone is above reproach, *the husband of one wife*. (Titus 1:5–6)

It is evident that only a man can be a "husband." In fact, the Greek term here, *anēr*, can mean either "man" or "husband," but with either meaning it is the Greek term that specifically designates a male human being. This means elders had to be men.

This is important because Paul is not restricting the office of elder to men in the city of Ephesus alone (assuming some kind of unique situation there), but elders were required to be men also in Crete, and not just at one or two locations in Crete but "in every town."

The phrase "husband of one wife" is best understood to mean that a polygamist could not be an elder in a church. Therefore this expression is not intended to rule out a single man (such as Jesus or Paul) from being an elder or to rule out someone who had been divorced and then remarried. Though polygamy was not common in the first century, it was practiced, especially among the Jews. The Jewish historian Josephus says, "For it is an ancestral custom of ours to have several wives at the same time," and several sections in rabbinic legislation regulated the inheritance customs and other aspects that would apply in cases of polygamy.[24]

2.3: The Relationship between the Family and the Church

In addition to those Scripture passages above, there are other arguments in favor of restricting the office of pastor and elder to men. One is that *the New Testament sees a close relationship between male leadership in the home and male leadership in the church.* This is in part because the church is viewed as a "family," and patterns of church life are imitated in the family, while patterns of family life are to be imitated in the church. Therefore Paul can say that a candidate for the office of elder (or overseer) "must manage his own household well, with all dignity keeping his children submissive, for if someone does not know how to manage his own household, how will he care for God's church?" (1 Timothy 3:4–5).

A little later Paul tells Timothy to relate to people in the church as he would relate to people in his own family:

---

23. For further discussion of the phrase "husband of one wife," see Grudem, *Systematic Theology* (1994), 916–17.
24. See Josephus, *Antiquities* 17.14; *Mishnah*, Yebamoth 4:11; Ketuboth 10:1, 4–5; Sanhedrin 2:4; Kerithoth 3:7; Kiddushin 2:7; Bechoroth 8:4.

> Do not rebuke an older man but encourage him ***as you would a father.*** Treat younger men ***like brothers***, older women ***like mothers***, younger women ***like sisters***, in all purity. (1 Timothy 5:1–2)

This indicates that male leadership in the home and in the church are closely tied together, and that in today's controversy, male leadership in the home and in the church will likely stand or fall together. If we begin to abandon the requirement for men to be pastors and elders in our churches, and if we begin establishing women in positions of teaching and governing authority over our churches, then we will likely see an erosion of male leadership in the home as well. For how can a man come to church and sit under the teaching and authority of his wife—teaching and authority that applies to all areas of life—and yet the minute he walks out the church door expect that he will be the head of his household and she will be subject to his authority? And such erosion of male leadership would affect not only the family of the woman doing the Bible teaching, but also (by implication and example) all the other families in the church.

The close connection in the New Testament between church and family is, therefore, another argument in favor of restricting to men some governing and teaching roles in the church.[25]

2.4: The Example of the Apostles

If Jesus had wanted to establish a truly egalitarian church, He could easily have chosen six men and six women to be apostles, and there would be no room for argument. While some people object that it would have been culturally offensive for Him to do this, if it had been Christ's intention for His church, then He would have done it, for He never hesitated to do culturally unpopular things when they were morally right.

But Jesus did not choose six men and six women as apostles. He chose twelve men (Matthew 10:2–4; see also Acts 1:24–26 where Matthias was chosen to replace Judas). These twelve apostles, under Jesus Christ as the head of the church, have the positions of highest authority in the church throughout its history. And they are all men. In fact, their authority will continue into the age to come, because Jesus tells these twelve, "Truly I say to you, in the new world, when the Son of Man will sit on his glorious throne, you who have followed me will also sit on twelve thrones, judging the twelve tribes of Israel" (Matthew 19:28).

The highest positions of human authority in the age to come are not given to six men and six women equally but to twelve men, the twelve apostles.

When we see the heavenly city, the book of Revelation tells us that we will see twelve men's names on the foundation of this city: "And the wall of the city had twelve foundations, and on them were the twelve names of the twelve apostles of the Lamb" (21:14).

---

25. See also Vern Poythress, "The Church as Family," in Piper and Grudem, *Recovering Biblical Manhood and Womanhood* (1991), 233–47.

Therefore, for all eternity, we will see that Jesus has called to Himself a great family of God's people in which the highest leadership positions are not distributed equally to men and to women, but are all held by men. From beginning to end, the Bible is simply not an egalitarian book.

2.5: The history of male teaching and leadership throughout the whole Bible

In claiming that some governing and teaching roles in the church should be restricted to men, we have looked at 1 Timothy 2:11–15, 1 Corinthians 14:33b–36, 1 Timothy 3:2, and Titus 1:6, as well as the relationship between the family and the church and the example of the apostles. But are there other passages than these?

Think of the Bible as a whole, from Genesis to Revelation. Where is there one example *in the entire Bible* of a woman publicly teaching an assembled group of God's people? There is none. Sometimes people mention Deborah in Judges 4, but she did not teach the people publicly, for people came to her privately to hear her wise decisions in disputed cases: "She used to sit under the palm of Deborah between Ramah and Bethel in the hill country of Ephraim, and the people of Israel came up to her for judgment" (v. 5). (See pp. 131–36 on Deborah.) In the Old Testament the priests were responsible to teach the people, and the priests were all men.[26]

Therefore, there is a consistent pattern in Scripture: Men teach and lead God's people. On rare occasions where women gained power as queens in Israel or Judah (such as Jezebel in 1 Kings 16–21 or Athaliah in 2 Kings 11), they led the people into evil, so they can hardly be used as positive examples of women having governing authority over the people of God.[27] In its consistant patterns of male governing and teaching, therefore, the entire Bible supports the idea of restricting to men the role of teaching and governing the assembly of God's people.

2.6: The history of the church

Throughout the history of the church, women's gifts and ministries have been valued and affirmed, but the dominant view by far has been that only men should govern and teach God's people in the role of pastors or elders (or in the role of priests in the Roman Catholic and Episcopal and Eastern Orthodox traditions). While this is not an argument directly from the Bible, and thus does not carry the same authority, it is nevertheless useful.

William Weinrich says that up until the nineteenth century "the only significant group that denied the continuing applicability of Paul's prohibitions was the Society of Friends (Quakers)....

26. See Leviticus 10:11; Malachi 2:6–7. Women prophets did not teach God's people: See the discussion in chapter 4, pp. 136–38.

27. See further discussion on women as queens in chapter 4, pp. 138–40.

George Fox (d. 1671), founder of the Quakers, and especially Margaret Fell (d. 1702) argued that the authority of the indwelling Spirit gave women equal right and obligation to speak, even in public assemblies."[28] He notes that John Wesley (d. 1791) expected that Methodists would follow the ordinary rule of discipline and women would be in subjection in the congregation, but he would allow from time to time for "an extraordinary impulse of the Spirit" that would allow a woman to speak in public on rare occasions. Otherwise, Weinrich says, "The Anabaptists, the Anglicans, the Puritans, and the Separatists all prohibited women from the public ministry of preaching and teaching. While groups that emphasized religious experience and interior calling did allow women to assume (more or less restricted) public preaching, not until the nineteenth century did women begin to make significant strides toward a ready acceptance of any public ministry. It has been only *in the last half of the twentieth century* that the major Protestant church bodies have begun to accept women as regular preachers and pastors."[29] In many of those cases, the leadership of those denominations was already in the hands of liberals who did not accept the full authority of the Bible as the inerrant Word of God.[30]

This of course does not prove that the complementarian position is correct, but it does mean that anyone who accepts the egalitarian position must conclude that the overwhelming majority of interpreters throughout the history of the church have all been wrong on this matter.[31] We would be justified in expecting very strong and persuasive reasons why the nearly unanimous understanding of the church throughout its history has been incorrect. Certainly this creates a strong presumption in favor of the complementarian position, unless compelling evidence can be produced on the other side.

---

28. William Weinrich, "Women in the History of the Church: Learned and Holy, but Not Pastors," in Piper and Grudem, *Recovering Biblical Manhood and Womanhood,* 278.
29. For further discussion see Weinrich, "Women in the History of the Church," 263–79. See also Tucker and Liefeld, *Daughters of the Church* (1987), and see also chapter 11 for further discussion of the roles of women in the history of the church. See also the extended comment from Richard John Neuhaus cited in chapter 11, pp. 468–69.
30. See the discussion of the relationship between liberalism and an egalitarian view of women in the church in chapter 13.
31. Sumner, *Men and Women in the Church,* claims that the idea that women are of equal worth in God's sight is also a novel view in the history of the church (47; and see 40–48, 55). She supports this claim with a small number of quotations from church history (Tertullian, Ambrose, Augustine, Aquinas), but even in these she fails to understand that when ancient authors spoke of someone being "inferior" or "superior" it often was with reference to rank or authority, not with reference to personal worth or value. She does not consider historical statements about the equal value of women, such as that of Chrysostom (AD 344/354–407), who wrote, "For what if the wife be under subjection to us? It is as a wife, as free, as equal in honor" (John Chrysostom, "Homilies on First Corinthians 26," in *Nicene and Post-Nicene Fathers [NPNF],* ed. Philip Schaff, ser. 1, 12:150). Such statements about women deserving honor and respect are common in Chrysostom's writings. Sumner herself also quotes Jerome (ca. 345–ca. 419) as a counterexample who honored women (*Men and Women in the Church,* 47n32).

    Sumner also claims that earlier writers taught that "Women were assigned to subordinate roles because women themselves were thought to be essentially inferior" (47). But her quotations do not prove this claim, and she fails even to mention, far less to evaluate on the basis of detailed historical study, the much more likely possibility that early writers taught that women should not lead men in the home or church *primarily because that was what the Bible taught.* I do not doubt that some in the history of the church held a wrongful view of women as inferior to

2.7: But what *should* women do in the church?

Probably the most frequent question I hear when I speak to Christian groups about this topic is this: "Okay, I agree with you that only men should be pastors and elders. But what about *other* activities in the church? What exactly do you think a woman should and should not do, according to the Bible?"

Sometimes people say, "Just where do you draw the line? Can women ever preach on Sunday morning? Can they teach adult Sunday school classes? What about serving communion? We want to follow Scripture, but we can't find any verses that talk about these specific things."

I think in most cases men and women who ask these questions genuinely want to encourage more opportunities for women in the overall ministry of the church. They sense that many evangelical churches have been too "traditional" and too restrictive on ministries available to women. They want to question "the way we have always done things" in the light of Scripture. But they also do not want to encourage anything that is contrary to Scripture.

In this section I will try to answer those questions, partly in the hope of encouraging churches to examine their traditions to see if there are more areas of ministry they could open to women as well as men. On the other hand, I also want to explain why I think certain kinds of activities are restricted to men.

For the purposes of this final section of this chapter, I will assume that readers agree that Scripture teaches *some* restriction on the roles women may fill in the church. Generally these restrictions fall in three areas, and almost all the questions of application pertain to at least one of these areas: (1) governing authority, (2) Bible teaching, and (3) public recognition or visibility. This is because Paul says, "I do not permit a woman to teach or to exercise authority over a man" and the other passages that speak of restrictions on women's roles in the church also deal with questions of governing and teaching (for example, 1 Corinthians14:33–35; 1 Timothy 3:1–7; Titus 1:5–9; Matthew 10:2–4). I have included the third area, public recognition or visibility, because it is a closely related question. There are some highly visible activities in the church that do not include governing or teaching authority, and people easily combinc and maybe confuse these in their minds. If we keep this area distinct, it helps us think more clearly about specific applications.

What follows here are three lists of activities. In List 1, I proceed from areas of greater governing authority to areas of lesser authority. In List 2, I proceed from areas of greater teaching

---

men in value or importance. But that alone does not establish Sumner's claim that that was the *premise* on which subordinate roles were based (it may instead have been the incorrect *conclusion* from those roles), nor does it demonstrate that that was the dominant view in church history. Finally, the fact that complementarians are willing to correct some errors of the past does not mean that our view is just as novel or just as ahistorical as the egalitarian view (see Sumner, *Men and Women in the Church,* 40–48), for in the most disputed question of exclusive male leadership in home and church, church history is overwhelmingly on the complementarian side, and the egalitarian view alone is novel.

responsibility and influence on the beliefs of the church to areas of lesser teaching responsibility and lesser influence on the beliefs of the church. In List 3, I proceed from areas of greater public recognition and visibility to areas of lesser visibility.

Before I give these lists, one word of caution is appropriate: These lists are *not* rankings of value or importance to the church! Paul tells us that *all* the members of the body are needed and that "the parts of the body that seem to be weaker are indispensable, and on those parts of the body that we think less honorable we bestow the greater honor" (1 Corinthians 12:22–23). And Jesus said, "Whoever would be great among you must be your servant" (Mark 10:43).

These statements remind us that when we talk about levels of governing authority, or levels of Bible teaching responsibility, or levels of public recognition, we are not talking about greatness or importance.

Then why talk about such levels at all? We must do so because Scripture tells us that *some* kinds of governing and teaching are inappropriate for women. In order to think clearly about what those roles are, we first must list the activities we are talking about. Then we can ask, in each case, if this was the kind of governing or teaching that Scripture intended us to understand in these passages. In short, we need to make such a list for purposes of clearer thinking on this issue.

Here then are the three lists. (The actual order of items on each list is approximate, and churches may think that some items should be moved up or down on the list according to the way they assess their own situations.)

List 1: Areas of Governing Authority: Which Offices or Activities Should Be Restricted to Men?

(listed in order of greatest to least amount of authority over men)

1. President of a denomination
2. Member of the governing board of a denomination
3. Regional governing authority (such as, district superintendent, bishop, or similar office)
4. Member of regional governing board
5. Senior pastor in local church (or associate pastor with many similar responsibilities to the senior pastor)
6. Member of governing board with authority over whole church (this would be the office of elder in many churches, while it would be the office of deacon or board member or church council member in others)
7. Presiding over a baptism or communion service (but see List 3 for serving communion or performing a baptism)

8. Giving spoken judgment on a prophecy given to the congregation (1 Corinthians 14:33–36)
9. Permanent leader of a fellowship group meeting in a home (both men and women members)
10. Committee chairman (or chairperson)[32]
11. Director of Christian education[33]
12. Sunday school superintendent[34]
13. Missionary responsibilities (many administrative responsibilities in missionary work in other countries)
14. Moderating a Bible discussion in a home Bible study group
15. Choir director
16. Leading singing on Sunday morning[35]
17. Deacon (in churches where this does not involve governing authority over the entire congregation)[36]
18. Administrative assistant to senior pastor
19. Church treasurer
20. Church secretary
21. Member of advisory council to regional governing authority
22. Meeting periodically with church governing board to give counsel and advice
23. Regular conversations between elders and their wives over matters coming before the elder board (with understanding that confidentiality is preserved)

---

32. I have put this item here because this activity and the following two have *some* kind of authority in the church, but it is less than the authority over the whole congregation that Paul has in mind in 1 Corinthians 14:33–36; 1 Timothy 2:12; 3; and Titus 1.
33. See footnote to item 10.
34. See footnote to item 10.
35. I understand that others may differ with me and may decide to list leading singing between 8 and 9. Such a decision would depend on how a church and the worship leader understand the degree of authority over the assembled congregation that is involved in leading a singing or worship time.
36. But see item 6 when "deacons" are the primary governing board over the congregation.

24. Formally counseling one man[37]
25. Formally counseling a couple together[38]
26. Formally counseling one woman[39]
27. Speaking in congregational business meetings
28. Voting in congregational business meetings[40]

List 2: Areas of Bible Teaching: Which Activities Should Be Restricted to Men?

(listed in order of greatest to least teaching influence over men in a group or congregation)

1. Teaching Bible or theology in a theological seminary
2. Teaching Bible or theology in a Christian college
3. Preaching (teaching the Bible) at a nationwide denominational meeting, or at a nationwide Christian conference
4. Preaching (teaching the Bible) at a regional meeting of churches, or at a regional Christian conference
5. Preaching (teaching the Bible) regularly to the whole church on Sunday mornings
6. Occasional preaching (teaching the Bible) to the whole church on Sunday mornings
7. Occasional Bible teaching at less formal meetings of the whole church (such as Sunday evening or at a midweek service)

---

37. I put items 24, 25, and 26 in this "Governing Authority" column (List 1) and also in the "Bible Teaching" column (List 2) because there is some amount of authority and some amount of Bible teaching involved in these counseling activities. I am not here commenting on whether it is ordinarily wise or most effective for one woman to counsel one man; I am just listing these activities according to the degree of governing or teaching authority they exhibit over the congregation of a church. I also realize that others may decide to put these activities at different places on these lists, depending on the style of counseling and the degree of authority they think attaches to it. It seems to me that these three items are quite similar to the positive example of Priscilla and Aquila together explaining to Apollos the way of God more accurately in a private setting in Acts 18:26.
38. See footnote to item 24.
39. See footnote to item 24.
40. Some may argue that when a woman votes she "exercises authority" over the congregation. I disagree. I believe she exercises some influence on the congregation, but so does everyone else who votes, and surely not everyone who votes is able or even qualified to exercise governing authority over the congregation. There is a huge difference between *exercising influence* through voting and *exercising authority* through governing the congregation (as an elder or a senior pastor would do). To take an analogy, an eighteen-year-old American can vote for the president of the United States, but cannot be president of the United States, and the authority residing in the office of president far exceeds the authority of any individual voter.

8. Bible teaching to an adult Sunday school class (both men and women members)
9. Bible teaching at a home Bible study (both men and women members)
10. Bible teaching to a college-age Sunday school class
11. Bible teaching to a high school Sunday school class
12. Writing a book on Bible doctrines[41]
13. Writing or editing a study Bible
14. Writing a commentary on a book of the Bible
15. Writing notes in a study Bible
16. Writing or editing other kinds of Christian books
17. Bible teaching to a women's Sunday school class
18. Bible teaching to a women's Bible study group during the week
19. Bible teaching to a junior high Sunday school class
20. Teaching as a Bible professor on a secular university campus[42]
21. Evangelistic speaking to large groups of non-Christians (for example, an evangelistic rally on a college campus)
22. Working as an evangelistic missionary in other cultures
23. Moderating a discussion in a small group Bible study (men and women members)
24. Reading Scripture aloud on Sunday morning
25. Reading Scripture to other, less formal meetings of the church
26. Giving a personal testimony before the congregation (a story of how God has worked in one's own or others' lives)

---

41. I have put four examples of writing activities here on the list because the author of a book is doing some kind of teaching, but it is different from the teaching of the assembled congregation that Paul prohibits in 1 Timothy 2. The teaching relationship of an author to a reader is much more like the one-to-one kind of teaching that Priscilla and Aquila did when they explained the way of God more accurately to Apollos in Acts 18:26. When I am reading a book, it is similar to having a private conversation with the author of the book. And there is another difference: Christians often read books they disagree with, but we do not expect the sermon on Sunday morning to be given by someone we fundamentally disagree with. One more difference is that authors of books do not think of themselves as having any governing authority over their readers.

42. I have put this here on the list because I see this task as essentially a combination of evangelism and teaching about the Bible as literature, mainly to non-Christians. Even though there may be Christians in some classes, the professor has no church-authorized authority or doctrinal endorsement, as there would be with a Bible teacher in a church or a professor in a Christian college or seminary. I realize that others would disagree with me on this point, and would think that this activity should be considered the same as item 2 on the list.

27. Participating in a discussion in a home Bible study (men and women members)
28. Formally counseling one man[43]
29. Formally counseling a married couple
30. Formally counseling a woman
31. Teaching children's Sunday school class
32. Teaching Vacation Bible School
33. Singing a solo on Sunday morning (a form of teaching since the lyrics often have biblical content and exhortation)
34. Singing to the congregation as a member of the choir
35. Singing hymns with the congregation (in this activity, sometimes we teach and exhort one another in some sense, see Colossians 3:16)

List 3: Areas of Public Visibility or Recognition: Which Activities Should Be Restricted to Men?

(listed in order of greatest to least public visibility or recognition in a local congregation)

1. Ordination as pastor (member of the clergy) in a denomination
2. Being licensed to perform some ministerial functions within a denomination
3. Paid member of pastoral staff (such as youth worker, music director, counselor, Christian education director)
4. Paid member of administrative church staff (such as church secretary or treasurer)
5. Performing a baptism (in churches where this is not exclusively the role of clergy or elders)
6. Helping to serve the Lord's Supper (in churches where this is not exclusively the role of clergy or elders)
7. Giving announcements at the Sunday morning service
8. Taking the offering
9. Public reading of Scripture
10. Public prayer

43. See footnote to item 24 in List 1 (above) for an explanation of why I put this item and the next two at this point in the list, and why I included these three items on both lists.

11. Prophesying in public (according to 1 Corinthians 11:5 and 14:29, where this is not understood as having authority equal to Scripture or Bible teaching)
12. Singing a solo on Sunday mornings
13. Giving a personal testimony in church
14. Giving a prayer request in church
15. Being a member of a prayer team that prays for people individually after the service.
16. Welcoming people at the door (a greeter)
17. Editing the church newsletter
18. Singing in the choir
19. Singing of hymns with congregation on Sunday morning
20. Participating in the responsive reading of Scripture on Sunday morning

Even such long lists are, of course, incomplete. For one thing, there are specialized ministries (parachurch organizations such as Campus Crusade for Christ, InterVarsity Christian Fellowship, the Navigators, Focus on the Family, or Prison Fellowship) that would have similar lists of activities but often with different titles.

In addition, this *list of activities* cannot include the *variation in attitudes* that can make a big difference in the actual level of governing authority in a specific situation. (Does a particular woman who chairs a committee have a domineering attitude or a gracious servant heart?) This list also cannot take into account any *variation in goals* that a person is trying to attain. (Is a woman seeking more and more authority over men, or is she genuinely seeking to use gifts for the benefit of the church?) Where churches see a borderline situation, it may be hard to decide the matter in advance, and the decision may well depend on variations in the attitudes and goals of the people involved.

Moreover, these lists cannot take into account the widely *varying situations* that occur in different churches. One church may have a college-age class of three students, while another may have a college-age class of five hundred. Surely what it means to teach and have authority over men applies differently in the two situations. In such borderline situations, churches will need to use mature wisdom and sound judgment to make a correct evaluation of what is appropriate in light of biblical principles. But I think these lists, though not exhaustive, are still helpful.

What is the solution?

These lists now present us with a dilemma: Everyone who agrees with the principles of the Danvers Statement[44] will agree that *some* of these uses of authority are appropriate for women, and some are not (List 1). They will also agree that *some* of these kinds of Bible teaching are appropriate for women, and some are not (List 2). And I think that everyone who agrees with the Danvers Statement will agree at least that ordination as a pastor is inappropriate for women, while there may be differences on whether the other areas of public visibility are appropriate (List 3). (Egalitarians, by contrast, would say *all* of the items on *all* of the lists should be open to gifted women as well as men.)

At this point I must state the obvious: *The Bible does not give us a specific verse on each of these situations.* But that is true about the entire Christian life. Each day we face thousands of decisions, very few of which are covered by a specific verse. We agree that it is wrong to steal, but can we use the office phone to make a personal call? May we take an unused bar of soap or a box of tissue from a hotel room? Surely not the towels or the table lamp! Between what is clearly right and clearly wrong we make decisions every day, seeking to be faithful to Scripture as we apply it to everyday life.

We must recognize that God in His wisdom has given us a Bible that specifies *many principles* for conduct and gives *some specific examples* of application. But by its very nature the Bible cannot speak directly to the thousands and even millions of real-life situations people will encounter throughout the centuries.

What then should we do? First, we should understand the principles that allow certain activities and understand the principles that prohibit other activities. Then between these parameters, we should attempt to make a mature judgment based on the wisdom God gives us and our knowledge of the situation. In many such situations, I have found the following chart useful:

A Spectrum of Different Actions

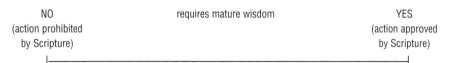

NO (action prohibited by Scripture)	requires mature wisdom	YES (action approved by Scripture)

44. See Appendix 1, pp. 537–40, for the Danvers Statement, which contains the fundamental statement of complementarian principles regarding the roles of men and women in marriage and the church.

Now regarding the question of women's activities in the church, what actions should we put on this scale? On the left side of the scale we can put verses such as 1 Timothy 2:12, where Paul does not permit a woman "to teach or exercise authority over a man," in the specific context that he is talking about. Since I think it is very evident from the context that Paul is talking about the *assembled congregation* in this passage (see 1 Timothy 2:8–10; 3:15), and that he is giving principles that apply to the entire congregation (see 1 Timothy 3:1–16), I think that the left end of the scale *prohibits women from teaching or having governing authority over the assembled congregation.*

What shall we put on the right end of the scale? Here we would put verses such as Acts 18:26, where, in a less formal setting apart from an assembled congregation, we find that Priscilla and Aquila were talking to Apollos, and "*they* took him and explained to him the way of God more accurately." This situation is similar to a small group Bible study in which both men and women are all participating and in that way all are in some way "teaching" one another. It is also similar to a woman talking to a man privately about the teaching of Scripture.

Another verse that we can put on the right end of the scale is Titus 2:4 which tells the older women to "train the young women to love their husbands and children."

Since Paul specifically prohibits women from teaching or having authority over *men,* we may also put on the right end of the chart the activity of teaching *children,* for surely both mothers and fathers teach their children, and it is appropriate that this family teaching activity extend into the Sunday school where women function as "mothers" of the church and teach other children as well as their own. So our scale would look like this:

NO (action prohibited by Scripture)	requires mature wisdom	YES (action approved by Scripture)
governing and Bible teaching authority over the assembled congregation	other kinds of governing and teaching activities	informal Bible instruction (as in a group of two or three) teaching women, teaching children

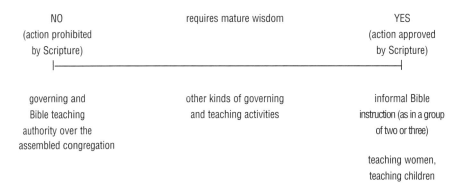

With such a scale in mind, we could place all the activities in the long lists above at one point or another on the scale. Some activities, such as serving as senior pastor in the local church, clearly fall on the "no" side of the scale, for the senior pastor teaches the Bible and exercises authority over the assembled congregation. Other activities, such as performing a baptism or leading a home fellowship group or chairing a committee, fall somewhere in the middle of the scale. And it is at those points that individuals and churches need to prayerfully consider just where they will "draw the line" in saying what activities are encouraged and what activities are prohibited for women in their local churches.

Application to List 1

Once we reach a conviction that Bible teaching and governing the assembled congregation are restricted to men, we can look again at List 1 (areas of governing authority). It seems clear that this principle would prohibit activities 1–8 for women, and probably also item 9: The office of senior pastor, and the office of elder (or equivalent), together with activities specifically connected to those positions, are not open to women. But all the other activities on the list, from item 10 to the end, are open to women.[45]

In my understanding, therefore, List 1 would look like this:

List 1: Areas of Governing Authority: Which Offices or Activities Should Be Restricted to Men?

(listed in order of greatest to least amount of authority over men)

Governing activities that should be restricted to men:

1. President of a denomination
2. Member of the governing board of a denomination
3. Regional governing authority (such as district superintendent, bishop, or similar office)
4. Member of regional governing board
5. Senior pastor in local church (or associate pastor with many similar responsibilities to the senior pastor)
6. Member of governing board with authority over whole church (this would be the office of elder in many churches, while it would be the office of deacon or board member or church council member in others)
7. Presiding over a baptism or communion service (but see List 3 for serving communion or performing a baptism)
8. Giving spoken judgment on a prophecy given to the congregation (1 Corinthians 14:33–36)
9. Permanent leader of a fellowship group meeting in a home (both men and women members)

45. See pp. 97–99 below for the somewhat broader perspective of the Danvers Statement.

Governing activities that should be open to both men and women:

10. Committee chairman (or chairperson)[46]
11. Director of Christian education
12. Sunday school superintendent
13. Missionary responsibilities (many administrative responsibilities in missionary work in other countries
14. Moderating a Bible discussion in a home Bible study group
15. Choir director
16. Leading singing on Sunday morning
17. Deacon (in churches where this does not involve governing authority over the entire congregation)[47]
18. Administrative assistant to senior pastor
19. Church treasurer
20. Church secretary
21. Member of advisory council to regional governing authority
22. Meeting periodically with church governing board to give counsel and advice
23. Regular conversations between elders and their wives over matters coming before the elder board (with understanding that confidentiality is preserved)
24. Formally counseling one man
25. Formally counseling a couple together
26. Formally counseling another woman
27. Speaking in congregational business meetings
28. Voting in congregational business meetings

I put item 9 in the first section because I do not think it appropriate for a woman to be a permanent leader of a home fellowship group, especially if the group regularly carries out pastoral care of its members and functions as a minichurch within the church. The leader of such a group carries a governing authority that is very similar to the authority over the assembled congregation that Paul mentions in 1 Timothy 2. Given the small size of churches meeting in homes in the first century, and given the pastoral nature of leading a home fellowship group, I think Paul would have included this in 1 Timothy 2:12, "I do not permit a woman to teach or to exercise authority over a man."

But that is my personal judgment. At one time I was a member of a church that had some women leading home fellowship groups. I disagreed with that decision, but I found that I could

46. See the footnotes to the first copy of each list earlier in this chapter for an explanation of why I have placed certain items (such as this one) where they are on the lists.

47. Some people may wish to restrict deacons to men based on 1 Timothy 3:12; see discussion on pp. 263–68.

in good conscience continue as an active and supportive member of the church. However, I don't think that I could have participated in a fellowship group in which a woman functioned in that pastoral role with regard to me and my wife.

So I would draw the line between items 9 and 10. From item 10 onward, I think it is right to encourage women to be involved in all the rest of the types of governing authority on the list. For example, I would approve of a woman as director of Christian education (item 11) or superintendent of the Sunday school (item 12), or as a committee chair (item 10). These activities do not carry the sort of authority over the whole congregation that Paul has in view in 1 Timothy 2, or when he specifies that elders should be men (1 Timothy 3; Titus 1).

Application to List 2

When we turn to areas of Bible teaching (List 2), my own personal judgment is that the line should be drawn between items 10 and 11. That means the list would look like this:

List 2: Areas of Bible Teaching: Which Activities Should Be Restricted to Men?

(listed in order of greatest to least teaching influence over men in a group or congregation)

Teaching activities that should be restricted to men:

1. Teaching Bible or theology in a theological seminary
2. Teaching Bible or theology in a Christian college
3. Preaching (teaching the Bible) at a nationwide denominational meeting, or at a nationwide Christian conference
4. Preaching (teaching the Bible) at a regional meeting of churches, or at a regional Christian conference
5. Preaching (teaching the Bible) regularly to the whole church on Sunday mornings
6. Occasional preaching (teaching the Bible) to the whole church on Sunday mornings
7. Occasional Bible teaching at less formal meetings of the whole church (such as Sunday evening or at a midweek service)
8. Bible teaching to an adult Sunday school class (both men and women members)
9. Bible teaching at a home Bible study (both men and women members)
10. Bible teaching to a college-age Sunday school class

Teaching activities that should be open to both men and women:

11. Bible teaching to a high school Sunday school class
12. Writing a book on Bible doctrines
13. Writing or editing a study Bible
14. Writing a commentary on a book of the Bible
15. Writing notes in a study Bible
16. Writing or editing other kinds of Christian books
17. Bible teaching to a women's Sunday school class
18. Bible teaching to a women's Bible study group during the week
19. Bible teaching to a junior high Sunday school class
20. Teaching as a Bible professor on a secular university campus
21. Evangelistic speaking to large groups of non-Christians (for example, an evangelistic rally on a college campus)
22. Working as an evangelistic missionary in other cultures
23. Moderating a discussion in a small group Bible study (men and women members)
24. Reading Scripture aloud on Sunday morning
25. Reading Scripture to other, less formal meetings of the church
26. Giving a personal testimony before the congregation (a story of how God has worked in one's own or others' lives)
27. Participating in a discussion in a home Bible study (men and women members)
28. Formally counseling one man
29. Formally counseling a married couple
30. Formally counseling a woman
31. Teaching children's Sunday school class
32. Teaching Vacation Bible School
33. Singing a solo on Sunday morning (this is a form of teaching, since the lyrics often have biblical content and exhortation)
34. Singing to the congregation as a member of the choir
35. Singing hymns with the congregation (in this activity, sometimes we teach and exhort one another in some sense, see Colossians 3:16)

There are several considerations that weighed in my decision of where to draw a line in List 2. As I mentioned when discussing List 1, there is a strong similarity between a home Bible study taught by a woman (item 9) and a local church meeting in a home in the ancient world. Therefore, I do not think it is appropriate for a woman to be the regular instructor in a home Bible study. On the other hand, I believe that moderating a discussion in a small group Bible study (item 23) is appropriate for women. The teaching and governing component is less than it would be if she were regularly teaching or had pastoral responsibility over the group, and does not resemble the teaching authority over the assembled congregation that Paul prohibits in 1 Timothy 2.

For similar reasons, I think it is inappropriate for a woman to be the Bible teacher in an adult Sunday school class (item 8). This looks so much like what Paul prohibited in 1 Timothy 2 that I cannot endorse it. (I have heard many stories of women doing such teaching effectively, but I don't want to base my decision on people's experiences. I am trying to decide how Scripture applies, and then let Scripture govern our experiences, not our experiences govern Scripture. It seems to me that teaching an adult Bible class is just what Paul is saying not to do—though God may bless His Word with good fruit at times even if women are disobedient to Scripture in teaching it to men.[48] The final question still must be what Scripture tells us to do and not to do.)

When do children become adults, and when does teaching *boys* become teaching *men*?[49] This will vary from society to society and from culture to culture. It may even vary from subculture to subculture. In our own culture, if children graduate from high school, move away from home, and begin to support themselves, then surely they are functioning as adults. A new household has been formed. In that case, the young men are adult men, and it would not be appropriate for a woman to teach a class with them as members.

Many college students also live away from home, support themselves at least in part, and function in our society in all other ways as independent adults. Most college students would be insulted if you called them children! For these reasons, I believe that a college-age Sunday school class (item 10) should have a male teacher.

The situation with a high school class is different, because high school students are still at home and still under the instruction of their mothers. Sunday school class might be seen as an extension of this home instruction, and therefore I do not think it is wrong for a woman to be a Bible teacher in a high school Sunday school class. However, many churches may think it *preferable* for a man to teach a high school class because of the modeling of male leadership in the church that these young adults will grow to appreciate and imitate. But I do not think having a woman teacher would be disobeying 1 Timothy 2:12.

The broad perspective of the Danvers Statement

When the founders of the Council on Biblical Manhood and Womanhood wrote the Danvers Statement in 1987, we realized that no brief statement could possibly include all the varieties of activities such as those in the list above. We wanted a brief statement that would apply broadly

48. See chapter 11, pp. 474–80, for a discussion of how God can bring some blessing to women when they do Bible teaching to groups of men and women, even though this is contrary to what Scripture directs.

49. A boy would not have been called an *anēr* ("man") in the ordinary use of Greek in Paul's time. A male child could be called a *brephos* ("infant"), a *nēpios* ("young child"), a *pais* ("child"), a *paidarion* ("youth"), a *teknon* ("child"), or a *huios* ("son"), but not an *anēr* ("man"). But in 1 Timothy 2:12, Paul speaks of not teaching or exercising authority over an *anēr*, a man.

across denominations and in all kinds of different churches. I think we came up with a helpful statement, though it is also a broad statement:

> In the church, redemption in Christ gives men and women an equal share in the blessings of salvation; nevertheless, *some governing and teaching roles within the church are restricted to men.* (Affirmation 6)

We intentionally wrote this statement to be somewhat broader in what it allowed than the personal convictions of many of us on the council at that time. We did this because we recognized that applying Scripture to specific situations not addressed by Scripture requires much wisdom and mature judgment, and Christians may differ in decisions about specific applications. Therefore we wanted to specify *what we thought the Bible at the very least requires of us.* In areas of difficulty in application, it is right for Christians to talk with each other and attempt to persuade one another about what God would have us do.

In saying that "*some* governing and teaching roles within the church are restricted to men," the Danvers Statement still draws a definite line and differs decisively with all egalitarians, because they simply could not agree with this statement. They would insist that *no* governing or teaching roles within the church should be restricted to men—that all should be open to women and men alike.

In this way the Danvers Statement draws a very broad circle. It asks only for what seems to so many evangelicals to be clearly affirmed in Scripture: that when the church assembles, there is a teaching and governing authority reserved for men. Christians who agree with this foundational principle agree with the Council on Biblical Manhood and Womanhood and agree with the Danvers Statement. People who differ with this put themselves in the egalitarian camp.

In spite of the many varieties of ways in which churches will work out this principle in their congregations and denominations, this phrase points to a decisive difference in understanding Scripture and in understanding how a church will function. This brief phrase, then, defines a foundational difference between egalitarians and complementarians over the role of women in the church.

Yet I realize that someone can subscribe to the Danvers Statement and approve of more activities for women than those I personally could endorse. For example, someone could subscribe to the Danvers Statement and still think it appropriate for a woman to be the permanent leader of a home fellowship group (List 1, item 9).

With regard to List 2 (areas of Bible teaching), the Danvers Statement draws a line that is broader than my personal judgment about what decisions are most consistent with Scripture. For example, a few evangelical leaders who identify themselves as complementarians have decided that Scripture allows women to occasionally preach to the whole church on Sunday morning (List 2, item 6). They argue that what Paul really has in mind in 1 Timothy 2:12 is the office of elder. First Timothy 2:12 focuses on governing authority and teaching in the church, and these are activities done by elders. As long as a woman does not *hold the office of elder* or *regularly perform the functions that an elder performs*, then 1 Timothy 2 does not prohibit her from occasional preaching, according to this view.

I disagree with this because Paul is speaking of *activities* and not the office of elder in 1 Timothy 2:12. He does not say, "I do not permit a woman to have the teaching or governing authority over men *that belongs to elders*," but rather he mentions certain activities in the assembled congregation that are prohibited to women: "I do not permit a woman to teach or to exercise authority over a man." For this reason, I cannot bring myself to think that Paul meant that women *could* teach and have authority over the congregation *occasionally*, but that they could not teach and have authority on a regular or permanent basis.

But I mention this difference because people who say women can do occasional Bible teaching to the church still *agree* with the broad language of the Danvers Statement that "*some* governing and teaching roles within the church are restricted to men." These people still think the office of elder is restricted to men, and the governing and teaching roles that belong to the office of elder are restricted to men. They are still complementarians, though we differ on some significant questions of application.

I hope that as we talk and pray and search Scripture more, we may come to greater agreement. But this kind of difference in specific application is inevitable in a world in which churches vary so widely in the nature of their church services and in their governing structures. In all areas of church life, differences on specific applications can occur without great harm if they occur within broader guidelines that we all agree on.

The same can be said with respect to items 7, 8, 9, and 10 on List 2 above. In a broad sense, people who say women can do these things are still within the broad parameters of the Danvers Statement, because they do affirm that "some...teaching roles within the church are restricted to men." But to me this position does not seem consistent with Scripture, because in 1 Timothy 2:12, Paul is writing about teaching in the context of an assembled group of Christians, and that is surely what these meetings are.

Application to List 3

As for List 3 (areas of public visibility or recognition), since Scripture indicates that the office of pastor/elder should be restricted to men, I draw the line after item 1, the ordination to the clergy, which in most or all denominations implies recognition of an ability to serve as senior pastor, is restricted to men. But all other items, from item 2 to the end, are open to women as well as men. So, for example, I think it is appropriate for women to hold other full-time positions on the "ministry staff" of the church (such as youth worker or music director or professional counselor).

The Danvers Statement draws the line in the same place here in List 3. By saying that "*some* governing and teaching roles within the church are restricted to men," it implies that the office of pastor or elder is restricted to men. But it allows for women to serve in all capacities from item 2 to the end of the list.

List 3: Areas of Public Visibility or Recognition: Which Activities Should be Restricted to Men?

(listed in order of greatest to least public visibility or recognition in a local congregation)

Public recognition that should be restricted to men:

1. Ordination as pastor (member of the clergy) in a denomination[50]

Public recognition that should be open to both men and women:

2. Being licensed to perform some ministerial functions within a denomination
3. Paid member of pastoral staff (such as youth worker, music director, counselor, Christian education director)
4. Paid member of administrative church staff (church secretary or treasurer, for example)
5. Performing a baptism (in churches where this is not exclusively the role of clergy or elders)
6. Helping to serve the Lord's Supper (in churches where this is not exclusively the role of clergy or elders)
7. Giving announcements at the Sunday morning service
8. Taking the offering
9. Public reading of Scripture
10. Public prayer
11. Prophesying in public (according to 1 Corinthians 11:5 and 14:29, where this is not understood as having authority equal to Scripture or Bible teaching)
12. Singing a solo on Sunday mornings
13. Giving a personal testimony in church
14. Giving a prayer request in church
15. Being a member of a prayer team that prays for people individually after the service
16. Welcoming people at the door (a greeter)
17. Editing the church newsletter
18. Singing in the choir
19. Singing of hymns with the congregation on Sunday morning
20. Participating in the responsive reading of Scripture on Sunday morning

---

50. I think this also includes ordination as a military chaplain; see chapter 9, p. 389.

Conclusion

I hope these guidelines will help many churches come to their own understanding of where to draw the line on what is appropriate for women and what is inappropriate. I realize that many churches will draw a more restrictive line than what I have proposed here, and others will be less restrictive. I simply encourage churches to be careful not to prohibit what the Bible doesn't prohibit, while they also attempt to preserve male leadership in the way Scripture directs.

What should be evident is that on all three lists, many activities are fully open to women. And these include a number of activities that have not traditionally been open to them.

In addition, I have not even mentioned hundreds of *other* kinds of ministries in a local church that both women and men are already carrying out, but that do not occur on any of these lists because they belong to other categories of activities.

I hope this controversy in the evangelical world will prompt churches to give earnest consideration to the possibilities of many more ministries for women than have been open to them in the past. It is the Council on Biblical Manhood and Womanhood's sincere desire to open the doors wide to all the areas of ministry that God intends for women to have. These areas of ministry may indeed be more numerous, more visible, and more prominent in the life of the church than we have previously thought. If that happens, this entire controversy will have served a wonderful purpose, and the church will be far stronger and far more pleasing to God as it carries out its ministry until Christ returns.

Chapter Three

Evangelical Feminist Claims from Genesis 1–3

Note to readers regarding format: Beginning with this chapter, most of the rest of the book follows a "Claims and Answers" format. I will first state an egalitarian (or evangelical feminist) claim, and then provide one or more responses to it. In each case, the egalitarian claim is put in boldface type, and each answer is also summarized in boldface. In this chapter, egalitarian claims are numbered 3.1, 3.2, 3.3, and so on. In chapter 4, egalitarian claims are numbered 4.1, 4.2, 4.3, etc. Answers to each egalitarian claim are then identified with lowercase alphabetical designations, so that the answers to claim 3.1 are listed as 3.1a, 3.1b, 3.1c, and so forth. With this layout, readers can choose to skim only the boldface headings to get a sense of the overall argument, or else to read the supporting material for a more detailed explanation.

In almost every case, I have quoted from some of the most responsible and influential evangelical feminist advocates of that position, and I have often given footnotes to additional egalitarians who take a similar position. In that way, readers who wish to read the egalitarian arguments for themselves can easily find them.[1]

Some of the material in chapters 3–12 overlaps with what I wrote in chapters 1–2. This is because I have tried to write so that each claim and answer can be read on its own.

In the first two chapters of this book, we have seen a detailed portrait of the Bible's teaching regarding men and women. God created us equal in His sight, equal in value and dignity, and equal in that we are both in the image of God. But He also created us with differences in roles, differences that find expression in the way we relate to each other in marriage and in the church. Therefore we have in Scripture a beautiful picture of *both equality and differences between men and women,* reflecting the equality and differences among the members of the Trinity.

1. If any egalitarian authors think I have not quoted or summarized their arguments accurately, I would appreciate knowing this. Comments can be sent to: wgrudem@phoenixseminary.edu

But this biblical teaching has been strongly challenged by evangelical feminists in the last thirty years. Can we continue to hold to the view presented in chapters 1 and 2 after considering the counterclaims of evangelical feminists? The remainder of this book is devoted to 118 claims that evangelical feminists have made, claims in which they object to the idea that the Bible affirms male headship in the home and in the church.

In this third chapter, we consider evangelical feminist (or "egalitarian")[2] claims regarding Genesis 1–3. If Adam and Eve were equal in God's sight, how could there be any difference in role or authority? And isn't male headship a result of sin and the Fall, and therefore something we should not perpetuate today? These and other egalitarian objections will be considered in this chapter.

EGALITARIAN CLAIM 3.1: CREATED EQUAL: IN GENESIS 1, ADAM AND EVE WERE CREATED EQUAL; THEREFORE, THERE COULD BE NO DIFFERENCE IN ROLE OR AUTHORITY BETWEEN THEM.

This is the fundamental egalitarian argument, and it is the unspoken assumption behind a large number of specific egalitarian arguments. The assumption is that equality is incompatible with difference in roles, and specifically with differences in authority. This argument was stated well by Linda Belleville in commenting on Genesis 1–2:

> Does being male and female distinguish who we are and what we can do in ways that are non-interchangeable and divinely ordered—a biblical manhood and womanhood so to speak? Although some are quick to say *yes*, the creation accounts offer no support. Instead, the note that is clearly sounded throughout Genesis 1 and 2 is that of *equality*. For one, there is an *equality* of personhood. Both male and female are created in the image of God.... There is also *equality* in the social realm.... There is likewise *equality* in the family realm.... Finally, there is *equality* in the spiritual realm.[3]

Aida Spencer also states this clearly, regarding Adam and Eve in Genesis 1–2:

> Their similar tasks necessitate the work of *equals*. Adam and Eve are *equal* in rank, *equal* in image. Genesis 2, like Genesis 1, declares and explains male and female *equality*, joint rulership, and interrelationship.[4]

---

2. I use the terms *evangelical feminist* and *egalitarian* interchangeably throughout this book.
3. Belleville, *Women Leaders and the Church* (2000), 99–101 (italics added). See also Groothuis, *Good News for Women* (1997), 122–23; Brown, *Women Ministers* (1996), 23; and several of the arguments of Bilezikian, *Beyond Sex Roles* (1985), 21–37.
4. Spencer, *Beyond the Curse* (1995), 29 (italics added).

Answer 3.1a: We must distinguish different senses of "equal." It is true that Adam and Eve were created equal in several ways, but equal value does not imply sameness in authority or roles.

I agree that Adam and Eve were created equal in many ways. They were equal in that both were "in the image of God" (Genesis 1:27). To be in the image of God means that they were like God and they represented God on the earth. This implies that men and women have *equal value* to God, and men and women deserve *equal honor and respect*. They were also *equal in their personhood*, their possession of the qualities that make a truly human person (though they no doubt *differed* in many of their abilities and preferences, as all human beings do). And Adam and Eve were *equal in their importance* to the human race, and importance to God. The human race, and God's plans for the human race, would not have gone very far if one of them had been missing!

But equal value and equal honor and equal personhood and equal importance do not require that people have the *same roles* or the *same authority*. A fundamental egalitarian error is constantly to blur the distinctions and to assume that being equal in the image of God means that people have to be equal (or the same) in authority. This assumption runs throughout Gilbert Bilezikian's treatment of Genesis 1–2,[5] but it is merely an unproven assumption, and it simply is not true.

Answer 3.1b: Many relationships among people involve equal value but difference in roles and authority.

To take a modern example, think of the 2001 World Series, which was won by the Arizona Diamondbacks while I was writing this chapter. Who was more valuable to the Diamondbacks, the manager Bob Brenly or the winning pitchers Randy Johnson and Curt Schilling? Of course, callers to a radio talk show could argue about that kind of question for hours. Some would say that Johnson and Schilling were most valuable, since they shared the Most Valuable Player award. Others would say that Brenly was most valuable, since he alone had the skill to coach a young team to the world championship. The argument is pointless, since the Diamondbacks needed both the coach and the pitchers, as well as many other players, to win. The truth is that Brenly, Johnson, and Schilling were equally valuable, and deserved equal honor.

But one thing is not in question: Bob Brenly had far greater *authority* than any player. He told Johnson and Schilling when they could play and when they had to come out of the game, and even if they didn't like it, they followed his instructions. Different roles, different authority, but equal value and importance.

In fact, greater authority did not result in greater honor in this case. Even though the manager had greater authority, the players got much more honor from fans. The players were

---

5. Bilezikian, *Beyond Sex Roles,* 21–37.

the true heroes in Arizona in 2001, and they were the ones who received the loudest cheers from the crowds.

The same holds true in many other human activities. In a university, the president and the board have greater authority than the faculty, but students come because of what they will learn from the professors. Both the administration and the faculty are valuable, at least equal in value, but they are not equal in authority or the same in their roles.

In a church, the elders (or other leaders) have greater authority, but all Christians are equal in value before God. In a church committee, the head of the committee has greater authority but no greater value as a person. In a family, the parents have authority over their children, but the children are just as valuable to God. In a city, the mayor has greater authority but no greater value to the city than many of the citizens.

So the fundamental egalitarian claim, "If men and women have different God-given roles and authority, then we can't be equal," is an unproven assumption and it just does not hold true in human experience.

Jesus taught the same thing:

> You know that the rulers of the Gentiles lord it over them, and their great ones exercise authority over them. It shall not be so among you. But whoever would be great among you must be your servant, and whoever would be first among you must be your slave, even as the Son of Man came not to be served but to serve, and to give his life as a ransom for many. (Matthew 20:25–28)

To have greater authority does not necessarily mean being great in God's sight. From the Bible's perspective, having authority over others and having value in God's kingdom are completely separate things.[6]

EGALITARIAN CLAIM 3.2: AUTHORITY DENIES EQUALITY: IF THERE WAS MALE AUTHORITY BEFORE THE FALL, THEN THE MALE WOULD BE SUPERIOR TO THE FEMALE AND THEY COULD NOT BE EQUAL.

This is the counterpart to the previous argument. If equality implies no difference in roles (from an egalitarian standpoint), then male authority must imply male *superiority*, a denial of equality. Aida Spencer writes, "Male and female share in power and authority, even as they share in dignity."[7] And immediately after Spencer says, "Adam and Eve are *equal* in rank, *equal* in

6. See chapter 10, sections 10.5–10.6, pp. 437–43, for a response to Rebecca Groothuis's claim that it is wrong to use analogies to other kinds of human subordination with equality, because the subordination of women to men is different: It is not based on ability or choice, and it is based on a woman's very being.
7. Spencer, *Beyond the Curse*, 23.

image," she then claims equality in authority: "God's original intention for women and men is that in work and in marriage they share tasks and share authority."[8]

Answer 3.2a: This blurs the discussion by using "equal" and "superior" in a vague, undefined way.

Of course Adam and Eve were not equal if equal is made to mean "the same," or if equal is made to mean "equal in authority." But the real question is whether they were equal in value, equal as creatures made in the image of God. They were equal in that way, but not in authority. The same is true of the word *superior*: if we are talking about superior authority, then Adam had superior authority. But if we are talking about superior value, then they were the same.

Answer 3.2b: This argument assumes that difference in authority implies difference in value, but we know that is not true in human relationships.

We already noticed above that many examples from everyday life show that people can have greater authority but not have greater value or importance. This is true with a baseball team's manager and his players, with parents and their children, with a mayor and the citizens in a town, and so forth. Adam had greater authority but not greater value.

Answer 3.2c: We also know that difference in authority does not imply difference in value among the members of the Trinity.

The Father, Son, and Holy Spirit are equal in value, in deity, and in all attributes. But the Father has an authority that the Son does not have, an authority as Father that is seen, for example, in the Father's direction of the Son and the Holy Spirit in their tasks in the creation of the universe and in saving human beings. Similarly, the Son has an authority greater than the Holy Spirit. (I discuss this subject at length in claims 10.2-10.5, below.) In the Trinity, then, there is genuine equality along with difference in role and authority.

EGALITARIAN CLAIM 3.3: BOTH TOLD TO RULE: ADAM AND EVE WERE BOTH TOLD TO RULE OVER THE CREATION. THEREFORE THERE WAS NO DIFFERENCE IN ROLE OR AUTHORITY BETWEEN THEM.

Gilbert Bilezikian makes this common egalitarian claim:

> Since both man and woman bear the image of God, they are both assigned the task of ruling the earth, without any reference to differentiation on the basis of sex. The text gives no hint of a division of responsibilities or of a distinction of rank in their adminis-

8. Ibid., 29.

tration of the natural realm. They are both equally entitled by God to act as His vice-regents for the rulership of the earth. The lack of any restrictions or of any qualifications in their participation in the task implies roles of equality for man and woman."[9]

Bilezikian adds that it would be natural to expect some indication of male authority in Genesis 1 if any existed, since Genesis 1 is a text that is "permeated with the concept of hierarchical organization" (p. 25).

Answer 3.3a: This claim takes something the Bible does say and adds to it something the Bible does not say.

True, the Bible says Adam and Eve were both told to rule over Creation:

> And God blessed them. And God said *to them*, "Be fruitful and multiply and fill the earth and subdue it and have dominion over the fish of the sea and over the birds of the heavens and over every living thing that moves on the earth." (Genesis 1:28)

But it does not say that they were to rule in the same way. And it does not say that they had the same authority.

This very verse tells both Adam and Eve to "Be fruitful and multiply and fill the earth," but that does not imply that they would act in the very same way in being fruitful and multiplying. Eve would have a role in bearing and nursing children that Adam could not have.

Answer 3.3b: The Bible does not teach everything in Genesis 1. The statements in Genesis 2 are also true.

This egalitarian claim wrongly assumes that something has to be taught in Genesis 1 in order to be true. But Genesis 2 teaches many things that are not found in Genesis 1, such as God forming the man "of dust from the ground" and breathing into man "the breath of life" (v. 7), and then putting the man in the Garden "to work it and keep it" (v. 15), as well as the tree of the knowledge of good and evil, Adam naming the animals, and God creating Eve from Adam's side. Therefore if Genesis 2 gives several indications of male authority or leadership, that is also part of the Bible and part of what we are to accept as true.

Bilezikian's claim that Genesis 1 is "permeated with the concept of hierarchical organization" is an exaggeration. The only mentions of authority or rule in Genesis 1 are statements about the sun and moon ruling over the day and night (vv. 16, 18) and about man having dominion over the plants and animals (vv. 26, 28–29). No details at all are given about the relationship between man and woman, for that is left for Genesis 2. And in Genesis 2, as we have already seen, we find that Adam and Eve were to relate to one another in different ways, with a leadership role given to Adam (see pp. 29–45, and the summary on p. 109). In fact, to turn

9. Bilezikian, *Beyond Sex Roles*, 24. See also Belleville, *Women Leaders and the Church*, 99–101; Groothuis, *Good News for Women*, 123; Spencer, *Beyond the Curse*, 22–23; Brown, *Women Ministers*, 23.

Bilezikian's argument back on him, we would expect to find material about the way Adam and Eve were to relate not in Genesis 1, but in Genesis 2, where their creation and their relationship is explained in much more detail.

Answer 3.3c: In other parts of Scripture, commands given to groups do not deny the authority and leadership patterns that exist within those groups.

The Great Commission, which commands us to "make disciples of all nations" (Matthew 28:19–20), is given to all Christians, but that does not deny the authority of elders in our churches. We don't say, "All Christians are told to proclaim the gospel, therefore there is no difference in role or authority between them." Moses commanded the people of Israel, "Go in and take possession of the land" (Deuteronomy 1:8), but that did not deny the authority of the leaders of the twelve tribes, or of the elders among them.

Egalitarian claim 3.4: Male Headship a Result of the Fall: In Genesis 1–3, male headship did not come about until after the Fall and is therefore a product of sin.

This is a fundamental claim of every egalitarian writer I know, and is even represented in titles like that of Aida Spencer's book *Beyond the Curse*. Spencer writes of Eve:

> Her curse was now to be ruled, perversely to long for her husband and he to rule over her. She would want to be dominated by her husband and he would submit to this desire.... The ruling is a consequence of Eve's longing and her fall.[10]

Gilbert Bilezikian likewise writes of Adam and Eve:

> Instead of meeting her desire and providing a mutually supportive and nurturing family environment, he will rule over her.... The clearest implication of this statement [Gen. 3:16], conferring rulership to Adam as a result of the fall, is that he was not Eve's ruler prior to the fall.[11]

And Rebecca Groothuis says,

> In fact, there is no mention of either spouse ruling over the other—until after their fall into sin, when God declares to the woman that "he will rule over you" (3:16). This is stated by God not as a command, but as a consequence of their sin.[12]

10. Spencer, *Beyond the Curse,* 36.
11. Bilezikian, *Beyond Sex Roles*, 55, and 264n12.
12. Groothuis, *Good News for Women*, 123. Many other egalitarian writers make similar statements. For example, see Brown, *Women Ministers*, 51, 55.

Answer 3.4a: There are at least ten arguments that prove there was male headship before the Fall.

I have explained these ten in Chapter 1. In summary form, they are:

1. *The order:* Adam was created first, then Eve (note the sequence in Genesis 2:7 and 2:18–23; 1 Timothy 2:13).
2. *The representation:* Adam, not Eve, had a special role in representing the human race (1 Corinthians 15:22, 45–49; Romans 5:12–21).
3. *The naming of woman:* Adam named Eve; Eve did not name Adam (Genesis 2:23).
4. *The naming of the human race:* God named the human race "Man," not "Woman" (Genesis 5:2).
5. *The primary accountability:* God called Adam to account first after the Fall (Genesis 3:9).
6. *The purpose:* Eve was created as a helper for Adam, not Adam as a helper for Eve (Genesis 2:18; 1 Corinthians 11:9).
7. *The conflict:* The Curse brought a distortion of previous roles, not the introduction of new roles (Genesis 3:16).
8. *The restoration:* Salvation in Christ in the New Testament reaffirms the Creation order (Colossians 3:18–19).
9. *The mystery:* Marriage from the beginning of Creation was a picture of the relationship between Christ and the church (Ephesians 5:32–33).
10. *The parallel with the Trinity:* The equality, differences, and unity between men and women reflect the equality, differences, and unity in the Trinity (1 Corinthians 11:3).

For further explanation of these points, see the discussion in chapter 1 (pp. 30–42). For egalitarian objections to these points, with answers to those objections, see the discussion in the rest of this chapter, and also chapter 10.

Answer 3.4b: It is true that oppressive male rule did not come about until after the Fall, but male headship and unique male authority in marriage did exist before the Fall.

As explained above (chapter 1, pp. 39–40), when God punished Adam and Eve after the Fall, His statement "he shall rule over you" (Genesis 3:16) indicated a rule by means of greater power, which among sinful human beings will often result in a harsh and oppressive rule. But this is part of God's curse following sin, and we should not support it or perpetuate it.

Instead of harsh, oppressive rule, the Bible restores the beauty of Adam and Eve's situation before the Fall when it says, "Wives, submit to your husbands, as is fitting in the Lord. Husbands, love your wives, and do not be harsh with them" (Colossians 3:18–19).

This is the beauty of the original relationship between Adam and Eve that the New Testament is restoring in our new creation in Christ.

Answer 3.4c: Some egalitarians deny the truth and purity of the words of the Bible in order to deny male leadership before there was sin in the world.

Some egalitarian writers go so far as to deny the truth or purity of God's words in the Bible. For example, Rebecca Groothuis denies that the meanings of the Hebrew words in Genesis 2 carry authority for us today (see Egalitarian claim 3.5), William Webb denies the historical accuracy of Genesis 2 (see Egalitarian claim 3.7), and Gilbert Bilezikian and Linda Belleville imply that Paul was wrong to reason from Adam's creation before Eve and make any application to the life of the church (see Egalitarian claim 3.12).

Egalitarian claim 3.5: Patriarchal Language: The Hebrew language of the Old Testament was "an expression of patriarchal culture."

Rebecca Groothuis says,

> We should note that the ancient Hebrew language was an expression of patriarchal culture. We cannot conclude, simply because the Bible was written under divine inspiration, that the languages in which the Bible was written were themselves created under divine inspiration. These languages were as male centered as the cultures they reflected and by which they were created. The fact that certain words in a language can be used to refer either to a male human or to humans in general reflects cultural concepts of gender; it says nothing about God's view of gender.[13]

Groothuis uses this statement to answer Raymond C. Ortlund's claim that male headship is hinted at when God calls the human race by the Hebrew equivalent of our word *man,* rather than by a Hebrew word that means *woman* or a word that would mean *person.*[14]

Answer 3.5a: All the meanings of the statements of Scripture are from God.

Groothuis uses this argument about language reflecting patriarchal culture in order to deny the meaning of some of the words of Scripture. She talks about "the languages in which the Bible was written" as if the debate were about words that occur *outside* of Scripture. But she glosses over the fact that the story of God's naming the human race *man* (Genesis 1:26–27; 5:2) is found in the Hebrew language *in the text of the Bible*. To say that these *words of the Bible* have a patri-

13. Groothuis, *Good News for Women,* 124.
14. See Ortlund, "Male-Female Equality," in Piper and Grudem, *Recovering Biblical Manhood and Womanhood* (1991), 98; see also pp. 34–36 above.

archal meaning that God did not intend, and in fact to say that these *words of the Bible* tell us "nothing about God's view of gender," is simply to deny the authority of this part of Scripture.

This approach is not a legitimate evangelical option. It fits a pattern of several egalitarian arguments that, upon examination, turn out to deny the authority of Scripture.

EGALITARIAN CLAIM 3.6: ANDROGYNOUS ADAM: ADAM WAS NOT MALE UNTIL EVE WAS CREATED, BUT WAS RATHER JUST "A SEXUALLY UNDIFFERENTIATED HUMAN."

Rebecca Groothuis writes,

> Some have suggested that before the woman was created, Adam was not a specifically male human, but was a sexually undifferentiated human. This idea seems to have some plausibility, given that the biblical text does not refer to Adam as male until after the woman is taken out of him.... [The text of Genesis 1:26–27 and 5:1–2] suggests that before the woman was taken out of the man, Adam had in himself, somehow, a capacity for both maleness and femaleness.[15]

Answer 3.6a: If Adam was not male, then Eve would not have been created as female.

Scripture says prior to the creation of Eve, there was not found for Adam "a helper fit for him" (Genesis 2:20). Then it says that God made Eve for Adam as a "helper fit for him," meaning one corresponding to and opposite to him. This means that Adam had sexual differentiation prior to the creation of Eve, and that Eve was created so that she would exactly complement Adam *as he existed prior to her creation.* Therefore Adam had to be male prior to Eve's creation. The egalitarian view represented here would destroy God's whole plan in making a "helper fit for" Adam.

Thus Groothuis is not correct when she says that "the biblical text does not refer to Adam as male until after the woman is taken out of him." The Hebrew term *'ādām* has the sense "man as opposed to woman" in Genesis 2:22, 23, 25; 3:8, 12, 17, 20, 21, but it is the same word used to refer to the man before Eve was created.[16]

Answer 3.6b: If Adam was not male or female, he could not be human.

If this egalitarian claim were true, then Adam was not a male human being or a female human being when he was first created, which means *he was not truly human* in the sense that anyone is today. There is no such thing as "a sexually undifferentiated human."

---

15. Groothuis, *Good News for Women,* 125.
16. BDB, 9.

Answer 3.6c: If Adam was not male, he could not have represented us.

Adam was alone when God gave him the command, "of the tree of the knowledge of good and evil you shall not eat" (Genesis 2:17, but Eve was not created until Genesis 2:22). This means that before Eve was created, Adam *as first created* has to be seen as our representative, and he represented us for a time without sinning. But if, as Groothuis suggests, Adam was created as "a sexually undifferentiated human," then he could not have represented us at the beginning, for he was not really like us "in every respect" (cf. Hebrews 2:17). This idea therefore contradicts the whole parallel between Adam and Christ (Romans 5:12–21; 1 Corinthians 15:21–22, 45–49) which Paul sees as essential to God's plan of salvation.

By implication, Groothuis's view also threatens Christ's maleness, for if Adam represented us for a time as "a sexually undifferentiated human," then why should Christ not also be "a sexually undifferentiated human"?

Answer 3.6d: The Bible gives no support to this idea.

This egalitarian proposal simply reads into the biblical text something that is not there. Groothuis says "the biblical text does not refer to Adam as male until after the woman is taken out of him," then adds, "In Genesis 1:26–27 and 5:1–2, we are told that God created Adam, that Adam was created in God's image, and that Adam was created male and female."

But Groothuis fails to understand a fundamental fact about translation: A word can take different senses in different contexts. The Brown-Driver-Briggs *Hebrew and English Lexicon of the Old Testament* gives three main meanings for the Hebrew word *'ādām*:

1. "*a man*… = human being" (and then it gives the sense "man as opposed to woman" for Genesis 2:22, 23, 25; 3:8, 12, 17, 20, 21).
2. "collective *man, mankind*" (and here it mentions Genesis 1:26, among other verses)
3. "proper name, masculine: Adam, first man" (and here it mentions Genesis 2:20; 3:17, 25, 5:1, 3, 4, 5).[17]

Groothuis has simply taken meaning 3 ("Adam" as a proper name) and imposed it on verses where it says God created "man" as male and female (meaning 2). But Groothuis's meaning "Adam" (as a proper name for a person) is impossible in Genesis 1:26–27 and Genesis 5:2, for several times the text specifies that it is referring to "them," to *plural* man and woman together:

> Then God said, "Let us make man in our image, after our likeness. And let *them* have dominion over the fish of the sea and over the birds of the heavens and over the livestock and over all the earth and over every creeping thing that creeps on the earth."

---

17. Ibid., 9. There is a fourth meaning, the proper name of a city in Joshua 3:16.

> So God created man in his own image, in the image of God he created him; male and female he created *them*. (Genesis 1:26–27)

It does not say "male and female he created *him*," which would be necessary for Groothuis's view. Similarly, we read:

> Male and female he created *them*, and he blessed *them* and named *them* Man when *they* were created. (Genesis 5:2)

Groothuis's view would have this text read, "Male and female he created *him* [or it?], and he blessed *him* [it?] and named *him* [it?] Man when *he* [it?] was created." The Bible does not say this.

And the Bible does not say that God first created "a human being" and then later made him into a male human being, but rather, "male and female he created them" (Genesis 1:27). Adam was male from the moment of his creation.

Answer 3.6e: Is this view an indication of deeper egalitarian hostility toward human sexuality?

When egalitarians labor to reject Adam's maleness, and thus go against the clear sense of Genesis 1–2 that people have understood for centuries, it makes me wonder if this doesn't reflect some deeper dislike of human sexuality in general, some hostility toward the very idea of manhood and womanhood. Why is it objectionable that God created Adam as a *man*?

Egalitarian claim 3.7: Genesis 1–2 Not Historically Accurate: The elements of male leadership or patriarchy seen in Genesis 1–2 do not actually portray the facts of the original Creation, but are a literary device that the author inserted into the Genesis story.

In a recent book that has had widespread influence, William Webb argues that the elements of male leadership that are in Genesis 2 do not reflect the actual historical situation in the Garden of Eden, but were inserted there as a literary device for possibly three reasons: (1) to anticipate the Fall, (2) to allow for better understanding by readers in the society and culture of Moses' time, or (3) to anticipate the agrarian society that would come into effect after the Fall.[18]

Webb agrees that "the practice of primogeniture in which the first born is granted prominence within the 'creative order' of a family unit"[19] is found in the narrative in Genesis 2. He sees this as support for male headship within the text of Genesis 2. He also thinks this is how it

---

18. See Webb, *Slaves, Women and Homosexuals* (2001). The back cover includes endorsements from Darrell Bock of Dallas Theological Seminary, Craig Evans of Trinity Western University, Craig Keener of Eastern Seminary, and Stephen Spencer of Dallas Theological Seminary (but now of Wheaton College).
19. Ibid., 135.

is understood by Paul when he says, "For Adam was formed first, then Eve" (1 Timothy 2:13). But Webb sees this primogeniture theme in Genesis 2 as a "cultural component" in that text.

But how could there be changing cultural influence in the pre-Fall Garden of Eden? Webb answers this question in three ways. First, he says these indications of male headship may be a *literary device that anticipates the Fall and God's subsequent curse*, rather than accurately recording what was in fact true in the Garden:

> A. . .question is how cultural features could possibly be found in the garden before the influence of culture. Several explanations exist. First, the whispers of patriarchy in the garden may have been placed there *in order to anticipate the curse.*[20]

Webb then claims that the literary construction of Genesis 2–3 includes at least one other example of "literary foreshadowing of the curse" in the pejorative description of the serpent as "*more crafty* than any of the wild animals" (Genesis 3:1). Webb then asks, "If the garden is completely pristine, how could certain creatures in the just-created animal kingdom reflect craftiness? Obviously, this Edenic material embraces *an artistic foreshadowing of events to come.*"[21]

Webb's analysis here assumes that there was no sin or evil in Genesis 3:1 *in actual fact*, but that by a literary device the author described the serpent as "crafty" (and therefore deceitful and therefore sinful), thus anticipating what he would be later, after the Fall. In the same way, he thinks the elements of male headship in Genesis 2 were not there in the Garden in actual fact, but were inserted as "an artistic foreshadowing of events to come."

Webb says further that "patriarchy" in Genesis 2 may have been inserted because it was a reflection of social categories familiar to readers at the time when Moses wrote Genesis, and that would have kept readers in Moses' time from being confused about the main point of the story (namely, that God made everything).

> Second, Eden's quiet echoes of patriarchy may be a way of *describing the past through present categories*. The Creation story may be *using the social categories that Moses' audience would have been familiar with*. God sometimes permits such accommodation in order not to confuse the main point he wants to communicate with factors that are secondary to that overall theme.[22]

Finally, Webb gives a third reason:

> Third. . .*the patriarchy of the garden may reflect God's anticipation of the social context into which Adam and Eve were about to venture*. An agrarian lifestyle. . .would

---

20. Ibid., 142–43 (italics added).
21. Ibid., 143 (italics added).
22. Ibid., italics added. Webb explains in a footnote that the "main point" of the creation narrative "is that Yahweh created the heavens and all that is in them, and Yahweh created the earth and all that is in it—God made everything" (143n46).

naturally produce some kind of hierarchy between men and women.... The presentation of the male-female relationship in patriarchal forms may simply be a way of anticipating this first (and major) life setting into which humankind would enter.[23]

Answer 3.7a: This argument assumes that several facts reported in Genesis 2 are not true.

Even in his analysis of the statement that the serpent was "crafty," Webb understands Genesis 3:1 to affirm something that he thinks was not true at that time, and thus Webb denies the truthfulness of a section of historical narrative in Scripture.

There is really no great difficulty in affirming that Genesis 3:1 is stating historical fact, and taking it at face value. Webb fails even to consider the most likely explanation: that there was sin in the angelic world sometime after the completion of the initial Creation (Genesis 1:31) but prior to Genesis 3:1.[24] Because of this rebellion in the angelic world (see 2 Peter 2:4; Jude 6), Satan himself was already evil and was somehow speaking through the serpent.[25] So Webb's claim that the crafty serpent in Genesis 3:1 must be "artistic foreshadowing of events to come" is not persuasive. It is better to take Genesis 3:1 as historically accurate and affirm that the serpent was in fact "crafty" and therefore deceptive and sinful.

Webb also denies the historical accuracy of Genesis 2 in all three of his explanations of why the narrative indicates male leadership (what he calls "patriarchy" and "primogeniture"). In reason (1), Webb claims that "the whispers of patriarchy in the garden may have been placed there in order to anticipate the curse."[26] Webb is saying that patriarchy did not exist in the garden *in actual fact*, but the author placed hints of it in the story as a way of anticipating the situation that would come about after there was sin in the world. This then is also an explicit denial of the historical accuracy of the Genesis 2 account.

In reason (2), Webb says that Moses, in the time he wrote, used "present categories" such as patriarchy to describe the past, and this was simply an "accommodation" by God "in order not to confuse the main point." That is, patriarchy did not actually exist in the Garden of Eden, but Moses inserted it there in Genesis 2 so as not to confuse his audience at a later time. Thus, Moses inserted false information into Genesis 2.

The same is true of Webb's reason (3). Webb believes that primogeniture (Adam being

---

23. Ibid., 144.
24. This is a fairly standard view among evangelical scholars, but Webb does not even consider it. See Grudem, *Systematic Theology* (1994), 412, and the relevant pages given for other systematic theologies on pp. 434–35.
25. The serpent, the act of deception, and Satan are connected in some New Testament contexts. Paul says, "I am afraid that as the serpent deceived Eve by his cunning, your thoughts will be lead astray from a sincere and pure devotion to Christ" (2 Corinthians 11:3, in a context opposing false apostles whom he categorizes as servants of Satan who "disguise themselves as servants of righteousness," v. 15). Revelation 12 describes Satan as "that ancient serpent, who is called the devil and Satan, the deceiver of the whole world" (v. 9). See also John 8:44 and 1 John 3:8, with reference to the beginning stages of history.
26. Webb, *Slaves, Women and Homosexuals*, 142–43.

created before Eve) occurs in Genesis 2, not because it reflected the actual situation in the Garden of Eden, but *because Adam and Eve after they sinned would enter into a situation where Adam had leadership over his wife*. This again is an explicit denial of the historical accuracy of the headship of Adam and his prior creation in Genesis 2. It was simply "a practical and gracious *anticipation* of the agrarian setting into which Adam and Eve were headed."[27]

Answer 3.7b: This egalitarian argument has to deny the historical truthfulness of a major section of Genesis 2.

It is important to realize how much Webb denies as historical fact in the Genesis narrative. He is not just denying that there was a "crafty" serpent who spoke to Eve (Genesis 3:1). He also denies the entire *theme of primogeniture* found in Genesis 2. That is, he denies the entire narrative structure that shows the man as created before the woman, for this is the basis for the primogeniture theme he sees Paul referring to in 1 Timothy 2:13, "For Adam was formed first, then Eve."

How much of Genesis 2 does that involve? How much inaccurate material has to be inserted into Genesis 2 either as a literary device foreshadowing the Fall (reason 1), or as an accommodation to the situation familiar to readers at the time of Moses (reason 2), or as an anticipation of an agrarian society that would be established after the Fall (reason 3)? It is no small amount.

- God placing the man (singular) in the Garden (v. 8),
- God putting the man in the Garden "to work it and keep it" (v. 15),
- God commanding the man that he may eat of every tree of the Garden but not of the tree of the knowledge of good and evil (vv. 16–17),
- God saying, "It is not good that the man should be alone; I will make him a helper fit for him" (v. 18),
- God bringing the beasts of the field and the birds of the heavens to the man to see what he would call them (v. 19),
- the man giving names to every living creature (v. 20),
- there not being found a helper fit for man (v. 20),
- God causing a deep sleep to fall upon the man and taking one of his ribs and forming it into a woman (v. 21–22).

This entire sequence, summarized by Paul in the statement "For Adam was formed first, then Eve," is merely a literary device that did not actually happen, according to Webb.

And all of this then enables Webb to say that Paul's appeal to the creation of Adam prior to Eve is not proof of a transcultural ethical standard.

---

27. Ibid., 145 (italics added); repeated on 151–55.

But if a theological argument has to deny significant portions of Scripture for its support, it should surely be rejected by evangelicals who are subject to the authority of the entire Bible as the Word of God.

EGALITARIAN CLAIM 3.8: *HELPER* IMPLIES EQUALITY: THE WORD *HELPER*, WHICH IS APPLIED TO EVE, IMPLIES THAT EVE IS EQUAL IN STATUS OR EVEN SUPERIOR TO ADAM.

Rebecca Groothuis says,

> If the term "helper" most frequently refers to God, whose status is clearly superior to ours...then there is no justification for inferring a subordinate status from the woman's designation as "helper."[28]

And Gilbert Bilezikian writes,

> It is now a matter of general knowledge that this Hebrew word for "helper" is not used in the Bible with reference to a subordinate person such as a servant or an underling. It is generally attributed to God when He is engaged in activities of relief or rescue among His people. Consequently, the word *helper* may not be used to draw inferences about subordinate female roles. If anything, the word points to the inadequacy and the helplessness of man when he was bereft of the woman in Eden. God provided him with a "rescuer."[29]

Stanley Grenz claims something similar:

> The debate over Genesis 2 verses 18 and 20 hinges on the meaning of the phrase *'ēzer kenegdô* (helper fit). Egalitarians not only dispute the complementarian claim that *helper* means "subordinate," but they also claim that the Hebrew designation clearly indicates the equality of the sexes. Alvera Mickelsen, for example, notes that in the Bible the word *'ēzer* (translated "helper") is *never* used of a subordinate.[30]

Answer 3.8a: The word *helper* (Hebrew *'ēzer*) is used of God, so the role of helper is an honorable one.

I agree with egalitarians that this Hebrew word is used most often to refer to God in the Old Testament. For example, "Our soul waits for the LORD; he is our *help* and our shield" (Psalm 33:20), or "My *help* comes from the LORD, who made heaven and earth" (Psalm 121:2).

28. Groothuis, *Good News for Women,* 134.
29. Bilezikian, *Beyond Sex Roles*, 28.
30. Grenz, *Women in the Church* (1995), 164. See also Brown, *Women Ministers*, 27.

Though the word can also be used in other ways, the fact that God calls Himself our "helper" imparts dignity and honor to this role and this title.

Answer 3.8b: The word *helper* (Hebrew *'ēzer*) cannot settle the question of superior or inferior authority or rank.

A person who helps can be superior to, equal to, or inferior to the person being helped. Sometimes God is called our helper (see above), and He is superior to us. On the other hand, the "helper" can be one of lesser rank or authority, as when God says about the prince of Jerusalem, "I will scatter toward every wind all who are around him, his *helpers* and all his troops, and I will unsheathe the sword after them" (Ezekiel 12:14). (This means that egalitarians are incorrect when they claim that this word is never used of someone of inferior status or rank.)[31] And the closely related feminine form of this noun can be used of an equal, as when one army helps another. For example, God said to the king of Judah, "Behold, Pharaoh's army that came to *help* you [literally, that came to you as a helper] is about to return to Egypt, to its own land" (Jeremiah 37:7).[32] If we expand our consideration to the related verb "to help" (*'āzar*), there are many more examples of someone with lesser rank or authority or power giving help (see for example 2 Samuel 21:17; 1 Chronicles 12:1).[33] So *helper* (*'ēzer*) itself cannot settle the issue for us; it has to be decided on other grounds.

Since the Old Testament deals almost entirely with various ways that God helps His people, it is not surprising that this word often refers to God as our helper. But that does not by itself imply that the helper is necessarily of greater authority or rank, any more than it implies that a helper is divine, or is Godlike, or anything else. The word just means that the helper is a person who helps, in whatever way the context specifies.

Answer 3.8c: Eve's creation as a "helper...*for* him" indicates a created role as helper who would bring benefit to Adam.

It is important to read the whole sentence in Genesis 2:18. As already noted in chapter 1, God made Eve to provide Adam with a helper, one who by virtue of Creation would function as Adam's helper.

> Then the LORD God said, "It is not good that the man should be alone; I will make him a helper fit for him." (Genesis 2:18)

---

31. Aida Spencer is incorrect when she says, "At no time does *'ēzer* indicate a subordinate helper unless the two references to 'helper' in Genesis 2:18, 20 are considered exceptions" (*Beyond the Curse*, 27). The statements by Bilezikian and Grenz (quoting Mickelsen) cited above are also incorrect.
32. Jeremiah 37:7 has the feminine form *'ezrāh*, but the lexicons show no difference in meaning between *'ēzer* and *'ezrāh* (see BDB, 740–41; *NIDOTTE* 3:378–79).
33. These verses were pointed out by Webb, *Slaves, Women and Homosexuals*, 128. Webb's own count indicates that when both noun and verb forms are included, in 18 percent of the cases the "helper" is of equal status, and in 10 percent, of lower status than the one being helped.

The Hebrew text can be translated literally, "I will make *for him* (Hebrew *le-*) a helper fit for him." The apostle Paul understands this accurately, because in 1 Corinthians 11 he writes, "Neither was man created *for* woman, but woman *for* man" (1 Corinthians 11:9). Eve's role, and the purpose that God had in mind when He created her, was that she would be "for him...a helper." Egalitarians regularly focus on the word *helper* by itself, which decides nothing, and fail to consider that the apostle Paul was emphasizing the relationship implied by the "for him" in the phrase "I will make for him a helper."

Yet, in the same sentence God emphasizes that the woman is not to help the man as one who is inferior to him. Rather, she is to be a helper "fit for him" and here the Hebrew word *kenegdô* means a help "*corresponding to him,*" that is "equal and adequate to himself."[34] So Eve was created as a helper, but as a helper who was Adam's equal, and one who differed from him, but who differed from him in ways that would exactly complement who Adam was.

EGALITARIAN CLAIM 3.9: *SUITABLE* IMPLIES SUPERIORITY: THE WORD *SUITABLE* IN THE PHRASE "A HELPER SUITABLE FOR HIM" (GENESIS 2:18) IMPLIES THAT EVE IS "IN FRONT OF" OR EVEN SUPERIOR TO ADAM.

Aida Spencer makes this unusual claim when she says, "The verse literally reads: 'And the Lord God thought it was not good for the Adam to be by himself; I will make for him a helper as if in front of him.'"[35]

She then says that the Hebrew term *kenegdô*, which is usually translated "suitable for" (NIV, NASB) or "fit for" (ESV, with margin "Or *corresponding to*"), actually means that God has made for Adam a helper "as if in front of him.... 'Front' or 'visible' seem to suggest superiority or equality.... The same preposition when converted into a noun (*nāgîd*) signifies 'a leader, ruler, prince, or king.'... 'In front of'...would symbolize equality (if not superiority!) in all respects."[36]

Answer 3.9a: It is true that some kind of equality is implied in this expression.

Spencer is correct to say that the expression *kenegdô* is made of combining *ke-*, "according to," and *neged*, "in front of," and the term is widely accepted to mean "according to what is in front of" or "corresponding to"[37] (the expression occurs only in Genesis 2:18 and 20). Spencer is correct to see significant implications of equality in this expression, but there is

34. BDB, 617.
35. Spencer, *Beyond the Curse*, 23. She does not explain why she thinks "thought" is a "literal" translation of *wayyō'mer*, which all standard English translations render as "said," in "and the Lord God *said*." Her translations of *hā'ādām* as "the Adam" rather than "the man" and her translation of *kenegdô* with the phrase "as if in front of" are also translations unique to Spencer; they are found in no English translation of the Bible.
36. Ibid., 24–25.
37. BDB, 617.

no implication of superiority. The term simply means "corresponding to" or "suitable for," and it shows that Eve was a suitable helper for Adam, one that "corresponded to" him in ways that the animals did not.

Answer 3.9b: But the word does not signify "equality...in all respects" or superiority.

Spencer goes beyond the evidence when she says that this expression signifies "equality (if not superiority!) in all respects." Surely it does not mean that Adam and Eve were exactly the same physically, for they were not—Eve "corresponded to" Adam in the exact way God intended, but that included differences! In the same way, the term itself neither implies nor excludes difference in roles in their relationship. It simply says that they would be "fit for" each other, "suitable for" each other, in many ways. That is consistent with appropriate differences in roles.

Spencer's claim that the expression may imply superiority because "The same preposition when converted into a noun (*nāgîd*) signifies 'a leader, ruler, prince, or king'" is just careless. The preposition *neged* does mean "in front of, in sight of, opposite to,"[38] and the noun *nāgîd* does mean "leader...ruler, prince." But that does not mean that the preposition *neged* means "ruler," for it has never been defined in this way. Spencer's mistake is to assume that a word takes all the meanings of other words related to it.[39] Raymond Ortlund shows the folly of such linguistic reasoning:

> By Spencer's line of reasoning we could argue that the English adjective "front" converts into the noun "frontier," suggesting that the word "front" connotes sparse habitation and primitive living conditions. This is simply invalid reasoning. Moreover, if *neged* means "superior to" then what are we to make of, say, Psalm 119:168? "All my ways are before (*neged*) you." Is the psalmist saying, "All my ways are superior to you, O Lord"? Not only is that an unbiblical notion, the whole burden of Psalm 119 is the excellency and authority of the law over the psalmist. The *neged* element in *kenegdô* merely conveys the idea of direct proximity or anteposition.[40]

38. Ibid.
39. Spencer here has gone beyond the linguistic error of "illegitimate totality transfer" (wrongly assuming that all possible meanings of a *single* word can be found in any one instance of that word) and has committed "illegitimate totality-of-related-words transfer" (assuming that all the meanings of a related or cognate noun are found in any one instance of a preposition).
40. Ortlund, "Male-Female Equality," 103–4. Examples showing this procedure to result in foolishness could be multiplied in English: If God creates Eve to "correspond to" Adam, does this mean that they write "correspondence" to each other? If Eve is "suitable for" Adam, does this mean that she wears a business suit? Or that she files a lawsuit against him?

To conclude, God made Eve as a "helper fit for him" and that means that Eve was created to "complement" or complete Adam in many ways. It does not mean that she would be the same as Adam in every way, or that their roles would be exactly the same, or that their authority would be equal. It surely does not mean that Eve would be superior to Adam. It just means that she would complement him in exactly the ways that God intended.

EGALITARIAN CLAIM 3.10: CREATION FROM ADAM'S SIDE: EVE'S CREATION FROM ADAM'S SIDE IMPLIES THAT THEY WERE EQUAL, AND THERE WAS NO UNIQUE AUTHORITY THAT ADAM HAD OVER EVE.

Gilbert Bilezikian writes:

> There is no justification for the derivation of Eve from the body of Adam to be viewed as a sign of her subordination to him. Such a theory might have had a chance of being true if she had been made out of the ground like the plants, the animals, and Adam himself. *But the story of Eve's creation teaches precisely the opposite lesson.* Unlike Adam, she was made out of human flesh already in existence. Humanity twice refined, *she is at least his equal.*[41]

Answer 3.10a: Paul thinks this is important.

In 1 Corinthians 11:8, the apostle Paul says, "For man was not made from woman, but woman from man," and he uses that to support his directions about wives wearing a head covering (which in the church at Corinth was a sign of submission to their husbands). Paul's reasoning differs from Bilezikian's at this point (see also p. 30, n. 13 above).

Answer 3.10b: Equality does not disprove differences.

Bilezikian's argument implies the same old egalitarian assumption: If Adam and Eve were equal, they could not be different in their roles.

Bilezikian is correct to see in Eve's creation from Adam's side an indication of equality in human nature, in personhood, in importance, and in the image of God. But such equality does not demand sameness in every respect. Adam and Eve were equal *and* different, and not only physically different, but also different in the roles they filled in their relationship (as we have seen from several other indications in Genesis).[42]

---

41. Bilezikian, *Beyond Sex Roles*, 29–30 (italics added). See also Brown, *Women Ministers*, 29.
42. See the discussion in chapter 1 about indications of Adam's leadership role in marriage before there was sin in the world, especially pp. 29–45.

Egalitarian claim 3.11: Prior Creation and Animal Rule: If prior creation gave authority to Adam, then the same logic would require that the animals rule over us, since they were created first.

This is a common egalitarian claim. Gilbert Bilezikian writes,

> As soon as primal origination becomes a norm that confers dominance to the first in line, both Adam and Eve fall under the rulership of animals. According to Genesis 1, animals were created before humans. Therefore, they should rule over humans. The absurdity of such a theory is evident. Temporal primacy of itself does not confer superior rank.[43]

Similarly, Linda Belleville says,

> The account in Genesis 2 certainly attaches no significance to the order of male then female. Indeed, the fact that the animals were created before the male should caution us against drawing a conclusion of this kind.[44]

Answer 3.11a: Authority relationships among human beings apply only to human beings.

The Bible clearly gives human beings authority to rule over the animal kingdom: "fill the earth and subdue it and have dominion over the fish of the sea and over the birds of the heavens and over every living thing that moves on the earth" (Genesis 1:28). So we see from Genesis itself that authority belonging to things created first is not an *absolute* rule that applies to everything ever created. It is a *limited* principle that applied to the creation of Adam and Eve, and that is clear because the Bible views it that way.

In fact, when the idea of primogeniture (the idea that leadership in a family belongs to the firstborn son) is applied in later Old Testament narratives, it is not an absolute principle either. It only applies to the oldest son, not to the firstborn daughter. It only applies within each family, not to children born earlier in neighboring families. And it surely does not apply to animals born in the household before the children! The concept is a limited principle that applies within human families, and there is no inconsistency in limiting its application in that way in the story of Adam and Eve. (See also pp. 67–69.)

Answer 3.11b: Paul views Adam's prior creation as important for the relationship between men and women.

Whether or not we think there is anything significant about the fact that Adam was created before Eve, the apostle Paul thought it significant enough to influence the way men and women should

43. Bilezikian, *Beyond Sex Roles*, 30.
44. Belleville, *Women Leaders and the Church*, 103. See also Brown, *Women Ministers*, 24–25.

relate to each other in the New Testament church age: "I do not permit a woman to teach or to exercise authority over a man.... *For* Adam was formed first, then Eve" (1 Timothy 2:11–12). To object, "Well that can't be right because then animals would rule over us," is to object to the reasoning of the Word of God itself. If we are going to remain subject to the authority of Scripture, then we should accept Paul's reasoning as valid.

EGALITARIAN CLAIM 3.12: ADAM'S FIRST CREATION INSIGNIFICANT: THE FACT THAT ADAM WAS CREATED BEFORE EVE IMPLIES NOTHING ABOUT MALE LEADERSHIP IN THE HOME OR THE CHURCH.

Gilbert Bilezikian makes this surprising assertion: "There is no evidence in the creation text for the temporal primacy of Adam to be interpreted as supremacy or rulership.[45] *Such a concept is present neither in the OT nor in the New.*"[46]

This is surprising because Paul explicitly makes this claim in 1 Timothy 2:12–13: "I do not permit a woman to teach or to exercise authority over a man.... *For* Adam was formed first, then Eve."

Bilezikian elsewhere explains that he thinks Paul is basing his reasoning in this passage not on temporal order (Adam created first), but rather on the fact that Eve did not receive the command not to eat the forbidden fruit directly from God, and therefore she was not as well trained, not as competent:

> If verse 13 is to stand alone as a reason, Paul never explains why Adam's having been created first should constitute an advantage for man, nor does he draw any implications from it. The fact that Adam was created first is meaningless for the ministry of teaching in the church.... Paul is establishing a principle based not on chronology but on competency.... "Adam was not deceived" ***because***, having been created first, he had received God's command in person.[47]

45. As on almost every page of his book, Bilezikian here uses pejorative terms to describe the position he opposes. I do not believe the Bible teaches male "supremacy" (which denies equality in the image of God) or male "rulership" (which carries the connotation of the kind of harsh rule implied in Genesis 3:16), rather than the loving headship taught in Ephesians 5:22–33. But I am responding to Bilezikian's argument here as if he were arguing not against these distortions, but against any kind of male leadership or headship, which I believe is a major intent of his book.
46. Bilezikian, *Beyond Sex Roles*, 30 (italics added). Bilezikian makes no reference on p. 30 to the obvious contradiction to his statement found in 1 Timothy 2:12–13, "I do not permit a woman to teach or to exercise authority over a man.... *For* Adam was formed first, then Eve." Finding his other statements on 1 Timothy 2:12–13 is a time-consuming task for the reader. On p. 30, Bilezikian refers to endnote 12 (found on p. 257), in which he says to see the discussion of 1 Timothy 2:11–15 on pp. 173–84. On those pages his only discussion of Adam's prior creation is his statement that Eve was not as well trained as Adam: Since "Eve was not created first or at the same time as Adam.... She was the one bereft of the firsthand experience of God's giving the prohibition relative to the tree" (180). However, a longer explanation of his position on 1 Timothy 2:12–13 is found in endnote 44 (pp. 296–98), which I have quoted in the following material.
47. Ibid., 296–97n44, to p. 180 (italics in original).

Linda Belleville writes,

> Although some have maintained that "Adam was formed first, then Eve" in 1 Timothy 2:13 denotes personal superiority (and so the male's headship), *first/then* usage elsewhere in the New Testament is clearly temporal in nature.... In fact, Paul uses it in this very way just ten verses later. Deacons, he states, must be tested "first" (*prōton*) and "then" *(eita)* let them serve (1 Tim. 3:10).[48]

Answer 3.12a: These objections assume in various ways that Paul was wrong. For example, Belleville's statement that "first/then" statements elsewhere in Paul are "temporal in nature" contains this reasoning:

1. Paul uses "first/then" statements elsewhere to speak of a temporal sequence with no implication of authority.
2. Therefore Paul's "first/then" in 1 Timothy 2:12–13 cannot have any implication of authority.

This reasoning is incorrect on several levels. (a) The main problem is that it says that Paul is wrong. It says that if he did not use "first/then" as a reason for authority elsewhere, he cannot use it as a reason for authority here either. But Paul's "for" (Greek *gar*) shows that that is exactly what he did. He used "Adam was formed first, then Eve" as a *reason* why he does not permit a woman to teach or have authority over a man in the assembled church. Belleville's objection that he did not use "first/then" elsewhere to make such an argument should not be used to say that such reasoning is incorrect.

In addition, (b) when Belleville says Paul's other "first/then" statements are temporal, and then offers that idea as an alternative to any teaching about authority, she simply misunderstands the fact that of course Paul's "first/then" statement in 1 Timothy 2:13 is also temporal. Paul is talking about a temporal sequence of events: "Adam was formed *first, then* Eve." But he is *reasoning* from that sequence to something else.

(c) Belleville fails to distinguish between the meaning of a phrase and the use an author makes of that phrase in different contexts. Here Paul uses the words "first/then" to mean a temporal sequence of events,[49] and then he applies that sequence to principles for male-female conduct in the church. Elsewhere he applies the phrase to the resurrection (1 Thessalonians

48. Belleville, *Women Leaders and the Church*, 193–94, in footnote 55 to p. 103. She then refers the reader to p. 179 for further discussion, and there she gives other examples of one thing happening before another "without any implication of superiority or authority." She concludes, "So *first/then* language need do no more than define a sequence of events or ideas." See also Brown, *Women Ministers*, 25.
49. But "first/then" statements need not always be temporal: see Jas. 3:17; Heb. 7:2; and perhaps 1 Cor. 12:28.

4:16–17), and to approving deacons (1 Timothy 3:10). He does not have to use "first/then" everywhere to talk about approving deacons (as Belleville's reasoning would have it), because an author does not have to talk about the same subject every time he uses a common phrase! But the main objection is that Belleville is saying that Paul's reasoning is incorrect.

Bilezikian's argument that verse 13 is invalid without an explanation—"Paul never explains why Adam's having been created first should constitute an advantage for man"—assumes that Paul has to explain his reasoning for it to be acceptable. But how dare we demand that the Bible give more explanation than it does or else we will not accept the reasoning?

When Bilezikian says, "nor does he draw any implications from it [Adam's being created first]," he simply denies the force of the conjunction "for" *(gar)* in 1 Timothy 2:13. Paul *does* draw an implication from Adam's being created first, and the implication is, "I do not permit a woman to teach or to exercise authority over a man." Bilezikian may disagree with Paul's implication, but it is not true to say that Paul does not draw any implication.

Answer 3.12b: This objection removes the reason Paul does give and replaces it with a reason Paul does not give.

Bilezikian's claim—"The fact that Adam was created first is meaningless for the ministry of teaching in the church.... Paul is establishing a principle based not on chronology but on competency"—assumes that Paul is reasoning as follows:

> I do not permit a woman to teach or to exercise authority over a man. *For* Adam heard God's command and was competent, but Eve did not hear the command, and was not competent.

But that is not what the Bible says. Paul does not mention anything about hearing a command from God or not hearing a command from God. He says, "For Adam was formed first, then Eve."

Moreover, how much competence does it take to understand that "of the tree of the knowledge of good and evil you shall not eat" (Genesis 2:17) means "of the tree of the knowledge of good and evil you shall not eat"? Bilezikian's argument assumes that Eve did not understand this simple command (even as told to her by Adam), and this in turn would imply that Eve was not responsible to obey it, and that she was not morally culpable for eating of the fruit! The argument is remarkably unpersuasive.

But most troubling of all is what Bilezikian's argument does with Scripture. He claims that what Paul says is not a good reason for what Paul commands; and then he substitutes a different reason for the one Paul actually gives. Are we free to treat Scripture this way, to change a verse we disagree with into something completely different, and then claim that that is what the verse really says? Is this the kind of treatment of God's Word that we want to allow and endorse in our churches?

Egalitarian claim 3.13: Man Leaves Father and Mother: The fact that a man leaves his father and mother shows there is no patriarchal system in view in Genesis 1–2.

Concerning the statement in Genesis 2:24, "Therefore a man shall leave his father and his mother and hold fast to his wife, and they shall become one flesh," Rebecca Groothuis writes that this is a "very nonpatriarchal statement."[50] Similarly, Gilbert Bilezikian says,

> The man's freedom of action in moving away and making his own choices does not reflect a family organization dependent on a father-ruler. Under a strictly patriarchal system, the father-ruler would be the one making those decisions; the new family would be aggregated to the patriarch's family, and it would remain under his authority....
>
> Singularly, nothing is said of the bride's relationship with her own parents. She seems to be a free agent, in command of her own life. In this verse [Genesis 2:24], the woman represents the stable point of reference. It is the man who moves toward her after leaving his parents. He attaches himself to the woman. She is not appended to his life. He is the one who adds his life to hers as he "cleaves" to her. The procedure of a man's separating from his father and cleaving to his wife reflects anything but a patriarch-dominated society.[51]

Answer 3.13a: Arguments against an extended patriarchal clan are "straw man" arguments.

When Groothuis and Bilezikian argue against an extended patriarchal clan with many adult sons and daughters under the authority of a "father-ruler," they are arguing against a position that no complementarian holds today. This is simply a "straw man" argument—it gives the appearance of defeating an opponent's position, but it is an illusion, because no real opponent holds the view they are arguing against.

These statements by Groothuis and Bilezikian have an appearance of persuasiveness because they blur two different meanings of *patriarchal* so that when they reject one meaning, readers think they have disproved the other meaning. The meaning they reject is the sense of "an extended clan with many adult children subject to the authority of one patriarch." The meaning they have not disproved is "any system with male headship in marriage."

---

50. Groothuis, *Good News for Women*, 123.
51. Bilezikian, *Beyond Sex Roles*, 34. See also Brown, *Women Ministers*, 33.

Answer 3.13b: This text shows that marriage establishes a new household and a new family.

Genesis 2:24 establishes a perspective on marriage according to which a man "shall leave his father and his mother," and that leaving signifies an end to the previous pattern of family relationships. When a man gets married, he is no longer a part of his father and mother's household, and no longer under their authority. A new household is established, a new family unit. This does disprove "patriarchy" in the first sense above, but not in the second sense.

Answer 3.13c: This text shows that man takes the initiative in establishing a new family.

Bilezikian is right to say that "The man takes the initiative to remove himself from his parents."[52] But this does nothing to deny male headship. In fact, it contains a hint of male headship, since it specifies that the man takes the initiative in establishing a new family.

Answer 3.13d: This text says nothing that argues against male leadership in marriage, unless foreign ideas are imported into the text.

In order to argue against male headship, Bilezikian imports several things into the text. The text says nothing about the man's bride being "a free agent, in command of her own life" (something unthinkable in the world of the Old Testament); it says nothing about her being a "stable point of reference"; and it says nothing about the man being the one who "adds his life to hers." It just says he shall "hold fast" to her and they will become "one flesh." The connection with verse 23, where the woman is taken from man's flesh and bone, gives the primary sense of an actual physical embrace.

So the text just says a man will leave his father and mother and embrace his wife, and they will become one flesh. That's it. Bilezikian's claims about her as a "free agent" and a "stable point of reference" are just foreign ideas he has imported into the text, adding to Scripture things that are not there.

Egalitarian claim 3.14: The Serpent's Strategy: The fact that the serpent approached Eve first rather than Adam implies that Adam did not have authority over Eve.

Gilbert Bilezikian claims that if Adam had a leadership role in the garden, the tempter would have attacked him first:

> If Adam was boss in the garden, it would have made more sense to go to him directly. By addressing himself to the lesser in command, the tempter would be taking the risk of Adam's interference as the authority figure, or of wasting his efforts in case Adam

52. Bilezikian, *Beyond Sex Roles*, 34.

> refused to participate in Eve's downfall. On the other hand, if Adam was indeed in command over Eve, the tempter would get both by obtaining his fall. If the tempter was facing a hierarchical situation between Adam and Eve, he obviously addressed himself to the wrong party. . . . Adam's willingness to follow Eve's example and to take of the fruit she gave him confirms the absence of predetermined roles in the garden. The alternative pattern of Adam's directing Eve's actions would have required the temptation to begin with him. . . . The tempter, being the most clever among his kind, rightly perceived that the greatest amount of resistance would come from the woman. So, he concentrated his attack upon her in the expectation that if she fell, Adam would follow suit.[53]

Answer 3.14a: This argument wrongly assumes that Satan has to attack the strongest person.

The false assumption running through Bilezikian's argument is that Satan (speaking through the serpent) would have attacked the strongest person, and thus would have attacked Adam if Adam had been in authority.

But the pattern of Scripture does not confirm this assumption. Peter writes, "Be sober-minded; be watchful. Your adversary the devil prowls around like a roaring lion, seeking someone to devour" (1 Peter 5:8). Lions often attack stragglers, weak animals who lag behind the herd. Similarly, people who have newly heard the gospel are objects of Satan's attack, for Jesus says, "And these are the ones along the path, where the word is sown: when they hear, Satan immediately comes and takes away the word that is sown in them" (Mark 4:15). Satan's temptations of Jesus occurred when Jesus was physically at his weakest point, after fasting for forty days (Matthew 4:2–3). And at the end of Jesus' life, the disciple whom Satan entered was Judas, not a strong, morally upright follower of Jesus, but one who "was a thief, and having charge of the moneybag he used to help himself to what was put into it" (John 12:6). Anyone with any pastoral experience knows that Satan does not always attack the strongest people in a congregation. Many (not all) of his evil attacks are against the weaker members.

So Bilezikian's assumption that the tempter would have attacked the strongest person (if Adam had been in authority) is incorrect. It makes Satan seem stronger and more courageous than he really is.

Answer 3.14b: This argument wrongly assumes that Satan would respect God's Creation order.

The original rebellion of Satan and his demons was against God's created order, against the authority structures that God had established:

---

53. Ibid., 42.

> And the angels who did not stay within their own position of authority, but left their proper dwelling, he has kept in eternal chains under gloomy darkness until the judgment of the great day (Jude 6)

> "How you are fallen from heaven,
> O Day Star, son of Dawn!
> How you are cut down to the ground,
> you who laid the nations low!
> You said in your heart,
> 'I will ascend to heaven;
> above the stars of God
> I will set my throne on high;
> I will sit on the mount of assembly
> in the far reaches of the north;
> I will ascend above the heights of the clouds;
> I will make myself like the Most High.'
> But you are brought down to Sheol,
> to the far reaches of the pit."
> (Isaiah 14:12–15)

It is one of Satan's characteristics to rebel, and to incite others to rebel, against the authority of God (as he did in Genesis 3:1–5). It fits this pattern for Satan to first try to persuade Eve to rebel against the authority structure God had established by deciding, independently of Adam, to listen to the serpent and follow his suggestion. Thus, Satan's activity elsewhere in Scripture suggests just the opposite of Bilezikian's claim that Satan would go to the strongest first and follow the authority structure God had established. It is more likely that he would go to the subordinate authority (Eve) and try to get her to undermine the male headship that God had established. In fact, that is the most persuasive explanation of what he did. And God hints at this when he judges Adam by saying, "***Because you have listened to the voice of your wife*** and have eaten of the tree...cursed is the ground because of you" (Genesis 3:17).

Conclusion

As explained more fully in chapter 1, there are at least ten arguments that male leadership existed alongside male–female equality before there was any sin in the world. It is appropriate to mention those ten reasons once again in summary form:

1. *The order:* Adam was created first, then Eve (note the sequence in Genesis 2:7 and Genesis 2:18–23; 1 Timothy 2:13).
2. *The representation:* Adam, not Eve, had a special role in representing the human race (1 Corinthians 15:22, 45–49; Romans 5:12–21).
3. *The naming of woman:* Adam named Eve; Eve did not name Adam (Genesis 2:23).
4. *The naming of the human race:* God named the human race "Man," not "Woman" (Genesis 5:2).
5. *The primary accountability:* God called Adam to account first after the Fall (Genesis 3:9).
6. *The purpose:* Eve was created as a helper for Adam, not Adam as a helper for Eve (Genesis 2:18; 1 Corinthians 11:9).
7. *The conflict:* The curse brought a distortion of previous roles, not the introduction of new roles (Genesis 3:16).
8. *The restoration:* Salvation in Christ in the New Testament reaffirms the Creation order (Colossians 3:18–19).
9. *The mystery:* Marriage from the beginning of Creation was a picture of the relationship between Christ and the church (Ephesians 5:32–33).
10. *The parallel with the Trinity:* The equality, differences, and unity between men and women reflect the equality, differences, and unity in the Trinity (1 Corinthians 11:3).

The egalitarian objections considered in this chapter have not been able to undermine those ten arguments. Nor have they made a persuasive case for an egalitarian position in Genesis 1–3. These egalitarian claims have included incorrect reasoning, incorrect statements of facts, incorrect claims for what the Bible says, incorrect procedures for interpretation, and incorrect denials of the truthfulness of the Bible.

It is best to conclude from Genesis 1–3 that God created Adam and Eve equal in personhood, importance, and dignity, but also different in role. As part of that difference in role God gave Adam a responsibility for leadership in the marriage before there was any sin in the world. Male leadership in marriage was not a result of the Fall, but was part of the original created order of which God said, "It was very good" (Genesis 1:31).

CHAPTER FOUR

Evangelical Feminist Claims from the Rest of the Old Testament

In the previous chapter we saw that egalitarian objections to a complementarian view of manhood and womanhood based on Genesis 1–3 were not persuasive. But what about the rest of the Old Testament? Doesn't Deborah's example show that women can assume leadership over men? And what about other women who were prophets in the Old Testament? Aren't there examples of women exercising leadership roles and being blessed by God?

This chapter considers those questions.

EGALITARIAN CLAIM 4.1: DEBORAH: DEBORAH'S LEADERSHIP IN ISRAEL (JUDGES 4) SHOWS THAT GOD CAN CALL WOMEN TO LEADERSHIP ROLES.

Egalitarian writers regularly appeal to the example of Deborah. Linda Belleville says:

> Deborah is called "prophetess" (Judg. 4:4 NIV), "judge" (Judg. 4:5 NRSV), and "mother in Israel" (Judg. 5:7). She held court in the hill country of Ephraim and all of Israel (men and women alike) came to her to have their disputes settled (Judg. 4:5). So respected was Deborah that the commander of her troops refused to go into battle without her (Judg. 4:8).[1]

Gilbert Bilezikian writes,

> As prophet, [Deborah] assumed spiritual leadership; as "judge" she exercised judicial and political power; and eventually she became involved in directing on the field the strategy for a decisively victorious battle. Probably because she was a spokesperson for God as a prophet, Deborah served also as a political guide and as a one-person supreme court (4:4–5).[2]

1. Belleville, *Women Leaders and the Church* (2000), 44.
2. Bilezikian, *Beyond Sex Roles* (1985), 70–71.

Stanley Grenz says,

> Deborah served as the highest leader of her people. Although she was married, her leadership role included the exercise of authority over men.... The example of Deborah confirms that neither God nor the ancient Hebrews found female leadership intrinsically abhorrent. On the contrary, a woman could—and did—exercise authority over the entire community, including men.[3]

Answer 4.1a: We should be thankful for Deborah.

In Judges 4–5, Deborah is a "prophetess" who faithfully delivered God's messages to Barak (Judges 4:6–7), courageously accompanied Barak to the place where Barak was assembling troops for battle (Judges 4:10), demonstrated strong faith by encouraging Barak that the Lord would be with him (Judges 4:14), and joined Barak in a lengthy song of praise and thanksgiving to God (Judges 5:1–31). She also must have spoken with much wisdom from God, because we read,

> Now Deborah, a prophetess, the wife of Lappidoth, was judging Israel at that time. She used to sit under the palm of Deborah between Ramah and Bethel in the hill country of Ephraim, and the people of Israel came up to her for judgment. (Judges 4:4–5)

For all these things, we should be thankful to God. For all generations, Deborah will serve as an example of faith, courage, worship, love for God, and godly wisdom. We must be careful not to let the disputes over Deborah cloud our appreciation for her or diminish the honor that Scripture accords to her.

Answer 4.1b: Deborah affirmed male leadership over God's people.

Deborah did not summon the people of Israel to battle, but encouraged Barak to do this (Judges 4:6–7, 14). Thus, rather than asserting leadership and authority for herself, she affirmed the rightness of male leadership. Then when Barak hesitated and insisted that Deborah accompany him to the battle (Judges 4:8), she announced a word of rebuke on Barak, and a loss of honor: "I will surely go with you. Nevertheless, the road on which you are going will not lead to your glory, for the LORD will sell Sisera into the hand of a woman" (Judges 4:9).[4] This implies that Barak should not have insisted that Deborah come with him. He should have acted like a man and led on his own.

---

3. Grenz, *Women in the Church* (1998), 68, 70. Others who see much significance in Deborah's leadership role include Jacobs, *Women of Destiny* (1996), 179–80; Brown, *Women Ministers* (1995), 104; and Grady, *Ten Lies the Church Tells Women* (2000), 37. Jacobs says, "Deborah *ruled* the nation as the senior judge of all the judges" (179).
4. Sumner, *Men and Women in the Church* (2003), 98, incorrectly understands Barak's insistence that Deborah accompany him as something the Bible views positively.

Answer 4.1c: The text does not say that Deborah ruled over God's people or taught them publicly or led them militarily.

It is important to examine the text of Judges 4 to see exactly what Deborah did and did not do:

1. She gave "judgment" (Hebrew *mishpāt*) to the people privately when they came to her. When the text says that "Deborah…was *judging* Israel at that time" (Judges 4:4), the Hebrew verb *shāphat,* "to judge," in this context does not mean "to rule or govern," but rather has the sense "*decide controversy,* discriminate between persons in civil, political, domestic and religious questions."[5] That is evident because the next verse tells how she was "judging": she "used to sit…under the palm tree of Deborah" and "the people of Israel came up to her for judgment." This is not a picture of public leadership like that of a king or queen, but private settling of disputes through both arbitration and judicial decisions.[6] If we decide to take this as an example for today, we might see it as justification for women to serve as counselors and as civil judges. But the text of Scripture does not say that Deborah ruled over God's people.
2. Deborah is never said to have taught the people in any assembled group or congregation. She gave private judgments when people came to her (Judges 4:5).
3. Deborah was never a priest, but in the Old Testament, it was the role of the priests to teach Scripture to the people. God told Aaron, as instruction for himself and for the priests to follow him, "and you are to teach the people of Israel all the statutes that the Lord has spoken to them by Moses" (Leviticus 10:11). And God spoke of His covenant with Levi, from whom all the priests descended,

   > True instruction was in his mouth, and no wrong was found on his lips. He walked with me in peace and uprightness, and he turned many from iniquity. For the lips of a priest should guard knowledge, and people should seek instruction from his mouth, for he is the messenger of the Lord of hosts. (Malachi 2:6–7)

4. Deborah refused to lead the people in military battle, but insisted that a man do this (Judges 4:6–7, 14). In fact, Tom Schreiner points out that Deborah is the only judge in the book of Judges who has no military function.[7]

---

5. BDB, 1047, 2.
6. The NIV is alone among standard translations in rendering Judges 4:4 as "Deborah…was *leading* Israel at that time." This is a rather loose paraphrase rather than lexically supported translation, since the meaning "lead" is not given for *shāphat* in BDB, 1047–48. Other standard translations all translate the verb *shāphat* in Judges 4:4 as "judging": ESV, NASB, KJV, NKJV, RSV, and NRSV. The Septuagint agrees, translating with *krinō*, "to judge."
7. Schreiner, "The Valuable Ministries of Women in the Context of Male Leadership," in Piper and Grudem, *Recovering Biblical Manhood and Womanhood* (1991), 216.

When Linda Belleville claims that Deborah "united" the tribes of Israel and "led them on to victory,"[8] her assertions are contrary to the text of Judges 4, which says that Deborah prophesied that God was commanding *Barak* to "gather your men" (v. 6). The text says that *Barak*, not Deborah, "called out Zebulun and Naphtali," and that "10,000 men went up at *his* heels" (v. 10), not Deborah's. It says that "*Barak* went down from Mount Tabor with 10,000 men following *him*" (v. 14), not Deborah. It says that "the LORD routed Sisera and all his chariots and all his army *before Barak* by the edge of the sword" (v. 15). Belleville actually speaks of the army of Israel as *Deborah's* troops ("her troops"),[9] but the Bible contains no such language. Belleville claims that Deborah "led them to victory," but the Bible says no such thing. Belleville is inserting into her reports of Scripture things that are not there. Deborah encouraged the male leadership of Barak, and the Bible says several times that he led Israel to victory.[10]

5. Deborah functioned as a "prophetess" (Judges 4:4). In this role, she delivered messages from God to the people, but this is a different role from the governing role of a king or the teaching role of a priest. (See Egalitarian claim 4.2 on women serving as prophets.)

Answer 4.1d: The Bible views Deborah's judgeship as a rebuke against the absence of male leadership.

Judges 4:4 suggests some amazement at the unusual nature of the situation in which a woman actually has to judge Israel, because it piles up a string of redundant words to emphasize that Deborah is a woman: translating the Hebrew text literally, the verse says, "And *Deborah*, a *woman*, a *prophetess*, the *wife* of Lappidoth, *she* was judging Israel at that time." Something is abnormal, something is wrong—there are no men to function as judge! This impression is confirmed when we read of Barak's timidity and the rebuke implied in his subsequent loss of glory: "the road on which you are going will not lead to your glory, for the LORD will sell Sisera into the hand of a woman" (Judges 4:9). Then in "The Song of Deborah and Barak" in the next chapter, Deborah expresses surprise that no man had stepped forward to initiate Israel's rescue from the oppressor, but that a *mother* in Israel had to do this:

> "The villagers ceased in Israel;
> they ceased to be until I arose;
> I, Deborah, arose *as a mother in Israel.*" (Judges 5:7)

8. Belleville, "Women in Ministry" (2001), 93.
9. Ibid.
10. Sarah Sumner similarly makes an inaccurate claim about what the Bible says when she writes, "Deborah is commended for leading ten thousand men into a battle against King Jabin and his army" (*Men and Women in the Church,* 109). Contrary to Sumner's claim, the Bible says that Deborah spoke to Barak, and Barak led the ten thousand men.

And the book of Judges treats Deborah somewhat differently from the other judges used by God to deliver Israel. In each case God or the Holy Spirit is specifically said to call or empower the judge: Othniel: "the LORD raised up a deliverer for the people of Israel, who saved them, Othniel the son of Kenaz" (Judges 3:9); Ehud: "the LORD raised up for them a deliverer, Ehud, the son of Gera, the Benjaminite, a left-handed man" (3:15); Gideon: "And the LORD turned to him and said, 'Go in this might of yours and save Israel from the hand of Midian; do not I send you?'" (6:14); Jephthah: "Then the Spirit of the LORD was upon Jephthah, and he passed through Gilead and Manasseh" (11:29); Samson: "And the woman bore a son and called his name Samson. And the young man grew, and the LORD blessed him. And the Spirit of the LORD began to stir him in Mahaneh-dan" (13:24–25). By contrast, we read of Deborah: "Now Deborah, a prophetess, the wife of Lappidoth, was judging Israel at that time" (4:4). It is not that God does not use her and speak through her, for He does. But something is not quite right: There is an absence of male leadership in Israel.

Does the story of Deborah then show that women can lead the people of God in churches where the men are passive and not leading? No, for Deborah did not do this. *The story of Deborah should motivate women in such situations to do what Deborah did: encourage and exhort a man to take the leadership role to which God has called him,* as Deborah encouraged and exhorted Barak (Judges 4:6–9, 14). Richard Schultz says that Deborah delivers the "divine declaration or decision" regarding the people's "call for help" in 4:3, and that "The divine response is indicated by her issuing the call to Barak to lead Israel into battle (4:6), thus designating him as the next individual to lead Israel."[11]

Barak finally did lead, and defeated the Canaanites. Then in subsequent biblical passages that speak of this period of the judges, Barak's leadership alone is mentioned: Samuel tells the people, "And the LORD sent Jerubbaal and *Barak* and Jephthah and Samuel and delivered you out of the hand of your enemies on every side" (1 Samuel 12:11). And the author of Hebrews says, "And what more shall I say? For time would fail me to tell of Gideon, *Barak*, Samson, Jephthah, of David and Samuel and the prophets" (Hebrews 11:32).

Answer 4.1e: We must use caution in drawing examples to imitate from the book of Judges.

The book of Judges has many examples of people doing things that we are not to imitate, such as Samson's marriage to a Philistine woman (14:1–4), or his visiting a prostitute (16:1), or

---

11. Richard Schultz, *NIDOTTE,* 4:216. Schultz also sees "and the people of Israel came up to her for judgment" in 4:5 as referring to a "a one-time act," seeking God's response to their cry for help in 4:3, and not to ongoing settling of disputes. This is contrary to the free paraphrase of the NIV, which specifies plural disputes in its translation, "the Israelites came to her *to have their disputes decided.*" The Hebrew text literally reads, "And the children of Israel came up to her for judgment," and the word for "judgment" *(mishpāt)* is singular, which gives some support to Schultz's view. The NIV's "she held court" (4:5; similarly, NLT) is also an interpretative paraphrase for the participle *yôshebet*, which simply means "she used to sit" (so ESV, NASB, RSV, NRSV, and similarly, NKJV; this very common verb *yāshab* simply means "sit, remain, dwell" [BDB, 442]).

Jephthah's foolish vow (11:30–31, 34–39), or the men of Benjamin lying in wait to snatch wives from the women dancing in the feast at Shiloh (21:19–23). The situation at the end of the book is summarized this way: "In those days there was no king in Israel. Everyone did what was right in his own eyes" (21:25).

This is not to deny the grace of God in working through Deborah! Surely the narrative in Judges shows God at work many times in spite of the failures and weaknesses of the people of Israel, and it affirms Deborah as an example of faith, courage, worship, love for God, and godly wisdom. But the unusual nature of Judges should also warn us that it is not a good source for examples of how the New Testament church should be governed. We should be cautious about drawing conclusions for leadership in the New Testament church from a book that primarily describes a breakdown of leadership among the people of God in the Old Testament.

EGALITARIAN CLAIM 4.2: WOMEN PROPHETS: OLD TESTAMENT EXAMPLES OF WOMEN PROPHETS LIKE MIRIAM, DEBORAH, AND HULDAH GIVE PRECEDENTS FOR WOMEN IN LEADERSHIP ROLES TODAY.

Once again, egalitarians commonly use this argument. Gilbert Bilezikian says,

> The prophetic ministry was the highest religious function in the Old Covenant.... Although statistically the majority of old-covenant prophets were male, the Bible refers to several prophetesses and describes them as exercising the same kind of authority in the religious sphere as their male counterparts (Miriam, Deborah, Huldah, and so on).[12]

After mentioning the prophetic ministries of Miriam and Deborah, Linda Belleville writes,

> Perhaps the best-known female prophet [during the period of monarchy] is Huldah, who was active during the time of Jeremiah and Zephaniah. It was to her that King Josiah sent a delegation to inquire about the Book of the Law that had been discovered while the temple was being renovated, and it was Huldah's warning to obey everything written in this book that brought about the well-known religious reforms of the seventh century BC (2 Kings 22; 2 Chron. 34:14–33).... There are also references to a number of unnamed women prophets. The prophet Isaiah, for example, was instructed to marry "the prophetess" (Isa. 8:3). And the prophet Ezekiel pronounced judgment against the daughters of Judah, who prophesied "out

12. Bilezikian, *Beyond Sex Roles*, 69.

of their own imagination" (Ezek. 13:17; see also vv. 18–24). These examples suggest that women were routinely called and readily accepted as prophets of Israel.[13]

Answer 4.2a: While there were women prophets in the Old Testament, no women taught God's people because there were no women priests.

The role of prophet is surely an honored role, and a vitally important one, for God speaks through a prophet to His people. But prophets and teachers have different roles in the Bible. A prophet is like a messenger who delivers a message but has no authority on his own to do more than that, such as explaining or applying the message: "Then Haggai, the *messenger* of the LORD, spoke to the people with the LORD's message, 'I am with you, declares the LORD'" (Haggai 1:13). A prophet could not add to the message anything of his own. Even Balaam admitted, "Must I not take care to speak what the LORD puts in my mouth?" (Numbers 23:12; see also 24:13, as well as the description of false prophets as those who speak when the Lord has given them no message in Jeremiah 14:14–15; 23:16–22; Ezekiel 13:1–3).

Why then could women prophesy but not teach the people? We may not be able to understand all the reasons, but it is clear that the two roles were distinct, and that God allowed women to be prophets but not teachers.

The priests, not the prophets, taught God's laws to the people. God told Aaron, as instruction for himself and for the priests to follow him, "And you are to *teach* the people of Israel all the statutes that the LORD has spoken to them by Moses" (Leviticus 10:11). Later, God spoke of His covenant with Levi, from whom all the priests descended,

> *True instruction was in his mouth*, and no wrong was found on his lips. He walked with me in peace and uprightness, and he turned many from iniquity. For the lips of a priest should guard knowledge, and people should seek *instruction* from his mouth, for he is the messenger of the LORD of hosts. (Malachi 2:6–7)

The role of teaching the people was reserved for the priests.

There is a similar situation in the New Testament. Women were able to prophesy in both the Old Testament and the New (see 1 Corinthians 11:5). They could deliver messages from God to His people. But women could not assume the role of teacher over God's people in either the Old or the New Testament (see 1 Timothy 2:12; 3:2; Titus 1:6 on New Testament teachers being only men, including the elders who did most of the teaching).[14]

---

13. Belleville, *Women Leaders and the Church*, 44–45. See also Brown, *Women Ministers*, 83, 93, 100; Grady, *Ten Lies*, 37–38.
14. See also the longer discussion in chapter 7, pp. 227–32, on why women could prophesy but not teach in New Testament churches.

In conclusion, prophets did not teach or govern God's people in either the Old Testament or the New Testament, and the roles of teaching and governing God's people were reserved for men, both in the Old Testament and the New.

Answer 4.2b: Women prophets always prophesied privately or prophesied to women.

It is significant that Miriam prophesied to the women of Israel:

> Then Miriam the prophetess, the sister of Aaron, took a tambourine in her hand, and *all the women went out after her* with tambourines and dancing. And Miriam sang to them:
>
> "Sing to the Lord, for he has triumphed gloriously;
> the horse and his rider he has thrown into the sea." (Exodus 15:20–21)

Rather than prophesying publicly, Deborah sent for Barak and gave a prophecy privately to him: "She sent and summoned Barak the son of Abinoam from Kedesh-naphtali and said to him, 'Has not the LORD, the God of Israel, commanded you, "Go, gather your men at Mount Tabor."'" (Judges 4:6).

And Huldah the prophetess gave her prophecy privately to a small group of five messengers from the king: "So Hilkiah the priest, and Ahikam, and Achbor, and Shaphan, and Asaiah went to Huldah the prophetess...and they talked with her" (2 Kings 22:14).

Women were able to prophesy in the Old Testament (as well as in the New; see pages 227–32), but in the Old Testament they always prophesied privately or to women. And prophecy consists of delivering messages from God to His people. It is different from teaching God's people and different from ruling God's people, neither of which women did with God's blessing in the Old or the New Testament.

EGALITARIAN CLAIM 4.3: WOMEN AS GOVERNMENTAL LEADERS: OLD TESTAMENT EXAMPLES OF WOMEN AS LEADERS OF THE GOVERNMENT OVER GOD'S PEOPLE GIVE PRECEDENTS FOR WOMEN IN ALL SORTS OF LEADERSHIP ROLES TODAY.

Linda Belleville writes, "Women in the ancient Near East provided political leadership. Some were heads of state. Athaliah, for example, ruled Israel from 842–836 BC."[15]

15. Belleville, "Women in Ministry," 94; see also her *Women Leaders and the Church*, 46. See also Brown, *Women Ministers*, 93.

Answer 4.3a: Instances where women seized ruling authority over God's people in the Old Testament are always viewed negatively.

Queens such as Jezebel (1 Kings 16:31; 18:4, 13; 19:1–2; 21:5–25) and Athaliah (2 Kings 11) led the people into evil when they gained power.[16]

It is amazing that Linda Belleville uses Athaliah as an example of "Women Leaders in Old Testament Times." She simply says that Athaliah "ruled Israel from 842–836 BC," but gives readers no Bible references so they can examine Athaliah's reign. Perhaps this is not so surprising, since Athaliah first led her son King Ahaziah into evil ("He also walked in the ways of the house of Ahab, for his mother was his counselor in doing wickedly" [2 Chronicles 22:3]), then, when Ahaziah was killed by Jehu, Athaliah "destroyed all the royal family" and became queen (2 Chronicles 22:10). The author of Chronicles calls her "that wicked woman" (2 Chronicles 24:7), and tells us that when she died, "all the people of the land rejoiced" (2 Chronicles 23:21). She should hardly be used as a positive example of women ruling over God's people.[17]

There were wise queens such as Esther, but she did not rule as a monarch, since the authority rested with Ahasuerus the king, and she was not queen over Israel, but over Persia.

Answer 4.3b: The Old Testament views the absence of male headship as a matter of shame and an indication of God's judgment on a society.

For example, note Isaiah's pronouncement of judgment against the people of Israel:

> For behold, the Lord GOD of hosts
> is taking away from Jerusalem and from Judah
> support and supply,
> all support of bread,
> and all support of water;
> the mighty man and the soldier,
> the judge and the prophet
> the diviner and the elder,
> the captain of fifty
> and the man of rank,
> the counselor and the skillful magician

---

16. However, the queen of Sheba (1 Kings 10:1–13) is viewed positively. As a foreign queen, she did not rule over God's people. Another foreign queen, the queen to King Belshazzar, gives wise counsel in Daniel 5:10–12.

17. Belleville says that there were not more women in public leadership roles because "domestic needs (especially the bearing and raising of children) left little time to pursue public roles" (*Women Leaders and the Church*, 46). But (1) this is inventing a reason the Bible nowhere gives; (2) this does not explain why there could be women prophets, as Belleville herself emphasizes; and (3) there were women who did not have children for a long time, such as Sarah and Hannah, and there were also many mature women whose children were grown, but even they did not assume teaching or governing roles over God's people.

> and the expert in charms.
> And I will make boys their princes,
> and infants shall rule over them. (Isaiah 3:1–4)

And a few verses later, with male leadership removed, God's judgment brings this result:

> My people—infants are their oppressors,
> and *women rule over them.*
> O my people, your guides mislead you
> and they have swallowed up the course of your paths. (Isaiah 3:12)

The absence of male leadership results in a desperate situation, with many women who have no male leadership or protection:

> And seven women shall take hold of one man in that day, saying, "We will eat our own bread and wear our own clothes, only let us be called by your name; take away our reproach." (Isaiah 4:1)

On a related theme, the absence of male might and protection is another sign of judgment against Nineveh:

> Behold, your troops
> are women in your midst.
> The gates of your land
> are wide open to your enemies;
> fire has devoured your bars. (Nahum 3:13; compare Jeremiah 50:37; 51:30)

Answer 4.3c: These Old Testament examples should not be used to discourage women from holding office in civil government today.

In the Old Testament, the *civil* government over the people of Israel was also the *religious* government over God's people. There was no distinction between civil government and church government as we have in the New Testament age. All the people who lived in Israel were also bound to obey all the religious laws about sacrifices and worship and serving the one true God. Therefore we cannot assume that the general pattern of restricting *civil government* leadership over the people of God to men would also apply to the New Testament age, where the civil government is separate from the government of the church.[18] The positive examples of women involved in civil leadership over nations other than Israel (such as Esther and the Queen of Sheba) should prevent us from arguing that it is wrong for women to hold a governing office.

---

18. I realize that in some cases, such as with the Church of England, the civil government retains some authority over the church. But the functions of governing the nation and governing the church can still be distinguished.

EGALITARIAN CLAIM 4.4: WOMEN PREACHERS: PSALM 68:11 AND ISAIAH 40:9 TALK ABOUT WOMEN WHO WERE PREACHERS, PROCLAIMING GOD'S GOOD NEWS.

Concerning these passages, Stanley Grenz writes,

> The psalmist later spoke of these women as public heralds of the word of God.... "The Lord announced the word, and great was the company of those who proclaimed it" (Ps 68:11 NIV). However, the feminine form of the Hebrew text is better translated, "great was the company of the women that heralded it...."
>
> Women could likewise be heralds of the word of God (Ps 68:11), a task associated with the prophetic office. Consequently, as the Hebrew construction of Isaiah 40:9 indicates, the prophet could freely use the feminine form to designate the herald who would one day announce the good tidings of God's powerful arrival: "You [feminine] who bring good tidings to Zion, go up on a high mountain.... Lift up your voice with a shout" (NIV).[19]

Answer 4.4a: Psalm 68:11 talks about women who announce a victory in battle.

The next verse tells the content of what the women are announcing, as is evident when the two verses are seen together:

> The Lord gives the word;
> *the women who announce the news* are a great host:
> "The kings of the armies—they flee, they flee!"
> The women at home divide the spoil. (Psalm 68:11–12)

Since these women who announce the good news[20] are "a great host," it seems that multitudes of women in various cities are joyfully proclaiming that God has intervened and their armies have won the battle.[21] There are echoes of the Song of Miriam (Exodus 15:20–21) and

19. Grenz, *Women in the Church,* 67–68, 70.
20. The proclamation of victory seems to be what was first announced by the "word" given by the Lord at the beginning of the verse, although whether through a male or female prophet it does not say. But the "great host" who subsequently announce the victory seem to be those who repeat the good news of victory throughout the cities of Israel.
21. We should also note that not all translations render the feminine participle in verse 11 as "the *women* who announce the news" (ESV). Grammatically feminine participles can be used to refer to "titles and designations of office," as *qōhelet* ("the preacher") in Ecclesiastes 1:1 (*Gesenius' Hebrew Grammar*, 2nd English ed., sec. 122r, 4:393). Thus, while the ESV, NASB, and NLT specify "women," and while this seems the more likely translation, several translations do not (NIV, RSV, NRSV, KJV, and NKJV). The Septuagint actually has a masculine plural dative participle, *tois euaggelizomenois.* Therefore, it is oversimplifying the situation to say, as Cindy Jacobs does, that "Any good translator can tell that the Hebrew is referring to women by using the feminine

the Song of Deborah and Barak (Judges 5), but the scene is also similar to 1 Samuel 18:6: "As they were coming home, when David returned from striking down the Philistine, the women came out of all the cities of Israel, singing and dancing, to meet King Saul, with tambourines, with songs of joy, and with musical instruments." Yes, women joyfully proclaimed the victories of the armies of Israel, but this is hardly a justification for women teaching God's Word to men in the New Testament age. Grenz has taken this verse out of its context.

Answer 4.4b: Isaiah 40:9 has feminine verbs because cities (like Jerusalem) are treated as grammatically feminine in Hebrew.

Most translations understand the feminine gender of the participle *mebassereth* (translated "herald") and the other feminine verbs in Isaiah 40:9 not to represent a woman who brings good news, but to indicate that *the city of Jerusalem,* which is also called Zion in this verse, is personified, and names of cities are regularly treated as grammatically feminine in Hebrew.[22]

> Get you up to a high mountain,
> *O Zion, herald* of good news;
> *lift up your voice* with strength,
> O Jerusalem, herald of good news;
> lift it up, fear not;
> say to the cities of Judah,
> "Behold your God!" (ESV; similarly NASB, RSV, NRSV, KJV, NKJV, NET)

Grenz shows no awareness of this standard grammatical feature in Hebrew, which explains why most English translations do not speak of a female herald here. At least two translations (the NIV and NLT) speak of one who brings good news *to Zion* (rather than speaking of Zion as the herald who brings good news to other cities), but even these translations give no indication that they think the feminine participle requires us to think of a female herald:

> You who bring good tidings to Zion,
> go up on a high mountain.
> You who bring good tidings to Jerusalem,
> lift up your voice with a shout,

---

gender.... The [KJV] translators simply could not believe that women could publish the good news, so they 'doctored' the passage according to their paradigm or worldview" (*Women of Destiny*, 195). She seems unaware that in Hebrew, participles that are grammatically feminine do not necessarily imply that women are being referred to, so the decision is not as simple as she indicates.

22. "The following classes of ideas are usually regarded as feminine.... (a) Names of *countries* and *towns*, since they are regarded as the mothers and nurses of the inhabitants" (*Gesenius' Hebrew Grammar*, 2nd English ed., sec. 122h, 4:391). A footnote to the same section in *Gesenius* mentions 2 Samuel 20:19 (which refers to the city of Abel as "a city that is a mother in Israel") and adds, "The comparison of Jerusalem to a woman is especially frequent in allegorical descriptions" (391n5, with reference to passages like Ezekiel 16:23 and Lamentations 1:1).

lift it up, do not be afraid;
say to the towns of Judah,
"Here is your God!" (NIV; similarly NLT)[23]

If the verse is taken in this way, it indicates a woman who proclaims the good news of the coming of the Lord, much as Miriam proclaimed victory (Exodus 15:20–21), as did Deborah (Judges 5), and much as women were the first to announce Jesus' resurrection (Matthew 28:1–10). It would be another example of women filling a prophetic office, but that is still different from the role of teaching which was reserved for the (male) priests, and different from the role of governing God's people. (See egalitarian claim 4.2 in this chapter (pp. 136–38) for a discussion of the role of women as prophets.)

Yet the "personification" view is favored by most translations, and has good reasons to support it.[24] The verse in any case provides no support for seeing women as "preachers" in the New Testament sense of those who teach the Word of God to an assembled congregation of believers.

EGALITARIAN CLAIM 4.5: MIRIAM AS LEADER: MIRIAM SERVED AS A LEADER OVER ISRAEL.

Linda Belleville makes high claims for Miriam's leadership role in Israel:

> Miriam, for example, was sent by the Lord (along with her two brothers) to "lead" (Masoretic text *he'elitîkā;* Septuagint, *anēgagon*) the people of Israel during the wilderness years (Micah 6:4). She was held in such high regard as a leader that the Israelites would not travel until she was at the helm (Num. 12:1–16).[25]

Answer 4.5a: Miriam did not "lead" the people of Israel.

Belleville's statements sound persuasive until we check the Hebrew and Greek text and find that this is not what Micah 6:4 says. Belleville has mistakenly applied to Miriam a Hebrew verb and a Greek verb that the Bible applies to God. Here is what the verse actually says:

> For I brought you up (Hebrew *he'elitîkā;* Septuagint, *anēgagon*; both verbs mean "to bring up") from the land of Egypt and redeemed you from the house of slavery, and I sent before you Moses, Aaron, and Miriam.

---

23. This possible reading is also given as an alternative in the margins of several other versions.
24. See the discussion in Young, *The Book of Isaiah* (1992), 3:36–37. The footnote in the *NET Bible* says, "Isaiah 41:27 and 52:7 speak of a herald sent *to* Zion, but the masculine singular form *mbsr* is used in these verses, in contrast to the feminine singular form *mbsrt* employed in 40:9, where Zion is addressed *as* a herald" (1293n3).
25. Belleville, "Women in Ministry," 93. See also Brown, *Women Ministers,* 100–101.

It says God brought them up from Egypt; it does not say that Miriam led them. Belleville has claimed something the verse does not say.

But doesn't the expression, "I sent before you Moses, Aaron, and Miriam," show that Miriam led Israel? Not really. The verse recalls that when Moses was leading the people of Israel, he was accompanied by his brother Aaron and his sister Miriam, so the three of them went "before" (Hebrew *lepānêka;* Septuagint *pro prosōpou sou*) the people of Israel. But that does not imply that Miriam had a leadership role (for nothing else in the Bible specifies this) or that Belleville is justified in saying that Miriam was "sent by the Lord" to "lead" the people of Israel.[26]

Answer 4.5b: The people of Israel did not insist that Miriam be "at the helm."

Belleville's claim that Miriam was "held in such high regard as a leader" that the Israelites would not travel until she was "at the helm" is another example of claiming something the Bible does not say. Readers who assume that Belleville is accurately reporting what is in Numbers 12:1–16 will be misled, for Numbers 12 is the story of God's judgment on Miriam and Aaron when they criticized Moses and attempted to intrude into the leadership role God had given him:

> Miriam and Aaron spoke against Moses because of the Cushite woman whom he had married.... And they said, "Has the LORD indeed spoken only through Moses? Has he not spoken through us also? And the LORD heard it.... And suddenly the LORD said to Moses and to Aaron and Miriam, "Come out, you three, to the tent of meeting."... And the LORD...called Aaron and Miriam, and they both came forward. And he said... "Why then were you not afraid to speak against my servant Moses?" And the anger of the LORD was kindled against them, and he departed.
>
> When the cloud removed from over the tent, behold, Miriam was leprous, like snow.... And Aaron said to Moses, "Oh, my lord, do not punish us because we have done foolishly and have sinned.... And Moses cried to the LORD, "Oh God, please heal her...." But the LORD said to Moses..."Let her be shut outside the camp seven days, and after that she may be brought in again." So Miriam was shut outside the camp seven days, and the people did not set out on the march till Miriam was brought in again. (Numbers 12:1–15)

The most this narrative says about Miriam's "leadership role" is that the Lord rebuked Miriam and Aaron for attempting to claim an equal leadership role with Moses. In fact, only Miriam, not

---

26. The NIV, alone among translations, says, "I brought you up out of Egypt and redeemed you from the land of slavery. I sent Moses *to lead you*, also Aaron and Miriam." But the translation "to lead you" is a very free interpretative paraphrase of the Hebrew text, which literally says, "I sent before you Moses, Aaron, and Miriam" (ESV; also NASB, RSV, NRSV, NKJV, KJV). Belleville's mistake in this verse was probably made first because she followed the NIV without checking the Hebrew of the end of the verse, and second because she then took the Hebrew and Greek verbs from the wrong part of the verse, leading her to attribute to Miriam what the Bible attributes to God.

Aaron, receives leprosy as a visible sign of God's displeasure. Where then is the evidence for Belleville's claim that Miriam "was held in such high regard as a leader"? It is not there. Where then is the evidence that the Israelites would not travel "until she was at the helm"? It is not there either. The Bible says that when Miriam tried to join Moses "at the helm" (to use Belleville's expression), God judged her with leprosy. The Bible says the opposite of what Belleville claims.

EGALITARIAN CLAIM 4.6: GODLY WOMEN: THERE ARE MANY GODLY WOMEN IN THE OLD TESTAMENT WHO SERVE AS EXAMPLES OF GOD'S BLESSING ON THE LEADERSHIP OF WOMEN.

I list this as a separate claim because egalitarian writers sometimes mention the numerous examples of godly women found in the Old Testament narratives, and from those examples they claim that the Old Testament gives approval to women leaders in general.[27]

Answer 4.6a: The Old Testament provides many examples of faithful women who received God's approval and blessing.

The Old Testament frequently honors women who are faithful to God and portrays them very favorably. Some examples are "Miriam the prophetess, the sister of Aaron" (Exodus 15:20; here she exercises a positive leadership role leading the women of Israel, in contrast to her mistake in Numbers 12), Deborah, who was "a prophetess" and a judge (Judges 4:4), and "Huldah the prophetess" who faithfully delivered the words the Lord had given her concerning King Josiah and the people of Judah (2 Kings 22:14–20; 2 Chronicles 34:22–28). In addition to these prophetesses, many other faithful, godly women are found in the Old Testament, such as Sarah, Rebekah, Ruth, Naomi, Abigail, Esther, and the godly wife of Proverbs 31.

Answer 4.6b: But the Old Testament never approves women taking authority over their husbands.

The godly women portrayed in the Old Testament are always seen as submissive to the leadership of their husbands. In fact, Peter sees a pattern in their behavior that Christian wives should imitate, for he says, "For this is how the holy women who hoped in God used to adorn themselves, by submitting to their husbands, as Sarah obeyed Abraham, calling him lord. And you are her children, if you do good and do not fear anything that is frightening" (1 Peter 3:5–6).[28]

---

27. See, for example, Brown, *Women Ministers*, 106.
28. For a discussion of Gilbert Bilezikian's claim that Abraham obeyed Sarah, and that Abigail took leadership over Nabal, see the discussion of egalitarian claims 4.8 and 4.9 (pp. 151–55).

Answer 4.6c: Instances where women seized ruling authority over God's people in the Old Testament are always viewed negatively.

Queens such as Jezebel (1 Kings 16:31; 18:4, 13; 19:1–2; 21:5–25) and Athaliah (2 Kings 11) led the people into evil when they gained power.[29]

There were wise queens such as Esther, a wonderful example of a godly woman, but she did not rule as a monarch, since the authority rested with Ahasuerus the king, and she was not queen over Israel, but over Persia. The Queen of Sheba (1 Kings 10:1–13) is also viewed positively, but as a foreign queen she did not rule over God's people.

Egalitarian claim 4.7: Male Leadership Caused Abuse: Old Testament examples of oppression and mistreatment of women were the result of male headship in the family (or patriarchy), and show male headship to be wrong.

Ruth Tucker writes, "Following the Fall into sin in Genesis 3, a new patriarchal order began, with the husband ruling over not only his wife but also the rest of his family."[30]

Tucker then describes a long list of abusive, destructive events, claiming at each point that they were the result of patriarchy (which to her is the entire system of male leadership in the family). When Abraham allows Sarah to be taken into Pharaoh's harem, it is an example of the "evils of patriarchy."[31] When a man in Sodom allows his concubine to be repeatedly raped and then killed (Judges 19:22–30), it "demonstrates the potential evil of the patriarchal system."[32] When David takes many wives, and then takes ten concubines and shuts them up under guard until the day of their death (2 Samuel 20:3), Tucker says, "Such were the evils of patriarchalism."[33] After noting that Solomon "made a game out of the custom [of polygamy], with his seven hundred wives and three hundred concubines (1 Kings 11:3)," Tucker observes, "Like other aspects of patriarchalism, polygamy had a very negative effect on women."[34] All these evils are blamed on a system of male leadership ("patriarchy") in the Old Testament.

But in the next chapter,[35] Tucker takes many positive examples from the Old Testament (such as Sarah, Ruth, Esther, and Deborah), and uses them not as positive examples of the patriarchal system, but as examples of how God worked positively through women in spite of "patriarchy." She says, "Indeed, for all the patriarchy manifested throughout the pages of the Old Testament, women are remarkably prominent."[36]

29. See further discussion of Athaliah earlier in this chapter, p. 139. Regarding Deborah, see pp. 133–34.
30. Tucker, *Women in the Maze* (1992), 57.
31. Ibid., 58.
32. Ibid., 59.
33. Ibid., 61.
34. Ibid., 61–62.
35. Ibid., 64–70.
36. Ibid., 64.

In a similar way, Gilbert Bilezikian takes something evil in the Old Testament, such as polygamy, and says it was the result of male authority in marriage:

> Evidently, the radical disruption of this family ordinance as it occurred at the fall opened the door wide to the monstrosity of polygamy *as husbands assumed the position of rulers over their wives*.[37]

He also claims that arbitrary divorces initiated by men were the result of male authority in marriage:

> The necessity for such a concession [divorce legislation in Deuteronomy 24:1–4] in the Mosaic Law illustrates *the vicious use to which the rulership principle was put by men*, as it gave them the power to dispose of their wives without concern for their desires and without retribution for their own injustice.[38]

Answer 4.7a: These evils were the result of sin and the abuse of male headship, not of male headship in itself.

If we read each of Ruth Tucker's examples in context, we see that they were seen as evil in themselves. *They are never viewed as the result of male headship*, but as a result of sinful human beings abusing their power. The Old Testament often rebukes men for their sins, but it never says, "You were wrong to think you should lead your family," or "Repent of your idea of male headship," or any similar thing. This is what Tucker and Bilezikian need in order to establish their claim that these evils were the result of patriarchy. But statements such as these are found nowhere in the Bible.

It is not legitimate to blame these evils on the system of male leadership that was assumed and affirmed in various ways in the Old Testament. Such an argument would be like saying, "These evils were the result of monotheism," since they all occurred among Israelites who held to monotheism. Of course, that is not a legitimate argument, but the reasoning process is similar to one of blaming all these sins on "patriarchy."

Answer 4.7b. This approach imposes a biased filter that leads to misinterpretation of the Old Testament.

This egalitarian filtering of the text may be summarized as follows:

37. Bilezikian, *Beyond Sex Roles,* 62 (italics added).
38. Ibid., 67.

If a text:	The egalitarian interpretation is:	How do we know this?
shows a **positive** example of prominence for women (such as Miriam, Deborah, Huldah)	God is gradually overcoming patriarchy because He wants to establish equal roles for men and women	because we know male leadership is wrong (assumption used to filter the text)
shows a **negative** example of oppression of women (such as rape, polygamy, adultery, arbitrary divorce)	God is showing the evil of patriarchy because He wants to establish equal roles for men and women	because we know male leadership is wrong (assumption used to filter the text)

A better approach is to stick to what the biblical text *actually says*:

If a text:	A better interpretation is:	How do we know this?
shows a positive example of prominence for women (such as Miriam, Deborah, Huldah)	God is affirming the valuable ministries of women in the context of male leadership	Scripture never says male leadership is wrong but rather affirms it (see 1 Peter 3:5–6 as a summary of OT passages; see also the uniform pattern that men should be priests and kings).
shows a negative example of oppression of women (such as rape, polygamy, adultery, arbitrary divorce) the Bible actually says.	God is showing the evil of abuses of male leadership itself. We should stick to what	Scripture condemns rape (Deuteronomy 22:25–27) and adultery (Exodus 20:17), but never condemns male leadership

A relevant example is David's abuse of power in committing adultery with Bathsheba (2 Samuel 11). God rebuked David through Nathan the prophet (2 Samuel 12:1–15), and there was trouble on David's house in subsequent years (2 Samuel 12:15–18:33). But God never says anything like, "This shows that it is wrong for a man to be king," or "This shows the evil of male leadership." David continues as king, and God keeps His promise that David's son (not his daughter) will be king (2 Samuel 7:12–16; 1 Kings 1:39).

Answer 4.7c: Polygamy was tolerated but not commanded by God in the Old Testament.

I agree with Bilezikian, Tucker, and others that polygamy was a departure from God's ideal of monogamous marriage established at Creation (Genesis 2:24). It was not commanded by God in the Old Testament, but neither was it explicitly prohibited. In the New Testament, elders and deacons in the church could not be polygamists (see "husband of one wife" in 1 Timothy 3:2, 12; Titus 1:6), and thus the practice was seen to be contrary to God's ideal.

But I disagree that Old Testament polygamy shows that male headship in marriage is wrong. The New Testament shows male headship in a relationship of one husband and one wife (Ephesians 5:22–33). Therefore polygamy is certainly not a necessary consequence of male headship. Polygamy was an *abuse* of male headship, and a result of sin; it was not a *result* of male headship.

Answer 4.7d: Gilbert Bilezikian maligns God's Old Testament laws on adultery, saying the laws were unfair.

In his zeal to show that male leadership in the Old Testament was an evil, Gilbert Bilezikian makes several statements about the Old Testament that are untrue. His purpose is to show that male leadership led to a "Double Standard on Adultery," a double standard that favored men. Consider Bilezikian's statements compared to the actual teaching of the Bible:

> The difference of status between men and women...would inevitably produce inequities in the area of sexual behavior. Such inequities are indeed reflected in the old-covenant legislation on adultery, which is summarized in Deuteronomy 22:13–30.[39]

Here Bilezikian says there were "inequities" in the Old Testament laws about adultery, specifically in Deuteronomy 22. But these are not man-generated laws. These are the laws God commanded Moses to teach the nation (see Deuteronomy 6:1). So Bilezikian is saying that there are "inequities" in God's laws given to Israel. He is saying that God's laws were unfair. But how can someone say this and still hold that God is fair and just and His words are true?

Bilezikian comments further on Deuteronomy 22:

> Since a married man was ruler over his wife, her unfaithfulness violated his property rights. It was a crime punishable by death. Therefore, an adulterous wife was put to death. (v. 22)
>
> Since a married woman was not ruler over her husband, she had no rights over him. Consequently, his adulterous behavior did not constitute a crime against her. As a result, *the old-covenant law prescribed no penalty against an unfaithful husband.* His extramarital relations were not considered an offense against his wife.[40]

But the very verse he cites says, "If a man is found lying with the wife of another man, *both of them shall die,* the man who lay with the woman, and the woman. So you shall purge the evil

39. Ibid., 64.
40. Ibid., 64–65.

from Israel" (Deuteronomy 22:22). How then can Bilezikian say, "The old-covenant law prescribed no penalty against an unfaithful husband"?[41] His statement is untrue.

And in the Ten Commandments we read,

> "You shall not commit adultery....
>
> You shall not covet your neighbor's house; *you shall not covet your neighbor's wife*, or his male servant, or his female servant, or his ox, or his donkey, or anything that is your neighbor's." (Exodus 20:14, 17)

The Old Testament law prohibited adultery. It even prohibited the coveting of "your neighbor's wife" that would lead to adultery. When it says, "your neighbor's *wife*," instead of "husband," the law is addressed directly to *men* (though it would have application also to a wife coveting her neighbor's husband).

Then Bilezikian says,

> The one-sided definition of adultery gave enough latitude to male permissive practices for prostitution to become a persistent affliction in the history of the old-covenant people.... *Nowhere is the practice of prostitution explicitly condemned or prohibited.*[42]

But is this true? Consider these verses:

> "Do not profane your daughter by making her a *prostitute*, lest the land fall into *prostitution* and the land become full of depravity." (Leviticus 19:29)

> "None of the daughters of Israel shall be a cult *prostitute*, and none of the sons of Israel shall be a cult *prostitute.*" (Deuteronomy 23:17)

> "You shall not bring the fee of a *prostitute* or the wages of a dog into the house of the LORD your God in payment for any vow, for both of these are an abomination to the LORD your God." (Deuteronomy 23:18)

---

41. After saying there was "no penalty against an unfaithful husband," Bilezikian goes on to say, "A man was subject to capital punishment if he had sexual relations with a married or betrothed woman" (p. 65). He does not appear to be troubled, or even show awareness, that this statement directly contradicts his earlier sentence about "no penalty against an unfaithful husband." He adds that "the violation of a single woman was not punishable by death..." (vv. 28–29), but fails to tell the reader that verses 28–29 do impose a penalty (a fine of "fifty shekels of silver") and require that he marry the woman, and that "He may not divorce her all his days." Bilezikian's statement that there was "no penalty against an unfaithful husband" is simply untrue.
42. Bilezikian, *Beyond Sex Roles*, 65.

> And behold, the woman meets him,
> dressed as a *prostitute*, wily of heart....
> All at once he follows her,
> as an ox goes to the slaughter,
> or as a stag is caught fast
> till an arrow pierces its liver;
> as a bird rushes into a snare;
> he does not know that it will cost him his life....
> Let not your heart turn aside to her ways;
> *do not stray into her paths.* (Proverbs 7:10, 22–23, 25)

> My son, give me your heart,
> and let your eyes observe my ways.
> For a *prostitute* is a deep pit;
> an adulteress is a narrow well.
> She lies in wait like a robber
> and increases the traitors among mankind. (Proverbs 23:26–27)

These passages contradict Bilezikian's statement, "nowhere is the practice of prostitution explicitly condemned or prohibited," and show it to be untrue.[43] In addition, prostitution violates God's fundamental command to guard sexual purity, "You shall not commit adultery" (Exodus 20:14). Of course prostitution is prohibited. In his attempt to portray male leadership in the Old Testament as evil, Bilezikian makes untrue statements about the Bible.

Egalitarian claim 4.8: Abraham Obeyed Sarah: The Old Testament shows that Abraham obeyed Sarah several times.

Gilbert Bilezikian writes,

> The Old Testament shows instances of wives who took over the leadership of their households, so that their husbands followed their orders and advice. Thus, Abraham, the man presented in Scripture as the model of faith for all believers, obeyed Sarah several times (Gen. 16:2, 6; 21:10–12)—even as Sarah is cited in the New Testament as an example of wifely obedience (1 Pet. 3:6).[44]

43. Bilezikian goes on to mention the "warnings" and "the few restrictions" placed on prostitution, such as the "prohibitions of...temple prostitutes," and says these "only emphasize its prevalence in Old Testament times" (*Beyond Sex Roles*, 65). But to say that "restrictions" proved the "prevalence" of prostitution is not the same as saying there are no restrictions! Indeed, God can very well prohibit something immoral that is common or prevalent (if it was common, which Bilezikian does not prove). Bilezikian seems unaware of the fact that to say prostitution is "nowhere...prohibited" and then to say that there are "warnings concerning the evils of prostitution" and "prohibitions of...temple prostitutes" is to affirm a contradiction.

44. Bilezikian, *Beyond Sex Roles*, 72. See also Brown, *Women Ministers*, 97.

Later Bilezikian writes,

> The use of Sarah as an example of obedience shows that Peter was not devoid of a sense of humor. In Genesis, Abraham is shown as obeying Sarah as often as Sarah obeyed Abraham—once at God's behest as he was told, "Whatever Sarah says to you, do as she tells you" (Gen. 16:2, 6; 21:11–12).... Sarah obeyed Abraham, but Christian wives, her spiritual daughters, are never told to "obey" their husbands neither here nor anywhere else in the Bible.[45]

Answer 4.8a: Sarah never led her household or ruled over Abraham.

The texts Bilezikian cites do not show Sarah taking over leadership of her household or Abraham obeying Sarah. Here are the verses he refers to:

> And Sarai said to Abram, "Behold now, the Lord has prevented me from bearing children. Go in to my servant; it may be that I shall obtain children by her." And Abram listened to the voice of Sarai. (Genesis 16:2)

> But Abram said to Sarai, "Behold, your servant is in your power; do to her as you please." Then Sarai dealt harshly with her, and she fled from her. (v. 6)

> So she said to Abraham, "Cast out this slave woman with her son, for the son of this slave woman shall not be heir with my son Isaac." And the thing was very displeasing to Abraham on account of his son. But God said to Abraham, "Be not displeased because of the boy and because of your slave woman. Whatever Sarah says to you, do as she tells you, for through Isaac shall your offspring be named." (21:10–12)

These are not examples of Abraham "obeying" Sarah, as Bilezikian claims. Genesis 16:2 is an example of a husband giving in to a wrongful request from his wife, resulting in disobedience to God, for in this verse Abraham gives in to Sarah's urging and soon he has a son by Hagar. For a husband to grant his wife's request surely does not prove that she has authority over him, any more than it shows a reversal of authority when God grants one of our requests, or when a parent grants a child's request. And when Abraham grants Sarah's wrongful request, with disastrous consequences, it proves even less. Bilezikian shows no awareness that the Bible does not hold up this incident of sin as a pattern for us to imitate.

In Genesis 16:6, Abraham does not obey Sarah but is clearly the family authority who (again wrongfully) gives in to Sarah's recriminations and allows her to mistreat Hagar and

45. Ibid., 191. Sarah Sumner takes a similar position, saying about Abraham that "God told him not to lead his wife Sarah but rather to listen to her and cooperate with her wishes" (*Men and Women in the Church,* 98).

Ishmael. Why does Bilezikian refer to these examples of sin as positive examples of a husband obeying his wife? To use such a procedure is to contradict the force of these passages.

In Genesis 21:11–12, God tells Abraham, "Listen to whatever Sarah tells you," but this was specifically about casting out Hagar and Ishmael. Abraham did what Sarah asked here not because he was obeying his wife but because at this specific point God told him to do what Sarah said. God used Sarah to convey His will to Abraham, but no pattern of husbands obeying their wives is established here. In fact, the exceptional intervention of God suggests that Abraham would not ordinarily have acceded to such a request from his wife.

Answer 4.8b: We are not free to take biblical statements and commands as a joke.

Bilezikian apparently takes Peter's statement as a joke, for he says, "The use of Sarah as an example of obedience shows that Peter was not devoid of a sense of humor."[46]

But to say that a straightforward biblical statement is an example of humor is simply an easy way to avoid the force of a verse whose plain meaning contradicts one's position. This is not the kind of argument that reflects submission to Scripture.

Answer 4.8c: We are not free to take Sarah's obedience as a negative example when Peter takes it as a positive example.

Bilezikian denies that Sarah is a model for Christian wives to follow, for he says:

> The point of Peter's reference to Sarah is that wives in the New Covenant can learn from their spiritual ancestress...who lived in the "dark side" of the old-covenant compromise, when she had to "obey" her husband.... Sarah obeyed Abraham, but Christian wives, her spiritual daughters, are never told to "obey" their husbands neither here nor anywhere else in the Bible.[47]

Whereas Peter uses Sarah as a positive example for Christian wives to imitate, Bilezikian uses her as a *negative* example, showing what Christian wives are not supposed to do.

Peter tells wives to act like "the holy women who hoped in God...by submitting to their husbands" (1 Peter 3:5), but Bilezikian says this was on the "dark side" of the "old-covenant compromise," implying that it should *not* be a pattern for women today.

Peter tells wives to act like Sarah, who "obeyed Abraham" (v. 6), but Bilezikian says that this verse does *not* tell wives to obey their husbands.

Readers should note carefully the result of Bilezikian's analysis of 1 Peter 3:1–7, because at several points he ends up denying what the text says and affirming what the text does not say. Peter says that wives *should* be submissive to their husbands, but Bilezikian says that the

46. Ibid.
47. Ibid.

motivations for a Christian wife's behavior should "have nothing in common with submission defined as obedience to authority."[48] Peter *does not say* that husbands should be submissive to their wives, but Bilezikian says that husbands should undergo a "traumatic role reversal" whereby "now it is husbands who must show consideration for their wives and bestow honor upon them, much like a servant to his master."[49] Peter says that *Sarah obeyed Abraham*, but Bilezikian claims that *Abraham obeyed Sarah*. Peter says that wives *should* follow the example of Sarah who obeyed her husband, but Bilezikian says that wives are *nowhere* told to be obedient to their husbands.

Bilezikian teaches just the opposite of what the Bible teaches regarding Sarah and Abraham. Under the guise of an alternative interpretation, we find a position that is repeatedly unwilling to submit to the authority of the actual words of Scripture, but simply changes the teaching of Scripture again and again.

EGALITARIAN CLAIM 4.9: ABIGAIL: THE STORY OF ABIGAIL (1 SAMUEL 25) SHOWS GOD'S APPROVAL OF A WIFE WHO ASSUMED AUTHORITY IN HER FAMILY.

After summarizing the story of David and Abigail, Gilbert Bilezikian writes:

> Obviously, the narrator of this account did not find it objectionable for a wife to take it upon herself to revoke her husband's orders, to dispose of household supplies without his permission.... David, as designated king (1 Sam. 16:1–13), commended Abigail for having acted independently, in contradiction to her husband's expressed will, and told her, "I have hearkened to your voice" (v. 35). David recognized Abigail's independent behavior as being in conformity to God's will (vv. 32–34). And when God Himself intervened, He did not punish Abigail for disobedience to her husband.... Such stories demonstrate that women were not always "subordinate authorities" in old-covenant times. Men could also be subordinated to their decisions.[50]

Answer 4.9a: Bilezikian reads into the text of Scripture things that are not there.

Bilezikian makes it appear as if Abigail disobeyed her husband, Nabal, but when we read the text, we find that nowhere in 1 Samuel 25 does Abigail disobey him, because nowhere does Nabal say one word to Abigail about David! In the text of Scripture, Nabal does not give any orders for Abigail to "revoke." Nabal speaks to "David's servants" (v. 10) and refuses their request

48. Ibid., 190.
49. Ibid., 192.
50. Ibid., 73. See also Brown, *Women Ministers*, 97.

for food, and then one of Nabal's servants goes and tells Abigail what has happened (v. 14). Thus, Bilezikian is wrong to call Abigail's action "disobedience to her husband," and to imply that God approved of such disobedience.

In fact, Abigail intervened with a gift of food to save her husband's life from certain death at the hands of David's four hundred soldiers (v. 13). When he found out about David's attack that had been avoided, he was apparently so afraid that "his heart died within him, and he became as a stone" (v. 37). Had he known of the impending attack, he very likely would have approved Abigail's action to save his life! I agree that Abigail in some sense acted contrary to the hostile intent behind Nabal's foolish words to David's servants, but she never directly disobeys Nabal, contrary to what Bilezikian says. And nothing in the text shows Nabal to be "subordinated to" the authority of his wife, as Bilezikian claims (he died from God's judgment in v. 38).

Yes, David says, "I have obeyed your voice" (1 Samuel 25:35), but he explains in the next phrase what he means by that: "I have granted your petition." This does not mean that David was "subordinated to" Abigail's decisions, for Abigail's request is delivered after she "fell before David on her face and bowed to the ground" (1 Samuel 25:23). This is hardly a picture of David submitting to the authority of a woman! David granted her request, much as a king might grant the request of one of his subjects.

As he has done with other passages, Bilezikian reads into the beautiful story of Abigail much that is simply not there. Once we examine the actual text of 1 Samuel 25, it is evident that this story cannot be rightly used as a model to encourage wives to disobey their husbands with God's approval, as Bilezikian's portrayal would have it. Bilezikian's claims are contrary to the text of 1 Samuel 25, and contrary to the teaching of the rest of Scripture.

EGALITARIAN CLAIM 4.10: THE PROVERBS 31 WIFE: THE DESCRIPTION OF "A GOOD WIFE" IN PROVERBS 31 OVERTURNS MALE LEADERSHIP IN THE FAMILY.

Gilbert Bilezikian says about Proverbs 31:

> This text...accomplishes a verse-by-verse demolition of the male-rulership system that issued from the fall, by showing God's ideal for women—to share fully in the responsibilities pertaining to the governance of community life in the family.[51]

In support of this contention, Bilezikian argues from Proverbs 31 by mentioning the verse reference but never quoting the whole verse.

---

51. Bilezikian, *Beyond Sex Roles*, 78. See also Brown, *Women Ministers*, 107.

Answer 4.10a: Bilezikian often inserts into the biblical text things that are not there.

We can see this by quoting Bilezikian's statements about several verses in Proverbs 31 and then quoting the actual verses themselves. In each case, what Bilezikian claims about the verse is not there. Here are some examples:

Bilezikian writes: *"Verses 11–12.* Her husband has confidence in her. He respects her judgment and her ***independent decisions.***"[52] But the verses actually say:

> The heart of her husband trusts in her,
> and he will have no lack of gain.
> She does him good, and not harm,
> all the days of her life. (Proverbs 31:11–12)

These verses do say her husband trusts her, but they say nothing about "independent decisions." Probably he does respect her judgment and her decisions, but to talk of "independent decisions" is to begin to drive a wedge into the harmony and interaction that God intends between husband and wife.

Bilezikian writes: "*Verse 15.* She is diligent and competent in the management of resources, personnel, and responsibilities in her house. She is ***the provider*** of food for the household."[53] But the verse actually says:

> She rises while it is yet night
> and provides food for her household
> and portions for her maidens. (Proverbs 31:15)

The problem with Bilezikian's statement is that calling her "*the* provider of food for the household" can easily be understood to mean that she is the primary breadwinner or primary provider of income for the household. This is the impression Bilezikian attempts to give, because he later says, "She manages for herself an independent career"[54] and "She is a 'working wife' as she combines career and housekeeping,"[55] while his view of the husband is anything but positive (see the next verse). The verse just means she puts out the food for the day.

Bilezikian writes: *"Verse 23.* This is the only reference to the 'activities' of the husband! The implication is that he is well respected in the community because of his wife's industry."[56] But the verse actually says,

---

52. Ibid., 76 (italics added).
53. Ibid.
54. Ibid.
55. Ibid., 77.
56. Ibid.

Her husband is known in the gates
when he sits among the elders of the land. (Proverbs 31:23)

In saying this verse describes the "activities" of the husband, Bilezikian portrays an idle husband supported by a working wife who brings in all the income and manages the household as well. But nothing in the text says that the husband does not work. To use a modern parallel, members of a city council will usually have other jobs that occupy most of their time. An idle, unproductive man would *not* have been respected among the elders in ancient Israel (see the statements about "the sluggard" earlier in Proverbs, such as in Proverbs 6:6, 9; 10:26; 13:4; 15:19; 19:24; 20:4; 21:25; 24:30–31). And while he probably was respected *in part* because of his excellent wife and her industry, the implication that he is lazy and is respected *only* because of her is inserting into the text ideas that are not there. To say that the Bible extols a picture of an idle husband supported by an industrious wife is to misrepresent the teaching of the Bible.

Bilezikian writes: "*Verse 27*. She is the vigilant supervisor of her household. The total list of her accomplishments indicates that she is the one responsible for making the managerial decisions affecting the life of her home."[57] But the verse actually says,

She looks well to the ways of her household
and does not eat the bread of idleness. (Proverbs 31:27)

The verse says she cares for her household and is not idle. But Bilezikian's language makes her sound like the head of the household ("*the* vigilant supervisor," and "*the one* responsible for making the managerial decisions"). The chapter praises the godly conduct of this wife, but it does not make her the head of the household or say anything about usurping her husband's authority. Bilezikian inserts into the biblical text ideas that are not there, and thus claims the Bible teaches things that it does not teach.

This is a wonderful chapter of the Bible but Bilezikian has made it out to be a sort of feminist manifesto. When Bilezikian says that Proverbs 31 "accomplishes a verse-by-verse demolition"[58] of male leadership in the family, he is distorting this chapter into something it never was and can never be.

57. Ibid.
58. Ibid., 78.

Conclusion

After Genesis 1–3, the rest of the Old Testament honors godly women in many ways, and shows that they as well as men could prophesy and could be courageous in risking their very lives to serve God by faith. But nothing in the Old Testament text indicates that women should be leaders over their husbands or lead or teach God's people. And several egalitarian claims to this effect insert into the text of the Bible many things that are not there.

CHAPTER FIVE

Evangelical Feminist Claims from the Gospels and Acts

Now we turn from the Old Testament to the New Testament. Jesus treated women with great honor and dignity. He surprised the Jewish people of His day in the way He interacted with and honored women as well as men, including several women among the group of disciples who followed Him. He even chose women to be the first witnesses to His resurrection. Don't Jesus' example and teaching show that He is overturning the patriarchal bias against women that was found in the Old Testament and in the Judaism of His day? Doesn't His example show that we should allow women and men equal access to all positions of leadership in the church?

And what about the early church? Perhaps Jesus appointed all male apostles because that was the only thing that would have been acceptable in His day. But doesn't Acts 2 show us that both men and women alike have gifts for ministry in the New Covenant Age? And aren't there examples of leading women, such as Priscilla, in the book of Acts?

It is questions like these that we consider in this chapter.

EGALITARIAN CLAIM 5.1: JESUS' TREATMENT OF WOMEN: JESUS UNDERMINED THE PATRIARCHAL NATURE OF FIRST-CENTURY JUDAISM THROUGH HIS POSITIVE TREATMENT OF WOMEN.

The Gospels give clear testimony that Jesus treated women with dignity and respect. Egalitarians see in Jesus' interactions with women a precedent for opening all ministry positions to women. Stanley Grenz writes,

> Jesus perhaps most notably departed from cultural norms by including women among his followers.... In contrast to many rabbis who considered it inappropriate to instruct women, Jesus readily taught them.... [By his response to Mary of Bethany

> in Luke 10:39] Jesus overturned the culturally determined priorities for women. He rejected the Jewish notion that household maintenance constituted the only appropriate role for women in society. And he defied the practice of excluding women from the study of the Torah. Our Lord set aside the customary prejudices of his day and restored the Old Testament injunction that both men and women apply themselves to learning God's law (Lk 11:27–28).[1]

Gilbert Bilezikian is quite sweeping in his conclusions:

> In multiple ways, Jesus established the principle of full access of both men and women to the responsibilities attendant to the harmonious functioning of the new community. Jesus taught his followers in word and deed to consider the gender difference irrelevant to the concerns and processes of the kingdom of God.[2]

J. Lee Grady adds:

> The strong church bias against women in leadership is peculiar when we examine Jesus' own inclusive attitudes toward the women who followed Him. As we have noted already, Jesus affirmed the equality of women in the midst of a culture that denied them basic human rights. He called them to be His disciples during a time when religious leaders taught that it was disgraceful even to teach a woman.... These women were not just stragglers who stayed at the back of Jesus' entourage watching Him from a distance while they cooked meals for the men. They were Jesus' disciples in the fullest sense, and we have every reason to believe that He commissioned them to minister in His name.[3]

Answer 5.1a: It is true that Jesus undermined abuses of male leadership found in some parts of Jewish society, and treated women with great respect and dignity.

There are numerous negative or demeaning statements about women in Rabbinic literature, some of which stem (in oral form at least) from the time of Jesus. These are documented extensively in several studies.[4] But the picture is not entirely negative. Ben Witherington notes,

---

1. Grenz, *Women in the Church* (1995), 74–75.
2. Bilezikian, *Beyond Sex Roles* (1985), 118.
3. Grady, *Ten Lies* (2000), 32–33.
4. For further study see the materials in Jeremias, *Jerusalem in the Time of Jesus* (1969), 359–76; Witherington, *Women and the Genesis of Christianity* (1990), 3–9, 251–53; Kittel and Freidrich, *Theological Dictionary of the New Testament (TDNT)* 1:781–84; and the extensive index of references in Rabbinic literature found in the index entry "Frau" in Strack and Billerbeck, *Kommentar zum Neuen Testament aus Talmud und Midrasch* (1926-1928), 4:2, 1226–27.

> It would be wrong to assume that a Jewish woman had no respect or *rights* in Jesus' day.... The Talmud instructs a man to love his wife as himself and to respect her more than himself.... There are even cases of women being taught the oral law and being consulted on its fine points.... Some women were able to become learned in both oral and written law and tradition.[5]

The overall picture, however, is that Jesus treated women as equals in a way that was surprising for first-century culture.

We should be thankful that Jesus honored women, and treated them as persons just as He treated men. He talked openly with women, to the amazement of His disciples (John 4:1–27), taught women (Luke 10:38–42), assumed that women as well as men could talk and reason about theological truths (Luke 10:38–42; John 4:7–26; 11:21–27), had women among the band of disciples who traveled with Him (Luke 8:1–3), accepted monetary support and ministry from them (Mark 15:40–41; Luke 8:3), and used women as well as men as teaching examples (Mark 12:41–44; Luke 15:8–10; 18:1–8). Jesus thus set a pattern that should forever challenge all cultures that treat women as second-class citizens, as it no doubt challenged and rebuked the culture of Jesus' day.

Answer 5.1b: But Jesus did not overthrow all male leadership, because He consistently called only men to the roles of governing and teaching God's people.

Jesus appointed only men to be His twelve apostles (Matthew 10:1–4). The apostles had governing authority over the early church. When a replacement was chosen for Judas, Peter said it had to be "one of the *men* who have accompanied us" (Acts 1:21). Yes, Jesus undermined the wrongful and abusive aspects of the patriarchal culture of that time, but he did not overturn a God-given pattern of male leadership in the household and male leadership among God's people.

EGALITARIAN CLAIM 5.2: JESUS AND MARY: WHEN JESUS PRAISED MARY AND CORRECTED MARTHA (LUKE 10:38–42), HE OVERTURNED THE EXPECTATIONS THAT A PATRIARCHAL CULTURE PLACED ON WOMEN.

Stanley Grenz writes,

> In contrast to many rabbis who considered it inappropriate to instruct women, Jesus readily taught them. Perhaps the most obvious example is Mary of Bethany, who sat at Jesus' feet (Lk 10:39).... By his response, Jesus overturned the culturally determined priorities for women. He rejected the Jewish notion that household maintenance

5. Witherington, *Women and the Genesis of Christianity*, 4–5, 7.

> constituted the only appropriate role for women in society. And he defied the practice of excluding women from the study of the Torah.[6]

And Aida Spencer says about Mary and Martha,

> Jesus has completely reversed the priorities and the consequences of those priorities in Jewish life. Not only does Jesus *not* think women are exempt from learning the Torah, but also they do *best* to learn God's law.... In choosing between a woman's role in homemaking and a woman's role in education, which Martha and Mary represent...Jesus has concluded that a woman's role as homemaker is *not* primary.... Apparently, Jesus thought women received more merit from attending the School of the Rabbis than sending men to the School of the Rabbis.[7]

Answer 5.2a: Jesus overturned some expectations, but the text does not say He overturned all expectations.

I am thankful that Jesus taught women and conversed openly with them about theological questions (as in John 4). But that does not mean that Jesus overturned *all* Jewish beliefs and customs about the roles of women and men! To say that is like arguing:

1. Jesus overturned Jewish expectations that people should take revenge, such as "an eye for an eye" (Matthew 5:38–42).
2. Therefore Jesus decreed that no criminals should ever be punished.

This argument is wrong because it takes a specific idea (no personal revenge) and broadens it into a general principle (no punishment for criminals), a principle that Jesus did not teach. This is adding to Jesus' teaching.

Similarly, it is like arguing:

1. Jesus overturned Jewish thinking by showing that lustful thoughts were sinful (Matthew 5:27–30).
2. Therefore, Jesus showed that all sexual desire is evil.

Again, the argument is wrong because it takes a specific statement Jesus made (lustful thoughts are sinful) and broadens it into a general principle (sexual desire is evil). But Jesus did not affirm this broad principle, for sexual desire within marriage, and sexual desire that leads to marriage, is viewed positively in Scripture (1 Corinthians 7:1–5). Similarly, in overturning some wrongful Jewish restrictions on women, Jesus did not overturn every Jewish idea or every Old Testament idea about male leadership.

---

6. Grenz, *Women in the Church,* 75.
7. Spencer, *Beyond the Curse* (1985), 60–61. Similarly, Sarah Sumner says, "Jesus was the first rabbi ever to accept a woman student" (*Men and Women in the Church* [2003], 125).

Answer 5.2b: This egalitarian argument imports ideas into the text that are not there.

Here is the actual story about Mary and Martha:

> Now as they went on their way, Jesus entered a village. And a woman named Martha welcomed him into her house. And she had a sister called Mary, who sat at the Lord's feet and listened to his teaching. But Martha was distracted with much serving. And she went up to him and said, "Lord, do you not care that my sister has left me to serve alone? Tell her then to help me." But the Lord answered her, "Martha, Martha, you are anxious and troubled about many things, but one thing is necessary. Mary has chosen the good portion, which will not be taken away from her." (Luke 10:38–42)

Jesus commended Mary for listening to *Him*. He said nothing about going to any "School of the Rabbis," as Spencer claims. He did not send His disciples to any school (they were "uneducated, common men," Acts 4:13), nor did He send Mary to any school. Jesus commended Mary for listening to *Him,* but Spencer, in her interpretation, has incorrectly made this into a treatise for formal theological education.[8] There is nothing about "a woman's role in education" being more important that "a woman's role as homemaker." Spencer and Sumner have read things into the text that are not there.

A related mistake in this kind of argument is to claim that sitting at Jesus' feet implied some kind of special status for Mary. Ruth Tucker and Walt Liefeld say,

> It is generally agreed that Jesus went far beyond the rabbis of his day in permitting this woman to assume the role of a disciple. This is certainly implied by Luke in portraying her as sitting "at the Lord's feet listening to what he said." Such a posture is described in the rabbinical literature...and Paul said that he was instructed "at the feet of Gamaliel" (KJV).[9]

They quote the *Mishnah, Aboth* 1.4, an example where people who learned from the rabbis sat at their feet. But everybody in Jewish society learned from the rabbis, so it is not clear how this citation proves anything special about Mary.[10]

---

8. I am not saying there is anything wrong with formal theological training (I have taught in two different theological seminaries for the last twenty-three years). Nor is there anything wrong with women as well as men receiving formal theological training. But I do not think much of an argument for it can be made from this incident of Jesus teaching Mary, and certainly Spencer has claimed more than the text justifies with her broad generalization that it is better for women to study theology than pursue homemaking. What is better for each person depends on God's specific calling.
9. Tucker and Liefeld, *Daughters of the Church* (1987), 26.
10. Their other supporting references on 474n22, refer to writings by Leonard Swidler, James Hurley, and Evelyn and Frank Stagg, but Hurley and the Staggs give no additional evidence, nor does Swidler. So where is the evidence?

The error here is an elementary logical fallacy. To take a common example:

1. All Rockefellers are rich.
2. That man is rich.
3. Therefore he is a Rockefeller.

The conclusion is false because the man may be Bill Gates or some other rich person. Similarly, these authors argue:

1. The rabbis' students sat at the feet of the rabbis.
2. Mary sat at the feet of Jesus.
3. Therefore Mary is Jesus' student in a "school of the rabbis."

But if people commonly sat at the feet of those who were teaching, the egalitarians are claiming more than the text supports. It just says that Mary sat at Jesus' feet and learned from Him.

Egalitarian claim 5.3: First Witnesses to Resurrection: Women were the first witnesses to the resurrection (Matthew 28:1–10), showing their reliability and suitability as messengers of the Lord. Therefore they can surely be pastors.

Aida Spencer writes,

> These very women...were chosen by Jesus to be the first witnesses to his resurrection.... Jesus...wanted women to learn and to testify before others about God's actions on earth. *He wanted these women whom he had taught to go on to take authoritative leadership positions themselves.* That is why they were chosen to be the first witnesses to the resurrection.[11]

And Stanley Grenz writes,

> The Gospel writers agree that the women were the first to receive the command to proclaim the resurrection gospel and that they obeyed that command (Mt 28:7; Mk 16:7; Jn 20:17–18). For the Evangelists this meant that in God's new economy, men *and* women are credible witnesses and capable messengers of the risen Lord.
>
> In the postresurrection community, women and men share in the proclamation of the good news. This new role for women forms a fitting climax to what developed throughout Jesus' life.[12]

---

11. Spencer, *Beyond the Curse,* 62, italics added.
12. Grenz, *Women in the Church,* 77.

J. Lee Grady also says,

> Because of cultural biases, Christ's male disciples did not believe the testimony of the women when they gave the astounding report about the open tomb. Yet Jesus appeared to the Twelve and confirmed the witness of the women, and by doing so He intentionally refuted the idea that women could not offer faithful testimony. Indeed, He affirmed the ministry of the women and challenged His narrow-minded male followers to do the same.
>
> After His resurrection, Jesus said to Mary Magdalene, "I ascend to My Father and your Father, and My God and your God" (John 20:17). Was He not affirming her as a witness of the gospel? Was she not commissioned by Christ Himself both to go and to speak for Him? Why then do we deny women the opportunity to carry the same message?[13]

Answer 5.3a: Yes, women were the first witnesses to Christ's resurrection, and this is a wonderful affirmation of the trustworthiness of women and their equal dignity as persons made in God's image, in contrast to some ideas in first-century culture.

We should be thankful to God for this wonderful affirmation of the trustworthiness of women as witnesses. Whereas first-century Judaism did not place confidence in the trustworthiness of women as witnesses in several kinds of legal cases, God decided that women would be the first witnesses to the most important event in all of history![14]

Answer 5.3b: But to give testimony as an eyewitness of a historic event is not the same as functioning as a teacher or elder in a church. Women did not do this in the New Testament.

We should not make the text say more than it says. In this case, the women ran and told the disciples, just as the angel had commanded them (Matthew 28:7–8) and as Jesus had commanded them (v. 10). But the text says nothing about teaching the assembled church or governing a local church. These same disciples did not establish these women as elders in early churches, and a few days after the resurrection Peter specified that "one of the *men*" should replace Judas among the eleven disciples (Acts 1:21, with the male-specific term *anēr*).

---

13. Grady, *Ten Lies,* 34–35.
14. After mentioning several categories of people who are not eligible to bear witness in court, the *Mishnah* then says, "This is the general rule: Any evidence that a woman is not eligible to bring, these are not eligible to bring" (*Rosh Hashanah* 1:8; quoted from Danby, *Mishnah*, 189); compare the comment in Blackman, *Mishnayoth* (1973), 2:387: "Certain kinds of evidence were accepted from a woman as for instance evidence regarding her husband's death or evidence concerning an unfaithful wife."

Egalitarian claim 5.4: Jesus' Humanity Is Important, Not His Maleness: Jesus' humanness, not His maleness, allowed Him to represent all humanity, both men and women.

Stanley Grenz summarizes a common egalitarian position:

> Although egalitarians acknowledge that the incarnation in the form of a male may have been historically and culturally necessary, they deny its soteriological necessity. To suggest otherwise would undercut Christ's status as representing all humans—male and female—in salvation.[15]

Grenz himself then gives a perplexing explanation of his view, in which he says that Jesus' maleness in fact *was* soteriologically necessary [that is, necessary for earning our salvation], but only because the culture of that day would only listen to a male:

> We cannot follow those who deny all soteriological significance to Jesus' maleness.... Because Jesus was a particular historical person, his maleness was integral to the completion of his task.... In the context in which he lived, Jesus' maleness was an indispensable dimension of his vocation. Only a male could have offered the radical critique of the power systems of his day.... A woman...would have been immediately dismissed solely on the basis of her sex.... Thus to be the liberator of both male and female, Jesus needed to be male.[16]

But Grenz is just saying that Christ's maleness was historically and culturally necessary. He concludes that today "we can best reflect the liberating significance of Jesus' incarnation as a male by following the principle of egalitarian mutuality that he pioneered." In other words, if both men and women are able to be pastors (for example), we will serve to liberate humanity from wrongful structures in our day.

Answer 5.4a: We are not free to pick and choose some attributes of Jesus' person as important and some as unimportant.

How can Grenz and others know that Jesus' manhood was not essential? It is Jesus as a whole person, and in fact as a *male* human being, who is our Savior.

Answer 5.4b: The pattern of male headship from the beginning of Creation argues for the importance of Jesus' maleness to represent all believers.

Adam *as a man* represented the human race, and this could not have been because sinful power structures in his culture would not accept female leadership! "For as by a man came death, by a

15. Grenz, *Women in the Church*, 207.
16. Ibid., 208–9. See also Grady, *Ten Lies*, 42.

man has come also the resurrection of the dead. For as in Adam all die, so also in Christ shall all be made alive" (1 Corinthians 15:21–22).[17] Eve did not represent the whole human race, but Adam did, and so did Christ. So Jesus' maleness was important to His role as a representative leader. And in that role, *as a man,* God ordained that He, like Adam before Him, would represent both men and women. To argue otherwise is to argue against a pattern established by God.

Answer 5.4c: Some complementarians argue that Christ's maleness shows that all pastors should be male as representatives of Christ. But all complementarians see Christ's maleness as indicating a pattern of male leadership among God's people.

Some complementarians, such as J. I. Packer, have argued that pastors (or priests or presbyters) should be male because they represent Christ, and Christ was male.[18] Others do not find this "pastors representing Christ" argument persuasive, or do not belong to a denominational tradition where the pastor is thought so strongly to represent Christ. But even for these people, the fact remains that Jesus, as head of the church, is a man, not merely a gender-neutral person.

EGALITARIAN CLAIM 5.5: SERVANT LEADERSHIP IS IMPORTANT, NOT AUTHORITATIVE LEADERSHIP: JESUS TAUGHT SERVANT LEADERSHIP, AND THIS IS INCONSISTENT WITH A MALE LEADERSHIP PATTERN OF USE OF POWER OVER OTHERS.

Stanley Grenz writes,

> The New Testament emphasis on facilitative leadership means that leaders of both genders best serve the church.... Many participants in the contemporary debate over women in ministry understand leadership as the exercise of power over others.... The chief flaw in this understanding of leadership, however, is that it sets aside our Lord's teaching. Jesus reveals in both word and deed that the divine way of life lies in humble servanthood.... To be a leader means above all to be a servant to others.... "Whoever wishes to be great among you must be your servant" (Mark 10:42–45).... Biblical, servant-oriented leadership...is best symbolized by men and women ministering together in this crucial dimension of church life.[19]

17. The Greek term for "man" here is *anthrōpos* (twice in v. 21), which can mean "person" or "man," depending on the context (BDAG, 80–82), but in cases where it refers to an actual male human being, readers would naturally understand the sense "man," and here Adam and Christ, who were men, are specifically named.
18. See J. I. Packer, "Let's Stop Making Women Presbyters," *Christianity Today* (February 11, 1991), 18–21. This is not Packer's only argument; he makes several others as well.
19. Grenz, *Women in the Church,* 216–18.

Answer 5.5.a: Jesus was both a servant and a leader with great authority.

Grenz and other egalitarians wrongly pit servant leadership against authority. Jesus came to serve, yes, and to give His life for us. But He was simultaneously Lord! He said, "You call me Teacher and Lord, and you are right, for so I am" (John 13:13), and "If you love me, you will keep my commandments" (John 14:15).

Answer 5.5b: Elders should likewise use authority with a servant heart.

Similarly, the New Testament tells elders to be "examples to the flock" (1 Peter 5:3), and all elders would do well to heed Jesus' words, "Whoever would be great among you must be your servant" (Mark 10:43). But this does not negate the authority given to elders, for the New Testament also says, "Obey your leaders and submit to them, for they are keeping watch over your souls, as those who will have to give an account" (Hebrews 13:17), and "Let the elders who rule well be considered worthy of double honor" (1 Timothy 5:17). If we are faithful to the whole New Testament, we will not pit authority against servanthood, but affirm both.

EGALITARIAN CLAIM 5.6: ANTICIPATE HEAVEN: SINCE JESUS TAUGHT THAT GENDER ISSUES WILL NO LONGER MATTER IN THE NEXT LIFE (MATTHEW 22:30), WE SHOULD DO WHAT WE CAN EVEN NOW TO ERADICATE MANY MALE—FEMALE DISTINCTIONS.

This claim is different from the others I treat in this book because in writing the book I could not locate any prominent egalitarian writer who advocated it. I could have left it out of the book, but I decided to include it (with this initial disclaimer) because (a) I think it sometimes functions as a subjective consideration that influences people's thinking whether or not it is made explicit; (b) it is a specific manifestation of an error called "over-realized eschatology" that theologians encounter with regard to many other topics; (c) I think I have read it previously in some egalitarian writing or heard it in some egalitarian speaking (but I cannot remember where!); and (d) if I state it and answer it here, perhaps it will keep others from adopting this argument in the future. Before any egalitarians accuse me of constructing a straw man argument at this point, let me say clearly that it is possible that none of them hold this view, and if they do not, then this will be a point on which we can agree.

Such a (possible) egalitarian argument might be constructed as follows: (1) Jesus taught, "In the resurrection they neither marry nor are given in marriage, but are like angels in heaven" (Matthew 22:30). (2) Therefore, we should work to eliminate gender-based role differences now, and thus become more like heaven in our churches today.

Answer 5.6a: We should obey the New Testament commands for the church age.

This argument (if anyone does make it) would ask us, in effect, to ignore the New Testament commands that were given *for us in this age* and to act on what we speculate might be true *in the age to come*. This is a kind of error called "over-realized eschatology" (that is, wrongly assuming that things that are not ours until heaven are ours already). If we were to try completely to act now as we will in heaven, we would have no hospitals or doctors, we would not spread the gospel, and we would no longer use the spiritual gifts that God intends for use in this age (1 Corinthians 13:8–13). Whatever we may find out in heaven, for this present life it is clear that our task is to obey God's Word.

Answer 5.6b: This reasoning would lead us to abolish marriage today as well.

If we follow this logic (which, as I said, I hope no egalitarian today holds), then when we read that in the age to come "they neither marry nor are given in marriage" (Matthew 22:30), we would have to adopt that policy too, no longer allowing marriage today. But that is not God's will for us in this age—in fact, to "forbid marriage" is called one of the "teachings of demons" in 1 Timothy 4:1–3.

Answer 5.6c: The Bible says people will not marry in heaven, but it does not say there will be no male or female in heaven.

We must be careful not to claim more than the Bible teaches. It says that in the resurrection people "neither marry nor are given in marriage," but nowhere does it say that we are not male or female in heaven. In some way we will be "like angels in heaven" (Matthew 22:30), but Jesus does not specify just how we will be like angels—except that we will not marry.

Several considerations argue that we will still be male and female in the age to come: Jesus was a man after His resurrection, and it is our own bodies that will, like Jesus' body, be raised from the dead on the last day. Moreover, our identity as male or female is something good, not part of sin or the curse, for "male and female" was part of the way God first created Adam and Eve and said they were "very good" (Genesis 1:31). So it seems that to be fully human requires that we be either man or woman. In the age to come, God will restore His Creation to what He first intended, by removing the effects of the Fall and the subsequent curse (Romans 8:18–25). But our identity as either male or female is so integral to our personhood that it seems unlikely that our gender will be abolished in the age to come.[20]

---

20. See further argument to this effect in John Frame, "Men and Women in the Image of God," in Piper and Grudem, *Recovering Biblical Manhood and Womanhood* (1991), 232, and Daniel R. Heimbach, "The Unchangeable Difference," in Grudem, *Biblical Foundations for Manhood and Womanhood* (2002), 275–89.

Egalitarian claim 5.7: Cultural Reasons for Male Apostles: The fact that Jesus appointed only men to be apostles was a mere concession to the culture of His time; it is not normative for us today.

Stanley Grenz writes,

> However, the maleness of the twelve apostles does not provide sufficient grounds from which to conclude that all ordained persons must be male. Such a conclusion fails to understand the foundational, unique and temporary role played by the Twelve, one that in the strict sense cannot be passed on to subsequent believers....
>
> In addition, the complementarian argument fails to understand the actual significance of Christ's choice of twelve men. The importance of this act does not lie in a permanent distinction of roles among his followers based on gender. Our Lord's selection was a symbolic act, understandable only in the context of Israel's history. His selection of twelve male apostles, reminiscent of the original patriarchs, was an eschatological sign denoting that Jesus was reconstituting the ancient people of God.[21]

Gilbert Bilezikian says,

> Because of the cultural constraints present in the Jewish world, the ministry of women apostles, or Samaritan apostles, or Gentile apostles would have been unacceptable. Therefore, the exclusion of women, Samaritans, and Gentiles was inevitable during the first phase of the fulfillment of the Great Commission. At a later date, when the gospel spread beyond the boundaries of Judaism, both men and women, Samaritans and Gentiles, became instrumental in carrying out the gospel mission.... Pragmatic considerations of accommodation determined the composition of the first apostolic group.[22]

Similarly, Aida Spencer objects that if the *maleness* of the twelve apostles requires male leadership in the church, the *Jewishness* of the twelve apostles requires Jewish leadership in the church:

> Jesus chose twelve among all his disciples to represent the original twelve tribes of Israel.... If Jesus' choice of twelve male disciples signifies that females should not be leaders in the church, then, consistently his choice also signifies that Gentiles should not be leaders in the church.[23]

---

21. Grenz, *Women in the Church*, 211–12.
22. Bilezikian, *Beyond Sex Roles*, 274.
23. Spencer, *Beyond the Curse*, 45.

Answer 5.7a: Jesus never compromised with the culture of His time in matters of moral right and wrong.

If Jesus had wanted to demonstrate that all church offices were open to women, He could easily have appointed six women and six men as apostles. That would have settled the leadership question for all time. But He did not.

Grenz is correct to point out that Jesus' choice of twelve disciples is an evident sign that He is replacing the twelve heads of the twelve tribes of Israel and setting up new leadership for the people of God. But that did not require twelve men, for six men and six women would also have constituted a new twelve-member leadership team. The fact is that Jesus intentionally and freely chose twelve men for these leadership positions.

To say that Jesus gave in to cultural pressures on this and thus failed to model and teach what He knew was God's ideal, is to call into question Jesus' integrity and courage. As James Borland writes,

> Jesus was not averse to breaking social customs when He felt it necessary. He criticized Pharisees to their face in public (Matthew 23:13–36), healed on the sabbath (Mark 1:21–27; Luke 13:14; John 5:8–10), and cleansed the temple (John 2:14–17; Matthew 21:12–13). Against custom, Jesus spoke to the Samaritan woman (John 4:7–9), ate with tax collectors and sinners (Matthew 9:11), and even ate with unwashed hands (Mark 7:1–23)! The point is that when moral issues were at stake, Jesus did not bend to cultural pressure. No, it was not social custom or cultural pressure that caused Jesus to appoint an all-male group of apostles.[24]

Nor did Jesus yield to cultural expectations when appointing His disciples. Matthew was a "tax collector" (Matthew 10:3), an unpopular figure (see Matthew 18:17; 21:31), and the disciples generally were "uneducated, common men" (Acts 4:13). Even Bilezikian, elsewhere in his book, says that Jesus

> took a *firmly countercultural stance on many issues,* not because of a volatile, reactionary character, but because His mission was to oppose that which violated the will of God. Consequently, on this issue of female roles and feminine identity, Jesus felt compelled by His convictions to affirm creation and to repudiate the fall.... Jesus solidly based His definitions of persons and His directives for male/female relations in the creation ideal. As a result, He fearlessly demonstrated in His actions, teachings, and example His rejection of the male-rulership principle. There is much evidence in the Gospels for Jesus' special concern for the restoration of women to the position of human dignity that Eve occupied in creation, before the fall.[25]

---

24. James A. Borland, "Women in the Life and Teachings of Jesus," in Piper and Grudem, *Recovering Biblical Manhood and Womanhood,* 120.
25. Bilezikian, *Beyond Sex Roles,* 81–82, italics added.

Precisely. So the argument that Jesus gave in to cultural pressure and gave preferential treatment to men as apostles, contrary to God's Creation ideals, is not correct. To think that Jesus "accommodated" His appointment of the apostles, a foundational and eternally significant action, to what would be acceptable for the time is not consistent with the rest of Jesus' ministry, and actually impugns Jesus' courage and character.

Answer 5.7b: The maleness of the apostles established a permanent pattern for male leadership in the church.

The highest human leadership among God's people in the New Covenant is simply not egalitarian. Even in the age to come, Jesus said, there will be a place of high authority for His twelve apostles: "Truly, I say to you, in the new world, when the Son of Man will sit on his glorious throne, you who have followed me will also sit on twelve thrones, judging the twelve tribes of Israel" (Matthew 19:28). And in the heavenly city we will see a permanent reminder of male leadership among God's people, for "the wall of the city had twelve foundations, and on them were the twelve names of the twelve apostles of the Lamb" (Revelation 21:14).

Grenz objects that the apostles are unique in their "foundational" and "temporary" role.[26] Of course they were unique. That is just the point. The most unique, foundational, authoritative leaders in the church were all men. At its very foundation, the church of Jesus Christ is not an egalitarian institution. It has 100 percent male leadership.

Answer 5.7c: But the Jewishness of the twelve apostles was only a temporary pattern because Jesus came first to the Jews.

Bilezikian, Grenz, and Spencer fail to recognize that the Jewishness of the twelve apostles was because in God's sovereign plan, *there were no Gentile men* in the church when it started. God's plan was to begin with the Jews and then include Gentiles, so Jesus started His work and ministry only among the Jews. He said, "I was sent only to the lost sheep of the house of Israel" (Matthew 15:24), and He told His disciples during His earthly ministry, "Go nowhere among the Gentiles and enter no town of the Samaritans, but go rather to the lost sheep of the house of Israel" (Matthew 10:5–6). Even at Pentecost, the people who heard and believed were Jews (Acts 2:5). There were no Gentiles among the earliest believers. By contrast, *there were women as well as men among Jesus' followers from the beginning*, and if Jesus had wanted to appoint women, He could have done so.

Once the gospel began to spread to Gentiles, *Gentiles were immediately included among the church leaders*, in accordance with Jesus' command to make disciples of "all nations" (Matthew 28:19).[27] Luke was a Gentile and he wrote two books of the New Testament, and

---

26. Grenz, *Women in the Church*, 211.
27. See also Acts 1:8, and note the appointment of elders in Gentile cities in Acts 14:23; note also that the requirements for elders in Titus 1 and 1 Timothy 3 do not include being Jewish.

Paul's companions Titus and Epaphroditus have Gentile names, not Jewish names. Gentiles had leadership roles in the New Testament, but women were not included in the role of elder.

The following chart shows this natural historical progression:

	Membership among God's people	**Authoritative leadership over God's people**
early in Acts	only Jews	Jewish men
later in Acts and epistles	Jews and Gentiles	Jewish and Gentile men

This pattern of male leadership continued throughout all periods of the New Testament.

Egalitarian claim 5.8: No Special Authority for Apostles: There was no special authority for the twelve apostles, nor was the original group of twelve very significant.

In an apparent attempt to minimize the importance of the maleness of Jesus' twelve apostles, Gilbert Bilezikian writes,

> Jesus pointedly does not replace Judas, the missing disciple. *The numerical integrity of the original group is unimportant to Jesus*, since disciples will multiply by the thousands. It was after Jesus' ascension and prior to the coming of the Holy Spirit at Pentecost that *the Eleven awkwardly attempted to select a twelfth member by resorting to the roll of the dice* (Acts 1:26). But, for Jesus, the preservation of the original unit was irrelevant, since the disciples would scatter and generate more disciples like themselves. The Eleven would eventually disappear among the multitudes of new disciples.... *New disciples who transmitted the teaching of Christ would become just as authoritative as the original disciples*. The authority resided in the message, not in the men and women who took it to the world.[28]

Answer 5.8a: The New Testament sees the original apostles as very significant.

Bilezikian's comments as quoted above are unfaithful to the text of Scripture in several respects. Far from *disappearing*, the Twelve will "sit on twelve thrones, judging the twelve tribes of Israel" (Matthew 19:28). And the twelve foundations of the heavenly city will have on them "the twelve names of the twelve apostles of the Lamb" (Revelation 21:14).

---

28. Bilezikian, *Beyond Sex Roles*, 114–15 (italics added).

Answer 5.8b: Jesus Himself chose a replacement for Judas.

The book of Acts is presented as a continuation of what "Jesus began to do and teach" as recorded in Luke (Acts 1:1). Therefore if something in Acts is viewed as a positive development in the growth of the church, we are to understand it as a result of Jesus' active lordship over the church. Jesus Himself had promised, "I will build my church" (Matthew 16:18), and the apostles are the "foundation" of that church (Ephesians 2:20). The choice of the twelfth apostle is an important first step in Christ's building of His church.

Moreover, the text presents the choice of Matthias to replace Judas as the fulfillment of the Scripture that says, "Let another take his office" (Acts 1:20, quoting Psalm 109:8). Then the disciples prayed to Jesus (as "Lord"), saying, "You, Lord, who know the hearts of all, show which one of these two *you have chosen* to take the place in this ministry and apostleship from which Judas turned aside" (Acts 1:24–25). Even the casting of lots repeats the frequent way the Lord made His will known in the Old Testament. The text gives no hint of divine disapproval in any of this. It is presented as something clearly under the direction of the risen Lord Jesus.

Therefore it is simply not true, and it is misrepresenting Scripture, to say as Bilezikian does, "The numerical integrity of the original group is unimportant to Jesus," and "the Eleven awkwardly attempted to select a twelfth member by resorting to the roll of the dice" (as if they did this on their own, not by the Lord's guidance), and to say, "for Jesus, the preservation of the original unit was irrelevant," and Jesus "does not replace Judas."

Answer 5.8c: The apostles had much greater authority than the rest of the church.

When Ananias lies to Peter, Peter says, "You have not lied to men but to God," and Ananias falls down dead (Acts 5:4–5). This is hardly ordinary authority. Paul says that "the things I am writing to you are *a command of the Lord*" (1 Corinthians 14:37), something ordinary Christians could certainly not say. And Peter speaks of "the commandment of the Lord and Savior *through your apostles*" (2 Peter 3:2). Paul could speak of "our authority, which the Lord gave for building you up and not for destroying you" (2 Corinthians 10:8). Bilezikian is simply incorrect to say that "New disciples who transmitted the teaching of Christ would become just as authoritative as the original disciples." The apostles had a unique authority that other Christians did not have, and with that authority they serve as an example of male headship in Christ's church.

Egalitarian claim 5.9: Gifts to All: Since the Holy Spirit is now poured out on all believers, both men and women (Acts 2:17–18), and since the Holy Spirit gives gifts to both men and women (1 Corinthians 12:7, 11; 1 Peter 4:10), there should be no restriction on the ministries available to both men and women.

Stanley Grenz writes,

> We have argued that the sovereignty of the Spirit in bestowing *charismata* on God's people clearly shows that God welcomes the ministry of both men and women in all aspects of church life, including the ordained office.[29]

He further states that

> The intimate relation between gifts and ministry has a crucial bearing on the issue of women in ministry. The fundamental conclusion resulting from our study is that the church must make room for all believers, whether male or female, to use their God-given gifts to build up the body of Christ. We must allow men and women to serve together with whatever gifts the Spirit bestows on them.[30]

J. Lee Grady writes that

> If preaching were to have been limited to men only, Joel would not have mentioned daughters in his prediction. He would have said instead, "In the last days, I will pour out My Spirit upon you, and your sons will prophesy while your daughters serve quietly in the background and pray for the men." That is not what the Bible says. It clearly states that women will preach. They will lead. They will be on the front lines of ministry. Like Deborah, they will take the church into enemy territory and watch as the Lord gives victory. Like Esther, they will not keep silent. Like Phoebe, they will co-labor with apostles to establish churches in unevangelized regions. If this is the clear mandate of Joel 2:28, why do churches that pride themselves on faithful adherence to a literal translation of the Bible reject it?[31]

Answer 5.9a: I agree that the Holy Spirit gives both men and women spiritual gifts in this age.

I am thankful that Peter declared that Joel's prophecy was fulfilled on the day of Pentecost:

---

29. Grenz, *Women in the Church*, 192.
30. Ibid., 190–91. See also Brown, *Women Ministers* (1996), 154.
31. Grady, *Ten Lies*, 44–45.

> "And in the last days it shall be," God declares,
> "that I will pour out my Spirit on all flesh,
> and your sons *and your daughters* shall prophesy,
> and your young men shall see visions,
> and your old men shall dream dreams;
> even on my male servants *and female servants*
> in those days I will pour out my Spirit, and they shall
> prophesy." (Acts 2:17–18)

This promise is fulfilled throughout the church today as both men and women alike are given spiritual gifts for the building up of the church. Paul includes every believer when he says, "To *each* is given the manifestation of the Spirit for the common good" (1 Corinthians 12:7), and Peter similarly says, "As *each* has received a gift, use it to serve one another, as good stewards of God's varied grace" (1 Peter 4:10). When the church is working properly, every woman as well as every man will be using at least one spiritual gift in ministry to others in the body of Christ.

Answer 5.9b: However, the Holy Spirit works within the boundaries laid down in His Word, the Bible.

We should never pit the work of the Holy Spirit against the Word of the Holy Spirit (2 Peter 1:21). He will never work in a way that contradicts His Word, the Bible. Within the Bible, the Holy Spirit has specified that the role of governing and teaching over the whole church, the role that is fulfilled by pastors and elders, is restricted to men. Therefore the gifts of the Holy Spirit to women will never require that they be used in ways that disobey these restrictions.

Answer 5.9c: Women who have teaching and administrative gifts should be able to use them in many ministries that do not include being an elder or doing Bible teaching to assembled groups of men and women.

As we saw in chapter 2, when women have Bible teaching gifts, they can use them with great effectiveness in ministries to other women, in writing ministries, in evangelistic ministries, and in ministries to children. Some of the women associated with the Council on Biblical Manhood and Womanhood in the U.S. have spoken to gatherings of several thousand women. Other women have had remarkable evangelistic ministries (and nothing in Scripture restricts women from doing evangelism or missionary work bringing the gospel to both men and women alike). Bible study books written by women speak to male and female readers one at a time, in something like the way Priscilla and Aquila spoke individually to Apollos (Acts 18:26), and thus I encourage women as well as men to write such books. Women with administrative gifts can often use them effectively in overseeing departments or specific ministries in local churches or in parachurch organizations. Women with wise insight into Scripture and its application to life can have effective counseling ministries. Women with gifts of intercession can use these gifts with the result of great blessing from God on various ministries and people.

In churches that allow other gifts, women with gifts of prophecy and healing will use them to minister to others with great benefit for the kingdom of God. And many other women with gifts similar to these will use them in less prominent but equally valuable ways in their local church fellowships. In these and other ways (see pp. 84–101), the gifts that the Holy Spirit gives to women can be used in ministries that are consistent with Scripture, ministries that make full use of their spiritual gifts and yet still protect and support the overall male leadership of the church, under male pastors and elders, according to what is taught in Scripture.

Egalitarian claim 5.10: Priscilla Taught Apollos: Since Priscilla and Aquila both "explained" to Apollos "the way of God more accurately" (Acts 18:26), women can teach men in the church.

This argument is made by a number of egalitarian writers. Aida Spencer writes,

> Priscilla...was herself an able teacher. In Acts 18:26 Luke records, "Having heard [Apollos], Priscilla and Aquila took him aside and more accurately expounded to him the way of God...." *Ektithēmai*...connotes a public declaration and exposition.[32]

Linda Belleville claims that this was the same type of teaching as done by Paul, because the same word is used:

> [In Acts 18:26] Luke says that Priscilla and Aquila "expounded" *(exethento)* the way of God to Apollos, but this is the same term Luke uses for Paul's teaching. "From morning until evening," Luke reports, "Paul expounded [*exetitheto*] and testified about the kingdom of God" (Acts 28:23 AT). So to draw a distinction between private and public forms of instruction or between informal and formal types at this stage in the church's development is simply anachronistic.[33]

Stanley Grenz denies that a valid distinction can be drawn between public and private instruction in this context:

> Contrary to complementarian opinion, the text of Acts will not allow us to transform this narrative into anything other than a clear indication of authoritative teaching by a woman in the church. The text gives no warrant to importing a distinction between private teaching in a home and authoritative teaching in the church. To pass by this

32. Spencer, *Beyond the Curse*, 107. (The ordinary lexical form of the verb is *ektithēmi.*)
33. Belleville, *Women Leaders and the Church* (2000), 59.

> incident as "*unofficial* guidance" as distinct from "*official* teaching leadership" is to draw too fine a line between authoritative and so-called nonauthoritative teaching among the people of God.[34]

Gilbert Bilezikian goes even further, for on the basis of one verse that reports one private conversation, he endows Priscilla and Aquila with the status of "seminary faculty":

> For all practical purposes, *Priscilla and Aquila acted as a seminary faculty* for a promising male pastoral student. They taught him those redemptive events of the life of Christ about which he had been left uninformed along with their theological significance.[35]

Answer 5.10a: Scripture encourages men and women to talk with each other about the Bible and Christian doctrine.

As I indicated in chapter 2, Acts 18:26 provides an excellent encouragement for women and men to talk with each other about the meanings of Bible passages in private discussions and in small group Bible studies, as Christians everywhere have done for centuries.[36] This has never been at issue.

Answer 5.10b: To say that there is no distinction between private and public teaching is to ignore the two fundamental factors of interpretation: the words of the text and the context.

When Belleville and Grenz deny that there is any difference between Priscilla's conversation with Apollos and public teaching by Paul, they ignore the specific words of the text. The narrative in Acts 18 is written in such a way that it guards us against understanding that they did this publicly, for it says, "When Priscilla and Aquila heard him, *they took him* and explained to him the way of God more accurately" (Acts 18:26). The phrase "they took him" indicates that they waited to speak to him until they could take him aside, out of public view.[37] And the context indicates that this is in contrast to the public speaking of Apollos in which "he began to speak boldly in the synagogue" (Acts 18:26a). When Grenz claims that "the text gives no warrant" for making such a distinction, he is not paying close attention to the words of the verse.

Belleville's assertion that the same word (*ektithēmi*) is used to refer to Paul's public preaching in Acts 28:23 confuses the meaning of a word with its use in different contexts. The

---

34. Grenz, *Women in the Church*, 82–83.
35. Bilezikian, *Beyond Sex Roles*, 201–2. See also Jacobs, *Women of Destiny* (1998), 194; Brown, *Women Ministers*, 177, 179. Sarah Sumner says, "Am I the only person to be stunned by this? Priscilla taught Apollos in Ephesus!" (*Men and Women in the Church*, 241).
36. See chapter 2, p. 75.
37. BDAG understand *proslambanō* in this verse to mean, "to take or lead off to oneself, *take aside*" (883).

word simply means "to convey information by careful elaboration, *explain, expound*"[38] and the context shows whether that is public or private explanation. Belleville's argument is somewhat like arguing,

1. In Acts 28:23 this word is used to refer to Paul's arguing about Jesus with the Jews in Rome from morning to evening;
2. Therefore, in Acts 18:26 the same word must mean that Priscilla argued about Jesus with the Jews in Rome from morning to evening.

The mistake is to think that we can import the context of a word used in one case into that word's use in another case. That is a fundamental error in interpretation. Surely a person can "explain" something either in private or in public. And the different contexts show that Acts 18:26 was private and Acts 28:23 was public.

Answer 5.10c: Priscilla's example does not give warrant for women to teach the Bible to the assembled church.

As we also saw in chapter 2, it is specifically in situations where the whole church is assembled that Paul restricts governing and teaching activities to men (see 1 Corinthians 14:33–36; 1 Timothy 2:11–15; see also the qualifications for elders in 1 Timothy 3 and Titus 1). The example of Priscilla and Aquila instructing Apollos privately in Acts 18:26 does not contradict this.

EGALITARIAN CLAIM 5.11: PRISCILLA IS NAMED FIRST: SINCE PRISCILLA'S NAME IS PUT BEFORE AQUILA'S NAME, ESPECIALLY WHEN THEY ARE IN MINISTRY SITUATIONS, THIS INDICATES THAT SHE WAS THE LEADER IN THEIR MINISTRY TEAM.

Linda Belleville argues:

> What is unusual, however, is that when Luke refers to their occupation as tent makers, the order is "Aquila and Priscilla" (Acts 18:2; cf. 1 Cor. 16:19), but when Luke and Paul speak from a ministry point of view, the order is always "Priscilla and Aquila." [Belleville mentions Acts 18:18, 26; Romans 16:3; 2 Timothy 4:19.] This would suggest that of the two, it was Priscilla who possessed the dominant ministry and leadership skills.[39]

---

38. Ibid., 310.

39. Belleville, *Women Leaders and the Church*, 68. See also Bilezikian, *Beyond Sex Roles*, 200–201; Grenz, *Women in the Church*, 82; Jacobs, *Women of Destiny*, 194–95, quoting Witherington, *Women and the Genesis of Christianity*, 220. See also Brown, *Women Ministers*, 175.

Bilezikian wrongly accuses the King James Version translators when he says they "followed a variant that inverted the names of Priscilla and Aquila in Acts 18:26, thus preferring to commit violence on the text of Scripture rather than face the fact that God calls qualified women to be teachers" (202). But he fails to mention that their

Answer 5.11a: It is difficult to know what, if anything, was meant by the order of names.

There is much speculation about what might be meant by the order of the names Priscilla and Aquila, but very little hard evidence to go on. Was the variation merely stylistic? Were the authors at times simply trying to give honor to the woman by naming her first? Leon Morris says, "Prisca is mentioned before her husband on four occasions out of six. . .from which some have deduced that she came from a higher social stratum, and others that she was more able than her husband."[40] F. F. Bruce says, "Paul generally put Prisca (Priscilla) before Aquila, her husband; this may have been due to her having the more impressive personality of the two, although some have inferred that her social rank was superior to his. She may have belonged. . .to. . .a noble Roman family, while he was a Jew from Pontus in northern Asia Minor."[41] Cranfield says that the more frequent placement of Priscilla's name first is more likely "due either to her having been converted before him (and perhaps having led her husband to faith in Christ) or to her having played an even more prominent part in the life and work of the Church than Aquila had," rather than to "her having been socially superior to him."[42]

Moreover, Belleville's claim that "when Luke and Paul speak from a ministry point of view, the order is always 'Priscilla and Aquila,'" is not correct. In 1 Corinthians 16:19, Paul reverses the order in connection with "the church in their house," which is surely a ministry connection: "Aquila and Prisca, together with the church in their house, send you hearty greetings in the Lord."[43]

In conclusion, it is difficult to say anything with certainty about the significance of the order of names. Belleville and others are simply claiming more than the text can prove.

---

policy throughout the New Testament was to follow the *Textus Receptus*, the Greek "received text" of that day, and they did so at this verse (which has Aquila first) as well as through the whole New Testament. They had few of the alternative texts available to them that we have today, and they did not count any other texts to be as reliable. This had nothing to do with their view of women teachers, and there was no "preferring" to "commit violence on. . .Scripture."

40. Morris, *The Epistle to the Romans* (1988), 531.
41. Bruce, *Romans* (1973), 271.
42. Cranfield, *Critical and Exegetical Commentary on the Epistle to the Romans* (1979), 2:784.
43. Bilezikian again reads into the Bible things that are not there when he says that "the epistle to the Romans was intended to have been read in the congregation(s) in Rome, obviously in the presence of Aquila and Priscilla and of the home-church that met in their house *and which they co-pastored*" (*Beyond Sex Roles*, 201 [italics added]).

Romans 16:3–5, to which Bilezikian refers, says, "*Greet Prisca and Aquila*, my fellow workers in Christ Jesus, who risked their necks for my life, to whom not only I give thanks but all the churches of the Gentiles give thanks as well. *Greet also the church in their house*." Not one word is said about "co-pastoring" a church.

EGALITARIAN CLAIM 5.12: TABITHA AS LEADER: PETER RAISED TABITHA FROM THE DEAD BECAUSE OF HER LEADERSHIP ROLE.

Gilbert Bilezikian claims that in Acts 9:36–43, the reason Peter raised Tabitha from the dead was because of her crucial leadership role in the church in Joppa.

> In...Joppa...when one of their numbers died...they refused to believe that she was gone. As a leader in the community (she is called a "disciple" in Acts 9:36), she had become indispensable to its life.... While listening to the mourners, Peter became convinced that at that point of time in the life of that community, Tabitha had become indispensable and irreplaceable. She was fulfilling such an *important dimension of leadership* that even God would not want her to be gone.... *Her leadership was important enough to the church* for it to send two men on a mission to fetch Peter, for Peter to interrupt a successful evangelistic campaign (v. 35) and...for Peter to decide that the only solution to the crisis created by her death was to bring her back to life.[44]

Answer 5.12a: Bilezikian is importing into the Bible things that are not there.

The text says nothing about any leadership role for Tabitha. It simply, beautifully says she was "full of good works and acts of charity" (9:36). It says nothing about any leadership role. Bilezikian is importing into his report of the Bible's story things that are not there in the text. If the story hints at any reason for the grief of the Christians in Joppa, it is their great love for Tabitha, and their thankfulness that she had ministered so generously to so many of them, as shown by the fact that when Peter came, "All the widows stood beside him weeping and showing tunics and other garments that Dorcas [her Greek name] made while she was with them" (9:39).

That Tabitha is called a "disciple" is not unusual; that term is used of Christians generally in Acts.[45] For example, Acts 6:1–2 says: "Now in these days when the *disciples* were increasing in number, a complaint by the Hellenists arose against the Hebrews because their widows were being neglected in the daily distribution. And the twelve summoned the full number of the *disciples* and said, 'It is not right that we should give up preaching the word of God to serve tables'" (see also Acts 6:7; 9:1; 11:26).

Bilezikian's claim about the reason for raising Tabitha, therefore, is not persuasive. Once again, he has imported into the Bible things that are not there.

---

44. Bilezikian, *Beyond Sex Roles*, 203–4.
45. To be more precise, the feminine noun *mathētria,* "disciple," used of Tabitha in Acts 9:36, is found nowhere else in the Bible (so it cannot be shown to be a technical term with any special meaning). But the cognate masculine term *mathētēs,* "disciple," is used several times in Acts to refer to Christians generally.

Conclusion

The Gospels and Acts show a wonderful, remarkable pattern of treating women as well as men with full respect and honor, and involving women in many crucial ministry roles for the early church. But the life of Christ and the story of the early church in Acts also show a pattern in which only men, such as Jesus' twelve apostles, were given teaching and governing roles over God's people.

CHAPTER SIX

Evangelical Feminist Claims About Marriage from the New Testament Epistles

Is it really possible to determine what the New Testament epistles teach about marriage? Of course there are passages that say the husband is the "head" of the wife (Ephesians 5:23), but isn't it possible that we have misunderstood *head,* and that it really means something else and does not indicate any special authority for a husband?

In addition, Galatians 3:28 says that now in the New Covenant, "there is neither male nor female, for you are all one in Christ Jesus," and doesn't that clear principle remove all gender-based distinctions in roles and show that we no longer need to follow outmoded ideas of male headship in marriage and the church? And doesn't Ephesians 5:21 teach "mutual submission" in which there is no unique authority for the husband in marriage?

Furthermore, we must recognize that ancient cultures were strongly patriarchal. Perhaps Paul said wives should be subject to their husbands so as not to give offense, especially to the Roman leaders he was hoping to evangelize. If that is true, wouldn't that mean those commands are no longer applicable today?

It is questions such as these that we now consider.

EGALITARIAN CLAIM 6.1: NO LONGER MALE OR FEMALE: GALATIANS 3:28—"THERE IS NEITHER JEW NOR GREEK, THERE IS NEITHER SLAVE NOR FREE, THERE IS NEITHER MALE NOR FEMALE, FOR YOU ARE ALL ONE IN CHRIST JESUS"—TEACHES THAT THERE IS FULL GENDER EQUALITY IN THE KINGDOM OF GOD.

This claim is probably the most common one made by egalitarian writers. Rebecca Groothuis is representative of many when she writes,

Of all the texts that support biblical equality, *Galatians 3:26–28 is probably the most important*. Unlike the New Testament proof texts traditionalists use to support hierarchical gender roles, this text is not a specific command directed toward a specific cultural situation. Rather, it is a broadly applicable statement of the inclusive nature of the New Covenant, whereby all groups of people, regardless of their previous religious status under the law, have now become one in Christ.[1]

Answer 6.1a: Galatians 3:28 teaches *unity* among diverse members in the body of Christ, but it does not teach that we are all *the same* or have all *the same roles*.[2]

Egalitarians frequently claim that if there is "neither male nor female," then distinctions in role based on our gender are abolished because we are now all "one in Christ Jesus."

The problem is that this is not what the verse says. To say that we are "one" means that we are *united*, that there should be no factions or divisions among us, and there should be no sense of pride and superiority or jealousy and inferiority between these groups that viewed themselves as so distinct in the ancient world. Jews should no longer think themselves superior to Greeks, freed men should no longer think themselves superior to slaves, and men should no longer think themselves superior to women. They are all *parts of one body* in Christ, and all share in equal value and dignity as members of one body in Christ.

But, as Richard Hove has demonstrated in detail elsewhere,[3] when the Bible says that several things are "one," it never joins things that are exactly the same. Rather, it says that things that are different, things that are diverse, share some kind of unity. So in Romans 12:4–5 we read, "For as in one body we have many members, and the members do not all have the same function, so *we*, though many, *are one body* in Christ, and individually members one of another."

Paul does not mean to say that all the members of the body are the *same*, for as anyone can see, a body has hands and feet and eyes and ears, and all the "members" are different and have different functions, though they are one body.

Similarly, Hove found that Paul, using the same construction,[4] can say, "*Now he who plants and he who waters are one*; but each will receive his own reward according to his own labor"

1. Groothuis, *Good News for Women* (1997), 25–26. See also Bilezikian, *Beyond Sex Roles* (1985), 126–28; Grenz, *Women in the Church* (1995), 99–107; Snodgrass, "Galatians 3:28: Conundrum or Solution?" in Mickelsen *Women, Authority and the Bible* (1995), 161–81, and the responses by Susie Stanley (181–88) and W. Ward Gasque (188–92); and Brown, *Women Ministers* (1996), 234–35.
2. Answers 6.1a and 6.1b are taken from chapter 1, pp. 25–61.
3. See Richard W. Hove, "Does Galatians 3:28 Negate Gender-Specific Roles?" in Grudem, *Biblical Foundations for Manhood and Womanhood* (1991), 105–43, and also his book, *Equality in Christ?* (1999).
4. Hove ran forty-five computer searches on Greek literature near the time of the New Testament. He reports finding sixteen examples of Greek expressions from the New Testament and other ancient literature that use the verb "to be" (*eimi*) plus the number "one" (Greek *heis/mia/hen*) and finds that the expression is never used to indicate unity among things that are identical, but always among things that are different and have different functions but that also share something in common that gives them a kind of unity (Hove, *Equality in Christ*, 72–76).

(1 Corinthians 3:8, NASB). Now planting and watering are two different activities done by different persons in Paul's example. They are not reduced to "sameness" nor are they required to act in exactly the same way, but they are still "one" because they have a unity of purpose and goal.

And so Galatians 3:28 simply says that we have a special kind of *unity* in the body of Christ. Our differences as male and female are not obliterated by this unity, but the unity is beautiful in God's sight particularly because it is a unity of different kinds of people.

Answer 6.1b: Galatians 3:28 cannot teach that all role distinctions are abolished, because the New Testament still gives different commands telling how men and women should obey God.

Surely this verse cannot abolish all differences between men and women, not only because Paul himself elsewhere commands husbands and wives to act differently according to their different roles, but also because marriage in Scripture from beginning to end is intended by God to be only between one man and one woman, not between one man and another man or one woman and another woman. If Galatians 3:28 truly abolished all differences between men and women, then how could anyone say that homosexual marriage was wrong? But homosexual conduct is surely forbidden by Scripture (see Romans 1:26–27; 1 Corinthians 6:9; 1 Timothy 1:10), and our egalitarian friends within the evangelical world agree that it is. Therefore Galatians 3:28 does not abolish differences in roles between men and women.

The egalitarian objection from Galatians 3:28, therefore, is not persuasive. Egalitarians are simply trying to make the verse say something it does not say and never has said and never will say. Galatians 3:28 tells us that we are united in Christ and that we should never be boastful or arrogant against others, and we should never feel inferior or without value in the body of Christ. But the verse does not say that men and women are the same or that they have to act the same.

Answer 6.1c: There are social implications in Galatians 3:28, but other texts in the New Testament explain what they are and are not.

Many egalitarians insist that "Social implications are necessarily involved" in Galatians 3:28,[5] and I agree. This text, and others like it, taught a new oneness in the way Christians should relate to one another, different from the wrongful stereotypes and discrimination that had characterized their past. The text had a powerful impact in the struggle to abolish slavery, because of the clear implication that it is wrong to divide the church into "slave" and "free," and to think of one group as superior to the other.

But we cannot follow the same path and say that marriage should be abolished as slavery was or that we should never again think of ourselves as "male" or "female." Just saying "There are social implications of this text," does not solve any questions about relationships between men and women in marriage and the church, because there are fundamental differences

5. Snodgrass, "Galatians 3:28," 177.

between the human institution of slavery (which should have been abolished) and the God-ordained institution of marriage (which should not be abolished).

Therefore, we need to realize that this is not the only text in the Bible on men and women. It is a true text, and it is a wonderful text, but it is not the only text, and we should not make it say more than it does. To determine the ways men and women should relate to each other in marriage and the church, and the roles men and women should fill in marriage and the church, we need the teaching of other texts. This is why Kline Snodgrass, writing on Galatians 3:28 in a collection of egalitarian essays, rightly says, "Galatians 3:28 does not spell out what roles and functions will look like where 'there is no male and female.'"[6]

Many other texts make clear that "there is neither male nor female" does not abolish all differences in roles between men and women.

Egalitarian claim 6.2: Seed Idea: Galatians 3:28 is a "seed idea" that would ultimately lead to the abolition of male headship once cultural changes made it possible to adopt a superior ethic to that of the New Testament.

This is an argument of William Webb, and it is found in the second of his eighteen proposed criteria for determining cultural relativity. Webb says, "A component of a text may be cultural if 'seed ideas' are present within the rest of Scripture to suggest and encourage further movement on a particular subject."[7]

Webb's conception of a "seed idea" is based on his claim that some New Testament commands are inconsistent with that seed idea, and those commands show only that "the biblical author pushed society as far as it could go at that time without creating more damage than good."[8] Webb claims that the "seed idea" is simply a pointer showing that there should be "further movement" toward a "more fully realized ethic" that is "more just, more equitable and more loving...a better ethic than the one expressed in the isolated words of the text."[9]

Webb thinks Galatians 3:28 is just such a "seed idea," that carries "social implications for the equality of women" today.[10]

Answer 6.2a: We should not think we can "move beyond" the ethic of the New Testament to a higher ethic.

We should not think it necessary to "move beyond" the ethic of the New Testament. It is not necessary to do this to argue for the abolition of slavery, for the New Testament never condones

6. Ibid., 179.
7. Webb, *Slaves, Women and Homosexuals* (2001), 83.
8. Ibid., 73.
9. Ibid., 36.
10. Ibid., 87.4

or approves of slavery as an institution, and never says it was created by God (as marriage was). The New Testament itself provides statements that would eventually lead to the abolition of slavery *based on the New Testament ethic itself*, not based on some "higher ethic" that would later be discovered.[11]

Similarly, Galatians 3:28 should not be seen as a "seed idea" pointing to some future, "higher ethic," but as a text fully consistent with other things the apostle Paul and other New Testament authors wrote about the relationships between men and women. If we take the entire New Testament as the very words of God for us in the New Covenant today, then any claim that Galatians 3:28 should overrule other texts such as Ephesians 5 and 1 Timothy 2 is a claim that Paul the apostle contradicts himself, and therefore that the Word of God contradicts itself.

EGALITARIAN CLAIM 6.3: NEW CREATION PATTERN: GALATIANS 3:28 IS A "NEW CREATION" PATTERN THAT OVERTHROWS THE "OLD CREATION" PATTERNS OF MALE LEADERSHIP IN THE HOME AND CHURCH.

William Webb says there are several "in Christ" statements like Galatians 3:28, which tells us that "there is neither male nor female, for you are all one *in Christ Jesus.*" These "in Christ" statements, he claims, "should be given prominence over the old-creation patterns" that include what Webb sees as "patriarchy." He says, "New-creation theology transforms the status of all its participantsinto one of equality.... [It] heavily favors an egalitarian position."[12]

Answer 6.3a: Male headship is part of the original good Creation, and it is also part of the new creation in Christ.

Webb fails adequately to take into account that the male headship in marriage that was found in the Garden was itself "very good" in God's sight. We should not look for some kind of morally superior ethic to replace it. Moreover, Webb overlooks other "new-creation" statements that affirm male headship in marriage, such as Colossians 3:18, "Wives, submit to your husbands, as is fitting *in the Lord.*" This command is part of the new "in Christ" or "in the Lord" creation, just as "children, obey your parents *in the Lord*, for this is right" (Ephesians 6:1) is part of the new creation in Christ. In fact, Paul's commands as an apostle for the New Testament church *are* part of the "new-creation" in Christ, and therefore "I do not permit a woman to teach or to exercise authority over a man" *is also part of that new creation*, because it is part of the teaching of the New Testament for the church after Pentecost.

11. For further analysis of Webb's system, see claims 9.3 (on slavery), 9.5, and Appendix 5, pp. 600–645.
12. Webb, *Slaves, Women and Homosexuals*, 152. See also Perriman, *Speaking of Women* (1998), 20, 23, 35.

Egalitarian claim 6.4: Mutual Submission: The New Testament writers urged the mutual submission of husbands and wives to one another (Ephesians 5:21). Therefore there is no unique leadership role for the husband.

Ephesians 5:21 says, "submitting to one another out of reverence for Christ."[13] Egalitarians say this verse teaches "mutual submission," and that means that just as wives have to submit to their husbands *so husbands have to submit to their wives*. Doesn't the text say that we have to submit "to one another"? And this means that there is no unique submission that a wife owes to her husband, and no unique authority that a husband has over his wife. Gilbert Bilezikian says,

> "Being subject to one another" is a very different relationship from "being subject to the other."... By definition, mutual submission rules out higher hierarchical differences. Being subject to one another is only possible among equals. It is a mutual (two-way) process that excludes the unilateral (one-way) subordination implicit in the concept of subjection without the reciprocal pronoun. Mutual subjection suggests horizontal lines of interaction among equals.[14]

Rebecca Groothuis, to take another example, says,

> The call to mutual reciprocal submission in Eph. 5:21 establishes the framework for the instructions to wives and husbands that follow.... Wives are to submit to their husbands in the same way that all believers are to submit to one another. This text is not advocating a unilateral female submission to male authority. Rather, it is presenting the submission of wives as one application of the basic principle of basic submission that is to be applied by all believers within the Body of Christ. [15]

Based on the idea of "mutual submission," egalitarians will sometimes say: "Of course I believe that a wife should be subject to her husband. And *a husband should also be subject to his wife*." Or an egalitarian woman might say, "I will be subject to my husband *as soon as he is subject to me*." And so, as egalitarians understand Ephesians 5:21, there is no difference in

---

13. I have quoted the ESV here, which rightly starts a new paragraph at verse 22 and keeps the string of Greek participles together in verses 19–21. (Verse 22 begins a new sentence in Greek, but verse 21 is the end of a long sentence running from verses 18 to 21). The question of whether to start a new paragraph with verse 21 or verse 22 is not crucial to either side's argument, however, since everyone agrees that verse 21 both modifies Paul's command to "be filled with the Spirit" in verse 18 and has implications for our understanding of the commands in 5:22–6:5. Sumner, *Men and Women in the Church* (2003), fails to understand this and claims that the dispute turns on where the paragraph breaks (155–9). The main difference is not where the paragraph begins but what the words translated "be subject" and "one another" actually mean.
14. Bilezikian, *Beyond Sex Roles*, 154.
15. Groothuis, *Good News for Women*, 164–65.

roles between men and women. There is no unique leadership role, no unique authority for the husband. There is simply "mutual submission."[16]

Answer 6.4a: If by "mutual submission" someone means that husband and wife should love one another and be considerate of one another's needs, this is surely a biblical idea, but it is not taught in this verse.

People can mean different things by "mutual submission." There is a sense of the phrase "mutual submission" that does not nullify the husband's authority within marriage. If "mutual submission" means *being considerate of one another*, and *caring for one another's needs* and *being thoughtful of one another* then of course I agree that "mutual submission" is a good thing (unless these ideas are used to nullify all unique authority for the husband). We can get these ideas from the Bible's commands to "love one another" (John 13:34) and from Paul's commands in Philippians 2:3–4, "Do nothing from rivalry or conceit, but in humility count others more significant than yourselves. Let each of you look not only to his own interests, but also to the interests of others."

But as we will see in the following discussion, it is doubtful that these ideas are taught in Ephesians 5:21. The Bible does not use the language of "being subject" to teach these things. In addition, egalitarians mean something so different by the phrase "mutual submission," and they have used this phrase so often to nullify male authority within marriage, that the expression "mutual submission" only leads to confusion.[17]

Answer 6.4b: In the context that follows Ephesians 5:21, Paul explains what he means by "submitting to one another": he means wives should submit to husbands, children to parents, and servants to masters.

The plain sense of "submitting to one another" in Ephesians 5:21 has been clear to Christians for centuries, simply from looking at the context. Paul explains in the following context that wives are to be subject to[18] their husbands (Ephesians 5:22–23), children are to be subject

---

16. In fact, our egalitarian friends have a journal called *Mutuality*, published by Christians for Biblical Equality.
17. When the Southern Baptist Convention was debating its statement on marriage and the family, I am told that there was a motion from the floor to add "mutual submission" to the statement. Dorothy Patterson, a member of the drafting committee for the statement and one of the original members of CBMW, spoke against the motion and explained how egalitarians have used it to deny any sense of male authority within marriage. The motion was defeated, and appropriately so. If "mutual submission" had been added to the Southern Baptist statement, it would have watered it down so much that people from almost any position could sign it, and it would have affirmed no unique male authority within marriage. (These events were reported to me by friends who were present when the statement was being debated on the floor of the Southern Baptist Convention in the summer of 1998.)
18. Sometimes people have objected that the verb "be subject to" (Greek *hupotassō*) is not actually found in verse 22. This is only partly true. A few significant Greek manuscripts lack *hupotassō* in this verse (p^{46}, B, and some church fathers), but many include it (Sinaiticus, A, D, 1739, many church fathers, and all the early versions in other languages). Whether or not it was there explicitly makes little difference to the context, for even if it is lacking, the idea "submit to, be subject to" from verse 21 would still be required for verse 22 to make sense, and *hupotassō* does occur explicitly in verse 24, "Now as the church *submits* to Christ, so also wives should submit in everything to their husbands."

to their parents (Ephesians 6:1–3), and slaves (or bondservants) are to be subject to their masters (Ephesians 6:5–8). These relationships are never reversed. He does not tell husbands to be subject to wives, or parents to be subject to their children (thus nullifying all parental authority), or masters to be subject to their servants.

Paul does not tell husbands and wives *generally* to be subject to each other, nor does he tell wives to be subject to *other people's husbands*. He says, "Wives, submit to *your own husbands*, as to the Lord" (Ephesians 5:22).[19]

What Paul has in mind is not a vague "mutual submission" where everybody is considerate and thoughtful of everybody else, but a specific kind of submission to an authority: the wife is subject to the authority of "her own husband." Similarly, parents and children aren't told to practice "mutual submission," but children are to be subject to (to "obey") their parents (Ephesians 6:1–3), and servants are told to be subject to (to "obey") their masters (Ephesians 6:5–8). In each case, the person in authority is not told to be subject to the one under authority, but Paul wisely gives guidelines to regulate the use of authority by husbands (who are to love their wives, Ephesians 5:25–33), by parents (who are not to provoke their children to anger, Ephesians 6:4), and by masters (who are to give up threatening their servants and remember that they too serve Christ, Ephesians 6:9). In no case is there "mutual submission"; in each case there is submission to authority and regulated use of that authority.

And then Paul says that the kind of submission wives are to exercise is like the submission of the church to Christ: "Now as the church submits to Christ, so also wives should submit in everything to their husbands" (Ephesians 5:24). This is surely not a "mutual submission," for the church is subject to Christ's authority in a way that Christ is not, and never will be, subject to us.

Answer 6.4c: The egalitarian view of "mutual submission" is a novelty in the history of the church.

Throughout the history of the church, I know of no author before 1968 who thought that "submitting to one another" makes the passage mean what egalitarians understand, namely, that there is no unique male headship and authority in marriage. For centuries it was understood that the passage teaches that we should all be subject to those God has put in authority over us, such as husbands, parents, or employers. Ephesians 5:21 was understood to restrain the authority of husbands, parents, and masters, but not to nullify it.

The clear meaning from the context is one reason why people didn't see "mutual submission" in Ephesians 5:21 as something that nullified a husband's authority. But feminist pressures in our culture led people to look for a way to avoid the force of Ephesians 5:22, "Wives, submit to your own husbands, as to the Lord."

---

19. The Greek text has the adjective *idios*, meaning "your own."

In previous generations some people did speak about "mutual submission," but never in the sense in which egalitarians today understand it.[20] In his study of the history of the interpretation of Ephesians 5:21, Daniel Doriani demonstrates that a number of earlier writers thought that there was a kind of "mutual submission" taught in the verse, but that such "submission" took very different forms for those *in authority* and for those *under authority*. They took it to mean that those in authority should govern wisely and with sacrificial concern for those under their authority. But Doriani found no author prior to the advent of feminism in the last half of the twentieth century who thought that "submitting to one another" nullified the authority of the husband within marriage.[21]

Answer 6.4d: Husbands are never told to be subject to their wives.

There is another fact that egalitarians cannot explain well when they propose "mutual submission" as an understanding of this verse. They fail to account for the fact that, while wives are several times in the New Testament told to be subject to their husbands (Ephesians 5:22–24; Colossians 3:18; Titus 2:5; 1 Peter 3:1–6), *husbands are never told to be subject to their wives*. Why is this, if Paul wanted to teach "mutual submission"?

The command that a husband should be subject to his wife would have been startling in an ancient male-dominated culture. Therefore, if the New Testament writers thought that Christian marriage required husbands to submit to their wives, they would have had to say that very clearly—otherwise, no early Christians would have ever known that was what they should do! But nowhere do we find such a command. It is surprising that evangelical feminists claim that the New Testament teaches this when it is nowhere explicitly stated.

Answer 6.4e: The egalitarian position depends on giving a Greek term a meaning it has never been shown to have.

When we look at the word Paul used when he said "submitting to one another" in Ephesians 5:21, we find that this word (Greek *hupotassō*) is always used of *submission to an authority*. No one has yet produced any examples in ancient Greek literature (either inside or outside the New Testament) where *hupotassō* is applied to a relationship between persons, and where it does not carry this sense of being *subject to an authority*.[22]

I have been asking a particular question for a number of years now (since I first asked it in the

---

20. Gilbert Bilezikian explains mutual submission with phrases like "help each other," "making themselves available to each other," "through love be servants [literally 'slaves'] of one another," "serving each other," and "a shared desire to serve others, to give of oneself, and to make a primary concern the interests and welfare of fellow believers" (*Beyond Sex Roles*, 154, 156).
21. See Doriani, "Historical Novelty of Egalitarian Interpretations of Scripture," in Grudem, *Biblical Foundations for Manhood and Womanhood*, 203–19.
22. With respect to persons, the BDAG gives the meanings, [active]: "to cause to be in a submissive relationship, to subject, to subordinate"; [passive]: "become subject...subject oneself, be subjected or subordinated, obey" (1042). Some, such as Gilbert Bilezikian, claim that the meaning of *hupotassō* is changed when the pronoun "to one another" (Greek *allēlōn*) is added to it. So Bilezikian says, "The addition...of the reciprocal pronoun 'to each other' changes its meaning entirely" (*Beyond Sex Roles*, 154).

plenary sessions of the 1986 meetings of the Evangelical Theological Society in Atlanta, Georgia), and I have not received an answer yet. The question is addressed to our egalitarian friends:

> Why should we assign to *hupotassō* in the New Testament a meaning (such as "defer to" or "be considerate of, be thoughtful of") that it is nowhere attested to have, and that no Greek lexicon has ever assigned to it, and that empties it of a meaning (onedirectional submission to an authority) which it always has when speaking of relationships between persons?

I do not believe the question has ever received a satisfactory answer. Linda Belleville attempted to answer it by saying that Ephesians 5:21 is unique:

> Christianity is by nature countercultural. Just because mutual submission was not the Greco-Roman way (and so not found in extrabiblical first-century texts) does not mean it was not the Christian way (and consequently found in biblical texts).... Every Greek lexicon I've consulted states that Ephesians 5:21 has no secular parallel.[23]

But this just confuses the issue. The question is not whether the ***teaching*** of the Bible is found in secular literature. Of course the Bible teaches hundreds of things that differ with secular culture. The question is whether the ***meaning of a specific word used to convey that teaching*** is found in ***any*** literature ***anywhere***, whether secular or Jewish or Christian.

We complementarians understand Paul to be using *hupotassō* in an ordinary, well-attested sense, "be subject to an authority." In using this word, Paul tells Christians to subject themselves to rightful authorities, which is itself a powerful teaching. But egalitarians have to claim a meaning for *hupotassō* that is found nowhere else, a meaning that empties the word of any idea of submission to an authority. So I wrote in 1998,

---

How can he claim that the meaning is changed? He says, "There are several words in the New Testament whose meaning is changed by the addition of the reciprocal pronoun *allēlōn*. Thus, the verb for "steal" becomes "deprive" with the addition of the reciprocal pronoun, without any idea of fraud (1 Corinthians 7:5). Likewise, the verb for 'worry' becomes 'care for each other' with the reciprocal pronoun (12:25)" (288n30).

However, his argument is incorrect for two reasons. First, the other examples he cites are not "changes of meaning" but are recognized, established alternative meanings of those words, supported in the standard Greek lexicons in the entries under words for "steal" and "worry." No meanings have changed, but words have a range or variety of meanings. By contrast, Bilezikian's "change of meaning" for *hupotassō* has no support in the lexicons. Second, his other examples are not parallel to the case of *allēlōn* with *hupotassō*. What he calls a change of sense in 1 Corinthians 7:5 is not due to the presence of the pronoun "to one another" but rather to the fact that it is a figurative usage of the word rather than a literal usage. It is the sense we would expect to attach to a figurative usage of the word applied to marital rights rather than to literal stealing of goods (see BDAG, 121). With regard to 1 Corinthians 12:25, Bilezikian's statement is simply incorrect: The meaning is not changed by the presence of a reciprocal pronoun, but 1 Corinthians 12:25 is just one of several examples in the New Testament where the sense of *merimnaō* is "to attend to, care for, be concerned about" (see BDAG, 632). The other verses where it has this sense do not even have the reciprocal pronoun.

23. Belleville, "Women in Ministry" (2001), 131.

> In every example we can find, when person A is said to "be subject to" person B, person B has a unique authority which person A does not have. In other words, *hupotassō* always implies a one-directional submission to someone in authority.[24]

Hupotassō does not mean "to be considerate and thoughtful of someone else," "to care for someone else," or "to put someone else's interests first" (meanings that are consistent with the egalitarian interpretation of "mutual submission"). It always means to be ***subject to someone else's authority***, in all Greek literature, Christian and non-Christian.

Though there are abundant examples of this sense in secular Greek literature, we don't have to seek examples from non-Christian literature to demonstrate this sense.

1. Jesus was "submissive to" the authority of His parents (Luke 2:51).
2. Demons were "subject to" the disciples (Luke 10:17). It is clear that the meaning "be considerate of, be thoughtful toward" cannot fit here, for the demons were certainly not considerate of or thoughtful toward the disciples!
3. Citizens are to be "subject to" or "in subjection" to the governing authorities (Romans 13:1, 5; Titus 3:1; 1 Peter 2:13).
4. The universe is "in subjection" to Christ (1 Corinthians 15:27; Ephesians 1:22).
5. Angels and other spiritual beings have been "subjected to" Christ (1 Peter 3:22).
6. Christ is "subjected to" God the Father (1 Corinthians 15:28).
7. Church members are to be "subject to" the elders in the church (1 Peter 5:5[25]).
8. Wives are told to be "subject to" their husbands (Ephesians 5:22, 24; Colossians 3:18; Titus 2:5; 1 Peter 3:5).
9. The church is to "submit to" Christ (Ephesians 5:24).
10. Servants are to be "submissive to" their masters (Titus 2:9; 1 Peter 2:18).
11. Christians are to be "subject to" God (Hebrews 12:9; James 4:7).

The meaning "be subject to an authority" is common, it is well attested, and it can be supported by dozens of other examples. This is the ordinary sense of the word, and Paul's readers would have understood the word in that sense.

The New Testament writers can use this ordinary Greek word to teach *ideas* that are not found in secular Greek literature, such as the idea that all things in the universe are subject to Jesus Christ, and that demons are subject to Jesus' disciples, and that Christ is subject to God the Father. The New Testament authors generally use ordinary Greek words and depend on the ordinary meanings of those Greek words to teach the unusual, world-changing content of the

---

24. Grudem, "An Open Letter to Egalitarians," *CBMW News* 3:1 (March 1998), 3.
25. First Corinthians 16:15–16 should also be placed in this category, because we know from 1 Clement 42:4, a letter written from Clement of Rome to the church of Corinth in AD 95, that the elders in the church at Corinth came from the household of Stephanas. Therefore, when Paul tells the Corinthians to be "subject to" the household of Stephanas, he is telling them to be subject to those who were elders in Corinth.

New Testament. This is not surprising, for they were communicating to ordinary Greek-speaking people in language they could understand.

But if the New Testament writers, including Paul, use *hupotassō* regularly to mean "be subject to an authority," then on what basis can Belleville claim that the word takes a different sense in Ephesians 5:21? On what basis can she claim that the word here means *something it has never meant anywhere else?* And how would Paul's readers ever have known that he wanted them to understand *hupotassō* in Ephesians 5:21 in a new sense, a sense it had never taken before? How could Paul's readers have known that this was the only time in all of ancient Greek that *hupotassō* was used to speak of one person being "subject" to another and it did not mean to be subject to the authority of that other person?

Now if there were other cases where *hupotassō* means "be considerate, be kind, be thoughtful toward someone," and there was no idea of *being subject to that person's authority,* then Belleville would be free to argue that *hupotassō* has two known senses, (1) be subject to someone's authority, and (2) be considerate, kind, thoughtful to someone else. She could then argue for sense (2) from the context of Ephesians 5:21. But has she given any examples to establish this other sense?

She cites two verses, saying that "Even a cursory look at Paul's writings shows that mutual submission is basic to his understanding of how believers are to relate to one another."[26]

> Philippians 2:4: "Let each of you look not only to his own interests, but also to the interests of others."
>
> Ephesians 5:21: "submitting to one another out of reverence for Christ."

But Philippians 2:4 does not contain *hupotassō*, so it cannot provide the needed evidence for the meaning of this word. This means that Belleville's sole proof for this unprecedented, unique meaning of *hupotassō* is Ephesians 5:21. Her argument takes the following form:

> *Question:* What example can you give from any other passage to show that *hupotassō* could take the unprecedented meaning you propose in Ephesians 5:21? *Answer:* My example is Ephesians 5:21.

This is tantamount to an admission that the meaning she claims for *hupotassō* in Ephesians 5:21 is not found anywhere else in Greek literature.

Then why should we accept her interpretation?

The reason to ask for other examples is that they give us a *range of meanings* that a word could take in the ancient world. Then from that known range of meanings, we look at the con-

26. Belleville, "Women in Ministry," 132.

text to decide what sense fits best. But if there are no examples of a new sense for a word, *we are not free to make up a new meaning on the spot,* one that supports the point we are anxious to establish. A basic principle of lexicography provides us with a helpful warning, one emphasized by John Chadwick in reflecting on his many years of work on the editorial team for the Liddell-Scott *Lexicon*:

> A constant problem to guard against is the proliferation of meanings.... It is often tempting to create a new sense to accommodate a difficult example, but we must always ask first, if there is any other way of taking the word which would allow us to assign the example to an already established sense.... As I have remarked in several of my notes, there may be no reason why a proposed sense should not exist, but is there any reason why it must exist?[27]

Belleville's claim that the meaning of *hupotassō* in Ephesians 5:21 is unique is similar to some responses I've received to my challenge to find an occurrence of *hupotassō* where it does not mean submission to an authority. The response is that the example of *hupotassō* that I am asking for is found in Ephesians 5:21, where *hupotassō* "obviously" means mutual submission and therefore it can't mean to be subject to an authority. Those who respond this way have not understood the question.

We are not free, in interpreting the Bible, to give a word any meaning we might think "fits." Words have established ranges of meanings that were familiar to native speakers of Greek in the ancient world and that allowed them to understand one another (that is how all language functions—speakers and hearers have in their minds "shared meanings" of thousands of words). Those established meanings are what are listed in dictionaries (or "lexicons") of ancient Greek. I am simply asking for some evidence that "be considerate of" with no idea of submission to an authority was an established, shared meaning of *hupotassō* in the ancient world. No one has produced any evidence.

To claim that *hupotassō* means something in Ephesians 5:21 that it nowhere meant at any other time or place in history would require (1) that Paul wrote a word with a new, secret meaning that Greek-speaking people had never known before, and (2) that Paul expected that all the Christians in all the churches to which the epistle to the Ephesians went would know this new, secret meaning and understand what he meant, and (3) that they would know that he did not mean by *hupotassō* what all Greek speakers everywhere had previously meant when they used it in conversation and even what Paul himself meant by it in all his other writings, and (4) that the meaning is now suddenly so "obvious" from the context that everyone should see it.

People may believe such a position if they wish, but it will be for reasons other than evidence or facts.

---

27. Chadwick, *Lexicographica Graeca* (1996), 23–24.

Answer 6.4f: The term translated "one another" often means "some to others" and not "everyone to everyone." That is the sense it has to have here.

The Greek term translated "one another" (the word *allēlōn*) can have two different meanings. Sometimes in the New Testament it means something like "everyone to everyone" as we see in verses like John 13:34, "A new commandment I give to you, that you *love one another*." Everyone agrees that this means that all Christians are to love all other Christians. It has the sense "everyone to everyone."

But egalitarians make a crucial mistake when they assume that because *allēlōn* means "everyone to everyone" in *some* verses, it must mean that in *all* verses. In many other contexts, the word doesn't mean "everyone to everyone," but "some to others."

For example, in Revelation 6:4, the rider on the red horse "was permitted to take peace from the earth, so that men should *slay one another*." This does not mean that every person first got killed and then killed the one who had murdered him! It simply means that *some* killed *others*. Here the word *allēlōn* does not mean "everyone to everyone" but "some to others."

We see a similar example in Galatians 6:2, "Bear *one another's* burdens, and so fulfill the law of Christ." Here Paul does not mean that everybody should switch burdens with everybody else, but only that some who are more able should bear the burdens of others who are less able to bear their burdens.[28] And in 1 Corinthians 11:33, Paul says, "When you come together to eat, wait for *one another*." This does not mean that those who come early should wait for those who are late and those who are late should wait for those who are there early. It means that those

---

28. Sarah Sumner says she is not persuaded by this argument regarding Revelation 6:4 and Galatians 6:2, because "since everyone has burdens, it's unrealistic to say that only 'some' of us should bear the burdens of 'others,'" and further, because "it's easier to imagine men killing each other than having 'some' kill 'others' without being killed themselves. In any battle, many of the slayers ultimately become part of the slain" (*Men and Women in the Church,* 156n3).

But Sumner misunderstands the point. I am not saying that people who kill in battle are never later killed themselves by someone else. I am saying that if person A kills person B in battle, then this is not "mutual killing," because person B does not rise from the dead and kill person A in turn! Even if someone else (say, person C) later kills person A, there is still no "mutual killing," because person A does not then rise from the dead and kill person C. In every single instance, *some kill others*, but people do not (generally) simultaneously kill each other.

For the parallel with the egalitarian claim of "mutual submission" to apply to "mutual killing," in a battle involving three hundred people every single person in the battle would have to kill all three hundred other people, and that person would also have to be killed three hundred times, once by every other "mutual killer" in the battle (which is nonsense). I agree that this is the sense that *allēlōn sometimes* takes, as in "love one another," which does in fact mean that in a church of three hundred every Christian is to love all three hundred others, and to be loved by three hundred others. My point is that this meaning "everyone to everyone" does not make sense in all cases, such as the case of killing in war.

The same is true with bearing burdens, or waiting for those who are late. Some bear the burdens of others, even though who are the burdened and who are the burden-bearers may vary from time to time. In a church of three hundred people, Paul did not intend that each person make a meal (for example) for every other person in the church (which would be 300 x 300 = 90,000 meals per day!), but that *some* in the church make a meal for *others* in the church in time of need. It would be nonsense to expect that the needy person would be waiting at the door with a meal to give in return whenever someone arrived to help. "Bear one another's burdens" means that in each case *some* should bear the burdens of *others*. It is the same with waiting: *Some* (who are on time) should wait for *others* (who are late). Similarly, *some* who are under authority should be subject to *others* who have authority over them. The word *allēlōn* does not require that everybody be subject to everybody.

who are early should wait for the others who are late. Here again, *allēlōn* means "some to others" (some are to wait for others). The New Testament has many other examples of this type (see, for example, Matthew 24:10; Luke 2:15; 12:1; 24:32). In these verses *allēlōn* means, "some to others." (The KJV often translated these passages, "one to another" or "one for another," as in 1 Cor. 11:33, "When ye come together to eat, tarry *one for another.*" Following this pattern, the KJV translated Ephesians 5:21, "submitting yourselves *one to another.*")

Therefore, "submitting to one another" in Ephesians 5:21 *can* take the sense "some be subject to others" if the context fits or requires this meaning. And, as we have seen above, the word translated "submitting to" (Greek *hupotassō*) requires this sense, because it is never used to speak of a reciprocal relationship between persons but always signifies one-directional submission to an authority.

Therefore we can paraphrase Ephesians 5:21 as follows: "Be subject to others in the church who are in positions of authority over you."[29]

Linda Belleville objects to this analysis. She says that the term translated "one another" (Greek *allēlois*; lexical form *allēlōn*)[30] "simply cannot bear any other lexical meaning but a reciprocal one," and therefore the verse must teach some kind of "mutual submission."[31]

In making this argument, Belleville fails to understand the actual issue under dispute. Everyone agrees that *allēlōn* has a "reciprocal" meaning. The question is what specific kind of reciprocal meaning the term implies. When a writer says that a group of people "love one another" or "care for one another," or that a group of people "were killing one another" or "were trampling on one another," the meaning is always in some sense reciprocal, because in every case *some in the group* do something to *others in the group.* In that sense the meaning of "one another" is reciprocal—the group acts upon itself, in contrast to saying that the group "loves *other* people," or that the group "was killing *other* people (outside the group)."

What Belleville fails to distinguish, however, is that sometimes *everybody* in the group does something to *everybody else* (loving one another, for example), and sometimes *some people* in the group do the action to *others* in the group (killing one another, when some are killing and others are being killed). In English we use "one another" for both senses, and we say they were "loving one another" or they were "killing one another." In Greek likewise, the term *allēlōn* can be used in both senses. The *kind of activity* involved determines the reciprocal sense of *allēlōn* that is intended.

---

29. It is interesting that the King James Version showed an understanding of the sense of *allēlōn* in this passage. It translated the verse, "Submitting yourselves *one to another* in the fear of God." When *allēlōn* takes the sense "some to others," the King James Version often signaled that by phrases such as "one to another."
30. The pronoun takes no singular (since it is always plural) and no nominative form (since it can never function as the subject of a sentence). In my earlier article I used the accusative plural *allelous* as the lexical form, from a habit learned from teaching Greek from J. W. Wenham's *The Elements of New Testament Greek* (1965), 205. However, the genitive plural *allēlōn* is used in the standard lexicons, and I have changed to it throughout the article as reproduced here.
31. Belleville, "Women in Ministry," 132.

My argument for Ephesians 5:21 is that "submitting to" someone in the sense intended by *hupotassō* is a one-directional activity. It is like the action of "killing one another"—in the nature of the action of killing, one person kills and the other is killed. The dead person does not rise from the dead after a few minutes and kill the other person, nor could every single person kill every single other person. Killing one another rather has the sense "some to others," in that some were killing others. Trampling on one another is a similar example: some trample on others, so the group can be said to be "trampling on one another." Waiting for one another when some people are late is the same idea: some wait, and some are waited for.

Belleville says she is unable to understand this distinction in meaning, and therefore she rejects it as a possibility:

> Wayne Grudem's claim that *allelous*...in Ephesians 5:21 takes the "common" meaning "some to others"...boggles the lexical imagination.... And how exactly Galatians 6:2 ("Carry *each other's* burdens"), 1 Corinthians 11:33 ("When you come together to eat, wait for *each other*"), and Revelation 6:4 ("To make the people [on earth] slay *each other*") support such a "common meaning" is likewise incomprehensible.[32]

But is it really that difficult to understand that Paul in Galatians 6:2 did not want every single person in the churches of Galatia to carry every other person's burden (each person would be carrying hundreds of burdens!), but that he wanted *some* to help *others* as they had need? Is it really "incomprehensible" that in 1 Corinthians 11:33, Paul wanted *some* (who were on time) to wait for *others* (who were late)? And is Belleville really unable to understand that in Revelation 6:4 some were killing and some were being killed (rather than the impossible idea that every single person was killing every single other person)? These are straightforward understandings of these passages.

Now with respect to Ephesians 5:21, our conclusion is (1) that *allēlōn* often takes the sense of "some to others" within a group, when the activity described is by nature a one-directional activity, and (2) that *hupotassō* always indicates a one-directional submission to an authority. Therefore we do not need to invent a new, unprecedented meaning for *hupotassō* in Ephesians 5:21. It takes a common, ordinary meaning, "be subject to an authority," and *allēlōn* takes a common, ordinary meaning, "some (in the group) to others (in the group)."

No idea of "mutual submission" is taught, then, in Ephesians 5:21. The idea itself is self-contradictory if *hupotassō* means here (as it does everywhere else) "be subject to an authority."

Answer 6.4g: Colossians 3:18, Titus 2:5, and 1 Peter 3:1 do not allow the egalitarian sense of "mutual submission."

One other fact warns us that the egalitarian claim of "mutual submission" should not be used as a magic wand to wave away any claims of male leadership in marriage: There is no statement

32. Ibid., 132n102.

about "submitting to one another" in the context of Colossians 3:18, Titus 2:5, or 1 Peter 3:1. Yet, as we saw earlier in this chapter, those verses also explicitly teach wives to be submissive to their husbands. They say nothing about husbands being submissive to their wives.

This leaves egalitarians in a dilemma. Nothing in these letters would have even hinted to Paul's original readers in Colossae, or to Titus and the church in Crete, or to Peter's readers in hundreds of churches in Asia Minor, anything like the "mutual submission" that egalitarians advocate. *But that means (from an egalitarian standpoint) that these three letters taught a wrong idea, the idea that wives should submit to the authority of their husbands in marriage.* Did the letters of the apostles Paul and Peter then lead the church astray? Would it have been sin for the original readers to obey the letters of Paul and Peter and teach that wives should be subject to their husbands? This would contradict our doctrine of Scripture as the inerrant, absolutely authoritative Word of God.[33]

Answer 6.4h: Conclusion: The egalitarian idea of "mutual submission" is not taught in this verse.

The egalitarian view has no sound basis in Scripture. The actual words of the text do not allow it. The text teaches that Christians should be subject to those in authority over them, whether husbands, parents, or masters. For all of these reasons, the egalitarian idea of "mutual submission" in Ephesians 5:21 should be discarded.

We can paraphrase Ephesians 5:21 as follows: "Be subject to others in the church who are in positions of authority over you." I do not believe any idea of "mutual submission" is taught in this verse. The idea itself is self-contradictory if *hupotassō* means here (as it does everywhere else) "be subject to an authority."

Answer 6.4i: Should "mutual submission" be put in churches' policy statements?

A word of advice to church leaders: If you want to add a statement on men and women in marriage to your church's governing document or publish it as a policy statement (as did the Southern Baptist Convention and Campus Crusade for Christ), and if in the process someone proposes to add the phrase "mutual submission" to the document, I urge you strongly not to

33. I agree that teachings in one part of the Bible can modify or refine our understanding of teachings in another part of the Bible. In this way the teachings of the different sections are complementary. But in the egalitarian claim that "mutual submission" nullifies a husband's authority and gives an entirely different sense to "submission," we are talking not just about a complementary teaching in another part of the Bible but something that fundamentally denies and even contradicts the meaning of these verses in Colossians, Titus, and 1 Peter. Even if we were to grant Bilezikian's claim that the addition of "to one another" to *hupotassō* "changes its meaning entirely," that would not help him in Colossians, Titus, and 1 Peter, where there is no statement about "one another," but just "wives, be subject to your own husbands." So would he say that readers in that day, and in this day, should obey those verses with the "unchanged" (according to his view) meaning of *hupotassō*? Or should people today *disobey* those verses? If the first, then the complementarian position is correct. If the second, then he is saying that people should disobey God's Word. Which will it be?

agree to it. In the sense that egalitarians understand "mutual submission," the idea is found nowhere in Scripture, and it actually nullifies the teaching of significant passages of Scripture.

How then should we respond when people say they favor "mutual submission"? We need to find out what they mean by it, and if they do not wish to advocate an egalitarian view, we need to suggest an alternative wording that speaks to their concerns more precisely. Some people who hold a fully complementarian view of marriage do use the phrase "mutual submission" and intend it in a way that does not nullify male leadership in marriage. Some people who want to use this language may have genuine concerns about men acting like dictators or tyrants in their marriages. If this is what they are seeking to guard against, then I suggest this alternative wording from the Campus Crusade for Christ statement:

> In a marriage lived according to these truths, the love between husband and wife will show itself in listening to each other's viewpoints, valuing each others' gifts, wisdom, and desires, honoring one another in public and in private, and always seeking to bring benefit, not harm, to one another.

Egalitarian claim 6.5: Preliminary Movement: The New Testament commands regarding male headship are only a "preliminary movement" to partially correct the culture at that time, and the New Testament ethic regarding male headship needs further improvement.

This is the claim of William Webb, who argues that the commands about wives submitting to their husbands in Ephesians 5:22–33 are not part of the "final ethic" that we should follow today, but are simply an indication of "where Scripture is moving on the issue of patriarchal power."[34]

Answer 6.5a: This denies the Bible's moral authority, for it assumes that the New Testament's ethical standards should not be ours today.

Webb's argument at this point is not persuasive because it depends on his assumption that the ethical standards of the New Testament are not God's ultimate ethical standards for us, but are simply one step along the way toward a kind of "ultimate ethic" that we should adopt today (pp. 36–39). Webb does not consider the moral commands of the New Testament to represent a perfect or final moral system for Christians. They are rather a pointer that "provides the direction toward the divine destination, but its literal, isolated words are not always the destination itself. Sometimes God's instructions are simply designed to get his flock moving" (p. 60).

34. Webb, *Slaves, Women and Homosexuals*, 80–1.

We should not find this position acceptable, because it essentially nullifies the moral authority of the New Testament for Christians today, not only with respect to Ephesians 5, but (in principle) with respect to all the moral commands of the New Testament. As I explain in more detail in another section of this book, Webb may in fact view some New Testament commands as representing an ultimate ethic, but even then he thinks we should obey them *not because they are taught in the New Testament*, but because Webb's system has filtered them through his eighteen criteria and then has found that what the New Testament teaches is also the moral standard that is found in his "ultimate ethic."[35]

EGALITARIAN CLAIM 6.6: *HEAD* MEANS "SOURCE" OR "PREEMINENT ONE": IN EPHESIANS 5:23, THE WORD *KEPHALĒ* ("HEAD") DOES NOT MEAN "PERSON IN AUTHORITY" BUT RATHER "SOURCE," AS IN "SOURCE OF A RIVER" (OR PERHAPS "PREEMINENT ONE").

In Ephesians 5:23, Paul makes this statement:

> For the husband is the *head* of the wife even as Christ is the *head* of the Church, his body, and is himself its Savior.

And in 1 Corinthians 11:3, he says:

> But I want you to understand that the *head* of every man is Christ, the *head* of a wife is her husband, and the *head* of Christ is God.

The most common egalitarian interpretation of these verses is that the word translated "head" (Greek, *kephalē*) does not mean "person in authority over" but has some other meaning, especially the meaning "source." Thus, the husband is the *source* of the wife (an allusion to the creation of Eve from Adam's side in Genesis 2), as Christ is the *source* of the Church.[36]

It is important to realize the decisive significance of these verses, and particularly of Ephesians 5:23, for the current controversy about male–female roles in marriage. If *head* means "person in authority over," then there is a unique authority that belongs to the husband in marriage, and it is parallel to Christ's authority over the church. If this is the true meaning of

---

35. See a fuller analysis of Webb's system in Appendix 5, pp. 600–645.

36. Egalitarian writings holding that *kephalē* means "source" are numerous. Some of the most influential are: Berkeley and Alvera Mickelsen, "What Does *Kephalē* Mean in the New Testament?" in *Women, Authority, and the Bible*, 97–110; Payne, "Response," in *Women, Authority, and the Bible*, 118–32; Bilezikian, "A Critical Examination of Wayne Grudem's Treatment of *Kepahlē* in Ancient Greek Texts," appendix to *Beyond Sex Roles*, 215–52; Kroeger, "The Classical Concept of *Head* as 'Source,'" Appendix 3 in *Equal to Serve*, 267–83; Fee, *First Epistle to the Corinthians* (1987), 501–5; Kroeger, "*Head*," in *Dictionary of Paul and His Letters*, 375–77; and Brown, *Women Ministers*, 213–15, 246. Many other egalitarian writers who have no advanced training in New Testament studies or in Greek simply quote one or more of these authors as proof of the meaning "source."

head in these verses, then the egalitarian view of marriage is wrong.[37] But if *head* means "source" here, then two Scripture texts significant to complementarians have been shown to have no impact on the controversy. Which view is right?

I will focus most attention on the meaning "source," and at the end add a comment about the alternative meaning "preeminent one."

Answer 6.6a: A word's meaning is found by examining its use in various contexts. *Kephalē* is found in over fifty contexts where it refers to people who have authority over others of whom they are the "head." But it never once takes a meaning "source without authority," as egalitarians would like to make it mean.

In 1985, I looked up 2,336 examples of *kephalē* in ancient Greek literature, using texts from Homer in the eighth century BC up to some church fathers in the fourth century AD I found that in those texts *kephalē* was applied to many people in authority (when it was used in a metaphorical sense to say that person A was the head of person or persons B), but it was never applied to a person without governing authority. Several studies took issue with part or all of my conclusions, and I have considered those in two subsequent studies, with my fundamental claims about the meaning of *kephalē* further established, it seems to me, by additional new evidence. Interested readers can find further details in those articles.[38] One of these articles (from 2001) is reprinted in the appendices to this book.[39]

To my knowledge, no one has yet produced one text in ancient Greek literature where a person is called the *kephalē* of another person or group *and that person is not the one in authority over that other person or group.* Nearly two decades after the publication of my 1985 study, the alleged meaning "source without authority" has still not been supported with *any* citation of *any* text in ancient Greek literature. Over fifty examples of *kephalē* meaning "ruler, authority over" have been found (they are listed in Appendix 3, pp. 544–51), but no examples of the meaning of "source without authority."

---

37. I realize that a few egalitarians claim that Paul's teaching only applied to his time in history, and is not applicable to us today. This position is not affected by disputes over the meaning of *head,* but it is very difficult to sustain in light of the parallel with Christ and the church, and in light of Paul's tying it to the statements about marriage before there was sin in the world (Ephesians 5:31–32, quoting Genesis 2:24).

38. For details, see Grudem, "The Meaning of 'Head' (*Kephalē*) in 1 Corinthians 11:3 and Ephesians 5:23," in *Biblical Foundations for Manhood and Womanhood,* ed. Wayne Grudem (2002), 145–202. That chapter is a reprint with only slight modifications, and the addition of interaction with Thiselton's commentary, to my article, "The Meaning of *kephalē* ('Head'): An Analysis of New Evidence, Real and Alleged," *Journal of the Evangelical Theological Society* 44/1 (March 2001): 25–65.

My two earlier studies on the meaning of *kephalē* were "The Meaning of *kephalē* ('Head'): A Response to Recent Studies," *TrinJ* 11 NS (Spring 1990): 3–72 (reprinted in *Recovering Biblical Manhood and Womanhood,* 425–68) and "Does *kephalē* ('Head') Mean 'Source' or 'Authority Over' in Greek Literature? A Survey of 2,336 Examples" in G. Knight, *The Role Relationship of Men and Women,* 49–80 (also printed in *TrinJ* 6 NS [Spring 1985] 38–59).

39. See Appendix 4, on pages 552–99, below.

Answer 6.6b. Verses that refer to Christ as "head" cannot rightly be used to deny the idea of authority.

It is surprising to see Linda Belleville using four New Testament verses that refer to Christ as responses to a request for examples of *kephalē* meaning "non-authoritative source." (She cites Ephesians 4:16 and 5:22–23; Colossians 1:18 and 2:19.)[40] Does she believe that Christ has no authority over His church? This is unlikely. But then why does she cite these in response to the question I posed in 1998: "Will you please show us one example in all of ancient Greek where this word for 'head' (*kephalē*) is used to say that person A is the 'head' of person or persons B, and means what you claim, namely, 'non-authoritative source'?"[41]

Far from answering the question, verses about Christ's role as *head* of the church support my earlier argument that wherever person A is called "head" of person (or persons) B, person A is in a position of authority over B. Belleville's first four verses here prove my point.[42]

Then Belleville gives one additional reference, a text from a Jewish work, *The Life of Adam and Eve* 19.[43] She writes, "In a Jewish work that is contemporary with Paul's writings, the author has Eve speaking of 'desire' as 'the source [*kephalē*] of every kind of sin."[44]

But this quotation does not prove Belleville's point either, because it does not give an example where *kephalē* is used to say that person A is the "head" of person or persons B, and means "non-authoritative source." This text does not even use *kephalē* to refer to a person, but rather says that "lust" is the "beginning (*kephalē*) of every sin."[45]

Belleville does not inform readers that the translation "source" here is her own, and that neither of the two standard English translations renders *kephalē* as "source" in this text.[46] In any case, it is not parallel to Ephesians 5:23, because it does not refer to a relationship between persons.

---

40. Belleville, "Women in Ministry," 138.
41. Grudem, "Open Letter to Egalitarians," *CBMW News* 3:1 (March 1998): 3.
42. Belleville notes that Christ "feeds and cares for" the church (Ephesians 5:29), which is surely true. In every relationship of authority between persons, the person in authority gives or provides some benefit to the person or group under authority (such as leadership, care, protection, example, teaching, love, or nourishment, depending on the nature of the relationship). But that does not mean that person A is the *source* of person B. Nor does it mean that *head* means "source" when applied to that relationship.

    To take a similar example from English, it makes sense to say that a school principal is the "head" of the school, since he or she has authority over the school. The principal also provides students with many things, such as leadership, discipline, and protection, so we could say that the principal is the "source" of leadership, discipline, and protection for the students. But we cannot say that the principal is the "source" of the students. They do not spring out of the principal. The principal is the "head" of the school only in the sense of being the "person in authority over" the school.
43. *The Life of Adam and Eve 19* is a pseudepigraphal Jewish work that can be dated to approximately 20 BC–AD 70. The Greek text is found in C. Von Tischendorf, *Apocalypses Apocryphae* 11 (1866), lines 1–2; English translations are found in R. H. Charles, *The Apocrypha and Pseudepigrapha of the Old Testament* (1913), 2:146; and James H. Charlesworth, *The Old Testament Pseudepigrapha* (1985), 2:279.
44. Belleville, "Women in Ministry," 137–38.
45. This is the translation of R. H. Charles, 146.
46. Charles renders it "beginning" and Charlesworth translates it "for coveteousness is the *origin* of every sin" (279), which he apparently also intends in the sense "beginning, first in a series of other sins," because in a footnote he explains, "Greek *kephalē* corresponds to the Heb. *rō'sh,* 'head' or 'first.'" This text is a bit unusual,

This example from *The Life of Adam and Eve 19* is not a special case, but is one of about seventy examples in ancient literature where *kephalē* takes the well-established sense of "beginning, first in a series." But to be the *first* or *beginning* is not the same as being the *source* of something. My oldest son is the first in a series of three sons, but he is not the source of my other sons. To take another example, in the English alphabet the letter *a* is the beginning of the alphabet, but *a* is not the "source" of the other letters in the alphabet. It is just the first in a series. So with *The Life of Adam and Eve* 19, the text affirms that coveting or desiring to sin is the *beginning* of every sin (for example, Eve first coveted, then she took the fruit, then she gave some to Adam, then she hid from God, then she denied responsibility), but it does not mean that coveting is the *source* of other sins. (In Old Testament thought, if anything can be said to be the source of sins, it is the human heart; see Genesis 6:5; 8:21; Exodus 4:21; Psalm 51:10; 139:23; 140:2; 141:4; Proverbs 4:23; 6:18; 26:24–25; Jeremiah 17:9; contrast Deuteronomy 6:5–6; 8:2; Psalm 19:14; 24:4; and in the New Testament, compare Mark 7:21–23).

My question therefore remains unanswered: Where is an example of *kephalē* where person A is the *kephalē* of person B and is not in authority over person B? There is none.

Answer 6.6c: A listing of several ancient texts where one person is the "head" of another makes clear the meaning "person in authority over another."

Here are several examples where *kephalē* is used to say that one person is the "head" of another, and the person who is called head is the one in authority:[47]

1. David as King of Israel is called the "head" of the people he conquered (2 Samuel [LXX 2 Kings] 22:44), "You kept me as the *head* of the nations; people whom I had not known served me"; similarly, Psalm 18 (LXX 17):43
2. The leaders of the tribes of Israel are called "heads" of the tribes (1 Kings [LXX 3 Kings] 8:1, Alexandrinus text), "Then Solomon assembled the elders of Israel and all the *heads* of the tribes" (similar statements in the second-century AD Greek translation of Aquila, Deuteronomy 5:23; 29:9 (English verse 10); 3 Kings [LXX 1 Kings] 8:1)
3. Jephthah becomes the "head" of the people of Gilead (Judges 11:11, "the people made him *head* and leader over them"; also stated in 10:18; 11:8, 9)
4. Pekah the son of Remaliah is the head of Samaria (Isaiah 7:9, "the *head* of Samaria is the son of Remaliah")
5. The father is the "head" of the family (Hermas, *Similitudes* 7.3; the man is called "the *head* of the house")

---

because both Charles and Charlesworth point out that the text is probably based on a pun in Hebrew where the words for "head" and "poison" have the same spelling, and the text is referring to poison that the serpent put on the forbidden fruit.

47. See Appendix 3, pp. 544–51, for additional references like the ones cited here. These texts are discussed in my 1985 and 1990 articles on *kephalē* (mentioned above, footnote 38).

6. The husband is the "head" of the wife (Ephesians 5:23, "the husband is *head* of the wife even as Christ is *head* of the church")
7. Christ is the "head" of the church (Colossians 1:18, "He is the *head* of the body, the church"; also in Ephesians 5:23)
8. Christ is the "head" of all things (Ephesians 1:22, "He put all things under his feet and gave him as *head* over all things to the church")
9. God the Father is the "head" of Christ (1 Corinthians 11:3, "the *head* of Christ is God")

In related statements using not metaphors but closely related similes, (1) the general of an army is said to be "like the head" in Plutarch, *Pelopidas* 2.1.3: In an army, "the light-armed troops are like the hands, the cavalry like the feet, the line of men-at-arms itself like chest and breastplate, and the general is like the *head*." Similarly, (2) the Roman Emperor is called the "head" of the people in Plutarch, *Galba* 4.3: "Vindix...wrote to Galba inviting him to assume the imperial power, and thus to serve what was a vigorous body in need of a *head*" (compare a related statement in Plutarch, *Cicero* 14.4). And (3) the King of Egypt is called "head" of the nation in Philo, *Moses* 2.30: "As the *head* is the ruling place in the living body, so Ptolemy became among kings."

Then there are the additional (somewhat later) citations from Chrysostom (c. 344/354–407 AD) quoted in my 2001 article,[48] where (1) God is the "head" of Christ; (2) Christ is the "head" of the church; (3) the husband is the "head" of the wife; (4) Christ is the "head" of all things; (5) church leaders are the "head" of the church; and (6) a woman is the "head" of her maidservant. In all six of these cases, he uses language of rulership and authority to explain the role of the "head," and uses language of submission and obedience to describe the role of the "body."

In addition, there are several statements from various authors indicating a common understanding that the physical head functioned as the "ruling" part of the body: (1) Plato says that the head "reigns over all the parts within us" (*Timaeus* 44.D). (2) Philo says, "the *head* is the ruling place in the living body" (*Moses* 2:30), "the mind is *head* and ruler of the sense-faculty in us" (*Moses* 2.82), "*head* we interpret allegorically to mean the ruling part of the soul" (*On Dreams* 2.207), and "Nature conferred the sovereignty of the body on the *head*" (*The Special Laws* 184). (3) Plutarch says, "We affectionately call a person 'soul' or '*head*' from his ruling parts" (*Table Talk* 7.7 [692.e.1]).

Clinton Arnold and Gregory Dawes, in extensive studies,[49] adduce other examples in ancient literature of the physical head seen as ruling or controlling the body. Though they find examples where the head or the brain is the source of something as well, they do not claim that

48. Grudem, "Meaning of *kephalē*" (2001)25–65.

49. Arnold, "Jesus Christ: 'Head' of the Church (Colossians and Ephesians)," in *Jesus of Nazareth*, ed. Joel Green and Max Turner (1994), 346–66; and Gregory Dawes, *The Body in Question: Meaning and Metaphor in the Interpretation of Ephesians 5:21–33* (1998), especially pp. 122–49 on "The 'Head' (κεφαλη) Metaphor."

these examples deny a simultaneous ruling or governing function to the physical head. If the physical head was a source of something like nourishment, it also was seen to have control and governance over the physical body.

Answer 6.6d: The meaning "source" makes no sense in key passages like Ephesians 5:23, "the husband is the head of the wife."

I am not the source of my wife in any meaningful sense of the word "source." And so it is with all husbands and wives. It is just not true to say, "the husband is the *source* of the wife as Christ is the source of the church." It makes the verse into nonsense.

Answer 6.6e: All the recognized lexicons (dictionaries) for ancient Greek, or their editors, now give *kephalē* the meaning "person in authority over" or something similar, but none give the meaning "source."

1. The standard lexicon for New Testament Greek, the Bauer-Danker-Arndt-Gingrich *Greek-English Lexicon* (BDAG) gives the meaning "in the case of living beings, to denote superior rank" (542). There is no meaning "source." Another New Testament lexicon, the *Greek English Lexicon of the New Testament Based on Semantic Domains* edited by Johannes P. Louw and Eugene E. Nida[50] lists for *kephalē* the meaning, "one who is of supreme or preeminent status, in view of authority to order or command—'one who is the head of, one who is superior to, one who is supreme over'" (vol. 1, p. 739), but they give no meaning such as "source, origin."
2. The standard lexicon for the Greek of the early Christian writers after the time of the New Testament, Lampe's *Patristic Greek Lexicon*, includes the following meanings:

> **B.** of persons; **1.** *head* of the house, Herm. *sim.* 7.3; **2.** *chief, head-man*... **3.** religious *superior*... **4.** of bishops, *kephalai ekklēsiōn* [other examples include "of the bishop of the city of Rome, being head of all the churches"]... **5.** *kephalē einai* c. genit. [to be head, with genitive] *take precedence of* (p. 749).

All five of these categories include leadership and authority attaching to the term *kephalē*.

3. The standard lexicon for all of ancient Greek, the Liddell-Scott *Greek–English Lexicon*,[51] does have an entry in which it mentioned the sense "source" of a river for *kephalē* (in plural, but "mouth" of a river for *kephalē* singular). But this sense is listed under the general heading "of things, extremity," and simply meant

50. Two vols. (New York: United Bible Societies, 1988).
51. LS, *Greek-English Lexicon* (1996), *945*.

> that the "source" and the "mouth" of a river were at the two "end points" of the river, and *kephalē* was taking an established meaning, "end point, extremity."

This was clarified in a letter from P. G. W. Glare, the current editor of the Liddell-Scott Lexicon *Supplement,* dated April 14, 1997:

> Dear Professor Grudem,
>
> Thank you for sending me the copy of your article on κεφαλή. The entry under this word in LSJ is not very satisfactory. Perhaps I could draw your attention to a section of *Lexicographica Graeca* by Dr John Chadwick (OUP 1996), though he does not deal in detail with the Septuagint and NT material. I was unable to revise the longer articles in LSJ when I was preparing the latest Supplement, since I did not have the financial resources to carry out a full-scale revision.
>
> I have no time at the moment to discuss all your examples individually and in any case *I am in broad agreement with your conclusions*. I might just make one or two generalizations. κεφαλή is the word normally used to translate the Hebrew *ro'sh*, and this *does seem frequently to denote leader or chief* without much reference to its original anatomical sense, and here it *seems perverse to deny authority. The supposed sense "source" of course does not exist* and it was at least unwise of Liddell and Scott to mention the word. At the most they should have said "applied to the source of a river in respect of its position in its (the river's) course."
>
> By NT times the Septuagint had been well established and one would only expect that a usage found frequently in it would come easily to such a writer as St. Paul. Where I would agree with Cervin is that in many of the examples, and I think all the Plutarch ones, we are dealing with similes or comparisons and the word itself is used in a literal sense. Here we are faced with the inadequacies of LSJ. If they had clearly distinguished between, for example, "the head as the seat of the intellect and emotions (and therefore the director of the body's actions)" and "the head as the extremity of the human or animal body" and so on, these figurative examples would naturally be attached to the end of the section they belong to and the author's intention would be clear. I hasten to add that in most cases the sense of the head as being the controlling agent is the one required and that *the idea of preeminence seems to me to be quite unsuitable*, and that there are still cases where κεφαλή can be understood, as in the Septuagint, in its transferred sense of head or leader.
>
> Once again, thank you for sending me the article. I shall file it in the hope that one day we will be able to embark on a more thorough revision of the lexicon.
>
> Yours sincerely,
> Peter Glare[52]

52. Personal letter from P. G. W. Glare to Wayne Grudem, April 14, 1997. Italics for emphasis have been added. Quoted by permission.

This statement comes from someone who, because of his position and scholarly reputation, could rightly be called the preeminent Greek lexicographer in the world.

In conclusion, the question for egalitarians is this: Why should we give *kephalē* in the New Testament a sense which it is nowhere attested to have, and which, when applied to persons, no Greek lexicon gives it?

Answer 6.6f: The meaning "one who does not take advantage of his body" is mentioned in no lexicon and proven by no ancient citation.

Sarah Sumner has a long discussion of the meaning of "head" in which she concludes (apparently) that "head" means "someone who does not compete with his body and does not take advantage of his body." She writes:

> We can now discern the meaning of the metaphor of Christ's headship of every man. It means that "every man"—relative to Christ—is a body, not a head.... The whole point of what Paul was saying about men and women being interdependent in the Lord is to inspire us to cooperate, not compete. Christ does not compete with every man. Indeed, he is not the man's competitor but his head. This is extremely significant because the same holds true for men and women. The man is the head of a woman, not the opponent of the woman. In other words, men and women are not designed to compete with one another.... Men need headship lessons.... Christ—as the head "of every man"—offers special lessons one-on-one to every man, so that he can learn not to take advantage of women.... Men are commanded to use their relative strength not to put women down but rather to lift women up. They lift women up not as an act of leadership but rather as an act of headship. For a head can't help but want its body to be honored because the head and body are one.[53]

Sumner thus proposes a meaning that has never been mentioned in any lexicon, any scholarly article, or any commentary at any time in history. She asks readers to believe that she has seen a meaning for *kephalē* that no one in history has seen before this. In her discussion she interacts with few of the relevant passages that use this word. Her proposed meaning would make nonsense of many examples of *kephalē* cited above.[54] For example, does the statement that David is "head" of the conquered nations (2 Samuel 22:44) mean that he takes no advantage of them? Does the statement that Pekah the son of Remaliah is the "head" of Samaria (Isaiah 7:9) mean that he takes no advantage of the people of Samaria? Does the statement that the Roman emperor is head of the empire (Plutarch, *Galba* 4.3) mean that he takes no advantage of the people in the empire? Does the statement that the king of Egypt is head of the nation (Philo, *Moses* 2.30) mean that he takes no

53. Sumner, *Men and Women in the Church*, 187–89.
54. See pp. 204–5 above.

advantage of the people of Egypt? Surely these are not obvious meanings that ancient readers would see in these passages, and therefore it comes as no surprise that Greek lexicographers throughout history have never thought of Sumner's proposed meaning.

On the other hand, the first part of Sumner's statement quoted above may indicate that she thinks *kephalē* just means "someone who is related to a body."[55] She in fact says in another place that "Metaphorically...Christ is the body of God."[56] But this meaning also makes no sense in many places where person A is said to be the *kephalē* of person or persons B. To take some examples from the previous paragraph, surely we are not to think that the conquered nations are David's body, or that Samaria is Pekah's body, or that Egypt is the king's body. To take another example, Paul says that God has made Christ to be "head over all things" (Ephesians 1:22) and that Christ is the "head of all rule and authority" (Colossians 2:10). Does this mean that the whole universe is Christ's body? Or that Christ's body is "all rule and authority"? Sumner recognizes the difficulty in Colossians 2:10 but in response proposes a novel, three-part picture of "Christ as the Head, the church as His body, and all things, including all rule and authority, as being 'under his feet.'"[57] She apparently sees no difficulty with the picture of a person having his own body under his feet.

Sumner, like Belleville and Bilezikian, tries to avoid the idea of authority, the one idea that is present every time person A is said to be the *kephalē* of person B, and invents her own new meaning that is unprecedented in the scholarly literature and inconsistent with many examples of the word itself. Will egalitarian attempts to invent new meanings for *kephalē* never end?

Answer 6.6g: The meaning "preeminent one" is likewise mentioned in no lexicon and proven by no ancient citation.

Perhaps because the objections against "source" were so strong, some recent writers have proposed another alternative meaning for *kephalē*, namely, "preeminent, prominent (person)." This view is advocated by Richard Cervin,[58] Andrew Perriman,[59] and, most recently, Anthony Thiselton, in his massive and erudite recent commentary *The First Epistle to the Corinthians*.[60] Thiselton translates 1 Corinthians 11:3:

---

55. This idea also runs through some of her discussion in *Men and Women in the Church,* 182–9.
56. Ibid., 182.
57. Ibid., 152.
58. Richard S. Cervin, "Does *kephalē* Mean 'Source' or 'Authority' in Greek Literature? A Rebuttal," *TrinJ* 6 NS (1989), 85–112. I responded to Cervin at length in "The Meaning of *kephalē* ('Head')," *TrinJ* 11 NS (Spring 1990), 3–72 (reprinted in *Recovering Biblical Manhood and Womanhood,* ed. Piper and Grudem 425–68).
59. Andrew Perriman, "The Head of a Woman: The Meaning of κεφαλη in 1 Corinthians 11:3," *Journal of the Evangelical Theological Society* 45:2 (1994) 602–22.
60. Thiselton, *First Epistle to the Corinthians* (2000), 800–822. I respond to Thiselton more fully in Grudem, *Biblical Foundations for Manhood and Womanhood*, 194–99 (reprinted below, pp. 592–96).

> However, I want you to understand that while Christ is preeminent (or *head*? *source*?) in relation to man, man is foremost (or *head*? *source*?) [sic] in relation to woman, and God is preeminent (or *head*? *source*?) in relation to Christ.[61]

What is surprising, even remarkable, about Thiselton's treatment is that in the end he (like Cervin and Perriman before him) advocates a meaning for *kephalē* that is found in no Greek lexicon at all! (Recall the statement from lexicographer Peter Glare, in the letter quoted above, "the idea of preeminence seems to me to be quite unsuitable.") Surely everyone agrees that a person's head is one prominent and visible part of the person (though one might argue that one's face is more prominent than the head), but that does not prove that *kephalē* would have been used as a metaphor for "prominent part" in ancient Greek. Surely if such a meaning were evident in any ancient texts, we could expect some major lexicons to list it as a recognized meaning. Or else we should expect these authors to produce some ancient texts where the sense of "prominence" *absent any idea of authority* is clearly demonstrated. But we find neither.

And we suspect that there is something strange about a translation that cannot translate a simple noun meaning "head" with another noun (such as "authority over" or even "source"), but must resort to the convoluted and rather vague adjectival phrases, "prominent in relation to" and then "foremost in relation to."[62] Such phrases do not allow readers to notice that even if we tried to translate the noun *kephalē* with a noun phrase representing his idea (for example, "prominent part"), it would produce the nonsensical statements, "Christ is the prominent part of man," and "the man is the prominent part of the woman," and "God is the prominent part of Christ." Once we render Thiselton's idea in this bare-faced way, parallel to the way we would say that "the head is the prominent part of the body," the supposed connection with the prominence of our physical heads on our bodies falls apart, for, while the head is a part of our physical body, a man is surely not a "part of a woman," nor is God a "part of Christ."

Moreover, while Thiselton rightly notes that metaphors usually carry multiple layers of meaning in any language, that is not true of his translation. The Greek text contains a metaphor of the head in relation to the body. But Thiselton "translates" not the mere word but the metaphor itself in a way that renders *only one* component of meaning (or what he claims is one component of meaning). In his rendering, there is no metaphor left for English readers, and no opportunity even to consider multiple meanings. But he says he cannot translate it simply as "head" because "in English-speaking contexts 'the head' almost always implies leadership and authority."[63] Indeed. But how is that different from Greek when *kephalē* is applied to persons?

---

61. Thiselton, *First Epistle to the Corinthians*, 800.

62. I realize there are times when a word used as a metaphor in another language cannot be translated directly into English without significant loss of meaning and significant addition of incorrect meaning, such as Philippians 1:8, where the RSV's "I yearn for you all with the *affection* of Christ Jesus" is necessary instead of the KJV's literal "I long after you all in the *bowels* of Jesus Christ." But even here, some roughly equivalent noun ("affection," or, in Philemon 7, "hearts") is able to provide the necessary substitute.

63. Thiselton, *First Epistle to the Corinthians*, 817.

In fact, Thiselton's translation "preeminent" creates more problems than it solves, because it imports a wrongful kind of male superiority into the text. To be "preeminent" means to be "superior to or notable above all others; outstanding."[64] Does the Bible really teach that the man is "superior to" the woman? Or "notable above the woman"? Or "outstanding in comparison to the woman"? All of these senses carry objectionable connotations of male superiority, connotations that deny our equality in the image of God. And when applied to the Father and the Son in the Trinity, they carry wrongful implications of the inferiority of the Son to the Father.

Perhaps most telling of all is the fact that the one idea that Thiselton labors so long to avoid—the idea of one person having authority over another—is the one idea that is present in *every* ancient example of the construction that takes the form "Person A is the *head* of person or persons B." No counter-examples have ever been produced, so far as I am aware (see brief summary in Answer 6.6a).

Of course, I agree with Thiselton that in each of these occurrences the person who is "head" is also "prominent" in some sense. That is because some sense of prominence accompanies leadership or authority. And that overtone or connotation is not lost in English if we translate *kephalē* as "head," for also in English the "head coach" or the "head of the company" or the "head of the household" has some prominence as well. But why must we try to *avoid* the one meaning that is represented in all the lexicons and is unmistakably present in every instance of this kind of construction, the idea of authority? One cannot prove that this great effort to avoid the idea of authority is because male authority in marriage is immensely unpopular in much of modern culture, but I cannot help but note that it is in this current historical context that such efforts repeatedly occur.

In short, Thiselton has advocated a meaning that is unattested in any lexicon and unproven by any new evidence. It fails fundamentally in explaining the metaphor because it avoids the idea of authority, the one component of meaning present in every ancient example of *kephalē* that takes the form, "person A is the head of person(s) B."

Egalitarian claim 6.7: 1 Corinthians 7:3–5: In 1 Corinthians 7:3–5, Paul establishes an egalitarian model within marriage.

This argument is made by William Webb. The text in question is 1 Corinthians 7:3–5, where Paul says,

> The husband should give to his wife her conjugal rights, and likewise the wife to her husband. For the wife does not have authority over her own body, but the husband does. Likewise the husband does not have authority over his own body, but the wife

64. *American Heritage Dictionary,* 1997 ed., 1427.

> does. Do not deprive one another, except perhaps by agreement for a limited time, that you may devote yourselves to prayer; but then come together again, so that Satan may not tempt you because of your lack of self-control.

Webb claims that the explanation John Piper and I gave for this text in *Recovering Biblical Manhood and Womanhood*,[65] nullifies all male headship within marriage. Webb says that Piper and Grudem's approach "ultimately abandons their own position" because "once one has eliminated any power differential and set up mutual deference and mutual consent as the basis for *all* decision making in a marriage (such as Piper and Grudem have done) there is nothing that makes the view substantially different from egalitarianism."[66]

Answer 6.7a: This text modifies and restrains, but does not nullify, a husband's authority in marriage.

Webb has misread the argument that John Piper and I made. In the very section he refers to, we say,

> What are the implications of this text for the leadership of the husband? Do the call for mutual yielding to sexual need and the renunciation of unilateral planning nullify the husband's responsibility for general leadership in the marriage? We don't think so. But this text...makes clear that his leadership will not involve selfish, unilateral choices.[67]

Thus, John Piper and I agree that 1 Corinthians 7:3–5 shows that there are areas of mutual obligation between husband and wife, and that we can extrapolate from that and say that the husband's leadership in the marriage should not be a selfish leadership that fails to listen to the concerns of his wife. But in that very context, and in dozens of places throughout the rest of the book, we argue that the husband has an authoritative leadership role in the marriage that the wife does not have. Piper and I qualify and modify the concept of authority, as Scripture does, in many places, but we nevertheless affirm it throughout the rest of the book.

Egalitarian claim 6.8: No Offense to Roman Leaders: Paul taught that wives should be subject to their husbands because he did not want to offend the patriarchal culture, and especially the Roman leaders, of that time.

This is the argument of my friend Craig Keener in *Paul, Women and Wives*. In commenting on Ephesians 5, Keener says,

65. Piper and Grudem, "An Overview of Central Concerns: Questions and Answers," in *Recovering Biblical Manhood and Womanhood* (1991), 87–88.
66. Webb, *Slaves, Women and Homosexuals*, 101.
67. Piper and Grudem, "Overview of Central Concerns," 88.

> Paul, awaiting trial in Rome, would have been contemplating strategies to appeal to the powerbrokers in Rome whose decisions could set precedents for policies toward Christians elsewhere in the empire. His household codes may represent a long-range response to basic Roman cultural objections to the gospel. Stressing the wife's submission would be important for evangelizing resistant elements in the Roman world and for resisting progressive cultural temptations for wives to affirm too much independence.[68]

Answer 6.8a: Paul does not appeal to expectations of "powerbrokers" in the Roman culture, but to the relationship between Christ and the church, and to the marriage of Adam and Eve before there was sin. Both of these are permanent reasons that transcend all cultures.

Here is Paul's statement in Ephesians 5:

> Wives, submit to your own husbands, as to the Lord. *For* the husband is the head of the wife *even as Christ is the head of the church*, his body, and is himself its Savior. (vv. 22–23)

This reason does not depend on the attitudes of powerful men in Rome at the time Paul was writing. It is a permanent description of God's purpose in marriage from the beginning. Paul's other statement is similar:

> "Therefore a man shall leave his father and mother and hold fast to his wife, and the two shall become one flesh." This mystery is profound, and I am saying that it refers to Christ and the church. (Ephesians 5:31–32)

Here Paul reaches all the way back to Genesis 2:24. It was originally written in the context of the marriage of Adam and Eve, but Paul applies it to "Christ and the church." Paul is saying that God created Adam and Eve so their relationship would picture the relationship between Christ and the church. Adam and Eve did not know it at the time, but that was the wonderful purpose God had in mind. And that was the purpose God had in mind for marriage in general ("Therefore a man shall leave his father and his mother and hold fast to his wife"). Every marriage that ever exists *should* reflect the relationship between Christ and His church. And that relationship is not egalitarian, for Christ has an authority over the church that we do not have over Christ. Paul does not base his teaching on the expectations of powerful non-Christian Roman leaders, as Keener claims. Paul bases his teaching on God's purpose in Creation.

---

68. Keener, *Paul, Women and Wives* (1992), 147.

Answer 6.8b: This argument assumes that Paul taught something wrong in order to advance the gospel, or else that he taught something and then contradicted it.

Some who claim that Paul was just appealing to the culture in effect say that it was not God's highest ideal for wives to be subject to their husbands, but Paul taught it anyway so the gospel could gain a hearing in that culture. But this casts a shadow over Paul's moral authority, and throws into question the morality of the Bible's teachings. If it was not God's ideal for wives to be subject to husbands, but Paul taught it with his apostolic authority writing to the church at Ephesus (and also taught it in Colossians and in Titus), then Paul was repeatedly teaching something wrong. And thus the Bible is teaching something wrong.

This is a misunderstanding of Paul's principle of becoming "all things to all people, that by all means I might save some" (1 Corinthians 9:22), for in the immediately preceding verse Paul affirms that this will not lead him to do wrong. He says he is not "outside the law of God but under the law of Christ" (1 Corinthians 9:21). He would not teach wrongful male headship in marriage just to advance the gospel.

Keener recognizes this, so he says that Paul also taught "mutual submission," that the husband also had to be subject to his wife.[69] But to demand that husbands be *subject* to their wives denies the very male headship Keener thinks was needed to advance the gospel, and thus it nullifies the strategy of not offending Roman leaders! This argument is caught in a self-contradiction.

As I explained above, the idea of "mutual submission" is a misunderstanding of Ephesians 5:21. But if Keener thinks Ephesians 5:21 teaches mutual submission in a way that nullifies a husband's authority in the marriage, then he no longer can argue that Paul's teaching is meant to gain the approval of pagan Roman men who wanted to preserve authority over their wives.

Egalitarian claim 6.9: Submission Only for Evangelism: The purpose for a wife's submission to her husband at the time of the New Testament was evangelism, and since this purpose is no longer valid, wives need no longer be subject to their husbands.

William Webb says that Peter "tells wives to obey their husbands so that unbelieving husbands 'may be won over without words'" (1 Peter 3:1), but that today the kind of "unilateral, patriarchy-type submission" that Peter advocates "may actually repulse [the unbelieving husband] and prevent him from being won to Christ." Webb concludes that "the stated evangelistic purpose of the text is not likely to be fulfilled in our contemporary setting."[70] He takes this as an indication

69. Ibid., 148, 169.
70. Webb, *Slaves, Women and Homosexuals*, 107–8.

that the command is "culturally bound,"[71] and says a wife can fulfill the evangelistic purpose today in other ways:

> A wife today can still achieve the evangelistic purpose statements within the biblical text by showing her husband deference and respect within a mutual-submission, rather than a unilateral-submission, framework.[72]

Answer 6.9a: This position says wives should not obey 1 Peter 3:1–2 today.

We should be very clear what Webb is saying here. He is saying there should be no unique authority for husbands in our modern culture. He is saying that wives with unbelieving husbands today should not obey 1 Peter 3:1–2, which says,

> Likewise, wives, be subject to your own husbands, so that even if some do not obey the word, they may be won without a word by the conduct of their wives—when they see your respectful and pure conduct.

Webb's assertion trivializes the testimony of thousands of Christian women even today whose unbelieving husbands *have* been won by the submissive behavior of their believing wives.

Answer 6.9b: This position makes Christian evangelism into a bait-and-switch technique.

A second problem with Webb's claim is that it makes first-century Christian evangelism into the ultimate "bait and switch" sales technique. Webb claims that Peter's command aimed to attract non-Christian husbands by the submissive behavior of their wives, but once these men became Christians and began to grow toward maturity they would discover the "seed ideas" for equality and mutual submission in texts such as Galatians 3:28, and then (according to Webb) they would learn that *this command for submission of their wives is a morally deficient pattern* that has to be abandoned in favor of an egalitarian position. Therefore, according to the logic of Webb's position, first-century evangelism was a deceptive maneuver in which the Word of God told people to use a morally deficient pattern of behavior simply to win unbelievers.

Answer 6.9c: This position will lead people to disobey other New Testament commands.

The third problem with Webb's explanation is that it opens the door for people to disobey many other New Testament commands if they think the reason for the command will no longer be fulfilled in our culture. For example, the command to be subject to human government is also based on an expected good outcome:

---

71. Ibid., 105.
72. Ibid., 108.

> Be subject for the Lord's sake to every human institution, whether it be to the emperor as supreme, or to governors as sent by him to punish those who do evil and to praise those who do good. For this is the will of God, *that by doing good you should put to silence the ignorance of foolish people.* (1 Peter 2:13–15)

But people today could say that being subject to government might not "put to silence the ignorance of foolish people," because some governments in some societies today are so hardened against the gospel that it will make no difference to them. Therefore (according to reasoning similar to Webb's) we would not have to obey that command either.[73]

Answer 6.9d: This position minimizes other reasons for submission given in the New Testament.

A fourth problem with Webb's approach is that it minimizes the *other reasons* given in the New Testament for a wife's submission to her husband.[74] Paul says,

> Wives, submit to your own husbands, as to the Lord. *For* the husband is the head of the wife even as Christ is the head of the church.... (Ephesians 5:22–23)

Similarly, when Paul talks about being subject to "the governing authorities" he does not give evangelism as the reason, but rather says that the agent of the government "is the servant of God, an avenger who carries out God's wrath on the wrongdoer. Therefore one must be in subjection, not only to avoid God's wrath but also for the sake of conscience" (Romans 13:4–5).

It is better to reject Webb's redemptive-movement hermeneutic and see the New Testament as the words of God for us today, words that contain God's morally pure standards for us to obey, and to obey *all* of the New Testament commands *simply because they are the words of God* who holds us responsible for obeying them. We do not have the right to take it upon ourselves to say, as Webb's position implies, "If a wife today submits to her unbelieving husband according to 1 Peter 3:1, I don't think that will help evangelism in our modern culture, so women should not follow that text today." That is setting up our own moral judgment as a higher standard than God's Word.

---

73. Webb says that we should be subject to the law today, not to political leaders (*Slaves, Women and Homosexuals,* 107), but Peter's admonition to be subject to "every human institution" surely includes both the law and the government officials. We are subject not just to the law, but to the people who enforce the law and who are representatives of the government and bear its authority today.

74. Webb admits, "There may be more than one purpose involved in giving a biblical command," and he allows for the "possibility" of other purposes for commands like this, but he names none, and he says if there were other purposes "one would be left with fulfilling a certain purpose but failing to fulfill others," and says there would then be a "modified application" (*Slaves, Women and Homosexuals*, 108). His next paragraph, on application, takes back even this hypothetical qualification, for it names no other purposes and it encourages wives to act as if the submission commands were not obligatory for them today.

EGALITARIAN CLAIM 6.10: YOUNG AND UNEDUCATED WIVES: WIVES WERE TO BE SUBJECT TO THEIR HUSBANDS AT THE TIME OF THE NEW TESTAMENT BECAUSE THEY WERE YOUNGER AND LESS EDUCATED THAN THEIR HUSBANDS, BUT THIS IS NOT TRUE TODAY, SO THE COMMAND NO LONGER APPLIES.

William Webb says that it made sense for wives to submit to their husbands in an ancient culture because of several "pragmatic factors": they had less education, less social exposure, less physical strength, and they were significantly younger than their husbands.[75] But most of these reasons, says Webb, no longer apply today,[76] and therefore the command for wives to be subject to their husbands should be seen as culturally relative. A wife today should just give some kind of "honor" and "respect" to her husband.[77]

Answer 6.10a: These are not the reasons Paul gives, and they would not apply to all wives.

Webb's argument here is not persuasive, however, because these are not the reasons the Bible gives for wives to be subject to their husbands. Two reasons the Bible gives are the parallel with Christ's relationship to the church (Ephesians 5:22–24) and the parallel with the relationship between the Father and Son in the Trinity (1 Corinthians 11:3). Another reason that Paul gives is that this is what "is fitting in the Lord" (Colossians 3:18). Yet another reason is that it is part of "what is good" (Titus 2:3–4), and another reason is that unbelieving husbands may be "won without a word by the conduct of their wives" (1 Peter 3:1).

By contrast, Webb's reasons here are merely speculative, and there is no indication that the biblical authors are taking these factors into account when they give these commands. Moreover, these New Testament commands apply to *all* wives, even those who were more intelligent than their husbands, or the same age as their husbands, or physically as strong as their husbands, or had as much social exposure and social rank as their husbands, or as much wealth as their husbands. Webb's reasons are simply not the reasons the Bible uses.

In short, Webb says that the Bible teaches a wife's submission because of Webb's own invented reasons. Then he removes these invented reasons for today's culture and concludes that we can count the command as culturally relative. It would be far better to heed the reasons that the Bible actually gives for wives to be subject to husbands.

75. Webb, *Slaves, Women and Homosexuals*, 213–14.
76. He says the only remaining difference is physical strength, and that is not so important today.
77. Webb, *Slaves, Women and Homosexuals*, 215.

Egalitarian claim 6.11: No Other Options: The Bible adopted male leadership because there were no competing options in society at that time, but there are other options today, so male headship in the family is not required.

William Webb says, "It is reasonably safe to assume, therefore, that the social reality of the biblical writers was the world of patriarchy.... This consideration increases the likelihood of patriarchy being a cultural component within Scripture."[78] Webb explains that an egalitarian position regarding marriage or the church was simply not an option, given the strongly patriarchal nature of the surrounding culture.

Answer 6.11a: The New Testament taught many things that were unpopular in the culture.

Webb's argument is not persuasive. The New Testament teaches many things that were not found in the surrounding culture. Before Jesus' earthly ministry, there were no people in the surrounding culture who believed that Jesus of Nazareth, the son of Joseph and Mary, was the Messiah. Even Webb admits that the idea that husbands should love their wives as Christ loved the church was revolutionary for the surrounding culture. The idea that there could be a church made up of Jews and Gentiles fellowshipping together on an equal basis was not an option in the surrounding culture.

Scripture often challenges and transforms the societies and cultures into which it speaks. Therefore, if a truly egalitarian model for marriage had been what God wanted for His people, He surely could have proclaimed it clearly through the pages of the New Testament and through the teachings of Jesus and the apostles. But (as Webb admits) the New Testament itself does not teach such a fully egalitarian position. According to Webb, we therefore have to move beyond the ethic of the New Testament to reach full egalitarianism.

It is interesting to see that Webb, whose system allows him to tell us that we do not have to obey the moral commands of the New Testament, does not mind admitting that the New Testament taught a complementarian view for its time. This is different from most egalitarians, who have not used Webb's system of interpretation and who therefore are still trying to prove the impossible—that the New Testament teaches an egalitarian view of men and women in marriage even for its own time.

---

78. Ibid., 154–55.

Conclusion

We have considered several major egalitarian objections to a complementarian view of marriage in this chapter. The egalitarian claims—(a) that Galatians 3:28 abolishes role differences between men and women, (b) that "mutual submission" in Ephesians 5:21 nullifies male headship, (c) that "head" actually means "source," (d) that Paul's teachings were given merely to advance the gospel for that time, and (e) that these commands were culturally relative—are all found to be unpersuasive, and do not represent the meaning of Scripture accurately. A complementarian view of male–female equality together with male headship is still the most persuasive understanding of the relevant New Testament texts.

CHAPTER SEVEN

Evangelical Feminist Claims About the Church from the New Testament Epistles

When we turn to the teachings about church leadership in the New Testament epistles, egalitarians propose many claims that would undermine the idea of restricting some leadership roles to men. For instance, aren't there women such as Phoebe and Junia who hold leading positions in the church? In addition, in 1 Corinthians 11, Paul clearly says that women could prophesy, and isn't that a leading role that indicates much influence in the church? Paul also had women as his coworkers in a number of cases, and perhaps there are indications of other women in leadership roles, such as deacons. In short, there are abundant evidences of women in leadership roles in the epistles.

Egalitarians propose several alternative ways of understanding passages such as 1 Corinthians 14:34 that seem to restrict the role of women. Perhaps these verses are a Corinthian quotation that Paul rejects? Or perhaps they are just applicable to a special situation in Corinth where women were shouting questions and disrupting the worship service?

In this chapter, we consider such egalitarian claims regarding the New Testament epistles' teaching about women in the church. However, the material on 1 Timothy 2:11–15 is so extensive that I have put it in a separate chapter, which follows this one.

EGALITARIAN CLAIM 7.1: PHOEBE AS LEADER: ROMANS 16:2 SAYS THAT PHOEBE WAS A "LEADER" OR "RULER" OF MANY PEOPLE, AND EVEN OF PAUL HIMSELF.

Romans 16:2 says that Phoebe "has been a *patron* (Greek *prostatis*) of many and of myself as well" (ESV). Other translations say that Phoebe was a "helper": The NASB says, "She herself has also been a *helper* of many, and of myself as well," and the NIV says, "For she has been a great *help* to many people, including me."

But Aida Spencer and several other egalitarians dispute this translation. Spencer says the verse means that Phoebe was a leader and ruler over Paul:

> The verb form of *prostatis*, which is *proistēmi*, literally signifies "to stand, place before or over."... Phoebe...is "a woman set over others" or "one who stands before." No other person is called a *prostatis* in the New Testament.... ***She has been a leader over many and even over Paul!***... The verb form *proistēmi*...with the genitive signifies "I am set over, I am the head of"..."I govern, direct," and "I stand before so as to guard".... The noun *prostatis* takes the genitive case of "many" and "me" to indicate these are the persons over whom Phoebe has been set. Phoebe is an explicit, commendable example of ***a woman set in authority over a man***, in this case, the great apostle Paul.[1]

Answer 7.1a: We should be hesitant to accept an interpretation that is found in no English translation.

A general word of caution that applies to many egalitarian claims discussed in this book is this: When an author claims a meaning for a word that is found in no English translation, and in fact is not even close to any meaning given in the text or margin of any English translation, we should require extensive evidence for such a meaning. That is the case here, for Spencer's translation "leader" is significantly different from "helper," "patron," "benefactor," and similar terms used in the common English Bible translations.[2]

In addition, when the interpretation creates an apparent conflict with other things found in the New Testament, it becomes even more doubtful. In this case, we recall that the apostle Paul did not think that even the Jerusalem apostles ruled over him. His apostleship, as did his message, came "not from men nor through man, but through Jesus Christ and God the Father, who raised him from the dead" (Galatians 1:1, 11–12). The status of "those who seemed to be influential" in the Jerusalem church was not greater than Paul, for he says, "what they were makes no difference to me; God shows no partiality" (Galatians 2:6), and he goes on to tell of how he rebuked Peter publicly (Galatians 2:11–14).

Spencer's argument therefore is inconsistent with the clear New Testament evidence that the apostle Paul did not consider himself subject to any human leader but to Jesus Christ alone.

---

1. Spencer, *Beyond the Curse* (1985), 115–16 (italics added). Spencer is quoted with approval by Tucker, *Women in the Maze* (1992), 100. See also Brown, *Women Ministers* (1996), 167; and Jacobs, *Women of Destiny* (1998), 181–82, who quotes, in support of the idea that Phoebe was a leader, a book by Trombley, *Who Said Women Can't Teach* (1985), 194–95. However, something has gone wrong with Jacobs's quote, because she quotes Trombley as basing the argument on "the verb *peritoneum*" in 1 Timothy 3:4–5, 12 (p. 182). There is no such Greek verb as *peritoneum*, nor does any Greek verb end with *-eum*. The verb *proistēmi* is found in those verses, however, and Trombley had *proistēmi* on p. 195.
2. The archaic KJV word *succourer* has a similar sense to these other translations. The other common English translations have "patron" (ESV), "helper" (NASB, RSV, NKJV), "help" (NIV), "has helped" (NLT), and "benefactor" (NRSV).

Answer 7:1b: Recent Greek lexicons show the meaning "patron" or "helper" to be most likely.

The two most recent Greek lexicons do not give the meaning "leader" for *prostatis*, which is the actual word used in Romans 16:2. The BDAG lexicon defines it as "woman in a supportive role, *patron, benefactor*" (885), and similarly defines the related masculine noun *prostatēs* as "one who looks out for the interest of others, *defender, guardian, benefactor*" (885). The Louw-Nida lexicon defines *prostatis* as "a woman who is active in helping—'helper, patroness...'" (1.459). While the older lexicon by Thayer did give the entry, "properly *a woman set over others*,"[3] that is apparently just an explanation of the word's connection to the masculine form *prostatēs*, and no actual examples are given. But the next meaning explains in what sense this is intended, because with specific reference to Romans 16:2 it says, "*a female guardian, protectress, patroness,* caring for the affairs of others and aiding them with her resources" (549).[4]

Answer 7.1c: Spencer has constructed a lexical "sleight of hand" argument, because she is not defining the noun *prostatis* but the related verb *proistēmi*, and words don't take all the meanings of all the other words that are related to them.

It is not legitimate to say "Word A is related to word B, and word B has a certain meaning, therefore, word A has this meaning as well."

Words just don't take all the meanings of related words. This is a simple fact of human language. For example, the word *butterfly* is related to *butter* and *fly*, but that does not mean that *butterfly* means "a pound of butter that has learned to fly." The word *conscience* is related to *science,* and the prefix *con* often means "with." But that does not mean that a "conscience" is only something that functions "with science." One meaning of *light* is "not heavy," but that does not mean that the word *enlighten* means "to make not heavy." Relationships among words are extremely complex, and we should put primary emphasis on *uses of a word itself,* not on related words.

Of course, words are often related in meaning to other words formed from the same root, but that is not always the case. *Autograph, automatic, automobile,* and *autopsy* do not mean the same thing, nor is an autopsy something one does on oneself! We cannot just take the meaning of one word and import it into another, related word (which is exactly what this argument does).

To take a Greek example, this argument follows the same logic as if someone argued that

3. Thayer, *Greek-English Lexicon of the 4ew Testament* (1901), 549.
4. The LS *Lexicon* defines *prostatis* as "feminine of *prostatēs*" (1527), but *prostatēs* takes a range of meanings, including not only "leader, ruler" but also "patron" (1527), and LS gives no discussion of which senses of *prostatēs* are also taken by the feminine form.

"crucifying once again" in Hebrews 6:6 really means "resurrect from the dead," because the word in Hebrews 6:6, *anastauroō*, is related to the word for "resurrection," which is *anastasis*. Both terms come from the prefix *ana* attached to a form of the verb *histēmi*, "to stand."[5] Such an argument is foolish, of course, but it is the same kind of argument being made by those who say that Phoebe was a "leader" based on Romans 16:2.

But if the noun *prostatis* is related to the verb *proistēmi*, then shouldn't we expect that their meanings will be at least somehow related? While it is not certain, we would expect that a noun and related verb will often have similar meanings. But even if we grant this, what Spencer (like others who use this argument) does not reveal to readers is that the related verb *proistēmi* can also mean, "to have an interest in, *show concern for, care for, give aid*" (BDAG, 870). And this seems to be the sense in which the noun *prostatis* is used in Romans 16:2. So even if we expect a related meaning, Spencer incorrectly depends on a selective citation of meaning for the verb *proistēmi* to explain the noun *prostatis*.

Romans 16:2 has another word built on the same *histēmi* root as *prostatis*, and Paul is probably making a play on words, for he says that the church should "help (*paristēmi*) her in whatever way she may require from you for she has been a helper (*prostatis*) of many and of myself as well" (Romans 16:2, RSV).

Egalitarian claim 7.2: Junia: There was even a woman apostle, Junia (Romans 16:7). If a woman can be an apostle, she can hold any other church office as well.

In Romans 16:7, Paul writes, "Greet Andronicus and Junias [or *Junia*], my kinsmen and my fellow prisoners, who are outstanding among the apostles, who also were in Christ before me" (NASB).

Egalitarians regularly claim that this refers to a woman named Junia, who was an apostle. Aida Spencer writes,

> Junia (and her male colleague Andronicus) would be Paul's counterpart in Rome. As an apostle, sent by God as an eyewitness to the resurrection of Jesus, Paul would lay the foundation for a church. Certainly authoritative preaching would have to be part of such a testimony. Junia, along with Andronicus, apparently laid the foundation for the churches at Rome.[6]

---

5. See Greenlee, *A New Testament Greek Morpheme Lexicon* (1983), 11:194–95, for a list of New Testament Greek words related to *histēmi*. Greenlee derived his lists from the designation of component parts of words in the abridged LS *Lexicon*, with help from more extensive works when necessary (see p. viii).
6. Spencer, *Beyond the Curse*, 102.

Similarly, Gilbert Bilezikian writes,

> Paul sends greetings in Rome to Andronicus and Junias, probably a husband-and-wife team of veteran missionaries, who are told to be "outstanding among the apostles" (Rom. 16:7).... The term apostle connoted the highest level of leadership and authority in the early church.... Even in its broader, more general use, it was an appellation of the highest distinction. Apparently, the openness of the early church to women in positions of leadership was such that their identification as "apostles" was received without difficulty.[7]

Answer 7.2a: The name that is spelled *iounian* in the Greek text of Romans 16:7 could be either a man's name or a woman's name simply according to the spelling.

Just as in English there are some names (such as Chris or Pat) that could be either a man's name or a woman's name, so in Greek, this name could be either masculine or feminine, and we cannot tell from the spelling alone.[8] Some translations have taken it as Junias (NIV, NASB, RSV, ASV), and some have taken it as Junia (KJV, NKJV, NRSV, NLT, ESV), usually indicating the alternative in the margin.

Answer 7.2b: In light of the most recent research in Greek grammar, the verse means, "Greet Andronicus and Junia(s)...well-known *to the apostles*."

The verse is best understood to say not that Andronicus and Junia(s) were "well-known *among* the apostles" but "well known *to* the apostles" (so ESV, NET Bible). Therefore it does not make much difference if this is a man's or a woman's name, because it does not say that Junia(s) was an apostle.

Prior to 2001, scholars had not done any significant computer-assisted research on the Greek construction (*episēmos* + dative) that is found in this verse, and therefore writings and translations before 2001 usually assumed that the meaning "well known *among*" was correct. But then in 2001, in an extensively researched technical article, the meaning "well known *to*" received strong support, with significant evidence from extrabiblical Greek.[9] A note to the NET

---

7. Bilezikian, *Beyond Sex Roles* (1985), 198. See also Keener, *Paul, Women and Wives* (1992), 241–42; Groothuis, *Good News for Women* (1997), 194–96; Brown, *Women Ministers*, 183; Jacobs, *Women of Destiny*, 184–86; Grady, *Ten Lies* (2000), 41; and Perriman, *Speaking of Women* (1998), 68–70. However, Belleville, *Women Leaders and the Church* (2000), 54–56, thinks that "apostle" here is not used in the same sense as it was with Paul and the Twelve, but in the sense of "church planter."
8. The ending *-an* is the accusative singular ending for a first declension masculine name ending in *-as (Iounias)* or for a first declension feminine name *(Iounia)* ending in *-a*.
9. M. H. Burer and D. B. Wallace, "Was Junia Really an Apostle? A Reexamination of Romans 16:7," *New Testament Studies* 47 (2001): 76–91.

Bible (in which Dan Wallace had significant influence after his research was underway, but prior to the publication of his article) explains, "in collocation with words of perception, (*en* plus) dative personal nouns are often used to show the recipients."[10]

The ESV (published in the fall of 2001) therefore translates the verse,

> Greet Andronicus and Junia [or *Junias*], my kinsmen and my fellow prisoners. They are *well known to the apostles* [or *messengers*], and they were in Christ before me.

This means that the verse does not even name Junia (Junias) as an apostle. It just says that the apostles know her (or him) well, and also Andronicus.[11]

Answer 7.2c: There is very little comment on this name in the first four hundred years after the New Testament, and the comments are mixed regarding the gender of the name.

Here are the dates of the earliest citations:[12]

WRITER	DIED	ROMANS 16:7
Origen	254	Junias[13]
Ambrosiaster	after 384	Junia
Epiphanius	403	Junias ("became bishop of Apameia of Syria")
Chrysostom	407	Junia
Rufinus	410 (once)	Junia
Jerome	419/420	Junia
Theodoretca of Cyrrhus	466	Junia

The quotation from the historian Epiphanius (315–403) is interesting: "Junias, of whom

10. *NET Bible*, note to Romans 16:7.

11. Keener writes, "Paul knows them well enough to recommend them without appealing to the other apostles, whose judgment he never cites on such matters" (Keener, *Paul, Women and Wives,* 242). Of course Paul did not have to appeal to the other apostles, but this does not mean he could not add the additional commendation that the apostles knew Andronicus and Junia(s) well.

12. Details of these citations can be found in Fitzmyer, *Romans* (1993), 737–38.

13. Origen (ca. 185–ca. 254) on Romans 16:7 understood *iounian* as masculine (in Migne 14.1280–81 and 1289; cited by Lightfoot, *The Epistle of St. Paul to the Galatians* [1957], 96, who refers to Origen on Romans 16:21 T. iv., p. 682D in Migne, and Origen on Rom. 16:39, ibid., p. 686E in Migne). Some have claimed that the text of Origen as recorded in the Migne edition is not reliable at this point (most refer to Brooten, "'Junia…outstanding among the Apostles,'" in *Women Priests*, 141). However, I have not been able independently to evaluate the evidence for Brooten's claim. The transcriptional error in the text recorded in Migne, if there was one, would have to have occurred in both places in Origen's commentary on Romans.

14. *Index discipulorum* 125.19–20. Epiphanius is a recognized ancient historian, but in the previous lines he refers to Prisca also as a man, which is puzzling and is not correct. In any case, in light of both the Origen quotes and the statement by Epiphanius, who claims knowledge of what happened to Junias, an absolute statement such as that of Linda Belleville is not true: Belleville says, "The fact of the matter is that no translator or commentator prior to the Middle Ages understood *Iounian* as anything other than feminine" (Belleville,

Paul makes mention, became bishop of Apameia of Syria."[14] If these citations from Origen and Epiphanius are accurate, two of the three earliest writers take Junia(s) as a man. However, both citations have been challenged as based on corrupted texts.[15]

From then on writers take it as a woman's name (Junia), but the relevance of a collection of these later patristic and medieval citations is minimal, for many writers could be simply imitating an earlier tradition. It is highly doubtful that they would have had any independent information about this person named only once in the New Testament, or any additional knowledge of the gender of a name that is rare in Greek in any case. And the increasing prominence of Latin over Greek, with the fact that Junia is a common woman's name in Latin, would have made it more likely that they would take it as a woman's name.

Answer 7.2d: However, evidence from Latin seems to favor the view that this was a woman's name, Junia.

Though Paul was writing in Greek, he was writing to Rome, and therefore many commentators favor the name Junia, which was a fairly common woman's name in Latin. But Junias (masculine) was unknown as a man's name. This common use of Junia as a woman's name in Latin has persuaded many commentators, and most recent commentators, to think of this as probably a woman's name.[16] Latin names would of course be common in Rome. However, this argument is not decisive, for Junias is possible as a shortened form of a man's name Junianus (like Silas for Silvanus; such shortened forms are common in the New Testament).[17] Overall, the evidence from Latin names seems to favor a woman's name here,[18] but even that only establishes a probability, not a firm conclusion.

Answer 7.2e: The word translated "apostles" could just mean "church messengers" here as it does elsewhere in Paul's writings.

A further uncertainty about this verse is the word translated "apostles." This same term

---

"Women in Ministry" [2001], 85). Many other writers make similar absolute claims, showing no knowledge of or interaction with the evidence from Epiphanius or the Migne manuscripts of Origen.

15. See the previous two footnotes.

16. This consideration was important to the translators of the English Standard Version, who put "Junia" in the text and "Or *Junias*" in the margin. See also Moo, *Epistle to the Romans* (1996), 921–24, with extensive discussion and bibliography. Moo takes the name as feminine ("Junia") and concludes that "apostle" here probably means "traveling missionary" (924). Andreas Köstenberger also concludes that "the meaning 'traveling missionary' is...most likely" ("Women in the Pauline Mission," in *The Gospel to the Nations*, 231).

17. For a long list of examples see A. T. Robertson, *A Grammar of the Greek New Testament in the Light of Historical Research* (1934), 172–73; also Blass and Debrunner, *A Greek Grammar of the New Testament* (1961), sec. 125, 1–2:67–8. Fitzmyer says that if this were a shortened form of a man's name, "such a name would indicate that he was at first a slave, then freed by a dominus named 'Junius'" (*Romans,* 738).

18. John Piper and I earlier argued that it should be taken as a man's name, based on the early citations and the fact that both names are rare in Greek. See Piper and Grudem, "Overview of Central Concerns," in *Recovering Biblical Manhood and Womanhood* (1991), 79–81. However, we did not give much weight to the evidence from Latin names in that earlier discussion.

(Greek *apostolos*) is used elsewhere in the New Testament to mean "messenger, one who is sent" when it refers to people who were not apostles in the sense of the Twelve or Paul: We see this use in John 13:16, "nor is a *messenger* greater than the one who sent him"; also 2 Corinthians 8:23, referring to the men who were accompanying Paul in bringing money to Jerusalem, "they are *messengers* of the churches"; and Paul tells the Philippians that Epaphroditus, who came to him, is "your *messenger* and minister to my need" (Philippians 2:25). Since Andronicus and Junia(s) are otherwise unknown as apostles, even if someone wanted to translate "well known *among*," the sense "well known among the messengers" would be more appropriate.[19]

Answer 7.2f: In conclusion, the feminist claim that there was an apostle named Junia is built upon one uncertainty (the gender of the name) on top of another uncertainty (the meaning of "apostle" in this verse) on top of an improbable meaning of a phrase ("well known among" rather than "well known to").

This is a highly speculative and flimsy foundation upon which to base any argument. It carries little weight against the clear teaching of exclusive male eldership and male apostleship in the rest of the New Testament.

EGALITARIAN CLAIM 7.3: WOMEN COULD PROPHESY: WOMEN COULD PROPHESY IN THE NEW TESTAMENT (1 CORINTHIANS 11:5), AND THIS IMPLIES THAT THEY COULD ALSO TEACH GOD'S WORD AND BE PASTORS OR ELDERS.

Many egalitarians make this argument. Gilbert Bilezikian writes,

> In Paul's graded scale of the "greater gifts" and of their corresponding ministries, prophecy is given second place after apostles (1 Cor. 12:28). According to Paul's teaching, both men and women had access to this ministry in the early church (1 Cor. 11:4–5).[20]

Linda Belleville says,

> Teaching was also a part of what a prophet did. "You can all prophesy in turn," Paul says to the Corinthians, "so that everyone may be instructed and encouraged" (1 Cor. 14:31; cf. 14:19 "to instruct," *katecheō*). Since there were women prophets in

19. Another alternative meaning, with a broader sense of "apostle," is "traveling missionaries," which Moo favors (see footnote 16 above).
20. Bilezikian, *Beyond Sex Roles*, 199.
21. Belleville, *Women Leaders and the Church*, 59.

Corinth (1 Cor. 11:5), instruction was most definitely part of their role.[21]

Aida Spencer says,

> The prophet functioned in the service as does a contemporary preacher.... The New Testament provides clear examples of women who are called prophets and described as prophesying. Prophets come second in Paul's list of the priority of gifts and second in his list of persons given to the church.[22]

Answer 7.3a: Prophecy and teaching are not the same. They are always viewed as separate gifts in the New Testament.

People who claim "prophesying was the same as preaching and teaching," or "if women can prophesy they can teach the Bible," fail to understand how clearly the New Testament distinguishes prophecy and teaching. They are always viewed as separate gifts:

> Romans 12:6–7: "Having gifts that differ according to the grace given to us, let us use them: if *prophecy*, in proportion to our faith; if service, in our serving; the one who *teaches*, in his teaching."

> 1 Corinthians 12:28–29: "And God has appointed in the church first apostles, second *prophets*, third *teachers*, then miracles, then gifts of healing, helping, administrating, and various kinds of tongues. Are all apostles? Are all *prophets*? Are all *teachers*? Do all work miracles?"

> Ephesians 4:11: "And he gave the apostles, the *prophets*, the evangelists, the pastors and *teachers*."

Answer 7.3b: Prophecy in the New Testament is reporting something God spontaneously brings to mind, while teaching is explaining and applying Scripture or the teachings of the apostles.

The authority of a prophet is unlike the authority of a teacher. Prophecy is always "reporting something God spontaneously brings to mind,"[23] as in 1 Corinthians 14:30–31, where Paul pictures one prophet speaking and then says, "If a *revelation* is made to another sitting there, let the first be silent. For you can all *prophesy* one by one." God suddenly brought something to someone's mind.

---

22. Spencer, *Beyond the Curse,* 103, 106. See also Brown, *Women Ministers,* 247; Grady, *Ten Lies,* 44; Perriman, *Speaking of Women,* 73, 83.
23. See my defense of this view of prophecy in Grudem, *Gift of Prophecy* (2000). A brief summary of my position is found in Grudem, *Systematic Theology*, 1049–61. (The difference between prophecy and teaching is also maintained by those who differ with my understanding of the gift of prophecy in the New Testament; see answer 7.3f below, pp. 231–32.)

Or in 1 Corinthians 14:25, if a stranger comes in and all prophesy, "the secrets of his heart are disclosed; and so, falling on his face, he will worship God and declare that God is really among you." God had suddenly brought to people's minds things they would not otherwise know.

As far as I can tell from the relevant passages, all New Testament prophecy was based on this kind of spontaneous prompting from the Holy Spirit. Agabus's prophecy of a famine had to be based on such a revelation (Acts 11:28), and so did his prediction of Paul's imprisonment in Jerusalem (Acts 21:10–11). The disciples at Tyre apparently had some kind of indication from God about the dangers Paul would encounter in Jerusalem (Acts 21:4). And even in John 11:51, when Caiaphas spoke unknowingly of Jesus' death for the people, he "prophesied." By contrast, no prophecy in New Testament churches is ever said to consist of the interpretation and application of texts of Scripture.

But teaching is different. In contrast to the gift of prophecy, no human speech called "teaching" (*didaskalia, didachē*) or an act done by a "teacher" (*didaskalos*), or described by the verb "teach" (*didaskō*), is ever said to be based on a "revelation" in the New Testament. Rather, teaching is usually an explanation and application of Scripture.

In Acts 15:35, Paul and Barnabas and "many others" are in Antioch "*teaching* and preaching *the word of the Lord*." At Corinth, Paul stayed one and a half years "*teaching* the *word of God* among them" (Acts 18:11). And the author of Hebrews tells his readers, "you need someone to teach you again the basic principles of the oracles of God" (Hebrews 5:12). Paul tells Timothy that "all *Scripture*" is "profitable for *teaching*" (2 Timothy 3:16). Since the apostles' writings had equal authority to the written Old Testament Scripture (see 2 Peter 3:2, 15–16), it is not surprising that Paul told Timothy to "command and teach" (1 Timothy 4:11) and to "teach and urge" (1 Timothy 6:2) Paul's instructions to the Ephesian church.

The difference with prophecy is quite clear here: Timothy wasn't to *prophesy* Paul's instructions; he was to *teach* them. Paul didn't prophesy his ways in every church; he taught them. The Thessalonians were not told to hold firm to the traditions that were "prophesied" to them but to the traditions they were "taught."

It was not prophecy but teaching that provided the doctrinal and ethical norms by which the church was regulated. An elder was to be "able to *teach*" (1 Timothy 3:2; cf. Titus 1:9), not "able to prophesy"! Timothy was to take heed to himself and to his "teaching" (1 Timothy 4:16), but he is never told to take heed to his prophesying. James warned that those who *teach*, not those who *prophesy*, will be judged with greater strictness (James 3:1).

So teaching in the New Testament epistles consisted of explaining and applying the words of Scripture or the equally authoritative teachings of Jesus and of the apostles. In the New Testament epistles, "teaching" was very much like what we call "Bible teaching" today.

Many charismatic and Pentecostal churches today understand this difference quite well: Prophecy, like other miraculous gifts, is subject to the governing authority of the elders or pastors of the church. Prophecy and teaching are different gifts.

Answer 7.3c. Therefore it makes sense to say that women could prophesy but not teach in the church.

Prophesying did not carry the same authority as teaching. Therefore it makes sense that Paul would allow women to prophesy but not to teach. It was those who taught, particularly the elders, who governed the church.

It also makes sense, therefore, for Paul to say that women could prophesy but could not speak out and judge prophecies in the church, for the judging of prophecies was assuming governing authority over the assembled congregation. (See claim 7.4 on 1 Corinthians 14:34–35, pp. 232–35.)

In the early church, the church father Tertullian (c. 160/170–c. 215/220) taught that women could prophesy but not teach in the church:

> In precisely the same manner, when enjoining on women silence in the church, that they speak not for the mere sake of learning (although that even they have the right of prophesying, he has already shown when he covers the woman that prophesies with a veil), he goes to the law for his sanction that woman should be under obedience.[24]

He also wrote,

> It is not permitted to a woman to speak in the church; but neither [is it permitted her] to teach, nor to baptize.[25]

This means that from a very early period in the history of the church, at least some recognized that women had a right to prophesy, but they were not allowed to teach in the church.

Answer 7.3d: The fact that people can learn from prophecies does not mean that prophets were the same as teachers.

It is true that people learn from prophecies, as is seen in 1 Corinthians 14:31: "For you can all prophesy one by one, so that all may *learn* and all be encouraged." But that does not mean that prophets are doing Bible teaching in the church. People can *learn* from many things—from a song, from a personal testimony, from someone's confession of sin, from someone's joy in the midst of trials, and so forth. But this does not mean that any of these activities, including prophecy, *is the same activity* as Bible teaching. The numerous verses above that clearly distinguish prophecy from teaching should make that clear.

Along this same line, Linda Belleville argues that the word "instruct" (*katecheō*) in 1 Corinthians 14:19 shows that prophets carried out a teaching function in the church.[26] But this is a slight-of-hand argument, because in her repeated references to this verse as a proof

---

24. Tertullian, "Against Marcion," 5.8.11, cited from *ANF* 3:446, col. 2.
25. Tertullian, "On the Veiling of Virgins" 9.1, cited from *ANF* 4:33, col. 1.
26. Belleville, "Women in Ministry," 97, 99–100.

that prophets could "instruct" or "teach,"[27] Belleville fails to tell her readers that this verse *does not mention prophecy!* She never actually quotes 1 Corinthians 14:19 so that readers would see this for themselves: "Nevertheless, in church I would rather speak five words with my mind in order to *instruct* (*katecheō*) others, than ten thousand words in a tongue."

Paul says nothing about prophecy in this verse. He is contrasting intelligible speech in the church with speaking in tongues. "Teaching" has already been mentioned in the context (v. 6), and that is most likely what Paul has in mind when he talks about speaking to "instruct others."

Answer 7.3e: Prophecy, like other spiritual gifts, was to be subject to the teaching authority of the elders.

The New Testament says, "Obey your leaders and *submit to them*" (Hebrews 13:17), and "you who are younger, *be subject to the elders*" (1 Peter 5:5), and "Let the elders who *rule well* be considered worthy of double honor, especially those who labor in preaching and teaching" (1 Timothy 5:17). Elders had governing authority in the early churches, and teaching authority belonged to the elders.

But prophecies had to be subject to the governing authority of the churches. Paul says, "Do not despise prophecies, but *test everything*; hold fast what is good" (1 Thessalonians 5:20–21). He says, "Let two or three prophets speak, and let the others weigh what is said" (1 Corinthians 14:29).

So the gift of prophecy did not involve either teaching authority or governing authority over the church. That is why women can prophesy but not teach in the assembled church.

Answer 7.3f: Those who believe that the New Testament gift of prophecy was the same as fully inspired prophecy in the Old Testament still see a difference between prophecy and Bible teaching.

Not all evangelicals agree with the understanding of the gift of prophecy that I presented above. Some claim that the gift of prophecy in the New Testament always involved declaring the very words of God, which had absolute authority and were never in error.[28] Those who hold this view still insist on a distinction between prophecy and teaching. The prophet would be like an ambassador who can deliver a message from the president but cannot add to or subtract from it. The teacher, on the other hand, brings much explanation and application *based on* the message, but does not deliver the original message. Another analogy is the difference between someone reading a Scripture passage in the church service and someone teaching on the basis of that passage. Most churches from time to time allow anyone—men or women, sometimes even children—to read Scripture aloud to the congregation. But they

27. Ibid., 87, 97, 100.
28. For example, this is the view of Richard Gaffin in his essays in *Are Miraculous Gifts for Today: Four Views* (1996), ed. Wayne Grudem, esp. 41–60.

do not allow all of those people to bring the sermon to the congregation. They recognize a difference between simply repeating a message that God has given in his own words, and teaching the church on the basis of that message.

Egalitarian claim 7.4: Nobody Obeys 1 Corinthians 14:34: Complementarians can't be consistent; 1 Corinthians 14:34 requires that women be silent in church, but everybody disobeys that command today, because women can sing, pray, read Scripture, and so forth. Similarly, other New Testament restrictions on women were for a particular circumstance, not for all time.

Paul wrote in 1 Corinthians,

> As in all the churches of the saints, *the women should keep silent in the churches.* For they are not permitted to speak, but should be in submission, as the Law also says. If there is anything they desire to learn, let them ask their husbands at home. For it is shameful for a woman to speak in church. (14:33b–35)

Although the argument that "nobody obeys 1 Corinthians 14:34 today" may not be explicitly made by any egalitarian writer, it is implicit in the thinking of many readers of the Bible who realize that no evangelical churches require complete silence of women today. So readers think, "This passage must be talking about a different situation than what we find in our modern church services. Maybe more of the Bible's commands concerning women in church are intended only for a specific situation as well." That is probably why William Webb included the statement, "Women should remain silent in the churches (1 Corinthians 14:34)" in his opening list of instructions from Scripture,[29] a list he asks readers to evaluate in order to decide which ones are "still in force for us today exactly as they are articulated 'on the page.'"[30] The expectation of course is that people will decide this verse is not in force for us today.

Answer 7.4a: The passage does not require women to be completely silent.

The passage never did require complete silence of women, even when Paul wrote it. This is evident because Paul says in 1 Corinthians 11, just three chapters earlier, that women who pray and prophesy should have their heads covered, which assumes that they could pray and prophesy aloud in church services. That passage says,

29. Webb, *Slaves, Women and Homosexuals* (2001), 14.
30. Ibid., 13.

> Every man who prays or prophesies with his head covered dishonors his head, but every wife who prays or prophesies with her head uncovered dishonors her head—it is the same as if her head were shaven. (1 Corinthians 11:4–5)

Therefore the question is, what kind of "silence" does Paul mean in 1 Corinthians 14:34? It cannot be silence of all speech, for it has to be speech that is not "in submission" to some authority, since Paul says, "they are *not* permitted *to speak*, *but* should be *in submission*, as the Law also says" (v. 34). As I suggest below, speech that involves judging prophecies fits this description, for it involves assuming the possession of superior authority in matters of doctrinal or ethical instruction.

A similar example of "silence" not meaning total silence but silence in one kind of speech, is found in this same context, where Paul says about those who speak in tongues, "But if there is no one to interpret, *let each of them keep silent in church* and speak to himself and to God" (1 Corinthians 14:28, just six verses before 14:34). Does Paul mean that people who had the gift of tongues could never say anything in church, never pray (in a known language) or read Scripture or sing aloud? Of course not. What Paul means is, "Let each of them *keep silent* in church *with respect to the topic I am discussing*, that is, do not speak in tongues." Speaking in tongues is what he is discussing in 1 Corinthians 14:27–28, but starting at verse 29, he turns to prophecies and the judging of prophecies.

Answer 7.4b: This passage requires women to be silent with respect to the activity under discussion, which is the judging of prophecies.[31]

What is the topic under discussion in the context 1 Corinthians 14:34? The topic in verses 29–33 has been prophecies and judging prophecies, beginning with verse 29, "Let two or three prophets speak, and let the others weigh what is said." In fact, verse 29 is a general principle about prophesying that divides itself into two halves, with (a) the first half talking about *prophesying* ("Let two or three prophets speak") and (b) the second half talking about *judging those prophecies* ("and let the others weigh what is said").

---

31. The interpretation followed here, that Paul is prohibiting women from passing spoken judgment on the prophecies given in church, was advocated by Hurley, *Man and Woman in Biblical Perspective* (1981), 188–94. It was defended by Grudem, *Gift of Prophecy,* 185–92, and defended in considerable detail by D. A. Carson, "'Silent in the Churches': On the Role of Women in 1 Corinthians 14:33b–36," in Piper and Grudem, *Recovering Biblical Manhood and Womanhood,* 140–53. The most recent, and most lengthy, defense of this view is Thiselton, *First Epistle to the Corinthians* (2000), 1146–61, with extensive interaction with other literature.

Another recent survey of views is J. Carl Laney, "Gender Based Boundaries for Gathered Congregations: An Interpretative History of 1 Corinthians 14:34–35," in *JBMW* 7/1 (Spring 2002), 4–13. Laney shows some sympathy for a view that 11:5 allows women to pray and prophesy in small group settings, but 14:34–35 forbids them to speak in the assembled congregation. However, it is doubtful that the early Christians, many of whom met in house churches, would have ever made such a distinction between home fellowships and assembled church meetings. Nor can I be persuaded that the Corinthians ever would have imagined that 1 Corinthians 11:2–16 referred to meetings in homes but verses 17–34 spoke of observing the Lord's Supper in a larger church gathering. Finally, this view would lead to the repressive situation where women would have no warrant even to pray aloud in an assembled congregation.

After giving this general principle in verse 29, Paul goes on to explain it: In verses 30–33a, he explains how to proceed with (a) "let two or three prophets speak," telling the Corinthians they should prophesy in turn, not all at once! Then in verses 33b–35, he explains how to proceed with (b) "let the others weigh what is said," and tells the Corinthians that women cannot speak aloud to pass judgment on the prophecies: "As in all the churches of the saints, let the women keep silent in the churches."

If someone gave a prophecy, for example, that Jesus was coming back "five days from now," there would need to be a correction given before the congregation because Jesus Himself taught that people can know "neither the day nor the hour" of His return (Matthew 25:13). But Paul says men should give such a correction, for in such a case, as is done "in all the churches of the saints,"[32] the women are to "keep silent in the churches" during that time. They are not to pass judgment out loud on the prophecies.

The rest of the passage gives further explanation. When Paul says, "For they are not permitted to speak, but should be in submission, as the Law also says," (v. 34b), he views speaking aloud to judge prophecies as a "governing" or "ruling" function in the congregation, the opposite of being submissive to male leadership in the church. (Paul is not quoting any specific Old Testament passage, but seems to be referring to the Old Testament generally as "the Law," probably especially the Creation order in Genesis 2, and understanding it as teaching a principle of male leadership among God's people.)

Then in verse 35, Paul adds, "If there is anything they desire to learn, let them ask their husbands at home. For it is shameful for a woman to speak in church." Here Paul anticipates an evasion of his teaching. He expects that there might be some women in Corinth who would say, "Okay, Paul, we won't stand up and pass judgment on any prophecies. But we just want to ask a few questions. What's wrong with that?" And Paul realizes that for some women, the questions would become a springboard for judgments, such as, "Your prophecy just said that Jesus

---

32. Grammatically it is possible to make "as in all the churches of the saints" modify the preceding clause, and thus the passage would read, "For God is not a God of confusion but of peace, as in all the churches of the saints." The KJV and NKJV do this, following the sentence division indicated by the Greek text they follow, the *Textus Receptus*; the NASB and NLT also break the sentences in this way, with the alternative in the margin.

However, this division of the sentences does not fit the sense of the passage. After saying something about the character of God, which is always the same, it would be pointless for Paul to add "as in all the churches of the saints," as if the Corinthians would have imagined that God would be a God of peace in some churches but not in others. But if "as in all the churches of the saints" modifies the following instructions about behavior in worship, it makes very good sense. The Corinthians should not deviate from the standards for worship that are followed by all churches everywhere. This is the way the sentences are divided in the NIV, RSV, NRSV, ASV, NEB, ESV, and the UBS and Nestle-Aland Greek texts. (It is possible for Paul to open a sentence with "As..." [Greek *hōs*], for he does this also in Ephesians 5:24 and Philippians 2:22.)

Does it matter that the verse division in our Bibles puts "as in all the churches of the saints" in verse 33, rather than verse 34? This should not influence our thinking, because verse divisions were not part of what Paul wrote, but were first inserted into an edition of the Greek New Testament in 1551 by the French editor and publisher Robert Estienne (in Latin, his last name is Stephanus), in an edition of the Greek New Testament in which he

would come back in five days. My question is, didn't Jesus Himself say that we can know neither the day nor the hour?"

In this way the question is really a judgment against the prophecy. So Paul rules out that evasion by saying, "If there is anything they desire to learn, let them ask their husbands at home." (He gives the general case, since most women would be married, and he assumes that the Corinthians can make appropriate applications for single women, who would no doubt know some men they could talk to after the service.)

Answer 7.4c: This passage is consistent with other New Testament passages that reserve the task of teaching and governing the whole congregation to men.

It is not surprising that Paul would say only men can give spoken corrections to prophecies. Such correction is part of the task of "teaching and having authority" over the congregation, the task that Paul reserves for men in 1 Timothy 2:12. For Paul to restrict this "doctrinal guardianship" job to men is entirely consistent with what he does in 1 Timothy 2, and also consistent with his expectation that elders are men ("husband of one wife" in 1 Timothy 3:2; Titus 1:6; compare "men" in Acts 20:30).

Egalitarian claim 7.5: 1 Corinthians 14:34–35 Not Part of Bible: 1 Corinthians 14:34–35 is a later scribal interpolation that does not belong in the Bible.

Gordon Fee, in his commentary on 1 Corinthians, argues that Paul did not write 1 Corinthians 14:34–35, but these verses were the addition of a later scribe.[33] He says,

> The case against these verses is so strong, and finding a viable solution to their meaning so difficult, that it seems best to view them as an interpolation.... One must assume that the words were first written as a gloss in the margin by someone who, probably in light of 1 Tim. 2:9–15, felt the need to qualify Paul's instructions even further.[34]

Fee's main reasons are that some later Greek manuscripts move these verses so that they follow verse 40, and, he says, the verses cannot be reconciled with 1 Corinthians 11:5 where Paul allows women to prophesy in the church.

---

inserted verse divisions while on a journey by horse from Paris to Lyons. (See Metzger, *Text of the New Testament* [1968], 104.) His verse division after "as in all the churches of the saints" eventually seems to have influenced the KJV of 1611 and through it the NKJV.

33. See Fee, *First Epistle to the Corinthians* (1987), 699–708. Groothuis, *Good News for Women*, 205, summarizes Fee's arguments as one possibility, but does not explicitly accept or reject them.

34. Ibid., 705.

Answer 7.5a: No Greek manuscripts of the New Testament lack these verses, and they do not necessarily contradict what Paul wrote elsewhere.

But Fee's arguments have been strongly rejected.[35] No Greek manuscript of any kind from any date lacks these verses (the Western manuscripts that move the verses to follow verse 40 are unreliable elsewhere in any case). And virtually all other interpreters in the history of the church have seen various ways to reconcile 14:34–35 and 11:5 (one fairly common way has been explained above), so Fee wrongly sees them as impossible to reconcile, and that is his primary argument against their authenticity. There are a number of well-known texts in the New Testament that at first reading seem difficult to reconcile with other texts, but upon more careful reading and study, they turn out to be consistent with each other. That is also the case here.

It should trouble evangelicals that Fee says these verses that are missing from no ancient manuscript are not part of the Bible and therefore "certainly not binding for Christians."[36] They have been part of the Bible in every copy that we know has ever existed. We cannot simply cut them out because they are difficult to interpret!

Answer 7.5b: This is a sophisticated academic procedure that results in removing the authority of part of the Word of God.

While some who read Fee may see this as merely a text-critical decision based on Fee's careful analysis of many different ancient manuscripts, two factors lead me to think of it rather as a different method of rejecting the authority of these verses for the church today. (I am not speaking of Fee's intention, which I do not know, but of the actual process he followed and the result he reached.)

First, out of the thousands of ancient New Testament manuscripts that exist today, not one has ever omitted these verses (though the verses are moved to follow verse 40 in a few Western manuscripts that are elsewhere unreliable in 1 Corinthians). This makes this passage significantly different from the other two examples Fee mentions where something not original has crept into the text tradition (John 5:3b–4 and 1 John 5:7).[37] In those cases the oldest and best manuscripts *lack* the added material, but in 1 Corinthians 14:34–35 *no* manuscript lacks this material. So Fee's procedure is different from every other text-critical decision made by editors of the Greek New Testament throughout history: he thinks we should exclude a passage from the

35. See the discussion in Thiselton, *First Epistle to the Corinthians*, 1148–50, with particular reference to an article by C. Niccum, "The Voice of the Manuscripts on the Silence of Women: The External Evidence for 1 Corinthians 14:34–35," *New Testament Studies* 43 (1997), 242–55. Thiselton says Niccum's article "seems overwhelmingly convincing" (1149n342). See also Carson, "Silent in the Churches," in Piper and Grudem, *Recovering Biblical Manhood and Womanhood,* 141–45.

36. Fee, *First Epistle to the Corinthians,* 708.

37. Fee, *First Epistle to the Corinthians,* 705.

New Testament that is *included* in every manuscript we have! In fact, this is not a highly doubtful text, but one that is given a "B" rating in the United Bible Societies' fourth edition of the Greek New Testament,[38] indicating that it is "almost certain."[39]

Second, the most decisive factor for Fee's conclusion is not the evidence from ancient manuscripts but rather that he thinks that these verses, which say that "the women should keep silent in the churches" (1 Corinthians 14:34), are impossible to reconcile with 1 Corinthians 11. This makes me think this is ultimately not a text-critical question, but an objection he has to the content of these verses. He says, "these verses stand in obvious contradiction to 11:2–16, where it is assumed without reproof that women pray and prophesy in the assembly."[40] But at this point Fee's procedure is different from that of all evangelical interpreters of Scripture. There are many passages in the Bible that on first reading seem difficult to reconcile with other passages in the Bible (think, for example, of the teaching of Paul and James on justification by faith, or the astounding claim that Jesus is God as well as the Father, when combined with the teaching that there is only one God). Historically interpreters with a high respect for the authority and consistency of Scripture have not decided that one set of verses stands "in obvious contradiction" to the other set and then thrown the difficult verses out of the Bible. Think of what would happen if we followed Fee's procedure in the Gospels, where we find some manuscript evidence of scribal attempts to "fix" the difficulty in almost every parallel passage that has details that are difficult to harmonize, just as Fee finds some manuscript evidence of scribal attempts to move 1 Corinthians 14:34–35 to another context. Rather, interpreters have returned to the difficult texts with the assumption that they have misunderstood something, and they have sought for interpretations that are fair to both texts and are not contradictory.[41]

Does Fee's solution to 1 Corinthians 14:34–35 then constitute evidence of a liberal tendency to reject the authority of the Bible? Readers will have to come to their own conclusions. It seems to me that Fee's recommendation that we should remove some hard verses from the Bible rather than seeking to understand them in a way that does not contradict other verses establishes a dangerous precedent. When the verses that he throws out of the Bible are missing from no manuscript, and also happen to be the very verses that show Paul's insistence on male governance of the church meetings "in all the churches of the saints," then it seems to me to be another example of a pattern in many egalitarian writings, a pattern of using sophisticated scholarly procedures in order to evade the requirement of submitting to the authority of the Word of God.

---

38. *The Greek New Testament*, 4th rev. ed., 601.
39. UBS^4, p. 3*.
40. Fee, *First Epistle to the Corinthians*, 702.
41. Fee himself lists—but then rejects—several ways people have interpreted 1 Corinthians 14:34–35 so as not to contradict 1 Corinthians 11.

Egalitarian claim 7.6: A Quotation That Paul Rejects: 1 Corinthians 14:34–35 are not Paul's words, but are a quotation from the Corinthians that Paul rejects.

Gilbert Bilezikian and Walter Kaiser,[42] followed by Judy Brown,[43] have argued that verses 34–35 are not Paul's teaching but a long quotation of the Corinthian position that Paul is surprised by and that he rejects by saying in verse 36, "What! Did the word of God originate with you?" (RSV). Their argument depends in large part on taking the little Greek word *ē* (rendered "What!" in the RSV, but most commonly translated "or") as an indication that Paul *rejects* what he has just said. Bilezikian writes, "It is worth noting that in 1 Corinthians more than in any of his other Epistles, Paul uses the *ē* particle to introduce rebuttals to statements preceding it."[44]

Answer 7.6a: It is precarious to consider a statement in the Bible a quotation that the author rejects unless we have strong evidence from the context.

The suggestion by Bilezikian and Kaiser is highly unlikely. Of course, it is always possible, when we are uncomfortable with a passage, to claim that "the Bible doesn't teach that but denies it" by saying it is a question or a statement that the author disagrees with. But *we need strong evidence in the context before we do this,* and in this case the evidence is not there. There is nothing that would make the original readers (or make us) think Paul is giving a quotation that he differs with. Paul can signal a quotation clearly when he wants to, as in "how can some of you say that there is no resurrection of the dead?" (1 Corinthians 15:12).[45] But here we have no such signal to the readers. We must use great caution in saying something is "a quotation that Paul rejects," for if we are wrong, we are negating something that is God's Word to us.

Answer 7.6b: These verses do not fit the pattern of other quotations from the Corinthians.

Most interpreters today think that Paul gives some short sayings from the Corinthians which he then interacts with, as in

> "All things are lawful for me," but not all things are helpful. "All things are lawful for me," but I will not be enslaved by anything. (1 Corinthians 6:12)

---

42. See Walter Kaiser, *Worldwide Challenge* 3 (1976), 9–12, and Bilezikian, *Beyond Sex Roles,* 286–88. Kaiser repeats his argument in Kaiser, *Toward an Exegetical Theology* (1981), 76–77, 119.
43. Brown, *Women Ministers*, 274–77, repeats Bilezikian's arguments with approval, concluding that "The best and perhaps the only correct understanding of the word in 1 Corinthians 14 is that verses 34–35 contain an error that Paul sharply challenges with the two sarcastic questions of verse 36."
44. Bilezikian, *Beyond Sex Roles*, 286.
45. Ancient Greek did not have quotation marks as we do today, but it used other means to introduce quotations, such as the words *You say that*... or similar expressions.

The quotation marks put in by modern translators indicate that they think the short quotation is something the Corinthians were saying, and Paul is responding to them. (Quotation marks were not used in ancient Greek, so we have to determine this from the context just as the original readers did.) But as D. A. Carson points out, the claim that 1 Corinthians 14:34–35 is also a quotation from the Corinthians does not fit the pattern of these other acknowledged quotations:

> It is very doubtful that verses 34–35 constitute a quotation, perhaps from the Corinthians' letter. During the last decade and a half, one notable trend in Corinthian studies has been to postulate that Paul is quoting the Corinthians in more and more places—usually in places where the commentator does not like what Paul is saying! That Paul does quote from the Corinthians' letter no one disputes. But the instances that are almost universally recognized as quotations (e.g., 6:12; 7:1b; 8:1b) enjoy certain common characteristics: (i) they are short (e.g., "Everything is permissible for me," 6:12); (ii) they are usually followed by sustained qualification (e.g., in 6:12 Paul goes on to add "but not everything is beneficial...but I will not be mastered by anything"—and then, following one more brief quotation from their letter, he devotes several verses to the principle he is expounding); (iii) Paul's response is unambiguous, even sharp. The first two criteria utterly fail if we assume verses 34–35 are a quotation from the letter sent by the Corinthians.[46]

Therefore these verses are unlike the other quotations from the Corinthians in this epistle. It may sound like a neat interpretative solution to claim that a passage one is uncomfortable with is a quotation that the author rejects, but such a procedure should only be used with great caution and with very strong evidence, lest we actually reject something that God intends us to take as His Word for us.

Answer 7.6c: Bilezikian's (and Kaiser's) argument for the word "or" (Greek *ē*) claims exactly the opposite of what the word means in contexts like this.

The first word in verse 36 is the common Greek word for "or."[47] Parallel examples (see below) show that *Paul wants the readers to deny verse 36* (the Word of God did *not* come forth from them, and they know it), and in that way he shows that *they should follow Paul's teaching in verses 34–35*. He wants them to see that they *should* do what is done "in all the churches of the saints"; namely, they should not have women speak in judgment on prophecies. They aren't the source of the Word of God and they can't make up their own rules contrary to all the other churches, and contrary to Paul.

46. Carson, "Silent in the Churches," in Piper and Grudem, *Recovering Biblical Manhood and Womanhood,* 148.
47. The KJV, followed by the RSV, translated it "What," but both the NKJV and the NRSV have replaced "What" with the more literal "Or." The ESV and NASB (margin) also translate it "Or," while the NIV, NASB (text), *NET Bible,* and NLT leave it untranslated.

But this means that Paul *affirms* verses 33b–35, he does not deny them. We can compare other examples where Paul uses the same construction. In all the other similar cases, Paul *affirms* the statement that comes before "or."[48]

> 1 Corinthians 6:15–16: "Do you not know that your bodies are members of Christ? Shall I then take the members of Christ and make them members of a prostitute? Never! *Or* do you not know that he who is joined to a prostitute becomes one body with her? For, as it is written, 'The two will become one flesh.'"

The form of the argument is this:

v. 15 Your bodies are members of Christ, so you should not make them members of a prostitute.
v. 16 *Or* do you not know that you will become one body with the prostitute?

Bilezikian has gotten it exactly wrong, claiming that the "or" makes readers *reject* what goes before. But Paul does not want them to reject the force of verse 15, he wants them to *accept* it: They should *never* make "the members of Christ" become "members of a prostitute."

Here is another example:

> 1 Corinthians 6:18–19: "Flee from sexual immorality. Every other sin a person commits is outside the body, but the sexually immoral person sins against his own body. *Or* do you not know that your body is a temple of the Holy Spirit within you, whom you have from God?"

The argument is:

v. 18 The sexually immoral person sins against his own body.
v. 19 *Or* do you not know that your body is a temple of the Holy Spirit?

Again, Paul wants the Corinthians to *accept* what he says in verse 18, not to reject it. Yet Bilezikian says that "in 1 Corinthians more than in any of his other Epistles, Paul uses the *ē* particle to introduce *rebuttals* to statements preceding it."[49] The fact of the matter is that Paul uses *ē* to introduce *affirmations* of the statements preceding it.

---

48. In the following examples, the Greek word *ē*, in the sense of "or," occurs in each verse. However, translations vary in how they render it from verse to verse. Some literally translate it as "or," while others at times attempt to bring out the force of it through use of some other syntax. Yet it should be clear from most or all English translations that in every case *Paul is not denying what he has just affirmed, but he is reaffirming it.* Bilezikian's summaries of these passages on pp. 286–87 do not quote the passages in whole, and therefore they do not represent the passages accurately. In most of the cases what Bilezikian claims the preceding verse is saying is some erroneous view that Paul is contradicting. But Paul himself is not affirming these errors! And the verses that precede the "or" do not affirm those errors. Bilezikian has repeatedly misrepresented what the verses are saying.
49. Bilezikian, *Beyond Sex Roles,* 286 (italics added).

> 1 Corinthians 9:4–6: "Do we not have the right to eat and drink? Do we not have the right to take along a believing wife, as do the other apostles and the brothers of the Lord and Cephas? ***Or*** is it only Barnabas and I who have no right to refrain from working for a living?"

Again, Paul wants the Corinthians to *accept* what he affirms in verses 4–5, that he has the right to food and drink and to be accompanied by a wife. The "or" shows that he wants them to *accept* what goes before; it is not a "rebuttal," as Bilezikian claims.

> 1 Corinthians 10:21–22: "You cannot drink the cup of the Lord and the cup of demons; you cannot partake of the table of the Lord and the table of demons. ***Or*** do we provoke the Lord to jealousy? We are not stronger than He, are we?" (NASB)

The point is the same: When Paul says "Or" in verse 22, it shows he wants them to *accept* what he affirms in verse 21, that they cannot drink the cup of the Lord and the cup of demons.

After a more extensive analysis of Bilezikian's treatment of the Greek *ē* in 1 Corinthians 14:36 and other examples, D. A. Carson writes,

> In every passage he treats on this matter, Bilezikian demonstrates, quite remarkably, that *he does not understand what he has cited.* In one instance (1 Corinthians 11:13), he refers to the particle *e* even though no Greek edition known to me includes that particle.
>
> All scholars make mistakes, I no less than others. But the sheer vehemence that has surrounded the treatment of this particle in recent years attests that we are facing more than an occasional lapse of exegetical judgment. We are facing an ideology that is so certain of itself that in the hands of some, at least, the text is not allowed to speak for itself. *The brute fact is this: in every instance in the New Testament where the disjunctive particle in question is used in a construction analogous to the passage at hand, its effect is to reinforce the truth of the clause or verse that precedes it.* Paul's point in 14:36 is that some Corinthians want to "deny or refute" what Paul has been saying in verses 34–35. So he continues, "Or [if you find it so hard to grant this, then consider:] did the word of God originate with you? Or are you the only people it has reached?" This is part and parcel of Paul's frequent insistence in this letter that the Corinthian church return to the common practice and perspective of the other churches (1:2; 4:17; 7:17; 11:16; 14:33) and to wholehearted submission to apostolic authority (14:37–38).[50]

---

50. Carson, "Silent in the Churches," in Piper and Grudem, *Recovering Biblical Manhood and Womanhood,* 150–51 (italics in first paragraph added).

Therefore the attempt by Bilezikian, Kaiser, and Brown to turn 1 Corinthians 14:33–34 into a quotation that Paul rejects turns out not to be supported by the evidence, and must itself be rejected.

Egalitarian claim 7.7: Disruptive Corinthian Women: Women in the Corinthian church were being noisy and disruptive, and that is the reason 1 Corinthians 14:34–35 tells women to be silent.

Probably the most common egalitarian position on 1 Corinthians 14:34–35 is that noisy or disorderly women were disrupting the worship service at Corinth, perhaps rudely shouting questions to their husbands (or to other men) seated across the room, or perhaps (according to a variant of this position) even giving loud shouts characteristic of near-ecstatic worship. Advocates of this interpretation say that Paul wanted to stop these disruptions and restore order to the service. Craig Keener says,

> We will turn to what seems to be the most likely interpretation of 1 Corinthians 14:34–35: Paul was addressing relatively uneducated women who were disrupting the service with irrelevant questions. The immediate remedy for this situation was for them to stop asking such questions; the long-term solution was to educate them.[51]

Stanley Grenz writes,

> The most widely held view among egalitarians claims that the problem in Corinth focused on certain women who were asking many questions that disrupted the worship services.... The women may have been recent converts...or perhaps they were uneducated women voicing irrelevant questions.... Or perhaps the women were interrupting either the Scripture exposition in the services or the evaluation of the prophetic messages.... Regardless of the actual details, the results were the same. The adamant questioning resulted in chaos. In response, Paul rules the women out of order.[52]

One detailed explanation of this view is from Linda Belleville, who says that married Corinthian women were less educated than their husbands, and were asking questions because they wanted to learn. She says, "It is likewise plain that the questions of these women were directed at men other than their husbands, for Paul instructs them to ask their *own* men."[53]

---

51. Keener, *Paul, Women and Wives,* 70.
52. Grenz, *Women in the Church* (1995), 123–24. See also Grady, *Ten Lies*, 61–64.
53. Belleville, "Women in Ministry," 116. See also Jacobs, *Women of Destiny*, 233; Brown, *Women Ministers*, 271–73.

Answer 7.7a: There is no evidence inside or outside the Bible to prove this theory.

The first thing to be said about this view is there are no facts to support it. There is nothing in 1 Corinthians that says women were being disruptive. And there is no evidence outside the Bible that women in the Corinthian church were disruptive. Some people have assumed this, but their position is just that: an assumption without evidence.

Craig Keener says that in 1 Corinthians 14:34–35 Paul "inserts here a brief digression related to order: the women must stop disrupting the service."[54] His footnote to this sentence lists twenty-six extrabiblical references,[55] and readers may assume this is overwhelming evidence of disorderly women in Corinth. But on closer inspection all these references are to Graeco-Roman and Jewish writings that talk about concerns for decency and order in public assemblies. Not one of them mentions women in the Corinthian church, or in any first-century church for that matter. Proving that Greeks and Romans and Jews had concerns for order in public assemblies does not prove that women in the church at Corinth were being disruptive or disorderly!

Yet Keener takes this unproven assumption as fact for much of the rest of his chapter. He speaks of "the probability that women were disrupting the church services at Corinth," and two pages later says, "once we have decided that the women are causing disturbances by their lack of appropriate silence, we must still ask what kind of disruptive speech Paul had in view." Then after considering various kinds of possible disruptions, he says, "What is almost certainly in view is that the women are interrupting the *Scripture exposition* with questions."[56]

What is the hard evidence for this? There is none.

Keener bases much on Paul's statement, "If there is anything they desire to learn, let them ask their husbands at home" (1 Corinthians 14:35). But that does not prove they were already asking disruptive questions, or any questions at all, during the worship service. It could just as well be Paul's way of heading off any possible attempts to evade his command that women not speak out and judge prophecies in the church service.[57]

Some interpreters have claimed that women were seated separately from men in early synagogues and churches, and this made it likely that women were shouting questions across the room to their husbands. But Keener rightly notes that there is no early historical evidence to support the idea that women sat separately from men, either in synagogues or in churches:

> But the evidence for this practice [separate seating for men and women] is problematic at best. Although the temple in Paul's day did not allow women into the court of Israel, there is no clear architectural segregation in the average local *synagogue*. The custom of gender segregation in the synagogue seems to have first arisen in the Middle

54. Keener, *Paul, Women and Wives,* 71.
55. Ibid., 89n4.
56. Ibid., 71, 73, 81.
57. See discussion on pp. 79 and 234–35.

> Ages, and earlier rabbinic literature presupposes that men and women met together there. Most ancient sites provide no clear indication of galleries, and if they did it would still not be clear that these were reserved for women. Still more problematic is the absence of architectural evidence that would allow any gender segregation in the homes; very unnatural dividers would have had to have been constructed.[58]

As far as other kinds of disruptive speech, such as frenzied, ecstatic behavior by women, one can find ancient literature that shows evidence of wild behavior by women in pagan religious rites at the time.[59] But there is also evidence of wild behavior by men! Therefore, it is illegitimate to use such evidence one-sidedly to claim that noisy women were a special problem at Corinth. This interpretation lacks solid historical support.

Belleville's assertion that married women were publicly asking questions of men *other than their husbands* is based on two basic errors in interpretation. First, Belleville says: "Here the context explicitly states that these women were married (*ei de* + the indicative ["and since they want" = the women of 14:34])."[60] But Belleville's claim that *ei de* + the indicative assumes that something is true involves a misunderstanding of Greek grammar.[61] Dan Wallace explains that a construction like this (the "first class condition") assumes something to be true *for the sake of argument*, but should not be taken to affirm that something is *actually the case*. This is not really complicated: both in Greek and in English such a statement begins with "if," and it points out something that the author is assuming to be true simply for the sake of showing the reasoning that would follow in the second half of the sentence if it were true. Therefore Belleville is incorrect to claim that the Greek text says the women were in fact married.

Second, when Paul says, "Let them ask their husbands at home" (1 Corinthians 14:35), it does not mean that they were asking *other* husbands. It simply means they are to ask their own husbands. When Paul says that wives should "submit to your own husbands, as to the Lord" (Ephesians 5:22), does that imply that the wives at Ephesus were all submitting to other women's husbands? Of course not. Belleville makes a fundamental mistake assuming that when Paul commends something, the opposite situation must already be occurring. But the text says nothing of the kind.

---

58. Keener, *Paul, Women and Wives,* 76.
59. See the helpful discussion, with several references, in Keener, *Paul, Women and Wives,* 77–78. Keener does not think the text points to frenzied behavior by women or by men in the church at Corinth, since he favors the "disruptive questions" view.
60. Belleville, "Women in Ministry," 115.
61. Dan Wallace says this idea that a "first class condition" (*ei* + indicative, which Belleville is talking about) assumes something to be true is incorrect. Wallace says, "This view is demonstrably false for conditional statements...there are thirty-six instances of the first class condition in the New Testament that cannot possibly be translated since...note the following illustrations. Matthew 12:27...if I cast out demons by Beelzebul, by whom do your sons cast them out?... 1 Corinthians 15:13...but if there is no resurrection, then Christ has not been raised." Wallace, *Greek Grammar Beyond the Basics* (1996), 690–91.

Answer 7.7b: This theory says Corinth is a special situation, but Paul applies his rule to "all the churches."

According to this view, noisy women were a special problem at Corinth. But Paul says, "*As in all the churches of the saints*, the women should keep silent *in the churches*" (1 Corinthians 14:33b–34), and there are strong reasons for thinking that even though the phrase "as in all the churches of the saints" comes at the end of verse 33, it really modifies "the women should keep silent in the churches."[62] And even if someone thinks that phrase goes with the preceding sentence, Paul still says, "the women should keep silent *in the churches*." Thus his rule cannot be restricted to one local church where there supposedly were problems.

This is very significant. It means that any explanation of this passage that limits its application to the situation at Corinth is unconvincing. But that is just what this "noisy Corinthian women" interpretation would have us believe—that noisy women at Corinth prompted Paul's directives. Instead, Paul directs the Corinthians to conform to a practice that was universal in the early church.

Keener says that the problem must have been specific to Corinth, because if Paul wanted to give general instructions that applied to all churches, "we can be sure that Paul would have already given these regulations during his extended stay with them (Acts 18:11, 18)."[63] But this argument is not convincing. For example, regarding the Lord's Supper, Paul tells the Corinthians he is just repeating what he had already taught them earlier: "For I received from the Lord what I also delivered to you, that the Lord Jesus on the night when he was betrayed took bread" (1 Corinthians 11:23). People can easily forget things, and they need to be reminded. People can start one pattern of conduct and then stray into another one, especially with new people continually coming into a church. If we follow the principle, "This instruction can't be for all churches, or Paul would have taught it in person, not by writing," then very little will be left in the Pauline epistles that applies to all churches. This is hardly a satisfactory approach to the New Testament Scriptures. Paul is telling the Corinthians to follow a practice "as in all the churches of the saints" (1 Corinthians 14:33).

Answer 7.7c: This "noisy women" theory does not make sense of Paul's solution.

If women were being disruptive, Paul would just tell them to act in an orderly way, not to be completely silent. In other cases where there are problems of disorder, Paul simply prescribes order (as with tongues or prophecy in verses 27, 29, 31, and as with the Lord's Supper in 1 Corinthians 11:33–34). If noise had been the problem in Corinth, he would have explicitly forbidden *disorderly* speech, not all speech.

---

62. See footnote 32 above for evidence that "As in all the churches of the saints" should go with what follows it.
63. Keener, *Paul, Women and Wives,* 73.

Answer 7.7d: This theory makes Paul's remedy unfair.

With this view, Paul would be punishing all women for the misdeeds of some. If there were noisy women, in order to be fair, Paul should have said, "The *disorderly* women should keep silent." But this egalitarian position makes Paul unfair, for it makes him silence all women, not just the disorderly ones. It is unlike Paul, or any other New Testament writer, to make unfair rules of this sort.

Also, Paul would be unfair to punish only the disorderly women and not any disorderly men. And to say that only women and no men were disorderly is merely an assumption with no facts to support it.

Answer 7.7e: Paul does not give noisy women as a reason, but gives the Old Testament law.

He says, "For they are not permitted to speak, but should be in submission, as the Law also says" (1 Corinthians 14:34). "Law" here most likely refers to teaching of the Old Testament in general on men and women, because Paul does not quote any specific Old Testament passage. He frequently uses "law" (Greek *nomos*) to refer to the Old Testament, and especially with this formula, "as the Law says" (see the other two instances in Romans 3:19 and 1 Corinthians 9:8).[64] It is unlikely that "law" refers to Roman law or to Jewish oral traditions, for Paul does not elsewhere use *nomos* in those ways.[65]

Paul therefore gives "the Law" as the reason for his statement, not noisy women. It is precarious to remove from our explanation the reason that Paul does give and replace it with a reason he does not give.

This is another reason why Keener's claim that Paul's concern was for order in the church services is unpersuasive. Paul here is not saying,

> "Let the women be silent because they should not be asking disruptive questions," or
>
> "Let the women be silent because God wants orderly worship services," but rather,

---

64. This was pointed out by Carson, "Silent in the Churches," in Piper and Grudem, *Recovering Biblical Manhood and Womanhood,* 148.
65. Linda Belleville says "law" here refers to Roman law ("Women in Ministry," 119). As evidence, she says, "Official religion of the Roman variety was closely supervised," but the only proof she gives is a reference to her book, *Women Leaders and the Church,* 36–38. On those pages, we look in vain for any reference to Roman law regulating anyone's conduct within any religious service. She mentions the Emperor Tiberias's attempt to abolish the Cult of Isis, but that proves nothing about attempts to regulate Christian conduct or any other religious activity within a worship service. Belleville asks us to believe, without proof, the rather remarkable position that Roman laws prohibited women from asking disruptive questions *within a worship service such as found in a Christian church.* And she gives not one shred of proof.

    Paul never uses "law" (Greek *nomos*) to refer to Roman law, but often uses it, as here, to refer to the teachings of the Old Testament taken as a whole.

    Kaiser, *Hard Sayings of the Old Testament* (1988), 36, claims that "the law" here means Rabbinic teaching, but he provides no supporting evidence, and, again, Paul does not use the word *law* in that way.

"As in all the churches of the saints, the women should keep silent in the churches. *For they are not permitted to speak, but should be in submission, as the Law also says.*" (1 Corinthians 14:33b–34)

Keener says Paul's main concern is order, but Paul himself says that his concern is the principle of submission—in this case, submission to male leadership among God's people.

Egalitarian claim 7.8: Women as Paul's Coworkers: Women such as Euodia and Syntyche (Philippians 4:2–3) were Paul's "coworkers" and therefore had significant leadership roles in the New Testament.

Linda Belleville writes,

> Women were actively engaged in evangelism during the early years of the church. Paul commends Priscilla and Aquila as "coworkers" (Rom. 16:3) and Tryphena, Tryphosa, and Persis as "those who work hard in the Lord" (Rom. 16:12). This is the language of missionary activity. In fact, *Paul uses exactly the same language of his own and other male colleagues' missionary labors.*... Euodia and Syntyche are the only women explicitly named as evangelists. They were Paul's coworkers, "who have contended 'by' his side in the cause of the gospel" (Phil. 4:2–3). Some would say these women did nothing more than provide hospitality, but the language does not in the least suggest this. For one, the term Paul uses of their role is a strong one.... Also, Paul says that they labored side by side with him and names them as partners.... There is more. The broader context shows that *these women were not only co-evangelists but key leaders of the Philippian church.* Why else would Paul publicly appeal to a third party (the enigmatic "yokefellow") to help these women work out their differences?[66]

Aida Spencer says,

> A "coworker" and possibly "worker" is someone whom Paul considers a colleague placed in a position of authority similar to his own position. Women certainly were called "coworkers."[67]

Stanley Grenz outlines several activities of Paul's coworkers, such as assisting in composing letters, carrying apostolic messages, encouraging believers on Paul's behalf, reporting to Paul on the status of congregations, and hosting house churches. Grenz then says,

---

66. Belleville, *Women Leaders and the Church*, 60.
67. Spencer, *Beyond the Curse*, 118–19. See also Bilezikian, *Beyond Sex Roles*, 198.

In view of this wide range of ministry, it would be ludicrous to deny that Paul's coworkers possessed authority in the churches. Some of those whom he described as "hard workers" provided oversight to a local congregation, a role which included the tasks of admonition (1 Thess. 5:12). Consequently, their leadership function obviously involved some form of authoritative speech, such as preaching and teaching.

Paul readily spoke of women, as well as men, as his coworkers. He never cautioned his recipients to view only the men as possessing authority or being worthy of honor. Rather, his readers were to "submit to...everyone who joins in the work, and labors at it" (1 Cor. 16:16 NIV).[68]

Answer 7.8a: It is true that women were Paul's coworkers, but the title "coworker" does not imply that they had equal authority to Paul, or that they had the office of elder, or that they taught or governed in any New Testament churches.

The Greek term translated "coworker" is *sunergos*. It means someone who worked with Paul, who helped him in his ministry. But to be a "fellow worker" or "coworker" does not mean that this person had governing or teaching authority in the churches. Paul calls many people "fellow workers," such as Prisca and Aquila (Romans 16:3); Urbanus (Romans 16:9); Epaphroditus (Philippians 2:25); Aristarchus, Mark, and Jesus who is called Justus (Colossians 4:10–11); Philemon (Philemon 1); Mark, Artistarchus, Demas, and Luke (Philemon 24); and others who are better known such as Titus (2 Corinthians 8:23); and Timothy (1 Thessalonians 3:2). John even applies the term *sunergos* to anyone who supports traveling missionaries or evangelists, for he writes, "Therefore we ought to support people like these, that we may be *fellow workers* (plural of Greek *sunergos*) for the truth" (3 John 8). But this surely does not mean that everyone who supported a traveling missionary had ruling authority over the churches!

Answer 7.8b: Some coworkers do things that other coworkers do not do.

It is true that some people who are called coworkers, such as Timothy and Titus, have considerable authority. But that does not mean that everyone who is called a coworker has similar authority or does the same thing.

Those who claim this are making an elementary mistake in logic:

1. *Some* coworkers had governing authority over churches.
2. Therefore *all* coworkers had governing authority over churches.

But it may not be true, for other people may be coworkers by helping in other ways (such as giving money in 3 John 8). The activity of *one* does not have to be duplicated in the activity of *all* unless it can be shown that such activities belonged to the essence of what it meant to be a

68. Grenz, *Women in the Church*, 84. See also Brown, *Women Ministers*, 176.

coworker (and it cannot, for their activities are too diverse). It is doubtful that Paul even thought of *coworker* as a technical term or a special category of person. He seemed generally willing to apply it to all who helped and worked with him to spread the gospel and build up the churches.

The fallacy of this egalitarian argument can be seen when we try to apply it to other characteristics of people who are called coworkers:

1. Some coworkers were women.
2. Therefore all coworkers were women.

Or we can try this one:

1. Some coworkers (such as Philemon) owned slaves.
2. Therefore all coworkers owned slaves.

Of course these conclusions do not follow.

The diverse use of *coworker* can also be seen in an example from English today. The president of a company or the owner of a business might easily refer to others in the company as his coworkers without in any way implying that they have similar authority.

Egalitarians are trying to make more out of a term than the term will bear. Paul's coworkers were simply those who worked with him in various ways, just as he called himself a coworker" (*sunergos*) with all the Christians at Corinth (2 Corinthians 1:24) and also called himself a coworker" (*sunergos*) with God (1 Corinthians 3:9). The term is not a technical term for any specific kind of responsibility in the early church.

Answer 7.8c: 1 Corinthians 16:16 does not tell Christians to be subject to every coworker.

Stanley Grenz and others make much of 1 Corinthians 16:15–16:

> Now I urge you, brothers—you know that the household of Stephanas were the first converts in Achaia, and that they have devoted themselves to the service of the saints—*be subject to such as these, and to every fellow worker and laborer.*

Grenz writes about this verse,

> Whatever their actual functions, Paul esteemed the labors of his female associates. In 1 Corinthians 16:16 (NIV) Paul instructs his readers "to submit…to everyone who joins in the work [*sunergounti*], and labors at it [*kopiōnti*]." The apostle employs these same words to describe the work of his male and female friends. All believers—including men—were to honor these women as leaders and submit to their authority.[69]

69. Ibid., 86.

But Grenz is mistaken when he says the apostle uses "these same words" to describe the work of his male and female friends. Paul does not use the same words, for this verse does not even use the noun "fellow worker" or "coworker" (Greek *sunergos*). Instead this verse has a related verb, *sunergeō*, which only occurs three other times in the New Testament and never elsewhere refers to those who work for the gospel:

> Romans 8:28: "And we know that for those who love God all things *work together* for good, for those who are called according to his purpose."
>
> 2 Corinthians 6:1: "*Working together* with him, then, we appeal to you not to receive the grace of God in vain."
>
> James 2:22: "You see that faith *was active along with* his works, and faith was completed by his works."[70]

Grenz does not tell his readers that 1 Corinthians 16:16 does not even have the noun *sunergos,* but a participle from the verb *sunergeō*. Though the words are related, it is no more true to say that everyone who "works together with" someone else (*sunergeō*) is a "coworker" (*sunergos*) than it is to say that everyone who is "sent" (*apostellō*) is an "apostle" (*apostolos*). This verse cannot rightly be used to draw any conclusions about what is meant by "coworker" where it does occur in Paul's writings.

What does this verse mean then? In 1 Corinthians 16:16, Paul must be referring to a more limited group whom the Corinthians would recognize as elders or leaders in the church, as indicated by the earlier phrases in these two verses. The passage specifically mentions "the household of Stephanas" and calls them the "first converts" (Greek *aparchē*, "firstfruits") of Achaia. It is likely that Stephanas and some others in his household were appointed elders in the church at Corinth, not only because Paul tells the church to be subject to them, but also because in 95 AD the epistle of 1 Clement (written *to Corinth* to encourage the church not to remove the elders whom the apostles had set in place) has a probable allusion to this verse. It says that the apostles "appointed their first converts [Greek *aparchē,* the same word used in 1 Corinthians 16:15]...to be bishops and deacons of the future believers" (1 Clement 42:4).[71]

70. The term is also used in Mark 16:20, a verse not in the oldest and best manuscripts: "And they went out and preached everywhere, while the Lord *worked with* them and confirmed the message by accompanying signs."

71. Cited from *The Apostolic Fathers*, trans. Kirsopp Lake (Loeb Classical Library, Cambridge: Harvard University Press, 1970), 2-vol. ed., 1:81. There are several quotations from 1 Corinthians in 1 Clement (see, for example, 1 Clement 13.1; 24.1; 34.8; 37.5; 49.5), and at one point the author even says, "Take up the epistle of the blessed Paul the apostle. What did he first write to you at the beginning of his preaching? With true inspiration he charged you concerning himself and Cephas and Apollos, because even then you had made yourselves partisans" (1 Clement 47:1–3). Therefore, the readers in Corinth would likely have understood 1 Clement 42:4 as a reference to 1 Corinthians 16:15.

Another reason for taking this passage in a restrictive sense is that Paul also tells them to be "subject to...every fellow worker *and laborer* [participle of Greek *kopiaō*]" (1 Corinthians 16:16). But surely Paul cannot mean they were to be subject to everyone referred to with the verb *kopiaō* in his epistles. For example, he uses the same word to say, "Let the thief no longer steal, but rather let him *labor*, doing honest work with his own hands, so that he may have something to share with anyone in need" (Ephesians 4:28).

Surely Paul cannot be saying that the Corinthians should be subject to every thief who stops stealing and starts earning a living! But on the same logic as Grenz uses for "fellow worker" (*sunergeō*) in 1 Corinthians 16:16, we would also have to say Christians have to be subject to everyone whom Paul says is "laboring." It is far better to think that in 1 Corinthians 16:16 "every fellow worker and laborer" means "everyone who works and labors with Stephanus and his household in the leadership of the church."

Such an understanding is confirmed by the fact that the prefix *sun-* on the verb *sunergeō* implies that there is someone in the context *with whom* the worker would be working. Translating the participles very literally, we would render this verse, "be subject to such as these, and to everyone *working with* and laboring."

The expression "working with" (the participle *sunergounti*, from *sunergeō*) causes the reader instinctively to ask, "Working with whom?" and to conclude, "Working with Stephanus and those like him who have leadership in the church." Readers would naturally read it as, "be subject to such as these, and to everyone *working with them* and laboring."

This means that Paul is referring in 1 Corinthians 16:15–16 to people whom the Corinthians would know as elders (and perhaps other church leaders), and this is consistent with his encouragement to be subject to "such as these." The verse does not even contain the term Paul uses elsewhere for coworker, and it is a mistake for Grenz to claim this verse as evidence that women had leadership or governing roles in the church.

Egalitarian claim 7.9: Women Elders: Women elders are mentioned in Titus 2:3, which speaks of "older women."

Some egalitarians have claimed that Paul is speaking of women elders in the following passage:

> Older men are to be sober-minded, dignified, self-controlled, sound in faith, in love, and in steadfastness. *Older women* likewise are to be reverent in behavior, not slanderers or slaves to much wine. They are to teach what is good, and so train the young women to love their husbands and children. (Titus 2:2–4)

Aida Spencer writes,

> Often little attention is given to the "old women" at Crete mentioned by Paul in Titus 2:3. However, the word "old" is the word *presbutis* or "female elder." The women could as easily be understood as "women elders" rather than "old women," especially in light of the fact that they are called "teachers" (*didaskalos*), "teachers of the good."[72]

Answer 7.9a: The parallels with other groups of older and younger persons make this interpretation unlikely.

The context of Titus 2:3 does not indicate or even hint at church offices (which Paul finished discussing in 1:5–9). Here Paul is simply talking about how Timothy should treat different groups of people. He talks about "older men" (v. 2), "older women" (v. 3), "young women" (v. 4), and "younger men" (v. 6).

In verse 2, the Greek word for "older men" is significant, because Paul does not use the Greek word *presbuteros* (which can mean either "elder" or "older man") but uses a different but related word, *presbutēs*, which only means an "old man" and is not used to refer to a church office.[73] Therefore verse 2 cannot be talking about men who are elders. Similarly, in Titus 2:3, Paul does not use a feminine form of the word that could mean "elder" in a masculine form (*presbuteros*), but uses a different word, *presbutis*, which means "old(er) woman" or "elderly lady."[74] The contrast with the "young women" whom the older women are to teach indicates that Paul is treating different categories of people according to age. He does not have church officers in mind in this context.

Moreover, he has just finished specifying that an elder must be "the husband of one wife" (Titus 1:6). This is hardly consistent with naming women elders in the next chapter.

Answer 7.9b: Spencer's interpretation is supported by no English translation and no lexicon.

Spencer defines the word *presbutis* as "female elder" but she does not tell the reader that this definition is not found in any Greek lexicon[75] or any English translation. The translation "older women" is found in the ESV, NASB, NIV, RSV, NRSV, NLT, and NKJV, with "aged women" in the KJV.

On what basis then are we supposed to believe that such an idiosyncratic position is a trustworthy translation? Unsuspecting readers may think that Spencer, as a New Testament professor, has defined the word accurately, but her translation is highly unlikely and, to my

72. Spencer, *Beyond the Curse*, 107.
73. BDAG, 863.
74. Ibid.
75. Ibid. The authors of this lexicon mention an article by Bernadette Brooten in which she claims that *presbutis* can mean either "elder" or "aged woman" on a burial inscription, but the lexicon gives no approval to that claim in the definition of the word.

knowledge, supported by no one outside the egalitarian camp. It is best to conclude that Titus 2:3 just speaks of "older women."[76]

Egalitarian claim 7.10: Hebrews 11:2: Women are included in the "elders" mentioned in Hebrews 11:2. Therefore there were women elders.

Cindy Jacobs claims that the term *elders* in Hebrews 11:2 shows that women could be called elders:

> From the book of Hebrews, we see that at least sometimes the term "elders" could also include women. In Hebrews 11:2 we read, "This faith is what the ancients were commended for" (NIV). The word "ancients" comes from the Greek word *presbuteroi* (plural of *presbuteros*) and has traditionally been translated into English by the terms "elders" (KJV, NKJV, ASV) and "men of old" (RSV, NASB). Yet among these "elders" mentioned, we find Sarah...Moses' mother...the women among "the people" who crossed the Red Sea...Rahab.[77]

Answer 7.10a: The meaning "elders" does not fit the context.

The problem with Cindy Jacobs's argument is that it fails to understand that the word *presbuteros* was sometimes used to mean "an older person" or "a person who lived long ago," and sometimes was used to mean "elder" in the sense of a church officer. The only question is what sense it takes in Hebrews 11:2. Clearly it takes the sense of "older person," or a person who lived a long time ago (defined as "*the men of old, our ancestors*" in BDAG, 862).

There is no hint of "elder" in the sense of a church office in this passage, nor would readers ever have thought that people like Abel and Enoch and Noah (vv. 4–7) were ever elders in the sense of officers in a local church. Therefore it is invalid to use the argument from Sarah and other women later in the chapter to say that women were sometimes called elders. The word *presbuteros*, like most words, has different meanings, and it is not legitimate to import one meaning of a word into a context where a different meaning is the one the author clearly meant.

---

76. The same arguments apply to 1 Timothy 5:1–2, where Paul says, "Do not rebuke an older man but encourage him as you would a father. Treat younger men like brothers, older women like mothers, younger women like sisters, in all purity." Groups of older and younger people, not church officers, are in view here. (Spencer does not argue from 1 Timothy 5:1–2, but some egalitarians may claim a similar argument here.)

77. Jacobs, *Women of Destiny,* 188.

Egalitarian claim 7.11: Author of Hebrews: It is very possible that a woman was the author of the book of Hebrews.

This argument is made by Gilbert Bilezikian, who writes,

> It is not inconceivable that Priscilla had been commissioned by some church leaders to address the issue of the relation of the two covenants.... Because of the anti-female bias of the Judeo-Christian congregations, she may have been requested to write anonymously.[78]

Answer 7.11a: The author's identity as a man is revealed in Hebrews 11:32.

In Hebrews 11:32, the author says, "And what more shall I say? For time would fail *me to tell* of Gideon, Barak, Samson, Jephthah, of David and Samuel and the prophets."

In English not much can be told about the author from this verse. But in Greek, the expression "to tell" is a participle (*diēgoumenon*) that modifies "me," and the participle is masculine (the feminine form would be *diēgoumenēn*). So the author identifies himself as male.

Someone could respond, "Well, that's just part of the disguise so that people won't know she is a woman." The problem with that argument is that it involves the author in dishonesty, saying something that she *intends* all Greek readers to take as an indication that she is a man. But in fact that is false. This is outright dishonesty, and it is unworthy of an author of Scripture.

Egalitarian claim 7.12: Elect Lady in 2 John: The "elect lady" in 2 John 1 is a woman in authority over a congregation.

The first verse in the short book of 2 John says, "The elder to the elect lady and her children, whom I love in truth, and not only I, but also all who know the truth."

Is this "elect lady" a woman elder in charge of a congregation? This is an argument made by Aida Spencer.

> If "elect lady" stands for a church, then who are "her children"? John calls the recipients of 1 John "my little children" (e.g. 2:1). A church would have to be called *either* elect lady *or* children in John's language scheme, not both. All the data is best understood if John were writing the letter to a woman who was the person in authority over a congregation.[79]

78. Bilezikian, *Beyond Sex Roles*, 302. Bilezikian gives several reasons why this theory seems plausible, but concludes that it is still a "very tentative theory" (305).

79. Spencer, *Beyond the Curse*, 110.

Answer 7.12a: It is much more likely that 2 John is addressed to a whole church. Thomas Schreiner has listed several factors that make it much more likely that 2 John is addressed to a whole church, and the "elect lady" is John's way of referring to the church metaphorically:

> Some have argued for women elders...from the "chosen lady" in 2 John.... The "chosen lady" in 2 John is almost certainly not an individual woman but a reference to the church. (1) John uses the second person plural in verses 6, 8, 10, and 12. The plural demonstrates that he is not writing to one person only; he is writing to an entire church. (2) Second John is much more general and less specific than 3 John. Third John was clearly written to an individual, Gaius, but the lack of specificity in 2 John suggests that a community is being addressed rather than an individual. (3) The description of the church as a "lady" accords well with the rest of Scripture. Paul and John both portray the church as Christ's bride (Ephesians 5:22–33; Revelation 19:7). The new Jerusalem is described as a bride (Revelation 21:2). In the Old Testament, Israel is often portrayed as a woman (Isaiah 54:1; Jeremiah 6:23; 31:21; Lamentations 4:3, 22). (4) The distinction between the "lady" and "her children" in 2 John does not suggest that she is distinct from her children. The "lady" is the church as a whole; the "children" are simply the individual members of the church.[80]

EGALITARIAN CLAIM 7.13: "THE WIDOWS" WERE WOMEN ELDERS: THE "WIDOWS" THAT PAUL DISCUSSES IN 1 TIMOTHY 5:3–16 WERE ACTUALLY FEMALE ELDERS.

Linda Belleville says, "What about female elders? There are good reasons for thinking that Paul is talking about just such a leadership role in 1 Timothy 5:9–10."[81]

Belleville gives four main reasons for seeing these widows as women elders: (1) "Paul limits the role to women age sixty or older (v. 9), which fits the primary Greek meaning of *presbuteros* as 'elderly.'"[82] (2) Paul "lists requirements that parallel the qualifications for elders found elsewhere in his writings. The widow must have been the wife of one husband, have raised her children well, be well-known for her good deeds, and have a reputation for offering hospitality."[83] (3) Widows were paid for their ministry: "Third, like an elder, she is to be remunerated for her ministry (v. 3), *timaō* = 'to reward,' 'to pay' (cf. 1 Tim. 5:17)."[84]

80. Schreiner, "Valuable Ministries of Women," 220.
81. Belleville, "Women in Ministry," 102.
82. Ibid.
83. Ibid., 102–3.
84. Ibid., 103.

(4) Paul's comment about women "saying things they ought not to" in 1 Timothy 5:13 "points to a teaching role."[85]

Answer 7.13a: Older people are not automatically "elders."

In her first reason, Belleville simply confuses two distinct meanings of a word. Just as in English we can speak of "elderly people" and we can also speak of church officers and call them "elders," so in Greek the term *presbuteros* can mean either (a) "pertaining to being relatively advanced in age, *older, old*" or it can mean (b) "an official. . .*elder, presbyter.*"[86] But Belleville confuses these two meanings, implying that older women should be thought of as church officers, as "elders"! This argument is the same as if I said, "I visited some elderly people in a nursing home last Sunday," and then someone replied to me, "Oh, you were visiting people who were 'elders' in their churches." Such a statement, of course, is nonsense because it confuses the meanings of the terms.

In addition, the term *presbuteros* (in either sense) does not even occur in the passage on widows (1 Timothy 5:3–16).

Answer 7.13b: The requirements for widows and elders are not the same.

Belleville claims the requirements for widows "parallel the qualifications for elders." But this is not true. Paul does not say an elder must be the "wife of one husband," but the "husband of one wife" (1 Timothy 3:2). The qualification for widows is similar, except for one important difference: it assumes that the widow is a woman, and it assumes that the elder is a man! In this sense the qualification is not parallel, but exactly the opposite.

Nor is Belleville's second qualification parallel, for Paul says that a widow has to be one who has "brought up children"[87] (1 Timothy 5:10), that is, cared for them physically and spiritually, a task one would expect of mothers in the first-century world. But Paul says that an elder "must manage his own household well, with all dignity keeping his children submissive, for if someone does not know how to manage his own household, how will he care for God's church?" (1 Timothy 3:4–5). Again, Paul assumes male leadership for the head of the household and for the one ultimately responsible for having submissive children, a qualification appropriate to the governing role of an elder and appropriate to that of a good father in the first-century church but different from the nurturing role expected of the widows at the time they were mothers of children.

Another qualification for an elder that is not a qualification for a widow is "able to teach" (1 Timothy 3:2). Belleville dismisses this qualification by saying that it "is only problematic for

85. Ibid., 92.
86. BDAG, 862.
87. The word translated "brought up" is *teknotropheō*, which means "bring up children, i.e., care for them physically and spiritually" (BDAG, 995).

those who would say that women in the early church were forbidden from teaching men" (p. 103), but she does not seem to realize that it is also very "problematic" for her argument that the qualifications for elders and widows are parallel, because the qualification "able to teach" is not found in the list of qualifications for widows.

To summarize, Belleville claims that the qualifications for widows are parallel to those for elders, but the actual facts are that though there are some similar qualifications pointing to godly character, there are also significant differences. An elder had to be a husband, had to keep his children submissive, had to manage his household well so he could care for God's church, and had to be able to teach. None of these things is required of widows.[88]

Answer 7.13c: Widows were given financial support because of need, not pay for ministry.

When Belleville claims that a widow "is to be remunerated for her ministry,"[89] she has taken something that the Bible does say and added to it something that the Bible does not say. It is true that Paul is talking about some kind of financial support in 1 Timothy 5:3–16. But Belleville has added that this is pay "for her ministry," which the Bible does not say. In fact, Paul cannot mean that they are being paid for their ministry, for if these widows have children or grandchildren, these children are supposed to support the widow: "but if a widow has children or grandchildren, let them first learn to show godliness to their own household and to make some return to their parents, for this is pleasing in the sight of God" (1 Timothy 5:4). Therefore widows were not being paid for some kind of ministry work, as Belleville claims. Rather, widows who had no believing relatives were being supported by the church because they had great need and no one else to support them.

Answer 7.13d: Wrongful gossip is not the same as rightful teaching.

When Belleville says the expression "saying things they ought not to" in 1 Timothy 5:13 "points to a teaching role,"[90] this is another slight-of-hand argument. This verse is not talking about those enrolled as older "widows" (who Belleville claims were actually elders), but is talking about younger widows whom Paul says should not be placed on the list of widows ("but refuse to enroll younger widows" [1 Timothy 5:11]). And the verse says nothing about carrying out

88. Paul does say that *younger* widows should "marry, bear children, manage their households" (1 Timothy 5:14), but the word translated "manage their households" is *oikodespoteō*, which means "manage one's household, keep house" (BDAG, 695). However, this is not a qualification for being enrolled as a widow, but something Paul says should be done by those who were not old enough to be placed on the list of widows, but who were younger and should remarry. Of course wives were to manage their households, but in the first-century world as Paul portrays it, that would have been a role they carried out under the leadership of their husbands, who would have overall management responsibilities for the household (1 Timothy 3:4–5 uses *proistēmi*, which means "to exercise a position of leadership, *rule, direct, be at the head [of]*") (BDAG, 870).

89. Belleville, "Women in Ministry," 103.

90. Ibid., 92.

Bible teaching before the assembled church, which is a responsibility of elders. Here is the actual verse, which is flimsy support indeed for women elders:

> Besides that, they [younger widows] learn to be idlers, going about from house to house, and not only idlers, but also *gossips and busybodies, saying what they should not*. So I would have younger widows marry, bear children, manage their households, and give the adversary no occasion for slander. (1 Timothy 5:13–14)

In conclusion, Belleville's argument that the "widows" in 1 Timothy 5 were actually elders would have us believe that the church at Ephesus was governed by a council of elderly grandmothers, dozens of widows who formed a matriarchal government over this large metropolitan church. But Scripture does not say what Belleville claims, for it does not say that these women are elders, it does not say that they had the same qualifications as elders did, it does not say that they were paid for their ministry, and it does not say that they carried out any teaching activity in the church.

Answer 7.13e: Belleville's claims that widows had pastoral responsibility and taught the basics of the faith are incorrect.

Belleville claims that in early church history widows had pastoral roles:

> *Ministering widows* flourished in the postapostolic period. The nature of their ministry was *decidedly pastoral*. Their duties included praying for the church and *teaching the basics of the faith*.... Clement of Alexandria ranked them after elders, bishops, and deacons (*Paidagogos* 3.12.97; *Homily* 9.36.2).[91]

Because the expression "decidedly pastoral" implies serving as a pastor in many readers' minds, and the phrase "teaching the basics of the faith" suggests some recognized teaching role, it is important to check Belleville's references to see if the documents she quotes support her claims. In footnote 36, page 92, she cites the following references:

1. *Canons of Hippolytus,* Canon #59,
2. *Didascalia Apostolorum,*
3. *Apostolic Constitutions* 2.35.2; 3.3.2,
4. B. Thurston, *The Widows: A Women's Ministry in the Early Church* (Minneapolis: Fortress, 1989), 54.

But these references do not support her claims.

91. Ibid; italics added.

1. The *Canons of Hippolytus* Canon #59 reads:

> Concerning the ordination of Widows. If a widow is ordained, she shall not be sealed, but be made by the name.... And the widow shall be ordained by word only, and she shall (then) be joined to the rest of the widows; and they shall not lay hands upon her, because *she does not offer the sacrifice, nor has she a (sacred) ministry*. For the sealing is for the priests because of their ministry, *but (the duty) of widows is about prayer*, which is the duty of all.[92]

This quotation explicitly distinguishes priestly ministerial functions from the functions of the widows, and says their ministry is prayer. There is nothing here about widows having pastoral ministries and "teaching the basics of the faith."

2. *The Didascalia Apostolorum*[93] says:

> Every widow therefore ought to be meek and quiet and gentle.... A widow should have no other care save to be praying for those who give, and for the whole Church. *And when she is asked a question by any one, let her not straightway give an answer, except only concerning righteousness and faith in God; but let her send them that desire to be instructed to the rulers*. And to those who question them let them [the widows] make answer only in refutation of idols and concerning the unity of God. But concerning punishment and reward, and the kingdom of the name of Christ, and His dispensation, *neither a widow nor a layman ought to speak*; for when they speak without the knowledge of doctrine, they will bring blasphemy upon the word.... For when the Gentiles who are being instructed hear the word of God not fittingly spoken...*and all the more in that it is spoken to them by a woman*—how that our Lord clothed Himself in a body, and concerning the passion of Christ: *they will mock and scoff*, instead of applauding the word of doctrine; and she shall incur a heavy judgment for sin.
>
> *It is neither right nor necessary therefore that women should be teachers*, and especially concerning the name of Christ and the redemption of His passion. *For you have not been appointed to this, O women, and especially widows, that you should teach*, but that you should pray and entreat the Lord God. For He the Lord God, Jesus Christ our Teacher, sent us the Twelve to instruct the People and the Gentiles; and *there were with us women disciples*, Mary Magdalene and Mary

92. English translation taken from the "The Apostolic Tradition of Hippolytus," appendix to Duchesne, *Christian Worship* (1927), 531. Parentheses are part of the original text, but italics are added. I am grateful to Linda Belleville for helping me to locate this text. The work is otherwise known as *The Apostolic Tradition* and probably dates from the 3rd century AD (see *Oxford Dictionary of the Christian Church*, 2nd ed., 76–77, 653).

93. This is a document on church order from the early 3rd century AD; see *Oxford Dictionary of the Christian Church*, 2nd ed., 401.

the daughter of James and the other Mary; *but He did not send them to instruct the people with us. For if it were required that women should teach, our Master Himself would have commanded these to give instruction with us.* But let a widow know that she is the altar of God; and let her sit ever at home, and not stray or run about among the houses of the faithful to receive. For the altar of God never strays or runs about anywhere, but is fixed in one place."[94]

3. In the *Apostolic Constitutions*,[95] the following statements are made about widows:

We do not permit our 'women to teach in the Church,' but only to pray and hear those that teach; for our Master and Lord, Jesus Himself, when He sent us the twelve to make disciples of the people and of the nations, *did nowhere send out women to preach,* although He did not want [lack] such. For there were with us the mother of our Lord and His sisters; also Mary Magdalene, and Mary the mother of James, and Martha and Mary the sisters of Lazarus; Salome, and certain others. *For, had it been necessary for women to teach, He Himself had first commanded these also to instruct the people with us.* For "if the head of the wife be the man," it is not reasonable that the rest of the body should govern the head. Let the widow therefore own herself to be the "altar of God," and let her sit in her house, and not enter into the houses of the faithful, under any pretence, to receive anything; for the altar of God never runs about, but is fixed in one place.[96]

4. Bonnie B. Thurston, *The Widows*, says:

[At the beginning of the second century AD:] In return for support, the widows were to lead a life of contemplation and intercession for the church. It is possible that some of the widows made charitable and pastoral house calls and taught younger women "what is good." As with so much about the order at this time, however, the duties, especially those of calling and teaching, are speculation on our part.[97]

[Origen, died ca. 254 AD:] While admitting that the women teach, Origen insists that their teaching should be addressed only to women.[98]

[In the *Didascalia Apostolorum*, early third century AD:] *The widows are strictly forbidden to teach or to baptize.... The writer is adamant...that they must neither teach nor baptize....* Furthermore, "teaching" is very

94. Chapter 15; taken from www.womenpriests.org/traditio/didasc.htm, citing R. H. Connolly, *Didascalia Apostolorum*. The Syriac Version translated and accompanied by the Verona Latin Fragments (Oxford, 1929). Italics added.

95. This is a collection of ecclesiastical law from the 4th century AD; see *Oxford Dictionary of the Christian Church*, 2nd ed., 75–76.

96. *Constitutions of the Holy Apostles*, in *ANF* 7, 427–28 (italics added).

97. Thurston, *The Widows* (1989), 54.

98. Ibid., 95 (italics added).

strictly understood. If a widow is questioned about the Christian faith, she is only allowed to reply to the most rudimentary issues.... *The writer clearly believes both that widows are incompetent to teach and that unbelievers would not take seriously teaching, or even opinions, of old women.*[99]

Why then does Belleville claim that the duties of widows included "teaching the basics of the faith"? The sources mentioned in her footnote prove that women, and in particular widows, were not allowed to teach. These sources prove the opposite of what Belleville claims.

EGALITARIAN CLAIM 7.14: WOMEN HOMEOWNERS AS OVERSEERS: WOMEN FUNCTIONED AS OVERSEERS OF THE CHURCHES THAT MET IN THEIR HOMES.

Linda Belleville claims that "Mary (Acts 12:12), Lydia (16:15), Chloe (1 Corinthians 1:11), and Nympha (Colossians 4:15)" were "overseers of house churches."[100] The reason Belleville gives for this is that "the homeowner in Greco-Roman times was in charge of any and all groups that met under their roof."[101] The example she gives is Jason, who was responsible to "post bond" in Acts 17:7–9.

Answer 7.14a: In this section, as frequently elsewhere, Belleville goes beyond the text of Scripture and claims far more than it actually says.

Jason was required by the city authorities to post some "money as security" (Acts 17:9), probably as a guarantee against any property damage or violence that the authorities suspected might happen. But that does not prove that Jason was ruling over the meetings of Christians in his house, and even over Paul and Silas when they conducted those meetings! Belleville would here have us believe that homeowners could bypass all the qualifications for elders in 1 Timothy 3 and Titus 1, and, simply by virtue of having a church meet in their home, become overseers or elders.[102]

99. Ibid., 99, 100–101 (italics added). Thurston adds a comment that the strength of the admonition not to teach "suggests that some of the widows must have been doing both" (99), but that is speculation on her part. In any case, if it was happening the document shows that it did not meet with general approval.

100. Belleville, "Women in Ministry," 95. See also Brown, *Women Ministers*, 170, 175, and Jacobs, *Women of Destiny*, 200. Jacobs says that the "presiding elder" of a house church "was also the head of the household where the church met." Therefore she concludes that "Lydia and Mary...and others very possibly functioned as 'presiding elders' (or at least the deacons) of the churches in their houses. In fact, if this is so, most of the house churches listed in Scripture were 'pastored' by women!" (200). A few pages earlier she quotes with approval a comment of C. Peter Wagner that there were no church buildings as we know them in the early church, and therefore meeting in private homes was the "norm" (197). Thus, reasoning from one unsubstantiated assumption about the role of a woman who owned a house, Jacobs suddenly has women pastors in "most" of the house churches in the New Testament.

101. Ibid., 83; also p. 96.

102. Belleville also claims as support the argument of Meeks, *The First Urban Christians* (1983), 76. However, what Meeks actually says in that passage is different from Belleville's statement that "the homeowner in Greco-Roman

She would also have us believe that Lydia, who was a brand new convert and who had just been baptized, became the overseer of the church at Philippi simply because she said to Paul, "come to my house and stay" (Acts 16:15). This claim is going far beyond the evidence in Scripture.

Answer 7.14b: A proliferation of unsubstantiated claims begins to look like grasping at straws.

The mention of Chloe as an overseer of a house church, together with a number of other arguments with similar lack of supporting evidence, makes the egalitarian position itself highly doubtful. Such arguments have so little factual support that they do seem to be grasping at straws. In fact, it seems that Belleville is unable to find any woman in Scripture whom she does not claim as a leader.

Only one verse in the whole Bible mentions Chloe: "For it has been reported to me by Chloe's people that there is quarreling among you, my brothers" (1 Corinthians 1:11).[103]

That is all it says. We do not know if "Chloe's people" means Chloe's friends or her relatives or her employees or some messengers sent by her or what. But in Belleville's essay, without a shred of evidence beyond this verse, Chloe is suddenly listed among the women who were "the overseers of house churches."[104]

This is not responsible biblical scholarship. It is not even responsible biblical interpretation at the lay level. It is simply wild speculation unsubstantiated by fact but presented in a sober essay by a professor of New Testament at North Park Theological Seminary. Unsuspecting readers who see Belleville's credentials, and who read the assessment of editors James Beck and Craig Blomberg that Belleville's essay falls "within the boundaries of sound New Testament scholarship" and does not include "the so-called hermeneutical oddities that some hierarchicalist authors have identified in the evangelical egalitarian literature,"[105] probably assume that Belleville has other

---

times was in charge of any and all groups that met under their roof" (83). What Meeks actually says is: "The household context also set the stage for some conflicts in the allocation of power and in the understanding of roles in the community. The head of the household, by normal expectations of the society, would exercise some authority over the group and would have some legal responsibility for it.... Yet, as we shall see, there were certain countervailing modes and centers of authority in the Christian movement that ran contrary to the power of the paterfamilias" (76).

Meeks himself sees certain "egalitarian" trends in early Christianity that would compete with the authority structure normally expected for a Roman household. But he also mentions "the kinds of power and leadership that rival and prevail over the position of the householder, either in the persons of the itinerant apostle and his fellow workers or in the charismatic figures in the local group" (77). Far from proving Belleville's assertion that the homeowner would be "in charge of any and all groups that met under their roof," Meeks says only that there would be "some authority" expected and "some legal responsibility," and he says it is impossible to tell how much competing views of authority and leadership within the Christian community would overcome these expectations.

103. The NIV says "some from Chloe's household," but the word *household* is not in the Greek text, which simply has a plural definite article with the genitive form of the name Chloe, and could be literally translated "those of Chloe."

104. Belleville, "Women in Ministry," 95.

105. Beck and Blomberg in *Two Views on Women in Ministry* (2001), 159.

scholarly reasons to claim that Lydia and Chloe were overseers. They probably assume this is just one more disputed point on which scholars cannot agree. And so the claim about Chloe is given some weight, along with many similar arguments, in favor of the egalitarian position: "It might be so; at least some scholars think it is so."

At some point in this debate, someone has to say clearly that not all scholarship is created equal, and not all scholarship is following the same principles of adherence to the facts of the biblical text and honesty in pointing out when an assertion is a novel view never before claimed by any responsible New Testament interpreter in the history of the Christian church.

EGALITARIAN CLAIM 7.15: WOMEN DEACONS: WOMEN SUCH AS PHOEBE (ROMANS 16:1) WERE DEACONS IN THE EARLY CHURCH, AND THIS SHOWS THAT ALL LEADERSHIP ROLES SHOULD BE OPEN TO WOMEN.

Linda Belleville says that in Romans 16:1, "Paul explicitly salutes Phoebe as a deacon of the church at Cenchrea."[106] And she says, "The Ephesian church most certainly had female deacons" (1 Timothy 3:11) since the qualifications for these women "are the exact duplicates of those listed for male deacons in 1 Timothy 3:8–10."[107]

Answer 7.15a: Many people think there were women deacons in the New Testament, while many others think there were not. But in either case, the office of deacon in the New Testament does not include the governing and teaching authority that is reserved for elders.

The two passages in question are Romans 16:1–2 and 1 Timothy 3:11. Romans 16:1–2 says,

> I commend to you our sister Phoebe, a servant of the church at Cenchreae, that you may welcome her in the Lord in a way worthy of the saints, and help her in whatever she may need from you, for she has been a patron of many and of myself as well.

106. Belleville, "Women in Ministry," 100. Keener, *Paul, Women and Wives,* 237–40 has an extensive discussion of Phoebe as a deacon, claiming that Paul applies the term *diakonos* "generally to a minister of the word" (238). But Keener has made a mistake in logic here, for the fact that some ministers of the word are called "deacons" or "servants" (*diakonoi*) does not mean that all "servants" (*diakonoi*) are ministers of the word. (To take another example showing the error of such logic, all the women in a certain church may be called Christians, but that does not mean that all who are called Christians in that church are women.)

107. Belleville, "Women in Ministry," 102. See also Brown, *Women Ministers*, 167. Whether or not we see women as deacons in 1 Timothy 3:11, Belleville's claim that the qualifications are the same is not the whole story, because verse 11 does not include some of the qualifications Paul mentions for men in verses 8–10, such as "not addicted to much wine," "not greedy for dishonest gain," and "they must hold the mystery of the faith with a clear conscience." In addition, in verse 12 Paul adds a qualification that could not be true of women: "Let deacons each be the husband of one wife, managing their children and their own households well," for a woman could not be a "husband," and the NT never uses *proistēmi* to speak of women "managing" or governing a household, but only of men. (BDAG, 870: "to exercise a position of leadership, *rule, direct, be at the head [of].*")

Some translations of this verse refer to Phoebe as a "deacon" instead of a "servant" (NRSV, TNIV, NLT), while others use the term "deaconess" (RSV, NIV margin). Other translations use "servant" (ESV, NIV, NASB, KJV, NKJV).

The Greek word *diakonos* can take both meanings. In Romans 13:4, it is translated "servant" (referring to the civil authority as the "*servant* of God") and in Romans 15:8 Christ is called a "*servant* to the circumcised to show God's truthfulness." The same word is used to refer to Apollos and Paul as "*servants* through whom you believed" in 1 Corinthians 3:5. But the term is also used to refer to the office of "deacon" in Philippians 1:1, 1 Timothy 3:8 and 12. And then it is translated "servant" again when referring to Timothy in 1 Timothy 4:6. In addition, the same term is translated "minister" in other verses (2 Corinthians 3:6; Ephesians 3:7; 6:21; Colossians 1:7, 23, 25; 4:7).[108]

With such a range of meaning, how are we to decide if Phoebe should be called "deacon" or "servant" in Romans 16:1? The question is whether Paul has a church office in view ("deacon") or is simply honoring Phoebe for her service to the church, and particularly (as most interpreters believe) for her work in carrying Paul's epistle to the church at Rome.

It does not matter very much to the argument of this book whether Phoebe is called a faithful "servant" or a "deacon" in Romans 16:1. In neither case does this passage show that she had any teaching or governing authority in the church. Teaching and governing the whole church are functions given to "elders," not deacons, in the New Testament (see 1 Timothy 3:2, 5; 5:17; Titus 1:9; also Acts 20:17, 28).

Sarah Sumner shows no knowledge of the differences in responsibilities between deacons and apostles in the New Testament when she argues that Phoebe was a *deacon* (*diakonos*, Romans 16:1), and Paul was also called a *diakonos*, and therefore Phoebe was a minister of the Word of God like Paul was. The flaw in reasoning is twofold. First, she is making the same mistake in logic as those who say that *some* coworkers had governing authority over the churches, therefore *all* coworkers had governing authority over the churches (see answer 7.8b). Here Sumner's reasoning is as follows:

1. Some people who are called *diakonos* were ministers of God's Word.
2. Therefore all people who are called *diakonos* were ministers of God's Word.

The error can be seen if we try a similar kind of reasoning with another characteristic:

1. Some people who are called *diakonos* were women (such as Phoebe).
2. Therefore all people who are called *diakonos* were women.

108. In the foregoing examples I am using the English Standard Version as a basis for comparison and to show the range of meanings of *diakonos*, but other translations would show similar variety in translating the word.

Of course the reasoning does not follow, because the term *diakonos* with the sense *servant* is applied very broadly in the New Testament, and not all who are called a *diakonos* have the same responsibilities.

The second flaw in Sumner's argument is more serious. Sumner presumably has enough knowledge of Greek to know that the common word *diakonos* (which appears twenty-nine times in the New Testament) can mean either "servant" or "deacon" (LS, 398) and is translated both ways in most English translations, depending on whether a church office is indicated in the context or not. However, she does not let her readers know this alternative sense of the word but merely quotes a number of verses that call Paul, Apollos, and others a *diakonos* and says "The word is exactly the same."[109] She does not quote Romans 13:4, for example, which says the civil magistrate is "God's *servant* for your good." Nor does she quote John 2:5, "His mother said to the *servants*, 'Do whatever he tells you,'" or other verses where the meaning *servant* and not *deacon* is required (such as Matthew 20:26; 22:13; Romans 15:8; 2 Corinthians 11:5; Galatians 2:17). She gives her readers no clue that a meaning other than "deacon" is possible, but just asserts,

> Some might argue that Phoebe was a deaconness, not a deacon. But the Bible says in Greek she was a deacon (*diakonos*). As a *diakonos*, Phoebe was a minister like Paul (Col. 1:23).... A *diakonos* is a leader who acts as a minister of God's Word.... Phoebe was a *diakonos* like Apollos (1 Cor. 3:5).... The word is exactly the same.[110]

The other passage at issue regarding whether women had the office of deacon is 1 Timothy 3:11. In the middle of a discussion about the qualifications and responsibilities of deacons, Paul says,

> Their wives [or "wives," or "women"; Greek, *gunaikas,* plural of *gunē*] likewise must be dignified, not slanderers, but sober-minded, faithful in all things.

Is Paul here giving qualifications for women who serve as deacons? Or is he talking about the qualifications for the wives of deacons? The question is complex, and both viewpoints are represented in *Recovering Biblical Manhood and Womanhood.* Tom Schreiner writes,

> With respect to women deacons, we need not come to a firm decision, for even if women were deacons this does not refute our thesis regarding male governance in

109. Sumner, *Men and Women in the Church* (2003), 242–43.

110. Ibid. At this point, rather than giving her readers any indication of responsible complementarian understandings of Phoebe, she trivializes any opposing view, saying, "How are we conservatives going to choose to respond to that? Are we going to tell ourselves, 'Well, it appears we have another exception on our hands'?... I can't do that anymore in good conscience" (243). If she is aware that complementarians point out different responsibilities for deacons and argue that *diakonos* could mean *servant* in Romans 16:1, then she is not being honest with her readers in failing to mention these alternatives. If she is not aware of these common alternatives, how can her book be taken as a responsible treatment of the issue?

the church. Even if women were appointed as deacons, they were not appointed as elders (1 Tim. 3:1–7; Titus 1:5–9). Two qualities demanded of elders—being apt to teach (1 Tim. 3:2) and governing of the church (1 Tim. 3:5)—are not part of the responsibility of deacons (cf. also 1 Tim. 5:17; Titus 1:9; Acts 20:17, 28 ff.). The deacon's tasks consisted mainly in practical service to the needs of the congregation. This is suggested by Acts 6:1–6, where the apostles devote themselves to prayer and the ministry of the Word (6:4), while the seven are selected to care for the practical concern of the daily distribution to widows. Elders were given the responsibility to lead and teach the congregation.[111]

Answer 7.15b: If the people who govern local churches are called "deacons," then women should not be deacons today.

In some churches today the deacons are the main governing board of the church. In that case, the deacons are functioning like elders functioned in the New Testament, and it is not appropriate for women to fill that role. But in other churches, deacons are simply what the Greek term first suggests, "servants" who carry out various activities in ministry to others, such as helping the needy (compare Acts 6:1–6), caring for the sick, or overseeing church activities such as youth work, finances, or prayer. In such cases, these activities do not involve teaching or governing activity over the whole church, and it seems appropriate for women as well as men to fill those roles.

There is room for legitimate differences of opinion over whether women could or could not be deacons in the early church, but in either case the office of deacon did not include the teaching and governing responsibilities that Paul reserves for men in 1 Timothy 2:12.

Answer 7.15c: There were women deacons in some parts of the early church, but they did not have teaching authority in the churches.

Belleville helpfully points out a number of writings from the early church fathers and other documents that give evidence of women serving as deacons in at least some parts of the early church.[112] But it is interesting that in her summary of their duties, she does not mention any teaching or governing authority over the church:

> The duties of female deacons in the postapostolic period were quite varied. They taught children and youth, evangelized unbelieving women, discipled new believers, visited the sick, cared for the ailing, administered communion to the shut-ins, and disbursed funds to the needy. In the worship service they served as doorkeepers,

111. Schreiner, "Valuable Ministries of Women," 220. Schreiner gives the argument in favor of women deacons on 213–14, and summarizes the arguments against women as deacons in 505n13.

112. Belleville, "Women in Ministry," 89–90.

assisted with the baptism of women, and administered communion as the occasion arose.[113]

The absence of teaching or governing responsibilities for women is confirmed when we look up some of the literature Belleville mentions. She says, "the *Didascalia Apostolorum* spells out their duties." Here is what it says:

> Wherefore, O bishop.... Those that please thee...thou shalt choose and appoint as deacons: a man for the performance of the most things that are required, but *a woman for the ministry of women*. For there are houses whither thou canst not send a deacon to the women, on account of the heathen, but mayest send a deaconess. Also, because in many other matters the office of a woman deacon is required.[114]

Belleville also says, "*Canon #15* of the Council of Chalcedon (fifth century) details the ordination process for women deacons and places them in the ranks of the clergy."[115]

It is true that this fifth-century AD document speaks of a "laying on of hands" to establish a woman in the role or office of deaconess, but there is no indication that this is parallel to what we today refer to as ordination for pastors or elders, and it is not true that this Canon places a woman "in the ranks of the clergy." Here is what it says:

> A woman shall not receive the laying on of hands as a deaconess under forty years of age, and then only after searching examination. And if, after she has had hands laid on her and has continued for a time to minister, she shall despise the grace of God and give herself in marriage, she shall be anathematized and the man united to her.[116]

An explanatory note to this canon refers the reader to an excursus on deaconesses that says,

> The principal work of the deaconess was to assist the female candidates for holy baptism. At that time the sacrament of baptism was always administered by immersion...and hence there was much that such an order of women could be useful in. Moreover they sometimes gave to the female catechumens preliminary instruction, but *their work was wholly limited to women*, and *for a deaconess of the Early Church to teach a man or to nurse him in sickness would have been an impossibility*. The duties of the deaconess are set forth in many ancient writings....
>
> [Then the author quotes Canon 12 of the Fourth Council of Carthage (398):] "Widows and dedicated women...who are chosen to assist at the baptism of women,

113. Ibid., 90.
114. Chapter 16; quotations taken from www.womenpriests.org/traditio/didasc.htm, citing R. H. Connolly, *Didascalia Apostolorum*. The Syriac Version translated and accompanied by the Verona Latin Fragments (Oxford, 1929). Italics added.
115. Belleville, "Women in Ministry," 90.
116. Quoted from *NPNF*, 2nd ser., 14:279.

should be so well instructed in their office as to be able to teach aptly and properly unskilled and rustic women how to answer at the time of their baptism to the questions put to them, and also how to live godly after they have been baptized."[117]

In light of this evidence, it is misleading for Belleville to say they were placed "in the ranks of the clergy." Women who were deacons in the early church were honored, and they performed valuable functions, but they did not teach or govern men, and they were not counted among the clergy.

EGALITARIAN CLAIM 7.16: ELDERS LACKED AUTHORITY: ELDERS AND OVERSEERS IN THE NEW TESTAMENT DID NOT HAVE AUTHORITY BECAUSE AUTHORITY BELONGED TO THE CHURCH, NOT TO PERSONS.

This is the rather unusual position of Linda Belleville, who writes,

> One is hard-pressed to find a biblical link between local church leadership and "authority" (*exousia*). The New Testament writers simply do not make this connection. In fact, no leadership position or activity in the New Testament is linked with authority.... It is the ***church*** that possesses authority and not particular individuals (or positions, for that matter).... Churches can, to be sure, choose individuals to represent their interests and to work on their behalf...but in no way do these individuals exercise authority over the congregation.[118]

Belleville gives four main reasons for this argument:

1. The term *exousia* ("authority") is not linked to people who have church leadership positions in the New Testament.
2. Passages that use the verb *proistēmi* to speak of the authority of church leaders have "no lexical basis" for associating this word with "exercise of rule" or "authority."
3. Hebrews 13:17 ("***Obey*** your leaders and ***submit to*** them") does not give authority to church leaders, because the key terms have been misunderstood. The verse means only that the readers "follow" their leaders and "yield to" them.
4. Finally, Belleville gives a new translation of 1 Peter 5:2–3: She says that Peter tells the leadership of Asian churches to be "shepherds of God's flock...***not*** ruling over [*katakurieuontes*] them but being examples to the flock."[119]

117. "Excursus on the Deaconess of the Early Church," unsigned article in *NPNF*, 2nd ser., 14:41 (italics added).
118. Belleville, "Women in Ministry," 104–6. Belleville says the only exception to her claim that "no leadership position or activity in the New Testament is linked with authority" (105) is 1 Corinthians 11:10, where Paul says a woman should have an "authority" (*exousia*) on her head. (See pp. 338–39 below for a discussion of 1 Corinthians 11:10.)
119. Ibid., 104–8.

Answer 7.16a: It is a mistake to say that because one specific *word* is missing, an entire *idea* is missing, because the New Testament authors are not limited to one specific Greek word to express the idea of authority in the church.

When Belleville objects that the word *exousia* is not linked to people who have church leadership, she is simply confusing a *word* with an *idea*. New Testament passages that talk about the authority of elders, for example, do not use this particular word, but they do use several other words to indicate governing authority over the congregation. Every language has synonyms, and it is an elementary mistake in interpretation to say, "Because word X is not used in relationship to this idea, this idea is not found in the New Testament." Several verses, such as 1 Thessalonians 5:12; 1 Timothy 5:17; Hebrews 13:17; and 1 Peter 5:3, show that there were specific people in positions of authority in the New Testament churches.

Answer 7:16b: It is not true that no leadership position in the New Testament is linked with authority.

And even with respect to the word *exousia*, Belleville's absolute claim that "no leadership position or activity in the New Testament is linked with authority"[120] is untrue. Paul says of his leadership position:

> For even if I boast a little too much of our *authority* (Greek *exousia*) which the Lord gave for building you up and not for destroying you, I will not be ashamed. (2 Corinthians 10:8)
>
> For this reason I write these things while I am away from you, that when I come I may not have to be severe in my use of the *authority* (Greek *exousia*) that the Lord has given me for building up and not for tearing down. (2 Corinthians 13:10)[121]

Answer 7.16c: It is not true that there is "no lexical basis" for associating *proistēmi* with exercise of rule or authority by elders.

Belleville claims that there is "no lexical basis" for associating the verb *proistēmi* in verses like 1 Thessalonians 5:12, 1 Timothy 3:4–5, and 1 Timothy 5:17 with "exercise of rule" or "authority" by church leaders.[122]

This is a remarkable assertion in light of what the lexicons actually say about *proistēmi*. Here are the passages that Belleville mentions regarding the authority of elders, with the words that correspond to *proistēmi* in italics:

---

120. Ibid., 105.
121. On the previous page, Belleville does restrict her claim to "local church leadership" (104), but the sentence on p. 105 is a broader, more general claim about "no leadership position or activity in the New Testament." In light of 2 Corinthians 10:8 and 13:10, this statement is not true.
122. Ibid., 104n53.

> We ask you, brothers, to respect those who labor among you and *are over you* in the Lord and admonish you. (1 Thessalonians 5:12)
>
> [An overseer or elder] must *manage* his own household well, with all dignity keeping his children submissive, for if someone does not know how to *manage* his own household, how will he care for God's church? (1 Timothy 3:4–5)
>
> Let the elders who *rule* well be considered worthy of double honor, especially those who labor in preaching and teaching. (1 Timothy 5:17)

Is Belleville correct in her claim that there is "no lexical basis" for understanding *proistēmi* to refer to rule or authority in these verses? The first meaning given in the BDAG lexicon is, "to exercise a position of leadership, ***rule, direct, be at the head (of)***."[123] The Liddell and Scott lexicon gives, among other meanings of this common verb, the following: "to be set over, be at the head of," "especially to be chief or leader of a party," "govern, direct."[124] It is difficult to understand how Belleville can say "there is no lexical basis" for such meanings.

Answer 7.16d: Hebrews 13:17 says to obey leaders, not just to follow them.

We read in Hebrews 13:17, *"Obey* your leaders and *submit to* them, for they are keeping watch over your souls, as those who will have to give an account."

Once again, it is surprising to see Belleville claim that this verse means only that the readers should "follow" their leaders and "yield to" them. And it is surprising to see her claim that "obey" is "not an accurate translation."[125]

Belleville gives readers no indication that in denying authority to church leaders in Hebrews 13:17 she is advocating a position that stands alone against all the main English translations of Hebrews 13:17:

> "Obey your leaders and submit to them" (ESV).
> "Obey your leaders and submit *to them"* (NASB).
> "Obey your leaders and submit to their authority" (NIV).
> "Obey your leaders and submit to them" (RSV).
> "Obey your leaders and submit to them" (NRSV).
> "Obey your leaders and submit to their authority" (REB).
> "Obey your spiritual leaders and do what they say" (NLT).

---

123. BDAG, 870. The verb *proistēmi* has a variety of meanings, including "show concern for, care for, give aid" (BDAG, 870), but the BDAG *Lexicon*, together with nearly all translations, places the verses in question in the first meaning, "to exercise a position of leadership, rule, direct," yet with some uncertainty about 1 Thessalonians 5:12. In any case, Belleville's statement that these meanings have "no lexical basis" is not true.

124. LS, 1482–83.

125. Belleville, "Women in Ministry," 108.

"Obey your leaders and submit to them" (NET BIBLE).
"Obey those who rule over you and be submissive" (NKJV).
"Obey them that have the rule over you, and submit yourselves" (KJV).

In addition, she is opposing the meanings of the key terms as given in the standard lexicons. The word "obey" is *peithō*, which takes the meaning "*obey, follow.*"[126] Belleville may claim that "obey" is "not an accurate translation," and readers who have no ability to check the Greek word for themselves may believe her because she is a New Testament professor, but her claim is not supported by the evidence, and it is not true.

In this same verse, the word "leaders" represents a participial form of *hēgeomai*, which means, "to be in a supervisory capacity, *lead, guide*"[127] and is used "of men in any leading position. . .*ruler, leader*. . .of princely authority. . .of military commanders [with many examples from historical literature outside the New Testament]. . .of heads of a Christian congregation."[128]

The term translated "submit" is *hupeikō*, which Belleville says means "to give way," "to yield."[129] She does not quote the BDAG lexicon, which says that *hupeikō* means "to yield to someone's authority, *yield, give way, submit.*"[130]

Answer 7.16e: 1 Peter 5:3 tells leaders not to be domineering. It does not tell them not to rule over people.

When Belleville translates 1 Peter 5:2–3 to say that elders should be "shepherds of God's flock. . .*not* ruling over [*katakurieuontes*] them," she fails to mention that she is again proposing an interpretation that is supported by none of the standard English translations, all of which give a pejorative sense to *katakurieuō* in this verse:

"not domineering over those in your charge" (ESV)
"nor yet as lording it over those allotted to your charge" (NASB)
"not lording it over those entrusted to you" (NIV)
"not as domineering over those in your charge" (RSV)
"do not lord it over those in your charge" (NRSV)
"not lording it over your charges" (REB)
"don't lord it over the people assigned to your care" (NLT)
"do not lord it over those entrusted to you" (NET BIBLE)
"nor as being lords over those entrusted to you" (NKJV)
"neither as being lords over *God's* heritage" (KJV)

---

126. BDAG, 792, 3b.
127. Ibid., 434.
128. Ibid.
129. Belleville, "Women in Ministry," 108n57.
130. BDAG, 1030.

The contrast, "not domineering over those in your charge, but being examples to the flock" makes this pejorative sense of domineering rule appropriate in the context.[131] Peter is not telling elders that they should not exercise any authority at all over the church, or that they do not have any authority, but that they should not use their authority in a distant and domineering way. In addition, two verses later, Peter says, "likewise, you who are younger, be subject to the elders" (1 Peter 5:5), thus reinforcing the idea of elder authority in the church.[132]

Answer 7.16f: Something is seriously wrong with an argument that changes the meanings of all the key terms in all the relevant passages to something not supported by any standard English translation.

Belleville takes each of the passages that refer to the authority of elders and redefines some of the key words, thus changing the meaning of these verses. But in each case she gives meanings that are her own unique interpretations and not consistent with the conclusions found in standard lexicons regarding these verses, and not consistent with the entire history of English translations. In addition, she gives unsuspecting readers no idea how idiosyncratic her interpretations are. Readers who ponder this may begin to wonder if there isn't something seriously wrong with such an argument, something profoundly flawed in such a procedure.

These verses on the authority of leaders should be enough to indicate that Belleville's claim that authority belonged to the church, but not to persons in the New Testament, is simply incorrect.

EGALITARIAN CLAIM 7.17: TEACHERS TODAY LACK AUTHORITY: TEACHERS TODAY DO NOT HAVE THE SAME AUTHORITY AS TEACHERS IN THE NEW TESTAMENT, BECAUSE WE HAVE THE WHOLE BIBLE NOW AND THE BIBLE IS REALLY OUR AUTHORITY.

This argument is stated by Gilbert Bilezikian, who says,

> The role of a teacher (either male or female) in our day has a significance entirely different from the ministry of teaching in apostolic times. Prior to the writing and the canonization of the books of the New Testament, teachers were the dispensers of Christian truth. Their authority was absolute and normative, provided that they were duly trained and authorized. With the formation of the New Testament canon, the locus of authority was displaced from the teacher to the teaching enscripturated in the New Testament. As a result, a current day teacher has no personal authority other than his or her competency. The authority rests in the text of the Bible and not in the person teaching the Bible. A teacher today is only a person *sharing* knowledge and

131. The BDAG *Lexicon* gives as one definition, "to have mastery, *be master, lord it (over), rule*" (519), indicating that the word can take a pejorative sense, and it includes this verse in that sense.

132. For evidence that Peter is referring to elders here, not just to older persons, see Grudem, *First Peter* (1998), 192.

insights from scripture. A sexless teaching machine may do as much without making any authority claims.[133]

Answer 7.17a: The authority of a teacher today is the same as at the time of the New Testament because Bible teaching always had to be based on the authority of the Bible, no matter how much of the Bible was available.

When Bilezikian says, "The role of a teacher (either male or female) in our day has a significance entirely different from the ministry of teaching in apostolic times," he is simply wrong. The authority of teachers at the time of the New Testament was based on the written words of God (or the authoritative words of the apostles, many of which would become part of the New Testament Scriptures). We see this pattern first in the life of Paul and those with him, because (as I mentioned in Answer 7.3b), in Acts 15:35, Paul and Barnabas and "many others" are in Antioch "*teaching* and preaching *the word of the Lord.*" At Corinth, Paul stayed one and a half years "*teaching the word of God* among them" (Acts 18:11).

With regard to other teachers, the author of Hebrews assumes that teachers ought to base their teaching on the words of God, for he says, "you need someone to teach you again the basic principles of the oracles of God" (Hebrews 5:12). And Paul tells Timothy that all "*Scripture*" is "profitable for *teaching*" (2 Timothy 3:16). Since the apostles' writings had equal authority to the Old Testament Scripture (see 2 Peter 3:2, 15–16), it is not surprising that Paul told Timothy to "command and teach" (1 Timothy 4:11) and to "teach and urge" (1 Timothy 6:2) Paul's instructions to the Ephesian church.

Similarly, Paul talks about an ordinary believer as "one who is taught the Word" (Galatians 6:6), showing that the Word of God forms the basis of the teaching. False teachers are those who desire "to be teachers of the Law" but who lack understanding (1 Timothy 1:7).

It is not true to say, as Bilezikian does, that "with the formation of the New Testament canon, the locus of authority was displaced from the teacher to the teaching inscripturated in the New Testament," because *all early teachers had the entire Old Testament* to base their teaching on. In addition, they had a growing collection of writings from the apostles themselves (or people such as Mark and Luke who were writing under the authorization of the apostles). So any Bible teacher even at the very beginning of the Christian church (apart from the apostles themselves) could base his teaching only on the authority of the Old Testament, and on the teaching of the apostles and the writings of the apostles as those became available. (Of course, a teacher could not base his teaching on the book of Philippians, for example, if he had not yet received the book of Philippians, but he would base his authority on as much Scripture as he had.) Therefore, Bilezikian's claim is incorrect.

---

133. Bilezikian, *Beyond Sex Roles*, 184.

Answer 7.17b: The authority of apostles was greater than that of teachers, and today the writings of the apostles (the New Testament) have taken the place of the living apostles in the New Testament church.

Paul tells the Corinthians, "The things I am writing to you are a command of the Lord" (1 Corinthians 14:37; see also Romans 2:16; 2 Corinthians 13:3; Galatians 1:8–9; 1 Thessalonians 2:13; 4:8, 15; 5:27; 2 Thessalonians 3:6, 14). And Peter tells readers to remember "the commandment of the Lord and Savior through your apostles" (2 Peter 3:2). Peter places Paul's writings in the same category as "the other Scriptures" (2 Peter 3:15–16), and Paul quotes the words of Luke 10:7 as "Scripture" (see 1 Timothy 5:17–18).

The apostles had a special office which ended around the time the New Testament writings were completed, and that office of apostle does not continue today.[134] But the office of apostle is different from that of teacher in the New Testament churches, because Paul lists them separately, as in 1 Corinthians 12:28 ("First apostles, second prophets, third teachers") and Ephesians 4:11 ("He gave the apostles, the prophets, the evangelists, the pastors and teachers"). Although there were only a very few apostles in the early church,[135] there were many teachers. In fact, James expected that there were teachers in every church he wrote to (see James 3:1).

Therefore when Bilezikian claims that the authority of teachers "was absolute and normative," he is mistaken, for that status applied only to the apostles and such authority is not claimed for anyone other than apostles.

Answer 7.17c: The primary authority for teachers today is the written Word of God. But in a secondary sense they have authority (a) because of congregational recognition of their trustworthiness as teachers, and (b) because of their own personal character qualities.

Bilezikian is also incorrect to say that a teacher's authority today is based only on competency, and a sexless teaching machine may "do as much" as a live teacher in sharing knowledge and insights from Scripture.

Are the character qualifications for elders (who did much of the Bible teaching) put in Paul's letters for nothing? The qualifications for elder included close attention to character traits having to do with high integrity, an exemplary moral life, and spiritual maturity (see 1 Timothy 3:2–7; Titus 1:6–9). Elders were not just "teaching machines"; their lives as well as their words taught the believers. Thus, Paul could tell Timothy and Titus that they should "*set the believers an example* in speech, in conduct, in love, in faith, in purity" (1 Timothy 4:12), and he told Titus, "Show yourself in all respects to be *a model of good works*" (Titus 2:7; compare 1 Corinthians 11:1; 2 Timothy 3:10–11).

134. For further discussion of this point, see Grudem, *Systematic Theology* (1994), 905–11.
135. See Grudem, *Systematic Theology*, 907–10.

When James says, "Not many of you should become teachers, my brothers, for you know that we who teach will be judged with greater strictness" (James 3:1), and when Paul talks about people who were "teachers" in the churches (1 Corinthians 12:28; Ephesians 4:11), they suggest that a certain group of people were established as teachers (this is especially true in Ephesians 4:11). The office of elder is frequently connected to public teaching in the church (see Ephesians 4:11; 1 Timothy 3:2; Titus 1:9; and especially 1 Timothy 5:17, "Let the elders who rule well be considered worthy of double honor, especially those who labor in *preaching and teaching*"). So there seems to have been an office of "teacher" in the early church, consisting of those who had been publicly recognized and established in that teaching role because of the church's willingness to publicly endorse the trustworthiness of these men. They were men of "recognized trustworthiness."

So teachers are more than "teaching machines." They are real people who, in the whole of their character and personhood, teach and model for the church. In this we can probably understand one of the reasons why the Bible restricts to men the roles of governing and teaching the church: The men who are teachers model the male leadership and male headship that God has established for our good in both the family and in the church. Such governing and teaching roles are most appropriate for those who model godly manhood.

Egalitarian claim 7.18: Paul Tells Women to Preach the Word: In 2 Timothy 4:1–2, Paul tells all Christians, including women, to "preach the Word."

This is the claim of Sarah Sumner in a long narrative reporting on the way her question about 2 Timothy 4:1–2 baffled an audience of women and they sat in stunned silence:

> A year or two ago, at a certain women's conference, I asked approximately four hundred Christian women to open their Bibles to 2 Timothy 3:16–17. Before I read it, I explained that the chapter and verse markings in Scripture were not inserted until the thirteenth century.[136] In other words, I told them that if Paul were alive today, he wouldn't know what was meant by "1 Timothy 2:12" because he never did see any chapters and verses superimposed upon his letters. Paul wrote and sent the letters as letters. In other words, his intention was for his letters to be read all at once. My intention at the conference was for the women to see what happens when we read 2 Timothy 3:16–17 with that in mind. As we already know, this text says, "All Scripture is inspired by God and profitable for teaching, for reproof, for correction, for training in righteousness that the man [Greek *anthrōpos*, "person"] of God may be adequate, equipped for every good work."

136. Sumner is three centuries off here regarding verses: Verse markings were inserted in 1551; see footnote 32, above.

At the conference, I asked the women, "Is everyone convinced that these two verses apply to all of us here today?" There were many nods of heads.

I posed the question again, "Everyone here is totally convinced that these two verses apply to you? You're *sure* the Bible is profitable to equip you, a woman, for every work?" The answer again was yes.

I repeated myself again, "None of you are doubtful that these two verses speak directly to you as women?"

The answer was so obvious that people were beginning to wonder what I had up my sleeve. I repeated again for a fourth time, and again for a fifth. I said, "Okay, this is the last call. Is there *anyone* in this room who believes that 2 Timothy 3:16–17 was not intended to apply to us?"

They all held their ground.

Then my eyes fell to the text where I begin to read the next two verses (2 Tim. 4:1–2), which explicitly say, "I solemnly charge you in the presence of God and of Christ Jesus, who is to judge the living and the dead, and by His appearing and His kingdom: preach the Word; be ready in season and out of season; reprove, rebuke, exhort, with great patience and instruction."

I looked up and paused for about one or two seconds. Then quietly I said, "Do these two verses *also* apply to you?"

Silence.

After a few more seconds, the room began to stir. There were nudgings and whispers and feelings of uncertainty and excitement. Everyone's interest was piqued.

But some of the women were disturbed. After the session one woman talked openly with me about some of her negative reactions.... She said, "By asking that question you made it sound as though women are supposed to go out and preach."

I didn't know what to say, so I said nothing. But I had a thought in mind: Am I the only one who makes it sound as though women are supposed to preach? Or does the Bible do that?[137]

---

137. Sumner, *Men and Women in the Church,* 217–20 (italics in original). This narrative is representative of much of Sumner's argument in the book, a method that could be called "argument by personal anecdote." At other key points she tells how as a professor she posed a particularly insightful question or gave a brilliant rejoinder to a question while speaking to a class or a lay audience, and the audience sat in stunned silence or even burst into amazed laughter (see 187, 195–96, 197).

Answer 7.18a: The commands in 1 Timothy 4:1–2 are all singular imperatives addressed specifically to Timothy.

What Sumner fails to tell her readers, and what she apparently failed to tell those four hundred women, is that the imperative verbs in 2 Timothy 4:1–2 are all singular: Paul is writing to Timothy, and he uses five second person *singular* aorist imperatives to tell Timothy:

> I charge you in the presence of God and of Christ Jesus, who is to judge the living and the dead, and by his appearing and his kingdom: *preach* the word; *be ready* in season and out of season; *reprove*, *rebuke*, and *exhort*, with complete patience and teaching.[138]

The original readers would have known that those singulars were addressed specifically to Timothy. Sarah Sumner, who earned a Ph.D. that required substantial competence in Greek, must know that also. But if she knows that the command "preach the Word" is a singular imperative addressed specifically to Timothy and not to all Christians, it is difficult to understand why she did not disclose it in such an extended and dramatic encounter with an audience of lay persons who have no access to the Greek text. She has withheld highly relevant information from her hearers (and her readers).

The singular imperative shows that the command "preach the Word" was a command specifically from Paul to Timothy. A correct modern application of it would say that it applies to all those who have responsibilities similar to Timothy in preaching and in church leadership. Among first-century hearers who understood Greek, no women who heard this singular command would have thought that Paul was telling them to "preach the Word." Why did Sumner not let her readers know this?

Conclusion

We have considered a large number of egalitarian arguments regarding women's roles in the church according to the New Testament epistles. Egalitarian authors have claimed that women prophets were the same as teachers, that Paul's coworkers were elders, that older women were elders, that women homeowners were elders, that women deacons governed the churches, and that specific women such as Phoebe and Junia had governing authority over the churches. But these claims have not turned out to be persuasive.

138. All of the italicized verbs in this quotation are aorist singular imperatives in Greek. The Greek text has no pronoun for "you" in the phrase translated "I charge you," so no argument about singular or plural can be made from that.

The egalitarian claims that 1 Corinthians 14:34–35 should not be part of the Bible, or is a quotation that Paul rejects, or was due to noisy, disruptive Corinthian women, also turned out not to be convincing. Nor were the claims that elders lacked authority, that teachers today lack authority, or that Paul's goal was simply not to offend the culture, found acceptable. Even before we look at 1 Timothy 2:11–15 in detail, the egalitarian claims from the rest of the New Testament epistles are not consistent with what the New Testament actually says. The New Testament consistently reserves certain teaching and governing roles in the church to men.

Yet whenever we say this we must remember that Jesus and the New Testament apostles gave much more affirmation to women's ministries and to women's value in the church than many churches have done historically. Several of these egalitarian objections have shown us that very clearly. These teachings of Scripture show us that in the midst of this controversy, we must continue to affirm and encourage multiple kinds of ministries by women throughout every aspect of the church's life. *Both* men and women are given spiritual gifts to be used for the common good, as the Holy Spirit intends.

Therefore we must be cautious of straying into liberalism or a denial of the authority of Scripture, while at the same time being cautious that we do not quench the Holy Spirit or unnecessarily restrict the gifts that the Holy Spirit has given to women and the ministries that He wants them to be involved in.

CHAPTER EIGHT

Evangelical Feminist Claims About the Church from 1 Timothy 2

Paul says in 1 Timothy 2:12, "I do not permit a woman to teach or to exercise authority over a man," but egalitarians propose several alternative explanations for this passage. They suggest that perhaps there was a unique situation in Ephesus in which women were teaching false doctrine, and Paul's command was relevant for that particular situation only. Others suggest that women were not well educated in the ancient world, and that is why Paul does not let them teach. Still others suggest that this command was restricted only to husbands and wives, or that it was a temporary command Paul gave only until women could be trained more fully.

Egalitarians also propose several alternative meanings to the word translated "exercise authority." Perhaps it means "domineer" or "misuse authority." Or perhaps it means "not commit violence" or "not proclaim oneself author of a man," or some other negative idea. Finally, some egalitarians propose that Paul was wrong in his teaching in 1 Timothy 2.

In this chapter, we consider these and other egalitarian objections to 1 Timothy 2:11–15.[1] I quote the entire passage here, beginning with verse 8:

> I desire then that in every place the men should pray, lifting holy hands without anger or quarreling; likewise also that women should adorn themselves in respectable apparel, with modesty and self-control, not with braided hair and gold or pearls or costly attire, but with what is proper for women who profess godliness—with good works. Let a woman learn quietly with all submissiveness. I do not permit a woman to teach or to exercise authority over a man; rather, she is to remain quiet. For Adam was

1. For lengthy, detailed, and fair treatments of this entire passage from a complementarian perspective, see Mounce, *Pastoral Epistles* (2000), 135–43, and the book-length treatment in Köstenberger et al., *Women in the Church: A Fresh Analysis of 1 Timothy 2:9–15* (1995). In that second book, for an analysis of detailed exegetical questions on this passage, see especially the essay by Schreiner, "Interpretation of 1 Timothy 2:9–15," 105–54. Many of the arguments I make in this chapter are made in more detail and with more extensive bibliography by both Mounce and Schreiner. (To read detailed treatments of this passage from an egalitarian perspective, see the egalitarian works that I refer to throughout this chapter.)

formed first, then Eve; and Adam was not deceived, but the woman was deceived and became a transgressor. Yet she will be saved through childbearing—if they continue in faith and love and holiness, with self-control.

EGALITARIAN CLAIM 8.1: WOMEN WERE TEACHING FALSE DOCTRINE: WOMEN IN EPHESUS WERE TEACHING FALSE DOCTRINE, AND THIS IS THE REASON PAUL PROHIBITS WOMEN FROM TEACHING IN 1 TIMOTHY 2:11–15. BUT THAT WAS A SPECIFIC COMMAND FOR THAT PARTICULAR SITUATION, AND THEREFORE IT IS NOT UNIVERSALLY BINDING ON US TODAY.

This view is commonly argued by egalitarians. Richard and Catherine Kroeger argue that women were teaching false doctrine, perhaps connected either to Gnosticism or to proto-Gnosticism:

> Our hypothesis will deal with the possibility that the false teachers were indeed Gnostics, proto-Gnostics, or some group with a mythology remarkably like that of the Gnostics.... We maintain that those involved with the false doctrines included both men and women, and that the women were involved in telling stories which contradicted the Scriptures.[2]

Craig Keener says, "Much of the false teaching in Ephesus was being spread through women in the congregation.... Presumably, Paul wants them to learn so that they could *teach.*"[3]

Gordon Fee writes (regarding 1 Timothy 2:12),

> It is probably because some of them have been so terribly deceived by the false teachers, who are specifically abusing the OT.... The word translated **authority**, which occurs only here in the NT, has the connotation "to domineer." In context it probably reflects again on the role the women were playing in advancing the errors—or speculations—of the false teachers and therefore is to be understood very closely with the prohibition against teaching.[4]

2. R. and C. Kroeger, *I Suffer Not a Woman* (1992), 65–66. Jacobs, *Women of Destiny* (1998), 240–41, shows sympathy for this "Gnostic heresy" view, depending only on the Kroegers for support. Grady, *Twenty-Five Tough Questions About Women and the Church* (2003), also agrees with the Kroegers' view, saying, "The Gnostics . . . concocted the notion that Eve was created before Adam.... It is possible that one or more female false teachers had invaded the church at Ephesus and were spreading this detestable doctrine" (144). Sumner, *Men and Women in the Church* (2003), also supports this view in her statement, "Perhaps the most insidious thing is that the false teachers, like Satan, were twisting the Scriptures, lying to the people by saying that Eve was created first and that Eve was not deceived" (259). Gnosticism was an early Christian heresy (from the second century AD) that taught that salvation came through special hidden knowledge (Greek *gnōsis*), and that created matter was evil. Gnostics denied that Jesus had a human nature.
3. Keener, *Paul, Women and Wives* (1992), 111–12.
4. Fee, *1 and 2 Timothy, Titus* (1998), 73.

And J. Lee Grady states,

> What is translated as "certain men" [in 1 Tim. 1:3] is the indefinite Greek pronoun *tisi*. An indefinite pronoun does not indicate gender. Paul is saying, "Instruct certain *people* not to teach strange doctrines." Later in 1 Timothy, it becomes evident that women were doing the teaching of these strange doctrines, at least in part. A major purpose of this entire epistle was to correct unbiblical teachings being presented by women.[5]

Don Williams says, "Could some of those teaching falsely be women? Quite probably so."[6]

Answer 8.1a: The only false teachers named at Ephesus are men, not women.

We have three passages that speak of false teachers in the church at Ephesus, and they all speak of men, not women, as doing the false teaching:

1. 1 Timothy 1:19–20: "some have made shipwreck of their faith, among whom are *Hymenaeus and Alexander*, whom I have handed over to Satan that they may learn not to blaspheme."
2. 2 Timothy 2:17–18: "Among them are *Hymenaeus and Philetus*, who have swerved from the truth, saying that the resurrection has already happened."
3. Acts 20:30: Paul warns the Ephesian elders that in the future, "from among your own selves will arise *men* speaking twisted things, to draw away the disciples after them." Here Paul specifically uses the term *anēr* (plural *andres*), which refers to male human beings, not to people generally. And he is speaking to the elders of the church at Ephesus, who were only men. He tells them that these false teachers will arise "from among your own selves."

So we have three passages that specify who the false teachers were (or would be in the future) at Ephesus, and in all three cases, the false teachers who are named are men, not women.[7]

---

5. Grady, *Ten Lies* (2000), 57. See also Perriman, *Speaking of Women* (1998), 141–2. I. Howard Marshall also thinks that behind 1 Timothy 2:12 "lies some particular false teaching by some women" (Marshall, *A Critical and Exegetical Commentary on the Pastoral Epistles, ICC* [Edinburgh: T & T Clark, 1999], 458).
6. Williams, *The Apostle Paul and Women in the Church* (1979), 111.
7. The Kroegers, after naming Hymenaeus, Alexander, and Philetus, do not dispute that these names refer to men. However, they then add, "We shall suggest that at least one of the individuals who was teaching a different doctrine was a woman" (59–60), but it does not appear that they are attempting to claim that any of these three names (which all have masculine gender forms in the Greek text) refers to a woman, and no later argument is made in their book (as far as I can tell) that one of these names refers to a woman. The statement must mean, rather, that their general argument *suggests* that there were one or more women *in addition to these three men* teaching false doctrine in Ephesus. But the fact remains that three men and no women are named. The Kroegers give no evidence to support their statement about an individual woman.

   Cindy Jacobs misunderstands the Kroegers' statement, for in reference to this passage in their book she writes, "The Kroegers suggest that at least one of these individuals was a woman and that 1 Timothy 2:12 forbids her to teach a heresy which was creating serious problems in the Church" (Jacobs, *Women of Destiny*, 235). But the names are all masculine in Greek and all refer to men.

Answer 8.1b: No clear proof of women teaching false doctrine at Ephesus has been found either inside the Bible or outside the Bible.

Sometimes egalitarians claim that various verses in 1 and 2 Timothy prove that women were teaching false doctrine, but the verses simply do not demonstrate that.

First Timothy 5:13 warns that younger women who do not marry again will become "gossips and busybodies, *saying what they should not*." But this does not indicate that any women were teaching false doctrine. To "gossip" means to spread "intimate or private rumors or facts,"[8] but spreading such personal details about other people, whether rumors or facts, is not the same as teaching false doctrine. Most of us can probably think of people in our local churches or communities who gossip, but they are not teachers of false doctrine! The two speech activities are quite distinct.

When Paul says in 1 Timothy 5:13 that such young women will become "*gossips* and busybodies, *saying what they should not*," the natural interpretation of "saying what they should not," is to take it as an expansion of what Paul means by "gossips." These younger widows who go from house to house will be saying things they should not say, spreading rumors and misinformation about other people. But this does not mean they are spreading false doctrine such as denying the resurrection of Christ, or saying that the resurrection is past already, or uttering blasphemies as Hymenaeus and Alexander did (1 Timothy 1:20), or speaking twisted things to gain a following as Paul predicted false teachers would do in Acts 20:30. There is good evidence that Paul was concerned about *gossip* becoming a problem among some women at Ephesus, but the needed evidence for women *teaching false doctrine* at Ephesus simply cannot be found in 1 Timothy 5:13.

However, my friend Rich Nathan depends on 1 Timothy 5:13 for his view that the most convincing solution regarding 1 Timothy 2 is that "the women in the Ephesian church had become the carriers of this false teaching," and he says that Gordon Fee's definition "to talk foolishness" or "to communicate false teaching" is a better translation than "gossips" for the word *phluaros* in 1 Timothy 5:13.[9] The reference he gives to Fee does not mention *phluaros*, so it is unclear what evidence Nathan is using to propose this new definition for the word.[10] The standard lexicons do not mention the sense, "to communicate false teaching," and such a verbal idea would be surprising to find for a definition of an adjective in any case. The BDAG definition is simply "*gossipy*,"[11] and LS says, "*silly talk, foolery, nonsense; tattler,*

8. *American Heritage Dictionary*, 3rd ed. (Boston: Houghton Mifflin, 1996), 783. The Greek term *phluaros* is an adjective meaning "gossipy" (BDAG, 1060).
9. Nathan, *Who Is My Enemy* (2002), 151.
10. Page 151n16 refers to p. 278, where Nathan cites Fee and Stewart, *How to Read the Bible for All Its Worth* (1993), 72–76. Though Nathan does not mention it, Fee's commentary on 1 Timothy does claim that *phluaros* is used of "speaking something foolish or absurd in comparison to truth" (Fee, *1 and 2 Timothy, Titus*, 122), but it is unclear on what basis Nathan or Fee can claim that the word means specifically to communicate false teaching. (Fee gives no evidence for his claim either.)
11. BDAG, 1060.

babbler."[12] No English translation known to me gives the sense "to communicate false teaching," and the sense "gossips" is the near-unanimous sense in modern translations (NASB, NIV, ESV, RSV, NRSV, NLT, NKJV). Thus, no nuance of "communicating false teaching" in 1 Timothy 5:13 has been proven by Fee or Nathan, and Nathan's claim that women were teaching false doctrine in Ephesus remains an assertion with no evidence to support it.[13]

Second Timothy 3:6–7 is another passage egalitarians sometimes use to claim there were women teaching false doctrine at Ephesus:

> For among them are those who creep into households and capture weak women, burdened with sins and led astray by various passions, always learning and never able to arrive at a knowledge of the truth.

This passage indicates that some women were *led astray* by false teachers. That is not surprising, for when false teaching comes into a church, some men and some women will be led astray—God does not give immunity from wrong belief to either men or women in general. But the passage does not say that the women were *doing the false teaching*; it simply says they were being led astray.

There is no proof that any woman or any group of women were engaged in teaching false doctrine at Ephesus. But even if that could be established, the egalitarian claim is not persuasive because it does not show that women were *primarily* responsible for spreading the false teaching—of which the only named proponents are men. And unless women were *primarily* responsible for spreading the false teaching, Paul's silencing of the women (in the egalitarian view) would not make sense.

Is there any other proof? Some have mentioned the passage about Jezebel in Revelation 2, where Jesus says to the church in Thyatira,

> But I have this against you, that you tolerate that woman Jezebel, who calls herself a prophetess and is teaching and seducing my servants to practice sexual immorality and to eat food sacrificed to idols. (v. 20)

Does this prove there were women teaching false doctrine at Ephesus? It does prove there was one woman in the church at Thyatira, a different church, teaching false doctrine and claiming to be a prophetess. And I do not deny that there have been women who taught false doctrine at various points in the history of the church. But *one woman teaching false doctrine at Thyatira* does not prove that there were *any women teaching false doctrine at Ephesus!* There

12. LS, 1946.
13. I am surprised to see Nathan, who is a careful thinker, advocate this position. It is kind of him to write, "My friend Wayne Grudem, a theologian, suggests that no external evidence exists of a feminist cult operating in Ephesus at the time of the writing of 1 Timothy, so how do we know that the apostle Paul was linking his prohibition to that particular problem?" (*Who Is My Enemy,* 150). Nathan offers no answer to this question. His interpretation is without basis in fact.

may or may not have been women teaching false doctrine at Ephesus. My point is simply that there is *no evidence* that women were teaching false doctrine at Ephesus. And so the claim turns out to be speculation without any hard evidence to support it. Should we base our interpretation of a passage on a claim with no supporting evidence and with substantial contrary evidence?

Answer 8.1c: Richard and Catherine Kroeger's claim of a Gnostic heresy that Eve was created before Adam has no persuasive historical basis.

Richard and Catherine Kroeger argue at great length for the presence of a Gnostic or proto-Gnostic heresy in Ephesus that taught that Eve was created before Adam and taught Adam spiritual knowledge.[14] To construct their case they have no proof from any first-century material outside the New Testament, but use *later sources* in such a way that has opened their work to significant criticism. They dismiss these concerns by saying,

> A substantive discussion of the sources, dating, and origins of Gnosticism is outside the purview of this book.... Our hypothesis will deal with the possibility that the false teachers were indeed Gnostics, proto-Gnostic, or some group with a mythology remarkably like that of the Gnostics.[15]

New Testament scholars with expertise in this area have not been positively impressed with the Kroegers' work. Thomas Schreiner summarizes much of the academic rejection of the Kroegers' speculative work in the following statement:

> Unfortunately, the Kroegers' reconstruction is riddled with methodological errors. They nod in the direction of saying that the heresy is "*proto-gnostic,*" but consistently appeal to later sources to establish the contours of the heresy. The lack of historical rigor, if I can say this kindly, is nothing less than astonishing. They have clearly not grasped how one should apply the historical method in discerning the nature of false teaching in the Pauline letters.[16]

Three other reviews of the Kroegers' work by New Testament experts offer deeply troubling evaluations. Stephen Baugh, New Testament professor at Westminster Seminary (California) whose PhD thesis is on the history of ancient Ephesus, wrote an extended review called "The

---

14. See especially R. and C. Kroeger, *I Suffer Not a Woman*, especially 59–66 and 119–25, with other additional historical material supposedly supporting this idea in the next several chapters.
15. Ibid., 65–66. (For an analysis of the Kroegers' claim that *authenteō* in 1 Timothy 2:12 means "proclaim oneself author of a man," in accordance with this alleged Gnostic heresy, see egalitarian claim 8.10.)
16. Schreiner, "Interpretation of 1 Timothy 2:9–15" (1995), 109–10. Schreiner adds, "For three devastating reviews of the Kroegers' work, see Robert W. Yarbrough, '*I Suffer Not a Woman:* A Review Essay,' *Presbyterion* 18 (1992): 25–33; Albert Wolters, 'Review: *I Suffer Not a Woman,*' *Calvin Theological Journal* 28 (1993): 208–13; S. M. Baugh, 'The Apostle Among the Amazons,' *Westminister Theological Journal* 56 (1994): 153–71." (See Appendix 6 for these reviews, pp. 646–74.)

    For an excellent brief summary of ancient Gnosticism and current scholarly viewpoints about it, with an extensive bibliography, see E. M. Yamauchi, "Gnosticism," *DNTB*, 414–18.

Apostle Among the Amazons."[17] As Baugh's title indicates, the Kroegers rely heavily on nonfactual myths (such as myths of Amazon "women warriors") to paint a picture of ancient Ephesus where women had usurped religious authority over men: a "feminist Ephesus" in the religious realm. But their historical reconstruction is just not true. Baugh says, "the Kroegers...have painted a picture of Ephesus which wanders widely from the facts" (p. 155). With his expertise in the history of Ephesus, Baugh affirms, "No one has established historically that there was, in fact, a feminist culture in first-century Ephesus. It has merely been assumed" (p. 154). He says the Kroegers' foundational claim that the religious sphere of life could be led by women, but not the social–civic spheres, "betrays an astonishing innocence of how ancient societies worked" (p. 160). After analyzing their data, he concludes, "It is difficult to imagine how such a momentous conclusion could have been erected upon such fragile, tottering evidence" (p. 161). Other evidence used by the Kroegers is "wildly anachronistic" (p. 163), and contains "outright errors of fact" (p. 165). On the other hand, "they virtually ignore a vast body of evidence of a historically much more reliable and relevant quality: the approximately 4,000 Ephesian inscriptions and the burgeoning secondary literature surrounding them" (p. 162).[18]

Another review of the book is by Albert Wolters, Professor of Religion and Theology/Classical Studies at Redeemer College in Hamilton, Ontario.[19] Wolters first summarizes the Kroegers' argument that 1 Timothy 2:12 should be translated, "I do not permit a woman to teach nor to represent herself as originator of man, but she is to be in conformity [with the Scriptures]," and that Paul was opposing a specific feminist heresy at Ephesus. He then says,

> their proposal, both philologically and historically, is a signal failure. In fact, it is not too much to say that their book is precisely the sort of thing that has too often given evangelical scholarship a bad name. There is little in the book's main thesis that can withstand serious scrutiny, and there is a host of subordinate detail that is misleading or downright false.[20]

---

17. Baugh, "Apostle Among the Amazons" (1994), 153–71.
18. The response to Baugh's analysis in the egalitarian journal *Priscilla Papers* by Alan Padgett is to say that Baugh "nowhere even considers, much less refutes, the idea that a small group of philosophers (like the Gnostics) might have been teaching the equality of women, contrary to the rest of society" Alan Padgett, "The Scholarship of Patriarchy (on 1 Timothy 2:8–15)," *Priscilla Papers* (winter 1997), 25–26. The word *might* in this statement reveals a desperate grasping at straws when there is no supporting evidence. I suppose someone could say there "might" have been people at Ephesus supporting all sorts of different doctrines, but a bare "might have been" in the absence of facts is hardly a sufficient basis on which to justify rejecting present-day obligations to obey the instructions of 1 Timothy 2:12. People can believe something that has no contemporaneous facts supporting it and hundreds of facts against it if they wish, but it will be for factors other than evidence and rational analysis.
19. Wolters, "Review: *I Suffer Not a Woman,*" 208–13.
20. Ibid., 209–10.

Citing several specific examples, Wolters observes that the Kroegers

> repeatedly misunderstand the sources they cite, and they fail to mention important recent literature which counts against their own interpretation.... Their scholarly documentation is riddled with elementary linguistic blunders.... Unfortunately, things are not much better with the Kroegers' historical argumentation. There is in fact no direct evidence that their postulated Gnostic sect ever existed in first-century Ephesus, or indeed that a Gnostic group fitting their description ever existed at all.[21]

He concludes that "the Kroegers have conspicuously failed to make their case.... It is very doubtful whether any serious commentary on 1 Timothy will ever adopt its basic thesis."[22]

Finally, the book was also reviewed by Robert W. Yarbrough, who was at that time Associate Professor of New Testament at Covenant Theological Seminary in St. Louis.[23] Yarbrough notes that the book's general method...is to build on one-sided statements, ignoring any research findings or even primary data that do not agree with its thesis. This makes for a convincing presentation, but only so long as one remains ignorant of the full range of pertinent data and dissenting scholarly opinion.[24]

Then Yarbrough issues warnings about the trend to interpret as culturally relative key teachings of Scripture:

> One may ask what the long-term outcome of the hermeneutics of an apparently growing stratum within evangelicalism is apt to be, assuming that the Kroegers' book is an example and harbinger. Is it possible to nibble away at the putative edges of the apostolic word about the sexes that was thought to be valid and authoritative for centuries without creating an appetite in some for larger and larger bites? If 1 Timothy 2:12 is simply cultural, why not (as many have already concluded) Eph 5:22 ("Wives, submit to your husbands...")? And if Eph 5:22, why not Eph 5:25ff., which teaches that husbands ought to be willing to lay down their lives for their wives like Christ did for the church?... What is noteworthy is to see ostensibly evangelical authors, apparently with little restraint from their evangelical publishers, urging with such aplomb such revisionist reading of apostolic teaching.[25]

In short, the Kroegers have carelessly cited much varied material from dates after 1 Timothy was written, often without giving readers a fair indication that they are quoting later material. They even appeal to stories from Greek mythology as if they were historical fact (such as the

---

21. Ibid., 211.
22. Ibid., 213.
23. Yarbrough, "*I Suffer Not a Woman:* A Review Essay," *Presbyterion* 18 (1992), 25–33.
24. Ibid., 27.
25. Ibid., 31–32.

myths about the Amazons, a race of female super-warriors). Their historical reconstructions are based on fanciful speculation and are not reliable.[26]

Few responsible egalitarian scholars have followed the Kroegers in this proposal. I. Howard Marshall says the Kroegers' reconstruction of the Ephesian background is "highly conjectural."[27]

Answer 8.1d: If the fact that some people were teaching false doctrine disqualified everyone of the same gender, then all men would have been disqualified from teaching.

The egalitarian argument (whether depending on the Kroegers' claim of a Gnostic myth, or on other claims that women were teaching false doctrine) simply is not consistent. Even if *some* women were teaching false doctrine at Ephesus, why would that lead Paul to prohibit *all* women from teaching? It would not be fair or consistent to do so. As we saw above, the only false teachers we know about with certainty at Ephesus are men, not women. Therefore if the egalitarian argument were consistent, it would have Paul prohibiting *all men* from teaching, just because some men were teaching false doctrine! But Paul does not do that, and this shows the inconsistency of the egalitarian argument.

Answer 8.1e: Paul gives the reason for his command, and it is the Creation order (1 Timothy 2:13–14), not any false teaching by women. It is precarious to substitute a reason Paul does not give for what he does give.

Paul does not mention false teaching by women as a reason for his command. He does not say, "I do not permit a woman to teach or to exercise authority over a man; rather, she is to remain quiet *for some women are teaching false doctrine there at Ephesus*." Rather, Paul's reason is the Creation order: "*For Adam was formed first, then Eve.*"

We should be reluctant to accept a position based on a reason Paul does not give, especially when it minimizes, ignores, or presents an eccentric interpretation of the reason Paul actually does give (as several egalitarian positions do).

Answer 8.1f: The argument that no men were even present with the women fails to consider the actual wording of this text.

Sarah Sumner proposes another explanation of why Paul said only women, not men, should be silent: perhaps there were no men present. She writes,

---

26. In addition, it should be troubling for evangelicals to see that the Kroegers do not think 1 and 2 Timothy were written by Paul, but were simply authorized by Paul and written by someone else after his death. They say, "We would argue for the involvement of at least one other hand in the composition. Possibly the epistle was written upon the instruction of the apostle Paul but completed after his death as his will and testament (*parathēkē*) to Timothy.... The author writes with the authority of Paul" (44). They then tell readers, "For convenience, the name *Paul* will at times be used to designate the writer of the Pastoral Epistles" (46).

27. Marshall, *Pastoral Epistles* (1999), 459.

> the women in Ephesus were talking when they should have been listening. Whether or not the men were present with them we do not know. If they weren't, that would constitute one plausible explanation of why Paul commanded women, not men, to be silent.[28]

This is indeed a novel proposal. The reason no one has proposed this before may be the difficulty of explaining why Paul commands these absent men to "pray, lifting holy hands without anger or quarreling" (1 Timothy 2:8), or why Paul would waste time telling women not to teach people who weren't there (v. 12). Sumner's argument is unsupported speculation.

EGALITARIAN CLAIM 8.2: WOMEN NOT EDUCATED: THE REFERENCE TO EVE'S DECEPTION IN 1 TIMOTHY 2:14 SHOWS THAT EVE WAS LESS EDUCATED THAN ADAM, JUST AS THE WOMEN IN EPHESUS WERE LESS EDUCATED THAN THE MEN. BUT WOMEN TODAY HAVE AS MUCH EDUCATION AS MEN; THEREFORE, 1 TIMOTHY 2:11–15 DOES NOT APPLY TO US TODAY.

Gilbert Bilezikian says,

> In the fateful story of the fall, it was Eve, *the lesser informed* person, who initiated a mistaken course of action and who led herself into error. Eve was not created first or at the same time as Adam. She was the late-comer on the scene. Of the two, she was the one bereft of the first hand experience of God's giving the prohibition relative to the tree. She should have deferred the matter to Adam, who was better prepared to deal with it since he had received the command directly from God.... Her mistake was to exercise an authoritative function for which she was not prepared....
>
> Paul's teaching in this passage has an absolute and universal relevance. The principle he lays down to protect the teaching ministry and the exercise-of-authority functions from incompetent persons is valid for all times and for all churches. Christian communities should always remain watchful to authorize in positions of leadership only those persons who have received adequate training.... According to Paul's principle, neither men nor women should be appointed to positions of leadership in the church until they can show evidence of maturity and competency.[29]

Craig Keener also thinks that the most likely reason for Paul's prohibition in 1 Timothy 2 against women teaching is their inadequate education:

---

28. Sumner, *Men and Women in the Church,* 250.
29. Bilezikian, *Beyond Sex Roles* (1985), 180–81. He elaborates on this on page 297: "Paul's understanding of the primacy of Adam as a safeguard against deception shows that he is concerned with competency. The reference to Eve...provides further evidence that Paul is establishing a principle based not on chronology but on competency" (p. 297). See also Jacobs, *Women of Destiny*, 230; Brown, *Women Ministers* (1996), 297–98; Perriman, *Speaking of Women*, 165–8; Nathan, *Who Is My Enemy,* 150, 153.

> The third possibility [which Keener thinks most likely] is that Paul intends to connect Eve's later creation to why she was deceived: She was not present when God gave the commandment, and thus was dependent on Adam for the teaching. In other words, she was inadequately educated—like the women in the Ephesian church.[30]

Answer 8.2a: Many men and many women had basic literacy skills in the first century, and very few men or women had education beyond this.

Steven Baugh, an expert in the history of ancient Ephesus, says about cultures like that of ancient Ephesus, "Few people in antiquity advanced in their formal education beyond today's elementary school levels, including men like Socrates, Sophocles, and Herodotus."[31] However, there is considerable evidence that *many women received basic literacy skills in the ancient world.* Baugh continues:

> Because women's education in antiquity usually took place privately, we get only a glimpse of it here and there. As for women's literacy, daughters of the upper classes needed some level of education for their duties in managing large households. And though they were not commonly found in fields like philosophy, women did read and write literature and poetry during this period.[32]

Baugh mentions that from Ephesus we have several examples of writing by women, including some poems and prayers.[33]

Other sources indicate that in Greek culture, the "Hellenistic school" form of education "endured with but slight changes to the end of the ancient world," and, "girls, too, were educated at all age levels. In some cases they came under the control of the same officials as the boys and shared the same teachers.... In other cases separate state officials were responsible for them."[34]

In Roman society, one of the factors of Roman schools was "the inclusion of girls in the benefits of education."[35] The *Oxford Classical Dictionary* notes that both Plato and Aristotle

30. Keener, *Paul, Women and Wives,* 116. In a similar way, Cindy Jacobs says (in her discussion of 1 Corinthians 14:34–35), "Also, at that time, most women were illiterate and hadn't had the privilege of an education" (Jacobs, *Women of Destiny*, 230). Grady agrees, claiming, "The women in Ephesus needed more instruction.... Women in this culture had been denied all educational opportunities. Except for some Roman women in the upper class, women in the Middle East and Asia Minor were sequestered at home and kept away from books and learning" (*Twenty-Five Tough Questions*, 141).
31. S. M. Baugh, "A Foreign World: Ephesus in the First Century," in Köstenberger, *Women in the Church,* 46, with reference to H. I. Marrou, *Education in Antiquity,* trans. George Lamb (New York: Sheed and Ward, 1956).
32. Ibid., 46.
33. Ibid., 47, footnote 140; additional evidence from several other sources is given on 46, notes 136, 138–39.
34. F. A. G. Beck, "Education" (1970), in the *OCD*, 2nd ed., 371.
35. Ibid., 372. The 3rd edition of the *OCD* reflects greater skepticism about the percentage of people educated in the ancient world but still says that "girls as we see from vase-painting, might be educated in all three elements [of gymnastics, music, and letters], as well as dancing, though not normally in the same schools as boys or to the same extent" (507), and in the Hellenistic period... "received more education than before...but cannot

"believed that men and women should have the same education and training."[36] And, with regard to women in earlier Greek society, "Papyri (private letters, etc.) show widespread literacy among the Greeks of Egypt" while in Rome, "upper-class Roman women were influential...many women were educated and witty."[37]

Even egalitarian Craig Keener, who argues that women were in general less educated than men, says,

> [In Greek and Roman culture] girls as well as boys were educated during this period, but, among those who could afford it, older students who went on to study philosophy or rhetoric were normally men.
>
> The contrast between men's and women's education is more dramatic...in ancient Judaism. The case should not, of course, be exaggerated. Women must have heard some Torah teaching regularly in the synagogues (Acts 17:4; 18:26), probably often learned some Bible teaching from their parents, and were presumably sometimes expected to join the father in teaching the children, especially when they were young. It was not unnatural for a wife or daughter of a rabbi to be able to cite Scripture accurately and effectively. But the rabbis did not normally feel that women needed Torah as much as men did.[38]

In *Women and Men in Ministry: A Complementary Perspective*,[39] Clinton Arnold and Robert Saucy report further evidence of the significant educational achievements of women in ancient Ephesus:

> In a very important recent study, Paul Trebilco has accumulated and presented the inscriptional evidence attesting to the role of women in civic positions in western Asia Minor....[40] It is frequently assumed in some of the literature that women in Ephesus (and in Asia Minor and the entire Roman world, for that matter) lacked education and the opportunity for an education. This has been drastically overstated....
>
> There is now inscriptional evidence that women served in some of the cities in a position that would be a close functional equivalent of our "superintendent of

---

have been educated everywhere as fully as boys. But how far one can really claim universal education among Greek children in the period (as Marrou) is controversial" (508). In Roman schools, "Elementary teachers of some kind were affordable to all but the poor," and in the schools, "boys were almost certainly in a majority but some girls did attend too" (510). Moreover, "some women could read and write...at least to the level needed for their role as guardians of the household stores...although there are many references to literary works by women, very few texts survive" (1623).

36. Walter K. Lacey, "Women" (1970), in the *OCD,* 2nd ed., 1139.
37. Ibid.
38. Keener, *Paul, Women and Wives,* 83, with many extrabiblical references given in the footnotes.
39. Saucy and TenElshof, eds., *Women and Men in Ministry* (2001).
40. Clinton Arnold and Robert Saucy at this point referred to Paul Trebilco, *Jewish Communities in Asia Minor* (1991), especially chapter 2, "The Prominence of Women in Asia Minor," on pp. 104–26. (Information taken from Arnold and Saucy, "Ephesian Background ," 366n4.)

schools," that is, in the capacity of a gymnasiarch (*gymnasiarchos*). The "gymnasium" was the center for education in a Greek city.... The "gymnasiarch" had oversight of the intellectual training of the citizens and for the general management of the facility. Inscriptions dating from the first to the third centuries attest to forty-eight women who served as gymnasiarchs in twenty-three cities of Asia Minor and the coastal islands. This suggests that *women not only had access to education, but also that in many places they were leading the educational system.*

This evidence stands in contrast to what we generally know of the plight of women at the beginning of the Roman Empire.... But beginning in the late republic (2nd Century BC) and early Imperial Period, a much greater array of opportunities opened up for women. The famous British classicist, Michael Grant, observed that "The Roman women of the late republic possessed a freedom and independence almost unparalleled until the present century."[41]

Arnold and Saucy conclude,

At the very least, the historical evidence we have presented demonstrates that some other reconstructions of the situation at Ephesus are far less likely. It is not probable that Paul was advocating a conformity to the prevailing culture on the issue of women's roles as a means of facilitating the evangelistic outreach of the church to the community. Those who have taken this position typically assume a far greater limitation on women than what appears to have been the case. *Nor is it likely that Paul was addressing a situation in which the women were uneducated and, therefore, were disqualified from teaching on that basis alone. Clearly, the women who attained civic offices were educated and, assuredly, a woman serving as a "superintendent of schools" was very well educated.*[42]

Answer 8.2b: The Bible never requires advanced degrees for people who teach God's Word or have governing authority in the church.

The fact that many women as well as men had basic literacy skills in Greek, Roman, and Jewish cultures is enough by itself to disprove the egalitarian claims about 1 Timothy 2. If absolutely *no* women and *only* men could read and write in ancient Ephesus, and if that practice had carried over into the church so that no Christian women learned the Bible, then the egalitarian claim would deserve some consideration. But that is simply not the case. Both women and men could read and write.

---

41. Arnold and Saucy, "The Ephesian Background of Paul's Teaching on Women's Ministry," in *Women and Men in Ministry*, 281–83 (italics added). The quotation from Michael Grant at the end of this statement has an endnote indicating that it was taken from Michael Grant, *A Social History of Greece and Rome*, 30–31.
42. Arnold and Saucy, "Ephesian Background," 287 (italics added).

Formal academic training in Scripture (as in a modern seminary or an ancient school for rabbis) was not required for leaders in the New Testament church. We even see that several of the apostles did not have formal biblical training or schooling as the rabbis did (see Acts 4:13). The ability to read and study Scripture was available to both men and women alike, and *both men and women learned and studied Scripture in the ancient church* (note Acts 18:26, where Priscilla and Aquila *together* instruct Apollos; also 1 Timothy 2:11 which encourages women to "learn," and Titus 2:3–4, where older women are to "teach what is good, and so train the young women"). This would have certainly been true in a major metropolitan center like Ephesus, where there would have been many literate, educated women in the church.

Answer 8.2c: It simply is not true that no women in the first-century churches were well enough educated to be teachers or rulers in the church, and therefore lack of education cannot be the reason for Paul's statement.

The New Testament shows several women who had a considerable level of understanding Scripture. Many women accompanied Jesus and learned from Him during His earthly ministry. (See Luke 8:1–3; 10:38–41; also John 4:1–27; 11:21–27). In this very passage in 1 Timothy, Paul says that women should "learn" (v. 11).

Perhaps the best example of a woman well trained in knowledge of the Bible is Priscilla. When Paul went to Corinth, he stayed with Aquila and Priscilla: "Because he was of the same trade he stayed with them and worked, for they were tentmakers by trade" (Acts 18:3). Paul stayed a year and six months at Corinth (Acts 18:11), and we may ponder just how much Bible and theology Priscilla would have learned while having the apostle Paul as a house guest and business partner during that time! Then Priscilla and Aquila went with Paul to Ephesus (Acts 18:18–19). It was at Ephesus in 51 AD that Priscilla and Aquila together "explained" to Apollos "the way of God more accurately" (Acts 18:26). So in 51 AD Priscilla knew Scripture well enough to help instruct Apollos.

After that, Priscilla probably learned from Paul for another three years while he stayed at Ephesus teaching "the whole counsel of God" (Acts 20:27; compare 1 Corinthians 16:19, where Priscilla is called Prisca, and Paul sends greeting to Corinth from Aquila and Prisca and the church that meets "in their house"). By the end of Paul's three-year stay in Ephesus, Priscilla had probably received four and a half years of teaching directly from the apostle Paul. No doubt many other women in Ephesus also learned from Paul—and from Priscilla!

Aquila and Priscilla went to Rome sometime later (Romans 16:3, perhaps around 58 AD), but they returned to Ephesus, for they were in Ephesus again at the end of Paul's life (in 2 Timothy 4:19, Paul writes to Timothy at Ephesus, "Greet Prisca and Aquila"). Now 2 Timothy was probably written in 66 or 67 AD (Eusebius says that Paul died in 67 AD), and 1 Timothy a short time before that, in perhaps 65 AD In addition, before he wrote 1 Timothy, Paul seems to have been in Ephesus and it seems he told Timothy to remain there when he left for Macedonia (see 1 Timothy 1:3: "As I urged you when I was going to Macedonia, remain in Ephesus..."). Therefore, both because 1 Timothy is near in time to 2 Timothy, and because Paul had last been in Ephesus to know who was there before he wrote 1 Timothy or 2 Timothy, it seems likely that Priscilla and Aquila were back in Ephesus by the time Paul wrote 1 Timothy, about 65 AD

What is the point of this? Not even well-educated Priscilla, nor any other well-educated women of Ephesus who followed her example and listened to Paul's teaching for several years, were allowed to teach men in the public assembly of the church. Writing to a church where many women had received significant training in the Bible from Paul himself for over three years, Paul said, "I do not permit a woman to teach or to have authority over a man" (1 Timothy 2:12). Paul's reason was certainly not lack of education.

Answer 8.2d: Lack of education is not the reason Paul gives for restricting teaching and governing roles to men. We should not deny the reason Paul gives and substitute a reason he does not give.

Paul does not say, "I do not permit a woman to teach or to exercise authority over a man; rather, she is to remain quiet, *for women are not as well-educated as men*." That is not the reason Paul gives. The reason he gives is the order that God established when He created Adam and Eve: "*For Adam was formed first, then Eve*; and Adam was not deceived, but the woman was deceived and became a transgressor" (1 Timothy 2:13–14).

Answer 8.2e: If lack of education were the reason, it would be unfair and inconsistent for Paul not to prohibit teaching by uneducated men.

Moreover, if lack of training was the reason that Paul prohibited women from teaching, then why did he not also prohibit untrained men from teaching? Surely there were untrained men in the congregations at Ephesus, including new converts and perhaps some poorly educated and illiterate slaves or day laborers. But Paul does not mention them. Why does he focus on women? The egalitarian position is inconsistent at this point, for it cannot explain why Paul excludes all women (even the well-educated ones) and does not exclude any men (even the poorly educated ones). Lack of education is not the reason for Paul's command.

Answer 8.2f: The phrase, "Adam was formed first, then Eve," cannot be made to mean that Eve had less education than Adam without doing violence to the text.

Sometimes egalitarians have tried to make Paul's statement, "For Adam was formed first, then Eve," into a statement about the education of Adam and Eve. For example, Walter Kaiser claims, "The verb is *plassō*, 'to form, to mold, to shape' (presumably in spiritual education), not, 'created first' (which in Greek is *ktizō*)." Kaiser says then that Paul's argument is based on the "orders of education," not the "orders of creation."[43]

43. Walter Kaiser, *Worldwide Challenge* 3 (1976), 9–12.

Gilbert Bilezikian says, "Eve. . .was the one bereft of the firsthand experience of God's giving the prohibition relative to the tree."[44] He then adds,

> Paul's understanding of the primacy of Adam as a safeguard against deception shows that he is concerned with competency. The reference to Eve, who was created after Adam and who therefore was vulnerable to deception, provides further evidence that Paul is establishing a principle based not on chronology but on competency.[45]

The problem with this "lack of education" interpretation of, "For Adam was *formed* first, then Eve," is that the Greek word that Paul uses, *plassō*, does not mean "educated" anywhere in the Bible. Paul is quoting the Greek translation of the Old Testament (the Septuagint) which uses the verb *plassō* four times in the very story of Creation Paul is referring to:

> Genesis 2:7: "Then the LORD God *formed* the man of dust from the ground."
> Genesis 2:8: "And the LORD God planted a garden in Eden, in the east, and there he put the man whom he had *formed*."
> Genesis 2:15 (Septuagint only): "And the LORD God took the man whom he had *formed* "[46]
> Genesis 2:19: "So out of the ground the LORD God *formed* every beast of the field and every bird of the heavens."

The word *plassō* is commonly used in the Septuagint to refer to God's act of Creation (thirty-one of forty-nine instances of *plassō* in the Septuagint refer to Creation). In no case in the Septuagint does this word mean "educate." So how could Paul mean "educate" when he knew the Septuagint used *plassō* in this very passage to refer to Creation?

When Paul in 1 Timothy 2 uses the very same Greek word the Septuagint used to speak of God *forming* the man from the dust of the ground, we should understand Paul's word *in the sense it has in the passage he is referring to*. There is no thought of "educating" Adam in these verses in Genesis, nor can that be the meaning for "formed" in 1 Timothy 2:13.[47]

The same considerations apply to Bilezikian's argument. Paul does not talk about education or training, and Paul does not mention Adam's receiving a command first, or anything like that. Bilezikian is reading into the text of 1 Timothy 2 things that are not there. Paul's words clearly and simply refer to the creation of Adam first, and then Eve, as the usage of *plassō* in the Greek translation of Genesis 2 indicates. That is surely what the original readers would have understood by Paul's words.

---

44. Bilezikian, *Beyond Sex Roles*, 180.
45. Ibid., 297.
46. This is my own translation of the Septuagint, which has *hon eplasen*; there is no equivalent for this in the Hebrew text, and it is not reflected in English translations.
47. The verb *plassō* can sometimes mean to "form by education, training, etc." (LS, 1412), but that meaning is not found in the Bible, and when it is found in literature outside the Bible, that meaning is made clear by specifications in the context that speak about forming or training the soul or forming or training the voice, and so forth. No such specifications are found in 1 Timothy 2:13.

But could Paul have meant that Eve's creation after Adam led to her misunderstanding the command not to eat from the tree of the knowledge of good and evil? Was Paul referring to Eve's lack of training? Deficient education cannot be the meaning because the prohibition was so simple. How many years of education does one need in order to understand the meaning of, "but of the tree of the knowledge of good and evil you shall not eat, for in the day that you eat of it you shall surely die" (Genesis 2:17). These are not difficult words in English or in Hebrew. There is no hint that any formal education or advanced training would have been necessary to understand that when God said that they should not eat of that tree, He meant they should not eat of that tree.

Therefore, the claim that "For Adam was formed first, then Eve" refers to lack of education ignores the plain force of the words and the meaning they have in the text that Paul is quoting, and is an interpretation that would have seemed foreign to the text and clearly wrong to Paul's original readers.

Egalitarian claim 8.3: Women Not Deceived Today: Women today are not as easily deceived as in the first century; therefore, 1 Timothy 2:12–14 does not apply to us today.

William Webb argues that women were more easily deceived in the ancient world because they were not as well educated as men, were younger, and had less social exposure and less knowledge.[48] He then goes to great lengths to demonstrate that these factors are not true of women today (he includes an appendix on research showing that gender plays a very small role in differences in ability to detect deception). Therefore he says 1 Timothy 2:14 is culturally relative and does not apply to women today:

> If it is true that relational people are more vulnerable to deceit, then why not choose men and women as leaders who are more rational and less relational?... The assumed link between "relational women" and "vulnerability to deception" has not been established.... The research shows that gender is not a significant issue in detecting deception.... Women in Paul's day were generally more easily deceived than men. Women in patriarchal societies generally married at a younger age than men, were not permitted the range of experiences and social exposure of men, and were often restricted in their formal education.... The best solution, then, is not to discount the historical teaching of the church but to say that the social data has changed from Paul's day to ours.... Applying 1 Timothy 2:14 today...requires that we...work with the underlying transcultural principle: *seek teachers and leaders who are not easily deceived.*[49]

48. Webb, *Slaves, Women and Homosexuals* (2001), 229.
49. Ibid., 229–30.

Answer 8.3a: Paul makes no reference to his current culture, but to a characteristic of Eve that he sees as relevant for all women in all cultures.

Webb's argument is not persuasive because it does not deal with what the text of Scripture actually says. It substitutes cultural analysis for the statements of Scripture.

Paul makes no reference to his culture or to women being susceptible to deception in the first century. Paul is talking about Adam and Eve, and he says that another reason women should not "teach" or "exercise authority over a man" is that "Adam was not deceived, but the woman was deceived and became a transgressor" (1 Timothy 2:12–14). However we understand that passage, it is evident that Paul is saying that something is true of Eve in relationship to Adam *that has transcultural significance for women and men generally in the New Testament church.*

Contrary to Webb's claim, Paul does not base his argument on education or age or social exposure or knowledge. Rather, he bases it on what he believes to be a transcultural principle that has application to men and women generally. Some complementarians understand this verse to be referring to the fact that Eve wrongfully took leadership in the family and made the decision to eat the forbidden fruit on her own, and other complementarians understand this to refer to a woman's "kinder, gentler nature" that makes her less likely to draw a hard line when close friends are teaching doctrinal error and relationships need to be broken.[50] Whatever interpretation we take, Paul is arguing from Eve's action at the Fall to a general truth about men and women teaching and governing the church; he is not arguing from any statement about women in his culture or any other culture.[51]

EGALITARIAN CLAIM 8.4: RESTRICTED TO HUSBANDS AND WIVES: 1 TIMOTHY 2:11–15 APPLIES ONLY TO HUSBANDS AND WIVES, MEANING ESSENTIALLY, "I DO NOT PERMIT A WOMAN TO TEACH OR HAVE AUTHORITY OVER HER HUSBAND."

This position was advocated by my friend Gordon Hugenberger in a 1992 article.[52] Hugenberger notes that the Greek word *anēr* can mean either "man" or "husband" and *gunē* can mean either "woman" or "wife." (To this point, Hugenberger is correct.) He then argues that in eleven

---

50. For discussion of this verse, see Schreiner, "Interpretation of 1 Timothy 2:9–15," 140–46; also 69–73, above.
51. In addition, it is not clear that Webb's tests of liability to deception (pp. 269–73) were even testing the kind of deception that Paul has in mind regarding Eve in the Garden. There, the deception involved analyzing certain doctrinal and ethical claims being made by a persuasive and deceptive false teacher (the serpent). Webb does not indicate how many of the studies he cites (if any) even dealt with the matter of analyzing whether certain doctrinal or ethical propositions, and certain matters of conduct, were consistent with an established body of doctrinal and ethical truth, as given by God. I am not sure how relevant such tests would be in any case (if any could be constructed), but the vagueness of Webb's descriptions of these studies gives no reason to think that the tests he mentioned were even about the same kind of deception.
52. Gordon Hugenberger, "Women in Church Office: Hermeneutics or Exegesis? A Survey of Approaches to 1 Timothy 2:8–15," in *Journal of the Evangelical Theological Society* 35:3 (September, 1992): 341–60.

other passages in Paul's writings, where the words *anēr* and *gunē* occur closely together, they mean "husband" and "wife." And then he says that the parallels between 1 Timothy 2 and 1 Peter 3:1–7 are "so impressive" that they "must be determinative for our exegesis of 1 Timothy 2."[53] Since 1 Peter 3:1–7 is discussing husbands and wives, Hugenberger argues, it is evident that 1 Timothy 2:8–15 must also be discussing husbands and wives. He argues that 1 Timothy 2 should be translated as follows:

> Therefore I want ***husbands*** everywhere to pray, lifting up holy hands without anger or disputing [with their wives]. Likewise I want ***wives*** to adorn themselves with proper dress, with decency and propriety.... A wife should learn in quietness and full submission. I do not permit a ***wife*** to teach—that is, to boss her ***husband***; she must be quiet. For Adam was formed first, then Eve. And Adam was not deceived but ***his wife*** was deceived and became a sinner. But she will be saved even through [the seemingly mundane work of] child rearing—that is, if they continue in faith, love, and holiness with propriety.[54]

However, several considerations argue against the idea that 1 Timothy 2:8–15 applies only to husbands and wives.

Answer 8.4a: It is true that the Greek words used here can mean either "man" or "husband" and either "woman" or "wife" according to the context. But all the other New Testament passages where the words mean "husband" or "wife" are different from this passage, because in those passages, the meanings "husband" and "wife" are made very clear from decisive clues in the context.

If we look at the other eleven passages that Hugenberger appeals to to claim that *anēr* and *gunē* mean "husband" and "wife" when they occur together, it is evident in every case that the subject under discussion is marriage, and there are decisive clues that require that meaning in those other contexts. Here are some examples:

Romans 7:2: "A ***married*** (*hupandros*) woman"

1 Corinthians 7:2: "Each man should have his ***own*** (*heautou*) wife and each woman her ***own*** (*idion*) husband"

1 Corinthians 7:12: "If any brother ***has*** (*echei*) a wife" (and the entire context of 1 Corinthians 7 is a discussion about marriage)

1 Corinthians 7:39: "A wife is bound to ***her*** (*autēs*) husband as long as he lives"

---

53. Ibid., 354–55.

54. Ibid., 355–56. Hugenberger's rendering of this passage inserts the Greek words at various points in order to show verbal parallels with 1 Peter 3, but these Greek words have been removed in order to give his English translation of the text itself.

Ephesians 5:22: "Wives submit to your *own* (*idiois*) husbands" (Some translations, such as the NIV, RSV, NRSV, and NLT, omit the word "own" but in doing so they fail to translate the Greek word *idiois*; in any case, everyone agrees that Ephesians 5 is talking about marriage.)[55]

Therefore, when Hugenberger mentions all these other contexts where *anēr* and *gunē* mean "husband" and "wife," he fails to recognize that this is nothing remarkable because those contexts are talking about marriage! But those contexts do not prove that marriage is in view in 1 Timothy 2, unless similar decisive clues are found there.

Hugenberger's claim that the parallels with 1 Peter 3:1–7 are especially important, even "determinative for our exegesis of 1 Timothy 2," is likewise unpersuasive. Peter starts out by saying, "Likewise, wives, be subject to your *own* (*idiois*) husbands." Immediately the context tells readers that marriage is in view.

In addition, 1 Peter 3:1–7 includes instructions on how husbands should act toward their wives (v. 7), something that is present whenever the New Testament authors discuss relationships between husbands and wives. But that is not the case in 1 Timothy 2. So Hugenberger's supposedly parallel passages are all significantly different in subject matter and in significant linguistic markers within those texts.

Answer 8.4b: No decisive clues from the context of 1 Timothy 2 would cause the original Greek readers to think that husbands and wives were meant here, and several clues would make them think of men and women in general.

If we look at the full passage in 1 Timothy 2, it is unlikely that Paul could mean that only "***husbands*** should pray, lifting holy hands without anger or quarreling," or that only "***wives*** should adorn themselves in respectable apparel, with modesty and self-control" (1 Timothy 2:8–9). Should not *single* men pray without anger or quarreling? Should not *single* women dress modestly? Paul's original readers would certainly have taken these directions to apply to *all* men and women, not just to husbands and wives, but that means that *in this very context*, their minds are already set on understanding *anēr* to mean "man" and *gunē* to mean "woman." Therefore it would take strong indications in the wording if the author wanted his readers to change their minds and begin thinking that the same words in this same context suddenly meant wives and husbands.

But nothing in the context gives such an indication.

Paul simply says, "Let a woman learn quietly with all submissiveness." He does not say (as he could easily have said), "Let a *married* woman learn quietly with all submissiveness." And he does not say, "I do not permit a woman to teach or exercise authority over *her own* husband" (as he could easily have done). He simply says, "I do not permit a woman to teach or exercise authority over a man."

---

55. More examples are given by Schreiner, "Interpretation of 1 Timothy 2:9–15," 116.

So the needed linguistic clues for a shift in meaning are absent, and other strong clues pointing to women and men generally are present.

Answer 8.4c: It is unlikely that Paul would insert instructions about family life in the middle of a context devoted to opposing false teaching and to choosing officers for the whole church (1 Timothy 1–3).

Paul begins this epistle by telling Timothy that he should "charge certain persons not to teach any different doctrine" (1 Timothy 1:3). He warns against some who "have made shipwreck of their faith," including "Hymenaeus and Alexander" (1 Timothy 1:19–20). In chapter 2 he talks about public prayer and teaching, then in chapter 3 he talks about church officers such as overseers (or bishops) and deacons. Then he tells Timothy that he has written these things so that Timothy "may know how one ought to behave in the household of God, which is the church of the living God" (1 Timothy 3:15). Then in chapter 4 he goes on to talk about false teachers who will devote themselves to "teachings of demons" (1 Timothy 4:1). Then he encourages Timothy, "devote yourself to the public reading of Scripture, to exhortation, to teaching" (1 Timothy 4:13). *The entire context has to do with concerns about the conduct of the church as a whole.*

This argues against the idea that 1 Timothy 2:12 is about the relationship between husband and wife (in the privacy of their home or in public). Paul's overall concern in these chapters is the public ministry of the church, and men and women in general.[56]

In short, the view that 1 Timothy 2:12 talks about a "wife" and a "husband" is not persuasive because all the other New Testament passages that use these words for wives and husbands have different contexts and different wording, and this context and this wording in 1 Timothy 2 contain several factors indicating that men and women generally are in view.

Egalitarian claim 8.5: Temporary Command: Paul's statement in 1 Timothy 2:12, "I do not permit" uses a present tense verb that shows it to be a temporary command. It could be translated, "I am *not now permitting* a woman to teach or to exercise authority over a man."

This egalitarian argument claims that Paul's command is temporary because there was an unusual situation in the church at Ephesus, probably one in which a number of women were taking the lead in teaching false doctrine. Because of that unusual situation, Paul *temporarily* said that women should not teach or have authority over a man, but that command, by its temporary nature, does not apply today. Gilbert Bilezikian represents this view:

56. For further evidence, see ibid., 117.

> Scholars have already pointed out that the present tense of Paul's "I do not permit..." has the force of "I do not permit *now* a woman to teach." But when these women will have learned sufficiently by sitting quietly and receptively under authorized teachers and when they "continue in faith, love, sanctification and discretion," there would remain no hindrance for them to serve as teachers.[57]

Similarly, Gordon Fee says that verse 12 is best translated, "I am not permitting," which, according to Fee, implies, "specific instructions to this situation."[58] Richard and Catherine Kroeger likewise say, "His use of the present tense may also indicate that his decree had to do with a situation contemporaneous with the writing of the epistle."[59]

Answer 8.5a: This argument misunderstands how Paul uses the present tense in commands.

Craig Blomberg rightly says about Paul's use of the present tense for "permit": "the present tense does not suggest Paul is making only a temporary ban; it is regularly used in a gnomic or timeless sense for proverbial instruction."[60]

Thomas Schreiner has done a helpful study of Paul's commands, showing how this egalitarian position cannot be defended in light of the pattern of Paul's other commands where he uses present tense verbs (actually, present indicatives that correspond to the present indicative *epitrepō*, "permit," in the phrase "I do not permit" (1 Timothy 2:12):[61]

> 1 Timothy 2:1: "I urge (*parakalō*, present indicative) that supplications, prayers, intercessions, and thanksgivings be made for all people." (This does not mean, "I temporarily urge that you pray, but this command has no relevance for future situations or future generations.")
>
> Romans 12:1: "I appeal (*parakalō*, present indicative) to you therefore, brothers, by the mercies of God, to present your bodies as a living sacrifice, holy and acceptable to God, which is your spiritual worship." (This does not mean, "I appeal temporarily to you readers in Rome in a special situation to present your bodies as a living sacrifice, but this command is not relevant for future years or future generations.")
>
> 1 Corinthians 4:16: "I urge (*parakalō*, present indicative) you, then, be imitators of me." (Not a temporary command.)

---

57. Bilezikian, *Beyond Sex Roles*, 180. This position was apparently first stated by Don Williams in *The Apostle Paul and Women in the Church*, 112. It is also held by Sumner, *Men and Women in the Church*, 240.
58. Fee, *1 and 2 Timothy, Titus*, 72.
59. R. and C. Kroeger, *I Suffer Not a Woman*, 83. See also Brown, *Women Ministers*, 296.
60. Craig Blomberg, "Neither Hierarchicalist nor Egalitarian: Gender Roles in Paul," in Beck and Blomberg, *Two Views on Women in Ministry*, 361.
61. Schreiner, "Interpretation of 1 Timothy 2:9–15," 125–27.

Ephesians 4:1: "I therefore, a prisoner for the Lord, urge (*parakalō*, present indicative) you to walk in a manner worthy of the calling to which you have been called." (This is not a temporary command.)

Titus 3:8: "I want (*boulomai*, present indicative) you to insist on these things, so that those who have believed in God may be careful to devote themselves to good works." (This is not a temporary command.)

Schreiner gives several other examples,[62] but the point should be clear. Appealing to the present tense or to Paul's use of first person, "I do not permit," cannot be used to argue that this is a temporary command. Such a claim misunderstands the force of the Greek present in Paul's commands. Of course, Paul is writing to specific situations, but Christians who believe Scripture to be the Word of God have rightly understood these to be *commands that are applicable for all Christians for all times.*[63] If we deny this, once again we end up denying a large number of the commands of the New Testament.

Answer 8.5b: This argument would soon lead people to avoid many of the commands of the New Testament. Here as elsewhere, egalitarians use a process of interpreting Scripture that will quickly nullify the authority of Scripture in the lives of Christians today.

Perhaps the danger of this egalitarian claim is not immediately evident. But when we realize that the New Testament epistles were written as *personal* correspondence to *specific churches* (in most cases) then we realize how much of the New Testament is threatened by any procedure that says, "This is just Paul's temporary command for that situation," or "This is just Paul's personal preference, not an abiding command for us today." In Paul's epistles alone, he uses the word *I* approximately 760 times.[64] To argue that the personal nature of these commands makes them temporary or invalidates their authority for us calls into question the authority of much of Paul's writings.

Similarly, Peter refers to his whole epistle by saying, "I have written briefly to you, exhorting and declaring [both of his verbs are present participles, explaining what Peter is doing in the epistle] that this is the true grace of God" (1 Peter 5:12). Surely we cannot make all of the epistle of 1 Peter a temporary command that applies only to a specific ancient situation! But the same procedure used by egalitarians in this objection could lead quickly to such a denial. And in this way the authority of much of the New Testament would be undermined.

---

62. See ibid., 126.

63. See chapter 9, 397–402, for a discussion of how we can know when some commands have specific applications that are culturally relative.

64. This is not an exact count because it is based on a search of one English translation, the English Standard Version, using Bible Works. In Greek, the personal pronoun "I" (Greek *egō*) is often unexpressed because its meaning is conveyed by the form of the verb. In addition, Paul uses the word *me* another 183 times (again merely using the ESV translation to give a rough idea of the frequency). And he sometimes refers to himself as "we."

If we compiled a long list of the commands given by the apostles in the New Testament, and crossed out all of those written in the first person with a present tense verb that said something like, "I command," or "I exhort," or "I do not permit," we would end up deleting large numbers of the commands in the New Testament. Once again, this egalitarian argument uses a procedure which not only leads to the wrong conclusion regarding the role of men and women in the church, but also threatens to undermine the authority of Scripture itself in our lives.

EGALITARIAN CLAIM 8.6: CREATION APPEALS NOT DECISIVE: PAUL'S APPEAL TO CREATION IS NOT DECISIVE, SINCE APPEALS TO CREATION CAN BE CULTURALLY RELATIVE.

This is an argument propounded by William Webb. He looks at Genesis 1–2 and claims that the complementarian appeal to Adam's leadership before the Fall is not convincing. The reason is that he claims there are several elements in the Creation account that are "culturally relative," and therefore the relationship between Adam and Eve before the Fall might also be culturally relative. Some of the culturally relative elements claimed by Webb are "farming as an occupation" and "ground transportation" and a "vegetarian diet."[65]

Answer 8.6a: Webb fails to realize what the apostle Paul realized, that the Bible nowhere limits us to these activities reported in the pre-Fall narrative.

Webb's list of "culturally relative" examples is hardly persuasive, because he fails to take account of the nature of the items that he lists. Surely nothing in the text suggests, and no responsible interpreter claims, that these activities are presented as the *only* activities human beings can do! So it is unclear why Webb thinks these can be counted as examples of "culturally relative" principles.

If Webb's reasoning is correct, then the apostle Paul is wrong. On the basis of Webb's argument, Paul could not have appealed to the Creation account in the first century either, because people in the first century were not limited to "farming as an occupation" (Paul was a tentmaker), and people in the first century were not limited to "ground transportation" (Paul traveled by sea), and people in the first century were not all married (both Jesus and Paul were single), and there was no requirement for everyone to have children (both Jesus and Paul were single), and there was no limitation to being a vegetarian (Paul approved the eating of meat, Romans 14:2–4; 1 Corinthians 10:25–27).

Paul was not persuaded by any of the factors that Webb claims to show cultural relativity in the Creation account. Paul knew that all those factors were there, yet he still believed that "Adam was formed first, then Eve" was valid ground for affirming an abiding, transcultural principle.

---

65. Webb, *Slaves, Women and Homosexuals*, 124–25.

Answer 8.6b: Webb fails to realize that everything before the Fall is morally good.

The point Webb overlooks is that everything in the Garden is *good* because God created it and declared it to be "very good" (Genesis 1:31). Therefore farming and gaining food from the earth are good. Walking through the garden is good. Vegetables are good. Bearing children is good. None of these things is later superceded by a "superior ethic" that would declare the goodness of these things to be culturally relative, so that farming would no longer be good, or walking on the earth would no longer be good, or vegetables would no longer be good, or bearing children would no longer be good.

Similarly, we have in the Garden male-female equality together with male headship in the marriage. That also is *good* and it is *created by God*, and we should not follow Webb in thinking that we can one day create a "superior ethic" that would declare male headship to be something that is *not* good or *not* approved by God.

Egalitarian claim 8.7: Why No Primogeniture Today? People who say 1 Timothy 2:13 is the basis for a transcultural principle should practice primogeniture today. But they don't, so one cannot base any transcultural principle on 1 Timothy 2:13.

William Webb also argues that if complementarians take Paul's argument seriously in 1 Timothy 2:13, then, to be consistent, we should practice primogeniture today as well. That would mean such things as giving the firstborn son a double portion of the inheritance and other significant rights and responsibilities of leadership.[66] He says,

> It is interesting that those who appeal to primogeniture in affirming the transcultural status of 1 Timothy 2:13 say very little about the sustained application of other primogeniture texts for our lives.[67]

Answer 8.7a: The Bible does not base any other commands on Adam's Creation before Eve, so we have no right to make up additional commands on our own.

In arguing that complementarians should practice primogeniture today if they are going to be consistent, Webb is simply confusing the issue. The Bible never says anything like, "All families should give a double portion of inheritance to the firstborn son, because Adam was formed first, then Eve." The Bible never commands any such thing, and Webb himself shows how the Bible

66. Ibid., 141–42. He gives a substantial list of "primogeniture" rights of the firstborn on p. 141.
67. Ibid., 142.

frequently overturns such a practice.[68] Webb has imported into the discussion an idea of "consistency" that is foreign to the Bible itself. Webb is basically arguing as follows:

1. The Bible makes one application from Adam's prior creation.
2. If you affirm that the Bible is correct in that first application, then you *have to* say that the Bible makes *other* applications from Adam's prior creation.

But that reasoning does not follow. We are not free to say that the Bible "should" make applications which it does not in fact make! That decision belongs in the hands of God, not us.

Consistency is simply affirming what the Bible says, and not denying the validity of any of the reasoning processes in Scripture (as Webb attempts to do with 1 Timothy 2:13), as well as not adding to the commands of Scripture (as Webb tries to push complementarians to do with this text). Consistency does not require us to make all sorts of applications of a biblical principle even when the Bible does not make those applications; rather, consistency is saying that the application Paul made from Genesis 2 is a valid and good one, and Scripture requires us also to affirm it as a transcultural principle today.

Paul says in 1 Timothy 2:12–13 that Adam's prior creation proves at least one thing: In the assembled church a woman should not "teach" or "exercise authority over a man" (1 Timothy 2:12). Are we to say that Paul was wrong?[69]

Egalitarian claim 8.8: "Not Domineer": "Not exercise authority" in 1 Timothy 2:12 means "not misuse authority" or "not domineer."

Egalitarian claim 8.9: "Not Murder or Commit Violence": "Not exercise authority" in 1 Timothy 2:12 means "not murder" or "not commit violence."

Egalitarian claim 8.10: "Not Proclaim Oneself Author of a Man": "Not exercise authority" in 1 Timothy 2:12 means "not proclaim oneself author of a man," in accordance with an ancient Gnostic heresy that Eve was created first.

I have listed these three egalitarian claims together because the answers to them will involve much of the same material. Each of these claims argues that 1 Timothy 2:12 does not mean

68. Ibid., 136–39.
69. Rich Nathan says that in the Bible "God often overrules the cultural laws of primogeniture" (*Who Is My Enemy*, 153). It is not clear how Nathan's point (which Paul also realized) would make 1 Timothy 2:12–13 culturally relative, because Paul is not arguing from some principle of primogeniture throughout the whole Bible but from the specific history of Adam's creation before Eve and what this creation pattern tells us about the way men and women should relate in the church for all time.

simply, "I do not permit a woman to teach or *to exercise authority* over a man," but rather has *some wrongful practice, some abuse of authority*, in view. The argument has to do with the specific word Paul used, the Greek verb *authenteō*. What did that verb mean?[70]

The most common alternative interpretation is that Paul is prohibiting some kind of *misuse* of authority. Thus David Scholer wrote,

> I am convinced that the evidence is in and that it clearly establishes *authentein*[71] as a negative term, indicating violence and inappropriate behavior. Thus, what Paul does not allow for women in 1 Timothy 2 is this type of behavior.... 1 Timothy 2 is opposing the negative behavior of women, probably the women mentioned in 1 Timothy 5:15 who follow and represent the false teachers 1 and 2 Timothy are dedicated to opposing.[72]

Similarly, Craig Keener at one point held, "Paul may here be warning against *a domineering use of authority*, rather than merely any use of authority."[73]

Rebecca Groothuis says this term includes a negative and harmful use of authority:

> Extensive recent research into Greek usage of this term suggests that at the time Paul wrote this letter to Timothy, *authentein*..."included a substantially negative element (i.e., 'dominate, take control by forceful aggression, instigate trouble')." Therefore, it seems forced and unreasonable to view 1 Timothy 2:12 as denying women the ordinary and appropriate exercise of authority. It appears far more likely that the prohibition refers to a negative and harmful use of authority—which...in this case probably referred specifically to the women who were teaching the heresy against which Paul had written 1 and 2 Timothy. Thus, Paul would not have intended this prohibition to exclude women for either the ministry of sound teaching or the legitimate exercise of ecclesiastical authority.[74]

---

70. Regarding Paul's use of the verb *authenteō* rather than the noun *exousia* ("authority"), see claim 8.12.
71. Throughout this book I normally cite Greek words with their lexical form (the form in which they occur in a Greek dictionary or lexicon) which in this case is *authenteō*. Some of the writers I quote cite this same word by using the infinitive form *authentein*. In both cases, the same word is being referred to.
72. David M. Scholer, "The Evangelical Debate over Biblical 'Headship,'" in Kroeger and Beck, *Women, Abuse, and the Bible* (1996), 50. Scholer says in his final footnote that this essay is a paper given at a conference on April 16, 1994, and his footnotes indicate interaction with literature up to 1993.
73. Keener, *Paul, Women and Wives,* 109; similarly, Fee, *1 and 2 Timothy, Titus,* 73. However, Keener later wrote that he found the evidence in Köstenberger et al., *Women in the Church,* to be persuasive for the view that *authenteō* has a neutral sense, referring to the exercise of authority, not a negative sense. He says in this later essay, "In contrast to my former position on this issue, however, I believe that Paul probably prohibits not simply 'teaching authoritatively,' but both teaching Scripture at all and having (or usurping) authority at all. In other words, women are forbidden to teach men—period" (Craig Keener, "Women in Ministry," in Beck and Blomberg, *Two Views on Women in Ministry*, 52–53).
74. Groothuis, *Good News for Women* (1997), 215. The quotation in the statement by Groothuis is taken from an article she refers to by Ronald Pierce, "Evangelicals and Gender Roles in the 1900's: 1 Timothy 2:8–15: A Test Case," *Journal of the Evangelical Theological Society* 36:3 (September, 1993), 349. Sumner, *Men and Women in the Church,* advocates the negative meaning "domineer over a man" (253).

And Leland Wilshire clearly advocates the meaning "instigate violence":

> The preponderant number of citations...have to do with self willed violence, criminal action, or murder or with the person who does these actions.... The issue may be...'instigating violence.... It was a problem not of authority but of violent self-assertion in a rhetorically defined form of instruction.[75]

J. Lee Grady thinks the term has some kind of negative connotation:

> Bible scholars have noted that *authentein* has a forceful and extremely negative connotation. It implies a more specific meaning than "to have authority over" and can be translated "to dominate," "to usurp," or "to take control." Often when this word was used in ancient Greek literature it was associated with violence or even murder.[76]

Another possible interpretation, related to Wilshire's idea of violence, has been proposed by Richard and Catherine Kroeger:

> *Authentēs* is applied on several occasions to those who perform ritual murder.... Such material does not allow us to rule out the possibility that 1 Timothy 2:12 prohibits cultic action involving actual or representational murder.... More likely than actual murder is the "voluntary death" or sham murder which played a significant part in mystery initiations.... It is at least possible that some sort of ritual murder, probably of a simulated nature, could be involved.[77]

And yet a third alternative has also been proposed by Richard and Catherine Kroeger. They argue that Paul here uses the word *authenteō* to mean, "proclaim oneself author of a man." The Kroegers then translate 1 Timothy 2 as, "I do not allow a woman to teach nor to proclaim herself author of man." The Kroegers understand this to be Paul's rejection of "a Gnostic notion of Eve as creator of Adam."[78]

Finally, Catherine Kroeger proposed a fourth alternative in 1979: that *authenteō* means "to thrust oneself" (in pagan sexual rituals). But this proposal has been almost universally rejected (see note 107 below).

But are these alternative meanings correct? Is Paul prohibiting the *misuse* of authority, or some other wrongful act, due to some problem unique to Ephesus at that time? If so, then someone might argue that 1 Timothy 2 applies only to that special situation and in ordinary situations women are free to teach and exercise authority over men. On the other hand, if

---

75. Leland Wilshire, "1 Timothy 2:12 Revisited," in *Evangelical Quarterly* 65:1 (1993), 47–48, 52.
76. Grady, *Ten Lies*, 58. See also Perriman, *Speaking of Women*, 171.
77. R. and C. Kroeger, *I Suffer Not a Woman*, 185–88.
78. Ibid., 103. See also Jacobs, *Women of Destiny*, 240–41, who finds the Kroegers' proposal persuasive. (For analysis of the Kroegers' claims that false teachers were promoting a Gnostic heresy about Eve being created first, see answer 8.1c, pp. 284–87.)

authenteō has an ordinary, neutral meaning such as "have authority," then it is more likely that Paul is making a general statement for all churches for all times. Rebecca Groothuis understands this, for she says, "All traditionalist interpretations, of course, require that *authentein* be defined in the sense of the normal, neutral exercise of authority."[79]

Answer 8.8a (these answers also apply to claims 8.9 and 8.10): The most complete study of this word shows that its meaning is primarily neutral, "to exercise authority over."

In 1995, H. Scott Baldwin published the most thorough study of the verb *authenteō* that had ever been done. Several earlier studies had looked at a number of occurrences of this verb, but no one had ever looked at *all* the examples that exist from ancient literature and ancient papyrus manuscripts.[80] Baldwin found eighty-two occurrences of *authenteō* in ancient writings, and he listed them all with the Greek text and English translation in a long appendix.[81] (Because such a list is not available anywhere else, I have reproduced Baldwin's list in an appendix to this book.)[82]

Baldwin pointed out that an earlier study by Leland Wilshire claimed to examine 314 citations, but the results were skewed because Wilshire did not limit himself to the verb *authenteō* but also incorrectly included other cognate words, including a noun, *authentēs*, which probably comes from a different root and in any case takes a far different meaning from the verb *authenteō* .[83] Baldwin found that in all uses of this verb, "the one unifying concept is that of *authority*."[84] Baldwin summarized his findings on the range of possible meaning for *authenteō* in the following table:[85]

The Meaning of *authenteō*

1. To rule, to reign sovereignly
2. To control, to dominate[86]

---

79. Groothuis, *Good News for Women*, 216. See also Brown, *Women Ministers*, 301.
80. H. Scott Baldwin, "A Difficult Word: *Authenteō* in 1 Timothy 2:12," in Köstenberger, *Women in the Church*, 65–80 and 269–305. (See Appendix 7 for Baldwin's entire list of eighty-two examples of *authenteō*.)
81. See Baldwin's list in Appendix 7, pp. 675–702.
82. I have listed only the English translation of Baldwin's examples. Full Greek texts can be found at www.EFBT100.com.
83. Baldwin refers to two articles by Leland Wilshire, "The *TLG* Computer and Further Reference to *AYTHENTEŌ* in 1 Timothy 2:12," *New Testament Studies* 34 (1988): 120–34; and, "1 Timothy 2:12 Revisited," 43–55. See the discussion below on the incorrect confusion of this verb and a noun with similar spelling.
84. Baldwin, "A Difficult Word," 72–73.
85. Ibid., 73.
86. Baldwin cautions readers that in accordance with standard English usage he uses "dominate" as a ***neutral*** term, not as a negative or pejorative term. By contrast, he uses "domineer" as a ***negative*** term meaning "to rule or govern arbitrarily or despotically...to exercise authority in an overbearing manner" (ibid). Sumner, *Men and Women in the Church,* ignores this distinction and quotes Baldwin's definition "dominate" on p. 252 but changes it to "domineer" in her conclusion on p. 253.

a. to compel, to influence someone/thing
b. middle voice: to be in effect, to have legal standing
c. hyperbolically: to domineer/play the tyrant (one example in Chrysostom, about 390 AD)
d. to grant authorization

3. To act independently
   a. to assume authority over
   b. to exercise one's own jurisdiction
   c. to flout the authority of (two examples, one from 690 AD and one from tenth century AD)
4. To be primarily responsible for or to instigate something
5. To commit a murder (unattested before the tenth century AD)

What should be evident from this chart is that there are no negative examples of the word *authenteō* at or around the time of the New Testament. Because language changes and meanings of words change over time, even the Chrysostom quotation from 390 AD, coming more than three hundred years after Paul wrote 1 Timothy, is of limited value in understanding the meaning of what Paul wrote.[87]

Baldwin's essay is especially helpful because he provides the full citation (usually in paragraph length) for each of these eighty-two examples, both in Greek and in English translation. Therefore anyone who questions his conclusions can simply read the examples in context to see if his reasoning is persuasive.

What is most striking about Baldwin's exhaustive study is the complete absence of some of the other meanings that have been proposed, meanings that are unrelated to the idea of using authority. I have included all eighty-two of Baldwin's examples in an appendix, so that readers can see for themselves how foreign to the general use of the word some of these egalitarian claims are.[88] To my knowledge, since Baldwin's study no additional examples of *authenteō* from ancient sources have been found or published by egalitarians, and one additional example confirming Baldwin has been found by David Huttar (see answer 8.8b), and two additional

---

87. Even that Chrysostom quote is capable of more than one interpretation. Chrysostom tells husbands, "Do not therefore, because thy wife is subject to thee, *act the despot*; nor because thy husband loveth thee, be thou puffed up" (translation found *NPNF,* ser. 1, 13:304; the full Greek text with the translation of the entire paragraph is also found in Baldwin's essay, p. 286). In the context, Chrysostom is telling husbands to love their wives. It is not certain that "misuse authority, domineer" is the sense. It is also possible that Chrysostom is telling husbands not to use their authority regularly or often, but rather to seek agreement and honest interaction and persuasion of one another. The sense could be, "Don't just give orders all the time because your wife is subject to you." The argument against a strongly negative sense here is that none of the other instances of this verb have a negative sense, and it is wise to avoid postulating a new sense if an established one fits the context. On the other hand, the parallel with telling the wife not to be puffed up (proud) argues for a negative sense for the verb in this instance. In any case, it is still over three hundred years after the time of the New Testament.

88. See Appendix 7, pp. 675–702, for all eighty-two examples of *authenteō*.

confirming examples have been found by Albert Wolters (see answer 8.8g). Therefore if egalitarians are going to find support for their argument in any ancient examples of *authenteō*, they will have to find it in the examples cited by Baldwin. And the evidence is simply not there.

Answer 8.8b: The meaning "to murder" is not supported by the ancient evidence.

Baldwin shows that there is no example of the verb *authenteō* with the meaning "to murder" until the tenth century AD! But this is nine hundred years after the time of the New Testament, and hardly counts as evidence of the meaning of a word in New Testament times. Baldwin writes, "The sometimes asserted meaning, 'to murder' (5), is not substantiated for any period even remotely close to the period of the writing of the New Testament."[89]

Now more recently David Huttar has argued, on the basis of careful examination of the manuscript tradition of Aeschylus, that the meaning "murder" even in this one late example was the result of a conjectural reading by an editor of a fragmentary manuscript. He thinks the supposed instance of *authenteō* meaning "murder" actually has the meaning "initiate an action," and does not mean murder. He now finds the meaning "murder" only in one linguistically erroneous manuscript from the thirteenth century:

> the meaning "murder" for *authentein* is not attested in any living, natural Greek used in ordinary discourse, but only in the ingenuity of an etymologizing hypothesis on the part of some comparatively late Byzantine scholar.[90]

But if the meaning "to murder" does not occur until twelve hundred years after the time of the New Testament, why have people claimed this meaning for the word? Apparently because they confused this verb with a noun that had a similar spelling but a vastly different meaning. Baldwin notes that the noun *authentēs* can mean "murderer."[91] In language generally there are examples where verbs do not take the same meaning as nouns with similar spelling, such as the verb *wind* (as in "to wind a clock") and the noun *wind* (as in "the wind was blowing"). Similarly, there is a difference between the noun *adult* and the verb *adulterate*.

The noun *authentēs* in fact has two very different meanings, (1) "master, one who has authority" and (2) "murderer" (LS, p. 275). Baldwin favors the explanation given in 1930 by J. H. Moulton and George Milligan,[92] where they say that the two senses of *authentēs* have come

---

89. Baldwin, "A Difficult Word," 76. The tenth-century quotation he refers to is in a marginal note (a "scholion") added to Aeschylus's play *Eumenides*, line 42a; see Greek text and English translation in Baldwin, p. 302.
90. David Huttar, "AYTHENTEIN in the Aeschylus Scholium," *Journal of the Evangelical Theological Society* 44 (2001), 625.
A similar conclusion was stated by Albert Wolters in a private letter to H. Scott Baldwin, which Baldwin quotes in "A Difficult Word": "The verb *authenteō* is attested only once in the meaning 'to murder,' and this anomalous use is best explained as a case of hypercorrection by an Atticist pedant, based on the noun *authentēs* meaning 'murderer' in Attic usage" (77n31).
91. See LS, 275.
92. J. H. Moulton and George Milligan, *Vocabulary of the Greek Testament Illustrated from the Papyri and Other Non-Literary Sources* (1972), 91.

from two different linguistic sources, but both words ended up with the same spelling.[93]

There is significant evidence for this difference in meaning between the verb *authenteō* and the noun *authentēs* from an ancient scholar named Hesychius of Alexandria (fifth century AD) who published a lexicon (or dictionary) of ancient Greek. In this lexicon, entries A8259 and A8260 give the following definitions:

> For the verb *authenteō*: "to exercise authority" (interestingly, he uses Greek *exousiazein* for this definition)
>
> For the noun *authentēs* he gives three meanings: (1) "person in authority," (2) "doer of a thing/one who kills himself," (3) "murderer."[94]

This difference between the meaning of the verb *authenteō* ("to have authority over") and the noun *authentēs* (which probably represents two different words that happen to be spelled the same way, one meaning "master," and one meaning "murderer") is also supported by the major dictionaries (lexicons) of ancient Greek.[95] In conclusion, what evidence is there that the verb *authenteō* could mean "to murder" at the time of the New Testament? There is no evidence at all. There is no lexicon that claims this meaning for this verb for anything near the time of the New Testament, and there is no citation from ancient Greek literature anywhere near the time of the New Testament that provides this meaning, either. We may safely say that the verb *authenteō* does not mean "to murder" in 1 Timothy 2:12.

Answer 8.8c: The meaning "to instigate violence" is not supported by the ancient evidence.

What we said about the meaning "to murder" can also be said about the suggestion from Leland Wilshire, that the meaning "instigating violence" was the best sense of *authenteō* at the time of the New Testament. Wilshire depended on other words, particularly the noun *authentēs*, but no Greek lexicon and no example of the verb *authenteō* from around the

93. See Baldwin, "A Difficult Word," 77n31. The same conclusion is reached by George W. Knight III "AYTHENTEIN in Reference to Women in 1 Timothy 2:12," *New Testament Studies* 30 (1984): 154, with reference to more detailed etymological explanations for how this came about.
94. These English translations of the meanings are from Baldwin, "A Difficult Word," 72n14, where the Greek text of Hesychius is also given.
95. The LS *Lexicon* under the verb *authenteō* gives the meaning "to have full power or authority over," and then also gives the meaning "commit a murder." But the only reference for that meaning is that same tenth-century AD reference from the scholion (marginal note) to Aeschylus's play, *Eumenides*, line 42a. However, LSJ does list the meaning "murder" for the noun (p. 275). The BDAG gives only the sense "to assume a stance of independent authority, *give orders to, dictate to,*" (150) for the verb. And Geoffrey Lampe's *Patristic Greek Lexicon* gives four meanings related to having authority, such as "hold sovereign authority, act with authority," and so forth, but indicates no meaning for murder (262, with many examples; note also the numerous examples of the noun *authentia* in the sense of sovereign power or supreme authority, 262–63).

time of the New Testament gives support to his claim. We may safely reject it as a claim without persuasive evidence.[96]

Answer 8.8d: Richard and Catherine Kroeger's claim that *authenteē* means "to proclaim oneself author of a man" (related to a Gnostic heresy that Eve was created first) is not supported by the ancient evidence.

In 1992, Richard and Catherine Kroeger argued that *authenteō* in 1 Timothy 2:12 means, "proclaim oneself author of man," and that we should translate 1 Timothy 2:12, "I do not allow a woman to teach nor *to proclaim herself author of man."*[97] The Kroegers say their translation would then answer a Gnostic heresy circulating at Ephesus, the idea that Eve was the creator of Adam. But several factors make this an impossible translation.

1. Not one of the eighty-two examples of *authenteō* quoted by Baldwin show the meaning "proclaim oneself to be the author of" (something).[98] Baldwin does give some examples where the verb means, "to be primarily responsible for or to instigate something"[99]), but no text shows the meaning, "*to proclaim oneself* the author of something"—there is nothing about proclaiming anything, for that matter.
2. The examples of the recognized sense, "to be primarily responsible for or to instigate something," all refer to being responsible for actions or activities (such as instigating a judgment), but none take the sense of *creating a person*, as in, "to proclaim oneself author of man." Therefore there are no actual quotations from any literature of any period that support the Kroegers' meaning.

   To take one example of their argument, the Kroegers claim Basil, *The Letters*, 51:24 as an example where *authenteō* can mean, "to proclaim oneself the author" (of something), but Baldwin refers to the "astonishing creativity" of such a translation, and notes that the Loeb Classical Library translation of this text renders the verb here "directing."[100] He also says that Lampe's lexicon lists this reference under the meaning, "be primarily responsible for."[101] So the Kroegers just inserted their novel idea, "*proclaim oneself* the author," into the Basil quotation, but no scholar before them had ever translated it with that sense or anything like it, and nothing in the context requires that sense.

---

96. See footnotes 75 and 83 above for the two Wilshire articles; his claim for the meaning "instigating violence" is in the second article from *Evangelical Quarterly* 65 (1993), 43–55. Except for the ninth or tenth-century AD citation from the scholia to Aeschylus, none of his unambiguous examples with the meaning "murder" are instances with the verb *authenteō*, but rely instead on the noun *authentēs* (see list on pp. 46–47).
97. R. and C. Kroeger, *I Suffer Not a Woman*, 103.
98. See all of Baldwin's eighty-two examples in Appendix 7, pp. 675–702.
99. Baldwin, "A Difficult Word," 73; see specific examples at p. 274, sec. 4.
100. Ibid., 323.
101. Baldwin also refers to the highly critical review of the Kroegers' claim for such a meaning by Albert Wolters in *Calvin Theological Journal* 28 (1993), 208–19.

3. No modern lexicon even hints a meaning such as "to proclaim oneself to be the author of."[102]
4. The Kroegers' claim that the meaning, "to represent oneself as the author, originator, or source of something" is in various older dictionaries:[103]

> In the late Renaissance, an era when scholars studied classical texts more thoroughly than is customary today and had at their disposal materials to which we no longer have access, another definition was cited by lexicographers: *praebo me auctorem*, to declare oneself the author or source of anything. *Authentein,* when used with the genitive, as it is in 1 Timothy 2:12, could imply not only to claim sovereignty but also to claim authorship. "To represent oneself as the author, originator, or source of something" was given in various older dictionaries, such as the widely-used work of Cornelis Schrevel and the still-fundamental Stephanus' *Thesaurus Linguae Graecae.* The earliest of these dates back to the Renaissance, the latest to the last century.[104]

But Professor Albert Wolters of Redeemer University in Ontario challenged the accuracy of the Kroegers' understanding of *authenteō*:

> The authors go to great lengths to argue that the verb *authentein* can mean "to represent oneself as originator of" or "to proclaim oneself author of" (p. 103), but their argument can hardly be taken seriously. Ignoring the fact that *authentein* is attested in New Testament times in the meaning "have authority over," they take their point of departure in the meaning "originate," a rare sense of the verb which is not

102. See the list of nine modern lexicons in Baldwin's article, pp. 66–67. The Kroegers also claimed that the meaning "to proclaim oneself the author of" (something) is found in Eusebius, *Life of Constantine the Great*, 2:48 (Kroegers, *I Suffer Not a Woman,* 103), but the meaning here is just "administrator," or "one primarily responsible for": see Baldwin, "A Difficult Word," 279–80, with the translation from *NPNF*, ser. 2, 1:512. The Kroegers also claimed Pope Leo I, Epistle #30, in a sentence that is quoted and translated by Baldwin, "A Difficult Word," 290–91, with the sense "instigated." Once again, the sense "to proclaim oneself the author of" is not demonstrated from these texts either, in spite of the novel translations offered by the Kroegers in their book. But if they can produce no citations of ancient texts that require this meaning, the claim is unconvincing.

103. The older Greek lexicons that they list are the following: George Dunbar, *A Greek-English Lexicon*, 3rd ed. (1850); Benjamin Hederich, *Graecum Lexicon Manuale* (1803); T. Morrell, *Lexicon Graeco-Prosodiacum* (1815); John Pickering, *Greek Lexicon* (1847); Johann Scapula (fl. 1580), *Lexicon Graeco-Latinum* (1653); Cornelis Schrevel, *Lexicon Manuale Graeco-Latinum et Latino-Graecum* (1823); *The Greek Lexicon of Schrevelius Translated into English with Many Additions* (1826); Stephanus, *Thesaurus Graecae Linguae* (1831–65). (From R. and C. Kroeger, *I Suffer Not a Woman*, 230n28.)

I did not have access to all of these lexicons, but the ones by Dunbar (p. 177) and Pickering (p. 179) do include this meaning as the Kroegers say. However, later lexicons did not support this meaning, and Albert Wolters argues that this sense was probably based on a misunderstanding of the Latin phrase in some of the earlier lexicons (see below).

104. R. and C. Kroeger, *I Suffer Not a Woman*, 102. The endnote at the end of this section adds, "This value disappeared from classical dictionaries about the time when the translation of 1 Timothy 2:12 was being challenged by feminists, in the mid-nineteenth century" (230n29).

> attested before the fourth century AD Moreover, for the Kroegers' overall proposal to work, they need to find evidence that the verb can mean "*claim to* originate." They find this evidence in the sixteenth-century Greek-Latin dictionary of Stephanus (and some of its derivatives), which states that *authenteō* means *praebeo me auctorem.* They then interpret this Latin definition to mean "to represent oneself as author," and go on to equate this with "asserting oneself to be the author or source of." Having established the sense in this way, they proceed to find this new meaning in three patristic texts of the fourth and fifth centuries (pp. 102–105).
>
> All of this makes an initial impression of great erudition, but masks the fact that the Latin idiom has been misunderstood (it simply means "behave as originator of," a Latin way of saying "originate"...; see under "praebeo" in the *Oxford Latin Dictionary* [5, b–c] or the *Thesaurus Linguae Latinae* [I,B,1 and II,B,I]; compare Calvin's Latin rendering of Heb. 5:2 and 2 Pet. 3:9) and that in the long history of classical scholarship the Kroegers are the first to find this sense in the three patristic texts cited.... (all three are listed under the meaning "be primarily responsible for, instigate, authorize" in Lampe, *Patristic Greek Lexicon*, s.v. 4). They even go so far as to suggest that Stephanus must have had access to Greek texts that are now lost (p. 102), and that the failure of contemporary Greek lexicons to list this sense has something to do with the rise of feminism (p. 230, note 29).
>
> Furthermore, although they cite a good deal of secondary literature on *authentein* and its cognates (p. 228, note 1), they repeatedly misunderstand the sources they cite, and they fail to mention important recent literature which counts against their own interpretation. For example, a Latin quote from Guillaume Budé is completely misunderstood on p. 102...(to make matters worse, the original is cited in a badly garbled form; see p. 230, note 27), and their mistranslation of a German citation about *authentein* shows similar incompetence (p. 101)....
>
> Philologically, it seems, the Kroegers are adept at making a Greek text say what they would like it to say, and their scholarly documentation is riddled with elementary linguistic blunders....[105] [Their] argument is a travesty of sound scholarship.[106]

In conclusion, the Kroegers have produced no ancient texts that require this meaning. The meaning has been universally rejected by modern lexicographers as a mistake, since it is not found as even a possibility in any Greek lexicon for the last one hundred years. It is a meaning without support in any ancient text or any modern lexicon.[107]

---

105. Wolters, "Review: *I Suffer Not a Woman,*" 210–11.
106. Ibid., 213.
107. The same arguments I made in this section about the absence of convincing evidence can also be applied to an earlier suggestion of Catherine Kroeger that *authenteō* really meant "to thrust oneself" (in sexually immoral practices in a pagan cult), and thus 1 Timothy 2:12 means, "I forbid a woman to teach or *engage in fertility practices* with a man" (Kroeger, "Ancient Heresies and a Strange Greek Verb," *The Reformed Journal*

Answer 8.8e: The grammatical structure of the sentence rules out any negative meaning (such as, "to misuse authority, to domineer, or to murder") and shows that the verb must have a positive meaning (such as "to exercise authority").

Another recent study of one hundred parallel examples to the sentence structure in 1 Timothy 2 has produced some important conclusions. Andreas Köstenberger found in the New Testament fifty-two other examples of the construction that is found in 1 Timothy 2:12, which we can summarize as: Neither [verb A] nor [verb B].[108]

The important point of Köstenberger's study is this: All of the examples fell into only two patterns:

Pattern 1: Two activities or concepts are viewed positively in and of themselves.
Pattern 2: Two activities or concepts are viewed negatively

Köstenberger found no exceptions to these patterns.

---

29 [March 1979]: 14; italics in original). This argument by Kroeger has been almost universally rejected by other writers from both complementarian and egalitarian camps (see Mounce, *Pastoral Epistles*, 127, and Marshall, *Pastoral Epistles*, 457, both with notes to other literature). So far as I am aware, she is suggesting a meaning for *authenteō* that has never been found in any lexicon, ever.

However, in spite of the fact that Kroeger's 1979 article has not withstood any scholarly scrutiny, I have been both amazed and disappointed to hear of a number of instances where this very article has been accepted as fact by unsuspecting lay persons who have no ability to check the actual ancient texts in which she claimed to find an erotic meaning for *authenteō*. When the texts she mentions are inspected, Kroeger's article turns out to be a bizarre proposal based on misrepresentation of obscure evidence that is accessible only to scholars. Full discussion of the texts can be found in Armin J. Panning, "AΨΥENTEIN—A Word Study," in *Wisconsin Lutheran Quarterly* 78 (1981): 185–91, and Carroll D. Osburn, "AΨΥENTE΄ (1 Timothy 2:12)," in *Restoration Quarterly* 25:1 (1982): 1–12.

Panning and Osburn note several problems: (1) Kroeger bases her claim on highly questionable meanings of texts, such as her own private translation of Wisdom of Solomon 12:6 in which she says it speaks of parents "engendering" children rather than the standard translation "murderers" of children (Panning, 189–90; this text has the noun *authentēs*, which everyone agrees can mean "murderer."); (2) Kroeger claims that a text refers to homosexual conduct but in fact there is no mention of homosexuality in the context, which is rather a speech by King Theseus of Athens praising the value of democracy, in which, when the people are the "master" (*authentēs*), "they rejoice in good young citizens" (Panning, 188); (3) Kroeger omits from a key quotation the second half of a sentence that disproves her meaning, a statement by Michael Glycas in which he criticizes the women of a certain tribe who "dominate" (*authenteō*) their men, fornicate as much as they please...and *carry on farming, build houses, and pursue all masculine activities*" (words in italics omitted by Kroeger) (Panning, 191); (4) Kroeger misunderstands the construction of a Greek sentence in Philodemus and wrongly claims grammatical parallel to a reference to sexual activity (Osburn, 5–6); (5) Kroeger misunderstands or incorrectly represents a comment on literary style, wrongly presenting it as a comment on the meaning of a word (the ancient lexicographers Moerus and Thomas Magister speak of *authenteō* being a more "vulgar" or "common" or "Koine" term (*koinoteron*) rather than a formal "Attic" Greek term, but no sexual nuance is meant) (Panning, 188–89). Although Osburn's evaluation is couched in polite academic language, the import is clear when Osburn says Kroeger's article is "more curious than substantive" (1), and must be taken "*cum grano salis*," (8), and that "Kroeger's hypothesis that the women teachers were offering sexual favors to their students has not a shred of evidence in its favor" (11). And Panning says, "It is the basic thesis of this study that the various passages cited by Catherine Kroeger do not require or support the meaning she suggests" (186).

108. Andreas Köstenberger, "A Complex Sentence Structure in 1 Timothy 2:12," in Köstenberger, *Women in the Church*, 81–103.

Some examples of pattern 1 are Matthew 6:28 (they neither labor nor spin); Matthew 13:13 (they neither hear nor understand, but both hearing and understanding are viewed as desirable activities); Luke 12:24 (they neither sow nor harvest); or Acts 4:18 (neither speak nor teach). These activities are all viewed positively in their contexts. Examples of pattern 2, where both activities are viewed negatively, are Matthew 6:20 (neither break in nor steal); John 14:27 (neither be troubled nor be afraid); Philippians 2:16 (neither run in vain nor labor in vain), and Hebrews 13:5 (neither leave nor forsake).

Köstenberger then considered forty-eight other examples of this kind of construction in literature outside the New Testament, from the third century BC to the end of the first century AD, and for all of these he lists both the Greek text and the English translation as well.[109] Again, the same pattern is found: either both activities are viewed positively (and negated for some other reason in the context), or both activities are viewed negatively. No exceptions were found.[110]

The importance for 1 Timothy 2:12 is this: One hundred other examples of the construction found in 1 Timothy 2:12 show that in ancient Greek writing, both activities in this construction must be viewed positively or else both activities must be viewed negatively. No exceptions were found. This means that if the activity of "teaching" is viewed positively in the context of 1 Timothy, then the activity of "having authority" must also be viewed positively.

Which is it? Köstenberger notes several cases where "teaching" is viewed positively in 1 and 2 Timothy, such as 1 Timothy 4:11, where Paul tells Timothy, "command and ***teach*** these things"; 1 Timothy 6:2, where Paul says, "***teach*** and encourage these things"; and 2 Timothy 2:2 where Paul says, pass on these things to faithful individuals "who will be able to ***teach*** others also." Certainly in 1 and 2 Timothy, the activity of Bible teaching is viewed as a positive one.[111]

But this means that "to have authority" must also be viewed as a positive activity in 1 Timothy 2:12. If 1 Timothy 2:12 follows the uniform pattern of one hundred other exam-

---

109. Ibid., 91–99.

110. Dan Doriani notes that when an activity that is viewed positively is joined with another viewed negatively, a different construction is used, for such activities are joined by *kai mē* ("and not"): He cites Matthew 17:7; John 20:27; Romans 12:14; 1 Timothy 5:16 (Doriani, *Women and Ministry* [2003], 179).

111. Sumner objects to this conclusion with the argument, "Alan Padgett has correctly pointed out Andreas Köstenberger's mistake of saying that the word *didaskein* "to teach" is always positive in Paul. As Padgett rightly shows, the word *didaskein* "to teach" is used negatively in Titus 1:11 and 1 Timothy 6:3.... See Alan Padgett, "The Scholarship of Patriarchy," *Priscilla Papers* (winter 1997), 24." (Sumner, *Men and Women in the Church*, 253n21; she refers to the word with the infinitive form *didaskein* while I have used the lexical form *didaskō*, but we are talking about the same word).

But these two verses are not counterexamples to Köstenberger's argument. In 1 Timothy 6:3 the word is not *didaskō*, "teach," but the compound word *heterodidaskaleō*, which means "to teach contrary to standard instruction, *give divergent*, i.e. *divisive, instruction*" (BDAG, 399), and which is therefore evidence that Paul needed some other word than *didaskō* to refer to a negative kind of teaching. Titus 1:11 says some people "are upsetting whole families by *teaching* (*didaskō*) for shameful gain *what they ought not to teach*," and thus the context supports Köstenberger's claim because it shows that Paul needed a contextual modifier ("what they ought not to teach") to turn the positive concept of "teaching" into a negative kind of destructive teaching. No such negative modifying phrase is found in 1 Timothy 2:12, however.

ples, then the verb *authenteō* in this verse cannot take any negative meaning such as "usurp authority,"[112] or "domineer," or "misuse authority."[113]

One further objection to Köstenberger comes from I. Howard Marshall. When Köstenberger says Paul would have used a negative term like ***heterodidaskalein*** if he had intended a negative action such as teaching false doctrine, Marshall responds that this "overlooks the fact that to say 'But I do not permit women to give false teaching' in this context would imply 'But I do allow men to do so'; in short, ***heterodidaskalein*** would be an inappropriate choice of word."[114]

But Marshall himself argues that *authenteō* has a negative nuance of "exercising autocratic power."[115] Marshall's argument essentially says, "Paul used negative word *A* because it would have been inappropriate for him to use *B*, since it was a negative word."

Marshall's same objection could be made against his own view in this way: to say, "But I do not permit women to exercise autocratic power" would imply, "But I do allow men to do so." But this is surely not Paul's meaning! By Marshall's own reasoning, therefore, his argument for a negative sense of *authenteō* is disproved.

Answer 8.8f: The grammar of 1 Timothy 2:12 shows that two activities are in view, teaching and having authority, not just one activity of "authoritative teaching."

My friend Craig Blomberg, who is not an egalitarian, adopts a surprising understanding of 1 Timothy 2:12. He says that "Paul is referring to one specific kind of authoritative teaching

---

What is surprising about Sumner's objection is that Köstenberger himself mentions these exact two verses as support for his case. He says, "If the writer had intended to give the term a negative connotation in 1 Timothy 2:12, he would in all likelihood have used the term *heterodidaskalein* (as in 1 Timothy 1:3; 6:3) or some other contextual qualifier specifying the (inappropriate or heretical) content of the teaching (as in Titus 1:11)" (Köstenberger, "Complex Sentence Structure," 103). It is unclear whether Sumner is unaware of what Köstenberger actually said or whether she just decided not to disclose it to her readers or respond to it.

Alan Padgett gives no additional argument in the article Sumner refers to, but merely mentions one additional verse. He writes, "Köstenberger is wrong to assert that 'to teach' is always positive in Paul, as Titus 1:11, 1 Timothy 1:7 and 6:3 make clear" (Padgett, "The Scholarship of Patriarchy," ***Priscilla Papers*** [winter 1997], 24). However, 1 Timothy 1:7 does not help Padgett's case either, because in that verse Paul views "teachers of the law" positively and criticizes those who wrongly seek that good task. (Moreover, Padgett fails to mention that the verb *didaskō* does not occur there, but the noun *nomodidaskalos*.) Padgett, like Sumner, fails to mention what Köstenberger had already said about these verses. Both Padgett and Sumner are unfair to their readers because they give the appearance of answering Köstenberger without letting their readers know what Köstenberger actually said about the objection they raise.

112. The King James Version in 1611 actually translated 1 Timothy 2:12 as "usurp authority," but this meaning has not been followed by any modern version, so far as I can tell. (The NKJV translates it "have authority.")

113. Köstenberger also demonstrates the inadequacy of a 1986 argument by Philip Barton Payne, in an unpublished paper, "***Oude*** in 1 Timothy 2:12," read at the 1986 annual meeting of the Evangelical Theological Society. Payne argued that the two verbs "convey a single coherent idea," and that the passage should be translated, "I do not permit a woman to teach in a domineering manner." But, as Köstenberger demonstrates (pp. 82–84), Payne's argument is seriously flawed because it assumes without proof that *authenteō* has the negative meaning "domineer," and Köstenberger's one hundred examples demonstrate that the verbs in such construction do not simply convey one "coherent idea," but refer to two activities that are related yet distinct.

114. Marshall, ***Pastoral Epistles***, 458.

115. Ibid.

rather than two independent activities."[116] Blomberg bases this interpretation on his claim that in 1 Timothy 2 Paul has a pattern "of using pairs of partly synonymous words or expressions to make his main points."[117] He lists twelve sets of what he says are such partly synonymous words or expressions, such as "peaceful and quiet" or "godliness and holiness" in 1 Timothy 2:2.

What is puzzling about this argument is that his twelve similar pairs of terms do not have even one pair that is really similar, for the syntax is different in all of them. First, the expression "God and Savior," which he claims for verse 5, is not there, and the expression "gold and silver," which he claims for verse 9, is not there (these are apparently oversights of a type uncommon in Blomberg's normally careful work). This leaves ten sets of expressions.

Of those remaining ten sets, two have no conjunction (petitions, prayers, etc. in 1 Timothy 2:1 and telling the truth, not lying in 1 Timothy 2:7). The other eight sets are all joined by the word *and* (Greek *kai*).

This means that of Blomberg's twelve examples, not one is parallel in syntax or in meaning to 1 Timothy 2:12, which has the expression "I do *not* permit a woman to teach *or* to exercise authority over a man," and uses the Greek construction *ouk...oude*. But *oude* is a negative conjunction, with a meaning that is opposite to that of *kai* ("and"). If Paul had said, "I do not permit a woman to teach *and* have authority over a man," it would provide the parallel that Blomberg claims. But Paul did not say that. So Blomberg has based an argument on twelve examples, not one of which is parallel to 1 Timothy 2:12.[118] His argument therefore is not persuasive.

Answer 8.8g: An extensive study of cognate words now confirms that the meaning of *authenteō* is primarily positive or neutral.

In addition to these earlier studies of *authenteō*, a massive, erudite study of the entire *authenteō* word group by Al Wolters has now appeared, encompassing and now surpassing all earlier studies in its scope.[119] After a detailed survey of all extant examples, not just of the verb *authenteō* but of several cognate words as well, Wolters concludes,

> First, the verb *authenteō* should not be interpreted in the light of *authentēs* "murderer," or the muddled definitions of it given in the Atticistic lexica. Instead, it should be understood, like all the other Hellenistic derivatives of *authentēs*, in the light of

116. Blomberg, "Neither Hierarchicalist Nor Egalitarian" (2001), 364.
117. Ibid., 363.
118. After we corresponded back and forth about what he had written in this section, Dr. Blomberg kindly sent me a prepublication copy of a revised form of his essay in which he drops the examples that had been included by mistake and rewords his claim to say, "While not always employing formal hendiadys and while using conjunctions other than *oude*, Paul seems to have a propensity to use pairs of largely synonymous words to say just about everything important twice" (p. 55 of unpublished paper sent to me). I appreciate this modification but I think it shows that my objection still stands: None of his proposed parallels are really parallel.
119. Albert Wolters, "A Semantic Study of *authentēs* and Its Derivatives," *Journal of Greco-Roman Christianity and Judaism* 1 (2000), 145–75 (this journal is so far only available on-line; see http://divinity.mcmaster.ca/pages/jgrchj/index.html). Although the publication date for this issue of the journal is 2000, I was only recently (in 2003) made aware of this article and I am unsure of the actual date it was published.

the meaning which that word had in the living Greek of the day, namely "master." Secondly, there seems to be no basis for the claim that *authenteō* in 1 Tim. 2:12 has a pejorative connotation, as in "usurp authority" or "domineer." Although it is possible to identify isolated cases of a pejorative use for both *authenteō* and *authentia,* these are not found before the fourth century AD. Overwhelmingly, the authority to which *authentēs* "master" and all its derivatives refer is a positive or neutral concept.[120]

Egalitarian claim 8.11: Gain Mastery: 1 Timothy 2:12 means, "I do not permit a woman to teach in order to gain mastery over a man."

Linda Belleville has yet another interpretation of 1 Timothy 2:12. She says that it means, "I do not permit a woman to teach *in order to gain mastery over a man*," or "I do not permit a woman to teach with a view to dominating a man."[121] Belleville's argument for this is that some other "neither...nor" constructions join to define "a related purpose or a goal." She gives the following examples:

> Matthew 6:20: "'where thieves neither break in nor steal' [that is, break in to steal]"
>
> Matthew 13:13: "'neither hears nor understands' (that is, hearing with the intent to understand)"
>
> Acts 17:24: "'neither dwells in temples made with human hands nor is served by human hands' (that is dwelling with a view to being served)."[122]

Answer 8.11a: Belleville has misrepresented her supporting verses and misunderstood Greek grammar.

Belleville has taken these three verses and made them say something they do not say. Then she uses these verses as a new "category" of meaning for "neither...nor" that she imposes on 1 Timothy 2:12.

There are perfectly good ways in Greek to say something like "to do x *in order to* do y." One way is to use the construction *eis* + infinitive. Another very common way is to use the word *hina*, usually followed by a subjunctive "to denote purpose, aim, or goal."[123] But none of these

120. Ibid., 170–71.
121. Belleville, "Women in Ministry" (2001), 127 (italics added).
122. Ibid., 126–27.
123. BDAG, 475.

verses that Belleville quotes uses such a construction! They simply say "neither x nor y" and purpose is not specified.

Moreover, it is not at all evident that the relationship is one of purpose. When Jesus says "where thieves do not break in and steal" (Matthew 6:20), He is saying two things. Sometimes thieves steal without breaking in (as in the public marketplace, or when people are traveling on an open highway, or elsewhere outdoors). Jesus is saying in heaven thieves neither break in nor steal, but Belleville reduces the two activities that Jesus specifies to one (they do not break in in order to steal).[124] This is not what Jesus said.

The same is true in Matthew 13:13. Jesus did not say that "they do not hear *in order to* understand," but, "they do not hear, *nor* do they understand." Those are two different things. Perhaps some were not hearing because they didn't want to understand, and perhaps some were not hearing for other reasons, or not understanding for other reasons. Jesus says that they didn't do either one.

The same is true in Acts 17:24–25. Paul did not say that God "does not live in temples made by man *in order to* be served by human hands," but rather Paul said two things: God "does not live in temples made by man, nor is he served by human hands," because God could be served by human hands in many areas of life outside a temple, and the Greek gods might live in temples not just to be served by human hands but for other purposes as well. Belleville is reductionistic in each case, because she takes two ideas and wrongly reduces them to one, with no justification in the Greek text. It is fair to conclude that she has established no new category of grammar, nor has she given any persuasive reason to support her view that 1 Timothy 2:12 permits only one activity, teaching in order to gain mastery over a man.

EGALITARIAN CLAIM 8.12: UNCOMMON WORD: IN 1 TIMOTHY 2:12, PAUL DOES NOT USE THE COMMON WORD FOR AUTHORITY (*EXOUSIA*), BUT USES A RELATIVELY UNCOMMON WORD, *AUTHENTEŌ*. SINCE THE WORD IS RARE, ITS MEANING CANNOT BE KNOWN WITH ANY CERTAINTY, AND WE SHOULD NOT PUT MUCH WEIGHT ON THIS VERSE.

Some egalitarian writers point out that in 1 Timothy 2:12 Paul uses the verb *authenteō* rather than the more common word for authority, *exousia*. They argue that *authenteō* occurs only one time in the New Testament and claim that its meaning is uncertain or unknown. Rebecca Groothuis says,

> It isn't even entirely clear what Paul was prohibiting. The word in verse 12 that is translated "authority" (*authentein*) is not the word used elsewhere in the New

124. The NASB is the most literal here with "not break in or steal," thus making the *ou*...*oude* construction visible in English (the KJV also shows this). Several other translations follow the RSV's "break in and steal."

> Testament to denote the positive or legitimate use of authority (*exousia*); in fact, this word occurs nowhere else in the New Testament. Moreover, it had a variety of meanings in ancient Greek usage, many of which were much stronger than mere authority, even to the point of denoting violence. Given that there is so much uncertainty concerning the word's intended meaning in this text, any definitive statement that Paul was forbidding women to exercise authority per se seems unwarranted.[125]

In 1985, Charles Trombley wrote,

> "To usurp authority" is the translation of a Greek verb, *authentein*. It's so rare that it's only found in one place in the Bible, and it was not a common word in secular usage. Why would Paul choose such an uncommon word to describe women usurping men's authority? Why did he use a rare verb that was considered vulgar and coarse?[126]

Answer 8.12a: Paul's use of a less common word does not mean that the word's meaning is uncertain or unknown.

Someone might think that if a word is uncommon in the New Testament, it is difficult to be sure what the word means. But that is not usually true. Because so much other Greek literature exists from the ancient world, a word that is uncommon in the New Testament may be quite common outside the New Testament. It is simply not the case that we have to be uncertain about words that occur only once in the New Testament. In fact, there are 1,934 words that occur only once,[127] and for the great majority of these, there are multiple examples of the word used in literature outside the New Testament, so that discovery of the meaning of the word is a process

125. Groothuis, *Good News for Women*, 215, with reference to Scholer, "The Evangelical Debate over Biblical 'Headship,'" 46. Scholer's survey of articles on the meaning of *authenteō* is on pages 44–50, but in a footnote Scholer says that his article is only a slightly revised form of a 1994 article (57n64). In any case, he does not take account of the definitive studies of *authenteō* published in 1995 by H. Scott Baldwin and Andreas Köstenberger (see notes 80 and 108 above). See also Keener, *Paul, Women and Wives,* 109.
    Nathan, *Who Is My Enemy,* writes, "The problem is that the connotation of the word *authentein* changed from classical Greek usage (where it meant to 'domineer over') to the time of the church fathers (where it meant merely 'to have authority over'). We simply don't have enough information regarding what Paul meant, based on the word's contemporary usage in the New Testament era, to conclusively state what the plain meaning of *authentein* is" (143). Nathan gives no support for his claim that *authentein* meant "to domineer over" in Greek usage before the time of the New Testament, nor does he show any awareness of the 1995 studies of this word by Baldwin and Köstenberger, so it is not clear what he bases his statement on. In actual fact, in Baldwin's exhaustive list of eighty-two examples of *authentein,* there is no example of the meaning "domineer" from classical Greek usage or anywhere near the time of the New Testament (see the list of examples in Appendix 7, pp. 675–702).
126. Trombley, *Who Said Women Can't Teach* (1985), 173. As support for the idea that the word *authentein* was "vulgar and coarse," Trombley quotes Catherine Kroeger, "Ancient Heresies and a Strange Greek Verb," *The Reformed Journal* (March, 1979). Not one of the eighty-two examples of *authenteō* that have been discovered (see Appendix 7, pp. 675–702) has a vulgar sense, and no lexicon gives any hint of support for this unusual claim. (See note 107 above regarding Catherine Kroeger's proposal of a sexual sense for *authenteō*.)
127. Robert Morgenthaler, *Statistik des Neutestamentlichen Wortschatzes* (1958), 165.

well grounded in hard evidence.[128] In 1 Timothy alone, there are 65 words that occur only once in the whole New Testament,[129] including the following:

> *diōktēs,* "persecutor" (1 Timothy 1:13)
> *antilutron,* "ransom" (1 Timothy 2:6)
> *neophutos,* "recent convert" (1 Timothy 3:6)
> *xenodocheō,* "show hospitality" (1 Timothy 5:10)
> *hudropoteō,* "drink water" (1 Timothy 5:23)
> *philarguria,* "love of money" (1 Timothy 6:10)

That these and other terms are "rare in the New Testament" does not make their meanings uncertain.

In the case of *authenteō*, we now have eighty-two other examples of this verb from Baldwin's study, which is a large base of information from which to draw fairly certain conclusions. In addition, we have evidence from several cognate words, and although I have argued above that such related words do not always accurately indicate a word's meaning, they often do, and in this case most of the evidence from related words also points to the idea of "authority" in some form, such as the noun *authentēs* in the sense of "master," and the noun *authentia*, meaning "absolute sway, authority."[130]

Of course, when the New Testament authors were writing, they had no way of knowing whether a word that seemed ordinary to them and to their readers would appear once or twice or five or ten times in the New Testament. They simply used words that conveyed clearly the meaning they intended, and they assumed their readers would understand that meaning. It is our task today to use all the available data that we have to understand the meaning of those words as precisely as we can.

Does it make any difference that Paul used *authenteō* rather than *exousia*? It is difficult to say much one way or the other. To begin with, *exousia* is a ***noun*** meaning "authority," but Paul used a verb *authenteō*, which means "to have or exercise authority." A simple reason for using *authenteō* may be that as Paul wrote he wanted a verb, not a noun, to express his meaning. There is a verb *exousiazō*, which means "to have the right of control, have the right/power for something or over someone," but it is not very common in the New Testament either, since it is used only four times (Luke 22:25; 1 Corinthians 6:12; 7:4 [twice]).

---

128. In fact, Morgenthaler lists on one page (177) the words that, at the time he published his book in 1958 (with a corrected reprint in 1973), were not known to exist in Greek before the time of the New Testament. This list consists of only 320 words, and only 246 of them are words that occur only once. Many of these words occur in literature shortly after the time of the New Testament, and many of them are compounds of or are clearly related in meaning to words that are well known.

129. See Andreas Köstenberger and Raymond Bouchoc, *The Book Study Concordance of the Greek New Testament* (2003), 1172. The following list of words is taken from that page.

130. LS, 275.

The noun *exousia* is quite common (102 times in the New Testament), but I see no reason why Paul had to be limited to using only common words or why anyone should say he should have used a noun in this verse. Nor can I see any reason why he should not be able to use words that were approximately synonymous, but had different nuances of meaning. There may have been nuances of *exousia* that he wanted to avoid, or nuances of *authenteō* that he wanted to include, but it is difficult for us to say what those might be. In any case, the verb he did use means "to have authority over," and that meaning now, in the light of much scholarly research, is established beyond reasonable doubt.

One more confirmation of the rightness of this understanding of *authenteō* is found in the very context in 1 Timothy 2. Paul says, "Let a woman learn quietly ***with all submissiveness.*** I do not permit a woman to teach or to exercise authority over a man; rather, she is to remain quiet" (1 Timothy 2:11–12). Here the activities of teaching and having authority are set in contrast to learning "with all submissiveness," and submissiveness is a fitting contrast to having authority.

EGALITARIAN CLAIM 8.13: JUST DON'T OFFEND THE CULTURE: PAUL'S MAIN POINT IN THESE RESTRICTIONS ON WOMEN TEACHING AND GOVERNING WAS NOT TO GIVE OFFENSE TO THE CULTURE OF THAT TIME. TODAY, SUCH ACTIVITIES BY WOMEN WOULD NOT GIVE OFFENSE TO OUR CULTURE, SO THE RESTRICTIONS DO NOT APPLY. WE HAVE TO DISTINGUISH BETWEEN THE MAIN CONCERN OF A WRITER AND THE OUTWARD FORM THAT HIS COMMAND TAKES.

This position was argued by my friend Grant Osborne.[131] Osborne says, first with regard to 1 Corinthians 14:34–36, "the normative aspect is the wife's subjection to her husband. The cultural application deals with the woman's silence in the assembly."[132] Similarly, in 1 Timothy 2:8–15, Osborne says, "we again see the balance between the normative principle (the woman's submissiveness) and the cultural application (not to teach but to be silent)."[133]

Osborne adds, "There are no biblical obstacles to [the ordination of women] in Western society where 'teaching' and 'speaking' in the church no longer have the implications they did in the first century. Attitudes today have changed."[134]

131. Grant Osborne, "Hermeneutics and Women in the Church," in *Journal of the Evangelical Theological Society* 20 (Dec. 1977): 337–52.
132. Ibid., 345.
133. Ibid., 347.
134. Ibid., 351–52. The possibility of disapproval from secular society on women teaching and governing the church in Ephesus is also given as a secondary reason for 1 Timothy 2:11–15 by Keener, *Paul, Women and Wives,* 111. (He thinks the primary reason is women's comparative lack of education.)

Answer 8.13a: The activities of teaching and governing the church are not merely a changeable outward form of some deeper principle, but they are the principles themselves because they represent fundamental activities essential to the life of the church.

The activities of teaching and governing the church are not like things such as a "holy kiss" (Romans 16:16; 1 Thessalonians 5:26) or head coverings for women (1 Corinthians 11:5), which are merely outward symbols or forms that can change from time to time and from culture to culture. You can have a church without holy kisses but you cannot have a church without teaching and governing functions. And you can have a church without women having their heads covered, but you cannot have a church without teaching and governing functions. These teaching and governing activities are fundamental to the life of the church, and thus they are not merely outward symbols. (For a discussion of how to know when a command is culturally relative, see the "Additional Note" at the end of chapter 9, pp. 397–402.)

Therefore, the distinction that Osborne makes between a "normative principle" and the "cultural application" does not properly apply in this case. Teaching and governing in the church are too fundamental to be merely culturally variable factors.

Answer 8.13b: Not offending the culture is not the reason Paul gives for his commands.

It is precarious to overlook the reason Paul gives (the created order of Adam and Eve) and emphasize a reason Paul did not give (offending the culture). Paul did not write, "I do not permit a woman to teach or to exercise authority over a man, *because that would be offensive to your culture*." Nor does he say anything like that. He says, "I do not permit a woman to teach or to exercise authority over a man; rather she is to remain quiet. *For Adam was formed first, then Eve*" (1 Timothy 2:12–13).

Answer 8.13c: This argument assumes that Paul taught something less than God's ideal in order to advance the gospel.

As I said earlier in response to Craig Keener's similar argument regarding marriage (see chapter 6, claim 6.8), this egalitarian argument is fraught with dangerous implications for the authority of Scripture, the moral integrity of the apostle Paul, and the words of God that Paul wrote. If in fact it was God's highest ideal for women as well as men to teach in the church, but Paul taught that women should not teach so as not to offend the culture, this casts a shadow over Paul's moral authority and throws into question the morality of the Bible's teachings. If it was *not* God's ideal for women to refrain from teaching and governing the church, but Paul taught it with his apostolic authority in writing to Timothy, then Paul was teaching something wrong.[135] And thus the Bible is teaching something wrong.

---

135. This would also be different from the example of polygamy, which God tolerated during the time of the Old Testament but never actually commanded.

This egalitarian approach misunderstands Paul's principle of becoming "all things to all people, that by all means I might save some" (1 Corinthians 9:22), for in the preceding verse Paul affirms that this principle will not lead him to do wrong. He says he is not "outside the law of God but *under the law of Christ*" (9:21). Paul would not have restricted teaching and governing in the church to men just to gain a hearing for the gospel or help make the gospel less offensive to the culture.

Answer 8.13d: Some women had prominent roles in pagan religions in Ephesus.

Paul Barnett points out,

> The most predominant citizen of Proconsular Asia, of which Ephesus was the leading city...was the *Archierus* of the Imperial Cult. This person...officiated at the numerous public festivals of the Cult of Rome. Inscriptional evidence reveals, quite remarkably, the existence of no less than fifteen *archiereiai* [= women high priests] over a period of two centuries and that these women high priests often held this high and prestigious office in their own right, quite independently of their husbands. Frequently their status derived from a distinguished father.[136]

Arnold and Saucy also point out considerable evidence from inscriptions[137] for women in various areas of civic and religious responsibility,[138] and thus the idea that women could not hold church office because it would have been unacceptable in that society does not square with the evidence:

> It is not probable that Paul was advocating a conformity to the prevailing culture on the issue of women's roles as a means of facilitating the evangelistic outreach of the church to the community. Those who have taken this position typically assume a far greater limitation on women than what appears to have been the case....
>
> We are left, then, with the recognition of a situation in Ephesus where women were converting to Christianity and desiring to attain leadership roles in the church similar to what they had in society. Aware of this situation, Paul addressed this issue because he did not want these churches to cave in to the cultural pressures of the day and violate a deep-set theological conviction about order between men and women.[139]

---

136. Paul Barnett, "Wives and Women's Ministry (1 Timothy 2:11–15)," in *Evangelical Quarterly* 61:3 (1989), 227. See also the evidence of Ephesian women in prominent civic and religious positions cited in Arnold and Saucy, "Ephesian Background," 281–87.
137. Inscriptions are writings that are carved or engraved on ancient tombs, monuments, coins, pottery, and other ancient stone and metal items.
138. Arnold and Saucy, "Ephesian Background," 282.
139. Ibid., 287. Arnold and Saucy refer to archaeological discoveries of Jewish inscriptions showing that there was at least one case, and perhaps several others, in which a woman had the role of "head of the synagogue" in

Egalitarian claim 8.14: Paul Was Wrong: Paul made a mistake in 1 Timothy 2 and reverted to his rabbinic background, failing to be consistent with his understanding of redemption in Christ.

In 1975 Paul King Jewett, a professor at Fuller Seminary, published *Man as Male and Female*,[140] which was (as far as I know) the first scholarly defense of an egalitarian viewpoint by an evangelical in modern times. In it he wrote,

> The apostle Paul was the heir of this contrast between the old and the new.... He was both a Jew and a Christian.... And his thinking about women...reflects both his Jewish and his Christian experience.... So far as he thought in terms of his Jewish background, he thought of the woman as subordinate to the man for whose sake she was created (1 Cor. 11:9). But so far as he thought in terms of the new insight he had gained through the revelation of God in Christ, he thought of the woman as equal to the man in all things.... Because *these two perspectives—the Jewish and the Christian—are incompatible, there is no satisfying way to harmonize the Pauline argument....*
>
> Paul...is assuming the traditional rabbinic understanding [of Gen. 2:18–23].... *Is this rabbinic understanding of Genesis 2:18f correct? We do not think that it is....*
>
> The difficulty is that Paul, who was an inspired apostle, appears to teach such female subordination in certain passages.... To resolve this difficulty, *one must recognize the human as well as the divine quality of Scripture.*[141]

Although few have followed Jewett in his claim that Paul made a mistake in what he wrote, Thomas Schreiner points out that a similar position was advocated by Clarence Boomsma as well.[142]

Answer 8.14a: This position is inconsistent with belief in the entire Bible as the Word of God, and is not a legitimate evangelical position.

Jewett's position allows the church today to disobey 1 Timothy 2:11–15, saying it was a mistake. But Christians who take the entire Bible as the Word of God and authoritative for

---

Smyrna (just north of Ephesus) in the second century, and other evidence that women had roles as "leader" or "elder" in various synagogue locations throughout Asia Minor (p. 286, with reference to studies by Paul Trebilco and Bernadette Brooten).

140. Paul Jewett, *Man as Male and Female* (1975).

141. Ibid., 112–13, 119, 134 (italics added).

142. Schreiner, "Interpretation of 1 Timothy 2:9–15," 107, with reference to Clarence Boomsma, *Male and Female, One in Christ* (1993). In a review of Boomsma's book, Albert Wolters writes, "I do not believe that anyone else in the Reformed tradition has ever dared to suggest that the scriptural argumentation of an apostle is clearly mistaken and unacceptable" (Albert Wolters, "Review of Boomsma, *Male and Female, One in Christ*," in *Calvin Theological Journal* 29 [1994], 285).

us today, do not have that option. This view refuses to take 1 Timothy 2 as God's truthful, divinely authoritative commands for Christians throughout the church age. This is not a legitimate position for an evangelical who believes that the entire Bible is "breathed out by God" (2 Timothy 3:16), and is thus the very Word of God.

EGALITARIAN CLAIM 8.15: THE NEW TESTAMENT MISINTERPRETS THE OLD TESTAMENT: IN SOME PASSAGES, SUCH AS 1 TIMOTHY 2:11–15, WE MAY FIND THAT OUR UNDERSTANDING OF THE OLD TESTAMENT IS SUPERIOR TO THAT OF A NEW TESTAMENT AUTHOR.

Asbury Seminary professor David Thompson claims there may be unusual times when we can carefully and cautiously differ with a New Testament author's interpretation of an Old Testament text. And one of those times is when we read Paul's interpretation of Genesis 2 in 1 Timothy 2.[143]

Thompson says that 1 Timothy 2:11–15 is hard to interpret (it poses "particularly complex problems hermeneutically") and, anyway, we might be able to reexamine Genesis 2 and disagree with Paul's interpretation of it: "We should take caution in immediately assuming that Paul's reading of Genesis 2 must, without further inquiry, be ours.[144]

Then he says that we should read the Genesis 2 account ourselves and understand it "on its own terms," and that our understanding of it can then be the "arbiter" of Paul's understanding: "It is entirely possible that at this point the Creation account, understood on its own terms, must be the arbiter of the more specifically confined reading given by Paul.[145]

Answer 8.15a: This procedure denies the absolute authority of Scripture for us today and sets us up as an authority greater than Scripture.

Thompson's procedure effectively denies the authority of Scripture for us today. Of course, Paul's use of Genesis 2 is a problem for egalitarians because Genesis 2 shows male headship in marriage before there was any sin in the world. Therefore it shows male headship as part of the way God created us as men and women. And then (to make things worse for the egalitarian position!), Paul *quotes* from Genesis 2 to establish male headship in the church (1 Timothy 2:13–14). This means that Paul sees male headship in the church as rooted in the way God created men and women from the beginning.

---

143. David L. Thompson, "Women, Men, Slaves and the Bible: Hermeneutical Inquiries," *Christian Scholar's Review* 25:3 (March, 1996), 326–49. For a full response to Thompson's article, see Wayne Grudem, "Asbury Professor Advocates Egalitarianism but Undermines Biblical Authority: A Critique of David Thompson's 'Trajectory' Hermeneutic" *CBMW News* 2:1 (December 1996), 8–12 (also available at www.cmbw.org). See also the discussion of Thompson's "trajectory hermeneutic" at claim 9.4, below.

144. Thompson, 346, 347.

145. Ibid., 347.

But Thompson has provided egalitarians with a new way to evade the force of that argument: With much caution, with careful study, with prayer, he says we should study Genesis 2 as twentieth-century interpreters. We should understand Genesis 2 "on its own terms." And when we understand the passage well enough, our understanding might (at times) enable us to reject Paul's interpretation. We can use Genesis 2 as the "arbiter" (or judge) of Paul's interpretation.

Note what has happened here. *We* are interpreting Genesis 2. And though Thompson may claim that *Genesis 2* is the judge of Paul's interpretation, the actual result (in the article) is that *Thompson's interpretation of Genesis 2* becomes the judge by which Paul's interpretation is pushed aside. Thompson's argument means that our interpretation can correct Paul's interpretation of Genesis 2—and, by implication, Paul's interpretation of other Old Testament passages as well.

Answer 8.15b: The New Testament's interpretations of the Old Testament are God's interpretations of the Old Testament.

If the Bible is the Word of God, then these interpretations are not just Paul's interpretations; they are also God's interpretations of His own Word. There might be times when I cannot understand an interpretation of the Old Testament by a New Testament author, but that does not give me the right to disagree with his interpretation. If I believe the Bible to be the very words of God, then I must believe that neither Paul nor any other scriptural author made mistakes in his interpretation of the Old Testament, or gave us interpretations of the Old Testament that we can reject in favor of better ones of our own.

Conclusion

For over thirty years, egalitarian interpreters have labored mightily to try to overcome the teaching of 1 Timothy 2 that women should not teach or exercise authority over a man in the assembled church. Literally thousands of pages have been written about this passage, and scholars have invested thousands of hours to research it.

But in the end the passage stands firm. Egalitarian attempts to discover another meaning for *authenteō* ("exercise authority") have been proven wrong again and again, and the more research that is done on this word, the more firmly the meaning "exercise authority" is established. In fact, the multiplication of novel proposed meanings reveals the futility of egalitarian efforts to establish a different meaning.

Attempts to claim that Paul was wrong, or that he misinterpreted the Old Testament, or that he was inconsistent in his application of his principles, have all proved to be unpersuasive. In addition, the claim that women were teaching false doctrine in Ephesus has not been supported by the evidence, all of which shows it was men who were promoting false doctrine. And more and more evidence shows that many women were quite well educated in Ephesus in the first century, so the claim that women were not well educated at the time does not accord with the facts either.

After giving detailed consideration to these various arguments, we have reason to be even more confident that 1 Timothy 2 teaches that certain governing and teaching roles in the church are reserved for men.

Yet we must continually remember, in the midst of this controversy, that Jesus and the New Testament apostles gave much more affirmation to women's ministries and to women's value in the church than many churches have. Therefore we must continue to affirm and encourage multiple kinds of ministries by women throughout every aspect of the church's life. *Both* men and women are given spiritual gifts to be used for the common good, as the Holy Spirit intends.

It is not enough, then, simply to oppose the egalitarian position. We have two responsibilities. We must be cautious of straying into liberalism or into a denial of the authority of Scripture, while at the same time being cautious that we do not quench the Holy Spirit or unnecessarily restrict the gifts that the Holy Spirit has given to women and the ministries that He wants them to be involved in.

CHAPTER NINE

Evangelical Feminist Claims About How to Interpret and Apply the Bible

Much of the controversy over men's and women's roles in marriage and the church has to do with how one interprets the Bible. There are significant differences over methods of interpretation in this controversy.

Egalitarians object that we don't follow the prohibitions about jewelry or braided hair for women today, nor do churches generally require head coverings for women. So why should we say that other restrictive verses about women's roles in the church are to be followed today?

In addition, haven't we discovered that some other teachings of the New Testament are culturally relative and not to be followed today? We don't teach that slavery is right today, so why should we teach that women's submission is required? Some egalitarians argue that the New Testament's ethical commands are not the final ethical standard God wants us to follow; they were simply one point in a "trajectory," and we can now see that the New Testament authors were taking significant steps toward a much higher ethic, an ethic that we can discern today, but that the New Testament authors did not reach in their lifetimes.

Other egalitarians say that the clear verses affirming women's ministries should be followed, not the obscure and debated passages (such as 1 Corinthians 14 and 1 Timothy 2), which nobody can finally agree about in any case.

With all the controversy on this issue, isn't it impossible to figure out what Scripture actually teaches about women in the church? And if it is impossible to decide what Scripture says, shouldn't we bless ministries of women that God is evidently blessing?

Other evangelicals today say it is acceptable for women to teach the Bible to both sexes if the woman is "under the authority of the pastor and elders." And still others say, "We are not a church, but a parachurch organization," and therefore they claim that it is acceptable for a woman to teach and govern mixed groups of men and women, because the New

Testament teachings on these issues *in the church* don't directly apply to their organizations.

Are these objections persuasive? They all have to do with questions about how the Bible should be interpreted and applied today.

EGALITARIAN CLAIM 9.1: NOBODY FORBIDS JEWELRY OR BRAIDS: COMPLEMENTARIANS ARE INCONSISTENT, BECAUSE THEY DON'T PROHIBIT WOMEN FROM WEARING JEWELRY OR BRAIDED HAIR, BUT THAT PROHIBITION IS FOUND IN THE VERY SAME PARAGRAPH IN THE BIBLE AS THE COMMAND ABOUT WOMEN NOT TEACHING OR HAVING AUTHORITY OVER MEN (1 TIMOTHY 2:9). WE SHOULD REALIZE THAT THE WHOLE SECTION WAS BINDING ONLY FOR THAT SITUATION AND CULTURE.

Paul says in 1 Timothy 2 that "women should adorn themselves in respectable apparel, with modesty and self-control, not with braided hair and gold or pearls or costly attire, but with what is proper for women who profess godliness—with good works" (vv. 9–10).

Alvera Mickelsen comments on this passage,

> Those who believe that verse 12 forever bars all women of all time from teaching or having authority over men usually ignore the commands in the other six verses in this section. This is a classic case of 'selective literalism.' If this passage is universal for all Christian women of all time, then no woman should ever wear pearls or gold (including wedding rings) or have braided hair or expensive clothing.[1]

Gilbert Bilezikian says,

> A warning must be voiced against the selective legalism which universalizes a local situation such as the ban on unqualified women teachers in Ephesus, but relativizes rules that are clearly given a universal relevance ("in every place"), such as hands lifted high in prayer and no braids, jewelry and fine apparel (2:8–9).... Consistency would require that both sets of ordinances be treated in the same manner.[2]

David M. Scholer comments,

> In view of this unity of 2:9–12 and the conclusion in 2:15, there is no exegetical, historical or hermeneutical basis to regard 2:9–10 as normatively different from 2:11–12. Nevertheless, most evangelicals, including those who see 2:11–12 as warrant for limiting women in ministry, take the injunctions against women's adornment

1. Alvera Mickelsen, "An Egalitarian View: There Is Neither Male nor Female in Christ," in Clouse and Clouse, *Women in Ministry: Four Views* (1989), 201.
2. Gilbert Bilezikian, *Beyond Sex Roles* (1985), 298–99n45 (referring to p. 181).

in 2:9–10 to be culturally relative and do not seek to apply them in the unqualified terms in which they are stated.[3]

Answer 9.1a: This passage does not prohibit jewelry or braided hair; it prohibits ostentation or excessive emphasis on jewelry or braided hair as a woman's source of beauty. Christian women should still obey that understanding of this passage today.

Thomas Schreiner points to a parallel passage in 1 Peter 3:3, where Peter says, "Do not let your adorning be external—the braiding of hair, the wearing of gold, or the putting on of clothing," and certainly Peter cannot be prohibiting all wearing of clothing in church![4] So Schreiner rightly says, "The proscription is not against all wearing of clothing, but luxurious adornment, an excessive devotion to beautiful and splendid attire." With regard to braided hair and gold and pearls, Schreiner says, "Paul's purpose is probably not to ban these altogether, but to warn against expensive and extravagant preoccupation with one's appearance.... In conclusion, the text does not rule out all wearing of jewelry by women, but forbids ostentation and luxury in adornment."[5]

Therefore complementarians are consistent, because they say (with most of the evangelical world) that these passages *are still relevant for us* and *must still be obeyed* today in largely the same sense that Paul and Peter intended 1 Timothy 2:9–10 and 1 Peter 3:3 to be obeyed by churches in their day. They were not legalistically prohibiting all use of jewelry, but were teaching the churches that women should exercise modesty and restraint rather than ostentation in their clothing.

Answer 9.1b: This egalitarian claim again comes dangerously close to denying the authority of Scripture.

Some egalitarians admit that we must obey these passages today, but the obedience takes a different form. They might say that jewelry in itself was ostentatious in the first century, and that the modern application is to avoid a kind of showy pride in one's clothing, though jewelry is allowed. This is a way of applying an ancient command to a slightly different modern situation *and still obeying it*.

But it is troubling to read the claims of other egalitarians who seem eager to find passages that they say we must disobey! Their reasoning goes as follows:

---

3. David Scholer, "1 Timothy 2:9–15 and the Place of Women in the Church's Ministry," in *Women, Authority and the Bible* (1995), 202. The same objections are raised by Sumner, *Men and Women in the Church* (2003), 213.
4. The NASB and KJV, along with the ESV which is quoted here, correctly translate *himatiōn* simply as "clothing" or "apparel" or "dresses." The NIV, as well as the RSV, NRSV, and NKJV insert the word "fine" before "clothes," but that is an interpretative addition because such a qualification is not represented in the Greek text.
5. Schreiner, "Interpretation of 1 Timothy 2:9–15" (1995), 119.

1. Of course we must disobey 1 Timothy 2:9 (about jewelry).
2. Therefore we should also disobey 1 Timothy 2:12 (about women teaching and having authority).

Such reasoning doubly rejects the authority of Scripture! Even if people say we should not follow 1 Timothy 2:9 in exactly the sense people followed it in the first century, our doctrine of Scripture as the Word of God requires us to obey 1 Timothy 2:9 *in some way or with some parallel application today*. And, similarly, we should have a way to understand 1 Timothy 2:12 that enables us to obey it in a similar way. But the egalitarian position (as represented by some) encourages disobedience to both passages. That practice could rapidly lead to a broader disintegration of the authority of the New Testament epistles in our lives today.

EGALITARIAN CLAIM 9.2: HEAD COVERINGS: JUST AS THE CHURCH HAS NOW LEARNED THAT WOMEN DO NOT HAVE TO WEAR HEAD COVERINGS AS COMMANDED IN 1 CORINTHIANS 11, SO IT NEEDS TO LEARN THAT WOMEN DO NOT HAVE TO SUBMIT TO THEIR HUSBANDS OR TO GIVE UP LEADERSHIP ROLES IN THE CHURCH TO MEN. ALL OF THESE WERE SIMPLY TRADITIONS PAUL WAS FOLLOWING IN THAT CULTURE.

Rich Nathan writes,

> Paul commands women in the church at Corinth to wear head coverings. Yet, most churches today (even the most traditional ones) don't require women to wear head coverings.... It is very rare, especially in America, for men to follow the explicit teaching of Scripture by kissing each other. We must admit that we all read the Bible with the understanding that the New Testament culture is different from ours.[6]

Such reasoning sounds plausible enough on first reading. When lay persons read that Paul required head coverings, and when they realize that few churches require head coverings for women today, it is easy to reason from (1) we don't require women to cover their heads as they did in the ancient world to (2) we don't need to exclude women from Bible teaching to the church, as they did in the ancient world.

The passage under discussion is as follows:

> Every man who prays or prophesies with his head covered dishonors his head, but every wife who prays or prophesies with her head uncovered dishonors her head—

---

6. Nathan, *Who Is My Enemy* (2002), 146. In this present section I deal only with the objection about head coverings, since it is used more often. Regarding the question of a holy kiss (Romans 16:16; 1 Corinthians 16:20; 2 Corinthians 13:12; 1 Thessalonians 5:26; 1 Peter 5:14), see the additional note at the end of this chapter, pp. 397–402.

> it is the same as if her head were shaven. For if a wife will not cover her head, then she should cut her hair short. But since it is disgraceful for a wife to cut off her hair or shave her head, let her cover her head. (1 Corinthians 11:4–6; see also vv. 10, 13)

(Some translations render the Greek word *gunē* in this passage as "woman" rather than "wife," and both meanings are possible for this word.)[7]

Answer 9.2a: Paul is concerned about head covering because it is an outward symbol of something else. But the meaning of such a symbol will vary according to how people in a given culture understand it. It would be wrong to require the same symbol today if it carried a completely different meaning.

No matter what people think about requiring head coverings for women today, all interpreters agree that head covering was a symbol for something else, and that Paul was concerned about it because of what that symbol meant. People have thought that head covering for women in the first century was a symbol of (a) a woman being in submission to her husband (or perhaps to the elders of the church), (b) being a woman rather than a man, (c) being a wife rather than an unmarried woman, or (d) having authority to pray and prophesy publicly in the church. There may be other explanations of the symbolism, but everyone agrees that Paul's concern is not to protect women from catching a cold or getting a sunburn on their head. Rather, he is concerned because of what wearing a head covering *symbolized* to people in Corinth.

So we should ask whether wearing a head covering symbolizes *any of these things* today. At least in twenty-first-century America, it symbolizes *none* of these things! When people see a woman wearing a hat, whether in church or outside of church, they don't immediately think,

- "Oh, I now know that woman is subject to her husband, because I see she is wearing a hat," or
- "Oh, I now realize that person is a woman and not a man, because she is wearing a hat," or
- "Oh, I now know that woman is married, not single, because she is wearing a hat," or
- "Oh, I now realize that woman has authority to pray and prophesy in the church, because she is wearing a hat."

Whatever we think a head covering symbolized in first-century Corinth, it does not symbolize the same thing today. And that means if Paul's concern was over what a head covering symbolized, then he would not want women to wear a head covering in a situation where a head covering did not carry the same symbolic meaning. Therefore, even if we cannot be sure what

7. For example, see section in Brown, *Women Ministers* (1996), 249–55.

the head coverings symbolized for women in the first century (for interpreters differ on this), the very fact that it does not symbolize much of anything to people today, even to Christians, is a strong argument that Paul would not have wanted us to follow it as sort of a meaningless symbol. I think it also means that God Himself does not intend us to follow this practice today, in a society and culture where it carries no symbolic meaning.

In fact, the response most people today are likely to have when they see a woman wearing a head covering in church is, "I suppose she's trying to be old fashioned, like someone from the 1950s or earlier. Well, she is free to do that if she wants, but it certainly looks strange." That is surely *not* the symbolic meaning that people attached to a woman's head covering in the first century.

Answer 9.2b: The most likely meaning of a woman wearing a head covering in first-century Corinth was to indicate that she was married. But no such meaning would be understood from a woman's head covering today.

The translators of the English Standard Version (quoted above) understood a woman's head covering in the first century to indicate she was married. Therefore in every verse in which head covering is mentioned, the ESV translates *gunē* as "wife." But the other verses it translates *gunē* as "woman," because these verses have more general statements about womanhood that Paul was using in order to discuss this specific application.

Evidence that head covering for a woman indicated that she was married is found both in literary sources and in archaeological discoveries of artwork portraying wedding scenes. Bruce Winter writes,

> The very mention of the word "veil" by Paul would automatically indicate to the Corinthians that the females under discussion in this passage were married.... The marriage ceremony involved what was called in Greek "veiling the bride" (*tēn numphēn katakalupsantes*). Both Tacitus and Juvenal describe the taking of "the veil of a bride" as one of the essential components of marriage. It was the social indicator by which the marital status of a woman was made clear to everyone.[8]

8. Bruce W. Winter, *After Paul Left Corinth* (2001), 127. Winter refers to a statement by Plutarch (born before AD 50, died sometime after AD 120) where the marriage ceremony is called "veiling the bride": "In Boeotia, after veiling the bride, they put on her head a chaplet of asparagus" [as part of the wedding ceremony], Plutarch, *Advice to the Bride and Groom*, 138D (quoted from *Plutarch's Moralia*, 301). The historian Tacitus (lived ca. AD 56 to ca. AD 118) described a marriage in which a man and woman "met for the avowed purposes of legitimate marriage," and where "the woman...assumed the veil," (*Annals*, 11.27; see also *Annals*, 15.37). Winter also refers to two statements from the Roman poet and satirist Juvenal (born sometime between AD 50 and AD 65), one in which a bride is "all prepared in her flaming veil" (*Juvenal* 10333–334), and another in which a man who holds his new bride is covered by her "long dress with veil" (*Juvenal* 2.124).

Artistic evidence is mentioned by Roy W. Christians in a recent study of 1 Corinthians 11:2–16.[9] Christians mentions a marble statue from Rome in what is clearly a wedding scene in which, "the man's head is uncovered and the woman's head is veiled."[10] Christians also mentions a similar scene in "a funerary relief from the Via Statilia outside Rome. Once again the husband has his head uncovered and the wife has her head covered."[11] He also refers to additional examples of similar archaeological evidence in the form of statues or other art objects that are discussed by David Gill in a 1990 article.[12]

Figure 9.1: British Museum Sculpture 2307: "The couple join hands, the man holds a scroll (the marriage contract), and the goddess Juno (between the couple) joins them in marriage."[13]

9. See Roy W. Christians, "The Permanent Relevance of 1 Corinthians 11:2–16 in Light of Recent Research into Its Historical and Cultural Background," paper given at the annual meeting of the Evangelical Theological Society, November 16, 2001, in Colorado Springs, Colorado. Christians's area of research for his PhD dissertation in New Testament is 1 Corinthians 11, and we may hope that the results of his research will be published in the near future.

   I realize that brides also veil their heads today in weddings without ongoing symbolism after the wedding, but the ancient literary evidence connecting veiling to the status of being married (see above) indicates a closer connection than we have today between veiling at the wedding and head coverings after the wedding.
10. An excellent photograph of this statue is found in Everett Ferguson, *Backgrounds of Early Christianity* (1993), 67.
11. Christians, "Permanent Relevance," 13.
12. See David Gill, "The Importance of Roman Portraiture for Head-Coverings in 1 Corinthians 11:2–16," *TynBul* 41 (1990), 253. Gill mentions the following evidence: S. Walker, *Memorials to the Roman Dead* (1985), 48–49, figure 39; B. F. Cook, *The Townley Marbles* (1985), 20–21, fig. 18; S. Walker, *Catalog of Roman Sarcophagi in the British Museum* (1990), 16–17, pl. 2, no. 4.
13. This is the description given by Ferguson, *Backgrounds of Early Christianity*, 67, for a nearly identical photo of a sarcophagus with a scene from a Roman wedding, 2nd century AD I wrote to Dr. Ferguson and got the information about the photo from him, and then wrote to the British museum for a photo of the same statue. However, the photo in Dr. Ferguson's book (p. 67) seems to be of the same couple and the same wedding, but with the heads of the bride, groom, and Juno in a slightly different position (the veil is much clearer in Dr. Ferguson's photo). The photos are so similar that I am unable to tell if they are two photos of the same statue taken from different angles, or photos of two different statues of the same wedding. In any case, the bride (far right) has a veil on her head and the groom (second from left) does not in both photos.

Therefore Bruce Winter appears to be correct in concluding, with regard to 1 Corinthians 11,

> Because any reference connecting a woman and a veil would immediately alert a first-century reader to the fact that she was a married woman, there are secure grounds for concluding that the issue here was married women praying and prophesying without their veil in the Christian meeting.[14]

But is it possible that a head covering in first-century Corinth was not a sign of being married, but was simply the way women dressed, and therefore a sign distinguishing women from men?[15] This does not seem likely in light of significant evidence connecting marriage and the veiling of a woman's head, but if it were true, it would not significantly affect our argument. If wearing a head covering in ancient Corinth was a symbol of being a woman, that is still not the meaning for a woman wearing a head covering in western societies today. And therefore head coverings should not be required for women today.[16]

Answer 9.2c: Today we obey the head covering commands for women in 1 Corinthians 11 by encouraging married women to wear whatever symbolizes being married in their own cultures.

In modern American society, a married woman wears a wedding ring to give public evidence that she is married. Just as Paul was concerned that women in Corinth not throw off their veils and thereby dishonor their husbands by not acting like married women in the church services, so married women today should not hide their wedding rings or otherwise publicly dishonor their marriage when they come to church. (There are probably a number of other symbols of being married in other cultures around the world, and the application of 1 Corinthians 11 to churches in those cultures is that married women [and men!] should not discard those symbols.)[17]

---

14. Winter, *After Paul Left Corinth*, 127.
15. This was the viewpoint I held, along with several other complementarians, before we were aware of the substantial evidence from ancient literature and from archaeology that connected marriage and wearing a veil in the first century. See, for example, Piper and Grudem, eds., *Recovering Biblical Manhood and Womanhood* (1991): "Paul is saying that...creation dictates that we use culturally appropriate expressions of masculinity and femininity, which just happened to be a head covering for women in that setting" (75), and "Paul wants the women to wear a head covering because such adornment appropriately distinguishes women from men" (Schreiner, "Valuable Ministries of Women" [1991], 135). In light of this new evidence, however, the earlier arguments in *Recovering Biblical Manhood and Womanhood* are strengthened rather than weakened. That is because the basic argument presented there would be the same: Head covering in ancient Corinth had a symbolic value that it no longer has today. But one detail in the argument is changed, and that is the explanation that head covering was a symbol, not of being a woman in general, but of being a married woman. The argument is stronger now, however, because of the significant amount of ancient evidence explaining just what was symbolized by the head covering.
16. For an analysis of the claim that *exousia* in 1 Corinthians 11:10 ("symbol of authority" or "authority") implies that women have the authority to speak or teach in the church, see answer 9.2f, below.
17. It is likely that a head covering symbolized not only being married but also being under the authority of one's husband in the ancient world (see answer 9.2f below). There may be no specific modern counterpart to this aspect of the symbolism other than a submissive demeanor and public words and actions that hint at the nature of the husband-wife relationship.

Notice that I am *not* saying that "we no longer have to obey 1 Corinthians 11." I am saying, rather, that the *outward form* in which we obey the passage may vary from culture to culture, just as the physical sign that symbolizes marriage varies from culture to culture. This is similar to the way that "you shall not covet your neighbor's...ox" (Exodus 20:17) applies today to not coveting our neighbor's car (or, in an agricultural society, his tractor).

Our approach here is very different from any egalitarian argument that says, "We don't have to obey the passage on head coverings, and we don't have to obey the passage on holy kisses, and we don't have to obey the passage on foot washing, so we probably don't have to obey the passages on male headship in marriage, either." That form of argument is particularly dangerous because it accumulates more and more sections of Scripture that "we don't have to obey today." But our submission to the authority of God as He speaks in His Word means that we have to obey *all* of these passages, though the *specific form* that obedience takes will vary from culture to culture, because the thing that God was concerned about in each case was not the outward form but the meaning conveyed by that form. (See the "Additional Note," pp. 397–402, on which commands take culturally variable forms of obedience.)

Answer 9.2d: The situation is far different with male headship in marriage and the church. These are not just outward symbols that can vary from culture to culture, but they are the reality itself.

It is easy enough to understand that a *physical object* can be a symbol of something else, such as a wedding ring or a head covering being a symbol of being married. (Similar physical symbols are a policeman's hat or badge as a symbol of his authority, or a crown as a symbol of royalty, or a chef's hat being a symbol of a preparer of fine foods, or a general's stars being a symbol of holding the rank of general in the army, or the black and white striped shirt of a referee being the symbol of the status of being a referee at a football game. These symbols could all change from culture to culture, but the underlying status that they represent would be the same.)

Similarly, we can understand how a *physical action* can be a symbol for an underlying reality. A kiss or a handshake or a hug can be a physical symbol for the reality of a warm greeting. But a similar kind of greeting might be conveyed by bowing in a Japanese culture. Sticking one's fingers in one's ears can be a symbol for not wanting to listen to something. (That symbol might be nearly universal.) And we understand quite well how the physical actions of baptism and partaking of the Lord's supper are physical symbols of deeper spiritual realities.

But "Wives, submit to your own husbands," and "Husbands, love your wives" (Ephesians 5:22, 25) are not mere symbols of some deeper reality. *They are the reality itself!* These commands are not physical items of clothing or momentary actions like a holy kiss, but they are fundamental, ongoing attitudes that should characterize the marriage relationship every hour of every day throughout one's married life. Similarly, leadership of the church by male elders (1 Timothy 2:12; 3:2) is not a temporary *symbol* of some deeper reality, *but is the reality itself.* It characterizes the ongoing leadership pattern of the church throughout all of its days.

Answer 9.2e: Christians who believe that 1 Corinthians 11 requires women for all times to have head coverings in church should obey this passage and not disregard it.

Some Christians today, particularly in countries outside the United States but also some in the United States, believe that 1 Corinthians 11 teaches that all Christian women in all churches for all times should have some kind of head covering. While I disagree with this understanding of the passage, it is right for Christians who hold this view to be consistent with their view in practice. If they think that God requires women to have their heads covered during the church service, then that is the practice they should follow. Not to follow it would be to disobey something one believes to be God's command.

Answer 9.2f: A woman's head covering in 1 Corinthians 11:10 is not a symbol of her authority to prophesy, but is a symbol of her husband's authority over her.

In an influential article in 1964, Morna Hooker argued that a woman's head covering was a symbol of her authority to prophesy publicly in church.[18] Hooker based her argument on 1 Corinthians 11:10: "That is why a wife ought to have a symbol of authority on her head, because of the angels."

In the Greek text, it does not literally say "a symbol of authority," but simply "authority," so we might literally translate, "A wife ought to have authority on her head." Hooker examines other examples of *exousia* ("authority") and finds that it always refers to a person's *own* authority, not the authority of someone else. Therefore, she argues, Paul must be saying that a woman's head covering symbolizes her authority to speak publicly in the worship service.

While I agree that Paul assumes that women can pray and prophesy publicly in church (see 1 Corinthians 11:5), I do not think this is the proper understanding of verse 10. The problem with Hooker's analysis is that most other examples of *exousia* refer to *authority itself*, not to something that is a *symbol of authority* (which her view also assumes for this verse). So most of the other examples are not really parallel.

In addition, Thomas Schreiner points out an interesting parallel from an ancient writer, Diodorus of Sicily, written sometime between 60 and 30 BC Diodorus describes a statue of the mother of King Osymandias as follows:

> There is also another statue of his mother standing alone, a monolith twenty cubits high, and *it has three kingdoms on its head*, signifying that she was both daughter and

18. See M. D. Hooker, "Authority on Her Head: An Examination of 1 Corinthians 11:10," *New Testament Studies* 10 (1964): 410–16.

wife and mother of a king (the word for "kingdoms" is *basileia*, "kingdom," not something like *stephanos* or *diadēma* which would represent a physical crown).[19]

The description clearly means in the context that the statue has three crowns, which are symbols of governing over kingdoms. But, as Schreiner points out,

> Here the three crowns (which Diodorus calls kingdoms) all represent someone else's authority—the authority of the woman's father (who was a king), husband (who was a king), and son (who was a king). In no case is the woman's own authority symbolized by the crowns she wears. Similarly, the head covering of the woman in 1 Corinthians 11 may well represent the authority of the man to whom she is subject in authority.[20]

Schreiner gives several other reasons why Hooker's argument is not persuasive, including the fact that in verses 3–9, head covering is what distinguishes women from men. But surely men had the authority to pray and prophesy as well, so it does not make sense to say that a head covering symbolized authority to pray and prophesy.[21]

It is best to conclude, then, that Paul sees a woman's veil on her head as a symbol of her husband's authority, and the fact that it is placed over her (on her head) is a rather transparent indication that she is under his authority.

Then what are we to make of the puzzling phrase, "Because of the angels" at the end of verse 10? It is difficult to be sure, but, as Schreiner says, "The best solution is probably that the angels...assist in worship and desire to see the order of creation maintained."[22]

EGALITARIAN CLAIM 9.3: SLAVERY: JUST AS THE CHURCH FINALLY RECOGNIZED THAT SLAVERY WAS WRONG, SO IT SHOULD NOW RECOGNIZE THAT MALE HEADSHIP IN MARRIAGE AND THE CHURCH IS WRONG.

This claim is frequently mentioned by egalitarian authors. Craig Keener says,

> Modern writers who argue that Paul's charge to wives to submit to their husbands "as to Christ" is binding in all cultures must come to grips with the fact that Paul even

19. Diodorus Siculus, 1.47.5. It is interesting, however, that the Loeb Classical Library translation renders it "three diadems on its head," in a manner similar to the way most English translations have rendered 1 Corinthians 11:10 not as "authority" but as "symbol of authority" (*Diodorus of Sicily*, trans. C. H. Goldfather, 1:168–69).
20. Schreiner, "Head Coverings, Prophecies, and the Trinity: 1 Corinthians 11:2–16," in Piper and Grudem, *Recovering Biblical Manhood and Womanhood*, 136.
21. See ibid., 135–36, for other objections to Hooker's view.
22. Ibid., 136. Schreiner adds that "uncertainty on this point does not affect the significance of the passage for today since the main burden of the text is quite clear" (487n26). He adds that other passages in the New Testament mention angels watching human activity, and this is viewed as a positive motive for obeying God's commands (see 1 Timothy 5:21; 1 Peter 1:12).

more plainly tells slaves to "obey" their masters "as they would Christ" (Eph 6:5). *If one is binding in all cultures, so is the other.*[23]

Rebecca Groothuis writes,

> The belief that people of African descent are inferior persons (not fit to be free) was slavery's logical concomitant. Likewise, the consensus of those who have advocated the subordination of women to men has historically been that women are inferior to men and hence, not fit to be free. The current traditionalist notion of a lifelong subordination that is determined by a person's inherent nature, but which does not imply inherent inferiority, is a historical, as well as a logical, anomaly.[24]

Answer 9.3a: Slavery is very different from marriage and from the church. Marriage was part of God's original Creation, but slavery was not. The church is a wonderful Creation of God, but slavery was not.

Egalitarians fail to realize the full implications of the wonderful differences between marriage and the church, on the one hand, and slavery on the other hand. Marriage and the church are good gifts from God. Slavery is not. It was right to abolish slavery. It is not right to attempt to abolish marriage or the church.

Slavery did not exist in God's original Creation in the Garden of Eden, but marriage did, and male headship did. It is something good and noble and right, something that God established before the Fall.[25]

Therefore, people who abolished slavery, *based on an appeal to biblical principles* (such as William Wilberforce in England and many Christians in the abolitionist movement in the United States) were abolishing something evil that God did not create. But Christians who oppose male headship in marriage and the church are attempting to abolish something good, something that God did create. The examples are simply not parallel.

Answer 9.3b: The New Testament never commanded slavery, but gave principles that regulated it and ultimately led to its abolition.

Paul says to slaves, "If you can gain your freedom, avail yourself of the opportunity" (1 Corinthians 7:21). And he tells Philemon that he should welcome his slave Onesimus back

---

23. Keener, *Paul, Women and Wives* (1992), 184 (italics added).
24. Groothuis, *Good News for Women* (1997), 62. See also Brown, *Women Ministers*, 198. David L. Thompson, "Women, Men, Slaves and the Bible" (1996), 340–46, argues that opponents of slavery in the nineteenth century could not use the Bible's texts on slavery but had to rely on broader biblical principles showing a "trajectory" toward which the New Testament was moving, a trajectory that would ultimately lead to the abolition of slavery. Thompson thinks a similar trajectory would lead to the abolition of teachings on women's submission to male leadership in marriage and the church today.
25. See the extensive discussion on male headship in Genesis 1–2, chapter 1, pp. 29–45.

"no longer as a slave but more than a slave, as a beloved brother" (Philemon 16), and that he should "receive him as you would receive me" (v. 17). Paul tells Philemon that if Onesimus owes him anything, Paul would pay it himself (vv. 18–19). Finally he says, "Confident of your obedience, I write to you, knowing that you will do *even more than I say*" (v. 21). This is a strong and not very subtle hint that Philemon should grant freedom to Onesimus. Paul's condemnation of "enslavers" (1 Timothy 1:10) also showed the moral wrong of forcibly putting anyone into slavery.

When we couple those verses with the realization that every human being is created in the image of God (see Genesis 1:27; 9:6; James 3:9), we see that the Bible, especially in the New Testament, contains powerful principles that would lead to an abolition of slavery. The New Testament never commands people to practice slavery or to own slaves; rather, it regulates the existing institution with statements such as, "masters, treat your slaves justly and fairly, knowing that you also have a Master in heaven" (Colossians 4:1).

The Bible does not approve or command slavery any more than it approves or commands persecution of Christians. When the author of Hebrews commends his readers by saying, "You joyfully accepted the plundering of your property, since you knew that you yourselves had a better possession and an abiding one" (Hebrews 10:34), that does not mean the Bible supports the plundering of Christians' property, or that it commands theft. It only means that *if* Christians have their property taken through persecution, they should still rejoice because of their heavenly treasure, which cannot be stolen. Similarly, when the Bible tells slaves to be submissive to their masters, it does not mean that the Bible supports or commands slavery, but only that it tells people who are slaves how they should respond.

The evangelical, Bible-believing Christians who ultimately brought about the abolition of slavery *did not modify or nullify any biblical teaching*, but that is what egalitarians want us to do with the teachings about men and women in marriage and in the church.[26]

Answer 9.3c: The fact that some Christians used the Bible to defend slavery in the past does not mean the Bible supports slavery.

Sometimes egalitarians seem to assume that if they can show that Christians used the Bible to defend slavery, that proves the Bible supported slavery, and this provides them a basis for arguing that we should "move beyond" other things the New Testament teaches as well.

William Webb sometimes appeals to the fact that proponents of slavery or proponents of monarchy in the past appealed to the Bible to prove their case. He says, "slavery proponents frequently argued from theological and christological analogies in the text,"[27] and that "in the past,

---

26. David Thompson fails to show awareness of this difference in the crucial section of his article on pp. 342–46.
27. Webb, *Slaves, Women and Homosexuals* (2001), 186.

the submission texts cited above were used by Christians to support monarchy as the only appropriate, God-honoring form of government."[28]

But the fact of the matter is that the Bible was used by more Christians to *oppose* slavery than to defend it, and eventually their arguments won and slavery was abolished. For example, Theodore Weld's, *The Bible Against Slavery* (1837) was widely distributed by abolitionists and frequently reprinted. Weld argues strongly against American slavery from Exodus 21:16, "He that stealeth a man and selleth him, or if he be found in his hand, he shall surely be put to death" (KJV) (13–15), as well as from the fact that men are in the image of God and therefore it is morally wrong to treat any human being as property (8–9, 15–17). He argues that ownership of another person breaks the eighth commandment, "Thou shalt not steal," as follows: "The eighth commandment forbids the taking of any part of that which belongs to another. Slavery takes the whole. Does the same Bible which prohibits the taking of any thing from him, sanction the taking of every thing? Does it thunder wrath against the man who robs his neighbor of a cent, yet commission him to rob his neighbor of himself? Slaveholding is the highest possible violation of the eighth commandment" (10–11). In the rest of the book he answers detailed objections about various verses used by slavery proponents. The whole basis of his book is that the moral standards taught in the Bible are right, and there is no hint that we have to move beyond the Bible's ethics as Webb would have us do.[29]

Answer 9.3d: The horrible abuses of human beings that occurred in American slavery made it an institution that was different in character from the first-century institution of being a "slave" or "bondservant" (Greek *doulos*).

When we hear the word "slavery" today, what comes to mind is what we have read in books, or seen in movies or on television, concerning the horrible abuses that occurred in American slavery during the nineteenth century and earlier. But if that is the picture that comes to mind when we read the word "slave" in the Bible, it is a distorted picture.

The person referred to as a "slave" or "bondservant" in the New Testament (Greek *doulos*) was legally "bound" to a certain master, almost always for a limited period of time until he could obtain his freedom. A detailed article in *The International Standard Bible Encyclopedia* explains,

> Persons in slavery under Roman law in the 1st cent. AD could generally count on being set free by age thirty.... Pertinent inscriptions indicate, however, that large numbers, approaching 50 percent, were set free prior to their thirtieth birthdays.[30]

---

28. Ibid., 107.
29. Weld, *The Bible Against Slavery* (1838; first published 1837), 8–17. See also several essays in *Against Slavery: An Abolitionist Reader* (2000), ed. Mason Lowance.
30. S. S. Bartchy, "Slavery," in *The International Standard Bible Encyclopedia* (1988), ed. Geoffrey W. Bromiley, 4:545.

Slaves in this sense had a higher social status and better economic situation than free day laborers who had to search for employment each day (see Matthew 20:1–7, where the master of a house goes into the marketplace to hire day laborers at different times during the day). By contrast, those who were "bondservants" (or "slaves") had greater economic security with a continuing job and steady income.[31]

Such slaves (in the first-century sense of "bondservants") worked in a variety of occupations:

> In Greco-Roman households slaves served not only as cooks, cleaners, and personal attendants, but also as tutors of persons of all ages, physicians, nurses, close companions, and managers of the household. In the business world, slaves were not only janitors and delivery boys; they were managers of estates, shops, and ships, as well as salesmen and contracting agents. In the civil service, slaves were not only used in street-paving and sewer-cleaning gangs, but also as administrators of funds and personnel and as executives with decision making powers.[32]

How then did people become slaves? While many were born into slavery, and while in earlier years up to the time of Caesar Augustus (63 BC to AD 14) the Romans had obtained slaves through conquest in war, by the time of the New Testament,

> Large numbers of people sold themselves into slavery for various reasons, above all to enter a life that was easier and more secure than existence as a poor, freeborn person, to obtain special jobs, and to climb socially....
>
> Many non-Romans sold themselves to Roman citizens with the justified expectation, carefully regulated by Roman law, of becoming Roman citizens themselves when manumitted....
>
> Certainly, capable slaves had an advantage over their free counterparts in that they were often given an excellent education at their owner's expense. Famous philosophers (Epictetus), teachers...grammarians...administrators (M.A. Felix, the procurator who was Paul's judge in Acts 23:24–24:27), artists, physicians, and writers were the result of this practice. These slaves and former slaves formed the broad "class" of intellectuals in the 1st century. Such slaves did not have to wait until manumission before they were capable of establishing friendships with their owners and other free persons as human beings....
>
> For many, self-sale into slavery with anticipation of manumission was regarded as the most direct means to be integrated into Greek and Roman society. As such, in

31. Ibid., 546: "To have turned all the slaves into free day laborers would have been to create an economy in which those at the bottom would have suffered even more insecurity and potential poverty than before." A. A. Ruprecht says, "Eighty-five to 90 percent of the inhabitants of Rome and peninsula Italy were slaves or of slave origin in the first and second centuries" ("Slave, Slavery," *DPL*, 881).

32. Bartchy, "Slavery," 544. A. A. Ruprecht agrees: see "Slave, Slavery," *DPL* 881–83.

> stark contrast to New World slavery in the 17th–19th cents., Greco-Roman slavery functioned as a process rather than a permanent condition.[33]

This is not to say that slavery was an ideal condition, for slaves looked forward to the time when they could purchase their freedom. They were still regarded by the law as things rather than persons according to their legal status. However,

> It was, of course, recognized that those in slavery, as many as one-third of the population in the large cities such as Rome, Ephesus, Antioch, and Corinth, were human beings if not "legal persons." As such they were protected by law against severe cruelty from their owners or others....
>
> A slave's property was entirely under the control of the slave, who could seek to increase it for use in purchasing legal freedom and in establishing a comfortable life as a freed person.[34]

So we must realize that first century "slavery" was for the most part much different in character from the horrible abuses that we commonly picture as "slavery" from our knowledge of American history. And yet we must recognize that the New Testament (a) never commanded this practice, (b) gave principles that regulated it while it was in existence, and (c) gave principles that ultimately led to the abolition of slavery itself.

Answer 9.3e: Defenders of slavery and modern day egalitarians are similar in one significant way.

While egalitarians claim that people who uphold differences in roles for men and women are like the people who used the Bible to defend slavery in the nineteenth century, it may be more accurate to say that modern egalitarians are like those defenders of slavery, at least in one important way: Both groups use verses from the Bible to justify something contrary to Scripture that is popular in their own culture.

---

33. Bartchy, "Slavery," 543–44. (In Matt. 25:15, slaves are entrusted with "talents"—immense amounts of money.)

34. Ibid., 544. It should be noted that some scholars differ with Bartchy and portray ancient slavery more negatively: see J. A. Harrill, "Slavery," *DNTB*, 1124–27, who says that the subject of ancient slavery has been a matter of "fierce scholarly debate" and this is "more controversial a subject than any other in the study of ancient literature and society" (1124). However, in support of Bartchy it should be noted that the article "Slavery" by M. I. Finley in the *OCD*, 2nd ed., 994–6, substantially agrees with Bartchy's assessment. This is significant because Finley, a highly respected Cambridge professor of history, was apparently the greatest modern historian of ancient slavery; all studies of this topic mention his monumental study *Ancient Slavery and Modern Ideology* (1980), along with several related works.

Scholars may debate for a long time exactly how evil first-century slavery was. No doubt there were many differences in a societal system that lasted so long and was so widely dispersed, and in such cases people can find data to support different views. What I am not willing to do is say that the institution of a *doulos* was inherently and pervasively so evil that the New Testament authors should have condemned it entirely, but they didn't, and therefore we can see that the New Testament's moral standards are inadequate. This would be to say that the New Testament actually teaches a defective moral standard, and I do not think that option is open for Christians who take the Bible as the flawless, pure Word of God.

In the nineteenth century, some Christians used the Bible to defend something widely accepted in their culture (slavery), and they failed to see that it was contrary to the Bible.

In our day, egalitarians use the Bible to defend something widely accepted in our culture (no gender based differences in men's and women's roles), and they fail to see that it is contrary to the Bible.

EGALITARIAN CLAIM 9.4: TRAJECTORY: PAUL AND OTHER NEW TESTAMENT AUTHORS WERE MOVING IN A TRAJECTORY TOWARD FULL INCLUSION OF WOMEN IN LEADERSHIP, BUT THEY DIDN'T QUITE REACH THAT GOAL BY THE TIME THE NEW TESTAMENT WAS COMPLETED. TODAY WE CAN SEE THE DIRECTION THEY WERE HEADING AND AFFIRM THE EGALITARIAN CONCLUSIONS THEY WERE HEADING TOWARD.

R. T. France, in his book *Women in the Church's Ministry: A Test Case for Biblical Interpretation*, takes this position. He argues that the Old Testament and Judaism in the time of Jesus were male-dominated and biased against women, but that Jesus began to overturn this system, and that the New Testament churches continued the process. We can now follow this "trajectory" to a point of full inclusion of women in all ministries. France explains:

> The gospels do not, perhaps, record a total reversal of Jewish prejudice against women and of their total exclusion from roles of leadership. But *they do contain the seeds from which such a reversal was bound to grow*. Effective revolutions are seldom completed in a year or two. In this, as in other matters, the disciples were slow learners. But the fuse, long as it might prove to be, had been ignited. [35]

France later comments on "there is no longer male and female" in Galatians 3:28,

> Paul here expresses *the end-point of the historical trajectory* which we have been tracing...from the male-dominated society of the Old Testament and of later Judaism, through the revolutionary implications and yet still limited actual outworking of Jesus' attitude to women, and on to the increasing prominence of women in the apostolic church and in its active ministry. At all points within the period of biblical history *the working out of the fundamental equality* expressed in Galatians 3:28 *remained constrained by the realities of the time*, and yet there was the basis, indeed the imperative, for the dismantling of the sexual discrimination which has prevailed since the fall. *How far along that trajectory it is appropriate and possible for the church to move* at any subsequent stage in history must remain a matter for debate, as it is today.[36]

---

35. R. T. France, *Women in the Church's Ministry: A Test Case for Biblical Interpretation* (1995), 78 (italics added).
36. Ibid., 91, italics added.

And he says that he has found his "basic position" regarding women in ministry

> not in these few texts [1 Corinthians 14:34–36 and 1 Timothy 2:11–15] but *in a trajectory of thought and practice developing through Scripture, and arguably pointing beyond itself* to the fuller outworking of God's ultimate purpose in Christ in ways which the first-century situation did not yet allow.[37]

A similar position is argued by Asbury Seminary professor David L. Thompson in a 1996 article in *Christian Scholar's Review:*[38]

> Sensing the direction of the canonical dialogue and prayerfully struggling with it, God's people conclude that they will most faithfully honor his Word by *accepting the target already anticipated in Scripture and toward which the Scriptural trajectory was heading* rather than the last entry in the Biblical conversation.... The canonical conversation at this point closed without final resolution. But *the trajectory was clearly set toward egalitarian relationships.*[39]

Answer 9.4a: This trajectory argument invalidates the Bible as our final authority.

Both France and Thompson admit that the New Testament authors did not teach the full inclusion of women in all forms of church leadership. As France says, the first-century situation "did not yet allow" this "fuller outworking of God's ultimate purpose," which they say should be our standard today.

But this means that the teachings of the New Testament are no longer our final authority. Our authority now becomes *our own ideas of the direction the New Testament was heading* but never quite reached.

Answer 9.4b: This trajectory argument denies the doctrine of Scripture and the principle of *sola Scriptura* as they have been believed in the major confessions of faith.

In order to guard against making our authority something other than the Bible, major confessions of faith have insisted that the words of God *in Scripture* are our authority, not some position arrived at after the Bible was finished. This is the Reformation doctrine of *sola Scriptura*, or "the Bible alone," as our ultimate authority for doctrine and life. The Westminster Confession of Faith says:

---

37. Ibid., 94–95.
38. Thompson, "Women, Men, Slaves and the Bible," 326–49. For a more detailed response to Thompson's article, especially his hermeneutical principles and his approach to the authority of Scripture, see Grudem, "Asbury Professor," *CBMW News* 2:1 (Dec 1996), 8–12 (also available at www.cmbw.org).
39. Thompson, "Women, Men, Slaves and the Bible," 338–39.

> The *whole counsel of God* concerning all things necessary for his own glory, man's salvation, faith and life, is either expressly set down in Scripture, or by good and necessary consequence may be deduced from Scripture: unto which nothing at any time is to be added, whether by new revelations of the Spirit, or traditions of men.[40]

More recently, the widely-acknowledged Chicago Statement on Biblical Inerrancy said:

> We affirm that God's revelation in the Holy Scriptures was progressive. We deny that later revelation, which may fulfill earlier revelation, ever corrects or contradicts it. We further deny that any normative revelation has been given since the completion of the New Testament writings.[41]

But this trajectory position would have the later standard (the supposed "goal" to which the New Testament was headed) contradict earlier revelation (which limited certain roles in the church to men).

The doctrinal statement of the Evangelical Theological Society says:

> *The Bible alone*, and the Bible in its entirety, *is the Word of God written*, and is therefore inerrant in the autographs.[42]

But this trajectory argument places authority ultimately in something beyond the New Testament writings.

Answer 9.4c: This trajectory argument fails to understand the uniqueness of the New Testament in distinction from the Old Testament.

France argues that we already see change from the Old Testament to the New Testament, and within the New Testament we see the apostles gradually growing in their understanding of the way Gentiles can be fully included in the church (as in the Jerusalem Council in Acts 15).[43] So why should we not allow change beyond what is in the New Testament?

This view fails to recognize the uniqueness of the New Testament. Yes, the New Testament explicitly tells us that we are no longer under the regulations of the Old Covenant (Hebrews 8:6–13), so we have clear warrant for saying the sacrificial laws and dietary laws are no longer binding on us. And we do see the apostles in a process of coming to understand the inclusion of the Gentiles in the church (Acts 15; Galatians 2:1–14; 3:28). But *that process was completed within the New Testament*, and the commands given to Christians in the New Testament say nothing about excluding Gentiles from the church. We do not have to progress on a "trajectory" beyond the New Testament to discover that.

---

40. Chapter 3, paragraph 6 (italics added).
41. Article V, *Journal of the Evangelical Theological Society* 21:4 (Dec 1978), 290–91.
42. www.etsjets.org.
43. France, *Women in the Church's Ministry*, 17–19.

Christians living in the time of Paul's epistles were living under the New Covenant. And we Christians living today are also living under the New Covenant. This is "the New Covenant in my blood" (1 Corinthians 11:25), which Jesus established and which we affirm every time we take the Lord's Supper. That means we are living in the same period in God's plan for "the history of redemption" as the first-century Christians. And that is why we can read and apply the New Testament directly to ourselves today.

To attempt to go beyond the New Testament documents and derive our authority from "where the New Testament was heading" is to reject the very documents God gave us to govern our life under the New Covenant until Christ returns.

Answer 9.4d: This trajectory argument is far different from later doctrinal formulations that were based on Scripture alone.

I agree that the church later formulated doctrines, such as the Trinity, that are not spelled out explicitly in the New Testament. But that is far different from what France and Thompson advocate, because Trinitarian doctrine was always *based on the actual teachings of the New Testament*, and its defenders always took the New Testament writings as their final authority. By contrast, France and Thompson do not take the New Testament statements as their final authority, but "go beyond" the New Testament to a "target" that *contradicts or nullifies* the restrictions on women's ministry given by Paul. No Trinitarian doctrine was ever built by saying we need a view that contradicts and denies what Paul wrote.

Answer 9.4e: This trajectory argument would lead the church to ethical chaos where no one could tell which view is right.

France and Thompson think the trajectory was heading toward egalitarianism. But this argument could be used in just the other way. Someone could take France's view of Galatians 3:28 and argue that the trajectory looks like this:

FROM PAUL'S EARLY WRITINGS	TO PAUL'S LAST, MORE MATURE WRITINGS	TO THE FINAL TARGET FOR THIS TRAJECTORY	APPLICATION TODAY
Galatians 3:28: women in all positions of leadership	1 Timothy 2–3; Titus 1: only men can teach or be elders	Women cannot participate in any ministry in the church	All ministry of all kinds must be done by men

This is a ridiculous conclusion, but if we accept the "trajectory" principle of France and Thompson, it would be hard to say it was wrong.

Or we could take a "trajectory" argument on divorce:

FROM JESUS' TEACHINGS	TO PAUL'S TEACHINGS	TO THE FINAL TARGET FOR THIS TRAJECTORY	APPLICATION TODAY
Only one ground for divorce: adultery (Matthew 19:6)	Two grounds for divorce: adultery or desertion (1 Corinthians 7:14)	Divorce for any hardship	God approves divorce for any hardship in marriage

We may think these trajectories are foolish, but they use the same process as France and Thompson in moving from earlier to later biblical writings. And these trajectories all have one thing in common: we no longer have to obey what the New Testament teaches. We can devise our own ideas about the direction things were heading at the end of the New Testament.

This method has no controls on it. It is subjective, and the final authority is not the Bible, but anyone's guess as to where the trajectory was heading.

Answer 9.4f: This trajectory argument is similar to the view of the Roman Catholic Church, which bases doctrine not only on the Bible but also on the authoritative teachings of the church that have come after the Bible was written.

One of the distinctive differences between historic, orthodox Protestants and the Roman Catholic Church has been that Protestants base doctrine on "Scripture alone" (in Latin, *sola Scriptura*), while Catholics base doctrine on Scripture *plus* the authoritative teaching of the church through history. This trajectory argument of France and Thompson is disturbingly similar to Roman Catholicism in this regard, because Roman Catholics place final authority not in the New Testament writings, but in their ideas of where that teaching was leading. Yet a Roman Catholic could argue that more reliable than their *speculation* on where the teaching was leading are the *historical facts* of where the teaching did lead. So the trajectory (which actually was fulfilled in church history) would look like this:

FROM JESUS' TEACHINGS	TO PAUL'S TEACHINGS	TO THE FINAL TARGET FOR THIS TRAJECTORY	APPLICATION TODAY
No local church officers or governing structure mentioned	Increased authority given to elders and deacons	Worldwide authority given to the Pope, cardinals, and bishops	We should submit to the authority of the Pope and the Roman Catholic Church

The Reformation principle *sola Scriptura* was formulated to guard against the kind of procedure France and Thompson advocate, because the Reformers knew that once our authority becomes "Scripture plus some later developments" rather than "Scripture alone," the unique governing authority of Scripture in our lives is lost.

On several grounds, then, this trajectory argument must be rejected as inconsistent with the view that "all Scripture is breathed out by God" (2 Timothy 3:16), and

> Every word of God proves true....
> Do not add to his words,
> lest he rebuke you and you be found a liar. (Proverbs 30:5–6)

Egalitarian claim 9.5: Redemptive-Movement Hermeneutic: William Webb's redemptive-movement hermeneutic shows that the submission texts and the male church leadership texts in the New Testament were culturally relative.

William Webb, in his book, *Slaves, Women and Homosexuals: Exploring the Hermeneutics of Cultural Analysis* (2001), proposes a system that he calls a "redemptive-movement hermeneutic," by which he argues that the New Testament texts about male headship in marriage and male church leadership are culturally relative.

In contrast to many egalitarians who argue that the New Testament does not teach that wives should be subject to their husbands or that only men should be elders, Webb takes a different approach: he believes that the New Testament *does* teach these things *for the culture in which the New Testament was written*, but he claims that in today's culture the treatment of women is an area in which "a better ethic than the one expressed in the isolated words of the text is possible."[44]

Webb admits that the Old and New Testaments improved the treatment of women when compared with their surrounding cultures, but he says,

> If one adopts a redemptive-movement hermeneutic, the softening of patriarchy (which Scripture itself initiates) can be taken a considerable distance further. Carrying the redemptive movement within Scripture to a more improved expression for gender relationships... [today] ends in either ultra-soft patriarchy or complementary egalitarianism.[45]

Later in the book, Webb defines "ultra-soft patriarchy" as a position in which there are no unique leadership roles for men in marriage or in the church, but men are given "a certain level

44. Webb, *Slaves, Women and Homosexuals*, 36 (italics added).
45. Ibid., 39.

of *symbolic* honor."[46] He defines "complementary egalitarianism" as a system in which there is full interdependence and "mutual submission" within marriage, and the only differences in roles are "based upon biological differences between men and women," so that Webb would favor "a greater participation of women in the early stages of child rearing."[47] Thus, Webb's "ultra-soft patriarchy" differs from his "complementary egalitarianism" only in the slight bit of "symbolic honor" that ultra-soft patriarchy would still give to men.

Because of its detail, novelty, and the complexity of its approach, this book deserves to be taken seriously by complementarians. It is the most sophisticated version of a "trajectory hermeneutic" (see claim 9.4) that has ever been published. However, because of concerns that are detailed below, I do not think the book succeeds in showing that male headship in the home and the church are culturally relative. Nor do I believe that the book provides a system for analyzing cultural relativity that is ultimately helpful for Christians to use today.[48]

Answer 9.5a: Webb's trajectory hermeneutic nullifies in principle the moral authority of the New Testament.

At first glance, it may not seem as though Webb "nullifies" the moral authority of the entire New Testament, because he agrees, for example, that homosexual conduct is morally wrong, and that the New Testament condemnations of homosexual conduct are transcultural.[49] He also affirms that the New Testament admonitions for children to be subject to their parents are transcultural.[50]

The important point to realize is the *basis* on which Webb affirms that these commands are transcultural. Most evangelicals read a text such as, "Children, obey your parents in the Lord, for this is right" (Ephesians 6:1), and conclude that children *today* are to obey their parents because the New Testament was written for Christians in the New Covenant age (the time between Christ's death and His return).

Most evangelicals reason similarly about the New Testament texts concerning homosexual conduct (see, for example, Romans 1:26–27; 1 Corinthians 6:9), and conclude that these are morally binding on us today, because we are part of the New Covenant age and these texts were written to New Covenant Christians.

But for Webb, the process is entirely different, and the basis of authority is different. The commands concerning children and homosexuals are binding on us today not because we are part of the New Covenant age, for which the New Testament was written (I could not find such a consideration anywhere in Webb's book), but rather *because these commands have*

---

46. Ibid., 243.
47. Ibid., 241.
48. For a detailed critique of Webb's book, see Appendix 5, pp. 600–645. See also the "Additional Note" at the end of this chapter, pp. 397–402, for an examination of guidelines for how we can determine which moral commands of Scripture are culturally relative.
49. Ibid., 39–41, 250–52, and many other places in the book.
50. Ibid., 212.

passed through the filtering system of Webb's eighteen criteria and have survived. Actually, the command for children to obey their parents has not entirely survived his filtering process, because Webb believes the command means that *adult* children should continue to be obedient to their parents throughout their adult lives, but this aspect of the command was culturally relative and need not be followed by us today.[51]

In this way, I believe it is fair to say that Webb's system invalidates the moral authority of the entire New Testament, at least in the sense that we today should be obedient to the moral commands that were written to New Covenant Christians. Instead, only those commands are binding that have passed through his eighteen-part filter.

According to Webb's system, then, Christians can no longer go to the New Testament, read the moral commands in one of Paul's epistles, and obey them. That would be to use a "static hermeneutic" that just reads the "isolated words of the text" and fails to understand "the spirit-movement component of meaning which significantly transforms the application of texts for subsequent generations."[52] Rather, we must realize that the New Testament teachings simply represent one stage in a trajectory of movement toward an ultimate ethic.

So how can Christians discover this "ultimate ethic"? Webb takes the rest of the book to explain eighteen fairly complex criteria (to which he gives names such as "preliminary movement," "seed ideas," "breakouts," and "competing options") by which Christians must evaluate the commands of the Bible and thereby discover the more just, more equitable ethical system the Bible was heading toward. Once that ultimate ethic has been discovered, it becomes the moral standard we should follow and obey.

What this means in actual practice, then, is that the moral authority of the New Testament is completely nullified, at least in principle. There may be some New Testament commands that Webb concludes actually do represent an ultimate ethic, but even then we should obey them *not because they are taught in the New Testament*, but because Webb's system has found that they meet the criteria of his "ultimate ethic."

The implications of this for Christian morality are extremely serious. It means that our ultimate authority is no longer the Bible but Webb's system. Of course, he claims that the "redemptive spirit" that drives his hermeneutic is *derived* from the biblical text, but by his own admission this "redemptive spirit" is not the same as the teachings of the Bible. It is derived from Webb's analysis of the interaction between the ancient culture and the biblical text.

---

51. Ibid. Webb does not consider the far simpler possibility that first-century readers would have understood the word *children* (Greek *tekna*) to apply only to people who were not adults, and so we today can say that Ephesians 6:1 applies to modern believers in just the same way that it applied to first-century believers, and no "cultural filters" need to be applied to that command.

52. Ibid., 34.

Answer 9.5b: Webb's authority is not the teaching of the New Testament but the goal he thinks the New Testament was moving toward.

Someone may object at this point, "Doesn't everyone have to use some kind of cultural filter like this? Doesn't everyone have to test the New Testament commands to see if they are culturally relative or transcultural, before deciding whether to obey them?"

There is a significant difference in approach. Most evangelicals (including me) believe we are under the moral authority of the New Testament and are obligated to obey its commands *when we are in the same situation as that addressed in the New Testament command* (such as being a parent, a child, a person contemplating a divorce, a church selecting elders or deacons, a church preparing to celebrate the Lord's Supper, a husband, a wife, and so forth). When there is no exact modern equivalent to some aspect of a command (such as, "honor the emperor" in 1 Peter 2:17), we are still obligated to obey the command, but we do so by *applying* it to situations that are essentially similar. Therefore, "honor the emperor" is applied to honoring the president or the prime minister. In fact, in several such cases the immediate context contains pointers to broader applications (such as 1 Peter 2:13–14, which mentions being subject to "every human institution" including the "emperor" and "governors" as specific examples). (For the small handful of slightly more difficult cases, such as a "holy kiss" and "foot washing," see the "Additional note to chapter 9" at the end of this chapter, pp. 397–402.)

But with Webb the situation is entirely different. He does not consider the moral commands of the New Testament to represent a perfect or final moral system for Christians. They are rather a *pointer* that "provides the direction toward the divine destination, but its literal, isolated words are not always the destination itself. Sometimes God's instructions are simply designed to get his flock moving."[53]

At the heart of Webb's system is what he calls a "redemptive-movement hermeneutic." He says that some may prefer calling his approach a "progressive" or "developmental" or "trajectory" hermeneutic, and he says that's fine. Webb explains his hermeneutic by what he calls "the X→Y→Z Principle." The letter Y indicates what the Bible says about a topic. Webb says, "The *central position* (Y) stands for where the isolated words of the Bible are in their development of a subject." The letter X represents "the perspective of the *original culture*," and the letter Z represents "an *ultimate ethic*," that is, God's final ideal that the Bible is moving toward.[54]

Therefore, what evangelicals have ordinarily understood to be the teaching of the Bible on particular subjects is in fact *only a point along the way* (indicated by letter Y) toward the development of a final or ultimate ethic (Z). Webb says,

53. Ibid., 60.
54. Ibid., 31.

> The X→Y→Z Principle illustrates how numerous aspects of the biblical text were *not* written to establish a utopian society with complete justice and equity. They were written within a cultural framework with limited moves toward an ultimate ethic.[55]

Therefore, Webb discovers a number of points where "our contemporary culture" has a *better* ethic than what is found in the Bible. Our culture has a better ethic today "where it happens to reflect a better social ethic—one closer to an *ultimate ethic* (Z) than to the ethic revealed in the isolated words of the biblical text."[56]

Answer 9.5c: Webb wrongly claims that the New Testament itself endorses slavery.

Webb's approach to Scripture can also be seen in the way he deals with biblical texts regarding slavery. While most evangelical interpreters say that the New Testament does not command or encourage or endorse slavery, but rather tells Christians who were slaves how they should conduct themselves, and also gives principles that would modify and ultimately lead to the abolition of slavery (1 Corinthians 7:21–22; Galatians 3:28; 1 Timothy 1:10; Philemon 16, 21), Webb *believes that the Bible actually endorses slavery*, however it is a kind of slavery with "better conditions and fewer abuses" (p. 37). He fails even to consider the strong anti-slavery arguments made by influential abolitionists such as Theodore Weld in his book, *The Bible Against Slavery* (see p. 342, above).

Webb's redemptive-movement hermeneutic approaches the slavery question by saying that the original culture (X) approved of "slavery with many abuses" (p. 37). Second, the Bible (Y) endorses "slavery with better conditions and fewer abuses" (p. 37). However, Webb believes that on the issue of slavery "our culture is much closer to an ultimate ethic than it is to the unrealized ethic reflected in the isolated words of the Bible" (p. 37). Today, the ethic of our culture, which is superior to that of the Bible, has "slavery eliminated and working conditions often improved" (p. 37). Webb believes our culture is much closer to an "ultimate ethic" (Z) in which we will see "wages maximized for all" (p. 37).[57]

At the end of the book, Webb recapitulates the results of his analysis regarding slavery:

> Scripture does not present a "finalized ethic" in every area of human relationship....
> To stop where the Bible stops (with its isolated words) ultimately fails to reapply the

55. Ibid.
56. Ibid. It is surprising to me that Webb's book has endorsements on the back cover by such recognized evangelical leaders as Darrell Bock of Dallas Seminary (who wrote the foreword), Stephen Spencer (formerly a theology professor at Dallas Seminary, but now teaching at Wheaton College), Craig Keener (of Eastern Seminary), and Craig Evans (of Trinity Western University). Sarah Sumner, *Men and Women in the Church,* says Webb's book is "the most helpful book I know" on discerning which passages are culturally bound and which are transcultural (213).
57. Webb does not explain what he means by "wages maximized for all," but readers might wonder if it means that profits and capital investment would be minimized in order for wages to be maximized? Or does it mean that all would have equal wages, since "all" would have maximized wages and this must mean that none would have lower wages than others? He does not make clear in what sense he thinks wages would be "maximized for all."

> redemptive spirit of the text as it spoke to the original audience. It fails to see that further reformation is possible.... *While Scripture had a positive influence in its time, we should take that redemptive spirit and move to an even better, more fully-realized ethic today.*[58]

Therefore, rather than saying that the New Testament does not endorse or command slavery, Webb believes that it *does* approve a system of slavery for the people at the time at which it was written. However, in its modifications and regulations of the institution of slavery, the Bible starts us along a trajectory which would lead to the ultimate abolition of slavery, though the New Testament never actually reaches that point. Thus, Webb's system gives us a morally deficient New Testament.

Answer 9.5d: Webb's trajectory argument denies the doctrine of Scripture and the principle of *sola Scriptura* as it has been believed in the major confessions of faith.

This is the same argument that was given in response to France and Thompson's "trajectory argument" (see section 9.4b).

Answer 9.5e: Webb's trajectory argument fails to understand the uniqueness of the New Testament in distinction from the Old Testament.

When Webb claims that "A redemptive-movement hermeneutic has always been a major part of the historic church, apostolic and beyond,"[59] and therefore that all Christians believe in some kind of "redemptive movement" hermeneutic, he fails to make one important distinction: Evangelicals have always held that the redemptive movement within Scripture ends with the New Testament! Webb carries it beyond the New Testament.

To attempt to go *beyond* the New Testament documents and derive our authority from "where the New Testament was heading" is to reject the very documents God gave us to govern our life under the New Covenant until Christ returns. (See section 9.4c for further discussion of this argument.)

Answer 9.5f: Webb's "trajectory argument" is far different from later doctrinal formulations that were based on Scripture alone.

This is the same argument that was given in response to France and Thompson's "trajectory argument." (See section 9.4d.)

---

58. Webb, 247 (italics added).
59. Ibid., 35.

Answer 9.5g: Webb's "trajectory argument" is similar to the view of the Roman Catholic Church, which bases doctrine not only on the Bible but also on the authoritative teachings of the church that have come after the Bible was written.

This is the same argument that was given in response to France and Thompson's "trajectory argument." (See section 9.4f.)

Answer 9.5h: Determining right and wrong in Webb's system is a subjective and indeterminate process that will lead to ethical chaos among Christians.

Here is Webb's key explanation of how his system works to discover the "redemptive spirit" within a text:

> The final and most important characteristic of a redemptive-movement hermeneutic is its focus on the spirit of a text.... The coinage "redemptive-movement hermeneutic" is derived from a concern that Christians apply the *redemptive spirit* within Scripture, not merely, or even primarily, its isolated words. *Finding the underlying spirit of a text is a delicate matter. It is not as direct or explicit as reading the words on the page.* In order to grasp the spirit of a text, *the interpreter must listen for how the text sounds within its various social contexts*. Two life settings are crucial: the broader, foreign ancient Near Eastern and Greco-Roman (ANE/GR) social context and the immediate, domestic Israelite/church setting. One must ask, what change/improvement is the text making in the lives of people in the covenant community? And, how does the text influence the larger ANE/GR world? Through reflecting upon these social-setting questions *the modern reader will begin to sense the redemptive spirit of the text*. Also, a third setting permits one another way of discovering the redemptive spirit, namely, the canonical movement across various biblical epochs.[60]

This paragraph is remarkable for the candor with which it reveals the subjective and indeterminate nature of Webb's ethical system. If the heart of the "most important characteristic" of his hermeneutic is discovered through "reflecting upon" the way the Bible interacts with ancient Near Eastern and Greco-Roman cultures, and through such reflection the interpreter will "begin to sense the redemptive spirit of the text," we have entered a realm so subjective that no two interpreters in the future will probably ever agree on where the "redemptive spirit of the text" that they are beginning to "sense" is leading, and what kind of "ultimate ethic" they should count as God's will for them. Ancient Near Eastern and Greek and Roman cultures were themselves diverse and complex, and different scholars will discover different trends and emphases in them. And then listening for "how the text sounds" within each culture is a process fraught with subjective judgments.

---

60. Ibid., 53 (italics added).

Those with a predisposition toward socialism will no doubt be delighted that Webb has begun to sense a redemptive spirit that will lead to "wages maximized for all."[61] But those more inclined to capitalism will no doubt begin to sense quite another redemptive spirit moving against the slavery and oppression of the ancient world, a redemptive spirit in which the dominant biblical themes of freedom and liberty and fair reward for one's labor lead to an "ultimate ethic" (Z) that encourages investment and a free enterprise system, one with maximization of profits for those worthy individuals who through their business activities best meet the material needs of mankind, and who also, by the high quality of goods they produce for others, best show that they love their neighbors as themselves.

No doubt Arminians will begin to sense the redemptive spirit of Arminianism moving against the fatalism of the ancient world in a much more Arminian direction than we find even in the New Testament. And Calvinists, through sober reflection upon the way the biblical text corrects the puny, weak gods in the Greek and Roman pantheon, will begin to sense the redemptive spirit of Calvinism moving through the New Testament toward an even higher emphasis on the sovereignty of God than we find in any current New Testament texts.

And on and on it will go. Baptists will begin to sense the redemptive spirit of believer's baptism as the New Testament corrects the all-inclusive nature of the religions of the ancient world, and paedobaptists will begin to sense the redemptive spirit of inclusion of infants in the covenant community, as the New Testament decisively corrects the neglect and abuse of children found in many ancient cultures. People seeking justification for their desire to obtain a divorce will begin to sense the redemptive spirit of more and more reasons for divorce, moving from the one reason that Jesus allowed (adultery—Matthew 19:9), to the increasing freedom found in Paul (desertion by an unbeliever—1 Corinthians 7:15), to many more reasons for divorce as we move along a trajectory toward an "ultimate ethic" (Z) where everyone should be completely happy with his or her spouse.

Now Webb may object that these hypothetical "redemptive spirit" findings could not be derived from a responsible use of his eighteen criteria. However, I have lived in the academic world for over thirty years, and I have a great deal of confidence in the ability of scholars to take Webb's set of criteria and make a case for almost anything they want. Whether or not my examples are the result of a proper use of Webb's criteria, the point remains: *the standard is no longer what the New Testament says, but rather the point toward which some biblical scholar thinks the Bible was moving*. Webb's redemptive-movement hermeneutic nullifies in principle the moral authority of the entire New Testament.

Webb's denial of the moral authority of the New Testament means that his system is not a legitimate option for evangelicals whose final authority is the Bible itself, rather than some better system for which the New Testament was only one step along the way.

61. Ibid., 37.

Egalitarian claim 9.6: Don't Mimic the First Century: The New Testament contains many elements of first-century culture that are descriptive rather than prescriptive. We should not try to "play first century" in our modern church setting.

This approach is taken by many egalitarians in many different forms. But probably the first statement of this viewpoint in the modern era was written by Krister Stendahl, who at the time of publication of the English translation of his argument was Academic Dean at Harvard Divinity School. In 1958, Stendahl wrote about a controversy over the ordination of women in the church of Sweden from 1951 to 1958. Scholars, clergy, and lay persons voiced strong opinions for and against women's ordination. Interestingly, Stendahl says, both sides in this debate agreed on the meaning of what Paul wrote in the New Testament:

> There is basic agreement between the exegetes who signed the Statement [opposing women's ordination] and the exegete of the Report [favoring women's ordination] with regard to the interpretation of the Pauline attitude: for Paul the question of the position of women was of fundamental significance.... The exegetes of both persuasions see it as their professional duty to assess the validity and the application of the ancient texts to the present situation. In the Statement this validity was affirmed; in the Report it had been denied. When these interpreters arrive at diametrically opposite results, although on the whole they accept the same understanding of the historical meaning of the texts, the problem must be one of application.... Thus it is a problem of hermeneutics rather than of exegesis. In other words, *it is the view of Scripture that is at issue.*[62]

Stendahl's own position is similar (in 1958!) to the "trajectory argument" of R. T. France in 1995 and David Thomson in 1996 (see previous section). Stendahl says,

> If the actual stage of implementation in the first-century becomes the standard for what is authoritative, then those elements which point toward future implementation become neutralized and absorbed in a static "biblical view".... The correct description of first-century Christianity is not automatically the authoritative and intended standard for the church throughout the ages. It has no means by which it can account for the ensuing centuries of church history as God's history. It becomes a nostalgic attempt to play "First-Century."[63]

62. Krister Stendahl, *The Bible and the Role of Women* (1966; first published in Swedish in 1958), 8–9 (italics added).
63. Ibid., 35–36.

This 1966 book by Stendahl (the English translation of his 1958 book in Swedish) is the precursor of much modern egalitarian thinking. Stendahl was not an evangelical in his view of the Bible. In fact, he was one of the most visible liberal theologians in the United States in 1966.

Stendahl's approach to Scripture (which I could briefly paraphrase as "Yes, this is what the New Testament commanded for its time, but we don't have to obey that today") is essentially the same as the approach to Scripture taken by France and Thompson and Webb in their "trajectory hermeneutic." The approach is not their novel invention, but was first taken by the liberal dean of Harvard Divinity School on the question of women's ordination in 1966.[64]

While many of the arguments I have made against the "trajectory hermeneutic" could also be applied to Stendahl's position, I give here three brief responses specifically to Stendahl.

Answer 9.6a: It is true that several elements of the New Testament are descriptive and we do not have to imitate them today, but these elements are usually reports of individual historical events and not moral commands given to whole churches.

For centuries, Christians have readily distinguished between *individual historical events* (such as Noah gathering the animals in the ark or Abraham offering his son Isaac on the altar or Jesus walking on the water or Paul sailing from Troas) and, on the other hand, patterns for us to imitate or *commands for us to obey* (such as Jesus' resisting the temptations of the devil or Jesus' welcoming of children and praying for them or His invitation to everyone, "Come to me, all who labor and are heavy laden, and I will give you rest" [Matthew 11:28], or Paul's command to "walk in love, as Christ loved us and gave himself up for us" [Ephesians 5:2]).

Within the very same chapter of one of Paul's epistles, Christians are able to see quite easily the distinction between (1) Paul's command to Timothy, "Always be sober-minded, endure suffering, do the work of an evangelist, fulfill your ministry" (2 Timothy 4:5), which has applicability to all Christians for all times, especially those who are in ministry positions, and (2) the situation-specific command just eight verses later, where Paul also says to Timothy, "When you come, bring the cloak that I left with Carpus at Troas, also the books, and above all the parchments" (2 Timothy 4:13). I am not aware of any Christians in the history of the church who have made it a practice year after year to try to find Paul's cloak and books at Troas so they could bring them to him in prison in Rome!

But once we have made a distinction between one-time historical events and abiding moral commands, when we return to 1 Timothy 2:12, "I do not permit a woman to teach or to exercise

---

64. I am grateful to David W. Jones for pointing out how much of current egalitarian argumentation was first stated by Stendahl in his small book. I remember reading Stendahl's book as an undergraduate at Harvard in 1967 or 1968 (it was being read by various students in the Harvard-Radcliffe Christian Fellowship) and thinking that he did not hold the same view of Scripture as the evangelicals on the Harvard campus. But I had forgotten about the book until David Jones called it to my attention and pointed out the similarities between Stendahl and many evangelical feminists today.

authority over a man," no elements in the text would make us think this is a temporary command similar to, "Bring the cloak that I left with Carpus at Troas" (2 Timothy 4:13). It is a moral command given to the whole church—in fact, to a collection of churches in and around the city of Ephesus—and it is explicitly based not on local circumstances or needs but on patterns found in Creation (1 Timothy 2:13–14).

Answer 9.6b: There are a few commands given to whole churches that we do not obey in exactly the same form today (such as head coverings and holy kisses), but we do still follow the principle of interpersonal relationships represented in even those commands.

Egalitarians make far too much of the fact that Christians today do not "greet one another with a holy kiss" (Romans 16:16; 1 Corinthians 16:20; 2 Corinthians 13:12; 1 Thessalonians 5:26).[65] Christians have realized for centuries that this form of greeting conveyed a certain positive meaning that was commonly understood in that culture, but the meaning today would be very different in several Western cultures. In many cases the action would be misunderstood and thought to be intrusive, offensive, or artificial rather than heartfelt, and would involve merely a formalistic compliance with some outward action rather than conveying the same positive meaning today. So the underlying meaning (Paul's concern that Christians greet one another warmly) is understood and conveyed by *other forms of warm greeting* that may vary from time to time and from culture to culture. The command still has some relevance for us, and we seek to obey it in modern forms as best we can.

That is far different from what egalitarians attempt to do with 1 Timothy 2:12. They imply that we no longer need to obey its restrictions at all! Rather than seeking to *apply* an ancient command in a modern form, and saying that our obedience has a somewhat different outward appearance today (as with the holy kiss), egalitarians often say that *we do not have to obey the command at all!* But that is not a proper interpretation or application of the commands of Scripture.[66]

Now, could it be that women not teaching or governing the church is merely the temporary "outward form" of the deeper principle, some principle such as not giving offense to the culture? As I argued above,[67] teaching and governing the church are not superficial forms or surface manifestations; they are fundamental activities themselves, essential to the life of a church. It is possible to have a fully functioning church without having holy kisses, but it is not possible to have a fully functioning church without people teaching and governing the church. These functions are essential to the life of a church, and are not culturally variable or optional. Therefore we should not see them as mere outward forms. They are the deeper principles and the deeper activities in themselves.

---

65. Rich Nathan, for example, argues on this basis (*Who Is My Enemy*, 146).
66. I am grateful to David Jones for pointing out this crucial difference in how commands are treated by many egalitarians.
67. See Chapter 8, claim 8.13, for a discussion of this topic (pp. 322–24).

Answer 9.6c: The New Testament commands about male leadership in the family and the church are not minor, incidental statements that might be culturally variable. They are grounded in fundamental truths about the nature of God, the nature of Christ's relationship to the church, and the nature of manhood and womanhood as God created it.

Christians also realize that things such as "holy kisses" are surface details, things that are less central to the life of a church. But when we talk about the relationship between a husband and wife in marriage (as discussed in chapters 1 and 6), and when we talk about men fulfilling teaching and governing functions in the church (as discussed in chapters 2, 7, and 8), we are talking about matters that are grounded in the nature of God, grounded in the nature of Christ's relationship to the church, and grounded in the nature of manhood and womanhood as God created it. These are fundamental truths, not subject to cultural variability.

EGALITARIAN CLAIM 9.7: CLEAR VERSES TRUMP UNCLEAR VERSES: WE SHOULD FOLLOW THE MAIN TEACHINGS OF SCRIPTURE WHEN THEY APPEAR TO CONFLICT WITH THE INCIDENTAL TEACHINGS. ON THIS ISSUE, WE MUST INTERPRET THE FEW ISOLATED, OBSCURE PASSAGES OF SCRIPTURE THAT APPEAR TO RESTRICT WOMEN'S MINISTRY IN LIGHT OF THE MANY CLEAR PASSAGES THAT OPEN ALL MINISTRY ROLES TO BOTH MEN AND WOMEN.

Egalitarians commonly claim there are only a few texts (such as 1 Timothy 2:12) that appear to restrict women's participation in all forms of ministry, and those texts are hotly debated and unclear. By contrast, the "inclusive" texts (such as Galatians 3:28) are clear and should take precedence.

Craig Keener writes,

> That the God of the Bible calls women to teach the Scriptures is, in my opinion, beyond dispute, supported by clear biblical evidence and challenged only by the interpretation of several comparatively ambiguous texts.[68]

W. Ward Gasque makes a similar argument:

> Galatians 3:28 is the necessary theological starting place for any discussion on the role of women in the church. Here is an unequivocal statement of absolute equality in Christ in the church.... Other texts must not be used to undermine this fundamental theological affirmation.[69]

---

68. Keener, *Paul, Women and Wives,* 11. See also Jacobs, *Women of Destiny* (1998), 233–34, quoting Dr. Jim Davis and Dr. Donna Johnson, *Redefining the Role of Women in the Church* (unpublished manuscript, p. 35).
69. W. Ward Gasque, "Response," in *Women, Authority and the Bible* (1986), 189.

Rich Nathan says,

> If 1 Timothy 2 is read as a universal restriction for all time on all women...then it stands entirely alone. I choose to read it in a manner congruent with the rest of the New Testament and to treat it as addressing a local problem in a first-century church.[70]

And Rebecca Groothuis writes,

> We need to widen the scope of the debate and look beyond the proof texts to the teaching of the whole of Scripture, to a theology of God and sexuality that is derived from Scripture, and even to the sciences.... Galatians 3:26–28 states that in Christ there is oneness and unity between male and female, Jew and Gentile, slave and free.[71]

Answer 9.7a: The Bible has to say something only once for it to be true and God's Word for us.

Even if one verse of the Bible restricted some governing and teaching roles to men, we would still be obligated to obey it, because the Bible is God's Word to us. There are several other commands in the New Testament that occur only once, but we still obey them. The command to examine ourselves before taking the Lord's Supper is found only in 1 Corinthians 11:27–32, but we consider it binding on us today. Paul's instructions about the value of being single for ministry and the value of being married for those who are not called to singleness occur only in 1 Corinthians 7, but we consider that teaching valid for today. Paul's allowance of divorce for desertion by an unbelieving spouse occurs only in 1 Corinthians 7:15, but we consider it valid for today. Paul's direction that speaking in tongues in the church service should be accompanied by interpretation occurs only once in the Bible, in 1 Corinthians 14:27–28, but churches that consider this gift valid for today still think this command is valid for today. The list of character qualifications for deacons occurs only once in the Bible, in 1 Timothy 3:8–13, but we consider it valid for today.

Therefore the argument that the restriction of some governing and teaching roles to men occurs in only a few passages, or in one passage, does not mean that we are free to disobey it. If the Bible teaches this in only one place, we are still obligated to obey it.

Answer 9.7b: The passages that prohibit women from being elders and from teaching or having authority over men in the assembled church are not isolated passages. They occur in the heart of the main New Testament teachings about church office and about conduct in public worship.

---

70. Nathan, *Who Is My Enemy*, 154.
71. Groothuis, *Good News for Women*, 232.

The main New Testament passages about how the church should act when it meets together are found in 1 Corinthians 11–14 and 1 Timothy.[72] And it is in 1 Corinthians 14:33–34 that we find the statement, "As in all the churches of the saints, the women should keep silent in the churches" (referring to the judging of prophecies, as explained earlier).[73] And it is in 1 Timothy, the book in which Paul writes more about church conduct, church officers, and church government than in any other book, that we find the statement, "I do not permit a woman to teach or to exercise authority over a man" (1 Timothy 2:12).

The egalitarian claim that these are "isolated" passages is incorrect. They are found at the heart of the New Testament material on how a church should function.

Answer 9.7c: The restriction of some church leadership functions to men is not based on just one or two passages, but on a consistent pattern of God's approval of male leadership throughout the Bible.

From Genesis to Revelation, God has established and approved male leadership for His people. The pattern began with the headship of Adam in the Garden of Eden in Genesis 2, and continued through the call of Abraham to be the father of a great nation through whom all nations would be blessed (Genesis 12). It was further seen in the call of Moses to lead God's people out of Egypt (Exodus 3), the call of David to be king (1 Samuel 16), and the call of many other kings as well as primarily male prophets and exclusively male priests in the Old Testament.

In the New Testament, we see the pattern of male leadership continue in Jesus Himself, the Son of God who became a man, and then in the twelve apostles whom Jesus appointed. We also see it continue in all the authors of New Testament books (who are all men), and in the appointment of male elders in governing positions over all the churches in the New Testament (1 Timothy 3:2; Titus 1:6; Acts 20:30; note the pattern of elders in every church in passages such as Acts 14:23; James 5:14; and 1 Peter 5:1). The pattern of male leadership is reflected even in the names of the twelve apostles inscribed on the foundations of the heavenly city in Revelation 21:14, and in the fact that the twelve apostles will sit on twelve thrones judging the twelve tribes of Israel in the age to come (Matthew 19:28). Even the names "Father" and "Son" used by the first and second members of the Trinity in their self-disclosure to us fit with the biblical pattern that governing authority over God's people is a male, not a female task. This is a consistent pattern from Genesis to Revelation.

Answer 9.7d: The passages that restrict some church leadership functions to men have not been thought to be obscure or difficult to understand by the vast majority of the church throughout its history. Obscurity in this case is not in the text of Scripture but in the eye of the beholder.

72. There is also material about public worship in other passages such as Colossians 3:16, but it is not as extensive. James 2:1–4 is about a specific problem of showing partiality to the rich.
73. See chapter 2, pp. 78–80, and chapter 7, pp. 227–46, on 1 Corinthians 14:34–35.

With very few exceptions, the church throughout its history has not found it difficult to understand that only men should be elders and have the role of teaching God's Word to the assembled church. After a survey of the history of interpretation of 1 Timothy 2:11–14, Daniel Doriani concludes:

> Throughout the ages the church has traditionally interpreted 1 Timothy 2:11–14 in a straightforward manner.... Women ought to learn, but in a quiet and submissive manner (2:11). They may teach informally, but may not hold teaching offices or formally authoritative positions in the church (2:12). Paul forbids that women teach both because of God's sovereign decree and because of the history and nature of man and woman (2:13–14).[74]

But suddenly, with the advent of modern feminism, many scholars have decided that these texts are obscure. Why has this happened? The texts did not change.

Thomas Schreiner has a telling observation on the way egalitarian scholars have understood 1 Timothy 2:13, in which Paul says that the reason women should not teach or have authority over a man in the church is, "For Adam was formed first, then Eve":

> Mary Evans says that the relevance of verse 13 for verse 12 is unclear, and that verse 13 merely introduces the next verse about Eve. Gordon Fee asserts that the verse is not central to Paul's argument. Timothy Harris says that the verse "is difficult to understand on any reading." Craig Keener thinks that the argument here is hard to fathom. David Scholer protests that the text is unclear, and that Paul cites selectively from Genesis. Steve Motyer says that logic and justice are nullified if the historic position of verses 13–14 is accepted.[75]

But Schreiner observes that these statements reflect on their authors more than on the text:

> It seems that unclarity is in the eye of the beholder, for the thrust of the verse has been deemed quite clear in the history of the church. The creation of Adam first gives the reason why men should be the authoritative teachers in the church.[76]

---

74. Doriani, "History of the Interpretation of 1 Timothy 2" (1995), 262. Alan Padgett objects to Doriani's claim about the historical understanding of the church by pointing out the egalitarian tract *Women's Speaking Justified,* published by the early Quaker Margaret Fell in 1667 (Alan Padgett, "The Scholarship of Patriarchy," *Priscilla Papers* [winter 1997], 25), but Doriani's survey already takes account of Fell's writing and rightly says that it "seems to have had little influence" (247; it did of course have significant influence within Quaker circles since Fell was married to Quaker founder George Fox, but its influence in other denominations and in academic writing was negligible).
75. Schreiner, "Interpretation of 1 Timothy 2:9–15," 136.
76. Ibid.

Answer 9.7e: By contrast, egalitarian claims that all church leadership roles should be open to women are based not on any direct teaching of Scripture but on doubtful inferences from passages where this topic is not even under discussion.

The most used egalitarian text is probably Galatians 3:28, "There is neither Jew nor Greek, there is neither slave nor free, there is neither male nor female, for you are all one in Christ Jesus." But this verse does not occur in a context talking about church government or church leadership, but in a context that talks about justification by faith, not by law. The story of Deborah (Judges 4) is not found in a passage about leadership in the New Testament church, but in an Old Testament narrative concerning a time when many unusual events occurred among God's people, including events the Bible does not intend us to imitate (such as several aspects in the story of Samson, and other events in Judges). We should surely be thankful for the prophetic ministries of Miriam (Exodus 15) and Huldah (2 Kings 22:14–20; 2 Chronicles 34:22–28), but they occur in contexts that clearly affirm male leadership over God's people, and they are not passages that discuss governing or teaching roles in the New Testament church.

Similarly, it is true that Priscilla and Aquila, in talking to Apollos, "explained to him the way of God more accurately" (Acts 18:26), yet this passage does not discuss governing or teaching roles over an assembly of God's people, but reports a private conversation. While Phoebe is named as a "servant" or "deacon" in the church in Cenchreae (Romans 16:1), and while we may conclude that she probably was the messenger who carried Paul's epistle to the church at Rome, once again this is not a passage that talks about teaching or governing authority in the New Testament church.

It is true that Philip's daughters prophesied (Acts 21:8–9), and it is true that women prophesied in the meetings of the early churches (1 Corinthians 11:5), but this is significantly different from governing or teaching the New Testament church.[77]

So where is there any example of women doing what egalitarians claim they should be able to do, that is, exercising governing or teaching authority over an assembled church? There is no example at all in the entire Bible.

Yet if God had wanted us to understand that women can fulfill this task, He surely could have made it clear by giving explicit examples and by specifying this in New Testament passages that teach us how the church should conduct its affairs. In reading the New Testament, we do not find this at all.

---

77. See the discussion on why the New Testament allows women to prophesy and not teach at claim 7.3 (pp. 227–32), and also at chapter 2, pp. 78–80.

EGALITARIAN CLAIM 9.8: NO ORDINATION IN NEW TESTAMENT: DEBATES OVER THE ORDINATION OF WOMEN ARE POINTLESS, SINCE THE NEW TESTAMENT NEVER SPEAKS ABOUT ORDINATION OF PASTORS.

This objection is expressed by Linda Belleville, after a discussion of New Testament passages about church leaders:

> Does this speak to the ordination of women? Unfortunately, it does not. Both the term and the concept are lacking in the New Testament—with respect to both men and women. The idea of "commissioning" (setting apart, dedicating) for a particular ministry is what we find (generally through the laying on of hands). For example, the church at Antioch commissioned Saul and Barnabas as missionaries (Acts 13:1–3), elders were commissioned at Ephesus (1 Tim. 5:22), Timothy was commissioned as an evangelist (1 Tim. 4:14; 2 Tim. 1:6), and Paul was commissioned as an apostle to the Gentiles (Acts 9:17–19; 22:12–16). But this is a far cry from how churches use the term "ordain" today.[78]

Ruth A. Tucker says,

> It may surprise many people that ordination—the issue that has caused more controversy regarding women than any other in the church today—is more a product of church tradition than of biblical precedent.[79]

Answer 9.8a: The idea of ordination is in the New Testament, even if the word is not.

Belleville's objection really gives much of the answer to that same objection. She points out several passages where people were "commissioned" or set apart for a particular ministry. This took place in a public ceremony where the leaders of the church would apparently lay hands upon the person being set apart and pray for that person.

Paul reminds Timothy of a time "when the council of elders laid their hands on you" (1 Timothy 4:14). And the sending out of Barnabas and Saul on their first missionary journey happened after the Holy Spirit commanded the church, "Set apart for me Barnabas and Saul for the work to which I have called them" (Acts 13:2). When the early church needed officers to distribute food to those in need, seven men were selected (often thought to be the first deacons) and we read, "These they set before the apostles, and they prayed and laid their hands on them" (Acts 6:6).

78. Belleville, "Women in Ministry" (2001), 109.
79. Tucker, *Women in the Maze* (1992), 206. Similarly, Sumner, *Men and Women in the Church,* 318-20.

On Paul's first missionary journey, he and Barnabas established elders in all the churches they planted: "And when they had appointed elders for them in every church, with prayer and fasting they committed them to the Lord in whom they had believed" (Acts 14:23). It wasn't any secret who the elders were in each church, because James could write to all the churches throughout the Roman Empire, "Is anyone among you sick? *Let him call for the elders of the church*" (James 5:14).

When we put these facts together, it seems evident that there was a public ceremony in which elders were recognized and established in their office in each church. From that point on, the whole congregation knew that these men had the right and responsibility to serve as elders.

Many churches today use *ordain* and *ordination* to refer to this process of establishing someone as an elder, sometimes as a part-time responsibility and sometimes as a full-time responsibility with the expectation that that person will do most of the formal Bible teaching in the church. Often the title "pastor" or "pastor-teacher" (see Ephesians 4:11) is attached to such responsibility.

Therefore, even though the term *ordination* is not found in the New Testament, the concept is surely evident in several passages. (Incidentally, there are other terms in English that refer to *concepts* in the New Testament, though the words themselves are not found in the Bible. These include words such as *Trinity, inerrancy, infallibility, sacrament,* and *church government*, to name a few.)

EGALITARIAN CLAIM 9.9: IT DEPENDS ON WHICH VERSES YOU EMPHASIZE: IT ALL DEPENDS ON WHICH TEXTS FROM THE BIBLE YOU DECIDE TO TAKE AS NORMATIVE. EGALITARIANS TAKE EQUALITY TEXTS AS NORMATIVE AND THAT LEADS TO AN EGALITARIAN CONCLUSION. COMPLEMENTARIANS TAKE SUBORDINATION TEXTS AS NORMATIVE AND THAT LEADS TO A COMPLEMENTARIAN CONCLUSION. BOTH APPROACHES ARE VALID, BOTH DEPEND ON THE BIBLE, AND BOTH SHOULD BE ALLOWED WITHIN EVANGELICALISM.

This egalitarian claim would have us believe that the whole issue is decided by which texts we decide to emphasize or rely on. For example, R. T. France says,

> We have seen that fundamental to this issue has been the question which among differing biblical texts or themes is considered to be basic.... Once we choose to begin at a given point, everything else will be viewed and interpreted in the light of that starting point.... There is no rule of thumb—that is precisely our problem. A judgment has to be made, and not all will make it in the same way. Probably we all have our 'canon within the canon' (by which we mean those parts of Scripture with

> which we feel comfortable, and which say what we would like them to say) which we regard as "basic." But those instinctive preferences are normally derived from the tradition within which we have been brought up, rather than from an informed and principled choice made on the basis of the texts themselves.[80]

Stanley Grenz adopts a similar view in a section in his book titled "The Question of Hermeneutical Priority":

> Yet one question remains: Which Pauline text(s) carry hermeneutical priority in our attempt to understand Paul's teaching about women in the church? Are we to look to the egalitarian principle the apostle set forth in Galatians 3:28 as the foundation for our understanding of the apostle's own position? Or do we begin with those passages which seem to place limitation on the service of women (1 Cor. 11:3–16; 14:34–35; 1 Tim. 2:11–15) and understand the Galatians text in the light of such restrictions?
>
> Egalitarians often claim that Galatians 3:28 deserves hermeneutical priority.... At this point, egalitarians, and not complementarians, are on the right track.... The seemingly restrictive texts complementarians cite...cannot be universal rules but Paul's attempts to counter the abuses of specific situations.[81]

Sarah Sumner says we have to decide "which verse(s) should take priority over the others," or "which verse stands in charge as the boss" (which she then calls the "boss verse").[82] Elsewhere she claims that we disagree because "we bring so many assumptions to the text," and if we bring egalitarian assumptions we will find egalitarian teaching in the text, but if we bring complementarian assumptions, we will find complementarian teaching in the text.[83]

Answer 9.9a: It is not true that the argument just depends on which texts we choose to take as "normative." All the texts in the Bible are God's words, and we cannot dismiss or choose to disregard any of them.

Nowhere in this book have I claimed that we must minimize or ignore so-called "egalitarian texts" on the basis of some kind of "hermeneutical priority" of other texts. I do not believe we should treat Scripture that way, because all of it is God's Word, and all of it is "profitable for teaching, for reproof, for correction, and for training in righteousness" (2 Timothy 3:16). I have attempted not to minimize but to treat these texts fairly and to remain subject to their authority, and this includes such (so-called) "egalitarian texts" as Galatians 3:28, and the passages about Deborah, Huldah, Phoebe, Priscilla, and Junia(s). Even if we studied all of these texts first and drew conclusions from them before we looked at any "complementarian texts"

80. France, *Women in the Church's Ministry,* 93–94.
81. Grenz, *Women in the Church* (1995), 106–7.
82. Sumner, *Men and Women in the Church,* 128; see also 256–57.
83. Ibid., 249; she also says that our viewpoints are often the result of traditional assumptions inherited from church history: See 275, 285, 292–93.

such as 1 Timothy 2:12, these "egalitarian texts" would not lead us to affirm that women could have governing and teaching roles over New Testament churches. The texts would not lead us to affirm that because they do not teach that. They surely honor the valuable ministries of women and their equality in value and dignity, but they do not tell us that women could govern or teach a New Testament church. They are not, therefore, truly "egalitarian texts."

But it is difficult to imagine that an egalitarian advocate could do the same with passages such as 1 Corinthians 14:33–36, 1 Timothy 2:11–15, the passages about male elders, and the passages about the twelve male apostles. It would be difficult to believe that an egalitarian could begin with only those texts and reach the conclusion that all roles in the church are open to women as well as men, because these texts set a pattern that so clearly affirms just the opposite.

I am not saying that we all emphasize every verse of the Bible equally. There will always be passages that a pastor will emphasize more in his preaching and teaching (he will probably spend more time teaching from Romans or 1 Corinthians than from Leviticus, for example), but that is not because this pastor thinks that Romans is part of a "canon within the canon" or that it has more authority. It is rather because Leviticus was written to a situation we no longer find ourselves in, the situation of God's people in the Old Covenant who had to follow ceremonial rules and regulations. But the New Testament epistles are written to people in the same situation we are in today—members of the New Testament church who live after Jesus' resurrection and before His second coming. Preaching from Leviticus is worthwhile and also "profitable for teaching, for reproof, for correction, and for training in righteousness" (2 Timothy 3:16), but its application to our situation is less direct and more difficult to understand, and it is not wrong to give it less emphasis in preaching than many of the New Testament books. This question of emphasis, however, is different from an egalitarian claim that implies we can effectively decide to be subject to some parts of Scripture and not others.

I am troubled by the egalitarian claim that it all depends on what texts we choose as basic, because that suggests there are other texts we can decide do not apply to us today and do not have authority over us today. Once again, that position weakens the authority of Scripture in our lives.

Answer 9.9b: The complementarian position understands the "equality texts" in a way consistent with their own wording and context, not in a way that contradicts subordination in roles.

The complementarian position does not "limit the application" of the so called "equality texts" in Scripture (such as Galatians 3:28), but understands them to be limited by their own contexts and subject matter and wording. That is what I have argued in detail throughout this book. I have argued in each case that this is not wrongly understanding these texts, but is understanding them according to the principles by which we should understand all texts. And we understand these texts in a way that does not require them to nullify or contradict other texts about male leadership in the church.

Answer 9.9c: It is not a question of choosing what kind of texts will "limit" and "expand" in application. Rather, it is a question of being faithful to the applications originally intended by the authors of the texts themselves.

The two positions are not the same in how they treat the texts they emphasize. Egalitarians *wrongly limit* the application of male leadership texts by saying they *don't apply today to the very same kinds of situations* they applied to when originally written (namely, conduct in the assembled church and the office of elder with governing authority over the church). But egalitarians *wrongly expand* the application of equality texts far beyond the kinds of situations they were originally written to address (as explained above, the "egalitarian texts" were not written to address situations of governing or teaching over the church).

By contrast, the complementarian position *rightly applies* the texts on male leadership to exactly *the same kind of situations* they applied to when originally written (governing and teaching God's people in the church). And the complementarian position *rightly applies* the "equality texts" to exactly *the same kinds of situations* they applied to when originally written (affirming all sorts of ministries for women except governing or teaching over the assembled church, and affirming the full dignity and value of women in God's sight and in the ministry of the church).

Thus, the two positions clearly differ in the way they interpret and apply biblical texts, not just in which texts they "choose as basic."

Answer 9.9d: This egalitarian claim dangerously hints at a new kind of liberalism in which people are free to "limit the application" of texts they dislike by appealing to vague principles such as equality, fairness, and justice.

This egalitarian claim looks dangerously similar to a procedure that has been used numerous times in the past to deny the authority of Scripture and allow all sorts of false doctrine into the church. For example, in the early part of the twentieth century, liberals routinely appealed to a vague general principle of the "love of God" in order to deny that God had any wrath against sin. And once they denied God's wrath, then it was easy to believe that all people everywhere would be saved (for God is a "God of love" and not of wrath). After that, it was also easy to believe that Jesus' death was not a substitutionary sacrifice for our sins—that is, He did not bear the wrath of God against our sins—but rather that His death was somehow an example for us. In this way a vague biblical principle ("God's love") was used to deny many specific passages of Scripture and to deny a major doctrine such as substitutionary atonement.

This is similar to the egalitarian claim that the *broad biblical principles* of equality and fairness require that women have access to the same governing and teaching roles in the church that men do. In this way, vague general principles are also used to weaken or nullify specific verses of Scripture.

EGALITARIAN CLAIM 9.10: IMPOSSIBLE TO FIGURE OUT WHAT SCRIPTURE TEACHES: NOBODY CAN CONCLUSIVELY FIGURE OUT WHAT THE BIBLE TEACHES ABOUT WOMEN IN THE CHURCH. IT IS A DISPUTED ISSUE THAT SCHOLARS WILL ARGUE ABOUT FOREVER, SOMETHING LIKE DIFFERENT VIEWS OF THE END TIMES. WE SHOULD THEREFORE AVOID THE DISPUTED VERSES AND MAKE A DECISION ON OTHER GROUNDS.

This is the view, for example, of Cindy Jacobs:

> As I've studied the so-called "difficult passages" about women, I have concluded that the differing interpretations are rather like that of teaching on end-time eschatology. Throughout the years I've heard excellent sermons on just about every position, all using Scripture, and all sounding as if they had merit![84]

A few pages later she affirms this principle regarding controversial passages of Scripture:

> Controversial passages lacking consensus from godly people of different persuasions usually mean that the passages are not clear enough to resolve with certainty. Therefore we must be tolerant on [sic] different views on those passages.[85]

A similar approach is taken by the Assemblies of God position paper on "The Role of Women in Ministry":

> We all agree that Scripture must be our final authority in settling questions of faith and practice. But when born-again, Spirit-filled Christians, following proper hermeneutical principles, come to reasonable but differing interpretations, we do well not to become dogmatic in support of one position.[86]

Sarah Sumner says,

> We don't know how to translate 1 Timothy 2, much less interpret it correctly or apply it appropriately today. That's why this passage is so humbling; to some extent it has stumped us all, scholars and practitioners alike.[87]

Rich Nathan writes,

> It is not at all plain what Paul meant to communicate to his original readers, plus it is even less plain how Paul's words should be applied today.... My files include at least

84. Jacobs, *Women of Destiny*, 175. Later she compares arguing about 1 Timothy 2:11–15 and 1 Corinthians 14:34–35 to arguing about "other obscure passages" such as "the verse that deals with baptism for the dead (see 1 Corinthians 15:29)" (234).
85. Ibid., 178 (Jacobs says she got this principle from Robert Clinton of Fuller Seminary).
86. Taken from http://ag.org/top/beliefs/position_papers/4191_women_ministry.cfm, paragraph 2.
87. Sumner, *Men and Women in the Church*, 248.

> fifteen very different interpretations of 1 Timothy 2.... To summarize, there is no common agreement on what these individual words mean in 1 Timothy 2:9-15.[88]

Answer 9.10a: Avoiding a decision on disputed passages effectively silences Scripture on this issue.

At the heart of this approach is the fact that sincere Christians like Cindy Jacobs, the Assemblies of God, Sarah Sumner, and Rich Nathan are saying that they cannot reach a decision on the meaning of 1 Corinthians 14, 1 Timothy 2, and the passages that say elders are to be the husband of one wife.[89] It is important to recognize what this does in this debate. It effectively prevents these passages from speaking to this question. If someone says, "Don't talk to us about those passages because nobody can figure out what they mean anyway," then he has essentially said that those passages cannot play a role in his decision about this question. And that means that *the passages that most directly speak to the question of women teaching and governing in the church are silenced and excluded from discussion on that very question.*

In essence, this approach guarantees that a decision about women teaching and governing in the church will be made without reference to the passages in the Bible that speak most directly to the topic. It is hard to think of an approach more likely to lead to a wrong decision.

Answer 9.10b: Avoiding disputed passages would never have kept false doctrine out of the church in the past, and it cannot keep it out today.

There is another serious problem with an approach that says we will not make decisions based on any "disputed" passages. If people really adopt this principle, they probably cannot rule out any major heresy in the church.

In the fourth-century controversy over the deity of Christ, the Arians (who denied the full deity of Christ) were apparently godly people *who disputed every major verse used by those who argued for the full deity of Christ.* That meant that all the passages on the deity of Christ were "disputed verses," with godly, praying scholars on both sides of the question. In the debate over biblical inerrancy, "godly people" vigorously debate the key verses used to support inerrancy. The "Oneness Pentecostals" who deny the Trinity hotly dispute all the verses brought to support the Trinity.

I wonder how many who take this "avoid disputed passages" approach have ever tried to discuss justification by faith alone with a born-again Roman Catholic. Within the Roman Catholic church are "godly people" *who make every verse on justification by faith alone a point of controversy.* This approach would mean we could never decide whether Catholics or Protestants are right about justification. On this principle of "avoiding disputed passages," no Christian could ever

---

88. Nathan, *Who Is My Enemy,* 142–44.

89. However, it is interesting that both Sumner and Nathan elsewhere say that they have decided that 1 Timothy 2:12 means that women who are teaching false doctrine in the church at Ephesus should be silent.

come to any conclusion about whether to baptize infants because "godly people" differ on whether infants should be baptized, and every verse is in dispute! To take yet another matter, the matter of spiritual gifts, all the key passages about miraculous gifts are vigorously "disputed" by sincere Christians. Must we say about all those passages, "These are disputed passages and evangelical scholars will never reach agreement, therefore, we cannot use these passages to decide what we think about miraculous gifts today?"

Once we begin to use the "avoid disputed passages" approach, we lose the ability to use hundreds of verses in God's Word that He gave us to understand, to believe, and to obey. And when that happens, our churches will be "tossed to and fro by the waves and carried about by every wind of doctrine" (Ephesians 4:14).

A better approach is to say that God has given us His Word so that it can be understood. Therefore we must pursue these "controversial texts" and follow the arguments on both sides, until we come to a satisfactory answer on what they mean. If a position is true to God's Word, it should not be based on "trust me" arguments from scholars who appeal to evidence that lay people cannot examine and evaluate, or who just quote the opinions of other authors to "prove" their points. Even when it involves arguments about Greek and Hebrew words, or ancient history, the evidence should be laid out in clear English, the examples of word usages should be given in English translation, and interested lay persons should be able to look at it and evaluate it for themselves. That is what I have tried to do in this book,[90] so that people can look at the evidence and come to their own conclusions about what the Bible says.

Answer 9.10c: Much of the confusion about the meaning of these disputed verses is caused by misinformation.

Much of the dispute on this question is not because the Scripture passages are difficult to understand. The "controversy" and "lack of consensus" over the key passages on women in ministry is in many cases caused by lack of information or by false statements being repeated again and again in egalitarian literature.

I am not asking you to take my word for this. You can check it out for yourself in the 118 egalitarian claims I have examined in this book. I have quoted from the highest quality and most responsible egalitarian literature time and again so that you can evaluate these egalitarian arguments for yourself.

With regard to most of the crucial questions, the supporting evidence is not something that is restricted to the realm of specialist scholars with technical knowledge. Even in those cases

90. See, for example, Appendixes 3 and 7 below (pp. 544–51 and 679–706) where I give in English translation over fifty examples of the word *kephalē* ("head") used to designate a person in authority and eighty-two examples of the word *authenteō* ("to exercise authority"). Readers can look over these examples and reach their own decisions on the meanings of these words. In addition, I have often quoted Bible passages in full so that readers can easily see what the verses actually say.

where the argument depends on the meaning of a Greek or Hebrew word, the relevant evidence from ancient literature can usually be presented in a clear and forthright way (in English translation) so that interested lay people have an opportunity to make an informed decision. Sadly, again and again I find that egalitarian interpretations are accepted *not* because people have *actually seen* the evidence that proves these views to be valid, but rather *because they have read the interpretation (not the actual evidence for it) in some evangelical writer whom they trust.* What readers don't realize is that often these writers are depending on the statements of other writers, and those writers on yet other writers, and in a number of cases the egalitarian scholar is advocating an extremely doubtful theory about the evidence that no one has ever before held. *But seldom is the actual evidence itself provided.* In many cases, that is because it simply does not exist. In other cases, the egalitarian scholar who is trusted has promoted an unusual understanding of the ancient world or a novel interpretation held by no other expert in the field before or since, yet the lay person believes and trusts the egalitarian scholar while having no idea how strange that scholar's views actually are.[91]

This consideration affects claims such as the idea that the Greek word for "head" could mean "source," the idea that Ephesians 5:21 teaches "mutual submission," the idea that there were women teaching false doctrine in Ephesus when Paul wrote 1 Timothy 2, the idea that the word translated "have authority over" in 1 Timothy 2:12 can mean "commit murder" or "proclaim oneself the originator of a man," or "thrust oneself," and so forth. For all of these points and more, there is no clear factual evidence from ancient literature (from word usage, similar grammatical constructions, etc.) to support the claims made. The necessary evidence does not exist and no egalitarian author has shown that it exists. (See the discussions on these points elsewhere in this book.) Yet thousands of people are making decisions based on these claims because they think the relevant evidence really does exist. In many cases they are believing a myth.

Answer 9.10d: Avoiding a decision on disputed passages essentially results in letting the egalitarian position win.

All that egalitarians want (for the moment at least) is the right for some women to become pastors and elders. If we avoid disputed passages and decide that "both views are acceptable," women will be established as elders and ordained as pastors, and encouraged to teach and have authority over men in the churches. If both views are acceptable, then there will be no

91. For one example, see Cindy Jacobs's statement about 1 Timothy 2:11–15: "In my study of this passage, I have found R. and C. Kroegers' book *I Suffer Not a Woman* (1992) particularly enlightening for understanding the historical and religious setting of Ephesus at the time 1 Timothy was written. Their study reveals a world of idolatrous paganism based upon a matriarchal society and goddess worship" (Jacobs, *Women of Destiny*, 235). Compare this statement to the scholarly analyses of the Kroegers' book found in chapter 8 above, pp. 280–88, and also in Appendix 6, pp. 646–74, and to the detailed criticisms of the accuracy of Catherine Kroeger's study of ancient word usage given in Appendix 4, pp. 552–99, for example.

effective way to prevent women from doing these things. Therefore avoiding the disputed passages is deciding that the egalitarian side has won the controversy, for all practical purposes.

But the process of change will not end there. The experience of the Presbyterian Church–USA and the current policy of Willow Creek Community Church, among others, have demonstrated that first egalitarians gain tolerance, then they gain majority control, then they exclude from the denomination or the church any who disagree with their position.[92]

Answer 9.10e: Do we really think that God does not want us to know what is right on this issue?

To say that we should be tolerant of different views about the end times is understandable. Whether someone is an amillennialist or a premillennialist, or a pretribulational or posttribulational premillennialist,[93] does not usually make very much difference in how he or she lives the Christian life. And since these views involve predictions of the future, they will continue to be impossible to resolve with certainty until the future arrives! It should not surprise us that God has left us with some aspects of mystery concerning the end times.

But the question of whether women should teach and govern churches is a different matter. Either we decide to have women pastors and elders or we do not. It is impossible to do both at the same time.

Do we think this topic is something that God cares about? Do we think it is something that He counts as a matter of obedience to Him? Or do we think that God does not really care what we do about this question?

The issue of roles of men and women in the church affects, to some degree, every Christian in the world, for it affects whom we choose as leaders in our churches, and it has a significant effect on what kinds of ministries the men and women in our churches carry out. When we say, "It is impossible to decide what the Bible teaches on this," *we imply that God did not think this to be an important enough issue to give us clear guidance in His Word.* We imply that God has left us instructions that are unclear or confusing on this issue. Do we really want to say this about God and His Word, on a topic that affects every church in the world every week of the year, for the entire church age until Christ returns?

I do not believe that this subject is unimportant to God. Nor do I believe that He has left instructions that are confusing or unclear. Yes, there is controversy about this matter today, but the controversy has come about because of other factors, not because God's Word is confusing or unclear.

---

92. See answer 9.11c, below, for details on these groups.
93. For an explanation of these terms, and the positions they represent, see Grudem, *Systematic Theology* (1994), chapters 54 and 55.

Answer 9.10f: The entire Christian church for nineteen hundred years did not think these passages were difficult or unclear.

Here is another difference between questions about the end times and questions about women's roles in the church. There have been controversies about the end times since the very early centuries of the church's history. But there have not been controversies about whether the roles of pastor and elder are reserved for men. As I explain in chapter 11 in more detail, apart from a few sectarian movements, the entire Christian church from the first century until the 1850s agreed that only men could be pastors and elders, and the vast majority agreed that only men could do public Bible teaching of men and women. From the 1850s until the 1950s in the United States, women pastors were a tiny minority, but over 98 percent of evangelical churches (over 99 percent of the Christian church if Roman Catholic and Orthodox groups are included) had only men as pastors.[94] The larger trend of allowing women to be ordained began with some liberal Protestant denominations in the 1950s and spread to a number of evangelical groups under the influence of evangelical feminism in the 1970s and 1980s. Before the advent of evangelical feminist writings in the 1970s, today's "disputed passages" on women in ministry were not thought to be unclear. This matter is much different from disputes over the end times.

Egalitarian claim 9.11: Stop Fighting About a Minor Issue: This is not a core issue, and it is not a major doctrine. We should stop fighting about this, allow different views and practices to exist in the church, and get on with more important ministries to a needy, hurting, lost world.

This objection is often heard when churches or organizations try to decide what their policy should be on men and women in the home and the church. This claim finds implicit voice in Ann Brown's statement,

> Why are there so many interpretations of Paul's letters? Is the apostle's teaching so confused and contradictory? I do not believe that it is, though *we* may be confused in expecting to discover dogmatic answers to questions which were not asked in the New Testament. Paul did not share the same ideological concerns as his twentieth-century readers.[95]

94. Even among those evangelical denominations that had women pastors, such as the Assemblies of God, the International Church of the Foursquare Gospel, and the Church of the Nazarene, women pastors constituted a small minority.

95. Ann Brown, *Apology to Women: Christian Images of the Female Sex* (1991), 157. The need to stop fighting about a relatively unclear and unimportant issue is a major theme in Brown's book, as indicated by her quotation from Milton which appears on the inside cover of her book (with archaic spelling preserved). It reads:

Regarding 1 Corinthians 14 and 1 Timothy 2, in answer to the question, "Why didn't Paul make it clearer?" Brown responds,

> I suspect that it is not clearer because it was not that important in the early church. Part of the problem is that we look at the New Testament through twentieth-century spectacles. I am not sure that the first-century church shared our preoccupation with ecclesiastical structures and status. Maybe they were too busy spreading the gospel to be concerned about precise job descriptions for women in their churches.[96]

William Webb proposes a "forum for harmony" in which he suggests that complementarians and egalitarians should reconcile their differences. He says of his proposals, "I hope they will awaken a spirit of reconciliation between egalitarians and partriarchalists."[97]

Answer 9.11a: The basic question underlying this controversy is obedience to the Bible. That is a major doctrine and it is a core issue.

Throughout this book, I have pointed out various ways in which egalitarian claims result in a rejection of the authority of the Bible over our lives. This happens through saying that certain passages no longer apply to us today, or saying that certain verses are not really part of the Bible, or saying Paul's reasoning from the Old Testament was wrong, or saying that the reason for Paul's command was something other than what he gave as the reason, or saying that the New Testament epistles are descriptive rather than prescriptive (and show us what was happening in the first century, not what we should do today), or saying that people can disobey what the Bible says if the elders or pastor give them permission, or saying that what we should obey is not what the New Testament says but our best guess as to where its "trajectory" was leading, and so forth.

But this repeated theme in the egalitarian position shows that *what is really at stake in this controversy is the authority of the Bible.* I am convinced that if the egalitarian position prevails, the principles it has used to interpret and apply Scripture will soon be broadened to many other areas of life, and no moral command of Scripture will be safe from its destructive procedures. Then the church will simply mimic the popular views of its culture in one issue after another, and Christians will no longer be subject to the authority of God speaking through His Word. I believe this is the direction egalitarianism is pushing the church. Therefore I believe this is an issue of major importance.

"Thus, they in mutual accusation spent / The fruitless hours, but neither self-condemning, / And of thir vain contest appeerd no end."

Similarly, Sarah Sumner, *Men and Women in the Church,* tells complementarians and egalitarians to "stop playing tug-of-war with each other" and to cooperate, not compete against each other (321).

96. Ibid., 159.

97. Webb, *Slaves, Women and Homosexuals*, 243. Unfortunately, the only two options offered in his "forum" are to capitulate 99 percent to egalitarian claims or to capitulate 100 percent egalitarian claims (see my analysis on pp. 639–40, below).

Answer 9.11b: The teaching of Scripture on men and women is not a minor or trivial issue, but has a massive effect on how we live our lives.

Is the teaching of the Bible on how men and women relate to each other in marriage a trivial issue? Is the teaching of the Bible about who should have authoritative leadership in the church a trivial issue? I do not believe so. The teaching of the Bible on men and women has a massive impact on marriages, families, and on children as they develop a sense of gender identity. And outside the realm of individual family life, feminism in our society, with its systematic denial of biblical roles for men and women, has had a massive impact in our educational system, our laws, our movies and TV and literature, our language, our military forces, our laws and expectations concerning sexual morality, and how we think of ourselves and relate to one another as men and women. Certainly some of these influences have been very good and brought about needed change (as I mentioned in the first chapter in this book), but many other changes have not been good and have not been consistent with biblical teachings. Whether we agree or disagree about specific changes, this matter is anything but a minor issue or one without consequence. The issue has massive consequences.

In addition, the influence of evangelical feminist teaching in our churches has been very significant, because in many churches the eldership and the ordained pastorate have been opened to thousands of women. Whether someone agrees with this change or not, the change is anything but minor or trivial. And I believe we will see increasingly significant consequences from this change. Over the next decade or two, I believe that including women as pastors and elders in evangelical churches will bring harmful effects as churches become more and more "feminized," resulting in a massive loss in male membership and male participation.[98] This has already happened in liberal Protestant denominations that adopted egalitarian views in the 1960s and 1970s. Leon Podles quotes several studies showing this trend:

> Lyle E. Schaller, an authority on church growth, observes that "In 1952 the adult attenders on Sunday morning in the typical Methodist, Presbyterian, Episcopal, Lutheran, Disciples, or Congregational worship service were approximately 53 percent female and 47 percent male, almost exactly the same as the distribution of the adult population. By 1986...these ratios were closer to 60 percent female and 40 percent male with many congregations reporting a 67–37 or 65–35 ratio." In 1992, 43 percent of men attended church, in 1996 only 28 percent. Patrick Arnold...notes, "some liberal Presbyterian or Methodist congregations are practically bereft of men." Kenneth Woodward reports that Protestant pastors "say that women usually outnumber the men three to one."[99]

---

98. For extensive documentation for how this has happened in liberal and Roman Catholic churches, see Leon J. Podles, *The Church Impotent: The Feminization of Christianity* (1999).
99. Ibid., 11–12.

Answer 9.11c: If we allow different views and practices on this issue to exist in the church, we are essentially admitting that both views are right. But that is all egalitarians want—at least until they attain majority control, and then the complementarian view is not allowed.

The plea that we should allow different views and practices to exist in the church is essentially a plea to stop saying that the egalitarian view is wrong and contrary to Scripture. But if we are convinced that it *is wrong*, and that it *is contrary to Scripture*, then we cannot support any policy that says we should allow both views and practices to exist in church, and just get along with our differences.

There are some doctrines on which Christians can "agree to disagree," such as details about the end times, and go on ministering together in the same church. Christians can differ on issues such as these *because they do not involve a rejection of the authority of Scripture on either side* and also *because differences do not have any significant effect on how we live or on how our church functions.*

But neither of those things is true with the question of women's roles in the church. As I mentioned in the previous section, it seems to me that the authority of Scripture *is* at stake in this controversy, because of the multiple ways in which prominent egalitarians adopt positions that reject the complete authority of Scripture. And either a church has women elders or it does not. Either it allows women to be ordained as pastors or it does not. You cannot have it both ways. For example, if a church were to ordain "a few" women as elders, the egalitarian position would have won, because this action would establish the validity of having women as elders.

I have also observed a regular pattern in which egalitarians first gain acceptance for their view, and then promote it more and more, and then force out the complementarians who still differ with them. I have seen this pattern, for example, in the United Presbyterian Church–USA, in which the ordination of women was approved in 1956 (in the north) and 1964 (in the south) but then in 1974 the denomination decided that it would require all candidates for ordination *to agree that they would participate in the ordination of women*. Here is one personal narrative of how this happened in the United Presbyterian Church–USA:

> Most felt that they were asked to leave their church, and that the most honorable way that this might be accomplished was to "peacefully withdraw." This action was precipitated by the popularly known "Kenyon Case" which began in the late Spring and ended in the late Fall of 1974. The watershed of this case had taken, and is taking place in 1975, even as this account is presently being penned.
>
> Mr. Walter Wynn Kenyon was an honors graduate of Pittsburgh Theological Seminary. In his trials for ordination, Mr. Kenyon, upon being asked his position on the ordination of women, stated that he could not in good conscience *participate* in the ordination of a woman. He said that it was his understanding of Scripture that

prevented such involvement, but went on to say that he would not stand in the way of such an ordination, if such was the desire of a church which he would happen to serve. Immediately there arose much dissent, and such dissent grew until the overwhelming majority of the church endorsed the judicial verdict which banned Kenyon and all future Kenyons from the pulpits of the UPCUSA. Furthermore, there was both explicit and implicit action which was taken against those men already ordained.

The Rev. Arthur C. Broadwick (and the Union UPCUSA of Pittsburgh) and the Rev. Carl W. Bogue, Jr. (and the Allenside UPCUSA of Akron) were already involved in litigations which involved this issue. And, in an even more pervasive way, the Stated Clerk of the UPCUSA (Mr. William P. Thompson), acting as the official interpreter of the Constitution of the UPCUSA, ruled that as one's answering the ordination/installation questions affirmatively was involved in the final decision in the Kenyon Case, any presently ordained pastor or ruling elder who held to the Kenyon views, could likewise never be placed in another pulpit or office unless he changed his views. The constitution of the UPCUSA clearly stated that men should exercise "forbearance in love" in situations where non-essentials of the presbyterian system of doctrine and polity were at stake. When the Permanent Judicial Commission of the UPCUSA ruled that Mr. Kenyon could not be ordained...it effectively elevated this doctrine concerning social relationships to the place of being a major doctrine of the church. Furthermore, by application, it appeared that this new essential would eclipse all others and become the *sine qua non* of "orthodoxy" test questions.

Such action by the Permanent Judicial Commission led to a crisis for all of those pastors and elders who held to the traditional views on this question and who were now considered heretics. Accordingly, to uphold the peace, unity and purity of the church, most of the men who made up the membership of the charter presbytery peaceably withdrew from the UPCUSA.

Respectfully and Humbly submitted, Richard E. Knodel, Jr.[100]

In a similar way, Willow Creek Community Church in South Barrington, Illinois, from at least 1997 has required that all members be willing to "joyfully sit under the teaching of women teachers at Willow Creek" and "joyfully submit to the leadership of women in various leadership positions at Willow Creek."[101]

---

100. This document can be read on-line at http://www.pcanet.org/history/findingaids/presbyteriesAM/ascension.html. See also Lois A. Boyd and R. Douglas Brackenridge, *Presbyterian Women in America* (1996), 138–39.
101. These quotations are from p. 3 of "The Elders' Response to the Most Frequently Asked Questions About Membership at Willow Creek," a paper distributed by the church and quoted in Wayne Grudem, "Willow Creek Enforces Egalitarianism," in *CBMW News* 2:5 (December 1997), 1.

So I am not persuaded that "allowing different views and practices to exist in the church" is where the egalitarian position will ultimately lead. In practice, it often leads to the exclusion of the other view.[102]

Answer 9.11d: When people say we should "stop fighting," it implies that complementarians are doing something wrong when we criticize egalitarians. But people who promote false doctrine will always say, "Let's stop fighting about this topic," because they want to stop the criticism.

It is not surprising that egalitarians say that Christians should "stop fighting" about this question, because to stop fighting means that any criticism of their view will be silenced, and their view will gain acceptance in the church. By calling the criticism of their view "fighting," they imply that the critics are doing wrong (for who wants to support fighting?). But using the term "fighting" is just giving a negative spin to what may well be very healthy and godly criticism of an incorrect position.

EGALITARIAN CLAIM 9.12: OKAY IF UNDER THE AUTHORITY OF PASTOR AND ELDERS: IF A WOMAN IS TEACHING "UNDER THE AUTHORITY OF THE PASTOR OR ELDERS," SHE MAY TEACH THE SCRIPTURES TO THE ASSEMBLED CONGREGATION.

This position is found frequently in evangelical churches. Many people who hold this position say they genuinely want to uphold male leadership in the church, and they say they are doing so when the woman teaches "under the authority of the elders," who are men (or of the pastor, who is a man).

This is not a commonly held view among egalitarian authors,[103] for they do not think only men should be elders, or that women need any approval from men to teach the Bible. But this view is often stated in phone calls or e-mails to the Council on Biblical Manhood and Womanhood office (www.cbmw.org), and I often hear it in personal conversations and discussions of church policies.

---

102. Someone could object that complementarians likewise eventually exclude egalitarians from influence in their churches. This does happen eventually, but often after a long period of allowing different views to be studied and taught. This is probably inevitable because the two views are mutually exclusive and only one side's position can be implemented (either a church has women elders or it does not). My own position is that the complementarian position is the right one and should be incorporated into governing documents of churches. At that point it takes on a status like other doctrines a church affirms, such as believer's baptism, for example. It is not that people can't read books and hear speakers who hold another view, but people who hold another view will not be given leadership roles in the church.

103. In fact, egalitarian author J. Lee Grady rejects this idea. He writes, in the context of talking about women who have public preaching ministries, "And in many cases, leaders have innocently twisted various Bible verses to suggest that a woman's public ministry can be valid only if she is properly 'covered' by a male who is present" (Grady, *Ten Lies* [2000], 89).

Is it true that a woman is obeying the Bible if she preaches a sermon "under the authority of the pastor and elders"?

Answer 9.12a: Pastors and elders cannot give someone permission to disobey the Bible.

The question here is, what does the Bible say? It does not merely say, "Preserve some kind of male authority in the congregation." It does not say, "A woman may not teach men unless she is under the authority of the elders." Rather, it says, "I do not permit a woman to teach or to exercise authority over a man" (1 Timothy 2:12).

Can a pastor or the elders of a church rightfully give a woman permission to disobey this statement of Scripture? Certainly not! Should any woman do what the Bible says *not* to do and excuse it by saying "I'm under the authority of the elders"? No.

Would we say that the elders of a church could tell people "under their authority" that they have permission to disobey *other* passages of Scripture? What would we think of someone who said, "I'm going to rob a bank today because I need money and my pastor has given me permission, and I'm under his authority"? Or of a person who said, "I'm committing adultery because I'm unhappy in my marriage and my elders have given me permission, so I'm still under the authority of my elders"? Or of someone who said, "I'm committing perjury because I don't want to go to jail and my pastor has given me permission, and I'm under his authority"? We would dismiss those statements as ridiculous, but they highlight the general principle that *no pastor or church elder or bishop or any other church officer has the authority to give people permission to disobey God's Word.*

Someone may answer, "But we are respecting the Bible's *general principle* of male headship in the church." But Paul did not say, "*Respect the general principle of male headship* in your church." He said, "*I do not permit a woman to teach or to exercise authority over a man*" (1 Timothy 2:12). We do not have the right to change what the Bible says and then obey some new "general principle of the Bible" we have made up.

Nor do we have the right to take a specific teaching of Scripture and abstract some general principle from it (such as a principle of "male headship") and then say that principle gives us the right *to disobey the specific commands of Scripture* that fall under that principle. We are not free to abstract general principles from the Bible however we wish, and then invent opinions about how those principles will apply in our situations. Such a procedure would allow people to evade any command of Scripture they were uncomfortable with. We would become a law unto ourselves, no longer subject to the authority of God's Word.

Answer 9.12b: Paul does not say, "I do not permit a woman to teach or to exercise authority over a man *unless she is under the authority of the elders*."

As with so many of these objections to 1 Timothy 2, this objection also would have us believe that the Bible says something a little bit different from what it actually does say.

Answer 9.12c: To add, "unless you are under the authority of your elders" to any of Paul's directions to churches would empty Paul's commands of their divine authority and reduce them to the level of advice that Paul hoped people would follow most of the time.

We could try this same procedure with some other passages. Would we think it right to say that the Bible teaches that men should pray "without anger or quarreling, *unless they quarrel under the authority of the elders*"? Or that women should adorn themselves "with modesty and self-control, *unless the elders give them permission to dress immodestly*"? Or would we say that those who are "rich in this present age" should "be generous and ready to share, *unless the elders give them permission to be stingy and miserly*"? (See 1 Timothy 6:17–19.)

But if we would not add, "unless the elders give permission to do otherwise under their authority" to any of the other commands in Scripture, neither should we add that evasion to 1 Timothy 2:12.

Answer 9.12d: This answer actually results in no differences between men and women regarding teaching the Bible to men.

If a woman says, "I will teach the Bible to men only when I am under the authority of the elders," she has become no different from men who teach the Bible. No man in any church should teach the Bible publicly unless he also is under the authority of the elders (or pastor, or other church officers) in that church. The general principle is that anyone who does Bible teaching in a church should be subject to the established governing authority in that church, whether it is a board of elders, a board of deacons, a church governing council, or the church board. Both men and women alike are subject to that requirement. Therefore this "under the authority of the elders" position essentially says there is no difference between what men can do and what women can do in teaching the Bible to men.

Do we really think that is what Paul meant? Do we really think that Paul did not mean to say anything *that applied only to women* when he said, "I do not permit a woman to teach or to exercise authority over a man" (1 Timothy 2:12)?

Egalitarian claim 9.13: We Are Not a Church: Because we are not a church, but rather a parachurch organization, New Testament restrictions against women teaching or having authority over men do not apply to us.

This argument is not usually made by egalitarian writers, because to make this argument someone has to assume that the New Testament restrictions on women in ministry *do* apply to a church situation. That is an assumption egalitarians are not willing to make.

But this argument is frequently made by people who claim to be complementarian and say they support male headship in the home and the church. Yet they say *because they are part of a parachurch organization* (such as a seminary, a mission board, or a campus ministry), the New Testament verses on women not teaching or having authority over men do not apply to their organization. I have listed this argument here as an "egalitarian claim" because it often functions in practice to advance egalitarian goals and to encourage women to function in ways contrary to New Testament teachings. However, as we shall see, there is also some truth in the argument and that also needs to be taken into account.

Answer 9.13a: The argument, "We are not a church," has some truth in it, but it is not the whole truth.

The truth is that parachurch organizations do not function in every way as churches do. Take, for example, some of the parachurch organizations I have been involved with. As far as I know, Phoenix Seminary, where I teach, has never

- baptized anyone
- ordained anyone to the ministry
- conducted a wedding or a funeral for anyone
- held morning Sunday school classes for children
- held Sunday morning worship services

Nor does Christian Heritage Academy of Northbrook, Illinois, a Christian school that my children attended, do such things. Nor does Multnomah Publishers, the publisher of this book. Nor does the Evangelical Theological Society, a professional academic society I have been a member of for many years. As a general practice, I do not think these activities are carried out by Campus Crusade for Christ or Focus on the Family or Promise Keepers or the Council on Biblical Manhood and Womanhood. These are all "parachurch" organizations in that they serve special purposes alongside the work of the church, and there are some "church" activities they do not do. If asked why they do not do these things, they will probably answer, "Because we are not a church." So there is some truth in the answer, "We are not a church," at least in some cases.

But that is not the whole story. In another sense, *there is only one church*, the worldwide Body of Christ, and these organizations are all part of it. They are just not part of any one local church or any one denomination.

In addition, these organizations seek to obey many commands that were first written to churches. They don't say, "First Corinthians was written to a church, and we are not a church, so we don't have to obey 1 Corinthians." In fact, if these organizations from time to time celebrate the Lord's Supper, they will probably read Paul's instructions in 1 Corinthians 11:23–29:

> For I received from the Lord what I also delivered to you, that the Lord Jesus on the night when he was betrayed took bread, and when he had given thanks, he broke it, and said, "This is my body which is for you. Do this in remembrance of me." In the same way also he took the cup, after supper, saying, "This cup is the New Covenant in my blood. Do this, as often as you drink it, in remembrance of me." For as often as you eat this bread and drink the cup, you proclaim the Lord's death until he comes. Whoever, therefore, eats the bread or drinks the cup of the Lord in an unworthy manner will be guilty of profaning the body and blood of the Lord. Let a person examine himself, then, and so eat of the bread and drink of the cup. For anyone who eats and drinks without discerning the body eats and drinks judgment on himself.

But these instructions were written to a church! So if people say, "We should not follow the New Testament instructions for churches because we are not a church," why do they read these instructions about the Lord's Supper? Or why do they even celebrate the Lord's Supper at all?[104]

All these organizations would probably think it important to follow the procedures of Matthew 18:15–17 in dealing with cases where one person sins against another. But these instructions assume they will be carried out by a church: "If he refuses to listen to them, *tell it to the church*" (Matthew 18:17).

The same is true of mission boards. If their missionaries baptize new converts they will think it important for the missionaries to obey the New Testament teachings on baptism (and not baptize people indiscriminately whether they profess faith or not, for example).[105] They do not

---

104. A few evangelicals say that parachurch organizations should never celebrate the Lord's Supper, for this very reason. Some even argue that parachurch organizations should not exist! I am not persuaded by this position, because even in the New Testament Paul and his missionary companions functioned as a sort of "parachurch organization." Though they were initially sent out by the church at Antioch (Acts 13:1–3), many (such as Timothy) who had no connection with Antioch later joined Paul, and Paul in his writings never identifies himself as sent from Antioch, but emphasizes that he was appointed by the Lord (Galatians 1:1). On his third missionary journey, he did not even return to Antioch (Acts 21:1–15). Therefore I see no good reason from Scripture to forbid or oppose parachurch organizations.

    But for those who say that parachurch organizations should never celebrate the Lord's Supper, I would respond that even they will agree that the procedure for church discipline that Jesus outlines for a "church" to follow in Matthew 18:15–17 should be followed in their organizations. So *some* things written to churches do apply to us.

105. Missionaries who hold to believer's baptism would baptize only those who make a profession of faith, and those who hold to infant baptism would also baptize the infant children of those who make a profession of faith, but in both cases they are seeking to follow what they think the New Testament teaches. No one is saying, "We are not a church, so what the New Testament teaches about baptism does not apply to us."

say, "We are not a church, so we don't have to follow the New Testament teachings about baptism, which were written to a church."

All of the New Testament epistles were written to churches (or to individuals such as Timothy and Titus and Philemon who were involved in local churches). Therefore the argument that "we are not a church, so we don't need to follow the instructions written to churches," taken to its logical conclusion, would mean that parachurch organizations do not have to obey anything written in the New Testament epistles! Surely that conclusion is wrong.

How then can we know when "we are not a church" is a valid reason and when it is not? I think the answer will be found as we look at a number of cases where the statement "we are not a church" is a good reason, and a number of other cases where it is not a good reason.

Answer 9.13b: The argument, "We are not a church," is a valid reason why parachurch organizations do not have to obey all the directions the New Testament gives to churches.

What follows is a list of some New Testament commands to churches (left column) and some examples of parachurch organizations that should *not* be expected to follow those commands (right column).

NEW TESTAMENT COMMAND	A PARACHURCH ORGANIZATION THAT WOULD NOT FOLLOW THIS COMMAND
Hebrews 10:25: "not neglecting to meet together, as is the habit of some, but encouraging one another, and all the more as you see the Day drawing near."	The Council on Biblical Manhood and Womanhood, whose members "meet together" once a year. (But going to church once a year is hardly the frequency of attendance this verse has in mind.)
Hebrews 13:17: "Obey your leaders and submit to them, for they are keeping watch over your souls, as those who will have to give an account."	The Evangelical Theological Society, a professional academic society. (When I was president in 1999, I don't think any of the twenty-five hundred members obeyed me for the entire year, or even considered it an option! Nor did I think that I had pastoral responsibility for their spiritual condition, as this verse assumes leaders will have in local churches.)
1 Corinthians 14:26: "When you come together, each one has a hymn, a lesson, a revelation, a tongue, or an interpretation."	My "Introduction to Theology" class at Phoenix Seminary, where I, not all the students, do the teaching when we "come together."
1 Timothy 3:2: "Therefore an overseer must be… the husband of one wife."	Bible Study Fellowship, an organization run entirely by women. (They do not require any of their leaders to be the "husband of one wife"!)
Titus 1:5: "This is why I left you in Crete, so that you might put what remained into order, and appoint elders in every town as I directed you."	Multnomah Publishers, a book publisher that has no intention of trying to appoint elders in every town in which they sell books, or even in every town in which they have employees.
Matthew 28:19: "Go therefore and make disciples of all nations, baptizing them in the name of the Father and of the Son and of the Holy Spirit."	Focus on the Family, a worldwide ministry through radio and other media (they do not attempt to baptize anyone who listens to their programs or calls them for advice, but they expect local churches to do that).

Answer 9.13c: But in *other* areas the argument, "We are not a church," does not allow parachurch organizations to avoid obeying New Testament commands to churches.

The following chart contains another list of New Testament commands (left column) and some examples of ways parachurch organizations should *not* ignore or disobey these commands, but should obey them (right column).

New Testament command	Example of situation where a parachurch organization should obey this command
1 Corinthians 11:27: "Whoever, therefore, eats the bread or drinks the cup of the Lord in an unworthy manner will be guilty of profaning the body and blood of the Lord. Let a person examine himself, then, and so eat of the bread and drink of the cup."	Whenever members of a parachurch organization celebrate the Lord's Supper. (For example, if the teachers and administrators of a Christian school celebrate the Lord's Supper at a retreat, they should not say, "We are not a church, so we don't have to follow this command, and people don't have to examine their lives before partaking.")
1 Corinthians 14:40: "But all things should be done decently and in order."	Whenever a group of Christians meets for worship, prayer, and study of the Bible. (For example, members of a Campus Crusade prayer meeting should not say, "All kinds of disorder and irreverent behavior are fine here, since we are not a church.")
1 Timothy 2:8: "I desire then that in every place the men should pray...without anger or quarreling."	Whenever men, or men and women, meet to pray in a group. (For example, a Promise Keepers prayer group should not say, "Anger and quarreling are okay here, since we are not a church").
1 Timothy 2:9: "likewise also that women should adorn themselves in respectable apparel, with modesty and self-control."	Whenever a group of Christian men and women meet to pray. (For example, members of an InterVarsity prayer meeting on a college campus should not say, "It's okay for women to dress immodestly here, and not to show self-control, since we are not a church.")
1 Thessalonians 5:20–21: "Do not despise prophecies, but test everything; hold fast what is good."	Whenever a group of Christians allows the gift of prophecy to function. (For example, a charismatic prayer group meeting at Regent University in Virginia Beach should not say, "We do not have to test prophecies, since we are not a church.")
1 Corinthians 14:27–28: "If any speak in a tongue, let there be only two or at most three, and each in turn, and let someone interpret. But if there is no one to interpret, let each of them keep silent in church and speak to himself and to God."	Whenever a group of Christians allows the gift of tongues to function. (For example, leaders of a charismatic worship service on some college campus should not say, "We are not a church, so it's okay if we have many messages in tongues with no interpretation.")
1 Timothy 3:2–3: "Therefore an overseer must be...sober-minded, self-controlled, respectable... not a drunkard, not violent but gentle, not quarrelsome, not a lover of money."	Whenever a parachurch organization chooses people for leadership positions. (For example, Campus Crusade for Christ should not say, "We can have staff members who are quarrelsome, violent, and occasionally get drunk, because we are not a church.")
2 Timothy 2:24–25: "And the Lord's servant must not be quarrelsome but kind to everyone, able to teach, patiently enduring evil, correcting his opponents with gentleness. God may perhaps grant them repentance leading to a knowledge of the truth"	Whenever a parachurch organization puts people in a teaching position. (For example, the leaders of Walk Thru the Bible should not say, "We can hire Bible teachers who are impatient and quarrelsome and harsh with people because we are not a church.")

In each of these cases, the members of a parachurch organization would be likely to use the very verses I quoted in the left column to correct any such abuses that might arise, even though all of those verses were written to a church, not to a parachurch organization.

What makes the difference then? How can we know when a New Testament command applies to a parachurch organization and when it does not? I think the solution is not a complex one, but is fairly straightforward (see the next section).

Answer 9.13d: Parachurch organizations should follow New Testament commands written to churches *when they are doing the same activities that the command is talking about.*

The principle that allows us to distinguish between commands that parachurch organizations should obey and those they do not need to obey is a simple one. It is a general principle that Christians often use, sometimes even instinctively, in the application of Scripture to all of life. The principle is *that we should obey the command when we are doing the same activity,* or a very similar activity, to what the command is talking about.

Therefore, Multnomah Publishers *should not* "appoint elders in every town" (Titus 1:5) where it sells books because it is not planting churches in a region, as Paul and Titus were. On the other hand, if a mission organization is planting churches in a region, it *should* make plans for how it could "appoint elders in every town" by raising up indigenous Christian leaders.

Similarly, the Evangelical Theological Society might never celebrate the Lord's Supper at one of its meetings. But if it did decide to celebrate the Lord's Supper, then it should follow Paul's directions in 1 Corinthians 11.

The principle then is simple: Parachurch organizations should follow New Testament commands written to churches *when those organizations are doing the same activities that the command is talking about.*

How then does that conclusion apply to women's roles in parachurch ministries? The following principles address that question.

Answer 9.13e: Organizations will need to seek God's wisdom to make the right decisions regarding the roles women fulfill within their organizations.

With all of the thousands of parachurch organizations in the world today, and the hundreds of thousands of activities carried out by those organizations, situations will vary widely. Before any decisions are made, leaders in each organization will need to ask for God's wisdom, according to James 1:5–8, in order to understand how their situations are *similar to* or *different from* the situations and activities found in the New Testament. Although in some cases it will be difficult at first to say how much the situation is similar and how much it is different, I believe in most cases the application of this principle will be quite clear.

Answer 9.13f: Bible teaching to assembled groups of Christian men and women outside the church is so similar to Bible teaching inside the church that it should be reserved for men.

As I explained in some detail in chapter 2,[106] teaching the Bible to an assembled group of men and women is so much like the situation Paul had in mind when he said, "I do not permit a woman to teach or to exercise authority over a man; rather, she is to remain quiet" (1 Timothy 2:12), that only men should do this. I believe that such a principle should apply not only to meetings in local churches, but also to Bible conferences, weekend retreats, and annual meetings held by parachurch organizations or denominations. For similar reasons, I do not think it appropriate for women to hold Bible teaching positions in Christian colleges and seminaries, because this responsibility is very similar to the Bible teaching role of elders in the New Testament, or even to the role of a mature, senior elder training younger elders.

Answer 9.13g: Serving as a military chaplain is so similar to serving as the pastor of a church that it should be restricted to men.

The activities and responsibilities that a military chaplain carries out are not significantly different from the activities and responsibilities carried out by a pastor/elder in a local church. Therefore, just as ordination to the pastorate is restricted to men, so appointment to the military chaplaincy, to be consistent, should also be restricted to men.[107]

However, if there are military chaplaincy roles that do not involve Bible teaching or governing authority over groups of Christian men, then such roles are appropriate for women as well as men.

Answer 9.13h: Serving on the governing board of a parachurch organization is often quite different from serving as an elder in a church, and therefore qualified men and women should both be encouraged to do this.

A member of an elder board in a church has great responsibility for the lives, conduct, and spiritual well-being of members of the church. Christians are to "be subject" to the elders (1 Peter 5:5), and the author of Hebrews says, "Obey your leaders and submit to them, for they are keeping watch over your souls, as those who will have to give an account" (Hebrews 13:17).

But the member of a parachurch governing board has authority over an *organization*, and over certain *activities* that people carry out within that organization, not over the entire lives of the members. So, for example, I consider myself to be subject to the authority of my pastor and the elders at Scottsdale Bible Church (of which I am a member), but I don't think of my life as

106. See pp. 95–97.

107. I realize that the military chaplaincy includes chaplains from many denominations, including those that ordain women. The military should accept such women chaplains if denominations send them, I think, because the decision to ordain and endorse them for the chaplaincy does not belong to the military but instead falls to the different denominations. Freedom of religion in a country includes freedom to hold different views on whether women should be ordained.

What I am advocating here, however, is that denominations that wish to be faithful to Scripture should not ordain or endorse women as chaplains, in my judgment.

subject to the authority of the governing board of the Council on Biblical Manhood and Womanhood (of which I am also a member). And the members of the board of a Christian school have authority over the school and its activities, but they do not have elder-like authority over the lives of the parents who make up the association that owns that school.[108] In fact, if an employee of a parachurch organization is involved in conduct that brings reproach on the organization (for example, if a Christian school teacher were discovered in sexual immorality), the organization would probably dismiss the employee, but the elder board at the teacher's church, not the school board, would ordinarily pursue church discipline for that teacher.

Therefore when Paul says, "I do not permit a woman to teach or to exercise authority over a man," the kind of authority he has in mind is *sufficiently different* from the kind of authority a governing board member generally has in parachurch organizations, and the argument, "We are not a church" is a helpful distinction in this situation.

Answer 9.13i: But serving as a direct supervisor over employees in a ministry role is similar enough to the role of a pastor or elder that the responsibility should be restricted to men.

To take a somewhat different example, the person serving as the academic dean in a theological seminary is supervising a number of men (the male faculty members) in their Bible teaching ministry. He does "exercise authority" over these men with respect to what they teach and their conduct as they teach and relate to students and to each other. His role is very much like that of a pastor or elder to these faculty members, and therefore it is appropriate for only men to have this role.[109]

To take another example, the campus director of a parachurch ministry on a college campus (such as Campus Crusade or InterVarsity) has a supervisory authority over the other staff

108. Theological seminaries have reached different decisions on this question. Both Trinity Evangelical Divinity School, where I taught for twenty years, and Phoenix Seminary, where I now teach, have women on their governing boards. I did not object to this, since governing the activities of a seminary is sufficiently different from governing a church. The boards met rather infrequently and made decisions regarding broad policies and budgets. They exercised almost no direct authority over me or over my conduct in the seminary, nor did I think of them as having the kind of pastoral responsibility for my life that I think my pastor and elders do. Some board members even attended an adult Sunday school class that I taught and where I was in charge. One board member was also a student in one of my classes, and neither of us ever thought there was any kind of elder-like authority functioning in that situation (except perhaps in a reverse sense, in that I as a teacher felt some responsibility for the spiritual lives of my students).

On the other hand, Westminster Theological Seminary in Philadelphia decided that the role of a board member was similar in many respects to the role of an elder in the church, and it decided to require its board members to consist only of people who had previously been ordained as elders in Presbyterian or Reformed churches, subject to the qualifications in 1 Timothy 3 and Titus 1. Within the conservative Reformed circles that Westminster serves, this rule effectively meant that all board members would be men. (The seminary at one point was threatened with loss of accreditation by the Middle States Accrediting Association unless it added women to its board. The seminary decided to fight this in court on First Amendment freedom of religion grounds, but before the matter could go to court, the accrediting agency, under pressure from the U.S. Department of Education, backed down.)

109. For example, Westminster Theological Seminary in Philadelphia specifies that their academic dean must be an ordained elder in a church.

members on that campus that is very similar to the role of a pastor or elder in a church, especially as the pastor or elder supervises other ministry activities in the church. Therefore, in my judgment, it is not appropriate for a woman to have the role of campus director and "exercise authority" in such a direct way over the men in that ministry. That would be doing what Paul said not to do.

On the other hand, supervisory positions in other types of organizations may be different. Are these roles mostly like the role of a pastor or elder, overseeing and supervising people's whole lives as they minister to others? Or are they more like the role of a supervisor in a secular workplace, overseeing only specific kinds of on-the-job activities? It will require godly wisdom to decide in each situation.

Answer 9.13j: The commands in the New Testament do not say that Christians should follow them "only in church settings."

This is a crucial point. Some New Testament commands do *not* apply to parachurch organizations *not* because they are not churches, but because *they are not performing the activity mentioned in those commands*. The Council on Biblical Manhood and Womanhood may never observe the Lord's Supper together, and therefore they will not have to follow the New Testament directions for the Lord's Supper. But *if they ever do observe the Lord's Supper*, then they will have to follow those commands. Whether CBMW is a church is not the crucial point. The crucial point is whether that organization is carrying out an activity for which the New Testament gives commands.

We must continue to insist strongly that the New Testament applies to *all* Christians in *all* societies and *all* cultures and *all* situations—and in *all* parachurch organizations! Its commands are valid whenever Christians carry out the activities included in those commands. I cannot imagine the apostle Paul writing to the Corinthians, "Follow these instructions if you are doing this as part of the church in Corinth, but if you are doing this as part of a Christian organization outside the church, then you do not have to obey my commands." The New Testament never speaks that way, or hints at any such way to "escape" from being accountable to obey it. This should make us cautious about ignoring commands that speak to the same kind of situations we are in.

Answer 9.13k: Right decisions about male leadership in parachurch situations will only be made by people who agree with and approve of the New Testament teachings about male leadership in the home and the church.

When members of a parachurch organization are making a decision about whether certain New Testament commands about men's and women's roles apply to their organization, it is important for them to be honest about their personal convictions regarding male leadership in the home and the church. Some members may be "closet egalitarians" who do not agree with the

New Testament restrictions of some governing and teaching roles to men *even in the church*. In their case, the argument, "We are not a church," is not their real concern, because even if it were a church situation, they would favor women teaching and having governing authority over men. When these people say, "We are not a church," it functions as a smoke screen because it is a quick slogan that can easily initiate a question that seems complex if people have not thought about it before, and thereby it distracts the discussion from the real issues.

On the other hand, for people who support male leadership in the home and the church, the consideration that "We are not a church" is a valid one to consider in light of the principle in answer 9.13d, and it is those people who are best qualified to make thoughtful, mature, biblically-faithful applications of these teachings to their own situations.

EGALITARIAN CLAIM 9:14: MALE HEADSHIP MUST APPLY EVERYWHERE OR NOWHERE: IT IS INCONSISTENT FOR COMPLEMENTARIANS TO APPLY THE PRINCIPLES OF MALE HEADSHIP ONLY TO THE HOME AND THE CHURCH.

Sarah Sumner makes this argument:

> If it's wrong for a woman to teach a man on the basis of the order of creation, then it has to be wrong for a woman to teach a man piano lessons. If her teaching him *per se* upsets the order of creation, then her teaching him anything must also be regarded as wrong. In other words, if it's wrong in principle for the second to teach the first, then it's wrong for a woman to teach a man.... It's illogical to believe that it's wrong to defy the order of creation only in "the household of God".... If the order of creation is a general principle, then it ought to be applied across the board. Instead, it's applied inconsistently and selectively.[110]

Answer 9.14a: Our standard must be what the Bible teaches, not some arbitrary idea of consistency.

Sumner's argument is based on a classic mistake in biblical interpretation, a mistake that takes one principle found in the Bible and attempts to maximize it above other things the Bible teaches, with the result that those other things are ultimately denied. The problem is that the principle of male headship is not the only principle in the Bible. There is another principle, and that is the principle of male-female equality in the image of God. By Sumner's own reasoning, someone might say, "It's inconsistent to apply the principle of equality only to things such as value, importance, and personhood. Consistency requires that men and women be equal in

110. Sumner, *Men and Women in the Church*, 227.

every way, including all the roles they fulfill in marriage and the church. The principle of equality requires that there be no differences!"

What is wrong with both the principle of "always follow male headship" and the principle of "always follow male-female equality" is that it is not up to us to decide in what ways these major principles in Scripture should be combined and applied in various situations. It is up to God, who has His own purposes and whose wisdom is infinitely greater than ours.

So how do we know which principles to apply? We are simply to obey the Bible in the specific application of these principles. What we find in the Bible is that God has given commands that establish male leadership in the *home* and in the *church*, but that other teachings in His Word give considerable freedom in other areas of life. We should not try to require either more or less than Scripture itself requires.

Sumner's argument is just another variety of the argument, "If men and women are different, they can't be equal, and if they are equal, they can't be different." I discussed this argument in chapter 3,[111] and it has come up again and again in various forms throughout this book.

EGALITARIAN CLAIM 9.15: INSECURE MEN FEEL THREATENED BY GIFTED WOMEN: THIS CONTROVERSY IS NOT REALLY ABOUT THE INTERPRETATION OF THE BIBLE, BUT DEEP DOWN IT IS ULTIMATELY A MATTER OF FEELINGS AND EMOTIONS. COMPLEMENTARIANS ARE REALLY INSECURE MEN WHO FEEL THREATENED BY STRONG, GIFTED WOMEN, AND THAT IS WHY THEY CONTINUE TO MAKE THIS ISSUE A MATTER OF CONTROVERSY.

This theme of weak, insecure men who are threatened by strong, gifted women runs through several parts of Sarah Sumner's book, *Men and Women in the Church*. The following quotations are representative of her frequent claim that insecure men have a problem relating to gifted women, and that the whole argument is really about feelings and emotions:

> As I see it, the confusion in the church *ultimately stems from a more fundamental question of relationships*. The church has not yet learned how to relate to Christian women who, in light of their ministry calling, have chosen to walk an unconventional path.... It seems that Christians also *feel uncomfortable* when a woman in the church begins to attain an excessive rolefulness, if you will.[112]

> Every generation produces gifted women who minister effectively to women and men. This book deals with the problem of relating to those women.[113]

---

111. See chapter 3, 103–6.

112. Sumner, *Men and Women in the Church,* 30. In all the quotations in this section, I have added italics to indicate Sumner's emphasis on feelings as the cause of this conflict.

113. Ibid., 49.

> [Summarizing her interpretation of John Piper's view:] Anytime a husband starts to doubt himself as a man or *feels that his manhood has been violated* by a woman's expression of strength, Piper says it's her responsibility to figure out a way to adjust.... My question has to do with why a man's "God-given sense of responsibility and leadership" is so *fragile and susceptible to offense*.[114]
>
> A few months ago I explained to five church leaders Piper's definition of biblical manhood.... *Intellectually* all five men saw the flaws in this definition. Yet they responded to it *emotionally* by saying to me, "You know what? We *like* this definition. And you know why? Because it's a definition! It's specific, and it makes us *feel secure*. It *feels so good* to be told what it means to be a man, *even if this definition isn't right*."[115]
>
> Dr. Ted Engstrom...said to me, "I am eighty-five years old now, so I have nothing to hide. *The problem is that we men are insecure.... We men are jealous and insecure*." A common formula for helping Christian men *feel* more solid and secure is to coach Christian women to hold back.[116]

---

114. Ibid., 88.

115. Ibid., 91 (italics added). This quotation makes these "five church leaders" sound irrational and foolish—they know something isn't right but they like it anyway. Sumner gives no location, date, time, or publicly accessible source with which readers could verify that she was quoting these "five church leaders" accurately. This procedure (supporting her points with personal anecdotes which are unverifiable and which readers cannot go back and check in context as they can with published writings) is common throughout Sumner's book. Such a procedure would not be allowed in academic writing, but apparently Sumner wants many sections of her book to be understood as a personal testimony and not as a verifiable, academically acceptable argument.

Dorothy Patterson has questioned the accuracy of Sumner's reports of private conversations. Patterson says, "Sumner continues taking words out of context, putting words in my mouth and even using quotation marks in the process!" (Dorothy Patterson, "Sarah Sumner's *Men and Women in the Church*: A Review Article," *JBMW* 8/1 [spring 2003], 42 [also available at www.cbmw.org]).

Patterson points out that Sumner incorrectly reported an incident where Anne Graham Lotz came to Southern Seminary in Louisville. Patterson says, "This misinformation was corrected for Sumner in her personal conversation with me almost two years before this volume was released. She not only ignored the correction, but also she did not check the information with Mrs. Lotz or SBTS president Dr. R. Albert Mohler Jr." (ibid.).

I noticed other inaccuracies with regard to facts known personally to me. For example, Sumner says, "In 1995 Wayne Grudem copioneered the Council on Biblical Manhood and Womanhood (CBMW)" (Sumner, *Men and Women in the Church*, 38). But CBMW was founded in 1987 and announced publicly in 1988, not in 1995. She also says, "Wayne Grudem is a Vineyard charismatic" (ibid.). It was strange for me to read this in a 2003 publication, because I have not been a member of a Vineyard church since 1994 (from 1994–2001 I was a member of a Southern Baptist Church, and from 2001 until today I have been a member of an independent Bible church). I also do not generally apply the term "charismatic" to myself because it includes nuances that I agree with and others I disagree with.

Sumner also says, "Dr. Ray Ortlund Jr. now serves as a senior pastor in Atlanta" (ibid., 42). But Ortlund has been a pastor in Augusta, Georgia, for several years, and has never been a pastor in Atlanta. The accumulation of these items makes me wonder: If Sumner has not been careful to be accurate in the details known to Dorothy Patterson and to me, then how can we be sure that she has taken care to be accurate in other details, especially the personal anecdotes she uses throughout the book? And how can we be sure that her memory of those conversations is accurate?

116. Ibid., 94. The quotation of Engstrom is another undocumented reference available to others in no publicly accessible form.

Another set of women told me they're *afraid* to unleash their strength. They said, "We're *afraid* because if we get involved in church leadership, then we are likely to go overboard and take full control of the men!" Men are *afraid*, and women are *afraid*. Men *feel* overly pressured to be perfect, and women *feel* overly pressured to hold back. Consequently both choke under the pressure of their *fears*.[117]

[In personal conversation a woman told Sumner that she was not going to teach the Bible "if any men are around":] "that way the men will *feel* like men."[118]

[Regarding a woman who came to Sumner's office and wept for thirty minutes "before she was able to talk":] All her life this woman had felt called into public ministry.... Her believing husband was well aware of this.... Yet her husband wasn't willing to accept it. For him it *felt embarrassing* to be the silent husband of a Bible-teaching wife. He *felt inferior* to her.... Her calling *undermined his sense of manhood*.... He couldn't trust God with regard to her. He didn't trust God for himself.[119]

Sometimes a husband...knows no other way *to protect his self-image* than to refuse to take the risk of sacrificing himself for the sake of his wife.... It is not uncommon for a Christian husband to *fear that his wife will upstage him*. He *feels afraid* that if his wife takes off, mounting up with wings like an eagle (Isa. 40:31), then he'll be left alone waddling around *feeling stupid*. The husband *feels* threatened.[120]

I am further convinced that *1 Timothy 2 does not lie at the heart of this debate*. The issue for conservatives is male headship.... At least for Piper and Grudem, *the underlying principle* in 1 Timothy 2 is...*for women to refrain in all times and all places from "offending" a man's "sense of" masculinity*.[121]

[Regarding one of her seminary professors who told her that he would not have her teach his class:] By this, I believe my professor was trying to tell me that the men in his class would not "*feel like men*" if I were to stand as their teacher. More specifically, I believe he was saying that *he* would not *feel like a man* if I were to teach his class.[122]

117. Ibid., 104.
118. Ibid., 109.
119. Ibid., 191–92.
120. Ibid., 205.
121. Ibid., 229.
122. Ibid., 230; see also 103, 143, 248, 300. In connection with a number of these quotations, Sumner mentions that gifted women have wrongly "held back" from doing what they felt God was calling them to do (73–74, 94, 104, and elsewhere in the book).

Answer 9.15a: This is an *ad hominem* argument.

In making this argument, Sumner commits another classic fallacy in argumentation. She is arguing against the person rather than against the argument that the other side makes (Latin *ad hominem*, "against the man"). She is saying that people who argue for a complementarian position have some personal defect in themselves, some emotional insecurity, that is the real basis for their position.

But how can Sumner presume to know that? Does she know the heart and the motive of every person who has argued a complementarian position in the last thirty years? Does she know the motive of the countless millions of Christians who have held a complementarian position throughout the history of the church?

Classes in debate and logic regularly teach students not to make *ad hominem* arguments because they fail to interact with the evidence, arguments, and logic of an opposing position. They shift the topic from the issue at hand to the character of the person on the other side. My claim throughout this book, and the claim made by many other complementarians, is that we hold our position because the Bible teaches it. When someone says that is not the real reason we hold our view, but we hold it because of personal insecurities, that also implies we are not telling the truth about the real reason for our position. People may believe this if they wish, but I would encourage readers to make their decisions by carefully considering the arguments on both sides about what the Bible actually teaches, not by listening to such *ad hominem* arguments.

CONCLUSION

We have considered many egalitarian objections in this chapter, but in the end none of them are persuasive in their attempts to overturn a complementarian understanding of the Bible's teaching on men's and women's roles in marriage and the church. We are not free to say that passages about head coverings for women or passages about wearing jewelry or braids *don't* apply to us today, but we should rather seek to understand the passages more accurately and therefore understand exactly *how* they apply to us today.

Contrary to egalitarian claims, the New Testament does not teach or command slavery, so the argument, "Just as we learned that slavery is wrong, so now we should learn that women's submission is wrong," does not provide a genuine parallel.

The "trajectory" arguments of R. T. France and William Webb deny the final authority of the New Testament for Christians today, and should not be considered a legitimate option for evangelicals. Similarly, claims that say we don't have to obey the "unclear" verses, or that we don't have to obey verses that we don't choose to emphasize, or that it is impossible to decide what the Scripture teaches, all likewise fail to be consistent with a belief in the complete authority of Scripture in our lives today. As for the claims that a woman can teach the Bible to men if she is under the authority of the elders, or if she is doing so outside of a church setting, these likewise turn out to be methods of avoiding obedience to the Bible, not methods of obeying what the Bible says.

Therefore these various egalitarian claims about how to interpret Scripture do not overturn the picture we saw in chapters 1 and 2 of our equality and differences as men and women created in the image of God.

ADDITIONAL NOTE TO CHAPTER 9: HOW CAN WE DETERMINE WHICH MORAL COMMANDS OF SCRIPTURE ARE CULTURALLY RELATIVE?

At several points in this chapter the question of the possible cultural relativity of some New Testament commands has come up. Most everyone agrees that we should not "greet one another with a holy kiss" today (at least in cultures where this is not a common greeting). But are there other commands like this, that were intended to be followed literally only in that particular culture? How should Christians determine which moral commands of the New Testament are culturally relative?

I originally wrote what follows as part of a review of William Webb's book, *Slaves, Women and Homosexuals*,[123] in which he claims that we need to move beyond the New Testament ethic to a higher ethic that we can discern today. But my comments here are applicable more broadly to the general question of how we can know what parts of the New Testament are culturally relative and what parts are still binding on us today.

I am concerned about the moral commands here. The question is not whether the historical sections of the Bible *report events* that occurred in an ancient culture, because the Bible is a historical book, and of course it reports thousands of events that occurred at an ancient time and in a culture significantly different from our own. The question rather is how we should approach the *moral commands* found in the New Testament. Are those commands to be obeyed by us today as well?

The question of which New Testament commands are culturally relative is really not a very complicated question. It is not nearly as complicated as Webb makes it out to be. The commands that are culturally relative are primarily—or exclusively—those that concern *physical actions that carry symbolic meaning*. When we look at the commands in the New Testament, I think there are only six main examples of texts about which people wonder if they are transcultural or if they are culturally relative:

1. Holy kiss (Romans 16:16; 1 Corinthians 16:20; 2 Corinthians 13:12; 1 Thessalonians 5:26; 1 Peter 5:14)

---

123. Webb, *Slaves, Women and Homosexuals* (2001). The remaining material in this "Additional Note" is taken from my review of Webb, which is reprinted in full (except for this section) in Appendix 5, pp. 600–645, below.

2. Foot washing (John 13:14; compare 1 Timothy 5:10, which is not a command)
3. Head covering for women or wives in worship (1 Corinthians 11:4–16)
4. Short hair for men (1 Corinthians 11:14)
5. No jewelry or braided hair for women (1 Timothy 2:9; 1 Peter 3:3)
6. Lifting hands in prayer (1 Timothy 2:8)

The first thing that we notice about this list is that *all of these examples refer to physical items or actions that carry symbolic meaning*. The holy kiss was a physical expression that conveyed the idea of a welcoming greeting. Foot washing (in the way that Jesus modeled it in John 13) was a physical action that symbolized taking a servantlike attitude toward one another. Head covering was a physical piece of clothing that symbolized something about a woman's status or role (most likely that she was a married woman, or possibly that she was a woman and not a man; others have proposed other interpretations, but all of them are an attempt to explain what the head covering symbolized). As Paul understands long hair for a man in 1 Corinthians 11:14, it is a "disgrace for him," because it is something that was distinctive to women (in that culture at least), and therefore it was a physical symbol of a man being like a woman rather than like a man.

For these first four examples, one can still find a few Christians who argue that we should follow those commands literally today, and that they are still applicable to us. But the vast majority of evangelicals, at least in the United States (I cannot speak for the rest of the world), have not needed Webb's "redemptive-movement hermeneutic" to reach the conclusion that the Bible does not intend us to follow those commands literally today. That is because they are not in themselves *fundamental, deep-level actions* that have to do with essential components of our relationships to one another (such as loving one another, honesty with one another, submission to rightful authority, speaking the truth and not lying about others, not committing adultery or murder or theft, and so forth). Rather they are outward, *surface-level manifestations* of the deeper realities that we should demonstrate today (such as greeting one another in love, or serving one another, or avoiding dressing in such a way as to give a signal that a man is trying to be a woman, or that a woman is trying to be a man). Therefore the vast majority of evangelicals are not troubled by these four "culturally relative" commands in the New Testament because they have concluded that *only the physical, surface manifestation is culturally relative*, and the underlying intent of the command is *not culturally relative* but is still binding on us today.

In seeing these outward manifestations as culturally relative (long before Webb's book was written), evangelicals have not adopted Webb's viewpoint that we need to move to a "better ethic" than that found in the New Testament commands. Evangelicals who take the Bible as the very words of God, and who believe that God's moral commands for His people are good and just and perfect, do not see these commands as part of a deficient moral system that is just a "pointer" to a higher ethic. They see these commands as a part of the entire New Testament ethic that they even today must submit to and obey.

For most people in the evangelical world, deciding that a holy kiss is a greeting that could be manifested in another way is not a terribly difficult decision. It is something that comes almost intuitively as people realize that there are different forms of greetings among different cultures.

The last two items on the list need to be treated a bit differently. When we rightly interpret the texts about jewelry and braided hair for women, I do not think that they prohibited such things *even at the time they were written*. Paul says that "women should *adorn themselves* in respectable apparel, with modesty and self control, not with braided hair and gold or pearls or costly attire" (1 Timothy 2:9). Paul is not saying that women should never wear such things. He is saying that those things should not be considered the source of their beauty. That is not how they should "adorn themselves."

This sense of the prohibition becomes even more clear in 1 Peter 3:3. The English Standard Version, which is very literal at this point, translates the passage as follows:

> Do not let your adorning be external—the braiding of hair, the wearing of gold, *or the putting on of clothing*—but let your adorning be the hidden person of the heart with the imperishable beauty of a gentle and quiet spirit, which in God's sight is very precious. (1 Peter 3:3–4)

If this passage forbids braiding of hair and wearing of gold, then it must also forbid "the putting on of clothing"! But surely Peter was not telling women they should wear no clothes to church! He was rather saying that those external things should not be what they look to for their "adorning," for their source of attractiveness and beauty to others. It should rather be the inner character qualities he mentions.[124] Therefore I do not think that the statements about jewelry and braided hair for women, when rightly understood, are "culturally relative" commands. They have direct application to women today as well.[125]

Finally, should men be "lifting holy hands" in prayer today? I think this may be transcultural and that we should consider restoring it to our practice of prayer (and praise) in evangelical circles today. Many Christians already do this in worship, and what influences my thinking is a frequent Old Testament pattern of lifting hands or stretching out hands to God in prayer (see, for example, Exodus 9:29; 1 Kings 8:38; Psalm 28:2; 63:4; 134:2; 143:6; Lamentations 3:41). On the other hand, since this is an outward, physical action (and thus

---

124. Some translations of 1 Peter 3:3 say that women should not put on "fine clothes" (so NIV; similarly RSV, NRSV, NLT, NKJV), but there is no adjective modifying "clothing" (Greek *himation*), and the ESV, NASB, and KJV have translated it more accurately.

125. I realize that others might argue that such braided hair and jewelry in the first century was recognized as an outward symbol of low moral character, and that was the reason that Paul and Peter prohibited it. I'm not persuaded by this because Peter still prohibits the "wearing of clothing," and I cannot think that only women of low moral character wore clothes in the first century. But if someone does take this position, it does not matter much for my argument, for this would then simply be one additional physical action that carries a symbolic meaning, and in this case also the prohibition would not be one that would apply in the same way to women who wanted to wear braided hair or jewelry today, since those things would not convey that meaning in modern society.

some may think that it falls in the same category as a holy kiss or the washing of feet), I can understand that others conclude that this is simply a variable cultural expression of an inward heart attitude toward God and dependence on Him and focus on Him in our prayers. It seems to me that there is room for Christians to differ on this question, but in any case it is not a complicated enough question that it requires Webb's entire "redemptive-movement hermeneutic" to encourage us to move beyond the ethic of the commands that we find in the New Testament.

Is it really that simple? Are the only matters in dispute about cultural relativity just these simple physical items or actions, all of which carry symbolic meaning? Perhaps I have missed one or two other examples,[126] but I suspect it really is that simple. I believe God has given us a Bible that He intends believers to be able to understand (what has traditionally been called the clarity or the perspicuity of Scripture). Surely the question is not as complex and confusing as Webb's book portrays it.

The general principle is this: *Some commands of Scripture concerning physical actions that carry symbolic meaning are rightly obeyed through different actions that still convey a similar meaning in each culture.* (I say "some commands" because baptism and the Lord's Supper are exceptions: They involve physical actions that are tied in many ways to the central events of redemptive history, and these actions should not be changed.)

Someone may object, what about all those other passages Webb lists at the beginning of his book (pp. 14–15), passages that people find so difficult to classify regarding the question of cultural relativity?

There are other widely accepted principles of biblical interpretation that explain why many other commands in the Bible are not binding today. These principles of interpretation, however, are far different from Webb's principles, because they argue that certain commands are not binding on Christians today because of *theological convictions about the nature of the Bible and its history*, not because of *cultural analysis* or because of convictions about *cultural relativity*, and surely not because of any conviction that the New Testament commands were simply representative of a transitional ethic beyond which we need to move as we find a better ethic in today's society.

The following list gives some kinds of commands in the Bible that Christians do not have to obey in any literal or direct sense today (a fact that is evident apart from Webb's "redemptive-movement hermeneutic"):

---

126. I am not saying that all physical actions with symbolic meaning are culturally variable, but most are. At least two are not, because the New Testament gives commands indicating that baptism and the Lord's Supper should be observed in the church for all time, since they are given by Jesus as abiding symbols (and more than symbols) to be observed by the New Covenant people of God.

1. The details of the Mosaic law code, which were written for people under the Mosaic covenant.[127]
2. Pre-Pentecost commands for situations unique to Jesus' earthly ministry (such as "go nowhere among the Gentiles" in Matthew 10:5).
3. Commands that apply only to people in the same life situation as the original command (such as "bring the cloak...and above all the parchments" in 2 Timothy 4:13, and also "no longer drink only water" in 1 Timothy 5:23). I would also put in this category Acts 15:29, which is a command for people in a situation of Jewish evangelism in the first century: "That you abstain from what has been sacrificed to idols, and from blood, and from what has been strangled" (note that Paul himself explicitly allows the eating of foods sacrificed to idols in 1 Corinthians 10).
4. Everyone agrees that there are some passages, especially in Jesus' earthly teaching, that are difficult to understand in terms of how broadly we should apply them. Passages like, "Do not refuse the one who would borrow from you" (Matthew 5:42) must be interpreted in the light of the whole of Scripture, including passages that command us to be wise and to be good stewards of what God has entrusted to us. But *these are not questions of cultural relativity*, nor do these difficult passages cause us to think that we must move beyond Jesus' teaching to some kind of higher and better ethic. We agree that we are to be subject to this teaching and to obey it, and we earnestly seek to know exactly how Jesus intends us to obey it.
5. There are differences among Christians today on how much we should try to follow commands regarding the miraculous working of the Holy Spirit such as, "Heal the sick, raise the dead, cleanse lepers, cast out demons" (Matthew 10:8). Some Christians think we should obey those commands directly, and they seek to do exactly what Jesus commanded. Other Christians believe that these commands were given only for that specific time in God's sovereign work in the history of redemption. But the important point here is that these differences are *theological*. This is not a dispute over whether certain commands are *culturally relative* because the point at issue is not one of ancient culture versus modern culture, but is rather a theological question about the teaching of the whole Bible concerning the working of miracles, and concerning God's purpose for miracles at various points in the history of redemption.

---

127. I realize that many people, including me, would argue that in various ways laws in the Mosaic law code give us guidance on the kinds of things that are pleasing and displeasing to God today. Trying to decide in what way these various laws should guide us, however, is one of the more difficult questions in biblical interpretation. But I know of no Christians who would say that Christians today are actually under the Mosaic covenant, and therefore bound to obey all of the commands in the Mosaic covenant, including the commands about sacrifices and clean and unclean foods, and so forth.

After we have made these qualifications, how much of the New Testament is left? Vast portions of the New Testament are still easily and directly applicable to our lives as Christians today, and many other passages are applicable with only minor changes to modern equivalents. As I was preparing to write this analysis of Webb's book, I read quickly through the New Testament epistles, and I was amazed how few of the commands found in the epistles raise any question at all about cultural relativity. (I encourage readers to try the same exercise for themselves.)

Where it is necessary to transfer a command to a modern equivalent, this is generally not difficult because there are sufficient similarities between the ancient situation and the modern situation, and Christian readers generally see the connection quite readily. It is not difficult to move from "the wages of the *laborers who mowed your fields*, which you kept back by fraud" (James 5:4) to "the wages of the *employees who work in your factory*, which you kept back by fraud." It is not difficult to move from "honor the *emperor*" (1 Peter 2:17) to "honor *government officials* who are set in authority over you." It is not difficult to move from "Masters, treat your *slaves* justly and fairly" to "Employers, treat your *employees* justly and fairly." It is not difficult to move from "*Slaves*, obey in everything those who are your earthly masters, not by way of eye-service, as people-pleasers, but with sincerity of heart, fearing the Lord" to "*Employees*, obey your employers" (with the general biblical principle that we are never to obey those in authority over us when obedience would mean disobedience to God's laws). It is not difficult to move from "food offered to idols" (1 Corinthians 8:10) to other kinds of things that encourage Christians to violate their conscience. And, to take one Old Testament example of a command that everyone believes tells us what God expects today, it is not difficult to move from "You shall not covet your neighbor's...ox" (Exodus 20:17) to "You shall not covet you neighbor's car or boat."

My suggestion, then, about the question of culturally relative commands, is that it is not that difficult a question. There are perhaps three to five "culturally relative" commands concerning physical actions that carry symbolic meaning (at least holy kiss, head covering, foot washing; perhaps short hair for men and lifting hands in prayer), but we still obey these by applying them in different forms today. There are other broad categories of commands (such as Mosaic laws) which are not binding on us because we are under the New Covenant. There are some fine points that require mature reflection (such as to what extent the details of the Old Testament show us what pleases God today). But the rest—especially the commands in the New Testament addressed to Christians in the New Covenant—were written for our benefit, and they are not for us to "move beyond," but to obey.

CHAPTER TEN

Evangelical Feminist Claims from Theology and from Ideas of Fairness and Justice

Some egalitarian claims are based on theological doctrines or on the general ideas of fairness and justice. For instance, doesn't the doctrine of the priesthood of all believers show that both men and women should be able to fill leadership roles in the church? And is the complementarian claim about parallels of subordination within the Trinity really valid? Might there not be a kind of "mutual submission" among the members of the Trinity? And wasn't Jesus' submission to His Father only for His time on the earth in any case?

With regard to questions of fairness, how can it be fair to prohibit a better-qualified woman from being a pastor just because she is a woman? And is it really fair to allow women to assume leadership roles on the mission field but prohibit them from taking these same roles here in the United States?

It is questions such as these that we consider in this chapter.

EGALITARIAN CLAIM 10.1: THE PRIESTHOOD OF ALL BELIEVERS: THE NEW TESTAMENT DOCTRINE OF THE PRIESTHOOD OF ALL BELIEVERS MEANS THAT BOTH MEN AND WOMEN ARE QUALIFIED TO FILL POSITIONS OF LEADERSHIP IN THE CHURCH.

The "priesthood of all believers" means that we no longer have to be represented before God by a priest. This is different from the situation in the Old Testament, where only priests from the tribe of Levi could enter the temple, and where only the high priest could enter the Holy of Holies, the inner part of the temple where God made His presence known among His people (Hebrews 9:6–7). In the New Testament we find that Jesus has become our great High Priest and that we belong to the New Covenant (Hebrews 9:11–12). Through Jesus all believers have access into the very presence of God (Hebrews 10:19–22), a spiritual truth vividly demonstrated when the curtain that closed off the Holy of Holies was torn in two from top to bottom when Jesus died (Matthew 27:51). Therefore Peter can say we are all a "holy priesthood" (1 Peter 2:5) and a "royal priesthood" (1 Peter 2:9). All believers are "priests" in the New Covenant.

But does this mean that everyone is qualified to be a pastor or elder in the church? Some egalitarians think so, such as Stanley Grenz:

> The sovereign Spirit calls different persons to various functions in the church, including oversight responsibilities. As the principle of *the universal priesthood of believers* indicates, the Spirit may base the choice on certain considerations. But gender is not an overriding factor that either qualifies or disqualifies a believer-priest for selection to the ordained office.[1]

Rebecca Groothuis writes,

> A viable and biblically consistent theology of sexuality must be firmly grounded in these biblical principles: the creation of man and woman as equally imaging God, *the priesthood of all believers*, the unique high priesthood of Christ, and the equality in spiritual status of women and men in Christ. The implications of these fundamental principles seem clearly to rule out any universal hierarchies or cosmic principles of male supremacy.[2]

Answer 10.1a: There is a difference between priesthood and the office of pastor or elder. Even though all believers are priests in the sense that we can draw near to God in prayer and worship without an earthly temple or a human priest, not every believer is qualified to be an elder or pastor or teacher in the church.

The office of elder (or pastor) has specific qualifications for leadership (for example, see 1 Timothy 3:1–7 and Titus 1:5–9). That is why churches don't say, "Anybody who wants to preach can preach a sermon next Sunday morning, since we hold to the priesthood of all believers," or "This morning we are passing around a sign-up sheet for elders, and anybody who wants to sign up can be an elder this year, since we hold to the priesthood of all believers." It is true that all believers are priests in that all can draw near to God (even children and brand new believers), but not all believers are qualified to be elders or pastors or teachers.

---

1. Grenz, *Women in the Church* (1995), 188 (italics added).
2. Groothuis, *Good News for Women* (1997), 232–33 (italics added). See also Brown, *Women Ministers* (1996), 191.

Answer 10.1b: The New Testament authors do not appeal to the priesthood of all believers when they discuss who is qualified to be a pastor or elder. They list several other qualifications, including maleness.

Both 1 Timothy 3:2 and Titus 1:6 require that an elder be a "husband of one wife." In addition, 1 Timothy 2:12 says a woman is not allowed "to teach or to exercise authority over a man," and these are the activities that are carried out by an elder or a pastor in the church. Therefore, New Testament authors do not think that the "priesthood of all believers" implies that women could be pastors or elders.

Answer 10.1c: We should never use one part of Scripture to draw conclusions that deny or contradict other parts of Scripture, but that is what this egalitarian claim does.

If the Bible is interpreted correctly, it will be seen to be internally consistent and its parts will not contradict each other. That is what Psalm 119 means when it says, "The *sum* of your word is truth, and every one of your righteous rules endures forever" (Psalm 119:160). The word *sum* indicates what results when we put various parts of God's Word together, when we combine them. The result is still "truth." In fact, if every part of the Bible is the Word of God, and if God is a God who "never lies" (Titus 1:2), then we would expect God's Word to be internally consistent and not self-contradictory.

But this egalitarian claim essentially asks us to use one truth of Scripture (the priesthood of all believers) to override or deny other passages of Scripture (1 Timothy 2:12; 3:2; Titus 1:6, along with other passages that establish a pattern of male leadership in the church). The result is to nullify the truthfulness or the authority of some parts of Scripture.

Egalitarian claim 10.2: No Eternal Submission of the Son: Complementarians mistakenly appeal to the Son being subject to the Father within the Trinity. First, this subjection existed only during Jesus' life on earth. Second, if the Son was eternally subject to the Father, then He could not be fully God. Third, scholars differ on this aspect of Trinitarian doctrine, so it is not certain anyway.

These objections to a parallel between the Father-Son relationship and the husband-wife relationship occur several times in egalitarian writings. Gilbert Bilezikian claims,

> It is much more appropriate, and theologically accurate, to speak of Christ's self-humiliation rather than of his subordination. Nobody subordinated him, and he was originally subordinated to no one....

> The frame of reference for every term that is found in Scripture to describe Christ's humiliation pertains to his ministry and not to his eternal state....
>
> Because there was no order of subordination within the Trinity prior to the Second Person's incarnation, there will remain no such thing after its completion. If we must talk of subordination it is only a functional or economic subordination that pertains exclusively to Christ's role in relation to human history.[3]

Rebecca Groothuis writes,

> If Christ's subordination is not limited to a specific project or function but characterizes his eternal relationship with God, then Christ is not merely functionally subordinate; he is by nature subordinate....
>
> It is by no means clear from Scripture that the members of the Godhead are related to one another in terms of an eternal structure of rule and submission. This is a debatable point of theology on which conservative scholars disagree.[4]

Answer 10.2a: There is substantial testimony in Scripture that the Son was subject to the Father before He came to live on earth.

Scripture frequently speaks of the Father-Son relationship within the Trinity, a relationship in which the Father "gave" His only Son (John 3:16) and "sent" the Son into the world (John 3:17, 34; 4:34; 8:42; Galatians 4:4). But if the Father shows His great love by the fact that He gave His Son, then He had to *be* Father *before* He could give His Son. The Son did not suddenly decide to become Son on the day He came to earth. The Trinity was not just Person A and Person B and Person C before Christ came to earth, for then there would have been no Father who could give and send His Son. The idea of giving His Son implies a headship, a unique authority for the Father *before* the Son came to earth. So even on the basis of John 3:16, the egalitarian claim that Jesus' submission to His Father was only during His time on earth is incorrect.

But the Father-Son relationship also existed *before* Creation.[5] The Father created through the Son, for "all things were made *through* him" (John 1:3), and "there is one God, the Father, *from* whom are all things...and one Lord, Jesus Christ, *through* whom are all things" (1 Corinthians 8:6). The Bible tells us that in these last days God "has spoken to us by his Son, whom he appointed the heir of all things, *through whom* also he created the world" (Hebrews 1:2). When the Bible discusses distinct actions of the members of the Trinity in Creation, this is the pattern: things were made "by" or "from" the Father and "through" the Son. But this also

---

3. Bilezikian, *Community 101* (1997), 190–91.
4. Groothuis, *Good News for Women*, 57.
5. Kevin Giles, *The Trinity and Subordinationism: The Doctrine of God and the Contemporary Gender Debate* (2002), incorrectly says that complementarians only argue from revelation concerning the Incarnation when they argue for the eternal subordination of the Son (17).

means that *before* Creation the Father was Father and the Son was Son. The Father had to *have* a Son before He could create a world *through* His Son. This means that they related as Father and Son before Creation. Again, the egalitarian claim that limits the Son's submission to the Incarnation[6] is incorrect.

In some places the Bible speaks of different roles for Father and Son *before* Creation. It was the Father who "predestined us" to be conformed to the image of His Son (Romans 8:29; compare 1 Peter 1:2). But if He "predestined us" to be like His Son, then, in the counsels of eternity in which predestination occurred, there had to be a Father who was predestining and a Son whom He decided we would be like. Paul also says that God the Father "chose us" in the Son "*before the foundation of the world*" (Ephesians 1:4). This means that before there was any Creation, before anything existed except God Himself, the Father was the one who chose, who initiated and planned, and, before creation, it was already decided that the Son would be the one to come to earth in obedience to the Father and die for our sins. Here is Paul's statement:

> Blessed be the God and Father of our Lord Jesus Christ, who has blessed us in Christ with every spiritual blessing in the heavenly places, even as he chose us in him *before the foundation of the world*, that we should be holy and blameless before him. In love he *predestined* us for adoption through Jesus Christ, according to the purpose of his will. (Ephesians 1:3–5)

Once again, the egalitarian claim that the Son's subordination to the Father was only for His time on earth is surely incorrect.

Bruce Ware adds a similar consideration from Revelation 13:8, which says, "and all who dwell on earth will worship [the beast], everyone whose name has not been written before the foundation of the world in the book of life of the Lamb that was slain." Ware writes,

> Revelation 13:8 likewise indicates that "the book of life" in which believers' names have been recorded is (1) "from the *foundation of the world*," and (2) is "of the *Lamb who has been slain*." Again we see clear evidence that the Father's purpose from eternity past was to send His Son, the Lamb of God, by which His own would be saved. The authority-obedience relation of Father and Son in the immanent Trinity is mandatory if we are to account for God the Father's eternal purpose to elect and save His people through His beloved Son.[7]

How do egalitarians answer these verses that show an eternal difference in role between the Father and Son before the world began? They ignore them. Most egalitarians who deny an eternal subordination of the Son to the Father do not treat these verses at all.

6. The word *Incarnation* refers to Christ's taking to Himself a human nature, like ours but free from sin.
7. Ware, "Tampering with the Trinity" (2002), 250.

Answer 10.2b: Christ was also subject to the authority of the Father while He was on earth as a man.

While Jesus was on earth, He was obedient to the commands of the Father, as many passages indicate.[8] In several of these verses there are also indications of a prior authority of the Father, an authority that reaches back before the Incarnation and indicates an eternal Father-Son relationship. Jesus says, "The Father is greater than I" (John 14:28). He says, "My food is to do the will of him who sent me and to accomplish his work" (John 4:34). He says, "I have come down from heaven, not to do my own will but the will of him who sent me" (John 6:38). But this means that prior to the Incarnation, there was a will of the Father that directed and guided what the Son would do when He came to earth.

Jesus also says, "The Father judges no one, but has given all judgment to the Son" (John 5:22). But if the Father *gave* the Son this authority to judge, then it had to be the Father's to give. There had to be a prior authority on the part of the Father, greater than the authority of the Son, by which the Father could have the ability and right to give judgment to the Son. One has to *have* authority before one can *delegate* authority. Similarly, Jesus says, "Truly, truly, I say to you, the Son can do nothing of his own accord, but only what he sees the Father doing. For whatever the Father does, that the Son does likewise" (John 5:19). Even when the Son prays to the Father and the Father grants what the Son asks (as in John 14:16), the relationship is the same, for the Son asks, and it is the Father's decision to grant or not to grant what is asked.

Answer 10.2c: What Christ gave up in coming to earth was glory and honor, not equal authority with the Father.

Gilbert Bilezikian claims that what Christ gave up in coming to earth was His equal authority with God the Father. Bilezikian says,

> One wonders where the equality came from that the Son let go in the *kenosis*. Eternal subordination precludes equality. The Biblical definition of the *kenosis* as the Son's refusal to exploit the status of equality he had with the Father attests to the fact that there was no subordination prior to the *kenosis*.[9]

Bilezikian's argument is as follows:

1. Christ gave up something when He "humbled himself" in Philippians 2:5–8 (this is what Bilezikian refers to as the *kenosis,* after the Greek word translated "made himself nothing" in Philippians 2:7).
2. What He must have given up was equal authority with the Father, since the passage says He "did not count *equality* with God a thing to be grasped" (v. 6).

---

8. Bruce Ware, for example, notes the following passages that indicate that Christ was sent to do the will of His Father: John 4:34; 5:23, 30, 37; 6:37–38, 57; 12:49 (Ware, "Tampering with the Trinity," 245).
9. Bilezikian, *Community 101,* 197.

3. Since the same passage says "he humbled himself *by becoming obedient* to the point of death" (v. 8), it implies that Christ was not obedient before the Incarnation.
4. Therefore He was not subordinate to the Father's authority prior to the Incarnation.

This argument is not convincing, however. Here is what Philippians 2:5–8 actually says:

> Have this mind among yourselves, which is yours in Christ Jesus, who, though he was in the form of God, did not count equality with God a thing to be grasped, but made himself nothing, taking the form of a servant, being born in the likeness of men. And being found in human form, he humbled himself by becoming obedient to the point of death, even death on a cross.

In response to Bilezikian, two things need to be said:

1. What Christ gave up was the honor and glory that was His in heaven. The text says nothing about giving up "equal authority" with the Father. The equality this passage talks about is *equality in glory and honor* in heaven, which Christ gave up in coming to earth. This glory and honor was restored to Him when God "highly exalted him" (v. 9).
2. The text does not say that Christ was *for the first time in all eternity* obedient to the Father when He became a man. It does not say that the Son was never obedient to the Father before that time. Rather, it focuses on what was new: obedience as a human being, and obedience to the point of death (v. 8).

Never before had the Son of God existed as a person who was also truly man. Never before had He humbled Himself to experience suffering and death as a result of obedience. This is what was new, but obedience to the Father was not new. Bilezikian's objection is not supported by Philippians 2.

Answer 10.2d: After Christ returned to heaven, He was still subject to the authority of the Father, and will be so forever.

In the future, the Son will be subject to the Father for all eternity. This is contrary to Gilbert Bilezikian's claim, "Because there was no order of subordination within the Trinity prior to the Second Person's incarnation, there will remain no such thing after its completion."[10] This is a baffling statement. It is baffling, first, because it talks about "no order of subordination within the Trinity prior to the Second Person's incarnation," but Bilezikian does not deal with any of those texts that speak of the Father predestining us in the Son or choosing us in the Son even "before the foundation of the world" (see above). How he can say "there was no order of subordination within the Trinity prior to the Second Person's incarnation" without dealing with those verses is unclear to me.

---

10. Ibid., 191.

Bilezikian's statement is also baffling because it says "there will remain no such thing after its completion." But what could Bilezikian mean by speaking of a time "after its completion" (that is, after the completion of the Incarnation)? If he means after Jesus returned to heaven in Acts 1, then many verses contradict him, for they say that Jesus ascended into heaven and assumed a place at the Father's right hand, which implies being subject to the Father's authority (for example, "Being therefore exalted at the right hand of God, and having received from the Father the promise of the Holy Spirit, he has poured out this that you yourselves are seeing and hearing," Acts 2:33; see more verses below). But if by the phrase "after its completion" Bilezikian means a time after Jesus ceases to be both fully man and fully God, then he has a strange view indeed of the Incarnation, for Scripture gives no indication that Jesus will ever cease to be both God and man: "Jesus Christ is the same yesterday and today and forever" (Hebrews 13:8). Jesus will remain both truly God and truly man forever, and it is troubling to see Bilezikian suggest otherwise, as if he thinks Christ's Incarnation will sometime come to an end.

There is much evidence in Scripture that after Christ returned to heaven, He was still subject to the authority of the Father. For example, the author of Hebrews says, "After making purification for sins, he sat down at the right hand of the Majesty on high" (Hebrews 1:3). To sit at the king's right hand in the ancient world indicated that one was second only to the king in authority, but it did not indicate authority equal to the king. For example, when the mother of James and John came to Jesus and asked, "Say that these two sons of mine are to sit, one at your right hand and one at your left, in your kingdom" (Matthew 20:21), she was not asking that they have authority equal to Jesus, but only that they be second to Him in authority. Jesus told James and John that that decision belonged to God the Father:

> He said to them, "You will drink my cup, but to sit at my right hand and at my left is not mine to grant, but it is for those for whom it has been prepared by my Father" (Matthew 20:23).[11]

In Psalm 110 there was a Messianic promise:

> The Lord says to my Lord:
> "Sit at my right hand,
> until I make your enemies your footstool." (v. 1)

This is not a promise that the Messiah would be equal to "the Lord" in authority, but that He would be second in authority, at the "right hand" of God. Jesus realized that He would fulfill that promise, for He quoted it in His conflict with the Pharisees (see Matthew 22:44). It indicated that He was to sit at the right hand of the Father.

---

11. See also Psalm 45:9: The queen is at the "right hand" of the king.

Why is this important? Because it shows that someone can be subordinate in authority to someone else but still be equal in being, equal in importance, equal in personhood. And if the Father and Son can be both equal and different in this way, then husband and wife in the image of God can be equal and different too. And thus the fundamental egalitarian objection, "If different, then not equal, and if equal, then not different," falls apart. This is why the debate about the Trinity is so important to this whole controversy.[12]

The promise that Jesus would sit at the Father's right hand is fulfilled after Jesus completes His work dying for us and rising from the dead. It is interesting to see how many times the Bible affirms that after Jesus' return to heaven He is still at the right hand of the Father, and therefore subordinate to the authority of the Father:

> Jesus said to him, "You have said so. But I tell you, from now on you will see the Son of Man seated *at the right hand of Power* and coming on the clouds of heaven." (Matthew 26:64)
>
> And Jesus said, "I am, and you will see the Son of Man seated *at the right hand of Power*, and coming with the clouds of heaven." (Mark 14:62)
>
> "But from now on the Son of Man shall be seated *at the right hand of the power of God.*" (Luke 22:69)
>
> "Being therefore exalted *at the right hand of God*, and having *received from the Father* the promise of the Holy Spirit, he has poured out this that you yourselves are seeing and hearing." (Acts 2:33)
>
> "God exalted him *at his right hand* as Leader and Savior, to give repentance to Israel and forgiveness of sins." (Acts 5:31)
>
> But he, full of the Holy Spirit, gazed into heaven and saw the glory of God, and Jesus standing *at the right hand of God*. And he said, "Behold, I see the heavens opened, and the Son of Man standing *at the right hand of God.*" (Acts 7:55–56)
>
> Who is to condemn? Christ Jesus is the one who died—more than that, who was raised—who is *at the right hand of God*, who indeed is interceding for us. (Romans 8:34)
>
> that he worked in Christ when he raised him from the dead and seated him *at his right hand* in the heavenly places. (Ephesians 1:20)

---

12. Nearly twenty-five years ago I wrote, "A proper understanding of the doctrine of the Trinity may well turn out to be the most decisive factor in finally deciding this current debate" (Grudem, review of Knight, *The New Testament Teaching on the Role Relationship of Men and Women*, for the *Journal of the Evangelical Theological Society* 22:4 [December 1979]: 375–76).

> If then you have been raised with Christ, seek the things that are above, where Christ is, seated *at the right hand of God.* (Colossians 3:1)

> He is the radiance of the glory of God and the exact imprint of his nature, and he upholds the universe by the word of his power. After making purification for sins, he sat down *at the right hand of the Majesty on high.* (Hebrews 1:3)

> And to which of the angels has he ever said, "Sit *at my right hand* until I make your enemies a footstool for your feet"? (Hebrews 1:13)

> Now the point in what we are saying is this: we have such a high priest, one who is seated *at the right hand of the throne of the Majesty in heaven.* (Hebrews 8:1)

> But when Christ had offered for all time a single sacrifice for sins, he sat down *at the right hand of God*, waiting from that time until his enemies should be made a footstool for his feet. (Hebrews 10:12–13)

> looking to Jesus, the founder and perfecter of our faith, who for the joy that was set before him endured the cross, despising the shame, and is seated *at the right hand of the throne of God.* (Hebrews 12:2)

> who has gone into heaven and is *at the right hand of God*, with angels, authorities, and powers having been subjected to him. (1 Peter 3:22)

Nowhere is this pattern reversed. Nowhere is it said that the Father sits at the Son's right hand. Nowhere does the Son give the Father the authority to sit with Him on His throne. The supreme authority always belongs to the Father. The egalitarian claim that Jesus was subject to the Father only during His life on earth is simply wrong.

Gilbert Bilezikian objects that other verses show the Son sitting *with* the Father on His throne.[13] This is true, as we see stated in various ways in the following verses:

> "The one who conquers, I will grant him to sit with me on my throne, as I also conquered and sat down with my Father on his throne." (Revelation 3:21)

> For the Lamb in the midst of the throne will be their shepherd,
> and he will guide them to springs of living water,
> and God will wipe away every tear from their eyes. (Revelation 7:17)

> She gave birth to a male child, one who is to rule all the nations with a rod of iron, but her child was caught up to God and to his throne. (Revelation 12:5)

---

13. A similar objection is made by Sumner, *Men and Women in the Church* (2003), 175.

> No longer will there be anything accursed, but the throne of God and of the Lamb will be in it, and his servants will worship him. (Revelation 22:3)

But these verses do not contradict the other verses that show Jesus at the right hand of God. Revelation 3:21 gives the answer: Just as we will sit *with* Christ on His throne, but He will still have the supreme authority, so Christ sits with the Father on His throne, but the Father still has supreme authority. (Bilezikian does not quote the first half of Revelation 3:21, which disproves his argument.) Both facts are true: Jesus sits with the Father on His throne, and Jesus is still at the right hand of the Father and the throne can still be called "his [that is, the Father's] throne." Similarly, Revelation 7, which refers to "the Lamb in the midst of the throne" (v. 17), also can say, "Salvation belongs to our God who sits on the throne, and to the Lamb!" (v. 10).

In addition to these there are passages that say that Christ in heaven "intercedes" for us—that is, He brings requests on our behalf to the Father:

> Who is to condemn? Christ Jesus is the one who died—more than that, who was raised—who is at the right hand of God, who indeed *is interceding for us.* (Romans 8:34)

> Consequently, he is able to save to the uttermost those who draw near to God through him, since *he always lives to make intercession for them.* (Hebrews 7:25)

These passages also indicate that the Father has greater authority than the Son, for the Son does not command the Father; rather, He brings requests, and these actions are appropriate to a relationship in which the Father is the one in authority over the Son.[14]

There is abundant testimony in Scripture that after Jesus returned to heaven, He was still subject to the authority of God the Father. His position is at the Father's right hand, and He intercedes for us before His Father. The very names "Father" and "Son" also attest to this, and those names have belonged to the Father and the Son forever. From eternity past to infinite eternity future the Son is subject to the Father's authority yet equal to Him in being, in value, in personhood, and in honor. Similarly in marriage as God created it, husbands and wives are equal in value and personhood, and should be equally honored as bearers of the image of God, but wives are also to be subject to the authority of their husbands. Equal *and* different. (See answer 10.2i, pp. 425–29, on the failure of egalitarians to deal with these verses.)

---

14. In both Romans 8:34 and Hebrews 7:25, the word *intercede* translates the Greek term *entugchanō*. This word is generally used in contexts of bringing requests or petitions before someone of greater authority. For example, Festus uses this word to say to King Agrippa, "You see this man about whom the whole Jewish people *petitioned* me" (Acts 25:24). Paul also uses it of Elijah when he "*appeals* to God against Israel" (Romans 11:2). In these cases the requests are made to the Roman governor or to God, that is, to someone in a position of high authority. Literature outside the New Testament provides further examples of *entugchanō* used in similar ways: See, for example, Wisd. 8:20 ("I *asked* the Lord, and made petition to him"); 1 Macc. 8:32; 3 Macc. 6:37 ("They *requested* the King, that he send them back to their home"); 1 Clem. 56:1; Epistle of Polycarp to the Philippians 4:3; Josephus, *Antiquities* 12:18; 16:170 (the Jews in Cyrene *petition* Marcus Agrippa concerning people in their land who are falsely collecting taxes). The word is used to refer to bringing requests to someone in greater authority.

Answer 10.2e: The Son will forever be subject to the authority of the Father.

The authority of the Father over the Son (and the Holy Spirit), an authority that never began but was always part of the eternal relationship among the members of the Trinity, will also never end. Paul tells us that after the last enemy, death, is destroyed, "the Son himself will also be subjected to him who put all things in subjection under him, that God may be all in all" (1 Corinthians 15:28).

Bilezikian's comment on this verse denies that it signifies anything eternal: "Any inference relative to an eternal state of subjection that would extend beyond this climactic fulfillment is not warranted by this text or any other Biblical text."[15] But this is not true, because this verse marks the beginning of the eternal state, where death, the "last enemy" (1 Corinthians 15:26), has been destroyed, and we live with God forever. This is at the end of the time during which Christ reigns "until he has put all his enemies under his feet" (v. 25). It is at "*the end*, when he delivers the kingdom to God the Father after destroying every rule and every authority and power" (v. 24).

Thus, in 1 Corinthians 15:28, Scripture shows us the beginning of the eternal state with the Son subject to the Father. Unless there is strong evidence in Scripture showing a later change in that situation (which there is not), the passage leads us to think that that situation will continue for eternity. Prior to the foundation of the world, the Son was eternally subject to the Father. In Creation, the Son was subject to the Father. During His time on earth, the Son was subject to the Father. When He returned to sit at the Father's right hand, the Son was subject to the Father. As He today intercedes for us, the Son is subject to the Father. When the last enemy, death, is finally destroyed, the Son will be subject to the Father. The relationship between Father and Son has always been that way, and it will be that way forever.

Does this mean that the Son is eternally inferior to the Father? No, He is equal to the Father in His being or essence, for He is fully God. It simply means that along with equality in attributes and deity and value and honor, there is also a subordination in role, and the Son is subject to the Father's authority.

This relationship between Father and Son that is seen in so many passages is never reversed, not in predestination before the foundation of the world, not in creation, not in sending the Son, not in directing what the Son would do, not in granting authority to the Son, not in the Son's work of redemption, not in the Son's return to sit at the Father's right hand, not in the Son's handing over the kingdom to God the Father, never. Never does Scripture say that the Son sends the Father into the world, or that the Holy Spirit sends the Father or the Son into the world, or that the Father obeys the commands of the Son or the Holy Spirit. Never does Scripture say that the Son predestined us to be conformed to the image of the Father. The role of planning, directing, sending, and commanding the Son belongs to the Father only.

---

15. Bilezikian, *Community 101*, 191.

And just as Father and Son are equal and different, so God has made husband and wife to be equal and different.

Answer 10.2f: The Christian church throughout history has affirmed both the subordination of the Son to the Father with respect to their roles, and the equality of the Son with the Father with respect to their being.

It is not responsible scholarship, nor is it fair to readers who may have little knowledge of church history, for Gilbert Bilezikian to claim that the position he holds is the historical doctrine of the Trinity, for it is not. Bilezikian first denies any subordination of the Son to the Father prior to the Incarnation:

> Because there was no order of subordination within the Trinity prior to the Second Person's incarnation, there will remain no such thing after its completion. If we must talk of subordination it is only a functional or economic subordination that pertains exclusively to Christ's role in relation to human history.

Then he says,

> Except for occasional and predictable deviations, *this is the historical Biblical trinitarian doctrine* that has been defined in the creeds and generally defended by the Church, at least the western Church, throughout the centuries.[16]

But when Bilezikian denies the eternal subordination of the Son to the Father (which exists along with equality in essence or being), he is denying the teaching of the church throughout history, and it is significant that he gives no quotations, no evidence, to support his claim that his view "is the historical Biblical trinitarian doctrine." This statement is simply not true. The vast majority of the church has affirmed equality in being *and* subordination in role among the persons in the Trinity, not simply during the time of Incarnation, but in the eternal relationships between the Father and the Son. The great, historic creeds affirm that there is an eternal difference between the Father and Son, not in their being (for they are equal in all attributes and the three persons are just one "being" or "substance"), but in the way they relate to one another. There is an ordering of their relationships such that the Father eternally is first, the Son second, and the Holy Spirit third.

The doctrine of the "eternal generation of the Son" or the "eternal begetting of the Son" found expression in the Nicene Creed (325 AD) in the phrase "begotten of the Father before all worlds," and in the Chalcedonian Creed (451 AD) in the phrase "begotten before all ages of the Father according to the Godhead." In the Athanasian Creed (4th–5th century AD) we read the expressions "The Son is of the Father alone: not made, nor created: but begotten"

16. Ibid., 191–92. For a discussion of the claims of Kevin Giles in his book *The Trinity and Subordinationism* (2002), see answer 10.2i (pp. 425–427).

and "the Son of God is...God, of the Substance of the Father; begotten before the worlds." It is open to discussion whether these were the most helpful expressions,[17] but it is not open to discussion whether the entire church throughout history has in these creeds affirmed that there was an *eternal* difference between the way the Son related to the Father and the way the Father related to the Son; that in their relationships the Father's role was primary and had priority, and the Son's role was secondary and was responsive to the Father; and that the Father was eternally Father and the Son was eternally Son.

We may describe this difference in relationship in other terms, as later theologians did (such as speaking of the eternal subordination of the Son with respect to role or relationship, not with respect to substance), and still say we are holding to the historic Trinitarian doctrine of the church. Yet we may not deny that there is *any* eternal difference in relationship between the Father and the Son, as Bilezikian and others do, and still claim to hold to the historic Trinitarian doctrine of the church.

Bilezikian gives no explanation of how he understands "begotten of the Father before all worlds" or "eternal generation" or "eternal begetting." It is remarkable that Bilezikian, in denying *any* eternal difference in relationship between the Father and the Son, gives no explanation for why he thinks he has not placed himself outside the bounds of the great Trinitarian confessions through history. And it is simply irresponsible scholarship to accuse all those who hold to the historic doctrine of the eternal subordination of the Son to the Father (in role, not in being) of "tampering with the doctrine of the Trinity" and coming close to Arianism and engaging in "hermeneutical bungee jumping."[18] It is Bilezikian, not complementarians, who is tampering with the doctrine of the Trinity. Bilezikian is certainly free to deny any eternal differences in the Father-Son relationship if he wishes, but he may not truthfully say that a denial of these eternal differences has been the historic doctrine of the church.

Here is a sampling of these creeds and the relevant expressions from them:

> Nicene Creed (325/ 381 AD):
>
> And in one Lord Jesus Christ, the only-begotten Son of God, *begotten of the Father before all worlds,* Light of Light, very God of very God, *begotten, not made*, being of one substance with the Father...and ascended into heaven, and *sitteth on the right hand of the Father*
>
> Chalcedonian Creed (451 AD):
>
> *begotten before all ages of the Father* according to the Godhead

17. For further discussion of the phrase "only begotten" and the Greek term *monogenēs* on which it is based, see Grudem, "The *Monogenēs* Controversy: 'Only' or 'Only Begotten'?" Appendix 6 in *Systematic Theology* (1994), 1233–34. (This appendix is in the revised printing only, from 2000 onward.)
18. For these accusations see Bilezikian, "Hermeneutical Bungee-Jumping," 57–68. The same article is found in Bilezikian, *Community 101*, 187–202.

Athanasian Creed (4th–5th century AD):

The Son is of the Father alone: not made, nor created: but *begotten*.... Our Lord Jesus Christ, the Son of God, is God and Man; God, of the Substance of the Father; *begotten before the worlds:* and Man, of the Substance of his Mother, born in the world.... He *sitteth on the right hand* of the Father God Almighty

Thirty-nine Articles (Church of England, 1571):

The Son, which is the Word of the Father, *begotten from everlasting of the Father*, the very and eternal God, and of one substance with the Father

Westminster Confession of Faith (1643–46):

the Father is of none, neither begotten, nor proceeding; *the Son is eternally begotten of the Father* (chapter 2, paragraph 3)

Bilezikian quotes no church historians, no creeds, no other recognized theologians when he affirms that his view is the historic doctrine of the church. But it is not difficult to find many theologians and historians of doctrine who differ with Bilezikian's unsubstantiated affirmation.

For example, concerning this inter-Trinitarian relationship between the Father and the Son, Charles Hodge (1797–1878), the great Princeton theologian whose monumental *Systematic Theology* has now been in print for 140 years, wrote about the Nicene Creed:

> The Nicene doctrine includes...the principle of the subordination of the Son to the Father, and of the Spirit to the Father and the Son. But this subordination does not imply inferiority.... The subordination intended is only that which concerns the mode of subsistence and operation.... The creeds are nothing more than a well-ordered arrangement of the facts of Scripture which concern the doctrine of the Trinity. They assert the distinct personality of the Father, Son, and Spirit...*and their consequent perfect equality*; and *the subordination of the Son to the Father, and of the Spirit to the Father and the Son, as to the mode of subsistence and operation*. These are scriptural facts, to which the creeds in question add nothing; and it is *in this sense they have been accepted by the Church universal.*[19]

The section in the Nicene Creed to which Hodge refers is this:

> And in one Lord Jesus Christ, the *only-begotten Son of God, begotten of the Father before all worlds*, Light of Light, very God *of very God, begotten, not made*, being of one substance with the Father.

---

19. Hodge, *Systematic Theology* (1871–73), 1:460–62 (italics added). A survey of historical evidence showing affirmation of the eternal subordination of the Son to the authority of the Father is found in Kovach and Schemm, "A Defense of the Doctrine of the Eternal Subordination of the Son" (1999), in *Journal of the Evangelical Theological Society*, 461–76. See also Grudem, *Systematic Theology*, 248–52.

Hodge is saying that in the phrases "only-begotten Son of God," and "begotten of the Father before all worlds," and "of very God," and "begotten, not made," the Nicene Creed is referring to an *eternal* distinction in relationship between the Father and the Son such that the Son was seen to be eternally "of" or "from" the Father (the Father was not "of" or "from" the Son). The Father has eternally been Father and the Son has eternally been Son. The expressions "only-begotten" and "begotten, not made," indicated to the authors of the Nicene Creed that there was a difference in the relationship between Father and Son such that the Son was the one "begotten" by the Father. But this difference in their relationship *never began* ("begotten of the Father before all worlds"), and it did not mean that the Son was created or derived His being from the Father ("begotten, not made"), because the Father and Son are of the same substance or essence ("of one substance with the Father"). It simply meant that the Father and Son *related* as Father and Son for all eternity. But that means there was an eternal difference in their roles, and it implies that the Father eternally was the one who initiated, planned, and directed, and the Son was the one who eternally responded to the Father and agreed to carry out the will of the Father, as He subsequently did in Creation and in redemption.

Other theologians in the history of the church have made similar affirmations, confirming Charles Hodge's statement that these concepts "have been accepted by the church universal."[20] Here is a sampling of some statements:[21]

Augustine (354–430):

> If however the reason why the Son is said to have been sent by the Father is simply that *the one is the Father and the other the Son* then there is nothing at all to stop us believing that the Son is equal to the Father and consubstantial and co-eternal, and yet that *the Son is sent by the Father*. Not because one is greater and the other less, but *because one is the Father and the other the Son*; *one is the begetter, the other begotten*; the first is the one from whom the sent one is; the other is the one who is from the sender. For *the Son is from the Father, not the Father from the Son*. In the light of this we can now perceive that the Son is not just said to have been sent because the Word became flesh, but that he was sent in order for the Word to become flesh, and by his bodily presence to do all that was written. That is, we should understand that it was not just the man who the Word became that was sent, but that the Word was sent to become man. For he was not sent in virtue of some disparity of power or substance or anything in him that was not equal to the Father, but *in virtue of the Son being from the Father, not the Father being from the Son.*[22]

---

20. Hodge, *Systematic Theology,* 1:462.
21. The following list of quotations was mostly compiled by my student Mark Stevenson at Trinity Evangelical Divinity School in March 1995, but I have made some additions to his list.
22. St. Augustine, *The Trinity*, vol. 5, IV.27, as quoted in Ware, "Tampering with the Trinity," 246; italics added. The same quotation can be found in *NPNF,* ser. 1, 3:83 (4.20.27).

Thomas Aquinas (1224–1274):

As the Father is not from another, it is in no way fitting for Him to be sent, but only for the Son and the Holy Spirit.[23]

John Calvin (1509–1564):

It is not fitting to suppress the distinction that we observe to be expressed in Scripture. It is this: ***to the Father is attributed the beginning of activity, and the fountain and wellspring of all things;*** to the Son, wisdom, counsel, and the ordered disposition of all things; but to the Spirit is assigned the power and efficacy of that activity. Indeed, although the eternity of the Father is also the eternity of the Son and the Spirit, since God could never exist apart from his wisdom and power, and we must not seek in eternity a *before* and *after*, nevertheless ***the observance of an order*** is not meaningless or superfluous, when the Father is thought of first, then from him the Son, and finally from both the Spirit.[24]

Charles Hodge (1797–1878):

Notwithstanding that the Father, Son, and Spirit are the same in substance, and equal in power and glory, it is no less true, according to the Scriptures, (a) That the Father is first, the Son second, and the Spirit third. (b) The Son is of the Father (*ek theou,* the *logos, eikōn, apaugasma tou theou*); and the Spirit is of the Father and of the Son. (c) The Father sends, and the Father and Son send the Spirit. (d) The Father operates through the Son, and the Father and Son operate through the Spirit. ***The converse of these statements is never found. The Son is never said to send the Father, nor to operate through Him; nor is the Spirit ever said to send the Father, or the Son, or to operate through them.*** The facts contained in this paragraph are summed up in the proposition: ***In the Holy Trinity there is a subordination of the Persons as to the mode of subsistence and operation. . . .***

There are some acts which are predominantly referred to the Father, others to the Son, and others to the Spirit. The Father creates, elects, and calls; the Son redeems; and the Spirit sanctifies. And, on the other hand, there are certain acts, or conditions, predicated of one person of the Trinity, which are never predicated of either of the others. Thus, generation belongs exclusively to the Father, filiation to the Son, and procession to the Spirit. This is the form in which the doctrine of the Trinity lies in the Bible. The above statement involves no philosophical element. It is simply an arrangement of the clearly revealed facts bearing on this subject. ***This is the form in which the doctrine has always entered into the faith of the Church,*** as a part of its religious convictions and experience.[25]

---

23. Thomas Aquinas, *Summa Theologica* 1a, 43.1 (as cited in Edmund J. Fortman, *The Triune God* [1982], 209).
24. John Calvin, *Institutes of the Christian Religion* (1960), 2-vol. ed., 1:13.18, 142–43.
25. Hodge, *Systematic Theology*, 1:444–45.

Under a section titled "The Mutual Relation of the Persons of the Trinity," Hodge writes:

On this subject the Nicene doctrine includes—

1. The principle of *the subordination of the Son to the Father,* and of the Spirit to the Father and the Son. *But this subordination does not imply inferiority.* For as the same divine essence with all its infinite perfections is common to the Father, Son, and Spirit, there can be no inferiority of one person to the other in the Trinity.... The subordination intended is only that which concerns the mode of subsistence and operation, implied in the Scriptural facts that the Son is of the Father operates through the Son, and the Father and the Son through the Spirit....

The creeds [Nicea and Constantinople] are nothing more than a well-ordered arrangement of the facts of Scripture which concern the doctrine of the Trinity. They assert the distinct personality of the Father, Son, and Spirit; their mutual relation as expressed by those terms; their absolute unity as to substance or essence, and their consequent perfect equality; and *the subordination of the Son to the Father, and of the Spirit to the Father and the Son, as to the mode of subsistence and operation. These are Scriptural facts to which the creeds in question add nothing; and it is in this sense they have been accepted by the Church universal.*[26]

B. B. Warfield (1851–1921):

There is, of course, no question that in "modes of operation," as it is technically called—that is to say, in the functions ascribed to the several Persons of the Trinity in the redemptive process, and, more broadly, *in the entire dealing of God with the world— the principle of subordination is clearly expressed.* The Father is first, the Son is second, and the Spirit is third, in the operations of God as revealed to us in general, and very especially in those operations by which redemption is accomplished.[27]

26. Ibid., 460–62.

27. B. B. Warfield, *The Works of B. B. Warfield* (1927), 10-vol. ed., 2:165ff. Warfield goes on to question how we can derive from Scripture any idea of an eternal subordination of the Son to the Father (163–67), but his purpose there seems mainly to be to guard against any idea that the Son is a lesser or different being from the Father, or that the Son has less power than the Father. Warfield does not deny the eternal subordination of the Son to the Father, but he also comes short of actually affirming it in this article. He does affirm (in the statement above) an eternal subordination with respect to all the activities of the Father and Son in the world (which would include not just redemption but also creation and providence and final judgment and the eternal state, and which thus differs with Bilezikian). In this article Warfield also fails to give any explicit consideration to those passages (such as Ephesians 1:4; Romans 8:29 and others cited above) that show a subordination of the Son to the Father before the world was made.

Augustus H. Strong (1836–1921):

> Father, Son, and Holy Spirit, while equal in essence and dignity, stand to each other in an order of personality, office, and operation.... *The subordination of the person of the Son to the person of the Father to be officially first, the Son second, and the Spirit third, is perfectly consistent with equality.* Priority is not necessarily superiority. *The possibility of an order, which yet involves no inequality, may be illustrated by the relation between man and woman.* In office man is first and woman is second, but woman's soul is worth as much as man's; *see 1 Cor 11:3.*[28]

Louis Berkhof (1873–1957):

> The only subordination of which we can speak, is a subordination in respect to order and relationship.
>
> d. The subsistence and operation of the three persons in the divine Being is marked by a certain definite order. There is a certain order in the ontological Trinity. In personal subsistence the Father is first, the Son second, and the Holy Spirit third. It need hardly be said that this order does not pertain to any priority of time or of essential dignity, but only to the logical order of derivation. The Father is neither begotten by, nor proceeds from any other person; the Son is eternally begotten of the Father, and the Spirit proceeds from the Father and the Son from all eternity. *Generation and procession take place within the Divine Being, and imply a certain subordination as to the manner of personal subsistence, but not subordination as far as the possession of the divine essence is concerned. This ontological Trinity and its inherent order is the metaphysical basis of the economical Trinity.*[29]

Church historian Philip Schaff (1819–1893) writes:

> The Nicene fathers still teach, like their predecessors, a certain *subordinationism*,[30] which seems to conflict with the doctrine of consubstantiality. But we must distinguish between a subordinationism of essence (*ousia*) and a *subordinationism of hypostasis, of order and dignity.* The former was denied, the latter affirmed.[31]

---

28. Strong, *Systematic Theology* (1907), 342, with references to other writers.
29. Berkhof, *Systematic Theology* (1939), 88–89.
30. Schaff uses *subordinationism* to refer not to the heresy by which the Son is thought to have an inferior *being* to the Father, but to the orthodox teaching that the Son has a subordinate *role* to the Father.
31. Philip Schaff, *History of the Christian Church* (1971), 3:681.

And historian J. N. D. Kelley similarly says, speaking of the Cappadocian father Gregory of Nyssa:

> It is clearly Gregory's doctrine that the Son acts as an agent, no doubt in subordination to the Father Who is the fountainhead of the Trinity, in the production of the Spirit.... As stated by the Cappadocians, however, the idea of the twofold procession from Father through Son lacks all trace of subordinationism, for its setting is a wholehearted recognition of the homoousion of the Spirit.[32]

Finally, church historian Geoffrey Bromiley writes:

> Eternal generation...is the phrase used to denote the inter-Trinitarian relationship between the Father and the Son as is taught by the Bible. "Generation" makes it plain that there is a divine sonship prior to the incarnation (cf. John 1:18; 1 John 4:9), that there is thus a distinction of persons within the one Godhead (John 5:26), and that between these persons *there is a superiority and subordination of order* (cf. John 5:19; 8:28). "Eternal" reinforces the fact that the generation is not merely economic (i.e. for the purpose of human salvation as in the incarnation, cf. Luke 1:35), but essential, and that as such it cannot be construed in the categories of natural or human generation. Thus it does not imply a time when the Son was not, as Arianism argued.... Nor does his subordination imply inferiority.... The phrase... corresponds to what God has shown us of himself in his own eternal being.... It finds creedal expression in the phrases "begotten of his Father before all worlds" (Nicene) and "begotten before the worlds" (Athanasian).[33]

This then has been the historic doctrine of the church. Egalitarians may differ with this doctrine today if they wish, and they may attempt to persuade us that they are right if they wish, but they must do this on the basis of arguments from Scripture, and they should also have the honesty and courtesy to explain to readers why they now feel it necessary to differ with the historic doctrine of the church as expressed in its major creeds.

32. J. N. D. Kelly, *Early Christian Doctrines* (1960), 263.
33. Geoffrey W. Bromiley, "Eternal Generation" (1984) in *EDT*, ed. Walter Elwell, 368.

Answer 10.2g: But the Son was also fully God. Therefore the very nature of the Trinitarian God shows that equality in personhood and value and abilities can exist along with being subject to the authority of another.

The subjection of the Son to the Father for all eternity, a subjection that never began but always existed, and a subjection that will continue eternally in the future, does not nullify the full deity of the Son. The Bible is very clear that the Son is fully God (see John 1:1–3; John 10:30; Romans 9:5; Titus 2:13; Hebrews 1:3, 8–10). Therefore the Son is both subject to the authority of the Father and at the same time equal to the Father in every attribute and in value and personhood forever. Equality in being and eternal differences in role exist together in the Trinity. Therefore equality in being and in value and in honor can exist together with differences in roles between husband and wife as well.

Bilezikian is unable even to admit that this historic view of the church is a possibility. Responding to Robert Letham, Bilezikian says,

> [Letham] gives lip service to the coequality of the members of the Trinity while, astoundingly, denying this equality in the same breath. One can appreciate the dilemma from his statement: "The coequality of the Father, Son and Holy Spirit in the unity of the one God takes the form of an order of subsistence." The confusion is flagrant.... It should be either equality and no hierarchy, or hierarchy and no equality.[34]

But what Bilezikian calls Letham's "confusion" is simply the historic view of the church: that the Father, Son, and Holy Spirit are equal in being and different in role. There is confusion here but it is not in the mind of Letham.

Sarah Sumner at first seems to affirm the orthodox doctrine of the subordination of the Son to the Father,[35] but then she modifies it with a novel proposal:

> So then, to whom is Christ finally subjected? God. Christ the Son is subject to the triune God of three persons. The Son is subjected to "the God and Father." And in that sense, the Son is subjected to himself. This is the doctrine of the Trinity.[36]

---

34. Bilezikian, *Community 101*, 196, quoting Robert Letham, "The Man-Woman Debate: Theological Comment," *WTJ* 52/1 (Spring 1990): 73.
35. Sumner, *Men and Women in the Church*, 177.
36. Ibid., 178. She returns to a similar theme later when she appeals to the doctrine of *perichoresis* or *circumincession* and says, "Circumincession also affirms that the action of one of the persons of the Trinity is also fully the action of the other two persons" (289n10). But Sumner misunderstands this doctrine. The term refers to the mutual indwelling of the persons of the Trinity in one another, and it may be used to affirm that the action of one person is the action of the being of God, but it should never be understood to deny that there are some things that one person of the Trinity does that the other persons do not do.
   Sumner (289n10) refers to Miroslav Volf, *After Our Likeness* (1998), to support her understanding of *perichoresis*, but Volf, unlike Sumner, is careful not to blur the distinctness of the persons: "Perichoresis refers to the reciprocal *interiority* of the Trinitarian persons...though...they do not cease to be distinct persons.... Perichoresis is 'coinherence in one another without any coalescence or commixture'" (209). (The quotations from Augustine that Sumner gives on p. 178 should not be understood to deny the distinctness of the persons in the Trinity, for Augustine does not do this.)

But this is not the doctrine of the Trinity. It sounds more like ancient modalism (the view that there is only one person in God) than Trinitarianism.[37] We should not understand the doctrine of the Trinity in a way that denies the distinctions between the Persons or that prevents us from saying that one Person in the Trinity does something the others do not do.

The Bible simply does not speak the way Sumner does. The Father did not send *Himself* into the world to become man and die for our sins; He sent the Son. The Father did not *Himself* bear the penalty for our sins (which is the ancient heresy of *patripassianism,* one form of modalism), nor did the Holy Spirit, but the Son did. The Son did not pray to *Himself*; He prayed to the Father. The Son does not sit at the right hand of *Himself* but at the right hand of the Father. And (contrary to Sumner) the Son is not subjected to *Himself*; He is subjected to the Father. To deny these distinctions is to deny that there are different persons in the Trinity, and thus it is to deny the Trinity.

This misunderstanding carries over into Sumner's statement about wives submitting to their husbands: She says, "the paradox of their oneness means that in submitting to her husband (with whom she is one), the wife ends up submitting to herself." She claims this is parallel to "Christ's submission to himself."[38] But Paul says husbands should love their wives "*as* their own bodies" (that is, in the same way as they love their own bodies),[39] and this is not because a husband's wife is identical with his own physical body, which would be nonsense.[40] If in submitting to her husband a wife is really just submitting to herself and not to a different person, then her husband has no distinct existence as a person. This also is nonsense.

Would Sumner say that when a wife disagrees with her husband, she should simply give in to him, since this is just giving in to herself?[41] This too is nonsense.

---

37. Modalism is also called modalistic monarchianism. See Craig Blaising, "Monarchianism," *EDT*, 727; also Grudem, *Systematic Theology*, 242.
38. Sumner, *Men and Women in the Church*, 198.
39. Ephesians 5:28. Greek *hōs* here is best understood to tell the manner in which husbands should love their wives. When Paul says later in that same verse, "He who loves his wife loves himself," he does not mean, "He who loves himself loves himself." He means that he who loves his wife will *also* bring good to himself as a result.
40. Sumner several times wrongly says that the wife *is* the husband's body (161, 167, 184). She derives this idea by drawing unjustified deductions from the metaphor of the husband being the "head" of the wife, but Scripture never says "the wife is the body of the husband." If the wife *is* the husband's body, then either he himself has two bodies, or he has no body and his wife is his body, and neither of these ideas can be true. Someone could draw all sorts of weird deductions from the metaphor of the husband as the head of the wife (she has no eyes, she can't see; she can't eat because she has no mouth; he can't walk, she is his feet and must walk for him; and so forth), but none of these are intended by the metaphor, which conveys the idea of authority and leadership but none of these other ideas. (See additional discussion of Sumner's understanding of *kephalē*, head, in chapter 6, pp. 208–9.)
41. Another novel theological concept of Sumner's is that "Mary was so human that Jesus got His male humanity from her.... Jesus received His humanity from Mary and His divinity from the Holy Spirit" (67). This is surely wrong, because Jesus did not "receive...His divinity" from anyone. He has eternally been the fully divine Son of God. Nor should we say that Jesus got His "male humanity" from Mary. If Jesus' human nature had been derived solely from Mary's physical body, He would have been her clone and would have had no Y chromosome, and therefore He would have been a woman. The doctrine of the Virgin Birth must be understood in a way consistent with Matthew 1:20, which says, "*that which is conceived in her* is from the Holy Spirit." What was conceived in Mary's womb was a human baby, and it was "from the Holy Spirit," which suggests (in light of our current understanding of how conception and growth occur) that half of the genetic material that Jesus received was miraculously created by the Holy Spirit, and half was from Mary.

Answer 10.2h: Egalitarians who claim that Christ's subordination to the Father was only for His time on earth still must agree that Christ's full deity existed along with subordination to the authority of the Father.

The egalitarian position is actually not helped very much by their claim that Christ's subordination to the authority of the Father was only during His time living on earth as a man. For even during that time, Christ was also fully God. For instance, even Gilbert Bilezikian says,

> So during his earthly life Christ remained a full participant in the Godhead, thereby retaining his divine subsistence. Paradoxically he also made himself subject to the Father when he assumed human personhood.[42]

But this means that during his time on earth Christ was both *equal in deity* to God the Father (equal in essence or being) and *subordinate in role* (He was obedient to the will of the Father). Even if we were to limit ourselves to those passages of Scripture that speak of Christ's obedience to His Father during His earthly ministry (and there are many such passages), it still proves that two persons can be equal in value and in their very being, and one can still be subordinate to the authority of the other. Thus it still provides a parallel to a husband and wife who are equal in the image of God but different in roles in marriage, and it still disproves the egalitarian claim that equality in the image of God cannot exist along with the idea that a husband has authority over his wife.

Answer 10.2i: Scholars who deny that the Son is eternally submissive to the Father do not prove their position from Scripture.

Regarding the eternal submission of the Son to the Father, Rebecca Groothuis says, "This is a debatable point of theology on which conservative scholars disagree." But egalitarian scholars who say that the Son was not eternally submissive to the authority of the Father *have not proven their position from Scripture*. Their general approach is to quote other theologians rather than dealing with the passages of Scripture that indicate such eternal differences in relationship within the Trinity. Usually they overlook or fail to deal with passages such as Ephesians 1:4, Romans 8:29, and 1 Peter 1:2, or passages such as John 1:3, 1 Corinthians 8:6, and Hebrews 1:2, which indicate that the Son was subject to the Father before the work of Creation began. Nor do they deal with 1 Corinthians 15:28 or the many passages in the epistles that indicate that the Son intercedes before the Father, that the Son is seated at the right hand of the Father, and that it is the Father's throne—passages that indicate that the Son will be subject to the authority of the Father for all eternity (see discussion of these passages on pp. 406-15, above).

42. Bilezikian, *Community 101*, 190.

The primary example of failure to argue from Scripture on this topic is Kevin Giles in *The Trinity and Subordinationism*. He tells readers that he will not argue from Scripture:

> In seeking to make a response to my fellow evangelicals who subordinate the Son to the Father, I do not appeal directly to particular scriptural passages to establish who is right or wrong.... I seek rather to prove that orthodoxy rejects this way of reading the Scriptures.[43]

Giles *does not think that citing verses from the Bible can resolve theological questions in general*. He thinks that the Bible can be read in different ways, and even though "given texts cannot mean just anything," he says that "more than one interpretation is possible."[44]

Giles even admits that it is possible to find evidence for the eternal subordination of the Son in Scripture: "I concede immediately that the New Testament *can* be read to teach that the Son is *eternally* subordinated to the Father."[45] But for him that is not decisive, because, as he tells us at the outset, "This book is predicated on the view that the Bible can often be read in more than one way, even on important matters."[46] Giles's fundamental approach should disturb evangelicals, for it means that appeals to Scripture can have no effect in his system. He can just reply, "Yes, the Bible can be read that way, but other readings are possible." And thus the voice of God's Word is effectively silenced.

How then does Giles think we should find out which view is right? The answer is found in church history: "In relation to the doctrine of the Trinity my argument is that the tradition should prescribe the correct reading."[47] For Giles then the tradition of the church becomes the supreme authority, an approach similar to Roman Catholicism but contrary to the Reformation doctrine of *sola Scriptura* ("Scripture alone"), and contrary to beliefs of evangelical Protestants.

Unfortunately, Giles's understanding of the historic view of the church on the Trinity is deeply flawed.[48] He continually blurs the distinction between the heresy of subordinationism (the view that the Son had a lesser being than the Father) and the orthodox view that the Son had a subordinate role but was equal in His being (this he also calls subordinationism, making the book simply a contribution to confusion on this topic).[49]

---

43. Giles, *The Trinity and Subordinationism* (2002), 25. The back cover identifies Giles as "vicar of St. Michael's Church (Anglican) in North Carlton, Australia."
44. Ibid., 10.
45. Ibid., 25.
46. Ibid., 9.
47. Ibid. He argues that the traditional view of the Trinity was right and should be followed, but the traditional view of male headship was wrong, and should not be followed, since on that matter no other reading was open to people in earlier centuries (9–10).
48. The book's title suggests that the whole book concerns the doctrine of the Trinity, but in fact only forty pages (32–71) contain discussion of the history of the doctrine of the Trinity prior to the nineteenth century. Pages 141–273 contain several other pieces he has written on men and women, on slavery, and on homosexuality.
49. Ibid., 16–17, 60–69. He even equates modern complementarians with ancient Arians who denied the deity of the Son (66), which is preposterous.

When he first deals with the Nicene Creed in his historical survey he does not even mention the crucial phrase "begotten of the Father before all worlds/ages."[50] He tries to show that the church historically has not held to the eternal subordination of the Son to the Father, and that theologians who claim otherwise are doing so only because they want to support their doctrine of male headship in marriage and the church (or, in the case of Princeton professor Charles Hodge, because they want to support their view of slavery).[51] If we are to accept Giles's thesis, we will have to believe that he is right and that world-renowned theologians and church historians such as Charles Hodge, Augustus Strong, Louis Berkhof, Philip Schaff, J. N. D. Kelley, and Geoffrey Bromiley have all misunderstood the history of the doctrine of the Trinity.[52] It seems more likely that Giles has misunderstood the historic view of the Trinity and has wrongly decided to believe that the teaching of the Bible cannot be used to settle doctrinal disputes.[53]

Another example of a failure to deal adequately with Scripture on this issue is Millard Erickson, in *God in Three Persons,*[54] where he argues against the eternal subordination of the Son. In dealing with the eternal relationships among the members of the Trinity, Erickson depends primarily not on Scripture but on several quotations from B. B. Warfield (some that are merely speculative statements in the original Warfield article, and several that simply show Warfield attempting to protect the doctrines of the Son and the Spirit from any thought of inferiority or derivation of being).[55] Erickson questions the idea of the eternal subordination of the Son to the Father,[56] but he fails to treat any of the passages just mentioned that indicate the Father's authority and primacy in the Father-Son relationship before the world was created (such as Ephesians 1:4; Romans 8:29; 1 Peter 1:2; John 1:3; 1 Corinthians 8:6; Hebrews 1:2). It is sur-

---

50. Ibid., 43–46. When he does mention the idea on p. 65 he misquotes the Nicene Creed as "eternally begotten of the Father," which is at best a free paraphrase of *ek tou patros gennēthenta pro panton ton aiōnōn*, "begotten of the Father before all ages." He mentions the expression there only to say that "eternally" opposed the Arian idea of the Son's creation in time, but fails to treat "begotten."
51. Ibid., 16, 74.
52. See pp. 417–22 above for quotations from these authors. Every one of these scholars has produced monumental works that have lasted or will last long beyond their lifetimes. Their names represent some of the highest scholarly achievements of evangelical scholarship in theology and in the history of doctrine in the nineteenth and twentieth centuries. This is significant because Giles differs with them not in the first instance over what people should believe today, but over a far simpler historical fact: What has the church believed throughout history? To claim that they have all been wrong about the history of a doctrine as central as the doctrine of the Trinity is a bold claim, to say the least.
53. An extensive and insightful review of Giles's book is Peter Schemm, "Kevin Giles's *The Trinity and Subordinationism*: A Review Article," *JBMW* 7/2 (Fall 2002): 67–78 (also available on-line at www.cbmw.org). Schemm points out several significant inaccuracies in Giles' reporting of the views of others (74), so his book should be read with caution. In addition, Mark Baddeley, "The Trinity and Subordinationism: A Response to Kevin Giles," *Reformed Theological Review* 63:1 (April 2004): 1-14, shows that Giles has quoted Karl Barth and Karl Rahner as saying exactly the opposite of what they actually say, and has seriously misrepresented the findings of the 1999 Sydney Anglican Diocese Doctrine Commission Report on the Trinity.
54. Millard Erickson, *God in Three Persons* (1995), 291–310.
55. See B. B. Warfield, "The Biblical Doctrine of the Trinity," in *Biblical Doctrines*, 164–67, as well as the discussion of Warfield in note 27, above.
56. Erickson, *God in Three Persons,* 309–10.

prising that Erickson can suggest that Christ's subordination to the Father while on earth is not representative of their relationship "before, or for that matter, after the earthly presence of the second person"[57] without dealing with any of these passages that talk about their relationship before Christ came to earth, or without dealing with 1 Corinthians 15:28, or the passages that talk about Christ being at the Father's right hand after His return to heaven.

Erickson writes, regarding Geoffrey Bromiley's summary of the doctrine of eternal generation as it has been held through the history of the church,

> Bromiley has correctly seen that generation, thought of as an eternal occurrence, involves subordination of the Son to the Father. His attempt to separate eternal subordination and superiority from inferiority seems to be a verbal distinction to which no real distinction corresponds. A temporal, functional subordination without inferiority of essence seems possible, but not an eternal subordination. And to speak of the superiority of the Father to the Son while denying the inferiority of the Son to the Father must be contradictory, unless indication is given of different senses in which these are being used.[58]

But this paragraph by Erickson is just stating the historic position of the church (which Bromiley correctly summarizes)[59] in apparently contradictory terms by leaving off the senses in which "superiority" and "inferiority" are intended. Bromiley specifies that it is a "superiority and subordination of order,"[60] similar to what I have here called "relationship." And yet there is no inferiority (or superiority) of being or essence: Father, Son, and Holy Spirit are each fully God and equal in all attributes.

Erickson's statement (that this is a "verbal distinction" but no "real distinction") is just another way of affirming the fundamental egalitarian claim that if there is equality there cannot be difference in role, and if there is difference in role there cannot be equality. Erickson himself admits that such a distinction is possible for a time ("a temporal, functional subordination without inferiority of essence seems possible"), but if it is possible for a time without denying the equality of the Son with the Father in essence, then why is it not possible for eternity? That is what many texts of Scripture (not treated by Erickson) lead us to believe.

As for Erickson's suggestion that the roles of the Father, Son, and Holy Spirit may have been voluntarily assumed by each person,61 the fact that this would have been an *eternal* decision (to which I think Erickson agrees62) implies that in all their interaction with the entire Creation for all eternity the Father, Son, and Holy Spirit have related to one another in ways that reflect the headship and authority of the Father, whom the Son and Spirit obey. So for all eternity we would

57. Ibid., 307.
58. Ibid., 309.
59. See Bromiley's statement above, p. 422.
60. Bromiley, "Eternal Generation," 368.
61. Erickson, *God in Three Persons,* 303.
62. Ibid., 310.

still have this voluntary decision and thus a relationship that indicates both *equality of being* and *subordination in role* with respect to actions in the Creation. This still provides a clear parallel to the headship of a husband over his wife (both equality and differences). Therefore, for the sake of the current argument there does not seem to be much difference between Erickson's view and one that holds to an eternal subordination of the Son to the Father in terms of relationship, together with equality in being. (However, I would affirm that the eternal relationships could not have been otherwise because the persons have eternally been Father, Son, and Holy Spirit, and those identities are appropriate to the differing eternal relationships that exist among them.)

Answer 10.2j: The idea of authority and submission never began; it existed forever in the very being of God.

The idea of authority and submission in an interpersonal relationship did not begin with the Council on Biblical Manhood and Womanhood in 1987. Nor did it begin with a few patriarchal men in the Old Testament. Nor did it begin with the Fall of Adam and Eve in Genesis 3. Nor did the idea of authority and submission to authority begin with the Creation of Adam and Eve in the Garden in Genesis 1 and 2. No, the idea of authority and submission has always existed in the eternal relationship between the Father and Son in the Trinity. And this means that the idea of authority and submission in interpersonal relationships *never began*—it has always existed in the eternal relationship between the Father and Son.

The doctrine of the Trinity thus indicates that equality of being together with authority and submission to authority are perhaps the most fundamental aspects of interpersonal relationship in the entire universe.

Egalitarian claim 10.3: Mutual Submission in the Trinity: Within the Trinity, the Father also submits to the Son, so there is no unique authority for the Father in relation to the Son.

Egalitarians such as Stanley Grenz now argue that there is mutual submission among the members of the Trinity:

> The argument from Christ's example often overlooks the deeper dynamic of mutual dependence within the Trinity.... The Father is dependent on the Son for his deity. In sending his Son into the world, the Father entrusted his own reign—indeed his own deity—to the Son (for example, Lk. 10:22). Likewise, the Father is dependent on the Son for his title as the Father. As Irenaeus pointed out in the second century, without

> the Son the Father is not the Father of the Son. Hence the subordination of the Son to the Father must be balanced by *the subordination of the Father to the Son.*[63]

In a later article Grenz repeated this analysis:

> The dynamic Origen referred to as "the eternal generation of the Son" moves in two directions. As the Church father Athanasius realized, this dynamic not only generates the Son but also constitutes the Father.... The Son is not the Son without the Father. But in the same way the Father...is not the Father without the Son.... We must balance the subordination of the Son to the Father with *the dependence of the Father on the Son*. In short, the eternal generation of the Son indicates that the first and second persons of the Trinity enjoy *a mutuality of relationship*. In a certain sense, each is dependent on the other for his own identity.[64]

Royce Gruenler has also made this argument from the Gospel of John. He claims to find there a theme of "mutual and voluntary subordination among the persons of the Triune Family,"[65] and says that in John 5:25–26 "Jesus makes it clear that he also shares equal authority with the Father to judge.... The Father willingly subordinates himself to the Son."[66]

Answer 10.3a: Grenz has confused the categories under discussion.

The question under discussion is the submission of the Son to the authority of the Father. All of the passages that I quoted above show the Father planning, initiating, directing, sending, and commanding, and they show the Son responding, obeying the Father, and carrying out the Father's plans. In order to show "mutual submission" in the Trinity or "the subordination of the Father to the Son" in a way that is parallel, Grenz would have to find some passages that show the Son commanding the Father, or the Son sending the Father, or the Son directing the activities of the Father, or the Father saying that He is obedient to the Son. But no verses like that are found.

So how does Grenz argue for the "subordination of the Father to the Son"? He changes the topic under discussion and confuses the categories. He says nothing about any submission of the Father to the Son's authority. He rather says, "without the Son the Father is not the Father of the Son." But this does not address the topic at hand. It is a linguistic sleight-of-hand argument that shifts the discussion to whether the Father would be Father without the Son (the answer is, of course not, but all that tells us is that if God were not a Trinity, He would not be a Trinity, or if God were different, He would be different). This statement tells us nothing about

63. Grenz, *Women in the Church,* 153–54. For a fuller discussion of this novel kind of egalitarian tampering with the doctrine of the Trinity see Ware, "Tampering with the Trinity," 233–53. Statements by Bilezikian affirming "mutual submission" in the Trinity are found in Bilezikian, "Hermeneutical Bungee-Jumping" (1997), 57–68.
64. Grenz, "Theological Foundations" (1998), 618 (italics added).
65. Royce Gruenler, *The Trinity in the Gospel of John* (1986), xvi.
66. Ibid., 38. (See pp. 541–43 below regarding egalitarians in England holding this view.)

who the true God is or about the relationships that *actually* exist among the persons of the Trinity. And it says nothing to show that the Father submits to the authority of the Son—which He never does.

Here is an example from family life that is parallel to Grenz's argument:

1. If I did not have a wife, I would not be a husband.
2. Therefore, I must have no unique authority as a husband, and there must be mutual submission in my marriage.

Or another example:

1. If I did not have a child, I would not be a parent.
2. Therefore, I must have no unique authority as a parent, and there must be mutual submission between my child and myself.

In both cases, the second statement does not follow. It has, in fact, no logical relationship to the first statement. Grenz has simply proven the obvious fact that there must be two people to have a relationship. But that says nothing about the nature of that relationship. And it certainly does not mean that there must be "mutual submission" in every relationship consisting of two people. Grenz has just confused the categories under discussion.

Answer 10.3b: No passage of Scripture and no recognized writer throughout the history of the church supports the idea of "mutual submission" in the Trinity. It is an egalitarian invention created to justify the egalitarian idea of mutual submission in marriage.

As far as I know, no recognized writer or teacher in the entire history of the church ever taught that there is "mutual submission" in the Trinity whereby the Father submits to the Son. No passage of Scripture says that the Father submits to the Son, or indicates that the Son has authority over the Father.

There are, I agree, several passages, such as the passage Grenz mentions, Luke 10:22, that indicate that the Father has entrusted considerable authority to the Son:

> All things have been handed over to me by my Father, and no one knows who the Son is except the Father, or who the Father is except the Son and anyone to whom the Son chooses to reveal him.

But that passage just proves the subordination of the Son to the Father. It is the Father who has delegated authority to the Son, so that people come to know the Father through the Son. But the Son did not have authority to hand over these things to the Father; rather, the Father "handed over" all things (presumably in context, this means "all things" pertaining to His Messianic role and mission) to the Son.

This is a fundamental confusion in Royce Gruenler's analysis as well. As Randy Stinson insightfully points out in an extensive review of Gruenler's claims,

> Part of Gruenler's argument that the Father submits to the Son, stems from his reading of [John] 5:22–23. He claims that since the Father gives the responsibility of judging to the Son, he is somehow submitting to the authority of the Son. This...betrays the proper understanding of delegated authority. The one who delegates does not make himself subordinate to the one to whom he delegates.... [Gruenler] has misunderstood the broader context of the Gospel of John.... The broader intention of John in his Gospel is to demonstrate the coequality of the Son with the Father while at the same time demonstrating the dependence of the Son on the Father.[67]

There are other passages that show the Son praying to the Father and asking things from the Father (Matthew 26:39; John 11:41–42; John 17:1–26). Even after He ascends into heaven, the Son prays to the Father for us (see Romans 8:34 and Hebrews 7:25). These actions are appropriate to a relationship in which the Father has supreme authority and the Son does not command Him but brings requests to Him.

Stinson discusses several of these passages, and then quotes with approval D. A. Carson's evaluation of such passages in John:

> The Father commands, sends, tells, commissions—and demonstrates his love for the Son by "showing" him everything such that the Son does whatever the Father does. The Son obeys, says only what the Father gives him to say, does only what the Father gives him to do, comes into the world as the Sent One—and demonstrates his love for the Father by such obedience. Not once is there any hint that the Son commissions the Father, who obeys. *Not once is there any hint that the Father submits to the Son or is dependent upon him for his own words and deeds.*[68]

Gruenler's portrayal of the Father-Son relationship in John, therefore, is hardly persuasive.[69]

In spite of a uniform pattern in Scripture showing an eternally past, a present, and an eternally future submission of the Son to the Father, and in spite of the absence of any recognized

67. Randy Stinson, "Does the Father Submit to the Son? A Critique of Royce Gruenler," in *JBMW* 6/2 (Fall 2001): 16. Sumner, *Men and Women in the Church,* makes a similar argument to Gruenler. She says that when the Father gave the Son authority to lay down his life and take it up again (John 10:18), it showed that the Father "deferred to the Son's authority" (177n10). She says that "to say that the Father commands the Son to act as though the Son has authority too is silly" (ibid.). Readers who have experience of delegating authority to others in the business world, for example, may be able to judge for themselves whether someone who *delegates* authority to another is really under the authority of that other person, or whether they think the idea of delegating authority is "silly." Sumner's argument does not understand the dynamics of delegating authority.

68. Ibid., 15, quoting D. A. Carson, *The Difficult Doctrine of the Love of God* (2000), 40 (italics added).

69. Gruenler's understanding of the text of John is strongly influenced by his clearly stated unwillingness to admit that the eternal subordination of the Son to the Father could possibly be consistent with eternal equality (see pp. xiii–xviii). This is just another form of the frequent egalitarian claim that if people are equal, they cannot have different roles, and if they have different roles, they cannot be equal.

teacher in the history of the church saying that the Father submits to the Son, and in spite of no passage in Scripture saying that the Father submits to the authority of the Son, so deep is the egalitarian commitment to "mutual submission" in marriage that they have invented a new doctrine of "mutual submission" in the Trinity to support it.

Answer 10.3c: If the Father also submitted to the authority of the Son, it would destroy the Trinity, because there would be no Father, Son, and Holy Spirit, but only Person A, Person A, and Person A.

The differences in authority among Father, Son, and Holy Spirit are the only interpersonal differences that the Bible indicates exist eternally among the members of the Godhead. They are equal in all their attributes and perfections, but for all eternity there has been a difference in authority, whereby the Father has authority over the Son that the Son does not have over the Father, and the Father and Son both have authority over the Holy Spirit that the Holy Spirit does not have over the Father and the Son. These differences, in which there is authority and submission to authority, seem to be the means by which Father, Son, and Holy Spirit differ from one another and can be differentiated from one another.

If we did not have such differences in authority in the relationships among the members of the Trinity, then we would not know of any differences at all, and it would be unclear whether there *are* any differences among the persons of the Trinity. But if there are no differences among them eternally, *then how does one person differ from the other*? They would no longer be Father, Son, and Holy Spirit, but rather Person A, Person A, and Person A, each identical to the other not only in being but also in role and in the way they relate to one another. This would be very troubling, for once we lose personal distinctions among the members of the Trinity, we sacrifice the very idea that personal differences are eternally and fundamentally good, and we no longer have in the being of God a guarantee that God will eternally preserve our own individual, personal distinctiveness either. (Probably egalitarians will not go that far in this generation, but that is the direction such ideas are heading.)

Egalitarian claim 10.4: No Parallel with Trinity: The comparison with the Trinity is invalid because Jesus' submission to the Father was voluntary and because there was never any disagreement among members of the Trinity.

This argument is made by Rebecca Groothuis, who writes,

> If, as traditionalists would have it, Christ's subordination within the redemptive program—which was a voluntary subordination—is to be considered indicative of his eternal subordination to the Father, then his eternal subordination must

also be regarded as voluntary. It must not be seen as the kind of subordination that is automatically assigned to or imposed upon a person regardless of that person's interests, inclinations, or abilities. Nor can it imply any need for one person to cast the deciding vote in case of disagreement, for there is always a perfect relational oneness among all three persons of the Godhead. Disagreements between humans are caused by sin (self-centeredness) and ignorance. The persons of the Trinity, however, are always perfectly loving, righteous, wise, and knowledgeable. Among such persons, there can be no occasion for discord or disagreement and hence no need for any "chain of command" or structure of authority that would ever require the subordinate person to act against his own judgment or preference.[70]

Answers 10.4a: The comparison with the Trinity is valid because the Bible appeals to women to decide to be subject to their husbands, and thus they, like Christ, should exercise a voluntary submission.

The Bible never tells husbands to attempt to force submission on their wives. Rather, it appeals to wives to decide voluntarily to be subject to their husband's authority and leadership:

> Wives, submit to your own husbands, as to the Lord. (Ephesians 5:22)
>
> Wives, submit to your husbands, as is fitting in the Lord. (Colossians 3:18)
>
> Likewise, wives, be subject to your own husbands, so that even if some do not obey the word, they may be won without a word by the conduct of their wives. (1 Peter 3:1; see also Titus 2:3–5)

In this way there is a parallel between a wife's submission to her husband and Christ's submission to His Father. He always delighted in doing the will of the Father, for He said, "My food is to do the will of him who sent me and to accomplish his work" (John 4:34) and, "I seek not my own will but the will of him who sent me" (John 5:30; see also John 6:38; 12:49–50; 14:31; 17:4; Hebrews 10:7).

Was it also this way before the Son came to earth as a man? As I noted above, there was an *eternal* subordination of the Son to the Father, not in existing as a lesser being, but in being subject to the will and direction and authority of the Father.[71] The Father–Son relationship, and the relationships of the Father and Son to the Holy Spirit, are part of the eternal being of God. Surely the Son and Holy Spirit *delight* in those eternal relationships, for they are part of the unsurpassed excellence of the being of God.

---

70. Groothuis, *Good News for Women*, 59.
71. See pp. 45–48 and 405–33, on the eternal subordination of the Son to the Father.

Answer 10.4b: But the comparison with the Trinity does not give justification for a wife to choose not to submit to her husband.

Does the voluntary nature of the Son's submission to the Father mean, as Groothuis suggests, that it is open to a wife to decide *not* to be subject to the authority of her husband? No, the Bible does not endorse any such decision. It just says, "Wives, submit to your own husbands, as to the Lord" (Ephesians 5:22). Could the Son have decided not to submit to the authority of the Father? No, for that would have been a rejection of His role as Son in relation to the Father.

So we must affirm that a wife's submission to her husband should be voluntary, and also that if she does not submit to her husband's authority, she is disobedient to Scripture and to God's will. How can it be voluntary then? In the same way that *all* of our obedience to God should be voluntary: We should actively *choose* to obey God each hour, each day of our lives. We should actively *choose* to obey God's moral laws in Scripture. And if we choose to disobey them, our choice is still wrong! To take another example, I should voluntarily and actively choose to tell the truth and not to lie. But if one day I do not feel like telling the truth, my desires do not make lying right! God's laws are not determined by my desires.

What should we say, then, if submission to a husband's authority is contrary to "a person's interests, inclinations, or abilities" (to quote Groothuis)?[72] What if a wife does not want to submit to her husband, and what if her leadership ability is greater than his? In that situation, we must distinguish between desires and ability. If she has greater leadership ability, that does not mean she should assume leadership in the family, because the Father's leadership in the Trinity is not based on greater ability (for Father, Son, and Holy Spirit are equal in attributes), but simply on the fact that He is Father. On the other hand, if she does not desire (or have "interests" or "inclinations") to be subject to her husband's authority, such desires do not make it right to reject her husband's authority. A desire that is contrary to Scripture does not show that Scripture should be changed or disobeyed, but rather that our desires need to be brought into conformity with God's Word. Such desires do not stem from the way God created woman from the beginning, but ultimately result from the Fall.[73]

To use the Son's voluntary submission to the Father in the Trinity as a justification for *disobeying* God's moral teaching in Scripture, as Groothuis seems to do, shows a profound misunderstanding of the unchangeable nature of God's moral laws, and a profound misunderstanding of the unchangeable and eternal Father-Son relationship within the Trinity.

Answer 10.4c: The appeal to the Trinity is valid because Christ's submission was grounded in His existence as Son for all eternity.

Why was the Son eternally subject to the Father? Simply because He eternally existed as Son, and submission to the Father was inherent in that relationship. Why should a wife be subject to her

72. Groothuis, *Good News for Women,* 59.
73. See the discussion of "desire" in Genesis 3:16 on pp. 37–41, above.

husband? Simply because she is a wife and he is a husband, she is a woman and he is a man. "Wives, be subject to your own husbands, as to the Lord" (Ephesians 5:22). "But I want you to understand that the head of every man is Christ, the head of a wife is her husband, and the head of Christ is God" (1 Corinthians 11:3). In the one case, submission is grounded in the Son's existence as Son. In the other case, submission is grounded in a wife's existence as a woman. This is a wonderful parallel between the submission (with equal dignity and value) of the Son of God to the Father and the submission (with equal dignity and value) of the wife to her husband.

Answer 10.4d: The appeal to the Trinity is valid because it shows that there is authority and submission even among sinless persons.

A common egalitarian mistake is to assume that authority and submission are only due to sin and ignorance. Groothuis's statement reveals this assumption:

> Disagreements between humans are caused by sin (self-centeredness) and ignorance. The persons of the Trinity, however, are always perfectly loving, righteous, wise, and knowledgeable. Among such persons, there can be no occasion for discord or disagreement and hence no need for any "chain of command" or structure of authority that would ever require the subordinate person to act against his own judgment or preference.[74]

Groothuis assumes that authority and submission must exist only when there is disagreement caused by sin or ignorance. But this is not true. Authority and submission to authority not only provide a means of subduing evil, they also provide a means of order and organization in interpersonal relationships. And they provide a means of division of labor and specialization in tasks, so that groups of people can work together on projects rather than each individual being on his own.

The example of the angels and archangels (1 Thessalonians 4:16; Jude 9) proves there is authority and submission among sinless creatures (for archangels are those with higher authority). The example of sinless angels being subject to God also proves it (Hebrews 1:14; 1 Peter 3:22). The example of Adam's headship in the Garden before sin also proves this (Genesis 2:7, 18–23; 3:9, 16; 5:1–2; 1 Corinthians 11:3; 15:22; Ephesians 5:31–32; Colossians 3:18–19; 1 Timothy 2:12–13).[75] The example of believers having authority over five cities and ten cities in the age to come proves this (Luke 19:17, 19). The example of kings of the earth who bring the glory and honor of their nations into the heavenly Jerusalem proves this (Revelation 21:24–26). And the example of eternal authority and submission in the Trinity proves this (1 Corinthians 15:28; Ephesians 1:4). Authority exists even where there is no sin.

---

74. Groothuis, *Good News for Women*, 59.
75. See discussion on the headship of Adam before there was sin in the world, pp. 29–45.

Groothuis may think there is "no need for any 'chain of command' or structure of authority" in the Trinity, but that just reveals a failure to understand that authority, and submission to authority, are in themselves good, though subject to distortion and abuse in a fallen world. Authority and submission to authority will exist forever in the new heavens and new earth, and they will not be evil nor will they be needed to suppress any evil. To think otherwise is to reflect the world's assumption that authority in itself is evil or else is necessitated by evil. But that is not the teaching of the Bible.

EGALITARIAN CLAIM 10.5: DIFFERENT SUBORDINATION: ANALOGIES WITH OTHER KINDS OF HUMAN SUBORDINATION ARE NOT VALID, BECAUSE THOSE ARE LIMITED IN FUNCTION AND DURATION AND ARE BASED ON HUMAN ABILITIES OR CHOICES. BUT THE SUBORDINATION OF WOMEN TO MEN TAUGHT BY COMPLEMENTARIANS IS UNLIMITED IN FUNCTION AND DURATION, AND IS BASED ON A WOMAN'S VERY BEING.

This argument is skillfully presented by Rebecca Groothuis, who says,

> The question then that must be addressed is not whether it is *possible* to be equal in being but different in role or rank (for it *is* possible), but whether it is logically and theologically appropriate to describe and defend the traditionalist understanding of women's subordination in these terms....
>
> Normally, functional subordination exists for the purpose of accomplishing a particular task or function, and applies only to a specific area of life for a limited period of time. It is determined on the basis of either the subordinated person's inferior ability in a particular area or his or her willingness to submit to leadership in order that a particular job be accomplished efficiently. Female subordination, on the other hand, is not limited to any one area of life, nor is it merely temporary. It is automatically assigned to every woman simply because she is a woman, and it cannot be justified on the basis of inferior ability, nor can it be explained as a mere expedient useful in dealing with a specific situation. It is, rather, a way of life, a definition of a woman's personhood.[76]

As examples of legitimate human subordination, Groothuis mentions a teacher and music student (unequal ability), or a chairperson chosen by an organization (voluntary choice for a specific purpose and limited time). But female subordination, she says, is different because it is not based on inferior ability or voluntary choice, and is not limited in scope or duration.

---

76. Groothuis, *Good News for Women*, 42–43. A similar view is expressed by Giles, *The Trinity and Subordinationism*, 17.

Answer 10.5a: All analogies are imperfect, but they can still illustrate some truth. The truth that other examples of human subordination teach is that equality in being can exist along with difference in roles.

Groothuis admits that it is "possible to be equal in being but different in role or rank."[77] She admits that this happens in some human activities, and in some human activities it is right. I agree.

But *the duration of a relationship does not affect this truth.* The members of a committee are subject to a committee chairman (or chairperson) for a short time, only as long as they serve on the committee. Children are subject to their parents for a longer time, as long as they live as children in their parents' home. Citizens are subject to government for their whole lives (Romans 13:1). Christians are subject to the leaders of the church for their whole lives (Hebrews 13:17). And wives are subject to their husbands for their whole lives (Ephesians 5:22–24). Duration is a difference, yes, but it is not a difference that affects the truth being illustrated—the truth that equality in being can exist together with differences in roles and authority.

The scope of the relationship does not affect this truth either. Committee members are subject to the committee chairman (or chairperson) for a limited number of functions, namely, only for the activities of the committee. Children are subject to their parents "in everything" (Colossians 3:20), and yet they are to put loyalty to Jesus even before obedience to father and mother (Matthew 10:37; 19:29). Citizens are subject to government in all their conduct in society, yet when conflict comes they must "obey God rather than men" (Acts 5:29). Wives are to be subject to their husbands "in everything" (Ephesians 5:24), yet they must put loyalty to God ahead of subjection to their husbands (Esther 4:16; 1 Peter 3:1). If subjection to authority can exist with equality in being for a few functions, then it can exist for many functions. The scope of the subjection can differ, yes, but it is not a difference that affects the truth being illustrated—the truth that equality in being can exist together with differences in roles and authority.

So these other analogies are valid. In fact, they are very helpful. Groothuis has not pointed out any differences that negate the validity of these analogies.

Answer 10.5b: The Bible sometimes bases roles on a person's "being" alone, not on ability or human choice. This contradicts the heart of the egalitarian position, which is that only ability or choice should determine roles in marriage and the church.

Groothuis rightly points out that in many examples of human subordination to authority, the subordination is based on differing ability or on voluntary choice. I agree that this is the case, for example, for the subordination of children to parents (different ability to direct the family), of employers to employees (voluntary choice to work at that job), of church members to church leaders (differing ability to lead, voluntary choice to be a member of the church, and often a voluntary choice of the leaders by the congregation), of citizens to government (at least where officials are elected), and so forth.

77. Ibid., 42.

But here we reach the heart of the egalitarian position. Is it right for a wife to be subject to her husband *simply because she is a woman*? Is it right for a husband to have authority in the family not because he is a better leader (ability) and not because husband and wife have agreed that the husband will lead (voluntary choice), but *simply because he is a man*?

Groothuis objects that if this is the case, then differing authority in marriage is based on a woman's very *being* (as a woman), and this necessarily implies that she is an inferior being to a man.

But Groothuis's error here is to assume that God has to base different roles on differing abilities, or else it is not fair. This assumption is untrue. Sometimes God assigns people to different roles because of His sovereign and wise choice, not based on any difference in abilities.

One example is the choice of priests in the Old Testament. There was no difference in *ability* among the men of the twelve tribes of Israel. The men of the tribe of Benjamin or the tribe of Reuben or the tribe of Simeon were surely strong enough and wise enough to perform priestly duties every day in the temple. But God did not choose them or allow them to do this. He chose only the men of the tribe of Levi, and specifically the descendants of Aaron (Exodus 28:1; 29:9)—not because they were stronger or wiser, and not because of any other ability, but simply because He chose them! Was this fair? It was what God did, and He is a just God, so by definition it was fair.

Another example is the choice of the people of Israel to be God's people. It was not based on their size (for there were many greater nations), or on any greater ability or merit, but simply because God decided to place His love on them (Deuteronomy 7:6–8).

The greatest example is seen among the persons in the Trinity.[78] The Father has authority that the Son does not have, not because He has greater ability to lead, but simply because He is Father. The Son submits to the authority of the Father, not because He is less wise or less powerful, but simply because He is Son. The distinction of persons cannot be based on different abilities, for there are no differing abilities among the persons of the Trinity, each of whom is fully God. And the Father is Father not because Person X in the Trinity one day "chose" to be Father and Person Y one day "chose" to be Son, but simply because the Father *has always been Father* and the Son *has always been Son*. If it were not so, the Father could not have chosen us in the Son, and predestined us to be conformed to the image of the Son, "before the foundation of the world" (Ephesians 1:4; see also Romans 8:29; 1 Peter 1:20). And if it were not so, God would not be the unchanging God, "with whom there is no variation or shadow due to change" (James 1:17).

Of course, the Father and Son delight in and continually will to fulfill their roles in this Father-Son relationship. But the roles they have as Father and Son are not theirs *because* they delight in them, but rather they delight in them *because* by nature they have always existed as Father and Son.

---

78. See egalitarian claim 10.4, pp. 433–37, on Groothuis's argument that parallels between the Trinity and male-female relationships are not appropriate.

So the differences in role and authority among the members of the Trinity are *not* limited in scope or duration, and are *not* based on ability or voluntary choice. They are just part of the being of God. Yet there is no inferiority of being, for the Son and Holy Spirit are also fully God, of the same nature as the Father. *Equal being* exists forever with *different functions* that are not based on ability or choice and are unlimited in scope and duration. Groothuis's argument therefore is invalid.

Now between men and women, it seems to be the case that God ordinarily gives to men some abilities and preferences that are appropriate to leadership (such as a more aggressive disposition and a sense of responsibility and rightness in leadership), and ordinarily gives to women some abilities and preferences that are appropriate to support that leadership (such as a more nurturing and caring disposition and a sense of rightness in fulfilling a supportive role for their husbands). Such abilities and preferences are appropriate to the roles God has established. But the Bible does not *base* male leadership on any such abilities or preferences.[79] It simply bases it on the fact that one person is the husband and one is the wife. The Bible does not say, "The husband is the head of the wife *in cases where he has greater ability to lead*," or "The husband is the head of the wife *if he chooses to lead and she chooses to submit to his leadership*," but rather, "The husband *is* the head of the wife even as Christ is the head of the church" (Ephesians 5:23), and "Wives, submit to your own husbands, as to the Lord" (Ephesians 5:22).

These verses are far different from the egalitarian view that only ability or voluntary choice should determine differences in role and authority. And they are far different from Groothuis's contention that different roles for men and women have to be based on ability or choice. That may be modern human thinking, but it is not the teaching of the Bible.

Sarah Sumner claims that the complementarian view does not consistently apply the parallel with the Trinity, because in the Trinity the Father and Son have exactly the same attributes and the same being, and "It is heresy to say that the Son is essentially distinct from the Father."[80] But then how can complementarians claim that men and women are different in their nature? She objects, "According to Piper *femininity* is not defined by an 'equality of essence and being'.... Masculinity and femininity are defined as essentially distinct from one another."

The answer is that we are not God, and we are not exactly the same as God. No one has said that the parallel with the Trinity is exact *in every respect.* The Father, Son, and Holy Spirit

79. Sumner, *Men and Women in the Church,* does not understand this difference, so she claims that the complementarian view is a "contradiction" (290), what she calls a "lack of logic" (295). She says, "It can't be true that the only reason why women are to assume inferior roles at church is because God said so, if indeed the permanent facts of nature also explain the reason why" (295). But it is not illogical to say that the *fundamental reason* God gives in Scripture for role differences is that one person is a man and one is a woman, and also to say that we see *confirmatory evidence* for the rightness of these role differences when we look at the abilities and tendencies that He gave us. It should not be surprising that God's wise commands correspond with His wise actions in creating us to be like we are.

80. Ibid., 288.

are one being, but husband and wife are surely not one being. We are distinct persons who are *different* beings, and no two created persons in the universe will ever share the unity of essence there is in the Trinity. Similarly, the analogy is not exact with regard to attributes. In the Trinity, the Father, Son, and Holy Spirit have exactly the same attributes. But men and women have different attributes—we have different gifts, abilities, and dispositions, and Sumner herself admits that we have physical differences.[81] So the analogy does not hold at every point (no analogy does), but that does not mean it is inconsistent. It is true in the ways we have claimed for it.

Egalitarian claim 10.6: Subordination in Essence: If female subordination is based on who a woman *is* (as female) rather than her ability or choice, then it is a subordination in essence. Therefore the complementarian position leads to the conclusion that women are lesser beings.

This objection is stated by Rebecca Groothuis:

> Regardless of how hierarchalists try to explain the situation, the idea that women are equal *in* their being, yet unequal *by virtue of* their being, is contradictory and ultimately nonsensical. If you cannot help but be what you are, and if inferiority in function follows inexorably from what you are, then you are inferior in your essential being.... A permanent and comprehensive subordination based on a person's essence is an essential (not merely a functional) subordination.[82]

Answer 10.6a: No, it is a subordination in function.

To state it again, the complementarian position is equality in being (in the sense of equal value, honor, personhood, and importance) with differences in authority. The complementarian position holds to subordination in function, not subordination in being.

Groothuis states our position in a misleading way, because her phrase "inferiority in function" carries connotations of lesser value. The complementarian position is that greater or lesser *authority* does not imply "*inferior* function" or "*superior* function," just *different* function.

Groothuis also states the position in a misleading way when she says, "the idea that women are equal *in* their being, yet unequal *by virtue of* their being, is contradictory and ultimately nonsensical."

The problem is that she uses "equal" and "unequal" with different meanings. If we reword her sentence so the meanings are explicit and the complementarian view is represented fairly, it

81. Ibid., 139–40.
82. Groothuis, *Good News for Women*, 55 (italics in original). See also Brown, *Women Ministers*, 8.

would say: "the idea that women are *equal in value and honor and personhood* but *unequal in authority* by virtue of their being *women* is contradictory and ultimately nonsensical."

But this idea is not at all contradictory and nonsensical. A contradiction would be to say, for example, "women are equal in value and women are not equal in value." That sentence takes the form, "A and not A," which is a contradiction. But to say, "women are equal in value and different in authority" is not at all a contradiction or nonsensical. Groothuis may disagree with that statement, but for her to use "equal" in two different ways and then call it a contradiction is simply a word trick.

Answer 10.6b: Women's submission to male headship is based on their having a *different* being, not an *inferior* being.

What Groothuis is really objecting to is women having different roles that are not based on ability or choice, but just on the fact that a person is a woman.

In fact, Groothuis herself does not object to the idea that people can be equal but different in some ways. She agrees, for example, that people can have different skills or social position and still be of equal value to God.[83] So she agrees that *some* kinds of differences are compatible with *some* kinds of equality.

But the only kinds of differences she allows are those based on ability or voluntary choice. This is evident when she assumes over and over again that, apart from voluntary choice, the only rightful submission to authority has to be based on inferior ability. She says, for example,

> Subordinating a woman solely by reason of her femaleness can be deemed fair and appropriate only if all females are, without exception, inferior to all males in their *ability* to perform the particular function for which they have been subordinated.[84]

That is just saying that *greater ability* is the *only* "fair and appropriate" basis for a husband to have leadership in the family. By contrast to Groothuis's idea of what is "fair and appropriate," the Bible never bases a husband's leadership on ability, but simply on the fact that he is a man. Are we to say that the Bible is not "fair and appropriate"? Are we to say that God's choice of the Levites to be priests, or of the Jews to be His people was not "fair and appropriate"? Are we to say that the eternal authority of God the Father over the Son and the Holy Spirit, based not on greater ability but just on being Father, is not "fair and appropriate"? Surely Groothuis is wrong here.

In the case of different roles for men and women in marriage, God can (and does) assign roles based on something other than abilities. He bases roles on the fact that one is a man and one is a woman ("the husband is the head of the wife even as Christ is the head of the church," Ephesians 5:23). God looks at these equal but different beings and assigns headship to the

83. Ibid., 46.
84. Ibid., 53 (italics added).

husband. And He bases it on the fact that they are different, not on any inferiority or superiority. Egalitarians may say, "That's not fair," or "I can't understand why God does this," but it still remains the decision God has made. And egalitarian opinions of whether God's actions are fair or reasonable need adjustment in light of the testimony of Scripture.

Egalitarian claim 10.7: Not a Caste System: We live in a free society where access to high status positions is based on ability and voluntary choice, not a caste society where some people are excluded by birth (as they are in a complementarian view).

Rebecca Groothuis allows for the validity of different roles based on personal choices (as with the leader of an organization) or on differing ability (as with recognizing different roles for a music student and teacher, or prohibiting weak or handicapped persons to sit by emergency exit doors on airplanes).[85] But Groothuis objects to determining different roles not on choice or ability, but merely on the basis of birth:

> Various versions of a caste system may permanently consign individuals of a certain race, sex, nationality, or socioeconomic class to limited roles and a subordinate status in society, regardless of each individual's abilities.... Although traditionalists do not acknowledge it, their prescribed gender roles belong in the final category of the "caste system"....
>
> On the one hand, there is the way of free societies, whereby individuals move in and out of leadership roles according to their experience and expertise. On the other hand, there is the way of the caste system, in which certain people are born into a permanently lower status and have no opportunity even to earn a higher-status position, regardless of their experience or expertise.[86]

Answer 10.7a: To frame the issue in terms of "higher status" and "lower status" skews the discussion and clouds the true issue.

The term "high status" imports considerations of honor and respect, which I agree that women should share in equally with men. This is not the issue.

85. Ibid., 50.
86. Ibid., 50–51.

Answer 10.7b: The real issue is authority and submission, which may or may not coincide with honor and respect, depending on the situation.

Authority is different from honor and respect (or "status," to use Groothuis's term).[87]

For example, when a child is born, the mother has the highest honor and respect. But the father still has highest authority in the family. Another example is Jesus' mother and father: Though Joseph functioned as leader in the family (see Matthew 2:13–14, 19–23), Mary has received much greater honor (Luke 1:48). Another example is seen in many athletic teams, where the manager and ultimately the owner have the authority, but players are often given higher honor.

Answer 10.7c: The caste system is an evil, dehumanizing system not commanded by God, but marriage and the church are good institutions created by God and regulated by His wise commands.

It is a blatant misrepresentation for Groothuis to compare the caste system to God's plans for marriage and the church. One is evil and the result of sin; the other is good and designed by God for our blessing.

Answer 10.7d: To say that both complementarianism and the caste system determine roles "by birth" misstates and clouds the true issue.

In a caste system, some people are denied opportunities for wealth, education, power, and prestige not exactly because of their birth (as Groothuis says), but specifically because of *who their parents are at the time of their birth*. If the parents belong to a lower caste, then the child belongs to a lower caste. By contrast, in biblical standards for manhood and womanhood, people are never assigned to roles because of *who their parents are*, but because of their *gender*, whether male or female. The reason Groothuis's comparison to a caste system initially sounds plausible is that we first identify gender at the time of birth, and people first identify caste at the time of birth. But the fact that two things are identified at the same time does not mean they are the same!

For example, children born in the U.S. usually become citizens of the U.S. In these cases, citizenship rights are determined *at the time of birth*. But should we then say, "Determining citizenship by birth is like the evil caste system, because caste is also determined by birth"? No, the comparison is incorrect, because the only similarity was the *time* at which something was made known (whether caste or citizenship). "Birth" by itself did not really determine either one, for *the caste of one's parents at the time of birth* determined caste but *the location of one's birth* determined citizenship. One system is evil; the other is not. The comparison is not valid, nor is Groothuis's comparison to the caste system valid.

---

87. See the discussion on the distinction between having more authority and having more honor or "status" in answers 3.1a and 3.1b, pp. 104–5.

Answer 10.7e: It is wrong to say that we should determine roles for men and women in marriage and the church according to the political theories of a "free society" rather than according to the Bible.

Groothuis speaks favorably of "the way of free societies, whereby individuals move in and out of leadership roles according to their experience and expertise." Complementarians do not deny this, for the Bible does not prohibit women from "leadership roles" in society, in government, in business, and so forth. Yet when it comes to marriage and the church, the Bible does give clear teachings, and we must follow those teachings rather than some human political theory.

As explained above,[88] the heart of the egalitarian position is that only ability and choice should determine roles in marriage and the church. It is not surprising that no biblical statements on marriage or the church are found in Groothuis's discussion at this point. In fact, her discussion here is based on political theory, and with respect to marriage and the church, it is far from the teaching of the Bible on manhood and womanhood. Again and again the Bible bases roles in marriage and the church on gender, not on ability or choice (though, as I mentioned above, God ordinarily gives some correlation between abilities and preferences and roles.[89])

Egalitarian claim 10.8: Society Today Rejects Gender Restrictions: In a society where women can attain any other position open to men, it is not fair to keep them from pastoral ministry.

Krister Stendahl, dean of Harvard Divinity School, expressed this sentiment in 1966:

> It would...be peculiar if the church...saw it as its duty to turn this biblical picture upside down by saying to its faithful: "in worldly affairs you may accept emancipation—and before God there is neither man nor woman—but in the church's life and its worship it is not so." Then one would have to go on to say: "in the world slaves are emancipated by now, but in the church that should not be so...etc., etc."
>
> The only alternative—so it seems to me—is to recognize the legal, economic, political, and professional emancipation of women, and that with joy and gratitude, as a great achievement.... If emancipation is right, then there is no valid "biblical" reason not to ordain women.[90]

---

88. See the earlier discussion in this chapter on the egalitarian refusal to consider any other basis for role differentiation than human abilities and human choices at claims 10.5 and 10.6, pp. 437–43.
89. See the discussion earlier in this chapter (answer 10.5b, pp. 438–41) on the connection between abilities and preferences of men and women and the roles God has assigned them.
90. Stendahl, *The Bible and the Role of Women* (1966), 40–41.

This claim is also made by authors such as Sarah Sumner. "It is logically inconsistent to think that women are designed to be subordinate to men in the home and church but not necessarily in society."[91]

Answer 10.8a: The Bible does not object to women in positions of leadership in other parts of society such as business, education, and government, but only restricts certain kinds of leadership to men in marriage and in the church.

We must be careful not to impose restrictions that the Bible does not support. The Bible does not extend its requirements for male leadership in the home and the church to any other areas of society. Whether or not we can understand God's reasons for this, it is not our place to say that He should have made rules that are more restrictive or less restrictive than what He did. He is God, and we are not!

However, people may have *different preferences* for having men in leadership, or for having women in leadership, in certain of these positions, and there is nothing wrong with that in principle. Some people may think that men in general are better suited for leadership positions in government, and they may generally vote for men who are running for office, but even they should be willing to make exceptions in cases where a woman is clearly better qualified and better suited to the role than the man she is running against. Alternatively, there may be situations where people think that a woman is better suited for a leadership position, such as academic dean where a large majority of the students and faculty are women, and there is nothing wrong with having a preference for a woman in such a position, even though an exception may be made if a particular man is the better choice. We can have preferences that allow for exceptions and that do not rise to the level of absolute moral requirements or matters of right and wrong.

No moral issue or matter of obedience to Scripture is at stake here. What would be wrong would be to insist that we must always have men in such positions, or that we must always have women in such positions, or (what is often assumed in modern culture) that the ideal is to have 50 percent men and 50 percent women in leadership positions in government, in business, in education, and so forth.

Finally, we may observe that in the United States, where the laws and the dominant media have advocated an egalitarian perspective for over thirty years, and where women as well as men have complete freedom to seek leadership roles throughout society, we still strongly favor having men fill a majority of leadership positions. As I write this paragraph, 85.8 percent of the members of Congress are men (out of 435 members of the House of Representatives, 62 are women, and out of 100 U.S. Senators 14 are women),[92] 88 percent of the fifty state governors

91. Sumner, *Men and Women in the Church*, 26.
92. This information can be read on-line at http://clerk.house.gov/members/congProfile.php.

are men (6 women governors out of 50 U.S. States)[93], and 98.9 percent of the CEOs of Fortune 1000 companies are men (there are 11 women CEOs out of *Fortune*'s listing of top 1000 companies).[94] This indicates that our society generally prefers men in positions of leadership, but does not consider male leadership in government or business a requirement or a necessity. This seems to me to be a healthy perspective in a free and open society.

Answer 10.8b: Our ideas of "fairness" must be determined by what the Bible teaches, not by what society might say about leadership roles in the church or in other areas of life.

God always does what is fair and just and right: "all his ways are justice. A God of faithfulness and without iniquity, just and upright is he" (Deuteronomy 32:4). As for God's commands, "The precepts of the LORD are right, rejoicing the heart" (Psalm 19:8). And God Himself said, "I the LORD speak the truth; I declare what is right" (Isaiah 45:19).

Therefore we must be very careful never to say or even to think that what God commands is unfair or unjust. What He commands is right, and He is the final standard of right and wrong. Moreover, what He commands is best for us. His commands do not demean women or harm or destroy women; His commands encourage and enable both men and women to be exactly what God created them to be.

But can we think of any reason why God might have decided that it was wise to preserve certain leadership roles for men in marriage and in the church, but not in the rest of society? The relationship between husband and wife pictures the relationship between Christ and the church (see Ephesians 5:22–33), and that is not true of the relationship between men and women in government or education or business. Therefore we can understand why it is appropriate to reserve leadership for the husband in marriage, for he represents Christ in this picture of Christ and the church.

With respect to the church, restricting the role of elder to men is part of a larger pattern in which the twelve apostles that Jesus chose were men, and the heads of the twelve tribes of Israel, who ruled over God's people in the Old Testament, were men as well. And Abraham, the father of the people of Israel, was a man, as was Moses, who led the people out of Egypt and gave them God's law. And all the priests were men. And Adam himself, as representative for the human race, was a man (see Romans 5:12–21; 1 Corinthians 15:21–22, 47–49). And the leadership roles in the Trinity belong to Father and Son, not to Mother and Daughter, nor does God identify Himself as Mother or Daughter.

What is the meaning of this? Perhaps that leadership positions as a general rule are most appropriately held by men, and that maleness is appropriate to leadership. For some reason, God

93. This information can be read on-line at http://www.nga.org/governors/1,1169,,00.html.
94. This information can be read on-line at http://www.fortune.com/fortune/specials/lists/women/game1.html.

deemed it wise to establish this not just as a general pattern, but as an absolute principle for the highest leadership roles over His people, whether in the Old Testament or the New Testament. Probably this is a reflection of the glory of the Father in His leadership role in the Trinity.

However, when God requires male leadership only in the home and the church, He at the same time allows women to have some high positions of leadership in other areas of society, and in this way He gives another manifestation of our equality in the image of God. When women have leadership positions in business or government, for example, we can see it as a reminder that we should never think that women *are unable* to fill these leadership roles, for some women fill these roles very well. In this way we see a reminder that we are equally in the image of God.

But at the same time as we observe some women functioning very well in many leadership roles in society, we remember that God has established exclusive male leadership roles in the home and in the church. We also observe a preponderance of males in leadership roles even in business or government,[95] and thereby we are reminded that God made us different, and one aspect of that difference is that maleness seems, in general, to be more suitable for such leadership roles and to fit more readily and naturally into them.

Answer 10.8c: Many kinds of full-time ministry are available to women as well as men, and we should encourage women in these ministries.

As I discussed in some detail in chapter 2, while I believe the office of elder and its equivalent (including the role of pastor) is restricted to men, many other kinds of ministries are appropriate for women as well as men (see pp. 84–101). These ministries include various kinds of teaching to large or small groups of women or children, leading women's Bible studies, writing ministries, ministries in counseling and music and Christian education, many kinds of missionary activities including Bible translations and evangelism, academic ministries of various kinds (except teaching Bible or theology in a Christian college or seminary), and all sorts of other ministries in the local church, including administrative ministries (that do not include elderlike authority over the whole church), and ministries of mercy and prayer, as well as many other ministries that could be added to this list. The presence and full acceptance of women in responsible positions in many areas of society should prompt the church to consider if we have done all we can to encourage all these kinds of women's ministries.

95. Note the unqualified claim of sociologist Steven Goldberg that "patriarchy is universal. For all the variety different societies have demonstrated in developing different types of political, economic, religious, and social systems, there has never been a society that has failed to associate authority and leadership in these areas with men. No anthropologist contests the fact that patriarchy is universal" (*The Inevitability of Patriarchy* (1973), 31–32). He interacts at length with writers who have claimed one society or another as an exception to this generalization.

Egalitarian claim 10.9: Necessary for True Equality: Women can never be considered truly equal to men unless they can also be pastors.

This claim is fundamental to the egalitarian position, and is expressed in various ways. Patricia Gundry put it this way in the opening chapter to the book *Women, Authority and the Bible*:

> There is but one central and watershed question in this conflicted issue: Are women fully human? All other questions and issues are peripheral to this question. If the answer is yes, then say a clear yes, not yes, but.... Yes, but is not yes...because yes, but...always carries restrictions and prohibitions that intrinsically deny that full humanity expression, opportunity or essence. Usually it denies all three.[96]

In the next chapter, Gretchen Gaebelein Hull went beyond Gundry's question and said,

> I suggest that we go further than Gundry did and ask this question: "Are women fully redeemed?"... Redeemed women are heirs of God and joint-heirs with Christ. Sisters can enter into that inheritance equally with brothers and can share equally in its administration.[97]

And Rebecca Groothuis says,

> In reserving leadership positions for men, traditionalists deny women the opportunity to demonstrate their equality of ability and maturity, and thereby to earn equality of status and social value.[98]

Answer 10.9a: It all depends on what is meant by "equal." This claim makes the mistake of thinking that "equality" has to mean "sameness" in every role. But we can be equal in many ways without being the same in every role.

The egalitarian claim depends on a certain meaning for "equal" (or "human" or "redeemed" in the first two quotes above). Groothuis specifies certain kinds of equality (ability, maturity, status, social value), and even the meaning of those could be debated. The point at issue is whether men and women can be different in some roles in marriage and the church *solely because of their gender*, and still be equal in many significant ways.

The complementarian position, as advocated in this book, takes issue with the egalitarian view of what is necessary for true equality. I argued in chapters 1 and 3 that men and women can be equal in value and dignity, equal in bearing the image of God, and equal in importance

96. Patricia Gundry, "Why We're Here," in Mickelsen, *Women, Authority and the Bible* (1986), 20.
97. Gretchen Gaebelein Hull, "Response," in Mickelsen, *Women, Authority and the Bible*, 24–26.
98. Groothuis, *Good News for Women*, 46.

in God's sight, without being the same in every way. We should not make the mistake of thinking that *equality* means that everyone has to have the same role.[99]

Rebecca Groothuis denies that egalitarians insist on "sameness" for men and women, but her discussion only reinforces the point, because the only differences that she says apply to all men and all women are the physical differences in our sexuality and the corresponding functions (such as bearing children) that result from those physical differences.[100]

Answer 10.9b: The Bible emphasizes that the body of Christ has many members, and all have *equal* value before God, but they have many *different* gifts and functions.

Paul does not think that we all have to have the same functions within the body of Christ in order to be of equal value. The wonderful metaphor he uses is that of the human body:

> The eye cannot say to the hand, "I have no need of you," nor again the head to the feet, "I have no need of you." On the contrary, the parts of the body that seem to be weaker are indispensable, and on those parts of the body that we think less honorable we bestow the greater honor, and our unpresentable parts are treated with greater modesty, which our more presentable parts do not require. But God has so composed the body, giving greater honor to the part that lacked it, that there may be no division in the body, but that the members may have the same care for one another. If one member suffers, all suffer together; if one member is honored, all rejoice together.
>
> Now you are the body of Christ and individually members of it. (1 Corinthians 12:21–27)

So it is with roles in the church. Some roles have greater prominence than others, but all have equal value, and all should be treated with honor.

Egalitarian claim 10.10: Qualifications: Why should a woman who is better qualified to be a pastor be ruled out simply because she is a woman?

This egalitarian claim is made by Rebecca Groothuis.

> Common sense tells us that it is counterproductive and unfair to pass over a qualified female for a leadership position and to install an incompetent male instead; yet this is what must sometimes be done when authority is deemed an exclusively male prerogative. Indeed, experience has proven women to be more than competent for leadership roles, both within and without the church.[101]

99. See the discussion of this question on pp. 104–6.
100. See Groothuis's discussion in *Good News for Women*, 47–49.
101. Ibid., 238.

Rich Nathan writes,

> Did Paul mean for us to. . .promote less qualified men above more qualified and gifted women because this honors God's plan in creation? I don't think Paul intended for us to adopt this utterly illogical perspective.[102]

Answer 10.10a: It is true that many women are gifted in teaching God's Word and have gifts of wisdom and maturity of judgment as well.

As I stated earlier,[103] the Bible highly honors the wisdom and knowledge that God gives to women, and gives many examples of significant ministry by women. When Paul says that older women should "teach what is good, and so train the young women" (Titus 2:3–4), he implies that many women have gifts of teaching and wisdom and knowledge. Because of this, in some cases a gifted woman has stronger teaching skills than her pastor.

Answer 10.10b: But God in His wisdom has said that one of the qualifications for teaching and governing over a church is to be a man.

Having certain skills or abilities is not the only thing that makes someone suitable for a certain role in God's eyes. For example, the Son has exactly the same abilities and perfections as the Father, but that does not mean He can take authority over the Father, or that He could have sent the Father into the world to die for our sins. The Son has the role of Son, and the Father has the role of Father as well as the leadership responsibilities that go with that role. Similarly, in the Old Testament, people from many different tribes would have had the ability to function as priests and carry out the sacrificial duties, but God commanded that only men from the tribe of Levi would have these responsibilities.

So we should not argue that teaching ability alone qualifies a woman to be a pastor. God has, in His wisdom, decided that one of the qualifications for being a pastor or elder is to be a man. And this is not an entirely arbitrary decision, but is appropriate to manhood. Some of the qualities essential to mature manhood are a disposition to lead and to provide for and to protect, and in the setting of a church these activities are carried out by elders and pastors. On the other hand, essential to mature womanhood is a disposition to support such male leadership.[104] So in requiring that elders be men, God has given a principle that also beautifully reflects the nature of men and women as He created them to be.

What then should we say if an egalitarian asks, "Would you rather have an incompetent male or a gifted female as a pastor?" The question is asking, "Would you rather have choice A that God

---

102. Nathan, *Who Is My Enemy* (2002), 152.

103. See pages 25–28, 49–50, 62–64, 75–78, 132, 145, 160–61, and 175–76 on the high value and honor the Bible gives to women.

104. See above, pp. 50, 440.

forbids or Choice B that God forbids?" The correct answer to such a question is "neither one."[105] An elder also has to be "able to teach" (1 Timothy 3:2).

Answer 10.10c: Therefore, on the basis of the teaching of the whole Bible, we can say that no woman is "better qualified" to be a pastor or elder, since one of the qualifications is to be a man.

We must not make the mistake of thinking that a woman's teaching ability is sufficient to qualify her to be a pastor or elder. The requirement that elders should be men is also part of the qualifications listed in Scripture.

Answer 10.10d: Women who have teaching gifts should be encouraged to use these in many other ways that are approved by Scripture.

I discussed in chapter 2 a number of ways that women with teaching gifts can teach hundreds or even thousands of other women, can have productive writing ministries, can carry on evangelistic activities aimed at both men and women (for this is not teaching or having authority over the church), can teach young people who are still under the instruction of their parents (and therefore "children" and not "men"), and can hold teaching positions in areas other than Bible and theology in Christian colleges and seminaries.[106]

EGALITARIAN CLAIM 10.11: IMAGE OF GOD: BOTH WOMEN AND MEN LEADERS ARE NEEDED TO FULLY REFLECT THE IMAGE OF GOD.

Stanley Grenz, writes,

> This understanding of the divine image constitutes a strong foundation for affirming the *participation of men and women in all areas of church life*. Because we are the image of God only as we share together in community, *we must welcome the participation and contribution of all individuals, both male and female*. Because men and women have unique contributions to make, the church must value the contributions of both sexes to the fulfillment of its task.[107]

Aida Spencer writes,

---

105. Even though he taught the logic of argumentation to Berkeley law students, Professor Phillip Johnson (whose writings on Darwinism I greatly appreciate) inappropriately offers us only two wrong choices when he writes in the foreword to Sarah Sumner's book, "I am certain that the overwhelming majority of faithful Christians agree with me that we would rather hear good teaching from a gifted woman than inferior teaching from a less gifted man" (*Men and Women in the Church,* 6). The question of which wrong choice we would prefer will not help us find the right choice.

106. See chapter 2, pp. 84–100.

107. Grenz, *Women in the Church,* 172 (italics added).

> God's original intention for women and men is that in work and in marriage they share tasks and share authority. Females as well as males are needed in positions of authority in the church to help people better to comprehend God's nature. *God's image needs male and female to reflect God more fully.*[108]

Cindy Jacobs writes,

> Without men and women working side by side, the Church will be ineffective. The complete image of God will only be manifested in its full expression when men and women stand side by side in the Church.[109]

Answer 10.11a: This claim would lead us to deny that Jesus could fully reflect the image of God.

If only men and women together can reflect the image of God, then Jesus, who was a man, could not fully reflect the image of God. But Scripture affirms that He fully reflects God to us:

> Jesus said to him, "Have I been with you so long, and you still do not know me, Philip? *Whoever has seen me has seen the Father.* How can you say, 'Show us the Father'?" (John 14:9)

> In their case the god of this world has blinded the minds of the unbelievers, to keep them from seeing the light of the gospel of the glory of *Christ, who is the image of God.* (2 Corinthians 4:4)

> *He is the image of the invisible God,* the firstborn of all creation. (Colossians 1:15)

> For in him all the fullness of God was pleased to dwell. (Colossians 1:19)

Therefore the egalitarian claim that both men and women leaders are necessary to fully reflect the image of God is false. If that were so, Jesus Himself could not be the leader of the church.

Answer 10.11b: One aspect of reflecting God's image is to reflect differences in authority in human relationships.

The egalitarian claim wrongly neglects an aspect of God that needs to be reflected in church life and in marriage: the difference in roles among the members of the Trinity. As Paul indicates in 1 Corinthians 11:3, "But I want you to understand that the head of every man is Christ, the head of a wife is her husband, and the head of Christ is God."

Thus, in a marriage relationship in which the husband has authority that his wife does not have, and in which the husband and wife are equal in value and dignity and personhood, there

---

108. Spencer, *Beyond the Curse* (1985), 29 (italics added).
109. Jacobs, *Women of Destiny* (1998), 153.

is a reflection of the equality and difference between Father and Son in the Trinity, a beautiful reflection of the image of God. And so it is with differences in role but equality in value and gifting in the church.

Answer 10.11c: The need to hear a woman's perspective on issues facing the church does not require that a church have women elders.

Related to the claim that both men and women are needed to fully reflect the image of God is the claim sometimes made that the elder board "needs to have a woman's perspective." Therefore (some egalitarians claim), it is right to have some women on the elder board.

However, as I mentioned in chapter 2 (p. 64), the men who are elders can and should frequently seek advice and counsel from their wives, as well as from other women in the church. This is analogous to the situation of a wise husband who often seeks counsel from and listens to the advice of his wife. If elders have frequent conversations with their wives and frequent opportunities to hear the perspectives of women in the church, they will gain the benefit of hearing women's perspectives without violating the biblical teachings that only men should have governing authority over the whole church. For example, I know of one wise pastor who meets once a month with eight to ten mature women of various ages in the church to listen to their concerns about various matters facing the church. Yet that church still has only men on its elder board.

The larger consideration here is again whether we will be subject to the authority of Scripture. God was not unaware of the value of hearing women's perspectives when making decisions about the direction of churches, but He still told us in Scripture that only men should be elders.

Egalitarian claim 10.12: Mission Field: It is inconsistent to restrict women from church leadership positions in the Western world and at the same time approve of women having such positions on the mission field.

I have heard this objection a number of times in personal conversation. Why should we allow women to plant churches, teach the Bible, and serve as pastors on the mission field while at the same time prohibiting them from such work here at home?

Rich Nathan writes, "How can churches justify women preaching the gospel and instructing men in other nations, while not allowing them to do the same here?"[110]

110. Nathan, *Who Is My Enemy,* 148.

Answer 10.12a: It is not right to say that the Bible is authoritative in one country and not in another.

We should never say that the Bible has authority in one country of the world and not in another! If anyone does this, he or she is being inconsistent and not respecting the authority of the Bible as the very Word of God. I would never want to support such a procedure.

Therefore whatever we decide the Bible teaches about women's roles in ministry, we should apply those principles consistently in every part of the world.

Answer 10.12b: Many kinds of women's ministries are approved by Scripture because they do not include teaching or governing over an assembled church or some equivalent activity.

As I pointed out in chapter 2, many ministries are entirely valid for women and are not prohibited by Scripture. For example, evangelistic ministry of various kinds is valid and should be encouraged for both men and women anywhere in the world.

More specifically, while people may have legitimate differences on whether it is wise for a mission board to send a single woman to evangelize an unreached group of people, I personally see no compelling objection to a woman doing evangelism in this way. Indeed, the history of missions is filled with the stories of courageous women who have carried out this kind of evangelism.

But what happens, time after time, is that as people become Christians, at first the woman missionary teaches the new converts in an informal way, analogous to the situation of Priscilla and Aquila teaching Apollos in Acts 18:26. Eventually, indigenous male leaders develop and a church is formed, and men in the village or tribe assume the leadership roles in the new church. This is a natural transition from an informal Bible study with a group of new Christians to an established church with men in leadership.[111]

Conclusion

We have considered several egalitarian claims based on theology and on the ideas of fairness and justice. The idea of the priesthood of all believers allows us all to have equal access before God without the necessity of a priest to intercede for us, but that does not guarantee that we are all qualified for every office in the church.

The parallel between the Son's submission to the Father, together with their equality in attributes and deity and honor, still provides an excellent parallel to the relationship between a husband and wife in marriage. The egalitarian claims that Jesus' submission to His Father was

---

111. See a specific example of this on pages 77–78.

only for His time here on earth are not consistent with numerous passages (largely ignored by egalitarians) that show an eternal Father-Son relationship, a relationship that never began and that eternally included the submission of the Son to the Father.

We also found that our ideas of fairness must be based on what God's Word teaches, because He is just and all that He tells us is just and fair.

As for the mission field, we should not have two standards, one for the mission field and one for our own country, but God's Word applies equally in all countries of the world.

Once again, the complementarian view of the equality of men and women in the image of God, together with their different roles in marriage and the church, is still seen to be valid and has not been overturned by the egalitarian objections we have considered in this chapter.

CHAPTER ELEVEN

Evangelical Feminist Claims from History and Experience

In this chapter we consider egalitarian objections based not on the Bible, but on observations of church history and contemporary experience. Haven't there been many women pastors and elders in the history of the church, giving us a precedent for women to be leaders in the church today? Haven't many denominations already approved women's ordination? And who are we to oppose the evident blessing of God on numerous women who currently serve as pastors and Bible teachers to men? Moreover, if a woman has a genuine call from God for pastoral ministry, how can we rightfully oppose that call?

Egalitarians also claim that many people with the gift of prophecy are calling for a new release of women into ministry today. Other people are saying that the full release of women into all aspects of ministry is necessary for such a unique time of worldwide revival as we see today, a time when God is bringing more people into the kingdom than at any other time in history. How can we refuse to have both men and women minister in the church at such a crucial time as this?

It is questions such as these that we consider in this chapter.

EGALITARIAN CLAIM 11.1: MANY HISTORICAL PRECEDENTS: THERE ARE MANY EXAMPLES OF WOMEN PASTORS AND WOMEN PREACHERS IN CHURCH HISTORY, SO THE EGALITARIAN POSITION IS NOT AS NOVEL AS SOME PEOPLE THINK.

This is the main argument of Janette Hassey's book *No Time for Silence*. She writes,

> In 1927, the Moody Bible Institute *Alumni News* proudly published a letter containing an astounding personal account of the ministry of Mabel C. Thomas, a 1913 MBI graduate. Thomas, called to the pastorate in a Kansas church, has preached, taught weekly Bible classes, and baptized dozens of converts. She concluded her letter with praise, since she "could not have met the many and varied opportunities for service without

the training of MBI" [Hassey's footnote indicates this is from *Moody Alumni News* (June 1927), 12].

Today, because of gender, female students at MBI and other Evangelical institutions are barred from pastoral training courses. Why has such an enormous shift occurred since the turn of the century? Why do many Evangelical groups who used women as pastors and preachers *then* now prohibit or discourage such ministry?...

How could Evangelicals a century ago hold high their inerrant, verbally inspired Bible in one hand while blessing the ministry of women preachers, pastors, Bible teachers, and evangelists with the other?...Those who endorsed women's public ministry were convinced that a literal approach to the Bible, and especially to prophecy, demanded such leadership by women.[1]

Hassey then details the history of women's involvement in public ministry in the United States. The first fully ordained woman was Antoinette Louisa Brown, who was ordained by the First Congregational Church of Butler and Savannah in Wayne County, New York, in 1853.[2] After 1853, Hassey reports the dates on which individual churches in various denominations first ordained women:

1865	Salvation Army (p. 53)[3]
1866	Advent Christians (p. 76)
1885	Seventh Day Baptists (p. 56)
1886	Free Will Baptists (p. 56)
1888	Disciples (p. 72)
1889	Cumberland Presbyterians (p. 77)[4]
1889	United Brethren (p. 51)
1890	Brethren (p. 58)
1897	Pilgrim Holiness (p. 53)
1903	American Baptists (p. 62)
1908	Nazarenes (p. 53)
1911	Mennonites (General Conference, p. 57)

In addition to these groups that ordained women, Hassey points out several other factors concerning evangelicalism in the United States:

1. Janette Hassey, *No Time for Silence* (1986), xi–xii.
2. Ibid., 69.
3. The Salvation Army was founded in 1865 and women had leadership roles at all levels from the beginning, so it is listed here even though installation in those roles may not have exactly paralleled "ordination" in other denominations.
4. However, this was revoked in 1894 (p. 78).

1. From Colonial days onward, there were some women Bible teachers and preachers in the United States. Until the mid-nineteenth century, these women preachers were mostly among the Quakers (p. 73), although there were also a few among some Baptist groups (p. 56). These women preachers became more numerous in the early 1900s[5] (several examples are given on pages 11–30).
2. In the early 1900s, many Bible institutes had both men and women students. While many of the students became missionaries, evangelists, and lay workers in churches, and many filled other non-pastoral roles (such as ministries of mercy and work with temperance and women's suffrage movements), some taught in Bible colleges and some became pastors, usually in smaller, rural churches where no trained men were available. The alumni publications of these Bible institutes (such as Moody Bible Institute in Chicago and Northwestern in Minneapolis) published the ministry reports of these women.[6]
3. Some early evangelical leaders in the United States supported the idea of women preachers, even if they were ambivalent on the idea of women's ordination as pastors. However, these leaders generally did not support an egalitarian view of marriage. Leaders who supported the right of women to preach included A. B. Simpson (founder of the Christian and Missionary Alliance), A. J. Gordon (prominent Baptist pastor, 1836–1895), and both Fredrik Franson and John Gustaf Princell (both influential in founding what became the Evangelical Free Church of America).[7]

What shall we make of Hassey's arguments? Do these historical facts indicate clear precedents that should lead us to think that the ordination of women is consistent with evangelical beliefs and especially with the conviction that the Bible is the inerrant Word of God? That is the intent of Hassey's book, and some have found the argument persuasive. But several other factors need to be considered before we reach such a conclusion.

Answer 11.1a: While Hassey has emphasized isolated examples, the entire history of the church, and the entire history of evangelicalism in America, looks far different: The vast majority of churches, and of evangelicals in particular, clearly rejected the idea of women as pastors throughout church history.

Several egalitarian books, in addition to Janette Hassey's book, provide helpful surveys of women who have played influential roles at various times in the history of the church. Probably the most comprehensive study is *Daughters of the Church: Women and Ministry from New Testament*

5. Hassey, *No Time for Silence,* 11–30, 56, 73.
6. Hassey quotes several of these reports on pp. 11–46.
7. Hassey discusses Simpson's views on pp. 15–16 and 19. A. J. Gordon's position is explained on pp. 20 and 105–8. Franson is discussed on pp. 84–86 and 108–10. Princell's views are reported on pp. 89–90.

Times to the Present by Ruth Tucker and Walter Liefeld.[8] A shorter summary of this study is found in Ruth Tucker's book *Women in the Maze*.[9] From a complementarian perspective, a helpful historical survey is the article by William Weinrich, "Women in the History of the Church: Learned and Holy, but not Pastors."[10] The most extensive scholarly history of the ordination of women in various American denominations is Mark Chaves, *Ordaining Women*.[11]

The conclusion from these studies is not in dispute: for the first eighteen hundred years of the history of the church, women played influential roles in evangelism, prayer, ministries of mercy, writing, financial support, political influence, private exhortation and encouragement and counsel, and teaching of women and children. But they never became pastors of churches, and rarely did they speak or teach publicly in mixed assemblies of men and women. When women did preach or teach the Bible to men, it was generally in "sectarian" movements such as the Quakers.[12] Tucker and Liefeld say: "Women were very prominent in church history...even though they were systematically denied positions of authority."[13]

Although early Methodism did not ordain women, John Wesley did allow women to speak in small informal groups,[14] and by the 1770s, Wesley would allow women to "exhort" but not to "preach" to larger groups of both men and women, arguing that it was allowed when they had "an *extraordinary* call" because he thought that "the whole work of God called Methodism is an extraordinary dispensation of His providence."[15]

After detailing other examples of women who spoke publicly in Baptist groups or among women who claimed extraordinary visions or revelations from the Holy Spirit,[16] Tucker and Liefeld conclude:

> The seventeenth and eighteenth centuries provided women with more opportunities for ministry than they had previously enjoyed, but only if they were willing to defy male leadership in the institutionalized churches or be associated with sectarian move-

8. Tucker and Liefeld, *Daughters of the Church* (1987).
9. Tucker, *Women in the Maze* (1992), 141–90.
10. Weinrich, "Women in the History of the Church," in Piper and Grudem, *Recovering Biblical Manhood and Womanhood* (1991), 263–79.
11. Mark Chaves, *Ordaining Women* (1997). Chaves gives a detailed list on pp. 16–17 of the date various denominations first granted full clergy rights to women. In a few cases his dates differ slightly from the list I have taken from Janette Hassey's book below, but these differences may be explained by the difference between an individual congregation ordaining a woman and an official denomination-wide decision to approve such ordination.
12. Margaret Fell, a leader among the early Quakers, published *Women's Speaking Justified, Proved and Allowed of by the Scriptures* in 1667 in London. She married George Fox, founder of the Quakers, in 1669. (See Tucker and Liefeld, *Daughters of the Church*, 227–32.) The Quakers (Society of Friends) had no ordained clergy of either sex, but supported women speaking publicly under the inspiration of the Holy Spirit. Hassey writes, "In Colonial America virtually all women preachers belonged to the Society of Friends" (*No Time for Silence*, 74).
13. Tucker and Liefeld, *Daughters of the Church*, 14–15.
14. Ibid., 240.
15. Ibid., 241.
16. Ibid., 220–24, 225–27.

> ments and endure the scorn of respectable society.... But...there was no room for debate in theological circles. Women were admonished to keep silent in the churches, and the vast majority did.[17]

William Weinrich says that prior to the Reformation, "there never was recognized ordained female ministry in the west (or east) that involved teaching in the assembly and ministering at the altar."[18] After the Reformation, within Protestantism, Weinrich says "the major Reformation and post-Reformation leaders assumed without question the practice of reserving the office of pastor and sacramental minister to men."[19] This was the conviction of Martin Luther and the Lutherans, John Calvin and the Reformed churches that followed his teaching, and of John Wesley and Methodism, who allowed women to speak under "an extraordinary impulse of the Spirit" but who did not allow women to be pastors or regular teachers or leaders of their congregations.[20] Then Weinrich adds:

> Other Reformation and post-Reformation groups largely concurred with the views of Luther, Calvin, and Wesley. The Anabaptists, the Anglicans, the Puritans, and the Separatists all prohibited women from the public ministry of preaching and teaching. While groups that emphasized religious experience and interior calling did allow women to assume (more or less restricted) public preaching, not until the 19th century did women begin to make significant strides toward a ready acceptance of any public ministry. It has been only in the last half of the 20th century that the major Protestant church bodies have begun to accept women as regular preachers and pastors.[21]

Some understanding of the extent of approval of female clergy can be gained from census numbers. In 1880 there were 165 female ministers in the whole United States. These women ministers constituted 0.3 percent of all the clergy in the U.S. By 1920 there were 1,787 women clergy in the United States, or 1.4 percent of the clergy.[22] But the number of women pastors in the major evangelical groups was much smaller, since presumably these numbers include all the female clergy among liberal groups such as Unitarians, Universalists, more liberal congregational churches, as well as women leaders in the Salvation Army and the Quakers. The 1920 number also includes any women clergy among early Pentecostal groups. But all of those combined made up only 1.4 percent of the total number of clergy in 1920. After we exclude a large proportion that were in liberal or sectarian groups, we find that the total number of women clergy in mainstream evangelical groups even in 1920 was exceptionally small.

---

17. Ibid., 243–44.
18. Weinrich, "Women in the History of the Church," 277.
19. Ibid.
20. Ibid., 278.
21. Ibid., 278–79.
22. Hassey, *No Time for Silence,* 9.

Answer 11.1b: Our authority must be what the Bible teaches, not what some Christians have done at various times in the past.

Even Janette Hassey, who favors full ordination for women, says at the end of her study:

> The undisputable fact that many Bible-believing evangelicals approved of female preachers, pastors and ordained ministers in the past does not necessarily make it right. The important question for Evangelicals is whether women's public ministry is biblical.[23]

This is the most important point about this study: The fundamental question is, What does the Bible teach about this? We may find it useful to read the arguments of evangelicals such as A. J. Gordon and Fredrik Franson to see if their interpretations of Scripture are persuasive (and Hassey helpfully summarizes their arguments on pages 95–121). But Christians who take the Bible as their supreme authority are not free to adopt a position simply because some evangelical leader in the past has held that position. The question is, How did they understand the key passages on this topic? And do we think they were correct in their understanding? Are we willing to defend that understanding as the correct understanding of Scripture today?

Moreover, it is amazing that Hassey and others can find so few early evangelical leaders who advocate women's ordination or women as preachers and Bible teachers. The history of evangelicalism in the United States includes many millions of believers and hundreds of denominations and viewpoints, and it is surprising how few and how hesitant are the advocates among evangelicals for any public ministry for women until the late 1970s.[24]

Answer 11.1c: Hassey's argument would have evangelicals today reject the godly wisdom of the majorities in these movements and adopt the rejected views of the minorities instead.

As Hassey herself points out, many of the denominations and institutions she examines later adopted policies that restricted the ordained pastoral ministry to men:

> Today, because of gender, female students at MBI and other Evangelical institutions are barred from pastoral training courses.... Why do many Evangelical groups who used women as pastors *then* now prohibit or discourage such ministry?[25]

Specifically, the Evangelical Free Church restricts ordination to men, in spite of the views of Franson and Princell. The Christian and Missionary Alliance restricts the eldership to men, in spite of the early views of A. B. Simpson. Many Bible colleges that formerly reported on women's

23. Ibid., 148.
24. Modern evangelical advocacy of an egalitarian position probably began in 1974 with the book by Letha Scanzoni and Nancy Hardesty, *All We're Meant to Be* (1974), which was followed quickly in 1975 by Paul Jewett's book, *Man as Male and Female* (1975).
25. Hassey, *No Time for Silence*, xi.

pastoral ministries (apparently favorably, according to Hassey) now teach that only men should be pastors and elders in churches.

What happened? In various ways, the majority of wise, godly leaders in those movements, after careful study and reflection on Scripture, decided to adopt such policies. They rejected the egalitarian tendencies Hassey discovered here and there in the early days of those movements. In the decision-making process, the egalitarians lost.

But *Hassey would have us go back and say the losers in the debate were right and the majority decision was wrong*. She would have us adopt the rejected views of the minority and reject the considered decision of the majority. But why? On what basis should the views of the minority be given privileged status and allowed to return now as established policy? Rather than respecting the wisdom and precedents of the vast majorities in earlier generations in these movements, Hassey's approach would have us reject that wisdom.

Answer 11.1d: Most early evangelical leaders who supported women's preaching were not egalitarians in the modern sense.

Modern egalitarians want evangelicals to go far beyond the views of the early leaders that Hassey quotes. Hassey points out that A. J. Gordon and Fredrik Franson were not egalitarian with respect to marriage, but supported "the husband's headship and wife's submission," as did Catherine Booth, who helped found the Salvation Army.[26] Though Franson encouraged women to preach, he did not write in support of women's ordination. Similarly, A. J. Gordon supported women's preaching but was unsure about women's ordination and women governing over congregations, thinking that 1 Timothy 2:12 might forbid such things.[27] And John Gustaf Princell also thought women could preach but was unwilling to advocate women in governing positions in churches.[28] Such positions are hardly the equivalent of modern egalitarian positions.

Answer 11.1e: There was great diversity and freedom in early American evangelicalism, along with a strong tradition of local church autonomy that allowed for the ordination of some women in specific local churches.

Freedom of religion has been a strong component of American history from its early days, and found expression in the First Amendment to the Constitution in 1789. Evangelicalism has spawned hundreds of denominations and various splinter groups and sects. In addition to the denominations with highly developed governmental structures and strong authority over local congregations (such as the Episcopalians, Presbyterians, and Methodists), there were many denominations that gave autonomy to local congregations to decide their own affairs, and this included the freedom to ordain whomever they wished. Denominations with a strong emphasis

26. Ibid., 109.
27. Ibid., 107, 109.
28. Ibid., 90.

on local church autonomy included many Baptist groups as well as many Free Churches. Hassey explains, "The Free Church congregational principle of the local autonomy of each church necessitated this openness to women."[29]

Where local church autonomy prevailed, it is not surprising that some small, rural churches would eventually have women pastors, especially if a church had a woman who had been trained at a Bible college and no men with similar training. But occasional cases like this, as Hassey reports, do not in themselves indicate denominational approval or majority assent, but rather an unwillingness to interfere with the strongly held principle of local church autonomy. In such cases, a denomination's decision to forbid women's ordination would ordinarily come only after the national governing structure had become more developed, and only after the denomination reached a consensus that this was a matter of enough importance to justify overriding the strongly held principle of local church autonomy.

Answer 11.1f: The vast majority of evangelical churches and institutions did not approve of the ordination of women at any point in American history. The trend among several major denominations to approve the ordination of women only began in the 1950s, well after liberal theology had gained controlling influence in those denominations.

In the late nineteenth century, the vast majority of evangelical groups, including several large denominations that would become liberal in the twentieth century, rejected women's ordination to the pastorate. But the roots of a trend toward women's ordination among liberal denominations can already be seen in the late nineteenth century. In 1889, J. T. Sunderland published *The Liberal Christian Ministry*, in which he said that one of the benefits of liberal Christianity, which rejected the view of the Bible as God's inspired Word, was that women had more freedom to minister in liberal churches. Hassey reports, "After praising Unitarian, Universalist, and Quaker female ministry, Sunderland wrote, 'no orthodox body has opened its regular ministry to women.'"[30]

A trend among liberal denominations to ordain women can also be seen in the extensive list compiled by Mark Chaves. Although there were a few exceptions prior to the 1950s, especially among some African-American, Baptistic, and Pentecostal groups,[31] the majority of large denominations in the United States did not approve women's ordination until 1956 or later,

29. Ibid., 91. Even today the Statement of Faith of the Evangelical Free Church of America says, "We believe that Jesus Christ is the Lord and Head of the Church, and that every local church has the right under Christ to decide and govern its own affairs" (Article 10).
30. J. T. Sunderland, *The Liberal Christian Ministry* (1889), as cited in Hassey, *No Time for Silence*, 2 and 222n6.
31. Among the larger denominations, the significant ones that ordained women prior to 1956 (according to Chaves's list) were Congregationalists (1853), Disciples of Christ (1888), the National Baptist Convention (1895), the Pentecostal Holiness Church (1895), the African Methodist Episcopal Zion Church (1898), the Northern Baptist Convention (1907), the Church of the Nazarene (1908), the Baptist General Conference (1918), the International Church of the Foursquare Gospel (1927), and the Assemblies of God (1935), Mark Chaves, *Ordaining Women* (1997), 16.

after most of them had come under the dominant influence of liberal theology (at least at their national leadership level). Here is the material from Chaves's chart:

Dates when major denominations began ordaining women in the United States:

Presbyterian Church in the USA (North)	1956
Methodist Church	1956
Church of the Brethren	1958
United Presbyterian Church, North America	1958
African Methodist Episcopal Church	1960
Presbyterian Church, US (South)	1964
Southern Baptist Convention	1964[32]
Evangelical United Brethren Church	1968
American Lutheran Church	1970
Lutheran Church in America	1970
Mennonite Church	1973
Free Methodist Church, North America	1974
Evangelical Covenant Church	1976
Episcopal Church	1976
Reformed Church in America	1979

Even as of 2003, a number of large and influential denominations within the United States do not ordain women. These include the Southern Baptist Convention, the Presbyterian Church in America, the Lutheran Church—Missouri Synod, the Evangelical Free Church of America (in spite of the views of Free Church forefathers Fredrik Franson and John Gustaf Princell), and the Christian and Missionary Alliance (in spite of the views of the founder, A. B. Simpson). In addition, there are thousands of Bible churches and independent churches, many of them with several thousand members, that do not ordain women.

Answer 11.1g: Early Bible institutes were founded to train lay workers, not pastors, although some women students later became pastors.

Hassey points out at several places that the early Bible institutes (such as Moody and Northwestern and others) were not formed as seminaries to train pastors. They were schools for training lay workers in the churches, and they naturally admitted both men and women as students.[33] Hassey notes that prior to the founding of Moody Bible Institute, Dwight L. Moody said,

32. This Southern Baptist policy was revoked in 1984, after conservatives recaptured leadership of the denomination; see Chaves, *Ordaining Women*, 35, 89.

33. Hassey, *No Time for Silence*, 14.

> I believe we need "gap men," men who are trained to fill the gap between the common people and the ministers. We are to raise up men and women who will be willing to lay down their lives alongside the laboring.[34]

Concerning the need for work among the urban poor, Moody said, "Give me women to work among this class of the population." Moody also wanted to solve the problem of "a chronic shortage of qualified Christian workers with a Bible education to assist in the inquiry room work connected with revivals."[35] With this purpose, Moody founded The Bible Institute of the Chicago Evangelization Society in 1889 (which was renamed Moody Bible Institute in 1900).

And Hassey notes that some early Bible institutes explicitly distinguished the purposes for which they were training women from those for which they were training men, with an assumption that only men would be pastors.[36]

Some women graduates of these institutes spoke widely in public meetings in opposition to drunkenness and support of the temperance movement.[37] Others began to preach, and some became pastors of churches.[38]

Hassey makes much of the fact that alumni publications from schools such as Moody reported the ministries of these women, but it is not clear that those reports indicated official endorsement of those ministries.[39] As Hassey says regarding Moody Bible Institute, "MBI leadership may not have explicitly encouraged women to preach, pastor, or seek ordination, but their implicit endorsement of women in these authoritative roles for over 40 years cannot be denied."[40]

Answer 11.1h: Early approval of women's preaching or women's ordination occurred more often in certain kinds of groups.

Hassey points out that among certain groups there was a higher likelihood that women's ordination would be approved. These groups included the following:

---

34. Ibid., 36.
35. Ibid.
36. Ibid. See p. 26 regarding Biola, and pages 27–29 regarding Philadelphia School of the Bible; she notes however that Moody, Northwestern, and other Bible institutes did not make such distinctions, at least not explicitly.
37. Ibid. See pp. 13, 22, 33.
38. Hassey tells interesting stories about various women, such as the discussion of several Baptist and congregational women on pp. 62–72.
39. To take one example, the *Moody Alumni News* for June 1927, pp. 12–13, does report the pastoral work of Mrs. Mabel C. Thomas, who continued serving as a pastor after her husband died, but it is just given in the midst of many pages of reports sent in by alumni and printed without comment. Hassey's claim in the first sentence of her book that in 1927 the *Moody Alumni News* "proudly published a letter containing an astounding personal account of the ministry of Mabel C. Thomas, a 1913 MBI graduate, called to the pastorate in a Kansas church," is an exaggeration. There is no indication that it was published any more proudly than the reports of dozens of other alumni from many graduating classes, listed by year of graduation. (To take another example, the Harvard alumni magazine also dutifully prints reports of my ministry that I send in from time to time, but Harvard University today would hardly endorse my defense of the Bible as the Word of God, of male headship in marriage, of Christ as the only way of salvation, and many other things.)
40. Hassey, *No Time for Silence,* 44. On pp. 38–45, she gives reports about a number of Moody graduates who became pastors.

1. Revivalist groups where experience of the Holy Spirit's anointing rather than formal training was the primary qualification for ministry. This includes the Quakers and the Cumberland Presbyterians (who voted to ordain women in 1892, but revoked the decision in 1894). Hassey says, "Revivalism…tended to loosen institutional structure and fostered informal, spontaneous worship; women experienced new opportunities to preach in such settings."[41]

   Historian George Marsden reaches a similar conclusion:

   > The fundamentalist movement generally allowed women only quite subordinate roles. When experiential emphasis predominated, the idea that Pentecost opened a dispensation when women would prophesy (as the prophet Joel suggested) might be accepted.[42]

2. Adventist groups that expected the imminent return of Christ and that thought that Joel's prophecy about the pouring out of the Holy Spirit in the last days opened new opportunities for women to minister.[43]
3. Lay movements where there was not as clear a distinction between clergy and laity.[44] Such lay movements did not immediately exclude women speakers, since everyone was thought of as a lay person, not a member of the clergy. However, as these movements matured, institutional structures developed and they established and ordained clergy. When that happened, a number of the movements decided they would not ordain women as members of the clergy.

   We could add that in other cases inter-church associations were formed, and some originally included groups that ordained women. One example Hassey gives is the group that eventually led to the Independent Fundamental Churches of America. When the association began in 1923 it included groups that allowed women's ordination, but it decided to eliminate groups that ordained women in 1930.[45]
4. Liberal groups or groups with significant liberal influence, such as the Congregationalists. Hassey notes that their Kansas City Declaration of 1913 "sharply contrasted with new fundamentalist creeds."[46]

In conclusion, given the incredible diversity of evangelicalism in America, and given the extensive religious freedom allowed in this country, it is not surprising that a few evangelicals

---

41. Ibid., 134.
42. George Marsden, *Fundamentalism and American Culture* (1980), 249–50.
43. Hassey, *No Time for Silence*, 76–77.
44. See Hassey, *No Time for Silence,* 93, on the beginnings of the Free Church as a lay movement, for example, in which men assumed the positions of pastors once more organized churches were developed.
45. Ibid., 79.
46. Ibid., 69.

supported women's preaching or women's ordination from time to time, or that there were some women preachers or even women pastors. But the overall picture that emerges is that these were the exceptions, and they constituted a tiny minority among all evangelicals in the United States, at least until the increasing influence of evangelical feminism in the 1980s. And even to this day, though it is difficult to ascertain exactly the number of ordained women in evangelical groups, it is certainly not very large.[47]

Answer 11.1i: A broader perspective from the worldwide Christian church shows that egalitarianism is an unusual development primarily confined to European and American Protestantism in the last half of the twentieth century and is by no means representative of the church through history or around the world.

Roman Catholic author Richard John Neuhaus offered a broader perspective on this question in some comments in *First Things* in March of 1996:

> Dr. Eugene Brand of the Lutheran World Federation (LWF)...addressing a recent consultation on women in Geneva...got carried away by the need to assure them that the LWF would "not sell out the ordination of women" to gain communion with the Roman Catholic or Orthodox churches. "We should not ask, 'Is it possible to ordain women?' We should ask, 'Is there any earthly reason why women should not be ordained?' The only answer to that question is no."
>
> The *only* answer? In fidelity to a tradition of almost two thousand years, the three bodies that hold to a sacramental view of ministry in apostolic succession—Catholic, Orthodox, and Anglican—unanimously answered the question otherwise. In 1994 and 1995 the Catholic Church again—this time in a form that clearly makes the teaching unchangeable in the future—declared that the Church is not authorized to ordain women to the priesthood. As much as we can say 'never' about anything in history, we can say that the Orthodox will never ordain women to the priesthood. The fact is that, among churches with a sacramental and apostolic view of ordination, the tradition was

---

47. To take one representative example, I think of the student body at Trinity Evangelical Divinity School, where I was a professor from 1981–2001. During that time Trinity admitted students from over a hundred denominations from the United States and abroad. We admitted both men and women students, and a number of faculty members (though not the majority) supported opening all ministry roles to women. Certainly there was no discrimination against women who wanted to enter the ministry.

Though the total number of women in the student body was around 22 percent, the number of women in the Master of Divinity program (the primary program for training pastors) remained steady at around 5 or 6 percent. And many of those women in the MDiv program were getting training as missionaries, counselors, wives of husbands who were planning to be pastors, or for further academic study. So not many of the women students in the MDiv program wanted to become pastors (though some did). That means that in one of the largest evangelical seminaries in the world, one which is representative of a broad cross section of evangelicalism, perhaps only 2 percent of the students were women who planned to become pastors. This is quite remarkable in the face of the avalanche of twenty-five years of evangelical feminist books and journal articles arguing vigorously for full participation of women in every aspect of ministry.

unbroken until 1974 when a few Episcopalian women were illegally ordained. The illegality was later regularized by the Episcopal Church in this country, and now the Church of England has followed suit. But the worldwide Anglican communion, counting fifty to sixty million members, is still divided on the question. The Catholic Church has more than a billion members, and the Orthodox approximately 200 million. It follows that, among the churches holding to a catholic view of ministry, those who have broken with the tradition—and that only within the last few years—claim about 3 percent of the membership. In addition, the great majority of Protestants who do not subscribe to a catholic view of priesthood (Baptist, Missouri Synod Lutherans, orthodox Calvinists, *et al.*) believe that ordaining women is precluded on biblical grounds. *The inescapable conclusion is that ordaining women is a very recent North American–European innovation accepted by a very small part of world Christianity.* Whether that very small part represents the wave of the future or a temporary aberration of our theologically confused times is a question about which people can disagree. But to say that no is the "only answer" to the question of whether there is any reason why women should not be (or cannot be) ordained is to write off two millennia of tradition and the practice of the overwhelming majority of Christians in the world today.... A small minority of Christians, and a much smaller minority of those holding to a catholic view of ministry, have in recent years decided that it is possible to ordain women to the priesthood. Through reasoned argument they can try to make the case for their innovation. Nobody's interests are served, and least of all is the interest of Christian unity served, by the *obiter dictum* that it is self-evident that everybody else is wrong.[48]

EGALITARIAN CLAIM 11.2: MANY DENOMINATIONS: MANY DENOMINATIONS HAVE STUDIED THIS ISSUE AND APPROVED WOMEN FOR ORDINATION. THIS PROVIDES A PATTERN FOR OTHERS TO FOLLOW.

This objection may not often be stated explicitly, but it is something to take into account, because there surely are more groups ordaining women today than there were thirty years ago.

Answer 11.2a: All theologically liberal denominations have approved women's ordination.

As I explained above, a trend began in the mid-1950s by which all of the theologically liberal denominations in the United States eventually approved the ordination of women. This includes the Methodist Church (1956), the Presbyterian Church—USA (1956 in the North and 1964 in

48. Richard John Neuhaus, "While We're At It," *First Things* 61 (March 1996), 69.

the South), the American Lutheran Church (1970), the Lutheran Church in America (1970; the ALC and LCA have now combined to form the Evangelical Lutheran Church in America), and the Episcopal Church (1976). I categorize these denominations as "theologically liberal" because the vast majority of those who hold denominational leadership positions or teach at denominational seminaries or run denominational publishing houses reject the idea that the Bible is the inspired and inerrant Word of God.

Answer 11.2b: Several denominations and organizations that are broadly tolerant of liberalism and that have leaders who have moved toward liberalism have approved women's ordination.

Included in this group are the Mennonite Church (which approved women's ordination in 1973), the Evangelical Covenant Church (1976), and the Reformed Church in America (1979). More recently, the Christian Reformed Church approved women's ordination in 1996 (it abandoned a formal commitment to the inerrancy of Scripture in 1974).[49] Though many members in these denominations hold to the complete truthfulness or inerrancy of Scripture as the very Word of God and are grieved at the increasing influence of liberalism among denominational leaders and seminary professors, the fact remains that these denominations encompass a wide variety in their views of the nature of Scripture.

The Southern Baptist Convention began in 1964 to allow women's ordination as it was practiced in individual congregations. These ordinations were not overturned by the denomination as a whole. But 1964 was a time when theological liberalism was gaining increasing influence in Southern Baptist seminaries and among denominational leaders. Then in 1984, after conservatives who held strongly to biblical inerrancy recaptured the leadership of that denomination, the Southern Baptist Convention reversed itself and revoked its approval of women's ordination.[50]

Another example is Fuller Theological Seminary in Pasadena, California. Though Fuller started as a conservative evangelical seminary, it removed the doctrine of biblical inerrancy from its statement of faith in 1971, and today, though it is still considered "evangelical" rather than "liberal," it has significant influence from theological liberalism among its faculty. Full-fledged advocacy of the ordination of women reigns on campus, and I doubt Fuller would hire anyone holding another position to teach there (or if someone were hired, I doubt that he would be allowed to express publicly his opposition to women's ordination).

Answer 11.2c: Women's ordination has also been approved by other groups that are not now theologically liberal but place extraordinary value on relating effectively to the culture, or place extraordinary value on the experience of effective ministry, and consequently place less value on maintaining doctrinal accuracy.

---

49. As reported in Chaves, *Ordaining Women,* 86.
50. Ibid., 35, 89.

The ability to relate effectively to modern culture was a foundational principle of Willow Creek Community Church in South Barrington, Illinois, especially because of its large emphasis on evangelism. To take another example, Fuller Seminary from its foundation in 1947 emphasized gaining approval and acceptance from the liberal academic world and gaining influence for evangelical convictions among liberal denominations.

Other groups have placed strong emphasis on the experience of effective ministry and in practice this seems to have had priority over what seemed (to them at least) to be controversial or confused doctrinal areas. This includes some Pentecostal groups, such as the International Church of the Foursquare Gospel and the Assemblies of God, both of which have ordained women as pastors for many decades (since its 1927 founding for the Foursquare denomination and since 1935 for the Assemblies of God).[51]

Answer 11.2d: But nearly all denominations and organizations that have refused women's ordination share some common characteristics: (1) They hold firmly to the inerrancy of the Bible; (2) they are strongly truth-based and doctrinally vigilant; and (3) in many cases their leaders have personally fought and won battles with liberalism.

After an extensive study of the history of women's ordination in the United States, Mark Chaves (who himself strongly favors the ordination of women) reports the following:

> Two groups of denominations are particularly resistant to women's ordination: ...denominations practicing sacramental ritual [by this he means the Roman Catholic Church and Eastern Orthodox and Episcopal churches] and denominations endorsing biblical inerrancy.... *Biblically inerrant denominations* are... resistant to formal gender equality.[52]

As I mentioned earlier, conservatives who held to inerrancy regained control of the Southern Baptist Convention over a ten or fifteen year period beginning in 1979.[53] The SBC in 2000 added this formal provision to its doctrinal statement: "The office of pastor is limited to men as qualified by Scripture" (Article VI of the Baptist Faith and Message).

Another example is the Lutheran Church—Missouri Synod, which in 1974 dismissed the president of Concordia Seminary in St. Louis, a measure that soon led to the angry resignation of forty-five of the fifty faculty members of the seminary, thereby removing most of the influence of theological liberalism that denied the complete truthfulness of Scripture.[54] The Missouri Synod does not ordain women.

---

51. Ibid., 16.
52. Ibid., 84–85 (italics added).
53. Conservatives regained control of the Southern Baptist Convention beginning with the election of Adrian Rogers as president of the denomination in 1979 (see Jerry Sutton, *The Baptist Reformation* [2000], 99).
54. More details on the Lutheran Church–Missouri Synod are given at p. 502n13.

Yet another example is the Presbyterian Church in America, which was formed when conservatives left the more liberal Southern Presbyterian Church in 1973. The PCA does not ordain women.

Current leaders in each of these three denominations remember their struggles with theological liberalism, and they remember that an egalitarian advocacy of women's ordination goes hand in hand with theological liberalism.

Another denomination that has refused to grant women's ordination is the Evangelical Free Church of America. Though it has not had to do battle with liberals for control of the denomination, it has maintained a strong doctrinal vigilance and a strong commitment to faithfully uphold the inerrancy of the Bible largely through the influence of Trinity Evangelical Divinity School.

Simply counting the number of denominations that approve women's ordination is not too helpful in resolving this question. But when we look at the historical pattern, it is evident that theological liberalism, indicated by a rejection of the authority of the Bible, in many cases precedes the approval of women's ordination. Therefore when we look more closely at the "many denominations" that have approved women's ordination, the trend can actually serve as a warning against following a similar path.

EGALITARIAN CLAIM 11.3: ARTWORK: ANCIENT ARTWORK SHOWS THE POSSIBILITY OF WOMEN BISHOPS IN THE ANCIENT CHURCH.

In a 1988 issue of the journal *Christian History*, Catherine Kroeger claims that a fresco on a Christian catacomb in Rome, dating from the late third century, shows a woman in "an amazingly authoritative stance, like that of a bishop." She adds, "the shepherds on either side may represent pastors, in which case the woman may be in the role of a bishop, blessing pastors in her charge."[55]

Answer 11.3a: No expert in the study of ancient Christian art supports Kroeger's interpretation.

The fresco in question is one example of a common kind of early painting called an *orant* or an *orans* (Latin, "one who prays"). The entry for "Orant" in the *Encyclopedia of Early Christianity* says,

> The posture symbolizing prayer, from Latin *orans* ("one who prays"). Typically, in early Christian art, the orant is represented by a standing female facing front, arms raised and extended outward from the body.... The figure is widely attested in the very

55. Comments by Catherine Kroeger in *Christian History,* 17 (1988): 2. The fresco is said to come from the Coemeterium Majus arcosolium in Rome.

> earliest Christian art...but there has been a long history of controversy surrounding its interpretation.... Because this image is often attested in funerary contexts, many interpreters have sought an eschatological-symbolic explanation: the orant is a symbol of the soul in paradise, or of the church (feminine) at prayer anticipating the next life.
>
> Other interpretations include a testimony to the piety and faithfulness of the deceased, or a portrayal of prayer for those still on earth.[56]

Nothing in any of these studies even hints that the person praying in these paintings is in "an especially authoritative stance," or might be a woman "bishop," or that the shepherds represent "pastors" in the care of a bishop, as Kroeger claims. These statements are pure speculation on Kroeger's part. A sense of fairness to one's readers should require that any author who makes such statements should at the very least include some kind of disclaimer, such as,

> This type of figure is common in early Christian art, and there are several competing theories about what these praying figures mean. My proposal is unusual, since no scholar who specializes in the study of ancient Christian art has ever proposed the interpretation I am giving, but it still seems right to me.

Then the author could give reasons and arguments for his or her interpretation. Such a procedure would be honest and fair to readers who have no opportunity to check the relevant sources for themselves. But Dr. Kroeger has not given any such disclaimer as this.

We might also expect that the editors of a journal such as *Christian History* would either have enough knowledge of the field themselves to know that Kroeger's statement was unprecedented in the history of scholarship concerning early Christian art, or that they would have access to reviewers who would have sufficient knowledge to tell them this so that at least readers would not automatically take Kroeger's interpretation as a reliable testimony from an expert in the field.[57] If Kroeger is unaware of this other scholarly work, then one wonders how she can be considered even minimally competent to write about it herself. If she is aware of this other scholarly work but fails to mention it to her readers, then she has not met fundamental demands of honesty in an article such as this.

The procedure followed in this egalitarian claim troubles me more than most of the other claims that I consider in this book. When no explanations or disclaimers are made alerting readers to the uniform lack of support from scholarly specialists for such an interpretation,

---

56. Paul Corby Finney, "Orant," in *Encyclopedia of Early Christianity* (1997), 831. In addition to Finney's article, see J. Beaudry, "Orans," in *New Catholic Encyclopedia* (2002), 621; A. M. Giuntella, "Orans," in *Encyclopedia of the Early Church* (1992), 2:615. All three articles include bibliographies of additional studies.

57. It is not clear to me that complementarian scholars had any opportunity for input in this issue of *Christian History*. The entire issue was devoted to the history of *Women in the Church*, and five of the six "contributing editors" were women who have been authors and leaders in the egalitarian movement: Patricia Gundry, Nancy Hardesty, Catherine Kroeger, Aida Spencer, and Karen Torjesen (p. 3).

this wild speculation (or so it seems to me, after reading these other articles) is taken as truth by unsuspecting readers. Cindy Jacobs, for example, simply trusts Kroeger's interpretation of this fresco as truthful, and counts it as evidence for women's participation in a high position of governing authority in the early church.[58] Thousands of readers of Jacobs's book also take it as true, thinking that since it has a footnote to a journal on church history, there must be scholarly support for the idea. And so something that is a figment of Catherine Kroeger's imagination, something that no scholar in the field has ever advocated before, is widely accepted as fact. The requirements of truthfulness should hold us to higher standards than this.

Answer 11.3b: This idea is contrary to what we know of the role of women in the early church.

Such "orant" paintings with different individuals portrayed on them are very common in early Christian art. If Kroeger's theory is correct, it would mean that women bishops were also very common in the early centuries of the church. But that is highly unlikely.

As far as I know, there is no historical record of any woman serving even as a pastor or an elder, to say nothing of a bishop, anywhere in the entire history of the early church (see the discussion earlier in this chapter). Probably the first woman to have such a recognized public role was Margaret Fell in the sectarian Quaker movement in 1667. If there ever had been a woman bishop in Rome in the late third century, as Kroeger supposes, it would have prompted widespread comment, and even opposition and conflict. In fact, the Roman Catholic church has a high interest in the historical succession of bishops in Rome! But there is no record of a woman bishop, to say nothing of dozens of women bishops, all of which also makes Kroeger's speculation highly unlikely.[59]

Egalitarian claim 11.4: Blessing on Ministry: God has evidently blessed the ministries of many women, including women pastors. Who are we to oppose what God has so clearly blessed?

Cindy Jacobs makes this argument:

> Women in numerous different ministries teach both men and women and are producing godly, lasting fruit for the Kingdom. Would that be happening if their work

58. Jacobs, *Women of Destiny*, 189, refers to Kroeger's interpretation of this fresco as evidence of women in leadership in the early church.

59. Someone might answer that the Catholic church has suppressed the evidence of these female bishops, but to say that is to admit that one has decided to believe something based on *no historical facts* even when that belief is contradicted by *many established historical facts*. People may believe such things if they wish, but such belief is based on something other than facts or evidence.

wasn't sanctioned by God? Wouldn't their ministries simply be dead and lifeless if God weren't anointing them?[60]

In personal conversation, people will sometimes say, "I heard Anne Graham Lotz preach and it changed my mind about women preaching." Or they will hear Beth Moore preach at a conference and think, "This is such good Bible teaching. How can it be wrong?"

But is this reasoning true? Does the evident blessing of God on some women pastors prove that what they are doing is right?

Answer 11.4a: Of course there will be some good results when a woman prays, trusts God, and teaches God's Word, because God's Word has power and because God in His grace often blesses us in spite of our mistakes. But that does not make the mistakes right, and God may withdraw His protection and blessing at any time.

It is not surprising to me that there is some measure of blessing when women act as pastors and teach the Word of God, whether in a local congregation, at a Bible conference, or before a television audience. This is because God's Word is powerful, and God brings blessing through His Word to those who hear it.

But the fact that God blesses the preaching of His Word does not make it right for a woman to be the preacher. God is a God of grace and there are many times when He blesses His people even when they disobey Him.

One example where God brought blessing in spite of disobedience is the story of Samson in Judges 13–16. Even though Samson broke God's laws by taking a Philistine wife (Judges 14), sleeping with a prostitute at Gaza (Judges 16:1–3), and living with Delilah, a foreign woman he had not married (Judges 16:4–22), God still empowered him mightily to defeat the Philistines again and again. This does not mean that Samson's sin was right in God's sight, but only that God in His grace empowered Samson *in spite of his disobedience*. Eventually God's protection and power were withdrawn, "but he did not know that the Lord had left him" (Judges 16:20), and the Philistines captured and imprisoned him (v. 21).

If God waited until Christians were perfect before He brought blessing to their ministries, there would be no blessing on any ministry in this life! God's grace is given to us in spite of our failings. But that does not mean that it is right to disobey Scripture, or that God will always give such blessing.

If a woman goes on serving as an elder or pastor, I believe she is doing so outside the will of God, and she has no guarantee of God's protection on her life. By continuing to act in ways contrary to Scripture, she puts herself spiritually in a dangerous position. I expect that

60. Jacobs, *Women of Destiny*, 176. Sumner, *Men and Women in the Church,* argues that "Every generation produces gifted women who minister effectively to women and men" (49), women whose ministry God blesses (and she frequently uses herself as the leading example): See 15, 17–19, 20–21, 49, 51–53, 73–74, 95–96, 104, 187, 195–97, 226, 308–9, 315.

eventually even the measure of blessing God has allowed on her ministry will be withdrawn (though I cannot presume that this will be true in every case).

One example of this is the tragic story of Aimee Semple McPherson (1890–1944) at the end of her ministry. Ruth Tucker recounts the story as follows:

> Aimee Semple McPherson, one of the most celebrated evangelists in the early decades of the twentieth century...was a crowd-pleaser who played up to her audiences with a dramatic flair, never seeming too concerned that her eccentricities might demean the cause of Christ. Nor was she particularly careful about her personal life: she left her first husband to go on the road as an itinerant evangelist, later remarried, and finally claimed to have been kidnapped—a story challenged by reporters, who insisted that she was hiding out with another man.... She cannot be excused for apparent moral lapses...but her ministry does demonstrate the power of God that often prevails despite sin and failure.[61]

There is no doubt that God accomplished much good through Aimee Semple McPherson, including the founding of the International Church of the Foursquare Gospel and of her church, the 5,300-seat Angeles Temple in Los Angeles. C. M. Robeck says, "She was undoubtedly the most prominent woman leader Pentecostalism has produced to date."[62] She was perhaps the most prominent woman leader in the entire history of Christianity in America.

But there was much personal tragedy after she began preaching widely around 1915, including a divorce in 1921, the scandal of her disappearance while swimming off Venice Beach in 1926, followed by her subsequent discovery in Mexico a month later, and allegations (never proven but widely believed) about an affair with a former employee, a nervous breakdown in 1930, another failed marriage in 1931, and death from "an apparently accidental overdose of a medical prescription" in 1944.[63]

Answer 11.4b: Arguments from the experience of blessing can go both ways: For two thousand years God has evidently blessed the ministries of millions of churches that have had only men as pastors and elders. Who are we to oppose what God has so clearly blessed?

Arguments based on experience are seldom conclusive. Even today, in the strongly egalitarian popular culture of the United States, by far the largest and most successful ministries (by any measure), the ministries that seem to have been most blessed by God, have men as senior pastors. Even those few large evangelical churches that have women as part of their pastoral team

---

61. Tucker, *Women in the Maze*, 187. (Tucker is an egalitarian who does not see the fact that McPherson was a woman pastor to be disobedience to God.)
62. C. M. Robeck Jr., "Aimee Semple McPherson," in *International Dictionary of Pentecostal and Charismatic Movements* (2002), 858.
63. Robeck, "McPherson," 856–59.

(such as Willow Creek Community Church) have a man (such as Bill Hybels) as the senior pastor and men do most of the preaching. And evangelical churches with women pastors are few in comparison to the large number of churches that have only men as pastors and elders.

This fact should not be lightly dismissed. If it really were God's ideal for men and women to share equally in eldership and pastoral leadership roles, then at some point in the last two thousand years, and especially today, would we not expect to see a remarkable and unmistakable blessing of God on many churches that have an equal number of men and women as elders and that share the main Bible teaching responsibilities equally between men and women pastors? And if the gender of pastors makes no difference to God, then why have we never seen God's evident blessing poured out abundantly on a church with *all women* pastors even once throughout the millions of churches that have existed in the last two thousand years?

Answer 11.4c: Liberal denominations that ordain women pastors have continually declined in membership and income.

Historian Ruth Tucker summarizes this trend:

> The role of women in the church in the twentieth century will perplex future historians.... Those historians who dig deeper will discover that the mainline churches that were offering women the greatest opportunities were simultaneously declining in membership and influence. Some of these churches, which once had stood firm on the historic orthodox faith, were becoming too sophisticated to take the Bible at face value. The gains that have been made, then, are mixed at best.[64]

Tucker's assessment can be supported by observing the membership trends in the large liberal denominations that have been the strongest proponents of women's ordination:[65]

Denomination	1971	1980	1990	2000
American Baptist Church	1,693,423	1,922,467	1,873,731	1,767,462
Evangelical Lutheran Church in America	5,500,687	5,273,662	5,226,798	5,113,418
Episcopal Church	3,024,724	2,823,399	2,445,286	2,314,756
Presbyterian Church—USA	4,649,440	4,012,825	3,553,335	3,141,566
United Methodist Church	11,535,986	11,552,111	11,091,032	10,350,629

64. Tucker, *Women in the Maze*, 184.
65. The information in this chart was compiled for me by my teaching assistants Travis Buchanan and Steve Eriksson from *Churches and Church Membership in the United States 1990* and *Religious Congregations and Membership in the United States 2000* (Nashville, TN: Glenmary Research Center, 2002), and from reference material compiled by Justin Taylor of Bethlehem Baptist Church, Minneapolis. Numbers for the Evangelical Lutheran Church in America use the combined totals for the American Lutheran Church and the Lutheran Church of America for 1971 and 1980.

Not all the churches in those denominations have women pastors, of course. And not all of the individual congregations within those denominations have adopted a liberal view of the Bible. Therefore this information must be used with caution. Anecdotal evidence over the years suggests that the congregations that have grown the most within those denominations also have the most conservative views of the Bible and have resisted the trend to have women pastors, but I do not have actual data to prove this (and I'm sure that people could point to exceptions).[66]

In any case, the argument that churches must ordain women pastors in order to do effective evangelism and grow in modern society simply is not supported by the evidence.

Answer 11.4d: Having women as pastors or elders erodes male leadership and brings increasing feminization of both the home and the church. It also erodes the authority of Scripture because people see it being disobeyed.

When people say there is "much blessing" from the ministries of women pastors, I do not think they are able to see all the consequences. Once a woman pastor and women elders are installed in a church, several other consequences will follow:

1. Many of the most conservative, faithful, Bible-believing members of the church will leave, convinced that the church is disobeying Scripture and that they cannot in good conscience support it any longer.[67]
2. Some of those who stay will still believe that the Bible teaches that women should not be elders, but they will support the leadership of the church. Many of them will think that the leaders they respect are encouraging a practice of disobedience to Scripture, and this will tend to erode people's confidence in Scripture in other areas as well.
3. Those who are persuaded that the Bible allows women as pastors will usually accept one or more of the methods of interpretation I discussed in previous chapters, methods that tend to erode and undermine the effective authority of Scripture in our lives. Therefore, they will be likely to adapt such methods in evading the force of other passages of Scripture in the future.

---

66. Others could object that such statistics are not conclusive because some Pentecostal and charismatic groups have seen rapid growth even though they ordain women. I agree that groups such as the Assemblies of God and the International Church of the Foursquare Gospel have experienced remarkable growth, but pastors within those groups also tell me that the larger and more rapidly growing churches in those denominations have men as pastors.
67. To take one example, I saw this happen at an influential evangelical church in Libertyville, Illinois, in 1996 and 1997. The pastor attempted over a period of months to add women to the governing board of the church, and as a result perhaps ten or more of the most conservative, most active families in the church left and joined the other main evangelical church in town, a Southern Baptist Church where I was an elder and where the pastor and church constitution clearly supported a complementarian position.

4. A church with female elders or pastors will tend to become more and more "feminized"[68] over time, with women holding most of the major leadership positions and men constituting a smaller and smaller percentage of the congregation.
5. Male leadership in the home will also be eroded, for people will reason instinctively if not explicitly that if women can function as leaders in the family of God, the church, then why should women not be able to function as well as men in leadership roles in the home? This influence will not be sudden or immediate, but will increase over time.

All this is to say that the "evident blessing" that God gives when women preach the Bible is not the only result of such preaching. There are significant negative consequences as well.

Answer 11.4e: What is right and wrong must be determined by the Bible, not by our experiences or our evaluation of the results of certain actions.

Determining right and wrong by means of results is often known as "the end justifies the means." It is a dangerous approach to take in ethical decisions, because it so easily encourages disobedience to Scripture.

In 1966, Joseph Fletcher published *Situation Ethics: The New Morality.*[69] He argued that people at times needed to break God's moral laws in the Bible in order to do the greatest good for the greatest number of people. But as these ideas worked their way through American society, the "new morality" of Fletcher's situation ethics brought about a tremendous erosion of moral standards and widespread disobedience to all of God's moral laws.

If I say that women should be pastors because it brings good results, *even if the Bible says otherwise*, then I have simply capitulated to situation ethics. What is right and wrong must be determined by the teachings of Scripture, not by looking at the results of actions that violate Scripture and then saying those actions are right.

Answer 11.4f: Determining right and wrong on the basis of human experience alone is the foundation of liberalism in theology. Feminism takes us in that direction.

J. I. Packer explains that one of the characteristics of theological liberalism is "an optimistic view of cultured humanity's power to perceive God by reflecting on its experience."[70] Thus, *experience*

---

68. See Podles, *The Church Impotent* (1999), who notes that in 1952 the adult attenders on Sunday morning in typical Protestant churches were 53 percent female and 47 percent male, which was almost exactly the same proportion of women and men in the adult population in the U.S. But by 1986 (after several decades of feminist influence in liberal denominations) the ratios were closer to 60 percent female and 40 percent male, with many congregations reporting a ratio of 65 percent to 35 percent (11–12). Podles focuses primarily on Roman Catholic and liberal Protestant churches in his study, and he concludes that, if present trends continue, the "Protestant clergy will be characteristically a female occupation, like nursing, within a generation" (xiii).
69. Joseph Fletcher, *Situation Ethics* (1966).
70. J. I. Packer, "Liberalism and Conservatism in Theology" in Ferguson and Wright, *New Dictionary of Theology* (1988), 385.

rather than the Bible becomes the ultimate standard in theology. If we decide that women and men can have all the same roles in the church primarily because we have seen blessing on the work of women preachers and Bible teachers, such an egalitarian argument leads us toward theological liberalism.

Answer 11.4g: Basing doctrinal decisions only on testimonies of personal experience will lead to all sorts of doctrinal errors.

I am not saying that experience or personal testimonies should be disregarded as we think about the teachings of the Bible. But experience and personal testimony can never prove something contrary to what the Bible teaches. If we begin to go in that direction, then we leave ourselves wide open to accepting such practices as praying to the saints based on some people's belief that those prayers have been answered, or accepting arguments and testimonies claiming that Christians should always be "healthy and wealthy." Basing our doctrine on experience alone can lead us in any direction.

Answer 11.4h: In this controversy, God is asking us to decide if the Bible or experience will be our standard of truth.

During the present controversy over women in leadership roles in the church, God has continued to allow a measure of blessing (for a time at least) on some churches that have women pastors and women elders, and on women who teach the Bible to congregations of men and women. This gives us an opportunity to decide whether we will follow His Word or allow ourselves to be led away from His Word by experiences that seem to bring blessing to people. Though not everyone will agree with me at this point, I believe this is a test of our faithfulness to God and to His Word in our generation. Eventually the consequences of each decision will become plain.

EGALITARIAN CLAIM 11.5: CALLING: IF A WOMAN HAS A GENUINE CALL FROM GOD FOR PASTORAL MINISTRY, WE HAVE NO RIGHT TO OPPOSE THAT CALL.

This argument is often made by women who believe that God has called them to become pastors. Millicent Hunter, whom *Charisma* magazine identifies as "pastor of 3,000-member Baptist Worship Center in Philadelphia," says that the current generation of women ministers is emerging with more boldness. "They are coming out of the woodwork with an 'I don't care what you think; this is what God called me to do' type of attitude."[71]

Sarah Sumner insists that God called her to be a theology professor:

---

71. Millicent Hunter, as quoted in *Charisma*, May 2003, 40.

> I didn't ask God to grant me the grace to enter seminary and complete my doctoral work. That was his idea. He designed the plan; he's the one who saw me through.[72]

She encourages other women to follow God's calling no matter what others may say:

> It is not Anne Graham Lotz's spiritual obligation to sit down with the leaders of the Southern Baptist Convention and convince them that God gave her as a preacher.... If God gave her as a preacher, then she is a preacher, even if someone claims that that's impossible....You are who you are no matter what.... God decides your calling. God decides your spiritual giftedness.... If the Spirit of God has given you as a pastor, you are a pastor, even if you're not employed as one.[73]

The following statement from a personal letter is typical of many that come to the office of the Council on Biblical Manhood and Womanhood:

> What will they answer, when before the throne of God, as to exactly why they didn't permit one that the Lord Himself *called* to teach, even a woman?... Am I any less called by God to do according to His purpose in my life because I am a woman?

Is this argument persuasive? Does God actually call some women to preach and teach His Word to men and women alike? Does He call some women to be pastors and elders?

Answer 11.5a: God never calls people to disobey His Word. Our decision on this matter must be based on the objective teaching of the Bible, not on some person's subjective experience, no matter how godly or sincere that person is.

This egalitarian claim is another form of the question, Will we take Scripture or experience as our ultimate guide?

I agree that people may have subjective experiences of God's presence and blessing that are genuine and real. But it is easy to make a mistake in understanding the meaning of those experiences. If a woman finds God's blessing and anointing when she preaches, then does that mean God is calling her to be a pastor, or does it mean that He is calling her to teach the Bible to women, in accordance with His Word, and that He will give much blessing in that task? If we had only the subjective experience alone to go on, it would be impossible to be certain that we had reached the right answer, because we would have only our own human interpretations of the event, not an interpretation given in God's own words. But in the Bible we have God's own words teaching us how to think about various ministries for women, and the Bible should be our guide in interpretive subjective experiences.

72. Sumner, *Men and Women in the Church,* 27.
73. Ibid., 318.

Answer 11.5b: What a woman perceives as a call from God to a pastoral ministry may be a genuine call to some other full-time ministry that is approved by Scripture.

Many ministries that include Bible teaching are open to women.[74] It may be that a strong sense of calling from God is in fact a calling from God to these kinds of ministries.

Egalitarian claim 11.6: Prophetic Voices: Many prophetic voices today are calling for a new release of women into ministry.

Cindy Jacobs, who speaks widely in charismatic and Pentecostal circles, writes,

> Of one thing I am certain: *God is calling women today in a greater way than He ever has before.* Major prophetic voices are prophesying all around the world that this is the time to find a way to release women into the ministry.[75]

Answer 11.6a: Prophecies today can be wrong.

Even if there are prophecies from other Christians saying that a certain woman is gifted in Bible teaching, or that she should become a pastor or elder, this does not mean we should accept these as genuine words from God. Paul commands that when Christians allow prophecies in the church, they are to "test everything" and to "hold fast what is good" (1 Thessalonians 5:20–21). This implies that some prophecies, and some things in some prophecies, are not good. Mature charismatic and Pentecostal leaders recognize that it is difficult, even for someone who has a prophetic gifting and has used it effectively for many years, to be sure whether any specific prophecy is from God, and whether all of it or just parts of it are from God. This is why Paul adds a provision for testing by others who hear the prophecy, both in 1 Thessalonians 5:20–21 and in 1 Corinthians 14:29.[76] Prophecies must be tested especially for their conformity to Scripture.

Answer 11.6b: Prophecies that contradict God's Word are wrong.

The people who give prophecies saying it is time to release women into ministries of teaching and having authority over men may be sincere, committed Christians. But it is possible for sincere, committed Christians to make mistakes, and even to be led astray by their own desires or by evil spirits masquerading as "angels of light" and giving a subjective impression that feels so much like a genuine prophetic impulse: "even Satan disguises himself as an angel of light. So it is no surprise if his servants, also, disguise themselves as servants of righteousness" (2 Corinthians 11:14–15).

---

74. See pp. 84–100.
75. Jacobs, *Women of Destiny,* 173.
76. I have written about the gift of prophecy at some length in *The Gift of Prophecy in the New Testament and Today* (2000). For a brief summary of my conclusions, see Grudem, *Systematic Theology* (1994), 1049–61.

The only safe way to guard against this is to test prophecies by Scripture. Prophecies that contradict Scripture are in error. We return to the fundamental question: What does the Bible teach? No genuine prophecy from the Holy Spirit is going to lead people to contradict or disobey His Word.

EGALITARIAN CLAIM 11.7: UNIQUE TIME: THIS IS A UNIQUE TIME IN HISTORY WHEN THE HOLY SPIRIT IS BRINGING ABOUT A WORLDWIDE REVIVAL. MORE PEOPLE ARE BECOMING CHRISTIANS TODAY THAN AT ANY TIME IN HISTORY. BECAUSE OF THIS UNIQUE TIME, GOD IS CALLING MEN AND WOMEN ALIKE TO PASTORAL MINISTRY.

This claim was made by John Arnott, senior pastor at the Toronto Airport Christian Fellowship:

> Women readers, be encouraged: your anointing will make room for you! The desperate need of the hour is not merely for people who are trained and educated, but for people of God who are anointed and can bring God's kingdom to a broken, hurting, desperate world through signs, wonders and the power of the Holy Spirit.
>
> All Christians must come to terms with the fact that about 85 percent of the world's population is lost. And the lost are really lost! Under these desperate conditions, why would anyone stand in the way of another who felt called of God to help bring in the harvest?[77]

In a similar vein Cindy Jacobs writes,

> As I have traveled around the world and seen great revivals in places such as Colombia and Argentina, I have seen churches in major revival so busy trying to get the converts discipled that they are happy for laborers—either men or women![78]

Answer 11.7a: The Bible was given to us as a guide for every period until Christ returns.

We are not free to say that "this is an unusual time, so we don't have to obey the Bible." God knew that these days would come, and He has made provision in His Word for every period of history up until the day Christ returns. We are not free to disregard it.

We should also realize that the period recorded in the book of Acts was a time of great revival and a great work of the Holy Spirit, yet there were no women pastors or elders. The Reformation in Europe and the Great Awakenings in the United States were times of great revival and blessing from God, yet they did not require Christians to disobey God's Word in this area.

---

77. John Arnott, "All Hands to the Harvest," in *Spread the Fire* 3:5 (October 1997): 1; this journal was published by the Toronto Airport Christian Fellowship: www.tacf.org.
78. Jacobs, *Women of Destiny,* 234.

Answer 11.7b: People who have said they can disobey God's Word because of unique circumstances have not been blessed by God.

Think, for example, of Saul, who disobeyed the words of the prophet Samuel and offered a burnt offering himself (1 Samuel 13:9) because he thought the circumstances were so pressing and he was going to lose the people who had gathered to him (see vv. 8, 11–12). As a result, Samuel told Saul, "Now your kingdom shall not continue" (1 Samuel 13:14).

Abram decided that he had waited long enough without a child and chose (at the prompting of his wife Sarai) to have a child with Hagar, Sarai's Egyptian servant (Genesis 16). But Abram's decision not to wait and trust God, but to take matters into his own hands because of the apparent urgency of the situation, was not blessed by God. His lack of faith resulted in the birth of Ishmael, whose descendants continue to be at enmity with the people of Israel to this day.

Answer 11.7c: This argument is just a way of saying that we are free to disobey Scripture in unusual times. That can never be right.

We keep returning to this question: What does the Bible say? If it forbids women from taking the office of pastor or elder, then we have no right to say this is a "unique time" when we can disobey what God's Word says. Continued blessing from God depends on continued obedience to God.

EGALITARIAN CLAIM 11.8: MANHOOD AND WOMANHOOD AREN'T REALLY DIFFERENT: EXCEPT FOR PHYSICAL DIFFERENCES, EVERYTHING THAT IS TRUE OF MEN IS ALSO TRUE OF WOMEN, AND EVERYTHING THAT IS TRUE OF WOMEN IS ALSO TRUE OF MEN.

This theme is found at several different places in Sarah Sumner's book. Many of her comments are framed as disagreements with the definitions of masculinity and femininity given by John Piper:

> At the heart of mature masculinity is a sense of benevolent responsibility to lead, provide for, and protect women in ways appropriate to a man's differing relationships.
>
> At the heart of mature femininity is a freeing disposition to affirm, receive and nurture strength and leadership from worthy men in ways appropriate to a woman's differing relationships.[79]

Sumner takes each part of these definitions and says that whatever complementarians claim to be true of men is also true of women:

> Sometimes it is wise for a man to lead and for a woman to affirm his leadership. Sometimes it is right for a man to protect a woman and a woman to nurture a man.

---

79. John Piper, "A Vision of Biblical Complementarity," in Piper and Grudem, *Recovering Biblical Manhood and Womanhood* (1991), 35–36.

> Sometimes it is best for a man to provide and a woman to receive. *But at other times, God wills the reverse.*[80]

Therefore Sumner does not want people to strive for biblical manhood and womanhood:

> It concerns me that...Piper's definitions guide people to think in terms of making it their goal to strive for "biblical manhood and womanhood." The Bible never commands us to strive for mature masculinity or mature femininity. Instead, the Word of God calls people to become like Christ. The right question is not "Am I fulfilling my call to become a biblical man or a biblical woman?" The right question is "Am I imitating Christ?"[81]

Sumner attempts to obliterate each of the differences that complementarians have spoken about between men and women. Do complementarians say that men should lead women? Sumner gives examples where women (such as herself) also lead men.[82] Do complementarians say that a husband should lead because he is the head of his wife? Sumner says that headship *does not mean leading* but rather it means that men are to use their strength to "lift women up." She says, "Men need headship lessons.... Christ...offers special lessons *one on one* to every man, so that he can learn not to take advantage of women."[83]

Do complementarians say that men should protect? Sumner says that women should also protect men.[84] Do complementarians say that men are warriors? Sumner says that women are also warriors: "The Lord is a warrior...and women, like men, are made in his warrior image."[85] Do complementarians say that women are weaker than men? Sumner says that men are also weak.[86]

Do complementarians say that women should learn from and submit to men? Sumner

---

80. Sumner, *Men and Women in the Church,* 98 (italics added).
81. Ibid., 86. Sumner also says, "The question 'What is manhood?' is not a fruitful one.... It is not from faith in God that anyone asks it" (93).
82. Ibid., 98. In a number of sections Sumner tells how she has found herself to be a better leader than the men she encounters, and her joy at triumphing in these encounters with men is transparent in her discussion. One narrative tells how she organized and taught a class for forty-two non-Christian men (no women allowed), and then asks, "Did the men in my class compromise their manhood by *submitting to a woman*?.... Most men are *delighted to follow a woman leader* as long as she honors them as men" (Sumner, *Men and Women in the Church,* 96–97, italics added). In another example she tells how she used her superior verbal skills to cause an entire classroom to laugh at a male student who tried to argue that a man would be the leader if a man were stranded alone on a desert island with a woman (ibid., 187). In another case she tells of a search committee that told her, "You emerged as our top candidate, and we want you to know that we're now looking for a male Sarah Sumner because you line up with our ideal profile person better than anyone else we know" (ibid., 21).
83. Ibid., 189.
84. Ibid., 91.
85. Ibid., 107.
86. Ibid., 135. Sumner looks at 1 Peter 3:7, which says that the woman is the "weaker vessel," and says, "The word is a comparative—weak*er*. The implication is that husbands are *weak* and wives are *weaker*.... The Greek word *asthenēs* literally means 'strengthless.' The implication, then, is that men are strengthless and women are yet more strengthless. The difference between men and women lies in the degree of their strengthlessness" (135).

    But Sumner misunderstands Peter's meaning here. The implied contrast in 1 Peter 3:7 is "stronger/weaker" not "weak/weaker." Her word studies on pp. 132–33 are not quite on the mark because she uses passages that have the absolute form of the adjective (*asthenēs*) rather than the comparative form of the adjective which is

says that men should also learn from and submit to women.[87] Do complementarians say that women should receive from men? Sumner says that men should also receive from women.[88] Do complementarians say that women are more relational than men? Sumner says that men should also be relational.[89] Do complementarians say that women should not *authentein* [exercise authority over] a woman (1 Timothy 2:12)? Sumner says, "In reality, it may be just as sinful for a man to *authentein* a woman as it is for a woman to *authentein* a man."[90] In other words, *every characteristic is reversible.*

Do complementarians say that only men should be ordained? Sumner says, "I do not hesitate to support men and women who either are already or are currently being ordained."[91] Do complementarians say that men should lead in the church? Sumner says, "The conclusion of this book is that *men and women should be leading the Christian community*, partnering as fathers and mothers. Whenever I preach at New Song [her church] I preach as a mother in the church."[92]

In this way, *Sumner's book is a thoroughgoing egalitarian book.* Although InterVarsity Press (USA) advertises it as "A biblical answer from a NONFEMINIST point of view,"[93] it is hard to see how it is "nonfeminist" except that it is written by an evangelical Christian, not an unbeliever. The overall argument of the book is not merely that there should be no differences in men's and women's *roles* except those based on physical differences, but it is even stronger than that: *except for physical differences, we should not even think there is any such concept as "masculinity" and "femininity,"* and it is wrong to encourage people to strive for such things.

So Sumner defines masculinity and femininity only in terms of our bodily characteristics: Masculinity is that "bodily characteristic that makes men less vulnerable than women." Femininity, then, is that "bodily characteristic that makes women more vulnerable than men."[94] But even secular feminists recognize that men's and women's bodies are different, so in terms of final conclusions it is hard to understand in what way Sumner's book is a nonfeminist book. There is no role in marriage or the church that Sumner reserves for men simply because they are men and not because of some physical difference.

Sumner expresses the physical differences in another way when she says, "We know that women have babies and men do not. But *other than that, the differences between men and women are not entirely clear.*"[95]

---

found in 1 Peter 3:7 (*astheneteros*, "weaker"). The comparative adjective is also used in 1 Corinthians 12:22 with the implied contrast "stronger/weaker."

87. Ibid., 95–96.
88. Ibid., 92, 98.
89. Ibid., 110.
90. Ibid., 249.
91. Ibid., 319n3.
92. Ibid., 323.
93. Advertisement in *World,* July 16, 2003, 31.
94. Ibid., 185. Elsewhere Sumner specifically defines that vulnerability as the susceptibility to rape: "Women are physically more vulnerable than men. Women can be raped" (136; see also 141).
95. Ibid., 265 (italics added). She discusses other physical differences on 139–41.

Answer 11.8a: This argument misunderstands the complementarian position.

The complementarian position does not speak of *absolute* differences between masculinity and femininity, but of *primary responsibilities,* and it points to *generalizations* that refer to characteristics and dispositions suitable to those primary responsibilities.[96] We do not say men should *always* protect and women can *never* protect in any way or in any sense, but rather that masculinity includes a sense of *primary responsibility* for protection, even though it is appropriate for women to help protect from time to time. We do not say that men should *always* lead and women should *never* lead in any circumstance, but rather that masculinity includes a sense of *primary responsibility* to lead, and that in the home and the church certain leadership roles are reserved for men, even though there are other contexts (such as some situations in business or civil government) in which it is appropriate for women to lead or to help to lead. We do not say that women *are* relational and men *are not* relational, but that women in general are *more relational* than men, even though there are still ways in which men should be relational as well.

The mistake Sumner makes again and again in the book is to assume that if she can find a single exception, it disproves a general truth about manhood and womanhood. But that is not the way generalizations function. For example, *in general* men are taller than women. This generalization is true, even though *some* women are taller than *some* men. In the same way, men *in general* are more aggressive and women *in general* are more relational; men tend to *seek leadership roles* and women tend to *affirm and support men in those roles*. Of course there are numerous exceptions, but the generalizations remain true.

Another way to understand this is to think of the top 10 percent of both men and women in any characteristic: The top 10 percent of men in height are taller than the top 10 percent of women in height, in any population. And the same holds true for the second 10 percent of men compared with the second 10 percent of women. Similarly, the strongest 10 percent of men are stronger than the strongest 10 percent of women (as is evident in professional athletics or the Olympic Games). But the examples that Sumner gives would be parallel to comparing a very tall

96. It is important to recognize that when complementarians define *masculinity* and *femininity* or *manhood* and *womanhood,* we speak in terms of general truths, dispositions, and primary responsibilities. We allow for many exceptions in individual cases. This is different from what we say about *specific roles in marriage and the church*. With regard to the Bible's teachings on specific roles, we say that Scripture requires that the husband *always* has a leadership role that the wife does not have, and that certain teaching and governing roles are *always* reserved for men in the church.

Why do we speak of absolute boundaries on role differences in marriage and the church, but only speak in generalizations about masculinity and femininity? Because in speaking about roles in marriage and the church, we have specific commands of Scripture and we should always be obedient to those commands. But in speaking of more general concepts such as masculinity and femininity or manhood and womanhood, we are drawing conclusions from what we observe in the pattern of biblical narratives and teachings, and in the patterns that we can discern by observing the way God has created us. (See also John Piper, "A Vision of Biblical Complementarity" in Piper and Grudem, *Recovering Biblical Manhood and Womanhood* [1991], 31–59.)

woman with a very short man and saying, "This shows that women are also tall, and therefore it is not true that men in general are taller than women in general."

Therefore Sumner's individual examples of women in various roles do not disprove Piper's claim that "a sense of benevolent responsibility to lead, provide for and protect women" is something essential to mature masculinity and should be encouraged as a worthy goal in all men. Nor does Sumner disprove Piper's claim that "a freeing disposition to affirm, receive and nurture strength and leadership from worthy men" is something essential to mature femininity and should be encouraged as a worthy goal in all women.

These dispositions are not the same, nor should they be the same, because manhood and womanhood are not the same, no matter how much Sumner and other egalitarians may strive to deny our differences. God has created men and women not only to be equal but also to be different, and it is right to seek to understand and strive to manifest those differences in our daily lives. Contrary to Sumner, it is right to guide people to make it their goal to strive for mature, biblical manhood and womanhood.

Answer 11.8b: The net result of this position is gender confusion.

The overall effect of reading a thoroughgoing egalitarian book like Sumner's[97] is to promote gender confusion among men and women. The only thing Sumner will allow us to tell boys and girls about their differences is that their bodies are different and that has some implications for how they should act toward each other. *This is nothing more than a secular feminist would say,* and it upholds no role differences between men and women other than those based on abilities and personal preferences.

What John Piper and I wrote in 1991 about the foundational statement "Men, Women and Biblical Equality" that Christians for Biblical Equality issued in 1989 can also be said of this position as represented by Sarah Sumner (we could substitute "Sumner" for "CBE"):

> The CBE statement says nothing positive concerning the special responsibilities that a person should bear by virtue of being a man or a woman. The silence of CBE on such implications for sexual differences is typical of egalitarians. It is one of the main reasons why so many young people today are confused about what it means to be a man or a woman. Readers are only told how their sexual differences *don't* count. They are not told in what sense they *do* count. We believe that the resulting confusion and frustration over male and female identity will be increasingly responsible for the precise negative effects that CBE aims to avert.[98]

---

97. Sumner's book does not promote itself as an egalitarian book but as a way of "building consensus on Christian leadership" (this is the subtitle of the book).

98. Piper and Grudem, "Charity, Clarity, and Hope," in Piper and Grudem, *Recovering Biblical Manhood and Womanhood* (1991), 416–17.

Conclusion

There have been women pastors and Bible teachers in the history of the church, but there were almost none up until 1850. There were very few from 1850 to 1950, although some charismatic groups and some groups that placed a high emphasis on personal calling and evidence of effective ministry (such as Wesleyans and Nazarenes) did have some women pastors.

The most significant increase in the number of women pastors occurred from 1950 to the present, and it has come largely in more liberal denominations. However, some evangelical groups have also been part of this trend, particularly since the 1970s and 1980s.

So in the last 150 years, there is some historical precedent for women pastors and Bible teachers, but it is not as strong as egalitarians would have us believe, and it is small compared with the entire history of the church. In any case, our final standard of what is right and wrong must be Scripture, not church history.

Claims of God's evident blessing on women's pastoral ministry, claims that God is calling certain women to be pastors and Bible teachers to be men, claims about the uniqueness of this time in history, and claims that manhood and womanhood aren't really different must be answered with the affirmation that the Bible alone is our final authority, not our experiences.

Therefore, the egalitarian claims in this chapter do have some interest, and they must be considered, but ultimately the answer to the controversy must be found in Scripture, not in evidence from history or personal experience.

CHAPTER TWELVE

Evangelical Feminist Claims That the Complementarian View Is Harmful

Sometimes egalitarians have claimed that the complementarian view of men and women is harmful, even to the point that it leads to abuse and repression of women in the home and in the church. In addition, it leads to a loss of workers at a time when the church needs all the help it can get. Finally, egalitarians sometimes point to tragic stories of men harming women, and claim that the complementarian view has led to such tragedies.

I consider claims such as these in this chapter.

EGALITARIAN CLAIM 12.1: ABUSE: MALE LEADERSHIP IN THE HOME AND IN THE CHURCH LEADS TO THE ABUSE AND REPRESSION OF WOMEN.

This claim is made several times in egalitarian literature. For example, it is evident in the title of the book by James and Phyllis Alsdurf, *Battered into Submission: The Tragedy of Wife Abuse in the Christian Home.*[1] This accusation is also the theme of *Women, Abuse, and the Bible: How Scripture Can Be Used to Hurt or to Heal.*[2] In the first chapter of that book, psychotherapist Carolyn Holderread Heggen writes,

> As I have listened to people in my clinical practice and interviewed hundreds of others for various research projects, I have come to identify certain religious beliefs that I believe are related to the abuse of women.... What are some of those beliefs?...
>
> God intends that men dominate and women submit.... The name for the social organization and set of beliefs that grant and sustain male dominance over women and children is *patriarchy*....

1. James and Phyllis Alsdurf, *Battered into Submission* (1989).
2. *Women, Abuse, and the Bible* (1996), ed. Catherine Clark Kroeger and James Beck.

> The inherent logic of patriarchy says that since men have the right to dominance and control, they also have the right to enforce that control....
>
> When...[a] woman told her pastor about her husband's abusive behavior, the pastor's response was: "No matter what he's doing to you...you owe it to him and to God to live in submission to your husband. You'll never be happy until you submit to him."... She was unhappy as a battered wife but had been told by her pastor that to be happy she must submit to her batterer....
>
> Women with strong religious backgrounds often are the least likely to believe that violence against them is wrong.... Battered women tend to hold traditional views about sex roles in the home....
>
> The longer I listen to stories of family abuse, the more I am convinced that we cannot both support patriarchy and stop domestic abuse. To stop violence among our families, we must stop holding up patriarchy as God's intention for us.[3]

Answer 12.1a: Abuse of wives by husbands is a horrible evil that should be opposed by all who believe the Bible to be the Word of God.

It is troubling to see egalitarians claim that belief in male headship in the home and church is a cause of violence against women. No one who takes the Bible as the Word of God should ever support or approve of abuse. All believers should insist with the apostle Paul that husbands are to love their wives as Christ loved the church (Ephesians 5:25). Christians should oppose and attempt to stop abuse whenever they become aware of it.[4]

Anyone who purports to hold to male headship in marriage should do so in a way consistent with the Bible. And the Bible teaches that such headship involves love and honor for one's wife. Distortions of this teaching both in the United States and in other cultures must be strongly and consistently opposed.[5]

---

3. Carolyn Holderread Heggen, "Religious Beliefs and Abuse," in Kroeger and Beck, *Women, Abuse, and the Bible* (1996), 15–17.
4. I am discussing abuse of wives by husbands throughout this chapter, because that is the more common form of physical abuse. However, I do not mean by that to imply that physical abuse of husbands by wives does not exist, because it is more common than most people realize. It can occur even when the husband is physically stronger but the wife still becomes hostile and aggressive, and the husband continues to receive the abuse but does not respond in kind. One study estimated that there are 1,500,000 female abuse victims and 835,000 male abuse victims in the U.S. each year ("Men Also Domestic-Abuse Victims," *Arizona Republic* [October 14, 2003], B1–B2, citing a 1998 National Violence Against Women Act survey sponsored by the federal Centers for Disease Control and Prevention and the National Institute of Justice). The *Arizona Republic* article (B2) referred to a book by broadcast journalist Philip Cook, *Abused Men: The Hidden Side of Domestic Violence* (1997). What I say in this chapter about the evils of abuse should also be understood to mean that abuse of husbands by wives is wrong in God's sight, and where it does occur, similar appropriate remedies to those I discuss in this chapter should be pursued.
5. Incidents of wife abuse are not limited to American culture, but can be found in many foreign cultures as well. I was shocked recently to hear someone who has taught at an evangelical seminary in an African country say that some of his seminary students (both husbands and wives) would argue openly in class that it is good for a wife to be beaten by her husband from time to time! Confirming a similar pattern, Cindy Jacobs writes, "A missionary

Answer 12.1b: It is not biblical male leadership but distortion and abuse of biblical male leadership that leads to the abuse and repression of women.

In the same chapter in which Paul says, "The husband is the head of the wife even as Christ is the head of the church," (Ephesians 5:23) and, "Wives, submit to your own husbands, as to the Lord" (v. 22), he also says, "Husbands, love your wives, as Christ loved the church and gave himself up for her" (v. 25). Elsewhere, where Paul says "Wives, submit to your husbands," he says in the next sentence, "Husbands, love your wives, *and do not be harsh with them*" (Colossians 3:18–19). Similarly, in the same chapter where Peter says, "Wives, be subject to your own husbands" (1 Peter 3:1), he also tells husbands, "Husbands, live with your wives in an understanding way, *showing honor to the woman* as the weaker vessel, since they are heirs with you of the grace of life, so that your prayers may not be hindered" (v. 7).

The Bible nowhere teaches male leadership in the family without at the same time teaching (or implying, as in 1 Corinthians 11:11–12) that husbands should love and care for and honor their wives.

Therefore any teaching that stresses a wife's submission to her husband without at the same time stressing the husband's obligation to love and care for his wife, and that men and women have equal value before God, is a distortion of the biblical teaching.

Answer 12.1c: It is cruel to tell wives who are being physically abused simply to stay and endure the suffering. Such advice will often lead to more violence and harm against them and their children.

Some studies indicate that when abused wives silently endure and seek to be more submissive to their abusive husbands rather than report the abuse and seek help from church or civil authorities, *such behavior often provokes even more violence from the abuser.*[6] Tragically, the Alsdurfs report case after case where an abused woman went to her pastor for help, only to have the pastor tell her he would not do anything to confront the husband (sometimes a leader in the church), and that the wife should stay and "submit" to her husband, even to his abuse.

This is a terrible misuse of Scripture. Yes, the Bible tells us there will be times when we must "suffer for righteousness' sake" (1 Peter 3:14), but several biblical examples show people escaping danger when they are able to do so. David fled from King Saul when Saul tried to kill him with

---

friend who was in a country in South America told me how he was once in a pastors' meeting where the discussion turned to whether it was all right to beat your wife. He said that the general consensus was that it was permitted as long as no one knew" (Jacobs, *Women of Destiny,* 218). Such teaching, even when it occurs in situations where wife beating is accepted by the general culture, is deeply evil and impossible to reconcile with "husbands, love your wives, as Christ loved the church and gave himself up for her" (Ephesians 5:25), and "husbands should love their wives as their own bodies" (Ephesians 5:28), and "husbands, love your wives, and do not be harsh with them" (Colossians 3:19).

6. See Alsdurf, *Battered into Submission*, 84–85. For example, they say one Bureau of Justice Statistics survey showed that 41 percent of married women who were attacked by their husbands or ex-husbands and did not call the police were attacked again within six months, compared with 15 percent of those who alerted the police (85).

a spear (1 Samuel 19:10). David did not "stay and remain submissive" to such violence. Paul escaped secretly from Damascus when the governor under King Aretas tried to kill him; he did not "stay and remain submissive" to the governor's plans of violence (2 Corinthians 11:32–33). Jesus escaped from an angry crowd at Nazareth that was planning to cast Him down a cliff (Luke 4:29–30), and He also hid and escaped from hostile Jewish leaders when they were making plans to kill Him before the completion of His ministry (John 8:59; 10:39). We should care for our bodies, which are the temples of the Holy Spirit (1 Corinthians 6:19–20), and not decide to follow a course of action that will probably result in physical harm to our bodies (unless God calls us to a dangerous situation, such as missionary work in hostile areas or military service to defend one's country). The book of Proverbs encourages us to be wise and to avoid physical danger when we can: "The prudent sees danger and hides himself, but the simple go on and suffer for it" (Proverbs 22:3; also 27:12).

Therefore when we become aware of a situation where a wife is being abused by her husband, we should take whatever steps we can to bring about personal confrontation and accountability for the abuser, church discipline, police protection and civil penalties in the court system, physical removal of the wife and children from the house for their protection, and other appropriate means in order to protect the abused and bring an end to the violence. "Rescue the weak and the needy; deliver them from the hand of the wicked" (Psalm 82:4). Jesus never teaches us to seek out or encourage suffering and persecution and hardship: we are to pray, "lead us not into temptation, but deliver us from evil" (Matthew 6:13).[7]

Answer 12.1d: Biblical male headship, rightly understood, protects women from abuse and repression and truly honors them as equal in value before God.

In a remarkably insightful article, Steven Tracy, academic dean at Phoenix Seminary, argues that the pattern of headship in the Trinity (in which the Father is the head of the Son, 1 Corinthians 11:3) demonstrates that a husband should honor and protect his wife even as the Father honors and protects (in a sense) the Son:

> One way men honor their wives is by protecting them. While protection is not explicitly noted in John 5:18–24, it is a logical application of loving and honoring. Furthermore, in the context of the final judgment, the Father does empower and protect the Son. This is particularly seen in Psalms 2 and 110, which speak of the Father's empowerment of the Son to triumph over his enemies. Is the protection of women explicitly linked to male headship in Scripture? Absolutely, for this is a dominant

7. Steven Tracy, who is both a New Testament professor and a professional counselor, has written an excellent paper dealing with the passages on suffering and showing that they cannot rightly be understood to promote the idea that wives should remain in a physically abusive situation and continue just to "submit" to it. (See Steven Tracy, "Domestic Violence in the Church and Redemptive Suffering in First Peter," paper read at the Evangelical Theological Society annual meeting, Toronto, Canada, November 20–22, 2002.)

biblical theme. Men are particularly called to protect and care for women and children (Deut. 25:5–10; Isa. 1:15–17; Jer. 22:2–3), for this is how God himself exercises his power and authority (Deut. 10:17–19).

Unfortunately, secular society and even the Christian church consistently fail to protect women, and often blame women for physical or sexual violence perpetrated upon them.... Pastors fail to take the husband's violence seriously and simply encourage wives to be submissive...a pastor must focus on confronting male abuses of power and protecting vulnerable women. Churches must begin to aggressively confront abusers, pursue all means possible to protect vulnerable women, and teach that male headship means protection, not domination.[8]

When the Council on Biblical Manhood and Womanhood was founded in 1987 to promote and defend a complementarian position regarding men and women, its statement of principles, the "Danvers Statement," indicated that the founders of CBMW were deeply concerned about "the upsurge of physical and emotional abuse in the family" (Rationale #6). Then in the affirmations of CBMW's principles, the Danvers Statement said, "In the family, husbands should forsake harsh or selfish leadership and grow in love and care for their wives" (Affirmation #6).

A more detailed statement on abuse was published in the August 1995 issue of *CBMW News* (p. 3).

CBMW's Statement on Abuse (adopted November 1994):

We understand abuse to mean the cruel use of power or authority to harm another person emotionally, physically, or sexually.

We are against all forms of physical, sexual and/or verbal abuse.

We believe that the biblical teaching on relationships between men and women does not support, but condemns abuse (Prov. 12:18; Eph. 5:25–29; 6:4; Col. 3:18; 1 Tim. 3:3; Titus 1:7–8; 1 Pet. 3:7; 5:3).

We believe that abuse is sin. It is destructive and evil. Abuse is the hallmark of the devil and is in direct opposition to the purposes of God. Abuse ought not to be tolerated in the Christian community.

We believe that the Christian community is responsible for the well-being of its members. It has a responsibility to lovingly confront abusers and to protect the abused.

We believe that both abusers and the abused are in need of emotional and spiritual healing.

We believe that God extends healing to those who earnestly seek him.

8. Steven Tracy, "Headship with a Heart: How Biblical Patriarchy Actually Prevents Abuse," *Christianity Today* (February 2003), 54.

> We are confident of the power of God's healing love to restore relationships fractured by abuse, but we realize that repentance, forgiveness, wholeness, and reconciliation is a process.
>
> Both abusers and abused are in need of on-going counseling, support and accountability. In instances where abusers are unrepentant and/or unwilling to make significant steps toward change, we believe that the Christian community must respond with firm discipline of the abuser and advocacy, support and protection of the abused.[9]
>
> We believe that by the power of God's Spirit, the Christian community can be an instrument of God's love and healing for those involved in abusive relationships and an example of wholeness in a fractured, broken world.

Therefore abuse is both contrary to Scripture and contrary to a complementarian view of the roles of men and women within marriage. It is wrong, and Christians have an obligation to attempt to stop it wherever they become aware that it is happening.

Answer 12.1e: Statistics claiming to connect male headship with abuse of women are misleading.

The problem with claims of a connection between belief in male headship and physical abuse is that those who claim this lump together in one group two very different kinds of people: (1) men who are violent and abusive and often not Christians at all, and who use male headship as a club to oppress their wives, and (2) genuine Christians who follow the Bible's teachings about loving and caring for their wives, and who would never strike or harm their wives.[10]

Any truth in the Bible can be taken out of context by someone and distorted and used in a harmful and destructive way. Even Satan himself quoted the Bible in trying to get Jesus to sin (see Matthew 4:1–11), but that does not prove that the Bible is evil, only that Satan was misusing it.

To take another example, someone might argue, "Belief in the authority of civil government leads to abuse and violence against citizens, because all abusive dictators argue that citizens

---

9. For specific suggestions, see Grudem and Rainey, eds., *Pastoral Leadership for Manhood and Womanhood* (2002), and especially two chapters: Ken Sande, "Church Discipline: God's Tool to Preserve and Heal Marriages," 161–85, and David Powilson, Paul David Tripp, and Edward T. Welch, "Pastoral Responses to Domestic Violence," 265–76.

10. For explanations of methodological errors in studies that connect violence to belief in male headship, see Donald G. Dutton, "Patriarchy and Wife Assault: The Ecological Fallacy," in *Violence and Victims* 9:2 (1994): 167–82. Dutton points out, for example, that Hispanic culture is more patriarchal than the general culture, but wife assault is about half the rate found among non-Hispanic whites (171). Dutton also asks, "What kind of causal weight does patriarchy have if 90 percent of the men raised under it are nonassaultive?" (172). Dutton's explanation is that belief in male headship does not have any causal relationship to abuse: He says, "Patriarchy does not elicit violence against women in any direct fashion" (176). Rather, he says, "Patriarchy...may provide the values and attitudes that personality-disordered men can exploit to justify their abuse of women" (176). Dutton published a book-length study on this topic in 1995: See Donald G. Dutton, *The Batterer* (1995).

 Now a major new study by University of Virginia sociologist W. Bradford Wilcox has shown that "evangelical Protestant men who are married with children and attend church regularly...have the *lowest* rate of domestic violence of any group in the United States" (*Christianity Today* [Aug., 2004], 44, with reference to Wilcox's book *Soft Patriarchs, New Men* [Chicago: Univ. of Chicago Press, 2004]).

should obey their governments." The answer to that argument is that the evil is found not in *belief in governmental authority* in itself, but in the *abuse* of governmental authority and in the failure to balance that authority with respect for the rights of citizens. Similar misleading arguments could be made about parents' authority over children (all abusers believe in authority, but that does not make parental authority wrong), or the use of authority by church leaders (all cult leaders who abuse authority believe they should have authority over people in their cult, but that does not make the authority of genuine elders and pastors in a church wrong).

Answer 12.1f: By contrast, feminism robs women of their femininity and womanhood as God created them, and is destructive to both men and women alike.

What position is it that is truly destructive to women? A fundamental problem with feminism is that it works in destructive ways in women's lives. It no longer allows them to be uniquely feminine and to be the women God created them to be. Feminism, at least in its radical forms, continually pushes women to be like men in every way, and the uniqueness and beauty of womanhood is lost. So it is ultimately not a complementarian view but a feminist view that is destructive to persons and families.

EGALITARIAN CLAIM 12.2: LOSS OF WORKERS: THE COMPLEMENTARIAN VIEW ROBS THE CHURCH OF HALF ITS WORKERS.

Sometimes egalitarians say that the needs of the church around the world are great, and it is a tragedy that the complementarian view robs the church of half its workers in a time of great need.[11]

Answer 12.2a: The complementarian view does not rob the church of any workers, but encourages everyone to use their gifts in accordance with Scripture.

Every Christian has spiritual gifts that are to be used in the various ministries of the church. "To *each* is given the manifestation of the Spirit for the common good" (1 Corinthians 12:7). Peter says, "As *each* has received a gift, use it to serve one another, as good stewards of God's varied grace" (1 Peter 4:10). Therefore we must continually affirm that *all women* as well as *all men* have been given gifts by the Holy Spirit to be used in the ministries of the church, and we should work hard to provide opportunities and encouragement for their various gifts to be used.

But these gifts must still be used *in accordance with Scripture* if we are to obtain God's fullest blessing on our work. Some of the many ministries that are available to women are mentioned in chapter 2.[12]

11. See also the discussion in chapter 11 under egalitarian claim 11.7, pp. 483–84.
12. See pp. 84–100.

EGALITARIAN CLAIM 12.3: MEAN TRADITIONALISTS: SOME TRADITIONALISTS ARE MEAN PEOPLE, AND SO THEIR VIEW IS WRONG.

This egalitarian "claim" is not actually made directly, but is sometimes implied when stories are repeated about abusive husbands or church leaders who "believed in male headship." For example, Patricia Gundry reports a horrible story about Eufame MacLayne in sixteenth century Scotland who was pregnant with twins and had a very difficult labor. She took a painkilling herb in order to survive the labor. Gundry describes what happened next:

> However, someone found out what she had done. Painkillers were forbidden to women in childbirth. It was against God's law. He wanted women to suffer in labor. The Bible said so, their punishment for Eve's sin.
>
> So Eufame was brought before those who decided punishment. And they could not of course let her go free (there was also the possibility of witchcraft, you see, because she had not relied solely on the grace of God for relief from her pain). So her babies were taken from her arms and given to someone else's care. Eufame was tied to a stake. Bundles of wood were laid at her feet. Then new mother Eufame was burned alive....
>
> Maybe you think things like that don't happen anymore. But I can still see Eufame there with tears running down her face.... I can see the heartless churchmen pronounce her doom in God's name.... They didn't think Eufame was fully human, because she was a woman. So it was all right to do that to her.[13]

Gundry follows this a few pages later with the story of the Chamberlen family of doctors in England who developed a tool, the obstetrical forceps, that made it possible to save many mothers and babies who otherwise would not have survived a difficult labor. Gundry explains that rather than making the forceps public for the benefit of women in all countries, the Chamberlen family kept this device a secret and used it for their own profit for almost one hundred years. At one point in the story she asks, "Did this compassionate, religious man share his lifesaving invention with others?... No, he did not."[14]

Stories like these make us angry at the cruel, hardhearted men responsible for such evils. But why are they found in egalitarian literature? Apparently to indicate some relationship between the cruelty of these men and a belief in male headship in the home and church.

---

13. Patricia Gundry, "Why We're Here" in Mickelsen, *Women, Authority and the Bible* (1986), 12–13.
14. Ibid., 18–20.

Answer 12.3a: An *ad hominem* argument is an invalid way of disproving another position.

An *ad hominem* argument is an argument "against the person" rather than against the position the person holds. Such arguments may have a powerful emotional impact on the hearers, but they are not a valid way of arguing against a viewpoint we disagree with.

We could take any Christian doctrine (or any denomination) and find some examples of mean people who hold to that doctrine (or belong to that denomination). We could then talk about that person as if he or she were *characteristic* of that viewpoint. For example, we could probably find an abusive husband who was a Baptist (or a Lutheran or a Catholic), and then say that example proves that Baptist doctrine (or Lutheran or Catholic) leads to abuse. But this is not an accurate or fair argument, because it does not argue against Baptist doctrine itself, nor does it show that the position *necessarily* led to this person's behavior. There are a lot of troubled and sinful people in the world. Sometimes they become associated with one viewpoint or another, but they should not be seen as representative of those viewpoints.

Similarly, we could, I suppose, find some evangelical feminists who are angry or belligerent or argumentative, but to hold them up as examples of evangelical feminism (unless they are in responsible leadership roles in that movement) is not right.

Answer 12.3b: It is only fair to evaluate a position, not on the basis of its worst representatives, but by the words and actions of its best representatives.

I have no objection to evaluating the complementarian position on the basis of writings published by organizations such as the Council on Biblical Manhood and Womanhood,[15] or on the basis of the actions of people who serve in leadership roles in CBMW or in similar complementarian organizations. This would be fair, for it would be evaluating a position based on its most responsible representatives, those who have been entrusted with visible leadership roles. But it is hardly fair to criticize the complementarian position because of the evil decision of some hardhearted men in the sixteenth century.

Egalitarian claim 12.4: Complementarians Are Troublemakers: Complementarians who keep talking about male leadership are just making trouble in the church. We should stop arguing about this issue and all get along with each other.

I treated this objection in section 9.11: "Stop Fighting About a Minor Issue," and what I said about that question serves as an answer at this point as well. (See pp. 376–81.)

15. See www.cbmw.org for information about the organization.

Conclusion

The claims that belief in male headship leads to abuse and repression of women are not well founded. It is not the Bible's teaching on male headship that leads to abuse, but a horrible distortion of the Bible's teaching, a distortion Christians have an obligation to oppose whenever they have opportunity to do so. Objections about specific harm complementarians have done in the past show that some evil and sinful people have held some parts of a complementarian view, but they certainly don't show that the view itself is wrong. The abuse of a complementarian view can lead to all sorts of evil, but these should not be counted as objections against the view itself.

Chapter Thirteen

Is Evangelical Feminism the New Path to Liberalism?

Some Disturbing Warning Signs

13.1: The connection between liberalism and an egalitarian view on women in the church

When we look at what happened in the last half of the twentieth century, quite a clear connection can be seen between theological liberalism and the endorsement of women's ordination.[1] In an important sociological study published by Harvard University Press, Mark Chaves traces the history of women's ordination in various denominations in the United States.[2] From Chaves's study, we can observe a pattern among the mainstream Protestant denominations whose leadership is dominated by theological liberals (that is, by those who reject the idea that the entire Bible is the written Word of God, and is therefore truthful in all it affirms).[3] Chaves notes the dates when ordination of women was approved in each of these denominations:

Methodist Church: 1956
Presbyterian Church—USA: 1956 (north), 1964 (south)
American Lutheran Church: 1970

1. For the sake of continuity of argument, much of the material in this first section on liberalism is repeated from chapter 11, section 11.2, (pp. 469–72). I have given more detail here, however.
2. See Mark Chaves, *Ordaining Women* (1997).
3. A more precise statement of a clear dividing line between liberals and evangelicals is found in the statement of faith of the Evangelical Theological Society, which says, "The Bible alone, and the Bible in its entirety, is the Word of God written and is therefore inerrant in the autographs."

Lutheran Church in America[4]: 1970
Episcopal Church: 1976[5]

Chaves notes an interesting example with the Southern Baptist Convention (SBC). In 1964 the SBC approved women's ordination (that is, a local congregation ordained a woman and this was not overturned by the denomination itself). But in 1964 the denominational leadership and the control of the seminaries were in the hands of "moderates" (the SBC term for those who did not affirm biblical inerrancy). However, in 1984, after conservatives recaptured control of the SBC, the denomination passed a resolution "that we encourage the service of women in all aspects of church life and work *other than pastoral functions and leadership roles entailing ordination.*"[6] This means that when the conservatives who held to biblical inerrancy recaptured the denomination, the denomination revoked its previous willingness to ordain women.[7]

Chaves lists some other denominations that are not completely dominated by theological liberalism, but that are broadly tolerant of liberalism and have seminary professors and denominational officials who have moved significantly in a liberal direction. (These categorizations of denominational doctrinal positions are not made by Chaves, who simply lists the denominations and the dates, but are my own assessment.) Consider the following denominations:

Mennonite Church: 1973
Evangelical Covenant Church: 1976
Reformed Church in America: 1979

Another example that occurred after Chaves finished his book was the Christian Reformed Church, which in 1995 approved the ordination of women.[8] Chaves does note, however, that the Christian Reformed Church "shifted its official position away from inerrancy only in 1972."[9]

Are there any types of denominations that are resistant to the ordination of women? Chaves indicates the following results of his study:

---

4. The American Lutheran Church and The Lutheran Church in America are presently combined into a single denomination, the Evangelical Lutheran Church in America (ELCA).
5. Chaves, *Ordaining Women,* 16–17. Chaves lists many other denominations, such as Baptist and Pentecostal denominations, that were ordaining women much earlier and were not affected by theological liberalism. Many of these other groups placed a strong emphasis on leading and calling by the Holy Spirit (such as Pentecostal groups) or placed a strong emphasis on the autonomy of the local congregation (such as many Baptist groups) and therefore these denominations were not adopting women's ordination because of theological liberalism. But my point here is that when liberalism was the dominant theological viewpoint in a denomination, from 1956 onward it became inevitable that that denomination would endorse women's ordination.
6. Chaves, *Ordaining Women*, 35.
7. A much stronger action than the resolution Chaves mentions was taken in June 2000, when the SBC added to "The Baptist Faith and Message" (its official statement of doctrine) the following sentence: "While both men and women are gifted for service in the church, the office of pastor is limited to men as qualified by Scripture" (added to Article VI, "The Church").
8. See "CRC Reverses Decision...Again" in *CBMW News* 1:1 (August 1995), 5.
9. Chaves, *Ordaining Women*, 86.

> Two groups of denominations are particularly resistant to women's ordination: denominations practicing sacramental ritual and denominations endorsing biblical inerrancy.... Biblically inerrant denominations are...resistant to formal gender equality.[10]

By "denominations practicing sacramental ritual" Chaves refers especially to Catholic, Eastern Orthodox, and Episcopalian denominations, who think of the priest as standing in the place of Christ at the Lord's Supper. Chaves thinks that explains why the Episcopal Church was rather slow in endorsing women's ordination in comparison to other denominations. But he notes that for "biblically inerrant denominations" the argument that the Bible prohibits the ordination of women is by far the most persuasive argument.[11]

I think that Chaves's observation that "denominations endorsing biblical inerrancy" are "particularly resistant to women's ordination" can be reinforced if we consider three influential evangelical denominations in the U.S.: the Lutheran Church—Missouri Synod (LCMS), the Presbyterian Church in America (PCA), and the Southern Baptist Convention (SBC). All three have the following characteristics in common:

1. they have fought major battles with liberalism recently enough that such conflicts are still part of the personal memories of current leaders
2. these leaders recognize that the liberal groups from which they are separate now aggressively promote women's ordination (the Evangelical Lutheran Church in America, the Presbyterian Church—USA, and the Cooperative Baptist Fellowship)
3. these leaders and their denominations are strongly opposed to women's ordination

In the Southern Baptist Convention, conservatives who held to inerrancy regained control of the denomination over a ten or fifteen year period beginning in 1979.[12] The SBC in 2000 added a formal provision to its doctrinal statement that "The office of pastor is limited to men as qualified by Scripture" (Article VI of the Baptist Faith and Message).

The Lutheran Church—Missouri Synod in 1974 dismissed the president of Concordia Seminary in St. Louis, a measure that soon led to the angry resignation of forty-five of the fifty faculty members of the seminary, thereby removing most of the influence of theological liberalism that denied the complete truthfulness of Scripture.[13]

---

10. Ibid., 84–85 (italics added).
11. Ibid., 89–91. Chaves strongly favors the ordination of women and goes on to argue that the Bible does not prohibit it.
12. Conservatives regained control of the Southern Baptist Convention beginning with the election of Adrian Rogers as president of the denomination in 1979 (see Jerry Sutton, *The Baptist Reformation* [2000], 99).
13. The Lutheran Church—Missouri Synod had been drifting toward a liberal view of Scripture for perhaps twenty or thirty years when conservatives within the denomination effectively regained control with the election of J. A. O. Preus as the denomination's president in 1969. The denominational convention in 1973 in New Orleans affirmed its clear adherence to biblical inerrancy and with this victory the denominational leadership suspended the president of Concordia Seminary in St. Louis, John Tietjen, on January 20, 1974. In February 1974, forty-five

Yet another example is the Presbyterian Church in America, which was formed when conservatives left the more liberal Southern Presbyterian Church in 1973.[14]

In each of these three denominations, people who currently hold positions of leadership remember their struggles with theological liberalism, and they remember that an egalitarian advocacy of women's ordination goes hand in hand with theological liberalism.

Another example of the connection between tendencies toward liberalism and the ordination of women is Fuller Theological Seminary in Pasadena, California. Though Fuller started as a conservative evangelical seminary, it removed the doctrine of biblical inerrancy from its statement of faith in 1971, and today there is significant influence from theological liberalism among its faculty. In addition, full-fledged advocacy of the ordination of women reigns on campus, and I doubt Fuller would hire anyone holding another position to teach there (or if someone were hired, I doubt that he would be allowed to express his opposition to women's ordination publicly).

As long ago as 1987, the egalitarian viewpoint was so firmly entrenched at Fuller that even a responsible academic statement of a complementarian view was effectively silenced by a barrage of protests. In May 1987, I received the following letter from a New Testament professor who had been invited to teach a course at Fuller on the Pastoral Epistles:

> What reminded me to write this letter was the class on the Pastorals that I am teaching at Fuller.... Boy did I get in trouble. One lady walked out, incredibly irate. The Women's Concerns Committee sent a letter to all my students, claiming that I should never have been allowed to teach this and that they would try to censor any further teaching along traditional lines of interpretation. So much for academic freedom and inquiry. I wrote to the dean and will be interested to see how the actual administration will react. I find it incredibly interesting, and inconsistent, that they allow the teaching of universalism...but our view of the women's passage must be banned.[15]

Two months later I received a follow-up letter from Dr. Mounce:

> For two and a half weeks I was slandered up and down campus. I was the major subject on the declaration board, etc. It was a real mess.... The vast majority of the letters were from students who were not in the class.... 2-1/2 weeks after the fact... Dean Meye finally called and we had dinner together.... He asked if I would be willing to retell the class what my actual intention was, and without groveling or backtracking, say that to whatever extent I was responsible for the misunderstanding, I apologize....

---

of the fifty faculty members at Concordia Seminary left in protest, but new faculty members were appointed, and the seminary and the denomination after that remained in the control of conservatives who held to biblical inerrancy. (See Harold Lindsell, *The Bible in the Balance* [1979], 244–74, especially 259–70.)

14. The Presbyterian Church in America was formed by conservatives who left the Presbyterian Church in the United States ("The Southern Presbyterian Church") in 1973 (see Susan Lynn Peterson, *Timeline Charts of the Western Church* [1999], 248).

15. Personal letter from William D. Mounce to Wayne Grudem, received May 14, 1987, quoted by permission.

> So I agreed and it went very well.... The next day Meye was deluged with letters and visits from my students who were very upset at the committee and his handling of the situation.... Meye never apologized, said that he or the school had behaved improperly, or that anything was mishandled except that I was allowed to teach what I thought. He accused me of such dastardly deeds as presenting my personal views with more force than the other views.... People need to be aware of what will happen at their schools if this situation is not dealt with properly.[16]

Endorsement of the ordination of women is not the final step in the process, however. Several denominations that approved women's ordination from 1956–1976, such as the United Methodist Church and the United Presbyterian Church USA, have large contingents pressing for (a) the endorsement of homosexual conduct as morally valid and (b) the approval of homosexual ordination. In fact, the Episcopal Church on August 5, 2003, approved the appointment of an openly homosexual bishop.[17] And on March 19, 2004, in the Pacific Northwest regional conference of the United Methodist church, a jury of clergy voted 11-0 (with two abstentions) to allow self-professed lesbian minister Karen Dammann to continue to serve as a Methodist minister. The denomination apparently cannot appeal the ruling.[18]

In more liberal denominations such as these, a predictable sequence has been seen (though only the Episcopal Church has followed the sequence to point 7):

1. Abandoning biblical inerrancy
2. Endorsing the ordination of women
3. Abandoning the Bible's teaching on male headship in marriage
4. Excluding clergy who are opposed to women's ordination
5. Approving homosexual conduct as morally valid in some cases
6. Approving homosexual ordination
7. Ordaining homosexuals to high leadership positions in the denomination

I am not arguing that all egalitarians are liberals. Some denominations have approved women's ordination for other reasons, such as a long historical tradition and a strong emphasis on gifting by the Holy Spirit as the primary requirement for ministry (as in the Assemblies of God), or because of the dominant influence of an egalitarian leader and a high priority on relating effectively to the culture (as in the Willow Creek Association).[19] But it is unquestionable that

---

16. Personal letter from William D. Mounce to Wayne Grudem, received July 23, 1987, quoted by permission.
17. See pp. 513–14 for more detail about the Episcopal Church's decision.
18. *World.* April 3, 2004, 29. However, two months later the denomination's general conference voted 674–262 to reaffirm their ban on ordaining practicing homosexuals, leaving Dammann's future status unclear (*World*, May 22, 2004). As for the Presbyterian Church (USA), on July 2, 2004, their legislative assembly rejected by 259–255 (or 50.4% to 49.6%) a proposal to allow ordination of homosexuals (AP dispatch, July 3, 2004, published in *Arizona Republic* at www. azcentral.com).
19. Fee, *First Epistle to the Corinthians,* 705.

theological liberalism leads to the endorsement of women's ordination. While not all egalitarians are liberals, all liberals are egalitarians. There is no theologically liberal denomination or seminary in the United States today that opposes women's ordination. ***Liberalism and the approval of women's ordination go hand in hand.***

13.2: Current egalitarian views that deny the authority of Scripture

In several sections of chapters 3 through 12 of this book, I have interacted with published egalitarian statements that either deny the complete truthfulness of Scripture or else deny the full authority of Scripture as the Word of God for us today. While those chapters give more detailed explanations of why such claims ultimately rest on a rejection of the authority of Scripture, it will be useful here to summarize those claims in brief form.

With respect to egalitarian writings on Genesis 1–3, this is true of Rebecca Groothuis's claims that the Hebrew language of the Old Testament reflects a wrongful patriarchy (claim 3.5), and William Webb's claims that parts of Genesis 1–2 are not historically accurate (claim 3.7).

With respect to egalitarian writings on the New Testament, a rejection of the final authority of Scripture for our lives today is found in William Webb's claim that Galatians 3:28 is a "seed idea" that would later lead to an ethic superior to that of the New Testament (claim 6.2) and also in Webb's claim that the New Testament commands regarding male headship are only a "preliminary movement" to partially correct the culture at that time, but that the New Testament ethic regarding male headship still needed further improvement (claim 6.5).

A different kind of problem is found in Gordon Fee's claim that 1 Corinthians 14:34–35 should not be considered part of the Bible and that these verses are "certainly not binding for Christians" (claim 7.5; see answer 7.5b, pp. 236–37, for reasons why I see this to be not merely an academic text-critical decision).

A liberal tendency to reject the authority of Scripture is also seen in Paul Jewett's and Clarence Boomsma's claims that Paul was wrong in his teaching in 1 Timothy 2 (claim 8.14), and in David Thompson's claims that Paul misinterprets Genesis 2, and that we can come to a better understanding of Genesis 2 than Paul did (claim 8.15).

Liberal tendencies in egalitarian procedures for interpreting the Bible include the claims of R. T. France and David Thompson that our authority is the point toward which the New Testament authors were progressing in a trajectory, not what the New Testament actually taught (claim 9.4). A similar rejection of the authority of the New Testament writings for our lives today is found in the redemptive-movement hermeneutic of William Webb, who says that the New Testament teachings on male headship in marriage and male leadership in the church were simply points along the path toward a superior ethic to that of the New Testament (claim 9.5). Related to this is the view of Kevin Giles that theological differences cannot be settled by appealing to the Bible, so the historical tradition of the church must be the basis for our decisions (discussed on pp. 426–27 under claim 10.2).

A different kind of problem is found when R. T. France, Sarah Sumner, and Stanley Grenz assert that our position on the roles of men and women simply depends on which verses we choose to emphasize, as if we were free to make such a decision to emphasize some verses and thereby have less obligation or no obligation to obey others (claim 9.9).

From a different perspective, Cindy Jacobs and the position paper of the Assemblies of God both claim that it is not possible to figure out what the Bible teaches on this issue, so our decision must be made on the basis of observing what kinds of ministries are effective today (claim 9.10). But this procedure effectively silences the ability of Scripture to speak to this controversy, so it is a different kind of rejection of the authority of Scripture.

Another liberal tendency to reject the authority of Scripture in our lives is found in the claim that a woman may teach Scripture to men if she does so "under the authority of the pastor or elders" (claim 9.12). I say this is indicative of a liberal tendency because on no other area of conduct would we be willing to say that someone can do what the Bible says not to do as long as the pastor and elders give their approval.[20] And yet another is the claim that since an organization is not a church, it does not have to follow the New Testament commands regarding such activities as women teaching the Bible to men (claim 9.13). The reason I say this is indicative of a liberal tendency to avoid the authority of Scripture is that, while we may agree that parachurch organizations are not required to do everything that the New Testament commands for churches, nevertheless, when a parachurch organization does those same things that the New Testament talks about for churches, it is required to follow the same rules that the New Testament lays down for churches. It is not as if we can set up a separate organization next door to a church and then say that the rules no longer apply to us. (See also pp. 384–92.)

Another procedure egalitarians use to avoid obedience to the New Testament directions concerning men and women is to place such a strong emphasis on experience that the teachings of Scripture no longer are the highest authority. This occurs when egalitarians such as Cindy Jacobs say that God's blessing on the ministries of women pastors shows that what they are doing is right (claim 11.4), and therefore objections based on what Scripture teaches are discarded. In a similar way, a liberal tendency to reject the authority of Scripture is seen whenever egalitarians claim that if a woman has a genuine call from God for a pastoral ministry, we have no right to oppose that call, and so the teachings of Scripture on this topic are nullified (claim 11.5).

Another liberal tendency to reject the supreme authority of Scripture is the claim of Cindy Jacobs and others who affirm that many contemporary prophecies are saying that God wants women to teach and preach to both sexes, or to be in pastoral leadership roles, and so the contemporary prophecies take precedence over the teaching of Scripture (claim 11.6). Yet another rejection of the ultimate authority of Scripture is found in claims like that of John Arnott of the Toronto Airport Christian Fellowship, that this is a unique time in history and therefore the old pro-

20. See the discussion at section 9.12 above, pp. 381–83.

hibitions against women being pastors or teaching the Bible to men no longer apply (claim 11.7).

There is another troubling matter regarding the approach to the Bible taken in some egalitarian claims. That has to do with alleged historical "facts" that often lead people to change their understanding of what the Bible says. But if those alleged facts are incorrect and people believe them anyway, then they will end up with mistaken ideas about what the Bible says, *and they will no longer believe or obey what it really says.* This is another way the effective authority of the Bible can be undermined in our churches.

A number of egalitarian claims trouble me in this regard, because they are promoted to unsuspecting readers as if they were established fact, when actually no proof for them has been found, and several of the claims are even contradicted by the facts we have. Our God is a God of truth (Proverbs 30:5; Titus 1:2; Hebrews 6:18), and He cares about truth (Exodus 20:16; 2 Corinthians 4:2; Ephesians 4:25; Colossians 3:9). Therefore it is of utmost importance that readers and authors on both sides of this controversy never fail to exercise the greatest care for accuracy regarding the historical or linguistic data that we depend on in interpreting the Bible.

As I explained in some detail in earlier chapters, some examples of egalitarian claims that are woefully lacking in historical proof, are claims that women were disrupting the worship service at Corinth (claim 7.7), that women homeowners were overseers in early churches (claim 7.14), that women deacons had governing authority in early church history (claim 7.15), that women were not educated in ancient Ephesus (claim 8.2), that women were teaching false doctrine in Ephesus (claim 8.1), that a Gnostic heresy about Eve being created first was influential in first-century Ephesus (claim 8.1, answer 8.1c), that the word *kephalē* ("head") often meant "source" (claim 6.6), that the word *authenteō* ("exercise authority") could mean "murder" or "commit violence," or "proclaim oneself author of a man," or could even have a vulgar sexual meaning (claims 8.8–8.10), that the doctrine of the eternal subordination of the Son is contrary to historic orthodox Christian doctrine (claim 10.2, especially answer 10.2f), and that catacomb paintings show an early woman bishop in Rome (claim 11.3). Many of these are promoted as fact but upon investigation they turn out to be only unsubstantiated speculation.

Not all of the 118 egalitarian claims in this book are effective rejections of the authority of Scripture in our lives. But a large number of egalitarian claims do fall in this category and indicate a deeply troubling trend toward a liberal rejection of the authority of the Bible. The claims that I have mentioned are promoted by influential egalitarian writers and published by leading evangelical publishers such as Baker Book House and InterVarsity Press.[21] Even those egalitarian authors who do not deny the authority of Scripture in these ways refrain from renouncing the approaches of those who do, and the influential egalitarian organization Christians for Biblical Equality promotes all of these books on their website.

---

21. By far the largest number of influential books promoting these claims have been from Baker Book House (see sections noted in the earlier chapters for books by Belleville, Bilezikian, Boomsma, Groothuis, and Kroeger) and IVP-USA (books by Giles, Grenz, Mickelsen, Sumner, Tucker, and Webb).

Therefore, I believe there are many egalitarian claims that directly deny the authority of Scripture, and many others that effectively undercut the authority of Scripture by leading people to think it teaches something other than what it actually does teach.

As evangelicals accept the validity of these claims one after the other, and as evangelical pastors preach sermons adopting the methods found in these claims, evangelicals are quietly and unsuspectingly being trained to reject this verse of Scripture and that command of Scripture, and this passage, and that teaching, here and there throughout the Bible. As this procedure goes on, we will begin to have whole churches who no longer "tremble" at the Word of God (Isaiah 66:2), and who no longer live by "every word that proceeds out of the mouth of God" (Matthew 4:4), but who pick and choose the things they like and the things they don't like in the Bible, using the very same methods they have been taught by these egalitarian writers. The church will thus be led step by step, often without knowing what is happening, to a new liberalism for the 21st century. And in this way the authority of God's Word, and the ultimate authority of God Himself over our lives, will be diminished and in principle rejected.

13.3: The disturbing destination: Denial of anything uniquely masculine

The egalitarian agenda will not stop simply with the rejection of male headship in marriage and the establishment of women as pastors and elders in churches. There is something much deeper at stake. At the foundation of egalitarianism is a dislike and a rejection of anything uniquely masculine.[22] This tendency is seen, for example, in Sarah Sumner's claim that even asking, "What is biblical manhood?" is asking the wrong question, and in her attempts to deny every one of the characteristics that we say distinguish men from women, and in her limiting "masculinity" and "femininity" only to differences in our physical bodies (claim 11.8). It is also seen in Rebecca Groothuis's suggestion that Adam was a sexually undifferentiated being when he was first created (claim 3.6). But why is it objectionable that God created Adam as a man? It makes one wonder if this idea doesn't reflect some deeper dislike of human sexuality in general, some hostility toward the very idea of manhood and womanhood.

This tendency is also seen in the emphasis that Jesus' humanity is what was really important for His incarnation, not His maleness (claim 5.4, advocated by Stanley Grenz). But one wonders again if this doesn't represent an underlying desire to reject anything uniquely male. Why should we object that Jesus came as a *man*?

A writer in the egalitarian publication *Mutuality* suggested (humorously) that a better title for John Gray's book *Men Are from Mars, Women Are from Venus* would be

> *Men Are from Mars, Women Are from Venus, But Some Men Are from Venus and Some Women Are from Mars, and All of God's Children Have Both Mars and Venus Qualities Within Them So Why Not Just Say that Men and Women Are from*

22. For further discussion of this trend, see Heimbach, "The Unchangeable Difference" (2002), in Grudem, *Biblical Foundations for Manhood and Womanhood*, 275–89, and Peter R. Jones, "Sexual Perversion: The Necessary Fruit of Neo-Pagan Spirituality in the Culture at Large" (2002), in that same volume, 257–74.

the Earth, and Let's Get About the Business of Developing the Unique God-Given Mars/Venus Qualities that God Has Given All of Us for the Sake of the Kingdom.[23]

When I read that, I realized that egalitarians seem to feel compelled to oppose any kinds of differences between men and women other than those that are purely physical. Even when egalitarian author Rebecca Groothuis tried to answer the charge that egalitarians think that men and women are the same, the only clear differences she could point to were the sexually based physical differences between men and women and abilities that flow directly from those physical differences.[24]

13.4: The next step: God, our Mother

Following the denial of male headship in marriage, and the denial of any restriction of leadership roles in the church to men, and the denial of anything uniquely masculine other than the physical differences among human beings, it is to be expected that egalitarians would begin to blur and then deny God's identity as our Father. This is exactly what has recently happened in egalitarian writings. Ruth Tucker, in her book *Women in the Maze*, encourages women to call God "Mother" in private prayer,

> We sing the words of John W. Petersen in worshipful praise, "Shepherd of love, you knew I had lost my way...." Would it be worse, or blasphemous, to sing something like "Mother of love..."? Both are figures of speech. But because of our fear of taking on the trappings of radical feminism or goddess worship, we dare not sing those words—except perhaps in our closets of prayer.[25]

We see a similar trend in literature sold by Christians for Biblical Equality through their website. Their egalitarian-advocacy website (www.cbeinternational.org) says that their bookstore contains books that further their mission: "Each resource we carry has first been evaluated by our team of reviewers to ensure that it furthers CBE's mission and vision."[26] Yet at least two books openly advocate praying to God as our Mother in heaven.[27]

---

23. Jim Banks article in *Mutuality* (May 1998), 3.
24. Groothuis, *Good News for Women* (1997), 47–49.
25. Tucker, *Women in the Maze* (1992), 20–21.
26. See www.cbeinternational.org in the "About CBE's Bookstore" section.
27. An extensive discussion of this tendency in egalitarian writings, and an analysis of why it is contrary to Scripture, is Randy Stinson, "Our Mother Who Art in Heaven: A Brief Overview and Critique of Evangelical Feminists and the Use of Feminine God-Language," *JBMW* 8/2 (fall 2003): 20–34. Stinson notes that there are several metaphors in Scripture that use feminine language to describe God in metaphorical ways, such as "the God who gave you birth" (Deuteronomy 32:18) or "As one whom his mother comforts, so I will comfort you" (Isaiah 66:13), or "For a long time I have held my peace; I have kept still and restrained myself; now I will cry out like a woman in labor" (Isaiah 42:14). But these never say God *is* a mother and they never *call God* by the name "Mother." Stinson writes, "There are...figures of speech: similes, metaphors, analogies, or personifications. There are no cases in which feminine terms are used as names, titles, or invocations of God. There are no instances where God is identified by a feminine term" (28). He quotes with approval John Cooper's statement,

The CBE bookstore carries a book by Paul R. Smith called Is It Okay to Call God "Mother": Considering the Feminine Face of God. In this book, Smith says, "In one sense I wrote this book so that our congregation could have a fuller explanation of why I believe it is important to call God "Mother" as well as "Father" in public worship."28

Smith introduces chapter 3 with a cartoon of Moses arriving in heaven, the Ten Commandments under his arm, saying to God, "Gee, I didn't expect you to be a soprano!" Later in the book, Smith asks the question, "Will the next thing be to say that Jesus should have been a woman?" and though he affirms that Jesus did come as a man, he says, "Something is wrong when we cannot conceive of the Messiah coming from a different cultural setting or being of a different race or gender." He says he has a sculpture of "a female Jesus hanging on the cross" and he admits that some people "have violent reactions" to it.[29]

Smith concludes this section by saying, "I personally try to avoid using masculine pronouns for the risen, transcendent Christ except when I am speaking of him during his time here on earth before his ascension."[30]

Smith does not explain how he can read the dozens or perhaps hundreds of passages in the New Testament epistles that refer to Jesus as "He" and "Him" after He ascended to heaven, using masculine singular pronouns in Greek, such as this passage from Colossians 1:

> He is the image of the invisible God, the firstborn of all creation. For by him all things were created, in heaven and on earth...all things were created through him and for him. And he is before all things, and in him all things hold together. And he is the head of the body of the church. He is the beginning, the firstborn from the dead, that in everything he might be preeminent. (vv. 15–18)

Or this statement from Philippians, talking about Christ after His ascension into heaven:

> Therefore God has highly exalted him and bestowed on him the name that is above every name, so that at the name of Jesus every knee should bow, in heaven and on earth and under the earth.... (Philippians 2:9–10)

How can Smith even read these passages if he tries to "avoid using masculine pronouns for the risen, transcendent Christ"? So eager is Smith to deny the masculinity of Jesus that he has come to the point where he avoids using language like the New Testament itself.[31]

"God is never directly said to be a mother, mistress, or female bird in the way he is said to be a father, king, judge, or shepherd" (ibid.). In short, we should not name God with names that the Bible never uses and actually avoids using. God's name is valued and highly protected in Scripture.

28. Paul R. Smith, *Is It Okay to Call God "Mother"?* (1993), 1.
29. Ibid., 134, 137, 140–41. Page 142 suggests that this sculpture, like another picture he has, is hanging on his office wall.
30. Ibid., 143.
31. Stinson also notes that Smith is an openly professing homosexual pastor, and cites Smith's writings on homosexuality ("Our Mother Who Art in Heaven," 25–26).

Another book sold on the CBE website is *God, A Word for Girls and Boys* by Jann Aldredge-Clanton.[32] This book teaches us to pray prayers like, "God, our Mother, we thank you that you love us so much to want the best for us. Thank you for trusting us enough to let us do things on our own.... Stay near us and help us to become all that we can be. Amen."[33]

In the introduction to the book, Aldredge-Clanton says,

> Masculine God-language hinders many children from establishing relationships of trust with God. In addition, calling God "he" causes boys to commit the sin of arrogance.... Calling the supreme power of the universe "he" causes girls to commit the sin of devaluing themselves. For the sake of "these little ones" we must change the way we talk about God and about human beings.[34]

Catherine Kroeger, one of the founders of Christians for Biblical Equality, has advocated calling God "Mother." In an article, "Women Elders...Called by God?," Richard and Catherine Kroeger write:

> So far we have referred to God as "He" and "Him" because most of us are used to employing these terms when we think of the Holy One. Indeed, it is sometimes asserted that those in holy office should be male to represent the Deity who is male. This is to ignore what the Bible has to say, for God is pictured as both male and female. Let us be clear that God does not possess sexuality—neither distinctive maleness nor femaleness; but to explain the love and work of God, both male and female imagery is used.
>
> Consider these scriptures carefully: Psalm 131:2–3; Deut. 32:18; Isa. 49:15, 66:9–13, 42:13–14; and Matthew 23:37. Among other passages is James 1:17–18, which first speaks of God as Father and then says God brought us forth as Mother. Job 38:28–29, Isa. 63:15 and Jer. 31:20 speak of the womb of God, surely a valuable image when we think of new birth. God's likeness to a mother is an important aspect of the divine nature. Can Christians neglect any aspect of God's being as it is revealed in Scripture? *There is good biblical reason, then, to speak of God as both Father and Mother, both "she" and "he."* This is particularly important for evangelicals to remember when they seek to witness to people turning to goddess worship in their desire for a deity with feminine attributes. It is also essential to remember when ministering to those with bad father images, who may have positive feelings about their mothers. Women as well as men are made in God's image! (Gen. 1:26–27, 5:1–2).[35]

---

32. Jann Aldredge-Clanton, *God, a Word for Girls and Boys* (1993).
33. Ibid., 23.
34. Ibid., 11.
35. This statement can be found at http://firstpresby.org/womenelders.htm. (italics added).

Liberal Protestants have traveled this route before. In 2002 the United Methodist Church published a supplement to its hymnal called *The Faith We Sing*, which included some new hymns such as "Bring Many Names," in which Methodists are to sing praise to "Strong Mother God, working night and day." The author of the lyrics, Brian Wren, professor of worship at Columbia Theological Seminary in Decatur, Georgia, supports these lyrics with an argument that sounds very much like the arguments egalitarians have used on other subjects. According to reporter Maura Jane Farrelly,

> Professor Wren says the Bible uses the word "Father" because it was written in a place and time when only men were in positions of authority. And because this isn't the case anymore in many Christian nations, Dr. Wren says there is no need to cling so literally to the "Father" image.[36]

A similar trend has been seen among disillusioned Southern Baptists who left the denomination in protest over the conservative control of the SBC and formed something called the Cooperative Baptist Fellowship (CBF).[37] At the CBF annual meeting that began June 28, 2001, in Atlanta, songs of praise to God as Mother were prominent:

> With songs and prayers to "Mother God," an auxiliary organization of the Cooperative Baptist Fellowship opened its annual meeting at the CBMW General Assembly Thursday with a clear message—the current controversy is about more than women pastors. The annual Baptist Women in Ministry breakfast was rife with stridently feminist God language, culminating in a litany read by BWIM members about their discomfort at calling God "Father," "Lord," and "King".... The group sang a hymn to "strong mother God".... Feminist language for God continued throughout the two-hour long business session and worship service. BWIM treasurer Sally Burgess told the crowd..."I believe God is good, and She knows what She's doing".... The CBF exhibit hall bookstore displayed a new Methodist "gender inclusive" hymnal...with a hymn written from the point of view of the earth entitled, "I am your Mother".... Preacher Elizabeth Clements read a sermon about her spiritual experiences in the presence of starry skies, winding rivers, and "trees older than Jesus."[38]

What then is the doctrinal direction to which egalitarianism leads? To an abolition of anything distinctively masculine. An androgynous Adam. A Jesus whose manhood is not

---

36. Maura Jane Farrelly, "Controversial Hymns Challenge U.S. Methodists' View of God," in *Voice of America News*, July 5, 2002 (www.voanews.com).
37. The Cooperative Baptist Fellowship was accepted into full membership as an independent denomination by the Baptist World Alliance in July of 2003, according to *World*, August 2, 2003, 23.
38. "'Mother God' Worshiped at Group's Gathering for CBF Annual Meeting," in *Baptist Press News*, June 29, 2001, (www.bpnews.net).

important, just his "humanity." A God who is both Father and Mother, and then a God who is Mother but cannot be called Father.

13.5: The final step: approval of homosexuality

No leading evangelical egalitarians up to this time have advocated the moral validity of homosexual conduct, as far as I know. And I'm thankful that the egalitarian organization Christians for Biblical Equality has steadfastly refused pressures to allow for the moral rightness of homosexual conduct.

However, we would be foolish to ignore the trend set by a number of more liberal Protestant denominations, denominations that from the 1950s to the 1970s approved the ordination of women using many of the same arguments that evangelical egalitarians are using today.[39] While the United Methodist Church, the Presbyterian Church—USA, and the Evangelical Lutheran Church in America have all resisted internal movements that attempted to pressure them to endorse homosexuality, they still have significant minorities within each denomination who continue to push in this direction (see p. 504, n18).

1. Episcopal Church

Most recently, the Episcopal Church in the United States has approved the appointment of V. Gene Robinson as its first homosexual bishop, by a vote of 62 to 45 in their House of Bishops.[40] As recently as 1998, this same denomination had approved a resolution calling homosexual activity "incompatible with Scripture."

Even secular newspapers pointed out that there were parallels to earlier decisions of the Episcopal Church. The *New York Times* reported:

> Bishop-elect Robinson's opponents said he would bring to the broader church schism, pain and confusion.... Other people called the warnings overblown. Look, they said, at other controversies that were also predicted to split the church like the ordination of women in 1976 and the ratifying of a woman, Barbara Harris, as Bishop, in 1989. This evening, Ms. Harris...said the church had survived and would once more. "I remember well the dire predictions made at the time of my election consent process," she said. "The communion, such as it is, a loose federation of autonomous provinces, has held."[41]

---

39. The widely influential book by Krister Stendahl, *The Bible and the Role of Women* (1966), contained many of the arguments that persuaded liberals to ordain women, and it is amazing to see how closely these arguments parallel the arguments being made by egalitarians today. (I am grateful to my former student, David Jones, for pointing out to me this parallel between Stendahl's writings and current egalitarian arguments.) See claim 9.6, pp. 358–61, for further discussion of Stendahl's argument.
40. "Episcopal Church Elects First Openly Gay Bishop," at www.foxnews.com, Tuesday, August 5, 2003.
41. *New York Times*, August 6, 2003, A12.

Therefore the advocates of homosexual ordination were not worried about a split in the church. Conservatives who did not leave when a woman was ordained as an Episcopal priest, and who did not leave when a woman was selected as a bishop, would probably not leave at the approval of a homosexual bishop either, or so the supporters of Bishop Robinson claimed.

A day after the House of Bishops approved this appointment, the leaders of the Episcopal Church approved a "compromise" resolution at the insistence of conservatives within the denomination. The compromise allowed local dioceses the option of whether to bless same-sex unions in their churches or not![42] But what this meant was that the denomination as a whole was allowing any local church to give a blessing to homosexual unions (they stopped short of officially calling it homosexual "marriage").

As I am writing this chapter, it remains to be seen whether conservatives will finally leave the denomination, or whether the worldwide Anglican communion will exercise disciplinary measures against the Episcopal Church in the United States. But what has happened in the denomination in the U.S. has still happened, and it is the culmination of a trend to reject the Bible's teachings on manhood and womanhood that began a few decades ago.

2. Presbyterian Church—USA

> At least 113 PCUSA congregations in 30 states have designated themselves "More Light Presbyterians" (MLP). Membership in the group, which seeks "full participation of lesbian, gay, bisexual, and transgender people of faith in the life, ministry, and witness of the Presbyterian Church (U.S.A.)," is up 20 percent from three years ago, according to retired MLP board member Gene Ruff.[43] (See also p. 504, n18, above.)

3. Evangelical Lutheran Church of America

Within the Evangelical Lutheran Church of America and other denominations, similar groups are growing:

> Meanwhile, 280 churches and 21 synods in the Evangelical Lutheran Church in America (ELCA) participate in a similar program called "Reconciling in Christ" (RIC). During RIC's first 18 years, 250 congregations across North America joined, but 30 new churches have joined this year alone. Other denominations have gay-affirming

---

42. "Episcopal Vote Allows Blessings of Gay Unions," www.washingtonpost.com, August 7, 2003, A-1.
43. "Go Forth and Sin: A Growing Mainline Movement Seeks to Affirm Homosexuality as Biblical," *World*, Aug. 2, 2003, 20. The same issue of *World* reports the results of a similar trend in Australia: "By a large margin, the 267 delegates to the national assembly of the 1.4 million-member Uniting Church of Australia (UCA) July 17 formally approved the ordination of homosexual men and women on a local-option basis by presbyteries and congregations. Evangelical clergy and congregations immediately began heading for the exits.... The UCA was formed by a merger of Presbyterian, Methodist, and Congregational churches in 1977, making it the country's third-largest denomination at the time" (*World*, August 2, 2003, 23).

programs such as the Rainbow Baptists, the Association of Welcoming and Affirming Baptists, and the United Methodist Reconciling Congregation Program.[44]

The ELCA has established a task force to formulate a recommendation regarding homosexuality, but some observers think the membership of the task force almost guarantees a liberalization of its current policy opposing homosexual activity:

> In April, the ELCA Task Force on Human Sexuality met in Chicago for its second conference. The denomination commissioned the task force "to guide" the ELCA's decision making on gay clergy and the blessing of same-sex relationships. But its expert panels may actually be a series of stacked decks....
>
> Roanoke College religion professor Robert Benne, a biblical conservative and task force panelist, told *World* the ELCA task force "certainly is weighted toward those who are open to revising basic teaching on homosexual relations." In addition, he said the presence of open homosexuals at every discussion "makes it difficult for folks who are uncertain or just plain nice to voice objections or even reservations about the revisionist agenda. Most church people like to be polite and accepting, so they often accept that agenda out of the desire to 'keep the peace in love.' "[45]

4. Christian Reformed Church

Nor is this movement confined to liberal denominations. The Christian Reformed Church (CRC) is still thought to be largely evangelical, and it was only in 1995 that the CRC approved the ordination of women. But now the First Christian Reformed Church in Toronto has "opened church leadership to practicing homosexual members 'living in committed relationships,' a move that the denomination expressly prohibits."[46]

In addition, Calvin College in Grand Rapids, Michigan, the college of the Christian Reformed Church, has increasingly allowed on its campus expressions of support for homosexuals to be evident on campus. *World* magazine reports:

> Calvin has since 2002 observed something called "Ribbon Week," during which heterosexual students wear ribbons to show their support for those who desire to sleep with people of the same sex. Calvin President Gaylen Byker... [said], "...homosexual-

44. Ibid., 20.
45. Ibid., 21.
46. "Reformed Congregation OKs Gay Leaders," *Christianity Today,* December 9, 2002, 19. In another development, on June 15, 2004, the Christian Reformed Church named the Rev. Robert DeMoor as editor of its denominational periodical, *The Banner.* DeMoor was a controversial choice because he had previously written in support of legal recognition of domestic partnership for homosexual couples. (Reported in the *Grand Rapids Press,* June 16, 2004, as accessed at http://www.mlive.com/news/grpress/index.ssf?/base/news_15/1087397677274730.xml).

> ity is qualitatively different from other sexual sin. It is a disorder," not chosen by the person. Having Ribbon Week, he said, "is like having cerebral palsy week."
>
> Pro-homosexuality material has crept into Calvin's curriculum.... At least some Calvin students have internalized the school's thinking on homosexuality.... In January, campus newspaper editor Christian Bell crossed swords with Gary Glenn, president of the American Family Association's Michigan chapter, and an ardent foe of legislation that gives special rights to homosexuals.... In an e-mail exchange with Mr. Glenn before his visit, Mr. Bell called him "a hate-mongering, homophobic bigot... from a documented hate group." Mr. Bell later issued a public apology.[47]

This article on Calvin College in *World* generated a barrage of pro and con letters to the editor in the following weeks, all of which can still be read on-line by interested readers.[48] Many writers expressed appreciation for a college like Calvin that is open to the expression of different viewpoints but still maintains a clear Christian commitment. No one claimed the quotes in the article were inaccurate, but some claimed they did not give a balanced view. Some letters from current and recent students confirmed the essential accuracy of the *World* article, such as this one:

---

47. "Shifting Sand?" *World,* May 10, 2003, 41–42.

48. See www.worldmag.com. A search for the phrase "Calvin College" turned up letters in the "Mailbag" section of *World* for June 7, June 14, June 21, June 28, and July 3, 2003. Calvin's president, Gaylen Byker, posted a response to the *World* article on the Calvin website, under "Calvin News" for May, 2003: see www.calvin.edu/news/releases/2002_03/calvin_letter.htm. He defends the diversity of the campus as well as its steadfast Christian orientation and academic excellence. He also says that the *World* article failed to give a balanced representation of the entirety of the college campus, which is excellent in many ways. Regarding homosexuality, he says, "Despite what *World*'s story might lead people to believe, homosexuality is not a preoccupation on Calvin's campus. We are working as a college to follow the call of our denomination's Synod (the Christian Reformed Church's highest ruling body) which in 1999 said the entire denomination is 'called as a Church to repent for our failures' in this area. 'Ribbon Week' is one way of reaching out with love and compassion to Calvin students who are gay...." He goes on to affirm that homosexual conduct is wrong. Interested persons may read the letter themselves and notice both what he says and what he does not say about the positions that are advocated on the campus.

In another letter responding to the *World* article, professor Quentin Schultze says, "The fact is that the Christian Reformed Church, which 'owns and operates' Calvin College, has encouraged the entire denomination to love gays and lesbians even while not accepting the sinful practices of some of them" (quoted from http://www.calvin.edu/news/releases/2002_03/schultze_letter.htm, Oct. 24, 2003). His expression "the sinful practices of some of them" seems consistent with the picture of Calvin College indicated by the other quotations in the article: The repeated theme is that there are some people who just "are" gays and lesbians, and if they refrain from putting their same-sex inclinations into practice, our attitude toward them should be one of love and acceptance. Hence, the campus-wide week-long emphasis on raising student awareness of gays' and lesbians' need for acceptance and support. At one level, who can object to showing love and support for any other human being? However, at another level, one suspects a larger agenda here on the part of homosexual advocates, an agenda of gaining acceptance by degrees. What would we think of a Christian campus, for example, that sponsored a week-long campaign to show acceptance and support of people who had lustful and adulterous desires, or were alcoholics, or who were addicted to gambling, or were always tempted to lie or curse, or who struggled with constant greed or envy? It seems from reading these comments from Calvin faculty, administrators, and students, that homosexuality is being made into a special cause at Calvin.

> I commend Lynn Vincent for writing "Shifting sand?" (May 10). As a sophomore at Calvin, I have been exposed firsthand to the changing of Calvin's foundation. Being a transfer student, I was not fully aware of the special events like "Ribbon Week." I asked a classmate what her purple ribbon meant and she said it's a sign of acceptance of all people. I later found out that "all people" meant gays, lesbians, and bisexuals. I have been appalled by posters advertising a support group for GLBs (as they are called) around campus. God condemned the practice, so why cannot God's judgment against GLB be proclaimed at Calvin? I am glad Calvin's lack of the morals it was founded on is being made known to the Christian community outside of Calvin. Much prayer and action is needed if a change is to take place.—Katie Wagenmaker, Coopersville, Mich.[49]

This does not indicate that the Christian Reformed Church has approved homosexuality (it has not), but it does indicate the existence of a struggle within the denomination, and the likelihood of more to come.

13.6: What is ultimately at stake: The Bible

As I have written this book and spent more and more time analyzing egalitarian arguments, I have become more firmly convinced that egalitarianism is becoming the new path to liberalism for evangelicals in our generation.[50]

The pioneers of evangelical feminism are liberal denominations. The arguments now being used by egalitarians were used by these liberal denominations when they were approving the ordination of women. Many of the current leaders of the egalitarian movement either advocate positions that undermine the authority of Scripture or at least advertise and promote books that undermine the authority of Scripture and lead believers toward liberalism. The hints we now have of the doctrinal direction in which evangelical feminism is moving predict an increasing emphasis on an abolition of anything that is distinctly masculine. Egalitarianism is heading toward an androgynous Adam who is neither male nor female, and a Jesus whose manhood is not important. It is heading toward a God who is both Father and Mother, and then only Mother. And soon the methods of evading the teachings of Scripture on manhood and womanhood will be used again and again by those who advocate the moral legitimacy of homosexuality.

The common denominator in all of this is a persistent undermining of the authority of Scripture in our lives. The title of this book is *Evangelical Feminism and Biblical Truth*. On the topic of manhood and womanhood, we have now analyzed extensively both evangelical feminism and biblical truth. My conclusion at the end of the study is that we must choose either evangelical feminism or biblical truth. We cannot have both.

---

49. "Mailbag," *World,* June 7, 2003, copied from www.worldmag.com on Oct. 23, 2003.
50. Mary Kassian issued a similar warning in 1992 when she wrote, "Many who once called themselves 'Biblical feminists' are now far from the Bible. This is because feminism and Christianity are antithetical" (*The Feminist Gospel* [Wheaton: Crossway, 1992], 239; see also 225–40, "The Slippery Slope.")

CHAPTER 14

The Current State of Evangelicalism Regarding Biblical Manhood and Womanhood

As I speak with people throughout much of the evangelical world, I find widespread awareness of an ongoing controversy over manhood and womanhood. In addition, there is much confusion both about what the Bible actually teaches and about how we should put these teachings into practice, whether in marriage or in the church. Yet I also sense a strong desire to know and to do God's will on these matters.

In this chapter I offer my assessment of the current state of evangelicalism on this question. Much of this material is scattered through previous sections of this book, but I repeat that information here in order to provide in one place an overview of what is happening in the evangelical world. For those who wish to see more detailed documentation for specific groups, I have included policy statements from various groups in an appendix.[1]

For the purposes of this chapter, the evangelical world can be divided into three groups: (1) complementarian, (2) egalitarian, and (3) undecided or uncommitted.

AN OVERVIEW OF COMPLEMENTARIAN, EGALITARIAN, AND UNDECIDED GROUPS TODAY

14.1: Complementarian groups

1. Two-Point Complementarian

There are two different groups among those who hold that the Bible teaches different roles for men and women. The first group I call "Two-Point Complementarian" because they hold that men and women are equal in value but have different roles in (1) the home and (2) the church.

1. See Appendix 8, pp. 703–66.

The other group, which I call "One-Point Complementarian," holds that men and women are equal in value but have different roles in (1) the home.

Three influential denominations are included among those that hold a Two-Point Complementarian position. The current leaders of these denominations have recently fought and won battles with liberalism, and they remember clearly that liberalism and women's ordination go hand in hand. These three denominations are the Southern Baptist Convention (at 16 million members, the largest Protestant denomination in the United States), the Lutheran Church—Missouri Synod (2.6 million members), and the smaller but very influential Presbyterian Church in America (316,000 members).[2]

Other Two-Point Complementarian groups include several denominations and organizations that historically have been strongly truth-based and doctrinally vigilant. Included in this group are the Evangelical Free Church of America, the Christian and Missionary Alliance, and the more recently formed Sovereign Grace Ministries (formerly PDI). Several seminaries also fall in this category, such as Westminster Seminary (Philadelphia and California), Reformed Seminary (Jackson, Orlando, and Charlotte), and Covenant Seminary in St. Louis, as well as Dallas Theological Seminary, The Master's Seminary, and now most or all of the Southern Baptist seminaries such as the Southern Baptist Theological Seminary in Louisville, Kentucky, and Southeastern Baptist Theological Seminary in Wake Forest, North Carolina.[3]

Many Bible colleges also fall in this category, such as Moody Bible Institute in Chicago, and Northwestern College in St. Paul, Minnesota, as well as some Reformed colleges, such as Covenant College in Lookout Mountain, Tennessee.

Thousands of independent churches and Bible churches across the United States also fall into this category.

In the publishing world, book publishers such as Crossway, Multnomah, Moody, and Presbyterian and Reformed will publish only complementarian books. Among periodicals, *World* magazine's editorial policy supports a complementarian position.[4]

Finally, the Council on Biblical Manhood and Womanhood (CBMW) is a parachurch organization whose purpose is to define, defend, and promote a Two-Point Complementarian position, which it has done since 1988.[5]

---

2. For more information on the recent history of these three denominations, see chapter 13, pp. 502–3.
3. I do not have as much specific information about the other three Southern Baptist seminaries (Southwestern in Ft. Worth, Texas; New Orleans Southern Baptist Seminary in New Orleans; and Golden Gate Seminary in San Francisco), but I believe their faculty members are also mostly or entirely complementarian. Paige Patterson moved from the presidency of Southeastern to become president of Southwestern in 2003, and he is a strongly committed complementarian, as is his academic dean Craig Blaising.
4. See the special issue of *World* on marriage and the family, May 20, 2000.
5. See www.cbmw.org.

2. One-Point Complementarian

An organization that holds a "One-Point Complementarian" position believes that men and women have equal value but they have different roles in (1) the home. In order to be in this category, an organization or group must be neutral regarding women as pastors or elders. (Those who advocate women's ordination I call egalitarian.) Many of these One-Point Complementarian groups may have leaders and members who are privately Two-Point Complementarians, but the official stance of the organization is only One-Point Complementarian.

Some parachurch organizations in this category are Focus on the Family and Promise Keepers. Both have decided not to take any official stand on the role of women in the church, but both uphold male headship in the home. In its official policies, Campus Crusade for Christ also falls in this category, since the organization has not taken any public stand on the role of women in ministry,[6] while Family Life, a division of Campus Crusade under the direction of Dennis Rainey, clearly teaches male headship in the home at its "Weekend to Remember" marriage conferences. Moreover, on July 28, 1999, a "Marriage and Family Statement" was distributed to five thousand staff at Campus Crusade's biannual staff conference on the campus of Colorado State University. The central section of that statement said:

> The husband and wife are of equal worth before God, since both are created in God's image. The marriage relationship models the way God relates to His people. A husband is to love his wife as Christ loved the church. He has the God-given responsibility to provide for, to protect, and to lead his family. A wife is to submit herself graciously to the servant leadership of her husband even as the church willingly submits to the headship of Christ. She, being in the image of God as is her husband and thus equal to him, has the God-given responsibility to respect her husband and to serve as his helper in managing the household and nurturing the next generation.
>
> In a marriage lived according to these truths, the love between husband and wife will show itself in listening to each other's viewpoints, valuing each other's gifts, wisdom, and desires, honoring one another in public and in private, and always seeking to bring benefit, not harm, to one another.[7]

Denominations generally do not fall in the One-Point Complementarian camp because in most cases they either approve or forbid the ordination of women. However, the Evangelical

---

6. In conversations with several people involved in Campus Crusade, I have been told that female campus directors are usually at an all-women's college or in cases where a male campus director has left in the middle of a year and the female associate director has taken over for the rest of the year. There may be other cases than these, but in the vast majority of cases the campus director has been a man and the associate campus director has been a woman. Above the level of individual campuses, the work of staff members is directed by regional teams that include both men and women who have been assigned different specific responsibilities.

7. For the 1999 statement, see Appendix 8, pp. 760–61.

Presbyterian Church's official policy allows members and clergy to hold differing views on women's roles in the church.[8]

14.2: Egalitarian groups

Egalitarian groups hold that men and women are equal in value, but all roles in the home and the church are determined by gifts, abilities, and preferences, not by gender. I have put organizations in this category if the egalitarian viewpoint is the dominant emphasis in the group, though in some organizations, some people still hold to a complementarian position, while in other organizations an egalitarian position is the only one allowed.

1. Liberal Denominations

When I call a denomination "liberal" here, I mean that liberalism is the dominant theological viewpoint, although in most or all of these groups there are more conservative believers who are saddened by the liberal direction of the denomination and stay to work for change. As I explained in chapters 11 and 13, egalitarianism is the dominant viewpoint in all theologically liberal denominations, and egalitarianism appears and gains strength as denominations move in a more liberal direction.[9]

By this I do not mean to say that all egalitarians are liberals. Some denominations have approved women's ordination for other reasons, which I will discuss in the following sections. But it is unquestionable that theological liberalism leads to the endorsement of women's ordination. While not all egalitarians are liberals, all liberals are egalitarians. There is no theologically liberal denomination or seminary in the United States today that opposes women's ordination.

2. Culturally Sensitive Egalitarians

Other egalitarian groups are not theologically liberal but are egalitarian for a variety of other reasons. One reason is that groups that emphasize *relating effectively to the culture* are attracted more strongly than other groups to the egalitarian trends in today's culture. Another characteristic of these groups is that, in their desire to have a positive influence on the culture, they place a higher value on effective results in ministry than they do on being sure they have correct doctrine or being sure they are faithful to the Bible in matters that seem to them to be second-order doctrines, not doctrines of primary importance (and they put controversies over women's roles in this category).

Examples of culturally sensitive egalitarian groups are Willow Creek Community Church[10] in South Barrington, Illinois, and Fuller Seminary in Pasadena, California (Fuller has had an

---

8. The EPC statement is in Appendix 8, p. 751.
9. See chapter 11, section 11.2, pp. 469–72, and chapter 13, pp. 500–505 for a discussion of the connection between liberalism and egalitarianism.
10. See Appendix 8, pp. 759–60, for the policy statement of Willow Creek Community Church.

emphasis on gaining acceptance and influence in liberal denominations and in the liberal academic world ever since its founding in 1947). Another predominantly egalitarian institution is Regent College in Vancouver, British Columbia, and it too places a high value on understanding and relating effectively to the culture, especially at the academic and professional level.[11]

3. Experience-Oriented Egalitarians

Included in this category are groups where *effective ministry* or *a strong calling from God* take priority (in practice at least) over what seem to these groups to be controversial or confused doctrinal areas (and they often put controversies about men and women in that category).

The Assemblies of God falls in this category, as does the International Church of the Four Square Gospel.[12] The Toronto Airport Christian Fellowship (formerly a Vineyard church) also falls in this category, with its strong emphasis on a personal experience of the power of the Holy Spirit. I also put *Charisma* magazine here because since at least 1997 or 1998, women pastors and women in ministry have often received emphasis in *Charisma* and its sister publication, *Ministries Today*.[13]

The Association of Vineyard Churches also falls in this category. When John Wimber was leading the Vineyard movement, he would not allow women to serve as elders in Vineyard churches.[14] However, after John Wimber's death in 1997, different churches and leaders had

---

11. Two complementarian faculty members, J. I. Packer and Bruce Waltke, are still affiliated with Regent College, but they are of retirement age and both teach part-time. Several students have reported to me that the egalitarian position of Gordon Fee, Stanley Grenz, and others has been the dominant viewpoint they hear in class (though Fee has also now retired and teaches only part-time, and Grenz no longer teaches at Regent).

In May 1994, at the invitation of the Regent College Student Council, I spoke on men's and women's roles in the church at a Saturday afternoon seminar on campus, with about eighty people in attendance. One prominent student leader said that my presentation was irenic enough that it made many friends, and, even more important, no enemies.

But later a small controversy arose when students invited me to return the following academic year. The administration now appeared unwilling to provide a forum in which I could speak. Over a hundred students signed a petition asking that I be allowed to speak on campus again, but by December 1994 it became clear to organizing students that the administration would not allow me or other outside speakers to address the issue of women in ministry.

12. See the statement on women in ministry from the Assemblies of God in Appendix 8, pp. 705–10, and notice how Scripture has effectively been neutralized for this question by the claim that there are differing views on these passages and it is not possible for the committee to decide between those different views. (See also pp. 371–76.)

13. See, for example, the article by Cindy Jacobs, "Women of God, Arise!" in *Charisma* (May 1998), 76-79, 110; Larry Keefauver, "Empower the Women," an editorial written by Keefauver as senior editor in *Ministries Today* (May/June 1998), 9; and the cover "Women of the Word" (March 1997). J. Lee Grady, the editor of *Charisma*, has published two books promoting an egalitarian position: *Ten Lies the Church Tells Women* (2000) and *Twenty-Five Tough Questions About Women and the Church* (2003).

14. See "Vineyard Restricts Elders to Men," in *CBMW News* 1:1 (August 1995), 9 (at www.cbmw.org), with quotations from the March/April 1994 edition of *Vineyard Reflections*, a publication sent to Vineyard leaders. Wimber wrote, "I believe God has established a gender-based eldership of the church. I endorse the traditional [and what I consider the *scriptural*] view of a unique leadership role for men in marriage, family, and in the church.... Consequently I personally do not favor ordaining women as elders in the local church." (However, Wimber also explained that he did allow for women to preach to mixed congregations under the authority of the local church elders.)

different views. On October 18, 2001, the national board published a statement saying that it had decided to allow each church to decide its own policy on this, effectively allowing women elders and pastors in the Vineyard movement.[15]

Other groups that place a high value on an experience of personal calling from God and experiences of fruitfulness in ministry are the Wesleyan Church, the Nazarene Church, and the Free Methodists.

4. Leader-Influenced Egalitarians

Other organizations within evangelicalism have adopted an egalitarian position primarily because of the influence of one or two strong leaders.

Included in this category is InterVarsity Christian Fellowship in the United States, which adopted a strong egalitarian position under the leadership of recent past president Steve Hayner. There are reports that InterVarsity staff members who held a complementarian position were not allowed to teach that position publicly under Hayner's leadership.[16] It appears from the books they publish that InterVarsity Press (USA) is also strongly egalitarian in its editorial policies. I do not think it has published a book from a complementarian position in the last twenty years, while it has published numerous egalitarian books.[17]

I also list Willow Creek Community Church in this category because of the strong influence of Dr. Gilbert Bilezikian, Wheaton College theology professor (now retired), who was an elder from the earliest beginnings of Willow Creek and whose book *Beyond Sex Roles* has been one of the most influential egalitarian books in the entire evangelical movement. (Willow Creek fits both this category and the earlier "culturally sensitive egalitarian" category.)

Finally, Christians for Biblical Equality (CBE) is a parachurch organization whose purpose is to define, defend, and promote an egalitarian position in the evangelical world, and it is thus a counterpart to the complementarian organization CBMW.

14.3: Undecided or uncommitted

Much of the rest of the evangelical world has not come to any clear conclusion on this issue, or has decided that it can allow both views to exist within the same organization. A number

---

15. See Appendix 8, p. 711, for this statement of the Vineyard's current policy. Two egalitarian books in the bibliography are by Vineyard pastors: Nathan, *Who Is My Enemy* (2002), and Williams, *The Apostle Paul and Women in the Church* (1979).
16. See "IVCF Affirms Egalitarianism," in CBMW *News* 1:1 (Aug. 1995), 4, with reference to Steve Hayner's position paper, "Women in the Ministries of InterVarsity," October 1993 (see also pp. 761-62.); Joe Maxwell, "Standing in the Gender Gap," *Christianity Today*, June 22, 1992, 69; and Jeff Robinson, "Louder Than Words," GenderNews.com, May 10, 2004.
17. See the bibliography for a list of InterVarsity Press books advocating an egalitarian position. One chapter in Edmund Clowney's book *The Church* (1995), 215–35, advocates a complementarian position, but this is only one chapter in one book, a book not primarily concerned with this question. I have been told that IVP is willing to publish a complementarian book on men and women, but I am not aware if any such book is scheduled. (In the United Kingdom, IVP-UK is a separate organization and it has not published several of the egalitarian titles published by IVP-US.)

of evangelical seminaries are in this category, such as Trinity Evangelical Divinity School in Deerfield, Illinois, where I taught for twenty years. Though a majority of the faculty hold a Two-Point Complementarian position, a significant minority hold an egalitarian position on women in ministry. Gordon-Conwell Seminary similarly allows both viewpoints on its faculty, though the presence of Aida Spencer (full-time) and Catherine Kroeger (adjunct) as New Testament professors means that the egalitarian viewpoint has a much stronger presence at Gordon-Conwell than at most other evangelical seminaries (Spencer and Kroeger are both influential egalitarian writers and speakers). Wheaton College in Illinois and Bethel College and Seminary in St. Paul, Minnesota, similarly have both egalitarians and complementarians on the faculty.

Many other evangelical organizations would also fit in this category.

14.4: Some personal observations on the current controversy

1. Male chauvinism has been the major problem through much of history.

For most cultures through most of history the most serious deviation from biblical standards regarding men and women has not been feminism, but harsh and oppressive male chauvinism. It still exists today, not only in some families in the United States, but also in a number of cultures throughout the world. Many non-Christian religions, such as Islam, tragically oppress women and fail to treat them as equals in the image of God.[18]

The first page of the Bible corrects this, in Genesis 1:27, where we find that God created both man and woman in His image.[19] Much of the rest of the Bible goes on to affirm the equal dignity and value of women in the sight of God, and that we must treat one another as equals in God's sight.

This truth has not always been fully recognized, even within the church. I believe that one of God's purposes in this present controversy is to correct some wrongful traditions and some wrongful assumptions of male superiority that have existed within churches and families in the evangelical world. In this and other issues, we should live with a constant expectation that over time the church will become more obedient to our Lord. I wrote in another context words that are also appropriate here:

> It has been about 1970 years since Pentecost, and during that time Jesus Christ has been gradually purifying and perfecting his church. In fact, Ephesians 5 tells us that "Christ loved the church and gave himself up for her, *that he might sanctify her,* having cleansed her by the washing of water with the word, that he might present the church to himself in splendor, without spot or wrinkle or any such thing, so that she might be holy and without blemish" (Ephesians 5:25-27). Throughout history, Jesus

18. See chapter 1, pp. 26–28 and 58–59.
19. See pp. 25–28, for a fuller discussion of this.

> Christ has been purifying the church, working toward the goal of a beautiful, holy, mature, godly church.
>
> Sometimes that process of purification has been marked by specific historical events; for example, in 325 and 381, the Nicene Creed; in 451, the Chalcedonian Creed; in 1517, Martin Luther's 95 theses; even in 1978, the International Council on Biblical Inerrancy's Chicago Statement on Biblical Inerrancy. At other times, there has been no one defining moment, but a gradual rejection of misunderstanding and a growing consensus endorsing Biblical truth in some area. For example: the rejection of the militarism of the crusades and their attempt to use the sword to advance the church; or the realization that the Bible does not teach that the sun goes around the earth; or, in the 16th and 17th centuries, the marvelous advances in doctrinal synthesis that found expression in the great confessions of faith following the Reformation; or, in the 17th and 18th centuries, the realization that the civil government could and should allow religious freedom; or in the 19th century, the growing consensus that slavery was wrong and must be abolished; or in the 20th century, the growing consensus that abortion was contrary to Scripture. Other examples could be given, but the pattern should be clear: Jesus Christ has not given up his task of purifying his church. The long-term pattern has not been nineteen centuries of decline in the purity and doctrinal and ethical understanding of the church, but rather a pattern of gradual and sometimes explosive increase in understanding and purity.[20]

The church learns and grows and is purified through controversy. After a controversy has gone on for some time, the main body of recognized teachers and leaders among Bible believing Christians will always make the right decision and will move forward with deeper understanding because Jesus Christ is Lord of His church, and He continues to protect and gradually to purify it. A minority will stick to wrong opinions and eventually become marginalized and then disappear, or they will have no significant, ongoing influence on the church.

And so I think this controversy will progress until the church reaches a right decision and incorrect views are left behind, just as they have been in past controversies.

However, in speaking of errors of male superiority in the past, I do not mean to imply that evangelical churches and families have been uniformly at fault. For example, one can read the Homilies of John Chrysostom (*ca.* 374–407) and find many beautiful admonitions about the love husbands should have for their wives and the dignity and respect with which they should treat them. Such emphases can be found in prominent writers throughout the history of the

20. These two paragraphs are taken from Grudem, "Do We Act As If We Really Believe That 'The Bible Alone, and the Bible in Its Entirety, Is the Word of God Written'?" ETS presidential address, 1999) *Journal of the Evangelical Theological Society* 43/1 (March 2000), 13.

church. And many denominations and ministries today promote and encourage valid ministries for women as well as for men.[21]

Nevertheless, as we seek to resolve this current controversy, those of us who are complementarians must continually be asking, can we do more to encourage and affirm the valuable ministries of women within scriptural guidelines? And in our hearts is there a genuine confidence in the equal value of men and women in the work of God's kingdom?

2. Egalitarianism is not advancing on the strength of exegetical arguments from Scripture.

As this controversy has progressed, more and more information has come to light. We have found more information about the meanings of words, about grammatical constructions, and about the larger biblical and historical backgrounds to the statements in Scripture.

These advances in scholarship have served to strengthen and confirm the complementarian position and to weaken the egalitarian position time and again. For example, the work of Andreas Köstenberger and H. Scott Baldwin was a significant advance in our understanding of the meaning of *authenteō* in 1 Timothy 2:12, showing that it means "have authority" or "exercise authority," rather than the negative meanings proposed by egalitarians.[22] The significant research of Richard Hove demonstrated that Galatians 3:28 ("There is neither male nor female, for you are all one in Christ Jesus") teaches the *unity* of *different persons with different roles,* not the *sameness* of men's and women's roles as egalitarians have claimed.[23] Steven Baugh and others have shown that there were well-educated women at Ephesus, contrary to the claim of some egalitarians that Paul prohibited women from teaching because they did not have enough education.[24]

Yet another advance in our understanding has come through the research of M. H. Burer and Daniel B. Wallace showing that the word *episēmos* in Romans 16:7 means that Junia(s) is "well known *to the apostles*" rather than "well known *among the apostles.*"[25] Another example would probably be my own work on the meaning of *kephalē* ("head"), which found over fifty examples where it means "person in authority." By contrast, no clear example has yet been produced of any text that says person A is the "head" of person B, and yet person A is not in a position of authority over person B (as the egalitarian position would require, in order to deny male leadership in those texts that say the husband is the head of the wife).[26]

---

21. I think of my local church, Scottsdale Bible Church, in Scottsdale, Arizona, which has a long history of promoting and encouraging valuable and visible ministries by women as well as men. Another example is Campus Crusade for Christ, which since its founding has had women as well as men in the front lines of campus ministry. And there are many other examples as well.
22. See pp. 307–16. The work of Köstenberger and Baldwin has now been supplemented by substantial new works by David Huttar and Albert Wolters (see pp. 309n90 and 317–18).
23. See pp. 184–85.
24. See pp. 289–91.
25. See pp. 224–25.
26. See pp. 202–11.

The overall result of research like this is that the complementarian position is becoming more firmly established through detailed academic work, while egalitarian arguments are crumbling. Since this is the case, how does the egalitarian position advance?

3. How does the egalitarian position advance?

In spite of numerous setbacks in academic research on the meaning of Scripture, the egalitarian position continues to advance on a number of fronts in the evangelical world. Why is this? As I have participated in and observed this controversy for over twenty years, I have concluded that the egalitarian position advances through the following methods.

a. Incorrect interpretations of Scripture. A significant number of egalitarian claims that I have responded to in this book fall in this first category. Egalitarians have claimed things about the meaning of Scripture that do not hold up on close examination of the text itself. Others may differ with me when I say that these egalitarian claims are based on incorrect interpretations, and they are free to do so. In fact, I have written this book so that people will be able to consider the egalitarian positions and my responses and decide for themselves which viewpoint is persuasive. Readers will have to examine the arguments and decide if they agree that these egalitarian claims are based on "incorrect interpretations of Scripture," as I have argued that they are.

b. Reading into Scripture things that aren't there. Several egalitarian claims are based on assertions that the Bible says something it actually does not say, such as the claim that Deborah led Israel into battle (claim 4.1), or that Miriam served as a leader over the people of Israel (claim 4.5), or that Abraham obeyed Sarah (claim 4.8), or that Proverbs 31 overturns male leadership in the family (claim 4.10), or that there was no special authority for the apostles in the New Testament church (claim 5.8), or that Peter raised Tabitha from the dead because of her leadership role (claim 5.12), or that the widows in 1 Timothy 5 were elders (claim 7.13), or that women who owned homes were the "overseers" who supervised churches that met in their homes (claim 7.14), or that elders in the New Testament churches did not have authority over the churches (claim 7.16), or that Paul tells women to "preach the Word" (claim 7.18).

c. Incorrect statements about the meanings of words in the Bible. Another category of egalitarian claims asserts that all of the English translations of the Bible are wrong, or that most or all of the standard Greek dictionaries are wrong, and that some new meaning should be accepted for key words that are in dispute in this controversy. One example is the claim that "a helper suitable for him" in Genesis 2:18 implies that Eve is superior to Adam (claim 3.9). Another is the claim that "head" means "source" in a sense that denies authority to the person who is called the "head" of someone else (claim 6.6). Another example is the claim that Romans 16:2 says that Phoebe was a "leader" or "ruler" of many (claim 7.1), and another is the claim that Ephesians 5:21 teaches that husbands and wives should "mutually submit" to one another (claim 6.4), or the claim that "have authority" in 1 Timothy 2:12 means "misuse authority" or "murder" or "commit violence" or "proclaim oneself author of a man" (claims

8.8, 8.9, 8.10), or the claim that 1 Timothy 2:12 means that Paul did not permit a woman to teach in order to gain mastery over a man (claim 8.11).

d. Incorrect statements about the history of the ancient or modern world. Over and over again, egalitarian writings claim things about the ancient world that are not true, such as that women were not well enough educated in the ancient world to serve as church leaders (claim 8.2). In fact, the more information we gain from the ancient world, the less plausible this assumption becomes. Or egalitarian writings claim things that have not been proven by any verses of Scripture or any established facts, such as the claim that women were teaching false doctrine at Ephesus (claim 8.1), or that women were disrupting the worship services at Corinth (claim 7.7). These claims are repeated over and over again, and people begin to believe them, thinking that scholars must have some evidence for them, yet remaining unaware that no hard evidence supports these claims.

Related to this is the misleading claim that male headship in the home and the church leads to abuse and repression of women (claim 12.1).

e. Methods of interpretation that reject the authority of Scripture and lead toward liberalism. Sometimes people say that this is "only a difference over Bible interpretation," and they conclude that both viewpoints should be allowed in the church. (I agree that with some egalitarian claims it is only a difference of interpretation, and I have argued specific points about those interpretations in this book.)

However, another class of interpretations by egalitarians is different from this, and it is deeply troubling. That is a class of interpretations that do not proceed on the same assumptions about the authority of Scripture in our lives.

As I mentioned in chapter 13, egalitarian claims that implicitly or explicitly deny the authority of Scripture include claims that the meanings of words in the Hebrew language of the Old Testament should not be an authority for us (claim 3.5), or that Genesis 1–2 is not historically accurate (claim 3.7), or that the New Testament ethic regarding male headship needs further improvement (claim 6.5), or that 1 Corinthians 14:34–35 is not part of the Bible (claim 7.5), or that the apostle Paul was wrong in what he said in 1 Timothy 2 (claim 8.14).

Another claim that fits this category is the idea that Paul and other New Testament authors were moving in a trajectory toward full inclusion of women in leadership, but they didn't reach that goal by the time the New Testament was completed; therefore, we should move beyond their teachings in the direction they were heading (claim 9.4). Similar to the trajectory hermeneutic position is the view of Kevin Giles that we cannot decide doctrinal questions by citing Scripture passages, so we must decide them instead according to what the church has historically held (at least in those cases where Giles thinks it held the right thing; see discussion at claim 10.2). Still other claims that deny the authority of Scripture include the idea that a "redemptive-movement hermeneutic" shows that the submission texts and the male church leadership texts in the New Testament were culturally relative (claim 9.5) or that one's decision on this matter all depends on which verses a person decides to emphasize (claim 9.9), or that it is impossible to figure out what the Bible teaches about this (claim 9.10), or that a woman can teach and have authority over men if she does so under the authority of the pastor and elders (claim 9.12), or that we do not have to obey certain New Testament commands even when we are engaged in the activities that they talk about simply because "we are not a church" (claim 9.13).

f. Rejecting Scripture as our authority and deciding this question on the basis of experience and personal inclination. Other egalitarian claims effectively place personal experience as a higher authority than Scripture. Included in this category are the arguments that we cannot oppose ministries that God has clearly blessed, so we should not waste time on obscure discussions about what the Bible might say about this (claim 11.4), or that we cannot deny the validity of a woman's ministry if she has a genuine call from God to be a pastor (claim 11.5), or that many prophetic voices today indicate that women should be allowed to teach the Bible to both sexes and to serve as pastors (again, without regard to the Bible's teaching on this matter) (claim 11.6), or that we are at a unique time in history where the old standards found in the Bible no longer apply (claim 11.7).

g. Suppression of information. On a number of occasions I have observed a pattern of conduct by which a pastor will lead a church in an egalitarian direction through the suppression of relevant information and a refusal to allow a fair opportunity for any competent expressions of a complementarian position. Typically a pastor will read some egalitarian books and become convinced that they are right. He will then seek out allies or work to establish allies for his position as a dominant group on the board of elders or the church governing board. Then he will preach a series of sermons promoting the egalitarian viewpoint. He may also promote occasions in which women actually teach the Bible to mixed groups.

If anyone objects to what he is doing, he and his fellow leaders label that person as "divisive" and say that he or she is wrongly opposing the church's leadership. If any church members ask for an opportunity to express a complementarian position, they are told that "people already know that viewpoint, and they don't need to hear it again," even though many may have never heard a responsible defense of a complementarian view that included thoughtful interaction with egalitarian claims. Therefore all that these "instinctive complementarians" have to support their view is an instinctive or traditional preference, but they have no persuasive arguments or facts with which to answer the fruits of thirty years of academic research by egalitarian scholars. When they try to cite Bible verses opposing the pastor's egalitarian agenda, he will answer with arguments from egalitarian scholars (such as those in this book). Often the pastor's arguments will not provide hard facts that people can inspect for themselves, but will take the form, "Scholar A and Scholar B say you are wrong, so you must be wrong." Such arguments seem hard to answer, because the instinctive complementarians lack technical training and lack the time and research facilities to find answers to the egalitarian scholars that the pastor quotes. In this way, the use of the Bible by the instinctive complementarians is effectively nullified.

It is thus a mismatch from the beginning. Even if opportunity is given for a forum to present a complementarian view, it may be at an inconvenient time or in a small room or will not be adequately publicized, and verbal commitments to allow such a meeting may be withdrawn or changed at the last minute. In every way possible, expression of a complementarian position will be minimized and marginalized and suppressed.[27]

4. Egalitarianism has two significant allies

As egalitarians attempt to gain influence in Christian organizations, they have two significant allies. The first is the secular culture, which in its more prominent expressions is strongly opposed to the authority of the Word of God, strongly opposed to the idea that any positions in society should be restricted to men, strongly opposed to the family as God created it to function, and (in many quarters) strongly opposed to authority in general. I recognize that not all people in our secular culture hold these positions, but a very influential part of our culture does, especially in the highly influential areas of the media, the entertainment industry, and secular universities.

The second ally of egalitarianism is a large group of Christian leaders who believe that the Bible teaches a complementarian position but who lack courage to teach about it or take a stand in favor of it. They are silent, "passive complementarians" who, in the face of relentless egalitarian pressure to change their organizations, simply give in more and more to appease a viewpoint they privately believe the Bible does not teach.

This is similar to the situation conservatives in liberal denominations face regarding homosexuality where too many people who think it is wrong will not take a stand. As Robert Benne, member of the task force on homosexuality in the Evangelical Lutheran Church in America said, the presence of open homosexuals at every discussion

> makes it difficult for folks who are uncertain or just plain nice to voice objections or even reservations about the revisionist agenda. Most church people like to be polite and accepting, so they often accept that agenda out of the desire to "keep the peace in love."[28]

One of the leaders who helped conservatives retake control of the Southern Baptist Convention after a struggle of many years told me privately, "Our biggest problem in this struggle was not the moderates who opposed us. Our biggest problem was conservatives who agreed with us and refused to say anything or take a stand to support us."

How different was the ministry of the apostle Paul! He did not lack courage to stand up

27. For an example of suppressing the complementarian view by rude heckling from the audience, see Wallace Benn, "How Egalitarian Tactics Swayed Evangelicals in the Church of England," *CBMW News* 2:3 (June 1997), 14, reproduced in Appendix 2, pp. 541–43.
28. *World,* Aug. 2, 2003, 21.

for unpopular teachings of God's Word. When he met with the elders of the church at Ephesus and recounted his three-year ministry among them, he was able to say with a clear conscience, "Therefore I testify to you this day that I am innocent of the blood of all of you, *for* I did not shrink from declaring to you the whole counsel of God" (Acts 20:26–27).

The word "for" indicates that Paul was giving the reason why he was "innocent of the blood of all of you." He said he would not be accountable before God for any failures in the church at Ephesus because he "did not shrink from declaring" to them *"the whole counsel of God."* He did not hold back from teaching something just because it was unpopular. He did not hold back from teaching something because it would have created opposition and struggle and conflict. In good conscience he proclaimed everything that God's Word taught on every topic, whether popular or not. He proclaimed "the whole counsel of God." And he stood before God blameless for his stewardship of the ministry to the Ephesian church.

If the apostle Paul were alive today, planting churches and overseeing leaders in those churches, would he counsel them to shrink back from speaking and teaching clearly about biblical roles for men and women? Would he counsel them to shrink back from giving a clear testimony of God's will concerning one of the most disputed and yet most urgent topics in our entire society? Would he tell pastors simply to be silent about this topic so that there could be "peace in our time" in our churches, and so that the resolution of the controversy would be left for others at another time and another place?

When Paul began to preach that people did not have to be circumcised in order to follow Christ, great persecution resulted, and his Jewish opponents pursued him from city to city, at one point even stoning him and leaving him for dead (Acts 14:19–23). But Paul did not compromise on the gospel of salvation *by faith alone in Christ alone*, not *by faith plus circumcision*. And when Paul later wrote to some of those very churches where he had been persecuted and even stoned and left for dead, he insisted on the purity of the gospel that he had proclaimed, and he said, "For am I now seeking the approval of man, or of God? Or am I trying to please man? If I were still trying to please man, I would not be a servant of Christ" (Galatians 1:10).

It is important for church leaders, in fact for all Christians, to ask themselves this same question.

14.5: Egalitarianism is an engine that will pull many destructive consequences in its train.

I have argued throughout this book that the complementarian position is confirmed in Scripture in many ways. And I have argued that this biblical position will lead Christian men and women to true joy and fulfillment as they live in accordance with the purposes God has given in His Word.

The other side of that teaching on the beauty and value of complementarianism is that the egalitarian position ultimately bears various kinds of destructive fruit in people's lives. I believe that an egalitarian position, with its constant blurring of the distinctions between men and women, will lead to a gender identity crisis in men and women, and especially in many of the children that they raise.[29] Men and women will be confused about what it means to be a man and what it means to be a woman, and how men and women should act in ways that are different from one another (topics that egalitarians will usually not teach on). Such a gender identity crisis will lead to increasing self-hatred in many people, to fear of marriage, to anger and violence that will stem from internal frustration (particularly in men), and to an increase in homosexual conduct.

As a result, I believe that the egalitarian position will lead to an increasing breakdown of families and a weakening and effeminization of the church.

In addition, egalitarianism will increasingly lead people to an acceptance of methods for interpreting Scripture that will then make it easy to relativize any of the unpopular moral commands of Scripture. If the many ways of denying the teaching of Scripture described in this book are applied to other unpopular teachings of Scripture, they can be readily dispensed with as well.

Therefore, I believe that ultimately the *effective* authority of Scripture to govern our lives is at stake in this controversy. The issue is not whether we *say* we believe the Bible is the Word of God or that we believe it is without error, but the issue is whether we *actually obey it* when its teachings are unpopular and conflict with the dominant viewpoints in our culture. If we do not obey it, then the effective authority of God to govern His people and His church through His Word has been eroded.

14.6: A strategy for complementarians

If you are a complementarian in a local church (or a parachurch organization) that has not decided this issue (or has decided it wrongly), here are my suggestions for practical things you can do, either alone or with the help of a few complementarian friends. If you think the Lord is calling you to prompt your church to make a policy decision regarding which leadership roles in the church are open to women and which are restricted to men:

1. Talk to your pastor (or president in a parachurch organization) and see where he stands. If he is undecided or uncertain, make available to him some complementarian books and literature. The most effective way to bring change in a church is if the pastor will preach a series of messages that teach the church about this issue. Many people in evangelical churches are not hostile to a complementarian position but are poorly informed about it.

---

29. By contrast, for a positive perspective on raising boys to be boys, see James Dobson's recent book *Bringing Up Boys* (2001). Dr. Dobson plans also to publish a book soon on bringing up girls. Many other excellent books on parenting are available from Focus on the Family (www.family.org) and from FamilyLife, a division of Campus Crusade for Christ (www.familylife.com).

2. Make available to church members a number of good books on this issue (see the bibliography at the end of this book for some ideas). People need to be well-informed if they are going to make a good decision.
3. Find out if your pastor is willing to support a process leading to a Two-Point complementarian addition to the church's constitution. If he will not support it and also will not oppose it, you can still go forward. But if he strongly opposes a complementarian position, you need to pray for wisdom about whether to proceed, because it will be exceptionally difficult to make a change. In most cases, attempting to push such a decision against the opposition of the senior pastor will lead to a major controversy that will result in either you or him having to leave the church (probably you). It may be God's will for you to drop the matter, stay in the church, and pray for a better opportunity to seek change in the future. Or it may be God's will for you to leave and find a complementarian church.
4. Find out the governing structure of your church and how it works. How are officers chosen? How are policy statements made?
5. Talk to current elders (or board members or deacons). Find out who will support you on this issue. Make available to them some complementarian books and literature.
6. If a majority of elders are not complementarian (or are unwilling to take a stand on this issue), see if you can find new candidates to stand for elder in the next election (or other process of elder selection). If you cannot get a majority of the elder board on your side, making a change will be extremely difficult, so you need again to pray for wisdom on whether to proceed or drop the matter for the present time.
7. Plan a process to inform the church about the need to address this issue, to hold informational meetings and discussions, and to get out information to people (including where they can find good materials from both sides that they can read). In many situations, especially if there are some vocal egalitarians in the church, it may be good to have one or more debates or forums where both sides can present their views and interact (but allow enough time—three or four hours anyway—because the issues are detailed and complex). An alternative is to allow one side to have an entire evening with a guest speaker and then allow the other side to have an entire evening with a guest speaker.[30]
8. Realize that you may be called divisive, insensitive, unloving, or other things. Be sure that these accusations are not true! Your viewpoint may be misrepresented

30. The CBMW office in Louisville, KY (phone 502-897-4065; or www.cbmw.org) can often suggest complementarian speakers for such events. I have not heard of any cases where the egalitarian position had gained ground as a result of an open and fair debate between speakers who were equally well prepared and who addressed an evangelical audience.

and your reputation may be attacked. Correct every misunderstanding and misrepresentation as soon as possible. Jesus always did, except in the unique events leading up to His death. Always follow 2 Timothy 2:24–25: "And the Lord's servant must not be quarrelsome but kind to everyone, able to teach, patiently enduring evil, correcting his opponents with gentleness. God may perhaps grant them repentance leading to a knowledge of the truth."

9. Propose a change in the church's constitution when it seems likely that you have enough support for a change. Then follow through until the change is made.
10. Don't back down at the last minute for the sake of friendship or just to keep someone from getting mad or leaving the church. Some people may attempt to manipulate the process by force of personality or by threats or dire warnings.
11. Continue to pray and commit the process to the Lord. Be kind. Do not violate the written procedures in the governing documents of the church.
12. If your proposal does not pass, remember that the matter is in the Lord's hands and continue to trust Him. Pray for wisdom about whether to leave the church or to stay and work for change at another time.
13. Remember that if your church does not establish a written policy with a Two-Point Complementarian position, it will not remain neutral. If it has no written policy, eventually the pressures of the culture will lead to ever-increasing compromises with an egalitarian position, and thus to increased tensions in the church. The issue will not just go away.

14.7: Expectations for the Future

I expect several different things will happen over the next ten years with this controversy.

1. The controversy will not go away until it has been resolved by the vast majority of evangelical groups and denominations. The pressures in the culture are so great that no church and no denomination and no parachurch organization can simply decide to avoid the controversy. Each group that has not done so will have to study this issue and reach a formal position on it. That position should then be spelled out in statements of faith (as with the Baptist Faith and Message statement of the Southern Baptist Convention), or in policy statements (many of which are found in an appendix at the end of this book).[31] But until a group adopts a formal written policy on the roles of men and women in ministry and in marriage, the controversy will not go away; it will just be postponed.

2. Once these written policies are established, change will be very difficult; the future direction of the group will be set. Many people who differ with the policy (whatever it is) will leave and find another church or organization, and more people who agree with the policy will

31. See Appendix 8, pp. 703–66.

join. Therefore, establishing a written policy (one way or the other) will usually bring the controversy to an end within each group, at least for many years. As I explained earlier in this book at several points, I fear that many sincere Christians will make erroneous decisions on these questions because they only were given misleading or incorrect information on various aspects of the Bible's teachings about this issue.

3. If a group endorses an egalitarian position, I believe that changes in traditionally held views in other areas of morality and doctrine will be rapid. The controversy over men and women is not the only controversy in the church. Other beliefs being challenged today are the truthfulness of the Bible in all that it affirms, the existence of hell and the eternal punishment of those who do not believe in Christ, the necessity to hear about Jesus Christ and trust in Him personally for salvation, the idea that God knows all future human choices, the doctrine that Christ bore the wrath of God that was due us for our sins (the doctrine of penal substitutionary atonement), and the belief that homosexual conduct is contrary to the moral standards of Scripture.

Those are only a few of the teachings of Scripture being challenged in various quarters today. Not every group that endorses egalitarianism will also abandon these doctrines, but the pressures to abandon them will be strong. If an egalitarian church begins to abandon some of these other doctrines as well, it will be a strong indication that the church is moving rapidly toward a new kind of liberalism. As I explained in the previous chapter, I believe that egalitarianism will usher in a liberal view of Scripture, and it will eventually result in the loss of a number of other doctrines, such as those I have just named.

4. However, I do not think for a minute that the egalitarian position will win in this controversy. Jesus promised, "I will build my church" (Matthew 16:18), and I believe He will protect and preserve His church and bring it to greater and greater purity and strength. Therefore I believe that the vast majority of the church will endorse a Two-Point Complementarian view of manhood and womanhood, yet one that is somewhat revised from traditional views because it will bring a new delight in the beauty of our masculinity and femininity as something God created as "very good" in His sight (Genesis 1:31). We will increasingly recognize, as men and women, that our differences as well as our similarities are "very good" and a cause of joy and delight—for us as well as for God.

I believe the complementarian view that will ultimately triumph in the church will result in a new honoring of women as truly equal partners in the family and in the work of the kingdom. I believe it will bring in a new openness toward different ministries for women and a new appreciation for the valuable ministries of women in the home and in the church, yet with "some governing and teaching roles...restricted to men."[32] And I believe it will also bring a new depth of understanding of what God intended when He created marriage and the family and the

32. Danvers Statement, Affirmation 6, p. 539 below.

church, and a new depth of understanding of God's wonderful purpose for us when we live according to His Word.

In this entire process, I believe that Jesus Christ will be purifying His church, according to His eternal and wise purpose,

> *That he might sanctify her,* having cleansed her by the washing of water with the word, *so that he might present the church to himself in splendor*, without spot or wrinkle or any such thing, that she might be holy and without blemish. (Ephesians 5:26–27)

He is the Lord of heaven and earth, and He will not fail.

The Danvers Statement[1]

Background: The Danvers Statement was prepared by several evangelical leaders at an early Council on Biblical Manhood and Womanhood meeting in Danvers, Massachusetts, in December 1987. It was first published in final form by the CBMW in Wheaton, Illinois, in November 1988.

Rationale

We have been moved in our purpose by the following contemporary developments, which we observe with deep concern:

1. The widespread uncertainty and confusion in our culture regarding the complementary differences between masculinity and femininity;
2. the tragic effects of this confusion in unraveling the fabric of marriage woven by God out of the beautiful and diverse strands of manhood and womanhood;
3. the increasing promotion given to feminist egalitarianism with accompanying distortions or neglect of the glad harmony portrayed in Scripture between the loving, humble leadership of redeemed husbands and the intelligent, willing support of that leadership by redeemed wives;
4. the widespread ambivalence regarding the values of motherhood, vocational homemaking, and the many ministries historically performed by women;
5. the growing claims of legitimacy for sexual relationships which have biblically and historically been considered illicit or perverse, and the increase in pornographic portrayal of human sexuality;
6. the upsurge of physical and emotional abuse in the family;
7. the emergence of roles for men and women in church leadership that do not conform to biblical teaching but backfire in the crippling of biblically faithful witness;
8. the increasing prevalence and acceptance of hermeneutical oddities devised to reinterpret apparently plain meanings of biblical texts;

1. The Danvers Statement can be obtained on-line at www.cbmw.org. More information about this and other issues related to biblical manhood and womanhood is available at that same website from the Council on Biblical Manhood and Womanhood.

9. the consequent threat to biblical authority as the clarity of Scripture is jeopardized and the accessibility of its meaning to ordinary people is withdrawn into the restricted realm of technical ingenuity;
10. and behind all this, the apparent accommodation of some within the church to the spirit of the age at the expense of winsome, radical biblical authenticity, which in the power of the Holy Spirit may reform rather than reflect our ailing culture.

Purposes

Recognizing our own abiding sinfulness and fallibility, and acknowledging the genuine evangelical standing of many who do not agree with all of our convictions, nevertheless, moved by the preceding observations and by the hope that the noble biblical vision of sexual complementarity may yet win the mind and heart of Christ's church, we engage to pursue the following purposes:

1. To study and set forth the biblical view of the relationship between men and women, especially in the home and in the church.
2. To promote the publication of scholarly and popular materials representing this view.
3. To encourage the confidence of lay people to study and understand for themselves the teaching of Scripture, especially on the issue of relationships between men and women.
4. To encourage the considered and sensitive application of this biblical view in the appropriate spheres of life.
5. And thereby

   - to bring healing to persons and relationships injured by an inadequate grasp of God's will concerning manhood and womanhood,
   - to help both men and women realize their full ministry potential through a true understanding and practice of their God-given roles,
   - and to promote the spread of the gospel among all peoples by fostering a biblical wholeness in relationships that will attract a fractured world.

Affirmations

Based on our understanding of biblical teachings, we affirm the following:

1. Both Adam and Eve were created in GodÕs image, equal before God as persons and distinct in their manhood and womanhood (Genesis 1:26–27; 2:18).
2. Distinctions in masculine and feminine roles are ordained by God as part of the created order, and should find an echo in every human heart (Genesis 2:18, 21–24; 1 Corinthians 11:7–9; 1 Timothy 2:12–14).

3. Adam's headship in marriage was established by God before the Fall, and was not a result of sin (Genesis 2:16–18, 21–24; 3:1–13; 1 Corinthians 11:7–9).
4. The Fall introduced distortions into the relationships between men and women (Genesis 3:1–7, 12, 16).

   - In the home, the husband's loving, humble headship tends to be replaced by domination or passivity; the wife's intelligent, willing submission tends to be replaced by usurpation or servility.
   - In the church, sin inclines men toward a worldly love of power or an abdication of spiritual responsibility, and inclines women to resist limitations on their roles or to neglect the use of their gifts in appropriate ministries.

5. The Old Testament, as well as the New Testament, manifests the equally high value and dignity which God attached to the roles of both men and women (Genesis 1:26–27; 2:18; Galatians 3:28). Both Old and New Testaments also affirm the principle of male headship in the family and in the covenant community (Genesis 2:18; Ephesians 5:21–33; Colossians 3:18–19; 1 Timothy 2:11–15).
6. Redemption in Christ aims at removing the distortions introduced by the curse.

   - In the family, husbands should forsake harsh or selfish leadership and grow in love and care for their wives; wives should forsake resistance to their husbands' authority and grow in willing, joyful submission to their husbands' leadership (Ephesians 5:21–33; Colossians 3:18–19; Titus 2:3–5; 1 Peter 3:1–7).
   - In the church, redemption in Christ gives men and women an equal share in the blessings of salvation; nevertheless, some governing and teaching roles within the church are restricted to men (Galatians 3:28; 1 Corinthians 11:2–16; 1 Timothy 2:11–15).

7. In all of life Christ is the supreme authority and guide for men and women, so that no earthly submission—domestic, religious, or civil—ever implies a mandate to follow a human authority into sin (Daniel 3:10–18; Acts 4:19–20; 5:27–29; 1 Peter 3:1–2).
8. In both men and women, a heartfelt sense of call to ministry should never be used to set aside biblical criteria for particular ministries (1 Timothy 2:11–15; 3:1–13; Titus 1:5–9). Rather, biblical teaching should remain the authority for testing our subjective discernment of God's will.

9. With half the world's population outside the reach of indigenous evangelism; with countless other lost people in those societies that have heard the gospel; with the stresses and miseries of sickness, malnutrition, homelessness, illiteracy, ignorance, aging, addiction, crime, incarceration, neuroses, and loneliness, no man or woman who feels a passion from God to make His grace known in word and deed need ever live without a fulfilling ministry for the glory of Christ and the good of this fallen world (1 Corinthians 12:7–21).
10. We are convinced that a denial or neglect of these principles will lead to increasingly destructive consequences in our families, our churches, and the culture at large.

We grant permission and encourage interested persons to use, reproduce, and distribute the Danvers Statement.

Printed copies of the Danvers Statement in brochure form are available for a small fee from the Council on Biblical Manhood and Womanhood at www.cbmw.org or 2825 Lexington Road, Box 926, Louisville, KY 40280, or phone 502-897-4065 or 888-560-8210.

How Egalitarian Tactics Swayed Evangelicals in the Church of England[1]

Wallace Benn[2]

November 1992 was a critical time for the Church of England. It was then that the General Synod voted in favour of women becoming priests/presbyters. Before the November vote, a preliminary discussion and vote was taken at the July synod. The Evangelical Group in General Synod (EGGS) arranged a debate and discussion about the whole issue. Everyone knew that it would be the evangelical vote that would cause the measure to succeed or fail, so the debate was important.

I was asked to be one of the speakers along with Colin Craston, a senior evangelical clergyman who is in favour of women priests. The debate had been carefully planned; we exchanged papers several months before and were meant to react to the final papers we each produced. It was set up to be as productive as possible and to minimise misunderstanding between us. However, on the Monday of the week of the debate Canon Craston pulled out, stating that he had to be at a meeting of the Synod Standing Committee, and without any consultation, he substituted for himself an able and popular laywoman theologian, Christina Baxter, the Dean of St. John's College, Nottingham. I respect and like Christina, but it was a clever debating substitution! Then Canon Craston arrived just after the debate started!

---

1. Reprinted from *CBMW News* 2:3 (June 1997), 14.
2. The Rev. Wallace Benn served as Vicar of St. Peter's Church, Harold Wood, Essex, England until May of 1997, when he became Bishop of Lewes in the English Diocese of Chichester. He is also a member of the CBMW Board of Reference.

We had a full, frank and irenic exchange of views that I hope and believe was helpful and instructive. Both positions were fully and fairly represented. What surprised me were several factors:

1. Although I am used in other contexts to being booed and heckled (at a University mission in the students' union, for example), to find oneself being treated like that by sisters and brothers in Christ was a surprising and difficult experience. Some evangelical feminists/egalitarians are just rude, and one feels that if men behaved like that we would be in deep trouble! Well, perhaps we have been rude or demeaning in the past too, but I was a bit surprised and shocked. I was very surprised to find someone like Elaine Storkey joining with others who were saying "Rubbish! Nonsense!" during my presentation.

During the discussion, I was also disappointed by the silence from many that held our position—although I do see that the tactic caused the other side to somewhat overstate their case.

2. I was very surprised by the patently selective use of material, and what looked like the dredging up of anything that would support a predetermined case. Let me give an example. One able minister in response to what I had said on Ephesians 5 made the point that "submit" was not present in the Greek text of Ephesians 5:22 so we did not need to bother about it! Mutual submission was all that is required! I was not allowed to respond, but I asked the chairman to ask him whether "submit" was in the text of verse 24 (which it is!). The answer was ducked, and one was left with the impression that either the person knew no Greek (patently not the case) or that selective use of the text was being made. This is frankly not worthy of us as evangelicals. I am loath to accuse and come to such conclusions, but I was deeply disturbed by what appeared to be on this occasion a lack of integrity in handling evidence.

3. What shocked me most of all was the response that I got when I talked about the "economic" view of the Trinity—that within the equality of the Trinity there was functional subordination, and that it was the delight of the Son to submit to the Father's will. This I said was the historic doctrine of the Trinity, which it is. At this a section of the one hundred present shouted "rubbish," "no," etc. At this point I asked Christina (who looked embarrassed) and others in the audience what alternative view they held. It materialised that they believed in mutual submission in the Trinity. I asked if I had understood them clearly, that is, that they believed that the Father submitted to the Son, the Father to the Spirit, the Son to the Spirit etc. They said I had understood them correctly. I then asked them for one piece of biblical evidence to substantiate this view. There was silence, and none was forthcoming! I then said gently that until some biblical evidence was forthcoming I would stick to the historic view for which there was lots of biblical support. More boos! I thought in my naïveté that the Trinity was unassailable amongst evangelicals until that day. But I now see more clearly that when one part of what Scripture teaches is abandoned then it is not long before other doctrines start being revised or adjusted. This is incredibly serious, as the erosion of the Trinity will lead to there being no distinctive persons in the Trinity, and therefore no distinctively Trinitarian doctrine! I was more

shaken by this aspect of the encounter than anything else, and deeply concerned at the erosion of fundamental doctrine amongst other respected evangelicals. Could they be so unaware of the seriousness of what was happening?

In the end, on November 11, 1992, the Ordination of Women as Priests Measure was just passed in each house of General Synod (bishops, presbyters, and laity) by the necessary two-thirds majority. I am told that the crucial determining vote was decided by two evangelical lay votes (out of 251 lay delegates voting) from people who changed their minds on the day of the vote!

Over Fifty Examples of *Kephalē* ("Head") Meaning "Authority Over/Ruler" in Ancient Literature[1]

E*xplanation:* I have listed here fifty-six examples from ancient literature where the Greek word kephalē ("head") is used to mean "authority over/ruler." Though egalitarians attempt to deny that kephalē carries this sense (see claim 6.6), this is the one meaning that is present in all of these examples, and no examples have ever been found where person A is called the "head" of person B and person A is not in a position of authority over person B. (In each case where the word *head* is in italics, it represents the Greek word kephalē.)

Detailed discussion of each of these passages can be found in my 1985, 1990, and 2001 articles, which are listed in the first footnote below. (All three articles are available at www.EFBT100.com and www.cbmw.org. The 2001 article is reprinted as Appendix 4.)

Examples of *kephalē* meaning "authority over/ruler" (where a person in

1. This appendix was compiled by Chris Cowan from the following articles: Grudem, "Does Kephalē ('Head') Mean 'Source' or 'Authority Over' in Greek Literature? A Survey of 2,336 Examples," *TrinJ* 10 NS (1985): 38–59 (reprinted as an appendix to George Knight's *The Role Relationship of Men and Women: New Testament Teaching,* 49–80); Grudem, "The Meaning of Kephalē ('Head'): A Response to Recent Studies," *TrinJ* 11 NS (1990): 3–72 (reprinted as an appendix to Piper and Grudem, *Recovering Biblical Manhood and Womanhood,* 425–68); Grudem, "Meaning of Kephalē ('Head'): An Analysis of New Evidence, Real and Alleged," *Journal of the Evangelical Theological Society* 44/1 (2001): 25–65 (reprinted in Grudem, *Biblical Foundations for Manhood Womanhood,* 145–202); Joseph Fitzmyer, "Another Look at Kephalē in 1 Corinthians 11:3," *New Testament Studies* 35 (1989): 503–11; Idem, "Kephalē in 1 Corinthians 11:3," *Interpretation* 47 (1993): 52–59.

authority is metaphorically called the *head* of others under his authority):

1. Deuteronomy 28:13, LXX: (in relationship to other nations) "And the Lord will make you the *head*, and not the tail; and you shall tend upward only, and not downward; if you obey the commandments of the Lord your God, which I command you this day" (compare with the following passage, where rule and authority are in view). (2nd cent. BC)
2. Deuteronomy 28:44, LXX: ("If you do not obey the voice of the Lord your God...," verse 15) "The sojourner who is among you shall mount above you higher and higher; and you shall come down lower and lower. He shall lend to you, and you shall not lend to him; he shall be the *head*, and you shall be the tail. All these curses shall come upon you." (2nd cent. BC)
3. Judges 10:18 (Alexandrinus), LXX: "And the people, the leaders of Gilead, said to one another, 'Who is the man that will begin to fight against the Ammonites? He shall be *head* over all the inhabitants of Gilead.'" (2nd cent. BC)
4. Judges 11:8 (Alexandrinus), LXX: "And the elders of Gilead said to Jephthah, 'That is why we have turned to you now, that you may go with us and fight with the Ammonites, and be our *head* over all the inhabitants of Gilead.'" (2nd cent. BC)
5. Judges 11:9 (Alexandrinus), LXX: "Jephthah said to the elders of Gilead, 'If you bring me home again to fight with the Ammonites, and the Lord gives them over to me, I will be your *head*.'" (2nd cent. BC)
6. Judges 11:11, LXX: "So Jephthah went with the elders of Gilead, and all the people made him *head* and leader over them." (2nd cent. BC)
7. 2 Kings (2 Samuel) 22:44, LXX: David says to God, "You shall keep me as the *head* of the Gentiles: a people which I knew not served me." (2nd cent. BC)
8. 3 Kings (1 Kings) 8:1 (Alexandrinus), LXX: "Then Solomon assembled the elders of Israel with all the *heads* of the tribes." (2nd cent. BC)
9. Psalm 17 (18):43, LXX: David says to God, "You will make me *head* of the Gentiles: a people whom I knew not served me." (2nd cent. BC)

10.–11. Isaiah 7:8, LXX: "For the *head* of Syria is Damascus, and the *head* of Damascus is Rezin" (on both cases "head" means "ruler" here: Damascus is the city that rules over Syria, and Rezin is the king who rules over Damascus). (2nd cent. BC)

12.–13. Isaiah 7:9, LXX: "And the *head* of Ephraim is Samaria, and the *head* of Samaria is the son of Remaliah." (2nd cent. BC)

14. Isaiah 9:14–16, LXX: (in the context of judgment) "So the Lord cut off from Israel *head* and tail...the elder and honored man is the head, and the prophet

who teaches lies is the tail; for those who lead this people lead them astray" [first instance of *head* only]. (2nd cent. BC)

15. Jeremiah 38 (31):7, LXX: "Rejoice and exult over the *head* of the nations." (2nd cent. BC)
16. Lamentations 1:5, LXX: [of Jerusalem] "Her foes have become the *head,* her enemies prosper, because the Lord has made her suffer for the multitude of her transgressions; her children have gone away, captives before the foe." (2nd cent. BC)

17.–19. 1 Corinthians 11:3: "I want you to know that the *head* of every man is Christ, and the *head* of the woman is the man, and the *head* of Christ is God." (1st cent. AD)

20. Ephesians 1:22: "He has put all things under his feet and has made him the *head* over all things for the church." (1st cent. AD)
21. Ephesians 4:15: "We are to grow up in every way into him who is the *head,* into Christ, from whom the whole body, joined and knit together by every joint with which it is supplied, when each part is working properly, makes bodily growth and upbuilds itself in love." (1st cent. AD)

22.–23. Ephesians 5:22–24: "Wives, be subject to your husbands, as to the Lord. For the husband is the *head* of the wife as Christ is the *head* of the church, his body, and is himself its Savior. As the church is subject to Christ, so let wives also be subject in everything to their husbands." (1st cent. AD)

24. Colossians 1:18: "He is the *head* of the body, the church." (1st cent. AD)
25. Colossians 2:10: "And you have come to fullness of life in him, who is the *head* of all rule and authority." (1st cent. AD)
26. Colossians 2:18–19: "Let no one disqualify you, insisting on self-abasement and worship of angels, taking his stand on visions, puffed up without reason by his sensuous mind, and not holding fast to the *Head,* from whom the whole body, nourished and knit together through its joints and ligaments, grows with a growth that is from God." (1st cent. AD)
27. Josephus, *War* 4.261: Jerusalem is the "*head* of the whole nation." (1st cent. AD)
28. Philo, *Moses* 2.30: "As the *head* is the ruling place in the living body, so Ptolemy [Ptolemy Philadelphos] became among kings." (1st cent. AD)

29.–30. Philo, *On Rewards and Punishments* 125: "The virtuous one, whether single man or people, will be the *head* of the human race and all the others will be like the parts of the body which are animated by the powers in and above the *head.*" (1st cent. AD)

31.–32. Plutarch, *Cicero* 14.4: Catiline says to Cicero, criticizing the Senate as weak and the people as strong, "There are two bodies, one lean and wasted, but with a *head,* and the other headless but strong and large. What am I doing wrong if I myself become a *head* for this?" In saying this, Catiline was threatening to become the head of the people and thus to lead the people in revolt against Cicero. Therefore, "Cicero was all the more alarmed." (1st/2nd cent. AD)

33. Plutarch, *Galba* 4.3: "Vindex...wrote to Galba inviting him to assume the imperial power, and thus to serve what was a vigorous body in need of a *head*." (1st/2nd cent. AD)
34. Hermas, *Similitudes* 7.3: The man is told that his family "cannot be punished in any other way than if you, the *head* of the house, be afflicted." (2nd cent. AD)
35. Aquila, Deuteronomy 5:23: " The *heads* of tribes." (2nd cent. AD)[2]
36. Aquila, Deuteronomy 29:10(9): " The *heads* of tribes." (2nd cent. AD)
37. Aquila, 3 Kings (1 Kings) 8:1: "Solomon assembled all the elders of Israel and all the *heads* of the tribes." (2nd cent. AD)
38. Aquila, Ezekiel 38:2: Gog is called the "ruling *head* of Meshech." (2nd cent. AD)
39. Theodotian, Judges 10:28: "He will be *head* over all the inhabitants of Gilead." (2nd cent. AD)
40. Athanasius, Work 005, 89.2.3 (*NPNF* ser. 2, 4:147; TLG, Athanasius, Work 005, 89.2.3.): He refers to "the bishops of illustrious cities," as "the *heads* of great churches." (4th cent. AD)
41. Chrysostom, *Homily 26 on 1 Corinthians* (*NPNF* ser. 1, 12:156; TLG Work 156, 61.222.49–61.222.54): "Consider nevertheless that she is a woman, the weaker vessel, whereas thou art a man. For therefore wert thou ordained to be ruler; and wert assigned to her in place of a *head*, that thou mightest bear with the weakness of her that is set under thee. Make then thy rule glorious. And glorious it will be when the subject of it meets with no dishonor from thee." (4th cent. AD)

42.–44. Chrysostom, *Homily 5 on 1–2 Thessalonians* (*NPNF* ser. 1, 13:397; TLG Work 163, 62.499.34–62.500.14): "For how is it not absurd, in other things to think thyself worthy of the preeminence, and to occupy the place of the *head*, but in teaching to quit thy station. The ruler ought not to excel the ruled in honors, so much as in virtues. For this is the duty of a ruler, for the other is the part of the ruled, but this is the achievement of the ruler himself. If thou enjoyest much honor, it is nothing to thee, for thou receivedst it from others. If thou shinest in much virtue, this is all thine own.

"Thou art the *head* of the woman, let then the *head* regulate the rest of the body. Dost thou not see that it is not so much above the rest of the body in situation, as in forethought, directing like a steersman the whole of it? For in the head are the eyes both of the body, and of the soul. Hence flows to them both the faculty of seeing,

2. Citations from Aquila are taken from F. Field, *Origenis Hexaplorum quae supersunt....* They are also listed in Edwin Hatch and Henry Redpath, *A Concordance to the Septuagint*, 2:762.

and the power of directing. And the rest of the body is appointed for service, but this is set to command. All the senses have thence their origin and their source. Thence are sent forth the organs of speech, the power of seeing, and of smelling, and all touch. For thence is derived the root of the nerves and of the bones. Seest thou not that it is superior in forethought more than in honor? So let us rule the women; let us surpass them, not by seeking greater honor from them, but by their being more benefited by us." (4th cent. AD)

45.–48. Chrysostom, *Homily 3 on Ephesians* (*NPNF* ser. 1, 13:62; TLG Work 159, 62.26.22–62.26.46): "'Which is His Body.' In order then that when you hear of the *Head* you may not conceive the notion of supremacy only, but also of consolidation, and that you may behold Him not as supreme Ruler only, but as *Head* of a body. 'The fullness of Him that filleth all in all,' he says.... Let us reverence our *Head*, let us reflect of what a *Head* we are the body—a Head, to whom all things are put in subjection" (the last "Head" in English is not italicized because it is not in the Greek text). (4th cent. AD)

49. Chrysostom, *Homily 13 on Ephesians* (*NPNF* ser. 1, 13:116; TLG Work 159, 62.99.22–62.99.29): "But now it is the very contrary; women outstrip and eclipse us [that is, in virtue]. How contemptible! What a shame is this! We hold the place of the *head*, and are surpassed by the body. We are ordained to rule over them; not merely that we may rule, but that we may rule in goodness also; for he that ruleth, ought especially to rule in this respect, by excelling in virtue; whereas if he is surpassed, he is no longer ruler." (4th cent. AD)

50.–52. Chrysostom, *Homily 20 on Ephesians* (*NPNF* ser. 1, 13:144; TLG Work 159, 62.136.33–62.136.51): "Let us take as our fundamental position then, that the husband occupies the place of the '*head*,' and the wife the place of the 'body.' Verses 23–24. Then, he proceeds with arguments and says that 'the husband is the *head* of the wife, as Christ also is the head of the church, being Himself the Saviour of the body. But as the church is subject to Christ, so let the wives be to their husbands in everything.' Then after saying, 'The husband is the *head* of the wife, as Christ also is of the church,' he further adds, 'and He is the Saviour of the body.' For indeed the head is the saving health of the body. He had already laid down beforehand for man and wife, the ground and provision of their love, assigning to each their proper place, to the one that of authority and forethought, to the other that of submission. As then 'the church,' that is, both husbands and wives, 'is subject unto Christ, so also ye wives submit yourselves to your husbands, as unto God'" (only the three examples of *head* placed in italics are counted in this paragraph because one other is not based on kephalē in Greek and the last example is not counted because it refers to the physical head in the body). (4th cent. AD)

53. Chrysostom, *Homily 20 on Ephesians* (*NPNF* ser. 1, 13:146–47; TLG Work 159, 62.140.51–62.141.13): "The wife is a second authority. Let not her then demand equality, for she is under the *head*; nor let him despise her as being in subjection, for she is the body; and if the head despise the body, it will itself also perish. But let him bring in love on his part as a counterpoise to obedience on her part.... Hence he places the one in subjection, and the other in authority, that there may be peace; for where there is equal authority there can never be peace; neither where a house is a democracy, nor where all are rulers; but the ruling power must of necessity be one. And this is universally the case with matters referring to the body, inasmuch as when men are spiritual, there will be peace" (second example not counted because it refers to physical head in the body). (4th cent. AD)
54. Chrysostom, *Homily 20 on Ephesians* (*NPNF* ser. 1, 13:149; TLG Work 159, 62.144.45–62.144.47): "Neither let a wife say to her husband, 'Unmanly coward that thou art, full of sluggishness and dullness, and fast asleep! Here is such a one, a low man, and of low parentage, who runs his risks, and makes his voyages, and has made a good fortune; and his wife wears her jewels, and goes out with her pair of milk-white mules; she rides about everywhere, she has troops of slaves, and a swarm of eunuchs, but thou hast cowered down and livest to no purpose.' Let not a wife say these things, nor anything like them. For she is the body, not to dictate to the *head*, but to submit herself and obey." (4th cent. AD)
55. Chrysostom, *Homily 6 on Ephesians* (*NPNF* ser. 1, 13:78; TLG Work 159, 62.47.55–62.47.59): "(for hear what he says writing to Timothy, [1 Timothy 5:20] 'Them that sin, reprove in the sight of all;') it is that the rulers are in a sickly state; for if the *head* be not sound, how can the rest of the body maintain its vigor? But mark how great is the present disorder" (church leaders are collectively called the *head* of the church). (4th cent. AD)
56. Chrysostom, *Homily 15 on Ephesians* (*NPNF* ser. 1, 13:12; TLG Work 159, 62.110.21–62.110.25): "'But,' say ye, 'The whole tribe of slaves is intolerable if it meet with indulgence.' True, I know it myself. But then, as I was saying, correct them in some other way, not by the scourge only, and by terror, but even by flattering them, and by acts of kindness. If she is a believer, she is thy sister. Consider that thou art her mistress, and that she ministers unto thee. If she be intemperate, cut off the occasions of drunkenness; call thy husband, and admonish her.... Yea, be she drunkard, or railer, or gossip, or evil-eyed, or extravagant, and a squanderer of thy substance, thou hast her for the partner of thy life. Train and restrain her. Necessity is upon thee. It is for this thou art the *head*. Regulate her therefore, do thy own part. Yea, and if she remain incorrigible, yea, though she steal, take care of thy goods, and do not punish her so much" (a woman is called the *head* of her maidservant). (4th cent. AD)

Head as a simile for leader

1. Plutarch, *Pelopidas* 2.1.3: In an army, "The light-armed troops are like the hands, the cavalry like the feet, the line of men-at-arms itself like chest and breastplate, and the general is like the *head.*" (1st/2nd cent. AD)
2. Plutarch, *Agis* 2.5: A ruler who follows popular opinions is compared to a serpent whose tail "rebelled against the *head*" and insisted on leading the body instead of it being led by the head. The serpent consequently harmed itself. The implication is that a ruler should be like the "head" of a serpent and thereby lead the people. (1st/2nd cent. AD)

Literal *head* said to rule over body

1. Although Plato does not use the word kephalē explicitly to refer to a human ruler or leader, he does say (in the text quoted earlier), that "the *head*. . .is the most divine part and the one that reigns over all the parts within us" (*Timaeus* 44D). This sentence does speak of the head as the ruling part of the body and therefore indicates that a metaphor that spoke of the leader or ruler of a group of people as its "head" would not have been unintelligible to Plato or his hearers. (5th/4th cent. BC)
2. Philo, *On Dreams* 2.207: " '*Head*' we interpret allegorically to mean the ruling part of the soul." (1st cent. AD)
3. Philo, *Moses* 2.82: "The mind is *head* and ruler of the sense-faculty in us." (1st cent. AD)
4. Philo, *The Special Laws* 184: "Nature conferred the sovereignty of the body on the *head.*" (1st cent. AD)

5.–6. Plutarch, *Table Talk* 6.7 (692.E.1): "We affectionately call a person 'soul' or '*head*' from his ruling parts." Here the metaphor of the head ruling the body is clear, as is the fact that the head controls the body in *Table Talk* 3.1 (647.C): "For pure wine, when it attacks the *head* and severs the body from the control of the mind, distresses a man." (1st/2nd cent. AD)

The meaning "ruler/authority" for *kephalē* in Greek lexicons

1. Bauer-Danker-Arndt-Gingrich, *A Greek-English Lexicon of the New Testament and Other Early Christian Literature*, 3rd ed., trans. from the 6th German ed.: "A being of high status, *head*, fig. 2a. In the case of living beings, to denote superior rank" (542).
2. Louw and Nida, *Greek-English Lexicon of the New Testament Based on Semantic Domains*, 2nd ed.: "One who is of supreme or preeminent status, in view of authority to order or command—'one who is the head of, one who is superior to, one who is supreme over'" (1:739).

3. Liddell-Scott-Jones, *A Greek-English Lexicon* (LSJ): The meaning "ruler/authority" was not listed. However, according to the current editor of the *Supplement* to Liddell-Scott, P. G. W. Glare, in a personal letter to Wayne Grudem, "The entry under this word in LSJ is not very satisfactory.... I have no time at the moment to discuss all your examples individually and in any case *I am in broad agreement with your conclusions*. I might just make one or two generalizations. Kephalē is the word normally used to translate the Hebrew ro'sh and this *does seem frequently to denote leader or chief* without much reference to its original anatomical sense, and here it *seems perverse to deny authority*." (From a personal letter from P. G. W. Glare to Wayne Grudem, April 14, 1997. Italics added. Quoted by permission.)
4. Lampe, *Patristic Greek Lexicon*: "B. of persons; 1. *head* of the house, Herm.*sim.* 7.3; 2. *chief, head-man*... 3. religious *superior*... 4. of bishops, kephalai... ekklesiōn [examples include "of the bishop of the city of Rome, being head of all the churches"]... 5. kephalē einai c. genit. [to be head, with genitive] *take precedence of*" (749).
5. Thayer, *A Greek-English Lexicon of the New Testament*: "Metaphorically anything supreme, chief, prominent; of persons, master, lord" (345).
6. Cremer, *Biblico-Theological Lexicon of New Testament Greek*: "The head is that part of the body which holds together and governs all the outgoings of life...and because of its vital connection stands in the relation of ruler to the other members" (354).

The Meaning of κεφαλή ("Head"): An Evaluation of New Evidence, Real and Alleged[1]

Wayne Grudem

The purpose of this article is to examine recent treatments of the meaning of the word κεφαλή ("head") as it pertains to certain passages in the New Testament,[2] focusing especially on new evidence cited by Catherine Kroeger in her article "Head" in the widely used *Dictionary of Paul and His Letters.*[3] Concerns will be raised about the level of care and accuracy with which evidence has been quoted in this reference book. In addition, some new patristic evidence on κεφαλή will be presented. Finally, the article will also cite new evaluations of the entry on κεφαλή in the Liddell-Scott lexicon from the editor of the *Supplement* to this lexicon and from another lexicographer who worked on this *Supplement.*

1. This article is taken from *Biblical Foundations for Manhood and Womanhood,* edited by Wayne Grudem, © 2002, 145–202, and is used by permission of Crossway Books, a division of Good News Publishers, Wheaton, Illinois. This article is identical to the article by the same title that I published in JETS 44/1 (March 2001), 25–65, with the exception of the added interaction with Anthony Thiselton's recent commentary on 1 Corinthians in section VIII (pp. 590–97).
2. The meaning of κεφαλή has attracted much interest because of its use in Ephesians 5:23, "The husband is the *head* (κεφαλή) of the wife even as Christ is the head of the church," and in 1 Corinthians 11:3, "the *head* of every man is Christ, the *head* of a wife is her husband, and the *head* of Christ is God." I previously wrote about the meaning of κεφαλή in 1985 and 1990: Wayne Grudem, "Does kephalē ('Head') Mean 'Source' or 'Authority over' in Greek Literature? A Survey of 2,336 Examples" (*Trinity Journal* 6 NS [1985], 38–59), and then, answering objections and arguing this in more detail, "The Meaning of kephalē: A Response to Recent Studies" (*Trinity Journal* 11 NS [1990], 3–72; reprinted as an appendix to *Recovering Biblical Manhood and Womanhood*, eds. John Piper and Wayne Grudem [Wheaton, IL: Crossway Books, 1991], 425–68). The 1990 article has references to several other studies of this word, and significant studies published after 1990 are mentioned near the end of this present article.
3. Edited by Gerald F. Hawthorne, Ralph P. Martin, and Daniel G. Reid (Downers Grove, IL, and Leicester, England: InterVarsity, 1993), 375–77.

I. The Striking Quotation from Chrysostom

When Dr. Kroeger's article appeared in 1993, it offered citations of a number of new references for the term κεφαλή and argued from these that κεφαλή primarily meant "source," not "authority over," and that it had that meaning not only at the time of the New Testament but also in the preceding classical period and in the subsequent patristic period in Greek literature. The most striking quotation in Dr. Kroeger's article was a statement from John Chrysostom (AD 344/354-407) that, if accurate, would appear to settle any dispute over whether κεφαλή meant "source" or "authority over," at least in the Christian world of the fourth century. Kroeger writes:

> In view of Scripture ascribing coequality of Christ with the Father (Jn. 1:1–3; 10:30; 14:9, 11; 16:15; 17:11, 21), John Chrysostom declared that only a heretic would understand Paul's use of "head" to mean "chief" or "authority over." Rather one should understand the term as implying "absolute oneness and cause and primal source" (PG 61.214, 216). (p. 377)

But is this what Chrysostom said? Kroeger claims (1) that Chrysostom is making a statement about the meaning of κεφαλή, (2) that Chrysostom denies that κεφαλή can mean "chief" or "authority over," and (3) that Chrysostom says that only a heretic would understand the word in that way.

Here is the quotation from Chrysostom:

> "But the head of the woman is the man; and the head of Christ is God." Here the heretics rush upon us with a certain declaration of inferiority, which out of these words they contrive against the Son. But they stumble against themselves. For if "the man be the head of the woman," and the head be of the same substance with the body, and "the head of Christ is God," the Son is of the same substance with the Father.[4] (Κεφαλὴ δὲ γυναικὸς ὁ ἄνηρ· κεφαλὴ δὲ Χριστοῦ ὁ Θεός. Ἐνταῦθα ἐπιπηδῶσιν ἡμῖν οἱ αἱρετικοὶ ἐλάττωσίν τινα ἐκ των εἰρημένων ἐπινοοῦντες τῷ Υἱῷ· ἀλλ' ἑαυτοίς περιπίπτουσιν. Εἰ γὰρ κεφαλὴ γυναικὸς ὁ ἀνὴρ, ὁμοούσιος δὲ ἡ κεφαλὴ τῷ σώματι, κεφαλὴ δὲ τοῦ Χριστοῦ ὁ Θεὸς, ὁμοούσιος ὁ Υἱὸς τῷ Πατρί.)

This is not a statement about the meaning of κεφαλή. Chrysostom is opposing the views of the Arians, who denied the deity of Christ. They did this by pointing to the statement, "the head of Christ is God" (in 1 Cor. 11:3) and saying that therefore the Son is a lesser being, not fully divine and not

---

4. Chrysostom, *Homily* 26 on 1 Corinthians (NPNF series 1, Vol. 12, p. 150.) The Greek text is from TLG Work 156, 61.214.18 to 61.214.23.
Where available, English quotations in this article have been taken from the *Ante-Nicene Fathers* series (ANF) and the *Nicene and Post-Nicene Fathers* series (NPNF) (reprint edition, Grand Rapids, MI: Eerdmans, 1969). Where no English translation was available, the English translations are mine, as indicated in each case. Greek citations have been taken from the *Thesaurus Linguae Graecae* (TLG), Disk E, except where no TLG reference is given, in which case I have cited the source of the Greek citation at each point.

equal to the Father in essence. Chrysostom counters their claim, but in doing so he does not say anything about the meaning of the word κεφαλή or say that only a "heretic" would take it to mean "chief" or "authority over" as Kroeger claims. Rather, from the idea that a head is "of the same substance (ὁμοούσιος) with the body," he affirms that the Son is "of the same substance (ὁμοούσιος) with the Father." There is no statement here saying that he disagrees with the Arians over the meaning of κεφαλή.

What comes next? In the following lines, Chrysostom says the "heretics" will counter by saying that the Son is subject to the Father and is therefore a lesser being:

> "Nay," say they, "it is not His being of another substance which we intend to show from hence, but that He is under subjection." (᾿Αλλ᾽ οὐ τὸ ἑτεροούσιον ἐντεῦθεν ἀποδεῖξαι βουλόμεθα, ἀλλ᾽ ὅτι ἄρχεται, φησί.)[5]

If Chrysostom had ever wanted to say that "head" could not mean "one in authority," here was the perfect opportunity. He could have answered these "heretics" by saying, as Dr. Kroeger apparently would like him to say, that κεφαλή did not mean "one in authority" and that "only a heretic" would understand Paul's use of "head" to mean "chief" or "authority over." But he does not say this at all. Rather, he assumes that κεφαλή *does* mean "authority over," because he *agrees* that the Son is obedient to the Father, and then he goes on to show that His obedience is not servile, like a slave, but free, like that of a wife who is equal in honor. Here are his words:

> For what if the wife be under subjection (ὑποτάσσω) to us? It is as a wife, as free, as equal in honor. And the Son also, though He did become obedient to the Father, it was as the Son of God, it was as God. For as the obedience of the Son to the Father is greater than we find in men towards the authors of their being, so also His liberty is greater...we ought to admire the Father also, that He begat such a son, not as a slave under command, but as free, yielding obedience and giving counsel. For the counselor is no slave....For with us indeed the woman is reasonably subjected (ὑποτάσσω) to the man.[6]

So is there any statement here about the meaning of κεφαλή? No, except the implication in the context that the Father is the "head" of the Son, and the Son is obedient to the Father. Chrysostom here does not deny that "head" means "one in authority" but assumes that "head" *does* mean this and explains what kind of authority that is with respect to the husband and with respect to God the Father.

Does Chrysostom differ with "the heretics" over the meaning of κεφαλή? No, he agrees with them. But they were saying that "the *head* of Christ is God" (1 Cor. 11:3) implied that the Son was a

5. Ibid., lines 23–25.
6. English translation from NPNF, Series 1, Vol. 12, p. 150. Greek text in TLG, Chrysostom, *Homilies on 1 Corinthians*, Work 156, 61.214.56 to 61.215.18.

lesser being than the Father, that He was not equal in deity. Chrysostom says that the Son is *equal* in deity and is *also subject to* the Father.

Interestingly, "the heretics" in this passage were reasoning in the same way that egalitarians such as Dr. Kroeger reason today they were saying that subordination to authority *necessarily implies* inferiority in a person's very being. They were saying that it is impossible for the Son to be equal to the Father in being (that is, equal in deity) and also subordinate in role. They used this reasoning as an argument to deny the deity of the Son. Egalitarians today use it as an argument to deny the unique, eternal subordination of the Son to the Father. But in both cases the fundamental assumption is that the Son cannot be *both* equal in deity and subordinate in role.

Chrysostom replies, however, that *both* are true. The Son is *equal* in deity (He, the "body," is ὁμοούσιος, of the same substance, as the "head"), and He also is *subordinate* to the authority of the head, and yet His submission is not forced (as a slave) but is voluntary, as a Son, and is similar to the submission of a wife to her husband.

Is there in this entire context any statement by Chrysostom that only heretics understand κεφαλή to mean "chief" or "authority over"? No. The quotation does not exist.[7] In this entire section Chrysostom himself understands κεφαλή to mean "chief"[8] or "authority over."[9]

---

7. I thought perhaps this reference in *Dictionary of Paul and His Letters* was a mistake. So I wrote to Dr. Kroeger saying that I could not find her quotation in that section of Chrysostom. She replied by sending me a printout (in Greek) of the exact passage that I cited at the beginning of this section. But the statement about only heretics using "head" to mean "chief" or "authority over" simply is not there. Chrysostom in fact said no such thing.
8. I myself would prefer not to translate κεφαλή as "chief," which too narrowly implies tribal relationships, but I am here using Kroeger's terminology.
9. It would have been nearly impossible for most readers of *Dictionary of Paul and His Letters* to discover that the striking quotation from Chrysostom did not exist. The only indication of the source of the quotation that Dr. Kroeger gave was "PG 61.214." This indicates a location in Migne, *Patrologia Graeca,* which took a considerable amount of time to locate and coordinate with an existing English translation (the standard English translation has a different numbering system). It is doubtful whether even 1 percent of the readers of *Dictionary of Paul and His Letters* would have enough ability to read patristic Greek to be able to find and understand this paragraph from Chrysostom. (Only very specialized research libraries have a complete set of the Migne collection of Greek and Latin texts of the writings of the church fathers. The set was published by Jacques Paul Migne in France in the mid-nineteenth century. *Patrologia Latina* [PL] was published in 221 volumes in Latin [1844–64], and *Patrologia Graeca* [PG] was published in 162 volumes in Greek with Latin translation [1857–66].)

   Of course, if no published English translation had existed, citing Migne alone would have been the only thing that could be done. But this material from Chrysostom exists in English translation in the *Nicene and Post-Nicene Fathers* series, which is widely available (the whole set is now in the public domain and is frequently reprinted). It is not clear to me why Dr. Kroeger did not give the reference for the English translation of this passage. If the citation had been given as "Chrysostom, *Homily 26 on 1 Corinthians* (NPNF 1:12, 150); Greek text in PG 61.214," it would have taken only a few minutes for a reader to locate it in almost any library. In a reference work intended for a general as well as an academic audience (as this volume is), it would seem appropriate to cite references in a way that enables others to look them up and evaluate them. Several other references in the article were much more difficult to locate than this one (see below).

II. Other Evidence from Chrysostom on the Meaning of κεφαλή ("Head")

Further evidence that Chrysostom did not in fact use κεφαλή to mean "source" and did not say that only heretics would use it to mean "authority over" is seen in the way he uses κεφαλή to mean "authority over" or "ruler" in the following examples:

1. *Homily 26 on 1 Corinthians (NPNF series 1, Vol. 12, p. 156; TLG Work 156, 61.222.49 to 61.222.54): Husband as head and ruler.*

> Consider nevertheless that she is a woman, the weaker vessel, whereas *thou art a man. For therefore wert thou ordained to be ruler; and wert assigned to her in place of a head*[10] (Διὰ γὰρ τοῦτο καὶ ἄρχων ἐχειροτονήθης, καὶ ἐν τάξει κεφαλῆς ἐδόθης), that thou mightest bear with the weakness of her that is set under thee. Make then thy rule glorious. And glorious it will be when the subject of it meets with no dishonor from thee.

2. *Homily 5 on 1–2 Thessalonians (NPNF series 1, Vol. 13, p. 397; TLG Work 163, 62.499.34 to 62.500.14): Husband as head to rule the rest of the body.*

> For how is it not absurd, in other things to think thyself worthy of the preeminence, and *to occupy the place of the head* (τὴν τῆς κεφαλῆς χώραν ἐπέχειν), but in teaching to quit thy station. The ruler ought not to excel the ruled in honors, so much as in virtues. For this is the duty of a ruler, for the other is the part of the ruled, but this is the achievement of the ruler himself. If thou enjoyest much honor, it is nothing to thee, for thou receivedst it from others. If thou shinest in much virtue, this is all thine own.
>
> *Thou art the head of the woman, let then the head regulate the rest of the body* (Κεφαλὴ τῆς γυναικὸς εἶ· οὐκοῦν ῥυθμιζέτω τὸ σῶμα τὸ λοιπὸν ἡ κεφαλή). Dost thou not see that it is not so much above the rest of the body in situation, as in forethought, directing like a steersman the whole of it? For in the head are the eyes both of the body, and of the soul. Hence flows to them both the faculty of seeing, and the power of directing. *And the rest of the body is appointed for service, but this is set to command* (Καὶ τὸ μὲν λοιπὸν τάττεται εἰς διακονίαν, αὐτὴ δὲ εἰς τὸ ἐπιτάττειν κεῖται). All the senses have thence their origin and

---

10. In this and several subsequent citations from ancient literature, I have added italics to enable readers to see more quickly the relevant section of the quotation.

Many of these patristic quotes contain expressions about the husband being "ruler" over his wife. I wish to make it clear that I am citing but not endorsing these statements. While many statements in the church fathers exhibit wonderful respect for women, at other points their language fails to show full understanding of the biblical teaching of men's and women's equality in value before God. Thus, rather than seeing the husband's authority as exhibiting itself in godly, loving leadership, they speak in harsher terms of "ruling" over one's wife. But my goal in this article is to report their language accurately, not to evaluate it.

their source (Πᾶσαι αἱ αἰσθήσεις ἐκεῖθεν ἔχουσι τὴν ἀρχὴν καὶ τὴν πηγήν·).[11] Thence are sent forth the organs of speech, the power of seeing, and of smelling, and all touch. For thence is derived the root of the nerves and of the bones. Seest thou not that it is superior in forethought more than in honor? So let us rule the women; let us surpass them, not by seeking greater honor from them, but by their being more benefited by us.

3. *Homily 3 on Ephesians (NPNF series 1, Vol. 13, p. 62; TLG Work 159, 62.26.22 to 62.26.46): Christ as head of the body, ruling over it, and head of all things.*

"Which is His Body." In order then that when you hear of the *Head* you may not conceive the notion of *supremacy* (ἀρχή)[12] only, but also of consolidation, and that you may behold Him not as *supreme Ruler* only, but as Head of a body. "The fulness of Him that filleth all in all" he says.... Let us reverence our Head, let us reflect of what a Head we are the body, —a Head, *to whom all things are put in subjection* (ᾗ πάντα ὑποτέτακται).

4. *Homily 13 on Ephesians (NPNF series 1, Vol. 13, p. 116; TLG Work 159, 62.99.22 to 62.99.29): Husbands as head ordained to rule over wives.*

But now it is the very contrary; women outstrip and eclipse us [that is, in virtue]. How contemptible! What a shame is this! *We hold the place of the head*, and are surpassed by the body. *We are ordained to rule over them*; not merely that we may rule, but that we may rule in goodness also (Ἄρχειν αὐτῶν ἐτάχθημεν, οὐχ ἵνα μόνον ἄρχωμεν, ἀλλ' ἵνα καὶ ἐν ἀρετῇ ἄρχωμεν); for he that ruleth, ought especially to rule in this respect, by excelling in virtue; whereas if he is surpassed, he is no longer ruler.

5. *Homily 20 on Ephesians (NPNF series 1, Vol. 13, p. 144; TLG Work 159, 62.136.33 to 62.136.51): Husband as head with authority; wife as body with submission.*

Let us take as our fundamental position then, that *the husband occupies the place of the "head," and the wife the place of the "body."* Ver. 23, 24. Then, he proceeds

---

11. It is significant here that when Chrysostom does want to speak of a "source," he does not use the word κεφαλή, "head," nor does he use the term ἀρχή, "beginning, origin," but he rather uses the ordinary Greek word for "source," namely, πηγή. If Chrysostom or any other writer had wanted to say clearly, "head, which is source," he could easily have used πηγή to do so. But I did not find any place in Chrysostom or any other author where κεφαλή is defined as meaning πηγή, "source."

12. Note here the word ἀρχή used in Chrysostom not to mean "source" but "supremacy," understood by the NPNF translator to imply rulership, since he translates the cognate term ἄρχων (ἄρχοντα) as "supreme Ruler" in the parallel expression in the next clause.

with arguments and says that "the husband is the head of the wife, as Christ also is the head of the Church, being Himself the Saviour of the body. But as the Church is subject to Christ, so let the wives be to their husbands in everything." Then after saying, "The husband is the head of the wife, as Christ also is of the Church," he further adds, "and He is the Saviour of the body." For indeed the head is the saving health of the body. He had already laid down beforehand for man and wife, the ground and provision of their love, *assigning to each their proper place, to the one that of authority and forethought, to the other that of submission* (ἑκάστῳ τὴν προσήκουσαν ἀπονέμων χώραν, τούτῳ μὲν τὴν ἀρχικὴν καὶ προνοητικὴν, ἐκείνῃ δὲ τὴν ὑποτακτικήν). As then "the Church," that is, both husbands and wives, "is subject unto Christ, so also ye wives submit yourselves to your husbands, as unto God."

6. *Homily 20 on Ephesians (NPNF series 1, Vol. 13, pp. 146–47; TLG Work 159, 62.140.51 to 62.141.13): Wife as body is subject to husband as head.*

The wife is a second authority (Ἀρχὴ δευτέρα ἐστὶν ἡ γυνή);[13] let not her then demand equality, for *she is under the head*; nor let him despise her as being in subjection, for she is the body; and if the head despise the body, it will itself also perish. But let him bring in love on his part as a counterpoise to obedience on her part.... Hence *he places the one in subjection, and the other in authority, that there may be peace; for where there is equal authority there can never be peace*; neither where a house is a democracy, nor where all are rulers; but the *ruling power*[14] must of necessity be one. And this is universally the case with matters referring to the body, inasmuch as when men are spiritual, there will be peace.

7. *Homily 20 on Ephesians (NPNF series 1, Vol. 13, p. 149; Greek portion in TLG Work 159, 62.144.45 to 62.144.47): Wife as body is to obey the husband as head.*

Neither let a wife say to her husband, "Unmanly coward that thou art, full of sluggishness and dullness, and fast asleep! Here is such a one, a low man, and of low parentage, who runs his risks, and makes his voyages, and has made a good fortune; and his wife wears her jewels, and goes out with her pair of milk-white mules; she rides about everywhere, she has troops of slaves, and a swarm of eunuchs, but thou hast cowered down and livest to no purpose." Let not a wife say these things, nor anything like them. *For she is the body, not to dictate to the head, but to submit herself and obey* (σῶμα γάρ ἐστιν, οὐχ ἵνα διατάττῃ τῇ κεφαλῇ, ἀλλ' ἵνα πείθηται καὶ ὑπακούῃ).

---

13. Note here the use of the term ἀρχή in Chrysostom to mean "authority, person in authority," not "source." With respect to governance of the household, Chrysostom says the wife is a second authority, under the authority of her husband.

14. Here also Chrysostom uses ἀρχή in the sense of "ruling power, authority."

8. *Homily 6 on Ephesians (NPNF series 1, Vol. 13, p. 78; TLG Work 159, 62.47.55 to 62.47.59): Church rulers as head of church.* In this passage, the "rulers" in the church are called the "head" of the church.

> (For hear what he says writing to Timothy, (I Tim. 5:20) "Them that sin, reprove in the sight of all;") it is that the *rulers* are in a sickly state; for if the *head* (κεφαλή) be not sound, how can the rest of the body maintain its vigor? But mark how great is the present disorder.

9. *Homily 15 on Ephesians (NPNF series 1, Vol. 13, p. 124; Greek portion in TLG Work 159, 62.110.21 to 62.110.25): A woman as head of her maidservant.* This is the only passage I found in Chrysostom—in fact, the only passage I have ever seen—where a woman is called the "head." This instance gives strong confirmation to the meaning "authority over, ruler," for here Chrysostom says that a woman is "head" of her maidservant, over whom she has authority.

> "But," say ye, "the whole tribe of slaves is intolerable if it meet with indulgence." True, I know it myself. But then, as I was saying, correct them in some other way, not by the scourge only, and by terror, but even by flattering them, and by acts of kindness. If she is a believer, she is thy sister. Consider that thou art her mistress, and that she ministers unto thee. If she be intemperate, cut off the occasions of drunkenness; call thy husband, and admonish her.... Yea, be she drunkard, or railer, or gossip, or evil-eyed, or extravagant, and a squanderer of thy substance, thou hast her for the partner of thy life. Train and restrain her. Necessity is upon thee. *It is for this thou art the head. Regulate her therefore*, do thy own part (διὰ τοῦτο κεφαλὴ εἶ σύ. Οὐκοῦν ῥύθμιζε, τὸ σαυτοῦ ποίει). Yea, and if she remain incorrigible, yea, though she steal, take care of thy goods, and do not punish her so much.

10. *The claim that* ἀρχή *means "source" in Chrysostom's Homily 26 on 1 Corinthians (NPNF series 1, Vol. 12, p. 151; TLG Work 156, 61.216.1 to 61.216.10).*

There is one more sentence to consider in Kroeger's claims about Chrysostom. Here again is the quotation from *Dictionary of Paul and His Letters* with which we began:

> In view of Scripture ascribing coequality of Christ with the Father (Jn. 1:1–3; 10:30; 14:9, 11; 16:15; 17:11, 21), John Chrysostom declared that only a heretic would understand Paul's use of "head" to mean "chief" or "authority over." Rather one should understand the term as implying "absolute oneness and cause and primal source" (PG 61.214, 216).[15]

15. Kroeger, "Head," 377.

In the last sentence, Kroeger claims that Chrysostom said we should understand κεφαλή as implying "absolute oneness and cause and primal source." She bases this idea on the second reference, PG 61.216, which reads as follows in the NPNF translation:

> Christ is called "the Head of the Church".... We should...accept the notion of a perfect union and the *first principle*, and not even these ideas absolutely, but here also we must form a notion...of that which is too high for us and suitable to the Godhead: for both the union is surer and the *beginning* more honorable. (NPNF Series 1, Vol. 12, p. 151)
>
> κεφαλὴ τῆς 'Εκκλησίας ὁ Χριστός·;.'Αφεῖναι μὲν ταῦτα ἃ εἶπον, λαβεῖν δὲ ἕνωσιν ἀκριβῆ, [καὶ αἰτίαν] καὶ *ἀρχὴν τὴν πρώτην*· καὶ οὐδὲ ταῦτα ἁπλῶς, ἀλλὰ καὶ ἐνταῦθα τὸ μεῖζον οἴκοθεν ἐπινοεῖν καὶ Θεῷ πρέπον· καὶ γὰρ ἡ ἕνωσις ἀσφαλεστέρα, καὶ ἡ *ἀρχὴ* τιμιωτέρα.[16]

The expression that the NPNF translator rendered "perfect union" Kroeger translated "absolute oneness," which is similar in meaning. Next Kroeger says "and cause," which accurately represents the words καὶ αἰτίαν, a textual variant that was not translated in the NPNF edition. But then where did she get the phrase "and primal source"? This was her translation of καὶ ἀρχὴν τὴν πρώτην, which was translated "first principle" in the NPNF translation (with no idea of "source"). Later in the same sentence the NPNF translation renders the word ἀρχή as "beginning," and the context shows that this refers back to the same word earlier in the sentence.

What Kroeger has done here (as elsewhere) is take one possible sense of ἀρχή—namely, the sense "source"—and not tell her readers that other senses of ἀρχή are possible. Nor has she mentioned that the commonly used English translation in the NPNF series translates this example not as "source" but as "principle" and then "beginning."

It is true that Lampe's *Patristic Greek Lexicon* lists "origin, source" as one of several possible senses for ἀρχή.[17] But the meanings "beginning," "principle," "foundation," "cause," "First Cause,"

---

16. TLG, Chrysostom, *Homilies on 1 Corinthians*, Work 156, 61.216.1 to 61.216.10. I have added the brackets to show the textual variant that is not translated by the NPNF translator.

17. P. 234. Note here, however, that we are now talking about ἀρχή, not about κεφαλή, for which the meaning "source" is not given in Lampe. As commonly happens with two different words, some of the senses of ἀρχή are shared with κεφαλή, and some are not.

An example from English may clarify this. I might say, "George Washington was the first head (that is, the first ruler) of the United States." Here "ruler" means "one who governs." But the term "ruler" has another meaning in American English, namely, "a straight-edged strip, as of wood or metal, for drawing straight lines and measuring lengths." The word "head" does not share that sense of "ruler" (I would not say, "I measured the margins of the page with my wooden head"). Similarly, the word "head" refers to a part of the human body, and the word "ruler" does not share that sense (I would not say, "I bumped my ruler on the door this morning").

Kroeger is making a methodological error to think that she can import all the senses of ἀρχή into the meaning of κεφαλή. Those specific meanings that she claims need first to be demonstrated for κεφαλή with clear evidence from lexicons and supported by persuasive citations from ancient literature where such meanings are required.

and "Creator" are also listed, as well as "rule, authority," "rulers, magistrates," "ecclesiastical authority," and "spiritual powers."[18]

It is difficult to understand why Kroeger took *one possible sense* of ἀρχή, one that the lexicons do not specifically use to apply to Christ, and did not tell the reader that this was a disputed translation unique to herself. Her writing sounds as if Chrysostom had defined κεφαλή as "source," whereas he had only used the term ἀρχή to explain how the head-body metaphor could apply both to the Father and the Son, and also to Christ and the church. He said it applied in a sense "suitable to the Godhead," in which the metaphor implied both the "perfect union" between the Father and Son and also that the Father is the "first principle" in the Trinity.[19] Chrysostom did not say that the Father was the "primal source" of the Son, and if he had said so he could be accused of Arianism, the heresy that said the Son was created by the Father. As with many other examples of Chrysostom's use of κεφαλή, no example of the metaphor "head" meaning "source" can be found here.

11. *Conclusion on Chrysostom's use of* κεφαλή.

Chrysostom uses κεφαλή to say that one person is the "head" of another in at least six different relationships: (1) God is the "head" of Christ; (2) Christ is the "head" of the church; (3) the husband is the "head" of the wife; (4) Christ is the "head" of all things; (5) church leaders are the "head" of the church; and (6) a woman is the "head" of her maidservant. In all six cases he uses language of rulership and authority to explain the role of the "head" and uses language of submission and obedience to describe the role of the "body."[20] Far from claiming that "only a heretic" would use κεφαλή to mean "authority over," Chrysostom repeatedly uses it that way himself.

I admit, of course, that fourth-century usage of a word by Chrysostom does not prove that word had the same sense in the first century; so this is not conclusive evidence for New Testament meanings. But since Dr. Kroeger appealed to patristic usage to argue for "source," it seemed appropriate to investigate this patristic evidence directly. This material is certainly of some value for New Testament studies, because the meanings of many words continued to be understood quite precisely by the church fathers, especially by those whose first language was Greek. If their date is clearly indicated, these new examples of κεφαλή in the sense "authority over" may be added to the more than

---

18. Lampe, 234–36.
19. The meaning "authority" is also legitimate for ἀρχή; so this passage could also be translated, "the notion of a perfect union, and the *first authority*." In fact, in light of Chrysostom's calling the wife a "second authority" elsewhere (see citation 6 above from his "Homily 20 on Ephesians," for example), the meaning "first authority" would be appropriate here, and the parallel would be that the Son is a "second authority" after the Father. Moreover, this is in the same sermon as the very first quotation from Chrysostom that I listed in this article (NPNF 1:12, p. 150; TLG 156, 61.214), where he sees the husband's role as "head" implying that the wife is "reasonably subjected" to him, and where he sees the Father's role as "head" as one in which the Son freely yields obedience to him.
20. This usage is so frequent in the passages I examined in Chrysostom, and receives so much emphasis, that I expect further examples could be found if one were to do an exhaustive examination of all his uses of κεφαλή, which I did not attempt.

forty examples cited in my 1990 article,[21] and they do show that the sense "authority over" continued to attach to κεφαλή at least until the end of the fourth century. But they also show an absence of the meaning "source" in this one church father, for Chrysostom does not use κεφαλή to mean "source" in any of the texts I found.

What then shall we make of Kroeger's statement that "John Chrysostom declared that only a heretic would understand Paul's use of 'head' to mean 'chief' or 'authority over'"? It is simply false.

III. Kroeger's Citations from Other Church Fathers

1. *Nine other patristic references.* Chrysostom is not the only church father whom Kroeger cites. In attempting to establish that the sense "chief" or "master" was "rarely" the sense "of the Greek kephalē in NT times," she writes:

> The contemporary desire to find in 1 Corinthians 11:3 a basis for the subordination of the Son to the Father has ancient roots. In response to such subordinationism, church fathers argued vehemently that for Paul *head* had meant "source." Athanasius (*Syn. Armin.* 26.3.35; *Anathema* 26. Migne PG 26, 740B), Cyril of Alexandria (*De Recte Fide ad Pulch.* 2.3, 268; *De Recte Fide ad Arcadiam* 1.1.5.5(2).63.), Basil (PG 30.80.23), Theodore of Mopsuestia (*Eccl. Theol.* 1.11.2–3; 2.7.1) and even Eusebius (*Eccl. Theol.* 1.11.2–3; 2.7.1) were quick to recognize the danger of an interpretation of 1 Corinthians 11:3 which could place Christ in a subordinate position relative to the Father.[22]

The first thing to note about this statement is the inaccurate equation of "the subordination of the Son to the Father" with "subordinationism" (which, in this context, Kroeger uses as a reference to a heresy the church rejected). The heresy commonly called "subordination*ism*" (italics added) is a denial that Christ is fully divine, a denial that He is "of the same substance" as the Father. The Arians whom Chrysostom was opposing in the citations quoted above would hold to subordinationism. But this is not the same as to say that 1 Corinthians 11:3 teaches the "subordination of the Son to the Father," for that language is an orthodox description of how the Son relates to the Father—He is *subject to* the Father, who creates the world *through* Him and sends Him into the world to die for our sins. To say that the Son is *subject to* the Father, or that He is *subordinate* in His relationship to the Father, has been orthodox teaching according to Roman Catholic, Eastern Orthodox, and Protestant theology through the whole history of the church at least since the Council of Nicea in AD 325, and Kroeger is simply mistaken to apply the name of the heresy "subordinationism" to it. But to say that the Son is not fully divine and thus to deny the deity of Christ would be subordinationism, and that the early fathers do not do.[23]

---

21. Grudem, "The Meaning of kephalē: A Response to Recent Studies" (see footnote 2 above).
22. Kroeger, "Head," 377.
23. Historian Philip Schaff, though he uses the term "subordinationism" in two senses, directly contradicts Kroeger's statement when he says, "The Nicene fathers still teach, like their predecessors, a certain *subordinationism*, which seems to conflict with the doctrine of consubstantiality. But we must distinguish between a

We can now examine these texts to see if they actually establish the idea that "church fathers argued vehemently that for Paul *head* had meant 'source,'" and if they show that these church fathers "were quick to recognize the danger" of understanding 1 Corinthians 11:3 to mean that Christ has a "subordinate position relative to the Father." The texts are given by Kroeger as follows:

1. Athanasius, *Syn. Armin.* 26.3.35
2. Athanasius, *Anathema* 26, MPG 26, 740B
3. Cyril of Alexandria, *De Recte Fide ad Pulch.* 2.3, 268.
4. Cyril of Alexandria, *De Recte Fide ad Arcadiam* 1.1.5.5(2).63.
5. Basil, PG 30.80.23
6. Theodore of Mopsuestia, *Eccl. Theol.* 1.11.2-3
7. Theodore of Mopsuestia, *Eccl. Theol.* 2.7.1
8. Eusebius, *Eccl. Theol.* 1.11.2-3
9. Eusebius, *Eccl. Theol.* 2.7.1

2. *The ambiguity of quotations that explain* κεφαλή *as* ἀρχή. The first thing to notice is that five of these nine references (numbers 2, 3, 4, and apparently 6 and 7 when corrected)[24] are

---

subordinationism of essence (οὐσία) and a *subordinationism of hypostasis, of order and dignity*. The former was denied, the latter affirmed." *History of the Christian Church* (3rd edition; Grand Rapids, MI: Eerdmans, 1971–72, reprinted from 1910 edition), Vol. 3, 680–681.

Several evangelical theologians speak of the subordination of the Son to the Father. For example, Charles Hodge says, "Notwithstanding that the Father, Son, and Spirit are the same in substance, and equal in power and glory, it is no less true, according to the Scriptures, (a.) That the Father is first, the Son second, and the Spirit third. (b.) The Son is of the Father (ἐκ θεοῦ, the λόγος, εἰκὼν, ἀπαύγασμα τοῦ θεοῦ); and the Spirit is of the Father and of the Son. (c.) The Father sends, and the Father and Son send the Spirit. (d.) The Father operates through the Son, and the Father and Son operate through the Spirit. *The converse of these statements is never found. The Son is never said to send the Father, nor to operate through Him; nor is the Spirit ever said to send the Father, or the Son, or to operate through Them*. The facts contained in this paragraph are summed up in the proposition: *In the Holy Trinity there is a subordination of the Persons as to the mode of subsistence and operation*." Charles Hodge, *Systematic Theology* (three volumes; reprint edition; Grand Rapids, MI: Eerdmans, 1970; first published 1871–73), Vol. 1, 444–445. (Italics for emphasis added in this and the other quotations in this footnote.)

Hodge continues later: "On this subject the Nicene doctrine includes, —1. The principle of *the subordination of the Son to the Father*, and of the Spirit to the Father and the Son. *But this subordination does not imply inferiority*" (ibid., 460). "The creeds [Nicea and Constantinople] are nothing more than a well-ordered arrangement of the facts of Scripture which concern the doctrine of the Trinity. They assert the distinct personality of the Father, Son, and Spirit; their mutual relation as expressed by those terms; their absolute unity as to substance or essence, and their consequent perfect equality; and *the subordination of the Son to the Father, and of the Spirit to the Father and the Son, as to the mode of subsistence and operation. These are Scriptural facts to which the creeds in question add nothing; and it is in this sense they have been accepted by the Church universal*" (ibid., 462).

See also B. B. Warfield: "There is, of course, no question that in 'modes of operation,'... *the principle of subordination is clearly expressed*" (*Works*, Vol. 2 [Grand Rapids. MI: Baker, 1991; reprint of 1929 edition], 165); similarly, A. H. Strong, *Systematic Theology* (Valley Forge, PA: Judson Press, 1907), 342, with references to other writers; also Louis Berkhof, *Systematic Theology* (4th edition, Grand Rapids, MI: Eerdmans, 1939), 88–89.

These statements, together with the patristic evidence cited in the following material, indicate that Kroeger's claim that church fathers denied the subordination of the Son to the Father is incorrect.

24. The references to Theodore of Mopsuestia are incorrect; see discussion below.

found in one paragraph on page 749 of Lampe's *Patristic Greek Lexicon*, II.B. 4, a paragraph that gives examples of κεφαλή used "as equivalent of ἀρχή." But ἀρχή is itself an ambiguous word and can mean "beginning" or "authority," as was indicated above, or in some cases "source."[25]

The distinction between the senses "source" and "beginning" is an important distinction because the beginning of something is not always the source of something. (For example, my oldest son is the "beginning" or "first" of my sons, but he is not the "source" of my other sons.) In the Bible itself we find several examples of ἀρχή used as "beginning" where the idea of "source" would not fit:

Genesis 1:1: In the beginning *(ἀρχή), God created the heavens and the earth.*

We could not say, "In the *source* God created the heavens and the earth."

Matthew 19:4: He answered, "Have you not read that he who created them from the beginning *(ἀρχή) made them male and female...?"*

We could not say, "He who made them from the *source* made them male and female." The same reasoning applies to other examples:

Mark 1:1: The beginning *(ἀρχή) of the gospel of Jesus Christ, the Son of God.*
Ἀρχὴ *τοῦ εὐαγγελίου Ἰησοῦ Χριστοῦ [υἱοῦ θεοῦ].*

This verse is not the "source" of the rest of Mark, but it is the starting point or "beginning" of Mark, the first in a series of many statements to follow.

John 1:1: In the beginning *(ἀρχή) was the Word, and the Word was with God, and the Word was God.*

John 2:11: This, the first *(ἀρχή) of his signs, Jesus did at Cana in Galilee, and manifested his glory. And his disciples believed in him.*

Colossians 1:18: He is the head of the body, the church. He is the beginning *(ἀρχή), the firstborn from the dead, that in everything he might be preeminent.*

Here Christ is said to be the "beginning" or "first in a series" of the people who would be raised from the dead. He is the first; others will follow.

25. Note that Lampe's *Lexicon* does not translate ἀρχή when it is used to explain κεφαλή in discussions of 1 Corinthians 11:3 but just says "as equivalent of ἀρχή." The difficulty of translation is partly due to the fact that both words can mean "ruler, authority," and both words can mean "beginning." But ἀρχή has several other possible meanings as well (see the above discussion in II.10, especially footnotes 17 and 19, pp. 560–61).

Revelation 22:13: "I am the Alpha and the Omega, the first and the last, the beginning *(ἀρχή) and the end."*

The idea "source" would not fit any of these examples. Nor is it the correct meaning in any other New Testament example. The BAGD *Lexicon* (pp. 111–112) does not list "source" as a possible meaning for ἀρχή in the New Testament or early Christian literature. It sometimes means "beginning." It sometimes means "authority" or "ruler," as in citations 3 and 6 from Chrysostom in the previous section of this paper. Therefore, to find examples of κεφαλή used as equivalent of ἀρχή does not prove that "church fathers argued vehemently that for Paul *head* had meant 'source.'" It would be just as legitimate on the basis of ἀρχή alone to say that they argued vehemently that for Paul *head* had meant "ruler" or *head* had meant "beginning."

IV. The Actual Patristic Citations

We can now look at these nine references cited by Kroeger, in which she says the church fathers "argued vehemently that for Paul *head* had meant 'source'" and denied that Christ is subordinate to the Father.

1. *Athanasius (ca.* AD *296–373), Syn. Armin. 26.3.35.* This is not actually a statement by a church father. This quotation is from an Arian creed, the "Macrostich" or 5th Confession of AD 344, which Athanasius quotes, along with several other Arian creeds, in order to show that they cannot even agree among themselves on what they teach. It is surprising that Kroeger cites this as evidence of what the "church fathers" taught, for Arianism was rejected as a heresy by the orthodox church, and this Arian creed does not represent what the recognized church fathers taught.

The quotation is as follows:

> Yet we must not consider the Son to be co-unbegun and co-ingenerate with the Father.... But we acknowledge that the Father who alone is Unbegun and Ingenerate, hath generated inconceivably and incomprehensibly to all; and that the Son hath been generated before ages, and in no wise to be ingenerate Himself like the Father, but to have the Father who generated Him as His *beginning* (ἀρχή); for "the Head of Christ is God."[26]

Here ἀρχή is used in the sense "beginning," according to the NPNF translator. In any case, the quotation of an Arian creed, with no subsequent comment on this word or phrase by Athanasius himself, is not reliable evidence on which to decide anything about the way κεφαλή was understood by Athanasius or other church fathers, as Kroeger claims. Nor does it provide any evidence that church fathers argued against the subordination of the Son to the Father.

---

26. The Greek text is in TLG Athanasius, *De synodis Arimini*, Work 010, 26, 3.3. The English translation is from NPNF, Second Series, Vol. 4, 463, with extensive notes on the Arian theology represented here.

2. *Athanasius (ca. AD 296–373), Anathema 26, MPG 26, 740B.* This quotation is not actually from an orthodox church father either. It is from another Arian creed, which Athanasius also quotes to show how the Arians cannot agree among themselves.

> Whosoever shall say that the Son is without beginning and ingenerate, as if speaking of two unbegun and two ingenerate, and making two Gods, be he anathema. For the Son is the Head, namely the beginning (ἀρχή) of all: and God is the *Head*, namely the beginning (ἀρχή) of Christ; for thus to one unbegun beginning (ἀρχή) of the universe do we religiously refer all things through the Son.[27]

Here again ἀρχή is used by the Arians in the sense of "beginning" to explain κεφαλή. But it does not show us how κεφαλή was understood by Athanasius or other church fathers, as Kroeger's article claimed.

In fact, Athanasius himself did not "argue vehemently" that for Paul, *head* meant "source," nor did he deny that κεφαλή could mean "authority over," for he refers to "the bishops of illustrious cities," for example, as "the *heads* of great churches" (κεφαλαὶ τοσούτων ἐκκλησιῶν).[28]

3. *Cyril of Alexandria (died AD 444), De Recte Fide ad Pulch. 2.3, 268.*

> ...the one of the earth and dust has become (γέγονεν) to us the first head of the race, that is ruler (ἀρχή) but since the second Adam has been named Christ, he was placed as head (κεφαλή), that is ruler (τουτέστιν ἀρχή) of those who through him are being transformed unto him into incorruption through sanctification by the Spirit. Therefore he on the one hand is our ruler (ἀρχή), that is head, in so far as he has appeared as a man; indeed, he, being by nature God, has a head, the Father in heaven. For, being by nature God the Word, he has been begotten from Him. But that the head signifies the ruler (ἀρχή), the fact that the husband is said to be the head of the wife confirms the sense for the truth of doubters: for she has been taken from him (ἐλήφθη γὰρ ἐξ αὐτοῦ). Therefore one Christ and Son and Lord, the one having as head the Father in heaven, being God by nature, became for us a "head" accordingly because of his kinship according to the flesh.[29]

In this quotation, κεφαλή is explained by ἀρχή, probably in the sense of "ruler," but the ambiguity of ἀρχή confronts us here, and the sense "beginning" or the sense "origin or source" for ἀρχή would also fit.

---

27. The Greek text is in TLG, Athanasius, *De synodis Arimini*, Work 010, 27.3,26 to 27.3,27. The English translation is from NPNF, Second Series, Vol. 4, p. 465.
28. The Greek text is in TLG, Athanasius, Work 005, 89.2.3. The English translation is in NPNF, Second Series, Vol. 4, p. 147. This text is also quoted by Joseph Fitzmyer, "kephalē in I Corinthians 11:3," *Interpretation* 47 (1993), 56, as evidence of the meaning "leader, ruler" for κεφαλή.
29. The Greek text is found in Eduard Schwartz, ed., *Acta Conciliorum Oecumenicorum* (Berlin: de Gruyter, 1927), 1.1.5, p. 28. The English translation is mine.

In 1990 I responded to Kroeger's citation of this passage[30] and said that even if the sense "source" were understood here, this is still not an instance of "source" apart from authority, for God and Christ and the husband are all in positions of authority.[31] Of course, if we took this passage in an isolated way, apart from its context in patristic writings and ancient Trinitarian controversies, and apart from previously established meanings for κεφαλή, there would be no strong objection to thinking that the meaning "source" would fit this passage as well, even though it would not be necessary for the sense of the passage. And it must also be recognized that it is an elementary fact of life that we receive our nourishment through our mouths, and thus in a sense through our heads, and this idea was plain to the ancient world as well; therefore, the idea that a metaphor would occur in which "head" meant "source" is not impossible.[32] But even if that sense were accepted here, it would scarcely be decisive for Pauline usage, since this passage comes four hundred years *after* Paul wrote.[33]

Yet several factors make me hesitate to jump to the meaning "source" here:

(1) First, a very similar connection between the man's headship and the woman's being taken from the man is made by an earlier Alexandrian writer, Clement of Alexandria (ca. AD 155-ca. 220), in *The Stromata* 4:8 (ANF 2, 420):

> "For I would have you know," says the apostle, "that the head of every man is Christ; and the head of the woman is the man: for the man is not of the woman, but the woman of the man (οὐ γὰρ ἐστιν ἀνὴρ ἐκ γυναικὸς, ἀλλὰ γυνὴ ἐξ ἀνδρός)."[34]

Such an explicit connection between man's headship and woman's being taken out of man might lead us to think that Clement of Alexandria would understand "head" to mean "source, origin" here, just as we might in the statement from Cyril of Alexandria. But this is not so, for later on the same page Clement explains:

> ***The ruling power is therefore the head*** (κεφαλὴ τοίνυν τὸ ἡγεμονικόν). And if "the Lord is head of the man, and the man is head of the woman," the man, "being the image and glory of God, is lord of the woman." Wherefore also in the

30. Grudem, "Meaning of kephalē: A Response to Recent Studies," 464–65.
31. Gregory W. Dawes, *The Body in Question: Metaphor and Meaning in the Interpretation of Ephesians 5:21–33* (Leiden: Brill, 1998), says that in analyzing this passage from Cyril of Alexandria, Grudem "suggests (rightly) that even here the term κεφαλή retains the sense of authority, and that a passage like this needs to be read in its historical context (the Trinitarian controversies of the early church)" (p. 128). However, Dawes differs with my hesitancy to see the meaning "source" as the most likely one here, saying that "different (metaphorical) senses of a word are possible in different contexts." He thinks that authority is present in the passage, but that it may be related to the idea of origin.
32. This is the point made by Dawes, as mentioned in the previous footnote.
33. Note the caution that was expressed above about the merely moderate relevance of the quotations from Chrysostom, who wrote over three hundred years after Paul.
34. The English translation in both quotations is that of the ANF series (2, 420). The Greek text is in the TLG, Clement of Alexandria, Work 4, 4.8.60.2.

> Epistle to the Ephesians it is written, "Subjecting yourselves one to another in the fear of God. Wives, submit yourselves to your own husbands, as to the Lord. For the husband is head of the wife. . . ."[35]

This means that Clement of Alexandria's first statement should be understood in the sense: the man has ruling authority over the woman *because* she was taken from him. Clement of Alexandria is simply connecting 1 Corinthians 11:3 with 1 Corinthians 11:8 and sees one as the reason supporting the other.

This means that a similar manner of reasoning would not be inappropriate for Cyril of Alexandria, writing later and coming from the same city: the man is the head of (that is, has ruling authority over) the woman *because* she was taken from him.

And there are several other factors that argue against the meaning "source" in Cyril of Alexandria, such as the following: (2) the way that a third writer, Theodore of Mopsuestia, who is contemporary with Cyril, so clearly connects the wife's obedience to her husband to the idea that she was taken from him in 1 Corinthians 11:7–8;[36] (3) the way other patristic writers so clearly understand κεφαλή to mean "authority over" in 1 Corinthians 11:3 and connect it to ἀρχή meaning "authority over";[37] (4) the fact that it says Adam "has become" (γέγονεν) first head of the race, which would be a strange notion for "source" (for a source is there from the beginning, and one does not later become a source, nor does one become a "first" source); and (5) the fact that "authority over" is a commonly understood and established meaning for κεφαλή, while "source" has yet to be demonstrated by anything other than ambiguous passages.

A factor related to (5) is (6) the absence of support from the lexicons for the meaning "source." This meaning is not given in Lampe's *Patristic Greek Lexicon*, the standard lexicon for this material, in the entry for κεφαλή, nor is it given in BAGD, the standard lexicon for New Testament Greek.[38] At this point sound lexicography should cause us to be cautious about adopting a new meaning for a word based on one difficult passage, or one passage where it "could" have that meaning. This point was emphasized by John Chadwick in reflecting on his many years of work on the editorial team for the Liddell-Scott *Lexicon*:

> A constant problem to guard against is the proliferation of meanings. . . . It is often tempting to create a new sense to accommodate a difficult example, but we must always ask first, if there is any other way of taking the word which would allow us to assign the example to an already established sense. . . . As I have remarked

35. ANF 2, 420; TLG, Work 4, 4.8.63.5 to 4.8.64.1.

36. See the material from Theodore of Mopsuestia below, in patristic citation 7a (section III.3.7a, pp. 570–71).

37. See the quotations from Chrysostom, above, and from Basil and Eusebius, below. For example, Joseph Fitzmyer speaks of "the many places in patristic literature where comments are made on I Corinthians 11:3. . . . In these places the sense of kephalē as 'leader, ruler, one having authority over' is clear" ("kephalē in I Corinthians 11:3").

38. The meaning "source" in the way Kroeger understands it is not given in the Liddell-Scott Lexicon either; see the discussion in section E below.

> in several of my notes, there may be no reason why a proposed sense should not exist, but is there any reason why it must exist?[39]

For these reasons, it seems to me that the established sense, "ruler, authority," best fits this passage in Cyril of Alexandria. By weighing these considerations on this and other passages, readers will have to form their own conclusions.

Yet one more point needs to be made. Cyril of Alexandria clearly did not deny the subordination of the Son to the Father, nor does his material support Kroeger's claim that these writers "were quick to recognize the danger of an interpretation of 1 Corinthians 11:3 which could place Christ in a subordinate position relative to the Father," for no denial of the Father's authority over the Son is found here. In fact, in his *Dialogues on the Trinity* Cyril of Alexandria has an extensive discussion of the subordination of the Son to the Father, explaining that it is a voluntary submission, like that of Isaac to Abraham, or like that of Jesus to His earthly parents, and that it does not show Him to be a lesser being but is consistent with His being of the same nature with His Father and thus fully God.[40]

4. *Cyril of Alexandria (died AD 444), De Recte Fide ad Arcadiam 1.1.5.5(2).63.*

> "But I want you to know that the head of every man is Christ, and the head of a woman is the man, and the head of Christ is God." The blessed Luke, composing for us the genealogy of Christ, begins (ἄρχεται) from Joseph, then he comes to Adam, soon speaking of God, placing as the beginning (ἀρχή) of man the God who made him. Thus we say Christ is the head of every man: for man was made through him and he was brought to birth, the Son not creating him in a servile way, but more divinely, as in the nature of a workman. "But the head of a woman is the man," for she was taken out of his flesh, and she has him even as (her) beginning (ἀρχή). And similarly, "the head of Christ is God," for he is from him according to nature: for the Word was begotten out of God the Father. Then how is Christ not God, the one of whom the Father, according to (his) nature, has been placed as head? Whenever I might say Christ appeared in the form of man, I understand the Word of God.[41]

This text gives an understanding of κεφαλή as ἀρχή, probably in the sense of "beginning," namely, the point from which something started. In both of these quotes from Cyril, someone might

---

39. John Chadwick, *Lexicographica Graeca: Contributions to the Lexicography of Ancient Greek* (Oxford: Clarendon Press, 1996), 23–24.
40. See Cyril of Alexandria, *Dialogues sur la Trinité*, ed. and trans. Georges Matthieu de Durand (Sources Chrétiennes 237; Paris: Cerf, 1977), 2:372–79 (with Greek text and French translation). Cyril's concern in this section is to show that submission does not negate the Son's deity, and so he emphasizes that, though the Son does submit to the Father, He remains equal with Him in "being" (οὐσία). He says it does not disturb the traits of the "substance" (τῆς οὐσίας) to give obedience "as a son to a father" (ὡς ἐξ υἱοῦ πρὸς πατέρα) (Durand, 374; 582.28–30). (I am grateful to my pastor Stephen E. Farish for saving me much time by quickly providing me with an English translation of many pages of the French translation of Cyril's intricate argumentation on the Trinity.)
41. The Greek text is found in Schwartz, *Acta Conciliorum Oecumenicorum*, 1.1.5, p. 76. The English translation is mine.

argue for the sense "source, origin," but the sense "authority" would fit as well (it seemed to be the sense in the earlier quote; however, here he could be making a different point). Yet "beginning" fits better than "source," because Cyril could have thought that "woman" had one man (Adam) as the starting point from which women began, but he would not have thought that any other women had subsequent men as their "source," for no woman since Eve has been taken out of a man. Cyril is tracing back a genealogy to its starting point and comes to Adam. "Beginning, starting point" therefore seems to fit this context. But the ambiguity of ἀρχή makes it difficult to decide.

5. *Basil (the Great, of Caesarea, c. AD 329–379), in Psalmum 28 (homilia 2), MPG 30:80 (TLG 53.30.80.23).*

> "And the beloved is as a son of unicorns" [LXX Ps. 28:6b]. After the opposing powers are raised up, then love for the Lord will appear plainly, and his strength will become evident, when no one casts a shadow over those in his presence. Therefore he says, after the [statement about] beating: "the beloved will be as the son of unicorns." But a unicorn is a *royal* (ἀρχικὸς, "royal, fit for rule") animal, *not made subject* to man, his strength *unconquerable* (ἀνυπότακτον ἀνθρώπῳ, τὴν ἰσχὺν ἀκαταμάχητον) always living in desert places, trusting in his one horn. Therefore the *unconquerable* nature of the Lord (ἡ ἀκαταγώνιστος τοῦ Κυρίου φύσις) is likened to a unicorn, both because of his *rule* (ἀρχή) upon everything, and because he has one *ruler* (ἀρχή) of himself, the Father: for "the head (κεφαλή) of Christ is God."[42]

This passage is significant, even though Basil's discussion is based on the Septuagint mistranslation of Psalm 28:6, "And the beloved is as a son of unicorns." But Basil uses this text as an opportunity to comment on the unconquerable nature of a unicorn and likens this to the supreme rule of Christ over everything. Then he adds that the Son has one ruler over himself, namely, God the Father. For our purposes, it is significant that for Basil "the head of Christ is God" meant "the ruler over Christ is God," and the word ἀρχή meant "ruler" when it was used as a synonym for κεφαλή.

6. *Theodore of Mopsuestia (ca. AD 350–428), Eccl. Theol. 1.11.2–3,* and

7. *Theodore of Mopsuestia (ca. AD 350–428), Eccl. Theol. 2.7.1.*

These two references do not exist.[43] The numbers were apparently copied by mistake from the Eusebius references below them (Eusebius, *Eccl. Theol.* 1.11.2–3 and 2.7.1). However, perhaps Kroeger intended to copy the reference to Theodore of Mopsuestia in the entry for κεφαλή in Lampe's *Lexicon.* That reference is as follows:

7a. *Theodore of Mopsuestia, 1 Cor. 11:3 (p. 187.12ff; M.66.888c):*

> This he wishes to say: that, on the one hand, we move forward from Christ to God

42. The Greek text is in TLG Basil, *In Psalmum 28 (homilia 2)*, Work 053, 30.80.12 to 30.80.23. The English translation is mine.

43. Theodore of Mopsuestia has no work with the title or abbreviation *Eccl. Theol.* (see Lampe, *Lexicon*, xli) .

> (ἀπὸ μὲν τοῦ Χριστοῦ ἐπὶ τὸν Θεὸν χωροῦμεν), out of whom he is, but on the other hand from man to Christ (ἀπὸ δὲ τοῦ ἀνδρὸς ἐπὶ τὸν Χριστόν): for we are out of him according to the second form of existence.... For on the one hand, being subject to suffering, we consider Adam to be head (κεφαλή), from whom we have taken existence. But on the other hand, not being subject to suffering, we consider Christ to be head (κεφαλή), from whom we have an unsuffering existence. Similarly, he says, also from woman to man (καὶ ἀπὸ τῆς γυναικὸς ἐπὶ τὸν ἄνδρα), since she has taken existence from him.[44]

This text at first seems ambiguous regarding the meaning of κεφαλή, perhaps because Theodore's commentaries exist only in fragments, and we may not have all that he wrote on this verse. The idea of "head" as "leader, ruler" seems possible, especially since he says we "advance" or "move forward"(χωρέω ἀπὸ [person B] ἐπὶ [person A]), in each case to the one who is "head," suggesting higher rank. But the idea of "beginning" (that is, the first one to exist in the condition specified) is also possible.

But Theodore's subsequent comments seem to tip the issue toward κεφαλή meaning "leader, authority over." This is because in 1 Corinthians 11:3 he connects man's headship with woman's being created from man, an idea that Theodore then explains when he comments on 1 Corinthians 11:7–8. These verses read as follows in the New Testament:

> *For a man ought not to cover his head, since he is the image and glory of God; but woman is the glory of man. (For man was not made from woman, but woman from man.)* (RSV)

When Theodore comments on this passage, he sees a woman's "glory" as consisting in her obedience to her husband:

> He calls the woman "glory" but surely not "image," because it applied faintly, since "glory" looks at obedience (εἰς τὴν ὑπακοήν), but "image" looks at rulership (εἰς τὸ ἀρχικόν).[45]

These subsequent remarks, coming just a few lines after his comment on 1 Corinthians 11:3, make the sense "authority over" most likely for κεφαλή in the 11:3 comment above. Theodore thinks that man is the authority over woman, since she was taken from him, and he says that this means she is his "glory" and should obey him, "since 'glory' looks at obedience, but 'image' looks at rulership."

---

44. The Greek text is found in Karl Staab, ed., *Pauluskommentare aus der griechischen Kirche* (Münster: Aschendorff, 1933), 187. The English translation is mine.
45. Greek text in Staab, *Pauluskommentare*, 188. The English translation is mine.

8. *Eusebius (ca.* AD *265–ca. 339), Eccl. Theol. 1.11.2–3.*

> And the great apostle teaches that the head of the Son himself is God, but (the head) of the church is the Son. How is he saying, on the one hand, "the head of Christ is God," but on the other hand saying concerning the Son, "and he gave him to be head over all things for the church, which is his body"? Is it not therefore that he may be *leader* (ἀρχηγός) and *head* (κεφαλή) of the church, but of him (the head) is the Father: Thus there is one God the Father of the only Son, and there is *one head*, even of Christ himself. But if there is one *ruler* (ἀρχή) and head, how then could there be two Gods? Is he not one alone, the one above whom no one is higher, neither does he claim any other cause of himself, but he has acquired the familial, unbegun, unbegotten deity from the *monarchial authority* (τῆς μοναρχικῆς ἐξουσίας),[46] and he has given to the Son his own divinity and life; who through him caused all things to exist, *who sends him, who appoints him, who commands, who teaches, who commits all things to him, who glorifies him, who exalts (him), who declares him king of all, who has committed all judgment to him. . . .*[47]

Far from demonstrating that the church fathers "were quick to recognize the danger of an interpretation of 1 Corinthians 11:3 which could place Christ in a subordinate position relative to the Father" (as Kroeger claims), this quotation from Eusebius shows that the Father as "head" has supreme authority, and that His authority over the Son is seen in many actions: He sends the Son, He appoints Him, He commands Him, He teaches Him, He commits all judgment to Him, and so forth. The Father's headship here means that He is the one in "authority over" the Son, and the Son's headship over the church means that He is the leader or ruler of the church.

9. *Eusebius (ca.* AD *265–ca. 339), Eccl. Theol . 2.7.1.*

> . . . but fear, O man, lest having confessed two substances, you would bring in two rulers (ἀρχή)[48] and would fall from the *monarchial* deity? Learn then thus, since there is one unbegun and unbegotten God, and since the Son has been begotten from him, there will be one ruler (ἀρχή), and one *monarchy and kingdom*, since even the Son himself claims his Father as ruler (ἀρχή). "For the head of Christ is God," according to the apostle.[49]

46. The Father's deity is said to come from His own supreme authority, His "monarchial authority."
47. The Greek text is found in TLG, Eusebius, *De ecclesiastica theologia*, Work 009, 1.11.2.4 to 1.11.3.11. The English translation is mine.
48. Here I have translated ἀρχή as "ruler," which is consistent with the previous Eusebius quotation from this same document, where this sense seems necessary.
49. The Greek text is found in TLG, Eusebius, *De ecclesiastica theologia*, Work 009, 2.7.1.1 to 2.7.2.1. The English translation is mine.

Again, Eusebius explains "the head of Christ is God" to imply that God the Father has supreme authority, and the Son is not another authority equal to Him.

Conclusion on patristic citations. Kroeger gave nine patristic references (in addition to the two from Chrysostom) to support her claims that "church fathers argued vehemently that for Paul *head* had meant 'source,'" and that they "were quick to recognize the danger" of understanding 1 Corinthians 11:3 to mean that Christ has a "subordinate position relative to the Father." Two of the citations (1, 2) were not statements of any church father but statements from heretical Arian creeds. Two more (6, 7) did not exist but may have been intended as a reference to Theodore of Mopsuestia in a commentary on 1 Corinthians 11 that relates the headship of the husband to his rulership and the wife's obedience. Three others (5, 8, 9) assumed that to be "head" of someone else implied having a position of authority or rule and thus supported the meaning "authority over." Two references from Cyril of Alexandria (3, 4) were ambiguous, due to ambiguity in the meaning of ἀρχή, since the meanings "authority," "beginning," or "origin" would all make sense in the contexts.

In none of the references did any church father "argue vehemently" that "for Paul *head* had meant 'source.'" And none of the references argued against an interpretation of 1 Corinthians 11:3 that placed Christ in a "subordinate position relative to the Father"; indeed, some of the references specify that Christ is obedient to the Father and that the Father rules over Him. In light of this evidence, it seems that Kroeger's assertion that church fathers "were quick to recognize the danger" of understanding 1 Corinthians 11:3 to mean that Christ has a "subordinate position relative to the Father" is also false.[50]

A failure to mention the way Lampe defines and does not define κεφαλή. Kroeger's apparent use of page 749 of Lampe's *Patristic Greek Lexicon* to find four of her actual eight patristic references is puzzling for two other reasons. First, she fails to mention that the meaning "source," which she claims was "vehemently" defended by the church fathers, is nowhere mentioned as a meaning for κεφαλή in this standard lexicon for patristic Greek. If the meaning "source" was "vehemently" defended by the church fathers, it is surprising that the editorial team of this definitive lexicon did not discover this fact as they worked through the writings of the church fathers for fifty-five years, from 1906 to 1961 (see Preface, iii). And it is inexcusable in a popular reference work to claim that a meaning was "vehemently" defended by the church fathers and fail to mention that that meaning simply is not listed in the standard Greek lexicon of the church fathers.

Second, it is troubling to see that Kroeger claims a nonexistent quote from Chrysostom to *deny* the meaning "chief" or "authority over" for the patristic period, but she does not mention that this is the essential meaning of the first five metaphorical definitions for κεφαλή (as applied to persons)

50. In direct contrast to Kroeger's claim, Joseph Fitzmyer mentions "the many places in patristic literature where comments are made on I Corinthians 11:3 or use of it is made. In these places the sense of kephalē as 'leader, ruler, one having authority over' is clear" ("kephalē in I Corinthians 11:3," 56).

that are given on the same page in Lampe's *Lexicon* (p. 749) from which she took several of her examples:

> **B**. of persons; **1**. *head* of the house, Herm.*sim*. 7.3; **2**. *chief, head-man*...**3**. religious *superior*...**4**. of bishops, κεφαλαὶ ἐκκλησιῶν [other examples include "of the bishop of the city of Rome, being head of all the churches"]...**5**. κεφαλὴ εἶναι c. genit. [to be head, with genitive] *take precedence of*

All five of these categories include leadership and authority attaching to the term κεφαλή. They show that κεφαλή meant "chief" and "authority over," according to the standard lexicon for patristic Greek. Since Kroeger's article depended so heavily on patristic evidence, and in fact (apparently) on this very page in this lexicon, these definitions from this standard patristic lexicon should have been mentioned. It is difficult to understand how she could claim that Chrysostom said that "only a heretic" would use this meaning when the standard lexicon for patristic Greek lists five different categories with this meaning in their entry on κεφαλή.

V. Evidence from Classical Literature

One other section from Kroeger's article deserves comment. In a section called "The Classical View of Head as Source," Kroeger attempts to demonstrate that kephalē meant "source" because it was equated with archē, which meant "source." She writes:

> By the time of Plato, adherents of Orphic religion were using kephalē with archē ("source" or "beginning"). (p. 375)

For support she gives the following references (with no quotations, no dates, and no further information).

1. Kern, Orph. Fr. 2. nos. 21 a.2., 168
2. Plato, Leg. IV.715E and sch
3. Proclus, In Tim. II 95.48 (V.322)
4. Pseudo-Aristides World 7
5. Eusebius, Praep. Ev. 3.9
6. Deveni Papyrus, col. 13, line 12
7. Stobaeus, Ecl. 1.23
8. Plutarch, Def. Orac. 436D
9. Achilles Tatius, fr. 81.29
10. Isaiah 9:14-15 (LXX)
11. Irenaeus, PG 7.496
12. Tertullian, Marc. 5.8
13. Philo, Congr. 61
14. Photius, Comm. 1 Cor. 11:3, ed. Staab 567.1

This looks like an impressive set of references to demonstrate "the classical concept of head as source." In fact, one review of *Dictionary of Paul and His Letters* pointed to C. Kroeger's article on "head" as one of the outstanding articles in the volume because it has "excellent Graeco-Roman material," deals with "the classical view of head as source," and "cites many primary references."[51] But do these fourteen references demonstrate that "head" meant "source," as Kroeger claims? Do they show examples of κεφαλή used with ἀρχή as "source" or "beginning" and so demonstrate the meaning "source" for κεφαλή? The first one is familiar to anyone following the previous discussions of κεφαλή:

1. *Kern, Orph. Fr. 2.nos. 21 a.2., 168 (5th cent.* BC*).*

> Zeus was first, Zeus is last with white, vivid lightning;
> Zeus the head (κεφαλή, but with ἀρχή as a variant reading), Zeus the middle,
> Zeus from whom all things are perfected
> (Ζεὺς κεφαλή, Ζεὺς μέσσα, Διὸς δ' ἐκ πάντα τέτυκται; *Orphic Fragments* 21a).[52]

The sense "beginning, first one" seems most likely for either κεφαλή or ἀρχή here, because of (1) the similarity to the idea of "first" and "last" in the previous line, and (2) the contrast with "middle" and the mention of perfection, giving the sense, "Zeus is the beginning, Zeus is the middle, Zeus is the one who completes all things." The *Oxford Classical Dictionary*, in discussing the basic tenets of Orphic religion, mentions a "common myth" in which "Zeus was praised as the beginning, the middle, and the end of all"[53] and so supports the sense "beginning" in this and similar texts. In any case, the meaning "source" cannot be established for κεφαλή from this passage.

2. *Plato (ca. 429–347* BC*), Leg. IV.715E and sch.*

> O men, that God who, as old tradition tells, holds the *beginning* (ἀρχή), the end, and the centre of all things that exist, completes his circuit by nature's ordinance in straight, unswerving course. (Plato, *Laws* IV.715E, LCL translation)

This text does not even contain κεφαλή; so it is not helpful for our inquiry. The term ἀρχή is here translated as "beginning" (not "source") by the LCL edition. It could not mean "source," because Plato would not say that God "holds" the source of all things. The best meaning would be "beginning," with the sense that God holds the beginning, the end, and the middle of all things that exist.

---

51. Aida Besançon Spencer, review of *Dictionary of Paul and His Letters* in *Themelios* 20:2 (Jan. 1995), 27–28. The review quotes as noteworthy Kroeger's quotation of John Chrysostom: "only a heretic would understand Paul's use of 'head' to mean 'chief' or 'authority over.'"
52. The Greek text is found in Otto Kern, *Orphicorum Fragmenta* (Berlin: Weidmannsche Verlagsbüchhandlung, 1922), 91); TLG, Orphica, Work 010, 6.13–14. The English is my translation.
53. *Oxford Classical Dictionary*, 2nd edition, eds. N. G. L. Hammond and H. H. Scullard (Oxford: Clarendon Press, 1970), 759.

Moreover, Kroeger claims that these texts show that κεφαλή was used *with* ἀρχή. But if κεφαλή does not even occur in this quotation, it cannot show that Plato was using κεφαλή *with* ἀρχή. In the absence of the term κεφαλή, this reference cannot be used as evidence for the meaning of that term.

3. *Proclus (AD 410–485), In Tim. II 95.48 (V.322).* This may be an incorrect reference, because Proclus *In Tim.* 2.95 ends at line 31, and line 48 does not exist.[54] Perhaps Kroeger meant to cite *In Tim.* 1.313.21, which has the same quote again about Zeus, this time in the form,

> Zeus the head, Zeus the middle, Zeus from whom comes all that is
> (Ζεὺς κεφαλή, Ζεὺς μέσσα, Διός δ' ἐκ πάντα τέτυκται).[55]

This reference gives no more support to the meaning "source" than the earlier passage in *Orphic Fragments*. It is difficult to understand why Kroeger includes this reference in a section on "The Classical View of Head as Source," since the classical period in Greek was prior to the time of the New Testament (the classical period in Greek literature is generally thought of as the period prior to 325 BC),[56] while Proclus was a Neoplatonist philosopher who lived from AD 410 to 485.

4. *Pseudo-Aristides World 7 (4th cent. BC?).* This is an incorrect reference, because there is no work called *World* written by Aristides or Pseudo-Aristides.[57]

However, the following quotation does appear in Aristotle (or Pseudo-Aristotle), *de Mundo* (*"On the Cosmos"* or *"On the World"*), section 7 (401a.29–30):[58]

> Zeus is the head, Zeus the centre; from Zeus comes all that is
> (Ζεὺς κεφαλή, Ζεὺς μέσσα, Διὸς δ' ἐκ πάντα τέτυκται).

Perhaps Kroeger found a reference to Ps-Arist., *World* 7 and understood Arist. to refer to Aristides rather than Aristotle. In any case, this is another quotation of the same sentence and adds no new evidence for the meaning of κεφαλή.

5. *Eusebius (ca. AD 265–ca. 339), Praep. Ev. 3.9.*

This text quotes followers of Orphic religion as saying,

> Zeus the head, Zeus the middle, Zeus from whom comes all that is

---

54. However, it is possible that Dr. Kroeger is citing some edition of Proclus with a numbering system different from that used in the standard text in the TLG database.
55. Proclus, *in Platonis Timaeum commentarii*, ed. E. Diehl, 3 vols, Leipzig (T.) 1903, 1904, 1906 (TLG, Proclus, *In Tim.* 1.313.21–22). The English is my translation in this and all subsequent citations of this sentence about Zeus, unless otherwise indicated.
56. *The Oxford Companion to Classical Literature*, comp. Paul Harvey (Oxford and New York: Oxford University Press, 1937), 106.
57. See LSJ, xix.
58. The text is found in the Loeb Classical Library edition of *Aristotle*, Vol. 3, 406.

(Ζεὺς κεφαλή, Ζεὺς μέσσα, Διὸς δ' ἐκ πάντα τέτυκται).[59]

This is a repetition of the same sentence again, with no additional evidence. Eusebius is also wrongly placed in this discussion of "The Classical Concept of Head," since he was a Christian historian who lived approximately AD 265–339.

6. *Deveni Papyrus, col. 13, line 12 (4th cent. BC).* This is a misspelled reference, and as a result it turned out to be very difficult to locate. It should read, *Derveni Papyrus*, col. 13, line 12.[60] It is from the late fourth century BC The text says:

> Zeus the head, Zeus the middle, Zeus from whom comes all that is
>
> (Ζεὺς κεφα[λή, Ζεὺς μέσσ]α, Διὸς δ' ἐκ [π]άντα τέτ[υκται]).[61]

This is a repetition of the same sentence. It provides no additional evidence.

7. *Stobaeus, Ecl. 1.23 (5th cent. AD).*

This text also quotes followers of Orphic religion as saying,

> Zeus the head, Zeus the middle, Zeus from whom comes (τέτυκται) all that is
> (Ζεὺς κεφαλή, Ζεὺς μέσσα, Διὸς δ' ἐκ πάντα τέτυκται).[62]

This is a repetition of the same sentence once again, with no additional evidence. Stobaeus is also wrongly placed in this discussion of "The Classical Concept of Head," since he lived in the fifth century AD.

8. *Plutarch (ca. AD 46–ca. 120), Def. Orac. 436D.* This text says:

> Zeus the beginning, Zeus the middle, Zeus from whom all things come about
> (Ζεὺς ἀρχὴ Ζεὺς μέσσα, Διὸς δ' ἐκ πάντα πέλονται).[63]

This text does not use κεφαλή but uses ἀρχή and therefore is wrongly included in this list. Plutarch is also incorrectly placed in this discussion of "The Classical Concept of Head," since he lived approximately AD 46–120.

9. *Achilles Tatius, fr. 81.29 (3rd cent. AD).* This is an incomplete reference, and it turned out to be very difficult to locate. The Loeb Classical Library edition of Achilles Tatius has only eight

---

59. TLG, Eusebius, *Praep. Evang.* 3.9.2.2.
60. The text was published in *Zeitschrift für Papyrologie und Epigraphik* 47 (1982), Appendix 8. Because of the misspelling of the name, I was unable to locate this until I received help from David Chapman, who was (in 1997) a graduate student at the University of Cambridge.
61. TLG, Orphica, *Fragmenta* (P. Derveni), Work 013, col 12.
62. TLG Joannes Stobaeus Anthologus, Work 001, 1.1.23.2–6.
63. TLG, Plutarch, Work 92, 436D.8–9.

chapters. No such document as "fr." (presumably "fragment") from Achilles Tatius is listed in the preface to Liddell and Scott.

However, this turns out to be a reference not to the better known Greek romantic writer Achilles Tatius (2nd century AD) found in the Loeb Classical Library series, but to another Achilles Tatius, a 3rd-century AD author with one surviving work, a commentary on the writings of Aratus. The citation of line 29 is not quite accurate, for the term κεφαλή does not occur in line 29. However, just three lines later, in lines 32–33, the text does contain ἀρχή in the following quotation:

> Zeus the beginning, Zeus the middle, Zeus from whom all things are perfected (Ζεὺς ἀρχή, Ζεὺς μέσσα, Διὸς δ' ἐκ πάντα τέτυκται).[64]

The word κεφαλή does not occur in this text; so it should not be included in this list. Nor is a third-century AD author useful evidence for the "classical" period in Greek.

10. *Isaiah 9:14-15 (LXX verses 13–14) (2nd cent. BC Greek translation).*

> So the LORD cut off from Israel *head* (κεφαλή) and tail, palm branch and reed in one day—the elder and honored man is the head (ἀρχή, "ruler"), and the prophet who teaches lies is the tail.

Far from establishing the meaning "source" for kephalē, this shows the sense "leader, one in authority," for it is the elder who is said to be "head."

11. *Irenaeus, PG 7.496 (ca. AD 175–ca. 195).* In describing the teaching of the Gnostics, Irenaeus reports this:

> They go on to say that the Demiurge imagined that he created all these things of himself, while in reality he made them in conjunction with the productive power of Achamoth.... They further affirm that his mother originated this opinion in his mind, because she desired to bring him forth possessed of such a character that he should be the head and source of his own essence (κεφαλὴν μὲν καὶ ἀρχὴν τῆς ἰδίας οὐσίας), and the absolute ruler (κύριος) over every kind of operation [that was afterwards attempted]. This mother they call Ogdoad, Sophia, Terra....(Irenaeus, *Against Heresies* 5.3 [ANF 1, 322–323])

Here the ambiguity about the meaning of ἀρχή confronts us again. The translator of the *Ante-Nicene Fathers* series rendered it "source," which is possible, but "ruler" or "beginning" are also possible. In any case, the text does not equate "head" with "source/ruler/beginning" but lists them as two items. So even if ἀρχή is translated "source," the phrase would still mean, "the head and

64. The text is found in Ernest Maass, *Commentariorum in Aratum reliquiae* (Berlin: Weidmann, 1898), 81, lines 32–33.

source of his own being," with "head" in the sense of "ruler." The text is ambiguous and does not provide convincing evidence of "head" meaning "source." Since Irenaeus wrote between about AD 175 and 195, this text should not be counted as evidence of a classical understanding of κεφαλή.

12. *Tertullian, Marc. 5.8 (ca. AD 160–ca. 220).*

> "The head of every man is Christ." What Christ, if he is not the author of man? The *head* here he has put for *authority*; now "authority" will accrue to none else than the "author." (*The Five Books Against Marcion*, book 5, chap. 8; ANF vol. 3, p. 445)

This text is translated from Latin, not Greek; so it is of little help in determining the meaning of kephalē, for the word does not occur here. If the text is counted as evidence, it supports not the idea of "source" but the idea of "head" as "ruler, one in authority." Since Tertullian lived ca. AD 160/170 to ca. 215/220 and wrote in Latin, this quotation is not from classical Greek but from patristic Latin.

13. *Philo (ca. 30 BC–AD 45), Congr. 61.* This quotation says:

> And of all the members of the clan here described Esau is the progenitor, the head as it were of the whole creature. (LCL, Vol. 4, 489; κεφαλὴ δὲ ὡς ζῴου πάντων τῶν λεχθέντων μερῶν ὁ γενάρχης ἐστὶν ʽΗσαῦ.)

Kroeger translates this "the progenitor" but fails to note that the ambiguity attaching to archē also attaches to genarchēs. The Liddell-Scott *Lexicon* gives two definitions for genarchēs: (1) "founder or first ancestor of a family," and (2) "ruler of created beings."[65] The quotation is ambiguous, and Philo, as is his custom, is constructing an allegory. In any case, it does not demonstrate any absence of the idea of authority from the "head," for Esau was surely the ruler of the clan descended from him.[66]

14. *Photius, Comm. 1 Cor. 11:3, ed. Staab 567.1 (9th cent. AD).* Finally, Kroeger adds a citation from Photius, not connecting κεφαλή with ἀρχή but saying "kephalē was considered by Photius to be a synonym for *procreator* or *progenitor* (Photius, *Comm. 1 Cor. 11:3*, ed. Staab 567.1)." This is the most egregious disregard of dating in all the citations that give the appearance of support for an early, "classical" view of head as source, because Photius is far from being a pre-New

---

65. LSJ, 342.

66. This text is not new but has been considered previously in studies of κεφαλή. As I wrote in my 1990 article: "The sense of 'head' here is difficult to determine. Payne suggests the meaning 'source of life' for head, a specific kind of 'source' that has never before been given in any lexicon. Yet it is possible that Philo thought of the physical head of an animal as in some sense energizing or giving life to the animal—this would then be a simile in which Esau (a representative of stubborn disobedience in this context) gives life to a whole list of other sins that Philo has been describing as a 'family' in this allegory. On the other hand, the word translated above as progenitor (genarchēs) also can mean 'ruler of created beings' (LSJ, 342). In that case the text would read: 'And Esau is the ruler of all the clan here described, the head as of a living animal.' Here the meaning would be that Esau is the ruler over the rest of the sinful clan and head would mean 'ruler, authority over.' It seems impossible from the context that we have to decide clearly for one meaning or the other in this text" (Grudem, "The Meaning of kephalē:, A Response to Recent Studies" 454–55).

Finally, Philo should not be cited as evidence for the "classical" view of a word, since he wrote in the first century AD.

Testament writer. He died in AD 891. This also makes him a highly dubious source for determining the New Testament meaning for κεφαλή. But Kroeger gives readers no indication of dates for any of what she claims as "classical" sources, thus leading the vast majority of readers (who have never heard of the ninth-century AD author Photius) to think that she has given evidence of an established meaning for κεφαλή prior to the time of the New Testament.

In any case, we can examine the Photius quotation, which says:

> On the one hand, the head of us who believe is Christ, as we are members of the same body and fellow partakers with him, having been begotten through the fellowship of his body and blood: for through him we all, having been called "one body," have him as head. "But the head of Christ is God" even the Father, as a begetter and originator and one of the same nature as him.[67] "And the head of the woman is the man," for he also exists as her begetter and originator and one of the same nature as her. The analogy is suitable and fits together. But if you might understand the "of every man" [1 Cor. 11:3] also to mean over the unbelievers, according to the word of the creation this (meaning) only is allowed: For having yielded to the man[68] to *reign* over the others, ***he allowed him to remain under his own unique authority and rule*** (αὐτὸν ὑπὸ τὴν ἰδίαν μόνον εἴασε μένειν ἐχουσίαν καὶ ἀρχήν) not having established over him another ruler and supreme authority.[69]

Kroeger is correct to say that the ideas of "procreator" and "progenitor" are contained in this ninth-century AD text, but it is not clear that these terms are used to *define* "head," any more than it would be to say that "head" *means* "of the same nature" (ὁμοούσιος), which is the third term used in this explanation. In all three terms (begetter, originator, of the same nature), Photius is using classical Trinitarian language to explain the Father's role as "head," saying it is "as" one who is begetter, originator, and of the same nature. This is standard Trinitarian language, and in dealing with 1 Corinthians 11:3, "the head of Christ is God," Photius maintains the orthodox definitions of the Father as the one who eternally begets the Son and eternally sends forth the Holy Spirit.

But this Trinitarian language does not establish Kroeger's claim in this section that there was a "classical" meaning of "source" for κεφαλή. Instead, the passage once again indicates that Photius understands "head" to mean "authority over." This is evident from the last two sentences

67. Photius is using language from prior Trinitarian controversies here. He says that the Father is "begetter and originator and of the same nature" as the Son. "Begetter" (γεννήτωρ) refers to the Father's eternal relationship to the Son, in what was called the "eternal generation of the Son." "Originator" (προβολεύς), according to Lampe's *Patristic Greek Lexicon*, was used in Trinitarian discussion particularly to refer to the Father's role with respect to the procession of the Holy Spirit (1140). And "of the same nature" (ὁμοούσιος) was the term used from the Nicene Creed onward to affirm the full deity of the Son.

68. Here "the man" refers to Christ as man.

69. The English translation is mine. The Greek text is from Karl Staab, *Pauluskommentare aus der griechischen Kirche* (Münster: Aschendorf, 1933), 567; TLG Photius, *Fragmenta in epistulam I ad Corinthias*, Work 15, 567.1–567.11.

in the citation, where we see how he relates "the head of every man is Christ" to "the head of Christ is God." Photius explains "the head of every man is Christ" to mean that Christ is appointed by the Father "to reign" even over unbelievers. This is consistent with the idea that the head of Christ is God, since Christ remains under God the Father's "own unique authority and rule." Once again, to be "head" is seen to mean that one is in the role of "authority over" another.

In any case, this obscure text from the ninth century AD is hardly relevant for Kroeger's section, "The Classical View of Head as Source," and hardly relevant for understanding the New Testament meaning of κεφαλή, since it came 800 years later.

Conclusion on Kroeger's section on "The Classical View of Head as Source." Of the fourteen references given by Kroeger in her section on "The Classical View of Head as Source," four (2, 8, 9, 12) did not contain the term κεφαλή and are not relevant for understanding the meaning of the term. Of the remaining ten, only three (1, 4, 6) were from the pre-New Testament "classical" period in Greek. All three of those were repeating the same sentence about Zeus, which means that the fourteen references in this section boil down to one piece of evidence. In that sentence, the meaning "source" is not proven, for the sense "beginning" best fits the context and follows the translation of the *Oxford Classical Dictionary*. This means that of the fourteen references in this section, none turned out to support the idea that classical Greek had a meaning "source" for κεφαλή.

If examples from all dates are included, however, then of the ten that contained κεφαλή, two (10, 14) clearly use κεφαλή to mean "authority over," and two others (11, 13) are ambiguous, since both the meaning "beginning" and the meaning "authority over" are possible. The remaining six (1, 3, 4, 5, 6, 7) use κεφαλή in the sense "beginning," all in the same sentence about Zeus. Once again, not one of the fourteen references turned out to support the meaning "source" for κεφαλή.

One more characteristic of these references should be noted. Kroeger's goal is to show that "source" is often the sense of κεφαλή in the New Testament *instead of* the meaning "authority over." She says at one point, "By the Byzantine era kephalē had acquired the sense of 'chief ' or 'master'...this was rarely true of the Greek kephalē in NT times."[70] In order to appreciate Kroeger's statement, we must realize that the Byzantine Age in Greek literature lasted from AD 529 to 1453,[71] and Greek usage during that time is of very little relevance for New Testament study. Thus Kroeger is implying, if not asserting, that "source" was a common and well-established sense for κεφαλή at the time of the New Testament, while "authority over" was a rare sense until about five hundred years after the New Testament.

But do any of her references prove this? It is significant to notice what kind of persons are called "head" in these quotations, both from patristic texts and from others:

70. Kroeger, "Head," 377.

71. *The Oxford Companion to Classical Literature*, comp. Paul Harvey (Oxford and New York: Oxford University Press, 1937), 83.

1. husband (head of wife)
2. God (head of Christ)
3. Christ (head of every man)
4. church leaders (head of church)
5. a woman (head of her maidservant)
6. Christ (head of the church)
7. Adam (head of human race)
8. Zeus (head of all things)
9. elders (head of Israel)
10. Gnostic Demiurge (head of his own being)
11. Esau (head of his clan)

In every case, ancient readers would have readily understood that the person called "head" was in a position of authority or rule over the person or group thought of as the "body" in the metaphor. Even in those cases where the sense "beginning" is appropriate, there is no idea of "beginning" without authority; rather, the person who is the "head" is always the one in authority. Therefore, it seems inevitable that the sense "authority" attaches to the metaphor when one person is called "head" (κεφαλή) of another person or group. The sense "authority over" for κεφαλή is firmly established.

VI. Dr. Kroeger's Response

I read an earlier version of this article as a paper at the 1997 annual meeting of the Evangelical Theological Society in Santa Clara, California.[72] Then at the 1998 meeting of the ETS in Orlando, Dr. Kroeger read a four-page response to my paper, entitled "The Use of Classical Disciplines in Biblical Research." In this response, she makes the following points:

(1) Although Photius wrote in the ninth century AD, his work as a lexicographer remains valuable to us, for he studied Greek literature from earlier centuries (p. 1).

(2) In the statements about "Zeus the head, Zeus the middle..." etc., the interchange of κεφαλή with ἀρχή as the quotation appears in various authors shows that "in the writers' minds they have the same semantic value and may be freely exchanged" (p. 2).

(3) Regarding erroneous citations in her article, she says, "Here my own effort to condense [sic] the lengthy citations led to the scrambling of a couple of references, although the majority were accurate" (pp. 2–3).

(4) The citation that I had been unable to locate (Achilles Tatius, fr. 81.29) was not from the commonly known Achilles Tatius (second century AD) but from a lesser known Achilles Tatius (third century AD), fragments of whose commentary on Aratus are published in Maass, *Commentariorum*

72. The paper contained all the substantive points of this present article except the survey of commentaries and journal articles in the last section, and the paper was distributed to all interested attendees at the conference. Dr. Kroeger was present and also received a copy of the paper.

in Aratum reliquiae (1898, repr. 1958). Dr. Kroeger says that my difficulty in finding this was because I "failed to recognize that in classical antiquity more than one writer might bear the same name" (p. 3).

(5) With respect to my critique of her article, she says that I "failed to differentiate between archōn, meaning ruler or commander, and the cognate archē meaning beginning, first principle or source. To be sure, archē can also indicate authority, rule, realm or magistracy. Almost never, however, does archē denote the person ruling. That sense is supplied by the cognate, archōn" (p. 3).

(6) Chrysostom held to the "commonly held anatomical views of antiquity, that the head was the source of the body's existence," and this led Chrysostom to "conventional metaphorical uses" for κεφαλή (by this she means the metaphor of "head" as "source") (p. 3).

(7) In Chrysostom's view, "as applied to the Trinity, kephalē must imply 'perfect oneness and primal cause and source.'" She concludes, "Indubitably he viewed one of the meanings of 'head' to be 'source' or 'origin' and deemed it theologically important" (p. 4).

In response to these seven items, the following points may be made:

(1) *Photius*: I agree that Photius' ninth-century AD lexicon has some value for scholarly work, but the fact remains that citing his commentary on 1 Corinthians (not his lexicon) in a section on "The Classical View of Head as Source" without giving readers any indication that he wrote eight hundred years after the New Testament or that he uses κεφαλή to mean "authority over" is misleading.

(2) *Statements about Zeus*: The fact that κεφαλή is used in some of the statements about Zeus and ἀρχή in others does not show that the words "have the same semantic value and may be freely exchanged," but only that they shared the one sense that fits that context, namely, "beginning, first in a series." In fact, one word (κεφαλή) signifies this meaning by means of a metaphor (the "head" as the end point, furthest extremity), and the other word (ἀρχή) means it literally. Therefore these quotes still fail to provide proof that κεφαλή could mean source. They just show what everyone has recognized all along, that κεφαλή in a meta-phorical sense could mean "beginning, first in a series, extremity, end-point."

(3) *Accuracy*: To say that she scrambled "a couple of references" is a rather low estimate. Of twenty-four key references to ancient literature, fourteen were accurate, but ten were not: Four did not contain κεφαλή, two had the wrong author listed, three had the wrong reference listed, and the one from Chrysostom did not exist at all. I agree with her that "the majority were accurate," since fourteen of twenty-four key references is more than half. But the standard of accuracy in scholarly works is not to get the "majority" of one's references right. They should all be right. This article fell far short of the standard of accuracy required for academic work.

(4) *Achilles Tatius*: I was glad at last to learn from Dr. Kroeger of the reference to the obscure Achilles Tatius, but to give a reference simply as "fr. 81.29," when the standard reference works (the preface to LSJ and the *Oxford Classical Dictionary*) do not list *any* work by *any* Achilles Tatius as "fr." is simply to consign all readers to the same kind of frustrating search of

libraries that I experienced.[73] I was also surprised to find, when I finally did consult the work, that it did not contain the term κεφαλή at all but used ἀρχή though that fact had not been mentioned in Dr. Kroeger's 1998 response when she named the volume in which the text had been published.

(5) *The term* ἀρχή: I do not think it is correct that ἀρχή "almost never" denotes the person ruling. See the citations from Chrysostom (above) where the wife is a "second authority,"[74] or from Basil and Eusebius, where the Father is the "ruler" of the Son;[75] see also BAGD, meaning 3, "ruler, authority" (p. 112).

(6) *Chrysostom on the function of the head in the body*: I agree that Chrysostom thought that the senses had their origin in the head. But that is not the issue. He also thought that the head ruled the body.[76] The question is not what meaning he *could have* given to "head" when used in a metaphorical sense, but what meaning he *actually did* give. The nine citations given earlier where the "head" is specified as the ruling part or the person in authority make clear that Chrysostom used κεφαλή with the sense "authority over" (which Kroeger still did not acknowledge).

Her citation from Chrysostom is interesting, however, in what it omits. Here is her exact statement and the quotation that she gave from Chrysostom in her response (p. 3):

> One of the points of disagreement between my colleague and my own work was over the treatment of the term by John Chrysostom, one of the earliest exegetes, a fourth century scholar whose first language was Greek. The commonly held anatomical views of antiquity, that the head was the source of the body's existence, led him to conventional metaphorical uses. From the head, he said, the senses "have their source and fount."
>
> In the head are the eyes both of the body, and of the soul....All the senses have thence their origin and their source. Thence are sent forth the organs of speech, the power of seeing, and of smelling, and all touch. For thence is derived the root of the nerves and of the bones. [*Commentary on I Thessalonians V:5,* p. 513]

This is one of the sections from Chrysostom that I quoted in the beginning of this paper—section B, citation (2) above. What is most interesting here is the material represented by the ellipsis

73. In this case I had also received help from David Chapman, a former student who was in Ph.D. studies at the University of Cambridge. He spent most of a day checking all the critical editions of Achilles Tatius, as well as papyrus fragments, but still found no work that could be identified as "fr. 81.29." We did not check the lesser-known Achilles Tatius because no reference work identified any work of his as "fr." I mention this only because the issue here is whether evangelical academic works should make it easy or hard for readers to check for themselves the sources quoted in an article.

74. Citation (6) from Chrysostom, above.

75. Patristic citations (5) and (8) above.

76. Clinton E. Arnold, "Jesus Christ: 'Head' of the Church (Colossians and Ephesians)," *In Jesus of Nazareth: Lord and Christ*, eds. Joel B. Green and Max Turner (Grand Rapids, MI: Eerdmans and Carlisle, England: Paternoster, 1994), 346–366 shows that in the ancient world the head was commonly understood to be both the ruling part and the source of nourishment for the body. Similar conclusions are reached in an extensive study by Gregory W. Dawes, *The Body in Question: Meaning and Metaphor in the Interpretation of Ephesians 5:21–33* (Leiden: Brill, 1998), 122–149.

in Dr. Kroeger's quotation of Chrysostom, as well as the two sentences immediately preceding this quotation and the two sentences immediately following it. This is highly relevant material that Dr. Kroeger omitted from this quotation in her attempt to argue that κεφαλή meant "source" and not "authority over." Here is the whole quotation, cited from the NPNF translation, with the words that Dr. Kroeger omitted underlined:

> *Thou art the head of the woman, let then the head regulate the rest of the body. Dost thou not see that it is not so much above the rest of the body in situation, as in forethought, directing like a steersman the whole of it?* For in the head are the eyes both of the body, and of the soul. *Hence flows to them both the faculty of seeing, and the power of directing. And the rest of the body is appointed for service, but this is set to command.* All the senses have thence their origin and their source. Thence are sent forth the organs of speech, the power of seeing, and of smelling, and all touch. For thence is derived the root of the nerves and of the bones. *Seest thou not that it is superior in forethought more than in honor? So let us rule the women; let us surpass them, not by seeking greater honor from them, but by their being more benefited by us.*[77]

The words missing from her quotation disprove the point she is trying to make, for they show the head regulating the body, directing it, and commanding it. Both at the beginning and the end of this quotation Chrysostom makes explicit the parallel with the husband's governing role as "head" meaning "one in authority." When the words that one leaves out of a quotation do not change the sense, no reader will object. But when the words that one leaves out are found to disprove the very point one is trying to make, readers will rightly conclude that one has not been truthful in handling the evidence.

(7) *Did Chrysostom understand* κεφαλή *as "source"?* Kroeger gives no further analysis of the quotation I listed above as Chrysostom (10), from *Homily 26 on 1 Corinthians* (TLG Work 156, 61.216.1–10). She simply repeats her translation of this section, except she changes "cause and primal source" to "primal cause and source." To put the matter plainly, this is assertion without argument, pure and simple. To reassert one's own idiosyncratic translation of a passage without further argument, and without giving reasons why it should be preferred to the commonly used NPNF translation of ἀρχή as "first principle" and also as "beginning" in this very passage, and without acknowledging that one's personal translation is a speculative one, hardly provides a reason for readers to be persuaded that she is correct.

(8) *What was not said*: What is interesting about this response is what was not said. No new evidence for κεφαλή as "source" was introduced. No objections were raised to my nine new citations of passages from Chrysostom where the meaning "authority over" was clear for κεφαλή. No answer

77. Chrysostom, *Homily 5 on 1-2 Thessalonians* (NPNF series 1, Vol. 13, 397). The relevant Greek portions are quoted at the beginning of this article in section II, citation (2), pp. 556–57.

was given for why she claimed a nonexistent quotation from Chrysostom to say that "only a heretic" would understand κεφαλή to mean "authority over." No explanation was given for why she said that the fathers vehemently argued for the meaning "source" when no reference she gave yielded any such vehement argument. No explanation was given for why she said the church fathers denied that Christ could be in a subordinate position relative to the Father when that very idea was seen several times in the actual references that she mentioned. No explanation was given for why she implied that the meaning "ruler, authority over" did not exist in the church fathers but failed to mention that Lampe's *Patristic Greek Lexicon* gave just this sense in its first five definitions of the metaphor as applied to persons. And no response was given to the important new letter from the editor of the Liddell-Scott *Lexicon: Supplement*, to which we now turn.

VII. Recent Lexicographical Developments Concerning κεφαλή

1. *The letter from the editor of the Liddell-Scott Lexicon.* There have been some other recent developments regarding the meaning of κεφαλή. Of considerable interest is a letter from the current editor of the *Supplement* to the Liddell-Scott *Lexicon*.

Most readers of this article will know that for several years a number of egalitarians have reinterpreted the verse, "for the husband is the *head* (κεφαλή) of the wife even as Christ is the head of the church" (Eph. 5:23). They were not inclined to agree that the husband's role as "head" meant he had authority to lead in the marriage. As an alternative interpretation that removed the idea of authority, they have said that "head" really means "source," because (they claimed) that is what the Greek word κεφαλή ("head") meant in ancient Greek literature. They went on to say that if the word "head" means "source," then there is no unique male authority in marriage and no male headship (in the commonly understood sense) taught in this verse or in the similar expression in 1 Corinthians 11:3.

A number of people did not find this explanation of "head" to be persuasive for Ephesians 5:23, because husbands are not the "source" of their wives in any ordinary sense of "source." But egalitarians continued to make this claim nonetheless and have said "source" was a common sense for κεφαλή in Greek.

The one piece of supporting evidence in Greek-English lexicons was claimed from the *Greek-English Lexicon* edited by H. G. Liddell and Robert Scott and revised by Henry Stuart Jones (ninth edition; Oxford: Clarendon, 1968, 945). This was important because this lexicon has been the standard lexicon for all of ancient Greek for over 150 years. Part of the entry for κεφαλή in the Liddell-Scott-Jones *Lexicon* (LSJ or simply Liddell-Scott) has the following headings:

II. 1. Of things, extremity
- a. In Botany
- b. In Anatomy
- c. Generally, *top, brim* of a vessel…*capital* of a column

d. In plural, *source* of a river, Herodotus 4.91 (but singular, *mouth*); generally, *source, origin*, *Orphic Fragments* 21a; *starting point* [examples: the head of time; the head of a month].

Even this entry did not prove the egalitarian claim that a *person* could be called the "source" of someone else by using κεφαλή, because the major category for this lexicon entry had to do with the end-point of "things," not with persons (but persons are in view in Ephesians 5:23, with Christ and a husband being called "head").

In an article written in 1985, I argued that the reason κεφαλή could be applied to either the *source* or the *mouth* of a river was that in these cases κεφαλη was used in a fairly common sense to mean the end-point of something. In this way, the top of a column in a building was called the "head," and the ends of the poles used to carry the Ark of the Covenant are called the "heads" of the poles in the Septuagint translation of 1 Kings 8:8. This is a natural and understandable extension of the word *head* since our heads are at the top or end of our bodies. In fact, this is what the editors of Liddell-Scott-Jones intended, for they placed the river examples as a subcategory under the general category, "of things, extremity." In 1990 I wrote on this again and attempted to answer objections that had been brought against my 1985 article by several authors.[78]

In early 1997 I sent a copy of my 1990 article on κεφαλή to the editor of the Liddell-Scott lexicon in Oxford, England, so that their editorial team might at least consider the evidence and arguments in it. The *Lexicon* itself is not undergoing revision, but a *Supplement* is published from time to time. The current editor of the Liddell-Scott *Lexicon: Supplement*, P. G. W. Glare, responded in a personal letter dated April 14, 1997, which I quote here with his permission (italics used for emphasis have been added):

> Dear Professor Grudem,
>
> Thank you for sending me the copy of your article on κεφαλή. The entry under this word in LSJ is not very satisfactory. Perhaps I could draw your attention to a section of *Lexicographica Graeca* by Dr John Chadwick (OUP 1996), though he does not deal in detail with the Septuagint and NT material. I was unable to revise the longer articles in LSJ when I was preparing the latest *Supplement*, since I did not have the financial resources to carry out a full-scale revision.
>
> I have no time at the moment to discuss all your examples individually and in any case *I am in broad agreement with your conclusions*. I might just make one or two generalizations. κεφαλή is the word normally used to translate the Hebrew ראשׁ, and this *does seem frequently to denote leader or chief* without much reference to its original anatomical sense, and here it *seems perverse to deny authority*.

78. Grudem, "Does kephalē ('Head') Mean 'Source' or "Authority Over' in Greek Literature?" 43–44; and Grudem, "The Meaning of kephalē: A Response to Recent Sutdies," 425–26, 432–33.

The supposed sense "source" of course does not exist and it was at least unwise of Liddell and Scott to mention the word. At the most they should have said "applied to the source of a river in respect of its position in its (the river's) course".

By NT times the Septuagint had been well established and one would only expect that a usage found frequently in it would come easily to such a writer as St. Paul. Where I would agree with Cervin is that in many of the examples, and I think all the Plutarch ones, we are dealing with similes or comparisons and the word itself is used in a literal sense. Here we are faced with the inadequacies of LSJ. If they had clearly distinguished between, for example, "the head as the seat of the intellect and emotions" (and therefore the director of the body's actions) and "the head as the extremity of the human or animal body" and so on, these figurative examples would naturally be attached to the end of the section they belong to and the author's intention would be clear. I hasten to add that in most cases the sense of the head as being the controlling agent is the one required and that *the idea of preeminence seems to me to be quite unsuitable*, and that there are still cases where κεφαλή can be understood, as in the Septuagint, in its transferred sense of head or leader.

Once again, thank you for sending me the article. I shall file it in the hope that one day we will be able to embark on a more thorough revision of the lexicon.

Yours sincerely,
Peter Glare[79]

This must be counted a significant statement because it comes from someone who, because of his position and scholarly reputation, could rightly be called the preeminent Greek lexicographer in the world.

2. *Other recent evidence.* The book to which Glare refers also provides evidence for the meaning "end point" and not "source" for κεφαλή—namely, John Chadwick's *Lexicographica Graeca: Contributions to the Lexicography of Ancient Greek*.[80] Chadwick, who before his recent death was a member of the Faculty of Classics at the University of Cambridge, says that his book "arose from working on the new supplement to Liddell and Scott as a member of the British Academy's Committee appointed to supervise the project" (p. v). He says, "kephalē can mean simply *either extremity of a linear object*" (p. 181) and then quotes the two examples where it can refer to either end of a river (what we would call its "source" or its "mouth"). He then says the same variety of usage is found with Greek archē, which can mean either "beginning" or "end." He explains, "in English a rope has two ends, in Greek two archai" (p. 181). Returning to kephalē, he mentions the quotation about

79. Personal letter from P. G. W. Glare to Wayne Grudem, April 14, 1997. Quoted by permission.
80. Oxford: Clarendon Press, 1996.

Zeus from the *Orphic Fragments* 21a and says, "On the same principle as the rivers, it may also mean the *starting point.*"[81]

This analysis from Chadwick is consistent with the methodological warning that I cited from him early in this article, a warning that is relevant for the few examples where the sense of κεφαλή is unclear from the immediate context. It may be tempting to allow the meaning "source" in such examples, even though the context does not require it, but Chadwick says:

> A constant problem to guard against is the proliferation of meanings.... It is often tempting to create a new sense to accommodate a difficult example, but we must always ask first, if there is any other way of taking the word which would allow us to assign the example to an already established sense.... As I have remarked in several of my notes, there may be no reason why a proposed sense should not exist, but is there any reason why it must exist?[82]

This does not mean that it is impossible that some persuasive examples of κεφαλή meaning "source" when used metaphorically of a person could turn up sometime in the future. If someone turns up new examples in the future, we will have to examine them at that point, to ask first whether they really mean "source," and second, whether they mean "source" with no sense of authority (which would be necessary for the egalitarian understanding of Ephesians 5:23). But Chadwick's warning does mean that our wisest course with a few ambiguous examples at the present time is to assign to them already established meanings if it is possible to do so without doing violence to the text in question. In the case of κεφαλή, the meanings "authority over" and "beginning" will fit *all* the ambiguous texts where "source" has been claimed as a meaning, and therefore (according to Chadwick's principle) we should not claim the meaning "source" when it is not necessary in any text and not an "already established sense."

Another analysis of κεφαλή from the perspective of modern linguistic principles is found in Max Turner, "Modern Linguistics and the New Testament," in *Hearing the New Testament.*[83] Turner, who is Director of Research and Senior Lecturer in New Testament at London Bible College, analyzes the texts where the meaning "source" has been claimed and shows that other, established senses are preferable in each case. He says that the meaning "source," as claimed by some, "is not recognized by the lexicons, and *we should consider it linguistically unsound*" (p. 167, italics added).

Finally, the primary lexicon for New Testament Greek, the Bauer-Arndt-Gingrich-Danker *Greek-English Lexicon of the New Testament and Other Early Christian Literature,*[84] has now been replaced by a new, completely revised third edition, based on the sixth German edition.

81. Chadwick, *Lexicographica Graeca*, 183, with reference to *Orphic Fragments* 21a; he also quotes in this regard *Placita,* 2.32.2.
82. Ibid., 23–24.
83. Joel Green, ed. (Grand Rapids, MI: Eerdmans, and Carlisle, England: Paternoster, 1995), 165–172.
84. 2nd edition; Chicago and London: University of Chicago Press, 1979. This is a translation based on the fifth German edition of Bauer's *Griechisch-Deutsches Wörterbuch* (1958).

Due to the extensive work of Frederick W. Danker, this third edition is known as the Bauer-Danker-Arndt-Gingrich *Lexicon*, as announced at the 1999 Society of Biblical Literature meeting in Boston. In that new lexicon the entry for κεφαλή includes these meanings: "a being of high status, *head*, fig. 2a. In the case of living beings, to denote superior rank.... 2b. Of things, *the uppermost part, extremity, end point*" (p. 542). No mention is made of the meaning "source."

3. *Is there any dispute in the lexicons about the meaning of* κεφαλή*?* Where does this leave us with regard to the dispute over κεφαλη in the ancient world? Up to this time, Liddell-Scott was the only Greek-English lexicon that even mentioned the possibility of the meaning "source" for κεφαλή.[85] All the other standard Greek-English lexicons for the New Testament gave meanings such as "leader, ruler, person in authority" and made no mention of the meaning "source" (see BAGD, 430; Louw-Nida, 1:739; also the older lexicons by Thayer, 345, and Cremer, 354; also TDNT, 3:363–372; as well as the sixth German edition of Walter Bauer, *Griechisch-deutsches Wörterbuch*,[86] 874–875; and most recently *A Greek-English Lexicon of the Septuagint*, edited by J. Lust, E. Eynikel, and K. Hauspie,[87] 254; similarly, for the patristic period see Lampe, *Patristic Greek Lexicon*, 749, as cited above).

But now the editor of the only lexicon that mentioned the meaning "source" in any connection says that κεφαλή "does seem frequently to denote leader or chief...and here it seems perverse to deny authority" and that "The supposed sense 'source' of course does not exist."

These recent developments therefore seem to indicate that there is no "battle of the lexicons" over the meaning of κεφαλή, but that the authors and editors of all the English lexicons for ancient Greek now agree (1) that the meaning "leader, chief, person in authority" clearly exists for κεφαλή, and (2) that the meaning "source" simply does not exist.

VIII. Other Recent Authors on κεφαλή

At the end of this treatment of κεφαλή, it is appropriate to mention some recent discussions in commentaries and articles. Among the commentaries, most recent writers have agreed that the meaning "authority over" is the correct sense of κεφαλή when used in a metaphorical way to refer to one person as the "head" of another or of others.[88]

85. Professor Al Wolters has pointed out to me in private correspondence (December 7, 1997), however, that the recognition that Herodotus 4:91 gives to the "sources" of the Tearus River with the plural of κεφαλή is rather standard in Greek lexicons in other languages than English. I agree that κεφαλή is applied to the sources of the river in the Herodotus passage, but I would also agree with the analyses of Glare and Chadwick that this is simply an *application* of the word to the geographical end-points of a river and fits the common sense "extremity, end-point" for κεφαλή and should not be counted as an example of a new meaning, "source." (Wolters himself thinks the Herodotus reference is a result of semantic borrowing from Persian and so has a rather un-Greek character. This is certainly possible and would not be inconsistent with my understanding of κεφαλή.)

86. Berlin and New York: de Gruyter, 1988.

87. Stuttgart: Deutsche Bibelgesellschaft, 1996.

88. Since I completed my 1990 article, the following commentaries have advocated the meaning "authority over" (or its equivalent) for κεφαλή in 1 Corinthians 11:3 or Ephesians 5:23: Andrew T. Lincoln, *Ephesians* (Word Biblical Commentary; Dallas: Word, 1990), 368–69 ("leader or ruler" in Eph. 1:22 and 5:23); Simon Kistemaker,

Among articles published since my 1990 analysis of κεφαλή, four in particular deserve mention. Joseph A. Fitzmyer, "kephalē in I Corinthians 11:3,"[89] thinks that the meaning "source" is appropriate in some extra-biblical passages, but he sees the meaning "leader, ruler, person in authority" as more frequent and thinks this is clearly the sense in 1 Corinthians 11:3. After citing significant patristic testimony to the meaning "leader, ruler" in this verse, Fitzmyer says,

> Given such a traditional interpretation of 1 Corinthians 11:3, one will have to marshall cogent and convincing arguments to say that Paul intended kephalē in that verse to mean "source" and not "one having authority over." Those who have claimed that "source" is the meaning intended by Paul have offered no other argument than their claim that kephalē would not have meant "ruler, leader, one having authority over" in Paul's day. The evidence brought forth above shows that it was certainly possible for a Hellenistic Jewish writer such as Paul to use the word in that sense. Hence, their argument has collapsed, and the traditional understanding has to be retained.[90]

Clinton E. Arnold, "Jesus Christ: 'Head' of the Church (Colossians and Ephesians),"[91] argues from first-century medical understanding that "the medical writers describe the head not only as the ruling part of the body, but also as the supply center of the body,"[92] which makes sense of the idea of the body being nourished through the head (as in Eph. 4:16) but in general supports the idea of "head" as "authority."

Gregory W. Dawes, *The Body in Question: Meaning and Metaphor in the Interpretation of Ephesians 5:21–33*,[93] has an entire chapter on "The 'Head' (κεφαλή) Metaphor" (122-149), in which he concludes that in Ephesians 1:22 and 5:22–24, the metaphor has the sense of "authority over." But in Ephesians 4:15 he thinks it conveys the sense of "source of the body's life and growth."[94] (He does not think the idea of authority is absent from that usage either.) He thinks the metaphor in which a person is spoken of as "head" is a live metaphor, and the sense has to be determined

---

Exposition of the First Epistle to the Corinthians (New Testament Commentary; Grand Rapids, MI: Baker, 1993), 365–67; Craig Blomberg, *1 Corinthians* (NIV Application Commentary; Grand Rapids, MI: Zondervan, 1994), 208–9; and Peter T. O'Brien, *The Letter to the Ephesians* (Pillar New Testament Commentary; Cambridge: Apollos, and Grand Rapids, MI: Eerdmans, 1999), 413–15. All of these commentators except O'Brien also say that the meaning "source" is a possible sense for κεφαλή but choose "leader, authority over" mainly from the force of the context in these passages. (Blomberg also notes that "authority" was the understanding of the vast majority of the church throughout history.) On the other hand, Walt Liefeld, *Ephesians* (IVP New Testament Commentary; Downers Grove, IL and Leicester, England: InterVarsity Press, 1997), 110, 144–45, is undecided among meanings "source," "ruler," and "prominent one," all of which he sees as possible.

89. "kephalē in 1 Corinthians 11:3," 52–59.
90. Ibid., p. 57.
91. *In Jesus of Nazareth: Lord and Christ*, eds. Joel B. Green and Max Turner (Grand Rapids, MI: Eerdmans and Carlisle, England: Paternoster, 1994), 346–66.
92. Arnold, ibid., 366.
93. Leiden: Brill, 1998.
94. He says that a live metaphor can take such a meaning in this context, "even if this sense is unusual" (147). Dawes says several times that one of the characteristics of a live metaphor is that it can take senses other than known, established senses, and in that way authors create new meaning.

from what first-century readers would normally have understood as the function of a literal head in relation to the body. He thinks the idea of leadership and control was clearly understood, and the idea of nourishment and provision was also understood.

Andrew Perriman, "The Head of a Woman: The Meaning of κεφαλή in 1 Cor. 11:3,"[95] argues that the meaning is "that which is most prominent, foremost, uppermost, preeminent." He raises several helpful objections against the meaning "source," but is less successful in removing the sense of authority from several passages in which he wants to see only "prominence," a sense that is not attested in the lexicons and not really required in any of the cases we have examined.

Anthony Thiselton,[96] in his massive and erudite recent commentary, *The First Epistle to the Corinthians*,[97] deals with κεφαλή in his treatment of 1 Corinthians 11:3. After an extensive review of the literature and the comment that "The translation of this verse has caused more personal agony and difficulty than any other in the epistle" (p. 811), he rejects both the translation "source" and the translation "head" (which, he says, has inevitable connotations of authority in current English). He says, "In the end we are convinced by advocates of a third view, even if barely" (p. 811)—namely, the idea of Perriman and Cervin that the main idea is that of "synecdoche and preeminence, foremost, topmost serving interactively as a metaphor drawn from the physiological head" (p. 816).[98] So Thiselton translates 1 Corinthians 11:3:

> *However, I want you to understand that while Christ is preeminent (or* head? source?*) in relation to man, man is foremost (or* head? source*) [sic] in relation to woman, and God is preeminent (or* head? source?*) in relation to Christ. (p. 800)*

His argument is that "head" (κεφαλή) is a "live metaphor" for Paul's readers, and therefore it refers to a "polymorphous concept," and that the word here has "multiple meanings" (p. 811). Since the actual physical head of a person is what is most prominent or recognizable about a person, the metaphor of "head," Thiselton thinks, would convey "the notion of *prominence*; i.e., the most conspicuous or *topmost* manifestation of that for which the term also functions as *synecdoche for the whole*" (p. 821).

What is surprising, even remarkable, about Thiselton's treatment is that after his extensive reporting of material on κεφαλή in articles and lexicons, in the end he (like Cervin and Perriman

95. *JETS* 45:2 (1994), 602–22.
96. The following material interacting with Thiselton's view has been added to this article since I first published it in *JETS* 44/1 (March 2001), 25–65.
97. Anthony Thiselton, *The First Epistle to the Corinthians*, NIGTC (Grand Rapids, MI: Eerdmans, and Carlisle, England: Paternoster, 2000), 800–22.
98. He also claims Dawes, *The Body in Question: Meaning and Metaphor in the Interpretation of Ephesians 5:21–33* in support of this view, but he minimizes the conclusion of Dawes (cited above) that the idea of rule or authority is present in all the relevant metaphorical uses that Dawes examines in Ephesians, which is the focus of his study. Thiselton, in contrast to Dawes, is seeking for a translation that does not include the idea of rule or authority.

before him) advocates a meaning for κεφαλή that is found in no Greek lexicon at all. Surely everyone would agree that in ordinary human experience a person's head is one prominent and visible part of the person (though one might argue that one's "face" is more prominent than the head generally); but in any case that does not prove that the word κεφαλή would have been used as a metaphor for "prominent part" in ancient Greek. Surely if such a meaning were evident in any ancient texts, we could expect some major lexicons to list it as a recognized meaning. Or else we should expect Thiselton to produce some ancient texts where the sense of "prominence" ***absent any idea of authority*** is clearly demonstrated. But we find neither.

And we suspect that there is something strange about a translation that cannot translate a simple noun meaning "head" with another noun (like "authority over" or even "source") but must resort to the convoluted and rather vague adjectival phrases, "prominent in relation to" and then "foremost in relation to."[99] Such phrases do not allow readers to notice the fact that even if Thiselton tried to translate the noun κεφαλή with a noun phrase representing his idea (for example, an expression like "prominent part"), it would produce the nonsensical statements, "Christ is the prominent part of man," "the man is the prominent part of the woman," and "God is the prominent part of Christ." Once we render Thiselton's idea in this bare-faced way, parallel to the way we would say that "the head is the prominent part of the body," the supposed connection with our physical heads and bodies falls apart, for while the head is a part of our physical body, a man is surely not a "part of a woman," nor is God a "part of Christ."

Moreover, while Thiselton rightly notes that metaphors usually carry multiple layers of meaning in any language, that is not true of his translation. The Greek text contains a metaphor of the head in relation to the body. But Thiselton "translates" not the mere word but the metaphor itself in a way that renders only one component of meaning (or what he claims is one component of meaning), yet he himself had said that the metaphor has "multiple meanings." In his rendering, there is no metaphor left for English readers, and no opportunity even to consider multiple meanings. But he says he cannot translate it simply as "head" because "in English-speaking contexts 'the head' almost always implies leadership and authority" (p. 817).

In fact, Thiselton's translation "preeminent" creates more problems than it solves, because it imports a wrongful kind of male superiority into the text. To be "preeminent" means to be "superior to or notable above all others; outstanding" (*American Heritage Dictionary*, 1997 edition, 1427). Does the Bible really teach that the man is "superior to" the woman? Or "notable above the woman"? Or "outstanding in comparison to the woman"? All of these senses carry objectionable connotations of male superiority, connotations that deny our equality in the image of God. And, when applied to the Father and the Son in the Trinity, they carry wrongful implications of the inferiority of the Son to the Father.

---

99. I realize there are times when a word used as a metaphor in another language simply cannot be translated directly into English without significant loss of meaning and significant addition of incorrect meaning, such as Philippians 1:8, where the RSV's "I yearn for you all with the *affection* of Christ Jesus" is necessary instead of the KJV's literal "I long after you all in the *bowels* of Jesus Christ." But even here, some roughly equivalent noun ("affection," or in Philemon 7, "hearts") is able to provide the necessary substitute.

Perhaps a realization of the objectionable connotations of male superiority in the word "preeminent" made Thiselton unable even to use it consistently in translating κεφαλή in his rendering of 1 Corinthians 11:3:

> However, I want you to understand that while Christ is preeminent (or *head? source?*) in relation to man, man is foremost (or *head? source?*) [sic] in relation to woman, and God is preeminent (or *head? source?*) in relation to Christ. (800)

But now what is gained by substituting the word "foremost"? Paul certainly cannot be speaking of location (as if a man always stands in front of a woman), for that would make no sense in this context. That leaves the sense "ahead of all others, especially in position or rank" (*American Heritage Dictionary,* 711). But if it means "the man is ahead of the woman in position or rank," then how has Thiselton avoided the sense of authority, except by cautious circumlocution that confuses more than clarifies?

Perhaps most telling of all is the fact that the one idea that Thiselton labors so long to avoid, the idea of one person having authority over another, is the one idea that is present in *every* ancient example of the construction that takes the form "Person A is the head of person or persons B." No counterexamples have ever been produced, so far as I am aware. It may be useful at this point to remind ourselves of what the ancient evidence actually says. Here are several examples:

1. David as King of Israel is called the "head" of the people he conquered (2 Sam. 22:44 [LXX 2 Kings 22:44]: "You shall keep me as the *head* of the Gentiles; a people which I knew not served me"; similarly, Psalm 18:43 (LXX 17:43).
2. The leaders of the tribes of Israel are called "heads" of the tribes (1 Kings [LXX 3 Kings] 8:1 (Alexandrinus text): "Then Solomon assembled the elders of Israel and all the *heads* of the tribes" (similar statements in Aquila, Deut. 5:23; 29:9 (10); 1 Kings [LXX 3 Kings] 8:1).
3. Jephthah becomes the "head" of the people of Gilead (Judg. 11:11, "the people made him *head* and leader over them"; also stated in 10:18; 11:8-9).
4. Pekah the son of Remaliah is the head of Samaria (Isa. 7:9, "the *head* of Samaria is the son of Remaliah").
5. The father is the head of the family (Hermas, *Similitudes* 7.3; the man is called "the *head* of the house").
6. The husband is the "head" of the wife (Eph. 5:23, "the husband is *head* of the wife even as Christ is *head* of the church"; compare similar statements found several times in Chrysostom as quoted above).
7. Christ is the "head" of the church (Col. 1:18, "He is the *head* of the body, the church"; also in Eph. 5:23).

8. Christ is the "head" of all things (Eph. 1:22, "He put all things under his feet and gave him as *head* over all things to the church").

9. God the Father is the "head" of Christ (1 Cor. 11:3, "the *head* of Christ is God").

In related statements using not metaphors but closely related similes, (1) the general of an army is said to be "like the head": Plutarch, *Pelopidas* 2.1.3: In an army, "the light-armed troops are like the hands, the cavalry like the feet, the line of men-at-arms itself like chest and breastplate, and the general is like the *head*." Similarly, (2) the Roman Emperor is called the "head" of the people in Plutarch, *Galba* 4.3: "Vindix. . .wrote to Galba inviting him to assume the imperial power, and thus to serve what was a vigorous body in need of a *head*" (compare a related statement in Plutarch, *Cicero* 14.4). And (3) the King of Egypt is called "head" of the nation in Philo, *Moses* 2.30: "As the *head* is the ruling place in the living body, so Ptolemy became among kings."

Then there are the additional citations from Chrysostom quoted earlier in this article, where (1) God is the "head" of Christ; (2) Christ is the "head" of the church; (3) the husband is the "head" of the wife; (4) Christ is the "head" of all things; (5) church leaders are the "head" of the church; and (6) a woman is the "head" of her maidservant. In all six of these cases, as we noted, he uses language of rulership and authority to explain the role of the "head" and uses language of submission and obedience to describe the role of the "body."[100]

In addition, there are several statements from various authors indicating a common understanding that the physical head functioned as the "ruling" part of the body: (1) Plato says that the head "reigns over all the parts within us" (*Timaeus* 44.D). (2) Philo says, "the *head* is the ruling place in the living body" (*Moses* 2:30), and "the mind is *head* and ruler of the sense-faculty in us" (*Moses* 2.82), and "'*Head*' we interpret allegorically to mean the ruling part of the soul" (*On Dreams* 2.207), and "Nature conferred the sovereignty of the body on the *head*" (*The Special Laws* 184). (3) Plutarch says, "We affectionately call a person 'soul' or '*head*' from his ruling parts" (*Table Talk* 7.7 [692.e.1]). Clint Arnold and Gregory Dawes, in the studies mentioned above, adduce other examples of the physical head seen as ruling or controlling the body in ancient literature. Though they find examples where the head or the brain are seen as the source of something as well, they do not claim that these examples can be understood to deny a simultaneous ruling or governing function to the physical head. If the physical head was seen as a source of something like nourishment, it also surely was seen to have control and governance over the physical body.

Regarding "head" as applied metaphorically to persons, to my knowledge no one has yet produced one text in ancient Greek literature (from the eighth century BC to the fourth century AD) where a person is called the κεφαλή ("head") of another person or group *and that person is not the one in authority over that other person or group.* The alleged meaning "prominent without authority," like the meaning "source without authority," now sixteen years after the publication of my

100. See my two previous articles on κεφαλή, mentioned at the beginning of this article, for additional references like the ones cited here.

1985 study of 2,336 examples of κεφαλή, has still not been supported with *any* citation of *any* text in ancient Greek literature. Over fifty examples of κεφαλή meaning "ruler, authority over" have been found, but no examples of the meaning of "source without authority."

Of course, I would agree with Thiselton that in all of these cases the person who is "head" is also "prominent" in some sense. That is because some sense of prominence accompanies the existence of leadership or authority. And that overtone or connotation is not lost in English if we translate κεφαλή as "head," for in English the "head coach" or the "head of the company" or the "head of the household" has some prominence as well. But why must we try to *avoid* the one meaning that is represented in all the lexicons and is unmistakably present in every instance of this kind of construction, the idea of authority? One cannot *prove* that this great effort to avoid the idea of authority is due to the fact that male authority in marriage is immensely unpopular in much of modern culture, but we cannot help but note that it is in this current historical context that such efforts repeatedly occur.

In short, Thiselton has advocated a meaning that is unattested in any lexicon and unproven by any new evidence. It fails fundamentally in explaining the metaphor because it avoids the idea of authority, the one component of meaning that is present in every ancient example of κεφαλή that takes the form, "person A is the head of person(s) B."

Finally, some treatments of κεφαλή in egalitarian literature deserve mention. Several treatments have been remarkably one-sided, particularly in their habit of failing even to mention significant literature on another side of this question.[101] Grace Ying May and Hyunhye Pokrifka Joe in a 1997 article, "Setting the Record Straight," say, "the word translated 'head' in Corinthians and Ephesians does not suggest male authority over women.... Paul...defines 'head' (kephalē in Greek) as the 'origin' of beings."[102] More remarkable is an article by Judy Brown, professor of church ministries at Central Bible College, Springfield, Missouri. Writing in the fall of 1999, Brown says of Ephesians 5:23, "the only thing that matters is the meaning of 'head' in first-century Greek, the language of Paul's letter. The evidence is overwhelming that the word meant 'source, supply' as in the 'fountainhead or headwaters of a stream or river.'"[103] Rebecca Groothuis in *Good News*

101. Kroeger herself is one example of this. Though she does cite my 1985 article in her bibliography, along with Richard Cervin's 1989 response to that study, she surprisingly does not mention my much longer 1990 study, which includes a lengthy response to Cervin, though the *Dictionary of Paul and His Letters* was published in 1993.

102. *Priscilla Papers* 11/1 (Winter 1997), 3. In their footnotes on p. 9, only articles on κεφαλή representing the "source" interpretation are even mentioned, in spite of the fact that this 1997 article was published long after my 1985 and 1990 articles, and after Fitzmyer's 1993 article. When a writer gives readers access to only one side of the argument, it does not suggest confidence that one's position would be more persuasive if readers knew about arguments on both sides.

103. Judy Brown, "I Now Pronounce You Adam and Eve," *Priscilla Papers* 13/4 (Fall 1999), 2–3. In the next sentence she refers readers to the literature on this question, but mentions only writings by Berkeley and Alvera Mickelsen (1986), Gilbert Bilezikian (1985), Gordon Fee (1987), and herself (1996). It is difficult to explain how Brown, as a college professor, could either be unaware of major studies on the other side of this question or else be aware of them and intentionally fail to mention them at all, and yet say that the evidence is "overwhelming" in favor of the meaning "source."

for Women ignores the most significant opposing literature in the same way.[104] However, not all egalitarian treatments have been one-sided in the literature they mention. For example, Craig Keener, *Paul, Women, and Wives*,[105] quotes significant treatments from both sides and says that "authority" is a possible sense for κεφαλή and thinks that would have been the acceptable sense in the culture to which Paul wrote.[106]

We may hope that articles and commentaries written in the future will take into account an increasing consensus in the major lexicons that the meaning "authority over" is firmly established for κεφαλή, and that the meaning "source," as Peter Glare says, "does not exist."

IX. A Note on Accuracy in Academic Work

One final comment should be made about the widely influential article on "head" with which we began. This article by Catherine Kroeger in *Dictionary of Paul and His Letters*, a major reference work, should be troubling to those who care about accuracy in scholarly work. The article is peppered with references to extra-biblical literature and therefore gives the appearance of careful scholarship. But only someone with access to a major research library, the ability to translate extensive passages from untranslated ancient Greek literature, and many days free for such research could ever have discovered that this is not careful scholarship. In fact, in several sections its disregard of facts is so egregious that it fails even to meet fundamental requirements of truthfulness.

With respect to patristic material, the striking new quotation that she said was from Chrysostom does not exist. Her claims for the meaning of κεφαλή in Chrysostom are proven false by numerous statements in Chrysostom's writings. The other patristic references that she cites either give clear support to the meaning "leader, authority over" or else are ambiguous. She fails to mention that Lampe's *Patristic Greek Lexicon*, on the page on which several of her references are found, does not give the meaning "source," which she claims for κεφαλή. She also fails to mention that the meaning "chief, superior" or its equivalent occurs five times on that same page as the primary metaphorical meaning that attaches to κεφαλή when it is used of persons.

With respect to classical Greek material, of the fourteen sources she cites to prove "the classical view of head as source," four do not even contain the term κεφαλή. Of the remaining ten, only three are from the pre-New Testament "classical" period in Greek. No dates were provided for any references, some of which came from the third, fifth, and even ninth century AD Several references were cited in such obscure ways that they took literally days to locate. Six of the references repeat the same sentence about Zeus, in which Zeus is seen as the "beginning" or "first in a series," but not as

---

104. Rebecca Groothuis, *Good News for Women* (Grand Rapids, MI: Baker, 1997) favors the meaning "source" (151) but does not even mention my studies or those of Fitzmyer in her endnotes (252–54, n. 13). Such oversight, whether intentional or accidental, does not inspire confidence that Groothuis's consideration of the matter has been thorough or careful.

105. Peabody, MA: Hendrickson, 1992.

106. Ibid., 34.

the "source." Two of the references actually speak of "head" as "leader, one in authority." Several of the sentences use κεφαλή with ἀρχή, but the ambiguity of ἀρχή makes them inconclusive as evidence, and the clear use of ἀρχή in Chrysostom and others to mean "ruler" suggests this as a possible meaning in the ambiguous texts as well. In sum, no evidence clearly demonstrated the meaning "source," and several pieces of evidence argued against it.

In terms of accuracy with sources, only fourteen of the twenty-four references cited were both accurate citations and contained the word κεφαλή, "head."

Then in her 1998 response to all of these concerns about accuracy, rather than correcting these errors, Dr. Kroeger gave yet another citation from Chrysostom that, when checked, showed that she had omitted contrary evidence that was at the beginning, middle, and end of the very passage she cited. Sadly, this is not the first time concerns have been raised about the trustworthiness of materials written by this author.[107]

People who read reference books have a right to expect that they will be basically trustworthy, and that where evidence is cited it will, if checked, provide clear support for the points being claimed. When one does check the evidence in an article and it turns out to be unreliable, that undermines confidence in the trustworthiness of the author, editors, and publisher who have produced the work. Because this topic has been so controversial, one would expect that those responsible for the volume would have taken particular care to ensure accuracy. But did anyone check any of this evidence? Did any editor at IVP?[108]

Yet the primary responsibility for this article rests with Dr. Kroeger, and the article is troubling at its core, not only for what it claims, but for the model of scholarly work that it puts forth. The scholarly task is an exciting one, especially in the area of biblical studies. But it is too large for any one person, and scholarship can be advanced in a helpful way when we are able to read and benefit from one another's work. Even when we disagree with the conclusions of an article, we should be able to expect that the citations of evidence are fundamentally reliable.

But the lack of care in the use of evidence as manifested in this article, if followed by others, would throw the scholarly process into decline. We would wonder if we could trust anything that was claimed by anyone else unless we checked the original data for ourselves. For most topics there would never be time to do this, and thus all the gains of scholarship in our major reference books would no longer be useful, for neither scholars nor laypersons would know if any reference works could be trusted.

---

107. See Albert Wolters's review of Catherine and Richard Kroeger, *I Suffer Not a Woman* (Grand Rapids, MI: Baker, 1992) in *Calvin Theological Journal* 28 (1993): "...their book is precisely the sort of thing that has too often given evangelical scholarship a bad name...there is a host of subordinate detail that is misleading or downright false" (209–10). See also Stephen Baugh's review of the same book in WTJ 56 (1994), 153–71, in which he says that the book "wanders widely from the facts" (155), is "wildly anachronistic" (163), and "contains outright errors of fact" (165).

108. The editorial work for this volume was done by InterVarsity Press in the United States. The volume was also published (but not edited) by Inter-Varsity Press in the United Kingdom (IVP-UK), a separate company.

Such a threat to the trustworthiness of facts cited in academic articles and reference books is a far more serious matter than the meaning of an individual Greek word, even a word as important as κεφαλή. We may differ for our whole lives on the *interpretation* of facts, for that is the nature of the scholarly task. But if our citations of the facts themselves cannot be trusted, then the foundations are destroyed.

Should We Move Beyond the New Testament to a Better Ethic? An Analysis of William J. Webb, *Slaves, Women and Homosexuals: Exploring the Hermeneutics of Cultural Analysis* (Downers Grove, IL: InterVarsity Press, 2001).[1]

Wayne Grudem

How can Christians today know which parts of the Bible are "culturally relative" and which parts apply to all believers in all cultures throughout history? William Webb has provided an entirely new approach to that question in a book that focuses specifically on slavery, men's and women's roles, and homosexuality, but that also provides a general approach to the question of cultural relativity, an approach that Webb hopes will prove useful for solving similar questions on other topics.

The book provides an extensive and rather complex system of cultural analysis that Webb calls a "redemptive-movement hermeneutic." As I explain more fully below, the essence of Webb's view is his claim that the ethical commands of the New Testament were a substantial improvement over the ethics of the surrounding culture (and sometimes an improvement over the ethics of the Old Testament), but the New Testament did not yet contain the "ultimate ethic," the goal toward which God was gradually moving His people. Today we need to discover what

1. This review article first appeared in *Journal of the Evangelical Theological Society* 47/2 (June 2004): 299–346, and is used by permission. One section of that review article has been moved to the "Additional Note" at the end of chapter 9 in this book, however (see pp. 397–402).

William Webb's book was published in the United Kingdom by Authentic Media, not by IVP-UK, which is a separate company from IVP-USA.

direction the "redemptive movement" of the New Testament was heading, and from that develop a set of ethical standards that is superior to what is commanded in the New Testament.

I expect that most readers will find Webb's explanation of why the Bible regulated but did not explicitly prohibit slavery to be a helpful analysis. Readers may also find helpful Webb's explanation of why the Bible's prohibitions against homosexual conduct are transcultural, not culturally relative. This is because Webb has read widely concerning slavery and homosexuality in the cultural backgrounds that surrounded the writers of the Old and New Testaments, and his book provides a helpful resource in those areas. However, as Thomas Schreiner pointed out in an earlier review,[2] Webb's opposition to homosexuality is a dangerously weak basis for evangelicals to use, because he fails to quote or discuss in any detail the strongest New Testament text on homosexuality, Romans 1:26–27, where Paul bases his argument on the natural order that God created (he gives the text only one paragraph on p. 109, lumping it together with Leviticus 18:22 and 20:13).[3] Webb never argues that homosexual conduct is wrong because the New Testament says so and the New Testament is God's final revelation to us in this age (to argue this way would be contrary to Webb's system; see below).

Regarding biblical roles for men and women, Webb's book provides a significant new challenge to those who believe that the Bible teaches that wives should be subject to their husbands today (according to several New Testament passages), and that some governing and teaching roles in the church, such as the office of elder or pastor, are restricted to men. In contrast to many egalitarians who have argued that the New Testament does not teach that wives should be subject to their husbands, or that only men should be elders, Webb takes a different approach: He believes that the New Testament *does* teach these things *for the culture in which the New Testament was written*, but that in today's culture the treatment of women is an area in which "*a better ethic than the one expressed in the isolated words of the text is possible*" (p. 36, italics added). (When Webb speaks of the "isolated words of the text," he does not mean the words interpreted in isolation from their immediate and broader context in the New Testament itself. He means the words interpreted in isolation from his system, in isolation from an application of his redemptive-movement hermeneutic to move us to a higher ethical standard than the New Testament.)

Webb admits that the Old and New Testaments improved the treatment of women when compared with their surrounding cultures, but, he says,

> If one adopts a redemptive-movement hermeneutic, the softening of patriarchy (which Scripture itself initiates) can be taken a considerable distance further. Carrying the redemptive movement within Scripture to a more improved expression

2. Thomas R. Schreiner, "Review of *Slaves, Women, and Homosexuals*," JBMW 7/1 (Spring 2002), 48–49, 51 (his review was originally published in *The Southern Baptist Journal of Theology* 6/1 (2002), 46–64).
3. Webb also includes Romans 1:26–27 in a list of verses in a footnote on p. 161, and it appears in the title of an article in the bibliography on p. 287.

for gender relationships... [today] ends in either ultra-soft patriarchy or complementary egalitarianism. (39)

Later in the book, Webb defines such "ultra-soft patriarchy" as a position in which there are no unique leadership roles for men in marriage or in the church, but men are given "a certain level of *symbolic* honor" (243). He defines "complementary egalitarianism" as full interdependence and "mutual submission" within marriage, and the only differences in roles are "based upon biological differences between men and women," so that Webb would favor "a greater participation of women in the early stages of child rearing" (241). Thus, Webb's "ultra-soft patriarchy" differs from his "complementary egalitarianism" only in the slight bit of "symbolic honor" which ultra-soft patriarchy would still give to men.

Because of its detail, novelty, and the complexity of its approach, this book deserves to be taken seriously by complementarians. However, because of concerns that are detailed below, I do not think that the book succeeds in showing that male headship in the home and the church is culturally relative. Nor do I believe that the book provides a system for analyzing cultural relativity that is ultimately helpful for Christians today.

Concerns related to the authority of Scripture and the finality of the New Testament.

1. Webb's trajectory hermeneutic nullifies in principle the moral authority of the entire New Testament and thus contradicts the Reformation principle of sola Scriptura.

At first glance, it may not seem as though Webb "nullifies" the moral authority of the entire New Testament, because he agrees, for example, that homosexual conduct is morally wrong and that the New Testament condemnations of homosexual conduct are transcultural (pp. 39–41, 250–2, and many other places in the book). He also affirms that the New Testament admonitions for children to be subject to their parents are transcultural (p. 212). Is Webb not then affirming that some aspects of New Testament ethics are transcultural?

The important point to realize is the *basis* on which Webb affirms that these are transcultural commands. Most evangelicals today read a text such as, "Children, obey your parents in the Lord, for this is right" (Ephesians 6:1), and conclude that children *today* are to obey their parents because the New Testament was written for Christians in the New Covenant age (after Christ's death). Since we Christians today are also in the New Covenant age (the period of time until Christ returns), this command is binding on us today.

Most evangelicals today reason similarly about the New Testament texts concerning homosexual conduct (see, for example, Romans 1:26–27; 1 Corinthians 6:9), and conclude that these are morally binding on us because these texts were written to New Covenant Christians, and we today are also part of the New Covenant.

But for Webb, *the process is entirely different*, and the basis of authority is different. The commands concerning children and homosexuals are binding on us today not *because they were written to New Covenant Christians* and we today are part of the New Covenant (I could not find such a consideration anywhere in Webb's book), but *because these commands have passed through the filtering system of Webb's eighteen criteria* and have survived. Actually, the command concerning children has not entirely survived his filtering process. Webb believes that the commands for children to obey their parents actually teach that *adult children* should continue to be obedient to their parents throughout their adult lives, but that this aspect of the command was culturally relative and need not be followed by us today (see p. 212).[4]

In this way, it is fair to say that *Webb's system invalidates the moral authority of the entire New Testament*, at least in the sense that we today should be obedient to the moral commands that were written to New Covenant Christians. Instead, only those commands are binding that have passed through his eighteen-part filter.

Someone may object, "Doesn't everyone have to use some kind of cultural filter? Doesn't everyone have to test the New Testament commands to see if they are culturally relative or transcultural before deciding whether to obey them?"

My response is that there is a fundamental difference in approach. Most evangelicals (including me) say that we *are* under the moral authority of the New Testament, and we are morally obligated to obey its commands when we are in the same situation as that addressed in the New Testament command (such as being a parent, a child, a person contemplating a divorce, a church selecting elders or deacons, a church preparing to celebrate the Lord's Supper, a husband, a wife, and so forth). When there is no exact modern equivalent to some aspect of a command (such as "honor the king" in 1 Peter 2:17), then we are still obligated to obey the command, but we do so by *applying* it to situations that are essentially similar to the one found in the New Testament. Therefore, "honor the king" is applied to honoring the president or the prime minister. In fact, in several such cases the immediate context contains pointers to broader applications (such as 1 Peter 2:13–14, which mentions being subject to "every authority instituted among men," including the "king" and "governors" as specific examples). (For the small handful of slightly more difficult cases, such as a "holy kiss" and "foot washing," see the additional note at the end of chapter 9.)[5]

But with Webb the situation is entirely different. He does not consider the moral commands of the New Testament to represent a perfect or final moral system for Christians. They are rather a pointer that "provides the direction toward the divine destination, but its literal, isolated words

---

4. Webb does not consider the far simpler possibility that first-century readers would have understood the word "children" (Greek *tekna*) to apply only to people who were not adults, and so we today can say that Ephesians 6:1 applies to modern believers in just the same way that it applied to first-century believers, and no "cultural filters" need to be applied to that command.

5. See chapter 9, pp. 397–402.

are not always the destination itself. Sometimes God's instructions are simply designed to get his flock moving" (60).

At the heart of Webb's system is what he calls a "redemptive-movement hermeneutic." He says that some may prefer calling his approach a "progressive" or "developmental" or "trajectory" hermeneutic and he says "that is fine" (31). Webb explains his hermeneutic by what he calls "the X→Y→Z Principle." The letter Y indicates what the Bible says about a topic. Webb says, "The *central position* (*Y*) stands for where the isolated words of the Bible are in their development of a subject" (31). The letter *X* represents "the perspective of the *original culture*," and the letter *Z* represents "an *ultimate ethic*," that is, God's final ideal that the Bible is moving toward.

Therefore in Webb's system, what evangelicals have ordinarily understood to be "the teaching of the Bible" on particular subjects is in fact only a point along the way (indicated by the letter *Y*) toward the development of a final or ultimate ethic (*Z*). Webb says,

> The X→Y→Z Principle illustrates how numerous aspects of the biblical text were *not* written to establish a utopian society with complete justice and equity. They were written within a cultural framework with limited moves toward an ultimate ethic. (31)

Therefore, Webb discovers a number of points where "our contemporary culture" has a better ethic than what is found in the words of the Bible. Our culture has a better ethic today "where it happens to reflect a better social ethic—one closer to an *ultimate ethic* (*Z*) than to the ethic revealed in the isolated words of the biblical text" (31).

Webb's approach to Scripture can also be seen in the way he deals with biblical texts regarding slavery. Most evangelical interpreters today would say that the New Testament does not command or encourage or endorse slavery, but rather tells Christians who were slaves how they should conduct themselves within that situation, and also gives principles that would modify and ultimately lead to the abolition of slavery (1 Corinthians 7:21–22; Galatians 3:28; Philemon 16, 21). By contrast, Webb believes that the Bible actually endorses slavery; however, it is a kind of slavery with "better conditions and fewer abuses" (37).

Webb's redemptive-movement hermeneutic approaches the slavery question by saying that the original culture (*X*) approved of "slavery with many abuses" (37). Partially correcting that original culture, the Bible (*Y*) endorses "slavery with better conditions and fewer abuses" (37). However, Webb believes that on the issue of slavery "our culture is much closer to an ultimate ethic than it is to the unrealized ethic reflected in the isolated words of the Bible" (37). Today, the ethic of our culture, which is superior to that of the Bible, has "slavery eliminated and working conditions often improved" (37). Webb believes our culture is much closer to an "ultimate ethic" (Z) in which we will see "wages maximized for all" (p. 37).[6]

6. Webb does not explain what he means by "wages maximized for all," but readers might wonder if it means that profits would be minimized and capital investment would be minimized, in order for wages to be maximized?

At the end of the book, Webb recapitulates the results of his analysis regarding slavery:

> Scripture does not present a "finalized ethic" in every area of human relationship.... To stop where the Bible stops (with its isolated words) ultimately fails to reapply the redemptive spirit of the text as it spoke to the original audience. It fails to see that further reformation is possible.... While Scripture had a positive influence in its time, we should take that redemptive spirit and move to an even better, more fully-realized ethic today. (247)

Therefore, rather than saying that *the New Testament* does not endorse or command slavery, Webb believes that it does approve a system of slavery for the people at the time at which it was written. However, in its modifications and regulations of slavery, the Bible starts us along a trajectory that would lead to the ultimate abolition of slavery, though the New Testament never actually reaches that point.

Webb asks why the Bible is this way:

> Why does God convey his message in a way that reflects a less-than-ultimate ethic...that evidences an underlying redemptive spirit and some movement in a positive direction, it often permits its words to stop short of completely fulfilling such a spirit? Why did God not simply give us a clearly laid out blueprint for an ultimate-ethic utopia-like society? How could a God of absolute justice not give us a revelation concerning absolute justice on every page? (57)

Webb's answer to these questions is to see this incomplete movement toward an ultimate ethic as a manifestation of God's wisdom. In showing us that the Bible was making progress against the surrounding culture, but not completely correcting the surrounding culture, we can see God's pastoral wisdom (58), His pedagogical skill (60), His evangelistic care for people who might not have heard the gospel if it proclaimed an ultimate ethic (63), and other aspects of God's wisdom (64–66).

According to Webb's system, then, Christians can no longer simply go to the New Testament, begin to read the moral commands in one of Paul's epistles, and believe that they should obey them. According to Webb, that would be to use a "static hermeneutic" that just reads the "isolated words of the text" and fails to understand "the spirit-movement component of meaning which significantly transforms the application of texts for subsequent generations" (34). Rather, we must realize that the New Testament teachings simply represent one stage in a trajectory of movement toward an ultimate ethic.

So how can Christians discover this "ultimate ethic"? Webb takes the rest of the book to

---

Or does it mean that all would have equal wages, since "all" would have maximized wages and this must mean that none would have lower wages than others? He does not make clear in what sense he thinks wages would be "maximized for all."

explain eighteen fairly complex criteria by which Christians must evaluate the commands of the Bible and thereby discover the more just, more equitable ethical system toward which the Bible was heading. Once that ultimate ethic has been discovered, that ultimate ethic is the moral standard that we should follow and obey.

What this means in actual practice is that the moral authority of the New Testament is completely nullified *at least in principle*. There may be some New Testament commands that Webb concludes actually do represent an ultimate ethic, but even then we should obey them *not because they are taught in the New Testament*, but because Webb's system has found that what they teach is also the moral standard found in his "ultimate ethic."

The implications of this for Christian morality are extremely serious. It means that our ultimate authority is no longer the Bible but Webb's system. Of course, he claims that the "redemptive spirit" that drives his hermeneutic for each area of ethics is derived from the biblical text, but by his own admission this "redemptive spirit" is not the same as the teachings of the Bible, but rather is derived from Webb's analysis of the interaction between the ancient culture and the biblical text. Here is his key explanation:

> The final and most important characteristic of a redemptive-movement hermeneutic is its focus on the spirit of a text.... The coinage "redemptive-movement hermeneutic" is derived from a concern that Christians apply the *redemptive spirit* within Scripture, not merely, or even primarily, its isolated words. *Finding the underlying spirit of a text is a delicate matter. It is not as direct or explicit as reading the words on the page.* In order to grasp the spirit of a text, *the interpreter must listen for how the text sounds within its various social contexts*. Two life settings are crucial: the broader, foreign ancient Near Eastern and Greco-Roman (ANE/GR) social context and the immediate, domestic Israelite/church setting. One must ask, what change/improvement is the text making in the lives of people in the covenant community? And, how does the text influence the larger ANE/GR world? Through reflecting upon these social-setting questions *the modern reader will begin to sense the redemptive spirit of the text*. Also, a third setting permits one another way of discovering the redemptive spirit, namely, the canonical movement across various biblical epochs. (53, italics added)

This paragraph is remarkable for the candor with which it reveals the subjective and indeterminate nature of Webb's ethical system. If the heart of the "most important characteristic" of his hermeneutic is discovered through "reflecting upon" the way the Bible interacts with ancient Near Eastern and Greco-Roman cultures, and through such reflection the interpreter will "begin to sense the redemptive spirit of the text," we have entered a realm so subjective that no two interpreters in the future will be likely to agree on where the "redemptive spirit of the text" that they are beginning to "sense" is leading, and what kind of "ultimate ethic" they should count as God's will for them.

Those with a predisposition toward socialism will no doubt be delighted that Webb has begun "to sense" a "redemptive spirit" that will lead to "wages maximized for all" (37). But those more inclined to capitalism will no doubt "begin to sense" quite another "redemptive spirit" in which the dominant biblical themes of freedom and liberty and fair reward for one's labor lead to an "ultimate ethic" (*Z*) that encourages investment and a free enterprise system, one with *maximization of profits* for those worthy individuals who through their business activities best meet the material needs of mankind, and thus by means of the high quality of goods they produce for others best show that they love their neighbors as themselves.

No doubt Arminians will "begin to sense the redemptive spirit" of Arminianism moving against the fatalism of the ancient world in a much more Arminian direction than we find even in the New Testament. And Calvinists, through serious and sober reflection upon the way in which the biblical text corrects the puny, weak gods in the Greek and Roman pantheon, will "begin to sense the redemptive spirit" of Calvinism moving through the New Testament toward an even higher emphasis on the sovereignty of God than we find in any current New Testament texts.

And on and on it will go. Baptists will "begin to sense the redemptive spirit" of believer's baptism as the New Testament corrects the all-inclusive nature of the religions of the ancient world, and paedobaptists will "begin to sense the redemptive spirit" of inclusion of infants in the covenant community, as the New Testament decisively corrects the neglect and abuse of children found in many ancient cultures. People seeking justification for their desire to obtain a divorce will "begin to sense the redemptive spirit" of more and more reasons for divorce, moving from the one reason that Jesus allowed (adultery in Matthew 19:9), to the increasing freedom found in Paul, who allows a second ground for divorce (desertion by an unbeliever in 1 Corinthians 7:15), along a trajectory toward many other reasons for divorce as we move toward an "ultimate ethic" (*Z*) where everyone should be completely happy with his or her spouse.

Now Webb may object that these hypothetical "redemptive spirit" findings could not be derived from a responsible use of his eighteen criteria. On the other hand, I have lived in the academic world for over thirty years, and I have a great deal of confidence in the ability of scholars to take a set of eighteen criteria and make a case for almost anything they desire. But whether or not my hypothetical suggestions are the result of a proper use of Webb's criteria, the point remains: *the standard is no longer what the New Testament says, but rather the point toward which some biblical scholar thinks the Bible was moving*. And that is why I believe that Webb's redemptive-movement hermeneutic nullifies in principle the moral authority of the entire New Testament.

Webb's system therefore constitutes a direct denial of the Reformation principle of *sola Scriptura,* the doctrine that "the Bible alone" is the ultimate authority for what we are to believe and do, and that its teachings constitute the norm to which all our beliefs and practices are to conform. In Webb's system the norm is no longer the teachings of the Bible but what we can discover about the "ultimate ethic" (*Z*) toward which the Bible was heading.[7]

This is extremely troubling because the principle of *sola Scriptura* is the principle that separated Protestantism from Roman Catholicism with respect to an ultimate authority. The Roman Catholic Church appealed both to Scripture *and to the tradition of the church as it developed after the time of the New Testament.* Martin Luther and the other Reformers struggled greatly to insist that the teachings of "the Bible *alone*" are our ultimate authority for doctrine and conduct. When Webb makes his "ultimate ethic" the product of ethical development *after* the New Testament, he advocates a system that is much more akin to Roman Catholicism than to historic Protestant belief.

2. Webb fails in nearly every section of the book to recognize that Christians are no longer bound by Old Covenant laws, and thus he neglects to use the fundamental structural division of the entire Bible (the difference between the Old and New Testaments) as a means of determining moral obligations for Christians today.

It is remarkable that in most of the sections of the book (not all), Webb fails to distinguish between the teachings of the Old Testament and the teachings of the New. Thus, in dealing with slavery, he often combines New Testament and Old Testament passages in the same list, without noticing any distinction between them (44, 74–76, 163–64, and elsewhere). He does the same thing with texts referring to women (46–47, 76–81, 160, 165–67), and primogeniture (94–95, 136–42), and with other elements of the Mosaic law code.

Although Webb occasionally gives limited attention to what he calls "canonical movement" from the Old Testament to the New (see pp. 77–78 for example), for him such development is just additional evidence that we should move beyond the New Testament even as the New Testament developed beyond the Old. He sees the Old and New Testaments as just two steps along the way toward further redemptive-movement in ethical development beyond the New

---

7. In a recent article Webb responded to Thomas Schreiner's criticism of him (in "Review of Slaves, Women, and Homosexuals") by affirming that he too believes that "for Christians the NT is most assuredly our final expression of canonical revelation.... We do not expect any further revelation until the coming of Jesus Christ.... The finality of the NT as the apex of revelation is not actually a point of disagreement between Schreiner and myself" (William Webb, "The Limits of a Redemptive-Movement Hermeneutic: A Focused Response to T. R. Schreiner," *Evangelical Quarterly* 75:4 [2003], 328–29). This sounds completely orthodox until we find what Webb means by these statements. He thinks the New Testament is our final revelation in that it shows that we must move beyond its moral teachings, and thus it proves his system to be correct. He says, "I would argue that the NT expresses an ultimate ethic in its underlying redemptive spirit (redemptive-movement meaning) but not in all of its concrete 'frozen in time' particulars" (329). He says the NT revelation is not final in its realization of ethical standards; it expresses "an incremental or developing (not ultimate) ethic in certain concrete particulars" (330). This is anything but the Reformation principle of *sola Scriptura*, in which the teachings and moral commands of the New Testament are themselves our final and ultimate authority. Webb's response to Schreiner is also significant because he simply repeats his previous evidence and arguments and does not introduce any new evidence or arguments in response to Schreiner's criticisms.

Testament. *He never considers the possibility that the development from Old Testament to New Testament is the end, and that the New Testament itself provides the final ethical standard for Christians in the New Covenant.*

When Webb claims that "a redemptive-movement hermeneutic has always been a major part of the historic church, apostolic and beyond" (35), and therefore that all Christians believe in some kind of "redemptive movement" hermeneutic, he fails to make one important distinction: Evangelicals have always held that the redemptive movement within Scripture ends with the New Testament! Webb carries it beyond the New Testament.

In doing this Webb fails to recognize the centrality of Jesus Christ for all of history. Yes, there is movement and development beyond the Old Testament, because in the Old Testament at many times and in many ways, "God spoke to our forefathers through the prophets." By contrast, "in these last days he *has spoken to us by his Son*, whom he appointed heir of all things, and through whom he made the universe" (Hebrews 1:1–2). In the writings of the New Testament we have a written record of the revelation that God gave us in Christ and the revelation that Christ gave to His apostles. We are not to look for doctrinal or ethical development beyond the teachings and commands of the New Testament, for that would be to look for development beyond the supreme revelation of God in His Son.

Yes, the New Testament explicitly tells us that we are no longer under the regulations of the Old Covenant (Hebrews 8:6–13), so we have clear warrant for saying the sacrificial laws and dietary laws are no longer binding on us. And we do see the apostles in a process of coming to understand the inclusion of the Gentiles in the church (Acts 15; Galatians 2:1–14; 3:28). But *that process was completed within the New Testament*, and the commands given to Christians in the New Testament say nothing about excluding Gentiles from the church! We do not have to progress on a "trajectory" beyond the New Testament to discover that.

Christians living in the time of Paul's epistles were living under the New Covenant. And Christians today are also living under the New Covenant. This is "the New Covenant in my blood" (1 Corinthians 11:25), which Jesus established and which we affirm every time we take the Lord's Supper. That means that we are living in *the same period in God's plan for "the history of redemption"* as the first-century Christians. And that is why we can read and directly apply the New Testament today.

To attempt to go *beyond* the New Testament documents and derive our authority from "where the New Testament was heading" is to reject the very documents that God gave us to govern our life under the New Covenant until Christ returns. It is to reject the Reformation doctrine of *sola Scriptura* and establish an entirely new basis of authority distinct from the Bible itself.

When Webb does touch on the relationship between the Old and New Testaments, he says that he is not going to decide how the Old Testament relates to the New. After saying that he rejects both the idea that "*only* those particulars of the Mosaic law that the New Testament *expressly sanctions* apply to New Testament believers," and the idea that "Christians are bound to obey *all* those particulars in the Mosaic law that the New Testament does not *expressly abrogate*," Webb tells us:

> Nor am I going to establish a more durable and alternative dictum about how the Old Testament relates to the modern Christian. Such is beyond the scope of this work. (205)

The problem is that throughout the book Webb uses dozens of examples from the Old Testament to establish and support the need to use his eighteen criteria in determining what is culturally relative, and to support the idea that we should abandon what he calls "biblical patriarchy" and move beyond it by "taking...a redemptive-movement approach to the present-day application of biblical patriarchy" (p. 172, after appealing to several Mosaic covenant laws regarding the treatment of women [165–67, for example]). Rather than saying, for example, that we should not follow the law that a woman was to be stoned if she was not a virgin at the time of marriage (Deuteronomy 22:20–21) *because we are under the New Covenant and no longer subject to the laws of the Mosaic covenant*, Webb uses this law about stoning as one of his examples showing that "the Christian who embraces the redemptive-movement hermeneutic will surely carry the redemptive spirit of *the biblical text* forward in today's setting" (167). What is telling in this statement (and dozens like it throughout the book) is his phrase "the biblical text." Anything found in any part of the Bible for Webb is simply part of "the biblical text," which is heavily affected by its ancient culture and which we need to move beyond today.

When Webb repeatedly gives long lists of Mosaic laws on slavery or wives, and then says it would be foolish to obey what "the Bible" says on these subjects today, unsuspecting readers may think that he has built a persuasive case for his eighteen criteria. But he has not, because the change from Old Covenant to New Covenant means that those dozens of Mosaic laws are not part of what "the Bible" requires of Christians today. We are not under the Mosaic law.[8]

Yet this fundamental omission is pervasive in Webb's book. If someone were to go through his book and remove all the examples he takes from the Old Testament, and all the implications that he draws from those examples, we would be left not with a book but with a small pamphlet.

Webb's failure to adequately take into account the fact that Christians are no longer bound by Mosaic covenant legislation is an omission of such magnitude as to nullify the value of this book as a guide for hermeneutics.

3. Webb denies the historicity of Genesis 2–3 in order to deny the contemporary validity of the male headship that he finds recorded in the text.

Another concern related to the authority of Scripture emerges from Webb's treatment of Genesis 2–3. Webb agrees that "the practice of primogeniture in which the first born is granted

8. Webb does at one point note that Christians are no longer bound to obey laws concerning Old Testament sacrifices, food laws, and circumcision (pp. 201–2), because these are explicitly discontinued in the New Testament, but the recognition of these specific points of discontinuity is nowhere else expanded into a general realization that New Testament Christians are not under the Mosaic law code.

prominence within the 'creative order' of a family unit" (135) is found in the narrative in Genesis 2. Webb sees this as support for male headship within the text of Genesis 2. He also thinks this is how it is understood by Paul when he says, "For Adam was formed first, then Eve" (1 Timothy 2:13). But Webb sees this "primogeniture" theme in Genesis 2 as a cultural component in that text.

But how could there be changing cultural influence in the pre-Fall Garden of Eden? Webb answers this question in three ways. First, he says these indications of male headship may be a literary device that anticipates events in the future rather than accurately recording what was in fact true in the Garden:

> A second question is how cultural features could possibly be found in the Garden before the influence of culture. Several explanations exist. First, the whispers of patriarchy in the Garden may have been placed there in order to anticipate the curse. (142–43)

Webb then claims that the literary construction of Genesis 2–3 includes at least one other example of "literary foreshadowing of the curse" in the pejorative description of the serpent as "*more crafty* than any of the wild animals" (Genesis 3:1). Webb then asks, "If the Garden is completely pristine, how could certain creatures in the just-created animal kingdom reflect craftiness? Obviously, this Edenic material embraces *an artistic foreshadowing of events to come*" (143, italics added).

Webb's analysis here assumes that there was no sin or evil in the Garden *in actual fact*, but that by a literary device the author described the serpent as "crafty" (and therefore deceitful and therefore sinful), thus anticipating what he would be later, after the Fall.

There are two problems here. First, it makes Genesis 3:1 affirm something that was not true at that time, and this denies the truthfulness of a section of historical narrative in Scripture. Second, it fails even to consider the most likely explanation, namely, that there was sin in the angelic world sometime after the completion of the initial Creation (Genesis 1:31) but prior to Genesis 3:1.[9] Because of this rebellion in the angelic world (see 2 Peter 2:4; Jude 1:6), Satan himself was somehow speaking through the serpent.[10] So Webb's claim that there must be "artistic foreshadowing of events to come" is not persuasive with respect to the serpent in Genesis 3:1.

The same should be said of his claim that "the whispers of patriarchy in the Garden may have been placed there in order to anticipate the curse" (142–43). Webb is saying that patriarchy

9. This is a fairly standard view among evangelical scholars, but Webb does not even consider it. See Wayne Grudem, *Systematic Theology,* 412, and the relevant pages given for other systematic theologies on pp. 434–35.
10. The serpent, the act of deception, and Satan are connected in some New Testament contexts. Paul says, "I am afraid that as the serpent deceived Eve by his cunning, your thoughts will be lead astray from a sincere and pure devotion to Christ" (2 Corinthians 11:3, in a context opposing false apostles whom he categorizes as servants of Satan who "disguise themselves as servants of righteousness," v. 15). Revelation 12 describes Satan as "that ancient serpent called the devil, or Satan, who leads the whole world astray" (Revelation 12:9). See also John 8:44 and 1 John 3:8, with reference to the beginning stages of history.

did not exist in the Garden *in actual fact*, but the author placed hints of it in the story as a way of anticipating the situation that would come about after there was sin in the world. This is also an explicit denial of the historical accuracy of the Genesis 2 account.

Webb goes on with a second explanation for the indications of male headship in Genesis 2:

> Second, Eden's quiet echoes of patriarchy may be a way of *describing the past through present categories*. The creation story may be *using the social categories that Moses' audience would have been familiar with*. God sometimes permits such accommodation in order not to confuse the main point he wants to communicate with factors that are secondary to that overall theme.[11] (143, italics added)

This is another way in which Webb denies the historicity of the Genesis 2 account. He says that Moses in the time he wrote used "present categories" such as patriarchy to describe the past, and this was simply an "accommodation" by God "in order not to confuse the main point." Patriarchy did not actually exist in the Garden of Eden, but Moses inserted it there so as not to confuse his audience. Thus, Moses inserted into Genesis 2 facts that were not true.

Finally, Webb gives a third reason:

> Third...*the patriarchy of the Garden may reflect God's anticipation of the social context into which Adam and Eve were about to venture*. An agrarian lifestyle...would naturally produce some kind of hierarchy between men and women.... The presentation of the male-female relationship in patriarchal forms may simply be a way of anticipating this first (and major) life setting into which humankind would enter. (144)

Again, Webb believes that the element of primogeniture (Adam being created before Eve) in Genesis 2 may have been written there, not because it reflected the actual facts of the situation in the Garden of Eden, but *because Adam and Eve after they sinned would enter into a situation where Adam as husband had leadership over his wife*. This again is an explicit denial of the historical accuracy of the headship of Adam and his prior Creation as found in Genesis 2. It was simply "a practical and gracious *anticipation* of the agrarian setting into which Adam and Eve were headed" (145, italics added; repeated on 151n55).

It is important to realize how much Webb is denying as historical fact in the Genesis narrative. He is not just denying that there actually was a "crafty" serpent who spoke to Eve (Genesis 3:1). He is also denying the entire *theme of primogeniture* in Genesis 2. That is, he is denying the entire narrative structure that shows the man as created before the woman, for this is the basis for the "primogeniture" theme that Webb sees Paul referring to in 1 Timothy 2:13, "For Adam was formed first, then Eve."

11. Webb explains in a footnote that the "main point" of the creation narrative "is that Yahweh created the heavens and all that is in them, and Yahweh created the earth and all that is in it—God made everything" (143n46).

How much of Genesis 2 does that involve? How much inaccurate material has to be inserted into Genesis 2 either as a literary device foreshadowing the Fall (reason 1), or as an accommodation to the situation familiar to readers at the time of Moses (reason 2), or as an anticipation of an agrarian society that would be established after the Fall (reason 3)? It is no small amount.

According to Webb's view, the entire narrative of God putting the man in the Garden "to work it and take care of it" (2:15) and commanding the man by himself that he may eat of every tree of the Garden but not of the tree of the knowledge of good and evil (2:16–17), and saying, "It is not good for the man to be alone. I will make him a helper suitable for him" (2:18), and bringing the beasts of the field and the birds of the heavens to the man to see what he would call them (2:19), and the man giving names to all livestock and all the birds of the heavens and every beast of the field (2:20), and there not being found a helper fit for man (2:20), and God causing a deep sleep to fall upon the man and taking one of his ribs and forming it into a woman (2:21–22). All of this sequence—summarized by Paul in the statement "For Adam was formed first, then Eve"—is a mere literary device that did not actually happen, according to Webb.

And all of this then enables him to say that criterion (7), "basis in original creation, section 2: primogeniture" is only a "moderately persuasive criterion" (123), so that he can then say that Paul's appeal to the creation of Adam prior to Eve is not proof of a transcultural ethical standard.

Concerns related to incorrect or highly unlikely interpretations of Scripture.

1. Webb repeatedly confuses events with commands, and fails to recognize that what the Bible reports as a background situation (such as slavery or monarchy, for example) it does not necessarily approve or command.

Again and again in his analysis Webb assumes that "the Bible" (in Webb's undifferentiated form, lumping Old and New Testament verses together) supports things such as slavery (see pp. 33, 36–37, 84, 106, 186, 202–3). He also uses monarchy as an example, assuming that the Bible presents monarchy as a favored form of government, one that people should approve or even say that the Bible requires (see, for example, pp. 107, 186, 203).

With respect to slavery, therefore, Webb says that

> a static hermeneutic [this is Webb's term for the hermeneutic used by everyone who does not use his redemptive-movement hermeneutic] would apply this slavery-refuge text by *permitting the ownership of slaves today*, provided that the church offers similar kinds of refuge for runaway *slaves.... Christians would dare not speak out against slavery*. They would support the institution of slavery. (33, italics added)

What is rather astonishing is that the only alternative that Webb acknowledges to his position is what he calls a "static hermeneutic." But then he affirms that such a "static hermeneutic" would have to support slavery:

> Even more tragic is that, in arguing for or *in permitting biblical slavery today*, a static hermeneutic takes our current standard of human rights and working conditions *backwards* by quantum leaps. We would shame a gospel that proclaims freedom to the captive.... A static hermeneutic would not condemn biblical-type slavery if that social order were to reappear in society today. (34, 36)

In his eyes there are only two choices: Do you support Webb's system or do you support slavery? Which will it be? He appears oblivious to the historical fact that for centuries many Christians have opposed slavery *from the text of Scripture itself*, without using Webb's new system of interpretation, and without rejecting the final moral authority of the New Testament. To say we have to choose between Webb's system and slavery is historically unfounded, is biblically untrue, and is astonishing in its failure to recognize other alternatives.

Webb sometimes appeals to the fact that proponents of slavery or proponents of monarchy in the past appealed to the Bible to prove their case. He says, "slavery proponents frequently argued from theological and christological analogies in the text" (186), and that "in the past, the submission texts cited above were used by Christians to support monarchy as the only appropriate, God-honoring form of government" (107). But the fact that some Christians in the past used the Bible to support slavery does not prove that the Bible supports slavery any more than one can prove that the Bible supports any number of false teachings (such as Arianism, or the Crusades, or the Inquisition, or salvation by works) that were supported in the past by people "using the Bible," but were ultimately rejected by the church. The devil himself even quoted the Bible to support his enticement to Jesus to throw Himself down from the top of the temple (Matthew 4:5–6), but that does not prove that the Bible actually supports the devil's ideas!

With regard to slavery, the Bible was used by more Christians to *oppose* slavery than to *defend* it, and eventually their arguments won, and slavery was abolished. But the fundamental difference from Webb is that the evangelical, Bible-believing Christians who ultimately brought about the abolition of slavery *did not advocate modifying or nullifying any biblical teaching*, or moving "beyond" the New Testament to a better ethic. They taught the abolition of slavery from the Bible itself.

Webb shows no awareness of biblical anti-slavery arguments such as those of Theodore Weld in *The Bible Against Slavery*,[12] a book that was widely distributed and frequently reprinted. Weld argued strongly against American slavery from Exodus 21:16, "He that stealeth

12. The following citations are from the 1838 edition: Theodore Weld, *The Bible Against Slavery* (4th edition, New York: American Anti-Slavery Society, 1838). The book was first published in Boston in 1837. See also several essays in Mason Lowance, editor, *Against Slavery: An Abolitionist Reader* (New York: Penguin Books, 2000).

a man and selleth him, or if he be found in his hand, he shall surely be put to death" (KJV) (pp. 13-15), as well as from the fact that men are in the image of God and therefore it is morally wrong to treat any human being as property (pp. 8-9, 15-17). He argued that ownership of another person breaks the eighth commandment, "Thou shalt not steal," as follows:

> The eighth commandment forbids the taking of *any* part of that which belongs to another. Slavery takes the *whole.* Does the same Bible which prohibits the taking of any thing from him, sanction the taking of *every* thing? Does it thunder wrath against the man who robs his neighbor of a *cent,* yet commission him to rob his neighbor of *himself*? Slaveholding is the highest possible violation of the eighth commandment." (pp. 10-11)

In the rest of the book Weld answered detailed objections about various verses used by slavery proponents. The whole basis of his book is that the moral standards taught in the Bible are right, and there is no hint that we have to move beyond the Bible's ethics to oppose slavery, as Webb would have us do.

The New Testament never commanded slavery, but gave principles that regulated it and ultimately led to its abolition. Paul says to slaves, "If you can gain your freedom, do so" (1 Corinthians 7:21). And he tells Philemon, regarding his slave Onesimus, that he should welcome him back "*no longer as a slave* but better than a slave, as a dear brother" (Philemon 1:16), and that he should "welcome him as you would welcome me" (v. 17), and that he should forgive anything that Onesimus owed him, or at least that Paul would pay it himself (vv. 18–19). Finally he says, "Confident of your obedience, I write to you, knowing that you will do *even more than I ask*" (v. 21). This is a strong and not very subtle hint that Philemon should grant freedom to Onesimus.

When we couple those verses with the realization that every human being is created in the image of God (see Genesis 1:27; 9:6; James 3:9; see also Job 31:15; Galatians 3:28), we then see that the Bible, and especially the New Testament, contains powerful principles that would lead to an abolition of slavery. The New Testament never commands people to practice slavery or to own slaves, but rather gives principles that would lead to the overthrow of that institution, and also regulates it while it is in existence by statements such as, "Masters, provide your slaves with what is right and fair, because you know that you also have a Master in heaven" (Colossians 4:1).

The Bible does not approve or command slavery any more than it approves or commands persecution of Christians. When the author of Hebrews commends his readers by saying, "You sympathized with those in prison and joyfully accepted the confiscation of your property, because you knew that you yourselves had better and lasting possessions" (Hebrews 10:34), that does not mean the Bible *supports* the plundering of Christians' property, or that it *commands theft*! It only means that *if* Christians find themselves in a situation where their property is taken through persecution, they should still rejoice because of their heavenly treasure, which cannot be stolen. Similarly, when the Bible tells slaves to be submissive to their masters, it does not mean that the Bible supports or commands slavery, but only that it tells people who are in a situation of slavery how they should respond.

Webb's mistaken evaluation of the Bible's teaching on slavery forms a fundamental building block in constructing his hermeneutic. Once we remove his claim that the Bible condones slavery, Webb's Exhibit A is gone, and he has lost his primary means of supporting the claim that we need his "redemptive-movement hermeneutic" to move beyond the ethic of the Bible itself.

2. Webb repeatedly assumes unlikely interpretations of Scripture in order to present a Bible that is so clearly wrong that it is impossible to believe and obey today.

In numerous sections Webb presents what he claims is the teaching of the Bible in order to build up a long list of culturally relative teachings, teachings to which readers will evidently respond by thinking, "Of course we cannot believe or obey those things today!" Webb then uses these lists of "impossible for today" teachings in order to show that his eighteen criteria are necessary and valid to determine cultural relativity.

The problem is, most evangelicals do not need Webb's "redemptive-movement hermeneutic" to know that the Bible does not teach these things. In fact, few if any responsible exegetes claim that the Bible teaches any of these things as ideas or ethical standards that should be followed by Christians today.

Here is a list of things that Webb assumes the Bible teaches:

(1) People should pursue farming as an occupation (124–25). Webb derives this from the fact that "in the Garden man was instructed to till the ground and eat of its produce" (124). The problem here is that Webb takes a *good* thing in the Bible (raising food from the ground) and wrongly makes it into *requirement for every person*, rather than seeing it as one among several responsibilities that God gave the human race. A more sound application of this text is to say that God still expects human beings to gain food from the ground, but the diversity of occupations within Scripture shows that this never was an expectation or a requirement of every single person.

(2) People should use only ground transportation. Webb says that "the mode of transportation within the Garden was walking," and he allows for extending that to "transportation by horse and other animals" (125). He says that the Creation pattern thus "squares nicely" with the lifestyle of those who restrict their transportation to horse and buggy today. But he says most Christians would see this as a "non-binding pattern within the creation texts" (125). The problem in this case is that even within the first two chapters of Genesis the commands to "subdue" the earth and "have dominion" over it imply an expectation that human beings would develop all sorts of products from the earth, including many different means of transportation. We do not need Webb's redemptive-movement hermeneutic to know that the Bible never presents "ground transportation" as the mode of transportation that people should use exclusively (think

of all the journeys by boats in the Bible), nor is this pattern of transportation ever used elsewhere as a basis for commands to God's people, nor does the Bible ever command people to use only ground transportation.

Webb has taken an event (Adam and Eve walking) and has mistakenly viewed it as a requirement that has to be overcome by Webb's redemptive-movement hermeneutic.

(3) Singleness is outside the will of God. Webb says, since Adam and Eve were married in the Garden of Eden, "if the creation material provides a tightly ordered paradigm for all of humanity to follow, one might get the impression that singleness was outside the will of God" (124). Here Webb has misread the Genesis narrative. Genesis 1–2 does not present a pattern where marriage is the only acceptable option, for God's command to Adam and Eve to "be fruitful and increase in number" (Genesis 1:28) envisions a situation where they would have children, and these children would have to be single for some time before they could be married. What we see rather from the Creation narrative is that God created marriage, that marriage is "very good," and that the relationship between Adam and Eve in marriage was not sinful but was good in God's sight. But to say that marriage is *good* does not imply that singleness is *bad*, or that marriage is *required* for every single individual, nor does the Genesis narrative imply those things.

(4) Women should be viewed as property. Webb says, "Within the biblical text one discovers an ownership mentality in the treatment of women. Women are frequently listed with the cattle and servants (Exodus 20:17; cf. Deuteronomy 5:21; Judges 5:30)" (165). But Webb oversimplifies when he assumes that listing "with" something implies a similar status. The main verse he cites is Exodus 20:17:

> "You shall not covet your neighbor's house. You shall not covet your neighbor's wife, or his manservant or maidservant, his ox or donkey, or anything that belongs to your neighbor."

This does not imply an "ownership mentality" toward women any more than it proves that people thought of women as houses! This amazing commandment actually establishes a high level of protection and honor for women and for marriage, for it addresses purity of heart.[13] People were not to covet someone else's house or wife or animals, but this surely also implies that wives were not to covet their neighbors' husbands, and surely the commandment does not also imply that husbands were viewed as property. Hearers could easily distinguish between houses, animals, and wives. Moreover, in the previous verses the seventh commandment (against adultery) is separate from the eighth (against stealing), thus clearly making a

13. Webb mentions other factors, such as a bride price paid to a father, and the fact that a husband is sometimes called a *ba'al* ("master"). But these things do not establish a view of women as property, for the bride price could simply be an expression of the honor and high value that the future husband was attributing to his bride, and the word *ba'al* can simply mean "husband" (BDB, 127).

distinction between husbands and wives, on the one hand, and property on the other. In any case, it is not hermeneutically legitimate to take aspects of the Mosaic law code as part of what the Bible teaches about women, for Christians are no longer under the Mosaic covenant. We do not need Webb's redemptive-movement hermeneutic to understand this, nor do these Mosaic covenant provisions demonstrate the legitimacy of Webb's hermeneutic.

(5) Families should practice primogeniture. Webb sees a system of primogeniture, in which the oldest son received "a double portion of the inheritance...led in military protection for the family...avenged wrongs done against family members...performed religious ceremonies" (141), and so forth, as a pattern that is found in the ethical system contained in the Bible. But he says primogeniture is culturally relative and should no longer be practiced today. But again Webb has mistakenly confused *events that are reported by the Bible* with *things that are required in the ethical system taught in the Bible.* Nowhere does the Bible command people to follow primogeniture customs (and Webb himself shows many examples where Scripture deviates from this pattern, pp. 136–39), and therefore we do not need a redemptive-movement hermeneutic to know that such a pattern is not required for people to follow, nor was it ever something that God required everyone to follow, even in the ancient world.

In addition to these five items, Webb claims that the Bible teaches a number of other objectionable things that few or no responsible evangelical scholars today would say are taught by the Bible. I do not need to comment on each one, but what is surprising is that Webb seldom shows awareness of, to say nothing of responding to, the reasoning of competent interpreters who argue that the Bible does not teach these things. Webb simply asserts that the Bible teaches the following:

(6) We should establish and support slavery (33, 36–37, 84, 106, 186, 202–3).

(7) People should establish and support monarchy as the right form of government (153, 186).

(8) People should wash each others' feet (204, 211).

(9) Adult children should obey their parents (212).

(10) The earth is the center of the universe. Webb says, "Scripture depicts a geocentric or earth-centered model of the universe. The earth is placed on a stationary foundation in a central location with other luminous bodies revolving above it" (221–22).

(11) The earth is flat. Webb says, "The church had difficulty accepting [that the earth was round]...because the Bible incorporated a 'flat earth' view of the world" (223). In this and the previous item Webb apparently thinks the Bible affirms things that are contrary to fact (in other words, in error).

(12) Wives should be subject to their husbands because husbands are older and better educated (213–16).

(13) Husbands should be allowed to physically discipline their wives (167, 189–90). Webb actually claims that the Bible gives approval to the idea that a husband should "strip his wife" and "physically confine" her (189). Webb bases this on his misinterpretation of Hosea 2:1–23. He claims that in this passage,

> unless Gomer puts away her sexual promiscuity, Hosea will take action against his wife:
>
> I [Hosea] will strip her [Gomer] naked
> and make her as bare as on the day she was born....
> Therefore I will block her path with thorn bushes;
> I will wall her in so she cannot find her way. (189)

What Webb does not disclose to readers is that the overwhelming majority of commentators understand this entire chapter to be speaking not of Hosea and Gomer but of God's judgment upon Israel. Speaking in prophetic imagery, as is common among the Old Testament prophets, God says that unless Israel abandons her sins, he will "strip her naked and make her as bare as on the day she was born" (Hosea 2:3), vividly portraying God's judgment on the nation.[14]

(14) People should greet one another with a holy kiss (203–4).

(15) Women are simply "reproductive gardens" and husbands provide 100 percent of the baby's new life. Webb says that the biblical picture is one in which

> a woman provides the "soil" into which a man planted the seed of the miniature child...to grow for nine months.... A tight agricultural analogy—the man provides the totality of the new life in seedling form while the woman provides only the fertile environment for its growth—reflects a culture-based component within the text. (223–24)

(16) The Bible approves obedience to many details of the Old Testament narrative and the Old Testament Mosaic laws, such as "polygamy and concubinage, levirate marriages, unequal value of men and women in vow redemption...the treatment of women as spoils of battle" and so forth (166–67).

---

14. Thomas McComiskey writes, "It is obvious that the lengthy address in 2:3–25 [English 2:1–23] is directed to the nation and not to Gomer personally" (Thomas McComiskey, "Hosea," in *The Minor Prophets*, 32). See also Keil and Delitzsch, *Commentary on the Old Testament, in loc.,* Douglas Stuart, *Hosea–Jonah,* Word Biblical Commentary (Waco, TX: Word, 1987), 42–48, and the section heading before chapter 2 in many English Bible translations, which say something similar to the NIV Study Bible heading, "Israel Punished and Restored" (1323). McComiskey points out that the phrase in v. 15, "as at the time when she came out of the land of Egypt," cannot apply to Gomer and indicates that the entire passage must have Israel primarily in mind. (Since the passage is an extended allegory, there are elements of it that of course could apply to the situation between Hosea and Gomer as well, but that does not mean that the primary reference is to Gomer, and it certainly does not mean that the passage provides justification for a husband to physically discipline his wife.)

If readers believe Webb when he says that the Bible teaches these things, then they will be inclined to agree with his argument that we need to go beyond the ethical system of the Bible and use Webb's "redemptive-movement hermeneutic" to move closer toward an "ultimate ethic."

But the Bible teaches and commands none of these things for Christians today. And that is not because Webb's "redemptive-movement hermeneutic" enables us to move *beyond* the ethics of the Bible. It is rather because New Covenant Christians know that the ethical system of the Bible itself does not support or require these things. Webb has given us a pot of stew mixed with Mosaic covenant laws that no longer apply, fragments of narrative history that were never commanded, cultural customs or habits the Bible never commanded us to follow, and phenomenological observations of the natural world which the Bible never presented as a description of the shape of the earth or the structure of the universe. We do not need a "redemptive-movement hermeneutic" to know that the Bible does not require these things of people today. We simply need the Bible itself, understood in each case with sensitivity to the immediate context and to the larger Old Covenant–New Covenant structure of redemptive history found within the Bible itself.

Concerns related to shifting the location of our moral norms from the objective commands of the New Testament to the subjective theories of contemporary scholars.

1. Webb creates an overly complex system of interpretation that will require a class of "priests" who have to interpret the Bible for us in the light of ancient Near Eastern and Greco-Roman culture.

At the heart of Webb's system is his requirement that the interpreter "must listen for how the text sounds within its various social contexts," especially "the broader, foreign ancient Near-Eastern and Greco-Roman (ANE/GR) social context and the immediate, domestic Israelite/church setting" (53).

How does one do this? Webb gives eighteen criteria which one must use in order to carry out his redemptive-movement hermeneutics properly. His first criterion is called "preliminary movement," and here is how he says it should happen:

> Assessing redemptive-movement has its complications. Without going into an elaborate explanation, I will simply suggest a number of guidelines: (1) the ANE/GR *real* world must be examined along with its *legal* world, (2) the biblical subject on the *whole* must be examined along with its *parts*, (3) the biblical text must be compared to a number of other ANE/GR cultures which themselves must be compared with each other, and (4) any portrait of movement must be composed of broad input from all three streams of assessment—foreign, domestic, and canonical. (82)

And this is just his procedure for the first of eighteen criteria! Who will be able to do this? Who knows the history of ancient cultures well enough to make these assessments?

Speaking from the perspective of over twenty-five years in the academic world, I will not say that only 1 percent of the *Christians* in the world will be able to use Webb's system and tell us what moral standards we should follow today. I will not even say that 1 percent of the *seminary-trained pastors* in the world will be able to follow Webb's system and tell us what moral standards we should obey today. I will not even say that 1 percent of the *seminary professors* will be able to have the requisite expertise in ancient cultures to use Webb's system and tell us what moral standards we should follow today. That is because the evaluation and assessment of any one ancient culture, to say nothing of all the ancient cultures surrounding the Bible, is a massive undertaking, even with 1 narrow subject such as laws concerning marriage and divorce, or property rights, or education and training of children. It is time-consuming and requires much specialized knowledge and an excellent research library. Therefore I will not even say that 1 percent of the *seminary professors who have academic doctorates in Old Testament or New Testament* will be able to use Webb's system and tell us what moral standards we should follow today. No, *in the end Webb's system as he describes it above can only be used by far less than 1 percent of the professors of New Testament and Old Testament in the Christian world today*, those few scholars who have the time and the specialized knowledge of rabbinic studies, of Greco-Roman culture, and of ancient Egyptian and Babylonian and Assyrian and Persian cultures, and who have access to a major research library, and who will then be able to use Webb's "redemptive-movement hermeneutic" in the way he describes in the paragraph just quoted. This tiny group of experts will have to tell us what moral standards God wants us to follow today.

And that is only for Criterion 1 in his list of eighteen criteria.

If the evangelical world begins to adopt Webb's system, it is not hard to imagine that we will soon require a new class of "priests," those erudite scholars with sufficient expertise in the ancient world that they can give us reliable conclusions about what kind of "ultimate ethic" we should follow today.

But this will create another problem, one I have observed often as I have lived and taught in the academic world: *Scholars with such specialized knowledge often disagree.* Anyone familiar with the debates over rabbinic views of justification in the last two decades will realize how difficult it can be to understand exactly what was believed in an ancient culture on even one narrow topic, to say nothing of the whole range of ethical commands that we find in the New Testament.

Where then will Webb's system lead us? *It will lead us to massive inability to know with confidence anything that God requires of us.* The more scholars who become involved with telling us "how the Bible was moving" with respect to this or that aspect of ancient culture, the more opinions we will have, and the more despair people will feel about ever being able to know what God requires of us, what His "ultimate ethic" is.

How different from Webb's system is the simple, direct teaching of the New Testament! Consider the following commands:

> Therefore each of you must put off falsehood and speak truthfully to his neighbor, for we are all members of one body. (Ephesians 4:25)
>
> He who has been stealing must steal no longer, but must work, doing something useful with his own hands, that he may have something to share with those in need. (Ephesians 4:28)
>
> Do not let any unwholesome talk come out of your mouths, but only what is helpful for building others up according to their needs, that it may benefit those who listen. (Ephesians 4:29)
>
> Get rid of all bitterness, rage and anger, brawling and slander, along with every form of malice. Be kind and compassionate to one another, forgiving each other, just as in Christ God forgave you. (Ephesians 4:31–32)
>
> But among you there must not be even a hint of sexual immorality, or of any kind of impurity, or of greed, because these are improper for God's holy people. (Ephesians 5:3)
>
> Do not get drunk on wine, which leads to debauchery. Instead, be filled with the Spirit. (Ephesians 5:18)
>
> Wives, submit to your husbands as to the Lord. (Ephesians 5:22)
>
> Husbands, love your wives, just as Christ loved the church and gave himself up for her. (Ephesians 5:25)
>
> Children, obey your parents in the Lord, for this is right. (Ephesians 6:1)
>
> Fathers, do not exasperate your children; instead, bring them up in the training and instruction of the Lord. (Ephesians 6:4)

I do not believe that God gave us a Bible that is so direct and clear and simple, only to require that all believers throughout all history should first filter these commands through a complex system of eighteen criteria before they can know whether to obey them or not. That is not the kind of Bible that God gave us, nor is there any indication in Scripture itself that believers have to have some kind of specialized academic knowledge and elaborate hermeneutical system before they can be sure that these are the things God requires of His children.

2. Webb creates a system that is overly liable to subjective influence and therefore is indeterminate and will lead to significant misuse.

A built-in liability to subjective influence is evident in Webb's treatment of several subjects, particularly his treatment of texts relating to the role of women in marriage and in the church. With few exceptions, *the selection of materials and the evaluation of the criteria are skewed in order that Webb can show again and again how male leadership in the home and in the church is a culturally relative idea*. For example, he places his first three criteria—(1)

Preliminary Movement, (2) Seed Ideas, (3) Breakouts—within the category of "persuasive criteria" (73), because all three of these *assume* that one needs to move to a higher ethic than that of the New Testament. These categories therefore allow him to say that the New Testament teachings on women are only "preliminary," and that the exceptions he finds in Galatians 3:28 and in Deborah and Junia are the truly "persuasive" examples that point to the far better "ultimate ethic" toward which the New Testament is heading.

By contrast, when he gets to Criterion 6, which is "Basis in Original Creation, Section One: Patterns" (123), Webb brings in several bizarre items such as "farming as an occupation" and "ground transportation," which no responsible interpreter would ever say the Bible requires for everyone today. Why does he do this? These allow him to claim that "original creation patterns do not provide an automatic guide for assessing what is transcultural within Scripture" (126). But when someone brings in such bizarre interpretations in order to be able to say that original Creation patterns of marriage are not clearly transcultural, then the reader rightly suspects that a subjective bias has entered into the selection of material.

Similarly, when we reach Criterion 14, "Basis in Theological Analogy" (185), the difficulty for egalitarians is going to be the fact that in Ephesians 5:22–33 Paul makes an analogy between the relationship of a husband and wife and the relationship between Christ and the church. How does Webb evade the force of the argument that this is obviously a transcultural comparison? He says there are other "theological analogies in Scripture that are not transcultural" and he says that slavery, monarchy, and "*right-handedness*" are also supported by "theological analogy" within Scripture (186–87). The problem is of course that the examples are not parallel. The Bible never says, "Support monarchy as the best system of government because God is a heavenly king," or "Support slavery as an institution because God is the ultimate slave owner in heaven," or "It is better to be right handed because Christ sits at God's right hand." So Webb's examples are not parallel to the example of Paul's statement,

> For the husband is the head of the wife as Christ is the head of the church, his body, of which he is the Savior. Now as the church submits to Christ, so also wives should submit to their husbands in everything.
>
> Husbands, love your wives, just as Christ loved the church and gave himself up for her. (Ephesians 5:23–25)

The fact that Webb brings in what he calls examples of "theological analogy" that are not really parallel is again evidence of subjective bias in the formulation and development of his criteria. Once he brings in these examples, he is able to classify "Basis in Theological Analogy" as an "inconclusive" criterion (185), one that really cannot rightly be used to prove that a wife's submission to her husband is transcultural.

Webb follows a similar procedure in Criterion 16, "Appeal to the Old Testament" (201).

In order to show that this also is an "inconclusive" criterion, Webb brings in examples that are not parallel to the Old Testament quotations about the role of women. Webb says that "several slave/master texts within the New Testament rely heavily on the Old Testament for their formulation for their ideas and words" (202), but the passages he mentions (such as 1 Peter 2:22–25) are simply used by the New Testament authors to show that Christians should trust in God when they are mistreated, and the passages in no way affirm that mistreatment of others is proper or that slavery is a morally right institution. In the same way, when Webb talks about "kings and subjects," he says, "The monarchy texts within the New Testament derive their message largely from the Old Testament" (203), and he mentions particularly 1 Peter 2:13–17 and Romans 13:1–5. But these passages do not support what Webb claims. They tell Christians to be subject to the ruling authority, but nowhere do they quote the Old Testament to prove that monarchy as an institution is required. Webb even goes so far in this section as to claim that the "holy kiss" and "foot-washing" are supported from the Old Testament (203–4), though no Old Testament verses are ever quoted to support them.

Once Webb has claimed that all these things are supported from the Old Testament but are not transcultural, it gives him the basis on which he claims that the New Testament teachings on the role of women are not transcultural just because they are supported by quotations from the Old Testament (he mentions 1 Corinthians 14:34; 1 Timothy 2:14–15 [sic]; 1 Peter 3:5–6 [204]). But because his examples like monarchy, slavery, and right-handedness are not really supported by Old Testament quotes, this argument has little force.

Why then is it that Webb brings in these examples that are not parallel in his Criterion 16, "Appeal to the Old Testament"? Readers may well suspect that a subjective bias has entered into the selection of material here. But the same criteria could easily be used by others, with other examples selected, to produce widely divergent results.

Webb fails to demonstrate that New Testament teachings on men and women in the home and in the church are culturally relative.

Throughout Webb's book he attempts to dismantle the complementarian arguments for male leadership in the home and the church by claiming that the biblical texts on male leadership are culturally relative. Yet in each case, his attempts to demonstrate cultural relativity are not persuasive. In the following section, I consider each of Webb's claims for cultural relativity in the order they occur in his book. (At several points in what follows I will briefly summarize arguments that have been made earlier in order to apply them to Webb's specific reasons for rejection of a complementarian view.)

1. Webb fails to show that New Testament commands regarding male headship are only a "preliminary movement" and that the New Testament ethic needs further improvement (Criterion 1).

Webb claims that the commands regarding wives submitting to their husbands in Ephesians 5:22–33 are not a final ethic that we should follow today, but are simply an indication of "where Scripture is moving on the issue of patriarchal power" (80–81). But this claim is not persuasive because it depends on his assumption that the ethical standards of the New Testament are not God's ultimate ethical standards for us, but are simply one step along the way toward an "ultimate ethic" that we should adopt today (36–39).

2. Webb fails to show that Galatians 3:28 is a "seed idea" that would ultimately lead to the abolition of male headship once cultural changes made it possible to adopt a superior ethic to that of the New Testament (Criterion 2).

Once again, Webb's conception of a "seed idea" is based on his claim that some New Testament commands are inconsistent with that seed idea, and those commands show only that "the biblical author pushed society as far as it could go at that time without creating more damage than good" (73). Webb claims that the "seed idea" is simply a pointer showing that there should be "further movement" toward a "more fully realized ethic" that is "more just, more equitable and more loving. . .a better ethic than the one expressed in the isolated words of the text" (36).

But, as I indicated above, it is not necessary to "move beyond" the ethic of the New Testament in order to argue for the abolition of slavery, for the New Testament never condones or approves of slavery and never says it was created by God (as marriage was). And the New Testament provides statements that would eventually lead to the abolition of slavery *based on the New Testament ethic itself*, not based on some "higher ethic" that would later be discovered. Similarly, Galatians 3:28 should not be seen as a "seed idea" pointing to some future "higher ethic" but as a text that is fully consistent with other things the apostle Paul and other New Testament authors wrote about the relationships between men and women. If we take the entire New Testament as the very words of God for us in the New Covenant today, then any claim that Galatians 3:28 should overrule other texts, such as Ephesians 5 and 1 Timothy 2, should be seen as a claim that Paul the apostle contradicts himself, and therefore that the Word of God contradicts itself.

3. Webb fails to show that 1 Corinthians 7:3–5 establishes an egalitarian model within marriage (Criterion 3).

In 1 Corinthians 7:3–5 Paul says,

> The husband should fulfill his marital duty to his wife, and likewise the wife to her husband. The wife's body does not belong to her alone but also to her husband. In the same way, the husband's body does not belong to him alone but also to his wife. Do not deprive each other except by mutual consent and for a time, so that you may devote yourselves to prayer. Then come together again so that Satan will not tempt you because of your lack of self-control.

Webb claims that the explanation that John Piper and I gave for this text in our book, *Recovering Biblical Manhood and Womanhood*,[15] nullifies all male headship within marriage. Webb says that Piper and Grudem's approach "ultimately abandons their own position" because "once one has eliminated any power differential and set up mutual deference and mutual consent as the basis for *all* decision-making in a marriage (such as Piper and Grudem have done) there is nothing that makes the view substantially different from egalitarianism" (101).

But Webb has misread our argument. In the very section to which he refers, we say,

> What are the implications of this text for the leadership of the husband? Do the call for mutual yielding to sexual need and the renunciation of unilateral planning nullify the husband's responsibility for general leadership in the marriage? We don't think so. But this text...makes clear that his leadership will not involve selfish, unilateral choices. (88)

Thus, Piper and I agree that 1 Corinthians 7:3–5 shows that there are areas of mutual obligation between husband and wife, and that we can extrapolate from that and say that the husband's leadership in the marriage should not be a selfish leadership that fails to listen to the concerns of his wife. But in that very context, and in dozens of places throughout the rest of the book, we argue that the husband has an authoritative leadership role in the marriage that the wife does not have. To say that the word *authority* is sometimes misunderstood is not to say that we deny the concept. We qualify and modify the concept of authority, as Scripture does, in many places, but we nevertheless affirm it throughout the rest of the book.

4. Webb fails to show that the only purpose for the wife's submission to her husband is evangelism, or that this purpose is no longer valid (Criterion 4).

In dealing with his Criterion 4, "Purpose/Intent Statements," Webb says that Peter "tells wives to obey their husbands so that unbelieving husbands 'may be won over without words' (1 Peter 3:1)," but that today the kind of "unilateral, patriarchy-type submission" that Peter advocates "may actually repulse him and prevent him from being won to Christ." Webb concludes that "the stated evangelistic purpose of the text is not likely to be fulfilled in our contemporary setting" (107–8).

We should be very clear what Webb is saying here. He is saying that wives with unbelieving husbands today do not need to obey 1 Peter 3:1–2, which says,

> Wives, in the same way be submissive to your husbands so that, if any of them do not believe the word, they may be won over without words by the behavior of their wives, when they see the purity and reverence of your lives.

15. John Piper and Wayne Grudem, eds., *Recovering Biblical Manhood and Womanhood* (1991), 87–88.

One problem with Webb's assertion is that it trivializes the testimony of thousands of Christian women whose unbelieving husbands *have* been won by the submissive behavior of their believing wives.

A second problem with Webb's claim is that it makes first century Christian evangelism into the ultimate "bait and switch" sales technique. Webb claims that Peter's command aimed to attract non-Christian husbands by the submissive behavior of their wives, but once these men became Christians and began to grow toward maturity, they would discover the "seed ideas" for equality and "mutual submission" in texts such as Galatians 3:28, and then (according to Webb) they would learn that *this command for submission of their wives is a morally deficient pattern* that has to be abandoned in favor of an egalitarian position. Therefore, according to the logic of Webb's position, first-century evangelism was a deceptive maneuver, in which the Word of God told people to use a morally deficient pattern of behavior simply to win unbelievers.

The third problem with Webb's explanation is that it opens the door for people to disobey many other New Testament commands if they think that the reason given for the command will no longer be fulfilled in our culture. For example, the command to be subject to human government is also based on an expected good outcome:

> Submit yourselves for the Lord's sake to every authority instituted among men: whether to the king, as the supreme authority, or to governors, who are sent by him to punish those who do wrong and to commend those who do right. For it is God's will *that by doing good you should silence the ignorant talk of foolish men.* (1 Peter 2:13–15, italics added)

But people today could say that being subject to government might not "put to silence the ignorance of foolish people," because some governments are just so hardened against the gospel that it will make no difference to them. Therefore (according to Webb's reasoning) we do not have to obey that command either.[16]

A fourth problem with Webb's approach is that it fails completely to consider the *other reasons* given in the New Testament for a wife's submission to her husband. Paul says,

> Wives, submit to your husbands as to the Lord. For the husband is the head of the wife as Christ is the head of the church, his body, of which he is the Savior. (Ephesians 5:22–23)

Similarly, when Paul talks about being subject to "the governing authorities" he does not give evangelism as the reason, but rather says that the agent of the government "is God's servant,

16. Webb says that we should be subject to the law today, not to political leaders (107), but Peter's admonition to be subject to "every human institution" would surely include both the law and the government officials. The fact is that we are subject not just to the law, but to the people who enforce the law and who are representatives of the government and bear its authority today.

an agent of wrath to bring punishment on the wrongdoer. Therefore, it is necessary to submit to the authorities, not only because of possible punishment but also because of conscience" (Romans 13:4–5).

It is better to reject Webb's redemptive-movement hermeneutic and see the New Testament as the words of God for us today, words that contain God's morally pure standards for us to obey, and to obey *all* of the New Testament commands *simply because they are the words of God* who holds us responsible for obeying them. We do not have the right to take it upon ourselves to say, as Webb's position implies, "If a wife today submits to her unbelieving husband according to 1 Peter 3:1, I don't think that will help evangelism in our modern culture, so women should not follow that text today." That is simply setting up our own moral judgment as a higher standard than God's Word.

5. Webb fails to show that Adam's naming of Eve in Genesis 2 indicates only equality (discussed under Criterion 5).

Webb claims that when Adam calls the woman ('ishshāh) in Genesis 2:23, because this word for "woman" sounds like the Hebrew word for man ('îsh) that shows that "Adam pronounces an affinity between the woman and himself. This act of naming places man and woman as partners in the dominion over the animal/plant kingdom" (116).

This argument is not convincing because the names for "man" and "woman" ('îsh and 'ishshāh) are somewhat the same and somewhat different. The words mean different things: 'îsh means "man" or "husband" (BDB, 35), and 'ishshāh means "woman, wife, female" (BDB, 61), and though the words look similar they are related to different roots (the BDB *Lexicon* speaks of "the impossibility of deriving 'îsh and 'ishshāh from the same root," 35). For Webb to say that this name *only* indicates equality is simply reductionistic—it is taking part of the truth and making it the whole truth. The names are similar and different, and they signify *both* similarity *and* difference.

Second, Webb fails to consider the strongest reason that this process shows male headship, and that is that throughout the Old Testament the one giving a name to someone else has authority over the one receiving that name. Therefore, just as Adam's prior activity of naming the animals indicated that he had the right to name them because he had authority over them, so Adam's giving a name to the woman is an indication that God had granted to Adam an authority or leadership role with respect to his wife.

6. Webb fails to show that there are culturally relative components in the pre-Fall Garden of Eden (Criterion 6).

First, Webb attempts to minimize the significance of the fact that God called Adam to account first after Adam and Eve had sinned (Genesis 3:9). Webb admits that this might qualify as "a quiet whisper of patriarchy" (130), but this is minimizing what is there in Scripture. If this is

God's action and *God's* call to Adam, it is anything but a whisper! This is the action of the sovereign God of the universe calling the man to account first for what had happened in his family (even though Eve had sinned first). It is an indication that God held Adam primarily responsible for what had happened (and this is confirmed by Paul's explanation that it was *Adam's* sin—not Eve's—that led to sin spreading to all people. See 1 Corinthians 15:22: "For as *in Adam* all die, so in Christ all will be made alive"; see also Romans 5:12–19).

With regard to the pre-Fall narrative itself, Webb claims to find some culturally relative elements within the account, such as "farming as an occupation" and "ground transportation" and a "vegetarian diet" (124–25). But this is hardly a persuasive list of examples, because Webb fails to take account of the nature of the items that he lists. Surely nothing in the text suggests, and no responsible interpreter claims, that these events are presented as the *only* activities human beings can do. So it is unclear why Webb thinks these can be counted as examples of "culturally relative" principles.

The point Webb overlooks is that everything in the Garden is *good* because it has been created by God and it was declared by Him to be "very good" (Genesis 1:31). Therefore farming and gaining food from the earth are good. Walking through the Garden is good. Vegetables are good. Bearing children is good. None of these things is later superseded by a "superior ethic" that would declare the goodness of these things to be culturally relative, so that farming or walking on the earth or bearing children would no longer be good!

Similarly, we have in the Garden male-female equality together with male headship in the marriage. That also is *good* and it is *created by God*, and we should not follow Webb in thinking that we can one day create a "superior ethic" that declares male headship to be *not* good or *not* approved by God.[17]

7. Webb fails to show that 1 Timothy 2:13, "For Adam was formed first, then Eve," is culturally relative (Criterion 7).

The reason egalitarians find 1 Timothy 2:13 particularly difficult is that Paul uses the order of Creation as the basis for saying, "I do not permit a woman to teach or to have authority over a man; she must be silent" (1 Timothy 2:12). If God's original creation of Adam and Eve was very good and free from sin (which it was), and if Paul sees in Adam's creation prior to Eve an indication that some teaching and governing roles in the New Testament church should be reserved for men (which Webb agrees is Paul's reasoning), then it is hard to escape the conclusion that the creation of Adam before Eve indicates a permanent, transcultural principle that supports some exclusively male teaching and governing roles in the church for all generations.

Webb attempts to avoid this by claiming there are some culturally relative things in

17. Some things that Webb claims are in the Garden, such as keeping the Sabbath, or a six-day work week (125–26) are doubtful interpretations and it is not evident that they were present in the Garden. Therefore they do not form a persuasive argument that some things in the Garden are culturally relative.

the original Creation account. But, as I indicated in the previous section, Webb fails to take into account that everything in the original creation is morally *good* and free from sin, and that includes Adam's headship in the marriage. In addition to that, if Webb's reasoning were correct, then Paul could not have appealed to the Creation account in the first century either, because people in the first century were not limited to "farming as an occupation" (Paul was a tentmaker), and people in the first century were not limited to "ground transportation" (Paul traveled by sea), and people in the first century were not all married (both Jesus and Paul were single), and there was no requirement for everyone to have children (both Jesus and Paul were single), and there was no limitation to being a vegetarian (Paul approved the eating of meat, Romans 14:2–4; 1 Corinthians 10:25–27). Therefore the apostle Paul himself did not think that any of Webb's supposedly "culturally relative" factors were found in the Creation account itself, or could be used to prove that it was invalid to appeal to the creation of Adam before Eve for transcultural principles that apply to conduct within the New Testament church. In short, Paul was not persuaded by any of the factors that Webb claims to show cultural relativity in the Creation account. Paul knew that all those factors were there, yet he still believed that "Adam was formed first, then Eve" was a valid reason for affirming an abiding, transcultural principle.

Webb's argument that the author of Genesis projected later circumstances back into the account of the Garden of Eden and thereby placed primogeniture in the Genesis 2 account (see discussion above) is also unpersuasive, because it denies the historical truthfulness of extended sections of the narrative in Genesis 2.

Finally, Webb objects that if complementarians take Paul's argument seriously in 1 Timothy 2:13, then, to be consistent, we should argue that primogeniture should be practiced today as well. He says, "It is interesting that those who appeal to primogeniture in affirming the trans-cultural status of 1 Timothy 2:13 say very little about the sustained application of other primogeniture texts for our lives" (142).

But here Webb is simply confusing the issue. The Bible never says, "All families should give a double portion of inheritance to the firstborn son, because Adam was formed first, then Eve." The Bible never commands any such thing, and Webb himself shows how the Bible frequently overturns such a practice (see pp. 136–39). Webb has imported into the discussion an idea of "consistency" that is foreign to the Bible itself. Webb is basically arguing as follows:

1.) The Bible makes one application from Adam's prior Creation.
2.) If you affirm that the Bible is correct in that first application, then you have to say that the Bible makes other applications from Adam's prior Creation.

But that reasoning does not follow. We are not free to say that the Bible *should* make applications that it does not make! That decision belongs to God, not us.

Consistency in this matter is simply affirming what the Bible says, and not denying the validity of any of the reasoning processes in Scripture (as Webb attempts to do with 1 Timothy

2:13), as well as not adding to the commands of Scripture (as Webb tries to push complementarians to do with this text). Consistency does not require that we make all sorts of applications of a biblical principle even when the Bible does not make those applications; rather, consistency says that the application Paul made from Genesis 2 is a valid and good one, and Scripture requires us also to affirm it as a transcultural principle today.

Paul is saying in 1 Timothy 2:12–13 that Adam's prior creation proves at least one thing: In the assembled church a woman should not "teach" or "have authority over a man" (1 Timothy 2:12). We are not free to adopt an interpretation that leads to the conclusion that Paul's reasoning process was incorrect even for his day.

8. Webb fails to show that Galatians 3:28 is a "new creation" pattern that overthrows the "old creation" patterns of male leadership in the home and church (Criterion 8).

Webb says there are several "in Christ" statements like Galatians 3:28, which tells us that "there is neither...male nor female, for you are all one in Christ Jesus." These "in Christ" statements, he claims, "should be given prominence over the old-creation patterns" that include what Webb sees as "patriarchy" within the "old-creation" patterns. He says, "New-creation theology transforms the status of all its participants...into one of equality.... It... heavily favors an egalitarian position" (152).

In this case again, Webb fails adequately to take into account that the male headship in marriage that was found in the Garden was itself "very good" in God's sight, and we should not look for some morally superior ethic to replace it. Moreover, Webb fails to take into account other "new-creation" statements that affirm male headship in marriage, such as Colossians 3:18, "Wives, submit to your husbands, as is fitting *in the Lord*" (italics added). This command is part of the new "in Christ" or "in the Lord" creation, just as "children, obey your parents *in the Lord*, for this is right" (Ephesians 6:1, italics added) is part of the new creation in Christ. In fact, Paul's commands as an apostle for the New Testament church *are* part of the "new-creation" in Christ, and therefore "I do not permit a woman to teach or to exercise authority over a man" *is also part of that new creation*, because it is part of the teaching of the New Testament for the church.

9. Webb fails to show that the Bible adopted male leadership because there were no competing options (Criterion 9).

Webb says, "It is reasonably safe to assume, therefore, that the social reality of the biblical writers was the world of patriarchy.... This consideration increases the likelihood of patriarchy being a cultural component within Scripture" (154–55). Webb explains that this is because an egalitarian position regarding marriage or the church was simply not an option, given the surrounding culture.

But this criterion is not persuasive. The New Testament teaches many things that were not found in the surrounding culture. No people in the surrounding culture believed in Jesus as the Messiah before He came. Even Webb admits that the idea that husbands should love their wives as Christ loved the church was revolutionary for the culture. The idea that there could be a church made up of Jews and Gentiles fellowshiping together was not an option in the surrounding culture.

Scripture often challenges and transforms the societies and cultures into which it speaks. Therefore, if a truly egalitarian model for marriage had been what God wanted for His people, He surely could have proclaimed it clearly through the pages of the New Testament and through the teachings of Jesus and the apostles. But (as Webb admits) the New Testament does not teach an egalitarian position. (According to Webb, we have to move beyond the ethic of the New Testament to reach full egalitarianism.)

10. Webb fails to show that the general principle of "justice" nullifies specific New Testament commands regarding male leadership (Criterion 13).

Webb asks, "Does the power inequality between men and women violate a theology of justice? Is there a hint of inequity or unfairness about the treatment of women in the Bible?" (181). Webb's answer is that "the general or broad principles of Scripture appear to favor movement from soft patriarchy to an egalitarian position" (184).[18]

The problem with Webb's analysis in this case is that it pits Scripture against Scripture. We are not free to take general principles like "justice" or "love" and say that they take priority over specific teachings of Scripture. Are we to say that the commands of the Bible in Ephesians 5 or 1 Timothy 2 were "unjust"?

Another problem with Webb's entire Criterion 13 (on specific versus general principles) is that it allows an interpreter to select any "general principle" he wants, and so drive the discussion in one direction or another. Webb chooses the general principles of "justice" and "equality," but why should these be the driving considerations? Why not choose the general principle of "the imitation of Christ" in His subjection to rightful authority and in his submission to the will of His Father? Why not choose the general principle of "submission to rightful authority," which is found in many levels of the Bible, and which is even found in the relationship of the Son to the Father in the Trinity? Of course, Webb does not select that general principle, for it would lead to a complementarian position.

This procedure of arguing that some broad principle overrides specific texts of Scripture is not a new idea with Webb. It is remarkably similar to the procedure used by liberals in the

18. What Webb calls "soft patriarchy" seems to be the position he thinks the New Testament taught for its time, because he thinks it is the position we should move "from." It is also essentially the position held by me and by the Council on Biblical Manhood and Womanhood, the position I have called a "complementarian" position (see Webb, pp. 26–27).

early part of the twentieth century when they appealed to the general principle of "the love of God" to override the specific teachings of the Bible about God's wrath, and particularly about God's wrath being poured out on His Son on the cross for our sins. In this way liberals commonly denied the heart of the atonement, that is, the doctrine of Christ's death as a substitute sacrifice in which He bore God's wrath against sin in our place (the penal substitutionary doctrine of the atonement).

Therefore this criterion (Webb's Criterion 13, "Specific Instructions Versus General Principles") is among the most dangerous of Webb's criteria, because it potentially can give legitimacy for people to find some "general principle" that will override texts of Scripture they find uncomfortable. The "love of God" principle could override the doctrine of hell, or could override the idea that not everyone will be saved. The "grace of God" principle could override the need for church elders to measure up to specific character traits. The "grace and forgiveness of God" principle could be used to override the specific teachings of the New Testament on divorce and remarriage. And so forth.

Webb himself says that this criterion is "susceptible to misuse" (183), to which I certainly agree. But then he says it is still "extremely helpful" (183), a statement with which I strongly disagree. Scripture does not contradict Scripture.

11. Webb fails to show that a wife's submission may be culturally relative because it is based on an analogy with Christ or with God (Criterion 14).

Webb argues that there are a number of culturally relative standards in the Bible, such as "slavery" or "monarchy" or "right-handedness" (186–87) that are based on an analogy with Christ or with God, and therefore it is not valid to say that New Testament teachings on male headship are transcultural because they are based on an analogy with Christ or with God. Specifically, Webb says that Ephesians 5:22–33 and 1 Corinthians 11:3 should not be seen as transcultural just because they depend on a "theological analogy" (188–89).

But once again Webb has mixed together things that are not parallel. First Corinthians 11:3 draws a parallel between the headship of the Father with respect to the Son and the headship of a husband with respect to his wife:

> Now I want you to realize that the head of every man is Christ, and the head of the woman is man, and the head of Christ is God.

But the Bible never makes statements like this regarding the other categories that Webb mentions. We do not find anywhere in Scripture statements like these:

> I want you to understand that right-handed people are superior to left-handed people, because Christ sits at the right hand of God.

> But I want you to understand that slavery is the best economic system, because God is the supreme slaveholder and you are all His slaves.

> I want you to understand that monarchy is the form of government that all nations should adopt, because God is the supreme king over the universe and you are all His subjects.

These are all ridiculous statements that the Scriptures would never make. Of course God *is* king over the universe and of course Jesus *does* sit at God's right hand, but the Bible never reasons from these things to the kinds of foolish statements it would have to make in order for Webb's argument to work.

Another problem with Webb's argument here is that it is once again based on his underlying assumption that it is possible to move to a "better ethic" (32) than the ethic of the New Testament. But consider 1 Corinthians 11:3 once again:

> Now I want you to realize that the head of every man is Christ, and the head of the woman is man, and the head of Christ is God.

Are we to understand that "the head of Christ is God" is only true for certain cultures at certain times? Are we to understand that "the head of every man is Christ" is true only for certain cultures and certain times? Certainly not (unless Webb also thinks these statements are culturally relative). But if the first and third parts of this verse are transcultural, then must we not also consider the second part to be transcultural, "the head of the woman is man"? Paul says there is a parallel between the eternal relationship of the Son to the Father and the relationship of a wife to her husband. And if Paul is correct that there is such a parallel, then the headship of a husband with respect to his wife is surely transcultural. Webb has shown no passages in the New Testament where such an argument is culturally relative.

The same considerations apply to Ephesians 5:22–23, where Paul says,

> Wives, submit to your husbands as to the Lord. For the husband is the head of the wife as Christ is the head of the church, his body, of which he is the Savior.

Paul bases his command on the fact that the relationship between a husband and wife is analogous to the relationship between Christ and the church. That is also a transcultural truth. Would Webb say that "Christ is the head of the church" is culturally relative? *Webb has produced no examples from the New Testament where a culturally relative command is similarly based on an appeal to the conduct of Christ or His relationship to the church.*

Contrary to Webb's claim on p. 186, 1 Peter 2:18–25 does not *endorse* slavery based on Christ's submission to suffering! First Peter 2 tells Christians *how to suffer* based on an imitation of Christ's example, but it does not thereby encourage persecution of Christians or say that such persecution or mistreatment is right. Similarly it does not argue, "Slavery is a morally good institution because Christ submitted to mistreatment." The New Testament never makes any such claim.

Webb's other response to Ephesians 5 and 1 Corinthians 11 is to say that if Paul had been addressing a different culture he would have commanded something different:

> If Paul had been addressing an egalitarian culture, he may have used the very same christological analogy (with its transcultural component) and reapplied it to an egalitarian relationship between husband and wife. He would simply have encouraged both the husband and the wife to sacrificially love one another. (188–89)

This amazing statement reveals how deeply committed Webb is to finding an egalitarian ethic that is "better than" the ethic taught in the New Testament. Even though he admits that *Paul did not teach an egalitarian view of marriage*, he says that *Paul would have taught an egalitarian view of marriage* had he been addressing a different culture, such as our egalitarian culture today! Webb is not at all bound by what Paul taught, but here as elsewhere feels free to use his speculation on what Paul "might have" taught in a different situation as a higher moral authority than what Paul actually did teach.

As I mentioned earlier (p. 619), Webb also claims that the Bible in Hosea 2 endorses the idea of a husband physically disciplining his wife after the analogy of God who disciplines the people of Israel (189–90). But here Webb is assuming a very unlikely view of Hosea 2, and he is surely assuming a morally offensive view of God and the Bible, because he is claiming that Hosea 2 could have rightly been used by husbands within Israel as a justification for stripping their wives naked and confining them physically as discipline for wrongdoing! This is something the Bible nowhere teaches, and certainly it is not taught in Hosea 2, but Webb claims it is taught there in order to find another "theological analogy" text that he can claim as transcultural. This one is a long stretch, and it is anything but persuasive.

12. Webb fails to show that New Testament submission lists have some culturally relative commands and some transcultural commands (Criterion 15).

Webb says that when he looks at the "submission lists" within the New Testament, two of the items are "culture bound" (monarchy and slavery), while two are "transcultural" (children/parents and congregation/elders) (196). Therefore he says it is uncertain whether the wife/husband submission command is cultural or transcultural, based on this criterion alone.

The problem with Webb's analysis here is the way he dismisses two of the commands in the New Testament as culturally relative. According to Webb, the command "Submit yourselves for the Lord's sake to every authority instituted among men: whether to the king, as the supreme authority, or to governors, who are sent by him to punish those who do wrong and to commend those who do right" (1 Peter 2:13–14) is "culturally relative" and we need to move to a better ethic than that of the New Testament, an ethic where we no longer have to submit to government leaders. But a better approach, and the one used by evangelicals who don't believe that we can move to a "better ethic" than that of the New Testament, is to say that we are still to *obey* that command, but we are to *apply it* to the closest parallel in our situation today, which is to be subject to government authorities. In fact, Peter allows for this when he talks about "every human institution," and Paul makes the same kind of general statement, not even mentioning an "emperor," but simply saying, "Everyone must submit himself *to the governing authorities*" (Romans 13:1). I see no reason why we should try to move beyond this New Testament teaching or see it as culturally relative.

In the same way, Christians today can obey the command, "Slaves, obey your earthly masters" (Ephesians 6:5) by *applying it* to the nearest parallel situation in our modern culture, namely, employees being subject to and obedient to their employers. The institution of "slave" (Greek doulos) was, in general, significantly different from the horrible abuses found in American slavery in the nineteenth century, and it was in fact the most common employment in the ancient world.[19] To make a parallel application to employees in their relationship to their employers is still to be subject to the ethic of the New Testament and obedient to it, and it is far different from Webb's system, in which we are no longer to obey this ethic but move toward a "better ethic" in which employees simply have to "fulfill the terms of their contract to the best of their ability" (38) in the hope that we will move toward Webb's "ultimate ethic" which has "wages maximized for all" (37; he nowhere explains this utopian platitude).

13. Webb fails to show that wives were to be subject to their husbands only because they were younger and less educated (Criterion 17).

Webb says that it made sense for wives to submit to their husbands in an ancient culture because they had less education, less social exposure, less physical strength, and they were significantly younger than their husbands (213–14). But these reasons, says Webb, no longer apply today, and therefore the command for wives to be subject to their husbands should be seen as culturally relative. A wife today should just give some kind of "honor" and "respect" to her husband (215).

Webb's argument here is not persuasive, however, because these are not the reasons the Bible gives for wives to be subject to their husbands. The reasons the Bible gives are the parallel with Christ's relationship to the church (Ephesians 5:22–24) and the parallel with the relationship between the Father and Son in the Trinity (1 Corinthians 11:3). Another reason that Paul gives is that this is what "is fitting in the Lord" (Colossians 3:18). Yet another reason is that it is part of "what is good" (Titus 2:3–4), and another reason is that unbelieving husbands may be "won over without words by the behavior of their wives" (1 Peter 3:1).

Webb's reasons here are merely speculative, and there is no indication that the biblical authors are taking these factors into account when they give these commands. Moreover, these New Testament commands apply to *all* wives, even those who were more intelligent than their husbands, or the same age as their husbands, or physically as strong as their husbands, or had

19. See the further discussion of slavery on pp. 339–45.

as much social exposure and social rank as their husbands, or as much wealth as their husbands. Webb's reasons are simply not the reasons the Bible uses.

In short, Webb says that the Bible teaches a wife's submission because of Webb's own invented reasons. Then he removes these invented reasons for today's culture and concludes that we can count the command as culturally relative. It is far better to heed the reasons the Bible actually gives, and to believe that these are the reasons that the Bible commands wives to be subject to husbands.

14. Webb fails to show that 1 Timothy 2:14, "Adam was not the one deceived; it was the woman who was deceived and became a sinner," is culturally relative (Criterion 18, "Scientific and Social-Scientific Evidence").

Webb argues that women were more easily deceived in the ancient world because they were not as well educated as men, were younger, and had less social exposure and less knowledge (229). But Webb goes to great lengths to demonstrate that these factors are not true of women today (he even has an appendix on research showing that gender plays a very small role in differences in ability to detect deception, 269–73). Therefore he says 1 Timothy 2:14 is culturally relative and does not apply to women today.

This argument is not persuasive because Paul makes no reference to his current culture or to women being susceptible to deception in the first century. Paul is talking again about Adam and Eve, and he says that another reason why women should not "teach" or "have authority over a man" is that "Adam was not the one deceived; it was the woman who was deceived and became a sinner" (1 Timothy 2:12–14). However we understand that passage, it is evident that Paul is saying that something is true of Eve in relationship to Adam *that has transcultural significance for women and men generally in the New Testament church*. Paul is not basing his argument on education or age or social exposure or knowledge (for no doubt there were many older and wiser women in the large church at Ephesus when Paul was writing to Timothy), but he is basing his argument on something that he sees to be a transcultural principle that has application to men and women generally. Some complementarians understand this verse to refer to Eve wrongfully taking leadership in the family and making the decision to eat the forbidden fruit on her own, and other complementarians understand this to refer to a woman's "kinder, gentler nature" and that she is therefore less likely to draw a hard line when close friends are teaching doctrinal error and relationships need to be broken.[20] Whatever interpretation we take, Paul is arguing from Eve's action at the Fall to a general truth about men and women teaching and governing the church; he is not explicitly arguing from any statement about women in his culture or any other culture.

---

20. For discussion of this verse, see Thomas Schreiner, "An Interpretation of 1 Timothy 2:9–15: A Dialogue with Scholarship," in *Women in the Church*, ed. Andreas Köstenberger, Thomas Schreiner, and H. Scott Baldwin (Grand Rapids, MI: Baker Book House, 1995), 140–46.

15. Webb fails to ask, "What if I am wrong?" about his entire system, but asks it only about one inconsequential point.

When readers see the title of Webb's last chapter, "What If I Am Wrong?" (236), they will likely expect, from the placement of this chapter at the end of the book, that Webb is raising the question, "What if I am wrong about my entire system?" But when we read this chapter carefully we find that is not at all what Webb is asking. *He does not even raise the possibility that his entire system about moving to a "better ethic" than the New Testament might be wrong.* He asks, "What if I am wrong?" about only one very small point, and that is whether Paul's appeal to primogeniture in 1 Timothy 2:13 should be viewed as transcultural rather than cultural. He says, "I am prepared to ask this chapter's reflective question about one aspect of my findings, namely, my assessment of 1 Timothy 2:13" (236). But he concludes that it does not really make much difference in the end, for even if one sees primogeniture as a transcultural factor, it is "light (not heavy) value in Scripture" (238), and it is significantly modified by other "culture-based factors" (238), and Galatians 3:28 still has "sociological implications that will modify the application even further" (240).

Therefore, even if Webb finds himself to be "wrong" on primogeniture in 1 Timothy 2:13, he says it will make very little difference. If he is right on 1 Timothy 2:13 being culturally relative, then he will end up with a "complementary egalitarianism" in which there is no "power differential based solely on gender" and no "role differentiation related to that power differential" (231). The only difference between the genders would be "based upon biological differences between men and women" and would include, for instance, "a greater participation of women in the early stages of child rearing" because of "the benefits of breast-feeding during early infant formation" (241).

But if Webb is wrong on 1 Timothy 2:13, then he thinks it would lead to an "ultra-soft patriarchy" in which there is "an equal power differential" between men and women in the home and in the church (243), but in which men would be granted "a certain level of *symbolic* honor for their firstborn status within the human family" (243).

Is there any difference then between Webb's two models, whether he is "right" or "wrong" on 1 Timothy 2:13? Webb himself says there is very little, because in either case,

> The application of 1 Timothy 2 is going to be very similar for both complementary egalitarians and ultra-soft partriarchalists. The only difference is whether there should be a dimension of *symbolic honor* granted to one gender over the other. (241)

What Webb is telling us then is that the only two options his system will allow are *both thoroughgoing egalitarian options*. In both cases, all teaching and governing roles in the church are open to women as well as men. In both situations, marriage is based on "mutual submission" and there is no unique leadership role or authority for the husband in the marriage. *The only difference is no real difference at all*, a mere question of whether some kind of "symbolic honor" should be given to men, a kind of honor that Webb does not further specify. I think it would be hard for anyone to see that "symbolic honor" as anything other than meaningless tokenism.

16. Webb proposes a misleading "forum for harmony" (243) which requires the abandonment of all gender-based leadership for men and asks that both sides begin to dialogue on the basis of a 99 percent capitulation to egalitarian claims.

At the end of his book, Webb says, "Complementary egalitarianism and ultra-soft patriarchy provide a forum for harmony and healing within the church" (p. 243). He says that his reflections in this final chapter have been included because, "I hope they will awaken a spirit of reconciliation between egalitarians and partriarchalists" (243).

What is the basis on which Webb proposes this "forum for harmony"? It is a forum to discuss whether we should adopt choice 1, "complementary egalitarianism" (which is Webb's title for a thoroughgoing egalitarian position), or whether we should adopt choice 2, "ultra-soft patriarchy" (which is Webb's other egalitarian option that gives a token "symbolic honor" to men).

Quite honestly, I find this somewhat insulting. I fail to understand how Webb expects his invitation to be taken seriously when the only two options offered in his "forum" are to capitulate 99 percent to egalitarian claims or to capitulate 100 percent to egalitarian claims. And even the 99 percent capitulation in what he calls "ultra-soft patriarchy" in the end is demeaning because it expects men to give up all male leadership roles in the home and the church and accept in return a token "symbolic honor."

In addition, complementarians will consider Webb's terminology offensive and confusing. As a cofounder of the Council on Biblical Manhood and Womanhood in 1987, and as a coauthor of the complementarian book *Recovering Biblical Manhood and Womanhood*, I wish to lodge a protest against Webb's use of two terms. His phrase "complementary egalitarianism," which he uses to describe a thoroughgoing egalitarian position, simply confuses the issues by using *complementary* for a position totally antithetical to what complementarians hold. In 1991, in the preface to *Recovering Biblical Manhood and Womanhood*, John Piper and I wrote,

> If one word must be used to describe our position, we prefer the term *complementarian*, since it suggests both equality and beneficial differences between men and women. We are uncomfortable with the term "traditionalist" because it implies an unwillingness to let Scripture challenge traditional patterns of behavior, and we certainly reject the term "hierarchicalist" because it overemphasizes structured authority while giving no suggestion of equality or the beauty of mutual interdependence. (xiv)

Since that time, *complementarian* has been the term we have consistently used to describe our position, and it has been widely (and courteously) used by others to describe our position as well. For Webb to apply it to an egalitarian position is to needlessly confuse the issues.[21]

For similar reasons, I find it objectionable that Webb consistently characterizes our position as "patriarchy." That term (which literally means "father-rule") almost uniformly has a pejorative connotation in modern society, and it carries nuances of an authoritarian father ruling over several generations of adults and children in an extended family in an ancient culture, none of which we are advocating today. The term by itself says nothing about the equal value that the Bible and our position attribute to men and women alike, nor does it say anything about a leadership role for the ***husband*** within the marriage (since it focuses on the role of the "father" or patēr, in the relationship). So it is an inappropriate, pejorative, and misleading term to refer to the position that we represent. It would seem more appropriate in academic debate, and indeed a simple matter of common courtesy, to refer to positions by the terms that the representatives of those positions choose for themselves rather than by pejorative terms that they reject.

Most of Webb's eighteen criteria for determining cultural relativity are unreliable guides for Christians today.

Webb's entire system is based on an assumption that the moral commands of the New Testament represent only a temporary ethical system for that time, and that we should use Webb's "redemptive-movement hermeneutic" to move beyond those ethical teachings to a "better ethic" (32) that is closer to the "ultimate ethic" God wants us to adopt. Since all of Webb's criteria are based on that assumption, the entire system is unpersuasive and inconsistent with a belief in the absolute moral authority of the teachings of the New Testament.

But at this point it is appropriate to comment specifically on each of the eighteen criteria that Webb produces, because in some cases his analysis produces helpful insight even though it is based on an underlying assumption with which I disagree.

In the following material, I offer only brief observations on each of the eighteen criteria.

---

21. Webb's objection that complementarians should not be able to use the term *complementarian* to describe their position because egalitarians also believe that men and women are "complementary" shows a failure to understand how specific words that indicate a special emphasis are commonly used as a convenient way to name different viewpoints and movements. Using Webb's logic, Presbyterians could say, "We should also be called Baptists because we too believe in baptism; therefore Baptists should not be the only ones called Baptists." Complementarians could say, "We should also be called egalitarians because we too believe that men and women are equal in many ways; therefore egalitarians should not be the only ones called egalitarians." In politics, Republicans could say, "We should also be called Democrats because we too believe in democracy; therefore Democrats should not be the only ones called Democrats." This procedure would introduce hopeless confusion into all conversation and make meaningful interaction almost impossible. CBMW chose the term *complementarian* as the single word that best represents our position in 1988 and we explained that decision in *Recovering Biblical Manhood and Womanhood* in 1991. We are not going to stop using *complementarian* to name our position, nor are we going to use it to refer to an egalitarian position. Confusion in terminology helps no one think clearly.

1. Preliminary Movement (73): I find this criterion unhelpful because it assumes that there can be "further movement" beyond the ethical teachings of the New Testament to a higher or better ethic. However, Webb's discussion is helpful as it applies to a number of Old Testament moral commands, which all interpreters I think would admit are a "preliminary" set of standards and not God's final moral standards for His people today. (All Christians of course see the Old Testament as preliminary to the New Testament, but that is far different from seeing the New Testament also as preliminary to further ethical development.) Another way of saying this is that all Christians agree there is "redemptive movement" from the Old Testament to the New Testament, but evangelicals have held that the movement stops with the New Testament. Prior to Webb, only Roman Catholics and liberal Protestants, not evangelicals, have taken developments beyond the New Testament as part or all of their ultimate authority.

2. Seed Ideas (83): I find this category unhelpful and unpersuasive because it assumes that some ideas in the New Testament (such as Galatians 3:28) are contradictory to other New Testament commands, and these "seed ideas" show us the direction we should look for a superior ethic to the New Testament.

3. Breakouts (91): I also find this category unhelpful and unpersuasive because it assumes that certain people in the Bible (such as Deborah or Junia) engage in activities that are contrary to the moral teachings in the biblical text, but that anticipate a movement to a higher ethic superior to that found in the Bible.

4. Purpose/Intent Statements (105): I find this category unpersuasive and troubling because it implies that we can disobey New Testament commands (such as the command for wives to be subject to their husbands) if we decide that the purpose specified in the command will no longer be fulfilled (for example, if we decide that wives being subject to their husbands will no longer help evangelism). This again assumes that we can move to a higher ethical level than that of the teachings of the New Testament. However, if Webb's analysis did not have the assumption that we could move to a higher ethical system than the New Testament, his explanation of the specific details of application today, such as his explanation of why we need not give a "holy kiss" (because it may not make people feel welcomed at all!), but should instead give some other kind of warm greeting, is a helpful explanation. (See the section at the end of chapter 9 for a discussion of the "holy kiss" and similar actions with symbolic purpose.)[22]

5. Basis in Fall or Curse (110): I agree with Webb's argument that moral commands based on the curse that God imposed in Genesis 3 are not valid as a standard for us to obey today. I also agree that the results of the curse continue in the present time, so that we are still subject to death, the ground still brings forth weeds, and women still experience pain in childbirth. I also agree with Webb that we should attempt to overcome these effects of the curse because I believe that has been the purpose of God in the history of redemption ever since He in justice imposed the curse.

22. See pp. 397–402, above.

6. Basis in Original Creation, Section 1: Patterns (123): I am not persuaded by Webb's argument that a component of a text only "may" be transcultural if it is rooted in the original Creation material (123), because I do not think he has discovered anything in the Garden before the Fall that is not morally good or that we should not see as morally good today. His attempts to find culturally relative components in the Genesis narrative are all based on a misreading of the purpose and intent of that narrative.

7. Basis in Original Creation, Section 2: Primogeniture (134): I find Webb's analysis here to be unpersuasive, both because his position is based on a denial of the historicity of Adam being created before Eve in Genesis 2, and because he thinks that the principle of primogeniture found in Adam's being created before Eve should not be taken as a transcultural principle unless people are willing to apply primogeniture in other aspects of society today. As I explained above, this assumes that Paul cannot properly make one application of a pattern found in Genesis 2 unless he also makes many other applications of a principle found in Genesis 2. I believe, in contrast to Webb, that it is up to God, not us, to decide what commands to give us based on principles in Genesis, and that we should simply follow the ones he gives.

8. Basis in New Creation (145): I find this criterion unpersuasive and unhelpful, not because I think that "new creation patterns" in the New Testament are wrong, but because Webb wrongly assumes that these patterns are in conflict with the pattern of male leadership found in God's original creation of Adam and Eve, and because Webb fails to consider other "new creation" commands that encourage wives to be subject to their husbands "in the Lord" (Colossians 3:18), and because Webb again assumes that the "new creation" statements in the New Testament are simply an indicator that leads us along the path to a higher ethical standard than that found in the commands of the New Testament itself.

9. Competing Options (152): I find this criterion helpful in Webb's discussion of why God did not immediately give commands to outlaw slavery (it would have caused massive and destructive economic upheaval), but rather gave principles that would lead to its abolition. But I find this criterion unhelpful in its assumption that the New Testament actually commanded or endorsed slavery, and also I find it unpersuasive in its claim that the New Testament could not have taught an egalitarian position at the time it was written (something Webb has failed to prove, and something that cannot be proven in light of the New Testament's willingness to challenge culture at many points).

10. Opposition to Original Culture (157): I find this criterion to be generally helpful, especially as it indicates the ways in which both Old and New Testaments oppose many current cultural attitudes and practices regarding slavery. I am not as sure that it is helpful for Webb's argument that the commands against homosexuality are transcultural because homosexuality was widely accepted in the ancient world, since I think that Webb underestimates the widespread moral disapproval of homosexual conduct in many sections of ancient society. And I think in this section Webb has not adequately considered the way the New Testament does oppose some cultural values regarding marriage when it strongly emphasizes the need for husbands to love their wives as Christ loved the church. But this shows that the New Testament was willing to stand against cultural views on marriage when it was something that was morally right.

11. Closely Related Issues (162): I find this category to be unhelpful and unpersuasive because Webb deals almost entirely with Mosaic laws regarding women while failing to take into account that Christians are no longer under the Mosaic covenant, and these laws are not what "the Bible" teaches for New Testament Christians in any case. Webb seems in this section to be on a fishing expedition to find deficient elements in Scripture, especially about the treatment of women, so that he can argue that we need to move to a higher ethic than that taught in the commands of the biblical text.

12. Penal Code (179): I found this section to be helpful in its observation that most actions that received the death penalty in the Old Testament still receive divine disapproval today (though there are a couple of exceptions regarding Sabbath breaking and cultic violations, so the analysis is not entirely convincing). This criterion does not have much application to the relationship between husbands and wives, as Webb himself admits (179).

13. Specific Instructions Versus General Principles (179): I found this section to be unpersuasive and actually quite dangerous for Christians today, because it could easily give legitimacy to disobedience to Scripture on any uncomfortable subject, simply by enabling people to find a "general principle" of Scripture that could be used to override a specific teaching.

14. Basis in Theological Analogy (185): I found this section to be deeply flawed, because it wrongly assumes that the Bible taught and approved slavery, monarchy, and even right-handedness! Then it argues that not all of these theological analogies are transcultural, and therefore the teachings on marriage in Ephesians 5 and 1 Corinthians 11:3 are not necessarily transcultural.

By use of this procedure Webb potentially nullifies all "imitation of Christ" passages in the New Testament. Webb's claim that a command based in theological analogy need not be transcultural is based on his claim that some culturally relative commands are based on similar theological analogies, but in fact he has produced no examples that are actually parallel to Ephesians 5 or 1 Corinthians 11:3.

15. Contextual Comparisons (192): I found this category to be unhelpful because Webb incorrectly assumes that the New Testament approves and endorses slavery and monarchy.

16. Appeal to the Old Testament (201): I found this analysis to be unpersuasive and unhelpful because Webb incorrectly brings in a number of texts that do not appeal to the Old Testament to prove the validity of slavery or monarchy, and also because he brings in a number of texts that do not appeal to the Old Testament at all but simply have parallels in the Old Testament (such as foot washing or the "holy kiss"). Therefore Webb wrongly dismisses texts regarding women that appeal to the Old Testament (such as 1 Corinthians 14:33, 36; 1 Timothy 2:11–15; 1 Peter 3:1–7).

In addition, Webb rightly sees that if the New Testament discontinues a practice, it is not required for Christians to obey (201). But he wrongly sees this as an evidence of cultural change rather than an evidence of a change from the Old Covenant to the New Covenant.

17. Pragmatic Basis Between Two Cultures (209): I found this criterion to be unpersuasive because in a number of cases (particularly with respect to husbands and wives) Webb assumed that he knew the reason for a command, then he used his assumed reasons (such as that wives were younger or less educated) to replace the actual reasons the Bible gave for a command. However, in the obvious example of why we do not wash other people's feet today, Webb's observation that we don't travel on dirt roads with sandals did express what people instinctively understand about this difference between ancient and modern culture.

18. Scientific and Social-Scientific Evidence (221): I found this entire section unpersuasive because Webb claims that the Bible teaches many things that it does not actually teach (such as a flat earth and a geocentric model of the universe). He then uses these examples to show that we have to abandon the teaching of the Bible because in a number of cases it goes contrary to present-day scientific evidence. Moreover, if Webb really believes that the Bible teaches these incorrect things, this indicates that he does not believe the Bible is inerrant in everything it affirms (and this is similar to his denial of the historicity of the creation of Adam prior to Eve in Genesis 2).

The difficult passages for determining cultural relativity are few, and most evangelicals have already reached a satisfactory conclusion about them.

Webb has made the question of determining when something is "culturally relative" into a much bigger problem than it actually is. The main question is not whether the ***historical*** sections of the Bible report events that occurred in an ancient culture, because the Bible is a historical book and it reports thousands of events that occurred at a time and in a culture significantly different from our own. The question rather is how we should approach the *moral commands* found in the New Testament. Are those commands to be obeyed by us today as well?

I have suggested in the final section of chapter 9 some guiding principles to help us answer that question, which is not nearly as complicated as Webb makes it out to be.[23]

Conclusion: Is William Webb's book a helpful guide for Christians today?

Although Webb raises many interesting and challenging questions regarding cultural relativity, I believe *Slaves, Women and Homosexuals: Exploring the Hermeneutics of Cultural Analysis* is a deeply flawed book that fundamentally contradicts the Reformation principle of *sola Scriptura* because it nullifies in principle the moral authority of the entire New Testament and replaces it with the moral authority of a "better ethic," an ethic that Webb claims to be able to

23. See the "Additional Note" to chapter 9, pp. 397–402 above, for the section, "How can we determine which commands of Scripture are culturally relative?"

discover through a complex hermeneutical process entirely foreign to the way God intended the Bible to be read, understood, believed, and obeyed. Because a denial in principle of the moral authority of the New Testament commands is at the heart of the whole system, and because the system denies the historical accuracy of the Creation account, I do not believe Webb's "redemptive-movement hermeneutic" should be accepted as a valid system for evangelicals today.

APPENDIX 6

Three Reviews of *I Suffer Not a Woman* by Richard and Catherine Kroeger

NOTE: This appendix contains three reviews of the Kroegers' book by S. M. Baugh, Albert Wolters, and Robert Yarbrough. Because the review by Baugh is so much longer and more detailed than the other two, I have placed it third in this appendix.

Albert Wolters, review of *I Suffer Not a Woman: Rethinking 1 Timothy 2:11–15 in Light of Ancient Evidence*, by Richard Clark Kroeger and Catherine Clark Kroeger[1]

In the current debate about women's ordination, 1 Timothy 2:11–15 continues to be one of the main bones of contention, and has occasioned a spate of exegetical studies (see the recent article by Gordon P. Hugenberger, "Women in Church Office: Hermeneutics or Exegesis? A Survey of Approaches to 1 Timothy 2:8–15," *JETS* 35 [1992], 341–60). In the present volume, the first book-length study of this disputed passage, Richard and Catherine Kroeger offer the most extensive presentation of their approach to this text, expanding on the briefer statements found in their joint article "Women in the Church" in the *EDT*, and in Catherine Kroeger's essay "1 Timothy 2:12: A Classicist's View" in *Women, Authority and the Bible,* 225–44. To a more limited extent, the book also carries forward themes found already in Catherine's first attempt to find an alternative to the traditional interpretation, published as "Ancient Heresies and a Strange Greek Verb" in the *Reformed Journal* 29.3 (March 1979), 12–15. The book is therefore an updating and an elaboration of more than a decade's work on these disputed verses.

Although the book is written for a general audience, it also makes a serious attempt to observe high standards of scholarship. The footnotes are replete with references to the

1. Reprinted from *Calvin Theological Journal* 28 (1993): 208–13. Used by permission.

ancient sources in their original languages, and to secondary literature up to 1990 in Latin, French, German, and Italian, as well as English. Clearly, the Kroegers are concerned to demonstrate to their evangelical readers that their proposal is based on extensive, solid, and up-to-date scholarship. They deplore the fact that "evangelical scholarship has not always been of a level of excellence that earned the respect of nonevangelicals" (38), and are evidently determined to present a case which can withstand scholarly scrutiny. In this review I intend to subject the Kroegers' book to just such a scrutiny, focusing on the exegetical, historical, and methodological aspects of their argument, and leaving to one side the rhetoric engendered by the women's ordination debate.

The Kroegers' basic thesis has a philological and a historical component. Philologically, they argue that verse 12 should be translated "I do not permit woman to teach nor to represent herself as originator of man, but she is to be in conformity [with the Scriptures] [or that she keeps it a secret]" (103), and maintain that "to teach" in this context means "to teach a wrong doctrine" (81). Historically, they argue that there had arisen in the first-century Christian community in Ephesus a Gnostic (or "proto-Gnostic") heresy characterized by the following teachings: 1.) Eve was the origin of Adam; 2.) Eve came before Adam; 3.) it was Adam that was deceived, Eve was in fact his enlightener; and 4.) childbearing is something religiously unworthy. If we put the philological and historical arguments together, it becomes clear that the apostle in 1 Timothy 2:12–15 contradicts each of these Gnostic teachings in turn: verse 12 counters 1.), verse 13 counters 2.), verse 14 counters 3.), and verse 15 counters 4.). In short, the passage is concerned to refute a specific heresy at a specific time and place, and we should not read it as a universal restriction on the role of women in the church.

It is clear that this bold and ingenious exegetical proposal has a claim to be taken seriously. After all, it is sound exegetical procedure to try to determine the specific historical situation to which a portion of Scripture was originally addressed, and there are certainly difficulties surrounding 1 Timothy 2:11–15 (both in terms of its detailed exegesis and its implications for Christian obedience today) that justify a reconsideration of the traditional interpretation. Moreover, the Kroegers have amassed a wealth of documentation in support of their interpretation that is impressive in its range.

Nevertheless, it needs to be said that their proposal, both philologically and historically, is a signal failure. In fact, it is not too much to say that their book is precisely the sort of thing that has too often given evangelical scholarship a bad name. There is little in the book's main thesis that can withstand serious scrutiny, and there is a host of subordinate detail that is misleading or downright false.

Consider, for example, their proposed new translation of verse 12. They are unable to adduce a single example, either from biblical or secular Greek, of didaskein meaning "to teach a wrong doctrine." (Nor does that meaning follow, as they suggest on p. 81, from the fact that this verb and its cognates in the Pastorals generally imply positive or negative content.) As for the interpretation of en hēsuchia einai as either "be in conformity [with the Scripture]" or "keep it a secret," this is equally arbitrary and unfounded. The fact that hēsuchia can on occasion have the connotation of "peace" or "harmony" hardly warrants the translation "conformity" (this simply trades on the ambiguity of the word *harmony* in English), much less the gratuitous insertion of "[with the Scriptures]" as part of the translation (103). Nor is there any warrant for the claim that en hēsuchia einai can mean "keep it a secret," a translation which seems to be based on a confusion with en hēsuchia exein ti (LSJ s.v. hēsuchia, 3).

The authors go to great lengths to argue that the verb authentein can mean "to represent oneself as originator of" or "to proclaim oneself author of" (103), but their argument can hardly be taken seriously. Ignoring the fact that authentein is attested in New Testament times in the meaning "have authority over," they take their point of departure in the meaning "originate," a rare sense of the verb which is not attested before the fourth century AD Moreover, for the Kroegers' overall proposal to work, they need to find evidence that the verb can mean "*claim to* originate." They find this evidence in the sixteenth-century Greek-Latin dictionary of Stephanus (and some of its derivatives), which states that authenteō means praebeo me auctorem. They then interpret this Latin definition to mean "to represent oneself as author," and go on to equate this with "asserting oneself to be the author or source of." Having established the sense in this way, they proceed to find this new meaning in three patristic texts of the fourth and fifth centuries (102–5).

All of this makes an initial impression of great erudition, but masks the fact that the Latin idiom has been misunderstood (it simply means "behave as originator of," a Latin way of saying "originate"; see under praebeo in the *Oxford Latin Dictionary* [5, b–c] or the *Thesaurus Linguae Latinae* [I,B,1 and II,B,I]; compare Calvin's Latin rendering of Hebrews 5:2 and 2 Peter 3:9) and that in the long history of classical scholarship the Kroegers are the first to find this sense in the three patristic texts cited (all three are listed under the meaning "be primarily responsible for, instigate, authorize" in Lampe, *Patristic Greek Lexicon*, s.v. 4). They even go so far as to suggest that Stephanus must have had access to Greek texts that are now lost (102), and that the failure of contemporary Greek lexicons to list this sense has something to do with the rise of feminism (230n29).

Furthermore, although they cite a good deal of secondary literature on authentein and its cognates (228n1), they repeatedly misunderstand the sources they cite, and they fail to mention important recent literature which counts against their own interpretation. For example, a Latin quote from Guillaume Budé is completely misunderstood on p. 102 (to make matters worse, the original is cited in a badly garbled form; see 230n27), and their mistranslation of a German citation about authentein shows similar incompetence (101). Conspicuous by its absence is any reference to the important article by L. E. Wilshire, "The TLG Computer and Further References to Authenteō in 1 Timothy 2:12," *NTS* 34 (1988), 120–34, which provides extensive evidence that supports the traditional interpretation of authentein in 1 Timothy 2:12. (They do quote other literature from 1988, and have at least five references to items published in 1990.) They also repeat the common mistake of asserting that the verb authentein means "to murder" in ancient Greek (86, 185, 203); in fact, this meaning is not attested for the verb (not to be confused with the noun authentēs) before the tenth century AD

Philologically, it seems, the Kroegers are adept at making a Greek text say what they would like it to say, and their scholarly documentation is riddled with elementary linguistic blunders. Further examples in the latter category are the assertion that parathēkē in the Pastorals refers to Paul's "will and testament" (44), an apparent confusion with diathēkē; and the made-up Greek sentence in which the accusative singular of anēr is given as andron (191).

Unfortunately, things are not much better with the Kroegers' historical argumentation. There is in fact no direct evidence that their postulated Gnostic sect ever existed in first-century Ephesus, or indeed that a Gnostic group fitting their description ever existed at all. The sect which, on their view, is the key to understanding 1 Timothy 2:11–15 is really nothing more than a hypothetical reconstruction based on disparate features of pagan religion in Ephesus and Anatolia, and on a few much later Gnostic documents. For example, for the Gnostic view that Eve precedes and creates Adam (points 1 and 2 above) they adduce only passages from the two related Nag Hammadi tractates called *The Hypostasis of the Archons* and *On the Origin of the World* (121), found in Egypt and dated to the third or fourth century AD. There is no evidence that any other Gnostic group ever held this view, despite the impression which the Kroegers seek to create on pp. 119–20. Since there was a plethora of such groups in the second century, it is very forced to appeal to these third-century documents from Egypt to establish a point about a hypothetical first-century sect in Ephesus.

Furthermore, the appeal to the two Nag Hammadi texts is itself seriously flawed. Even if we grant that the passages cited (*Hyp. Arch.* 89.12–18; *Orig. World* 115.30–116.8) do refer to Eve *creating* Adam, and not just rousing him from sleep (which seems the much more likely reading), it needs to be pointed out that the Eve in question is the *heavenly* Eve, which the Gnostics distinguished from the earthly Eve who was Adam's human partner. Consequently, even if this *could* be shown to be the view of the Kroegers' hypothetical Ephesian Gnostics, it would not be refuted by Paul's statement in 1 Timothy 2:13 that "Adam was formed first, then Eve," since Paul is clearly referring to the earthly Eve of the biblical story.

Space does not permit a discussion of the Kroegers' attempt to find evidence in Gnostic writings of the views numbered 3 and 4 above. It is enough to say that they can find that evidence only by picking and choosing *from* a number of different Gnostic groups, from different times and places. It is significant that they can find no group which holds all four of the required doctrines, and that none of the Gnosticisms adduced has any connection with first-century Ephesus. Furthermore, it seems to have escaped the Kroegers that view number

4 contradicts their earlier assertion that their hypothetical Gnostic group "acclaimed motherhood as the ultimate reality" (112).

Perhaps even more damaging is their failure to refer to the extensive ancient sources which do refer directly to the Christian church in late first-century Ephesus—none of which supports the presence there of the kind of Gnosticism that the Kroegers postulate. (Note that they consider the Pastorals to be post-Pauline, but date them before AD 100; see p. 44). They make no mention, for example, of the works of Polycarp, Papias, or Ignatius. Nor do they make any reference to the Gospel of John, which was in all likelihood written in Ephesus in the late first century. Presumably the Kroegers are silent about these sources because they do not support the hypothesis that the authors are advocating. For a recent synthesis of the relevant evidence, see Thomas A. Robinson, *Orthodoxy and Heresy in Western Asia Minor in the First Christian Century* (PhD dissertation, McMaster University, 1985), especially chapter 2: "Ephesus and Western Asia Minor: The Key Christian Centre, 70–100 C.E."

The Kroegers' silence about the fourth Gospel is especially telling, because Irenaeus claimed that John wrote his Gospel specifically against Cerinthus, an early Gnostic who was active in Ephesus. One would think that they would have seized upon this bit of evidence as support for their basic hypothesis of a Gnostic group in Ephesus at that time. However, they mention Cerinthus only in passing (65, 101). How are we to account for their reluctance to pursue this line of inquiry? No doubt the reason is once again the fact that this evidence, on closer examination, does not support their theory. The Cerinthian Gnostics seem not to have espoused the doctrines which the Kroegers need to make their case.

Another reason may have to do with Cerinthus' use of the Greek word authentia as the name of his supreme deity. This is a word meaning "absolute sway, authority," and might be taken as evidence that Gnostics in first-century Ephesus would have connected the cognate verb authentein with the notion of authority. This, however, is a suggestion which the Kroegers are at some pains to avoid. As it happens, authentia (and its adjectival cognate authentikos) figures quite prominently in the vocabulary of many Gnostic groups, and scholars are generally agreed that it conveys the notion of sovereignty or authority. The Kroegers, however, although they cannot avoid referring repeatedly to this common Gnostic term and its adjective, generally refrain from translating them (see 101, 110, 118, 152, 222) or else use the word *power,* which is less likely to give people the wrong idea about authentein (87, 90, 100, 213).

In addition to all of this, there are innumerable minor errors throughout the book. There is the consistent misspelling of the Greek name Hygieia as "Hygeia" (131, 162, 163, 248), and of aretalogy as "aretology" (158, 159 *bis,* 231, 245), the astonishing claim that 2 Corinthians was written "from Asia, probably from Ephesus" (163), the amusing failure to recognize the phrase "perform the rites of Venus" as a seventeenth-century euphemism for sexual intercourse (198), and much more. This review is not the place to list them all.

It is clear from the foregoing that, in the opinion of this reviewer, the Kroegers have conspicuously failed to make their case. No doubt the book will have considerable influence in the evangelical world, but it is very doubtful whether any serious commentary on 1 Timothy will ever adopt its basic thesis. (It is very telling that the authors' display of erudition is contained in a popular book aimed at a broad evangelical audience, not at their academic peers in classical and biblical scholarship.) The book will do its work within the context of current ecclesiastical debates, but its argumentation is a travesty of sound scholarship.

"*I Suffer Not a Woman:* A Review Essay" by Robert W. Yarbrough[1]

Controversy over how certain Pauline texts of old ought to be applied today continues to rage in evangelical circles. At the center of debate are passages that appear to mandate equally important but functionally distinct roles of service, in both home and church, for all women and men alike who recognize the authority of Christ and Scripture over their lives. One of the more warmly contested verses is 1 Timothy 2:12: "I permit no woman to teach or to have authority over men; she is to keep silent" (RSV). How should this verse be understood in the modern setting?

A new book by Richard Clark Kroeger and Catherine Clark Kroeger, *I Suffer Not a Woman: Rethinking 1 Timothy 2:11–15 in Light of Ancient Evidence,* attempts to give a satisfactory response to that question. This essay will comment on the book's positive features along with some apparent deficiencies. It will conclude by reflecting on the possible importance of the book as an indicator of evangelicalism's theology, hermeneutic, and future.

Argument and methodological weaknesses

First, to the book's central argument: The authors assert that the best translation of 1 Timothy 2:12 is, "I do not allow a woman to teach or proclaim herself author of man" (192). That is, women preaching or teaching in church should neither teach nor preach that women are the source of men or mankind. The Kroegers claim that in first-century Ephesus, Anatolian, female-dominated religious views had merged with Jewish and Gnostic traditions about Eve. The result was that women, who according to the Kroegers were elders, teachers, and even apostles in the Pauline churches just like men were, might tend to ape indigenous cultural belief by teaching its unscriptural views of human origins in the churches. They might teach that "female activity brought man into existence" (113). Paul forbids them to teach this because it does not square with the claim in Genesis that Adam was created first.

---

1. Reprinted from *Presbyterion* 18/1 (1992):25–33. Used by permission.

Positive features of the book are several. First, the reader does not have to waste time wondering what the authors' point of view is: They are avowedly feminist in sympathy and are convinced from the outset that traditional readings of 1 Timothy 2:12 must be rejected. While more nuance in conviction might have made for more convincing argumentation, its lack contributes to the book's intense focus. Second, the book displays a certain erudition. Its arguments are supported by hundreds of references to scores of primary sources. As it notes, "evangelical scholarship has not always been of a level of excellence that earned the respect of nonevangelicals" (38). The Kroegers' aim to redress this grievance is commendable. Third, it appears to be comprehensive in scope. It leaves few stones, of certain kinds anyway, unturned in its effort to sustain its central argument. Some seven appendixes, a few of them lengthy, augment claims made in various chapters. Despite its semipopular tone and target audience, the book has every appearance of scholarly rigor and weight.

Still, precisely in the name of scholarly rigor serious questions may be raised regarding the book's method and content.

First, regarding method, three broad representative deficiencies seem worth probing. Anyone of them alone might cast a distinct shadow on the book's claims; together they render its primary argument dubious.

1.) The book gives the impression that certain findings are true when they are in fact widely, and plausibly, contested. This belies the claim that the authors strive for "a thorough knowledge of the exegesis of other scholars including those with whom we disagree" (38). If the Kroegers possess this knowledge, they do not often factor it into the arguments of this book.

E.g., on p. 112 it is avowed that the Greek word for "head" meant "source" rather than "authority." No reference whatsoever is made, not even in a footnote, to the extensive literature both secondary and primary which attests cogently to the contrary.[2] Other examples along this line are not lacking, as when a statement in the apocryphal Gospel according to the Egyptians is alleged to furnish the background for understanding Paul's statement about women being saved through childbirth (176f.). What is the evidence that either this heretical group or the community that produced this document existed alongside apostolic Christianity in Ephesus during Paul's lifetime?

Or again, the book states, "The earliest writer to lay at Eve's door the blame for the advent of sin and death into the world is Ben Sirach in the second century BCE." (144). This seems to overlook Moses (Genesis 2 and 3), yet is stated as a categorical fact. Or again, Paul allegedly "glosses over the fact that Adam...had sinned knowingly" (123). One might have expected more caution in imputing deceit to an inspired apostolic writer who appears to have shared

2. For another, perhaps more serious example of this method, see n. 6 below. On the debate over the meaning of "head" (kephalē), see Grudem, "Meaning of Kephalē ('Head'): A Response to Recent Studies," in J. Piper and W. Grudem, eds., *Recovering Biblical Manhood and Womanhood* (Wheaton, IL: Crossway Books, 1991), 425–68.

something of Jesus' own divine insight into Moses' writings. Yet there is no discussion or qualification of this weighty charge.

Or again, the word anthrōpos (person, man) "does not specifically denote gender" (69). Yet in various New Testament passages it is used synonymously with anēr, a word that means "male" or "husband" and not just "person" (see, e.g., Luke 6:6, 8; 8:27, 29). In John 3 anthrōpos is used to refer to Nicodemus; does this exclude his gender? Acts 19:35 makes clear that in first-century Ephesus anthrōpos can be a subset of anēr: "Men [andres, plural of anēr] of Ephesus, what man [anthrōpos] is there among you..."

The point is that the book's general method, not at every juncture but at many, is to build on one-sided statements, ignoring any research findings or even primary data that do not agree with its thesis. This makes for a convincing presentation—but only so long as one remains ignorant of the full range of pertinent data and dissenting scholarly opinion.

2.) The book mixes data from various centuries, millennia, cultures, and religions in a generally indiscriminate manner. Too little prudence, control, or methodological discipline is exercised in explaining the context of 1 Timothy 2:12 in the light of traditions, whether historical or mythological, from hundreds if not thousands of years before or after the first century. Samuel Sandmel's "Parallelomania" is by now a dated article,[3] but its strictures still cast timely doubt over the soundness of many of the book's comparative observations.[4] How likely is it, for example, that Paul's call for women to dress modestly and let good works be their adornment (1 Timothy 2:9–10) was "a warning to women who sometimes disrobed during worship" (74)? While it is no doubt true that frescoes in Pompeii show female worshipers of Dionysius being immodest in their religious revelry, can we take seriously the suggestion that as Timothy's male parishioners in Ephesus raised their hands in prayer, women might have been inclined to raise their skirts to the waist (75) as a tribute to fertility, so that Paul had to urge them instead to modesty? Here and elsewhere, an uncritical use of comparative material leads to arguments that might furnish comic relief were they not adduced with such gravity, and built on with so little tentativeness.

3.) The book falls prey to a number of linguistic fallacies. A troubling underlying tendency that permeates the entire discussion involves willingness to traffic in currently fashionable appeals to the indeterminacy of meaning: "We need to bear in mind that one of the distinctives of the Pastorals is the use of expressions which may be construed variously" (189; cf. 104).

From this starting point, which the Kroegers use to legitimize an aggressive aproach to linguistic experimentation, the word authentein (translated "have authority over" in 1 Timothy 2:12) is examined against the background of all possible meanings in all possible contexts in all possible parts of speech (noun, adjective, adverb) and cognate forms in all extant literature. But the question is what the word as a verb means in this specific literary, historical, cultural,

3. *Journal of Biblical Literature* 81 (1962): 1–13.

4. A more recent discussion of the great care needed in extrapolating from Paul's remarks within a given situation, to a reconstruction of that situation, and then back to the situation and the Pauline text itself, is available in J. M. G. Barclay, *Obeying the Truth: Paul's Ethics in Galatians* (Minneapolis: Fortress, 1991), 36–74.

and theological context, not what a related form means as another part of speech or cognate form in other contexts. It is surely unlikely, for example, that 1 Timothy 2:12 is forbidding cultic murder (or "ritual castration"; see p. 94) of men by women, even though authentein does mean murder or suicide in certain contexts. Yet the Kroegers insist that we cannot "rule out the possibility" that this is Paul's intent (185). But one might just as well argue that Pharoah's daughter's servant did not "take up" Moses' basket from the bulrushes but rather "destroyed" it (Exodus 2:5, LXX), or that Moses did not "kill" but simply "picked up" the Egyptian he slew (Exodus 2:14, LXX). After all, the same Greek verb *(anairō)* is the root in both cases. Readers who know Greek know the difference. (Similarly, literate English speakers can distinguish between the contrasting meanings of "save" in the sentence, "God's grace will save all sinners save those who spurn His grace." The first "save" connotes inclusion and acceptance, the second exclusion and rejection. But one is not free to interchange them, at least not without realizing that to do so yields a meaning that would stand the Christian gospel on its head.)

A related example of unsound linguistic practice regarding authentein is found on p. 99, where appeal is made to "the original sense" and a supposed "most basic" meaning of the word. When phrases like this crop up, can illegitimate totality transfer be far behind? There is by now surely no need to rehearse the timeworn criticisms of such diachronic etymologies and root fallacies as this, which brought trenchant protests against the likes of Kittel's theological dictionary decades ago (see, e.g., James Barr, *The Semantics of Biblical Language,* and more recently Don Carson, *Exegetical Fallacies,* or Moises Silva, *God, Language, and Scripture).*

In a word, the Kroegers have failed to show either the necessity or the plausibility of some other rendering of authentein in this context.[5] Their methods have often led them down a path where firm linguistic footing appears to be signally lacking.

Representative specific questions

So much for an overview of methodological deficiencies. More specific problems of content deserve mention as well. Three samples must suffice.

1.) With reference to Paul's statement that Phoebe "has become [egenēthē] a helper to many" (Romans 16:2, RSV), the Kroegers claim that ginomai (to become, to be, to happen) in this verse means "appointed or ordained," since this verb "is identical to that used when Paul says, 'I was made [or ordained] minister' (Ephesians 3:7; Colossians 1:23) and to indicate that Christ was appointed (or ordained) high priest (Hebrews 5:5)" (91). Both this claim and the

5. Here is another instance where ignoring pertinent literature both secondary and primary vitiates the argument: see Leland Wilshire, "The *TLG* Computer and Further Reference to AΨΥENTE´ in 1 Timothy 2:12," *New Testament Studies* 34 (1988): 120, 134. Wilshire examines an exhaustive database and concludes: "Sometime during the spread of koine, the word authenteō went beyond the predominant Attic meaning connecting it with murder and suicide and into the broader concept of criminal behaviour. It also began to take on the additional meanings of 'to exercise authority/power/rights' which became firmly established in the Greek Patristic writers to mean 'to exercise authority'" (131). It is doubtful that the Kroegers do justice to either this argument or its underlying evidence.

logic underlying it are insupportable. Nor is this meaning to be found in either Bauer's dictionary of New Testament Greek or Liddell and Scott's of classical Greek. Yet Phoebe's alleged eldership looms large in the Kroegers' reconstruction of a first-century, apostolic church whose offices were equally as open to women as to men.

2.) The general picture of women's prominence and egalitarian status along with men in the early church given on pp. 91–92 is vastly overstated. It is one thing to argue that women should serve in precisely the same capacities as men in the Western church and world today. It is another to project that ideal back *onto* the earliest decades of the church. But that is what the Kroegers do—the "older women" in Titus 2:3 becoming now "female elders" in their reading (91), for example, or the women whose homes housed Christian meetings now becoming the ordained presiding officers of the churches in their cities (92).

3.) Most fundamentally, the book raises doubts by its basic premise that the so-called traditional rendering of 1 Timothy 2:12 stands in contradiction to other Pauline letters. The Kroegers arrive at this putative finding, which controls the book's discussion throughout, by assuming that the implication of Galatians 3:28 ("neither male nor female") is that men and women filled exactly the same offices and roles in the early church (see, e.g., pp. 39f.). If women were originally pastors, teachers, and apostles right alongside men, then any verses like 1 Timothy 2:12 that seem to restrict such activity must be either mistranslations, locally or temporally limited, or both. If, on the other hand, Galatians 3:28 cannot be used in this way,[6] and if women's unique giftedness in the apostolic church was not seen as merely egalitarian imitation of men's calling and function, then the problem the Kroegers diagnose vanishes, and 1 Timothy 2:12 becomes part of an overall church structure in which one's sexuality, when relevant at all, was viewed as part of a sovereign God's divine bestowal and enablement through which to serve Christ, rather than as a hindrance to evade or transcend. Moreover, the so-called traditional rendering once more comports well with other Pauline statements—including 1 Timothy 2:11 ("Let a woman learn in silence with all submission"), a key verse to which the Kroegers' reading of the passage fails to do justice, calling their overall thesis into question sheerly on contextual grounds.

Concluding reflections

The book as a whole points to more basic issues underlying debate about sex roles in evangelical Christian churches today. Observations along two broad lines may be offered in conclusion.

First, Bible-believing Christians of all persuasions must realize that 1 Timothy 2:12 presents

6. S. Lewis Johnson Jr., e.g., contends that "there is no reason to claim that Galatians 3:28 supports an egalitarianism of function in the church. It does plainly teach an egalitarianism of privilege in the covenantal union of believers in Christ. The Abrahamic promises, in their flowering by the Redeemer's saving work, belong universally to the family of God. Questions of roles and functions in that body can only be answered by a consideration of other and later New Testament teaching" ("Role Distinctions in the Church: Galatians 3:28," in Piper and Grudem, eds., *Recovering Biblical Manhood and Womanhood,* 164).

an interpretative challenge. To this extent the Kroegers' book is justified, as was that of Sharon Hodgin Gritz which appeared a year ago but came to somewhat different conclusions.[7] Groups that have traditionally placed great stress on restricting women's activities, or allowed men to exercise unbiblical dominance over sisters in the faith (including wives), would do well to regard books like the Kroegers' as reminders that it is as easy to be too strict, inhuman, and unchristian in applying Paul's teaching, whatever its precise applications, as it is to be too lax and worldly. Groups with scruples regarding women's roles in Christian life and ministry dare not stop short of applying the whole counsel of God, but they also dare not "think beyond what is written" (1 Corinthians 4:6). There is no question that some modern conservative Protestant perceptions of what is universally appropriate for women in church and home find as little basis in Scripture as some avant-garde feminist views. Moreover, there is no support in the Bible for the lamentable triumphalist tendency of some (usually male) conservative Protestants to assume that women, not only in the church but in society generally, should be content to submit to men, to suffer gladly as their coffee-making secretaries toiling under glass ceilings, and to put up with sexist jokes, stereotypes, and other harassment. When a verse like 1 Timothy 2:12 is used as support, vigorous denial, corrective teaching, and transformation of thought and deed is called for. Books like the Kroegers' might find less appeal if those who failed to give women their due in home, church, and world did not so often misappropriate the Bible in justifying themselves. Paul's statement from another context comes to mind: "If we would judge ourselves, we would not be judged" (1 Corinthians 11:31).

Second, the Kroegers' book may be seen as not so much about women's (and men's) roles as about God's Word. Does it mean what it says, and can we still trust it today? Or are we free to reconstrue it, rationalizing innovative interpretations by a great show of ostensible erudition?[8]

Or perhaps the real question is even whether the book may point to covert evangelical ambivalence about the nature of God Himself. A century ago liberalism revolutionized the doctrine of God in (at that time still largely "conservative") North American churches, as the notion of a fatherly God presiding over a good society of nice people came to displace orthodox belief in a God of both love and judgment who called all persons to repent and cling to the bloody cross of the divine Christ as their only hope in both this world and the next. "God" was redefined from the top down, so to speak, by a frontal assault on the Bible's teaching about Him.

Today's evangelicals, heirs of forefathers who steadfastly resisted the shift to liberalism, show little sign of abandoning their orthodox view of God—though some claim to see a dark cloud the size of a man's hand on the horizon. Still, one may ask what the long-term outcome of

---

7. Sharon Hodgin Gritz, *Paul, Women Teachers, and the Mother Goddess at Ephesus: A Study of 1 Timothy 2:9–15 in Light of the Religious and Cultural Milieu of the First Century* (Lanham, MD: University Press of America, 1991).
8. Still much to the point regarding this danger are Adolf Schlatter's remarks in "The Theology of the New Testament and Dogmatics," *The Nature of New Testament Theology*, ed. Robert Morgan (London: SCM, 1973), pp. 149ff.

the hermeneutics of an apparently growing stratum within evangelicalism is apt to be, assuming that the Kroegers' book is an example and harbinger. Is it possible to nibble away at the putative edges of the apostolic word about the sexes that was thought to be valid and authoritative for centuries without creating an appetite in some for larger and larger bites? If 1 Timothy 2:12 is simply cultural, why not (as many have already concluded) Ephesians 5:22 ("Wives, submit to your husbands...")? And if Ephesians 5:22, why not Eph 5:25ff., which teaches that husbands ought to be willing to lay down their lives for their wives like Christ did for the church? If secular Western society's egalitarian turn this century has pre-evangelized the church to accept a new reading of its own charter documents when these touch on sex roles, perhaps society is also pointing the way for churchgoing men and women in terms of no-fault divorce, abortion on demand, nonpayment of child support by absentee parents, extramarital infidelity, interchangeability of sexual preference, and any number of other policies or behaviors that Christians used to think the Bible forbade, but that start to make sense once the "myth" of distinct, God-ordained sexual natures, roles, and responsibilities is abandoned, whether outright or by radical reinterpretation. It might then be not only a short but inevitable step, having thoroughgoingly modified old doctrines of persons, to modify the doctrine of God. (Some think this is already underway, as when Christ is no longer so much "head" as "source" in keeping with recent feminist lexicographical claims.) Feuerbach was, after all, fundamentally correct (though ironically anticipated in his insight by the Bible itself) that mankind's inveterate tendency is to make God in its own image.

Of course, in mainline Protestantism this is exactly what has happened, to various extents in various quarters.[9] What is noteworthy is to see ostensibly evangelical authors, apparently with little restraint from their evangelical publishers, urging with such aplomb such revisionist reading of apostolic teaching. While the historian's maxim that history never repeats itself cautions us against presuming that North American evangelicalism's immediate future will of necessity bear some resemblance to its vicissitudes of a century or more ago, only the historically naive, or perhaps the ideologically blinded, would insist on suppressing consideration of the possibility.

According to the Kroegers, "Contemporary readers find it difficult to imagine the easy manner in which people in the first century adopted many elements from various religious systems" (69). Given the apparent inroads of elements from various ideological systems on this book, discerning readers may now find such syncretistic tendencies less difficult to imagine.

We also learn that "in the ancient world, theology often had to accommodate itself to myths that were already current" (127). Today such myths as human autonomy, unisex anthropology, and

---

9. See the recent and important study by Mary A. Kassian, *The Feminist Gospel: The Movement to Unite Feminism with the Church* (Wheaton, IL: Crossway, 1992), with its trenchant warnings to evangelicals.

androgynous divinity, while under fire among some neo-conservatism, are still quite the rage in mainline centers of thought, exerting some considerable influence, it appears, on how the Bible is handled in evangelical quarters. Paul's first epistle to Timothy at Ephesus may, then, be simultaneously more distant from, and more pertinent to, our current setting than the Kroegers suppose.

* Robert Yarbrough holds a PhD in New Testament from the University of Aberdeen and is Associate Professor of New Testament at Covenant Theological Seminary.

"The Apostle Paul Among the Amazons"
S. M. Baugh Review[1]

Richard Clark Kroeger and Catherine Clark Kroeger, *I Suffer Not a Woman: Rethinking 1 Timothy 2:11–15 in Light of Ancient Evidence* (Grand Rapids, MI: Baker Book House, 1992). Some abbreviations used in this review are: *OCD* for *The Oxford Classical Dictionary* (eds. N. Hammond and H. Scullard; 2d ed.; Oxford: Clarendon, 1970); *IEph* for the (repertorium) collection of Ephesian inscriptions: *Die Inschriften von Ephesos* (eds. Wankel, Merkelbach, et al.; 8 vols.; Bonn: Rudolf Habelt, 1979–84); JÖAI for Jahreshefte des Österreichischen Archäologischen Institutes in Wien; ZPE for Zeitschrift für Papyrologie und Epigraphik; and New Docs for the series *New Documents Illustrating Early Christianity* (eds. G. H. R. Horsley and S. R. Llewelyn; 6 vols.; Macquarie University, 1981–92). Abbreviations of ancient authors and their works, when used, are those of the *OCD*.

Not long ago, Marcus Barth said in regard to Pauline Ephesus: "The cult of the Great Mother and the Artemis temple stamped this city more than others as a bastion and bulwark of women's rights."[2] Echoes of this speculation have formed the foundation of a popular egalitarian argument that the prohibition of women "teaching and exercising authority over a man" in 1 Timothy 2:12 was only designed to correct a radical situation at Ephesus (cf. 1 Timothy 1:3).[3] "The gospel [was] struggling in Ephesus with Gnostic-influenced

1. Reprinted from *Westminster Theological Journal* 56:1 (Spring 1994): 153–71. Used by permission.
2. M. Barth, *Ephesians 4–6* (AB 34; 2 vols.; Garden City: Doubleday, 1974) 2.661; see also id., "Traditions in Ephesians," *NTS* 30 (1984): 16.
3. See, for example, Sharon Hodgin Gritz, *Paul, Women Teachers, and the Mother Goddess at Ephesus: A Study of 1 Timothy 2:9–15 in Light of the Religious and Cultural Milieu of the First Century* (Lanham, New York, and London: University Press of America, 1991).

women trumpeting a feminist reinterpretation of Adam and Eve as precedent for their own spiritual primacy and authority."[4] In other words, because "the Ephesian women were radical feminists and trying to dominate men,"[5] Paul merely objects to *Ephesian* women teaching and exercising authority.

Up to this point, no one has established historically that there was, in fact, a feminist culture in first-century Ephesus.[6] It has merely been assumed.[7] Enter Richard and Catherine Kroegers' *I Suffer Not a Woman: Rethinking 1 Timothy 2:11–15 in Light of Ancient Evidence*. As the subtitle suggests, the chief purpose of this book is to support the egalitarian restriction of 1 Timothy 2:12 to a feminist climate at Ephesus through presentation of a wide range of archaeological and ancient literary material. (Mrs. Kroeger speaks from her twin vantage points as a classicist and founder of an evangelical feminist organization.)[8]

The actual argument of *I Suffer Not a Woman* has many parts; its main lines run as follows. The Kroegers begin from what is now a standard egalitarian assumption that all distinctions

---

4. Bruce Barron, "Putting Women in Their Place: 1 Timothy 2 and Evangelical Views of Women in Church Leadership," *JETS* 33 (1990): 451–9. Cf. Kenneth E. Bailey ("Women in/of the New Testament: A Middle Eastern Cultural View," [unpublished study paper, n.d.]): "What kind of female attitudes would have developed in a town centered on a fertility goddess whose worship was exclusively led by women and eunuchs.... It does not take too much imagination to fill in the spaces between the lines of 1 Timothy...A group of powerful women appear [sic] to have seized control of the council of elders.... The author of 1 Timothy means, 'I do not permit women in the church to exercise unlimited brutalizing power over men such as happens in the cult of Artemis in Ephesus'" (17, 19).
5. John Cooper, *A Cause for Division? Women in Office and the Unity of the Church* (Grand Rapids: Calvin Theological Seminary, 1991), 50.
6. Gritz's *Paul, Women Teachers, and the Mother Goddess at Ephesus* may appear to be an exception, but her work is flawed by similar methodological problems as *I Suffer Not a Woman*. Gritz fails to use any of the abundant archaeological and epigraphical sources from Ephesus (with very slight exceptions). How else could she have relied so heavily on the mistaken notion that the priestesses of Artemis Ephesia engaged in sacred prostitution (pp. 39–41)? Compare Richard Oster, "The Ephesian Artemis as an Opponent of Early Christianity," *JAC* 19 (1976): 24–44, esp. p. 28, where he points to ancient evidence for "the sexual purity of the priests of Artemis, and the absolute exclusion of prostitutes from the temple of Artemis." The priestesses of Artemis of the Imperial era were maiden daughters of the Ephesian elite or wealthy matrons known to have husbands and children, for example: Stertinia Marena (*IEph* 411; 4123), Claudia Trophime (*IEph* 508), Hordeonia Pulchra (*IEph* 984; see *IEph* 20 for her famous father), Hordeonia Paulina (*IEph* 981; see *IEph* 690 for her son), Auphidia Quintilia (*IEph* 637 who honored her husband), Claudia Crateia Veriane (*IEph* 980), Vipsania Olympias (*IEph* 987), Ulpia Euodia Mudiane (*IEph* 989), and many others. Plutarch likened the priestesses of Artemis to the vestal virgins of Rome (*An seni respublica gerenda sit* 24 [795d–e]; cf. *IEph* 990). They were not sacred prostitutes! (The Kroegers also refer to sacred prostitution as "widely practiced in the temples of Asia Minor" [98]; this too is mistaken for the NT era.) Even Gritz's title begs an important question: Was Artemis Ephesia truly a mother goddess? See below.
7. The worship of a female goddess, even a fertility goddess, does not *ipso facto* imply a feminist culture as Barth and others assume. Did the worship of Astarte create a feminist culture in Old Testament Israel or her neighbors? Athene was the chief deity in Athens, but no historian would dream of describing Athenian culture as feministic, where a woman's greatest fame was "to be least talked about by men" (Thucydides 2.44). Cf. *Women's Life in Greece and Rome: A Source Book in Translation* (ed. M. Lefkowitz and M. Fant; Baltimore: Johns Hopkins, 1982), 12–20; Eva Cantarella, *Pandora's Daughters: The Role and Status of Women in Greek and Roman Antiquity* (Baltimore: Johns Hopkins, 1987); David Cohen, "Seclusion, Separation, and the Status of Women in Classical Athens," *Greece and Rome* 36 (1989): 3–15.
8. See also Catherine Kroeger, "1 Timothy 2:12—A Classicist's View," in *Women, Authority and the Bible* (ed. A. Mickelsen; Downers Grove, IL: InterVarsity, 1986): 225–44.

between men and women are erased in Christ. When Paul forbade women from exercising the authority of the pastoral and teaching office ("to teach or to have authority over a man," 1 Timothy 2:12), he was addressing only the Ephesian situation because of its feminist religious culture where women had usurped religious authority over men. Paul's real purpose was only to prevent *Ephesian* women from teaching men. More specifically, he was only forbidding women from teaching a particular Gnostic notion concerning Eve.[9]

They conclude in light of this scenario that women should be ordained to pastoral ministry.

There are already reviews of *I Suffer Not a Woman* which subject the book's handling of the Bible and its speculations on Gnosticism to searching criticism.[10] Therefore, this essay will not cover the same ground (with one exception). Instead, I will concentrate upon the Kroegers' attempt to substantiate matriarchy at ancient Ephesus, since the cultural and religious background is less familiar to NT students and has not received specialized investigation in this connection to date.[11]

In my opinion, the Kroegers (and others mentioned above) have painted a picture of Ephesus which wanders widely from the facts. Yet because the Kroegers cite a number of ancient authors, their portrait of Ephesus and of the cult of Artemis Ephesia may appear to be more plausible than it actually is. One must recognize, though, that their portrayal of Ephesus is inspired by an eccentric reading of 1 Timothy 2:12. In order to illustrate this point, let us look briefly at their treatment of this key passage.

In general, the Kroegers show a tendency to interpret biblical passages idiosyncratically without offering defense for their understanding.[12] Their interpretation of 1 Timothy 2:12 is defended, but it is confused and confusing at best. Their translation is: "I do not allow a woman

9. "In this book, we shall suggest that 1 Timothy 2:11–15 is not a decree of timeless and universal restriction and punishment but a corrective: a specific direction as to what women should not teach and why" (23). That Paul grounds his teaching upon the created order (1 Timothy 2:13; cf. 1 Corinthians 11:8–9) rather than upon a post-lapsus "punishment" does not enter into the authors' consideration.
10. For example, Albert Wolters' review in *Calvin Theological Journal* 28 (1993) 208–13; and Robert Yarbrough, "*I Suffer Not a Woman:* A Review Essay," *Presbyterion* 18 (1992): 25–33.
11. I am preparing a more technical discussion of Ephesian society and its mythical gynecocracy for a different forum: "A Foreign World: Ephesus in the First Century," in *Women and the Church: A Fresh Analysis of 1 Timothy 2:11–15 in Its Literary, Cultural, and Theological Contexts* (ed. S. Baldwin and T. Schreiner; Grand Rapids: Baker, forthcoming).
12. For example, they cite Titus 2:3 as evidence of "female elders" (p. 91) who taught men in the NT church (p. 81), but these are clearly "older women" (versus "older men," v. 2) who are to disciple "younger women" "to be homemakers, kind, subject to their own husbands" (Titus 2:5). And they take 1 Timothy 5:5–10 as referring to women "who are to be enrolled as members of the clergy" (p. 91), although this list clearly refers to financial support in context (5:16; cf. James 1:27; Acts 6:1). And does Timothy's instruction in the faith by his mother and grandmother really act as warrant for ordination to the pastoral office (17)?

The Kroegers follow a familiar egalitarian line by taking Phoebe as an example of an ordained "overseer" in the NT church (17). But if the term προστατιθ in Rom 16:2 refers to the office of elder or pastor, Paul would be saying that Phoebe exercised spiritual rule over himself as well: "she was προστατιθ of many even of myself also." Perhaps to avoid this problem, but still to retain Phoebe as an example of a female overseer, the Kroegers resort to what can only be called a desperate translation of Romans 16:2: "For she has been appointed, actually by my own action, an officer presiding over many." But there is no grammatical defense for taking the genitive "of myself also" as expressing agency: "by my own action." The preposition̹ πο is required at least.

to teach nor to proclaim herself author of man but she is to be in conformity (with the Scriptures) (or that she keeps it a secret)" (103, 189, et al.). In the discussion that follows, we will focus upon their interpretation of the first two infinitive clauses.[13]

In the authors' rendering and interpretation, the lead verb "I do not allow" has two parallel, infinitive complements: "to teach" and "to proclaim herself author of." The authors clearly wish to *interpret* the second infinitive as indirect discourse (37, 190–92, et al.), even though their translation expresses it as a complement. If the second infinitive functions as indirect statement, the rendering would be: "I do not allow a woman to teach *that* she is the originator of man" (191, italics added), which ignores the conjunction o[δϵ. Although they confuse the reader at this point, the authors seem to recognize that the Greek does not allow taking the second infinitive as indirect discourse after all,[14] yet they adopt this interpretation anyway: "We can understand the content of the forbidden teaching as being the notion that woman was responsible for the creation of man" (103).[15]

The Kroegers claim justification for their interpretation of 1 Timothy 2:12 by taking α[υϵντϵιν as an act of speech: "to *proclaim* oneself author of," a highly questionable meaning for this verb at best.[16] (And it does *not* function as indirect discourse with this meaning!) But what is most interesting in the authors' philological treatment is that they come up with a classic case of "illegitimate totality transfer," which becomes programmatic for their historical investigation: "Authentēs and authentein sometimes occur in contexts in which both sex and murder are present" (95). "Possibly [Paul] wished to evoke more than one image [with authentein]" (79). "It is strange indeed that our target verse should include a pivotal word

13. The Greek of 1 Timothy 2:12 has one main verb ("I do not allow") with three infinitive complements; it woodenly reads: "I do not allow a woman to be engaged in teaching nor (do I allow her) to be exercising authority over a man, but (I command her) to be in silence" (cf. NIV, "she must be silent"). The Kroegers' eccentric translation of the last infinitive clause misfires in both options they give: 1.) "in conformity (to the Scriptures)" for the phrase rν 'σψξια, "in silence" or "quietly," is forced at best, and 2.) to take the infinitive "to be" as the content of the teaching ("but I do not allow a woman to teach...that she keep it a secret") ignores the adversative conjunction and makes the clause unintelligible.

14. To take the second infinitive as indirect discourse would require taking the third infinitive in the same way, yielding nonsense: "I do not allow a woman to teach that she is the originator of man but (to teach) that she should be silent." The o[;o[δϵ series has two meanings: 1.) to mark a parallel statement: "For we did *not* bring anything into the world, *neither* can we take anything out of it" (1 Timothy 6:7; cf. 6:17–18; 1 Corinthians 15:13, 16; Galatians 1:12; Philippians 2:16; etc.); and 2.) to mark the negation of a concession: "There is *no* righteous person, *not even one*" (Romans 3:10; cf. 8:7). (The notion that "*oude* indicates that authentein explains what sort, or what manner, of teaching is prohibited" [84] is never this word's semantic function.) It is easier to see how clear Paul's point is—not the Kroegers'—if we put 1 Timothy 2:12 positively: "I allow a woman to teach *and* to exercise authority" or "I allow a woman to teach, *even* to exercise authority" (cf. analogous Matthew 8:21; Mark 10:4; 1 Timothy 2:4; 5:4, 14; Titus 3:1–2; etc.). See esp. 1 Corinthians 14:34 for a syntactically and lexically close parallel to 1 Timothy 2:12.

15. "Bearing in mind that oude can introduce an infinitive of indirect discourse.... The word didaskein (to teach) is frequently accompanied by an infinitive which defines what was taught" (191). And see the anecdote on pp. 37–38.

16. I will defer analysis of this much-discussed verb to what should prove to be the definitive treatment: Scott Baldwin's contribution in *Women and the Church* (forthcoming); cf. Leland Wilshire, "1 Timothy 2:12 Revisited," *Evangelical Quarterly* 65 (1993): 43–55 for bibliography in the meantime.

which has implications of killing, beginning, and copulating, as these all were elements of the mystery religions practiced in Asia Minor" (87).

I Suffer Not a Woman is filled with efforts to find "sex reversal," "female dominance," and "sex and death" motifs in Ephesian society, because the Kroegers believe that, in the end, all these things are implied in Paul's prohibition that women should not α[υεντειν. It is no wonder that L. E. Wilshire, even though he shares the egalitarian outlook, says: "This is a breathtaking extension into (pre-) Gnostic content yet an interpretation I do not find supported either by the totality of their own extensive philological study, by the NT context, or by the immediate usages of the word authenteō and its variants."[17]

If a sympathetic reader is not convinced by the Kroegers' interpretations, one may wonder why further discussion of their book is necessary. May we not quietly consign it to the curiosity shop, expecting it to find its way eventually to the bookshelf of some restaurant? I think not, because of Wilshire's further remarks on *I Suffer Not a Woman*: "Its finest sections are those analyzing the culture of Ephesus and Asia Minor along with the pagan literature and religions of the first-century era. The appendixes on ritual murder, grammar, ancient novels, and the Gnostic use of sex are extremely valuable."[18] Since others may share Wilshire's high estimation of this book's value as a guide to Ephesian culture, presentation of more facts in this area is warranted, especially if Richard Oster is right about "the neglect of ancient Ephesus in current New Testament scholarship."[19] The present review will show that a different picture of Ephesian society than found in *I Suffer Not a Woman* is more credible.

There are a few indications in the NT itself that Ephesus was a typically Hellenistic culture in regard to female roles in family and society. For instance, we have no direct evidence that women taught in any official or public capacity at Ephesus (or elsewhere).[20] In line with this, the false teachers mentioned in the Pastorals are said to be men "who worm their way into homes and gain control over weak-willed women" (2 Timothy 3:6; cf. 1 Timothy 1:6–11). And

17. "1 Timothy 2:12 Revisited," 54. Wilshire observes that his earlier study on α[υεντειν (*NTS* 34 [1988] 120–34) is missing in the Kroegers' book, although it is normally cited in discussions of this verb. "The omission," he says, "would seem to be deliberate" (53).
18. Wilshire, "1 Timothy 2:12 Revisited," 54.
19. Oster, *A Bibliography of Ancient Ephesus* (ATLABS 19; Metuchen and London: Scarecrow, 1987), xxii. Greg Horsley's recent survey was designed to be "consciousness-raising" for NT scholars: "The Inscriptions of Ephesus and the New Testament," *NovT* 34 (1992) 105–68. More limited in scope is Peter Lampe, "Acta 19 im Spiegel der ephesischen Inschriften," *BZ* 36 (1992) 59–76. For my work relating to Ephesus, see "Paul and Ephesus: The Apostle Among His Contemporaries" (PhD diss., University of California, Irvine, 1990); "Phraseology and the Reliability of Acts," *NTS* 36 (1990) 290–94; and "'Savior of All People': 1 Timothy 4:10 in Context," *WTJ* 54 (1992) 331–40.
20. Public involvement of women in Roman society is sometimes interpreted as evidence for a more "egalitarian attitude" than was found in Greek cities (Gritz, *Paul, Women Teachers, and the Mother Goddess at Ephesus*, 16); but compare Tacitus's nasty remarks about Agrippina's public appearances (*Ann.* 12.37). Regarding Roman women and their intellectual pursuits, one cannot help recalling Calpurnia, Pliny the Younger's wife, who did listen to his public recitals—discreetly behind a curtain (*Ep.* 4.19). Compare Ramsay MacMullen, "Woman in Public in the Roman Empire," *Historia* 29 (1980): 208–18.

Ephesian women do not appear as the sophists, rhetors, teachers, philosophers, or their disciples in our ancient sources, whereas several men do.[21]

Furthermore, the evidence of Acts hints that men took a leading role in economic, civil, and religious affairs at Ephesus; no Ephesian women are mentioned in these connections. Demetrius the silversmith and his guild (whom he addresses as ζνδρεθ, "men") were in the marketplace deriving a lucrative profit from the Artemisium tourist trade (Acts 19:24–27). Luke also mentions the (male) Asiarchs who were members of the premier social circles in the province of Asia (Acts 19:31).[22]

When we look further into Acts 19, we find hints of male involvement in Ephesian religious affairs. It was the Secretary of the People (γραμματεψθ), certainly a man,[23] who defused the excited mob in the theater by defending the goddess's honor (Acts 19:35–40). The Secretary mentions that Ephesus itself was "νέκοροθ of the great goddess" (Acts 19:35). This term, νέκοροθ, is frequently used for the individual or group charged with the oversight of a cult.[24] Since women were not citizens of Greek πολειθ like Ephesus,[25] it was the male citizen body of Ephesus—acting through its municipal officers, the γραμματεψθ and the all-male βοψλη ("State Council")—who claimed the oversight of the cult of Artemis Ephesia. We can safely infer from this slight NT evidence alone that religious affairs at Ephesus were not exclusively in the hands of women as the authors of *I Suffer Not a Woman* allege.

Turning to the Kroegers' main thesis, we might mistakenly think that they hope to establish that Ephesian society *in toto* was "a *society* that looked upon the feminine as primal source" (105, italics added). They say that "for millennia the matriarchal goddesses reigned supreme" and that "the maternal aspect was glorified in a manner almost unknown farther west" (50). Hence, this "divine maternal principle" was "the concept underlying *the political, economic,*

21. Examples of male sophists, rhetors, etc. are T. Flavius Damianus (*IEph* 672a–b, 676a, 678a, 735, 811, 2100, 3029, 3051, 3080–81; *VS* 2.23); P. Hordeonius Lollianus (*IEph* 20 and 984; *VS* 1.23); Tib. Claudius Flavianus Dionysius (*IEph* 426 and 3047; *VS* 1.22); Soterus the "Chief Sophist" (*IEph* 1548; *VS* 2.23); Hadrianus of Tyre (*IEph* 1539); L. Vevius Severus (*IEph* 611); [-ius] Secundinus of Tralles (*IEph* 4340); and Ofellius Laetus (*IEph* 3901). Ephesus was "a center of philosophical and rhetorical studies" (*VS* 8.8; also Tacitus, *Dial.* 15.3); cf. Knibbe and Iplikçioglu, "Neue Inschriften aus Ephesos VIII," *JÖAI* 53 (1981/82) 136–40 and 149–50.
22. See still Baugh, "Paul and Ephesus" (esp. ch. 6, "Paul and the Asiarchs") despite the continuing debate over identification of the Asiarchate with the provincial high priesthood (e.g., Kearsley in *New Docs* 4, pp. 46–55). My point—that the Asiarchs were the social elite at Ephesus—is not affected by this debate.
23. Perhaps this was Alexander Memnon, son of Artemidorus (*IEph* 261), who served as γραμματεψθ in the mid-first-century AD.
24. An inscription identifying Ephesus as "the νέκοροθ of Artemis" is often mentioned in Acts commentaries; for instance, Foakes-Jackson and Kirsopp Lake, *The Beginnings of Christianity: The Acts of the Apostles* (London: MacMillan, 1933), 4.250; cf. Colin Hemer, *The Book of Acts in the Setting of Hellenistic History* (Tübingen: J. C. B. Mohr [Paul Siebeck], 1989), 122.
25. Notice that the Secretary addressed the mob as the ρκκλησια of male citizens: ζνδρεθ ρφεσιοι, "Men, Ephesians" (Acts 19:35, 39). In this connection, Galatians 3:28–29 is all the more revolutionary, but as a reference to legal and political standing touching one's own right of inheritance; it cannot be pressed for implications on church office.

and social existence of Ephesus" (57, italics added). This certainly is the force of Marcus Barth's and others' understanding noted above.

Yet, conversely, the Kroegers also say quite explicitly that Ephesus was *not* a "matriarchal" society! "Nevertheless there is no evidence that women took an ascendant role over the men in civil life" (92).

> Modern scholarship tends to find that female dominance is not attested in the civil affairs of western Asia Minor, and that matriarchy can be found with certainty only in the religious realm of Bronze Age Crete.[26] Nevertheless the tradition of a religiously-based rule of men by women is incontestable.... The Lycians were said to have been ruled by women from ancient times. They claimed descent through their mothers, honored women more than men, and bestowed the inheritance on daughters rather than sons. (193–94)[27]

The Kroegers are trying to establish a careful distinction despite their hazy statements about "Ephesus' strong emphasis on *the maternal principle*" (55, italics added).[28] They are aware that historians are unanimous: There were no matriarchal (or gynecocratic) societies in antiquity. So, in order to establish their thesis about the background and interpretation of 1 Timothy 2:9–15, they need some type of matriarchy at Ephesus. The answer? Although women were not dominant in *civil* affairs, they say: "Religious affairs were significantly different within its (Asia Minor's) temple systems and especially in the mysteries, matriarchy prevailed" (92). Hence, they would have us believe that "Ephesus stood as a bastion of feminine supremacy *in religion*" (54, italics added).

Now, the notion that any ancient culture could maintain a matriarchy only in the religious sphere but not in the social-civic spheres of life betrays an astonishing innocence of how ancient societies worked. It is a commonplace in the study of antiquity that all areas of life were interconnected, evidenced in that "a magistrate was usually a priest as a part of his official functions" in Hellenic cities.[29] To separate these spheres of existence and to assert patriarchy or something

26. To support matriarchy in Minoan Crete, the Kroegers cite two articles by Simon Pembroke, despite the fact that Pembroke refutes this notion (240n7). "As Simon Pembroke has shown, there is no evidence whatever for the existence of matriarchal societies in the ancient world" (Mary Lefkowitz, "Influential Women," in *Images of Women in Antiquity* [ed. A. Cameron and A. Kuhrt; Detroit: Wayne State, 1983], 49). See Pembroke, "Last of the Matriarchs: A Study in the Inscriptions of Lycia," *Journal of Economic and Social History of the Orient* 8 (1965): 217–47; and idem, "Women in Charge: The Function of Alternatives in Early Greek Tradition and the Ancient Idea of Matriarchy," *Journal of the Warburg and Courtauld Institute* 30 (1967): 1–35. For other denials of matriarchy in Minoan civilization see, for example, Stella Georgoudi, "Creating a Myth of Matriarchy," in *A History of Women in the West* (ed. P. Pantel; Cambridge, MA: Belknap/Harvard University Press, 1992), 1.460; and Cantarella, *Pandora's Daughters*, 14–15.
27. Does the last statement seem self-contradictory? They say there was no matriarchy except in Minoan Crete (ca. 3000–1500 BC), but the Lycians (south central Asia Minor) had "rule by women."
28. The Kroegers fail to distinguish *gynecocracy* (actual rule of women), *matriarchy* (priority or rule of mothers), *matrilinearity* (tracing descent through one's mother), and *feminism* (an ideology and a modern movement). All gets mixed up as this vague "maternal principle" and whatnot. These distinctions are rightly insisted upon by Pembroke ("Women in Charge," 1).
29. "Priests," *OCD*; cf. Burkert, *Greek Religion (Cambridge: MA: Harvard University Press, 1985),* 95–98.

similar in the civil sphere and matriarchy in the religious sphere is *prima facie* implausible. Accordingly, we must look carefully at the arguments the Kroegers advance to support their idea.

Our authors' argumentation is quite complicated actually, so I will try to reproduce its main points in this simpler form:

Premise 1: First-century worship of Artemis Ephesia embodied an ancient Anatolian sex-reversal principle. Hence, Pauline Ephesus may be characterized as the "bastion of a strongly developed theological system" (58) of female dominance in religion ("matriarchy").

Evidence A: The Anatolian religious situation was begun by the Amazons (mythical gynecocrats) and preserved in their myths (47, 52, 93, 193–96).

Evidence B: There is a myth that Hercules was forced into submission to Lydian women as one of his labors (194–95).

Evidence C: Herodotus mentions matrilinearity in fifth-century BC Lycia (109, 194).[30]

Evidence D: It is assumed that Artemis was syncretized to the Anatolian Great Mother and given the nature of a fertility goddess (50–54).

Evidence E: Eunuch priests and hermaphrodites were part of Artemis Ephesia's entourage according to the authors (196).

Evidence F: Women had greater religious status at Ephesus as "principal mediators of the gods" (71; see pp. 70–74). In line with this, Artemis's "high priest" (a misnomer) was replaced by a "high priestess" (another misnomer) in the first century AD (71, 89, 196).

Evidence G: "Sex and death" is a theme of second- or third-century AD novels set in Ephesus (Appendix 4, pp. 197–202).

Premise 2: Gnostic teaching on the reversal of the role of Eve in Creation was popular in Pauline Ephesus.[31]

---

30. It is never made clear how this piece of evidence relates directly to the Kroegers' argument, but I am guessing that it has something to do with their idea that "Lydian women appear to have been especially active in the cult of the Ephesian Artemis" (p. 70; cf. pp. 193–94). Of course, one may ask for evidence of specifically "Lydian women" in the first-century AD Artemis cult. The Kroegers present references to "Lydian maidens" dancing in honor of Artemis Ephesia from two Athenian comic poets writing from 450 to 500 years earlier! (Lydia back then was still remembered as the kingdom of the legendary Croesus, but that was all ancient history by NT times.) How anachronistic poetic references to Lydian dancing girls connect another anachronistic reference to Lycian matrilinearity is a mystery (Lydia and Lycia were separate regions of Asia Minor). And how this all relates to thoroughly Hellenistic-Roman Ephesus of the first century AD (which was in the region of *Ionia*) is an even graver mystery.

31. The Gnostic question is not addressed in this review, yet I might note in passing that the Kroegers' historical method in their search for Gnosticism at Pauline Ephesus leaves much to be desired. For example, in chap. 15, "The Veneration of the Serpent and Eve," they use representations of snakes found at Ephesus as partial support for the presence of Gnosticism there. But the snake was a very *widespread* religious symbol in the pagan world, as the Kroegers observe (p. 161). These Ephesian snakes, if they were truly religious symbols, could very well have represented Greek household deities or the equivalent Roman *lares* from the home of a Latin merchant living at Ephesus (e.g., "*qui in statario* [the slave-market] *negotiantur*," *IEph* 646 and 3025). More likely, they stood for the god of healing, Asclepius. Ephesus possessed a well-known medical college whose chief-doctor (zρξιατροθ) also served as priest to Asclepius (cf. snakes on modern medical symbols). As an interesting sidelight, one of these chief-doctors was Jewish (*IEph* 1677). A snake symbol is unlikely to indicate the presence of Gnosticism without solid, corroborating evidence.

Conclusion: First Timothy 2:9–15 is merely countering this theological matrix of the Artemis cult and Gnosticism combined: "In 1 Timothy 2:5–15 [sic] Paul addresses the notion that women were necessary to communicate ultimate truth. He is as well combating the willingness of women to assume that they had a monopoly on the divine enlightenment" (73). "We suggest that the writer of the Pastorals was opposing a doctrine which acclaimed motherhood as the ultimate reality" (112).[32]

It is difficult to imagine how such a momentous conclusion could have been erected upon such fragile, tottering evidence. And what is more egregious than the Kroegers' reliance upon such implausible information is the fact that among their "enormous amount of supplemental material" (14) they virtually ignore a vast body of evidence of a historically much more reliable and relevant quality: the approximately four thousand Ephesian inscriptions and the burgeoning secondary literature surrounding them.[33]

Furthermore, evidence from materials they do utilize but which contradicts the authors' position often goes unmentioned by them. For instance, the second-century novel by Achilles Tatius is discussed by the Kroegers in Appendix 4 (200–02). It challenges the authors' theses in three ways. 1.) A male priest appears as the head of the Artemisium at Ephesus and no priestess appears in the novel; however, this fact goes unnoticed in place of some (fanciful) interpretations of "sex and death" motifs. 2.) Artemis Ephesia herself is presented in this novel as the classic Greek "goddess of purity" and "the Virgin," yet this does not detour the authors from taking her as a fertility goddess dedicated to "sex-reversal." 3.) Tatius writes: "From ancient days this temple [the Artemisium] had been forbidden to free women who were not virgins. Only men and virgins were permitted here. If a non-virgin woman passed

32. "Such a pagan element, based upon sex hostility and reversal of gender roles, may well have found a place in a cult practice among the dissidents in the congregation at Ephesus. The apostle who taught that in Jesus there is neither male nor female would surely have condemned it. If this is the case, the condemnation [i.e., 1 Timothy 2:12] is not directed against women participating in leadership but rather against a monopoly on religious power by women. Such a monopolistic attitude in the church is wrong, whether arrogated to themselves by men or women" (93).

33. For a recent bibliography on Ephesus see Oster, *Bibliography*. The inscriptions were collected and published from 1979 to 1984 in the "*IEph*" volumes. Newer inscriptions are periodically published by Dieter Knibbe et al. in *JÖAI*. Discussion of Ephesian material occupies much of *New Docs* volumes 4 through 6 and occurs frequently in *ZPE* and in the newer *Epigraphia anatolica*. Some Ephesian inscriptions can be found in English translation, for example, Naphtali Lewis, *Greek Historical Documents: The Roman Principate: AD 27– AD 285* (Toronto: Hakkert, 1974), passim. Only two inscriptions are actually quoted (pp. 52 and 89 [repeated on p. 202]) and the following statement is made: "By the first century C.E., it appears from inscriptional evidence that the function of the male high priest had been supplanted by that of the high priestess. Two inscriptions tell of the performance of the mysteries in the cult of Artemis by a priestess, but we know of none in which the officiant is a male" (89). Since identification of these inscriptions is not provided, it is difficult to know exactly what they are talking about; there was neither a "*high* priest" nor a "*high* priestess" of Artemis (see below). As for their latter statement, it is true that "fulfilled the mysteries" is used by priestesses of Artemis (on more than two inscriptions), but it is not true that officiants were all female when one considers the male κοψρητεθ et al. (see below). The famous Salutaris inscription from Ephesus provided endowments to various civil and religious officials to defray the cost of their participation in the annual festival of Artemis. See the full analysis of this inscription by Guy M. Rogers, *The Sacred Identity of Ephesos* (London and New York: Routledge, 1991).

inside, the penalty was death."[34] If non-virgins (e.g., mothers) were specifically barred from access to Artemis Ephesia's temple, it would seem to undermine the idea that "within [Asia Minor's—including Ephesus's] temple systems and especially in the mysteries, ***matriarchy*** prevailed" (92, italics added).

As one can now guess, I believe that each piece of evidence noted above (Evidence A–G) is open to the gravest of doubts. But rather than give a detailed response to each point *seriatim*—which would tax the reader's patience beyond limits—let me respond in a general way and then take up specific points in varying degrees of detail.

Please observe, first, how few genuinely historical facts support the Kroegers' elaborate argument: Artemis the Virgin's worshippers lifting their skirts in worship as part of fertility rites (74–75)? This is at best sheer imagination, when, in fact, Artemis's female devotees prided themselves on their modest piety. Take Laevia Paula, for example, who died a few decades before Paul was in Ephesus. She was the wife of M. Antonius Albus, "the patron [προσστατιθ] of the temple of Artemis" (*IEph* 614c)—notice again male involvement in the cult. At Laevia's funeral a herald proclaimed: "The Council and People crown Laevia Paula daughter of Lucius, who lived a modest and decorous life" (*IEph* 614b).[35]

Note also the Kroegers' heavy reliance upon mythology as historical sources. Amazons?[36] Hercules? (Evidence A–B.) Were we to analyze modern American society, would we rely on myths of Paul Bunyan and his blue ox, Babe, or on tales of Johnny Appleseed? Certainly the ancients did not all take their myths very seriously: "The bards tell many lies" was proverbial by Plutarch's day (ca. AD 50–120).[37]

Other evidence for matriarchy adduced by the Kroegers is wildly anachronistic, and some is historically unreliable even for its own day. For instance, they rely upon Herodotus (fifth century BC; pp. 109, 194); Autocrates (fourth century BC; p. 70); and Aristophanes (fifth century BC; pp. 70–71). Let us look briefly, for example, at the evidence from Herodotus (Evidence C).

A Greek man would normally state his full name as "So-and-So, son of So-and-So" (his father).[38] But, says Herodotus, a Lycian "will say that he is the son of such a mother, and recount

---

34. Tatius, "Leucippe and Clitophon," in *Collected Ancient Greek Novels* (trans. J. Winkler; ed. B. P. Reardon; Berkeley: University of California, 1989), 267.
35. The phrase "modest and decorous life" is σ́φρονα και κοσμιον;βιον, reminiscent of 1 Timthy 2:9: σωφροσψνηθ κοσμειν Wαψταθ, "to adorn themselves with modesty."
36. Scholars today see the Amazon myths not as an indication of ancient gynecocratic ideology, but rather as an attempt "to indicate how bad things could be when women got the upper hand" (Lefkowitz, "Influential Women," 49). Cf. "Amazons" in *OCD*; Lorna Hardwick, "Ancient Amazons—Heroes, Outsiders or Women?" *Greece and Rome* 37 (1990): 14–36.
37. *Quomodo adul.* 16A. Plato, similarly, would censor the poets' myths in his ideal πολιθ (*Resp.* 376e–378e).
38. A quote from Aristophanes, *Thesm.* 622. Greek women, likewise, would give their lineage from their fathers (or their husbands); e.g., Artemoi (daughter of) Artemidorus (*IEph* 3031; AD 4–14). The Roman practice is similar: "C. Iulius C. f. Caesar" means "Gaius Julius Caesar son of Gaius" and "Claudia C. f. Secunda" means "Claudia the second daughter of Gaius." Cf. "Names, Personal" in *OCD*; Arthur E. Gordon, *Illustrated Introduction to Latin Epigraphy* (Berkeley, Los Angeles, and London: University of California, 1983), 17–30; and Colin Hemer, "The Name of Paul," *TynBul* 36 (1985): 179–83.

the mothers of his mother" (1.173; LCL). Now, let us accept the veracity of Herodotus's remark for the moment.[39] How is this statement relevant? Tracing lineage through one's mother does not itself prove *matriarchy*. But more critically, how can Herodotus's distant statement carry any weight in light of all the abundant names on first-century AD Ephesian inscriptions that conclusively demonstrate that Ephesians listed their father's name, not their mother's?[40] Herodotus's statement is not only anachronistic and irrelevant, but goes contrary to more germane, lavish evidence.

The Kroegers' argument relies heavily on two key points: 1.) that Artemis Ephesia was a manifestation of the Anatolian mother goddess; and 2.) that fertility practices and ideologies were therefore connected to Artemis's cult (Evidence D). Both of these crucial questions are begged by the Kroegers, and both are most implausible for Artemis the Unbroken Virgin.[41] Although she may have originated from the Anatolian Great Mother in pre-Hellenic times, the identification of Artemis Ephesia with the Great Mother *in historical times* is most unlikely according to Richard Oster, a specialist in this area. He writes:

> The nature and essence of the cult of Artemis was open, as all religions are, to change and flux. Even if the eunuch priests known as Megabyzi [who disappeared after the first century BC] suggest fertility rites similar to the Mother Goddess of Asia Minor, it is necessary to remember that *this part of the cult vanished in the period*

39. Simon Pembroke (whom the Kroegers cite [240n7]) casts doubts on the accuracy of Herodotus's statement. Some Lycian men list their father's name, their mother's name, and even their uncle's name. Pembroke explains the instances where a mother's name was used as remarriage situations, illegitimacy, adoption, or fosterage ("Last of the Matriarchs," passim). As for Herodotus, Pembroke concludes: "What the Greeks knew about their past, and about their neighbors, turns out to be very little" ("Women in Charge," 35). Nevertheless, the Kroegers take Herodotus as reliable evidence of Lycian matriarchy somehow relevant for NT Ephesus (which had no direct ties to Lycia anyway—it was in Ionia).

40. For instance, evidence from *New Docs* 4 (7, 74–82, 127) shows only patronymics: T. Aelius Marcianus Priscus son of Aelius Priscus, who was "the leader of the festival (in honor of Artemis) and president of the athletic games" (Horsley's translation); Heliodoros son of Philippos and grandson of Philippos, a sacred official of Artemis (νεοποιοθ); and Claudia daughter of Erotion. Since the Kroegers quote from Horsley's volume (52 [224n5]), one would expect this evidence to enter into their discussion; it does not. More example names, from the hundreds possible, come from the fishery customs-office inscription (*IEph* 20; AD 54–59). There are eighty-eight legible names, of whom forty-four have Roman and forty-four have Greek names. Of the men with Greek names, twenty-seven clearly give their filiation from their father (e.g., Heraclides son of Heraclides son of Heraclides), sixteen give no filiation (e.g., Didymus Theuda), and the rest are too fragmentary to be of help. But no Greek (or Roman) gives his mother's name in his lineage. (See Baugh, "Paul and Ephesus," Appendix 2; and Horsley, *New Docs* 5, pp. 95–114, who reads eighty-nine names.)

41. Homer, *Od.* 6.109 (as cited by Burkert, *Greek Religion*, 150). For Artemis of Ephesia as "the Virgin," see Oster, "Opponent," 28; see also the statue of a classically Hellenic Artemis found in an Ephesian home (A. Bammer et al., *Führer durch das archäologische Museum in Selçuk-Ephesos* [Vienna: Österreichisches Archäologisches Institut, 1974], photo no. 9). We should not interpret the other, very oriental statues of Artemis Ephesia too hastily. As Stella Georgoudi warns in connection with Minoan Crete: "To deduce the existence of a matriarchal society from such images in the absence of related myths, to write history on the basis of iconographic sources alone, is a risky business that can lead only to the most dubious conclusions" ("Myth of Matriarchy," 460). The "breasts" on these statues were probably some kind of ornamentation. After careful study, Robert Fleischer concludes, "Bezüglich der Bedeutung der 'Brüste' scheint es auch heute noch nicht möglich, über Spekulationen hinauszukommen" (*Artemis von Ephesos und Verwandte Kultstatuen aus Anatolien und Syrien* [Leiden: Brill, 1973] 87; see esp. plates 58 and 138–41 for similar ornaments on Zeus [!] and Cybele).

> *of the early Roman Empire*.... A final argument against a fertility interpretation of the goddess in the Roman Empire is the deafening silence from all the primary sources. None of the extant myths point in this direction, neither do the significant epithets of the goddess.[42]

If the Kroegers' argument is based upon shaky interpretations of doubtful evidence so far, we should also point out the outright errors of fact (Evidence E). For example, we have the following statement of evidence: "The inclusion of castrated priests and hermaphrodites in the official retinue of the Ephesian Artemis further suggests the presence of sex reversal. The assumption of ultimate power in the cult by a high priestess rather than a high priest again indicates that the primary religious power lay with women by the first century C.E." (196).[43]

First, the Kroegers have derived these "castrated priests and hermaphrodites" from the well-known "Megabyzus," a eunuch priest who served as head of a hierarchy of maiden priestesses according to Strabo (*Geog.* 14.1.23). But our evidence indicates that this priesthood was discontinued toward the end of the first century BC[44] Not only have the Kroegers multiplied this one eunuch into many (and invented hermaphrodites!), but they tacitly affirm that this priesthood was discontinued—the Megabyzus was the only discontinued Ephesian priesthood of which I know—and was replaced by a "high priestess." This fact, therefore, cannot support their argument for "sex reversal" in Pauline Ephesus. If anything, the formerly Persian character of Artemis's retinue was being conformed to traditional Graeco-Roman standards by this time.

Similarly, the replacement of a eunuch priest by a "high priestess"[45] by the first century (Evidence F) would seem to undermine the Kroegers' point that Artemis Ephesia's character as a fertility goddess is derived from the previous cult of the Anatolian Great Mother. If "primary

---

42. Oster, "Ephesus as a Religious Center under the Principate, I. Paganism Before Constantine," *ANRW* 2.18.3 (1990): 1725–26 (italics added); see also his "Opponent," 28; and "Artemis" in *OCD*. Note that the Great Mother had a separate cult at Ephesus into the Roman era: Oster, "Ephesus as a Religious Center," 1687–88; and Dieter Knibbe, "Ephesos—nicht nur die Stadt der Artemis: die 'anderen' ephesischen Götter," in *Studien zur Religion und Kultur Kleinasiens* (ed. S. Sahin, E. Schwartheim, and J. Wagner; 2-vol. ed.; Leiden: Brill, 1978): 2.490–91. For related chthonic cults, see, for example, *IEph* 902 (26–19 BC), which mentions "Isidorus son of Apollonis son of Apollonis, the priest of Fruitful Earth" (καρποφοροθ γη).

43. "By the first century C.E. the high priestess had replaced the high priest as the chief functionary of the cult, both at Ephesus and at neighboring Sardis. Women were assuming greater status as principal mediators of the gods" (71).

44. Note that Strabo himself (late first-century BC) speaks in the past tense: "They used to have eunuch priests, whom they would call 'Megabyzoi'" (*Geog.* 14.1.23). Cf. Oster, "Ephesus as a Religious Center," 1721–22.

45. As mentioned, neither the term "high priest" nor "high priestess" occurs in reference to the Artemis cult. The Kroegers have evidently confused the high priesthood of the provincial cult of the emperors ("High Priest of Asia" and "High Priestess of Asia") with the priesthood of the separate Artemis cult (see *I Suffer Not a Woman*, 92–93). In the inscriptions, sometimes the term "high priestess" without the qualifier "of Asia" is used for a provincial high priestess (e.g., *IEph* 810), and "priestess" without "of Artemis" occurs (e.g., *IEph* 508). See, for instance, *IEph* 994, where the offices are distinguished: "(daughter of) a priestess and κοσμητειρα of Artemis and of a high priestess of Asia." One should also note that there were significantly more high priests of Asia than high priestesses; see now: Steven J. Friesen, *Twice Neokoros: Ephesus, Asia, and the Cult of the Flavian Imperial Family* (Leiden, New York, Köln: Brill, 1993), 76–113, and the comprehensive list of officers in Appendix 1. In any case, this is another example of the Kroegers' apparent lack of facility with Ephesian historical material.

religious power" lay with women because of a centuries-old principle of female dominance, as they argue, why would the rise of a "high priestess" only occur by the first century? We would have expected women to hold the reigns of "religious power" from the earliest period.[46]

But the truth is, the presence of a "priestess of Artemis" in the cult of Artemis Ephesia—evidenced by a fair number of inscriptions—does not nullify the fact that "religious power" at Ephesus was firmly in the hands of: a.) the Roman government; b.) the municipal magistrates and council (see on Acts 19 above); and c.) various sacred offices filled primarily by men. This assertion is easy to validate from several sources, but let us look closely at only one, the edict of the Roman proconsul of AD 44, Paullus Fabius Persicus, which reads in part:

> The temple of Artemis herself—which is an adornment to the whole province because of the magnificence of the building, the antiquity of the worship of the goddess, and the abundance of the incomes granted to the goddess by the Emperor—is being deprived of its proper revenues. These had been sufficient for the maintenance and for the adornment of votive offerings, but they are being diverted for the illegal wants of the *Koinon's* leaders,[47] according as they consider will bring them profit... While using the appearance of the divine temple as a pretext, they sell the priesthoods as if at public auction. Indeed, they invite men of every kind to their sale, then they do not select the most suitable men upon whose heads the crown would fittingly be placed. (Instead) they restrict incomes to those who are being consecrated to as (little) as they are willing to accept, in order that they themselves might appropriate as much as possible. [The edict goes on to regulate other matters. *IEph* 17, 1–20.]

From the fact that a.) the Roman proconsul (possibly acting for Claudius) pronounced on the election of priests of Artemis, and that b.) certain incomes were granted to the goddess by the emperor as an exercise of his *auctoritas*,[48] we can conclude that the Roman government was quite willing to believe that it held the ultimate religious power in Ephesus (and in other provincial cities).[49] And we know that the Ephesians sometimes acknowledged this Roman overlordship in the religious realm.[50]

---

46. That "religious power" is attendant with priesthoods in the Greek world is a misunderstanding of the nature of Hellenic priesthoods anyway. I daresay, of the Christian ministry as well.
47. These are magistrates in either the provincial or municipal government. See Baugh, "Paul and Ephesus," 159–61.
48. Income from fish ponds and farmlands were granted to the goddess by the emperor; the latter is indicated on boundary stones which read, "*Imp. Caesar Augustus fines Dianae restituit*" (*IEph* 3501–2); cf. Dieter Knibbe et al., "Der Grundbesitz der ephesischen Artemis im Kaystrostal," *ZPE* 33 (1979) 139–46.
49. Augustus also limited the boundaries of the asylum area of the Artemisium (Strabo, *Geog*. 14.1.23; Dio Cassius 51.20.6). For other provinces, see, for example, Pliny's and the Emperor Trajan's correspondence regarding relocation of the temple of the Great Mother in Nicomedia (*Ep*. 10.49–50), the consecration of burial ground (*Ep*. 10.68–69), and the sanctity of a neglected shrine to Claudius (*Ep*. 10.70–71). Trajan was consulted in the latter two cases as *pontifex maximus*; cf. A. N. Sherwin-White, *The Letters of Pliny: A Historical and Social Commentary* (Oxford: Clarendon, 1966), 632, 655–59.
50. The Ephesians petitioned the Roman proconsuls for permission to perform mysteries to Demeter "with all

But what were the priesthoods which these men (ζνυρωποι) were "buying"? The title "priest of Artemis" does occur on early imperial inscriptions. C. Julius Atticus was "priest of Artemis *Soteira* (and) of the family of Caesar" (*IEph* 1265), and Apollonius Politicus was "the priest of Artemis" who dedicated a local altar.[51] C. Stertinius Orpex (whose daughter was a priestess of Artemis) says that he donated five thousand denarii "to the Council of the Ephesians and to the priests" (*IEph* 4123; under Nero). Although "priest of Artemis" is not a commonly mentioned title, these few occurrences are enough to show that women did not exclusively hold priesthoods of Artemis Ephesia in the imperial era.[52]

The Kroegers make no mention of male priests of Artemis. Instead, they present a quite different scenario, such as this:

> In Ephesus women assumed the role of the man-slaying Amazons who had founded the cult of Artemis of Ephesus.... The female dancers at the temple of the Ephesian Artemis clashed their arms, so lethal weapons were part of the priestesses' religious accoutrements. There are reasons to suspect that the dances may have contained a simulated attack on males, especially as they were performed with spears.... They would surely have inspired terror; and this, Strabo tells us, was one of the purposes of the dance. (186–87)

Now, Strabo says that this ritual act—he does not call it a "dance"—was performed by the κοψρητεθ.[53] The Kroegers have identified them as priestesses of Artemis. The only problem is that we have honorary lists naming κοψρητεθ on over fifty extant Ephesian inscriptions.[54] On first-century AD inscriptions alone there are over one hundred κοψρητεθ named (*IEph* 1001–20, 1047). These κοψρητεθ are ***all men***. For example, a list dating to AD 54–59 reads:

---

sanctity and lawful customs" (*IEph* 213; AD 88–89) and to celebrate festivals throughout a whole month in honor of Artemis (*IEph* 24; AD 162–64). (Both these inscriptions are discussed by Horsley [*New Docs* 4.74–82, 94–95]). Ephesian inscriptions usually give an emperor's full titles, including his high priesthood; for example: "To Tiberius Claudius Caesar Augustus Germanicus, son of D[rusus], *pontifex maximus* (*archiereus megistos*)" (*IEph* 259b).

51. Knibbe and Iplikçioglu, "Neue Inschriften aus Ephesos IX," *JÖAI* 55 (1984): 120–21.

52. Possibly another "priest of Artemis" occurs on *IEph* 4337, and note also the priest of Artemis in "Leucippe and Clitophon," mentioned above. Oster lists twenty-three sacerdotal and honorary offices connected to the cult of Artemis ("Ephesus as a Religious Center," 1722); most were held by men. We should mention especially the important (male) ζνυρωποι who functioned something like a board of trustees for the Artemisium and its property (*IEph* 27, 1570–90b, 2212, etc.; cf. Horsley, *New Docs* 4.127–29). There were also professional guilds (e.g., "Association of the Sacred Taste") which managed the banking, real estate, and agricultural resources of the Artemisium (Baugh, "Paul and Ephesus," 39–42).

53. Here is the passage in Strabo: "Above the grove (Ortygia) lies Mt. Solmissus, where, it is said, the Curetes [κοψρητεθ] stationed themselves, and with the din of their arms frightened Hera out of her wits.... A general festival is held there annually; and by a certain custom the youths vie for honour, particularly in the spendour of their banquets there. At that time, also, a special college of the Curetes [κοψρητεθ] holds symposiums and performs certain mystic sacrifices" (*Geog*. 14.1.20 [LCL]).

54. See Dieter Knibbe, *Forschungen in Ephesos. 9.1.1. Der Staatsmarkt. Die Inschriften des Prytaneions. Die Kureteninschriften and sonstige religiöse Texte* (Vienna: Österreichischen Akademie der Wissenschaften, 1981). Most of the inscriptions analyzed by Knibbe are given in vol. 4 of the *IEph* collection (ca. *IEph* 1001–80). See also the brief treatment in *New Docs* 6.196–202.

> When Tiberius Claudius Hermias, son of Ari_os, Quirinian tribe, was prytanis, the loyal, pious κοψρητεθ were: Halys son of Ari_os, Dionysius son of Charesios son of Mithridatus, Ti. Claudius Erastus son of Hermias, Antiochus son of Antiochus, Trypho Assklas son of Trypho (son of Trypho); Marcus was victim-inspector, Menodotus was sacred herald, Olympicus was incense-bearer, (and) Metras was flautist of the drink offering. (*IEph* 1008)[55]

Somehow, the Kroegers turn the male κοψρητεθ into women, and use these phantom priestesses as evidence for Amazonian religious power! Since many of these κοψρητεθ inscriptions were published as long as a century ago, are we wrong to expect them to have entered into the Kroegers' purview?[56]

That women were involved in the cult of Artemis Ephesia is not in question. But the Kroegers interpret the fact that there was a priestess of Artemis as an indication that "the primary religious power lay with women by the first century" (196). Let us ignore for the moment the previously discussed involvement of Roman and Ephesian men in the cult. Do the authors not know that priestesses were a common phenomenon throughout the Graeco-Roman world where no matriarchy was present? Although it is not invariable, "a priestess very commonly officiates for goddesses and a priest for gods" in Greek cults.[57] The fact that Artemis Ephesia had a priestess does not at all act as evidence of "matriarchy," "sex-reversal," or "primacy of the maternal." Instead, it shows that this cult had typical Hellenic features where men still might play a leading role.[58]

The social and religious role of the priestess of Artemis is hard to discern precisely. Sometimes the title "priestess" is joined with the title κοσμητειρα, "adorner" (*IEph* 892, 983–84, 989, et al.), suggesting that the priestesses were involved with clothing the cult statue of Artemis, since we know that sacred clothing was part of her cult.[59] Their role may have been much like the girls and priestesses who made and helped present an ornate new robe (πεπλοθ) to Athene during the Panathenaia procession of Athens.[60] Such processions were not only "very

55. Many κοψρητεθ on the surviving lists served also on the city council, further evidencing the connection between the municipal government and the Artemis cult mentioned above.

56. "If our love of God demands hard mental effort, let us not forget also to love God with all our strength. It is our responsibility to exercise the most serious scholarly endeavor of which we are capable" (38).

57. Burkert, *Greek Religion*, 98. For one example of each, notice: "the priest of Zeus" at Lystra in Acts 14:13 and the well-known priestess of Athene Polias (e.g., Pausanias 1.27). Michael Grant observes: "Athenian women acted as priestesses in more than forty cults" (*A Social History of Greece and Rome* [New York: Scribner, 1992], 8). For Rome, recall the important Vestal Virgins (e.g., Pliny, *Ep.* 4.11; Tacitus, *Ann.* 11.32). We should mention that apart from the priestesses of Artemis and of Hestia, most Ephesian cults (of gods or goddesses) were served by male priests (e.g., *IEph* 702, 902, 1210, 1213, 1235, 1239, 3239, and 4337).

58. I must once again ask the reader to consult my forthcoming study sketching Ephesian society in *Women and the Church* noted above. In the meantime, Oster's "Ephesus as a Religious Center" is an excellent, authoritative overview.

59. *IEph* 2; cf. F. Sokolowski, "A New Testimony on the Cult of Artemis of Ephesus," *HTR* 58 (1965): 427–31.

60. H. W. Parke, *Festivals of the Athenians* (London: Thames and Hudson, 1977) 33–50; Burkert, *Greek Religion*, 232–33.

prominent features of Greek festivals" in general (*OCD*) but are explicitly mentioned in connection with Artemis Ephesia.[61]

The priestesses of Artemis may have had not only a ceremonial part in Ephesian pageants, but were probably expected to underwrite some of its expenses also. As evidence, one first-century priestess, Vipsania Olympias, says that she not only "served as priestess circumspectly," but she "wreathed the temple and all its precincts in the days of the goddess' manifestations" (*IEph* 987). Another priestess, Ulpia Euodia Mudiane, daughter of Mudianus and Euodia "performed the mysteries and made all expenses through my parents" (*IEph* 989), showing, by the way, that she was undoubtedly an unmarried girl.[62] But that these Ephesian girls and matrons carried spears and performed "simulated attacks on males" is, frankly, incredible. They may have resembled "Rose Bowl Queens" in Artemis Ephesia's parades more than Amazon warriors!

Finally, the Kroegers' Evidence G consists of a creative, abstract use of ancient "gothic novels" to establish that there was "sex and death in an Ephesus-oriented context" (200). But are not "sex and death" everywhere present in ancient (and modern) literature? Look at *The Iliad*: sex and death. Plato's *Symposium*: sex; his *Apology*: death. Suetonius' *Nero*: lots of sex and death. Shakespeare's "Romeo and Juliet": sex and death on stage. Any modern novel or television program: sex and death *ad nauseam*. What exactly is the point?

We could find much more to critique in *I Suffer Not a Woman*,[63] but the reader has probably seen enough to gather that the Ephesian religious and cultural situation was not, in fact, marked by matriarchy of any sort. And it seems quite clear to me after prolonged study of the issues that 1 Timothy 2:9–15 is an appropriate mandate in any ancient (or modern) city or culture.

However, despite my negative evaluation of *I Suffer Not a Woman*, I should mention that I sincerely agree with the authors' stated purpose: "Our purpose is to maintain on the basis of

---

61. *IEph* 1577 mentions a procession under the supervision of two men connected to the Artemisium's rent office (cf. *IEph* 26 and 221). Various processions are also detailed in the famous Salutaris foundation (*IEph* 27–37; AD 104), the subject of Rogers's *Sacred Identity*; cf. I. Ringwood, "Festivals of Ephesus," *AJA* 76/1 (1972) 17–22. Such a procession in Ephesus opens the second-century (?) romance by Xenophon of Ephesus ("An Ephesian Tale," in *Collected Greek Novels*, 128–69). The heroine of this tale, Anthia, is called a "priestess" by the Kroegers (197), but this is an example of their overly imaginative reading of the ancient novels. Anthia, a fourteen-year-old, simply led the contingent of marriageable girls, since, says Xenophon, "It was the custom at this festival to find husbands for the girls and wives for the young men" ("Ephesian Tale," 129). For similar participation of girls and young women in Greek festivals, see Louise Bruit Zaidman, "Pandora's Daughters and Rituals in Grecian Cities," in *A History of Women*, 338–76.

62. See also a Flavia Chrysanthe who "fulfilled the myster[ies] *generously*" (second to third centuries AD; Knibbe and Iplikçioglu, "Neue Inschriften IX," 123, no. 4261); and a stone from ca. AD 165 which reads: "[name lost] served as priestess of Artemis piously and generously...and gave five thousand denarii to the city in accordance with the Council's vote" (Knibbe, Engelmann, and Iplikçioglu, "Neue Inschriften XI," 176, no. 4521). There may have been a set fee for serving as priestess of Artemis, and the βοψλη controlled the office. Also, that these priestesses served for a limited duration (annually?) shows the characteristically Hellenistic, not Anatolian, nature of the cult of Artemis Ephesia, contra the Kroegers.

63. For instance, their association of the "mysteries" of the Artemis cult with the so-called mystery religions far overruns the evidence. The "mysteries [better, 'rites'] and sacrifices" at Ephesus probably had nothing to do with bizarre sexual practices as the Kroegers suggest.

Scripture that both men and women are equally called to commitment and service, wherever and however God may lead" (14). But let us be clear that the point at issue between us is in defining the areas of "commitment and service" into which God leads women. The ordination issue is not about whether women may "teach or make decisions" as the Kroegers put it (17), but whether or not God calls women to the office(s) of elder or pastor-teacher.

The Kroegers adduce NT examples of women active in service to Christ in support of women's ordination. But are not these merely illustrations of the general office of believer? In order for discussions to advance among evangelicals, one would hope that writers such as the Kroegers will begin by clarifying their views of gifts and church office—which would have been highly desirable in *I Suffer Not a Woman*.

Furthermore, let us discuss these issues of church office from known ecclesiastical positions. For the Kroegers to speak vaguely about their opponents as "traditionalists," or worse, anecdotally as "those who justify the abuse of women by citing Scripture" (38), is itself an abuse of one's brothers and sisters who, we trust, are motivated by the love of God and His truth rather than by "a monopolistic attitude" (93). Let us discuss this issue without rancor or prejudice. But let us discuss it clearly, with a competent grasp of the issues and of the historical facts. On the latter point, let the notion that Ephesus was a "bastion of women's rights" or "matriarchy" be dropped once and for all. It was not.

And let us further be clear about the consequences of the women's ordination debate. If God does not call women into the pastoral office, they are in danger of acting like non-Levites who would presumptuously handle the tabernacle equipment (Numbers 1:51; 2 Samuel 6:6–7). God does not take the office of pastor-teacher lightly: "Not many of you should presume to be teachers, my brothers, because you know that we who teach will be judged more strictly" (James 3:1).

APPENDIX 7

Complete List of Eighty-Two Examples of *Authenteō* ("to exercise authority") in Ancient Greek Literature

Explanation: The following pages contain H. Scott Baldwin's exhaustive list of eighty-two examples of the term authenteō ("to exercise authority") in ancient Greek literature. This appendix is reproduced from H. Scott Baldwin, "Authenteō in Ancient Greek Literature," Appendix 2 in *Women in the Church: A Fresh Analysis of 1 Timothy 2:9–15*, edited by Andreas Köstenberger, Thomas Schreiner, and H. Scott Baldwin (Grand Rapids, MI: Baker Book House, 1995), 269–305. Used by permission of Baker Book House. However, to save space and because of the difficulty of typesetting hundreds of lines of Greek text, Baldwin's citations of the actual Greek texts have been removed from this appendix. Baldwin's original appendix, including Greek texts, may be viewed online at www.EFBT100.com or www.cbmw.org.

Readers who wonder if authenteō took the meanings that egalitarians claim, such as "to murder," "to instigate violence," "to proclaim oneself author of a man," "to thrust oneself," or "to misuse authority," see for themselves if the egalitarian case is convincing.

Further discussion of these examples is given in H. Scott Baldwin, "A Difficult Word: Authenteō in 1 Timothy 2:12," in *Women in the Church*, 65–80. Regarding the list reproduced here on the following pages, Baldwin writes, "All currently known occurrences of the verb authenteō are given in Appendix 2.[1] In analyzing this material, it becomes evident that the one unifying concept is that of *authority*."[2] (Baldwin has updated and clarified his analysis in a forthcoming second edition of *Women in the Church*.)

1. Baldwin qualifies this by saying that he omitted over twenty examples in the church fathers that were just quotations of 1 Timothy 2:12 and therefore of less help in defining the meaning of the term. He also omitted ten examples from a manuscript of doubtful origin and date called *The Alexander Romance* (Baldwin, "Difficult Word," 72n17). Since Baldwin's appendix was published, three more examples of authenteō have been noted in other articles, all confirming Baldwin's conclusions: see above, chapter 8, p. 308, n. 90 and p. 317, n. 119, for the articles by Huttar and Wolters.
2. Ibid, 72–73. Baldwin uses *domineer* as a negative term implying "misuse or abuse of authority," but he uses *dominate* as a neutral term implying "to bear rule" or "to have a commanding influence" (p. 73, n. 19).

αὐθεντεαω in Ancient Greek Literature

H. Scott Baldwin

I. The Meanings of αὐθεντεαω in Ancient Greek Literature

1. To rule, to reign sovereignly

[1st cent. BC] Philodemus, *Rhetorica*, "those in authority" {ptc}
[c. AD 325] Eusebius, *On Ecclesiastical Theology*, "the Father ruling" {ptc}
[AD 375] Epiphanius, *Medicine Chest Against All Heresies*, "the Son…ruling" {ptc}
[c. AD 390] John Chrysostom, *On the Holy Pentecost*, "exercising authority" {finite}
———, *Homily on Psalm 92*, "do I reign" {finite}
———, *The Heavenly Reign*, "rule absolutely" {finite}
———, *About Martha, Mary, and Lazarus*, "reigns…reign" {finite/finite}
———, *On the Resurrection of the Lord*, "rules" {finite}
[AD 446] Proculus Constantinopolitanus, *Oration #6*, "rules" {finite}
[5th cent. AD] Ammonius Alexandrius, *Fragments of Acts*, "exercised authority" {inf}
[6th cent. AD] Romanus Melodus Hymnographus, *Hymn 20*, "you…do reign" {finite}
———, *Hymn 22*, "I rule" {finite}

2. To control, to dominate

[2nd cent. AD] Ptolomey, *Tetrabiblos*, "dominates Mercury and the moon" {ptc}
[AD 370] Saint Basil, *The Letters*, "directing the bold deed" {ptc}
———, *The Letters*, "exercise full authority in this matter" {inf}
[c. AD 390] John Chrysostom, *Homily on Genesis*, "being in charge" {finite}
———, *Homilies on the Gospel of Saint Matthew*, "authority over her Son" {finite}
———, *Homilies on the Acts of the Apostles*, "as having been put in charge of them" {finite}
———, *When All Things Are Subject to Him*, "rules the will" {finite}
[4th cent. AD] Didymus the Blind, *Commentary on Job*, "control my flood of tears" {ptc}
———, *Dialogue between a Montanist and an Orthodox*, "to control…controlling men" {inf/ptc}
[5th cent. AD] Eusebius of Alexandria, *Sermons, #5*, "to exercise authority over the people" {inf}
[c. AD 520] Joannes Philoponus, *About the Rational Soul*, "ignorance rules the soul" {finite}

[6th cent. AD] *PMasp 67151*, "to have authority in any fashion" {inf}

[AD 790] *Second Council of Nicea*, "Take the leading part " {finite}

[12th cent. AD] Michael Glycas, *Annals*, "exercise authority over the men" {finite}

[Ms from 15th cent. AD] Ptolemy, Codicum Parisinorum, "exercises authority over all" {ptc}

a. To compel, to influence someone/something

[27 BC] *BGU 1208*, "I exercised authority over him" {ptc}

[c. AD 350] Athanasius, *Testimonies from Scripture*, "the Spirit sovereignly compels" {finite}

[c. AD 390] John Chrysostom, *Sermons in Genesis*, "exercised authority wrongly" {finite}

———, *About Martha, Mary, and Lazarus*, "this One compelling" {ptc}

[5th cent. AD] Ammonius, *Fragments of Acts*, "all did compel others" {finite}

[AD 690] Joannes Malalas, *Chronicles*, "put pressure on the governor" {ptc}

b. Middle voice: to be in effect, to have legal standing

[d. AD 235] Hippolytus, *On the End of the World*, "have legal authority over" {finite}

[7th cent. AD] *Chronicon Paschale*, "be authoritative" {inf}

[7th cent. AD] *Chronicon Paschale*, "be valid" {inf}

c. Hyperbolically: to domineer/to play the tyrant

[c. AD 390] John Chrysostom, *Homilies on Colossians*, "act the despot" {finite}

d. To grant authorization

[c. AD 350] Athanasius, *The Synod of the Arians in Italy*, "the Father authorizing" {ptc}

[AD 451] Emperor Marcian, *Letter to Leo, #1*, "you granting authorization" {ptc}

[AD 451] Council of Chalcedon, *Pulcheria to Leo*, "you granting authorization" {ptc}

[post AD 450] Socrates Scholasticus, *Church History*, "granting authorization" {ptc}

[d. AD 638] Sophronius Palestrinus, trans. of *On Illustrious Men*, "granting the authorization" {ptc}

3. To act independently

[c. AD 390] John Chrysostom, *Homilies on Saint Matthew,* "acted by His own power" {ptc}

———, *Homilies on the Gospel of Saint John*, "act with authority" {finite}

———, *Homilies on Romans*, "have even that [be] independent" {inf}

———, *Homilies on Colossians*, "to have your own way" {inf}

———, *On the Holy Passover*, "exercise my own authority" {finite}

[AD 451] Council of Chalcedon, *Eleventh Session*, "exercised their own initiative" {finite}

[5th cent. AD] Ammonius Alexandrius, *Fragments of Acts*, "to act independently" {inf}

[6th cent. AD] *PLond 1708*, "acted on his own authority" {inf}

a. To assume authority over

[c. AD 390] John Chrysostom, *By the Lake of Genesareth*, "take charge!" {finite}
[post AD 450] Socrates Scholasticus, *Church History*, "taking charge" {ptc}
[6th–7th cent. AD] *BGU 103*, "assume authority over the matter…assume authority" {finite/finite}
[9th cent. AD] Photius, *Chronicles*, "took charge" {ptc}

b. To exercise one's own jurisdiction

[2nd cent. AD] Moeris, *Attic Lexicon*, "to have independent jurisdiction" {inf}
[c. AD 450] Olympiodorus, *Excerpts*, "exercising his own authority" {ptc}
[AD 451] Council of Chalcedon, *To Makarios and Mt. Sinai*, "assumed his own jurisdiction" {finite}
[5th cent. AD] Victor Antiochenus, *Chains in Mark*, "assumes his own authority" {finite}
[c. AD 560] Joannes Lydus, *On the Magistracies of Roman Constitution*, "of its own initiative" {ptc}
[6th cent. AD] Leontius Heir., *Against the Nestorians*, "act on our own authority" {finite}
[AD 600] Evagrius Scholasticus, *Letter to a Vigilant Tutor*, "assuming his own jurisdiction" {ptc}
[AD 690] John Malalas, *Chronicles*, "exercised their own authority" {ptc}
———, *Chronicles*, "on his own authority" {ptc}
———, *Chronicles*, "on his own initiative" {ptc}
[AD 817] Theophanes, *The Chronicle*, "exercising their own authority" {ptc}
[9th cent. AD] Photius, *Library*, "exercising his own authority" {ptc}
———, *Library*, "exercised his own authority" {ptc}
[10th cent. AD] Constantine VII, *About Virtues and Vices*, "exercised their own jurisdiction" {ptc}
[13th–14th cent. AD] Thomas Magister, *Attic Sayings*, " = to be with independent jurisdiction" {inf}

c. To flout the authority of

[AD 690] John Malalas, *Chronicles*, "overruling the senate" {ptc}
———, *Chronicles*, "flouting the authority of the senate" {ptc}
[10th cent. AD] Constantine VII, *About Strategy*, "flouting the authority of the senate" {ptc}

4. To be primarily responsible for or to instigate something

[c. AD 325] Eusebius, *The Life of Constantine*, "God is himself the administrator of judgment" {finite}
[c. AD 350] Athanasius, *Letter to Rufinius*, "instigating unrighteousness" {finite}
[AD 449] Leo I, *Epistle 30*, "a certain dispute instigated by Eutyches" {ptc}
[AD 790] *Second Council of Nicea*, "originate" {ptc}
[10th cent. AD] Scholia Vetera on Homer's *Iliad*, "the one originating the writing" {ptc}
[10th cent. AD] The Suda Lexicon, "be responsible for" {ptc}

5. To commit a murder

[10th cent. AD] Scholia Vetera on Aeschylus' *Eumenides*, "murder" {ptc}

II. Occurrences of αὐθεντεαω in Ancient Greek Literature (Texts)

Literary Greeks (1st cent. BC–2nd cent. AD)

[1st cent. BC] Philodemus, Rhetorica {ref: 133.14}

Text: Philodemus, *Philodemi: Volumina Rhetorica*, vol. 3, ed. S. Sudhaus (Leipzig, 1896), 133.

Translation:[3] H. H. Hubbell, "The Rhetorica of Philodemus," *Transactions of the Connecticut Academy of Arts and Sciences* 23 (1920): 306.

To tell the truth the rhetors do a great deal of harm to many people, and incur the enmity of powerful rulers, whereas philosophers gain the friendship of public men by helping them out of their trouble. Ought we not to consider that men who incur the enmity of *those in authority* are villains, and hated by both gods and men?[4]

[2nd cent. AD] Ptolemy, *Tetrabiblos* {ref: III.13}

Text: W. G. Waddell, ed., *Manetho*, and F. E. Robbins, ed., *Ptolemy Tetrabiblos*, combined volume, Loeb Classical Library (London, 1964), 338.

Translation: same

If Saturn alone is ruler of the soul and *dominates*[5] Mercury and the moon, if he has a dignified position with reference to the universe and the angels, he makes his subjects lovers of the body...but if his position is the opposite and without dignity, he makes them sordid.

[2nd cent. AD] Moeris, *Attic Lexicon*

---

3. Throughout the appendix I have provided English translations by someone other than myself wherever they are available.
4. Several issues bear on this perplexing text. First, while it is true that Philodemus produced "elegant but often indecent love epigrams" (Hammond and Scullard, *The Oxford Classical Dictionary*, 2nd ed. [Oxford: Clarendon, 1970], 818), even a cursory review of this prose work shows that it is a serious treatise in seven books concerning the nature and effect of rhetoric. This particular section, book 5, deals with the negative effects of rhetors and rhetoric. The assertion of C. C. Kroeger ("Ancient Heresies and a Strange Greek Verb," *Reformed Journal* [Mar. 1979]: 12–14) that the word here must have an erotic sense because it was "penned by the rhetorician and obscene epigrammatist" is inapposite.
   Second, the text as given is a reconstruction by Sudhaus. It is entirely possible that αὐθεντουCσιν could be read as αὐθενταιασιν, the Old Attic dative plural of a αὐθεαντης, in which case it is a noun and not a verbal form at all.
   Third, it should be remembered that Hubbell is not giving a precise translation but a paraphrase. However, C. J. Vooys, *Lexicon Philodemeum. Pars Prior* (Purmerend [The Netherlands]: Muusses, 1934), 53, accepts Sudhaus's reconstruction and gives the Latin equivalent, dominor, for the Greek verb, indicating the meaning, "to be lord and master." Similarly DGE lists this passage with the meaning "ejercer la autoridad" [= "exercise authority over"].
5. E. A. Sophocles, *Greek Lexicon of the Roman and Byzantine Periods* (New York: Scribner's, 1887), 276, lists this use under "be in power over, to have authority over."

Text: Moeris, *Lexicon Atticista*, ed. Johannes Pierson and Georg Koch (Lipsiae: Sumptibus, 1830; reprint, Hildesheim: Olm, 1969), 54.

Translation: my own

Αὐτοδικεῖν, Attic. αὐθεντεῖν, Hellenistic[6]

Nonliterary Papyri (1st cent. BC*–7th cent.* AD*)*

[27 BC] *BGU 1208* {ref: line 38}

Text: F. Schubart et al., eds., *Äegyptische Urkunden aus den königlichen Museen zu Berlin*, vol. 4 (Berlin: Weidmannsche, 1912), 351.

Translation: John R. Werner, Wycliffe Bible Translators, International Linguistic Center, Dallas, Tex., letter as quoted by George W. Knight III, "ΑΨΥΕΝΤΕ´ in Reference to Women in 1 Timothy 2:12," *NTS* 30 (1984): 143–57.

I *exercised authority over him*, and he consented to provide for Calatytis the Boatman on terms of full fare, within the hour.[7]

[6th cent. AD] *PLond 1708* {ref: line 38}

Text: H. I. Bell, ed., *Greek Papyri in the British Museum. Catalogue, with Texts*, vol. 5 (London: British Museum, 1917), 119.

Translation: my own

But the aforementioned Psates, who is our elder brother, not only took to himself all the paternal and maternal inheritance and defrauded us, his own brothers, but even *acted on his own authority* and leased[8] our ancestral home and collected rents and appropriated them to himself.

6. The editors note that the verbs should be taken as infinitives: αὐτοδικεῖν, αυθεντεῖν.
7. The translation of this text is disputed. G. W. Knight, 145, gives Werner's translation here. F. Preisigke, *Wörterbuch der griechischen Papyrusurkunden*, vol. 1 (Berlin: Erben, 1925), 235, lists this under "herr sein, fest auftreten" ("be master, to act confidently"). Liddell, Scott, Jones, *A Greek-English Lexicon, with Supplement* (Oxford: Clarendon, 1968) list this under "to have full power or authority over." P. B. Payne, "ʺοὐδεα in 1 Timothy 2:12" (unpublished paper presented at the ETS annual meeting November 21, 1986), implies that the translation of Paul D. Peterson is superior: "when I had prevailed upon him to provide." Of Payne's arguments the last is the most important—the use of προας. Payne writes that this use is "'denoting a hostile or friendly relationship—a. hostile against, with after verbs of disputing, etc.' (BAG, 717; cf. LSJ, 1497). This passage is about a hostile relationship; his action is called 'insolence' in the text. None of the other uses of προας in the over three columns devoted to it in BAG seem to fit the text." It is difficult to evaluate the strength of Payne's argument. For all extant uses of verbal αὐθεντεαω that are transitive in the Greek—nearly all are followed by a genitive noun, only twice by an accusative noun, once by the preposition περια, once by the preposition εἰs, and here alone by the preposition προas. However, the meaning of "compel" does seem appropriate.
8. This phrase given by Bell himself in a footnote. Preisigke lists this reference, along with *PMasp 67151.174* below, under "verfügungsberechtigt sein" ("having legitimate authority to dispose" [of something]).

[6th cent. AD] *PMasp 67151* {ref: line 174}

Text: Jeanne Maspero, ed., *Papyrus Grecs d'Époque Byzantine, Catalogue Général des Antiquités Égyptiennes du musée Caire*, vol. 2 (Cairo: Imp. de l'institute francois d'archéologie orientale, 1913; reprint: Osnabruck: Otto Zeller, 1973).

Translation: my own

I will and command my wife, my nobleborn life partner, to have authority over her own things and solely over the dowry given by me to her in the hour of our suitable wedding before our union; and that she be content with these things and not to be able to seek anything further with regard to my heirs of any kind or joint heirs neither *to have authority* in any fashion to detach outright goods of any kind from any manner of my estate.[9]

[6th cent.–7th cent. AD] *BGU 103* {ref: lines 3 & 8}

Text: F. Schubart et al., eds., *Äegyptische Urkunden aus den königlichen Museen zu Berlin,* vol. 1 (Berlin: Weidmannsche, 1895), 122.

Translation: John R. Werner, Wycliffe Bible Translators, International Linguistic Center, Dallas, Tex., letter as quoted by George W. Knight III, "in Reference to Women in 1 Timothy 2:12," NTS 30 (1984): 143–57.

Since the brothers of the blessed Enoch have come to us saying, "We want to go to law with his wife," please be so good, Your (*pl.*) Godhelp, if you will *assume authority*[10] over the matter and receive them in the city, and they will come to terms with each other; but if not, please be so good as to have both sides come here and we shall have them come to terms in accordance with justice and in accordance with the custom of Creation. But do not defer, Your (*pl.*) Piety-to-the-Father, because of a deposit, to send them forth; but if, again, you *assume authority* and receive them into the city, fine.

The Church Fathers (4th cent. AD*)*

[d. AD 235] Hippolytus, *On the End of the World* {ref: 7.5}

Text: Hippolytus, *De consummatione mundi, in Hippolyt's kleinere exegetische und homiletische Schriften*, ed. H. Achelis in *Die griechischen christlichen Schriftsteller*, 1.2 (Leipzig: Himrichs, 1897), 289–309.

Translation: my own

9. This translation is at variance with that of C. C. and R. C. Kroeger, *I Suffer Not a Woman: Rethinking 1 Timothy 2:11–15 in Light of Ancient Evidence* (Grand Rapids: Baker, 1992), 89, who translate it "not to claim as her own [authentein] in any manner anything of my various possessions to detach it altogether from my estate." Two factors mitigate the Kroegers' translation: (1) Preisigke, renders the key passage "noch soll er berechtigt sein, irgend ein Bermögenstuck an sich zu reißen" ("neither should she be entitled to appropriate to herself any piece of property"), which is plainly "have authority to detach for herself"; and (2) the meaning "claim as one's own" is otherwise completely unattested.

10. Preisigke lists this under "beherrschen" ("rule, control, or dominate") and notes concerning the situation of the citation, "falls die Sache zu deinem Geschäftsreise gehört" ("in case the matter belongs to your business trip").

Therefore, everyone will walk according to his own desire, and the children will lay hands upon their parents, a wife will hand over her own husband to death and a man his own wife to judgment as deserving to render account. Inhuman masters will *have legal authority* over their servants and servants shall put on an unruly disposition toward their masters.[11]

[c. AD 325] Eusebius, *On Ecclesiastical Theology* {ref: 3.5.22.1}

Text: *Eusebius, De Ecclesiastica Theologica*, ed. Kosterman and Hawsen, vol. 4 of *Eusebius Werke*.

Translation: my own

Therefore, to the holy and thrice-blessed Trinity alone this One [the Holy Spirit] belongs. Through no other means, seeing he has carefully arranged it, should the mystery of regeneration for all those who believe in him from among the Gentiles be handed over from the Savior to his apostles. Neither should there be without him baptizing "them in the name of the Father and Son and Holy Spirit,"—of the Father *ruling* and giving grace, of the Son who is being served by this (for "grace and truth came through Jesus Christ"), of the Holy Spirit, clearly the Comforter, himself being the provision according to distinctions of his gifts, for, "to some through the Spirit he gives a word of wisdom, to another a word of knowledge according to the same Spirit, to another faith in the same Spirit" and other verses can be reckoned with these likewise.

———, *The Life of Constantine* {ref: 2.48.1.8}

Text: Eusebius, Vita Constantini, ed. F. Winkelman, vol. 1.1 of *Eusebius Werke*.

Translation: Eusebius, *Church History, Life of Constantine the Great, and Oration in Praise of Constantine*, trans. E. C. Richardson, A Select Library of Nicene and Post-Nicene Fathers of the Christian Church Series, ed. Philip Schaff and Henry Wace (reprint; Grand Rapids: Eerdmans, 1952), 512.

11. A. Roberts, in Hippolytus, *Discourse on the End of the World*, The Ante-Nicene Fathers of the Christian Church Series, vol. 5, ed. Philip Schaff and Henry Wace (reprint; Grand Rapids: Eerdmans, 1952), 243, translates this passage: "Wherefore, everyone all shall walk after their own will. Children will lay hands on their parents. The wife will give up her own husband to death, and the husband will bring his own wife to judgment like a criminal. Masters *will lord it over* their servants savagely, and servants will assume an unruly demeanor toward their masters."

Arguably, Roberts has missed the translation here for two reasons: (1) ἀπααvθρωποι is an adjective that modifies δεσποαται, not an adverb; (2) he has missed the importance of the middle voice. In the other two instances of the middle voice it means "to be in force, to have legal authority over" (see [the *Chronicon Paschale*, below). Sophocles held the middle to indicate "to be in force." If so, ours is a better translation. The case cannot be decided with certainty. The structure of the sentence does not provide the parallelism expected. If Roberts' translation of the middle voice were correct, we should expect to see (morally negative adjective—"inhuman") + (morally neutral noun—"masters") + (morally negative verb—"lord it over") paralleled by (morally negative adjective—"factious" or "rebellious" or "lazy", etc.) + (morally neutral noun—"servants") + (morally negative verb). But as it is "servant" is not modified. Therefore, the choice to translate αὐθεvτουα μαιν a morally neutral sense in this passage cannot be validated or invalidated from the structure of the passage. On balance then, the rare use of the middle, if the evidence from the *Chronicon* is taken as normative, suggests itself as the most significant factor, and αὐθεvτεαω should be taken here as "have legal authority over."

Accordingly no wise man will ever be surprised when he sees the mass of mankind influenced by opposite sentiments. For the beauty of virtue would be useless and unperceived, did not vice display in contrast with it the course of perversity and folly. Hence it is that the one is crowned with reward, while the most high God is himself *the administrator*[12] *of judgment* to the other.

[c. AD 350] Athanasius, *The Synod of the Arians in Italy and Seleucia of Isauria* {ref: 27.3.26}

Text: Athanasius, *De Synodis Arimini in Italia et Seleuciae in Isauria*, ed. H. G. Opitz, in Athanasius Werke, vol. 2.1 (Berlin: de Gruyter, 1940). This text reappears in *Athanasius, Symboule Sirmium, Anathema XVIII*, MPG 26:737(XVIII).

Translation: Athanasius, *Selected Treatises of S. Athanasius, Archbishop of Alexandria, in Controversy with the Arians*, trans. J. H. Parker (Oxford: J. H. Parker, 1842), 121.

Whosoever hearing that the Father is Lord and the Son Lord and the Father and Son Lord, for there is Lord from Lord, says there are two Gods, be he anathema. For we do not place the Son in the Father's order, but as subordinate to the Father; for He did not descend upon Sodom without the Father's will, not did He rain [fire] from Himself, but from the Lord, that is the Father *authorizing it*. Nor is He of Himself set down on the right hand, but He hears the Father saying, "Sit thou on My right hand."

———, *Letter to Rufinius* {ref: 78.8}

Text: Athanasius, *Epistulae ad Rufinium, in Fascido IX. Discipline général antique (ii e –ix e s.)*, vol. 2, *Les canons des pères grecs*, ed. P. Joannou (Rome: Italo-Orientale, 1963), 76–80.

Translation: my own

And indeed he strove in this manner to please much in this and every way, so as on the one hand to make allowance upon their repentance for the ones who had fallen and the ones being directors of impiety, but not to give to them a place among the clergy. But to the ones not *instigating* unrighteousness,[13] but being sweeping away because of force and violence, he deemed to give to them lenient judgment, and even to have a place among the clergy, especially because they made a credible apology, and these he somehow deemed as having become part of the household again.

12. Here the sense of "be primarily responsible for" is apposite.

13. Sophocles uses this citation as one of two (the other is the Second Council of Nicea) to substantiate a meaning of "to be the originator of anything" for αὐθεντεαω. Lampe lists this under "be primarily responsible for, instigate, authorize."

———, *Testimonies from Scripture (The Essential Community of Father and Son and Holy Spirit)* {ref: 28.41.31}[14]

Text: Athanasius, *Testimonia e Scripturia (de communi essentia patris et filii et spiritus sancti)*, in H. G. Opitz, *op cit.*

Translation: my own

Concerning the Spirit in the Acts [of the Apostles] it says, "The ones sent out by the Holy Spirit came to Seleucia." If therefore the act of being called is of God, why does the Spirit through the prophet say, "Thus says the Lord?" And again the Spirit [says] to the saints in Antioch, "Set aside for me Paul and Barnabas to the work which I have called them." Learn therefore the power of the Trinity. The Father gives the law, the Son commands, the Spirit sovereignly *compels*. Hear the one speaking of God, "The ones preaching good news will come, whom the Lord has called."

[AD 370] Saint Basil, *The Letters* {ref: #51, line 24}

Text: Saint Basil, *The Letters*, vol. 3, ed. Roy J. Deferrari, Loeb Classical Library Series (Cambridge, Mass.: Harvard University Press, 1952), 322.

Translation: Ibid., 323.

Tell me, did I anathematize the most blessed Dianius? For this is the charge they made against us. Where or when? In whose presence? On what pretext? Was it bare words or in writing? Was I merely quoting others, or myself originating and *directing* the bold deed?[15] Oh, the shamelessness of those who are ever ready to say anything!

———, *The Letters* {ref: #69, line 45}

Text: Saint Basil, *The Letters*, vol. 4, ed. Roy J. Deferrari, Loeb Classical Library Series (Cambridge, Mass.: Harvard University Press, 1952), 40, 42.

Translation: Ibid., 41, 43.

It has seemed to us advisable in the circumstances, moreover, to write to the bishop of Rome, that he may examine into the state of affairs here, and give us his opinion, so that, as it is difficult to send men from Rome by a general synodical decree, he may himself *exercise full authority* in this matter, selecting men capable of enduring the hardships of a journey.

14. This is believed not to be one of the genuine works of Athanasius, and therefore may be of a much later date.
15. Kroegers, *I Suffer Not a Woman,* 103, render this "profess himself to be its author." On the astonishing creativity of the rendering "profess him to be," see A. Wolters, review of *I Suffer Not a Woman,* by C. C. and R. C. Kroeger, in *Calvin Theological Journal* 28 (1993): 210. Lampe lists this under "be primarily responsible for, etc."

[AD 375] Epiphanius, Bishop of Salamis (Constantia), *Medicine Chest Against All Heresies* {ref: 224.2}

Text: Epiphanius Constantiensis, *Panarion*, in *Epiphanius*, vol. 2, ed. K. Holl (Leipzig, 1922), 224.

Translation: my own

For we see even here [i.e., in this passage] concerning with the Son himself, it says, "when he shall hand over the kingdom to the God and Father, then shall he make powerless all rule and authority and power." This means the Son himself is handing over the kingdom and rendering powerless all rule. The next, "He must reign until he should put all his enemies under his feet," means the Son is doing all things and *ruling* and exercising authority and handing over to the Father the ones who are in submission along with the kingdom."

[c. AD 390] John Chrysostom, *On the Holy Pentecost* {ref: 50:464.35}

Text: John Chrysostom, *De Sancta Pentecosta*, MPG 50: 453–70.

Translation: my own

And Paul cries out saying, "All these the one and the same spirit works, distributing to each one just as he wills." "Just as he wills," he says, not "just as it has been determined"; "distributing," not "being distributed"; *"exercising authority,"* not "being subject to authority." For where Paul bears witness to the Father of his own authority, he attributes it even to the Holy Spirit.

———, *Sermons on Genesis* {ref: 54.594.52}

Text: John Chrysostom, *In Genesium* (Sermons), MPG 54:581–630.

Translation: my own

Concerning this hear how Paul speaks of subordination, in order to teach again old and new [women believers] harmony. "Let a woman," he says, "learn in silence in all submission." See even he puts the woman in submission to the man. But he anticipates the reader should hear the reason. Why "in all submission"? For "A woman," he says, "I do not allow to teach." Why? Because she once taught Adam wrongly. "Neither to have authority over men." Why not at any time? Because she once *exercised authority wrongly*. "But to be in silence." Again he speaks the reason. "For Adam," he says, "was not deceived, but the woman after being deceived became the transgressor." [Notes: Here Chrysostom adds Kakōs, "wrongly," when he wishes to speak of wrongful authority.—WG]

———, *Homily on Genesis* {ref: 56.533.20}

Text: John Chrysostom, *In Genesium*, MPG 56:525–38.

Translation: my own

"Who told you that you are naked, except that you ate from the tree of which I commanded you, 'This alone you shall not eat?'; You forsook, me the one who molded you, and went over to the enemy; You let go of me, the one who was the craftsman, and joined the one who strayed. I commanded you of this one only not to eat and you have become co-conspirator with the devil." Adam said, "The woman which you gave to me, she gave to me of the tree and I ate." What unreasonable pretext! What excuse not worthy of being spoken! What bitter locution not justifying the speaking! The woman was given to you as a helper, not *as being in charge*; as one who agrees, not as the mistress of the manor; as of one mind, not as tutor; as yoked together, not ruling; as subject to, not highest over; as being in concert with you, not as prevailing over you.

———, *Homily on Psalm 92* {ref: 55.615.4}

Text: John Chrysostom, *In Psalum 92*, MPG 55:611–16.

Translation: my own

Why did you teach me to sew together a bunch of fig leaves? Why did you lead me to the ensnaring fruit, Bewitching Woman, saying, "Take, eat of the fruit begrudged to you, but if you eat of it, in that day your eyes will be opened, and you will be as God, knowing good and evil?" What have you done, Woman? I am blinded, I can not see. I did evil and turned away from the good. Just like the sunbeam, I toil—but not like God *do I reign.* Disobedient One, Woman, do you not know who you are?

———, *Homilies on the Gospel of Saint Matthew* {ref: 57.239.50}

Text: John Chrysostom, *In Mattaeum*, MPG 57:13–772

Translation: John H. Parker, *The Homilies of S. John Chrysostom on the Gospel of St. Matthew* (Oxford: J. H. Parker, 1843), 225.

For this cause He who had raised thousands of the dead with a word only, when He was calling Lazarus, added also a prayer; and then, lest this should make Him appear less than Him that begat Him, He, to correct this suspicion, added, "I said these things, because of the people which standeth by, that they may believe that Thou hast sent Me." And neither doth He work all things as one who *acted by His own powe*r, that He might thoroughly correct their weakness; nor doth He all things with prayer, lest He should leave matter of evil suspicion to them that should follow, as though He were without strength or power: but He mingles the latter with the former, and those again with these.

———, *Homilies on the Gospel of Saint Matthew* {ref: 57.465.1}

Text: John Chrysostom, *In Mattaeum*, MPG 57:13–772.

Translation: John H. Parker, *The Homilies of S. John Chrysostom on the Gospel of St. Matthew* (Oxford: J. H. Parker, 1843), 608.

[In reference to Matt. 12:46–49 and Mary:]

For in fact that which she assayed to do, was of superfluous vanity; in that she wanted to shew the people, that she *hath power and authority over her Son*, imagining not as yet any thing great concerning him; whence also her unseasonable approach.

———, *Homilies on the Gospel of Saint John* {ref: 59.367.45}

Text: John Chrysostom, *In Joannen*, MPG 59:23–482.

Translation: John H. Parker, *The Homilies of S. John Chrysostom on the Gospel of St. John* (Oxford: J. H. Parker, 1842), 587.

[In reference to John 12:21:]

When the report concerning him was imparted to them, they say, "We would see Jesus." Philip gives place to Andrew as being before him, and communicates the matter to him. But neither doth he at once *act with authority*; for he heard that saying, "Go not into the way of the Gentiles": therefore having communicated with the disciple, he refers the matter to his Master. For they both spoke to Him.

———, *Homilies on the Acts of the Apostles* {ref: 60.37.13}

Text: John Chrysostom, *In Acta Apostelorum*, MPG 60:13–384.

Translation: John H. Parker, *The Homilies of S. John Chrysostom on the Gospel of St. John* (Oxford: J. H. Parker, 1841), 43.

[In reference to Acts 1:15–26 and Peter:]

For observe, they were an hundred and twenty, and he asks for one out of the whole body: with good right, as *having been put in charge* of them: for to him had Christ said, "And when thou art converted, strengthen thy brethren."

———, *Homilies on Romans* {ref: 60.525.41}

Text: John Chrysostom, *In Epistulam ad Romanos*, MPG 60:391–682.

Translation: John H. Parker, *The Homilies of S. John Chrysostom on the Epistle of St. Paul to the Romans* (Oxford: J. H. Parker, 1841), 587.

[With reference to Rom. 8:14:]

Now this is again a much greater honor than the first. And this is why he does not say merely, "as many as live by the Spirit of God," but, "as many as are led by the Spirit of God," to shew that he would have Him use such power over our life as a pilot doth over a ship, or a charioteer over a pair of horses. And it is not the body only, but the soul, itself too, that he is for setting under reins of this sort. For he would not *have even that independent*, but place its authority also under the power of the Spirit.

———, *Homilies on Colossians* {ref: 62.366.29}

Text: John Chrysostom, *In Epistulam ad Colossenses*, MPG 62:299–392.

Translation: John H. Parker, *The Homilies of S. John Chrysostom on the Epistle of St. Paul to the Philippians, Colossians, and Thessalonians* (Oxford: J. H. Parker, 1879), 294–95.

To love therefore is the husbands' part, to yield is theirs. If then each one contributes his own part, all stands firm. For from being loved, the wife too becomes affectionate; and from her being submissive, the husband becomes gentle. And see how in nature also it hath been so ordered, that the one should love, the other obey. For when the governing party loves the governed, then every thing stands fast. Love from the governed is not so requisite, as from the governing to the governed; for from the other obedience is due. For that the woman hath beauty, and the man desire, shews nothing else than that for the sake of love it hath been made so. Do not therefore, because thy wife is subject to thee, *act the despot;* nor because thy husband loveth thee, be thou puffed up. For this cause hath He subjected her to thee, that she may be loved the more. For this cause He hath made thee to be loved, O wife, that thou mayest easily bear thy subjection.

———, *Homilies on Colossians* {ref: 62.376.1}

Text: John Chrysostom, *In Epistulam ad Colossenses*, MPG 62:299–392.

Translation: John H. Parker, *The Homilies of S. John Chrysostom on the Epistle of St. Paul to the Philippians, Colossians, and Thessalonians* (Oxford: J. H. Parker, 1879), 309.

But let us see the wisdom of Paul. "Walk in wisdom," he saith, "towards them that are without, redeeming the time." That is, the time is not yours, but theirs. Do not then wish *to have your own way* (i.e. in the world, as men of the world), but redeem the time. And he said not simply, "Buy," but "redeem," making it your own after another manner.

———, *The Heavenly Reign* {ref: 59.583.46}

Text: John Chrysostom, *In Illud: Regnum Caelorum Patri Filius*, MPG 59:577–86.

Translation: my own

[The householder of Matt. 20 addresses the others about the eleventh-hour worker.]

Therefore, am I not unable not to honor, by every honor and with all diligence, the one desiring me thus, the one believing in me thus? As you believed, he believed; as you abounded, he abounded; as you worshipped, he worshipped; as you reigned, he reigned; as you were afflicted, were we not afflicted? But I, by grace, will fill up what is lacking. Is it not lawful for me to do, what I will among my own? Do I take what is yours? I provide out of my own resources. For not by means of your property do I seek glory. I *rule absolutely* by means of my own. For I did not appoint you as a guardian of my opinion. I received you as a hireling from the beginning. For I did not appoint you as lord of my authority. As a lover of mankind I share with my own.

———, *About Martha, Mary, and Lazarus* {ref: 61.706.19, 20}

Text: John Chrysostom, *In Martham, Miriam et Lazarus*, MPG 61:705–10.

Translation: my own

[Elijah cries out:]

"Set me free me, Lord, from this mob! He put around me gawkers. He placed around me disgraceful ones. He brought upon me much tribulation. Give life and I will supply the rain. Give full measure of bereavement and I will irrigate the land with tears. Give the old manner of discipline and I will stir up the tongue for a shower of tears." These things occurred rather, for the sake of prophecy of the resurrection of Lazarus and the controversy with the Jews—because another Lord *reigns* and another servant raises the dead. Elijah raised the dead, but nevertheless he did not *reign*.

———, *About Martha, Mary, and Lazarus* {ref: 61.706.57}

Text: John Chrysostom, *In Martham, Miriam et Lazarus*, MPG 61:705–10.

Translation: my own

Who is this one who is calling? Who is *this one compelling*? Who is this one forming again the one shamefully cast into a sepulchre? Who is this one waking the dead as from sleep? Who is the one sundering the adamantine gates? Who is this one crying, "Lazarus, come out!" The voice sounds like a man, but the power is the power of God. Who is the one calling? It is not man; it is the form of man, but the voice of God.

———, *By the Lake of Genesareth* {ref: 64.52.15}

Text: John Chrysostom, *In lacum Genesarth et in Sanctum Petrum Apostolum*, MPG 64:47–52.

Translation: my own

Moses insulted him, but Christ healed. Thus he is healed, and there the gift of treating the sick is command to come forth. Why? In order that love of mankind by the Lord Jesus should be made known and the incessant love of money of the Jews should appear. Why the infamous reproach of the leper, "Lord, if you wish you are able to heal me"? I do not say, "comfort!," but "*take charge*!"; I do not say "to pray!" but "to heal!" To heal his own by God's own will, but not by another spirit. "Lord, if you will, you are able to make me clean." For he heard the word of the prophet, "Our God does what ever he has willed in heaven and all earth."

———, *On the Holy Passover* {ref: line 25}

Text: John Chrysostom, C. Baur, "Drei unedierte Chrysostums-Text, bzw," *Traditio 9* (1953): 108–10.

Translation: my own

"Destroy this temple and in three days I will raise it." He did not say, "The Father will raise it," in order that you, Ares, do not pounce upon the word; But, "I will raise it. I, not being commanded, *exercise my own authority.*" But why not immediately instead of after three days? You ask, "Why does he not rise immediately, but after three days?" In order that he should not vitiate the type of Jonah the prophet.

———, *When All Things Are Subject to Him* {ref: 160.25}

Text: John Chrysostom, *In Illud: Quando ipsi subicietomnia*, ed. S. Haidacher, "Drei unedierte Chrysostomus-Texte einer Baseler handscrift," *Zeitschrift für Katholische Theologie* 31 (1907): 150–67.

Translation: my own

But nothing of this did the Savior say to the one who came to him sincerely, but after praising him for the sincerity of his faith, pure and genuine, he gave him salvation. "You have come to me faithfully. Receive faithfully the remedy. By my will you inscribe the good deed, from my will receive salvation." "Lord, if you will, you are able to make me clean." "I will be clean." Do not stand with the factious at the borders of impiousness; You see that he is subject to the word, but for the members of the Household, he *rules* the will; but when I say these things, I bring in and do not exclude from the Son the will of the Paternal Will.

———, *On the Resurrection of the Lord* {ref: line 42}

Text: John Chrysostom, *In Resurrectionen Domini*, ed. C. Datema and P. Allen, "Text and Tradition of Two, etc," *Jahrbuch der österreichischen Byzantinistik* 30 (1981): 94–97.

Translation: my own

Today we celebrate the universal feast together, fulfilling likewise the law and confirming grace, "because the law was given through Moses, but grace and truth came through Jesus Christ." Where there is a servant, there is a "was given"; but where there is freedom, there is a "came," because the servant serves, but the Lord *rules*.

[4th cent. AD] Didymus the Blind, *Commentary on Job* {ref: 285.4}

Text: Didymus Caecus, *Didymos der Blinde. Kommentar zu Hiob*, pt. 3, ed. U. Hegendorn, D. Hagendorn, and L. Koenen (Bonn: Habelt, 1968), 2–220.

Translation: my own

But this thing he does not ignore, but he makes plain the plot. It says, "Thus changing again marvelously you destroy me." It proves that even if I should be hunted like a lion, having been surrounded by such ones, they themselves do not *control* my deliverance.

———, *Dialogue Between a Montanist and an Orthodox* {ref: 457.2; 457.8}

Text: Didymus Caecus, Dialexis Montanistae et orthodoxi, in "Widerlegung eines Montanisten," *Zeitschrift für Kirchengeschichte* 26 (1905): 449–58.

Translation: my own

We do not shun the prophecies of women. Even the holy Mary prophesied saying, "From now on all generations will bless me." And even as you say the holy Philip had prophesying daughters, and Miriam, the sister of Aaron, prophesied. But we do not allow them to speak in church nor *to control* men so that books be written in their name. For this is "uncovered": for women to pray and to prophesy, but not to dishonor the head, that is, the man. For the holy Mother of God, Mary, was not unable to write a book under her own name; but she did not do it in order not to dishonor the head by *controlling* men.

[AD 446] Proculus Constantinopolitanus, *Oration #6* {ref: 65.816 A}

Text: Proculus Constantinopolitanus, *Oratio VI*, MPG 65:692ff.

Translation: my own

How much is the difference between law and grace! How the one condemns, but the other unites; the one punishes, but the other saves completely; the one serves, but the other *rules*; the one afflicts with sin, but the other utterly destroys sin.

[AD 449] Leo I, Pope, *Epistle #30 (To Pulcheria)* {ref: 54.788 A}

Text: Leo Magni, *Epistulae XXX*, MPL 54.788ff.

Translation: my own (Cpr. *Epistle XXXI*, trans. C. L. Feltoe, in *The Nicene and Post-Nicene Fathers*, Second Series, ed. P. Schaff and H. Wace, [Grand Rapids: Eerdmans, 1979]).

You have been taught by this vaunting Holy Spirit. To him you have submitted your authority. Through his gifts and his favors you rule. Hence, seeing that, I knew through the report of my brother and fellow bishop Flavian, a certain dispute, *instigated* by Eutyches, in the Church of Constantinople, has arisen against the pure faith of Christianity.

[c. AD 450] Olympiodorus, *Excerpt from the History of Olypiodorus* {ref: 456.3}

Text: Olympiodorus, *Ex Historia Olympiodori Excerpta, in Dexippi, Eunapii, Petri Patricii, Prisci, Malchi*, et al., ed. B. G. Niebuhre, I. Bekker, et al. (Bonnae: Weberi, 1829), 456.

Translation: my own

The second part begins here: For Jobinos, making his own brother Sebastian king, contrary to the wishes of Adaulfo, made Adaulfo his enemy. And Adaulfo sent ambassadors to Honorios, and he promised to bring peace—and the heads of the tyrants. They returned and promised with oaths, and the head of Sebastian was sent to the king. But being besieged by Adaulfo, Jobinos surrendered himself, and he was sent to the king. Dardanos, the governor, *exercising his own authority*, killed him.

[post AD 450] Socrates Scholasticus, *Church History* {ref: 2.30.63}

Text: Socrates' *Ecclesiastical History*, 2nd ed., ed. W. Bright (Oxford: Clarendon, 1893), 1–330.

Translation: my own [compare J. H. Parker's translation of Athanasius, *Controversy with the Arians* (above)]

For the Son does not dictate to the Father, but is in submission to the Father. Neither does he descend to a body without the Father's will; nor did he rain [sic] from himself, but from the Lord, that is, the Father *granting authorization*.

———, *Socrates* {ref: 2.34.6}

Text: *Socrates' Ecclesiastical History*, 2nd ed., ed. W. Bright (Oxford: Clarendon, 1893), 1–330.

Translation: my own

So that, not long after, his spy was detected by Constantine. For Domitian, *taking charge*, confined the then commander of the East and Magnos, the quaestor, informing the king about his spy.

[AD 451] Emperor Marcian, *Letter to Leo, #1* {ref: 54.900 B}

Text: Marcianus Imperator, *Epistulae ad Leonem, I,* MPL 54.900ff.

Translation: my own

On account of our application, and the existence of all the foregoing matters, so that, every unrighteous wanderer having been put away through the well-disciplined ones of this synod, *you granting authorization*, great peace with respect to the bishops of the catholic faith will come about, and the pollutions of all will be clean and spotless.

[AD 451] Council of Chalcedon, *Letter of Empress Pulcheria to Leo I* {ref: 2, 1, 1.9.34.}

Text: *Concilium universale Chalcedonese anno 451*, vol. 2.1.1–2.1.2, ed. E. Schwartz (Berlin: de Gruyter, 1933; reprint, 1962).

Translation: my own

In order that all, even every bishop of Anatolia, Thrace, and even Illyricum, just as indeed it pleases our most holy king, should appear to my yoke fellow in one city of the region of Anatolia, and there convene a synod concerning the Catholic Confession and concerning these bishops who have separated themselves from it, just as faith and Christian piety demand and they should determine, you *granting authorization*.

———, *Eleventh Session of Chalcedon,*[16] 29 October 451 {ref: 2, 1, 3.48.12}

The Most Pious Bassianos said, "When was I ever in Evazae or went out of it? But I was declared bishop by violence! The canons are the manifest authority. The Fathers would say, 'If there is a preference, it is for the election to office, not for the vacating of it.' These would say, 'We know the canons.' I exhort you, listen to me. While this reckless deed was being done, they *exercised their own initiative* and broke into my room and seized me. Even then we only sought the priesthood. But they acted as if violence were sought!" The Most Pious Stephen said, "Worthy are the canons to be read which say that the election to office in one city is without force in another."

———, *Letter to Bishop Makarios and the Monastery on Mt. Sinai* {ref: 2, 1, 3.131.26}

Then gathering to himself multitudes of the deceivers and acquiring as allies the ignorant-of-the-simple-truth-as-it-is-spoken, he overran the Ailiean city, burning homes, murdering righteous men, committing the rash deeds which were condemned in the last indictment. During these acts, hunting down the notably pious as dangerous criminals, he *assumed his own jurisdiction* and broke into the prisons in order to put in his power the facility to release those subject to trial, that is to say, to offend the guiltless.

[5th cent. AD] Ammonius Alexandrius, *Fragments of Acts* {ref: 85:1537 B}

Text: Ammonius Alexandrius, *Fragmenta* Acti, MPG 85:1524ff.

Translation: my own

And when they called, they were inquiring if Simon, the one called Peter, were a guest there. But while Peter was thinking over the vision, the Spirit spoke to him. One must note that it is not necessary for one *to act independently* by himself[17] and to lead into innovations in the faith; whereas Peter was at a loss after such a vision, the Spirit turned his ear to him.

———, *Fragments of Acts* {ref: 85:1549 A}

Text: Ammonius Alexandrius, *Fragmenta Acti*, MPG 85:1524ff.

Translation: my own

Because such things were of profit to them through the word, the Antiochenes did not shrink from sending to Jerusalem to ask concerning these matters. And these were not issues of the original Deity, or of the fleshly nature of the Son, or concerning the Spirit, or angels, or rulers, or heaven, or another such living creature, but concerning circumcision, an infinitesimal, unseemly part of the body of man. For it was necessary that one jot and one tittle of the

16. The text titles this section ""πραξις ιβ" = Twelfth Session." C. J. Hefele, *History of the Councils of the Church*, vol. 3 (Edinburgh: T. & T. Clark, 1895), 321, records this defense as occurring in the eleventh session.

17. Lampe lists this under "assume authority, act on one's own authority."

spiritual law be fulfilled. The disciples of Antioch *exercised authority*. But they considered such things—even the evaluation of nakedness—to be the subject of inquiry. For just so they sent Barnabas and Paul from Antioch to ask those who were in Jerusalem.

———, *Fragments of Acts* {ref: 85:1552 A}

Text: Ammonius Alexandrius, *Fragmenta Acti*, MPG 85:1524ff.

Translation: my own

For it seems to us who are of one accord, Semeioteos, that neither James nor Peter was audacious to judge it to be good, apart from all of the church, to decree the things concerning circumcision. Wherefore, neither did all *compel others*, unless they were persuaded that it seemed so also to the Holy Spirit. They determined this authority in the epistle saying, "It seemed good to the Holy Spirit and to us," to Barnabas and to Paul, to men who handed over their lives for the sake of the Lord.

[5th cent. AD] Eusebius of Alexandria, *Sermons, #5* {ref: 86.348 D}

Text: Eusebius Alexandrini, *Sermones, V*, MPG 86:309ff.

Translation: my own

And finally I will set forth the word concerning deacons. The deacon ought to accomplish everything in accordance with the intention of the elder, and for the rules and for the needs of the church; not *to exercise authority over* the people, but to do everything by the command of the elder. But the elder being at hand, neither does he have authority to banish or to do the like.

[5th cent. AD] Victor Antiochenus, *Chains in Mark* {ref: 292.29}

Text: Victor Antiochenus, *Catenae in Evangelia S. Matthaei et S. Marci ad fidem Codd. MSS.*, vol. 1 of *Catenae Graecorum Patrum in Novum Testamentum*, ed. J. A. Cramer (Oxford, 1840; reprint Hildesheim: Olms, 1967).

Translation: my own

He [Jesus] naturally recalled David, who reckoned he should not live according to the law when he took the priestly food and gave it to the ones with him, in order that he [Jesus] should multiply the shame of the one snitching on the Apostles. "For if a prophet *assumes his own authority* against the law, being led to it by the wants and needs of the followers who indeed are under the law, if you see my disciples on account of not having bread, setting a table with a meal of seeds for themselves, should you be vexed and judge the law? Or do you not know that David was a servant of the law?—but I, the Son of Man, am Lord of the Sabbath."

The Byzantines (6th cent. AD–12th cent. AD)

[c. AD 520] Joannes Philoponus, *About the Rational Soul* {ref: 487.12}

Text: [c. AD 520] Joannes Philoponus, *De Anima*, ed. M. Hayduck, vol. 15, *Commentaria in Aristoelem Graeca* (Berlin: Reiner, 1897).

Translation: my own

But the cause of this is the inexperience and the dimness of soul in the matter. For just as, when the healthy ones are in a pestilential country, they suffer many things, so ignorance rather than knowledge *rules the soul* in birth. Since therefore we are deceived, it was necessary for him to discourse more concerning guile. For neither did Empedocles form the opinion "not to be beguiled." For this opinion, the saying "not to be beguiled," was refuted by Plato.

[c. AD 560] Joannes Lydus, *On the Magistracies of the Roman Constitution* {ref: 3.42}

Text: Joannes Lydus, *Ioannis Lydi, De Magistratibus Populi Romani, vol. 3*, ed. R. Wünsch (Leipzig, 1903), 131.

Translation: T. F. Carney, *Bureaucracy in Traditional Society: Romano-Byzantine Bureaucracies Viewed from Within*, 3 vols. in 1, no. 3, "John the Lydian, On the Magistracies of the Roman Constitution" (Lawrenceville, Kans., 1971).

For the emperor was prevailed upon to write with his own hand a law that stripped the prefecture of all authority. For the magistracy which but recently *of its own initiative*[18] both lightened the tribute and made additional grants to the cities for foodstuffs, lighting, shows and renovations of public works, was not capable hereafter (and did not dare to do so) of making anyone a grant of at least some tiny recompense.

[6th cent. AD] Leontius Hierosolymitanus, *Against the Nestorians, Book 5* {ref: 86:1720 D}

Text: Leontius Hierosolymitanus, *Adversus Nestorianos, Lib. V*, MPG 86:1400ff.

Translation: my own

We will not *act on our own authority* to call the Mother of Jesus, "Theotokos,"[19] the Holy Scriptures nowhere addressing her thus, nor any one of the Fathers.

[6th cent. AD] Romanus Melodus Hymnographus, *Hymn 20* {ref: 13.6}

Text: Romanus, *Romanos le Mélode. Hymnes*, vol. 2, ed. J. Grosdidier de Matons (Paris: Cerf, 1965).

Translation: my own

All the earth we ruled, all booty we have;
But you as a great sovereign

---

18. Plainly the sense here is that of "relying on its own authority."
19. Lampe lists this under "presume on one's own authority."

coming upon them, *do reign*, leading us away
who are completely the property of the master.

———, *Hymn 22* {ref: 17.8}

Text: Romanus, *Romanos le Mélode. Hymnes*, vol. 3, ed. J. Grosdidier de Matons (Paris: Cerf, 1965).

Translation: my own

I am powerful and I will to save,
Therefore I command, I *rule* and I say, "I will, be clean."

[AD 600] Evagrius Scholasticus, *Letter to a Vigilant Tutor* {ref: 86.2564 E}

Text: Evagrius Scholasticus, *Epistula ad Vigilium Papam*, MPG 86:2416ff.

Translation: my own

For this fellow took upon himself the communion, in order to neglect the many, being of the same mind as the Eutychians, having been legally deposed by his own bishop—the one we among the saints think of as our father, even the archbishop Flavian—*assuming his own jurisdiction* without regulation in order to receive communion before sitting in council in Ephesus with the God-loving bishops.

[d. AD 638] Sophronius Palestrinus, Greek translation of the Latin work, Hieronymus Stridonensis, *On Illustrious Men*.

Text: Hieronymus Stridonensis, *De viris illustribus*, in O. von Gebhart, *Texte und Untersuchungen zur Geschichte der Altchrislichen Literatur (Leipzig)*, 14^{1b} (1896), as quoted by G. W. H. Lampe, *Patristic Greek Lexicon* (Oxford: Clarendon, 1961), 262.

Translation: my own

Mark. . .briefly composed a gospel, which thing Peter, approved, and *granting authorization*, he published what will be read by the church.

[AD 690] Joannes Malalas, *Chronicles* {ref: 257.15}

Text: Joannes Malalae, *Chronographia* (Bonnae: Weberi, 1831).

Translation: Elizabeth Jeffreys, Michael Jeffreys, and Roger Scott, *The Chronicle of John Malalas: A Translation* (Melbourne: Australian Association for Byzantine Studies, 1986), 136.

The emperor Nero sent an expedition against Judea and Jerusalem and treated all the inhabitants badly, killing many in a pitched battle, since they had behaved rebelliously and had shouted insults against Nero, because he had beheaded Pilate to avenge Christ. Pilate had come before Nero for no other reason than that they had *put pressure on*[20] their governor when they

20. Sophocles lists this under the heading "to compel." Here, as in BGU 1208, the idea of "to compel/influence" is in view.

had crucified Christ. So Nero was angry with them because they were rebels.

———, *Chronicles* {ref: 291.12}

Text: *Chronographia.*

Translation: Jeffreys, *Malalas*, 155.

During his reign the senator Albinos rebelled. The army, which had been sent by the previous emperor Didius to fight against the Gepids, proclaimed Albinus emperor, *overruling* the senate. Severus pursued him into Thrace, captured him, and put him to death.

———, *Chronicles* {ref: 341.15}

Text: *Chronographia.*

Translation: Jeffreys, *Malalas*, 185.

After the reign of Valentinian the Great, the Ruthless, the army made a man named Eugenios emperor, *flouting the authority* of the senate. He reigned twenty-two days and was immediately assassinated.

———, *Chronicles* {ref: 359.13}

Text: *Chronographia.*

Translation: Jeffreys, *Malalas*, 196.

At that time the Alexandrians, given free rein by their bishop, [*exercising their own authority*[21]] seized and burnt on a pyre of brushwood Hypatia the famous philosopher, who had a great reputation and who was an old woman.

———, *Chronicles* {ref: 416.14}

Text: *Chronographia.*

Translation: Jeffreys, *Malalas*, 235–36.

He [Theodotos, a city prefect] was appointed during the first indication and restored order over the rioting among the Byzantines by punishing many of the rioters at the emperor Justin's command. Among these he arrested a certain Theodosios, nicknamed Ztikkas, who was very wealthy and held the rank of illustris. Theodotos, *on his own authority*, put him to death without reporting this to the emperor. This met with the emperor's anger and he was dismissed from office, deprived of his rank, and ordered into exile in the East.

21. The translators evidently did not find it necessary to translate the participle here. But it seems that αὐθεντησαντες refers to an action by the Alexandrians distinct from λαβοαντες παρρησιααν. One could wish for more context here to decide how Malalas viewed their action. Unfortunately there is none.

———, *Chronicles* {ref: 462.12}

Text: *Chronographia.*

Translation: Jeffreys, *Malalas*, 270.

The Roman magister[22] came to Hierapolis, and learnt that the Persians had encamped on Roman territory. He went off to Belisarios who was near the Persians at the city of Barbalissos, together with Stephanos and Apskal, the exarchs, and the dux Simmas, with 4,000 men. Belisarios was angry with Sounikas because he had attacked the Persian army *on his own initiative*. When the Roman magister arrived he reconciled them, urging them to advance on the Persians.

[7th cent. AD] Anonymous, *Chronicon Paschale* {ref: 619.9}

Text: anonymous, *Chronicon Paschale*, ed. Dindorf (Bonnae: Weberi, 1832).

Translation: anonymous, *Chronicon Paschale*, ed. Michael and Mary White (Liverpool: Liverpool University Press, 1989), 110.

Indication 7, year 2, sole consulship of Decius. In this year the Justinianic Codex was completed and it was ordered that it *be authoritative* from the 16th day before Kalends of April [17 March] of the current tax period 7.

In this year in accordance with God's clemency there occurred the Great Death.

———, *Chronicon Paschale* {ref: 634.1}

Text: anonymous, *Chronicon Paschale*, ed. Dindorf (Bonnae: Weberi, 1832).

Translation: anonymous, *Chronicon Paschale*, ed. Michael and Mary White (Liverpool: Liverpool University Press, 1989), 110.

And it was ordered that, the previous edition being made void, it should *be valid* from the 4th day before Kalends of January [29 Dec], in indication 13.

[AD 789] Second Council of Nicea {ref: 721 D}

Text: Nicolao (Sebastian) Coleti, ed., *Sacrosancta Concilia ad Regium Additionem exacta*, vol. 8 (Venice, 1728–33).[23]

Translation: *The Seventh General Council, The Second Council of Nicaea*, ed. John Mendham (London: Painter, undated).

"However, let this same Epistle to Rufinius be read once more." And the following passage was read which declares:—"That they who had so fallen as to become very leaders of impiety should, indeed, be pardoned on repentance, but should no longer have any place among the clergy; but that, in respect of those who had not *taken any leading part*, but had been constrained

22. Minister in charge of miscellaneous administrative duties in the imperial house-hold and especially foreign affairs (cf. Jeffreys, *Malalas*, 316).

23. Note that this is a near quotation of Athanasius's *Letter to Rufinius*.

by force or violence, that they should not only meet with pardon, but should retain their place among the clergy, especially if they had a fair excuse to make for themselves. . . ."

"For the Father does admit to the Priesthood those who, not having *originated* heresy, were seduced or violently drawn aside; while he excludes those only who were the actual originators or violent promoters of the same."

[AD 817] Theophanes, *The Chronicle* {ref: 372.13}

Text: Theophanes, *Chronicon* (Bonnae: Weberi, 1839).

Translation: my own

In that same year the Theodosians and the Gaianitians in Alexandria began to create an assembly, and the Gaianitians *exercising their own authority* elected Elpidios, their archdeacon, as bishop for them. The king had arranged for the replacement to come about; but coming to Sigrin he died. And the Theodosians elected Dorotheon as bishop for themselves secretly by night.

[9th cent. AD] Photius, *Library* {ref: 80.59a.11}

Text: *Photius, Bibliothèque*, ed. R. Henry (Paris: Les Belles Lettres), as cited by T. L. G.

Translation: my own [Note: Photius has reproduced Olympiodorus's account (above) exactly.]

The second part begins here: For Jobinos, making his own brother Sebastian king, contrary to the wishes of Adaulfo, made Adaulfo his enemy. And Adaulfo sent ambassadors to Honorios, and he promised to bring peace—and the heads of the tyrants. They returned and promised with oaths, and the head of Sebastian was sent to the king. But being besieged by Adaulfo, Jobinos surrendered himself, and he was sent to the king. Dardanos, the governor, *exercising his own authority,* killed him.

———, *Photius* {ref: 80.62b.31}

Text: *Photius, Bibliothèque*, ed. R. Henry (Paris: Les Belles Lettres), as cited by T. L. G.

Translation: my own

For Honorios, stricken by a dropsy-like disease, died six days before the kalends of September [= 27 August]. And letters were sent to the East announcing the death of the king. Meanwhile a certain Joannes *took charge and ruled* tyrannically. Upon him the public proclamation was spoken just as a certain prediction had indicated.

———, *Photius* {ref: 238.317b.7}

Text: *Photius, Bibliothèque*, ed. R. Henry (Paris: Les Belles Lettres), as cited by T. L. G.

Translation: my own [cpr. Josephus Antiquities 20.199–201]

For Ananus, son of Ananus, receiving the High Priesthood—Joseph [Joseph Cabi] being deprived of it—was rash and even more reckless. He followed the party of the Sadducees. Now these were more headstrong in judgment than all others. So this Ananus, Festus having completed his term in Judea and Albinus not yet having assumed his, *exercised his own authority* and convened the Sanhedrin. And James, the Lord's brother, along with others, he charged illegally, procuring their execution by stoning.

[10th cent. AD][24] Scholia Vetera on Aeschylus's *Eumenides* {ref: line 42a}

Text: O. L. Smith, ed., *Scholia Graeca In Aeschylum Quae Exstant Omnia*, vol. 1 (Leipzig: Tübner, 1976), 45. [For text of *Eumenides* itself, see Aeschylus, *Aeschylus*, ed. Herbert W. Smyth, Loeb Classical Library (Cambridge, Mass.: Harvard University Press, 1963), 275.]

Translation: of Scholia: my own; of Aeschylus: H. W. Smyth

[Eumenides lines 39–45:]

TEXT: I was on my way to the inner shrine, enriched with many a wreath, when, on the centrestone, I beheld a man defiled before Heaven occupying the seat of the supplicants. His hands were dripping gore; he held a sword just drawn and a lofty olive branch reverently crowned with a tuft of wool exceeding large—white was the fleece; for as to this I can speak clearly.

SCHOLIA: Dripping} indicating clearly a recent *murder* occurs.

[10th cent. AD] Scholia on Homer, *Scholia on the Iliad* {ref: Book 10, entry 694}

Text: *Scholia Graeca in Homeri Iliadem*, vol. 2, ed. H. Erbse (Berlin: de Gruyter, 1971) [For text of *The Iliad* itself, see Homer, *The Iliad*, ed. A. T. Murray, Loeb Classical Library (Cambridge, Mass.: Harvard University Press, 1924), 432.]

Translation: of Scholia: my own; of Homer: A. T. Murray

[The Iliad, IX, line 694]

TEXT: For full masterfully did he address their gathering.

SCHOLIA: This verse is from another place. For now it does not fit properly. For then it was wont to be mentioned when *the one originating* the writing had set forth something astounding.[25]

[10th cent. AD] Emperor Constantine VII Porphyrogenitus, *About Strategy* {ref: 159.33}

Text: Constantinus VII Porphyrogenitus, *De Insidiis*, ed. C. de Boor (Berlin: Weidmann, 1905), 1–228.

Translation: my own

For his wife slayed the deceased King Marion, who was not proclaimed king publicly by the assembly because the army, *controlling the assembly*, made him king.

---

24. This scholion is repeated with slight variations in several MSS from 10th–16th cents. AD However, the oldest, given here, is from the 10th cent. AD. Smith indicates that all extant scholia vetera on Aeschylus originate from a pre-10th-cent. AD manuscript no longer extant. Although it is known that many of the scholia vetera date back into the Hellenistic period, the 10th cent. AD is the earliest sure dating possible for this scholion.

25. Murray says in a note, "Line 694 was rejected by Zenodotus, Aristophanes, and Aristarchus."

———, *About Virtues and Vices* {ref: 1.160.18}

Text: Constantinius VII Porphyrogenitus, *De virtutibus et vitiis*, vol. 2, pt. 1, ed. T. Büttner-Wobst and A. G. Roos (Berlin: Weidmann, 1906), 1–361.

Translation: my own

For the Emperor Decius was a Christ-hating Roman. In his time there was a great persecution of the Christians. He set up his godless image so that the ones finding those called Christians *exercised their own jurisdiction*[26] and murdered them and seized all their goods with impunity. Also many Christians were murdered by the crowds of each city who happened upon them and hauled them before the praetors.

[10th cent. AD] The Suda Lexicon {ref: A 4426}

Text: *Svidae Lexicon*, pt. 1, ed. A. Adler (Reprint: Stuttgart: Tübner, 1971), 412.

Translation: my own

Αὐθεαντης· The one who does a thing with his own hand or the one executing a thing. Therefore with Isocrates, "αὐθεαντης." Lysias himself listed it for "The 30." And indeed in others it serves for "τougs φοανους" [the murderers]. For "ὁ αὐθεαντης" indicates "ὁ αὐτοαχειρ" and "αὐθεντηασαντα" equals "κυαριος γενοαμενος" [be lord over]. Αὐθεντηασαντα itself does not require that one wear the sword himself. For Mithridates [c. 87 BC] set out in battle order to conquer the Romans. He sent a letter having the royal seal to the cities. In one day he arranged it and immediately what was written was carried out, so that some would not find out before hand and be on guard. For he ordered them to kill whatever Roman they should find. And he carried out his strike not only by means of the murderous slaying of the soldiers dressed for battle, but even the people they killed along with them, so that multitudes were put to death. And he assigned great punishments for some of those who spared others.

[12th cent. AD] Michael Glycas, *Annals* {ref: 270.10}

Text: Michael Glycas, *Michaelis Glycae Annales*, ed. I. Bekker (Bonn, 1836), 270.

Translation: my own

The women from the Agilians *exercise authority over*[27] the men and they do evil as they desire, not being jealous of men, but achieving in agriculture, and in construction, and in all manly things.

[12th–14th cent. AD] Thomas Magister, *Attic Sayings* {ref: 18.9}

Text: Thomas Magister, *Ecloga vocum Atticarum*, ed. F. Ritschel (Halle, 1832; reprint: Hildesheim/New York: Georg Olm, 1970).

26. Or perhaps, "took justice into their own hands and. . . ."

27. The Latin of this diglot edition of the text renders this phrase "apud Agilaeos feminae sua viros in potestate habent." G. W. Knight, 149, translates with the assistance of S. Kistemaker, "have in their own power (authority)."

Translation: my own

Say autodikein [= "to be with independent jurisdiction"[28]] not authentein, for it is more vulgar.[29]

[Ms from 15th cent. AD] Ptolemy, *Codicum Parisinorum: Catalogus Codicum Astrologorum Graecorum* {ref: 1.777.7}

Text: Ptolemy, *Codicum Parisinorum: Catalogus Codicum Astrologorum Graecorum*, vol. 7–1, ed. F. Cumont (Brussels, 1929), 177.

Translation: John R. Werner, Wycliffe Bible Translators, International Linguistic Center, Dallas, Tex., letter (Apr. 8, 1980) as quoted by George W. Knight III, "ʼΑΥΘΕΝΤΕΩ in Reference to Women in 1 Timothy 2.12," *NTS* 30 (1984): 143–57.

But if [Mercury is] in the regions of Saturn, [that signifies that the newborn baby will be] one who lives by his wits with theft or waterside activities. But if the Beneficent Ones are in the quartile aspect, [that signifies that the newborn will be] the *one who exercises authority over* all [others who are in the trade and pays no consequences (or, acquires nothing)].

28. LSJ, 280, also give "to have one's own courts."

29. Additional note: "Vulgar" here means "ordinary, common" language as opposed to elegant or refined language. It does not mean "obscene" or "offensive" (it translates the word koinoteron, "more common"). —Note added by Wayne Grudem.

Policy Statements of Selected Denominations and Parachurch Organizations Regarding Women in Ministry[1]

Compiled by Travis Buchanan,
Phoenix Seminary, Scottsdale, Arizona

Contents

DENOMINATIONS

1. We arrived at this list of denominations mostly by using the list titled "Enrollment by Religious Affiliation" in the back of the 2000-01 catalog of Trinity Evangelical Divinity School in Deerfield, Illinois (TEDS), where I taught from 1981 to 2001. The statements are current as of 2004. Since TEDS draws students from a wide spectrum of evangelical denominations, I thought such a list would be representative of most of the major denominations in the evangelical world in the United States today. I did not include denominations from other countries or denominations that had only a very few students at TEDS. My assistant Travis Buchanan then compiled this list by contacting each denomination either directly or through its website. Groups that wish to add or update their policy statements may send them to office@cbmw.org. —Wayne Grudem

Denominations

Assemblies of God USA[2]

Supernatural manifestations and gifts of the Holy Spirit have played a distinctive role in the origin, development, and growth of the Assemblies of God. From the earliest days of our organization, spiritual gifting has been evident in the ministries of many outstanding women. Divine enablement has also been seen in the spiritual leadership of women in other Pentecostal groups. The Pentecostal movement believes that the 20th-century outpouring of the Spirit is a true fulfillment of the scriptural prediction, "Your daughters shall prophecy...and upon the handmaids in those days will I pour out my Spirit" (Joel 2:28, 29).

The Bible as Final Authority

The history and current practice of the Assemblies of God give demonstration that God can and does bless the public ministry of women. Yet there is currently much debate concerning the proper role of women in spiritual leadership. So it is appropriate to ask if Scripture describes any limits to this public ministry. We all agree that Scripture must be our final authority in settling questions of faith and practice. But when born-again, Spirit-filled Christians, following proper hermeneutical principles, come to reasonable but differing interpretations, we do well not to become dogmatic in support of one position. We affirm the inerrancy and authority of Scripture. We desire to know for certain what God expects of us. When we come to a sure understanding of His divine Word, we are committed to declaring and obeying those clear instructions. But we also exercise caution in giving authoritative importance to interpretations that do not have indisputable support from the whole of Scripture. Although the Holy Spirit may be active in the work of translation and interpretation, we cannot claim inerrancy for interpretations (even of extant Hebrew or Greek texts).

Historical and Global Precedent

In the early days of most revivals, when spiritual fervor is high and the Lord's return is expected at any time, there is often a place for, and acceptance of, the anointed ministry of women. Over time, however, concerns about organization and lines of authority begin to emerge, and the group moves toward a more structured ministry. As institutional concerns come to the forefront, the spiritual leadership of women is accepted less readily, and church leadership becomes predominately male. The experience of the Assemblies of God has been no exception to this progression.

---

2. The following information may be read on-line at http://ag.org/top/beliefs/position_papers/4191_women_ministry.cfm. This statement has been used with permission.

Twentieth-century practice among Pentecostals around the world reveals evidence of a genuine struggle to apply biblical truth in various cultural contexts. In some settings, female spiritual leadership is readily accepted; in others, though women may have limited ministry, leadership posts are withheld from them. At times there is inconsistency between the leadership a female missionary has at home and that which she has on the field, or between her opportunities and those of a national female. Indeed, culture has influenced the extent of leadership a woman has been allowed to share. The Church must always be sensitive to cultural concerns, but it must look to Scripture for the truth that applies to all times and cultures.

Biblical Examples of Women in Ministry

Old Testament history includes accounts of strong female leadership. Miriam was a prophet, one of the triumvirate of leaders God sent to Israel during the Exodus period (Exodus 15:20). Deborah, as prophet and judge, led the army of the Lord into successful combat (Judges 4–5). Huldah, also a prophet, authenticated the scroll of the Law found in the temple and helped spark the great religious reform in the days of Josiah (2 Kings 22; 2 Chronicles 34).

The New Testament also records ministering women in the Church Age. Tabitha (Dorcas) is called a disciple and had a ministry of helps (Acts 9:36). Philip had four virgin daughters who prophesied (Acts 21:8–9). Euodia and Syntyche were Paul's coworkers who shared in his struggle to spread the gospel (Philippians 4:2–3). Priscilla was another of Paul's exemplary "fellow workers in Christ Jesus" (Romans 16:3–4, NIV). In Romans 16, Paul greets a multitude of ministering persons, a large number of them women.

Phoebe, a leader in the church at Cenchrea, was highly commended to the church at Rome by Paul (Romans 16:1–2). Unfortunately, biases of modern English translators have sometimes obscured Phoebe's position of leadership, calling her a "servant" or "helper," etc. Yet Phoebe was diakonos of the church at Cenchrea. Paul often used this term for a minister or leader of a congregation and applied it specifically to Jesus Christ, Tychicus, Epaphras, Timothy, and to his own ministry. Depending on the context, diakonos is usually translated "deacon" or "minister." Though some translators have chosen the word deaconess (because Phoebe was a woman), such a distinction is not in the original Greek. It seems likely that diakonos was the designation for an official leadership position in the Early Church.

Junia was identified by Paul as an apostle (Romans 16:7). But many translators and scholars, unwilling to admit there could have been a female apostle, have since the 13th century masculinized her name to Junias. The biblical record shows that Paul was a strong advocate of women's ministry.

The instances of women filling leadership roles in the Bible should be taken as a divinely approved pattern, not as exceptions to divine decrees. Even a limited number of women with scripturally commended leadership roles should affirm that God does indeed call women to spiritual leadership.

A Biblical Survey of the Role of Women in Ministry

Of primary importance in defining the scriptural role of women in ministry is the biblical meaning of "ministry." Of Christ our great model, it was said, "For even the Son of man came not to be ministered unto, but to minister, and to give his life a ransom for many" (Mark 10.45). New Testament leadership, as modeled by Jesus, portrays the spiritual leader as a servant. The question of human authority is not of primary significance, though it naturally arises as organization and structure develop.

Genesis 2:18–25

Some expositors have taught that all women should be subordinate to adult men because Eve was created after Adam to be his helper ("help meet," KJV). Yet the word ezer ("helper") is never used in the Hebrew Bible with a subordinate meaning. Seventeen out of the twenty times it is used, it refers to God as the helper. Instead of being created as a subordinate, Eve was created to be a "suitable" (kenegdo) helper, or one "corresponding to" Adam.

Some argue that God created men and women with different characteristics and desires, and that these differences explain why leadership roles should be withheld from women. Others attribute these perceived differences to culture and social expectations imposed on children from birth to adulthood. Physical differences and distinctive biological functions are obvious; but it is only by implication that gender distinctives can be made to suggest leadership limitations.

Paul's Emphasis on Charismatic Ministry

Ministry in the New Testament is charismatic in nature. It is made possible and energized as the Holy Spirit sovereignly distributes spiritual gifts (charismata) to each member of the body of Christ (Romans 12:6–8; 1 Corinthians 12:7–11, 27–28; Ephesians 4:7–12; 1 Peter 4:10–11). While some gifts are a spontaneous work of the Spirit and others are recognized ministry gifts to the Body, all are given for service without regard to gender differentiation. For example, the gift of prophecy is explicitly for both men and women: "Your sons and your daughters shall prophesy" (Acts 2:17). That women received and exercised this gift of the Spirit is well attested in the New Testament (Acts 21:9; 1 Corinthians 11:5).

If Peter found certain statements by Paul hard to understand (2 Peter 3:16), then it is no surprise that we, who are removed by 1900 additional years of history, would share his struggle in interpreting some Pauline passages. And we, like Peter (2 Peter 3:15), must respect and love our brothers and sisters who hold alternative interpretations on issues that are not critical to our salvation or standing before God. We only request that those interpretations be expressed and practiced in love and consideration for all of God's children, both men and women.

First Corinthians 11:3–12

The statement that "the man is the head of the woman" has for centuries been used to justify the practice of male superiority and to exclude women from spiritual leadership. Two alternative translations for kephale ("head"), debated widely by contemporary evangelical scholars, are (1) "authority over" and (2) "source" or "origin." Both meanings can be found in literature of Paul's time.

Taking the passage as a whole, the second meaning fits as well as or better than the first meaning, leading to the summary statement of verse 12: "As the woman is of the man, even so is the man also by the woman; but all things [are] of God." Even the relationship between the eternal Son and the Father—"the head of Christ is God" (11:3)—fits better as "source" than "authority over" (cf. John 8:42). Without attempting to resolve this debate, we do not find sufficient evidence in *kephale* to deny leadership roles to women (in light of biblical examples of women in positions of spiritual authority, and in light of the whole counsel of Scripture).

First Corinthians 14:34–36

There are only two passages in the entire New Testament which might seem to contain a prohibition against the ministry of women (1 Corinthians 14:34 and 1 Timothy 2:12). Since these must be placed alongside Paul's other statements and practices, they can hardly be absolute, unequivocal prohibitions of the ministry of women. Instead, they seem to be teachings dealing with specific, local problems that needed correction.

There are various interpretations of what Paul was limiting when he said, "Let your women keep silence in the churches: for it is not permitted unto them to speak" (14:34). Options include (1) chatter in public services, (2) ecstatic disruptions, (3) certain authoritative ministries (such as judging prophecies), and (4) asking questions during the service. Yet, Paul does allow women to pray and prophesy in the corporate service (1 Corinthians 11:5).

Although we may not solve all the difficulties of this chapter, we do conclude that this passage does not prohibit female leadership, but like the rest of the chapter, it admonishes that "all things be done decently and in order" (1 Corinthians 14:40).

First Timothy 2:11–15

The meaning and application of Paul's statement, "I suffer not a woman to teach, nor to usurp authority over the man" (1 Timothy 2:12), have puzzled interpreters and resulted in a variety of positions on the role of women in ministry and spiritual leadership. Is the prohibition of women teaching and exercising authority a universal truth, or was Paul reporting his application of divine truth for the society and Christian community to which he and Timothy ministered?

From the above survey of passages on exemplary women in ministry, it is clear that Paul recognized the ministry of women. Yet there were some obvious problems concerning women in Ephesus. They were evidently given to immodest apparel and adornment (1 Timothy 2:9).

The younger widows "learn to be idle,... and not only idle, but tattlers also and busybodies, speaking things which they ought not" (1 Timothy 5:13). In his second letter to Timothy, Paul warned against depraved persons (possibly including women) who manipulated "weak-willed," or "gullible," women (2 Timothy 3:6, NIV).

A reading of the entire passage of 1 Timothy 2:9–15 strongly suggests that Paul was giving Timothy advice about dealing with some heretical teachings and practices involving women in the church at Ephesus. The heresy may have been so serious that he had to say about the Ephesian women, "I am not allowing women to teach or have authority over a man." But we know from other passages that such an exclusion was not normative in Paul's ministry.

First Timothy 3:1–13

This entire passage has been held by some to confirm that all leaders and authorities in the Early Church were intended to be, and indeed were, males. It is true that the passage deals primarily with male leadership, most likely because of majority practice and expectations. When there were women leaders, like Phoebe, they would be expected to meet the same standards of character and behavior.

Translations of verse 11 present evidence of the translator's choice based on personal expectations. The word gunaikas can be translated as either "wives" or "women," depending on the translator's assumptions concerning the context. One rendering leaves the impression that these are qualifications for deacons' wives; the other suggests this exhortation is addressed to female spiritual leaders.

Although the first-century cultural milieu produced a primarily male church leadership, this passage along with other biblical evidence of female spiritual leadership (e.g., Acts 21:9; Romans 16:1–15; Philippians 4:2–3) demonstrates that female leadership was not prohibited, either for Paul's day or for today. Passages which imply that most leaders were male should not be made to say that women cannot be leaders.

Galatians 3:28

Those who oppose allowing women to hold positions of spiritual leadership must place contextual limitations on Galatians 3:28: "There is neither Jew nor Greek, there is neither bond nor free, there is neither male nor female: for ye are all one in Christ Jesus."

Some interpreters restrict the meaning of this triad to salvation by faith or oneness in Christ. That truth is certainly articulated throughout Scripture. Yet the verse carries a ring of universal application for all our relationships, not just an assurance that anyone can come to Christ. "Neither Jew nor Greek...neither bond nor free...neither male nor female"—these are basic relationship principles to which faithful followers of Christ must give highest priority.

The God of the Bible has "no respect of persons" (Romans 2:11; cf. also 2 Samuel 14:14; 2 Chronicles 19:7; Acts 10:34; Ephesians 6:9). He calls whom He will and gives gifts and ministries as He chooses; man must not put limitations on divine prerogatives. In Christ we are truly set free from sin and its curse, which separate from God and elevate or demean according to race, social standing, or gender.

Therefore We Conclude

After examining the various translations and interpretations of biblical passages relating to the role of women in the first-century church, and desiring to apply biblical principles to contemporary church practice, we conclude that we cannot find convincing evidence that the ministry of women is restricted according to some sacred or immutable principle.

We are aware that the ministry and leadership of women are not accepted by some individuals, both within and outside the Christian community. We condemn all prejudice and self-promotion, by men or women. The existence in the secular world of bigotry against women cannot be denied. But there is no place for such an attitude in the body of Christ. We acknowledge that attitudes of secular society, based on long-standing practice and tradition, have influenced the application of biblical principles to local circumstances. We desire wisely to respect yet help redeem cultures which are at variance with Kingdom principles. Like Paul, we affirm the Great Commission takes priority over every other consideration. We must reach men and women for Christ, no matter what their cultural or ethnic customs may be. The message of redemption has been carried to remote parts of the world through the ministry of dedicated, Spirit-filled men *and* women. A believer's gifts and anointing should still today make a way for his or her ministry. The Pentecostal ministry is not a profession to which men or women merely aspire; it must always be a divine calling, confirmed by the Spirit with a special gifting.

The Assemblies of God has been blessed and must continue to be blessed by the ministry of God's gifted and commissioned daughters. To the degree that we are convinced of our Pentecostal distinctives—that it is *God* who divinely calls and supernaturally anoints for ministry—we must continue to be open to the full use of women's gifts in ministry and spiritual leadership.

As we look on the fields ripe for harvest, may we not be guilty of sending away any of the reapers God calls. Let us entrust to these women of God the sacred sickle, and with our sincerest blessings thrust them out into the whitened fields.

COMMISSION MEMBERSHIP

Gordon Anderson
Zenas, J. Bicket, chairman
Robert L. Brandt
Richard Dresselhaus
Harry Faught
William A. Griffin
Stanley M. Horton
Edgar R. Lee
Paul Lowenberg
Jesse Miranda
Robert D. Ross
Wesley W. Smith
Hardy W. Steinberg

Association of Vineyard Churches[3]

October 18, 2001
The Ordination of Women

The Board of Directors of The Association of Vineyard Churches, having recognized that individuals deeply committed to Jesus Christ and the authority of Scripture have arrived at different conclusions regarding the propriety of the ordination of women, have agreed that this issue should be settled in each local church as they endeavor to live under the lordship of Jesus Christ. To help thc local churches work through this issue we requested that leaders and pastors in the Vineyard present papers to the board which would be posted on the website for ninety days. Attached are the papers we have received. For further dialogue on these matters, please contact the authors of the papers.

American Baptist Churches USA,[4] and American Baptist Women in Ministry

AMERICAN BAPTIST RESOLUTION ON THE EMPOWERMENT OF WOMEN IN THE AMERICAN BAPTIST CHURCHES

WHEREAS, Jesus, who came to bring salvation to all persons and set at liberty all those who are oppressed, calls us to work for the liberation of all persons;

WHEREAS, the empowerment of women is one of the most important issues facing the church today, and the mission of the church of Jesus Christ requires the talents of women as well as men;

WHEREAS, the American Baptist Churches in 1969 urged its affiliated organizations and churches to:

1.) Reverse the declining number of positions held by professionally trained women in local churches, states, cities, and regional and national staffs;

2.) Establish policies and practices in electing and appointing persons to offices, committees, and boards to ensure more adequate opportunities for women;

3.) Give equal status to women in positions of major responsibility (deacons, moderators, trustees, etc.) within the local church;

WHEREAS, the General Board, in December 1976, adopted a Policy Statement on Human Rights which states that the American Baptist Churches in the USA will support programs and measures to assure the following rights:

3. The following statement may be read on-line at http://www.vineyardusa.org/news/articles/vineyardusa_articles.htm (with several other position papers also posted) and has been used with permission.
4. The following information may be read on-line at http://www.abc-usa.org/resources/resol/empwomen.htm.

The right to develop skills and abilities, to utilize these in economic, political, social, intellectual, and religious institutions, and to receive a just return for one's labor;

The right to human dignity, to be respected and treated as a person, and to be protected against discrimination without regard to age, sex, race, class, marital status, income, national origin, legal status, culture, or condition in society; and

WHEREAS, the General Board established the American Baptist Churches Task Force on Women in February 1974, as a "channel for creating a climate in which each person has the opportunity to take the risks to become the full person God intended and to use fully her or his God-given gifts":

1.) RESOLVED, that the General and National Boards instruct their staffs to accelerate actions which will eliminate institutional sexism and empower women within the national and general corporations of the ABC; and

2.) RESOLVED, that the General Board encourage the staff of all Covenanting and Affiliating Organizations and American Baptist-related institutions to initiate actions which will work toward the elimination of institutional sexism and empower women within their respective organizations.

Section 1 is directed to the Office of the General Secretary, Offices of National Boards, and administratively related organizations.

Section 2 is directed to Regions, States, Cities, schools and colleges, homes and hospitals.

Adopted by the General Board of American Baptist Churches—December 1977
Updated for SCOR language—October 1981
Continued by the General Board for another four years—June 1982
Modified by the Executive Committee of the General Board—December 1990
Modified by the Executive Committee of the General Board—March 1995

There is also the following statement available from American Baptist Women in Ministry[5]:

A Brief Description of American Baptist Women in Ministry

Who are American Baptist Women in Ministry?

We are women who have answered God's call to ministry, serving in local churches and in other ministry settings.

You may know us as:

- Ordained, licensed, and lay pastors
- Educators
- Pastoral counselors
- Evangelists
- Chaplains
- Camp staff
- Missionaries
- Musicians
- Professors
- Administrators
- Area, region, and national staff

5. The following information may be read on-line at http://www.abwim.org/information.asp.

How does ABWIM function?

The Women in Ministry Program began as the shared vision of concerned women and men in the early 1970s. The WIM program works to:

- Represent women in ministry on various boards, task forces, and committees to educate and advocate regarding the role of women in church leadership.
- Build bridges of acceptance, to increase visibility and placement of women in ministerial leadership with American Baptist churches, seminaries, and organizations.
- Advocate for women throughout the denomination as a liaison for individuals and institutions who support women in ministry.
- Establish and strengthen networks of support, increase multicultural dialogue, and develop partnerships among women in ministry and their constituencies.
- Plan and administer national and regional conferences for encouragement, renewal, and equipping.

How do the American Baptist Churches support women in ministry?

American Baptist Churches supports women in ministry by:

- Affirming a historical commitment to women in seminary or in vocational lay ministry.
- Calling women to lead in congregations; seminaries; national, regional, and area staffs; and in other professional ministries.
- Supporting American Baptist Women in ministry through a variety of ongoing educational, financial, and spiritual resources.
- Demonstrating good stewardship of women's spiritual gifts through the maintenance of the ABWIM offices, and the inclusion of women in the American Baptist profile system for ministry placement.

What do American Baptists believe about ministry?

- All persons are created in the image of God. (Genesis 1:27)
- Every person who confesses faith in Jesus Christ is called to discipleship and ministry. (1 Corinthians 12:12–13)
- God gives every Christian gifts for ministry. (1 Corinthians 12; 1 Corinthians 14:26; Romans 12:1–8; Ephesians 4:11–16; 1 Peter 4:10–11; Acts 2:14–21)
- God calls the church to the ministry of reconciliation through Christ, by whom we are a new creation. (2 Corinthians 5:16–21)
- The ministry of word and reconciliation belongs to all persons regardless of gender. (Galatians 3:26–29)
- God's spirit empowers all of God's people for prophetic ministry. (Joel 2:28; Acts 2:17)

Baptist General Conference

No statement.

Conservative Baptist Association of America[6]

CONSERVATIVE BAPTISTS AND WOMEN IN MINISTRY

The practice of Conservative Baptist Churches as related to women in ministry varies widely. A few churches do not permit a woman to speak from behind the pulpit. Other CB churches include women on the pastoral staff and actively encourage and train women for leadership roles in the church. The practice of the majority of CB churches falls somewhere between these two positions.

While not included in the Conservative Baptist Statement of Faith, CBAmerica counsels member churches to reserve the position of senior pastor for men only. Though this is not a unanimous position, it expressed the position and practice or the vast majority of Conservative Baptist pastors and leaders.

General Association of Regular Baptists[7]

Resolution #10, the ordination of women

Passed June 26, 1975

WHEREAS a growing number of religious bodies are ordaining women to the ministry, such actions receiving considerable notice in the public media; and wide acclaim by many in our society who view this as a step of progress, an evidence of enlightenment, and a sign of increasing liberation for women, and

WHEREAS proponents of the ordination of women either deliberately reject the plain prohibitions of Scripture regarding this practice, or else dismiss them as a cultural bias of the New Testament writers, thus reflecting upon the doctrine of biblical inspiration,

BE IT RESOLVED that we, the messengers of the churches in fellowship with the General Association of Regular Baptist Churches, meeting in annual conference at Winona Lake, Indiana, June 23–27, 1975, declare our conviction that the New Testament clearly teaches that women cannot be ordained to the gospel ministry, nor can they properly serve as deacons of a local church, and for them to serve in such capacities is in violation of divine revelation, and

BE IT FINALLY RESOVED that, while accepting these restrictions upon the service of women, we also rejoice in the many and varied ministries in which Christian women can and do

---

6. The following information was received in a personal e-mail to Travis Buchanan on February 19, 2004, from Jack Estep, executive administrator of CBAmerica. It is used with permission.
7. The following information was received in a personal fax sent to Travis Buchanan on October 9, 2003, from Daria Greening with the General Association of Regular Baptist Churches. It is used with permission.

engage, exercising their God-given spiritual gifts, and that we give gratitude to God in particular for the dedicated women in our Regular Baptist churches who make such a vital contribution to the work of the Lord.

Resolutions Passed at the General Association of Regular Baptist Churches 53rd Annual Conference, Seattle, Washington, June 25–29, 1984

All resolutions passed by unanimous vote except #3, which passed by an overwhelming majority vote.

Resolution #2

WOMEN'S ROLE IN THE CHURCH AND HOME

Whereas the ordination of women to the Christian ministry is being advocated in both liberal and evangelical circles; and

Whereas women's subordination to male authority in the church and home has become a subject of controversy; and

Whereas there is outright rejection by a number of evangelicals of some of Paul's teaching in the New Testament regarding women, calling his instructions rabbinical and erroneous; and

Whereas some of the evangelical women's caucases [sic] have both misinterpreted Scripture and also objected to the revealed names of God in the desire to eliminate gender-specific language;

Be it resolved that the messengers of the General Association of Regular Baptist Churches, meeting in Seattle, Washington, June 25–29, 1984, affirm their adherence to the New Testament teaching that women are not legitimate candidates of ordination and that God has committed to men the important responsibility of leadership and authority in the church and in the home (1 Corinthians 11:3; Ephesians 5:21–24; 1 Timothy 2:11–15; 3:1–7).

Be it further resolved that we recognize Christian women's spiritual equality with Christian men (Galatians 3:26–29), affirming that subordination is not equivalent to inferiority (was not Christ equal to and yet subordinate to the Father?), and that women's role in the church and home has its own unique function and dignity.

MALE-ONLY PREACHERS

WHEREAS, this past March the Church of England admitted women to its priesthood for the first time since King Henry VIII created the Church of England in the sixteenth century; and

WHEREAS, on that so-called historic day twelve hundred women deacons and their supporters packed the Bristol Cathedral for the ordination of thirty-three women by Bishop Barry Rogerson; and

WHEREAS, in so doing, the Church of England joined twelve of the twenty-eight self-governing provinces of the worldwide Anglican community, as well as many other Protestant church bodies in what has become an ever-widening popular action;

BE IT THEREFORE RESOLVED that we, as messengers of the churches in fellowship with the General Association of Regular Baptist Churches, meeting for our 63rd annual conference in Bellevue, Washington, on June 25–29, 1994, state by way of general consensus and belief that the clear teaching of Scripture allows only men in the offices of pastor and deacon, and that such biblical phrases as "Look out among you seven men of honest report," and "I suffer not a woman to teach, nor to usurp authority over the man, but to be in silence" clearly establish God's gender limitation for these offices.

BE IT FURTHER RESOLVED that we do not believe God's commandments are grievous but rather wise, and that in His wisdom He calls for men to be spiritual leaders, thereby guaranteeing the continuance of this role in the church and home, which leadership need not depreciate or cancel the many necessary and valuable contributions of women in most spheres of life.

BE IT FURTHER RESOLVED that we generously express our gratitude for those women who, like Mary of Romans 16:6, bestow much labor in Christ's church at the local level, in Christian organizations, and on the mission fields of the world.

Southern Baptist Convention[8]

Women participate equally with men in the priesthood of all believers. Their role is crucial, their wisdom, grace, and commitment exemplary. Women are an integral part of our Southern Baptist boards, faculties, mission teams, writer pools, and professional staffs. We affirm and celebrate their Great Commission impact.

[In addition to the above statement, on June 14, 2000, the Southern Baptist Convention adopted a revised summary of the Southern Baptist faith, including the following:]

> While both men and women are gifted for service in the church, the office of pastor is limited to men as qualified by Scripture.
>
> The husband and wife are of equal worth before God, since both are created in God's image. The marriage relationship models the way God relates to His people. A husband is to love his wife as Christ loved the church. He has the God-given responsibility to provide for, to protect, and to lead his family. A wife is to submit herself graciously to the servant leadership of her husband even as the church willingly submits to the headship of Christ. She, being in the image of God as is her husband and thus equal to him, has the God-given responsibility to respect her husband and to serve as his helper in managing the household and nurturing the next generation.[9]

8. The following information may be read on-line at http://www.sbc.net/aboutus/pswomen.asp.
9. *The Baptist Faith and Message*, VI, "The Church," and XVIII, "The Family." (See www.sbc.net/bfm/bfm2000.asp.)

Calvary Chapel[10]

No statement.

Christian and Missionary Alliance[11]

Women may fulfill any function in the local church which the senior pastor and elders may choose to delegate to them consistent with the Uniform Constitution for Accredited Churches and may properly engage in any kind of ministry except that which involves elder authority.

Christian Churches and Churches of Christ

No response received to requests for a statement.

Church of the Nazarene[12]

The official position of the Church of the Nazarene is established by the denomination's General Assembly, our highest legislative body and highest court of appeals. By General Assembly action, there has been a paragraph on women in ministry in the denomination's Manual since 1980. That statement was amended in 1993 and expanded in 2001. Here is the statement as it was amended in 2001 and stands today:

Paragraph 904.6 Women in Ministry

The Church of the Nazarene supports the right of women to use their God-given spiritual gifts within the church, affirms the historic right of women to be elected and appointed to places of leadership within the Church of the Nazarene, including the offices of both elder and deacon.

The purpose of Christ's redemptive work is to set God's creation free from the curse of the Fall. Those who are "in Christ" are new creations (2 Corinthians 5:17). In this redemptive community, no human being is to be regarded as inferior on the basis of social status, race, or gender (Galatians 3:26–28).

Acknowledging the apparent paradox created by Paul's instruction to Timothy (1 Timothy 2:11–12) and to the church in Corinth (1 Corinthians 14:33–34), we believe interpreting these passages as limiting the role of women in ministry presents serious conflicts with specific passages of Scripture that commend female participation in spiritual leadership roles (Joel 2:28–29; Acts 2:17–18; 21:8–9; Romans 16:1, 3, 7; Philippians 4:2–3), and violates the spirit and practice of the Wesleyan-holiness tradition. Finally, it is incompatible with the character

---

10. In a personal e-mail sent to Travis Buchanan on November 6, 2003, Carl Westerlund, an associate pastor with Calvary Chapel Costa Mesa, said, "We do not issue policy statements on various subjects. As a practice, we do not have women as senior pastors." (He asked that the statement be attributed to him, and not Calvary Chapel itself.)
11. The following information may be read on-line at http://www.cmalliance.org/resources/books/manual.jsp.
12. The following information was received in a personal e-mail sent to Travis Buchanan on July 21, 2003, from Stan Ingersol, Denominational Archivist for Church of the Nazarene.

of God presented throughout Scripture, especially as revealed in the person of Jesus Christ (*Manual* 904.6).

The Church of the Nazarene has ordained women from its beginning. Indeed, nearly all of the Wesleyan-holiness parent bodies who joined to form the Nazarene denomination ordained women prior to their coming together. This reflected a common commitment to a specific doctrine of the ministry that was closely associated with the Wesleyan evangelical tradition, and it is likely that throughout the 1920s, 1930s, and 1940s the Church of the Nazarene supported more ordained women in ministry than any other American denomination. In 1955, for instance, over 250 Nazarene congregations in the U.S. were pastored by women. Throughout the twentieth century, our church has ordained thousands of women to the ministry. These have served as pastors, evangelists, missionaries, and theological educators in our denomination. This has been cross-cultural as well. Some of our strongest female ministers have been pastors or evangelists in Africa and in Latin America.

The first woman ordained by one of our parent bodies was Anna S. Hanscomb, who was ordained in 1892 by the Central Evangelical Holiness Association, a small holiness body in New England. A Southern group, the New Testament Church of Christ, also ordained several women before the twentieth century, including Mary Lee Cagle (the subject of my doctoral dissertation at Duke University) and her friend Mrs. Elliott J. Sheeks. A paper on Cagle that I read at the 1991 session of the Wesleyan Theological Society is available on the Web at this address: http://wesley.nnu.edu/WesleyanTheology/theojrnl/26-30/28-7.htm.

Several websites at Nazarene.org have materials on the church's acceptance of women clergy:

http://www.nazarene.org/ssm/adult/women/clergy/index.html
http://www.nazarenepastor.org/womenclergy/nazarene.shtml.

Conservative Congregational Christian Conference[13]

Statement regarding ministerial standing of women

The Conservative Congregational Christian Conference affirms certain doctrines and principles as basic to its existence and, therefore, nonnegotiable in its practice. Among these are its commitment to the full Divine inspiration and authority of the Bible; the autonomous polity of our local churches; and the importance of maintaining unity without denying diversity. Each of these three affirmations has been considered as vital to our position with regard to the ministerial standing of women in our Conference.

A significant amount of study has been done by evangelicals on this subject in recent years. It appears evident to us that Christians, equally committed to the authority of Holy Scripture, may disagree on whether or not the Scriptures allow for the ordination of women. We recognize that

13. The following information may be read on-line at http://ccccusa.ccccsitelaunch.com/index.cfm/method/content.A695BB21-4911-4AB1-9325E65B8BD305E4.

some defenders of women's ordination do so upon principles which sacrifice biblical authority. We in no way support such efforts. We affirm that persons who are firmly committed to the authority of God's Word, though they differ in their interpretations of the Word on this subject, are welcome to hold their convictions with clear conscience within our fellowship.

No church, within our Conference, is required to teach and practice a viewpoint, with regard to ordaining women, which is against the conviction of that particular assembly. Each congregation ordains whom it freely chooses, thus preserving its own autonomy. Whoever is duly ordained in a local church, whether male or female, may apply to the CCCC Credentials Committee and, if qualified, be recognized as ordained. This should not be understood as Conference approval nor disapproval of the ordination of women, but rather as recognition of the conscientious action of an autonomous congregation.

We urge, in this issue as in others, that members of the Conference relate to one another in a spirit of love and unity. Members are not asked to compromise their own convictions, but are asked to respect the rights of others, who are also devoted to the Head of the church and to His Word, to hold their own convictions as well.

Episcopal Church[14]

Women began being ordained in the Episcopal Church in 1976. A brief statement of that event:

The Road to Minneapolis

Pro- and anti-groups proliferated in the final months prior to the 1976 Convention in Minneapolis. The issue was debated, often hotly, in many diocesan conventions. The intensity ratcheted up because the final stage of prayer book revision was underway at the same time. As controversial as ordaining women, the 1979 Book of Common Prayer was to be presented in Minneapolis.

The day came, September 16, 1976. In an intensely charged atmosphere, the House of Deputies adopted a resolution already approved by the House of Bishops, calling for a new section in the church's canon law:

> The provisions of these canons for the admission of Candidates, and for the Ordination to the three Orders, Bishops, Priests and deacons, shall be equally applicable to men and women.[15]

14. More information may be obtained on-line at http://www.episcopalarchives.org/.
15. This information may be read on-line at http://www.episcopalchurch.org/WOMEN/two/25yearsagao.htm.

Committee on the Status of Women[16]

The Committee on the Status of Women is appointed by the Presiding Bishop and The President of the House of Deputies to report to the General Convention. Created through a 1988 General Convention resolution, its mission arises out of the Baptismal Covenant. Informed by the work of its predecessor, the Committee for the Full Participation of Women in the Life of the Church, the CSW has established the following overall goals: 1.) to monitor the status of all women and promote their full participation in the life of the church; 2.) to monitor the effects of sexism, racism, and all other forms of discrimination on the status of women in the United States; 3.) to advise and recommend to the General Convention and to the church policy and program which will improve the status of women. In addition, the committee is actively engaged in task of ending violence against women and is striving to make the "Episcopal Church a truly safe place for all God's people."

Contact: Sally Bucklee, 10450 Lottsford Road, Mitchellville, MD 20721
(301) 925-7363, e-mail: s.bucklee@worldnet.att.net
Website: www.episcopalchurch.org/gc/ccab/ecsw/default.html

Official Canons (Laws) of the Episcopal Church:

Resolution Number: 1976-B005

Title: Amend Canon III.9 and Renumber Accordingly
Legislative Action Taken: Concurred As Submitted
Final text:

Resolved, the House of Deputies concurring, that a new Section 1 of Title III, Canon 9, be adopted, with renumbering of the present Section 1 and following, the said Section 1 to read as follows:

Section 1. The provisions of these canons for the admission of Candidates, and for the Ordination to the three Orders: Bishops, Priests and deacons, shall be equally applicable to men and women. (General Convention, *Journal of the General Convention of the Episcopal Church, Minneapolis, 1976* [New York: General Convention, 1977], C-52.)

Resolution Number: 1976-D029

Title: Promote Programs Concerning Discrimination Against Women in the Church
Legislative Action Taken: Concurred as Submitted
Final Text:

Resolved, the House of Bishops concurring, that the 65th General Convention affirms Christ's teaching of full humanity and new life for all by urging that the Executive Council promote

16. The following information may be read on-line at http://www.episcopalchurch.org/WOMEN/one/committee_women.htm.

through its office of Christian Education and its Lay Ministries Task Force on Women programs that deal with the church's past role in the discrimination against women, the church's present anxiety about changing social roles resulting from the emergence of women and the necessity of future action by the church in the liberation of both men and women, and be it further

Resolved, that this 65th General Convention commends appropriate study and action by individual members through their several congregations and dioceses. (General Convention, *Journal of the General Convention of the Episcopal Church, Minneapolis 1976* [New York: General Convention, 1977], C-111.)

Resolution Number: 1985-D027

Title: Appoint a Group to Study the Participation of Women in Church Life
Legislative Action Taken: Concurred as Submitted
Final text:

Resolved, the House of Bishops concurring, that this 68th General Convention request the Presiding Bishop to implement the Executive Council's recommendation to appoint a broadly representative group from across the church to study women's participation in congregational, diocesan, provincial, and national church bodies and to review, evaluate, plan and propose policy on women's full participation in the life of this church, taking into consideration the study being made by the Triennial Committee and availing itself of information from the Council for Women's Ministries and other agencies of this church, the Anglican Communion, and ecumenical bodies concerned with women's ministries. (General convention, *Journal of the General Convention of the Episcopal Church, Anaheim, 1985* [New York: General Convention, 1986], 269.)

Resolution Number: 1988-A077

Title: Request the Presiding Bishop to Appoint a Committee on the Status of Women
Legislative Action Taken: Concurred as Submitted
Final Text:

Resolved, the House of Bishops concurring, that this 69th General Convention request the Presiding Bishop to appoint a Committee on the Status of Women, which would report to Executive Council. Its responsibilities would include:

- supporting and advising the Presiding Bishop on matters affecting the participation of women in the church, including assisting in the identification of women for appointment to various church bodies;
- serving as advisory body to the Office of Women in Mission and Ministry;
- maintaining advocacy for women's ministries, and for the justice issues which particularly affect women; and
- continuing the monitoring and analysis of patterns of women's participation in the church; and be it further

Resolved, that the committee be composed of not more than twelve (12) members, appointed by the Presiding Bishop and confirmed by Executive Council, with its members reflecting the diversity of the worshipping community of the Episcopal Church, and including a Bishop, Priest(s), deacon(s), and lay persons with specific interest in and concern for the participation of women in the mission and ministry of the church. (General Convention, *Journal of the General Convention of The Episcopal Church, Detroit, 1988* [New York: General Convention, 1989], 308.)

Evangelical Covenant Church of America[17]

A biblical and theological basis for women in ministry

At its 1976 Annual Meeting the Evangelical Covenant Church voted to go on record as favoring the ordination of women. At the 1981 Annual Meeting a motion to rescind that action was overwhelmingly defeated. However, some Covenant people still have questions about the role of women in the ordained ministry. Were the decisions made legitimately or were they merely a reflection of new movements in our society?

The changes affecting women in the modern era have obviously influenced the church's thinking, but the ministry of women is neither derived from society's ideas nor a partner to its extremes. For a tradition that is based on the question "Where is it written?" only one foundation is satisfactory for having women minister in the name of Jesus Christ. Women ought to minister not because society says so but because the Bible leads the church to such a conclusion. A legitimate biblical and theological basis for women in ministry is, therefore, crucial to the ongoing implementation of the Covenant's decision regarding the ordination of women.

Biblical passages on the ministry of women

Usually when people speak of biblical texts on the ministry of women, they refer to only two texts, the two that appear opposed to the idea. These texts will need to be treated justly, but all of the Bible must be included in the discussion, not just two verses. Moreover, as with the interpretation of all Scripture, these two texts must be understood in their proper historical and biblical contexts. The Bible is not like a flat landscape, but is more like varied terrain, and each part must be dealt with in its own right. This is not to suggest that some parts may be ignored or are more important than others, but merely to stress that all the Bible must be treated fairly.

The issue of women in ministry is primarily a New Testament discussion, but there are Old Testament texts that deserve attention. Genesis 1:26–28 indicates that man and woman were created together in the image of God and that dominion was given to both of them. In various contexts (such as Exodus 38:8 and 1 Samuel 2:1–10) women are mentioned as playing a part in Israel's worship. More important are the women who functioned in leadership roles and con-

17. The following information may be read on-line at http://www.covchurch.org/cov/resources/pwomenmin.html.

sequently provide an Old Testament basis for women in ministry. Miriam and Huldah are both referred to as prophetesses who had significant roles in God's purposes (Exodus 15:20–21 and 2 Kings 22:14–20). Deborah is also referred to as a prophetess, but she is best remembered for her activity as a judge of Israel and a leader in a time of conflict (Judges 4–5). These texts do not legitimate the ministry of women by themselves, but they do provide important precedents.

The New Testament texts referring to women present a view that is markedly different from the negative view of women predominant in ancient societies. Women in biblical times usually were not educated, and rabbis warned against teaching the law to females. The limited information from ancient sources indicates that women who were considered respectable did not take part in public life. Rather, such women were expected to spend most of their lives within the confines of the home. Women were viewed as temptations to sin. They were not counted in the number of persons needed to have a synagogue, nor was their testimony accepted in a court of law. But Jesus' attitude and practice was in direct contradiction to that of his contemporaries. He initiated conversation even with unrespectable females like the Samaritan woman at the well (John 4). Because of her witness, many of the townspeople believed in Jesus. Jesus had women disciples who accompanied him from Galilee to Jerusalem and helped finance His ministry (Mark 15:40–41 and Luke 8:1–3). Jesus taught Mary and defended her choice to learn (Luke 10:38–42). Women were the last at the cross and the first at the tomb. After His resurrection Jesus appeared first to women and gave them the task of telling the good news to the disciples (Matthew 28:7).

The newfound freedom and role of women in Christ is clear also in the writings of the early church. The book of Acts frequently mentions the presence and activity of women in the founding of the church. From the praying in the upper room (1:14) to the persecution by Saul (8:3) to the reception of the gospel by Greeks (17:12), women were involved. Of major importance is the quotation of Joel 2:28–32 which is used in Acts 2:17–21 to explain the pouring out of the Spirit at Pentecost. With this event the promise had been fulfilled that God would pour out His Spirit so that both sons and daughters would prophesy. The church at Philippi was founded on women, and one of them, Lydia, obviously played an important role in the origin and growth of this church. The four prophesying daughters of Philip, who are mentioned in Acts 21:9, are further examples of the ministry of the Holy Spirit through women.

The ministry of women becomes even clearer in the writings of Paul. In Christ racial, societal, and sexual barriers have been broken down so that all are made one. "There is neither Jew nor Greek, there is neither slave nor free, there is not male and female, for you all are one in Christ Jesus" (Galatians 3:28). This newly found oneness does not refer merely to our standing before God or to a oneness to be found at Christ's second coming. It refers also to the present, for it is the basis of Paul's rebuke of Peter's hypocrisy in no longer eating with Greeks in Antioch (Galatians 2:11–21). In the American Civil War era some people argued that this verse had no social implications for the question of slavery, but most Christians have come to see the error of this judgment. There is nothing in Christianity that relates only to our salvation; our faith relates to all of life, including the roles of male and female. The issue is whether our attitudes concerning race, social class, and gender will be determined by our oneness in Christ in the new age or by the barriers and values of the old age.

In Paul's letters we encounter a significant number of women who were engaged in the work of the gospel. We are not told the details of what any of these women did in their ministries, but the same language that Paul used of himself and his male helpers is used of them. Romans 16 mentions ten different women who were engaged in various kinds of ministries. Phoebe, who was probably the person who delivered the letter to the Romans, is described with the Greek word diakonos (which can be translated as "deacon" or "servant") and as one who helped many, including Paul (Romans 16:1–2). Prisca, also referred to as Priscilla, is called a fellow worker of Paul in 16:3. She and Aquila, her husband, had a church in their house, and the two of them instructed Apollos in Christian doctrine (Acts 18:26). Mary, Tryphaena, Tryphosa, and Persis were all women that Paul described as ones who labored in the Lord (Romans 16:6 and 12). It is also probable that Romans 16:7 refers to a woman, Junia, as an apostle, rather than to a man named Junias as in many translations of this text. (Since there is no evidence of this name being used for a man, the charge of a male bias in some translations is difficult to avoid.) In Philippians 4:2–3 two other women, Euodia and Syntyche, are said to have struggled along with Paul and his other fellow-workers in the gospel. Such evidence cannot be discounted.

First Corinthians 11:5 is one of the most important passages regarding women in ministry. This text is often overlooked because of other questions, but it is clear that women were praying and prophesying in the early church. The only concern about their activity was for proper decorum in the way they dressed. We cannot easily argue that women were allowed to prophesy but were not allowed to preach or teach. The New Testament does not make such a distinction between prophesying and teaching (see 1 Corinthians 14:3 and 31).

Biblical passages used against the ministry of women

One of the beneficial aspects of the discussion of women in ministry is that it has helped us to become more conscious of the way we understand and apply Scripture. Our concern in interpreting any part of Scripture must go beyond a superficial reading that violates the original intention of the passage. Our focus should be on *why* the words of the text were written. Only if we understand why a text was written will we be able to apply it appropriately. For proper interpretation texts must be read in context and in light of the rest of Scripture. To isolate texts from their contexts or to deal only with passages suitable to our ideas leads to distortion. In such instances we may do justice to the letter of Scripture without ever discerning its spirit.

A case in point is the way some people have viewed 1 Timothy 3:1–7 as a barrier to women in ministry because it states that an "overseer" (or bishop) should be the husband of one wife.

To suggest that this injunction excludes women from ministry is to ignore the text's intention. The passage focuses on the necessity of fidelity in a monogamous relationship as one of several tests of the moral character of an overseer. There is no attempt to provide an eternal decree that overseers should always be married men. Certainly no attempt has been made on the basis of this verse to exclude single men from ministry. Nor has the guideline that an overseer should rule his own house well (verse 4) been automatically used to prevent fathers of rebellious children from ministering. A literalistic interpretation is inappropriate.

First Corinthians 14:34–36 and 1 Timothy 2:11–12 are of a different character, however, and must not be brushed aside. These two texts are well-known for their imposition of silence on women, and clearly seem contradictory to the passages supporting women in ministry.

With regard to 1 Corinthians 14:34–36, how can we understand the fact that within the one epistle, 1 Corinthians, Paul both gave directions for proper dress when women were praying and prophesying and asked for their silence? People have often attempted to explain away either 1 Corinthians 11:5 or 14:34–36 to remove the difficulty. They have suggested that two different kinds of service were in mind or that one of the texts was added by someone else later or that Paul did not really mean what he said in one or the other of the texts. None of these explanations will do, and justice must be done to both passages. We cannot allow ourselves to ignore the texts that do not fit with our preconceived ideas.

The context of 1 Corinthians 14:34–36 begins with verse 26, and it is clear that the worship of the early church was different from our usual services. When the church met for worship, all the people were encouraged to make a contribution to the service by offering some item for praise or instruction. Paul's concern in 14:26–36 is the disruption of the service. Women are not the only ones asked to be silent. Anyone who was going to speak in tongues is told to keep silent if no interpreter was present (14:28). Also, if one prophet was speaking and revelation came to someone else, the first prophet should be silent (14:30). Nor were women the only ones told to be in submission. The various prophets were to be submissive to each other as well (14:32). The service was to be orderly because God is a God of peace (14:33 and 40). The last part of verse 33 ("as in *all* the churches of the saints") should probably be read with the rest of verse 33, rather than with verse 34 as in some translations.

The issue with regard to women is clearly within the context of the disruption of the worship service. The new-found freedom of women in Christ no doubt caused difficulties in the Corinthian church and elsewhere, as passages like this and 11:2–16 show. Apparently married women were disrupting the service by asking questions of their husbands, so they were instructed to wait and ask their questions at home. It seems from 14:36 that this disruption of the service was one of several ways that pride was manifesting itself in the Corinthian church. This activity was considered shameful, particularly in an ancient culture where any public exposure of women was considered a disgrace.

There are still unanswered questions about this text, such as which Old Testament passage is referred to with "as the law says" in 14:34. But regardless of such questions, clearly this passage says what it does because of problems in the Corinthian church and attitudes in the ancient world and not because women should never speak in church. To suggest otherwise removes 1 Corinthians 14:34 from its context and creates an insurmountable contradiction with 11:5.

The text in 1 Timothy 2:11–12 is more difficult to understand, but the issues are the same. There is no question that in this passage women were prohibited from teaching men. The question is "Why?" Were there reasons in this circumstance why women were prohibited from teaching, or were women never to teach men? If the latter, there are blatant contradictions between this text and other texts like 1 Corinthians 11:5. A commitment to the unity of Scripture, and indeed an assumption of the unity of Paul's thought (assuming some form of Pauline authorship), requires a closer analysis of this passage.

There *are* specific indications as to the reason why women were prohibited from teaching in this circumstance. Clearly the Pastoral Epistles were not written to be manuals of church government. Rather they were written to combat false teaching and heresy. Approximately one-fifth of the two hundred and forty-two verses in the Pastorals explicitly treat false teaching. If false teaching is a concern of the Pastorals, it is *the* concern of 1 Timothy. Immediately in 1 Timothy 1:3 the concern to prevent false teaching is expressed as the reason Timothy was left in Ephesus. Speculations about myths and genealogies, along with emphasis on knowledge and asceticism, had led many astray. Some of the best successes of the false teachers were among women. First Timothy 5 treats a number of problems caused by women in connection with false teaching. The concern in 5:13 is not merely for gossiping, but for spreading the false teaching which has "turned some aside to follow Satan" (5:15). Second Timothy 3:6–7 speaks of false teachers who creep into houses and take captive "silly women" who are ever learning and never able to come to the knowledge of the truth.

The whole of 1 Timothy 2 must be interpreted within this context of false teaching. The focus of the whole chapter is prayer, but the concern over false teachers is clear in 2:8, where men are told to pray *without wrath and disputing,* and in 2:14, where the issue is fear of deception.

Even with this recognition of the context of false teaching, 1 Timothy 2:8–15 still has several debated issues. In 2:9 it is preferable to understand that women are to pray with proper decorum in the way they dress, which is the same subject as in 1 Corinthians 11:5. Alternatively, some translations would suggest that the concern is merely for the way women dress with no thought about their praying. (The issue is whether with "likewise" in 2:9 the meaning is "likewise I desire women to pray" or "likewise I desire.") Also some translations say in 2:11 that a woman should learn "in silence," but "in quietness" would be more appropriate. The same root word is used in 2:2 with regard to the quiet and tranquil life that all are to lead. The desire is that both men and women pray and that women in Ephesus learn in submission and quietness, as indeed is expected of all Christians.

The most difficult part of this passage is 2:12, which is usually translated as: "I do not permit a woman to teach or to have dominion over a man, but to be in quietness." The problem is with the word translated "have dominion over" *(authentein* in Greek), for it does not occur anywhere else in the New Testament. This is not the usual word for authority. Outside the Bible the word is used of murder, suicide, having dominion over, and, some argue, of sexual offenses. The original idea seems to have been "to thrust oneself." The uses of the word for murder and suicide obviously are not pertinent for this text. If the reference is to authority, as seems likely, the negative connotations of this word would require a translation such as "domineer." Whatever the meaning, what is prohibited of women with this word seems so negative that it would not be permitted of men either.

The words of 1 Timothy 2:13–15 are difficult on any understanding of the text, but they seem to be caustic comments directed at women influenced by false teachers to leave their responsibilities. The only other reference to Eve in the New Testament is in 2 Corinthians 11:3 which is also concerned with seduction by false teachers. Elsewhere when the fall of humanity is discussed, reference is always to the disobedience of Adam. In a society where women were not educated and had not previously been full participants in everyday life, without doubt women would have been easy targets for false teachers.

There is no need, therefore, to see a contradiction between 1 Corinthians 11:5, where women are viewed as praying and prophesying, and 1 Timothy 2:12 where women are prohibited from teaching men. The prohibition in 1 Timothy 2 was required by conditions in that time and place. Specifically the prohibition was required because false teachers had led women to leave their domestic responsibilities, to be disruptive, and to be nonproductive in the community. These words should not be used as a universal prohibition of teaching by women.

Those who are quick to argue against women in ministry on the basis of texts like 1 Corinthians 14:34–36 and 1 Timothy 2:11–12 need to ask why they do not imitate the kind of church service described in 1 Corinthians 14:26–36 or why they do not institute widows' roles and care for widows according to the instructions of 1 Timothy 5. Using proof-texts out of context and using only the parts of the text that we like are not suitable practices for a church claiming to believe the Bible. Likewise, we ought not to set some texts against others as if to suggest that we may choose the one group and ignore the others.

Further theological considerations

In addition to a discussion of the relevant biblical texts, there are several theological issues that are decisive for the position one takes on women in ministry. Often assumptions are made about these topics that are informed more from our society or traditions than by the Bible and the gospel. A reconsideration of these topics can lead to the removal of many of the barriers to effective ministry in our time.

Authority

Often when people are opposed to women in ministry, the real issue is not the Bible, but authority. They argue that women ought not be in positions of authority. Such people need to ask themselves what authority really is and why men may have it and women may not. Misunderstood texts dealing with husband-wife relationships have wrongly been applied to the question of women in ministry. For example, people have viewed the term "helpmeet" in Genesis 2:18 as a basis for arguing for the inferiority of the woman. The words in question, however, mean "a helper suitable for him" and do not suggest inferiority, for the same word *helper* is also used of God (Deuteronomy 33:7). Similarly, people argue that women are not to be in positions of authority because in Genesis 3:16 Eve was told that her husband would rule over her. However, these words are descriptive of life after the Fall, not descriptive of what God had intended for humanity.

The biggest offense is that people have assumed this world's understanding of authority and applied it to the church, but in Christ authority must be understood differently. The classic text dealing with authority is Matthew 20:25–28 in which Jesus instructed His disciples that the world's views on authority and greatness ought not be their view. Rather than leaders lording over and having authority over others, the leaders should be their servants. This teaching is valid, not only for the ministry, but for family relationships and all other kinds of leadership roles.

Ephesians 5:22, however, is often used to argue that women should not be in authority since wives should be in submission to their husbands. It is questionable whether texts dealing with the marriage relationship should be applied to the question of women in ministry. But apart from that, the more important point is that Ephesians 5:22 is one of the most abused texts in the Bible. The submission of wives must be seen only as one example of the mutual submission that is required of all Christians in 5:21. In fact, in the manuscripts of 5:22 followed by most editions of the Greek New Testament, the word *submit* is not even present; it is assumed from verse 21. From this world's perspective mutual submission does not make sense but it is merely another way of expressing the point of Matthew 20:25–28. In the context of the ancient world, wives were instructed to submit to their husbands because Christianity with its call of total commitment to Christ was viewed as a threat to the family. In Titus 2:5 wives are asked to submit *so that the Word of God is not blasphemed.* Husbands are referred to as "head" in Ephesians 5, but only to place greater responsibility on the husband in caring for the wife. He is to give himself for her in *love* as Christ gave Himself for the church. Both in the family and in the church *mutual submission* is the controlling principle.

In recent times some people have granted that women may minister, but argue that women ought not be in positions of ultimate authority. Such a distinction cannot be defended, for no biblical texts indicate two levels of authority in ministry. We do not need a view of authority that will keep women from functioning in ministry. We need a view of ministry that subverts what this world understands by authority. Mutual submission is the gospel in action.

Ministry

Often when people are opposed to women in ministry, their opposition is based on their view of ministry. Particularly if the Old Testament priesthood is taken as the model for ministry, women will hardly be accepted as pastors since only men were priests in the Old Testament, and only men who were Levites at that. Even in the Old Testament, however, the original intention was that the Israelites should be a kingdom of priests (Exodus 19:6), and this idea becomes important in the New Testament. While there are some parallels between the Old Testament priesthood and Christian ministry, the former is not an appropriate model for the latter. As Protestants, we do not have priests; rather, we stress the priesthood of all believers. Stress on the priesthood of all believers ought to *require* the ministry of women.

Focus on passages such as Ephesians 4:12 has rightly emphasized that ministry is the task of the church and not just the task of the clergy. Distinctions of value, sanctity, and privilege between clergy and laity ought to be rejected, and the ministry of women is one way to emphasize the ministry of all the church.

Ordination, because it has been viewed as conferring special status on pastors, has often functioned as a barrier both to the ministry of women and to the ministry of the laity. This practice of ordaining certain people for ministry has antecedents in the New Testament, but it is not taught explicitly. This is not to argue against ordination and certainly not to argue against a professional clergy, but the church needs to discuss what ordination means and make sure that ordination does not become more hindrance than help in proclaiming the gospel. Ministry is not some privilege to which the few are called. It is the task of all Christians as they identify with the ministry and love of Jesus Christ.

A gifted church

Closely related to the discussion of the ministry of all the church is the focus on the variety of gifts in the body of Christ. By recognizing the diversity of gifts within its fellowship the church recognizes that the Spirit of God functions in different ways in different people. A person's task in the ministry of the church is determined by the way the Spirit is manifested in that person's life and actions (1 Corinthians 12:11). Whether a woman or a man is granted the privilege of serving the church as a pastor is not based on that person's choice to do so, but on the recognition that the Spirit of God has led and empowered that person for pastoral ministry. The requirement for pastoral ministry is manifestation of the Spirit not being a male. Nowhere in the New Testament are the gifts of the Spirit determined by gender. If women are encouraged to affirm their gifts for ministry, the church will have new resources for evangelism, service, and discipleship. Such a new power for the spread of the gospel could be decisive for the growth and health of the church.

The development of doctrine

Some people have opposed women in ministry merely because the church rarely has had women ministers before. There were exceptions, but basically this is true. Still it is not a valid objection. While tradition should be valued, only the Scriptures are authoritative. At numerous times in the history of the church Christians have realized that the gospel in their time required new thoughts, definitions, and actions that had not been expressed in earlier times. The doctrine of the Trinity is an obvious example of such developing theology. In the sixteenth century the understanding of salvation and the role of the church were redefined. In the last century the abolition of slavery in the United States took place as a result of the application of the gospel in new ways. In focusing on the authority of Scripture, we do not believe that God is prohibited from doing new things. Our God is alive and continually leads his people to apply the gospel to their own time. The gospel does not change, but the way that it is applied in a particular time and place may.

Final considerations

Our society faces numerous problems, many of them related to sexual roles and distinctions. These problems are also problems in the church. The extremes in our society create fears about a deterioration of family structures or other changes that might occur. The encouragement of women in ministry does not derive from these extremes and should not contribute to the fears. Women in ministry not only will release the energies of the church for the proclamation of the gospel, but having women in ministerial roles will also help the church deal honestly and much more wholly than before with what it means to be a man and with what it means to be a woman.

The ministry of the church is an enormous and sometimes difficult task. The gifts and abilities of women are needed as much as those of men. Women will encounter the same kinds of problems that men do, but the church cannot afford to erect additional obstacles that will inhibit their ministry. It is time to let the Spirit of God work through all of God's people, including women. Enjoying the freedom of the Spirit will not only mean that women are allowed to minister, but that God's people will also allow themselves to be ministered to by all those who are gifted and called by God.

This statement was prepared for the Board of the Ministry of the Evangelical Covenant Church by a committee consisting of Robert Johnston, Jean Lambert, David Scholer, and Klyne Snodgrass. The original draft, biblical translations, and the subsequent editing were done by Klyne Snodgrass. The statement was approved by the Board on October 19, 1984, and was subsequently revised after discussion with the Covenant Ministerium and then was approved again by the Board of Ministry on February 12, 1987. Covenant Publications, 3200 W. Foster Avenue, Chicago, IL 60625.

Evangelical Free Church of America[18]

The EFC does not ordain women. This is stated explicitly in our Steps Toward Credentialing booklet (p. 4, IV.A.1, "The ordination credential may be issued to candidates who 1.) are male in gender").

Women can and do, however, serve in ministry, and the EFC recognizes this by being willing to grant a Christian Ministry License to those engaged in vocational ministry. (This license, by the way, is not just for women but also available for men who are in ministry and are not ordained.) These are the only official statements made by the general conference of the EFCA.

Independent Fundamental Churches of America[19]

IFCA International was founded in 1930 at Cicero, IL, as the Independent Fundamental Churches of America. The founders were J. Oliver Buswell, M. R. DeHaan, and Billy McCarrell. Members have included through the years men like William Pettingill, Louis Talbot, Charles Feinberg, J. Vernon McGee, John Walvoord, Merrill Unger, Charles Ryrie, Kenneth Gangel, and John MacArthur. Today we are a fellowship of one thousand independent local churches and twelve hundred pastors and Christian workers who all ascribe to the IFCA International Doctrinal Statement.

Each year we gather in an annual convention where, among other things, we pass resolutions expressing our consensus on the issues of the day. In this way we inform our Fellowship and alert ourselves to theological, ecclesiastical, and cultural trends.

We give and receive information and then pass resolutions to help solidify our position concerning the issues.

At the 1975 and 1992 Annual Conventions we passed two resolutions of interest to you [see below for both statements]: "The Ordination of Women" (1975) and "The Role of Women in the Local Church" (1992).

An unedited listing of IFCA International Convention Resolutions may be found on our website at www.ifca.org/Resolutions/index.html.

We are right now in the process of adding to that index every Convention Resolution passed since 1955. So if you go to that address, you will find postings being added regularly until we have them all.

Resolution on the ordination of women

WHEREAS, our society is witnessing an unbiblical position ascribed to women; and

WHEREAS, the Scriptures clearly teach that in Christ there is no distinction between the

18. The following information was received in a personal e-mail sent to Travis Buchanan on August 8, 2003, from Greg Strand with the EFCA. This statement has been used with permission.
19. The following information was received in a personal e-mail sent to Travis Buchanan on August 21, 2003, from Les Lofquist, IFCA International Executive Director. This statement has been used with permission.

man and the woman, and that they share equally all spiritual blessings in the family of God as heirs of the grace of life; and

WHEREAS, the Scriptures further teach that within the family of God a certain order is established in which the woman is not to exercise authority over the man,

BE IT THEREFORE RESOLVED, that this 46th Annual Convention of the Independent Fundamental Churches of America assembled at Portland, Oregon, June 21–27, 1975, goes on record and communicates to our churches that the Bible teaches that only male members be considered as candidates for ordination to the ministry of the gospel.

The role of women in the local church

WHEREAS, the age in which we live is one in which society's attitudes toward women are in a state of change, thus creating a growing uncertainty regarding the ministry of women in the local church; and,

WHEREAS, evangelical feminism and other similar movements have erred in their efforts to redefine the role of women in the church and, in fact, have succeeded in leading many away from the biblical teaching regarding the distinction between the roles of men and women; and,

WHEREAS, many churches, some even within our movement, have been negligent in recognizing the potential of women for ministry and of encouraging women to become involved in significant ministries, thus failing to utilize a God-given resource to the church, and also have been negligent to show proper appreciation for what women are doing in the church; and,

WHEREAS, the Holy Spirit gives spiritual gifts to men and women of God (1 Corinthians 12:7–11), and the Scripture teaches that men and women are to use those spiritual gifts in ministry, which is edifying to the body of Christ and that such ministry is crucial to the effective functioning and growth of the local church (1 Peter 4:10; 1 Corinthians 12:12–26);

BE IT THEREFORE RESOLVED, that the members and delegates present at the 63rd National Convention of the Independent Fundamental Churches of America, meeting in Orlando, Florida, June 22–26, 1992, affirm that Scripture does not provide for women to serve in the office of elder or deacon (or any office of equivalent authority), not by reason of some inferiority, but by reason of God's ordained order pertaining to leadership in the church (1 Timothy 2:11–14; 3:2, 12; Galatians 3:28); and,

BE IT FURTHER RESOLVED, that we acknowledge the valid questions and positive contributions of those who have called our attention to some of the injustices and insensitivities toward women in the church; and,

BE IT FINALLY RESOLVED, that we encourage our churches to make a deliberate effort to recognize the potential of women for ministry, to encourage women to become involved in significant ministries, to utilize this God-given resource, and to demonstrate appreciation for their ministry in the local church.

International Church of the Foursquare Gospel[20]

Women in Ordained Leadership Ministry

A Position Statement for the International Church of the Foursquare Gospel

Throughout seven decades the Foursquare Church has recognized the equality of men and women as they have served the Lord and their church as members, ministers, and as leaders. The Foursquare Church has followed the biblical pattern of mutual partnership and submission in the family. It is our conviction that while men and women are equal in the sight of God, He has gifted each individual with spiritual and natural abilities as He has pleased. These gifts differ, as do personalities and the destinies which God has placed before them.

The purpose of this paper is not to present an exhaustive study of how women in ministry fulfill their calling. Rather, it is to answer a consistent stream of inquiries as to the Foursquare Church's attitude toward the biblical right of women to serve in ministry and leadership, even to the extent of holding ecclesiastical position. It will also serve as a reminder to women desiring to enter the ministry of their God-given privilege to "be all they can be," for the glory of God and the good of our Church.

The International Church of the Foursquare Gospel affirms the place of women in ordained ministry and leadership. This belief affords women positions in all capacities in the local church, on the mission field, and at all levels of government in the Foursquare corporate structure. Currently, there are extensive examples of women effectively serving at the local church level as senior pastors, associate and assistant pastors, youth and Christian education ministers, council members, elders, deacons, teachers, prophets, and administrators. Through the Foursquare corporate structure, women may serve as district supervisors, district and divisional leaders, and corporate officers.

The Foursquare movement has husbands and wives who each feel a distinct call, as well as those women who serve, officially and unofficially, as partners in their husband's assignment. Women, unmarried and married, serving in official Foursquare ministry and leadership, have been endorsed and encouraged by statements approved and passed as sanctioned Foursquare resolutions. The 1975 official organization statement, "Women in Public Ministry," reads:

> A close study of the Word of God, both Old and New Testament, indicates that God has seen fit to use women in His service in virtually every way He has employed men. We, therefore, see nothing that should restrict God-ordained and Spirit-filled ministry of women in any capacity or office of the Church in keeping with the Word of God which guides men and women alike.

---

20. The following information was received in a personal e-mail from Ron Williams, Special Counsel to the Office of the President (ICFG), to Travis Buchanan on April 8, 2004. This statement is used with permission.

A 1988 declaration was unanimously passed by the Board of Directors. It reads:

> The present and historical position of the Foursquare Church affirms the biblical truth that women are called of God to a role of leadership and public ministry. We hereby reaffirm and encourage the ministry of women throughout the International Church of the Foursquare Gospel.

To gain a more comprehensive understanding of our movement's affirmation of women in leadership roles, we will address: 1) The General Biblical Position; 2) The Ministry of Jesus; 3) The Ministry of Women in the Early Church; and 4) The Ministry of Women in the Foursquare Church.

1) General Biblical Position

Prophets

- Miriam (Exodus 15:20–21; Numbers 12:1–15; 20:1; 26:59; Deuteronomy 24:9) "I brought you up from the land of Egypt, I redeemed you from the house of bondage; And I sent before you Moses, Aaron, and Miriam" (Micah 6:4).
- Huldah (2 Kings 22:14–20; 2 Chronicles 34:22–33)
- The wife of Isaiah (Isaiah 8:3)
- Anna (Luke 2:36)
- Philip's four daughters (Acts 21:9)
- Early church women (1 Corinthians 11:5)

Judges/Military Leaders

- Deborah (Judges 4–5)

Diplomats

- Abigail (2 Samuel 25:1–42; 2 Samuel 2:2)
- Esther (Book of Esther)
- Phoebe, deacon and minister (Romans 16:1–2)
- Junia, apostle (Romans 16:7)
- Priscilla, early church teacher (Acts 18:2, 24–26; Romans 16:3; 1 Corinthians 16:19)
- Euodia and Syntyche, preachers and coworkers with Paul (Philippians 4:2–3)
- Unnamed intercessors and prophetic women (1 Corinthians 11:2–16)
- Nympha, pastor (Colossians 4:15)

2) The Ministry of Jesus

Certainly the words "subordinate" and "inferior" could well describe the cultural status of women during the time of Jesus. Our Lord, however, by His teaching and actions, affirms the worth and value of women as persons to be included, along with men, in God's love and service. Note these examples of Jesus relating to women:

The woman at the well (John 4:4–42)
Mary and Martha (Luke 10:38–42)
Mary Magdalene (Mark 16:9)
The widow of Nain (Luke 7:11–17)
The woman with the issue of blood (Mark 5:25–45)
Peter's mother-in-law (Luke 4:38–39)
Jesus' teaching about "one flesh" (Matthew 19:3–9)

Jesus' example of ministry to women shows that He received them, cared about them and had compassion on them. Jesus gives the same spiritual privileges to women that He gives to men. The gospel message elevates women along with men.

Jesus also honored women by allowing them to minister to Him.

Mary anointed Jesus' head (John 12:1–8).
Jesus' feet were anointed by a sinful woman (Luke 7:36–50).
Women were followers of Jesus and ministered to Him (Luke 8:1–3).

Women stood at the foot of the Cross and remained there until His body was taken down (Mark 15:40–41, 47).

Women were first at the tomb on resurrection morning, for they had come to anoint His body for burial (Mark 16:1–3).

Women were first to give the message that Jesus is raised from the dead (Matthew 28:7–8).

Jesus models the inclusion of women; His life and teaching powerfully affirm God's view of women.

3) The Ministry of Women in the Early Church

The early Church included both men and women in membership and leadership ministry. There were women at the first early Church meeting (Acts 1:14–15, most likely the women noted in Luke 8:1–3; 23:49, 55; 24:10) where they waited for the promise of the Holy Spirit.

Acts 2:11—There were women present at the Spirit's outpouring.
Acts 2:17—There is the prophecy about "daughters prophesying."
Acts 9:36–41—Tabitha (Dorcas), a devoted disciple, was raised from the dead.
Acts 16:15; 18:1–3; 21:8–9; Philemon 22—Hospitable women opened their homes to missionaries and as centers of outreaches.
Acts 16:15, 40—There were churches in women's homes.

A text which gives validity to women in ministry is Joel 2:28, quoted in Acts 2:16–18, "And it shall come to pass in the last days, says God, that I will pour out of My Spirit on all flesh; your sons and your daughters shall prophecy." Aimee Semple McPherson, founder of the International Church of the Foursquare Gospel, frequently referred to this text as the basis for God empowering both men and women to believe for supernatural manifestations and gifts of the Holy Spirit today. This text's encouragement of women to minister has served as a biblical basis for our own (and many other) denominations to include, rather than exclude, women from leadership ministry.

Women are "the redeemed of the Lord," gifted and called to minister on His behalf. Neither a prophetic call nor the anointing of the Lord are based on gender, ethnicity or social class. God has poured out His Spirit upon all, and He is not a respecter of persons.

4) The Ministry of Women in the Foursquare Church

Because the history of the Foursquare Church is relatively short, we are privileged to have living sources to provide insight into the historic place women have held in the Foursquare Church. In reference to our founder and the men and women who served with her, there are the following observations:

It was a woman, Aimee Semple McPherson, who founded the International Church of the Foursquare Gospel. God gave her the plan for the "mother" church and the faith to build the now historic landmark, Angelus Temple. Sister McPherson based her right to preach on the prophecy of Joel 2:28–29 and the example of other Bible women.

While capable men and women of faith served with Sister McPherson, it was God's anointing on her that caused Angelus Temple to be a revival center where tens of thousands came to know Christ and experience the infilling of the Holy Spirit. When Sister McPherson was not preaching, she would have women and men preach in her place. Among the women were Roberta Semple (her daughter) and evangelist Reba Crawford.

The Foursquare Training Institute and later LIFE Bible College were founded by Sister McPherson. Three-fourths of the institute's first students were women. Of the institute's 16 original graduates, 14 were women. The first dean of the college was Harriet Jordan. She held that office until 1937.

Strong women of faith with unique spiritual dedication have pioneered Foursquare churches, evangelized, served as missionaries and have done administrative work. Women preachers are a definable part of the Pentecostal and Foursquare heritage (The Vine and the Branches, Nathaniel Van Cleave).

The list of Foursquare credentialed women and leaders in the present is also extensive. In recent years in the United States, women have made up approximately one third of all active credentialed Foursquare ministers, one of the highest proportions of women ministers of any church in the world. In other nations hundreds of women also serve in Ephesians 4 giftings.

It must be noted that not all women ministers serve as the primary overseer of a church or ministry. Yet, the sheer number of women who have been credentialed reveals that Foursquare women regard themselves as true ministers and leaders of the gospel in every way. They hold credentials because they currently do the work of the ministry and desire to minister in an even greater manner. They are not afraid to take on the burden of serving people, nor to call themselves leaders. In fact, it is quite common today to find couples who minister together, with the church recognizing them as co-pastors.

Women in ministry have made a significant contribution to global impact. Certainly, women have contributed greatly to the spread of the Foursquare Gospel to the more than 90 nations where it thrives today.

Women have served diligently in fields all over the world, some alongside their husbands, and some whose husbands are not in vocational ministry. Single women have also served with distinction, including high profile positions in Bible colleges and Christian education. Each year, through missions teams, hundreds of women from Foursquare churches minister in other countries as team members. Currently, in many countries, women serve on national boards, as district supervisors and as pastors, teachers, prophets and evangelists (Ephesians 4:11). Cultural barriers to women in ministry are being addressed and women are being released to fulfill their God-given roles. They are exercising their Spirit-ordained gifts.

Conclusion:

There are cultural issues associated with being a woman in ministry. Our commitment to the authority of Scripture and quality biblical interpretation requires that we attempt to define what is cultural and what is biblical. Women, like men, must be diligent to study the Scriptures and understand God's calling on their lives.

Foursquare history is filled with women and men who have found productive ministry, not based on gender, but based on God's gifting and calling (Proverbs 18:16; 2 Peter 1:10).

This brochure is intended as a companion document to the fuller excursus, Women in Ordained Ministry, available from the National Church Resource Center of the ICFG (213) 989–4481.

We are grateful to Gary Matsdorf, Committee Chairperson; committee members John Amstutz, Vickie Becker, Sheri Benvenuti, Beverly Brafford, Eloise Clarno, Jeanie Cosby, Jack Hayford, Don Long, Ed Stanton, Ivy Stanton, and Ron Williams.

Evangelical Lutheran Church in America[21]

Ordination of women has not been an issue in the ELCA, which came into existence in 1988 as a result of a merger. The three predecessor church bodies had begun ordaining women as early as 1970, so women have been considered full partners in ministry for the lifetime of this church without restrictions. At present, 15 percent of our clergy are women (the percentage is higher among clergy still serving, and even higher in seminary enrollments) and seven of our sixty-six bishops are women.

Lutheran Church—Missouri Synod[22]

In addition to the moral and vocational qualifications required of those divinely placed into this high office in the church (1 Timothy 3:1–7; Titus 3:5–9), the Scriptures teach that the incumbent of the pastoral office must be a man. On the basis of Old Testament Scripture, St. Paul taught that "the women should keep silence in the churches. For they are not permitted to speak, but should be subordinate, as even the law says" (1 Corinthians 14:34). Understood within its context, this passage means that women ought not lead the public worship service, specifically carry out the teaching-preaching aspects of the service. In 1 Timothy 2:12 St. Paul instructs the church, "Let a woman learn in silence with all submissiveness. I permit no woman to teach or have authority over man; she is to keep silent."

Again on the basis of scriptural arguments, the apostle holds in this text that women are not to take the position of one who is assigned responsibility for the formal, public proclamation of the Christian faith.

In summary, Scripture teaches that women should not hold the formal position of the authoritative public teaching office in the church, that is, the office of pastor.

Evangelical Mennonite[23]

The official position of the Evangelical Mennonite Conference is quoted below (taken from the Constitution, last revised 1994):

For pastors: "The pastor or leading minister of a local church should be a male."

For ministers: "Ministers may be elected from the male members and ordained or commissioned by the church."

For deacons: "Married couples or individuals may be called to serve in appropriate areas of ministry."

According to the conference position, women can be called as deacons, but not as ministers or pastors. Aberdeen EMC and Fort Garry EMC (both in Winnipeg, MB) have both had a

21. The following information was received in a personal e-mail sent to Travis Buchanan from Miriam L. Woolbert, with the ELCA Department for Communication. This statement has been used with permission.
22. The following information may be read on-line at http://www.lcms.org/ctcr/docs/pdf/servwom.pdf.
23. The following information was received in a personal e-mail sent to Travis Buchanan on August 7, 2003, from Becky Buhler, administrative assistant EM Conference office. This statement has been used with permission.

woman on staff in a pastoral role. These women, however, though they are recognized in their local church, are not recognized at the conference level and are not considered part of the EMC Ministerial. They may attend meetings and, in fact, would be encouraged to attend, but would not be able to vote. Some churches also have women serving on their local ministerial, but again, these women would not be recognized at the conference level. However, women who are called as deacons and go through the conference examination process would be considered part of the ministerial.

The ministerial consists of all ministers and deacons within the Conference. Ministers and deacons become members of the ministerial when they have been processed and approved by the Board of Ministers and deacons. Because the conference position does not allow women to be ministers or pastors, they would not be processed by the conference and therefore cannot be accepted into the ministerial. The conference position allows women to be deacons, and so, once processed by the conference, a deaconess would be considered part of the ministerial.

The issue of women in leadership was raised several years ago. Three papers laying out different positions were discussed at the July 1999 Conference Council meeting. We are now into the fifth year of a five-year moratorium on this issue, so the issue may be addressed again at the Conference Council meeting in July 2004 or later.

Some women missionaries to foreign countries do serve in pastoral roles. These women have been processed by the Board of Missions (which shows conference support for their role) but would not be considered part of the conference ministerial since they have not been processed by the Board of Ministers and deacons.

Recommendation regarding Women and Church Leadership

Preamble

We recognize that the question of women and church leadership is an important one. As a Conference we have wrestled with the question periodically in the past, and particularly this past year. We are also aware of the divisive potential of this issue and the possibility of this deterring us from enjoying the common ground we share on so many issues, as well as hindering us from carrying out our mandate of proclaiming the gospel at home and abroad. We are, by the grace of God, committed to fulfill the purpose of the Conference as outlined in our Constitution. In connection with the issue under discussion we call attention to purpose #4: "building and maintaining community among member churches" (Constitution, p. 30). It is our prayer that this will happen as we deal with this issue.

In response to the July 1998 request from Region 7 to register a woman pastor to officiate at weddings, it was decided to study the issue and then seek to come to a decision in one year. The Board of Ministers and deacons sponsored a study conference on the topic *Women and Church Leadership*. In addition, there has been discussion of the topic through letters to the editor in *The Messenger*.

The issue, as we see it, is not women's ministry in general. God has gifted women in many ways and uses them in His kingdom. As a Conference we have been blessed by the ministry of women in the Conference. Many of the questions about women's ministry roles in the church were answered when we revised the Constitution in 1992. The focus of the current discussion is the question of ordination of women. As a Conference we limit ordination and/or licensing as ministers to men. We recognize there may be exceptional circumstances where the accepted pattern is temporarily modified.

Another issue that seems to create confusion is the terms used in connection with the office of a minister. The Conference has two rites or rituals it uses to set individuals apart for a particular service or ministry (Constitution, pp. 24–29; Conference Handbook, viii. 2).

First, we practice the licensing of a minister. Licensing is a Conference ceremony whereby a man is given the full rights and responsibilities of a minister in the Conference for a specific period of time.

Second, we practice ordination as a ceremony whereby a man is set aside as a minister for life. For life usually implies a review at the age of sixty-five, unless other factors dictate an earlier review.

Only men are licensed and/or ordained. Both, being licensed or ordained, involve being registered to officiate at weddings, but both do not necessarily demand or require it. Ordinarily, the Conference registers those who are licensed or ordained.

Registration to officiate at weddings is a government requirement and procedure whereby individuals are granted the authority to officiate at marriages. Usually a person is recommended by a group to the government in order to receive the registration. Therefore there is a distinction between being licensed, ordained, and registered to officiate at marriages.

The General Board Executive, in consultation with the Board of Ministers and deacons, has sought to take into consideration all the efforts that have been put forth in discussing this issue. The following recommendation was developed to resolve the issue.

We recommend:

- that we do not engage in a Constitutional revision on women in church leadership but maintain our current position on male ministerial (pastors and ministers) leadership; and
- that we consider the request from Region 7 as an exceptional circumstance, and therefore grant the request to register the individual to officiate at marriages; and
- that in our July 1999 decision we commit to lay this issue to rest for a minimum time period of five years.

Mennonite Brethren (North America)[24]

Resolution adopted August 10, 1981, by the Mennonite Brethren Conference of North America:

"Resolution on the Ministry of the Women in the Church"

1.) We should be careful not to take our models for the husband/wife relationship and for the place of the woman in the church from the current feminist movement, which is largely secular in orientation. We recognize, of course, that movements in society at times force students of the Bible to ask whether they have understood the Scriptures correctly, but the church must always hold a critical stance toward such movements, including also Christian interpretations which have denied Christian women their rightful place in family, church, and society.

2.) We would caution against those modern currents of thought which tend to minimize the significance of a woman's high calling to be a wife and a mother to her children, and we should do all that we can to strengthen the family and to establish it on biblical principles.

3.) We, as men, confess that we have not always loved our wives and honored them as we should. However, we believe that the Scriptures teach that "the husband is the head of the wife," and that a wife's submission to a loving husband is in no way demeaning. True fulfillment comes to both husband and wife when they seek to serve one another, and to be submissive one to another (Ephesians 5:21, "and be subject to your own husbands, as to the Lord"), rather than in the desire for equality or even superiority. This, however, does not mean that we condone any form of oppression (either of men or women) in our society.

4.) We recognize that the language of Scripture reflects the patriarchal societies in which the Bible emerged. We should not, however, sit in judgment over Scripture, for God's Word was given for all times and all cultures. It should be understood that when words such as "brother," "brotherhood" and the like are used for the believers that these terms include also the sisters. Therefore, we should not accuse those who use this biblical patriarchal language in teaching and preaching, of being antifeminist. On the other hand, we should avoid using sexist language that offends.

5.) We encourage our churches to free and affirm women for ministries in the church, at home and abroad, in decision-making, evangelizing, teaching, counseling, encouragement, music, youth, visitations, etc.

6.) We do not hold that the reciprocal relationship between male and female, as established in creation, has been annulled by redemption. We do believe that the Bible's teaching on the headship of the husband has bearing on the place of woman in the church. We do not hold that the passages in the New Testament (such as 1 Corinthians 14 and 1 Timothy 2), which put restrictions on the Christian woman, have become irrelevant, even though they were given in a

24. The following information was received in a personal e-mail sent to Travis Buchanan on July 22, 2003, from Donna Sullivan with the Mennonite Brethren (North America).

different cultural context and, therefore, do need to be reapplied. And while we recognize that women played a significant role in the early church—something we would encourage them to do in our day as well—we encourage our sisters to be involved in all ministries of the church as they are gifted by God and called by the church, with the exception of the senior pastor position.

African Methodist Episcopal

No response received to requests for a statement.

African Methodist Episcopal Zion

No response received to requests for a statement.

Free Methodist Church of North America[25]

Women in ministry

The General Conference of 1974 passed a resolution "giving women equal status with men in the ministry of the church" (General Conference Minutes, p. 388). According to the General Conference report in *Light & Life* magazine, the vote was unanimous. That vote, in the minds of many, settled the issue and they turned their attention to other concerns.

During the intervening twenty years, the denomination's position has not changed. However, outside the denomination, the voices opposing women in ministry and limiting the leadership roles of women in the local church have become more assertive. Some of those voices are respected evangelical leaders (e.g., refer to J. I. Packer below) who seem to be ignorant of Wesleyan/holiness church history, inferring that anyone who differs from them is playing fast and loose with Scripture. This is confusing to many.

On the other hand, within the denomination there is growing concern over the fact that, though women officially have access to full ordination and any role in the church, few women are in leadership positions. At a time when women are entering formerly male-dominated professions in increasing numbers and providing community leadership, the percentage of women among Free Methodist pastors, especially senior pastors, and in church and conference leadership roles, is not growing as would be expected.

Given these concerns, the Study Commission on Doctrine believes it is time to articulate anew the church's position on women in ministry. In the following pages we will examine the historical support for ordaining women, the appropriate principles of biblical interpretation, and the scriptural bases for releasing the daughters of God in leadership and ministry.

---

25. The following information was received in a personal e-mail sent to Travis Buchanan on October 15, 2003, from Janet Duncan, Board of Bishops office, Free Methodist Church of North America. This statement, entitled "Women in Ministry," explains the Free Methodist church view on the role of women in ministry and was adopted by the 1995 General Conference of the Free Methodist Church of North America.

Our history

Writing in *Christianity Today*, J. I. Packer claimed that the call for the ordination of women is a modern concern resulting in part from social changes since World War I. He also stated that "Bible-based evangelical communities of all denominational stripes within Protestantism agree in opposing this trend" (Packer, p. 18). Packer apparently has no awareness of Wesleyan/holiness history or the status of women within Wesleyan/holiness denominations. The Salvation Army, the Anderson Church of God, and the Church of the Nazarene, all founded in the last decades of the nineteenth century, have ordained women since their beginnings (Dayton, pp. 94, 97–98).

Believing it is God who must place the call on any minister, they have accepted that God could choose to call women as well as men. Since its founding, women, called and empowered by the Holy Spirit, have ministered in the Free Methodist Church.

As early as 1861, when the church was just one year old, the minutes of the Genesee Convention report the discussion of women preaching (see Richardson, p. 53). Bishop B. T. Roberts believed strongly in the equality of men and women. He argued that women should be working shoulder to shoulder with men in building the kingdom of God. He tried to lead the denomination toward the ordination of women.

The General Conference of 1874 established a class of ministers called evangelists. They were persons called of God to preach the gospel and promote revival but not called to a pastoral charge. Both "brothers and sisters" could be licensed as evangelists. Thus, women were licensed and ministered as lay preachers in the church.

To the General Conference of 1890, "B. T. Roberts offered the following resolution: that the gospel of Jesus Christ, in the provision which it makes, and in the agencies which it employs for the salvation of mankind, knows no distinction of nationality, condition, [or] sex: therefore, no person who is called of God, and who is duly qualified, should be refused ordination on account of sex, or race or condition" (1890 General Conference Minutes, p. 131). After much debate, the motion lost by a vote of 37 to 41. Deeply grieved by this action, Roberts took up his pen. In 1891 he published *On Ordaining Women—Biblical and Historical Insights.* In the preface Roberts states the purpose for his writing: "that truth may prevail, Christ be glorified, and His kingdom be advanced on earth" (Roberts, p. 8). Unfortunately, Roberts died in 1893 without seeing women fully released to build the kingdom of God through the Free Methodist Church.

Although the 1890 General Conference refused to grant ordination to women, a step of progress was made for women. *The Free Methodist* (the denominational magazine) for October 22, 1890, reported, "Two of the lay delegates having seats in the General Conference [sic] are ladies.... Both are doing some committee work. Most of our readers will be glad to know that the question of admitting ladies as lay delegates did not in the least disrupt the equanimity of the conference." Throughout its history, the Free Methodist Church has not officially limited the role of women in the church except in the case of ordination.

The General Conference of 1894 again addressed the place of women in ministry. It added a paragraph to the section on evangelists. "When women have been licensed by the Annual Conference, and have served two successive years under appointment as pastors, they may...have a voice and vote in the Annual Conference; and in the transaction of Conference business they shall be counted with the preachers" (see Hogue, vol. 1, p. 218). Though Evangelists were supposed to be lay, nonpastoral preachers, the church acknowledged that women evangelists were pastoring.

Ordination was finally granted to women by the 1911 General Conference. But it was a limited ordination. They could be ordained deacon, "provided always that this ordination of women shall not be considered a step toward ordination as elder" (Hogue, vol. 1, p. 218). Women could preach and pastor, but they were barred from senior leadership in the church until 1974.

In the foreword to the 1992 reproduction of *On Ordaining Women,* John E. Van Valin says, "For the last 132 years, the Free Methodist Church has with honor taken her place among many other groups within the Christian faith who accord to women honor and respect in ministry. For our church this honor is in part symbolized by...ordination.... The reprinting of this centenarian volume signals not so much a new era in the life of the church but a presentation of her cherished heritage."

Interpreting Scripture

In the search for truth, Free Methodists want to know what the Bible says on any issue. Scripture is the ultimate authority on which we depend. But Scripture must be interpreted to ascertain God's message for us. How one approaches the task of interpretation makes a great deal of difference in the meanings discovered. Before examining the biblical bases for women in ministry, let us identify the principles which should guide interpretation.

W. Ward Gasque in his article "The Role of Women in the Church, in Society and in the Home" identifies several principles which need to guide our study of biblical texts. First, *the contextual principle*. What is the author discussing in the surrounding verses? How does the verse under study relate to the theme and logic of the whole passage? The context provides insight on the meaning.

Second, *the linguistic principle*. The Bible was written in Hebrew or Greek. Translating meaning from language to language is a challenge. Understanding God's Word for us requires an honest examination of a passage in its original language. What meanings might words have carried? Is that meaning accurately and fully translated into the English? Have translators used different English words for the same Greek or Hebrew word in different passages? For example, in Romans 16:1 Phoebe is called a "servant." The Greek word used here is usually translated "deacon" or "minister" in verses speaking of men. Why is Phoebe not similarly called a "deacon" or "minister"?

Third, *the historical principle*. Without an understanding of the historical setting in which biblical authors were writing, we often miss the revolutionary nature of Scripture in contrast to pagan ways. Reading Paul's letters to the churches without knowing the historical setting is like listening to one side of a telephone conversation. Our interpretation may be distorted if we do not seek to understand the heresies being spread in the early church and the lifestyle issues which infant Christians brought into the church.

Fourth, *interpret a particular text within the context of an author's writing as a whole.* To discern Paul's views on women, one must wrestle with all that he said on the subject and make sense of the whole. When there seem to be contradictions, the historical and contextual principles may help unravel the mystery.

Fifth, *the principle of the analogy of faith.* Christians assume the consistency of Scripture as a whole. Any individual text must therefore be interpreted in the light of the whole. Understanding the flow of Scripture is important in discovering its consistency. Gilbert Bilezikian in *Beyond Sex Roles* suggests that creation—fall—redemption summarize the flow of Scripture (Bilezikian, pp. 15ff.). In Genesis 1 and 2 we find God's creation design; Genesis 3 records the Fall and the rest of the Old Testament tells of God's first covenant with fallen human beings. The New Testament proclaims the story of redemption and the New Covenant through which persons can be redeemed and empowered by God's Spirit to live in accordance with God's will—the creation design. When interpreting specific Scripture passages it is important to distinguish between the creation design, descriptions of God working patiently with fallen humanity under the first covenant, and God's vision for those who are redeemed.

It is interesting to note that where persons begin their study of what the Bible has to say about women impacts their final conclusions. Some begin with statements from Paul and Peter which seem to limit the role of women in the church and make them subservient to men in the home. They then see the rest of Scripture through these verses. Others begin with Genesis 1–3 and move on through Scripture. They are amazed by Jesus' treatment of women, thrilled by Acts 2:16 and Galatians 3:28. They celebrate the equality the Bible portrays for women and men. In the light of the whole, they wrestle with the difficult passages and discover the harmony of these verses when sound interpretive principles are used (see Gasque, p. 1).

The last principle mentioned by Gasque is the *history of biblical interpretation.* For centuries Christians used Scripture to prove the rightness of slavery. Finally, principles similar to those identified above were applied to the verses referring to slaves and nineteenth-century evangelical Christians began to call for the abolition of slavery. Their approach to biblical interpretation also led them to support the ordination of women (see Dayton, p. 90). It is interesting to note that in the first chapter of *On Ordaining Women* Roberts states, "If those who stood high as interpreters of Reason and Revelation, and who expressed the prevailing sentiments of their day, were so greatly mistaken on [the slavery issue]...is it not possible that the current sentiment as to the position which WOMAN should be permitted to occupy in the church of Christ may also be wrong?" (Roberts, p. 11). Sound principles of interpretation are needed to clear up misunderstandings and destructive error.

Biblical support for women in ministry

In recent years, many excellent books have been written to articulate the biblical perspective on the place of women and men in the church and home. Many of the insights presented by these modern writers had already been anticipated by Roberts in his brief book. Since we are here addressing Free Methodists, we will turn first to Roberts for help in seeing what the Bible says about women in ministry and amplify his work with insights from other scholars. The bibliography at the end of this article provides resources for further study.

Old Testament insights

Roberts begins his biblical study with Genesis 2:18, "The Lord said, 'It is not good for the man to be alone. I will make a helper suitable for him.'" Some use this verse to prove that women are simply to "help" men, to serve them. Roberts reads this verse to mean that "woman was created, not as the *servant* of man, but as his *companion, his equal.*" Adam Clarke, he notes, understood the Hebrew to imply "that the woman was to be a perfect resemblance of the man, possessing neither inferiority or superiority, but being in all things like and equal to himself." The word translated "helper" in Genesis 2:18 appears nineteen times in the Old Testament. Fifteen times it refers to God helping needy people. It therefore carries no connotation of inferiority (see Evans, p. 16).

To both man and woman, God gave the order to be fruitful and to take dominion over the world (Genesis 1:28). There is no hint of woman's subjection before the Fall. Roberts notes that when Jesus was asked about divorce in Matthew 19:3, he based his response on Genesis 2:24, "For this reason a man will leave his father and mother and be united to his wife, and they will become one flesh." Why did Jesus refer back to the time before the Fall? "To reenact the law enacted then. Thus Christ restored the primitive law. He said nothing about the subjection of women—not one word.... Christ came to repair the ruin wrought by the Fall" (Roberts, pp. 35–36). Christ calls redeemed humanity to live out the Creation design.

The Old Testament tells of two categories of religious leaders: priests and prophets. All the Hebrew priests were male. With the coming of Christ as our great high priest, the order of priests ended. The prophets are therefore more the Old Testament counterparts of contemporary Christian ministers. And there were women prophets including Miriam (Exodus 15:20), Deborah (Judges 4:4), and Huldah (2 Kings 22:14). The Scripture presents their stories, making no issue of their gender. Women judges and prophets are both recognized.

Roberts concludes his review of the Old Testament by stating "There is nothing in the creation of woman or in her condition under the law which proves that no woman should be ordained as a minister of the gospel" (Roberts, p. 37).

New Testament insights

Jesus shocked His world by the way in which He treated women. He respected them, taking time to talk with them (John 4), heal them (Luke 8:48), forgive them (John 8:11), engage them in theological discussion (John 4:19–26; 11:23–27), and welcome them as disciples—i.e., learners (Luke 10:39, 42). He drew into His teaching parables from their experiences (Luke 15:8–10). No other rabbi of Jesus' time did such things. Jesus' treatment of women was revolutionary. He even commanded a woman to be the first witness to the resurrection (John 20:17). Moreover, Jesus made no statements limiting women in their ministry for Him.

But, some may say, the twelve apostles were all men. Does that not indicate church leaders should be men? To this objection Roberts responded, "If *gentiles* are to preach, why did [Jesus] not choose a *gentile* among the twelve? Why were the twelve *Jews*, every one of them? The example is as binding in the one case as the other" (Roberts, p. 37).

The key text on women's ministry for the nineteenth-century holiness movement was Acts 2:16–18, "This is what was spoken by the prophet Joel: 'In the last days, God says, I will pour out my Spirit on all people. Your sons and daughters will prophesy, your young men will see visions, your old men will dream dreams. Even on my servants, both men and women, I will pour out my Spirit in those days, and they will prophesy.'" One Methodist woman preacher declared Pentecost as "Woman's Emancipation Day." A new age began with Pentecost, an age in which the Holy Spirit anointed daughters as well as sons to preach and prophesy (Malcolm, pp. 120, 127).

For Roberts, Galatians 3:28 was the key verse which settled the question of whether or not women could be ministers, "There is neither Jew nor Greek, slave nor free, male nor female, for you are all one in Christ Jesus." Some claim that this verse refers only to salvation. To this objection Roberts replied, "If this verse referred *only to salvation by faith*, the *female* would not be specified.... In the many offers of salvation made in the New Testament, woman is not specially mentioned.... 'He that believeth and is baptized shall be saved' included woman as well as man. Everyone so understood it.... We must understand [Galatians 3:28] to teach, as it actually does, the perfect equality of all, under the gospel, in *rights and privileges*, without respect of *nationality*, or condition, or sex. If this gives to *men* of all nations the right to become ministers of the gospel, it gives *women* precisely the same right" (Roberts, pp. 37–39).

But, you may be asking, what about the verses that seem to limit women's involvement in the church? Are they in conflict with the rest of the Bible, or is there a way of understanding them which is in harmony with the flow of Scripture? Two such passages are 1 Corinthians 14:34–35 and 1 Timothy 2:11–12.

In 1 Corinthians 11:5, Paul talks about women covering their heads when they pray and prophesy. Those instructions would not be needed if all "women should remain silent in the churches" (1 Corinthians 14:34). Paul's theme in chapter 14 is orderly worship. Verses 26–35 identify three groups of persons who apparently were creating disorder and needed to be silent: persons speaking in tongues when there was no interpreter (v. 28), those who continued to speak when someone else received a revelation (v. 30), and women who were speaking out during worship (v. 34). John Bristow notes that the word translated "speak" in verse 34 is laleo, which of all the verbs that may be translated "speak" is the only one that can simply mean talk to one another (Bristow, p. 63). The Corinthian women were told not to interrupt the church service by conversing together; if they had questions about the topic at hand, they should wait and discuss them at home (v. 35). Probably these women were experiencing new liberties as Christians. They were not accustomed to being in public gatherings. Paul is calling, not for the silencing of women preachers, but for the silencing of women who disrupted worship with their conversations and questions, along with the silencing of others whose behavior detracted from worship (see further Evans, pp. 95–108).

We have already noted that Free Methodists historically have not silenced women in the church. Women have testified, sung, preached, and taught in the church. But for over one hundred years the leadership and authority of women were limited by denying full ordination. One speaker in the 1890 General Conference debate declared, "We would give her the same educational advantages, and the same property rights as man. We would acknowledge her to be the equal of man in intellect, equal in ability, but not equal in authority" (see Gramento, p. 77).

Persons holding such a view would probably quote 1 Timothy 2:12 as their biblical support, "I do not permit a woman to teach or to have authority over a man; she must be silent." A look at linguistics and the historical context can help shed light on the meaning of this passage. In verse 12 Paul uses the Greek word authentein for authority, rather than the common word he uses in all such cases. Authentein carries the idea of autocratic or totally self-directed behavior, of usurping authority or domineering. Paul forbids women to usurp authority that is not rightly theirs (Evans, p. 103). The word translated "man" in this verse is the Greek word often translated "husband." Some scholars believe verse 12 speaks to husbands and wives as they relate to one another in the worshipping community and not to the role of women in general.

Pastor Timothy was dealing with false teaching in Ephesus. Paul was concerned that Timothy not allow men or women to teach false doctrines (1 Timothy 1:3). In the context of this concern, Paul stated that women "should learn in quietness and full submission" (1 Timothy 2:11). The call for an attitude of quiet submission on the part of the learner probably reflected first-century educational ideas rather than limitations prescribed for women. But the significant point in verse 11 is that Paul wanted women to be learning. In our day of education for all, we miss the radical nature of Paul's statement (Evans, p. 102).

At the end of her study on 1 Timothy 2:11–12, Mary Evans concludes, "While the prohibition [to teach and have authority] is not absolute, it remains a prohibition. No believer, male or female, has an automatic right to teach. Any, particularly women, who are untaught and easily deceived, must continue to concentrate on learning rather than on usurping an authority which had not been given them" (Evans, p. 106). When viewed in their literary and historical context with insights from the Greek, these passages do not contradict what we find elsewhere in Scripture.

Conclusion

What does the Free Methodist Church believe the Scriptures teach about the place of women in the church? Bishop Roberts summarized those beliefs well:

- Man and woman were created equal, each possessing the same rights and privileges as the other.
- At the Fall, woman...became subject to her husband.
- Christ reenacted the primitive law and restored the original relation of equality of the sexes.
- The objections to the equality of man and woman in the Christian church, based upon the Bible, rest upon a wrong translation of some passages and a misinterpretation of others.
- We come, then, to this final conclusion: The gospel of Jesus Christ, in the provisions which it makes, and in the agencies which it employs, for the salvation of humankind, knows no distinction of race, condition, or sex. (Roberts, pp. 103–4)

With these beliefs, women should be encouraged to take their place in all areas of church leadership and ministry. Jesus calls us all, women and men, to make disciples and build the kingdom of God.

United Methodist Church

Women and men[26]

We affirm with Scripture the common humanity of male and female, both having equal worth in the eyes of God. We reject the erroneous notion that one gender is superior to another, that one gender must strive against another, and that members of one gender may receive love, power, and esteem only at the expense of another. We especially reject the idea that God made individuals as incomplete fragments, made whole only in union with another. We call upon women and men alike to share power and control, to learn to give freely and to receive freely, to be complete and to respect the wholeness of others. We seek for every individual opportunities and freedom to love and be loved, to seek and receive justice, and to practice ethical self-determination. We understand our gender diversity to be a gift from God, intended to add to the rich variety of human experience and perspective; and we guard against attitudes and traditions that would use this good gift to leave members of one sex more vulnerable in relationships than members of another.

---

26. The following information may be read on-line at http://www.umc.org/interior.asp?mid=1725.

Rights of women[27]

We affirm women and men to be equal in every aspect of their common life. We therefore urge that every effort be made to eliminate sex-role stereotypes in activity and portrayal of family life and in all aspects of voluntary and compensatory participation in the church and society. We affirm the right of women to equal treatment in employment, responsibility, promotion, and compensation. We affirm the importance of women in decision-making positions at all levels of church life and urge such bodies to guarantee their presence through policies of employment and recruitment. We support affirmative action as one method of addressing the inequalities and discriminatory practices within our church and society. We urge employers of persons in dual career families, both in the church and society, to apply proper consideration of both parties when relocation is considered.

Missionary Church USA[28]

The role of women in ministry

The important role of women in ministry is clearly affirmed in both the Old and New Testaments (see Judges 4–5; Esther 1–9; Acts 18:14–28; 21:8–9; and Romans 16:1–2) and is a vital part of the heritage of the Missionary Church. We believe that it is consistent with both Scripture and our heritage that the Missionary Church clearly affirm her understanding with regard to that role.

As members of the body of Christ, all women have been given spiritual gifts (1 Corinthians 12). Furthermore, God has uniquely gifted certain women for administrative and leadership roles. We recognize that it is God's will that these women engage in church and parachurch ministries, such as serving on boards and committees, teaching Sunday school classes that may include men, speaking in services, and serving on ministerial staffs.

We affirm the essential equality of men and women with regard to their standing before God and the inherited blessings of salvation (1 Corinthians 11:11; Galatians 3:28). At the same time, there is a functional difference reflected in 1 Timothy 3:1–7 and Titus 1:5–9. This difference does not deny the essential equality of men and women, just as God being the head of Christ does not deny the essential equality of the Father and the Son (1 Corinthians 11:3).

We believe that the New Testament words *elder, overseer,* and *pastor-teacher* refer, with differing implications, to the same office (1 Timothy 3:1–7; Titus 1:5–9; Ephesians 4:11; compare 1 Timothy 2:12). These New Testament references indicate that this office should be filled by men. The position of the pastor in a church with one pastor or the senior pastor in a church with multiple staff is the contemporary equivalent of this New Testament office. In addition, denominational and district executives who serve as overseers of the church generally or local

---

27. The following information may be read on-line at http://www.umc.org/interior.asp?mid=1751.

28. The following information was received in a personal e-mail sent to Travis Buchanan on November 4, 2003, from Diane Rodocker with MCUSA. Their complete constitution is available on-line at mcusa.org under the link labeled "Beliefs."

churches specifically shall be men. In situations of need and for the duration of that need, a woman may serve in the role and perform the ministries of a pastor-teacher. In 1 Timothy 2:12 in the Greek, Paul says that a woman should not "continue" as the official teacher of a congregation nor "continue" having authority over men. He does not forbid her doing such altogether.

We believe what the New Testament teaches about the role of women in ministry is God's continuing will for His people in every era.

—Adopted by the 1989 General Conference

Evangelical Presbyterian Church[29]

Position paper on the ordination of women

The Evangelical Presbyterian Church does not believe that the issue of the ordination of women is an essential of the faith. The historic Reformed position on the scriptural doctrine of government by elders is believed to be that form needed for the perfecting of the order of the visible church, but has never been considered to be essential to its existence. The *Westminster Confession of Faith* makes it clear that the church Catholic is sometimes more, sometimes less visible according to the purity of the church at a particular time. Also, the purest churches under heaven are subject both to mixture and error.

Nonetheless, in spite of such failures to be all God wants His church to be, the *Westminster Confession of Faith* affirms that "there shall always be a church on earth to worship God according to His will."

Thus, while some churches may ordain women and some may decline to do so, neither position is essential to the existence of the church. Since people of good faith who equally love the Lord and hold to the infallibility of Scripture differ on this issue, and since uniformity of view and practice is not essential to the existence of the visible church, the Evangelical Presbyterian Church has chosen to leave this decision to the Spirit-guided consciences of particular congregations concerning the ordination of women as elders and deacons, and to the presbyteries concerning the ordination of women as Ministers.

It is in this context that the Evangelical Presbyterian Church states in its *Book of Government*, chapter 7, entitled "Rights Reserved to a Particular Church," that "the particular church has the right to elect its own officers" (7-2). This right is guaranteed in perpetuity.

Finally, the motto of our church summarizes our stance: "In essentials, unity; in nonessentials, liberty; in all things, charity."

—Adopted by the 4th General Assembly. June, 1984

29. The following information may be read on-line at http://www.epc.org/about-epc/position-papers/ordination-women.html.

Orthodox Presbyterian Church[30]

"The Orthodox Presbyterian Church does not ordain women to the office of minister, ruling elder, or deacon. The OP Form of Government says, 'Our Lord continues to build His church through the ministry of men whom He calls and endues with special gifts for teaching, ruling and serving'" (FG V:2) (Chapter V is entitled "Offices in the Church").

Additionally, Chapter XXV of the Form of government of the OPC says the following in Section 1:

1. Every congregation shall elect ruling elders and deacons, except in extraordinary circumstances. Those elected must be male communicant members in good and regular standing in the church in which they are to exercise their office.

Presbyterian Church in America

Women, like men, are created in the image of God. In the PCA we have a national organization known as Women in the Church (WIC) which functions under the aegis of the committee of Christian Education and Publications. The PCA has consistently held the distinction between office and function. The office of ordained elders and ordained deacons are reserved for qualified men only. We believe this is a scriptural teaching—specifically, in the Old Testament the office of the priesthood was open only to the Aaronic line of men. Others, including other Levites, were not permitted to exercise this office. In the New Testament, the apostles were appointed by Christ, and they in turn appointed elders, who were qualified men, to the office. Women may teach and assist the officers by exercising all kinds of functions. But the authoritative roles of elders and deacons in the body of Christ is reserved to men.[31]

It therefore follows simply that women are not called to be nor may they be ordained as elders. To do so would explicitly violate 1 Timothy 2:12 and cannot be permitted by those who would submit themselves to the Word of God.[32]

Quotations from the Book of Church Order

Chapter 16: Church Orders—The Doctrine of Vocation.

16-2. The government of the Church is by officers gifted to represent Christ, and the right of God's people to recognize by election to office those so gifted is inalienable. Therefore no man can be placed over a church in any office without the election, or at least the consent of that church.

---

30. The following information was received in a personal e-mail sent to Travis Buchanan on December 4, 2003, from Donald J. Duff, the Stated Clerk of the General Assembly of the Orthodox Presbyterian Church. These statements have been used with permission.
31. From the document, "Twenty Questions and Answers About the Presbyterian Church in America."
32. *Documents of Synod: Study Papers and Actions of the Reformed Presbyterian Church, Evangelical Synod—1965–1982,* ed. Paul R. Gilchrist (Lookout Mountain, TN: Reformed Presbyterian Church, Evangelical Synod), 430.

16-3. Upon those whom God calls to bear office in His Church He bestows suitable gifts for the discharge of their various duties. And it is indispensable that, besides possessing the necessary gifts and abilities, natural and acquired, every one admitted to an office should be sound in the faith, and his life be according to godliness. Wherefore every candidate for office is to be approved by the court by which he is to be ordained.

Chapter 17: Doctrine of Ordination.

17-3. As every ecclesiastical office, according to the Scriptures, is a special charge, no man shall be ordained unless it be to the performance of a definite work.

Chapter 18: Candidates for the Gospel Ministry.

18-1. A candidate for the ministry is a member of the Church in full communion who, believing himself to be called to preach the Gospel, submits himself to the care and guidance of the Presbytery in his course of study and of practical training to prepare himself for this office.

Chapter 24: Election, Ordination and Installation of Ruling Elders and Deacons

Election

24-1. Every church shall elect persons to the offices of ruling elder and deacon in the following manner: At such times as determined by the Session, communicant members of the congregation may submit names to the Session, keeping in mind that each prospective officer should be an active male member who meets the qualifications set forth in 1 Timothy 3 and Titus 1.[33]

Presbyterian Church in the U.S.A.[34]

Clergywomen's Experiences in Ministry: Realities and Challenges

History

Women have always been central to the life and mission of the Presbyterian denomination. However, women's leadership has not always been appropriately acknowledged, not universally sought within church structures.

Basic assumptions about men, women, roles, and equality were significantly challenged in the 1960s. A new vision of partnership for women and men began to transform the Christian community's self-awareness as a whole people of God in the 1970s. Groups within the church began to assert their conviction that the church should model in its corporate life a concern for justice and equality for all God's people.

33. Excerpted from the *Book of Church Order,* chapters 16–18, 24, available online at http://www.pcanet.org/BCO/BCO16-19.htm.

34. The following information may be read on-line at http://www.pcusa.org/women/history.htm.

During the 1970s, many "task forces on women" began to be formed in the church to explore new ways of gender partnerships. More and more women began to take their places beside their brothers to teach and preach, to chair committees, and make policy decisions.

Through the 1980s, a new presence emerged, as women increasingly became biblical scholars and theologians. Many in the church were beginning to see the Bible, theology, and the world through women's eyes. Since 1986, we have recognized strong women leaders through the Women of Faith Award.

In 1983, reunion of the Presbyterian Church (U.S.A.) resulted in a new structure and the formation of the Women's Ministry Unit. The church structure has evolved and since 1993, the Women's Ministries Program Area continues as a part of the National Ministries Division. Together we seek to serve Jesus Christ and to proclaim the good news on behalf of women!

In 2005, we will celebrate the 75th anniversary of the ordination of women as elders and in 2006 the 50th anniversary of women to the Office of Word and Sacrament.

Additional information from the PCUSA:[35]

The Advocacy Committee for Women's Concerns calls upon the church at every level to raise awareness about gender-discrimination in the church and recommends that the 215th General Assembly (2003) do the following:

1. Instruct General Assembly entities and request middle governing bodies and seminaries to encourage congregations to call clergywomen from various racial ethnic backgrounds as well as Caucasian clergywomen.

2. Instruct the Advocacy Committee for Women's Concerns (ACWC) to research current programs and support for clergywomen, particularly racial ethnic and single clergywomen, and to bring recommendations to the 216th General Assembly (2004).

3. Instruct Churchwide Personnel Services and request middle governing bodies, seminaries, and congregations to address the difficulties frequently encountered in the position of associate pastor.

4. Request that presbyteries and congregations review their policies and practices in relation to clergywomen, including salaries, pension, Social Security, health insurance, dependent care, family leave, and other benefits, and correct any deficiencies or inequities found.

5. Request committees on ministry, committees on preparation for ministry, and congregations to emphasize the importance of integrating self-care and care of family with the demands/expectations of the practice of ministry, for clergy and for candidates.

6. Call congregations to new openness in considering clergywomen for positions of pastoral leadership, especially as solo pastors and heads of staff.

7. Call upon PC(USA) seminaries to develop courses addressing the importance of holistic health as it relates to the demands/expectations of the practice of ministry.

---

35. This information may be read on-line at http://www.pcusa.org/ga215/business/singles/comm0401.pdf.

8. Affirm the biblical and theological background and policy proposals incorporated in the study papers "All the Livelong Day: Women and Work" (1995) and "Vocation and Work" (1990).

9. Instruct the Advocacy Committee for Women's Concerns and the Women's Ministries program area to partner with the General Assembly Committee on Representation and the racial ethnic caucuses to monitor clergywomen's call processes and equity issues related to terms of call.

10. Instruct ACWC to provide a forum at future General Assemblies for clergywomen to comment on issues raised in the 2002 ACWC survey and offer continuing feedback to the church.

11. Instruct the Stated Clerk's office to make this report and any follow-up information available to the church electronically.

Christian Reformed Church[36]

Women in Ecclesiastical Office

Position

Women may be ordained to all ecclesiastical offices in the Christian Reformed Church. Women may be ordained as deacons in any church and as elders, ministers, and evangelists in churches belonging to classes that have declared the word *male* inoperative in Church Order Article 3-A. In classes that have not approved opening all the offices to women, individual congregations may still elect women as elders. The church's position is in effect until 2005, when it will again be reviewed. The biblical-theological argumentation that undergirds the CRC's approach to this issue can be found in Agenda for Synod 2000, pp. 355–73.

History

The CRC began to deal with this issue in 1970, when synod appointed a committee to examine the practice of excluding women from the various ordained offices in the church in response to discussions in the Reformed Ecumenical Synod (RES), of which the CRC is a member. This first study committee reported to Synod 1973, concluding that excluding women from ecclesiastical office cannot be defended on biblical grounds, but synod decided to appoint another committee to study the matter. The second study committee on the same topic came to the same conclusion in 1975, but, judging that the church was not ready for women in office, synod appointed two more committees—one to help the churches make all possible use of women's gifts and another to study hermeneutical principles and apply them to relevant Scripture passages. The first committee was given an expanded mandate in 1977 and was renamed the Service Committee for the Use of Members' Gifts. The second committee reported in 1978 and recommended that women be ordained as deacons. Synod agreed, provided that the work of deacons be distinguished from that of elders.

36. This information may be read on-line at http://www.crcna.org/crbe/crbe_pos_womenoffice.htm and has been used with permission.

Synod 1979 deferred ratification of the change in the Church Order required for women to be deacons as well as implementation of that decision and instead appointed another committee to study the whole issue. Synod 1981 received the report of the study committee, which recommended that women be ordained as deacons, but synod again decided to defer the decision of 1978 and appointed another committee to study the issue of the headship of men over women in marriage and its implications for the church. The headship study committee finally reported in 1984 and made the same recommendation that synod had passed six years earlier—that women be ordained as deacons provided their work is distinguished from that of elders. Synod agreed and finally ratified the necessary change in the Church Order.

Synod 1985 declared that the headship principle prohibits women from being elders and ministers, disallowed the use of adjunct elders, and appointed a committee to study the authority and function of elders and deacons. Synod 1987 distinguished between a church's consistory (elders), diaconate (deacons), and council (both elders and deacons); decided that deacons may not be delegated to classis meetings; and appointed yet another committee to study the headship principle. Synod 1989 instructed some churches that were ordaining women as elders to cease doing so and declared that unordained adjunct positions are allowable for women.

In 1990 the second headship study committee recommended that all the offices—elder, minister, and evangelist—be open to women, after finding that the headship principle does not transfer from marriage to the church. Synod agreed and opened all the offices to women but deferred implementation and ratification of the necessary Church Order change until 1992. Synod 1991 appointed a small ad hoc committee to gather biblical grounds for the decision of 1990. That committee reported in 1992, but synod decided against ratification. Synod 1992 did encourage the church to use the gifts of women, in teaching, expounding the Word of God, and providing pastoral care, all under the supervision of the elders.

Synod 1993 decided to revise the 1992 decision by allowing local churches the option of ordaining women as elders, ministers, and evangelists. It also decided to delete the word *male* from Article 3 of the Church Order, which gives the requirements for elders, ministers, and evangelists, but left it to Synod 1994 to decide on the advisability of ratification. Synod 1994 did not ratify the change but maintained the original language of the Church Order, claiming that the clear teaching of Scripture prohibits women from holding those offices. It instructed all churches that had ordained women as elders to release them. It also appointed a committee to clarify the meaning of "expounding the Word of God" from the decision of Synod 1992.

Synod 1995 recognized that there are two different perspectives and convictions on this issue, both of which honor the Scriptures as the infallible Word of God, and decided to give classes the option of declaring the word *male* in Church Order Article 3 inoperative, thereby allowing their churches to ordain women to all the offices. Synod 1995 also passed a set of regulations to be in effect until 2000 that restricted women from serving as delegates to synod or as synodical deputies or to be appointed by synodical agencies to ordained positions. The regulations also prevented any synodical delegates, synodical deputies, or seminary board members from being required to vote, against their consciences, on women candidates or nominees. Synod also decided that, in classes that do not declare the word *male* inoperative, churches may still choose to ordain women as elders. These decisions constitute the current position of the CRC on women in ecclesiastical office. Synod 1995 also received the report of the committee on expounding but did not alter the 1992 decision. Subsequent synods have not acceded to overtures attempting to change the 1995 decision. Synod 2000 extended the church's position on women in office for another five years, to 2005, when the issue will again be revisited. Women were first approved as candidates for the ministry of the Word in the CRC at Synod 1996. By 2000, eighteen of the forty-seven classes had declared the word *male* inoperative in Church Order Article 3-A, thereby opening the offices of elder, minister, and evangelist to women in those classes.

Reformed Church in America[37]

History of women's involvement in the RCA

Women have made vital contributions to the Reformed Church in America throughout its 375-year history.

Women's involvement in church activities began as early as the year 1800. Sarah Doremus, a member of South Dutch Church in New York City, organized the Women's Union Missionary Society, which spurred other Reformed churches to collaborate.

In 1869 the Reformed Church in America sent its first female missionary, Mary Kidder. She served as a schoolteacher in Japan and founded a seminary there.

Between 1875 and 1900, the newly established Women's Board of Foreign Mission raised nearly $750,000 to be used to support women missionaries, girls' schools, and seminaries. With auxiliaries in nearly every congregation in 1890, the women of the Reformed Church were better organized for mission than were the men.

In 1932 the denomination opened the offices of deacon and elder to women, and by 1979 women were accepted for ordination as ministers of Word and sacrament.

Today, women in the RCA serve as pastors, elders, and deacons. They also contribute their time and resources through the Office of Women and the Commission for Women and in countless local ministries.

Sovereign Grace Ministries[38]

All members of the church universal are to be a vital and committed part of a local church. In this context they are called to walk out the New Covenant as the people of God and demonstrate the reality of the kingdom of God. The ascended Christ has given gift ministries to the church

37. The following information may be read on-line at http://www.rca.org/lead/women/history.php.
38. This information may be read on-line at http://www.sovereigngraceministries.org/about/faith.html#church.

(including apostles, prophets, evangelists, pastors, and teachers) for the equipping of Christ's body that it might mature and grow. Through the gift ministries all members of the church are to be nurtured and equipped for the work of ministry. Women play a vital role in the life of the church but in keeping with God's created design, they are not permitted "to teach or to have authority over a man" (1 Timothy 2:11). Leadership in the church is male. In the context of the local church, God's people receive pastoral care and leadership and the opportunity to employ their God-given gifts in His service in relation to one another and to the world.

United Church of Christ[39]

The United Church of Christ (UCC) is pleased that its forebears were the first to ordain a woman to ministry. We ordained Antoinette Brown to ministry in 1853. This was so controversial in 1853 among fellow church members that Brown wrote in a letter to a friend, "People have stopped laughing and are starting to get mad." Today, approximately 30 percent of active ordained UCC clergy are women. The UCC has a commitment to inviting all people to Christ's table for full participation because we believe that all belong body and soul not to ourselves but to our Lord and Savior Jesus Christ. We tend to believe that there is no room for exclusion based on race, sex, sexual orientation, creeds, opinions, and many other matters at Christ's table.

Wesleyan Church[40]

We do not have a statement in our Discipline that speaks to this. It is so much a part of who we are that we simply assume the ordination of women. The only official statement is on our website...a reaffirmation of the position we have held."

Women in leadership[41]

In spite of some forces which seek to undo our long-standing position on the ordination of women, we refuse to budge on this issue—we will not tolerate the blocking of a person's ordination due to their gender, for we believe that both men and women are called to the ministry and thus should be ordained. Furthermore, we condemn any practice of exclusive male-only leadership on boards and committees in the church, excluding women from these positions by either public policy or unofficial behind-the-scenes agreed-upon policy, for we believe that when it comes to God's gifts, graces, and callings, there is neither male nor female. (1966 General Conference)

---

39. The following statement was officially given by the spokesperson for the national setting of the United Church of Christ (UCC), Ron Buford, in a personal e-mail sent to Travis Buchanan on July 29, 2003. This statement has been used with permission. More information may be obtained on-line at www.stillspeaking.com.
40. From a personal e-mail sent to Travis Buchanan on July 15, 2003, by Ron Kelly, general secretary with the Wesleyan Church. This statement has been used with permission.
41. The following information may be read on-line at http://www.wesleyan.org/about/issues.htm#rights.

Willow Creek Community Church

Statement on Women and Men in Ministry[42]

We believe the Bible teaches that men and women were created by God and equally bear His image (Genesis 1:27). God's intention was for them to share oneness and community (Genesis 2:23–24), even as the Godhead experiences oneness within the Trinity. Each had a direct relationship with God and they shared jointly the responsibilities of rearing children and having dominion over the created order (Genesis 1:26–28). However, human oneness was shattered by the Fall. The struggle for power and the desire to "rule over" another is part of the result of human sin. Genesis 3:16 is a prediction of the effects of the Fall rather than a prescription of God's ideal order.

However, God has acted in Christ to redeem the human race, and to offer to all people the opportunity to be part of the New Community, His church. It is God's intention for His children to experience the oneness that exists between the Father and the Son (John 17:11, 20–23). This means that old divisions and hierarchies between genders and races are not to be tolerated in the church, where all are "one in Christ Jesus" (Galatians 3:28).

In the formation of the church at Pentecost, the Holy Spirit was poured out on women and men alike, as had been predicted long before the coming of Christ (Joel 2:28; see also Acts 2:18). In the New Testament, women as well as men exercise prophetic and priestly functions (Acts 2:17–18; 1 Corinthians 11:4–5; 1 Peter 2:9–10). Further, the Spirit bestows gifts on all members of the New Community sovereignly, without giving anyone preferential treatment based on gender (Acts 2:1–21; 1 Corinthians 12:7, 11). Every believer is to offer her or his gifts for the benefit of the body of Christ (Romans 12:4–8; 1 Peter 4:10–11). To prevent believers from exercising their spiritual gifts is to quench the work of the Spirit.

In all attempts to understand and put into practice appropriate relationships between genders in the body of Christ, our sole authority is the will of God as expressed in Scripture. A few isolated scriptural texts appear to restrict the full ministry freedom of women. The interpretation of those passages must take into account their relation to the broader teaching of Scripture and their specific contexts. We believe that, when the Bible is interpreted comprehensively, it teaches the full equality of men and women in status, giftedness, and opportunity for ministry.

Therefore, in our attempts to live together as a biblically functioning community, we are committed to the following values:

To provide opportunity for ministry based on giftedness and character, without regard to gender.

To pursue the kind of purity and loyalty in relationships between genders that led New Testament writers to describe them in terms of family: "brothers and sisters."

---

42. This is an excerpt from the Participating Membership Manual, © 1995 Willow Creek Community Church (version 1.0).

To use sensitivity in language that reflects the honor and value God desires for maleness and femaleness and to encourage the use of translations of Scripture that accurately portray God's will that His church be an inclusive community.

To be intentional where appropriate in overcoming sexist elements of our culture and to offer encouragement to women in areas where their giftedness has been traditionally discouraged.

To teach and model these values to members of our community, to the church, and to the world at large.

For further study and more complete discussion of the key scriptural passages pertaining to this issue, we recommend:

Barton, Ruth, *Becoming a Woman of Strength,* Shaw
Bilezikian, Gilbert, *Beyond Sex Roles*, Baker
Hull, Gretchen, *Equal to Serve*, Fleming H. Revell
Keener, Craig, *Paul, Women and Wives*, Hendrickson
Ogden, Greg, *The New Reformation*, Zondervan
Spencer, Aida, *Beyond the Curse*, Hendrickson

Parachurch Ministries

Campus Crusade for Christ

Campus Crusade for Christ policy statement on the family: July 1999[43]

God has ordained the family as the foundational institution of human society. It is composed of persons related to one another by marriage, blood, or adoption.

Marriage is the uniting of one man and one woman in covenant commitment for a lifetime. It is God's unique gift to reveal the union between Christ and His church, and to provide for the man and the woman in marriage the framework for intimate companionship, the channel for sexual expression according to biblical standards, and the means for procreation of the human race.

The husband and wife are of equal worth before God, since both are created in God's image. The marriage relationship models the way God relates to His people. A husband is to love his wife as Christ loved the church. He has the God-given responsibility to provide for, to protect, and to lead his family. A wife is to submit herself graciously to the servant leadership of her husband even

43. This policy statement was announced by Bill Bright and distributed to Campus Crusade staff members at a biannual staff conference, July 28, 1999, at Colorado State University, Fort Collins, Colorado. The statement was reported in a Religion News Service dispatch July 30, 1999, a Baptist Press story by Art Toalston on July 29, 1999 (www.baptistpress.com, under archives for July 29, 1999), an article in *World* magazine, Sept. 11, 1999 (p. 32), and it was also quoted in full in James Dobson's monthly newsletter *Family News from Dr. James Dobson* (Sept., 1999, pp. 1–2). The statement is also reproduced and discussed in Dennis Rainey, *Ministering to Twenty-First Century Families* (Nashville: Word, 2001), 39–56.

as the church willingly submits to the headship of Christ. She, being in the image of God as is her husband and thus equal to him, has the God-given responsibility to respect her husband and to serve as his helper in managing the household and nurturing the next generation.

In a marriage lived according to these truths, the love between husband and wife will show itself in listening to each other's viewpoints, valuing each other's gifts, wisdom, and desires, honoring one another in public and in private, and always seeking to bring benefit, not harm, to one another.

Children, from the moment of conception, are a blessing and heritage from the Lord. Parents are to demonstrate to their children God's pattern for marriage. Parents are to teach their children spiritual and moral values and to lead them, through consistent lifestyle example and loving discipline, to make choices based on biblical truth. Children are to honor and obey their parents.

InterVarsity Christian Fellowship[44]

The current practice of InterVarsity reflects not only our historical commitment to empower the ministries of women according to their gifts, but also to promote women staff wherever possible within InterVarsity's structure....

When discussions are held both internally and externally with regard to women in positions of leadership in InterVarsity, two key questions frequently arise:

1. Does a woman have biblical freedom to have a teaching ministry in relation to both men and women?
2. Does a woman have biblical freedom to exercise positions of authority over men in roles such as chapter president, campus staff member, staff director, or departmental manager?

Those who take a more restrictive view would say that the Bible prohibits women from all ministry roles associated with positions of authority over men.... Those within InterVarsity have more often taken one of the following positions:

1. The Bible prohibits women from certain ministry roles within a local church but allows greater freedom to women in missionary endeavors that supplement the ministry of a local church.
2. The Bible permits women to be in any ministry for which they are gifted, qualified, and duly appointed.

There is little which would distinguish these two positions within the staff practice of the Fellowship and frequently InterVarsity staff are unaware of which position a colleague might hold.

---

44. The following has been excerpted from "Women in the Ministries of InterVarsity," © 1998, by Stephen A. Hayner, president of InterVarsity Christian Fellowship 1988 to 2001. Pages 8–11. This statement has been reprinted here with the permission of Bill McConnell, assistant to the president at IVCF, who sent these pages in a personal e-mail to Travis Buchanan on July 30, 2003.

However, those who take the first position, tend to see biblical parameters on the ministries of women as more restrictive, but justify InterVarsity's practice on the basis that we are a mission agency and not an ecclesiastical structure. Those who take the second position, accept women's unrestricted scope of ministry in InterVarsity on the basis of their understanding of Scripture without reference to church polity....

While many churches would view restrictions on women in ministry and leadership as a more central distinctive of biblical faith, especially in this historical moment, we do not view it as such. We recognize that there are Scriptures which have led some churches to question the propriety of women in certain leadership positions, yet we also see evidence in Scripture of women affirmed for their gifts of teaching and leadership.

Because ecclesiastical office is not an issue which seems central to our ministry as a mission organization, and because of disagreement among biblical scholars on the interpretation or biblical teaching on the subject, we have never been willing to let gender be the determining factor which qualified some for leadership selection, especially above the criteria of gifts, character, essential theological faithfulness (as defined by our Basis of Faith), and experience.

Navigators

No statement.

Young Life[45]

Women in the Young Life Ministry

Young Life believes that men and women together reflect the wholeness of Christ and that God calls and gifts both men and women to serve at every level in this mission.

As a mission, Young Life:

- Celebrates that from its inception, men and women have worked together in this ministry.
- Believes that kids, volunteers, and staff—both men and women—deserve to see models of women living out their call to ministry in a variety of leadership positions.
- Honors women who have been called to the single life of ministry as well as those who have been called to marriage and ministry, or marriage, motherhood, and ministry.
- Offers women the flexibility to move in and out of Young Life as they respond to God's call during the various seasons of their lives.
- Pledges to provide opportunities that will encourage women because any minority within a larger group has the need for special support.

45. The following paper is reflective of Young Life's position on this issue and is used with permission. It was received from Young Life Communications Services in a personal e-mail sent to Travis Buchanan on August 5, 2003, via Sarah Knott, assistant to Terry Swenson, vice president, Young Life.

- Refuses to tolerate the exclusion of women from activities (e.g., speaking in club) or roles (e.g., camp director) because of their gender.
- Expects that in opposite-gender supervision, boundaries will be appropriate and professional, with the primary focus being on coaching for ministry.
- Celebrates the selection in recent years of more and more women to roles of line authority as area directors, department heads, leaders at properties, regional directors, and vice presidents.
- Anticipates with hope that this great mission will increasingly reflect the diversity of the kingdom of God.

Position Paper: Women in the Young Life Ministry
Spring 2002

Introduction

The mission of Young Life is to introduce adolescents to Jesus Christ and help them grow in their faith. It is the historic calling of Young Life, as a mission of the church, to carry out the Great Commission to a rather narrow target: adolescents, particularly unchurched or disinterested adolescents. In essence, Young Life staff and volunteer leaders are missionaries to the adolescent culture. While Young Life is part of the historic, larger church, it is essentially a sending organization that facilitates those who have a unique calling to present Christ to kids.

Historical perspective

From the inception of Young Life, Jim Rayburn's incredible vision and winsome style attracted both men and women to the "Young Life Campaign." The task was enormous, and their commitment was all encompassing. Early staff spent hours at contact work, "earning the right to be heard" by the adolescents of the 1940s, in order to present the truth of Jesus Christ to them. Men and women worked alongside one another in gender roles quite typical of that decade.

Over the years, Young Life experienced rapid growth, adding service center and property staff to the already expanding number of field staff. Women continued to join the mission, some serving as paid staff, others as volunteer leaders and many as staff spouses, all committed to sharing Christ with kids. The task was daunting, but men and women joined together tirelessly to expand Young Life's outreach to adolescents.

There came a day, however, when Young Life recognized that gifted women needed encouragement as well as more opportunities to use their talents. So, over time, the mission continued to define and refine its position on women in this ministry. In the 1980s Young Life commissioned a paper to be written on the topic of women in ministry, and the Field Management Team adopted the affirmation: "Within Young Life, men and women alike have the opportunity and responsibility to exercise their God-given gifts throughout the mission." In the 1990s, the Mission Field Team further clarified Young Life's position: "No staff person or volunteer leader will be excluded from any position, ministry role, or leadership opportunity in the mission on the basis of gender."

2002 position statement

Young Life believes that men and women together reflect the wholeness of Christ and that God calls and gifts both men and women to serve at every level in this mission.

Scripture as our basis

The basis for these affirmations, as in any position that Young Life takes on an issue, flows out of our understanding of Scripture. Article I of the Young Life Statement of Faith indicates that we believe that the Scriptures of the Old and New Testaments, having been given by divine inspiration, are the Word of God, the final and supreme authority in all matters of faith and conduct. Further, Young Life believes that it is the total witness of Scripture that must inform our thinking and our actions on any particular issue, not isolated passages taken out of context.

The Old Testament

The Creation account in Genesis indicates that God not only created both male and female in His own image, but gave to both of them authority over and responsibility for His creation.

Overall, the Old Testament holds a number of examples of women filling significant leadership roles, leading both men and women (Deborah, Miriam, Esther, Ruth). References are made to these women without any indication that they are fulfilling abnormal roles even though the culture of that day was decidedly patriarchal.

The Gospels

The Gospels certainly affirm that Jesus offered dignity to women, which was in contrast to the cultural norms of the day. He included women among His close friends (Mary, Martha, Mary Magdalene), encouraged women to become His followers, and selected women to be the first announcers of His resurrection. Although He did not speak specifically to the topic of women in ministry, His actions certainly ushered in a kingdom community in which men and women would be affirmed both by God and by each other.

The early church

The book of Acts informs us that after the ascension of Jesus, the group that waited and prayed in Jerusalem included both men and women. When the promised Holy Spirit did come, Peter stepped forward to declare that what was happening that day had been predicted by the prophet Joel: "In the last days," God said, "I will pour out my Holy Spirit upon all mankind, and your sons and daughters shall prophesy..." (Joel 2:28). That women did indeed exercise the gift of prophecy is attested to in Acts 21:7–9 by the reference to Philip the evangelist's four daughters "who had the gift of prophecy."

Paul's letters

Paul makes numerous references to women as coworkers in spreading the gospel, thereby indicating that women as well as men were very much a part of the ministry and growth of the early church. In Romans 16, Paul mentions several women in this capacity: Phoebe (who had been "a great help to many people"), Priscilla (along with Aquila referred to as "my fellow workers in Christ Jesus"), Mary (who "worked very hard for you"), Persis, Tryphena, and Tryphosa (who all worked hard in the Lord). In his letter to the Philippians, Paul mentions Euodia and Syntyche (albeit in reference to their well-known quarrel) as coworkers in sharing the gospel.

The references to these many women as ministers with him in spreading the gospel must be kept in mind as one considers Paul's injunctions in 1 Corinthians 14 and 1 Timothy 2 that women should remain silent in the church and should not teach or have authority over a man. Disagreement over the interpretation of these passages for the church is not about to cease, but Young Life believes that they were written to restore order in the midst of apparent chaos, and that they must be considered in light of Paul's larger context of seeing a number of women as his teammates in ministry.

Paul summarizes this biblical view in his concluding remarks to the Galatians when he deals with barriers that had been established because of race, ethnicity, economics, or gender. He implores us to live above such divisions and declares, "You are all one in Christ Jesus" (Galatians 3:28).

Conclusion

Young Life seeks to create a climate in which both staff and volunteers will live out this oneness in Christ, increasingly reflecting kingdom diversity in all arenas and at all levels of this mission.

Youth for Christ[46]

In YFC we believe the following:

Youth for Christ men and women must be able to advance to the level of responsibility and/or position appropriate to the gifts given them by God.

1. As believers in Christ, we are of the same spirit. Scripture states in Joel 2:28–29, "I will pour out my Spirit on all mankind...on the male and female servants" (Acts 2:16–18). Galatians 3:28 further states that we are one in Christ.
2. God's Word also tells us that each one of us has been given spiritual gifts for the good of the body of Christ; "We have different gifts, according to the grace given us, let each exercise them accordingly" (Romans 12:6; 1 Corinthians 12:4–6).

46. The following information may be obtained by contacting the training department at Youth for Christ USA / PO Box 2288822 / Denver, CO 80222.

3. It is our responsibility as Christians to cultivate and use our gifts to edify the body which, in turn, glorifies Christ (1 Timothy 4:14). We must use our gifts to minister to the body; failure to do so causes disfavor with Christ (Matthew 25:14–29; Luke 12:42–48).

Both men and women have the responsibility to use their gifts to benefit the body of Christ. Therefore, a woman in Youth for Christ must be enabled and encouraged to advance to any position that her gifts allow her. This we believe is in accordance with Scripture.

Bibliography

The literature on this topic is immense, and I have not attempted to make this an exhaustive bibliography. I have included the most commonly used academic books from both positions, a few that focus on practical application for marriage, and only the articles that I cited in this book.

One helpful source for further bibliographical information is the *Journal for Biblical Manhood and Womanhood (JBMW)* (2825 Lexington Road, Box 926, Louisville, KY 40280). Beginning with *JBMW* issue 6/1 (spring 2001), managing editor Rob Lister has published annually an extensive annotated bibliography for gender-related articles appearing in the previous year, using the categories "complementarian," "egalitarian," "non-evangelical," and "undeclared," and giving a one-paragraph summary of each article. *JBMW* is available online at www.cbmw.org.

For books by evangelical authors that are clearly complementarian or egalitarian, I have designated them with a boldface [comp.] or [egal.] after each entry.

Books

Akin, Daniel. *God on Sex*. Nashville, TN: Broadman and Holman Publishers, 2003. **[comp.]**

Aland, Barbara, et al., eds. *The Greek New Testament*, 4th rev. ed. Stuttgart: Deutsche Bibelgesellschaft and United Bible Societies, 1994.

Aldredge-Clanton, Jann. *God, a Word for Girls and Boys.* Louisville, KY: Glad River Publications, 1993. **[egal.]**

Alsdurf, James and Phyllis. *Battered into Submission: The Tragedy of Wife Abuse in the Christian Home.* Downers Grove, IL: InterVarsity Press, 1989. **[egal.]**

Baldwin, Joyce. *Women Likewise*. London: Falcon Booklets, Church Pastoral Aid Society, 1973. **[egal.]**

Barclay, J. M. G. *Obeying the Truth: Paul's Ethics in Galatians.* Minneapolis: Fortress, 1991.

Barth, M. *Ephesians 4–6.* AB 34, 2-vol. ed. Garden City: Doubleday, 1974.

Beck, James R. and Craig L. Blomberg, eds. *Two Views on Women in Ministry*. Grand Rapids, MI: Zondervan, 2001.

Belleville, Linda L. *Women Leaders and the Church: Three Crucial Questions.* Grand Rapids, MI: Baker Book House, 2000. **[egal.]**

Benton, John. *Gender Questions: Biblical Manhood and Womanhood in the Contemporary World.* Darlington, England: Evangelical Press, 2000. **[comp.]**

Berkhof, Louis. *Systematic Theology*, 4th ed. Grand Rapids, MI: Wm. B. Eerdmans Publishing Co., 1939.

Bilezikian, Gilbert. *Beyond Sex Roles: What the Bible Says About a Woman's Place in Church and Family*, 2nd ed. Grand Rapids, MI: Baker Book House, 1985. **[egal.]**

———. *Community 101.* Grand Rapids, MI: Zondervan, 1997. **[egal.]**

Blackman, Philip. *Mishnayoth*, 7-vol. ed. Gateshead, U.K.: Judaica, 1973.

Blass, F., and A. Debrunner, *A Greek Grammar of the New Testament and Other Early Christian Literature.* Trans. Robert W. Funk. Chicago: University of Chicago Press, 1961.

Blomberg, Craig. *1 Corinthians,* NIV Application Commentary. Grand Rapids, MI: Zondervan, 1994.

Boldrey, Richard and Joyce Boldrey. *Chauvinist or Feminist? Paul's View of Women*. Grand Rapids, MI: Baker Book House, 1976. **[egal.]**

Bolt, Peter, and Mark Thompson, eds. *The Gospel to the Nations*. Leicester, England: IVP, 2000.

Boomsma, Clarence. *Male and Female, One in Christ: New Testament Teaching on Women in Office.* Grand Rapids, MI: Baker Book House, 1993. **[egal.]**

Booth, Catherine. *Female Ministry: Woman's Right to Preach the Gospel.* New York: The Salvation Army, 1975. (First published London, 1859.) **[egal.]**

Boyd, Lois A., and R. Douglas Brackenridge, *Presbyterian Women in America: Two Centuries of a Quest for Status*, 2nd ed. Westport, CN: Greenwood Press, 1996.

Bristow, John Temple. *What Paul Really Said About Women: An Apostle's Liberating Views on Equality in Marriage, Leadership, and Love.* San Francisco: HarperCollins, 1991. **[egal.]**

Bromiley, Geoffrey W., ed. *The International Standard Bible Encyclopedia*, rev. ed., 4 vols. Grand Rapids, MI: Wm. B. Eerdmans Publishing Co., 1978–1988.

Brooten, Bernadette. *Women Priests: A Catholic Commentary on the Vatican Declaration.* New York: Paulist Press, 1977. **[egal.]**

Brown, Ann. *Apology to Women: Christian Images of the Female Sex.* Downers Grove, IL: InterVarsity Press, 1991. **[egal.]**

Brown, Judy L. *Women Ministers According to Scripture*. Kearney, NE: Morris Publishing, 1996. **[egal.]**

Bruce, F. F. *Romans*. TNTC; London: Tyndale Press, 1973.

Burgess, Stanley M., and Eduard van der Maas, eds. *International Dictionary of Pentecostal and Charismatic Movements*, rev. and expanded ed. Grand Rapids, MI: Zondervan, 2002.

Burke, H. Dale. *Different By Design*. Chicago: Moody Press, 2000. **[comp.]**

Burkert, Walter. *Greek Religion*. Cambridge, MA: Harvard University Press, 1985.

Bushnell, Katherine C. *God's Word to Women: One Hundred Bible Studies on Woman's Place in the Divine Economy*. North Collins, N.Y., n.d. (First published 1919, with no date indicated on the publication.) **[egal.]**

Calvin, John. *Institutes of the Christian Religion*, 2-vol. ed., trans. Ford Lewis Battles. Philadelphia: Westminster, 1960.

Campbell, Ken. *Marriage and Family in the Biblical World.* Downers Grove, IL: InterVarsity Press, 2003.

Carson, D. A. *The Difficult Doctrine of the Love of God.* Wheaton: Crossway Books, 2000.

Chadwick, John. *Lexicographica Graeca: Contributions to the Lexicography of Ancient Greek.* Oxford: Clarendon Press, 1996.

Chappell, Bryan. *Each for the Other*. Grand Rapids, MI: Baker Book House, 1998. **[comp.]**

Charles, R. H. *The Apocrypha and Pseudepigrapha of the Old Testament,* 2-vol. ed. Oxford: Clarendon Press, 1913.

Charlesworth, James H., ed. *The Old Testament Pseudepigrapha,* 2-vol. ed. London: Darton, Longman & Todd, 1985.

Chaves, Mark. *Ordaining Women: Culture and Conflict in Religious Organizations*. Cambridge, MA: Harvard University Press, 1997. **[egal.]**

Clark, Stephen B. *Man and Woman in Christ: An Examination of the Roles of Men and Women in Light of Scripture and the Social Sciences.* Ann Arbor, MI: Servant Books, 1980. **[comp.]**

Clouse, Bonnidell and Robert G. Clouse, eds. *Women in Ministry: Four Views*. Downers Grove, IL: InterVarsity Press, 1989.

Clowney, Edmund. *The Church.* Downers Grove, IL: InterVarsity Press, 1995. **[comp.]**

Cook, B. F. *The Townley Marbles.* London: British Museum of Publications, 1985.

Cook, Philip W. *Abused Men: The Hidden Side of Domestic Violence.* Westport, CT: Praeger, 1997.

Cooper, John. *A Cause for Division? Women in Office and the Unity of the Church*. Grand Rapids, MI: Calvin Theological Seminary, 1991. **[egal.]**

Cottrell, Jack. *Feminism and the Bible: An Introduction to Feminism for Christians.* Joplin, MO: College Press, 1992. **[comp.]**

Crabb, Larry. *Men and Women: Enjoying the Difference*. Grand Rapids, MI: Zondervan, 1991. **[comp.]**

Cranfield, C. E. B. *A Critical and Exegetical Commentary on the Epistle to the Romans, ICC*. Edinburgh: T&T Clark, 1975, 1979.

Cyril of Alexandria. *Dialogues sur la Trinité*, ed. and trans., Georges Matthieu de Durand. Sources Chrétiennes 237; Paris: Cerf, 1977.

Danby, Herbert. *The Mishnah*. Oxford: Oxford University Press, 1933.

Davis, Philip G. *Goddess Unmasked: The Rise of Neopagan Feminist Spirituality.* Dallas: Spence Publishing, 1998.

Dawes, Gregory W. *The Body in Question: Meaning and Metaphor in the Interpretation of Ephesians 5:21–33.* Leiden: Brill, 1998.

DeMoss, Nancy Leigh, ed. *Biblical Womanhood in the Home*. Wheaton, IL: Crossway Books, 2002. **[comp.]**

———. *Lies Women Believe and the Truth that Sets Them Free.* Chicago: Moody Press, 2001. **[comp.]**

———. *Walking in the Truth*. Chicago: Moody Press, 2002. **[comp.]**

DiBerardino, Angelo, ed. *Encyclopedia of the Early Church*. Trans. Adrian Walford, vol. 2. New York: Oxford University Press, 1992.

Dobson, James. *Bringing Up Boys*. Wheaton, IL: Tyndale House Publishers, 2001. **[comp.]**

Doriani, Dan. *The Life of a God-Made Man.* Wheaton, IL: Crossway Books, 2001. **[comp.]**

———. *Women and Ministry: What the Bible Teaches*. Wheaton, IL: Crossway Books, 2003. **[comp.]**

Duchesne, L. *Christian Worship: Its Origin and Evolution*. Trans. M. L. McClure, 5th ed. London: S.P.C.K., 1927.

Dunbar, George. *A Greek-English Lexicon*, 3rd ed. Edinburgh: MacLachlan and Stewart, 1850.

Dutton, D. G. *The Batterer: A Psychological Profile.* New York: Harper Collins, 1995.

Edwards, Brian, ed. *Men, Women and Authority: Serving Together in the Church*. Kent, England: Day One Publications, 1996. **[comp.]**

Elwell, Walter, ed. *Evangelical Dictionary of Theology*. Grand Rapids, MI: Baker Book House, 1984.

Erickson, Millard. *God in Three Persons.* Grand Rapids, MI: Baker Book House, 1995.

Evans, Mary J. *Women in the Bible: An Overview of All the Crucial Passages on Women's Roles.* Downers Grove, IL: InterVarsity Press, 1983. **[egal.]**

Farrar, Steve. *Anchor Man.* Nashville: Thomas Nelson Publishers, 1998. **[comp.]**

———. *Point Man: How a Man Can Lead His Family.* rev. ed. Sisters, OR: Multnomah, 2003. **[comp.]**

Fee, Gordon D. *The First Epistle to the Corinthians*. New International Commentary on the New Testament. Grand Rapids, MI: Wm. B. Eerdmans Publishing Co., 1987. **[egal.]**

———. *1 and 2 Timothy, Titus*. New International Biblical Commentary. W. Ward Gasque, New Testament ed. Peabody, MA: Hendrickson Publishers, 1988. **[egal.]**

Fee, Gordon, and Douglas Stuart. *How to Read the Bible for All Its Worth,* 2nd ed. Grand Rapids, MI: Zondervan, 1993.

Ferguson, Everett, ed. *Encyclopedia of Early Christianity*, 2nd ed. New York and London: Garland, 1997.

Ferguson, Everett. *Backgrounds of Early Christianity*, 2nd ed. Grand Rapids, MI: Wm. B. Eerdmans Publishing Co., 1993.

Ferguson, Sinclair B., and David F. Wright, eds. *New Dictionary of Theology.* Leicester, UK: InterVarsity Press, 1988.

Field, F. *Origenis Hexaplorum quae supersunt*... Hildesheim: Georg Olms, 1964.

Finley, M. I. *Ancient Slavery and Modern Ideology*. New York: Viking Press, 1980.

Fitzmyer, Joseph A. *Romans: A New Translation with Introduction and Commentary*, Anchor Bible. New York: Doubleday, 1993.

Fletcher, Joseph. *Situation Ethics: The New Morality.* Philadelphia: Westminster Press, 1966.

Foh, Susan T. *Women and the Word of God: A Response to Biblical Feminism.* N.p.: Presbyterian and Reformed, 1980. **[comp.]**

Fortman, Edmund J. *The Triune God.* Grand Rapids, MI: Baker Book House, 1982.

France, R. T. *Women in the Church's Ministry: A Test Case for Biblical Interpretation.* Grand Rapids, MI: Wm. B. Eerdmans Publishing Co., 1995. **[egal.]**

Garland, Diana R. *Family Ministry: A Comprehensive Guide.* Downers Grove, IL: InterVarsity Press, 1999. **[egal.]**

George, Elizabeth. *A Woman's High Calling.* Eugene, OR: Harvest House Publishers, 2001. **[comp.]**

Gilder, George. *Men and Marriage.* Gretna, LA: Pelican Publishing, 1986.

Giles, Kevin. *The Trinity and Subordinationism: The Doctrine of God and the Contemporary Gender Debate.* Downers Grove, IL: InterVarsity Press, 2002. **[egal.]**

Goldberg, Steven. *The Inevitability of Patriarchy: Why Biological Differences Between Men and Women Always Produces Male Domination.* New York: William Morrow and Company, 1973.

Grady, J. Lee. *Ten Lies the Church Tells Women: How the Bible Has Been Misused to Keep Women in Spiritual Bondage.* Lake Mary, FL: Creation House, 2000. **[egal.]**

———. *Twenty-Five Tough Questions about Women and the Church: Answers from God's Word That Will Set Women Free.* Lake Mary, FL: Charisma House, 2003. **[egal.]**

Gray, John. *Men Are from Mars, Women Are from Venus.* New York: HarperCollins, 1992.

Green, Joel, ed. *Hearing the New Testament.* Grand Rapids, MI: Eerdmans, 1995.

Green, Joel B. and Max Turner, eds. *Jesus of Nazareth: Lord and Christ.* Grand Rapids, MI: Wm. B. Eerdmans Publishing Co., and Carlisle, England: Paternoster, 1994.

Greenlee, J. Harold. *A New Testament Greek Morpheme Lexicon.* Grand Rapids, MI: Zondervan, 1983.

Grenz, Stanley, J. *Women in the Church: A Biblical Theology of Women in Ministry.* Downers Grove, IL: InterVarsity Press, 1995. **[egal.]**

Gritz, Sharon Hodgin. *Paul, Women Teachers, and the Mother Goddess at Ephesus: A Study of 1 Timothy 2:9–15 in Light of the Religious and Cultural Milieu of the First Century.* Lanham, MD: University Press of America, 1991.

Groothuis, Rebecca Merrill. *Women Caught in the Conflict: The Culture War Between Traditionalism and Feminism.* Grand Rapids, MI: Baker Book House, 1994. **[egal.]**

———. *The Feminist Bogeywoman: Questions and Answers about Evangelical Feminism.* Grand Rapids, MI: Baker Book House, 1995. **[egal.]**

———. *Good News for Women: A Biblical Picture of Gender Equality.* Grand Rapids, MI: Baker Book House, 1997. **[egal.]**

Grudem, Wayne, ed. *Are Miraculous Gifts for Today? Four Views.* Grand Rapids, MI: Zondervan, 1996.

———, ed. *Biblical Foundations for Manhood and Womanhood.* Wheaton, IL: Crossway Books, 2002. **[comp.]**

———. *First Peter.* Leicester, England: InterVarsity Press, and Grand Rapids, MI: Wm. B. Eerdmans Publishing Co., 1988.

———. *The Gift of Prophecy in the New Testament and Today,* rev. ed. Wheaton, IL: Crossway Books, 2000.

———. *Systematic Theology: An Introduction to Biblical Doctrine.* Leicester, England: InterVarsity Press, and Grand Rapids, MI: Zondervan, 1994.

Grudem, Wayne and Dennis Rainey, eds. *Pastoral Leadership for Manhood and Womanhood.* Wheaton, IL: Crossway Books, 2002. **[comp.]**

Gruenler, Royce. *The Trinity in the Gospel of John.* Grand Rapids, MI: Baker Book House, 1986.

Gundry, Patricia. *Woman, Be Free!* Grand Rapids, MI: Zondervan, 1977. **[egal.]**

Hammond, N. G. L. and H. H. Scullard, eds. *Oxford Classical Dictionary*, 2nd ed. Oxford: Clarendon Press, 1970.

Hardenbrook, Weldon M. *Missing from Action: Vanishing Manhood in America.* Nashville: Thomas Nelson Publishers, 1987. **[comp.]**

Harper, Michael. *Equal and Different: Male and Female in Church and Family.* London: Hodder and Stoughton, 1994. **[comp.]**

Harris, Paul R. *Why is Feminism So Hard to Resist?* Decatur, IL: Repristination Press, 1998. **[comp.]**

Harvey, Paul, comp. *Oxford Companion to Classical Literature*. Oxford and New York: Oxford University Press, 1937.

Hassey, Janette. *No Time for Silence: Evangelical Women in Public Ministry Around the Turn of the Century.* Grand Rapids, MI: Zondervan, 1986. **[egal.]**

Hatch, Edwin, and Henry Redpath. *A Concordance to the Septuagint*, 2-vol. ed. Graz, Austria: Akademische Druck-und-Verlagsanstalt, 1954.

Hederich, Benjamin. *Graecum Lexicon Manuale*. London: Wilks and Taylor, 1803.

Heimbach, Daniel R. *Pagan Sexuality: At the Center of the Contemporary Moral Crisis*. Southeastern Baptist Theological Seminary, 2001. **[comp.]**

———. *Counterfeit Sexuality: Defending Biblical Sexual Morality from Four Threats to God's Design for Biblical Sexual Behavior.* Colorado Springs: A Special Report from Focus on the Family, n.d. **[comp.]**

Hodge, Charles. *An Exposition of 1 and 2 Corinthians*. Wilmington, DE: Sovereign Grace, 1972; first published 1857.

———. *Systematic Theology,* 3-vol. ed., reprint. Grand Rapids, MI: Wm. B. Eerdmans Publishing Co., 1970; first published 1871–73.

Hopko, Thomas, ed. *Women and the Priesthood.* Crestwood, NY: St. Vladimir's Seminary Press, 1983. **[comp.]**

Hornblower, Simon, and Antony Spawforth, eds. *Oxford Classical Dictionary.* Oxford University Press, 1996.

House, H. Wayne. *The Role of Women in Ministry Today*. Grand Rapids, MI: Baker Book House, 1995. (Reprinted: Nashville: Thomas Nelson Publishers, 1990.) **[comp.]**

Hove, Richard. *Equality in Christ? Galatians 3:28 and the Gender Dispute.* Wheaton, IL: Crossway Books, 1999. **[comp.]**

Howe, Margaret E. *Women and Church Leadership*. Grand Rapids, MI: Zondervan, 1982. **[egal.]**

Hughes, Barbara. *Disciplines of a Godly Woman*. Wheaton, IL: Crossway Books, 2001. **[comp.]**

Hughes, R. Kent. *Disciplines of a Godly Man.* Wheaton, IL: Crossway Books, 1991. **[comp.]**

Hull, Gretchen Gaebelein. *Equal to Serve: Women and Men Working Together Revealing the Gospel.* Old Tappan, NJ: Revell, 1987, 1991. **[egal.]**

Hunt, Susan. *By Design*. Wheaton, IL: Crossway Books, 1994. **[comp.]**

———. *Spiritual Mothering*. Wheaton, IL: Crossway Books, 1992. **[comp.]**

Hunt, Susan and Peggy Hutcheson. *Leadership for Women in the Church*. Grand Rapids, MI: Zondervan, 1991. **[comp.]**

Hunt, Susan and Barbara Thompson. *The Legacy of Biblical Womanhood.* Wheaton, IL: Crossway Books, 2003. **[comp.]**

Hurley, James B. *Man and Woman in Biblical Perspective*. Grand Rapids, MI: Zondervan, 1981. **[comp.]**

Inrig, Elizabeth. *Release Your Potential: Using Your Gifts in a Thriving Women's Ministry.* Chicago: Moody Press, 2001. **[comp.]**

Jackson, F. J. Foakes, and Kirsopp Lake. *The Beginnings of Christianity: The Acts of the Apostles.* 5 vols. London: MacMillan, 1933.

Jacobs, Cindy. *Women of Destiny: Releasing You to Fulfill God's Call in Your Life and in the Church.* Ventura, CA: Regal Books, 1998. **[egal.]**

James, Carolyn Custis. *When Life and Beliefs Collide: How Knowing God Makes a Difference.* Grand Rapids, MI: Zondervan, 2001.

James, Sharon. *God's Design for Women: Biblical Womanhood for Today*. Darlington, England: Evangelical Press, 2002. **[comp.]**

Jepsen, Dee. *Women: Beyond Equal Rights*. Waco, TX: Word Books, 1984. **[comp.]**

Jeremias, Joachim. *Jerusalem in the Time of Jesus.* English translation. London: S. C. M. Press, 1969.

Jewett, Paul K. *Man As Male and Female: A Study in Sexual Relationships from a Theological Point of View.* Grand Rapids, MI: Wm. B. Eerdmans Publishing Co., 1975. **[egal.]**

Kaiser, Walter. *Hard Sayings of the Old Testament.* Downers Grove, IL: InterVarsity Press, 1988.

———. *Toward an Exegetical Theology*. Grand Rapids, MI: Baker Book House, 1981.

Kassian, Mary A. *Women, Creation and the Fall.* Wheaton, IL: Crossway Books, 1990. **[comp.]**

———. *The Feminist Gospel: The Movement to Unite Feminism with the Church.* Wheaton, IL: Crossway Books, 1992. **[comp.]**

Kautzsch, F., ed. *Gesenius' Hebrew Grammar*. Trans. A. E. Cowley. Oxford: Clarendon Press, 1910.

Keener, Craig S. *Paul, Women and Wives: Marriage and Women's Ministry in the Letters of Paul.* Peabody, MA: Hendrickson, 1992. **[egal.]**

Kelly, J. N. D. *Early Christian Doctrines,* 2nd ed. New York: Harper & Row, 1960.

Kern, Otto. *Orphicorum Fragmenta.* Berlin: Weidmannsche Verlagsbüchhandlung, 1922.

Kimmel, Tim. *Basic Training for a Few Good Men*. Nashville: Thomas Nelson Publishers, 1997. **[comp.]**

Kistemaker, Simon. *Exposition of the First Epistle to the Corinthians.* New Testament Commentary. Grand Rapids, MI: Baker Book House, 1993.

Knight, George W. III. *The Role Relationship of Men and Women: New Testament Teaching*. Chicago: Moody Press, 1985. **[comp.]**

———. *The Pastoral Epistles*. New International Greek Testament Commentary. Grand Rapids, MI: Wm. B. Eerdmans Publishing Co., 1992. **[comp.]**

Köstenberger, Andreas, and Raymond Bouchoc. *The Book Study Concordance of the Greek New Testament.* Nashville: Broadman and Holman, 2003.

Köstenberger, Andreas J., Thomas R. Schreiner, and H. Scott Baldwin, eds. *Women in the Church: A Fresh Analysis of 1 Timothy 2:9–15*. Grand Rapids, MI: Baker Book House, 1995. **[comp.]**

Kroeger, Catherine Clark and James R. Beck, eds. *Women, Abuse, and the Bible: How Scripture Can Be Used to Hurt or Heal.* Grand Rapids, MI: Baker Book House, 1996. **[egal.]**

Kroeger, Catherine Clark and Mary J. Evans, eds. *The IVP Women's Bible Commentary*. Downers Grove, IL: InterVarsity Press, 2002. **[egal.]**

Kroeger, Richard Clark and Catherine Clark Kroeger. *I Suffer Not a Woman: Rethinking 1 Timothy 2:11–15 in Light of Ancient Evidence*. Grand Rapids, MI: Baker Book House, 1992. **[egal.]**

Lake, Kirsopp, trans. *The Apostolic Fathers.* 2 vols. Loeb Classical Library. Cambridge: Harvard University Press, 1970.

Lepine, Bob. *The Christian Husband.* Ann Arbor, MI.: Servant Publications, 1999. **[comp.]**

Lewis, Robert. *Real Family Values: Leading Your Family into the 21st Century with Clarity and Conviction.* Sisters, OR: Multnomah Publishers, 2000. **[comp.]**

———. *Raising a Modern-Day Knight*. Colorado Springs: Focus on the Family, 1997. **[comp.]**

Lewis, Robert and William Hendricks. *Rocking the Roles: Building a Win-Win Marriage*. Colorado Springs: NavPress, 1991. **[comp.]**

Liefeld, Walter. *Ephesians.* IVP New Testament Commentary. Downers Grove, IL, and Leicester: InterVarsity Press, 1997.

Lightfoot, J. B. *The Epistle of St. Paul to the Galatians.* Reprinted Grand Rapids, MI: Zondervan, 1957; first published 1865.

Lincoln, Andrew T. *Ephesians.* Word Biblical Commentary; Dallas: Word, 1990.

Lindsell, Harold. *The Bible in the Balance.* Grand Rapids, MI: Zondervan, 1979.

Lowance, Mason, ed. *Against Slavery: An Abolitionist Reader.* New York: Penguin Books, 2000.

Lundy, Daniel G. *Women, the Bible and the Church: Currents of Change in the Evangelical World.* Richmond Hill, Ontario: Canadian Christian Publications, 1993. **[comp.]**

Lutz, Lorry. *Women as Risk-Takers for God: Finding Your Role in the Neighborhood, Church, and World.* Grand Rapids, MI: Baker Book House, 1997. **[egal.]**

Maass, Ernest. *Commentariorum in Aratum reliquiae.* Berlin: Weidmann, 1898.

Mahaney, Carolyn. *Feminine Appeal: Seven Virtues of a Godly Wife and Mother.* Wheaton, IL: Crossway Books, 2003. **[comp.]**

Malcolm, Kari Torjesen. *Women at the Crossroads: A Path Beyond Feminism and Traditionalism*. Downers Grove, IL: InterVarsity Press, 1982. **[egal.]**

Marsden, George, *Fundamentalism and American Culture.* New York: Oxford University Press, 1980.

Marshall, I. Howard. *A Critical and Exegetical Commentary on the Pastoral Epistles, ICC*. Edinburgh: T&T Clark, 1999. **[egal.]**

Marthaler, Berard L., ed. *New Catholic Encyclopedia*. Washington, DC: Catholic University of America, 2002.

Martin, Faith. *Call Me Blessed: The Emerging Christian Woman*. Grand Rapids, MI: Wm. B. Eerdmans Publishing Co., 1988. **[egal.]**

Martin, Francis. *The Feminist Question: Feminist Theology in the Light of Christian Tradition.* Grand Rapids, MI: Wm. B. Eerdmans Publishing Co., 1994.

McComiskey, Thomas, ed. *The Minor Prophets.* Grand Rapids, MI: Baker Book House, 1992.

Meeks, Wayne. *The First Urban Christians: The Social World of the Apostle Paul.* New Haven, CT: Yale University Press, 1983.

Metzger, Bruce M. *The Text of the New Testament: Its Transmission, Corruption, and Restoration,* 2nd ed. Oxford: Clarendon Press, 1968.

Mickelsen, Alvera, ed. *Women, Authority and the Bible: Some of Today's Leading Evangelicals Seek to Break Through a Critical Impasse.* Downers Grove, IL: InterVarsity Press, 1986. **[egal.]**

Mitchell, Patrick. *The Scandal of Gender: Early Christian Teaching on the Man and the Woman.* Salisbury, MA: Regina Orthodox Press, 1998. **[comp.]**

Mollenkott, Virginia. *Women, Men, and the Bible*. Nashville: Abingdon Press, 1977. **[egal.]**

Moo, Douglas. *Epistle to the Romans*, NICNT. Grand Rapids, MI: Wm. B. Eerdmans Publishing Co., 1996.

Morgan, Robert, ed. *The Nature of New Testament Theology.* London: SCM, 1973.

Morgenthaler, Robert. *Statistik des Neutestamentlichen Wortschatzes*. Zurich: Gotthelf, 1958.

Morrell, T. *Lexicon Graeco-Prosodiacum*. Cambridge: J. Smith, 1815.

Morris, Leon. *The Epistle to the Romans,* PNTC. Grand Rapids, MI: Wm. B. Eerdmans Publishing Co., 1988.

Moulton, J. H., and George Milligan. *The Vocabulary of the Greek Testament Illustrated from the Papyri and Other Nonliterary Sources*. Grand Rapids, MI: Wm. B. Eerdmans Publishing Co., 1972 reprint; first published 1930.

Mounce, William D. *Pastoral Epistles*. Word Biblical Commentary, vol. 46. Nashville: Thomas Nelson, 2000. **[comp.]**

Nathan, Rich. "Is the Feminist My Enemy?" *Who Is My Enemy?* Grand Rapids, MI: Zondervan, 2002. **[egal.]**

Neuer, Werner. *Man and Woman in Christian Perspective*. Trans. Gordon Wenham. London: Hodder and Stoughton, 1990. **[comp.]**

Nicole, Roger. "A Tale of Two Marriages." *Standing Forth: Collected Writings of Roger Nicole*. Rosshire, Great Britain: Christian Focus, 2002. **[egal.]**

O'Brien, Peter T. *The Letter to the Ephesians.* Pillar New Testament Commentary. Cambridge: Apollos, and Grand Rapids, MI: Wm. B. Eerdmans Publishing Co., 1999. **[comp.]**

O'Leary, Dale. *The Gender Agenda: Redefining Equality*. Lafayette, LA: Vital Issues Press, 1997. **[comp.]**

Orthodox Church in America. *Women and Men in the Church: A Study of the Community of Women and Men in the Church*. Syosset, New York: Department of Religious Education, 1980.

Osburn, Carroll D., ed. *Essays on Women in Earliest Christianity.* Volumes 1 and 2. Joplin, MO: College Press Publishing Company, 1995. **[egal.]**

———. *Women in the Church: Refocusing the Discussion.* Abilene, TX: Restoration Perspectives, 1994. **[egal.]**

Oster, Richard. *A Bibliography of Ancient Ephesus,* ATLABS 19. Metuchen and London: Scarecrow, 1987.

Otto, Donna. *The Stay-at-Home Mom.* Eugene, OR: Harvest House Publishers, 1991. **[comp.]**

Pantel, P., ed. *A History of Women in the West.* Cambridge, MA: Belknap/Harvard University Press, 1992.

Passno, Diane. *Feminism: Mystique or Mistake? Rediscovering God's Liberating Plan for Women.* Wheaton, IL: Tyndale House Publishers, 2000. **[comp.]**

Patterson, Dorothy. *A Woman Seeking God.* Nashville: Broadman and Holman Publishers, 1992. **[comp.]**

Patterson, Dorothy and Rhonda Kelley, eds. *The Woman's Study Bible.* Nashville: Thomas Nelson Publishers, 1995. **[comp.]**

Paul, John II. *On the Dignity and Vocation of Women.* Boston: St. Paul Books and Media, 1988.

Peace, Martha. *The Excellent Wife.* Bemidji, MN: Focus, 1999. **[comp.]**

Perriman, Andrew. *Speaking of Women: Interpreting Paul.* Leicester, England: InterVarsity Press, 1998. **[egal.]**

Peterson, Susan Lynn. *Timeline Charts of the Western Church.* Grand Rapids, MI: Zondervan, 1999.

Pickering, John. *Greek Lexicon.* Boston: Wilkins, Carter, and Co., 1847.

Piper, John and Wayne Grudem, eds. *Recovering Biblical Manhood and Womanhood: A Response to Evangelical Feminism.* Wheaton, IL: Crossway Books, 1991. **[comp.]**

Plutarch. *Plutarch's Moralia.* Trans. Frank Cole Babbitt, Loeb Classical Library, vol. 2. New York: G. P. Putnam's Sons, 1928.

Podles, Leon J. *The Church Impotent: The Feminization of Christianity.* Dallas: Spence Publishing, 1999.

Rainey, Dennis. *A Call to Family Reformation.* Little Rock, AR: Family Life, 1996. **[comp.]**

———. *Ministering to Twenty-First Century Families.* Nashville: Word, 2001. **[comp.]**

———. *One Home at a Time.* Colorado Springs: Focus on the Family Publishing, 1997. **[comp.]**

Rainey, Dennis and Barbara. *The New Building Your Mate's Self-Esteem.* Nashville: Thomas Nelson Publishers, 1995. **[comp.]**

Robertson, A. T. *A Grammar of the Greek New Testament in the Light of Historical Research.* Nashville: Broadman, 1934.

Rosberg, Gary and Barbara. *Divorce-Proof Your Marriage.* Wheaton, IL: Tyndale House Publishers, 2002. **[comp.]**

Saucy, Robert L. and Judith K. TenElshof, eds. *Women and Men in Ministry: A Complementary Perspective.* Chicago: Moody Press, 2001. **[comp.]**

Scanzoni, Letha and Nancy Hardesty. *All We're Meant to Be.* Waco, TX: Word Books, 1974. **[egal.]**

Scapula Johann. *Lexicon Graeco-Latinum.* Oxford: Clarendon, 1653.

Schaff, Philip. *History of the Christian Church.* Original 1910, reprint. Grand Rapids, MI: Wm. B. Eerdmans Publishing Co., 1971.

Schrevel, Cornelis. *Lexicon Manuale Graeco-Latinum et Latino-Graecum.* Edinburgh: Bell and Bradfute, 1823.

Schwartz, Eduard, ed. *Acta Conciliorum Oecumenicorum.* Berlin: de Gruyter, 1927.

Smith, F. LaGard. *Men of Strength for Women of God.* Eugene, OR: Harvest House Publishers, 1989. **[comp.]**

Smith, Paul R. *Is It Okay to Call God "Mother"? Considering the Feminine Face of God.* Peabody, MA: Hendrickson Publishers, 1993. **[egal.]**

Spencer, Aída Besançon. *Beyond the Curse: Women Called to Ministry.* Nashville: Thomas Nelson Publishers, 1985. **[egal.]**

St. Augustine, *The Trinity.* Trans. Edmund Hill, vol. 5 of *The Works of St. Augustine.* Brooklyn, NY: New City Press, 1991.

Staab, Karl, ed. *Pauluskommentare aus der griechischen Kirche.* Münster: Aschendorff, 1933.

Stendahl, Krister. *The Bible and the Role of Women: A Case Study in Hermeneutics.* Trans. Emilie T. Sanders. Philadelphia: Fortress Press, 1966, 1st Swedish ed., 1958. **[egal.]**

Stephanus. *Thesaurus Graecae Linguae.* Ed. W. and L. Dindorf. Paris: Didot, 1831–1865.

Storkey, Elaine. *Origins of Difference: The Gender Debate Revisited.* Grand Rapids, MI: Baker Book House, 2001. **[egal.]**

Strack, Hermann, and Paul Billerbeck. *Kommentar zum Neuen Testament aus Talmud und Midrasch*, 4-vol. ed., Munich: C. H. Beck, 1926–1928.
Strauch, Alexander. *Biblical Eldership*. Littleton, CO: Lewis and Roth Publishers, 1995. **[comp.]**
———. *The New Testament Deacon: Minister of Mercy*. Littleton, CO: Lewis and Roth Publishers, 1992. **[comp.]**
Strong, Augustus. *Systematic Theology*. Valley Forge, PA: Judson Press, 1907.
Sumner, Sarah. *Men and Women in the Church: Building Consensus on Christian Leadership*. Downers Grove, IL: InterVarsity Press, 2003. **[egal.]**
Sunderland, J. T. *The Liberal Christian Ministry*. Boston: G. H. Ellis, 1889.
Sutton, Jerry. *The Baptist Reformation: The Conservative Resurgence in the Southern Baptist Convention*. Nashville: Broadman and Holman, 2000.
Tannen, Debra. *You Just Don't Understand: Women and Men in Conversation*. New York: Ballantine Books, 1990.
Thayer, Joseph Henry. *Greek-English Lexicon of the New Testament*. Edinburgh: T. & T. Clark, 1901.
Thiselton, Anthony. *First Epistle to the Corinthians, NIGTC*. Grand Rapids, MI: Wm. B. Eerdmans Publishing Co., 2000. **[egal.]**
Thurston, Bonnie B. *The Widows: A Women's Ministry in the Early Church*. Minneapolis: Fortress Press, 1989.
Trebilco, Paul. *Jewish Communities in Asia Minor*, SNTSMS 69. Cambridge: Cambridge University Press, 1991.
Trombley, Charles. *Who Said Women Can't Teach?* South Plainfield, NJ: Bridge Publishing, 1985. **[egal.]**
Tucker, Ruth A. *Women in the Maze: Questions and Answers on Biblical Equality*. Downers Grove, IL: InterVarsity Press, 1992. **[egal.]**
Tucker, Ruth A. and Walter Liefeld. *Daughters of the Church: Women and Ministry from New Testament Times to the Present*. Grand Rapids, MI: Zondervan, 1987. **[egal.]**
Van Leeuwen, Mary Stewart. *Gender and Grace: Love, Work and Parenting in a Changing World*. Downers Grove, IL: InterVarsity Press, 1990. **[egal.]**
Volf, Miroslav. *After Our Likeness*. Grand Rapids, MI: Wm. B. Eerdmans Publishing Co., 1998.
Von Tischendorf, C. *Apocalypses Apocryphae*. Leipzig: Mendelssohn, 1866.
Walker, S. *Memorials to the Roman Dead*. London: British Museum of Publications, 1985.
———. *Catalog of Roman Sarcophagi in the British Museum*. London: British Museum of Publications, 1990.
Wallace, Daniel B. *Greek Grammar Beyond the Basics*. Grand Rapids, MI: Zondervan, 1996.
Warfield, B. B. *The Works of B. B. Warfield*, 10-vol. ed., original 1927. Grand Rapids, MI: Baker Book House, 1991 (reprint).
Webb, William J. *Slaves, Women and Homosexuals: Exploring the Hermeneutics of Cultural Analysis*. Downers Grove, IL: InterVarsity Press, 2001. **[egal.]**
Weber, Linda. *Mom, You're Incredible*. Colorado Springs: Focus on the Family Publishing, 1994. **[comp.]**
———. *Woman of Splendor*. Nashville: Broadman and Holman Publishers, 1999. **[comp.]**
Weber, Stu. *Four Pillars of a Man's Heart*. Sisters, OR: Multnomah Publishers, 1997. **[comp.]**
———. *Tender Warrior*. Sisters, OR: Multnomah Publishers, 1993. **[comp.]**
Weld, Theodore. *The Bible Against Slavery*, 4th ed. New York: American Anti-Slavery Society, 1838.
Wenham J. W. *The Elements of New Testament Greek*. Cambridge: CUP, 1965.
Williams, Don. *The Apostle Paul and Women in the Church*. Ventura, CA: Regal Books, 1979. **[egal.]**
Winter, Bruce W. *After Paul Left Corinth*. Grand Rapids, MI: Wm. B. Eerdmans Publishing Co., 2001.
Witherington, Ben III. *Women and the Genesis of Christianity*. Cambridge: Cambridge University Press, 1990.
Witherington, Ben III. *Women in the Earliest Churches*. Society for New Testament Studies Monograph Series. G. N. Stanton, general editor. Cambridge: Cambridge University Press, 1988.
Young, Edward J. *The Book of Isaiah*, NICOT. Grand Rapids, MI: Wm. B. Eerdmans Publishing Co., 1992.

Articles

Arnold, Clinton. "Jesus Christ: 'Head' of the Church (Colossians and Ephesians)," in *Jesus of Nazareth: Lord and Christ,* ed. Joel B. Green and Max Turner (Grand Rapids, MI: Wm. B. Eerdmans Publishing Co. and Carlisle, England: Paternoster, 1994), 346–66.

Arnold, Clinton and Robert Saucy. "The Ephesian Background of Paul's Teaching on Women's Ministry," in *Women and Men in Ministry: A Complementary Perspective,* ed. Robert L. Saucy and Judith K. TenElshof (Chicago: Moody Press, 2001), 279–90.

Arnott, John. "All Hands to the Harvest," in *Spread the Fire,* Oct. 1997, 1. (Also found at the Toronto Airport Christian Fellowship web site, at www.tacf.org/stf/archive/3-5/arnotts.html.)

Baddeley, Mark. "The Trinity and Subordinationism: A Response to Kevin Giles." Reformed Theological Review 63:1 (April, 2004), 1–14.

Baldwin, H. Scott. "Authenteō in Ancient Greek Literature," in *Women in the Church: A Fresh Analysis of 1 Timothy 2:9–15,* ed. Andreas J. Köstenberger, Thomas R. Schreiner, and H. Scott Baldwin (Grand Rapids, MI: Baker Book House, 1995), 269–305.

———. "A Difficult Word: Authenteō in 1 Timothy 2:12," in *Women in the Church*, 65–80.

Barnett, Paul. "Wives and Women's Ministry (1 Timothy 2:11–15)," in *Evangelical Quarterly* 61:3 (1989): 225–38.

Barron, Bruce. "Putting Women in Their Place: 1 Timothy 2 and Evangelical Views of Women in Church Leadership," *JETS* 33 (1990): 451–59.

Bartchy, S. S. "Slavery," in *International Standard Bible Encyclopedia,* 4 vols., ed. Geoffrey W. Bromiley (Grand Rapids, MI: Wm. B. Eerdmans Publishing Co., 1979–1988), 4:539–46.

Baugh, S. M. "The Apostle Paul among the Amazons," *Westminister Theological Journal* 56 (1994): 153–71.

———. "A Foreign World: Ephesus in the First Century," in *Women in the Church: A Fresh Analysis of 1 Timothy 2:9–15,* ed. Andreas J. Köstenberger, Thomas R. Schreiner, and H. Scott Baldwin (Grand Rapids, MI: Baker Book House, 1995), 13–52.

Beaudry, J. "Orans," in *New Catholic Encyclopedia*, ed. Berard L. Marthaler (Washington, D.C.: Catholic University of America, 2002), 621.

Beck, F. A. G. "Education," in *Oxford Classical Dictionary*, 2nd edition, ed. N.G.L. Hammond and H.H. Scullard (Oxford: Clarendon Press, 1970), 369–73.

Belleville, Linda. "Women in Ministry," in *Two Views on Women in Ministry,* ed. James R. Beck and Craig L. Blomberg (Grand Rapids, MI: Zondervan, 2001), 75–154.

Benn, Wallace. "How Egalitarian Tactics Swayed Evangelicals in the Church of England." *CBMW News* 2:3 (June 1997), 14.

Bilezikian, Gilbert. "A Critical Examination of Wayne Grudem's Treatment of Kephalē in Ancient Greek Texts," appendix to Gilbert Bilezikian, *Beyond Sex Roles: What the Bible Says about a Woman's Place in Church and Family*, 2nd ed. (Grand Rapids, MI: Baker Book House, 1985), 215–52.

———. "Hermeneutical Bungee-Jumping: Subordination in the Godhead," *JETS* 40/1 (March 1997): 57–68; also reprinted as appendix in *Community 101* (Grand Rapids, MI: Zondervan, 1997).

Blaising, Craig. "Monarchianism," in *EDT*, 727.

Blomberg, Craig. "Neither Hierarchicalist nor Egalitarian: Gender Roles in Paul," in *Two Views on Women in Ministry,* ed. James R. Beck and Craig L. Blomberg (Grand Rapids, MI: Zondervan, 2001), 329–72.

Borland, James A. "Women in the Life and Teachings of Jesus," in *Recovering Biblical Manhood and Womanhood,* ed. John Piper and Wayne Grudem (Wheaton, IL: Crossway Books, 1991), 113–23.

Bromiley, Geoffrey W. "Eternal Generation," in *Evangelical Dictionary of Theology*, ed. Walter Elwell (Grand Rapids, MI: Baker Book House, 1984), 368.

Brown, Judy. "I Now Pronounce You Adam and Eve," *Priscilla Papers* 13/4 (Fall 1999): 2–3.

Burer, M. H. and D. B. Wallace, "Was Junia Really an Apostle? A Re-examination of Rom. 16.7," *New Testament Studies* 47 (2001): 76–91.

Carson, D. A. "'Silent in the Churches': On the Role of Women in 1 Corinthians 14:33b–36," in *Recovering Biblical Manhood and Womanhood,* ed. J. Piper and W. Grudem (Wheaton, IL: Crossway Books, 1991), 140–53.

Cervin, Richard. "Does Kephalē Mean 'Source' or 'Authority' in Greek Literature? A Rebuttal," *TrinJ* 6 NS (1989): 85–112.

Christians, Roy W. "The Permanent Relevance of 1 Corinthians 11:2–16 in Light of Recent Research into Its Historical and Cultural Background," paper given at the annual meeting of the Evangelical Theological Society, November 16, 2001, in Colorado Springs, Colorado.

"CRC reverses decision…again" in *CBMW News* 1:1 (August 1995): 5.

Doriani, Dan. "A History of the Interpretation of 1 Timothy 2," in *Women in the Church: A Fresh Analysis of 1 Timothy 2:9–15,* ed. Andreas J. Köstenberger, Thomas R. Schreiner, and H. Scott Baldwin (Grand Rapids, MI: Baker Book House, 1995), 213–67.

———. "Historical Novelty of Egalitarian Interpretations of Scripture," in *Biblical Foundations for Manhood and Womanhood,* ed. Wayne Grudem (Wheaton, IL: Crossway Books, 2002), 203–19.

Dutton, Donald G. "Patriarchy and Wife Assault: The Ecological Fallacy," in *Violence and Victims* 9:2 (1994): 167–82.

Farrelly, Maura Jane. "Controversial Hymns Challenge U.S. Methodists' View of God," in *Voice of America News,* July 5, 2002 (www.voanews.com).

Finley, M. I. "Slavery," in *OCD,* 2nd ed. (Oxford: Clarendon Press, 1970), 994–96.

Finney, Paul Corby. "Orant," in *Encyclopedia of Early Christianity,* second edition, ed. Everett Ferguson (New York and London: Garland, 1997), 831.

Fitzmyer, Joseph. "Another Look at Kephalē in 1 Corinthians 11:3," *NTS* 35 (1989): 503–11.

Foh, Susan T. "What is the Woman's Desire?" *Westminster Theological Journal* 37 (1975): 376–83.

Frame, John. "Men and Women in the Image of God," in *Recovering Biblical Manhood and Womanhood,* ed. John Piper and Wayne Grudem (Wheaton, IL: Crossway Books, 1991), 225–32.

Gasque, W. Ward. "Response," in *Women, Authority and the Bible,* ed. Alvera Mickelsen (Downers Grove, IL: InterVarsity Press, 1986), 188–92.

Gill, David. "The Importance of Roman Portraiture for Head-Coverings in 1 Corinthians 11:2–16," *Tyndale Bulletin* 41 (1990): 245–60.

Giuntella, A. M. "Orans," in *Encyclopedia of the Early Church* (New York: Oxford University Press, 1992), 2:615.

Grenz, Stanley J. "Theological Foundations for Male-Female Relationships," *Journal of the Evangelical Theological Society* 41/4 (December 1998): 615–30.

Grudem, Wayne. "Asbury Professor Advocates Egalitarianism but Undermines Biblical Authority: A Critique of David Thompson's 'Trajectory' Hermeneutic." *CBMW News* 2:1 (Dec. 1996): 8–12.

———. "Do We Act As If We Really Believe the 'The Bible Alone, and the Bible in Its Entirety, Is the Word of God Written?'" *Journal of the Evangelical Theological Society* 43/1 (March 2000): 5–26.

———. "Does Kephalē ('Head') Mean 'Source' or 'Authority Over' in Greek Literature? A Survey of 2,336 Examples," *TrinJ* 10 NS (1985): 38–59.

———. "The Key Issues in the Manhood-Womanhood Controversy, and the Way Forward," in *Biblical Foundations for Manhood and Womanhood,* ed. W. Grudem (Wheaton, IL: Crossway Books, 2002), 19–68.

———. "The Meaning of Kephalē ('Head'): A Response to Recent Studies," *TrinJ* 11NS (Spring 1990): 3–72. Reprinted in *Recovering Biblical Manhood and Womanhood* (Wheaton, IL: Crossway Books, 1991), 425–68.

———. "The Meaning of Kephalē ('Head'): An Analysis of New Evidence, Real and Alleged," *JETS* 44/1 (March 2001): 25–65.

———. "The Monogenes Controversy: 'Only' or 'Only Begotten'?" Appendix 6 in Wayne Grudem, *Systematic Theology: An Introduction to Biblical Doctrine* (Leicester, England: InterVarsity Press, and Grand Rapids, MI: Zondervan, 1994), 1233–34.

———"The Myth of Mutual Submission as an Interpretation of Ephesians 5:21," in *Biblical Foundations for Manhood and Womanhood,* ed. Wayne Grudem (Wheaton, IL: Crossway Books, 2002), 221–31.

———. "An Open Letter to Egalitarians: Six Questions That Have Never Been Answered," *CBMW News* 3:1 (March 1998): 1, 3–4.
———. "Review of George W. Knight III, *The New Testament Teaching on the Role Relationship of Men and Women," JETS* 22:4 (Dec. 1979): 375–76.
———. "Willow Creek Enforces Egalitarianism: Policy Requires All Staff and New Members to Joyfully Affirm Egalitarian Views," in *CBMW News* 2:5 (Dec. 1997): 1, 3–6.
Gundry, Patricia, "Why We're Here," in *Women, Authority and the Bible,* ed. Alvera Mickelsen (Downers Grove, IL: InterVarsity Press, 1986), 10–21.
Hayner, Steve. "Women in the Ministries of InterVarsity," © 1998, 8–11.
Heggen, Carolyn Holderread. "Religious Beliefs and Abuse," in *Women, Abuse, and the Bible: How Scripture Can Be Used to Hurt or Heal,* ed. Catherine Kroeger and James R. Beck (Grand Rapids, MI: Baker Book House, 1996), 15–27.
Heimbach, Daniel R. "The Unchangeable Difference," in *Biblical Foundations for Manhood and Womanhood,* ed. Wayne Grudem (Wheaton, IL: Crossway Books, 2002), 275–89.
Hooker, M. D. "Authority on Her Head: An Examination of I Cor. xi.10," *New Testament Studies* 10 (1964): 410–16.
Hove, Richard W. "Does Galatians 3:28 Negate Gender-Specific Roles?" in *Biblical Foundations for Manhood and Womanhood,* ed. Wayne Grudem (Wheaton, IL: Crossway Books, 2002), 105–43.
Hugenberger, Gordon. "Women in Church Office: Hermeneutics or Exegesis? A Survey of Approaches to 1 Timothy 2:8–15," in *Journal of the Evangelical Theological Society* 35:3 (September 1992): 341–60.
Hull, Gretchen Gaebelein. "Response," in *Women, Authority and the Bible,* ed. Alvera Mickelsen (Downers Grove, IL: InterVarsity Press, 1986), 22–27.
Huttar, David. "AΨTHENTEIN in the Aeschylus Scholium," *Journal of the Evangelical Theological Society* 44 (2001): 615–25.
"IVCF Affirms Egalitarianism," in *CBMW News* 1:1 (Aug. 1995), 4.
Jacobs, Cindy. "Women of God, Arise!" in *Charisma,* May 1998, 76–79, 110.
Johnson, Gregg. "The Biological Basis for Gender-Specific Behavior," in *Recovering Biblical Manhood and Womanhood: A Response to Evangelical Feminism,* ed. John Piper and Wayne Grudem (Wheaton, IL: Crossway Books, 1991), 280–93.
Johnson, S. Lewis Jr. "Role Distinctions in the Church: Galatians 3:28," in *Recovering Biblical Manhood and Womanhood,* ed. John Piper and Wayne Grudem (Wheaton, IL: Crossway Books, 1991), 154–64.
Jones, Peter R. "Sexual Perversion: The Necessary Fruit of Neo-Pagan Spirituality in the Culture at Large," in *Biblical Foundations for Manhood and Womanhood,* ed. Wayne Grudem (Wheaton, IL: Crossway Books, 2002), 257–74.
Keener, Craig. "Is Subordination Within the Trinity Really Heresy? A Study of John 5:18 in Context," *TrinJ* 20 NS (1999): 39–51.
———. "Women in Ministry," in *Two Views on Women in Ministry,* ed. James R. Beck and Craig L. Blomberg (Grand Rapids, MI: Zondervan, 2001), 25–73.
Keefauver, Larry. "Empower the Women," editorial written by Keefauver as senior editor in *Ministries Today* (May/June 1998): 9.
Knight, George W. III. "AΥTHENTEIN in Reference to Women in 1 Timothy 2:12," *NTS* 30 (1984): 154.
Köstenberger, Andreas. "A Complex Sentence Structure in 1 Timothy 2:12," in *Women in the Church: A Fresh Analysis of 1 Timothy 2:9–15,* ed. Andreas J. Köstenberger, Thomas R. Schreiner, and H. Scott Baldwin (Grand Rapids, MI: Baker Book House, 1995), 81–103.
———. "Saved Through Childbearing: A Fresh Look at 1 Timothy 2:15 Points to Protection from Satan's Deception," in *CBMW News* 2:4 (Sept. 1997): 1–5.
———. "Women in the Pauline Mission," in *The Gospel to the Nations*, eds. Peter Bolt and Mark Thompson (Leicester, England: InterVarsity Press, 2000), 221–47.

Kovach, Stephen D. and Peter R. Schemm Jr., "A Defense of the Doctrine of the Eternal Subordination of the Son," in *Journal of the Evangelical Theological Society* 42/3 (Sept. 1999): 461–76.

Kroeger, Catherine Clark. "Ancient Heresies and a Strange Greek Verb," *The Reformed Journal* 29 (March 1979): 12–15.

———. "The Classical Concept of Head as 'Source,'" Appx. 3 in Gretchen Hull, *Equal to Serve: Women and Men Working Together Revealing the Gospel* (Old Tappan, NJ: Fleming H. Revell, 1987, 1991), 267–83.

———. "First Timothy 2:12–A Classicist's View," in *Women, Authority and the Bible,* ed. Alvera Mickelsen (Downers Grove, IL: InterVarsity Press, 1995), 225–44.

———. "Women's Roles?" in *Christian History*, Issue 17 (1998): 2.

Lacey, Walter K. "Women," in the *OCD,* 2nd ed. (Oxford: Clarendon Press, 1970), 1139–40.

Laney, J. Carl. "Gender-Based Boundaries for Gathered Congregations: An Interpretative History of 1 Corinthians 14:34–35," in *Journal for Biblical Manhood and Womanhood* 7/1 (Spring 2002): 4–13.

Letham, Robert, "The Man-Woman Debate: Theological Comment," *WTJ* 52/1 (Spring 1990): 65–78.

McComiskey, Thomas. "Hosea," in *The Minor Prophets,* ed. Thomas E. McComiskey (Grand Rapids, MI: Baker Book House, 1992), 1–237.

Mickelsen, Alvera. "An Egalitarian View: There Is Neither Male Nor Female in Christ" in *Women in Ministry: Four Views,* ed. Bonnidell Clouse and Robert G. Clouse (Downers Grove, IL: InterVarsity Press, 1989), 173–206.

Mickelsen, Berkeley and Alvera. "What Does Kephalē Mean in the New Testament?" in *Women, Authority and the Bible,* ed. Alvera Mickelsen (Downers Grove, IL: InterVarsity Press, 1986), 97–110.

Moo, Douglas. "What Does It Mean Not to Teach or Have Authority Over Men? 1 Timothy 2:11–15" in *Recovering Biblical Manhood and Womanhood,* ed. John Piper and Wayne Grudem (Wheaton, IL: Crossway Books, 1991), 179–93.

Neuhaus, Richard John. "While We're At It," *First Things* 61 (March 1996): 69.

Niccum, C. "The Voice of the Manuscripts on the Silence of Women: The External Evidence for 1 Cor 14:34–35," *New Testament Studies* 43 (1997): 242–55.

Ortlund, Raymond Jr. "Male-Female Equality and Male Headship: Genesis 1–3," in *Recovering Biblical Manhood and Womanhood,* ed. John Piper and Wayne Grudem (Wheaton, IL: Crossway Books, 1991), 95–112.

Osborne, Grant. "Hermeneutics and Women in the Church," in *Journal of the Evangelical Theological Society* 20 (Dec. 1977): 337–52.

Packer, J. I. "Let's Stop Making Women Presbyters," *Christianity Today* (Feb. 11, 1991), 18–21.

———. "Liberalism and Conservatism in Theology" in *New Dictionary of Theology*, ed. Sinclair B. Ferguson and David F. Wright (Leicester, UK: InterVarsity Press, 1988), 384–86.

Padgett, Alan. "The Scholarship of Patriarchy (On 1 Timothy 2:8–15)," *Priscilla Papers* (Winter 1997).

Patterson, Dorothy. "The High Calling of Wife and Mother in Biblical Perspective," in *Recovering Biblical Manhood and Womanhood,* ed. J. Piper and W. Grudem (Wheaton, IL: Crossway Books, 1991), 364–77.

———. "Sarah Sumner's *Men and Women in the Church*: A Review Article" *JBMW* 8/1 (Spring 2003), 39–50.

Payne, Philip. "Response," in *Women, Authority, and the Bible,* ed. Alvera Mickelsen (Downers Grove, IL: InterVarsity Press, 1986), 118–32.

Perriman, Andrew. "The Head of a Woman: The Meaning of κεφαλη in 1 Cor. 11:3," *Journal of the Evangelical Theological Society* 45:2 (1994): 602–22.

Pierce, Ronald. "Evangelicals and Gender Roles in the 1900's: 1 Tim. 2:8–15: A Test Case," *Journal of the Evangelical Theological Society* 36:3 (September 1993): 343–55.

Piper, John. "A Vision of Biblical Complementarity," in *Recovering Biblical Manhood and Womanhood,* ed. John Piper and Wayne Grudem (Wheaton, IL: Crossway Books, 1991), 31–59.

Piper, John and Wayne Grudem. "Charity, Clarity, and Hope," in *Recovering Biblical Manhood and Womanhood,* ed. John Piper and Wayne Grudem (Wheaton, IL: Crossway Books, 1991), 403–22.

———. "An Overview of Central Concerns: Questions and Answers," in *Recovering Biblical Manhood and Womanhood,* ed. John Piper and Wayne Grudem (Wheaton, IL: Crossway Books, 1991), 60–92.

Powilson, David, et al. "Pastoral Responses to Domestic Violence," in *Pastoral Leadership for Manhood and Womanhood,* ed. Wayne Grudem and Dennis Rainey (Wheaton, IL: Crossway Books, 2002), 265–76.

Poythress, Vern Sheridan. "The Church as Family: Why Male Leadership in the Family Requires Male Leadership in the Church," in *Recovering Biblical Manhood and Womanhood,* ed. John Piper and Wayne Grudem (Wheaton, IL: Crossway Books, 1991), 233–47.

Ramsey, George W. "Is Name-Giving an Act of Domination in Genesis 2:23 and Elsewhere?" *Catholic Biblical Quarterly* 50 (1988): 24–35.

Robeck Jr., C. M. "Aimee Semple McPherson," in *International Dictionary of Pentecostal and Charismatic Movements*, revised and expanded edition, ed. Stanley M. Burgess and Eduard van der Maas (Grand Rapids, MI: Zondervan, 2002), 856–59.

Ruprecht, A. A. "Slave, Slavery," *DPL*, 881–83.

Sande, Ken. "Church Discipline: God's Tool to Preserve and Heal Marriages," in *Pastoral Leadership for Manhood and Womanhood,* ed. Wayne Grudem and Dennis Rainey (Wheaton, IL: Crossway Books, 2002), 161–85.

Schemm, Peter. "Kevin Giles's *The Trinity and Subordinationism*: A Review Article," *Journal for Biblical Manhood and Womanhood* 7/2 (Fall 2002): 67–78.

Scholer, David. "The Evangelical Debate over Biblical 'Headship,'" in *Women, Abuse, and the Bible: How Scripture Can Be Used to Hurt or Heal,* ed. Catherine Kroeger and James R. Beck (Grand Rapids, MI: Baker Book House, 1996), 28–57.

———. "First Timothy 2:9–15 and the Place of Women in the Church's Ministry," in *Women, Authority and the Bible,* ed. Alvera Mickelsen (Downers Grove, IL: InterVarsity Press, 1995), 193–224.

Schreiner, Thomas R. "An Interpretation of 1 Timothy 2:9–15: A Dialogue with Scholarship," *Women in the Church: A Fresh Analysis of 1 Timothy 2:9–15,* ed. Andreas J. Köstenberger, Thomas R. Schreiner, and H. Scott Baldwin (Grand Rapids, MI: Baker Book House, 1995), 105–54.

———. "Head Coverings, Prophecies, and the Trinity: 1 Corinthians 11:2–16," in *Recovering Biblical Manhood and Womanhood,* ed. John Piper and Wayne Grudem (Wheaton, IL: Crossway Books, 1991), 124–39.

———. "Review of Webb, *Slaves, Women, and Homosexuals*," *JBMW* 7/1 (Spring 2002): 41–51.

———. "The Valuable Ministries of Women in the Context of Male Leadership," in *Recovering Biblical Manhood and Womanhood,* ed. John Piper and Wayne Grudem (Wheaton, IL: Crossway Books, 1991), 209–24.

Snodgrass, Klyne. "Galatians 3:28: Conundrum or Solution?" in *Women, Authority and the Bible,* ed. Alvera Mickelsen (Downers Grove, IL: InterVarsity Press, 1995), 161–81.

Sokolowski, F. "A New Testimony on the Cult of Artemis of Ephesus," *HTR* 58 (1965): 427–31.

Stinson, Randy. "Does the Father Submit to the Son? A Critique of Royce Gruenler," in *Journal for Biblical Manhood and Womanhood* 6/2 (Fall 2001): 12–17.

———. "Our Mother Who Art in Heaven: A Brief Overview and Critique of Evangelical Feminists and the Use of Feminine God-Language," *JBMW* 8/2 (Fall 2003): 20–34.

Thiselton, Anthony. "Supposed Power of Words in the Biblical Writings," *Journal of Theological Studies*, N.S., vol. XXV, pt. 2 (October 1974): 283–99.

Thompson, David L. "Women, Men, Slaves and the Bible: Hermeneutical Inquiries," *Christian Scholar's Review* 25:3 (March 1996): 326–49.

Tracy, Steven. "Domestic Violence in the Church and Redemptive Suffering in 1 Peter," paper read at the Evangelical Theological Society annual meeting, Toronto, Canada, November 20–22, 2002.

———. "Headship with a Heart: How Biblical Patriarchy Actually Prevents Abuse," in *Christianity Today* (Feb. 2003), 50, 52–54.

Turner, Max. "Modern Linguistics and the New Testament," in *Hearing the New Testament: Strategies for Interpretation,* ed. Joel B. Green (Grand Rapids, MI: Wm. B. Eerdmans Publishing Co., and Carlisle, England: Paternoster, 1995), 165–72.

Ware, Bruce A. "Male and Female Complementarity and the Image of God," in *Biblical Foundations for Manhood and Womanhood,* ed. Wayne Grudem (Wheaton, IL: Crossway Books, 2002), 71–92.

———. "Tampering with the Trinity: Does the Son Submit to His Father?" in *Biblical Foundations for Manhood and Womanhood,* ed. Wayne Grudem (Wheaton, IL: Crossway Books, 2002), 233–53.

Warfield, B. B. "The Biblical Doctrine of the Trinity," in *Biblical Doctrines* (Grand Rapids, MI: Baker Book House, 1991, reprint of 1929 edition), 133–72.

Webb, William. "The Limits of a Redemptive-Movement Hermeneutic: A Focused Response to T. R. Schreiner," *Evangelical Quarterly* 75:4 (2003): 327–42.

Weinrich, William. "Women in the History of the Church: Learned and Holy, But Not Pastors," in *Recovering Biblical Manhood and Womanhood,* ed. John Piper and Wayne Grudem (Wheaton, IL: Crossway Books, 1991), 263–79.

Wilshire, L. E. "The TLG Computer and Further Reference to AYTHENTEO in 1 Timothy 2:12," *NTS* 34 (1988): 120–34.

———. "1 Timothy 2:12 Revisited: A Reply to Paul W. Barnett and Timothy J. Harris," *Evangelical Quarterly* 65 (1993): 43–55.

Wolters, Albert. "A Semantic Study of authentēs and Its Derivatives," *Journal of Greco-Roman Christianity and Judaism* 1 (2000): 145–75.

———. "Review: I Suffer Not a Woman," *Calvin Theological Journal* 28 (1993): 208–13.

———. "Review of Clarence Boomsma, *Male and Female, One in Christ: New Testament Teaching on Women in Office"* in *Calvin Theological Journal* 29 (1994): 278–85.

Yamauchi, E. M. "Gnosticism," *DNTB*, 414–18.

Yarbrough, Robert W. "The Hermeneutics of 1 Timothy 2:9-15," in *Women in the Church: A Fresh Analysis of 1 Timothy 2:9–15,* ed. Andreas J. Köstenberger, Thomas R. Schreiner, and H. Scott Baldwin (Grand Rapids, MI: Baker Book House, 1995), 155–96.

———. "*I Suffer Not a Woman:* A Review Essay," *Presbyterion* 18/1 (1992): 25–33.

Scripture Index

Note: Page numbers in **bold** *indicate more extensive treatment of a passage.*

2 Corinthians

Galatians

Name Index

Note: Biblical names, ancient names, and modern names are all combined in this single index.

Subject Index

(including index of egalitarian claims)